THE OXFORD HANDBOO

THE HISTORY OF CRIME AND CRIMINAL JUSTICE

THE OXFORD HANDBOOKS IN CRIMINOLOGY AND CRIMINAL JUSTICE

GENERAL EDITOR: MICHAEL TONRY

The *Oxford Handbooks In Criminology And Criminal Justice* offer authoritative, comprehensive, and critical overviews of the state of the art of criminology and criminal justice. Each volume focuses on a major area of each discipline, is edited by a distinguished group of specialists, and contains specially commissioned, original essays from leading international scholars in their respective fields. Guided by the general editorship of Michael Tonry, the series will provide an invaluable reference for scholars, students, and policy makers seeking to understand a wide range of research and policies in criminology and criminal justice.

Other titles in this series:

WHITE-COLLAR CRIME
Shanna R. Van Slyke, Michael L. Benson, and Francis T. Cullen

ORGANIZED CRIME
Letizia Paoli

CRIMINOLOGICAL THEORY
Francis T. Cullen and Pamela Wilcox

CRIME PREVENTION
Brandon C. Welsh and David P. Farrington

THE OXFORD HANDBOOK OF

THE HISTORY OF CRIME AND CRIMINAL JUSTICE

Edited by

PAUL KNEPPER

and

ANJA JOHANSEN

OXFORD

UNIVERSITY PRESS

OXFORD
UNIVERSITY PRESS

Oxford University Press is a department of the University of Oxford. It furthers
the University's objective of excellence in research, scholarship, and education
by publishing worldwide. Oxford is a registered trade mark of Oxford University
Press in the UK and certain other countries.

Published in the United States of America by Oxford University Press
198 Madison Avenue, New York, NY 10016, United States of America.

Library of congress cataloging in publication data
The Oxford handbook of the history of crime and criminal justice / edited by Paul Knepper
and Anja Johansen.
pages cm.—(The Oxford handbooks in criminology and criminal justice)
Includes bibliographical references and index.
ISBN 978-0-19-935233-3 (hardcover : alk. paper); 978-0-19-094737-8 (paperback : alk. paper)
1. Criminology—History.   2. Crime--History.   3. Criminal justice, Administration of—History.
I. Knepper, Paul, editor.   II. Johansen, Anja, 1965- editor.
HV6021.O94 2016
364.9—dc23
2015033526

Contents

PART THREE: CRIME, GENDER, AND ETHNICITIES

PART FOUR: CULTURAL REPRESENTATIONS OF CRIME

PART FIVE: RISE OF CRIMINOLOGY

PART SIX: LAW ENFORCEMENT AND POLICING

PART SEVEN: LAW, COURTS, AND CRIMINAL JUSTICE

PART EIGHT: PUNISHMENT AND PRISONS

Contributors

Marcelo F. Aebi is Professor of Criminology and Criminal Law at the University of Lausanne.

Constance Bantman is Lecturer in French at the University of Surrey.

David G. Barrie is Associate Professor of History at the University of Western Australia.

Gray Cavender is Professor of Justice and Social Inquiry in the School of Social Transformation at Arizona State University.

Elizabeth Dale is Professor of History and Affiliate Professor of Law at the University of Florida.

Margo De Koster is Lecturer in Historical Criminology at the Vrije Universiteit Amsterdam.

Catherine Denys is Professor of Early Modern History at the University of Lille III.

Markus D. Dubber is Professor of Law at the University of Toronto.

Joachim Eibach is Associate Professor for Early Modern and Modern History at the University of Bern.

Clive Emsley is Emeritus Professor of History at the Open University.

Mark Finnane is Professor of History in the School of Humanities at Griffith University.

Magaly Rodríguez García is assistant professor of the research unity Modernity & Society 1800–2000 in the Department of History at the University of Leuven.

Stephen Garton is Professor of History at the University of Sydney.

Barry Godfrey is Professor of Social Justice at the University of Liverpool.

Kali N. Gross is Associate Professor of African and African Diaspora Studies at the University of Texas at Austin.

Manon van der Heijden is Professor of Comparative Urban History at Leiden University.

Anja Johansen is Senior Lecturer in Comparative European History at the University of Dundee.

Nancy Jurik is Professor of Justice and Social Inquiry at Arizona State University.

Paul Knepper is Professor of Criminology at the University of Sheffield.

Sharon A. Kowalsky is Associate Professor of History at Texas A&M University–Commerce.

Paul Lawrence is Senior Lecturer in History at the Open University.

Antonia Linde is Lecturer in the Department of Law and Political Science at the Universitat Oberta.

Hamish Maxwell-Stewart is Professor of History at the University of Tasmania.

Randall McGowen is Professor of History at the University of Oregon.

Richard Mc Mahon is Assistant Professor of History at Trinity College Dublin.

Michael Meranze is Professor of History at the University of California–Los Angeles.

Pablo Piccato is Professor of History at Columbia University.

Herbert Reinke is Senior Researcher at The Humboldt University, Berlin.

Sandra Scicluna is Senior Lecturer of Criminology at the University of Malta.

Heather Shore is a Reader in History at Leeds Beckett University.

Haia Shpayer-Makov is Professor of Modern British and European History at the University of Haifa.

Daniel Siemens is Assistant Professor of History at Bielefeld University.

Pieter Spierenburg is Emeritus Professor from the Erasmus University, Rotterdam.

Carolyn Strange is Senior Fellow in the School of History at Australian National University.

Tammy Whitlock is Assistant Professor of History at the University of Kentucky.

John Carter Wood is Professor of History at the Leibniz Institute of European History, Mainz.

Per Jørgen Ystehede is Senior Executive Officer in the Department of Criminology and Sociology of Law at the University of Oslo.

THE OXFORD HANDBOOK OF

THE HISTORY OF CRIME AND CRIMINAL JUSTICE

INTRODUCTION

PAUL KNEPPER AND ANJA JOHANSEN

THE history of crime and criminal justice refers to an interdisciplinary field of research into the past that engages a variety of topics, methods, and theories. What was until the 1960s the preserve of scholars working on legal-institutional history today involves historians from many sections of social and cultural history, as well as gender studies, urban history, and colonial history. Yet crime and criminal justice in past societies has also attracted the attention of scholars well beyond the traditional historical discipline. These include researchers from criminology, socio-legal studies, and other social sciences, as well as cultural studies and philosophy—not to mention individuals writing local history, popular history, and even historical crime fiction.

Given the exchange between historians and social scientists during the past four decades, it is difficult to meaningfully describe research on crime and criminal justice in the past within the study of "history." There are statistical models of crime trends, micro-histories of murder, and genealogies of punishment in society; police history, historical criminology, and postcolonial studies of law. This interdisciplinarity presents newcomers with a bewildering array of concepts and methods, discussions and debates that range across the social sciences and humanities. We therefore recognized the value of a systematic and comprehensive guide to the historical study of crime and criminal justice, although the diversity of subject matter and rapid development of the field makes this a challenge. In this introduction, we discuss the purpose, structure, and conceptual issues related to how we assembled *The Oxford Handbook of the History of Crime and Criminal Justice*.

The main purpose of putting together the *Handbook* is to bring together researchers who work on crime and criminal justice in the past with an emphasis on how the interaction between history and social sciences has shaped the field. Historians and social scientists claim much of the same territory and regularly make use of each other's work. Collectively, they share many concepts and methods, as well as disagreements and controversies, and they contribute to a core of knowledge about crime and criminal justice As a result, it is necessary to talk about historical or social science "approaches" rather than the formal disciplinary affiliation of individual scholars, because many historians employ social science methods or apply social theory, and many social scientists engage traditional methods of historical research or make use of conclusions obtained through traditional methods of historical research.

The interaction between historians and social scientists has taken place in several areas. One of these has been social theory. Developed on the basis of observations of society in the present, social theories have provided new insights into the past. Historical research has also repeatedly challenged social theories that have claimed to be universally applicable but have been undermined by being measured against past realities. In other cases, historical studies, inspired by insights from the past, have challenged social scientists to inquire about the present. Edward Thompson, Eric Hobsbawm, Douglas Hay, and the Warwick School sparked the modern history of crime and criminal justice when they brought Marxist theory to the examination of law and society in the eighteenth century. Their application of theory implied that similar processes of elite control over legal institutions, as well as resistance from the lower orders of society, continued through time and should be relevant for studies on criminal justice in the present (Lea 1999). At the same time, historians have borrowed ideas from social theory. Theories and concepts from sociology such as "social control" (Nye 1958) and "moral panic" (Cohen 1972; Hall et al. 1978) have guided much historical exploration into implicit control mechanisms and functions in criminal justice practices and institutions, as well as into popular perceptions of crime and the manufacturing of public fears by the media.

Michel Foucault has influenced studies on criminal justice, past and present, at many levels. In the first place, he challenged historians to fundamentally rethink the optimistic narrative of "ever-growing enlightenment and rationality" that had dominated interpretations of development in criminal justice since the eighteenth century. In Foucault's version of poststructuralism, most notably his work *Discipline and Punish* (1979), he critically analyzed criminal justice discourse and institutions in Europe since the eighteenth century and established the prison as a major subject of historical inquiry. Many historians rejected Foucault's methodology; it was philosophical rather than historical, as well as unsystematic and selective in its handling of historical sources (Evans 1997). Nevertheless, the Foucauldian challenge provoked historians to closely analyze penal institutions. While this reevaluation corrected Foucault on many details, it also led many historians to appreciate the deeper logic and function of penal institutions as attempts to discipline and "reconstruct" awkward individuals into conforming members of society. Rather than illustrating another strand of humanism, the development of criminal justice in Europe and North America became a narrative about knowledge, power, and control.

Historians and social scientists have shared in critical examinations of perceptions and images of the past circulated by the media, by politicians, or by other historians, all of which shape popular myths and justify criminal justice policies in the present. Police historians—led by Vic Gatrell, Robert Storch, and Clive Emsley—have challenged the myth of the gentle and honest British bobby who enforced the law in communities by consent of the local population and without political favoritism or class bias

(Williams 2011). They have shown that "a golden age of British policing" never existed, an insight that has profound implications for the legitimizing rhetoric of contemporary British police forces, which have already lost much of their reputation for honesty and integrity as a result of reports into institutional racism (the Stephen Lawrence case) and revelations of systematic police coverups of embarrassing failings (during the Hillsborough disaster).

Many representations of crime in the past possess significance beyond crime and criminal justice as such; they involve images of national identity or of victims and villains in the historical process. Detailed studies of the past, research on the historical origins of institutions, and comparisons between different countries have questioned established myths by placing them in proper historical context. Randolph Roth (2009) and Robert Dykstra (1996) have both investigated the extent to which the American "Wild West" was really criminal and violent. Although they come to different conclusions, their disagreement concerns not just historical evidence, but also the much larger narrative about the role of cowboys on the western frontier in the formation of modern American society. Historical research on Australia's convict origins similarly has significance beyond the practice of transportation (Garton 1991). Given the importance of convicts and their descendants in the founding of Australia, historians—starting with George Wood in the 1920s—have discussed whether the first convicts to arrive from Britain belonged to the "criminal class" or were simply "working class." Feminist historians, such as Joy Damousi (1997) and Kay Daniels (1998), joined the conversation by challenging the idea that most of the first British women to settle Australia were passive victims of historical processes, and instead portrayed the female convicts as feisty, spirited personalities who resisted the roles men tried to create for them.

Some historians have been more interested in borrowing social science techniques than applying social theory. The fascination with quantification in the 1970s, encouraged by access to mainframe computers, led to much important statistical research, but also to fierce debates about the reliability of the underlying statistical data (Gatrell & Hadden 1972; Tobias 1979). Douglas Greenberg (1974) and Eric Monkkonen (1975) pioneered the use of computerized statistical techniques for analyzing historical "data sets" in studies of urban crime, policing, and criminal justice processing. Since then, projects like the digitization of the Proceedings from the Old Bailey by Bob Shoemaker, Tim Hitchcock, and Clive Emsley (followed by the website "London Lives 1690–1800: Crime, Poverty and Social Policy in the Metropolis") have proved a major success, attracting users far beyond members of the academic community. The Digital Panopticon project, led by Barry Godfrey, Robert Shoemaker, Hamish Maxwell-Stewart, and Deborah Oxley, aims to develop techniques for mining genealogical, biometric, and criminal justice records by collating information from Britain and Australia for 90,000 people sentenced at London's Old Bailey in the 1870s.

There is, then, undeniable overlap between historians and social scientists working on crime and criminal justice in the past. Rather than describing this as a move toward "convergence" in research by historians and social scientists (Godfrey, Lawrence, & Williams 2008, p. 19), we see "twin knowledges" preserved by university organization,

academic journals, societies, and most of all, different intellectual reasons for exploring the past. For historians, the nature of crime in the past, as well as long-term change
and persistence in criminal justice, has intrinsic intellectual worth. Historians aim to
understand crime and criminal justice in the wider social, political, and cultural context of previous experience. In contrast, social scientists interested in past crime and
criminal justice pursue a deeper understanding of problems in the present by questioning the historical origins of practices and institutions. They value the past as background for reflection about approaches to crime in the present; the past is useful for
reform or critique of current policies, a tool to inform current practices or suggest
alternatives. Many historians, like social scientists, see their work as having relevance
for understanding crime and criminal justice in the present. But historians study crime
and criminal justice to contribute to historical knowledge, and social scientists study
the past to build social science knowledge (e.g., sociological knowledge, criminological
knowledge, socio-legal knowledge, etc).

The essays in the first section of this book address the interaction between history
and social science. Paul Lawrence examines the major theoretical frameworks, and
Barry Godfrey explains methods of historical research. As Lawrence explains, crime
became a subject for historical study in the 1970s with the arrival of the "new social
history." The new social history brought concepts and methods from the social sciences to historical inquiry. This fusion of social science and history has produced a
great deal of useful work, but also generated a lot of discussion about the reliability and
possible use of statistical data from courts and police, particularly from the nineteenth
century. Godfrey discusses the potential limitations and pitfalls of these methods and
approaches for historical research. Marcelo Aebi and Antonia Linde discuss the modeling of crime trends, problems in interpretation of crime statistics, and the issue of
long-term decline in violence across Europe. Richard Mc Mahon (in a later section)
also discusses the secular trend toward declining levels of interpersonal violence, particularly the methodological challenges involved in establishing reliable figures from
the medieval and early modern period.

The impact of the urban space on patterns of crime has preoccupied scholars and
social commentators since the nineteenth century, originally from the presumption
that large urban areas were inherently more criminogenic and violent than village societies because of their concentration of people and more limited possibilities for the
social control of thousands of unaffiliated and mobile individuals with little interest
in respecting law and order. Yet while the nature and relative distribution of crime
between rural and urban areas are scarcely studied and often poorly understood, one
aspect has been questioned and challenged by both historians and social scientists,
namely, the idea of modern urban spaces as inherently criminogenic and violent.

Starting in the 1960s as an attempt to understand modern urban violence, Ted R. Gurr
(1981) formulated a model of European trends in violence that has attracted a great deal
of discussion about the long-term decline in criminal violence. In a similar vein, Eric
Monkkonen (1981) and Roger Lane (1986) have argued that levels of crime and violence
in cities declined in the nineteenth century. The message of this work is that nothing is

inherent in cities that generates crime and disorder; therefore, it was not processes of urbanization in themselves that made violence inevitable. Instead, urban violence had specific causes that could be effectively addressed through government policies. Other researchers, particularly those drawing on cultural history and urban geography, have been more cautious, noting how available evidence has been influenced by popular perceptions (Kalifa 2004). Peter King's studies on homicide rates in rapidly urbanizing areas compared to remote rural areas of England, Wales, and Scotland have presented a very mixed picture. King argues that it was not the urban space in itself but numerous differentiated factors that led to high levels of registered violence and homicide in Glasgow during the early decades of industrialization, but that this trend passed within a few decades (King 2010).

Catherine Denys's essay on the geography of crime examines this debate. She focuses on crime in rural and village settings in relation to the transition toward urbanization. Heather Shore deals with organized crime and the cultural concept of the urban underworld, and Magaly Rodríguez García's review of prostitution looks at forms of crime that have traditionally been associated with urban areas. Nevertheless, as Shore's essay makes clear, our understanding of rural banditry could benefit from the insights of studies on urban organized crime. The same applies to prostitution; our knowledge of this practice in traditional village societies is very sparse. Tammy Whitlock's essay looks at retail theft, a form of crime that is unquestionably modern and urban. All of this work may help to identify whether any particular features characterizes modern, urban crime as ontologically distinct from traditional rural crime.

Approaches to crime have also been profoundly influenced by cultural assumptions about crime and violence in relation to gender, and the interaction between social theory and history has produced much useful research in this field. The feminist sociologist Frances Heidensohn argued in the 1960s that criminal or violent women are conceptualized and treated by criminal justice systems as "doubly deviant" (Heidensohn 1968). In the 1980s, Nicole Rafter and others introduced gender to crime history as a specific social category and examined expectations for women with reference to their social roles. While male violence breached social norms, this was nevertheless understood as reflecting men's intrinsic nature. In contrast, violent and criminal behavior by women not only transgressed social norms, but also contradicted what was presumed to be "female nature." Lucia Zedner (1991) and Shani D'Cruze (1998) have engaged this discussion with reference to Victoria-era Britain, as has Ann-Louise Shapiro (1996) with her look at "crimes of passion" in France. Further research has explored gender perspectives on leniency by criminal justice systems in relation to infanticide and the use of "criminal insanity" verdicts.

Yet whether courts sometimes penalized women more severely or leniently, the overall evidence from European and North American courts and police across the centuries has consistently shown that women constitute a relatively small portion of criminal justice populations. Traditionally this observable fact fitted well with prevailing cultural notions of violence and crime being predominantly male, and women not being naturally prone to violence or crime. In order to avoid perpetuating interpretations based on gender prejudice, historians have questioned whether the nature and proportion of crime for men and women are constants or whether they have fluctuated over time. Using records from London's Old Bailey, Malcolm Feeley and Deborah Little (1991) revealed a marked decrease in women's criminal involvement over the course of the eighteenth and early nineteenth centuries—what they termed the "vanishing female"—thus challenging the notion that crime has always been a male activity. From an opposite perspective, Martin Wiener (2004) provocatively argued that too much attention has been focused on femininity and patriarchy, and suggests that the criminalization in the nineteenth century of natural masculine reactions explains both the vanishing female and changing crime patterns.

In this volume, Joachim Eibach discusses the changing cultural meaning and social function of male violence as a cultural construction of masculinity, and Manon van der Heijden addresses the question about violence and culture from the perspective of female violence. Another consequence of the research on gender as a social category has been acceptance of the impossibility of attributing any single identity to women. Rafter's analysis of "partial justice" (1985) presents gender in relation to class and race/ethnicity as organizing principles for prisons. The essays in this volume by Margo De Koster and Herbert Reinke on policing minorities and by Kali Gross on black women, crime, and justice examine the interaction of gender, race/ethnicity, and class.

Other scholars, guided less by social science models or history than by cultural analysis, see the history of crime as a suitable arena for a broader societal critique. During the 1980s, the social science model that animated crime history came under attack from the "new cultural history." Using techniques from linguistics, Foucault championed an alternative approach to studying the past that denied that "society," particularly in the past, was an entity that could be studied, and maintained that "science" did not offer legitimate methodologies to examine the past. Only discourse and individual viewpoints could be studied. David Garland's studies of prison and welfare in Britain and the death penalty in the United States offered broad cultural critique of punishment in contemporary society. Garland does not specifically argue for the abolition of the prison or the death penalty, but instead rejects the values on which institutions and policies are based through examination of their emergence and development. Following Foucault's argument that the treatment of people at the margins reveals the essential nature of governance in any society, Garland contends that the purpose of cultural analysis is to encourage a wider examination of the values and emotions on which contemporary institutions, policies, and practices are based (Garland 1985; Garland 2010).

Foucault's cultural history is not the only version of cultural history, nor is every cultural historian necessarily interested in his version of discourse analysis. But he was the single most important figure in initiating the "cultural turn" in historical inquiry, and accordingly cultural history has become increasingly part of the history of crime. Foucault encouraged the expansion of crime and criminal justice history to include print media, crime fiction, and material culture. This *Handbook* includes work on media and crime by John Carter Wood; on crime, criminology, and the crime genre by Gray Cavender and Nancy Jurik; and on detective and murder fiction by Pablo Piccato.

It also includes Per Jørgen Ystehede's essay on crime museums, which reflects the overlap of crime history, cultural history, and the history of memory.

Foucault also encouraged the history of criminology. Prior to the 1980s, there was little interest in this area, and what was written tended to follow a history of science approach resting on assumptions about continuous progress in insight and knowledge. Hermann Mannheim's *Pioneers in Criminology* (1960) celebrated the achievements of individuals that led to the formation of criminology as a discipline. Robert Nye (1976) emphasized the achievements of the French school of criminology over the Italian school. But following Foucault, all this changed. Critical inquiries appeared that dealt with questions about how criminology formed in relation to criminal justice institutions, as well as about criminology and criminal justice as forms of social control. Garland (1985) presented prisons as an "institutional surface" and an "experimental laboratory" in which the new science of criminology could develop. More recently, historians have questioned the presentation of criminology as a science of "the other." Re-reading the texts of early founders reveals systems of thought very different from those described by Foucault (Vyleta 2006). The *Handbook* includes contributions from Pieter Spierenburg on the founders of criminology, Stephen Garton on psychiatric approaches, and Sharon A. Kowalsky on the role of women in Soviet criminology.

The *Handbook* covers "crime" and "criminal justice," terms that have been subject to considerable disagreement among those writing history. What is meant by "crime"? Geoffrey Elton has pointed out that even as late as the eighteenth century, crime lacked a precise legal meaning in English law. There was a category of offenses, the "real crimes," he said, that comprised treasons and felonies, punishable by death. These included murder, arson, and forms of theft, such as appropriating the cargo from a shipwreck. There was also a series of acts identified as illicit, such as beatings, cheating, and nuisances (Elton 1983, p. 290). James Sharpe, however, has challenged the claim that there was anything such as "real crime" that could be the subject of historical investigation. While serious crime might appear more real, he advised against narrowing the subject to felonies. In modern English society, petty crime was more common, typical, and entitled to be known as "real" crime. "Our aim," Sharpe wrote, "when studying crime in the past, therefore, must be to take as wide a view of the phenomenon as possible" (Sharpe 1999, p. 10).

Historians and social scientists have nevertheless paid more attention to certain violations of the law than others. The discussion about the decline of violence in Europe has been based on homicide, as trends in homicide are regarded as more precisely counted and indicative of wider trends in criminal violence (Johnson & Monkkonen 1996; Roth et al. 2008). However, whether we ought to spend as much time on homicide compared to theft is part of a wider debate on how much importance we should assign to the legal definition of crime. François Ploux (2008) has insisted that too little attention has been paid to the implications of studying crime through the "prism of categories used in judicial thought." The problem with regarding crime as a legal issue is the tendency to see all violations of the law, whether homicide, theft, or sexual offenses, as coming from a single, coherent motivation. He advocates replacement of the statistical approach, with its emphasis on legal categories, with an emphasis on deviant acts in relation to social categories constructed by the researcher, such as family relationships, attempts to defend honor, and so on. In selecting topics for the *Handbook*, we have relied on a wide definition of crime that encompasses both the crime as a legal offense and sociology of deviance approaches, with the understanding that "crime history" includes a wide range of activities. We include not only Richard Mc Mahon on homicide and Tammy Whitlock on retail theft, but also Magaly Rodríguez García on prostitution (which was in many countries not a criminal act), Heather Shore on the underworld, Constance Bantman on anarchist violence, and Paul Knepper on drug trafficking.

Like "crime," the term "criminal justice" is difficult to nail down. We have included sections on police, courts, and prisons—implying that these are major components of this concept—but the question of what constitutes criminal justice, and how the modern system came to be the way it is, is far from simple. When, why, and how people decide to set up institutions for responding to crime, what these institutions actually do versus what they are meant to do, and the experience of criminal justice versus what the founders claimed it would look like remain challenging. In contemporary Western cultures, police, courts, and prisons function together as components of the "criminal justice system," but this is a recent idea, and it is easy when writing about the past to conceptualize criminal justice in an anachronistic and unhistorical way.

One solution is to start in the present and examine how current criminal justice institutions came to be. Garland (2014) has explained how writing the history of punishment in society begins with critical observations of present-day practices. The historian then works backward to trace the genealogy of contemporary institution; to chart the decline or emergence of present practices out of struggles of power that have been neglected. The "history of the present" has had considerable appeal, particularly in historical criminology, in which the goal is to encourage evaluation of policies and practices. However, one particular challenge with imagining responses to crime in the past as a series of trajectories or pathways to the present is, as John Braithwaite (2003) has pointed out, what to do with institutions that did not survive. The history of punishment contains a great many institutions and practices that do not have representation in the present. The section on prisons and punishment in the *Handbook* includes an essay on the modern prison by Michael Meranze and on the death penalty by Randall McGowen, as well as essays about the forms of other institutions and practices, including work on the asylums, workhouses, and hospitals of the early modern era by Sandra Scicluna and on transportation by Hamish Maxwell-Stewart.

Within criminal justice history, "models" have been particularly important. In *Popular Justice* (1980) Samuel Walker took on the challenge of writing a history of American criminal justice; he did this by distinguishing the legal response to crime and delinquency from private initiatives. But to construct American criminal justice out of fifty state versions and many more local varieties, he relied on a favorite device of historians of criminal justice: the idea that the founders established model institutions in cities and states that were replicated across the country (Walker 1980). Questions of what constitutes a "model" and how the process of "modeling" took place have remained.

This has been the case in the history of policing, as examined in Anja Johansen's essay on police and the public and in Mark Finnane's essay on the origins of modern policing. The policing section also includes David Barrie on forms of policing before professionalization, Haia Shpayer-Makov on detectives and forensic science, and Clive Emsley on crime and policing in wartime.

Given the role of social history in crime history, more attention has been focused on police and prisons than on courts. More than twenty years ago, Allen Steinberg prefaced his study of private prosecution in Philadelphia during the nineteenth century with the observation that criminal justice history emerged with the histories of police and prisons (Steinberg 1989). While there have been histories of courts and legal practices, it remains the case that relatively more histories concern police and prisons than courts. Furthermore, the role of courts, as examined in legal history, has not been integrated into criminal justice history. One of our objectives in putting together the *Handbook* has been to incorporate legal history. Markus Dubber examines interpretive frameworks used in law and history. Elizabeth Dale develops a wider approach to legal history in her essay on "everyday justice," as does Daniel Siemens in his discussion of criminal trials in the public imagination. Carolyn Strange explores the meaning of criminal justice in her discussion of discretion by probation, parole, and the death sentence.

There were, in assembling the *Handbook*, additional issues to be decided: time frame, geography, and historiography. Time frame—what period the volume should cover—invites a larger question about when "crime history" begins. When, so to speak, was the first crime committed? Xavier Rousseaux (2013) has proposed an early date. The concept of crime, he wrote, originated in ancient Roman law and developed in ecclesiastical institutions in cities across Europe during the medieval period. He observed that a virtually new concept of crime emerged in the fifteenth century that encompassed new types of crime and new populations of criminals. Alternatively, Pieter Spierenburg (1985) has proposed a later date, placing the beginning of the history of crime in the sixteenth century because crime presupposes the existence of an authority, the state, that is interested in identifying and punishing offenses. Drawing on theory from Norbert Elias, Spierenburg held that the state had an important role in the "monopolization of violence" (Spierenburg 1985, pp. 64–66). The issue of origins or beginnings is tied to the conceptualization of crime; when crime history begins depends on the theoretical perspective in use. The early date suits researchers more inclined to a "sociology of deviance" perspective, while the later date appeals to those who prefer a more legalistic definition.

Then there is the other side of the question: When does "crime history" end? Or, to put it another way, when does history end and social science begin? Criminologists (and other social scientists) are interested in the recent past and regularly investigate shifts in policy and practice over the past few decades. Ian Loader and Richard Sparks (2005) have examined crime policy in England and Wales during the last thirty years of the twentieth century and have encouraged criminologists attracted by the idea of writing a "history of the present" to "think seriously about the past" (Loader &

Sparks 2005, p. 15). Yet in describing their work as "historical sociology" rather than a "history" or even "historical analysis," they signal a difference between the study of crime and criminal justice in history and that of the recent past. This is a matter of methodology. Access to living persons affords a range of data collection methods that social scientists prefer to use: written surveys, interviews, observation, and so on. Archival materials, where they exist, are restricted; privacy laws and ethics review boards prevent researchers from writing about people in 1995 in the same way as people in 1895. But the larger difference—to return to our earlier discussion—has to do with the different purposes of history and social science. Criminologists recall activities and events in recent decades to contribute to criminological knowledge, not historical knowledge. For the *Handbook*, we decided to concentrate on the eighteenth, nineteenth, and twentieth centuries (1700–2000)—three centuries that have been the focus of a great deal of crime history.

On the whole, the contributions discuss the Western world, particularly Europe and the United States. Europe and the United States, it might be said, represent the "known world" of crime history, and much of what has been written derives from these parts of the globe. But we also invited contributors prepared to discuss the situation on the edge of familiar geography: Pablo Piccato on Mexico, Sharon A. Kowalsky on Soviet Russia, and Sandra Scicluna on Malta. It is also worth emphasizing that the geography of crime history has in recent years expanded toward Central and South America, as well as India, China, and Japan. As these essays indicate, crime historians are leaving the familiar settings of Europe and North America to write the history of crime and justice around the world. Ricardo Salvatore, Carlos Aguirre, and Pablo Piccato have been writing the history of crime and criminal justice in Central and South America, extending and reexamining European-based explanations for urban crime and the development of police and prisons to Argentina, Mexico, Uruguay, Peru, and other countries (Johnson 1990; Piccato 2001; Salvatore & Aguirre 1996). Recent interest in the British Empire, driven by the new imperial history and postcolonial studies, has encouraged studies of crime and criminal justice outside of Europe and the United States (Godfrey & Dunstall 2005; Brown 2014)

Much crime history has been written in national or more local contexts, and expanding the geography of crime history is important for crossing conceptual borders. The "nationalist" tendency in crime history equates society and nation, and explains crime and criminal justice as the effect of causes occurring at this level. Elizabeth Dale (2011) has examined how criminal justice in the United States became national, with a look at the role of the federal government vis-à-vis states. But other historical writing has yet to recognize the significance of the state. Despite very different roles of the state in the Anglo-American and continental European traditions, many historians have invoked a simple model, formed more by a priori assumptions than by empirical research.

Finally, there is the issue of history versus historiography. All of the contributors to this volume locate their discussion with reference to historical scholarship on the topic, although some essays devote more space to what other historians have said than others. This is partly a reflection of the topic—the literature on some topics has been built up over decades, while other topics have emerged only in the past few years. The issue of historiography raised by *Handbook* contributions involves the larger issue of language. A great deal of work has been written in languages other than English. Italian micro-history, German modernization theory, and (especially) the second-generation Annales School all have something to offer crime history, although such work has not been integrated into the Anglo-American tradition. We invited contributors familiar with work published in other languages to include this where appropriate.

Our thanks to each of the contributors for making *The Oxford Handbook of the History of Crime and Criminal Justice* possible. We would also like to thank Michael Tonry for suggesting the project, and James Cook for seeing it through.

REFERENCES

Braithwaite, John. 2003. "What's Wrong with the Sociology of Punishment?" *Theoretical Criminology* 7:5–28.

Brown, Mark. 2014. *Penal Power and Colonial Rule.* New York: Routledge.

Cohen, Stanley. 1972. *Folk Devils and Moral Panics.* London: MacGibbon & Kee.

Dale, Elizabeth. 2011. *Criminal Justice in the United States, 1789–1939.* Cambridge: Cambridge University Press.

Damousi, Joy. 1997. *Depraved and Disorderly: Female Convicts, Sexuality and Gender in Colonial Australia.* Cambridge: Cambridge University Press.

Daniels, Kay. 1998. *Convict Women.* St Leonards, New South Wales, Australia: Allen & Unwin.

D'Cruze, Shani. 1998. *Crimes and Outrage: Sex, Violence and Victorian Working Women.* London: University College London Press.

Dykstra, Robert. 1996. "Field Notes: Overdosing on Dodge City." *Western Historical Quarterly* 27:505–14.

Elton, G. R. 1983. *Studies in Tudor and Stuart Politics and Government,* Vol. 3. Cambridge: Cambridge University Press.

Evans, Richard. 1997. *In Defence of History.* London: Granta.

Feeley, Malcolm, & Deborah Little. 1991. "The Vanishing Female: The Decline of Women in the Criminal Process, 1687–1912." *Law and Society Review* 25:719–58.

Garland, David. 1985. *Punishment and Welfare: A History of Penal Strategies.* London: Gower.

Garland, David. 2010. *Peculiar Institution: America's Death Penalty in an Age of Abolition.* Cambridge, MA: Belknap Press.

Garland, David. 2014. "What Is a 'History of the Present'? On Foucault's Genealogies and Their Critical Preconditions." *Punishment and Society* 16:365–84.

Garton, Stephen. 1991. "The Convict Origins Debate: Historians and the Problem of the 'Criminal Class.'" *Australian and New Zealand Journal of Criminology* 24:66–92.

Gatrell, Vic, & Tom Hadden. 1972. "Criminal Statistics and Their Interpretation." In *Nineteenth-Century Society: Essays on the Use of Quantitative Methods for the Study of Social Data,* ed. E. A. Wrigley, 336–95. Cambridge: Cambridge University Press.

Godfrey, Barry, & Grame Dunstall, eds. 2005. *Crime and Empire, 1840–1940: Criminal Justice in Local and Global Contexts.* Cullompton, Devon, UK: Willan.

Godfrey, Barry, Paul Lawrence, & Chris A. Williams. 2008. *History and Crime.* Los Angeles: Sage.

Greenberg, Douglas. 1974. *Crime and Law Enforcement in the Colony of New York, 1691–1776.* Ithaca, NY: Cornell University Press.

Gurr, Ted R. 1981. "Historical Trends in Violent Crime: A Critical Review of the Evidence." *Crime and Justice: An Annual Review of Research* 3:295–353.

Hall, Stuart, Chas Critcher, Tony Jefferson, John Clarke, & Brian Roberts. 1978. *Mugging, the State, and Law and Order.* New York: Holmes & Meier.

Heidensohn, Frances. 1968. "The Deviance of Women: A Critique and an Enquiry." *British Journal of Sociology* 19:160–72.

Johnson, Eric, & Eric Monkkonen. 1996. *The Civilization of Crime: Violence in Town and Country since the Middle Ages.* Urbana: University of Illinois Press.

Johnson, Lyman. 1990. *The Problem of Order in Changing Societies: Essays on Crime and Policing in Argentina and Uruguay.* Albuquerque: University of New Mexico Press.

Kalifa, Dominique. 2004. "Crime Scenes: Criminal Topography and Social Imaginary in Nineteenth-Century Paris." *French Historical Studies* 27:175–94.

King, Peter. 2010. "The Impact of Urbanization on Murder Rates and the Geography of Homicide in England and Wales, 1780–1850." *Historical Journal* 53:671–98.

Lane, Roger. 1986. *The Roots of Violence in Black Philadelphia, 1860–1900.* Cambridge, MA: Harvard University Press.

Lea, John. 1999. "Social Crime Revisited." *Theoretical Criminology* 3:307–25.

Loader, Ian, & Richard Sparks. 2005. "For an Historical Sociology of Crime Policy in England and Wales since 1968." In *Managing Modernity: Politics and the Culture of Control,* ed. Matt Matravers, 5–32. London: Routledge.

Mannheim, Herman. 1960. *Pioneers in Criminology.* London: Stevens & Sons.

Monkkonen, Eric. 1975. *The Dangerous Class: Crime and Poverty in Columbus, Ohio, 1860–1885.* Cambridge, MA: Harvard University Press.

Monkkenon, Eric. 1981. "A Disorderly People? Urban Order in Nineteenth and Twentieth Century American." *Journal of American History* 68:539–59.

Nye, Ivan F. 1958. *Family Relations and Delinquent Behavior.* New York: John Wiley.

Nye, Robert. 1976. "Heredity or Milieu: The Foundations of Modern European Criminological Thought." *Isis* 67:334–55.

Piccato, Pablo. 2001. *City of Suspects: Crime in Mexico City 1900–1931.* Durham, NC: Duke University Press.

Ploux, François. 2008. "Violence in France's Past: An Anthropological Approach." In *Violence in Europe: Historical and Contemporary Perspectives,* ed. Sophie Body-Gendrot & Pieter Spierenburg, 65–78. New York: Springer.

Roth, Randolph. 2009. *American Homicide.* Cambridge, MA: Harvard University Press.

Roth, Randolph, Douglas L. Eckberg, Cornelia Hughes Dayton, Kenneth Wheeler, James Watkinson, Robb Haberman, & James M. Denham. 2008. "The Historical Violence Database: A Collaborative Research Project on the History of Violent Crime and Violent Death." *Historical Methods* 41:81–97.

Rousseaux, Xavier. 2013. "A History of Crime and Criminal Justice in Europe." In *The Routledge Handbook of European Criminology,* ed. Sophie Body-Gendrot, Mike Hough, Clara Kerezsi, Rene Levy, & Sonja Snacken, 38–54. London: Routledge.

Salvatore, Ricardo D. and Carlos Aguirre. 1996. *The Birth of the Penitentiary in Latin America: Essays on Criminology, Prison Reform and Social Control, 1830–1940.* Austin: University of Texas Press.

Shapiro, Ann-Louise. 1996. *Breaking the Codes: Female Criminality in Fin-de-Siècle Paris*. Stanford, CA: Stanford University Press.

Sharpe, James A. 199. *Crime in Early Modern England, 1550–1750*, 2nd ed. London: Longman.

Spierenburg, Pieter. 1985. "Evaluation of the Conditions and Main Problems Relating to the Contribution of Historical Research to the Understanding of Crime and Criminal Justice." In *Historical Research on Crime and Criminal Justice*, ed. European Committee on Crime Problems, 51–95. Strasbourg: Council of Europe.

Steinberg, Allen. 1989. *The Transformation of Criminal Justice: Philadelphia, 1800–1880*. Chapel Hill: University of North Carolina Press.

Tobias, John. 1979. *Crime and Police in England, 1700–1900*. Dublin: Gill & Macmillan.

Vyleta, Daniel. 2006. "Was Early Twentieth-Century Criminology a Science of 'the Other'? A Re-Evaluation of Austro-German Criminological Debates." *Cultural and Social History* 3:406–23.

Walker, Samuel. 1980. *Popular Justice: A History of American Criminal Justice*. New York: Oxford University Press.

Wiener, Martin. 2004. *Men of Blood: Violence, Manliness and Criminal Justice in Victorian England*. Cambridge: Cambridge University Press.

Williams, Chris A. 2011. *Police and Policing in the Twentieth Century*. Farnham, UK: Ashgate.

Zedner, Lucia. 1991. *Women, Crime and Custody in Victorian England*. Oxford: Oxford University Press.

PART ONE

HISTORIANS,
INTERPRETATIONS,
METHODOLOGIES

CHAPTER 1

......

THE HISTORIOGRAPHY OF CRIME AND CRIMINAL JUSTICE

......

PAUL LAWRENCE

INTRODUCTION

> If some fairy gave me the power of seeing a scene of one and the same
> kind in every age of history . . . I would choose . . . a trial for murder,
> because I think that it would give me so many hints as to a multitude of
> matters of the first importance.
>
> —Frederic Maitland, *Collected Papers of
> Frederic William Maitland*, Vol. 3

POPULAR interest in noteworthy crimes of the past, particularly violent ones, is peren-
nial. Debates about crime rates—and whether they are going up or down in comparison
with the past—have been staple aspects of public life since at least the early nineteenth
century. However, criminal justice history as a specialist field of academic endeavor is
of relatively recent advent in the United Kingdom, as elsewhere in Europe. As Clive
Emsley, one of the pioneers of the field, has noted, "in 1975, the history of crime, criminal justice, penal policy and penal institutions . . . was a subject scarcely explored by
academics" (2005, p. 2). This essay does not seek to provide a comprehensive, chronological, or bibliographical summary of the development of the field. There have been
various perceptive overviews during the last twenty years (Innes & Styles 1986; Emsley
1996; King 1999; Emsley 2005; Smith 2007; Williams 2008a; Churchill 2014), but inevitably, these become dated over time, and the field is now so large that an attempt to
consider all works would be impossible. Instead, this essay argues that it is possible to
trace the development of four conceptual approaches to the writing of criminal justice
history and examines the main contours of these different ways of studying crime and

its control in the past. Some reference will be made to works focused on other European countries, but, in the main, this overview will concentrate on the literature devoted to the United Kingdom, where (arguably) the historiography is the most mature.

It will be posited that four distinct ways of writing criminal justice history (positivist/empirical, theoretical, social, and cultural) developed broadly consecutively over the course of the twentieth century. These did not necessarily develop in a linear fashion, with earlier approaches being superseded by later ones and a single approach to the topic being generally accepted at any given point in time. Rather, all four can be seen to have overlapped and intertwined to form a diverse but mature and methodologically sophisticated field of endeavor. The development of these four stages in the writing of criminal justice history map fairly closely onto developments in the field of history—and to some extent criminology—more broadly. While this framing environment cannot be discussed in detail, key points of contact will be outlined as appropriate. Overall, the broad thrust of the essay is an attempt to explain why particular types of crime and criminal justice history have been written at particular times and places, and how these have then gone on to influence subsequent works in the field. The full range of methods, approaches, and topics within the field are, of course, discussed in much greater detail in the essays that follow this one.

The essay is divided into five sections. The first covers early forays into criminal justice history by both historians and criminologists during the first half of the twentieth century. It argues that these first works were primarily positivist/empirical, in that authors often viewed the sources they drew on as largely unproblematic reflections of social reality and wrote from a standpoint of belief in the superiority of contemporary forms of crime control. The second section shows how these positivist/empirical approaches were challenged during the 1960s and 1970s by more theory-driven accounts of criminal justice history that sought to link changes in crime and criminal justice to the development of the modern state. While, ultimately, this new wave of research did not lead to the development of a field underpinned by theory and its exposition, it had a lasting influence in directing criminal justice historians' gaze toward the state and the exercise of its power to watch and punish.

The third section views the expansionist period of modern criminal justice history, the later 1970s and 1980s, as profoundly influenced by the research agendas of left-wing social history. While the legacy of empirical and theoretical approaches remained, much new research was prompted by a desire to understand the lived experience of ordinary citizens—whether criminals, victims, police officers, court officials, or the general public—and to elaborate and challenge prior notions of the primacy of the state in the field of crime control. The fourth section characterizes a set of more recent work since the 1990s as primarily informed by a "cultural" history approach. Crime is often viewed in this work as a social construct, rather than a self-evident and coherent category of social action. Such research has focused on, *inter alia*, topics such as the role of the press and other media in the "construction" of crime, changing notions of crime and criminals over time, and the influence on "crime" of changing cultural norms related to masculinity, femininity, and honor.

The final section of the essay sets out recent developments in the field. It traces the evolution of historical criminology but argues that the fields of history and criminology remain divergent in the ways in which they seek to narrate the past. It also discusses the increasing influence of large-scale digitization projects in the field, identifies underresearched areas, and posits some new avenues for research. Throughout, the essay seeks to make links to broader developments in the fields of criminology and history, and to highlight how debates about crime and its control are primarily debates about power and its distribution within societies over time. The references given refer to exemplars of the particular trends and approaches discussed, rather than to the totality of works on a particular topic.

I. Positivist/Empiricist Approaches to Criminal Justice History

While Gatrell has questioned whether a "crime problem"—as a general category of public debate—really existed before the later eighteenth century (1990, p. 248), it is certainly true that there is a centuries-old tradition of writing about past crimes in morality tales intended to encourage social cohesion and good conduct. This tradition continued into the early nineteenth century, and in one sense newspapers as they developed in that period might be viewed as providing "histories" of specific crimes. Certainly, the print media can be read as a conceptual space for public reflection on crime and its control, an exercise often carried out through the use of examples from the past (Lemmings 2012). However, narratives of crime written prior to the early nineteenth century tended to be based on singular events, and were not attempts to conceptualize and analyze "crime" *sui generis*. Moreover, although criminal and judicial statistics began to be recorded during the early part of the nineteenth century, other records, such as written police and court records, were much more limited. The bureaucracy associated with contemporary crime control did not yet exist, and, of course, criminals tended not to keep tidy sets of written records. Hence, extant writing addressing crime trends over time and developments in the administration of justice was often anecdotal, or based on personal opinion and very limited data (Colquhoun 1800).

Crime and its control had undoubtedly become a key feature of parliamentary and public debate by the early nineteenth century (Dodsworth 2014), but it was not until toward the end of the century that academic research and publication on aspects of crime and criminal justice history began. Early works tended to draw heavily on official sources such as government statistics and House of Commons reports. These were often used in an uncritical fashion, and data that now appear crude and partial were seen as conclusive and unproblematic. Many publications were also imbued with the notion of "progress" from a chaotic, unregulated past to a controlled and orderly present. Legal historians were among the first to trace, in this empirical and positivist fashion, the development of state efforts to delineate and control crime (Stephens 1883; Maitland 1911; Holdsworth 1903–1938). While legal history is now vastly more sophisticated, and many historians have also written about the legal system, debates do still remain as to whether the contemporary proponents of "black letter" legal history (focussed primarily on the development of laws and legal processes) give sufficient weight to the social context within which the law operates (Charlesworth 2007).

Early criminal justice historians, too, often implicitly accepted and reproduced the narratives presented in government sources, which identified rising crime and disorder in the latter part of the eighteenth century and gradual improvements in crime control ever since. Charles Reith, for example, argued that orderliness was "almost non-existent" in London in the eighteenth century and that it was an "unquestionable historical fact" that it was only the "successful establishment of the police institution" that remedied this situation (1943, p. 3). Other writers wrote in a similar vein. T. A. Critchley, for example, concurred that there had been a danger of "a total relapse into barbarity" at the start of the nineteenth century, which was only averted by effective police reformers (1967, p. 22). While now seen as crude and partial, the tendency of early works such as these to focus on official processes and structures when writing the history of crime and policing, and to see this history as an unproblematic process of improvement and progress, did shape the field in the early years. Such a viewpoint is perhaps unsurprising given that many writers were themselves involved in the official administration of criminal justice. Critchley, for example, was a Home Office civil servant, as was Jenifer Hart in her early career (1955).

The pioneers of interwar criminology, too, often took a similar empirical, positivist approach to criminal justice history. Leon Radzinowicz's first project, for example, after arriving at Cambridge University at the end of the 1930s, was an analysis of the nineteenth-century "Blue Books" (government compilations of largely statistical information) in relation to the evolution of criminal justice policy in England. He believed this historical approach was "vital" for anyone wishing to analyze "English penal thought, legislation and policy" (Radzinowicz 1999, p. 156). Radzinowicz's labors eventually resulted in his mammoth five-volume history of the English criminal justice system from 1750 to the present (1948–1986). Clearly, the direct "use" of history to explain the present and inform future policy was not conceived of as problematic within criminology at the time, and other pioneering criminologists were also open to such approaches. On arriving at the London School of Economics—also during the later 1930s—Hermann Mannheim gave a course of lectures that considered the aims and history of punishment (Rock 1988, p. xviii). Also adopting this approach was Max Grünhut, whose opus *Penal Reform* (1948) was a historical and comparative study of penal thinking and policy extending over 150 years. In clear contrast to the preexisting medical/penal approaches to criminology present in the United Kingdom at the time (Garland 1988), all three of these pioneering interwar criminologists shared the belief that discussions of contemporary policy and institutions could and should be informed by a consideration of the historical conditions out of which they had grown.

While Smith (2007, p. 607) has argued, convincingly, that Radzinowicz's work was far more sophisticated than that of Reith, Critchley, and other early police historians, early historical criminology nonetheless shared with the works of these authors a desire to trace a rational process of progressive "reform" within the administration of criminal justice. It is this aim, alongside the focus on official processes and structures, and the predominant use of official sources and data, that leads to the characterization of the major works of criminal justice history of the early part of the twentieth century—and beyond in some cases—as positivist/empirical.

One facet of the use of official sources that characterized these early works was a reliance on government statistics of crime, and a desire to trace levels of crime over time has been an enduring preoccupation of criminal justice historians ever since. As Emsley (2004, p. 21) has noted, "many of the key questions, certainly many of the most popular questions about crime, are quantitative. How much was there? Was it increasing or decreasing? Which types of crime were most prevalent at particular periods or in particular places?" In fact, the validity—or otherwise—of criminal and judicial statistics is a topic that has generated significant debate among historians adopting empirical approaches to criminal justice history. While early proponents had, as already discussed, a tendency to use official statistics uncritically, a range of approaches has been adopted since then. Williams delineates three basic positions (2008a). Some authors have taken a "positivist" approach, believing that while there are significant problems with historical crime statistics, they can nonetheless on some occasions be indicative of trends in actual crime over time (Gatrell & Hadden 1972). Others have taken what Williams labels an "interactionist" approach, arguing that while crime statistics cannot reveal anything of actual rates of offending, they are a good guide to activity within the criminal justice system, as well as indicative of some of the deeper structural factors influencing offending (Beattie 1986). Finally, some authors have taken a "pessimistic" view, claiming that historical crime statistics are entirely useless. Taylor (1998), for example, has argued that such statistics were even on occasion entirely fabricated for political reasons. While this claim has been critiqued (Morris 2001), it remains true to say that criminal justice historians have, at best, an ambiguous relationship with statistics. That said, statistics are employed extensively at times, particularly in studies of violence and violent crime over the *longue durée* (Eisner 2003; Spierenburg 2008), and their use in many works is aligned with the positivist/empirical belief that they can, if used with caution, reveal something about actual practices of offending in the past.

Overall, while early works of criminal justice history were few in number, their foundational influence was long felt. Their primary focus on the development of official structures of criminal justice and their use of government sources in a highly empirical—and, at times, uncritical—manner remained the dominant approach for decades. And when a new approach to criminal justice history did develop, it defined itself in outright opposition to this first mode of research and writing.

II. Theoretical Perspectives

Starting in the mid-twentieth century, a number of theoretical analyses of policing and criminal justice emerged, many written from a Marxist perspective. Georg Rusche and Otto Kirchheimer's *Punishment and Social Structure* (1939) is a significant starting point, as it was to become highly influential in the later development of both criminal justice history and radical criminology. Essentially, they provided one of the first structuralist interpretations of punishment, arguing that forms of punishment are determined by the means of production prevailing in a given historical epoch. In this model, punishment—and, by implication, policing—is seen as a tool of class domination, its form changing in different epochs, but always directed primarily against the economically dispossessed. The book was "largely ignored for 30 years" (Garland 1990, p. 106), but in the later 1960s it became widely known and influential. While it has been critiqued for historical inaccuracies and for being overly reductive, it undoubtedly heralded a wave of theoretically inspired analyses of criminal justice history.

Alan Silver (1967), for example, argued that the modern police were introduced primarily to relieve elites within society of their customary duties in relation to policing and justice. Rather than the personal, customary authority of the premodern era, in the "policed society" of the capitalist age control of the populace became, of necessity, bureaucratic, diffuse, and hence more efficient. Similarly, Spitzer and Scull agreed that it was the rise of capitalist market relations in the early nineteenth century that led to the management of crime being "rationalised and transformed into a responsibility of the state" (1977, p. 281). Raeff, too, focused on the role of elites and the state in creating the institutional prerequisites for the transition to modern forms of justice (1975; 1983).

Perhaps the most influential proponent of the theory that the rise of the modern state necessitated a wholesale transformation in the administration of justice has been Michel Foucault (1975). Foucault's work is hard to summarize, but his central concern is with power. Where Rusche and Kirchheimer related criminal justice to modes of economic production, Foucault linked it to changing forms of government. In early modern absolutist forms of government, the king had absolute power over his subjects and demonstrated this "ownership" visibly via gruesome punishment of the body. In the new nation-states of the nineteenth century, the individual, Foucault argued, was the property of society as a whole, and hence punishments such as the prison were designed not to damage individuals but to retain their economic productivity. For Foucault, in the new, bureaucratic criminal justice mechanisms, power rested not with individuals, but within institutions and their abstract knowledge. Or, as he put it, "power . . . is not possessed as a thing, or transferred as a property; it functions like a piece of machinery. . . . It is the apparatus as a whole that produces 'power'" (1975, p. 177).

Foucault's work has been inspirational to many subsequent analyses of criminal justice history. Michael Ignatieff, for example, drew extensively on it in his analysis of the nineteenth-century prison, tracing a new desire to discipline both mind and body, and for the state to reserve to itself the prerogative to punish workers (1978). That said, Foucault's theories have also been critiqued extensively. Ignatieff himself revised his own earlier work significantly (1983), and Spierenburg (1991), *inter alia*, has pointed out that Foucault, because he produced his theory without recourse to archival sources, is wrong in dating the birth of the prison primarily to the nineteenth century. Many authors have observed that while Foucault does describe transformations in the administration of criminal justice well, he does not really provide a particularly convincing explanation of them.

Thus, as Williams (2008a, p. 35) notes, "Foucault's impact ... has been paradoxical: his work generated much fruitful research, but the outcome of this was largely critical of his central arguments about changing penal practice." That said, the theoretical work of Foucault and others in turn led to further works of criminal justice history that, while not primarily "theoretical" per se, certainly drew on the notion of a long-term shift away from community sanctions toward "official" modes of criminal justice administration that were coincident with the rise of the modern state and a capitalist mode of production (Gatrell, Lenman, & Parker 1980). The conceptual dichotomy of premodern/modern and customary/bureaucratic modes of criminal justice is a legacy of early theory that has only recently begun to be dismantled.

Of course, not all structuralist approaches to the study of criminal justice history have been Marxist-inspired, or even written from a left-wing perspective. Another influential work of theory, also published in the same year as Rusche and Kirchheimer's (1939) and also not gaining maximum influence until its publication in English decades later, was Norbert Elias's *The Civilising Process* (1969). Elias did not write explicitly about crime per se, but rather about the way in which, starting within the medieval court and with the evolution of courtly etiquette, European standards regarding violence, manners, and speech all were modified by changing thresholds of shame and repugnance, that is, mental and physical aversion to certain types of actions. He argued that, as the state became the only legitimate source of power and authority over a territory and became stable—as happened in Europe in the late seventeenth and early eighteenth centuries— citizens developed modes of behavior that assisted in the formation of a capitalistic economy. For example, because they increasingly had to interact socially and commercially with strangers, they developed agreed understandings of how to behave and less aggressive ways of settling disputes—usually bringing in new state agencies such as the police or taking civil action in the courts. Elias's work has been extensively critiqued (Schwerhoff 2002) but has also inspired many subsequent authors, particularly those interested in the study of criminal violence, such as Spierenburg (1998), Eisner (2003), and Wood (2004).

A more recent theoretical perspective, evolutionary psychology, has also had an impact on criminal justice history, again particularly on those studying violent crime. Essentially, proponents of evolutionary psychology argue that some aspects of modern behavior are patterned by evolution rather than being culturally specific. The potential advantages of this view to the study of criminal justice history having been outlined by Wood (2007), some historians have now begun to investigate the possibility that elements of criminal behavior that appear relatively constant over time (e.g., the frequency with which young men commit impulsive violent acts) might be in some ways patterned by evolution. Randolph Roth (2012), for example, in examining historical murder rates in the United States, has claimed that when people are discontented with the society in which they live—as demonstrated by political discontent—levels of violence go up. For Roth, evolutionary psychology provides the key to understanding this correlation. Under supportive environmental circumstances, biological processes promote thought and behavior characterized by trust and cooperation. By contrast, low levels of political legitimacy—interpreted by individuals as adverse environmental circumstances—prompt a tendency toward anger, retaliation, and aggression. While still controversial, work drawing on evolutionary theory to help explain patterns of criminal violence is opening up interesting new avenues of research.

Overall, the theoretical/structuralist approaches to the history of crime and criminal justice that were first developed during the 1960s and 1970s provided a useful correction to the optimism and naïveté of prior positivist/empiricist approaches. However, it is true to say that criminal justice history has firmly resisted any movement toward becoming a heavily "theorized" discipline. Some authors, as noted, have fruitfully taken particular theoretical standpoints as helpful starting points for more archival or empirical studies, but the majority of scholars working in the field today only sparsely engage with any of the major theoretical perspectives discussed previously. That is not to say, however, that these works have had no impact on the field. What they have undoubtedly imparted is a general awareness of power and its uneven social distribution as a key theme to be considered when studying the construction and control of "crime." This theme was developed extensively by the next wave of criminal justice historians, as described in the next section.

III. Crime History as a Subset of Social History

During the 1970s, a group of historians including Edward Thompson (known as the "Warwick School") conceived of a new form of social history that aimed to write "history from below," addressing the lived experience of the working class. Some of the scholars involved in this project—Thompson himself, but also Christopher Hill and Eric Hobsbawm—had previously been part of the Communist Party Historians Group (c. 1946–1956), but by the 1970s the main legacy of this Marxist background was a view of class and class struggle as central to an analysis of eighteenth-century society. Many within the Warwick School, drawing on Thompson's aim to rescue the working class from "the enormous condescension of posterity" (1963, p. 12), came to view the criminal justice system as an arena for the exercise and negotiation of class power within society. Their research did not aim to substantiate or develop particular theoretical models, however, and was on occasion avowedly antitheoretical. In this, they mirrored the thinking of many within the historical profession opposed to the ascendancy of sociology as a university discipline during the period (Elton 1977). Rather, they sought to move away from earlier political and economic approaches to the study of history, to focus on everyday life and the detailed workings of social relations on a daily basis.

This new wave of criminal justice history was focused initially on the eighteenth century, and it resulted in a series of debates as to whether the criminal courts functioned primarily as a mechanism of elite power. Douglas Hay (1976) initially argued that the assize courts combined terror and the discretionary use of mercy so as to preserve elite hegemony, but this position was soon challenged by Brewer and Styles, who maintained that the law and the courts were in fact "a multiple-use right available to most Englishmen" (1980, p. 20). John Langbein too (1983) asserted that a wide range of social groups used the law to gain redress during the later eighteenth century, and other works on this theme combined to underline the picture of the law as a multi-use right. While the framing of criminal laws and the daily operation of the courts were certainly weighted in favor of the elites within society who were most closely involved in its administration, the law was available to the lower orders in a multitude of ways. King (2000), for example, has demonstrated convincingly how poorer citizens could subvert the legal system in imaginative ways—initiating cases but not turning up to court, for example, thus putting the accused to considerable expense and inconvenience. The lower (magistrates') courts were also often used for conflict resolution on a daily basis by the poorer members of society in London and elsewhere (Davis 1984).

Recent studies on the workings of the court system, and on the law more broadly, has also been done using a primarily social history approach. The summary (lower) courts and their role in the regulation of local daily life since the 1750s have been explored in great detail (Shoemaker 1991; King 2004; Gray 2009), with authors concluding that they were the main context in which eighteenth-century Britons encountered the legal power of the state—and tested its limits. Equally, scholars of legal history have sought to show how legal concerns and procedures came to permeate eighteenth-century society (Landau 2005). Even research conducted by those working primarily in a legal studies context came to no longer be divorced from social context. Scholarly analysis of the presumption of innocence in the English legal system, for example, still demonstrated—if *en passant*—the extent to which the courts' implementation of particular trial processes impacted upon the daily life of the lower classes (Smith 2005, pp. 149–54).

Likewise, scholars working on the history of punishment also turned away during this period from interpretations based either on the notion of progressive humanitarianism/professionalization or on reductive theories of control. While some were focused more on the history of institutions and policy (e.g., McConville 1981) others sought to debate the social aspects of punishment, investigating how it was understood and interpreted by those administering and observing it (Gatrell 1994; McGowen 1994; Wiener 1994). More recently, a micro-historical social history approach has been apparent in studies of the prison (Brown 2003) and of transportation (Anderson 2007).

Criminal justice historians who began to apply a social history approach to the study of the police were initially focused more on the nineteenth century than the eighteenth. Earlier, reductive histories of the police were quickly dismissed (Robinson 1979), and authors took up the theme of the impact of a changing criminal justice system—and particularly the advent of the "New Police"—on the daily life of the working classes. Robert Storch, for example, argued that the New Police "had a broader mission in the nineteenth century . . . to act as an all-purpose lever of urban discipline" (1976, p. 481). In a detailed study of working-class life in the north of England, he concluded that the police came to act as "domestic missionaries," involved in the regulation of a host of noncriminal activities ranging from street trading to fairs, from the operation of common lodging houses to licensing. Others took up this theme, also concluding that the nineteenth century witnessed the construction of a "policeman-state" that allowed "better off people to discipline their inferiors" (Gatrell 1990, p. 258).

As with the work on the courts outlined previously, however, this overtly class-based analysis quickly became more nuanced, with later authors stressing how the broad aims of reformers and elites were always tempered by the practical constraints of enforcing laws on the ground (Emsley 1987; 1991). For example, most nineteenth-century police officers had working-class backgrounds, and hence had a degree of sympathy and tolerance for those living in the poorer areas they often policed, a fact that necessarily infused their use of discretion in deciding who to arrest and which elements of legislation to enforce rigorously (Lawrence 2004). Such foci were also apparent in work published elsewhere in Europe (see, e.g., Berlière 2008). Policing in the nineteenth century thus also came to be seen as a multi-use right—weighted in favor of elites but available to all but the poorest within society.

Since the 1990s, the basic contours of police history have continued to be fleshed out, usually drawing on a broad social history approach. A focus on everyday policing, informed by detailed local studies grounded in time and place, has been prevalent. The false divide between "old" and "new" forms of policing—with the old parish constable system seen as inefficient and amateur and the new police forces set up in the nineteenth century viewed as effective and professional—has been convincingly dismantled (Reynolds 1998; Beattie 2012). A new focus on eighteenth-century policing has also become apparent in work focused on other European countries (Denys 2002; Milliot 2011). Equally, the existence of private forms of policing has been elaborated (Godfrey 2002), and other nonstate forms of conflict resolution have also been explored (McGowen 2005; Locker 2005). A social history approach can also be seen in the rich research on the police as an employer (Shpayer-Makov 2002) and on the lived reality of working as a police officer (Weinberger 1995; Klein 2010). Even those studying the upper levels of the police service have tended to locate their subjects firmly within the local social structures in which they operated (Wall 1998).

Overall, the "social history" approach to criminal justice history has sought to combine a recognition of the significance of top-down, state reform processes with detailed archival work exposing the complex mechanisms of resistance, accommodation, and acceptance that are apparent in local studies of crime and its control. Underpinning all such works is the belief that through detailed archival work the historian can both reconstitute the impact of criminal justice processes on daily life and lived experience and uncover something of the functioning of society as a whole. The flow of power, the construction of authority, the nature of interpersonal relations, and the agency of those often presumed powerless are all key themes that have been taken up by authors adopting this approach to criminal justice history.

IV. Cultural Approaches to Criminal Justice History

In many ways the questions about the empirical, historical method that were raised by postmodernism during the final quarter of the twentieth century were met with "rank indifference rather than outright hostility" in much of the historical profession (Joyce & Kelly 1991, p. 205). Certainly, the field of criminal justice history was largely untouched by the vicissitudes of the postmodernist challenge. That said, it is possible to discern, from the 1990s onward, a new approach to the writing of criminal justice history, one concerned very much with the notion of crime as a constructed social and cultural discourse. Of course, criminal justice historians had recognized for some decades that "crime" was not a self-evident category of behavior and regulation, but rather a cultural classification that changed and shifted according to prevailing social norms. The notion of "social crime"—wherein some actions defined as illegal actually enjoy considerable popular support—had been debated since the 1960s (Hobsbawm 1969).

However, a more avowedly cultural approach to the study of criminal justice history has become apparent over the last two decades. While not replacing the prevalent social history approach, three new foci of interest can be identified. Some historians have sought to investigate the cultural construction of notions of crime and criminality, studying how perceptions of gender, class, and ethnicity have shaped the way in which certain behaviors have typically been explained and regulated. Others have looked at how long-term changes in cultural norms surrounding concepts such as honor have impacted the perception and incidence of some potentially criminal behaviors. Finally, a number of recent studies have considered the historical role of the media (particularly newspapers) in the construction of public knowledge about crime.

Turning first to consider works that have addressed the culturally constructed nature of crime and criminals, a number of authors have provided historical analyses of the phenomena we now term "moral panics" (Davis 1980; Pearson 1983; King 2003). This work has convincingly revealed the cultural mechanisms through which intense public concern over relatively minor threats can lead to swift—but usually ineffective—legislative change. Further work on "social crime" has highlighted how changing definitions of private property, particularly in the workplace, also fed into notions of what constituted criminal behavior (Rule 1997; Godfrey 1999), although some such work has found that the notion of "social" crime is far more problematic than initially thought (Archer 1999). In a similar vein, many historians have been interested in the historical evolution of notions of middle-class or white-collar crime, demonstrating how certain forms of criminal behavior commonly went entirely unregarded during the nineteenth century, as their perpetrators did not match prevailing cultural stereotypes of criminals (Sindall 1983; Robb 2002). Alongside this, however, other work has shown a remarkable continuity of focus on the poorer members of society as a criminal, or at least problematic, "underclass" (Welshman 2005). Overall, such cultural approaches to the study of crime have helped highlight further ways in which, as a category of social behavior, "criminality" is always contingent and evolving rather than self-evident and perpetual.

Building on this type of research, a particularly rich theme in cultural criminal justice history has been the study of gender and crime. Historians have considered why adult men have been the primary concern of the criminal justice system, questioning whether this could really have been due to a persistent lack of criminal behavior among the female population. Adopting the notion of "separate spheres"—the idea that during industrialization women and men became separated both spatially and culturally, with women more likely to remain within the home and men more likely to be active in professional and public spaces—some have argued that these broader social changes could explain "the vanishing female" (Feeley & Little 1991). Others, however, have been more interested in the cultural aspects of this posited "disappearance" from the criminal statistics. Zedner (1991), for example, argued that during the nineteenth century certain categories of female action came to be seen culturally as properly belonging to the medical sphere rather than the criminal. Conversely, there has also been work considering why women have been particularly associated with certain types of crimes. Poisoning, for example, was viewed in the nineteenth century as a quintessentially "female" offense (Watson 2004). The culturally constructed associations made between women and sexual danger/deviance during the nineteenth century have also been explored in interesting ways (Walkowitz 1992; D'Cruze 1998; D'Cruze & Jackson 2009).

Obviously, work on gender and crime has not solely focused on women. Wiener, for example, has argued that the prevalence of the notion that there were separate spheres of action for men and women had the effect of criminalizing certain forms of male violence (2004). In his view, the development of cultural stereotypes of the innocence or weakness of women led in turn to more severe sentences for men who injured and killed women. By contrast, Ballinger (2000) has argued that many women convicted and executed for murder were denied clemency precisely because they too had broken the cultural norms attached to notions of femininity/masculinity. More broadly, there have been a number of surveys looking at how the changing social construction of masculinity—in particular the appropriateness or otherwise of interpersonal violence between men—may have affected both perceptions and incidence of violent crime (Shoemaker 2001; Wood 2004; Emsley 2007). A developing strand of work has considered how violence in fact infused many aspects of popular culture during the Victorian period (Crone 2012).

Compared to this work on gender and crime, there has been limited research into ethnicity as a culturally dependent categorization important to the study of crime and criminal justice. Significant work on the Irish in England—the largest immigrant group during the nineteenth century—has shown how popular cultural perceptions of migrant Irish workers as prone to drinking and fighting led inevitably to their overrepresentation in crime statistics (King 2013). There has also been some historical work on the cultural aspects of racial bias in twentieth-century policing (Whitfield 2004), but relatively little else has been done on the impact of constructions of ethnicity on the criminal justice systems of the nineteenth and early twentieth centuries.

A final strand of the recent cultural approach to criminal justice history is typified by a tranche of works considering the role of the press and other media in the cultural construction of criminality. This work covers a broad sweep of time, demonstrating interesting continuities in press agendas across the centuries. It has been argued, for example, that the shift from published trial reports to early newspaper coverage of crime at the end of the eighteenth century was associated with, and reinforced, a growing tendency to see crime as the preserve of a distinct "criminal class," rather than as an unfortunate temptation to which any citizen could fall prey (Devereaux 2007; Shoemaker 2008). Ward (2014) concurs with this contention, but has also argued that the press during this period generally sought to reinforce a positive view of the role of the criminal justice system for public consumption. During the nineteenth century, press coverage of crime news grew enormously, but historians have debated the significance of this growth. Snell (2007), for example, has argued that newspapers had a significant influence on readers' perceptions of crime and criminality, while King (2007) has claimed that nineteenth-century press narratives were too contradictory to have significant influence on perceptions of crime at a population level.

Turning to the twentieth century, very interesting work has been done tracing the development of sensationalist press coverage of crimes involving women during the interwar period (Wood 2012; Wood 2014). Wood has concluded that the 1930s was a formative period in the making of the modern popular press and that "human interest" crime-related narratives were a key element in this process. Wood has also looked at how particular cultural tropes—the phrase "the third degree" in relation to police interrogation techniques, for example—gained cultural purchase and currency during this time (2010). Not all work on the cultural construction of crime has been related to the press, of course. There have also been important studies of topics as varied as the early development of the "idea" of the police (Dodsworth 2008; Dodsworth 2014) and the significance of crime fiction in shaping public perceptions of criminal justice (Shpayer-Makov 2011). Such trends can also be identified in a European context (Müller 2005; Kalifa 2005; Kalifa 2013). Overall, cultural approaches to the study of criminal justice history have always remained anchored in an empirical source base and a desire to uncover and situate the cultural as an aspect of the social. That said, this recent approach has contributed to the field a sophisticated analysis of the cultural bases of perceptions of crime and criminality, and an awareness of the contingency of these during any given historical period.

V. Recent Trends

In the early twenty-first century, three emergent trends are apparent in the field of criminal justice history. Historical criminology (research at the interface between history and sociological criminology) has been a topic of considerable interest. Large digitization and record linkage projects are generating both an enthusiasm for quantitative studies and new possibilities for qualitative work. Finally, criminal justice historians who have spent decades elaborating state systems for crime control and punishment are now working hard to show how these systems blur, and interface at the edges, into informal and semiformal mechanisms of social ordering.

For much of the twentieth century, research into the history of crime by historians and by sociologically trained criminologists was often—despite congruence in subject matter and sources—conducted and published separately. There were occasional calls for a closer working relationship (Davies & Pearson 1999), but relatively little work genuinely mixed the approaches of the two disciplines (Lawrence 2012). That said, recent works have sought to set out the advantages of "historical criminology" (Bosworth 2001; Knepper & Scicluna 2010), and there is evidence of growing interest in collaborative work across the disciplines. It might be argued that criminologists are increasingly looking to the past to answer questions about the present (Zedner 2006; Loader 2006), realizing, perhaps, that the 1950s—the starting point for many traditional analyses—are actually an atypical point in the long-term history of crime and its control. Historians, too, have been moving their research further into the twentieth century (Williams 2014) and seeking increasingly to answer contemporary questions using data from the past.

The early twenty-first century has also seen the large-scale digitization of archival records pertaining to criminal justice history (Crone 2009). The Old Bailey Online 1674–1913 was the first of these, providing a digitized and enhanced version of the printed court transcripts of London's main criminal court from this period. The database enabled online searches of particular words and phrases, or using a variety of variables, and performed certain statistical functions automatically on request. More recently, London Lives 1690–1800 has extended the same approach, linking a variety of different preexisting datasets to provide online access to some 250,000 archival and printed records from eight London archives, many related to the history of criminal justice. The Digital Panopticon project is currently attempting to bring together online a range of records pertaining to the roughly 90,000 individuals sentenced at the Old Bailey between 1780 and 1875. Even digital humanities projects that are not focused on crime and its control can contain much relevant data. The 19th Century British Library Newspapers and John Johnson Collection of Printed Ephemera collections also contain much of interest to criminal justice historians, with the latter having recently created a "Crime, Murders and Executions" section.

In some ways, of course, these new digital resources enable historians to conduct research in innovative ways—tracking individuals as they move through a series of engagements with different institutions of justice and control, for example—that were only previously possible by serendipity, given the extent of the records to be surveyed. Large datasets also enable the easy counting of offenders and crimes. But, on the other hand, it is not clear at this point whether these resources will actually lead to new modes of research, or if they will simply enable more or quicker research in the current mode. There is the possibility that these sophisticated search tools will lead historians to neglect the need to research their sources rigorously. The Central Criminal Court (which the Old Bailey became in 1834) was very different from its predecessor in terms of operation and catchment area. A digital interface can make source comparison easy, but knowledge of what is being counted, analyzed, or compared remains vital. These projects also, of course, have the potential to direct researchers' gazes back to London, where the large datasets are focused, just at a time when many have been realizing how little is known of criminal justice in rural and peripheral areas. Their potential is incredible, but their impact is only just being seen.

A final trend perhaps becoming apparent is a move to see crime and its control as part of a much broader field of social regulation (Churchill 2014). There has been, for example, debate over the extent to which private forms of policing have always coexisted alongside state processes (Zedner 2006; Williams 2008b). The historical development of the concept of "security," and the development of the modern security industry alongside official law and order mechanisms, has also begun to receive scrutiny (Moss 2011; Churchill 2015).

Overall, the discipline of criminal justice history has developed over the course of a century into a mature and vibrant academic community. All four of the different approaches outlined in this essay are currently in use in blended form, and the discipline today is characterized by its firm rejection of any single methodology. There is much research as yet undone. The early modern period remains underexamined, and there has been a tendency to privilege major towns and cities in research over rural and peripheral areas. This essay has concentrated on English-language research, but, of course, there has been significant work in other national contexts, particularly in Europe (Rousseaux 1993; Reinke 2009). A key next step for the field will be to build on early work by adopting a comparative approach that spans borders (Knepper 2011). That said, it is now impossible to write convincingly about crime and its control in the present without some awareness of the past, and the field has proved beyond doubt that both the definition of crime and the mechanisms of its control are always intricately bound up in the exercise of power. Evaluating this intimate connection will remain central to our understanding of modern states and modern societies.

REFERENCES

Anderson, Clare. 2007. "Sepoys, Servants and Settlers: Convict Transportation in the Indian Ocean, 1787–1945." In *Cultures of Confinement: The Prison in Global Perspective*, ed. Frank Dikötter & Ian Brown, 185–220. Ithaca, NY: Cornell University Press.

Archer, John. 1999. "Poacher Gangs and Violence: The Urban-Rural Divide in Nineteenth-Century Lancashire." *British Journal of Criminology* 39 (1): 25–38.

Ballinger, Anette. 2000. *Dead Woman Walking*. Dartmouth, UK: Ashgate.

Beattie, John. 1986. *Crime and the Courts in England, 1660–1800*. Oxford: Clarendon Press.

Beattie, John. 2012. *The First English Detectives. The Bow Street Runners and the Police of London, 1750–1840*. Oxford: Oxford University Press.

Berlière, Jean-Marc, Catherine Denys, Dominique Kalifa, & Vincent Milliot. 2008. *Métiers de police. Être policier en Europe, XIVIIIe–XXe siècle*. Rennes, France: Presses Universitaires de Rennes.

Bosworth, Mary. 2001. "The Past as a Foreign Country? Some Methodological Implications of Doing Historical Criminology." *Theoretical Criminology* 41 (3): 431–42.

Brewer, John, & John Styles. 1980. *An Ungovernable People: The English and Their Law in the Seventeenth and Eighteenth Centuries*. London: Hutchinson.

Brown, Alyson. 2003. *English Society and the Prison*. London: Boydell Press.

Charlesworth, Lorie. 2007. "On Historical Contextualisation: Some Critical Socio-Legal Reflections." *Crimes and Misdemeanours: Deviance and the Law in Historical Perspective* 1 (1): 1–40.

Churchill, David. 2014. "Rethinking the State Monopolisation Thesis: The Historiography of Policing and Criminal Justice in Nineteenth-Century England." *Crime, History and Societies* 18 (1): 131–52.

Churchill, David. 2015. "Lock-Picking Competitions and the Emergence of the British Security Industry in the Mid-Nineteenth-Century." *History Workshop Journal* 80 (1): 52–74.

Colquhoun, Patrick. 1800. *A Treatise on the Police of the Metropolis*. London: C. Dilly.

Critchley, T. A. 1967. *A History of Police in England and Wales, 900–1966*. London: Constable.

Crone, Rosalind. 2009. "Crime and Its Fabrication: A Review of New Digital Resources in the History of Crime." *Journal of Victorian Culture* 14 (1): 125–33.

Crone, Rosalind. 2012. *Violent Victorians: Popular Entertainment in Nineteenth-Century London*. Manchester: Manchester University Press.

Davies, Andrew, & Geoffrey Pearson. 1999. "Introduction." *British Journal of Criminology* 39 (1): 1–9.

Davis, Jennifer. 1980. "The London Garrotting Panic of 1862." In *Crime and the Law: The Social History of Crime in Western Europe since 1500*, ed. Vic Gatrell, Bruce Lenman, & Geoffrey Parker, 190–214. London: Europa.

Davis, Jennifer. 1984. "A Poor Man's System of Justice? The London Police Courts in the Second Half of the Nineteenth Century." *Historical Journal* 27 (2): 309–35.

D'Cruze, Shani. 1998. *Crimes of Outrage: Sex, Violence and Victorian Working Women*. London: Routledge.

D'Cruze, Shani, & Louise Jackson. 2009. *Women, Crime and Justice in England since 1660*. London: Palgrave Macmillan.

Denys, Catherine. 2002. *Police et Sécurité au XVIIIe Siècle, dans les villes de la frontière Franco-Belge*. Paris: L'Harmattan.

Devereaux, Simon. 2007. "From Sessions to Newspapers? Criminal Trial Reporting, the Nature of Crime, and the London Press, 1770–1800." *London Journal* 32 (1): 1–27.

Dodsworth, Francis. 2008. "The Idea of Police in Eighteenth-Century England: Discipline, Reformation, Superintendence, c.1780-1800." *Journal of the History of Ideas* 69(4): 583–605.

Dodsworth, Francis. 2014. *The "Idea" of Policing*. London: Pickering and Chatto.

Eisner, Manuel. 2003. "Long-Term Historical Trends in Violent Crime." In *Crime and Justice: A Review of Research*, ed. Michael Tonry, 83–142. Chicago: University of Chicago Press.

Elias, Norbert. 1969. *The Civilising Process*. Volume 1, *The History of Manners*. Oxford: Blackwell.

Elton, Geoffrey. 1977. "Presidential Address: The Historian's Social Function." *Transactions of the Royal Historical Society* 5 (27): 197–211.

Emsley, Clive. 1987. *Crime and Society in England, 1750–1900*. London: Longman.

Emsley, Clive. 1991. *The English Police*. London: Longman.

Emsley, Clive. 1996. "Albion's Felonious Attractions: Reflections upon the History of Crime in England." In *Crime History and Histories of Crime: Studies of the Historiography of Crime and Criminal Justice in Modern History*, ed. Clive Emsley & Louis Knafla, 67–83. London: Greenwood.

Emsley, Clive. 2005. "Filling in, Adding up, Moving on: Criminal Justice History in Contemporary Britain." *Crime, History and Societies* 9 (1): 117–38.

Emsley, Clive. 2007. *The English and Violence since 1750*. London: Bloomsbury.

Feeley, Malcolm, & Deborah Little. 1991. "The Vanishing Female: The Decline of Women in the Criminal Process, 1687–1912." *Law and Society Review* 25 (4): 719–59.

Foucault, Michel. 1975. *Discipline and Punish: The Birth of the Prison*. Paris: Gallimard.

Garland, David. 1988. "British Criminology before 1935." *British Journal of Criminology* 28 (2): 1–17.

Garland, David. 1990. *Punishment and Modern Society*. Oxford: Clarendon Press.

Gatrell, Vic. 1990. "Crime, Authority and the Policeman-State." In *The Cambridge Social History of Britain*, Vol. 3, ed. Vic Gatrell, Bruce Lenman, & Geoffrey Parker, 243–310. Cambridge: Cambridge University Press.

Gatrell, Vic. 1994. *The Hanging Tree*. Oxford: Oxford University Press.

Gatrell, Vic, & T. B. Hadden. 1972. "Criminal Statistics and Their Interpretation." In *Ninteenth-Century Society: Essays in the Use of Quantitative Methods for the Study of Social Data*, ed. E. A. Wrigley, 336–96. Cambridge: Cambridge University Press.

Gatrell, Vic, Bruce Lenman, & Geoffrey Parker, eds. 1980. *Crime and the Law: A Social History of Crime in Western Europe since 1500*. London: Europa.

Godfrey, Barry. 1999. "The Impact of the Factory on Workplace Appropriate in the Nineteenth-Century." *British Journal of Criminology* 39 (1): 56–71.

Godfrey, Barry. 2002. "Private Policing and the Workplace: The Worsted Committee and the Policing of Labor in Northern England, 1840–1880." In *Policing and War in Europe*, ed. Louis A. Knafla, 87–107. Westport, CT: Greenwood Press.

Gray, Drew. 2009. *Crime, Prosecution and Social Relations: The Summary Courts of the City of London in the Late Eighteenth Century*. Basingstoke, UK: Palgrave Macmillan.

Grünhut, Max. 1948. *Penal Reform: A Comparative Study*. Oxford: Clarendon.

Hart, Jenifer. 1955. "Reform of the Borough Police." *English Historical Review* 70:411–27.

Hay, Douglas, Peter Linebaugh, John Rule, & Edward Thompson. 1976. *Albion's Fatal Tree*. London: Allen Lane.

Hobsbawm, Eric. 1969. *Bandits*. New York: Delacorte Press.

Holdsworth, William. 1903–1938. *A History of English Law*, 13 vols. London: Methuen.

Ignatieff, Michael. 1978. *A Just Measure of Pain: The Penitentiary in the Industrial Revolution, 1750–1850*. New York: Columbia University Press.

Ignatieff, Michael. 1983. "State, Civil Society and Total Institutions: A Critique of Recent Social Histories of Punishment." In *Legality, Ideology and the State*, ed. David Sugarman, 183–211. London: Academic Press.

Innes, Joanna, & John Styles. 1986. "The Crime Wave: Recent Writings on Crime and Criminal Justice in the Eighteenth Century." *Journal of British Studies* 25 (4): 380–435.

Joyce, Patrick, & Catriona Kelly. 1991. "History and Post-Modernism." *Past and Present* 133: 204–13.

Kalifa, Dominique. 2005. *Crime et culture au XIXe siècle*. Paris: Perrin.

Kalifa, Dominique. 2013. *Les Bas-Fonds. Histoire d'un imaginaire*. Paris: Éditions du Seuil.

King, Peter. 1999. "Locating Histories of Crime: A Bibliographical Study." *British Journal of Criminology* 39 (1): 161–74.

King, Peter. 2000. *Crime, Justice and Discretion in England, 1740–1820*. Oxford: Oxford University Press.

King, Peter. 2003. "Moral Panics and Violent Street Crime, 1750–2000: A Comparative Perspective." In *Comparative Histories of Crime*, ed. Clive Emsley & Barry Godfrey. Cullompton, UK: Willan.

King, Peter. 2004. "Summary Justice and Social Relations in Eighteenth-Century England." *Past and Present* 183:125–72.

King, Peter. 2007. "Newspaper Reporting and Attitudes to Crime and Justice in Late-Eighteenth- and Early-Nineteenth-Century London." *Continuity and Change* 22 (1): 73–112.

King, Peter. 2013. "Ethnicity, Prejudice, and Justice: The Treatment of the Irish at the Old Bailey, 1750–1825." *Journal of British Studies* 52 (2): 390–414.

Klein, Joanne. 2010. *Invisible Men: The Secret Lives of Police Constables in Liverpool, Manchester and Birmingham, 1900–1939*. Liverpool: Liverpool University Press.

Knepper, Paul. 2011. *International Crime in the 20th Century*. London: Palgrave.

Knepper, Paul, & Sandra Scicluna. 2010. "Historical Criminology and the Imprisonment of Women in 19th-Century Malta." *Theoretical Criminology* 14 (4): 407–24.

Landau, Norma. 2005. "Summary Conviction and the Development of the Penal Law." *Law and History Review* 23 (1): 173–89.

Langbein, John. 1983. "Albion's Fatal Flaws." *Past and Present* 98:96–120.

Lawrence, Paul. 2004. "Policing the Poor in England and France, 1850–1900." In *Social Control in Modern Europe, Volume 2, 1800–2000*, ed. Clive Emsley, Pieter Spierenburg, & Eric Johnson, 210–25. Athens: Ohio University Press.

Lawrence, Paul. 2012. "History, Criminology and the 'Use' of the Past." *Theoretical Criminology* 16 (3): 313–28.

Lemmings, David. 2012. *Crime, Courtrooms and the Public Sphere in Britain, 1700–1850*. Farnham, UK: Ashgate.

Loader, Ian. 2006. "The Fall of the 'Platonic Guardians': Liberalism, Criminology and Political Responses to Crime in England and Wales." *British Journal of Criminology* 46 (4): 561–86.

Locker, John. 2005. "Quiet Thieves, Quiet Punishment: Private Responses to the 'Respectable' Offender, c. 1850–1930." *Crime, History and Societies* 9 (1): 9–31.

Maitland, Frederic. 1911. *The Collected Papers of Frederic William Maitland, Volume 3*, ed. H. A. L. Fisher. Cambridge: Cambridge University Press.

McConville, Seán. 1981. *A History of English Prison Administration, Volume 1, 1750–1877*. London: Routledge and Kegan Paul.

McGowen, Randall. 1994. "Civilizing Punishment: The End of the Public Execution in England." *Journal of British Studies* 33:257–82.

McGowen, Randall. 2005. "The Bank of England and the Policing of Forgery, 1797–1821." *Past and Present* 186 (1): 81–116.

Milliot, Vincent. 2011. *Un policier des Lumières*. Seyssel, France: Champ Vallon.

Moss, Eloise. 2011. "Burglary Insurance and the Culture of Fear in Britain, c. 1889–1939." *Historical Journal* 54 (4): 1039–64.

Müller, Philipp. 2005. *Auf der Suche nach dem Täter: Die öffentliche Dramatisierung von Verbrechen im Berlin des Kaiserreichs*. Frankfurt am Main, Germany: Campus.

Pearson, Geoffrey. 1983. *Hooligan: A History of Respectable Fears*. Basingstoke, UK: Macmillan.

Radzinowicz, Leon. 1999. *Adventures in Criminology*. London: Routledge.

Raeff, Marc. 1975. "The Well-Ordered Police State and the Development of Modernity in Seventeeth- and Eighteenth-Century Europe: An Attempt at a Comparative Approach." *American Historical Review* 80 (5): 1221–43.

Raeff, Marc. 1983. *The Well-Ordered Police State: Social and Institutional Change Through Law in the Germanies and Russia, 1600–1800*. New Haven, CT: Yale University Press.

Reith, Charles. 1943. *The British Police and the Democratic Ideal*. London: Oxford University Press.

Reinke, Herbert. 2009. "Crime and Criminal Justice History in Germany. A Report on Recent Trends." *Crime, History and Societies* 13 (1): 117–37.

Reynolds, Elaine. 1998. *Before the Bobbies: The Night Watch and Police Reform in Metropolitan London, 1720–1830*. Basingstoke, UK: Macmillan.

Robb, George. 2002. *White-Collar Crime in Modern England: Financial Fraud and Business Morality, 1845–1929*. Cambridge: Cambridge University Press.

Robinson, Cyril D. 1979. "Ideology as History: A Look at the Way Some English Police Historians Look at the Police." *Police Studies* 2:35–49.

Rock, Paul. 1988. *A History of British Criminology*. Oxford: Oxford University Press.

Roth, Randolph. 2012. *American Homicide*. Cambridge, MA: Harvard University Press.

Rousseaux, Xavier. "Criminality and Criminal Justice History in Europe." *Criminal Justice History* 14:159–81.

Rule, John. 1997. "Social Crime in the Rural South in the Eighteenth and Nineteenth Centuries." In *Crime, Protest and Popular Politics in Southern England, 1740–1850*, ed. John Rule & Roger Wells, 153–68. London: Hambledon.

Rusche, Georg, & Otto Kirchheimer. 1939. *Punishment and Social Structure*. New York: Columbia University Press.

Schwerhoff, Gerd. 2002. "Criminalized Violence and the Process of Civilisaion: A Reappraisal." *Crime, History and Societies* 6 (2): 103–26.

Shoemaker, Robert. 1991. *Prosecution and Punishment: Petty Crime and the Law in London and Rural Middlesex, c. 1660–1725*. Cambridge: Cambridge University Press.

Shoemaker, Robert. 2001. "Male Honour and the Decline of Public Violence in Eighteenth-Century London." *Social History* 26:190–203.

Shoemaker, Robert. 2008. "The Representation of Crime and Criminal Justice in Eighteenth-Century London." *Journal of British Studies* 47:574–75.

Shpayer-Makov, Haia. 2002. *The Making of a Policeman*. Aldershot, UK: Ashgate.

Shpayer-Makov, Haia. 2011. "Revisiting the Detective Figure in Late Victorian and Edwardian Fiction: A View from the Perspective of Police History." *Law, Crime and History* 2:165–93.

Silver, Allan. 1967. "The Demand for Order in Civil Society: A Review of Some Themes in the History of Urban Crime, Police and Riot." In *The Police: Six Sociological Essays*, ed. David J. Bordua, 1–24. New York: John Wiley and Sons.

Sindall, Rob. 1983. "Middle-Class Crime in Nineteenth-Century England." *Criminal Justice History: An International Annual* 4:23–40.

Smith, Bruce. 2005. "The Presumption of Guilt and the English Law of Theft, 1750–1850." *Law and History Review* 23 (1): 133–71.

Smith, Bruce. 2007. "English Criminal Justice Administration, 1650–1850: A Historiographical Essay." *Law and History Review* 25 (3): 593–364.

Snell, Esther. 2007. "Changing Discourses of Crime: Representations of Criminality in the Eighteenth-Century Newspaper Press." *Continuity and Change* 22 (1): 13–47.

Spierenburg, Pieter. 1991. *The Prison Experience*. New Brunswick, NJ: Rutgers University Press.

Spierenburg, Pieter, ed. 1998. *Men and Violence: Gender, Honor, and Rituals in Modern Europe and America*. Columbus: Ohio State University Press.

Spierenburg, Pieter. 2008. *A History of Murder*. Cambridge: Polity Press.

Spitzer, Steven, & Andrew Scull. 1977. "Social Control in Historical Perspective: From Private to Public Responses to Crime." In *Corrections and Punishment*, ed. David F. Greenberg, 265–86. London: Sage.

Stephens, James. 1883. *A History of the Criminal Law of England*, 3 vols. London: Macmillan.

Storch, Robert. 1976. "The Policeman as Domestic Missionary: Urban Discipline and Popular Resistance in Northern England, 1840–57." *International Review of Social History* 20:61–90.

Taylor, Howard. 1998. "Rationing Crime: The Political Economy of Criminal Statistics since the 1850s." *Economic History Review* 49 (3): 569–90.

Thompson, Edward P. 1963. *The Making of the English Working Class*. London: Victor Gollanz.

Walkowitz, Judith. 1992. *City of Dreadful Delight. Narratives of Sexual Danger in Late-Victorian London*. Chicago: University of Chicago Press.

Wall, David S. 1998. *The Chief Constables of England and Wales. The Socio-Legal History of a Criminal Justice Elite*. Aldershot, UK: Ashgate.

Ward, Richard. 2014. *Print Culture, Crime and Justice in 18th-Century London*. London: Bloomsbury.

Watson, Katherine. 2004. *Poisoned Lives: English Poisoners and Their Victims*. London: Hambledon.

Weinberger, Barbara. 1995. *The Best Police in the World: An Oral History of English Policing*. Aldershot, UK: Scolar Press.

Welshman, John. 2005. *Underclass: A History of the Excluded, 1880–2000*. London: Hambledon & London.

Whitfield, James. 2004. *Unhappy Dialogue: The Metropolitan Police and Black Londoners in Post-War Britain*. Cullompton, UK: Willan.

Wiener, Martin. 1994. *Reconstructing the Criminal: Culture, Law and Policy in England, 1830–1914*. Cambridge: Cambridge University Press.

Wiener, Martin. 2004. *Men of Blood: Violence, Manliness and Criminal Justice in Victorian England*. New York: Cambridge University Press.

Williams, Chris A. 2008a. "Ideologies, Structures and Contingencies: Writing the History of British Criminal Justice since 1975." *Revue Française de Civilisation Britannique* 14 (4): 59–84.

Williams, Chris A. 2008b. "Constables for Hire: The History of Private 'Public' Policing in the UK." *Policing and Society* 18 (2): 190–205.

Williams, Chris A. 2014. *Police Control Systems in Britain, 1775–1975*. Manchester: Manchester University Press.

Wood, John C. 2004. *The Shadow of Our Refinement. Violence and Crime in Nineteenth-Century England*. New York: Routledge.

Wood, John C. 2007. "The Limits of Culture? Society, Evolutionary Psychology and the History of Violence." *Cultural and Social History* 4 (1): 95–114.

———. 2010. "'The Third Degree': Press Reporting, Crime Fiction and Police Powers in 1920s Britain." *Twentieth Century British History* 21 (4): 464–85.

———. 2012. *The Most Remarkable Woman in England: Poison, Celebrity and the Trials of Beatrice Pace*. Manchester: Manchester University Press.

———. 2014. "The Constables and the 'Garage Girl': The Police, the Press and the Case of Helene Adele." *Media History* 20 (4): 384–99.

Zedner, Lucia. 1991. *Women, Crime and Custody in Victorian England*. Oxford: Clarendon.

———. 2006. "Policing Before and After the Police: The Historical Antecedents of Contemporary Crime Control." *British Journal of Criminology* 46 (1): 78–96.

CHAPTER 2

THE CRIME HISTORIAN'S *MODI OPERANDI*

BARRY GODFREY

INTRODUCTION

"For historians the sources they exploit (whether archival, oral, or visual) *are* the methodology" (Godfrey 2011, p. 159). Sources provide data that are always mediated and manipulated in some way using a variety of methods, so the archival collection or digital recovery of data is always followed by some kind of analysis—anything else would be a simple antiquarian reproduction of historical data with little purpose. For some historians the analysis may consist simply of putting things together in their heads, and therefore they do not see any point in discussing methods. Others, especially those who have carried out their doctorates since the 1990s, may use simple quantitative analysis, even if this just means dabbling in Excel to create a database or dipping their toe into SPSS to carry out some limited quantitative inquiries. As will be discussed in this chapter, discourse and narrative analysis of one kind or another have been widely employed by researchers, and biographical methods and data-linkage projects are also now becoming mainstream methods. It is undoubtedly the case, however, that many historians are wary, disinterested, or even completely uninterested in describing and discussing the methods of inquiry that have preceded their analysis and, ultimately, have produced their research findings. The following sections may help to explain why this is the case, and, in doing so, the essay will hopefully raise a number of interesting methodological questions for us—and maybe even some fundamental questions about the integrity and utility of our everyday practices as crime historians.

This essay examines the available evidence, the repertoire of techniques, and the investigative strategies used in the study of the history of crime and criminal justice. This is a large and constantly expanding topic, of course, and, although the chapter will chart some of the major methodological approaches, reading the literature referenced within the essay will add greater depth. The essay begins by describing the sources and databases available to us, and how they have been used to shape the direction of crime history. Accordingly, we will look at how and in what ways historians have used government statistics, newspaper material, reports of commissions and visitors, legislative inquiries, and oral/autobiographical reminiscences. It will also consider the newer methodological techniques that accompany digital resources, as well as the cultural, gender, biographical, and spatial "turns" of recent years. It will then attempt to answer some questions that are rarely raised in "methods" chapters but have nonetheless remained implicit in general discussions in the historiography. A reflexive response to these questions will help us to understand how methodology relates to theory and will identify underlying philosophies about the role, capacity, and impact of crime history. For example, we can ask, Is crime history an art, or is it a science? Are crime historians attempting to paint a picture of the past that engages and entertains as well as informs the reader, or are we attempting to scientifically prove hypotheses to policymakers using historical data—and, in either case, who are our audiences for that kind of work? Are the tools that we have at our disposal sufficient for that task? Are the new sources that have emerged in the last twenty years, and the associated new ways of exploiting them, better than the traditional tools that crime historians employed in the last quarter of the twentieth century? Have biographical data-linkage methodologies and micro-histories replaced statistics? Have longitudinal or digitally enabled research methods established a new baseline, pushing large collaborative projects toward which research councils are moving more and more to eclipse the sole scholar working on one or two documents? And if they do, what will the new ways of working be? What new techniques and methodologies will need to be developed, and how will they be new and better? Last, as history and the social sciences move toward a closer relationship, will crime historians have to interact with the ethics committees and research governance systems that watch over criminological, psychological, health, and sociological research? Will standards governing ethical action toward our subjects apply to us? The next section explains the diversity of sources, methods, approaches, and philosophies that characterize crime history.

I. Two Crime Historians Walk into a Bar . . .

As Paul Lawrence's chapter in this volume has shown, there have been a multiplicity of approaches to researching the history of crime, and "crime historians" should never be considered a homogeneous group, despite the tendency of its members to share similar interests and concerns. The likelihood is that two historians taking about their subject in a bar are likely to approach their conversation about crime from a variety of theoretical positions—say, feminist, or Marxist, or possibly even neoliberal or New Right (though the ranks of the latter group are thinner on the ground than they used to be). They are also likely to hold different opinions about the correct methodological approach that will allow them to interrogate their subject, answer their research questions, and, perhaps to a lesser extent, preserve the integrity of their theoretical stance. Although methods and theory are different, theoretical positions and methodological approaches are often intricately connected. For example, the trend toward "history from below" that originated in the 1970s and 1980s went hand in hand with the development of oral history and the search for the "ordinary" voice within the official records of crime. This search extended the range and type of sources that crime historians—and, more broadly, social historians—were prepared to use. As social historians, we have all benefited (see Fairburn 1999; Godfrey 2011) from the "sources revolution" that has taken place, massively enlarging the documentary, visual, filmic, and other sources that we can now draw upon reflexively and unapologetically.

Ironically, however, while the sources base has broadened, the academic base has perhaps somewhat narrowed. Crime historians of the 1970s and 1980s—although that label was then barely acknowledged—emerged from, and were still partly in the worlds of, geography, psychology, sociology, information sciences, criminology, English literature, as well as from a variety of political and social historical backgrounds. No wonder those academics who were working in crime history at that time—and a few of whom still are—were accepting of a framework in which different sources of knowledge came together to investigate the social history of crime and, with it, varying ideas on methodology, from textual analysis of broadsides to geographic information systems (GIS) analysis, architecture, and the analysis of photographs and early cinema. As crime history becomes more of a fixture in modern history courses, and in criminology and sociology syllabuses, are the times now perhaps a-changing?

In some respects, the scope of crime history appears to be narrowing. Doctoral students studying the history of policing, punishment, offenders, and other related topics now tend to have already completed crime history modules at the undergraduate or master's level and are supervised by academics who have themselves completed doctorates in crime history. In the past, it would have been rare for someone supervising a thesis on, say, the history of policing or prisons to have a great wealth of knowledge specifically on that topic. More likely a social historian of some kind, or possibly a criminologist or geographer, would have served as supervisor. This gave crime history a broad and ecumenical foundation that allowed a range of methods to be employed. However, just as criminology—and before that sociology and psychology—started to narrow its focus as generations of researchers refined the parameters of their discipline, crime history may start to do the same. If that happens, and an idea of what can and cannot be included as "crime history" is created, it is entirely possible that methodological approaches will go through the same narrowing process. The expansion of available sources may be accompanied by a rise in orthodoxy on how to use and interpret them. Before we start to ask whether a narrower set of approved methods should be adopted or the diversity of methodological approaches preserved, or even increased, the following sections will explore the methods that have predominantly been and are now currently used by crime historians: our *modi operandi*, as it were.

II. THE FOUNDATIONAL METHODS
OF CRIME HISTORY

Counting was the foundational methodology of our discipline. Statistical indices of offending seem to have provided Victorian and Edwardian policymakers with an accurate real-world view of the amount of crime that occurred, and the success of the criminal justice system in combating it, and it also provided historians with a relatively easy gauge to assess their efforts too. If the figures were accurate and revealed real offending levels as well as prosecution and sentencing trends, then it should be easy to relate contemporary policy and innovations in regulating criminal behavior to these trends. However, as is now well known, the criminal statistics published annually since 1856 need very careful handling, and any simple positivistic reading of them is doomed to failure. Criminologists have queued up to list the severe limitations of both the national and the local series of criminal statistics (see Maguire 2012 for a review of debates), and historians have proved that the inaccuracies and disorienting changes in the ways that crimes were reported, recorded, and categorized have long beleaguered the analysis of criminal statistics. In 1972 Tobias noted that "one basic problem confronting all who seek to think constructively about crime is that it is very difficult to determine, even approximately, the number of crimes committed in any given period or place" (p. 81; see also later critiques of criminal statistics in Gatrell 1980; Weaver 1995; Williams 2001; Godfrey, Williams, & Lawrence 2007; and Godfrey & Lawrence 2014). The people who were responsible for compiling the statistics were also aware of these problems by the 1890s but persisted in trying to produce rational and accurate measures of crime (Godfrey 2014, pp. 18–30).

Historians too have seen value in treating the statistics not as reliable measures of real offending, but as indicators of a combination of socioeconomic conditions, public anxieties, police practice, and governmental policy (see Gatrell & Hadden 1972; Godfrey, Lawrence, & Williams 2007, pp. 35–39). Radzinowicz's magnificent studies of the development of criminal justice in the United Kingdom written between 1948 and 1990 are drawn principally from published governmental sources, such as select committee reports, governmental inquiries, and published annual reports of crime, offending, and policing. He managed to integrate a sensitive reading of the official and statistical measures with an understanding of contemporary policy landscapes, economic conditions, the development of criminal justice agencies, legislative changes, and so forth, and to thereby show that official reports and statistics require contextualization but should not be ignored (Beattie 1986; King 1984; Davis 1980; Davis 1984).

Other historians have constructed their own statistical indices using official statistics as a base but not an endpoint—see, for example, Sharpe's (2011) work using quarter sessions and coroners' data, or King's (2010; 2011) work on homicide and violence in Cornwall and Scotland. Zedner (1991) used criminal statistics to show apparent gender and class biases within the criminal justice system. Finding that women were gradually removed from the prosecution process toward the end of the nineteenth century, Zedner concluded that middle-class women were able to avoid prosecution, or, if convicted, custodial sentences. However, the statistics appeared to show that working-class women who could not demonstrate their respectability in court were considered doubly deviant—first, for breaking the law, and second, for not living up to dominant conceptions of femininity. Godfrey, Farrall, and Karstedt (2005) disputed Zedner's conclusions but, like many others, also used the criminal statistics as a base for their own work. In the future, international as well as national statistical comparisons will be more readily achievable. Statistical databases (such as the Historical Violence Database of the Criminal Justice Research Centre at Ohio University https://cjrc.osu.edu/research/interdisciplinary/hvd and the Quetelet Project http://www.fundp.ac.be/en/research/projects/page_view/03299003/) will no doubt be joined by databases from other European and non-European nations. The broader geographical base that these kinds of statistical databases provide will form a sounder platform for understanding the epistemological and ontological construction of criminal statistics—what they can and cannot show—but even then it will never convince all historians that the statistics offer anything more than a fatally flawed picture of crime.

Howard Taylor mounted the most serious assault on official statistics of crime in the 1990s, alleging that even the "gold standard" of judicial figures—the homicide rates—are effectively "decided" by Home Office statisticians (Taylor 1998a; Taylor 1998b; Williams 2000; Morris 2001). Although historians have tried and failed to find empirical evidence to support Taylor's theories, doubts about the veracity and completeness of the crime statistics remain, and the whole debate about the validity of using criminal statistics seems curiously unresolved. Whether derided and ignored or contextualized and used as a base for further study, criminal statistics still seem to sit outside of the theoretically driven methodological work that has characterized much of crime history since the 1970s.

III. Crime History Methods and Interaction with Theory

A wave of Marxist and socialist-minded historians profoundly altered the field after the publication of Edward Thompson's *The Making of the English Working Class* ([1963] 2013) and *Whigs and Hunters* (1975), together with Douglas Hay et al.'s *Albion's Fatal Tree* (1975) and Bob Storch's (1975; 1976) studies of the introduction to and operation of policing in northern England. Together these scholars introduced new sets of records into the vocabulary of crime history sources. The sources they used were as "official" as those used by Radzinowicz—assize trial court records, quarter session indictments, the pardons and remarks of judges when pronouncing sentence on the condemned—but they were read "against the grain." (For a full discussion of these sources, see Gatrell 1994, as well as the guides to official crime history records held by the United

Kingdom's national repository, http://www.nationalarchives.gov.uk/). For Hay and others, the records of the courts were the records of a ruling elite who used the law to curtail and inhibit the rights of free-born Englishmen, and to criminalize customary entitlements (King 2000; Godfrey 2013). This group of researchers replaced the rather implicit conservatism of postwar historians with a more directly acknowledged theoretical frame, and their theoretical and methodological stances were mutually reinforcing. Documents can only be read against the grain if one assumes that the authors were determined to obfuscate their intentions and that criminal records have a hidden meaning (Gilligan & Pratt 2003). This view and approach is so deeply ingrained in the training of crime historians today that many tend to take this kind of methodology for granted. Indeed, the approach of counterintuitive reading only began to fracture once the textual and discourse analysis methods promoted by Michel Foucault gained prominence and different kinds of discourse analysis were promoted by different historians and social scientists.

Michel Foucault published *Discipline and Punish: The Origin of the Prison* in the same year that *Albion's Fatal Tree* (1975) appeared, and arguably, his work has had greater influence than *Albion*. His treatise on technologies of power used discourse analysis—the textual deconstruction of official and nonofficial documents, speeches, literature, and so on—to reveal underlying constructions of power that were not "owned" by particular groups in society, as Marxists would claim, but that drew their power from underlying assumptions evident in the language used by institutions created in the eighteenth and nineteenth centuries. For Foucault, power and knowledge were inextricably linked, and this could be seen in the intertextual communications between penal and other institutions. After Foucault, all texts—written and oral—became potential source material, and a number of Foucauldian followers expanded on his methods to produce theories to explain the intertextual links among knowledge, power, and the criminal justice system (Leps 1992). The ease with which Foucault's methodology could be applied to a number of disparate sources expanded the range of crime history considerably. Court documents, contemporary newspapers and literature, and even prison timetables could all be unlocked with the power of discourse analysis, and the "cultural turn" that Foucault and his followers initiated in the 1990s was exploited most fully in studies of intimate violence and gender relations, becoming in itself a new "gender turn."

IV. SEX CRIME: METHODS AND MADNESS

In their book *Methods, Sex and Madness*, Davidson and Layder (1994) attempted to make discussion of methods more attractive to researchers by exploring methodological issues with reference to classic studies of mental illness and sexual activity:

> Our aim is to provide a very general introduction to the main techniques used by social researchers and the philosophical and methodological problems associated

with them, but to do so in a reasonably engaging way. We do this primarily through a focus on research into human sexuality and madness. . . . By exploring both technical and conceptual problems in the work of Freud and Kinsey, and by considering the difficulties faced by researchers concerned with phenomena such as rape, witch hunts and prostitution, this book makes methodological issues both interesting and accessible. (p. i)

Sex sells, perhaps even in the academic market, but more importantly, the study of sex and intimate human relationships has been at the forefront of work utilizing new forms of historical data. Indeed, it is in the arena of intimate violence (i.e., domestic abuse, sexual offenses against women and children) that we have seen some of the most innovative research methods developed in recent years, such as the use of divorce records by Hammerton (1995) and the use of the records kept by charities and faith organizations by Jackson (2010). D'Cruze (1998) used police occurrence books (which recorded the daily activities of police officers on the beat) and petty sessions' minute books (which recorded cases of domestic violence dealt with in the magistrates' courts) to show that the violence that women experienced in their homes was downplayed or ignored by the police, and therefore never reached the courts (D'Cruze 1999). The newspaper trial reports that D'Cruze analyzed subsequently revealed that those cases of sexual and domestic violence that overcame police prejudices and actually did end up being prosecuted in the courtroom were then ignored or disregarded by magistrates. Without access to and use of these sources of data, the gendered mechanisms of the Victorian criminal justice system would have remained hidden.

Other types of records usually analyzed by cultural or political historians now feature as part of the crime history methodological menu. For example, we now have access to a wide range of working-class as well as elite autobiographies. From the late nineteenth century on, it became popular for police officers, prison officers, and other officials to comment in print on their lives, their jobs, and wider thoughts about crime in general, and these can be placed alongside published and unpublished autobiographies of offenders and prisoners (see Benney 1936, among many others). Oral histories are another important source that reaches into the general everyday experience of crime and victimization. Offering even more possibilities, many of the hundreds of oral history collections formed in the 1980s and the secondary analysis of transcribed interviews can extend the reach of historians of crime back to the 1920s. *The Oral History Reader* (Perks & Thompson 1998) provides a good overview of the problems faced by researchers using oral evidence. Both Judith Walkowitz's (1992) and Drew Grey's (2010) studies of sexual danger in Victorian London drew upon contemporary newspapers and literature to explore the narrative structure of contemporary moral scripts. In doing so, they used print media not only as a source of factual information, but also to examine the gendered nature of moral messages surrounding risk in the nineteenth-century city. One advantage available to modern researchers of crime is that many of these sources, particularly newspapers and contemporary literature, are increasingly becoming available in digital form.

V. DIGITAL ARCHAEOLOGY?

The digitization of archived newspapers has picked up pace recently, with some individual newspaper series stretching back in time considerably. The *Times Online*, for example, includes copy from 1785; the *Guardian and Observer Digital Archive* is available from 1791; and the *Daily Mirror Archive* (http://www.ukpressonline.co.uk) includes full-page images for every issue of the *Daily Mirror* from 1903. Digital companies such as ProQuest and Gale Cengage have collected together groups of regional newspapers that give very good if not total national coverage, and there are also international collections that can be found in such repositories as Trove https://trove.nla.gov.au/newspaper for Australia, ProQuest for the *New York Times*, and Gale Cengage for other nineteenth-century American newspapers).

The most complete collection that is available to most researchers working or studying in a university is the 19th Century British Library Newspapers collection that contains full runs of a number of regional newspapers from the nineteenth century (http://www.britishnewspaperarchive.co.uk). The popular press—penny papers—are represented alongside the quality elite broadsheets, and there is a good geographical spread of titles. There are still many gaps, however, and the microfilm and microfiche reels held in local studies collections and county records offices can be used to provide data from newspapers that have not been digitized due to the expense of the process. They are likely to fulfill this role for decades to come. In addition to newsprint, cartoons have been made digitally available, including the *Punch* cartoons (http://www.punchcartoons.com) and lithographs published in the *Illustrated London News, Police Gazette*, and other popular journals of the time that show contemporary attitudes toward crime and offending.

For the earlier period, good electronic broadsides can now be found in Harvard's online repository (http://broadsides.law.harvard.edu/) and the National Library of Scotland's collection of 2,000 broadsides with a searchable index (http://digital.nls.uk/broadsides/). Statistics of crime and official government reports are also available digitally (for a summary, see http://www.parliament.uk/business/publications/parliamentary-archives/archives-electronic/).

All in all, then, a vast digitized repository of trial reports, editorials, and images is available to researchers. The technical preparation of the data—optical character recognition (OCR) reading, processing, and so on—requires the skills of experts, but the methods required to use the data are scarcely different from those needed to plow through hundreds of issues of various newspapers, or scroll through microfilms at the British Newspaper Library. Certainly, the speed with which relevant digitalized data can be found through electronic searches and filters is much enhanced. However, the most influential digital projects are those that have the capacity to do more than reproduce statistical indices or the text of parliamentary reports or speed up the finding of newspaper crime reports.

Bob Shoemaker, Tim Hitchcock, and Clive Emsley, in partnership with the Humanities Research Institute, created the website http://www.oldbaileyonline.org/, which went live in 2003 and made available, in a searchable, full-text online database, the records of cases from 1674 to 1913 heard in London's Central Criminal Court or Old Bailey, as well as the Accounts of the Ordinary of Newgate, the cleric who recorded the life stories of many of the condemned between 1679 and 1772. The site also provides explanatory essays about the Old Bailey itself, its workload, and the way the website renders online data to researchers. In total it contains nearly 200,000 trial details and some biographical details of 2,500 men and women. Because the website provides digital images of all 190,000 original pages of the Old Bailey Proceedings, 4,000 pages of the Central Criminal Court's Ordinary's Accounts, advice on methods of searching this resource, information on the historical and legal background to the Old Bailey and its Proceedings, and a feature whereby simple analysis can be performed, the website has been widely used by researchers and undergraduate students to carry out their own research inquiries. Even so, the site has probably still not reached its full potential, and it will only do so when the data it contains are linked to other data sets in order to provide biographical data that can form cradle-to-grave records of those who appeared in the courtrooms and prisons, or who were transported across the seas for their crimes.

In 2010 a new digital resource project called the Digital Panopticon was initiated (scheduled to go live in 2018) linking the Old Bailey Online website to the Founders and Survivors website (http://foundersandsurvivors.org), which contains the records of 73,000 convicts transported to Tasmania (Van Dieman's Land), including employment details, convict indents, height and biometric data, details of punishment, and reports on individuals' progress in the penal colony. These two large databases will be linked to other data sources and a number of other databases to produce a mega-digital resource that will bring together genealogical, biometric, and criminal justice datasets held in the United Kingdom and Australia in order to explore the impact of the different types of penal punishments on the lives of approximately 90,000 people sentenced at the Old Bailey between 1780 and 1925. The handling of such large amounts of biographical and biometric data for thousands of people will require new methods to be developed (see the discussion of the biographical turn later in this chapter), and may also require historians to rethink their ethical stance. Because one strand of the Digital Panopticon project traces the geographical mobility of convicts—and, when possible, that of their children too—as well as their social mobility, the project will allow researchers to carry out their own inquiries about the geographies of crime and resettlement after punishment using GIS data, mapping systems, and so on. However, the project in itself is not as fundamentally spatially orientated as some recent studies of offending have been.

VI. Lost in Space?

Similar to those conducted as part of the Digital Panopticon, mapping exercises have recently been conducted that have led to new approaches to answering questions about the importance of place and location in the character and organization of criminal activities. For example, Joyce's (2003) study of literary geographies of crime in Victorian

London (see esp. pp. 13–59); Houlbrook's (2001) study of illicit homosexual liaisons in London; Chamberlain's (2012) study of prostitution in interwar Liverpool; Jackson and Bartie's (2011) study of the policing of youth leisure in English and Scottish cities; and Adey, Godfrey, and Cox's (2015) study of wartime Merseyside, which mapped prosecutions for black-out offenses against actual bombsites. These projects have literally "re-placed" crime within its spatial as well as social context, and it is likely that GIS and digital visualization will combine together to produce interactive maps that can be used to analyze crime in much more interesting and productive ways in the future.

VII. New Sources, New Possibilities?

Is it time to stop now? From the previous paragraphs we could reasonably assume that we have become a fractured discipline that has allowed the discovery of new sources and methods of analysis to overwhelm us. If we consider the few dominant sources used by Leon Radzinowicz or Edward Thompson to construct truly magisterial sweeps of law, working-class communities, and society, and then consider the huge variety of records and sources of data swept up into quite modest articles upon this or that, perhaps we should ask whether we have become too all-encompassing of new data sources, too ready to search for new methods, and too myopic in our vision of the power of law over people's lives.

Before the introduction of tens and now hundreds of TV channels, workplace and schoolyard conversations were facilitated by the fact that nearly everyone watched the same shows, and a debate could take place about their merits. We had a common base from which to compare. The situation was the same for crime historians, whose debates about the accuracy and validity of, say, criminal statistics or quarter sessions documents could be informed by the same knowledge and concerns. Now, like multi-channel TV, it is more and more difficult to get a grip on the various types of sources that are available, let alone to be in a position to compare them in any meaningful way: does, for example, a select committee report on policing or the TV series *Dixon of Dock Green* offer the more accurate portrayal of postwar policing? Put simply, the question is, Should we now refocus on a few authoritative sources, forget the rest, and write the type of historical studies that A. J. P. Taylor or Geoffrey Elton would consider worth reading? Or should we take advantage of the wealth of sources and methodological approaches we have at our disposal and produce the multilayered and complex histories that address the needs of our time? The methods we employ, of course, as well as the writing style and dissemination of our work, will depend on what we see as the needs of our time, and the audiences we are writing for.

VIII. Is Crime History Art or Science?

As history and sociology/criminology move closer together it is likely that we will see the continuing conflation of research methods from the two areas. Often the disciplines sit in the same university administrative units, history of crime essays are published in mainstream criminology journals, and doctoral students of each subject take the same training modules. In truth, the social sciences' use of qualitative interviews is similar to historians' use of oral history, and the methods of statistical, visual, and documentary analysis used by both are the same, so, in terms of methods, there is little difference in many ways between social history and social science (Brown & Barratt 2002; Godfrey, Williams, & Lawrence 2007). However, as previously discussed, historians of crime also emerged from a literary as well as a historical background, and many fine histories have been written with a more artistic and literary bias than a social scientific one, such as Colley's *Captives* (2003) or Larson's *Devil in the White City* (2003). Taking the study of transportation of convicts to Australia as an example, we can see the application of a whole range of methodological approaches, from those recognizable to social scientists to those more closely linked with literary representations.

The eighteenth-century origin of the convict transportation was the decision of the government to send to the farthest outpost of the British Empire those criminals who had escaped the gallows but were viewed as too dangerous to remain in society (Finnane 1997). Because Australia was far enough away to discourage convicts from returning, and offered a strategic advantage to British naval and trade interests in that region, eventually 168,000 men and women were sent there to serve their sentences. However, when the colonies began to grow into viable economic and social communities, the colonists successfully agitated to end transportation. The experiment thus came to an end, but it has interested historians and criminologists ever since. There is also, of course, a considerable interest among historians, and among the Australian general public, about the origins of this society. Robert Hughes's 1987 work *The Fatal Shore* on the subject has come to be regarded as something of a reference point. Hughes's methods are recognizable: he examines the documentary evidence, private letters, public correspondence, journals, diaries, and contemporary as well as modern publications on the topic, and in every way his approach conforms to the methodological norms of most social historians writing at that time. However, his writing style is more engaging and accessible than that of his contemporaries:

> Denied its voice as history, convict experience became the province of journalists and novelists. The general public never lost its curiosity about these "dark" years in which so many of its roots lay tangled; and a vivid, trashy Grand Guignol, long on rum, sodomy and the lash, but decidedly short on the more prosaic facts about how most convicts actually lived and worked, sprang up to supply its demands. . . .
> All the popular literature of transportation focused on the horrors of the System, the outer penal settlements to which recidivists were condemned—Port Arthur, Macquarie Harbor, Moreton Bay and especially Norfolk Island. It presented convict life as a wretched purgatory, relieved only by stretches of pure hell. (p. xiii)

This is not a completely different form of writing than that seen in the work of, say, Hamish Maxwell-Stewart, who has engagingly written about Maria Island (2008). However, it reveals a different type of methodological approach than that used by

Maxwell-Stewart (2012), who quantitatively analyzes the health and longevity of convicts and former convicts in order to establish a scientific basis for understanding how their experiences of punishment affected the body. Whether we favor the artistic approach or the scientific one, choosing it tactically to maximize dissemination and impact, or because we naturally incline to artistic and literary forms, it hardly matters. The value of each of the two approaches has been proved over time, and although their writing styles and underlying philosophies are different, the soundness of their methodological bases is paramount (Eisner 1981).

Hughes (1987, pp. 158–203), Maxwell-Stewart (2001) and colleagues (Frost & Maxwell-Stewart 2001; Maxwell-Stuart & Hood 2001), and others (Dunstan 2000) have all used biographical data to analyze the life histories of convicts, and have been instrumental in taking new directions within our discipline—ones that explore episodes or events in order to interrogate a wider picture or use individuals' biographical/biometric data to investigate wider social issues.

IX. Have Micro-Histories and Biographical Data Linkage Replaced Statistical and Documentary Methods of Analysis?

Historians have always used key events to illustrate significant shifts in policy or culture, and these micro-histories, or what we might call a concentration of more discrete historical episodes, can then be used to illustrate wider historical phenomena (Gatrell 1994; Shore 2002). Recent work has shown the utility of a methodology that collects together all available data on one event, or one series of events, such as Alyson Brown's (2013) micro-historical study of the 1932 Dartmoor Prison riot. Brown demonstrates how this one key event can tell us much more about the penal estate and its aims and operations than a grand sweep covering the history of imprisonment. In her book, she advocates a micro-history which:

> entails extensive examination and reconstruction of individual and family social relationships within a restricted geographical space and episodic which entails meticulous scrutiny of an event or encounter in order to illuminate aspects of a past society and culture that resist disclosure through more unconventional historical methods. (p. 133)

The methodologies employed in micro-histories are quite similar to those used in biographical analysis, in which data are assembled from official printed documents and, where they exist, reports, newspapers, and private papers and correspondence.

However, biographical approaches often take the person as the reference point, rather than any particular episode. For example, Godfrey, Cox, and Farrall(2007; 2010) examined the lives of people who at some point found themselves before the courts. It would have been equally as valid to study only these individuals' interactions in court or prison, and relate those to wider penal philosophies or historical changes in criminal justice systems. However, Godfrey and colleagues were interested in examining people's onset into criminality, their experiences under punishment, and their subsequent desistence from or persistence in criminal activities. This necessitated a cradle-to-grave study of the people themselves: they became the subject. Biographical research therefore requires additional data in order to compile information across the whole lifetime of a person: census data; birth, marriage, and death registers; military records; work records—which are sometimes, but not usually, available—and any other civil or criminal information that is available. These data are usually entered into life-grids, which sequentially order the events in a person's life by year and type, making "reading" them a little easier, before the data are entered into a machine-readable database. There are some limitations to this methodology, since it relies on official documents, which may omit detail and are always shaped by the needs of the institution they were written for, not for the historian who reads them.

However, this approach seems useful for understanding the progress of a person's life and how his or her offending related to life events such as marriage, having children, or periods of punishment and supervision. Biographical methods, which have long been used in health research (see the essays in Ziebland et al. 2013), have now been taken up by a raft of doctoral students as well as established researchers, and therefore we can expect this approach to continue to be used for a good while longer. Has this methodology replaced other forms of inquiry though?

Simple statistical analysis may not be as popular as it once was, but longitudinal quantitative analysis again appears to be moving to the forefront of crime history methods. Some of the most exciting work of late—particularly on violence—has used long runs of data, contextualized by documentary analysis, to produce well-crafted and detailed work. For example, David Courtwright's (1996) analysis of the history of violence in the United States stretches from the violence of conquering the West, to the tragic experiences of the American Civil War, to street violence today. Roth (2012), too, has used long statistical runs to explore homicide over the same period (both use psycho-dynamic explanations to explain the rise and fall in levels of violence, but their theories rest on statistical measures of homicides and murders). So, while positivistic statistical explanations have receded, quantitative history—some of which relies on official statistics, some of which uses biographical or biometric data—may yet usher a new "quantitative turn" into the crime history methods lexicon.

Researchers using statistical and quantitative analysis have never in themselves been subject to rigorous ethical scrutiny, although the means by which they collect the data that they "crunch" has. Historical data—and historians, too—seem to escape ethical review. However, the conflation of quantitative analysis of biographical/biometric data at the individual level may necessitate more robust ethical review. Indeed, it is worth considering whether all of our research methodologies are conforming to modern standards of ethical research.

X. Ethical Researching—Can We Actually *Be* Unethical?

Historians deal with the body in the library. The people they study are usually, but not always, long dead. Historians cannot be held legally responsible for maligning the people they describe in their articles and books, and although they can be criticized for giving an unfavorable impression of their subject's actions while they were alive, they will never be hauled before the courts for doing so. One cannot libel the dead. I doubt it is for that reason that we historians tend to be a little glib about ethics. It is more likely that we do not see ethics as playing any part in our work: we simply see ourselves as separate from the social and other scientists who work with live subjects, and who therefore have to spend a considerable amount of time and thought considering and negotiating university or National Health Service ethics committees. Do we take ethics for granted because it does not make any sense to apply them to dead people, or because we consider ourselves to be, in essence, ethical researchers?

For the most part, historical research need not trouble the ethics panels. The methods we use are non-intrusive and, in the main, do not involve live subjects. Oral history, of course, is an exception to this rule, and some have attempted to make an ethics regime designed for the sciences and health researchers "fit" the humanities, though with some difficulty, or to request a new hybrid approach:

> The blurring of disciplinary boundaries involves a re-thinking of ethical guidelines and points to a need for development of shared guidelines between history and social science. There may be a need for a different kind of ethical practice which considers areas such as how we conceive of participants, whether living or dead and a distinction between codes of ethics and personal morality. (Richardson & Godfrey 2003; see also Godfrey & Richardson 2004, p. 150)

As a research method, biographical and micro-historical research can impact not the dead, but their living descendants. The same is true—and indeed, the risks are much greater—for digitally rendered data. The speed at which nominal data linkage can take place on the Web means that a huge amount of "sensitive" material on individuals can be accumulated very quickly. As yet, we have very little guidance available for students or academic researchers on how and in what circumstances we should use these personal data. In some respects, it is the republishing of these data that is problematic, particularly as it is not always possible to control the audience for one's work. Indeed, it is not always possible to get *any* kind of audience for one's research. The following section discusses how some research methods lend themselves to an increased visibility for research findings.

XI. Writing Crime History Badly

In 2013, Michael Billig published *Learn to Write Badly: How to Succeed in the Social Sciences*. His argument was that technical academic terms and theoretical jargon obfuscate the meaning of much published work, and that criticism could easily apply to historical as well as social science publications. Too many history books are read solely by academics within their very small field, and there is an almost total lack of deep methodological description that explains how the writers came to their views, because the methods used in the research are implicitly accepted by those within that small academic circle. As this essay has tried to make clear, this approach to methods is simply not sustainable, and it ignores key debates about the direction of our subject. Nevertheless, it may be that in one, and only one, area of study, the lack of a methodological section is desirable: public and campaigning history.

Some rigorously researched books with robust methodologies have broken through to a wider market and had success in changing public opinion and public policy. During the late 1970s and 1980s, the overpolicing of young black/minority ethnic groups led to riots and to criticism of police tactics in Hall et al.'s *Policing the Crisis* (1978). This book was influential, to an extent, and fed into debates about new forms of community policing that were thought to be less abrasive. On the other end of the political spectrum, Windschuttle's *The Killing of History* (1996), with its controversial and flawed research methodology, ironically caused conservative Australian politicians to acknowledge past crimes against the indigenous community. Davies's (2009) work on gangs has been published in academic journals, but also in a more popular-format book, and has been featured in theater productions and on television. This work has therefore had a much greater visibility than it would have had if it had been solely found on the bookshelves of university libraries. Davies's work has therefore had greater capacity to change public opinion toward young people and crime.

In the future, planning the methods for our work will also need to include plans for producing the work in more popular formats: on television and the Web, and maybe even in semi-fictional novels. We might need to think how we can produce methodologically sound work that translates into popular history. Should we just not reveal the sources and methods we have used, or should we find a more accessible way of explaining our research strategies to a wider audience in order to write crime history "well"?

Conclusion

Counting (statistics), reading (discourse analysis), looking (visual sociology), typing (digital resources), and linking (micro-histories and biographical research): that is the history of research methodology for our discipline. We have spent considerable time trying to distinguish between sources and methods, and have concluded that while the sources explosion has created an ever-expanding range of things to be collected, considered, and analyzed, the methods we use to do those tasks are remarkably stable, and even conservative. Even the newer techniques of nominal data linkage and micro-historical research would be recognizable to Radzinowicz or Thompson. That is not to say that we should be complacent in devising new ways of producing our research findings; indeed, it may be the very reason why we have to do so much more in that regard. Methodological innovation has played a part in developing the biographical and cultural turns that have enriched and pushed forward our discipline, and it may well be the key to developing the next set of "turns" in crime history.

REFERENCES

Adey, Peter, Barry Godfrey, & David Cox. 2015. *Crime, Regulation, and Control: Protecting the Population of a Blitzed City, 1939–1945*. London: Bloomsbury.

Beattie, John. 1986. *Crime and the Courts in England, 1660–1800*. Oxford: Clarendon.

Benney, Mark. 1936. *Low Company: Describing the Evolution of a Burglar*. London: Peter Davies.

Billig, Michael. 2013. *Learn to Write Badly: How to Succeed in the Social Sciences*. Cambridge: Cambridge University Press.

Brown, Alyson. 2013. *Inter-War Penal Policy and Crime in England: The Dartmoor Convict Prison Riot, 1932*. Basingstoke, UK: Palgrave Macmillan.

Brown, Alyson, & David Barratt. 2002. *Knowledge of Evil: Child Prostitution and Child Sexual Abuse in Twentieth-Century England*. Collumpton, UK: Willan Publications.

Chamberlain, Kerry. 2012. "Prostitution in Inter-War Liverpool." Ph.D. diss., Keele University.

Colley, Linda. 2003. *Captives: Britain, Empire and the World, 1650–1800*. London: Pimlico.

Courtwright David. 1996. *Violent Land: Single Men and Social Disorder from the Frontier to the Inner City*. Cambridge, MA: Harvard University Press.

Davidson, Julia, & Derek Layder. 1994. *Methods, Sex and Madness*. London: Routledge.

Davies, Andrew. 2009. *Gangs of Manchester*. London: Milo Books.

Davis, Jennifer. 1980. "The London Garroting Panic of 1862." In *Crime and the Law: The Social History of Crime in Western Europe since 1500*, ed. Vic Gatrell, Bruce Lenman, & Geoffrey Parker, 190–213. London: Europa.

Davis, Jennifer. 1984. "A Poor Man's System of Justice? The London Police Courts in the Second Half of the Nineteenth Century." *Historical Journal* 27 (2): 309–35.

D'Cruze, Shani. 1998. *Crimes of Outrage: Sex, Violence and Victorian Working Women*. London: University College London Press.

D'Cruze, Shani. 1999. "Sex, Violence and Local Courts: Working-Class Respectability in a Mid-Nineteenth-Century Lancashire Town." *British Journal of Criminology* 39 (1): 39–55.

Dunstan, David. 2000. *Owen Suffolk's Days of Crime and Years of Suffering*. Melbourne: Australian Scholarly Publishing.

Eisner, Elliot W. 1981. "On the Difference Between Scientific and Artistic Approaches to Qualitative Research." *Review of Research in Visual Arts Education* 13 (Winter): 1–9.

Fairburn, Miles. 1999. *Social History: Problems, Strategies and Methods*. London: Palgrave Macmillan.

Finnane, Mark. 1997. *Punishment in Australian Society*. Melbourne: Oxford University Press.

Foucault, Michel. 1975. *Discipline and Punish: The Origin of the Prison*. London: Penguin.

Frost, Lucy, & Hamish Maxwell-Stewart. 2001. *Chain Letters: Narrating Convict Lives*. Melbourne: Melbourne University Press.

Gatrell, Vic. 1980. "The Decline of Theft and Violence in Victorian and Edwardian England." In *Crime and the Law: The Social History of Crime in Western Europe since 1500*, ed. Vic Gatrell, Bruce Lenman, & Geoffrey Parker, 238–370. London: Europa.

Gatrell, Vic, & Toby Hadden. 1972. "Criminal Statistics and Their Interpretation." In *Nineteenth Century Society: Essays in the Use of Quantitative Methods for the Study of Social Data*, ed. Edward Anthony Wrigley, 336–96. Cambridge: Cambridge University Press.

Gilligan, George, & John Pratt. 2003. *Crime, Truth and Justice: Official Inquiry, Discourse, Knowledge*. Cullompton, UK: Willan.

Godfrey, Barry. 2003. "Counting and accounting for the decline in non-lethal violence in England, Australia and New Zealand, 1880-1920," *British Journal of Criminology* 43(2): 340–53.

Godfrey, Barry. 2011. "Historical and Archival Research Methods." In *The Handbook on Criminology Research Methods*, ed. David Gadd, Susannah Karstedt, & Steve Mesner, 159–75. New York: SAGE.

Godfrey, Barry. 2014. *Crime in England, 1880–1945: The Rough, the Policed, and the Incarcerated*. London: Routledge.

Godfrey, Barry, David Cox, & Stephen Farrall. 2007. *Criminal Lives: Family, Employment and Offending*. Oxford: Oxford University Press.

Godfrey, Barry, David Cox, & Stephen Farrall. 2010. *Serious Offenders: A Historical Study of Habitual Offenders*. Oxford: Oxford University Press.

Godfrey, Barry, & Paul Lawrence. 2014. *Crime and Justice since 1750*. London: Routledge.

Godfrey, Barry, Paul Lawrence, & Chris Williams. 2007. *History and Crime*. London: Sage.

Godfrey, Barry, & Jane Richardson. 2004. "Loss, Collective Memory and Transcripted Oral Histories." *International Journal of Social Research Methodology* 7 (2): 143–55.

Grey, Drew. 2010. *London's Shadows: The Dark Side of the Victorian City*. London: Continuum.

Hall, Steve, Charles Critcher, Tony Jefferson, John Clarke, & Brian Roberts. 1978. *Policing the Crisis: Mugging, the State and Law and Order*. London: Macmillan.

Hammerton, James. 1995. *Cruelty and Companionship: Conflict in Nineteenth Century Married Life*. London: Routledge.

Hay, Douglas, Peter Linebaugh, John Rule, Edward Thompson, & Chris Winslow. 1975. *Albion's Fatal Tree: Crime and Society in Eighteenth-Century England*. London: Allen Lane.

Houlbrook, Matthew. 2001. "Towards a Historical Geography of Sexuality." *Journal of Urban History* 2 (4): 497–504.

Hughes, Robert. 1987. *The Fatal Shore: A History of the Transportation of Convicts to Australia, 1787–1868*. London: Collins Harvill.

Jackson, Louise. 2010. "The Geography of Everyday Life: Spatial and Ethnographic Approaches to the History of Crime and Policing." Paper presented at the British Crime Historians Symposium 2, Sheffield, UK, September 2–3.

Jackson, Louise, & Angela Bartie. 2011. "'Children of the City': Juvenile Justice, Property and Place in England and Scotland, 1945–1960." *Economic History Review* 64 (1): 88–113.

Joyce, Simon. 2003. *Capital Offenses: Geographies of Class and Crime in Victorian London*. Charlottesville: University of Virginia Press.

King, Peter. 1984. "Decision Makers and Decision-Making in the English Criminal Law, 1750–1800." *Historical Journal* 27:25–58.

King, Peter. 2000. *Crime, Justice and Discretion, Law and Social Relations in England, 1740–1820*. Oxford: Oxford University Press.

King, Peter. 2010. "The Impact of Urbanization on Murder Rates and on the Geography of Homicide in England and Wales, 1780–1850." *Historical Journal* 53:1–28.

King, Peter. 2011. "Urbanization, Rising Homicide Rates and the Geography of Lethal Violence in Scotland, 1800–1860." *History* (July): 231–59.

Larson, Erik. 2003. *Devil in the White City*. London: Random House.

Leps, Marie-Christine. 1992. *Apprehending the Criminal: The Production of Deviance in Nineteenth-Century Discourse*. Durham, NC: Duke University Press.

Maguire, Mike. 2012. "Criminal Statistics and the Construction of Crime." In *The Oxford Handbook of Criminology*, ed. Mike Maguire, Rod Morgan, & Robert Reiner, 206–45. Oxford: Oxford University Press.

Maxwell-Stewart, Hamish. 2008. *Closing Hell's Gates: The Death of a Convict Station*. London: Allen and Unwin.

Maxwell-Stewart, Hamish. 2012. "Isles of the Dead: Convict Death Rates in Comparative Perspective." *Historic Environment* 24 (3): 28–34.

Maxwell-Stewart, Hamish, & Susan Hood. 2001. *Pack of Thieves?: 52 Port Arthur Lives*. Port Arthur, Australia: Port Arthur Historic Site Management Authority.

Morris, Robert. 2001. "Lies, Damned Lies and Criminal Statistics: Reinterpreting the Criminal Statistics in England and Wales." *Crime, History and Societies* 5 (1): 111–27.

Perks, Robert, & Alistair Thompson. 1998. *The Oral History Reader*. London: Routledge.

Radzinowicz, Leon. 1948–1986. *A History of the English Criminal Law and Its Administration from 1750* (4 vol.). London: Stevens & Sons.

Radzinowicz, Leon, & Roger Hood. 1990. *A History of the English Criminal Law and Its Administration from 1750*, Vol. 5, *The Emergence of Penal Policy*. Oxford: Clarendon Press.

Richardson, Jane, & Barry Godfrey. 2003. "Towards Ethical Practice in the Use of Transcribed Oral Interviews." *International Journal of Social Research Methodology* 6 (4): 200–14.

Roth, Randall. 2012. *American Homicide*. Cambridge, MA: Harvard University Press.

Sharpe, James, & John Dickinson. 2011. "Coroners' Inquests in an English County in the Late Seventeenth and Eighteenth Centuries: A Preliminary Survey." *Northern History* 48:25–46.

Shore, Heather. 2002. *Artful Dodgers: Youth and Crime in Early Nineteenth-Century London*. London: Boydell Press.

Storch, Robert. 1975. "The Plague of Blue Locusts: Police Reform and Popular Resistance in Northern England, 1840–57." *International Review of Social History* 20:61–90.

Storch, Robert. 1976. "The Policeman as Domestic Missionary: Urban Discipline and Popular Culture in Northern England, 1850–1880." *Journal of Social History* 9:481–511.

Taylor, Howard. 1998a. "Rationing Crime: The Political Economy of Criminal Statistics since the 1850s." *Economic History Review* 49 (3): 569–90.

Taylor, Howard. 1998b. "The Politics of the Rising Crime Statistics of England and Wales." *Crime, History & Societies* 1 (2): 5–28.

Thompson, Edward. [1963] 2013. *The Making of the English Working Class*. London: Penguin Modern Classics.

Thompson, Edward. 1975. *Whigs and Hunters: The Origins of the Black Act*. London: Allen Lane.

Tobias, John. 1972. *Nineteenth-Century Crime: Prevention and Punishment*. Newton Abbot, UK: David & Charles.

Walkowitz, Judith. 1992. *City of Dreadful Delight: Narratives of Sexual Danger in Late-Victorian London*. London: Virago.

Weaver, John. 1995. *Crimes, Constables and Courts: Order and Transgression in a Canadian City, 1816–1970*. Montreal: McGill-Queen's University Press.

Williams, Chris. 2000. "Counting Crimes or Counting People: Some Implications of Mid-Nineteenth Century British Police Returns." *Crime, History & Societies* 4 (2): 77–93.

Windschuttle, Keith. 1996. *The Killing of History. How Literary Critics and Social Theorists Are Murdering Our Past*. San Francisco, CA: Encounter Books.

Zedner, Lucia. 1991. *Women, Crime and Custody in Victorian England*. Oxford: Oxford University Press.

Ziebland, Susan, Angela Carter, Joseph Calbrese, & Louise Locock, eds. 2013. *Understanding and Using Health Experiences*. Oxford: Oxford University Press.

CHAPTER 3

LONG-TERM TRENDS IN CRIME

Continuity and Change

MARCELO F. AEBI AND ANTONIA LINDE

INTRODUCTION

ASSESSING the state-of-the-art research on long-term crime trends in Western industrialized countries, Johnson and Monkkonen (1996b) conclude that until the late 1970s, researchers considered it almost impossible to obtain reliable estimates of the levels of crime in earlier times. As a consequence, they were less interested in crime rates and trends than in "everything surrounding crime-legal institutions from the penal system to modes of enforcement, popular and elite attitudes, court systems and crimes coming to courts" (Johnson & Monkkonen 1996b, p. 2). This state of affairs changed during the following twenty years in such a way that by the mid-1990s it was "assumed that crime—in particular personal violence—in the Western world has declined since the early Middle Ages until very recently. This simple statement encompasses the two aspects of crime that scholars expected never to approach: international comparison and lengthy trends" (Johnson & Monkkonen 1996b, p. 4).

The goal of this chapter is to introduce the reader to the available research on long-term trends in crime, paying special attention to its historical development and the methodological challenges it involves, and presenting its main findings and their possible interpretations. The reader will thus discover that Johnson and Monkkonen (1996b) are right about the general consensus on the long-term decrease of interpersonal violence in Western Europe and the United States, but also that international comparisons have been a key element of research in criminology since the origins of this social science. We start the chapter with a short overview of the historical development of comparisons of crime rates and crime trends. On that basis, we present a classification of the types of research that have been conducted according to their unit of analysis, time span, and offenses analyzed. This leads us to analyze the way in which crime has been defined and measured by researchers, putting the accent on the use of homicide as a proxy for violent offenses. Then we present the main sources of data for research on crime trends and discuss their validity and reliability. We also examine the pitfalls involved in the process of interpretation of the trends shown by such sources. Finally, we provide an overview of the main theories proposed by researchers to explain the trends observed.

I. Historical Development of Research on Crime Trends

Science is based on comparisons; therefore, as soon as data were available for more than one year or more than one country, researchers and journalists started comparing them. Hence, when the first *comprehensive* national judiciary statistics were published in France in 1827, the data included in them—which referred back to the year 1825—were immediately compared to the figures available for other countries, such as England, for which data existed but were not as rich in detail as the brand-new French statistics (Aubusson de Cavarlay 1998). Two years later, when the Netherlands—which at that time included Belgium—published its first criminal statistics, Adolphe Quételet (1829) accompanied them with an essay in which he included comparisons with the French statistics as well as his first observations about the regularity of crime across time. Thus, analyzing the French figures for 1825 and 1826—the only two years available at that time—he mentioned the "frightening regularity" (*effrayante regularité*) with which the same crimes were committed. For example, he pointed out that there had been 250 crimes against relatives in 1825, and 244 in 1826; 613 forgeries in 1825, and 610 in 1826; and 4,841 thefts in 1825, against 4,489 in 1826 (Quételet 1829, p. 28). Later, he extended his observations to slightly longer series and observed the same "remarkable consistency" (*constance étonnante*) (1833, p. 20) not only in the number of crimes, but also in the characteristics of the accused offenders in terms of age and gender (Quételet 1831; Quételet 1835). It is on the basis of the 1842 English translation of his 1835 *Treatise on Man and the Development of His Faculties* that this remark, which gave birth to the illusion of stable crime trends, a conclusion supported also by Guerry (1833), has been quoted for one and a half centuries, from Buckle (1864) to Hagan (2013), to name only two researchers at both ends of that time frame.[1]

Although Quételet (1829) contrasted the figures from the first Dutch criminal statistics with the French ones, he believed that they could not be compared to the data from England, because, among other reasons, the latter only included indictable offenses. The comparison with France was possible because the data had been collected in a similar way and both countries applied the same law. The reason for that similarity was that the Netherlands, during its time under the rule of Louis Napoleon as the Kingdom of Holland (1806–1810), had adopted the French civil and penal codes with only minor modifications. At the time of Quételet's comparison, the main difference between the two systems was that the jury had been abolished in the Netherlands (1829, p. 26).

This shows that since the beginning, the commentators of criminal statistics have been aware of many of the problems related to cross-national comparisons, such as the differences in the definitions of offenses, criminal codes and criminal proceedings codes, and ways of collecting data. Some of them, like Quételet or Mittermaier (1830), have mentioned these problems but considered that some types of comparisons could still be made, while others, like Alphonse De Candolle (1987 [1830]; 1987 [1832]), have been extremely reluctant to engage in international comparisons. As we will see throughout this chapter, these two positions can still be found among contemporary researchers. In addition, we will see, in the subsection on homicide as a proxy for violent offenses, that also since the beginning researchers have been complaining about the way in which the press compares levels of crime across nations.

Back in 1829, the Grand Duchy of Baden also published its conviction statistics, which were compared by Mittermaier (1829) to the data on convictions available from England as well as some regions of Switzerland, the United States, and other German states (see Reinke 1998). Then, in 1835, Ducpetiaux published a book including data from four Western European countries that seems to be the first one completely dedicated to cross-national comparisons of crime statistics.[2] Since then, the interest in comparative criminology has never ceased.

Among the most influential works of the second half of the nineteenth century, we can mention the first German doctoral dissertation based on criminal statistics, in which Georg von Mayr (1865) compared different states of Germany and established crime trends since the 1830s (Reinke 1998), as well as the studies conducted by researchers from the French and the Italian schools of criminology. Hence, in France, Gabriel Tarde (1886) published the classic book *Comparative Criminality* (*La criminalité comparée*), in which he analyzed recorded crime across countries and regions since the beginning of the statistical series in the mid-1820s. Tarde paid particular attention to the negative effects of industrialization on levels of crime in the cities compared to those in rural areas, which he considered healthier. It took almost a century to find data showing that interpersonal violence was indeed higher in the countryside (Johnson & Monkkonen 1996b). At the same time, Ferri (1895) produced his *Atlas of Homicide* spanning nations across Europe, which showed higher levels of homicide in the southern regions than the northern ones, and led to a debate on the influence of climate—a factor previously mentioned by Quételet (1835)—on delinquency. Ferri (1892, p. 256) was also among the first researchers to establish long-term homicide and suicide trends—covering in some cases several decades of the nineteenth century—for a series of European countries.

During the first half of the twentieth century, Verkko compared homicides across nations, but he published in Finnish, and despite Ekelund's (1942) efforts to summarize in English some of his main ideas, his work remained relatively unknown to the scientific community until he was translated in the second half of the century (see, e.g., Verkko 1967). Rusche and Kirchheimer (1939) also studied crime trends for different offenses in several European countries and during different periods of the nineteenth and early twentieth centuries, including data from police, conviction, and prison statistics, and giving a predominant role to the relationship between unemployment and crime.

In the 1960s, two different tendencies can be observed. Sociologists of deviance rediscovered the limits of criminal statistics (Kitsuse & Cicourel 1963) and became more interested in the social reaction to crime than in crime itself. At the same time, some historians started looking for data on crime from the years before the publication of the first criminal statistics. Among the latter, Pierre Chaunu directed in France a series of studies based on the analysis of ancient criminal proceedings that allowed the construction of time series and the development of the hypothesis known as "violence to theft"—which will be discussed later—to explain them (Boutelet & Chaunu 1962). Another group of French historians who specialized in punishment in the nineteenth century were interested in the development of the prison system. In 1975, the publication by philosopher Michel Foucault of *Discipline and Punish* presented an innovative view of the birth of prisons. Foucault (1975) believed that prisons became the main form of punishment in the late eighteenth and early nineteenth centuries in the context of the development of a disciplinary society. They thus were part of a carceral system that included schools, hospitals, psychiatric asylums, factories, and similar institutions whose aim was to discipline the bodies of the persons within them in order to control them. Nevertheless, Foucault in his analysis followed a heterodox method that was severely criticized by contemporary historians of punishment in a special issue of a French specialized journal.[3] This group asked Foucault "essentially, whether his dichotomies between *l'age classique* and *l'age moderne* do not reproduce the 'traditional-modern' schematization which has so bedeviled the historical genealogy of the industrial world" (Ignatieff 1982). They also criticized his idea of presenting France as having become a disciplined society by 1850 and were skeptical about the possibility of a hidden plan developed by the bourgeoisie to establish the prison system: "Who exactly was responsible for putting the carceral archipelago in place?" (Ignatieff 1982). Although later Foucault (2009) moderated his position, he is traditionally quoted according to his ideas of the mid-1970s.

In the meantime, and for reasons related to an increase in crime since the 1960s that will be developed more deeply in the next section, researchers became particularly interested in establishing long-term crime trends. Thus, by the end of the 1970s, there was enough empirical evidence to affirm that violent crime had been declining in Europe since the Middle Ages (Gurr 1981). Additionally, researchers started questioning the conclusions of the nineteenth-century authors who had considered that urbanization was related to an increase of crime (Lodhi & Tilly 1973). They also casted serious doubts on many classic ideas of that century, such as those related to the relationship among change, strain, and disorder, which suddenly seemed to lack empirical support (Tilly 1984, p. 53). The validity of these findings was enhanced by the fact that similar results were found in different regions of Western Europe, such as the Netherlands (Spierenburg 1994) and the Scandinavian countries (Österberg 1992), as well as in the United States (for an overview, see Johnson & Monkkonen 1996a).

In that context, European data became particularly relevant, as the study of long-term crime trends in the United States has been problematic because of the lack of national crime statistics until the development of the Federal Bureau of Investigation's Uniform Crime Reports in 1930. Before that, many U.S. states produced their own statistical collections, but only prison statistics were collected at the national level. Since the beginning of the twentieth century, Robinson (1910; 1911; 1920) had denounced such a situation and pleaded for the development of national statistics based on convictions. Nevertheless, court statistics at the national level were never fully developed.[4] Indeed, Robinson highlighted many of the drawbacks that are still mentioned by contemporary researchers, who usually are forced to establish long-term trends on the basis of data for specific cities or regions of the United States (Roth 2009). As a consequence, most of the research currently produced in that country focuses on crime rates after the Second World War.

II. Varieties of Contemporary Research on Crime Trends

The recent literature on crime trends admits at least three broad classifications based, respectively, on the unit of analysis, the type of offense studied, and the time span covered by the analysis. According to their unit of analysis, studies can be divided into those covering crime trends in a particular country and those adopting a comparative perspective including two or more countries. According to the type of offenses analyzed, studies that examine a single country or cover short periods of time typically contain analyses of several types of crime. On the contrary, the overwhelming majority of comparative studies, and especially those covering long periods of time, are dedicated to homicide trends. Other violent offenses, such as assault and robbery, have received less attention, while property offenses and cybercrime are seldom studied. Finally, according to the time span of the analysis, two types of studies can be distinguished. The first includes research covering the evolution of crime after the Second World War and has been written mainly by criminologists. The second includes research covering crime trends since the late Middle Ages and has been written by researchers from different fields including history, sociology, political science, philosophy, and, of course, criminology. Both approaches search for causal explanations of crime trends; however, the kind of analysis that can be conducted for each period is heavily conditioned by the available data. Research based on post-1945 trends can take advantage of the multiplication of macro-level indicators and indexes that are useful as independent variables. Hence, authors usually proceed to study the correlations between different crime measures and a series of socioeconomic, political, and cultural variables. These analyses have become increasingly sophisticated with the availability of statistical packages that allow the application of econometric models, although quite often there are serious doubts as to whether the data available are accurate enough for such models. On the opposite end of the spectrum, research covering long periods of time for which few independent variables are available tends to be more descriptive, as well as speculative, regarding the explanations of the trends observed.

In that perspective, the temporal distribution of studies on crime trends conducted during the last fifty years shows two peaks: one at the turn of the 1980s and the other at the turn of the 2000s, coinciding, respectively, with an upward and a downward trend in crime in the United States and Western European countries. At the time of the first peak, criminologists were trying to explain the rise in crime that followed the Second World War, and some researchers reacted by showing that such an increase was preceded by a long-term decrease. During that period, the most well-known example of an article written by criminologists, based on national data covering the period after the Second World War, including several offenses, and in which crime trends were tested against a series of independent variables is the study by Cohen and Felson (1979) that introduced the routine activities approach. At the same time, the most-quoted example of the work of a political scientist, covering several centuries, focused on violence, and including several countries is a 1981 paper by Ted Robert Gurr. It was published in the context of the debate on crime trends in Western societies, and it stressed that the increase in the 1960s and 1970s was preceded by a much longer downward trend, in such a way that the evolution of serious crime depicted a distended U-shaped curve. Gurr (1981) also drew a distinction between trends in the United States and those in Western Europe, and introduced the ideas of Elias (2000 [1939]) and the civilizing process to explain the evolution of crime since the early modern period.

At the turn of the 2000s, research on crime trends peaked again as criminologists started proposing explanations for the decrease in crime observed in the United States since 1992. Curiously enough, even after similar declines have been observed in other countries, many of the U.S. explanations are still focusing on local causes for such a decline (Goldberger & Rosenfeld 2008; Rosenfeld 2014), a situation that Tonry (2014, p. 3) describes as "at least a little parochial." In a comparative perspective, nonetheless, researchers placed this new decrease in the context of the well-known long-term downward trend in interpersonal violence (Eisner 2001; Eisner 2003). Thus, the upward trend observed from the 1960s to the early 1990s came to be viewed as an exception for which different explanations have been proposed (Aebi & Linde 2014c).

Hence, after almost 200 years of research, it can be said that the hypothesis of stable crime trends has been falsified, and the same is true for the correlation between urbanization and violent crime. Indeed, "rural societies of the distant past were far more violent than the predominantly urban societies of both the recent past and the present" (Johnson & Monkkonen 1996b, p. 7). The present state of knowledge has been reviewed by Pinker (2011), who produced a general overview of the decline of interpersonal violence, gathering information from prehistoric times to the twenty-first century. He shows that researchers currently tend to agree on the fact that, in the context of a civilizing process, violence has been decreasing in industrialized Western societies since the late Middle Ages (i.e., 1300–1500 C.E.), and that such a decrease was particularly important in the seventeenth and eighteenth centuries. In Western European countries, this decline has only been interrupted in three historical periods, during which the available data suggest an upward trend of homicide rates. The first one took place in the last decades of the sixteenth century, the second one at the turn of the nineteenth century (i.e., before and just after 1800), and the third one from the 1960s to the early 1990s (Eisner 2001, p. 633). In the United States, where the period of observation is shorter, there have been "three great surges of violent crime which began ca. 1850, 1900, and 1960" (Gurr 1981, p. 295). Nevertheless, it must be mentioned that a major objection to the concept of the civilizing process is that in order to accept it, one has to focus on the periods of peace and leave aside the genocides, mass killings, and homicides that took place in the same countries where the process was taking place (as exemplified in acts against members of native nations or ethnic or religious minorities), in their colonies, or in the territories where they were fighting wars in which many of the victims were civilians. This leads us to concentrate on the types of offenses that have been studied by researchers.

III. Defining Crime

A. Property and Violent Offenses

Gottfredson and Hirschi (1990) define crime as "acts of force or fraud undertaken in pursuit of self-interest" (p. 15). This wide-ranging definition, inspired by the classic principles of Roman law, presents the advantage of easily generating consensus. However, the main challenge for researchers interested in comparative crime trends is to identify the operational definitions of crime used across time and space.

From that perspective, property offenses are particularly problematic. Even if the basic principle remains the same—taking something that belongs to someone else against his or her will—the concepts of property and its distribution across the population have undergone so many changes that it is practically impossible to follow the evolution of theft through time and space. For example, large-scale economic crime has been documented since the times of the Roman Empire (Huisman et al. 2015, p. 3), but until recent times it had not been measured in terms of rates that could be used to establish trends and comparisons across nations. In the case of petty property offenses, Romantic literature of the nineteenth century conveys the image of the thief who steals to avoid starving. Its archetype is the main character of Victor Hugo's *Les Misérables*, who is punished for stealing bread. At that time, poverty was so extreme that the houses of the poor seldom included suitable targets for theft.[5] Hence, authors like Beccaria (2009 [1764]) seem to have taken for granted that the rich were the victims of theft, while thieves came mainly from the deprived classes.[6] Indeed, the link between poverty and property offenses seems profoundly engraved in the collective consciousness. This could explain why the basic version of anomie theory—a concept developed by Merton

(1938) during the Great Depression based on the distance between economic goals and the legitimate means to achieve them—is intuitively perceived as plausible by the public, even if the empirical evidence on it is still a matter of discussion among researchers.

In highly industrialized Western countries, the situation started to change in the second half of the twentieth Century with the development of a market economy, the generalization of access to consumer goods, and the miniaturization of electronic devices. At that moment, households started to be filled with suitable targets for theft. At the same time, the development of alternative crime measures, particularly crime victim surveys, helped researchers better understand the evolution of property crime in such a context and led to the development of new theories such as the lifestyle (Hindelang, Gottfredson, & Garofalo 1978) and routine activities (Cohen & Felson 1979) theories. The problem is that researchers still have not found reliable indicators of theft for the previous centuries and therefore have been unable to establish consistent long-term crime trends. As the same is true for white-collar crime, researchers specializing in long-term crime trends have concentrated their efforts on the study of the evolution of violent offenses.

The World Health Organization (WHO) defines violence as "the intentional use of physical force or power, threatened or actual, against oneself, another person, or against a group or community, that either results in or has a high likelihood of resulting in injury, death, psychological harm, maldevelopment or deprivation" (WHO 2002, p. 4). From this definition, the WHO devised a typology of three broad categories of violent acts: *self-directed violence* (which includes self-abuse and suicide); *interpersonal violence* (which includes family and intimate partner violence and community violence); and *collective violence* (subdivided into social, political, and economic violence).

Durkheim, one of the founding fathers of sociology, dedicated a full book to the study of suicide (1897 [2007]), but he also covered some forms of interpersonal violence. Probably because in some countries suicide was considered an offense until quite recently—in England and Wales, for example, it was decriminalized only by the Suicide Act of 1961—criminologists continued to pay attention to it during the twentieth century. However, their main focus of research has been the evolution of interpersonal violence. Initially they principally studied community violence, defined as "violence between individuals who are unrelated, and who may or may not know each other, generally taking place outside the home" (WHO 2002, p. 5). However, since the last quarter of the twentieth century, family and intimate partner violence has also been the object of many studies.

Once more, it is the operationalization of the concept of violence that complicates the picture. First of all, there is currently a general consensus that the perception of what is a violent act has changed throughout the centuries. In particular, industrialized Western societies have become more sensitive to violence. To name but one example, physical punishment of children by their parents was tolerated without much discussion until the second half of the twentieth century. This means that an offense such as assault has undergone a lot of modifications in its definition. Rape has also been redefined, and robbery, as we have seen before, is affected by the availability of suitable targets.

As a consequence, in order to operationalize violence, most studies concentrate on homicide, which is usually defined as the intentional killing of a person. With this definition, this behavior is probably the only one whose interdiction seems stable across time, even if exceptions can be found under specific circumstances such as war. The question then becomes: Is homicide a good proxy for violent offenses?

B. Homicide as a Proxy for Violent Offenses

Every year, the publication of crime statistics by Eurostat or the Council of Europe is followed by a series of press articles that compare figures across countries. Generally, such comparisons are performed in an inadequate way and produce misleading conclusions. That is why serious newspapers usually add comments by experts that warn the reader about the risks of such comparisons.[7] The idea of progress is seriously undermined when one reads De Candolle (1987 [1832]) and finds out that the same debates were taking place almost 200 years ago.[8] A classic mistake, for example, is to compare the total number of recorded offenses or convictions imposed, as these are the worst indicators for such comparisons because they amplify the problems linked to the recording of each particular type of crime. Already in the 1820s, Quételet (1829) had mentioned the debate generated by the fact that the number of persons accused of crimes in England was six times higher than in France, and had explained that the comparison was inadequate because data for England included not only felonies (*crimes*) but also misdemeanors (*affaires correctionnelles*). In order to solve this problem, he was probably the first researcher to suggest comparing similar crimes—in particular, murder (Quételet 1829, p. 25).[9]

A century and a half later, Gurr (1981) took into account the results of the first victimization surveys—which showed that the correspondence between police and victimization data increased with the seriousness of the offense (Skogan 1976)—to highlight the relevance of murder for the study of trends in interpersonal violence. If the more serious crimes are the ones that are most often reported to the police, then "murder is the most accurately recorded violent crime" (Gurr 1981, p. 298). Similarly, analyzing the validity of conviction statistics as measures of homicide, Gurr concluded that "because homicide usually has been committed by people known to the victim (as evinced by many microstudies) and in Western societies usually has attracted close official attention, the slippage between act and court record is probably less for homicide than other crimes against persons" (1981, p. 299).

Hence, Gurr (1981) and later Eisner (2003) and Pinker (2011) used homicide trends as a proxy for trends in interpersonal violence. The fact that homicide and nonlethal violent offenses followed similar trends in English-speaking countries during the second half of the twentieth century and into the 2000s (Tonry 2014) reinforced that use. However, in continental Western Europe, assault and homicide had opposite trends—with assault increasing and homicide decreasing—from the 1990s to the mid-2000s (Aebi & Linde 2010; Aebi & Linde 2012). Tonry (2014, p. 39) suggests that the difference could be artificial, reflecting "major shifts in cultural thresholds of tolerance of violence." According to him, "nonlethal violence should be probabilistically associated with lethal violence in the same way that traffic deaths are with vehicle miles driven. Both sets of outcomes are products of the law of large numbers. . . . Deaths should be probabilistically associated with the total number of potentially violent incidents" (Tonry 2014, p. 39).

Nevertheless, there is no definitive empirical evidence about such a relationship in Western continental Europe, and the situation is more complicated when the sample includes countries from other regions of the world. Thus, comparing fifty-eight countries around the world using the International Crime Victim Survey (ICVS), the United Nations Office on Drugs and Crime (UNODC) (2011) found that, in general, many of the countries with high homicide rates also showed high robbery rates. Taking into account that ICVS rates are not affected by the validity and reliability problems of official statistics, and that homicide is the offense most effectively recorded by the latter, the authors concluded that homicide can be considered "a reasonable proxy for violent crime in general" (UNODC 2011, p. 15). However, there is no association between homicide and other violent offenses included in the ICVS such as assault (including threats) and rape. Consequently, the UNODC also recognizes this significant variation across nations: "There are countries in which there is an abundance of violent crime that does not result in homicide and others where homicide appears high in comparison to general levels of non-lethal violence" (2011, p. 15).

Hence, recent data suggest that the correlation between homicide and other violent offenses varies across countries. The characteristics of that correlation during previous periods of the history of humankind remain unknown. The reason is that although one can find indirect indicators of homicide for different periods (Pinker 2011), it is almost impossible to find them for crimes such as assault, rape, or robbery—which, incidentally, is considered a property offense in civil law countries. In sum, there is a tendency among researchers to consider homicide as a reasonable proxy for violent offenses, even if the empirical evidence for that correlation is not conclusive.

IV. Measuring Long-Term Crime Trends

A. Sources for Research on Long-Term Crime Trends

Studies covering the current level of crime or its short-term evolution are mostly based on criminal justice statistics—which correspond to those collected by police, prosecution, court, and prison authorities and are usually known as "official" statistics—victimization surveys,[10] and, for youth samples, self-reported delinquency studies. The limitations of these sources have been thoroughly studied, and there is consensus among researchers that while none of them produces an accurate picture of the levels and trends in crime, their combination can increase our understanding of them. Other statistics and specific surveys can also be useful. In particular, public health data are often considered the most reliable source for data on homicide victimization (LaFree 2005) and are part of the mortality statistics that countries elaborate according to the International Classification of Diseases developed by the WHO.

The situation is harder to solve for studies covering long-term trends because most of the measures of crime mentioned previously are relatively new. Self-reported delinquency surveys did not become a usual measure of crime until the second half of the twentieth century, and victimization surveys only reached wide usage in the last quarter of it. In the case of police statistics for Western nations, "rarely do the records antedate the establishment of modern police forces in the mid to late nineteenth century" (Gurr 1981, p. 298). For example, in England and Wales, police data—in the form of indictable offenses reported to the police—have only been available since 1857, when the country started publishing comprehensive national criminal statistics (Maguire 2007, p. 244). Prison statistics have existed since the nineteenth century, but, as they mainly reflect the levels of punishment within a society, their relationship with crime trends is only indirect. For example, studies about the long-term evolution of prison populations in Belgium (Vanneste 2003) and Italy (Melossi 2009) have usually found a relationship between trends in homicide and trends in the prison population, even if they were inspired by the work of Rusche and Kirchheimer (1939) and were mainly testing the relationship between imprisonment and unemployment. The exceptions to this scarcity of indicators are Sweden and Finland (which was a part of Sweden until 1809), which disposed of mortality statistics since the middle of the eighteenth century.

In sum, in Western European countries, conviction statistics are the main official source of crime data for research covering trends during the last two centuries. As we mentioned in the introduction, conviction statistics started to be published in some European countries in the late 1820s.[11] Indeed, such publications usually combined what are nowadays called "prosecution statistics" with conviction statistics. That is why Gurr (1981, p. 299) states that "most studies of nineteenth-century crime, and virtually all earlier ones, use data on indictments/committals or convictions."

For all these reasons, researchers interested in long-term trends keep searching for alternative measures of crime, and one can say that they are particularly imaginative. In a review of the literature, Rousseaux (1993) identifies studies conducted on the basis of the sentences pronounced by the courts of specific jurisdictions, medical sources such as coroners' records of homicides and death registration data in England and Wales, and the minutes taken when a dead body was found in Amsterdam and Normandy. For non-state societies, the two main sources of data for homicides have been the records of ethnographers—who registered the deaths that occurred in the societies they were studying—and "forensic archaeologists, who sift through burial sites or museum collections with an eye for signs of foul play . . . such as . . . a spearhead or arrowhead embedded in a bone . . . bashed-in skulls, cut marks from stone tools on skulls or limbs, and parry fractures on ulnar bones" (Pinker 2011, p. 48). These sources allow the production of rough estimates of the percentage of deaths caused by violence.

It is also interesting to note here that, among its many privileges, the aristocracy also historically benefited from detailed records of its demography. Hence, using data from Hollingsworth (1965), Clark (2007, p. 122) has estimated the net reproduction rate and the life expectancy for males at birth and at age twenty for English aristocrats (kings and dukes), as well as the fractions of death from violence among them, which decreased from 26 percent in the period 1330–1479 to 4 percent in the period 1780–1829.

Finally, trying to measure the evolution of intolerance to violence, researchers have used indicators such as the abolition of judicial torture, which took place from the 1750s to the 1850s in most continental countries, although it was first abolished in England in 1640 and in Scotland in 1708 (Hunt 2007; Mannix 1964). Nevertheless, there have been setbacks in this development. For example, on January 20, 2015, U.S. president Barack Obama stated in his State of the Union address before Congress: "As Americans, we respect human dignity, even when we're threatened, which is why I have prohibited torture."[12] Also in the United States, another indicator of increased sensitivity to violence used by researchers is the decrease in execution rates since the beginning of the seventeenth century (Pinker 2011, pp. 151). In Europe, one of the conditions for membership in the Council of Europe—which currently counts forty-seven member-states—is to have abolished the death penalty or at least introduced a moratorium on its application. However, once more we must mention that the idea of a civilizing process, which includes the abolition of torture, has been seriously damaged by the clearly established fact that torture has been reintroduced during colonial wars, national liberation wars, dictatorship regimes, and the contemporary combat against terrorism. And, of course, the validity and reliability of all of the abovementioned measures of crime and violence remain a matter of endless discussion, as we will briefly see in the next section.

B. The Validity of the Sources for Research on Long-Term Crime Trends

None of the available sources for research on long-term crime trends is perfectly valid. In this section we summarize the problems related to the use of conviction statistics, which provide the longest historical series of crime data. However, most of the problems related to the use of conviction statistics are similar to the ones found when using other types of criminal justice statistics (see, e.g., Aebi 2010).

As we have seen, although some criminologists tend to consider Kitsuse and Cicourel (1963) the discoverers of both the dark figure and the limitations of criminal statistics (Ouimet & Tessier-Jasmin 2009), the fact is that both these concepts were identified by the first researchers, and in particular by Alphonse De Candolle (1987 [1830]; 1987 [1832]), in the early 1830s, immediately after the publication of the French national judiciary statistics. De Candolle (1987 [1830]) mentioned that such statistics did not include the offenses that had not been discovered by their victims and those that the victims decided not to report. As Beirne (1993, p. 105) points out, this is probably the first mention of the dark figure of crime. De Candolle (1987 [1830]) also noted that conviction statistics based on the number of persons convicted do not include those cases in which the author of the crime is unknown of those in which the legal procedure does not lead to a sentence by a court. He identified some of the methodological problems related to the study of crime trends, mentioning that sudden changes in them could be due to changes in prosecution activity (De Candolle 1987 [1830]). Similarly, he rejected the idea proposed by Quételet (1831) of a constant proportion between the total number of offenses committed and the number of offenses known and tried by a judicial authority, stating that such a proportion could vary across time, hence affecting crime trends (De Candolle 1987 [1832]). He was also reluctant to engage in cross-national comparisons because the number of unknown crimes varied from one country to another (De Candolle 1987 [1830]) and because there were important differences across national criminal justice systems (De Candolle 1987 [1832]). In that context, he paid particular attention to the presence or absence of a jury, which he considered the main cause of mistakes in comparisons. He also identified varying legal definitions of offenses and procedural systems as major sources of distortions. Finally, he suggested that if cross-national comparisons were to be made, they should be based on the number of accused persons instead of on the number of sentenced persons (De Candolle 1987 [1832]). The reason was that many offenses known to the prosecution authorities do not lead to a conviction.

As can be seen, De Candolle anticipated by 100 years the so-called Sellin's dictum, which states that "*the value of a crime rate for index purposes decreases as the distance from the crime itself in terms of procedure increases*" (Sellin 1931, p. 346, emphasis in the original). If the *validity* of a crime measure is defined as its capacity to measure efficiently the phenomenon under study—that is, crime—this means that conviction statistics are less valid than police statistics because the latter are closer to the offense itself. On the other hand, if the *reliability* of a crime measure is defined as its capacity to provide measurements that are intersubjective and reproducible—that is, to reach the same result independent of the person who manipulates the instrument—conviction statistics can be seen as more reliable than police statistics. The reason is that conviction statistics are based on a decision made by a judge that relies on much more information than was available to the police officers who recorded the offense. Also, if different judges arrive at different sentences in similar cases, a superior court will intervene in order to unify the jurisprudence.[13] Thus, many authors consider conviction statistics to be a useful indicator of crime trends (von Hofer & Lappi-Seppala 2014).

The problems related to the counting unit of conviction statistics identified by De Candolle are still a matter of concern. Thus, when conducting cross-national comparisons, it is essential to identify whether the statistics of the countries being compared are based on convictions or on persons convicted, and whether they apply a principal offense rule implying that an offender convicted for several offenses is counted only once and for the most serious offense. Another source of differences across countries relates to the point at which data are collected for the statistics, as some countries record court decisions before any appeal is made, while others record them after the appeals have been exhausted (Aebi et al. 2010, pp. 165–66).

As far as divergences in the definition of offenses are concerned, intentional homicide provides a good example. It has been mentioned before that this crime is often used for international comparisons because it is supposed to be defined in a similar way across nations. However, there are several sources of distortion, including the way in which this crime is distinguished from negligent homicide and manslaughter, and the more subtle distinctions that can exist among intentional homicide, murder, assault leading to death, and nonnegligent manslaughter. These differences can be even more important in a historical perspective. For example, in France during the *Ancien Régime*—from the fifteenth century to the start of the French Revolution in 1789—the intention to kill was not taken into account, and each act capable of causing death was considered a homicide (Rousseaux 1993). Finally, the way in which attempted homicides are recorded can also introduce major differences. For example, across European nations, the percentage of attempted homicides recorded by the police can vary from 10 percent to 90 percent of the total recorded homicides (Aebi 2010). In the case of conviction statistics, the influence of the ratio between completed and attempted offenses on cross-national comparisons is less well known because most countries provide an overall total of persons convicted for murder, which include attempts at murder, but are unable to indicate the percentage of the total the latter comprises.

In sum, multiple problems can affect the comparability of crime measures, and researchers interested in comparative criminology must be aware that they will spend a good part of their time trying to find ways of dealing with such problems. Whenever it is possible, a comparison of different sources for the same phenomenon is a good starting point to identify potential complications and improve time series. In Sweden, for example, von Hofer (1990) compared homicides during the nineteenth and twentieth centuries according to mortality statistics—available since the 1750s—and according to conviction statistics—available since the 1830s. He found that even if the statistics were based on different counting units—victims of homicide in the case of mortality statistics, and persons sentenced for homicide in the case of conviction statistics—the trends were quite similar. In similar cases, Monkkonen (2001) recommends comparing both series using the *capture-recapture* technique of the Chandra-Sekar-Deming method, which can be a useful tool for identifying homicides omitted or unrecorded in the original sources.

V. Pitfalls of Theoretical Interpretations of Crime Trends

Once the data have been found, the researcher faces the challenge of establishing appropriate hypotheses and interpretations of the trends that can be established. Some of these challenges are similar to those usually found in criminological research, but others are specific or take a particular turn when applied to the study of crime trends. This section focuses on four of these specific issues: the problem of the denominator, chronocentrism, parochialism, and causationism.

A. The Problem of the Denominator

It is well known that absolute numbers are useless for comparative research. For example, the number of thefts in a given city does not provide any information on the number of potential targets for such thefts, security measures, population, or geographic characteristics of the city. An additional problem for comparative criminologists is that all these variables fluctuate across time and space. Homicides are usually presented as rates per 100,000 inhabitants, but the population of cities and countries during remote periods of time is extremely difficult to estimate. For example, in the case of the rates of murders in the United States before the first census of 1790, not only is it difficult to establish the numerator (i.e., the number of murders), but "the denominator, too, is often no better than an educated guess" (Lane 2011). In small towns, changes in the denominator can drastically modify rates, while in big cities it is sometimes difficult to establish whether the number of homicides recorded includes those committed in adjacent regions—for which authors of such crimes may have been judged in the closest capital—whose estimated population is not taken into account in the computation of the rates. Hence, Monkkonen (2001) posits that homicide rates in medieval cities, such as those calculated by Hammer (1978) for Oxford, could be highly overestimated. In order to solve that problem, he suggests following the example of demographers by using the capture-recapture method to estimate the population (i.e., the denominator) of each place studied. The structure of the population must also be taken into account in the computation because, historically, the rate of homicides has been related to the percentage of young males in the general population, and this percentage has changed widely throughout history under the influence of variations in infant mortality, waves of immigration—mostly composed of young males—and infant mortality. Thus, Monkkonen (2001) has shown how the use of age-standardized homicide rates can change the picture of homicide in several cities in the 1880s and early 1890s.

B. Chronocentrism

The concept of chronocentrism (from the Greek *chrono*, time, and *kentron*, center) has been applied to criminology by Rock (2005), who took it from (Morson 1996) and defined it as "the unsubstantiated, often uninspected, almost certainly untenable but powerful doctrine that what is current must somehow be superior to what went before" (Rock 2005, p. 474). Although this author uses the concept to show how the younger generations of criminologists tend to forget what was written by the previous generations, it is also possible to apply it in a more general sense.

In that perspective, quite often the current generation considers that they are at the end of some sort of evolutionary process. For example, in *The End of History and the Last Man*, Fukuyama (1992) concludes that liberal democracies are the final form of government and represent the final point in the sociocultural evolution of humanity. Even if the author used his title with some irony, and probably a good sense of marketing, there is no doubt that, twenty years later, history continues its course and the map of the world continues to change. In the case of crime trends, researchers working in the 1980s talked about a "distended U-shaped curve" to explain the evolution of violence from the early modern period to the 1970s (Gurr 1981, p. 296) because they could not anticipate the future evolution of it. Thirty years later, the increase in violence from the 1960s to the 1990s can be seen as an exception to a long-lasting decreasing trend. Thus, Pinker (2011, p. 106), who applies Elias's (2000 [1939]) idea of a civilizing process to explain such trends, talks about "de-civilization" in the 1960s and "re-civilization" in the 1990s. When the next upward trend arrives, researchers will probably start to think about a curvilinear evolution of violence since the Second World War.

C. Parochialism

The online Oxford *British and World English Dictionary* defines parochialism as "a limited or narrow outlook, especially focused on a local area; narrow-mindedness." In the context of research on crime trends, parochialism can assume two forms. The first one consists of analyzing trends in one country and proposing local explanations for them without taking into account what is going on in similar countries. Thus, the researcher loses the opportunity of testing whether there are common trends that would require general instead of local explanations. The second form, which can also be seen as a light form of ethnocentrism, consists of extrapolating the trends found in one country to other countries without studying the latter.

Many of the explanations given to the crime drop observed in the United States from 1992 onward can be seen as parochial—according to the first form of parochialism presented in the prior paragraph—because they focus on local explanations that could not be applied to other countries experiencing similar trends in crime (Eisner 2008; Tonry 2014). A well-known illustration of this pitfall can be seen in the presentation of the first edition of *The Crime Drop in America*, a book by Blumstein and Wallman (2000), at the American Society of Criminology conference of 2000 in San Francisco. The session was summarized by Young (2004), who mentions that "the first question, from a Canadian woman, was something of a revelation. She pointed out, ironically, how Canadians were supposed to be condemned to culturally lag behind their American cousins, but that they too had had a drop in violence, despite the fact that they had not experienced such a period of rapid prison expansion, that zero-tolerance policing was not de rigueur and that Canada had only a small problem of crack-cocaine" (Young 2004, pp. 27–28). The "Canadian woman" was the well-known criminologist Rosemary

Gartner (Laub 2001), and her remarks were taken into account for the second edition of the book (Blumstein & Wallman 2006).

The second type of parochialism is often a consequence of the fact that long-term crime data are currently available for only a small group of highly industrialized Western countries. Thus, the trends observed in these countries are sometimes extrapolated to other regions of the world for which data are not available. This approach takes a more subtle form when the classification of countries into nonindustrialized (developing), in transition, and industrialized—even if many of the latter have relocated their industries in offshore countries—is seen as a sort of ordinal and longitudinal scale. Then it is inferred that the current situation in nonindustrialized nations corresponds to that experienced by industrialized countries 100 or 200 years ago, and it is supposed that the former will follow the same evolution of the latter, not only in terms of industrialization, but also in terms of crime trends. For example, according to LaFree (2005, p. 192), "an important underlying assumption of contemporary modernization theorists ... is that nations evolve through similar developmental stages, as lesser-developed nations gradually adopt the characteristics of more developed nations." This idea was first developed by Shelley (1981), who later modified her position in consideration of the fact that industrialization and urbanization are not always accompanied by political and social modernization (Howard, Newman, & Pridemore 2000; Shelley 1986). In practice, this idea remains active, and quite often it is suggested that the high rates of crime observed in nonindustrialized nations will tend to decline with modernization. Incidentally, the same suggestion can be made when crime trends are explained through the theory of the civilizing process (Elias 2000 [1939]).

D. Causationism

Causationism is the "doctrine or theory that every event is the result of a prior and adequate cause."[14] Criminologists, sociologists, economists, and other social scientists regularly show their inability to make accurate predictions of future macro-level trends in their disciplines. Instead, quite often they act as historians, concentrating on previous trends and providing different causal explanations for them. Thus, in the same way that economists did not predict the financial crisis of 2008 but have provided several explanations for it, criminologists did not predict the crime drop in the United States but have proposed, and continue to propose, different explanations for it. The latter are essentially causal explanations. To name but a few, the drop in crime in the United States has been partially attributed to an increase in imprisonment (Levitt 1996), the legalization of abortion (Donohue & Levitt 2001), an increase in the number of police officers (Levitt 2004), the end of the crack epidemic (Blumstein & Rosenfeld 1998), and changes in demographics and economic opportunities (Blumstein & Wallman 2006).

However, even when trying to explain the past, social scientists do not always reach consensus. Thus, while some authors continue to quote the legalization of abortion as one of the causes of the homicide drop, others consider such an explanation to not be appropriate (Joyce 2004). Both groups show correlations between homicide, abortion, and other variables, but none can definitely prove that they are completely right and the others are completely wrong. That is why the reader usually chooses the explanation that better fits her or his *Weltanschauung*, or the one that is presented in the most convincing way from a rhetorical point of view.

We have reached here the main inner limitation of social sciences: they leave a significant margin of interpretation that, unfortunately, is sometimes filled with ideology. That is why there are no real scientific revolutions in the social sciences. Social theories are seldom falsified and tend to cumulate. Thomas S. Kuhn was fully aware of that fact, and, already in the preface of the book in which he introduced the concept of scientific revolutions, he stated that he was "struck by the number and extent of the overt disagreements between social scientists about the nature of legitimate scientific problems and methods" and "the controversies over fundamentals that today often seem endemic among, say, psychologists or sociologists" (Kuhn 1970, p. vii).

In the case of crime trends, this paradox has been well summarized by Hanns von Hofer (2012), who was intrigued by the number and diversity of explanations proposed for the evolution of crime in Europe after the Second Word War. In particular, he wondered whether it was really possible to talk about "crime trends" (and consequently to propose substantial explanations for such trends), or whether we were facing a "random walk" (in other words, if the evolution observed is purely accidental). According to him, "it becomes clear that yearly crime data from the post-war period (presently about 60 observations) in many instances cannot form a robust empirical basis to decide whether we observe causal trends or random patterns in the data. Many criminological time series studies comprise an even shorter time period" (p. 86).

VI. THEORETICAL EXPLANATIONS OF CRIME TRENDS

Two main theories have usually been used to explain long-term crime trends: the Durkheimian modernization perspective and civilization theory. For shorter periods of time, particularly for crime trends since the Second World War, the ecological opportunity perspective is also quoted quite frequently. Finally, the Marxian world system perspective has mainly been used to explain cross-sectional differences across nations or the changes that take place inside a country during the transition toward a market economy. The four perspectives will be presented here. The reader must be aware that they were developed ex post facto, that is, that they were produced to explain trends that were already apparent and not to predict future trends. As a consequence, they tend to fit well the trends they are supposed to explain. For example, civilization theory was developed in the late 1930s to explain the changes observed in European societies since the Middle Ages; the Marxian world-system perspective took form in the

1970s and reflects the conflictive period in which it was produced, characterized by the national liberation wars, the Vietnam War, the dictatorships supported by some core nations across the world, and the Cold War; the ecological opportunity perspective was developed at the end of the 1970s to explain the crime trends shown by victimization surveys; and, finally, the Durkheimian modernization perspective finds its remote origins in the second half of the nineteenth century, when several researchers were trying to propose explanations for the changes they observed related to modernity. Curiously enough, we will see that research conducted in the second half of the twentieth century found that the crime trends that the Durkheimian modernization theory tried to explain had been calculated incorrectly—in particular, finding erroneously that old rural societies were more violent than the new metropolises—and therefore it could be considered the only theory to have been falsified. However, and probably to the great despair of Karl Popper, the theory was consequently modified, and since then continues to be one of the most quoted and tested perspectives.[15] Old theories die hard.

A. The Durkheimian Modernization Perspective and Its Derivatives

Most of the cross-national studies conducted by criminologists since the 1970s apply the Durkheimian modernization perspective to explain variations in levels of crime, particularly homicide, across nations (Neuman & Berger 1988; Nivette 2011). Basically, this perspective "suggests rapid societal and structural change to be the primary source of deviance within a society" (Kick & LaFree 1985; LaFree 1999; Nivette 2011). As its name indicates, this perspective finds its inspiration in the work of Emile Durkheim (1893 [1997]), who studied the consequences for social cohesion of the transition from the so-called traditional to modern society in France during the second half of the nineteenth century. Durkheim (1893 [1997]) first focused his approach on the interdependence among individuals created by the division of labor, considering that such a division could pacify the relationships among individuals, but could also adopt pathological forms. It is in this context that he mentioned the *anomic* division of labor that could lead to behaviors going against the social rules. Durkheim borrowed the term *anomie* from Jean-Marie Guyau, who had coined it from the Greek *a-nomos* (absence of rules) in 1885 (Boudon & Bourricaud 1989). Later, in his work on suicide, Durkheim (1897 [2007]) characterized anomie as a sentiment of alienation that can emerge in periods of transition, when old values are replaced by new ones. In that context, individuals cannot control their desires, which are unlimited, and suffer a sickness of infinity, which may lead to suicide. This concept is quite close to the *spleen* immortalized by Charles Baudelaire in *Les Fleurs du mal* (1993 [1857]).

In the 1930s, during the Great Depression in the United States, the concept of anomie was redefined by Merton (1938) and became less sophisticated than its original formulation. In this form, it started referring to the distance between institutionalized means and cultural goals, which can be particularly far away from each other in a period of economic crisis (Merton 1938). Later, Shelley (1981) adapted this theory for use in comparative criminology. Since then, studies finding higher homicide rates in nonindustrialized countries than in the industrialized ones usually justify their findings by saying that the former are undergoing a process of modernization, suggesting that such rates will decrease as industrialization is fully achieved. Thus, nowadays Durkheim is usually interpreted as having predicted that crime would rise in periods of transition, but if that is the case, then one of the most striking results of research on long-term trends in homicide is that it has proven that Durkheim was wrong (Killias 1991). Western European societies underwent their major cultural and socioeconomic change in the past 250 years, including the rise of industrialization and big cities, the development of the proletariat, and the spread of science and education, but did not react to such strain with an increase of interpersonal violence. As Eisner (2008, p. 302) puts it: "If anything, modernity was associated with decreasing homicide."

Indeed, the success of the Durkheimian modernization perspective among criminologists is inversely proportional to its rejection by historians since the 1990s. Sharpe, for example, has said:

> I have always been a little unhappy with the concept of "modernization," and it was never as widely adopted in Britain as it seems to have been in the United States a decade or two ago: indeed, the English Marxist historian Edward Thompson once referred to modernization theory as "a pseudo-knowledge that has prestige on a few American campuses." It seems to me that if we accept "modernization" as a useful shorthand term, it is another way of stating the main lines of development formulated by classical sociology: Marx's concept of a transition from feudalism to capitalism, Weber's notion of the transition from a "traditional" to a "rational" society, or that other old friend, the shift from *Gemeinschaft* to *Gesellschaft* traced by Tönnies. All of these thinkers (and, one suspects, a number of others who were influential in the decades around 1900 but who are now more or less forgotten) were concerned with exploring the problematic of the great transition from a stable, rural, preindustrial society to an unstable, urban, and industrial one. (1996, p. 20)

The most well-know derivative of modernization theory in the field of long-term crime trends is the violence to theft hypothesis developed by Pierre Chaunu and his colleagues in France in the early 1960s (Boutelet & Chaunu 1962). Studying a sample of criminal proceedings in Normandy, they found that most of the criminals sentenced in the seventeenth century were violent offenders, malnourished and incapable of controlling themselves during the summer harvest. On the contrary, in the eighteenth century, most of the sentenced criminals were reasoning criminals who tried to steal from and deceive others (Boutelet & Chaunu 1962). These scholars suggested that the delinquency treated by the courts had shifted from violent offenses to property offenses as a result of changes in mental structures, self-control, and lifestyles. This hypothesis was quite popular in the 1960s, a period in which many European intellectuals sympathized with a Marxist analysis of society that considered property the main cause of crime. Nevertheless, the vast majority of empirical analyses have rejected this hypothesis. According to Johnson and Monkkonen (1996b, pp. 6–7), "the popular *de la violence au vol* (from violence to theft) 'modernization' thesis does not hold up to empirical verification. . . . Hence the perceived decline in violence over the long term was in fact real and not merely a spurious correlate of a growing interest in prosecuting property crimes in bourgeois society. Whereas violence certainly did decrease over the centuries, there is no solid evidence that property crimes actually increased."

B. Civilization Theory

Norbert Elias introduced the concept of a civilizing process in 1939, but his work remained almost confidential until the 1960s before becoming a classic at the turn of the 1980s, when he was rediscovered by researchers trying to explain the decline in homicide since the late modern period. In a nutshell, Elias (2000 [1939]) suggested that since the Middle Ages, Western European societies have experienced a series of changes related to the division of labor and the monopolization of the use of violence by the state, which also led to the development of the modern state. These changes increased the interdependence among individuals and were mirrored by a change in their *habitus* and an increase in self-restraint. The process described by Elias fits perfectly well the long-term decline in interpersonal violence observed by researchers such as Gurr (1981), Eisner (2003), and Pinker (2011), who consequently have adopted it as their main theoretical framework.[16]

In the mid-1990s, Johnson and Monkkonen (1996b) tried to explain why this idea of Elias had not commonly been accepted during the past fifty years: "Elias's work has many substantive implications that historians would have found unacceptable thirty years ago: first, that control of violent behavior emanated from courts; second, that urban centers would have more 'civilized' behavior; third, that areas where state systems had not yet penetrated would be more impulsively violent; and, fourth, that, over time, violence would decline." Furthermore, they stated, Elias' work ran contrary to the persuasive argument "that, with the breakdown of family and community (*Gemeinschaft*) and the rise of mass society (*Gesellschaft*), especially through urbanization, industrialization, and the class alignment of capitalist societies, crime has increased" (Johnson & Monkkonen 1996b, p. 5). Indeed, until the turn of the 1980s, explanations of crime trends were mostly based on modernization theory and its derivatives, among which the so-called violence to theft thesis (Boutelet & Chaunu 1962) played a major role. It was not until then that Gurr (1981) introduced the ideas of Elias to the criminological scientific community as an explanation of long-term crime trends, while Cohen and Felson (1979) proposed the routine activities approach to explain short-term crime trends.

C. The Ecological Opportunity Perspective

The ecological opportunity perspective refers mainly to the routine activities approach developed by Cohen and Felson (1979) and sometimes called opportunity theory (Cohen, Kluegel, & Land 1981). When it was first proposed by Cohen and Felson (1979), the routine activities approach suggested that the socioeconomic improvements that took place in the United States after the Second World War had led to an increase in crime because they provided further opportunities to engage in criminal behaviors. Thus, the increase in the average income of the population meant that more consumer goods were bought and could be stolen, while technological improvements meant that smaller portable devices were produced that could easily be stolen. Opportunities for burglary, for example, increased as single households proliferated, females were fully incorporated into the job market, and increasing household income allowed people to spend more time outside their homes. Thus there was a decrease in the number of capable guardians who could protect the houses, which were empty during longer periods of time. The postwar period therefore saw an increase of suitable targets and a decrease of capable guardians, and this led potential offenders to find more opportunities to commit crime (Cohen & Felson 1979; Felson 1987). In their original analysis of crime rates in the United States from 1947 to 1974, Cohen and Felson (1979) included homicide, forcible rape, and aggravated assault as indicators of violent offenses. They suggested that their rise was due to the growth of the nonhousehold-nonfamily activities that we have just described, which had increased the risk of personal victimization. In a similar perspective, the latter was explained by *lifestyle theory*—which was proposed almost at the same time—which focused on the increasing amount of time individuals spent in public places, particularly at night (Hindelang, Gottfredson, & Garofalo 1978). The routine activities and lifestyle theories have also been used to explain crime trends in Europe, including homicide victimization from 1960 to 2010 (Aebi & Linde 2014c). However, as far as we know, the ecological opportunity perspective has not been applied to explain long-term crime trends, as defined in this article. The reason may well be that the main indicator of such trends used by researchers are victimization surveys, which were not available before the 1970s. Eisner (2008) has argued that ecological opportunity theory cannot explain long-term trends in homicide because several potential drivers of violence in public space, like alcohol consumption and leisure time, were increasing at the beginning of the twentieth century, while homicide was decreasing. However, it seems an interesting challenge to try to find alternative indicators for a theory that fits well the evolution of crime since the 1950s.

D. Marxian World System Perspective

The Marxian world system perspective, sometimes called simply conflict theory (LaFree 2005), can be seen as a "synthesis of Marxian criminology and world system theory" (Neuman & Berger 1988, p. 284). Contrary to the previous theories, it was not proposed by a single author, but is the result of the works of several and therefore is not exempt from contradictions. For this reason, LaFree, Curtis, and McDowall (2015) refer to it using the plural denomination of "conflict perspectives."

The premise of the Marxian world system perspective is that the uneven expansion of the market economy has created three categories of countries: *core nations*, which are industrialized and take advantage of the natural resources of *semi-periphery nations*— most of which are their former colonies, rich in natural resources—and *periphery nations*, which are underdeveloped and are at the mercy of the core and periphery nations (Howard, Newman, & Pridemore 2000)

From a cross-sectional point of view, some of the premises of this perspective can be tested through a comparison of crime in these three types of nations. Such analyses have shown, for example, that homicide rates are much higher in the peripheral nations of Central America and Africa than in the core nations of Western Europe (UNODC 2014). From a longitudinal point of view, which is relevant to the discussion in this chapter, this theory has mainly been used to explain the consequences of the development of capitalism in precapitalist societies and its negative effects on social relationships. However, the literature on this topic has to face the lack of reliable indicators for establishing long-term trends. Moreover, it has been produced mainly by political scientists, anthropologists, and sociologists, and, as a consequence, criminological issues are treated only in a superficial way (Howard, Newman, & Pridemore 2000). An additional inconvenience comes from the fact that there seems to be no theoretical consensus on the way crime should develop in the long run, especially as countries achieve their transition from one economic category to another. For example, in the 2010s, the former Soviet republics that joined the European Union are considered transition economies, while some Asian and American nations have joined the category of newly industrialized countries, but conflict perspectives do not provide a clear hypothesis about the future evolution of crime in these countries.

Finally, recent empirical analyses of short-term trends in homicide show that, since the beginning of the 1990s, wealthy nations have shown decreasing trends, while non-wealthy nations have shown increases (LaFree, Curtis, & McDowall 2015). This increase has affected in particular several Central and Southern American nations (Baumer & Wolff 2014).

CONCLUSION

Criminologists have been interested in cross-national comparisons of levels and trends in crime since the beginning of the publication of criminal statistics in the 1820s. Currently, most of their studies concentrate on trends after the Second World War and often apply sophisticated statistical models. However, quite often the data available at the international level are not as reliable as expected and do not fulfill the requirements for such analyses. At the same time, there is a limited number of researchers interested in the history of crime who have been collecting the different indicators available since the Middle Ages, and sometimes even before that. These researchers come from different fields, and the data they collect are usually not appropriate for statistical time series analyses.

On the basis of the data collected by these researchers, there is currently a major consensus that interpersonal violence has declined in western Europe since the late Middle Ages and in the United States since the seventeenth century, with a few interruptions to this downward trend. This decrease has been mainly explained as the effect of a civilizing process, characterized by the monopolization of violence by the state and the growth of self-restraint among individuals, which resulted in an increased sensitization to interpersonal violence. However, these conclusions are based on a very small set of nations. Moreover, in order to fully accept them, one has to ignore the periods of war that occurred during this time, as well as the genocides, mass killings, and homicides of civilians committed by some of these nations in their own countries, their former colonies, and the places where they were fighting a war. Finally, the long-term evolution of crime in most regions of the world, such as Asia, Africa, Oceania, Eastern Europe, and Central and South America, is relatively unknown.

Researchers interested in long-term crime trends are confronted by a series of methodological problems. First of all, the definitions of offenses vary across time and space. Changes in definitions are related to the perception of delinquent behavior by the given society. In particular, the decrease in interpersonal violence seems related to an increased sensitivity toward such violence by members of the society, which in turn is reflected in the enlargement of the definition of violence by the criminal law and an increased enforcement of this law. In addition, data covering several centuries are not easily available, and whenever absolute numbers are found, they still have to be put in relation to the general population to which they refer—in order to express them as figures per 100,000 inhabitants, for example—which is not an easy task. In particular, official crime statistics are only available for a period of roughly two centuries in Western European countries, while surveys were developed mainly in the second half of the twentieth century. As a consequence, researchers have searched for alternative sources of information. In that context, those who specialize in long-term crime trends have concentrated their efforts on the study of the evolution of violent offenses, and particularly homicide, for which it is possible to find indirect measures, such as medical records or findings from ethnographers and archaeologists. As a result, and quite often without a solid empirical basis, homicide has been used as a proxy for violent offenses. Whether this is really the case is still a matter of discussion.

Researchers are constantly involved in discussions about the different crime measures used for the study of trends, and such discussions will probably continue endlessly. The replication of similar findings with different measures seems to be the best indicator of a relatively reliable finding. The interpretation of those findings is another delicate issue, as researchers can easily fall into the traps of chronocentrism, parochialism, and causationism. Such problems can also affect the theories developed to explain crime trends, among which the most well known are the Durkheimian modernization perspective, the Marxian world system perspective, the ecological opportunity perspective, and the already-mentioned civilization theory. Indeed, one of the main advantages of long-term crime trends research is that it can prove that some theories and explanations that seem valid for relatively short periods of time—such as the transition to modernity or the aftermath of the fall of the Soviet Union—are indeed false.

NOTES

1. Inspired by Quételet and the available statistics, Buckle went as far as affirming that "the fact is, that murder is committed with as much regularity, and bears as uniform a relation to certain known circumstances, as do the movements of the tides, and the rotations of the seasons" (1864, p. 18).
2. The title of the book can be translated as *Comparative Criminal Statistics in France, Belgium, England and Germany* (Ducpetiaux 1835).
3. *Annales historiques de la Révolution française* 228 (July–September 1977), under the direction of Maurice Agulhon. This publication led to an animated debate whose results were published in a book edited by Michelle Perrot (1980), which includes transcripts of the debate, a series of articles, a critique of Foucault by Jacques Leonard, and Foucault's answer to it.
4. See http://www.courtstatistics.org/.
5. Throughout history, painters have portrayed mainly the households of the most powerful people, those who could afford the cost of a painting. The same is true for the first photographs, which were extremely expensive. Thus, most of our pictorial testimony depicts the way of life of families with a high socioeconomic status. In contrast, many of the forensic pictures taken in households where crimes took place at the beginning of the twentieth century by Rodolphe Archibald Reiss (1875–1929), founder of the School of Criminal Sciences of the University of Lausanne, provide firsthand testimony of the austerity of working-class homes (see Champod et al., 2009)
6. "Here, more or less, is the reasoning of a thief or an assassin, who has no counterweight for not violating the laws except for the gallows or the wheel. . . . Why should I respect laws that leave so great a gap between me and the rich man? He denies me the small change that I look to him for, and his excuse is to order me to toil at work of which he knows nothing. Who has made these laws? Rich and powerful men, who never deign to visit the squalid huts of the poor, who have never divided moldy bread among the tears of their wives and the innocent cries of their starving children" (Beccaria 2009 [1764], pp. 73–74).
7. For example, a selection of the press articles that followed the publication of the Council of Europe Annual Penal Statistics (SPACE) in 2015 can be found at http://wp.unil.ch/space/space-i/annual-reports/.
8. "If one goes through the daily newspapers, they are full of conclusions as accurate as the following: In England they commit so many more crimes than in France; this means, some say, that the criminal law and the police are vicious there; others say it means that education is not, as it was supposed, so favourable to morality, etc. They nearly go as far as making an argument against the Catholic religion because there are more murders in Spain than in England or Geneva; or against the Protestant religion because one steals more in these two countries than in France or Belgium. The number of crimes that come to the attention of the courts, compared from one period to another, from one province

to another, from the city to the countryside, or from one country to another, has become an endless arsenal of two-edged weapons, of overarching arguments, which leave more than one speechless because of their numerical form. However, before putting an implicit faith in figures, one must know what they represent, whether they are accurate, whether they are comparable, and whether the facts enumerated had been correctly classified. Finally, it is only after these figures are properly controlled, when one starts searching for the causes of the established facts, that all the difficulties are found. It is then that all the paths that one follows have forks and become darker" (De Candolle 1987 [1830], p. 352; our translation).

9. Quételet (1829, p. 25) was perfectly aware that even comparisons of murder can be misleading and suggested also taking into consideration the death sentences pronounced and those effectively enforced.

10. During the last quarter of the twentieth century, many countries started conducting periodic general victimization surveys that now provide an alternative source for the study of crime trends. Some of them also developed specific surveys, such as those focusing on violence against women (Aebi & Linde 2014b). At the international level, the ICVS is the main instrument for comparisons of victimization across nations.

11. For a presentation of the development of conviction statistics across Europe following the redefinition of European borders by the Treaty of Vienna in 1815, see Aebi & Linde (2012); Aebi & Linde (2014a).

12. The text of this speech is available on the website of the White House, at https://www.whitehouse.gov/the-press-office/2015/01/20/remarks-president-state-union-address-january-20-2015 (accessed May 31, 2015).

13. For a more detailed presentation of this discussion, see Aebi & Linde (2012).

14. According to the definition provided by the *Webster's New Universal Unabridged Dictionary*.

15. See, for example, the recent test by LaFree, Curtis, and McDowall (2015), which includes an overview of other recent research applying modernization theory.

16. Eisner (2014) has also used the concept of models of conduct of life developed by Max Weber (1982 [1920]) to explain the role of the Protestant disciplinary ethos in the growth of self-discipline, and he has paid particular attention to the link between macro-level changes in self-control and long-term trends in homicide.

References

Aebi, M. F. 2010. "Methodological Issues in the Comparison of Police-Recorded Crime Rates." In *International Handbook of Criminology*, ed. S. G. Shoham, P. Knepper, & M. Kett, 211–27. Boca Raton, London, & New York: CRC Press, Taylor & Francis Group.

Aebi, M. F., B. Aubusson de Cavarlay, G. Barclay, B. Gruszczyńska, S. Harrendorf, M. Heiskanen, V. Hysi et al. 2010. *European Sourcebook of Crime and Criminal Justice Statistics—2010*, 4th ed. Den Haag: Boom Juridische Uitgevers.

Aebi, M. F., & A. Linde. 2010. "Is There a Crime Drop in Western Europe?" *European Journal on Criminal Policy and Research* 16 (4): 251–77.

Aebi, M. F., & A. Linde. 2012. "Conviction Statistics as an Indicator of Crime Trends in Europe from 1990 to 2006." *European Journal on Criminal Policy and Research* 18 (1): 103–44.

Aebi, M. F., & A. Linde. 2014a. "Conviction Statistics as Measures of Crime." In *Encyclopedia of Quality of Life and Well-Being Research*, ed. A. C. Michalos, 1,276–81. New York: Springer.

Aebi, M. F., & A. Linde. 2014b. "National Victimization Surveys." In *Encyclopedia of Criminology and Criminal Justice*, ed. G. Bruinsma & D. Weisburd, 3,228–42. New York: Springer.

Aebi, M. F., & A. Linde. 2014c. "The Persistence of Lifestyles: Rates and Correlates of Homicide in Western Europe from 1960 to 2010." *European Journal of Criminology* 11 (5): 552–77.

Aubusson de Cavarlay, B. 1998. De la statistique criminelle apparente à la statistique judiciaire cachée. *Déviance et société* 22 (2): 155–80.

Baudelaire, C. 1993 [1857]. *The Flowers of Evil*. Oxford: Oxford University Press.

Baumer, E. P., & K. T. Wolff. 2014. "Exploring the Breadth and Sources of Contemporary Cross-National Homicide Trends." *Crime and Justice* 43: 231–87.

Beccaria, C. 2009 [1764]. *On Crimes and Punishments*, 5th ed. Trans. and ed. by Graeme R. Newman & Pietro Marongiu. New Brunswick & London: Transaction.

Beirne, P. 1993. *Inventing Criminology: Essays on the Rise of "Homo Criminalis."* Albany: SUNY Press.

Blumstein, A., & R. Rosenfeld. 1998. "Explaining Recent Trends in U.S. Homicide Rates." *Journal of Criminal Law and Criminology* 88 (4): 1175–1216.

Blumstein, A., & J. Wallman. 2000. *The Crime Drop in America*. Cambridge & New York: Cambridge University Press.

Blumstein, A., & J. Wallman. 2006. *The Crime Drop in America*, 2nd ed. Cambridge & New York: Cambridge University Press.

Boudon, R., & F. Bourricaud. 1989. *A Critical Dictionary of Sociology*. London: Routledge.

Boutelet, B., & P. Chaunu. 1962. "Etude par sondage de la criminalité dans le bailliage du Pont-de-l'Arche (XVIIe–XVIIIe siècles)." *Annales de Normandie* 12 (4): 235–62.

Buckle, H. T. 1864. *History of Civilization in England*, Vol. 1. New York: D. Appleton and Company.

Champod, C., D. Girardin, L. Lebart, P. Margot, J. Mathyer, N. Quinche, & E. Sapin, E. 2009. *Le théâtre du crime: Rodolphe A. Reiss, 1875–1929*. Lausanne: Presses polytechniques et universitaires romandes.

Clark, G. 2007. *A Farewell to Alms: A Brief Economic History of the World*. Princeton, NJ, & Oxford: Princeton University Press.

Cohen, L. E., & M. Felson. 1979. "Social Change and Crime Rate Trends: A Routine Activity Approach." *American Sociological Review* 44 (4): 588–608.

Cohen, L. E., J. R. Kluegel, & K. C. Land. 1981. "Social Inequality and Predatory Criminal Victimization: An Exposition and Test of a Formal Theory." *American Sociological Review* 46 (5): 505–24.

De Candolle, A. 1987 [1830]. "Considérations sur la statistique des délits." *Déviance et société* 11 (4): 352–55.

De Candolle, A. 1987 [1832]. "De la statistique criminelle." *Déviance et société* 11 (4): 356–63.

Donohue, J. J. I., & S. D. Levitt. 2001. "The Impact of Legalized Abortion on Crime." *Quarterly Journal of Economics* 116 (2): 379–420.

Ducpetiaux, É. 1835. *Statistique comparée de la Criminalité en France, en Belgique, en Angleterre et en Allemagne*. Belgium: Haumann.

Durkheim, E. 1893 [1997]. *The Division of Labor in Society*. New York: Simon and Schuster.

Durkheim, E. 1897 [2007]. *Suicide: A Study in Sociology*. New York: Free Press.

Eisner, M. 2001. "Modernization, Self-Control and Lethal Violence: The Long-Term Dynamics of European Homicide Rates in Theoretical Perspective." *British Journal of Criminology* 41 (4): 618–38.

Eisner, M. 2003. "Long-Term Historical Trends in Violent Crime." *Crime and Justice* 30: 83–142.

Eisner, M. 2008. "Modernity Strikes Back? A Historical Perspective on the Latest Increase in Interpersonal Violence (1960–1990)." *International Journal of Conflict and Violence* 2 (2): 288–316.

Eisner, M. 2014. "From Swords to Words: Does Macro-Level Change in Self-Control Predict Long-Term Variation in Levels of Homicide?" *Crime and Justice* 43: 65–134.

Ekelund, E. 1942. "Criminal Statistics: The Volume of Crime." *Journal of Criminal Law and Criminology* 32 (5): 540–47.

Elias, N. 2000 [1939]. *The Civilizing Process: Sociogenetic and Psychogenetic Investigations.* Ofxord: Blackwell.

Felson, M. 1987. "Routine Activities and Crime in the Developing Metropolis." *Criminology* 25 (4): 911–32.

Ferri, E. 1892. *L'omicidio-suicidio: Responsabilità giuridica*, 3rd ed. Torino, Italy: Fratelli Bocca Editori.

Ferri, E. 1895. *Atlante antropologico-statistico dell'omicidio.* Torino, Italy: Fratelli Bocca Editori.

Foucault, M. 1975. *Surveiller et punir: Naissance de la prison.* Paris: Gallimard.

Foucault, M. 2009. *Security, Territory, Population: Lectures at the Collège de France 1977–1978.* Houndmills, UK: Palgrave Macmillan.

Fukuyama, F. 1992. *The End of History and the Last Man.* New York: Free Press.

Goldberger, A. S., & R. Rosenfeld, eds. 2008. *Understanding Crime Trends: Workshop Report.* Washington, D.C.: National Academies Press.

Gottfredson, M. R., & T. Hirschi. 1990. *A General Theory of Crime.* Stanford, CA: Stanford University Press.

Guerry, A.-M. 1833. *Essai sur la statistique morale de la France.* Paris: Chez Crochard.

Gurr, T. R. 1981. "Historical Trends in Violent Crime: A Critical Review of the Evidence." *Crime and Justice* 3: 295–353.

Hagan, F. E. 2013. *Introduction to Criminology: Theories, Methods, and Criminal Behavior*, 8th ed. New York: SAGE.

Hammer, C. I. J. 1978. "Patterns of Homicide in a Medieval University Town: Fourteenth-Century Oxford." *Past and Present* 78: 3–23.

Hindelang, M. J., M. R. Gottfredson, & J. Garofalo. 1978. *Victims of Personal Crime: An Empirical Foundation for a Theory of Personal Victimization.* Cambridge, MA: Ballinger.

Hollingsworth, T. H., ed. 1965. *The Demography of the British Peerage.* London: Population Investigation Committee, London School of Economics.

Howard, G. J., G. Newman, & W. A. Pridemore. 2000. "Theory, Method, and Data in Comparative Criminology." *Criminal Justice* 4: 139–211.

Huisman, W., J. van Erp, G. V. Walle, & J. Beckers. 2015. "Criminology and White-Collar Crime in Europe." In *The Routledge Handbook of White-Collar and Corporate Crime in Europe*, ed. J. van Erp, W. Huisman, G. V. Walle, & J. Beckers, 1–21. Abingdon & New York: Routledge.

Hunt, L. A. 2007. *Inventing Human Rights: A History.* New York: Norton.

Ignatieff, M. 1982. "Review: *L'Impossible Prison: Recherches sur le système pénitentiaire au XIXe siècle* by Michelle Perrot." *Social History* 7 (2): 227–29.

Johnson, E. A., & E. H. Monkkonen. 1996a. *The Civilization of Crime: Violence in Town and Country since the Middle Ages.* Urbana & Chicago: University of Illinois Press.

Johnson, E. A., & E. H. Monkkonen. 1996b. "Introduction." In *The Civilization of Crime: Violence in Town and Country since the Middle Ages*, ed. E. A. Johnson & E. H. Monkkonen, 1–13. Urbana & Chicago: University of Illinois Press.

Joyce, T. 2004. "Did Legalized Abortion Lower Crime?" *Journal of Human Resources* 39 (1): 1–28.

Killias, M. 1991. *Précis de criminologie*. Bern, Switzerland: Staempfli.

Kitsuse, J. I., & A. V. Cicourel. 1963. "A Note on the Uses of Official Statistics." *Social Problems* 11 (2): 131–39.

Kuhn, T. S. 1970. *The Structure of Scientific Revolutions*, 2nd ed. Chicago: University of Chicago Press.

LaFree, G. 2005. "Evidence for Elite Convergence in Cross-National Homicide Victimization Trends, 1956 to 2000." *Sociological Quarterly* 46 (1): 191–211.

LaFree, G., K. Curtis, & D. McDowall. 2015. "How Effective Are Our 'Better Angels'? Assessing Country-Level Declines in Homicide since 1950." *European Journal of Criminology* 12 (4): 482–504.

Lane, R. 2011. "Taking the Mystery Out of Murder Rates: Can It Be Done?" *Ohio State Journal of Criminal Law* 8 (2): 553–81.

Laub, J. H. 2001. "Review: *The Crime Drop in America*, Edited by Alfred Blumstein and Joel Wallman." *American Journal of Sociology* 106 (6): 1820–22.

Levitt, S. D. 1996. "The Effect of Prison Population Size on Crime Rates: Evidence from Prison Overcrowding Litigation." *Quarterly Journal of Economics* 111 (2): 319–51.

Levitt, S. D. 2004. "Understanding Why Crime Fell in the 1990s: Four Factors that Explain the Decline and Six that Do Not." *Journal of Economic Perspectives* 18 (1): 163–90.

Lodhi, A. Q., & C. Tilly. 1973. "Urbanization, Crime, and Collective Violence in 19th-Century France." *American Journal of Sociology* 79 (2): 296–318.

Maguire, M. 2007. "Crime Data and Statistics." In *The Oxford Handbook of Criminology*, 4th ed., ed. M. Maguire, R. Morgan, & R. Reiner, 241–301. Oxford: Oxford University Press.

Mannix, D. P. 1964. *The History of Torture*. Sparkford, UK: Sutton.

Mayr, G. V. 1865. *Statistik der Bettler und Vaganten im Königreiche Bayern*. München: J. Gotteswinter & Mössl.

Melossi, D. 2009. *Controlling Crime, Controlling Society: Thinking about Crime in Europe and America*. Cambridge: Polity Press.

Merton, R. K. 1938. "Social Structure and Anomie." *American Sociological Review* 3 (5): 672–82.

Mittermaier, C. J. A. 1829. "Der französische Compte général de l'administration de la justice criminelle pendant l'année 1827. Dargestellt und verglichen mit den Nachrichten über den Zustand der Verbrechen in Nordamerika, England, der Schweiz, Baiern, Würtemberg und Baden, mit Untersuchung der Ursache der Verbrechen." *Annalen der deutschen und ausländischen Criminal-Rechts-Pflege* 3:154–80, 354–86.

Mittermaier, C. J. A. 1830. "Beiträge zur Criminalstatistik, mit vergleichenden Bemerkungen über die Verhältnisse der Verbrechen und der Criminaljustiz in Frankreich, England, den Niederlanden, der Schweiz, Baiern, Baden und Lippe-Detmold." *Beiträge der Ausländischen Criminal-Rechts-Pflege* 7–8:197–232/190–218.

Monkkonen, E. H. 2001. "New Standards for Historical Homicide Research." *Crime, History & Societies* 5 (2): 5–26.

Morson, G. S. 1996. *Narrative and Freedom: The Shadows of Time*. New Haven, CT: Yale University Press.

Neuman, W. L., & R. J. Berger. 1988. "Competing Perspectives on Cross-National Crime: An Evaluation of Theory and Evidence." *Sociological Quarterly* 29 (2): 281–313.

Nivette, A. E. 2011. "Cross-National Predictors of Crime: A Meta-Analysis." *Homicide Studies* 15 (2): 103–31.

Österberg, E. 1992. "Criminality, Social Control, and the Early Modern State: Evidence and Interpretations in Scandinavian Historiography." *Social Science History* 16 (1): 67–98.

Ouimet, M., & J.-M. Tessier-Jasmin. 2009. "Policer la violence: analyse du taux de déclaration et du taux d'enregistrement des victimisations criminelles au Canada en 1999 et 2004." *Canadian Journal of Criminology and Criminal Justice* 51 (2): 227–53.

Perrot, M. 1980. *L'impossible prison: Recherches sur le système pénitentiaire au XIXe siècle.* Paris: Seuil.

Pinker, S. 2011. *The Better Angels of Our Nature: Why Violence Has Declined.* New York: Penguin Books.

Quételet, A. 1829. *Recherches statistiques sur le royaume des Pays-Bas: Mémoire lu à la séance de l'Académie du 6 décembre 1828.* Bruxelles: M. Hayez.

Quételet, A. 1831. *Recherches sur le penchant au crime aux différens âges.* Bruxelles: M. Hayez.

Quételet, A. 1833. *Recherches sur le penchant au crime aux différens âges,* 2nd ed. Bruxelles: M. Hayez.

Quételet, A. 1835. *Sur l'homme et le développement de ses facultés ou essai de physique sociale.* Paris: Bachelier.

Reinke, H. 1998. "Une 'bonne' statistique pour la lutte contre la criminalité? Observations sur les origines de la statistique criminelle en Allemagne au XIXe et au début du XXe siècle." *Déviance et Société* 22 (2): 113–25.

Robinson, L. N. 1910. "A Plan for the Reorganization of Criminal Statistics in the USA." *Journal of the American Institute of Criminal Law and Criminology* 1 (1): 44–49.

Robinson, L. N. 1911. *History and Organization of Criminal Statistics in the United States.* Boston: Houghton Mifflin.

Robinson, L. N. 1920. "The Improvement of Criminal Statistics in the United States." *Quarterly Publications of the American Statistical Association* 17 (130): 157–63.

Rock, P. 2005. "Chronocentrism and British Criminology." *British Journal of Sociology* 56 (3): 473–91.

Rosenfeld, R. 2014. "The Crime Trends Roundtable." *Criminologist* 39 (1): 1–4.

Roth, R. 2009. *American Homicide.* Cambridge, MA & London: Belknap Press of Harvard University Press.

Rousseaux, X. 1993. "Civilisation des moeurs et/ou déplacement de l'insécurité? La violence à l'épreuve du temps." *Déviance et société* 17 (3): 291–97.

Rusche, G., & O. Kirchheimer. 1939. *Punishment and Social Structure.* New York: Columbia University Press.

Sellin, T. 1931. "The Basis of a Crime Index." *Journal of Criminal Law and Criminology* 22 (3): 335–56.

Sharpe, J. A. 1996. "Crime in England: Long-Term Trends and the Problem of Modernization." In *The Civilization of Crime: Violence in Town and Country since the Middle Ages,* ed. E. A. Johnson & E. H. Monkkonen, 17–34. Urbana & Chicago: University of Illinois Press.

Shelley, L. I. 1981. *Crime and Modernization: The Impact of Industrialization and Urbanization on Crime.* Carbondale: Southern Illinois University Press.

Shelley, L. I. 1986. "Crime and Modernization Reexamined." *International Annals of Criminology* 24 (1–2): 7–21.

Skogan, W. G. 1976. "Citizen Reporting of Crime: Some National Panel Data." *Criminology* 13 (4): 535–49.

Spierenburg, P. 1994. "Faces of Violence: Homicide Trends and Cultural Meanings: Amsterdam, 1431–1816." *Journal of Social History* 27 (4): 701–16.

Tarde, G. 1886. *La criminalité comparée*. Paris: Félix Alcan.

Tilly, C. 1984. *Big Structures, Large Processes, Huge Comparisons*. New York: Russell Sage Foundation.

Tonry, M. 2014. "Why Crime Rates Are Falling Throughout the Western World." *Crime and Justice* 43:1–63.

United Nations Office on Drugs and Crime (UNODC). 2011. *2011 Global Study on Homicide: Trends, Context, Data*. Vienna: UNODC.

United Nations Office on Drugs and Crime (UNODC). 2014. *Global Study on Homicide 2013: Trends, Context, Data*. Vienna: UNODC.

Vanneste, C. 2003. *Les chiffres des prisons: Des logiques économiques à leur traduction pénale*. Paris: L'Harmattan.

Verkko, V. 1967. "Static and Dynamic 'Laws' of Sex and Homicide." In *Studies in Homicide*, ed. M. E. Wolfgang, 36–44. New York: Harper & Row.

von Hofer, H. 1990. "Homicide in Swedish Statistics, 1750–1988." In A. Snare (Ed.), *Criminal Violence in Scandinavia: Selected Topics*, ed. A. Snare, 11:28–45. Oslo: Norwegian University Press.

von Hofer, H. 2012. "Crime Trends vs. Random Walk: Piftalls of Ad Hoc Chart Reading. In *Nordic Criminal Statistics, 1950–2010*, ed. H. von Hofer, T. Lappi-Seppala, & L. Westfelt, 79–88. Stockholm: Kriminologiska institutionen, Stockholms universitet.

von Hofer, H., & T. Lappi-Seppala. 2014. "The Development of Crime in Light of Finnish and Swedish Criminal Justice Statistics, circa 1750–2010." *European Journal of Criminology* 11 (2): 169–94.

World Health Organization (WHO). 2002. *World Report on Violence and Health: Summary*. Geneva: WHO.

Young, J. 2004. "Mayhem and Measurement in Late Modernity." In *Crime and Crime Control in an Integrating Europe: Plenary Presentations Held at the Third Annual Conference of the European Society of Criminology, Helsinki 2003*, ed. K. Aromaa & S. Nevala, 18–31. Helsinki: HEUNI.

....

CHAPTER 4

GEOGRAPHY OF CRIME

Urban and Rural Environments

....

CATHERINE DENYS

INTRODUCTION

....

HISTORIANS no longer accept the idyllic image of village life in the past, when interaction between inhabitants may have generated effective informal social control, in contrast to the image of the corrupting and anomic modern city (Emsley 2007, pp. 135–59). On the contrary, during the period 1750–1950 violence seems to have declined more rapidly in urban societies than in the countryside. Moreover, the process of social pacification and how it varied between regions or countries continues to be an object of debate. Evidently, the pace of the long-term declines in urban and rural violence was not the same everywhere, and the different progressions of this decline did not necessarily coincide. If the modern city did indeed lead to more peaceful behavior, how do we reconcile this civilizing effect with the brutality in social relationships that accompanied the massive and rapid urbanization of the period of industrialization? What was the role played by the state in these processes, at a time when popular challenges to public authority were as strong as attempts to enforce law and order? Should we consider other explanations, such as cultural or even anthropological factors, to shed light on the geography of crime? As historical studies currently stand, these questions have given rise to fascinating analyses, but a definitive synthesis has yet to be written.

This essay analyzes four key aspects of the geography of crime. First, it examines the historical transformation in the distribution of crime between town and rural areas in the West between 1750 and 1950, which remains a complex issue that is still not well understood. Second, it explores how certain types of crime were influenced directly by the environment in which the criminals lived, before turning to other types that seem to have been independent of their surroundings or simply a transposition of the same phenomena from rural to urban settings. Finally, as there is no consensus among historians as to the long-term changes in the relative distribution of violence perpetrated by urban and rural populations, it discusses the difficulty of suggesting comprehensive explanations that take into account the associated phenomena of urbanization, industrialization, and modernization.

I. A Relatively Unexplored Issue Leading to Ambiguous Analysis

While historians of crime and justice are indeed very interested in variables such as age and gender in the establishment of criminal typologies, the study of crime locations has yet to benefit significantly from the "spatial turn" that has influenced many other historical fields. While rural crime during the period 1750–1950 has been examined slightly more often than urban crime during the same period, the latter has also been the subject of extensive research. However, works on rural and urban crime have rarely been viewed in parallel across long time periods, and regional monographs as well as national syntheses often limit themselves to briefly addressing a comparison of the two sets of data, if these do indeed exist.

Even when the title of a study introduces "urban and rural crime," these two phenomena are studied side by side; comparisons are much rarer. In the subtitle to their introduction of the volume entitled *The Civilization of Crime* (1996), editors Eric A. Johnson and Eric H. Monkkonen address the issue that interests us here, "Violence in Town and Country since the Middle Ages," but only four of the ten contributors (Egmont, Diederiks, Weinberger, and Johnson) tackle it head-on. In the very thorough article by Manuel Eisner (2003) on "Long-Term Historical Trends in Violent Crime," the town and country are only approached through a geo-historical reconstruction. The article compares northwestern Europe, which was more rapidly urbanized and saw an early decline in homicide in the sixteenth and seventeenth centuries, to Mediterranean and Eastern Europe, which remained rural for a longer period and where the decisive decline in homicide did not occur until the late nineteenth century. Eisner attributes the gap that he identifies between the northern and southern regions of Italy and France to the same differences in levels of urbanization and industrialization. However, when it comes to explanations, he calls upon familiar social, economic, and cultural factors without returning to the role of the rural or urban environment, as if it were irrelevant. For example, he does not discuss whether the growing power of the state was manifested in the same way, at the same pace, and with the same effects in towns and in the countryside. Most recently, Peter King (2013) has addressed this problem with regard to the nineteenth century, beginning with the United Kingdom before extrapolating his findings to Europe as a whole. He challenges the notion of the pacifying city by noting a sharp rise in crime in the newly industrialized regions of England and Scotland between 1820 and 1850. Industrialization and the accompanying rapid urbanization brought about a reversal in the centuries-long decline in violence in the early nineteenth century; however, this reversal would prove temporary, and, from 1850 onward, rates began to fall again very quickly. The industrial cities therefore seem to have been more criminogenic, at least in the early phase, a phenomenon that has also been observed in Sweden (Österberg 1996) and, very recently, in Marseille (Regnard-Drouot 2009). Nevertheless, this trend does not seem to hold true for Germany (Johnson 1996). Conversely, in the late nineteenth century, the gap between crime rates in rural and in urban areas in Europe tended to narrow, as if the environment no longer had any effect on violent behavior. The case of France is more problematic; on the one hand, the heavily urbanized and industrial regions of the north had higher crime rates than the rural regions of the center, which seems to support the conclusions of Peter King (2013); yet at the same time, the rural regions of the south, and Corsica in particular, displayed even higher crime rates than the north. Urbanization cannot therefore be the only factor, nor perhaps even an important factor, in these regional differences, a point to which we will return after an overview of the crimes and misdemeanors committed in town and country.

II. Rural Crime versus Urban Crime

A. Wood and Crop Theft and Poaching: The Essence of Rural Crime

The theft of wood, petty theft from crops or gardens, the theft of small livestock, and hunting or fishing in private areas may not seem particularly serious today. This has not always been the case, however, as these offenses constituted vital levies before the advent of the consumer society and gave rise to profound conflict in rural society (Archer 1990; Schulte 1994; Ager 2014).

Forest crimes in particular have interested historians working on France, England, and Germany of the eighteenth and nineteenth centuries. They all stress the contrast between the rights to collective usage as understood by villagers and a "modern" concept of individual property championed by feudal lords and the king, or, rather, by the new owners of the land. In eighteenth-century France, clashes between villagers and forest wardens working for the local lord or the king were innumerable, as were the fines imposed by the manorial courts or the royal *Maîtrise des Eaux et Forêts*. These disputes could become more serious as the result of several factors. Rapid demographic growth of the rural populations made survival more difficult for those who could not find work in the towns. The use of the forest with varying degrees of legality was therefore essential to the survival of the poorest: collecting dead wood was the only way to keep warm; game and wild berries were a welcome dietary supplement; and, finally, the access to grazing herds of pigs or goats in the woods allowed those without land to rear a few animals. The growing demand for firewood and other forms of fuels, such as peat and charcoal, created a real shortage, which forced woodcutters and coalmen to penetrate farther and farther into the forest. Industrial development encouraged black-smiths and glassmakers to move closer to their raw materials. But this overexploitation of the forest caused the game to flee and prevented large trees from reaching maturity. The forest lost its value for its owners, whether they were using it for the extensive hunts enjoyed by monarchs and nobles, or whether they relied on it simply for the sale of timber.

Disputes between landowners and villagers over the ownership of woodland became more serious whenever the landowners in question tried to restrict rights to collec-tive usage or sought to reinstate long-forgotten feudal privileges. Woods, like marshes and moors, were indeed often undivided "common land." This "feudal reaction" pro-voked violent clashes between the population and forest wardens. Whenever these wardens increased restrictions on the use of common resources, villagers reacted with collective—and sometimes spectacular—opposition. In the 1720s, the royal and eccle-siastical forests of Windsor and Hampshire were ransacked by armed gangs of horse-men with blackened faces. The "Blacks" killed a considerable number of deer belonging to the royal estate, emptied the lakes of fish and water, and destroyed crops and live-stock. These gangs created an almost insurrectional climate, released prisoners, and threatened to kill the wardens and burn down properties. According to E. P. Thompson (1975), this radicalization of violence was a response to the destruction of a balance between the users and the owners of the forest. Other forms of delinquency were con-tained thanks to individual agreements negotiated between the villagers and the repre-sentatives of the landowners. Wherever attempts were made to replace such agreement with rigorous enforcement of property rights, this triggered protests from all those whose survival depended on such arrangements. Landowners with connections to the parliamentary Whig Party ensured the criminalization of forest delinquency to the extent that with the Black Act of 1723 the simple acts of carrying arms or blackening one's face in the forest became punishable by death.

France experienced very similar outbreaks of violence over forest rights, despite royal legislation in place since 1669 that aimed more at protecting timber than at favor-ing landowners (Corvol 1987). The first "Guerre des Demoiselles" broke out in 1765 in the Forest of Chaux in Franche-Comté: gangs of peasants with blackened faces and dis-guised as women attacked the forest wardens and set fire to their homes (Nicolas 2002). Royal authorities were increasingly powerless against this resistance, with the situation reaching its peak in the late eighteenth century. After the Revolution, French forests were probably in the worst state in their history. The monarchy of the Restoration era reacted with the passage of the new Rural Code of 1827, which marked a new stage in the restriction of collective rights in favor of private property. This again provoked collective opposition, some of which included earlier traditions of disguise, such as that waged by the new Guerre des Demoiselles in Ariège (Baby 1972; Sahlins 1994). Similarly, the introduction of hunting licenses in 1844 resulted in repeated clashes between peasants and wardens.

However, forest crimes should not be attributed exclusively to the defense of collective rights and the survival of the poorest. Some of the removed wood and poached game was sold directly to urban populations, supplying a well-organized black market. During the terrible winter of 1740, 4,000 to 5,000 people ravaged the Bois des Célestins near Versailles for several weeks. The Parisian bourgeoisie came out to observe the devastation and to purchase looted wood (Nicolas 2002, p. 442). Some unscrupulous traders fueled the demand for game, and quasi-professional poachers were commonplace figures in rural crime, diametrically opposed to the gamekeepers or forest wardens who tried to catch them in the act. In nineteenth-century England, poaching was directly related to the demand for cheap meat in the towns, although it declined with the development of new production and distribution channels for foodstuffs toward the end of the century (Archer 1999).

B. Multidimensional Rural Violence: The French Example

France provides a rich case study for the development of rural crime during the nineteenth century because the rural exodus was slow and the urban population did not overtake the rural population until 1930. Moreover, rural France has come under particular scrutiny from various historical schools. Crime in the countryside included acts that varied greatly in severity, from petty theft to gruesome homicides and armed rebellion. It is not possible to disentangle the consequences of interpersonal violence from those of collective movements here. Depending on the legal disputes studied or the theoretical assumptions made, historians have focused on different types of violence and have constructed explanatory models that overlap but are not exhaustive.

With this in mind, the first studies of collective violence in the countryside of nineteenth-century France interpreted these acts as echoes of the great political debates of the period. Influenced by the seminal work of Georges Lefebvre on the "Great Fear" (1932)—the collective panic that seized the countryside at the beginning of the French Revolution—historians have looked for early symptoms or the aftermath of regime changes in the rural movements of 1815, 1840–1850, and 1870. Violence has therefore been interpreted as one of the ways political debates penetrated the rural world and as an indicator of the emergence of political awareness among the rural masses. Maurice Agulhon's *La République au village* (1970) marks a major historiographical turning point toward a focus on local approaches to national phenomena, and it paved the way for two historiographical currents.

Inspired by Eugen Weber's (1977) thesis on the slow integration of the French peasant world into the nation, one line of research particularly focused on rural rejection of the growing constraints imposed by the state (Soulet 1988; Thibon, 1988). Forest crimes, opposition to the payment of taxes and conscription, and rebellion against police authority (Lignereux 2008) were all interpreted as signs of the difficulties experienced by rural communities in adapting to the national framework.

A second current of historiography, inspired by an anthropological approach, went to the very heart of rural communities in order to dissect the systems of alliance, inheritance, and hierarchy that determined the social equilibrium (Claverie & Lamaison 1982; Chauvaud 1995). Violence was in this context viewed as part of the reconfiguration of these balances. Challenges in the form of attacks on livestock, arson, and assaults aimed at reasserting the position of individual inhabitants within the village hierarchy. This led to reprisals and revenge from their targets, who viewed such responses as necessary for retaining their rank. At the same time, this violence had to remain within certain limits, and peaceful settlement of disputes continued to be possible through these ritualized negotiations.

A synthesis of the two approaches shows how political issues became part of the local rivalries and complex games through which social positions were constantly changing within the village. At a regional level, the same honor and revenge mechanism resulted in fierce and bitter "village brawls" that repeatedly broke out at festivals and fairs (Ploux 2002), and in which violence contributed to the internal cementation of groups (Lenclud 1983). Judicial authorities were often perplexed by the brutality of the rural world, while the villagers themselves exploited justice to pursue their own ends.

Yet violence, in its most extreme forms, can also be interpreted in exactly the opposite way, as the population's ultimate response to the disintegration of community links, and as an uncontrolled reaction to a threat that is all the more disturbing because it is misjudged. In the context of the fear felt throughout society after the fall of the Second Empire and the Prussian invasion, the simple presence of a young nobleman at the cattle market in a small village in the Dordogne on 16 August 1870 triggered a horrific lynching (Corbin 1990).

Such an extreme should not, however, conceal the sharp decline in rural crime in the nineteenth century. It should also be noted that the regions that have been most studied, such as the Pyrenees or the Auvergne, were also very isolated and far from the areas that were regularly crossed by travelers and therefore more open to change. In the late nineteenth century, the most traditionally rural crimes—such as arson, ritual abuse, and social unrest—disappear from court records. Rather than simply resulting from the process of civilization or from the absorption of these populations into the national mold, it is more likely that the rural exodus and devitalization of the countryside played the key role in the decline of village violence. Only Corsica appears to have resisted, maintaining a revenge-based system that resulted in a homicide rate exceptional in late nineteenth-century France.

C. Crowds and Urban Disorder

Large-scale rural revolts belonged mainly to the sixteenth and seventeenth centuries. In the eighteenth and nineteenth centuries, the political authorities turned their attention to the towns with their restless crowds, ready to run amok. Food riots still dominated during the major part of the eighteenth century, developing at marketplaces and triggered whenever grain was scarce or prices reached unusual heights. Women often played a leading role. Crowds did not engage in indiscriminate looting, sought to prevent grain from leaving the local area and targeted merchants with monopolies. These monopolists were accused of being involved in a hypothetical "famine conspiracy" in which they exacerbated shortages and speculated in the rise and fall of prices. Often, the rioters paid for the grain they seized at the price they considered fair, according to an understanding of the "moral economy," which contrasted with the mechanisms of the liberal economy (Thompson 1971). The liberalization of the grain trade advocated by Turgot, minister of finance under Louis XVI, when combined with crop failures, resulted in the "Guerre des Famines," a series of riots in Paris and neighboring towns in the spring of 1775. On this occasion, these initially unremarkable market riots worsened because the minister was determined to reject the usual amicable settlements between the crowd and the local authorities, including agreements over what the population saw as fair bread prices, or "popular taxation." The lieutenant general of the Paris police and the commanders of constabularies at the provincial level also opposed the full liberalization of the market, which made the situation uncontrollable and destroyed the traditional balance between the police and urban society (Kaplan 1996; Milliot 2011, pp. 403–04).

The authorities were fearful of urban crowds, who were all too eager to be stirred up to violent protest. In the streets, passersby gathered spontaneously to release people arrested by the police. The slightest disputes between two neighbors could trigger bystanders to collectively take sides, with blows quickly following insults. In 1750 a series of kidnappings of beggars terrified working-class families in Paris, who rose up against police officers and spies (Farge & Revel 1988). Shoemaker (2004) refers to the eighteenth-century "London mob," the crowd always ready to mobilize in order to rowdily express their approval or disapproval of government policies. These chaotic incidents, often accompanied by a party atmosphere with bonfires, illuminations, and comic processions, were feared by foreigners but tolerated by the municipal authorities in the name of English liberties. Toward the late eighteenth century, however, the excesses of the mob became much less acceptable to the authorities, and the scale of massacres and devastation caused by the Gordon Riots of June 1780 marked the end of this tolerance. Shortly afterward, the successive "journées révolutionnaires" in France confirmed the worst fears among the wealthy that the political mobilization of crowds was linked to extreme violence.

In the nineteenth century, fear shifted from the capitals to the great industrial centers and their restless working-class populations, which rose up in such incidents as the silk workers' revolt in Lyon (1831) or the Chartist agitation of the Bull Ring Riots in Birmingham (1839). In the second half of the nineteenth century, workers' movements became more organized, while spontaneous outbursts became less frequent. At the same time the violence of the repression often exceeded that of the demonstrators (e.g., the Peterloo Massacre in Manchester on 18 August 1819, the Bloody Week of the Paris Commune from 21 to 28 May 1871, and the shooting at Fourmies on 1 May 1891).

Despite this relative pacification, the industrial towns of the nineteenth century were still marked by serious collective violence, with recent immigrants pitted against the more well-established workers, or with sectarian and ethnic clashes in the cities. In Liverpool, where Irish immigration was extremely widespread, as in Marseille, with its high level of Italian immigration, clashes between the communities, as well as sectarian or xenophobic riots, happened regularly (Neale 1988). Any conspicuous manifestation of affiliation to a community (Orange parades or Catholic processions) was taken as a provocation and risked triggering confrontation. This was the case of the so-called Skeleton Army Riots of the 1880s, which opposed Salvation Army propaganda in the south of England (Bailey 1977).

D. Urban Underworlds

The very existence of an urban underworld, a sort of counterculture that saw criminals of all kinds gather in impenetrable places, is questionable. The urban underworld was essentially an ideological construct that reflected social fears. However, the absence of such a formal association did not prevent the existence of differing degrees of organized crime that were directly linked to the conditions of urban life.

In the eighteenth century, neither the authorities nor society in general seemed particularly concerned about organized crime in towns and cities despite myths about the *Cour des Miracles*—a slum district of Paris known as the "Courtyard of Miracles" because cripples returning to them would "miraculously" regain their full bodily capabilities once on their home turf—and the celebrity of certain thief-gang leaders (e.g., Jonathan Wild, executed in 1725, and Cartouche, executed in 1721). Court records reveal contacts between thieves, but attempts by police officials to draw attention to the existence of networks involving thieves and receivers of stolen goods do not seem to have been mirrored in society. Thieves and beggars were one of the minor inconveniences of urban life, like dirty streets or the overcrowding in the homes of poor families. Depictions of the alleged dangers of the streets and the lack of safety for citizens emanated for the most part from reformers, who painted a bleak picture of the situation to justify the founding or development of police institutions (Denys, Marin, & Milliot 2009).

In the nineteenth century, on the other hand, genuine social anxiety, mixed with increasing fascination with crime and criminals, surfaced with regard to the *bas fonds*, or back streets. The growth of suburbs and working-class areas, now scrutinized by attentive observers—with the help of new administrative statistics and medical topographies—revealed to the expanding middle classes a disturbing picture of poverty from which they sought to distance themselves. In the increasingly influential bourgeois ideology, working-class neighborhoods were perceived as dens of vice and their inhabitants as criminals in the making, as described by some social observers and police practitioners. Criminals were no longer individuals defying society by personal choice, but representatives of the morally and physically degraded classes. The "working classes" became synonymous with the "dangerous classes" (Chevalier 1958), while a particular form of literature provided an image that was all the more convincing because it was based in part on reality. The social construction of an urban criminal class was strongly supported by the development of an imaginary world in literature inspired by real events, including novels by writers such as Eugène Sue and Charles Dickens; the life stories of police officers such as Vidocq, in Paris; or press reports of gory crime and detective stories (Kalifa 1995). The boundaries between fiction and reality disappeared, not only in the eyes of the general public, who readily believed that Sherlock Holmes really existed, but also in the heart of the community of historians, who struggled to establish a relationship between myth and reality (Chassaigne 2005; Shore 2010). All these scholars, however, mention the proximity in time between waves of urban redevelopment (e.g., Haussmann's transformation of French cities during the Second Empire of 1850–1870, the establishment of new, fashionable districts organized around open squares in English cities, the ubiquitous building of sewer networks, the extension of street lighting) and the horrific descriptions of slums and rookeries. The emphasis on the impenetrable, labyrinthine character of these neighborhoods, their foul stench and repulsive, unhealthy dirt, reflected both the challenge that developers faced in terms of uncontrolled growth of cities and their desire to regulate the urban organism.

The attention paid to prostitution in the nineteenth century reveals the same ambivalence. While luxury brothels frequented by high-society figures reached their peak between 1850 and 1870, the police hounded the women who worked the streets. The fight against the spread of syphilis was combined with a desire to clean up the city's moral fiber and to root out vice. Prostitutes were viewed not only as women who had strayed from the straight and narrow, but also as a link to the criminal classes (Corbin 1979; Walkowitz 1980). The murder of five prostitutes in Whitechapel by Jack the Ripper in 1888 temporarily focused public attention on the dangers of prostitution, but did not lead to a decline in a phenomenon that was fueled by poverty. Although rural prostitution also existed in isolated inns, industrial and border regions, and near military camps (Luddy 2007), prostitution remained a largely urban activity that escaped any attempt at regulation and control by the police, medical authorities, or moral and religious entrepreneurs.

III. Surprising Similarities Between Urban and Rural Crime

A. Rural and Urban Gangs

Like the urban underworld, banditry played a similar role in fiction but is not supported by historical and social evidence. Between the groups of destitute vagabonds driven to the roads by the recurrent crop crises of the pre-industrial era and the more flamboyant figures of organized crime after the Second World War, subtle gradations make the picture complex. Even the seemingly simplest division into bandits and gangsters, with the former operating in the countryside and the latter in towns and cities, needs to be qualified. Some points do unite these various aspects of organized crime, however. First, bandits worked in groups and were not isolated criminals. Gangs of bandits may have had differing degrees of organization and hierarchy, but bandits always had associates. Some gangs consisting of former soldiers were organized along military lines. The famous Mandrin, who organized the smuggling of tobacco and cloth between Savoy and France in 1754–1755, was able to act in broad daylight and directly attack the *Ferme générale* because he led a company of disciplined soldiers. However, at the same time, small-scale smuggling was widely practiced by border populations, with little overall organization. Cartouche, famous for leading an extremely large gang of thieves in Paris during the Regency period at the beginning of Louis XV's reign (1715–1723), spent time in the army and willingly recruited former soldiers and deserters. At the time of his execution in 1721, nearly 300 accomplices had been brought to justice, although plenty of thieves probably remained in the streets of the French capital (Péveri 1997).

Apart from a few well-known cases of fearsome organized gangs, the concept of a network is often more appropriate in any discussion of this type of crime, as bandits would pass information backward and forward, meet up at rallying points (e.g., cabarets, inns, and fairs), and use the same receivers of their stolen goods. These receivers were also a crucial point of contact between urban and rural crime because most stolen goods passed through their hands. They were under police surveillance, but their illegal activities are difficult to disentangle from the practice of reselling, which was extremely widespread before 1950. These bandits preferred to operate on roads that passed through woods, but gangs that lived in forests or caves were rare, particularly during the winter, when their spoils allowed them to live much more comfortable and happy lives in the city.

Comparisons are sometimes made between more astute criminals in towns and cities, organized into ingenious and skillful gangs of cutpurses or pickpockets, and more violent and expeditious banditry in the countryside. The atrocious practice of *chauffeurs*, or stokers, who tortured their victims to find out where they kept their savings, captured the imagination. But rural robbers also knew how to use women and children to find out about the security methods used by isolated farms or potential loot. Urban gangs—like their rural counterparts—did not hesitate to murder their victims. The areas of operation could be either urban or rural, with some groups specializing in attacks on farms and others focusing on horse rustling or highway robbery by ambush. Nevertheless, the most active gangs often operated both in towns and cities and in the countryside: Cartouche attacked carriages between Versailles and Paris, while Mandrin attacked the offices of the *Ferme générale* in the cities of southeastern France.

In fact, the most important characteristic of gangs was precisely this mobility, which allowed them to evade pursuit and attack wherever they were least expected. The geography of their crimes does not point to a simple dichotomy between town and countryside, but rather to the control of a territory, varying considerably in size, inside which they operated. There were local gangs with limited areas of influence that essentially relied on their detailed knowledge of micro-local conditions, with the result that their crimes cannot be easily separated from other forms of economic, political, and social violence mentioned previously. On the other hand, gangs that operated on an extremely large scale, knowing everything there was to know about communication networks, also existed (Ortalli 1986; Danker 2001).

Some historians have noticed the international and cross-border nature of certain gangs. Xavier Rousseaux (2000) has demonstrated how the wars of the French Revolution and the Napoleonic Empire created favorable conditions for the emergence of gangs with considerable areas of influence by shifting borders and weakening law enforcement. The "Bande d'Orgères," for example, terrorized the farmers of the Paris Basin and Normandy between 1785 and 1792 (Zysberg 1985; Cobb 1972). During the era of the French Directory (1795–1799), judicial disorganization gave free rein to highly mobile gangs, such as the so-called Flemish gang that operated between Luxembourg and the Flemish coast (Rousseaux 2013). Salembier, the leader of a gang of garrotters active between 1795 and 1801, operated between Normandy and Flanders. The Schinderhannes gang and their associates systematically plundered the Rhineland between 1792 and 1803.

Immigration from Europe's poor or troubled regions also encouraged the formation of ethnic or international gangs. Florike Egmond (1993) has demonstrated the existence of Jewish and gypsy networks—the former more urban, the latter more rural—in the Netherlands during the eighteenth century. She highlights the contrasts between the practices of different rural bandits depending on the varying features of the countryside where they operated. In the most rural parts of Brabant, the gangs were more indigenous, living in villages and carrying out violent attacks on farms, but were also linked to small-scale rural crime, such as begging combined with threats and opportunistic petty theft. These gangs had few connections to the towns and cities. On the other hand, in Holland, where the population density was much greater and there were many more towns and cities, rural gangs were much more international and closely linked to the towns, where they spent part of their time, even if their criminal operations were conducted in the country. They differed, however, from strictly urban criminals, who did not form organized gangs but joined into small operational groups that came together from time to time to commit theft and burglary.

Interpretations of banditry have given rise to historiographical debates. For Eric Hobsbawm (1969), the "social bandit," an individual who was well-integrated into the local population, embodied the proletarian resistance to the wealthy, and banditry was an archaic form of political struggle (Hobsbawn, 1959). These bandits, heroes to the poor, should therefore not be confused with ordinary criminals. Forty years after Hobsbawm's work, historians of banditry have observed more ambiguous relationships between peasants and bandits, and have found that positive legends about eighteenth- and nineteenth-century Robin Hoods came about mostly after those individuals' deaths, while court records tell of the crimes that were actually committed by them (Sharpe 2005; Kwass 2014, pp. 262–83). It has admittedly been firmly established that judges and the authorities often used the threat and fear created by bandits among the wealthy to sustain and further repressive policies. It is also clear that more than one state consciously promoted the conflation of rebellion—political or social—and actual banditry in order to discredit the former. Xavier Rousseaux has recently demonstrated this practice with reference to the Belgian territories between the mid-eighteenth century and the First World War (2013). During the French Revolution, opponents to the Republic were automatically treated as bandits, resulting in a heavy military crackdown in the Vendée and elsewhere. However, this political use of banditry did not turn all bandits into defenders of the people. During the repression of the "Guerre des Paysans," or peasant war of 1798 in the Belgian *départements* recently annexed by France, official statements treated all opponents as dangerous bandits, but military judges clearly distinguished between political rebels, *chauffeurs*, and other garrotters. The anthropologist and historian Anton Blok (1991), who focused on the "Bokkerijders," a group organized as a secret society that was active in the Lower Meuse between 1730 and 1778, went so far as to emphasize a peasant attitude toward these bandits that was ambiguous to say the least. For him, the Bokkerijders were a movement similar to the Mafia, making up a counterculture in which its members lived apparently normal lives but came together secretly to commit their crimes.

B. Gangs, Gangsters, Mafias: From the City to the World

In the second half of the nineteenth century, concern about rural gangs diminished only to shift to more urban organized crime. By the 1850–1860s, several incidents in London of thefts accompanied by the strangling of victims had given rise to a "garroting panic," magnified by the press in English towns and cities (Sindall 1987; Sindall 1990). Concern about an underworld that controlled the "other side" of society spread in the industrial cities. The latest incarnation of the urban criminal, the gangster, developed at the very end of the nineteenth century and in the early twentieth century. The figure of the gangster was an amalgamation of various types of criminals who were in reality very different from each other. On the one hand, the term was used to refer to the gangs of young people that would hang around on street corners displaying worrying behavior, including a taste for gratuitous violence. On the other hand, it evoked the hardened criminal, a member of a secret association controlling vast swathes of an illegal economy in the process of globalization.

Although eighteenth-century cities already had their *coureurs de nuit*, night runners (Pitou 2000), and other types of youth who refused regular work, such as Liverpool's "cornermen" starting around 1860, it was not until the 1880s–1900s that growing concern developed with regard to the young, unoccupied men who conspicuously occupied the urban space. To mark themselves out and distinguish between one another, London's hooligans, like Paris's apaches, adopted dress codes and haircuts. The principal characteristics of these gangs were territoriality and youth (Taylor 2010; Perrot 1979). These "street gangs," which took the names of specific streets, strived to control a neighborhood using intimidation and violence toward the police and particularly rival gangs. However, beyond occasional recruitment activities, these street gangsters do not seem to have had close ties to the real world of organized crime. As noted, the attention paid to them is historically linked to the development of social concern about young people being in danger and the emergence of the category of adolescence as distinguished from childhood and adulthood (Yvorel 2005; Shore 1999).

Criminal organizations of the late nineteenth and early twentieth centuries were more closely linked to the global expansion of the economy than to urban or rural territory. The gangsters of this period were in fact characterized by high levels of mobility made possible by modern forms of communication. Their targets were also linked to changes in the economy (e.g., attacks on city banks or railway convoys). Magnified by the press, the "exploits" of these gangsters reconnected with the earlier theme of banditry as challenging society and its norms, and colored these crimes with an air of anarchy (e.g., in the case of the Bonnot Gang in 1911–1912) at a time when genuine political anarchists had increased their attacks on European rulers and social unrest was reflected by harsh strikes.

At the turn of the nineteenth century, the Mafia or mafias represented the upper level of this new landscape of organized crime. Their activities were originally both rural and urban, as one of their features was precisely this flexible adaptation to socio-economic developments. Since the 1990s, following the work of Salvatore Lupo (1993), a number of myths and previously held beliefs have been swept aside by genuinely historical analysis. Fantastical, ancient, or medieval origins have been abandoned, as well as culturalist assumptions that referred to southern Italy as a socially fixed archaism. The explanation of the Mafia phenomenon as stemming from the poverty of overpopulated regions and the agrarian structure of the *latifundia* does not hold up to a precise examination of the development of the Mafia in the prosperous villages and towns of western Sicily. The Sicilian and Neapolitan Mafia was born in the 1860s against the very particular backdrop of Italy's struggle to emerge as a unified country. Its link with political secret societies, including the Carbonari, has been proved. The primary objective of the Mafia was therefore political, with a secret and violent nature that was present from the very beginning. The political instability of the 1860s, combined with the vulnerable structure of agricultural production (the wealth of Palermo, for example, was based on the citrus orchards that surrounded it, which depended closely on the distribution of water and the orange-selling networks), facilitated the use of private armed guards and methods of intimidation against economic competitors or political adversaries. Violence became a regular mode of social relations and fostered a widespread climate of fear beneath the appearance of order. Law enforcement by state authorities was paralyzed by links between Mafia leaders and local political elites, with the latter needing the support of the former to accede to or remain in power. Under the guise of protecting producers and traders, the Mafia imposed widespread racketeering and directly threatened those who attempted to oppose it. At the start of the twentieth century, encouraged by mass immigration to America, an Italian Mafia was established in major cities across the United States, including the Mano Nera in New York. The debate over its origins continues: Was it an extension of the Sicilian Mafia or an independent phenomenon? In any case, the more organized Italo-American Mafia rapidly overtook other urban gangs in controlling illegal activities, prostitution, gambling, and the sale of alcohol and drugs.

C. The Great Refusal of Machinery

A final rural/urban parallel might be drawn with regard to the unrest linked to the mechanization of agricultural and industrial labor. In the countryside of the south and east of England in the 1830s–1840s, poor peasants attacked the new threshing machines that had deprived them of work. They dismantled machinery as well as threatened owners with the burning of crops if salaries were not increased. These threats were expressed in letters signed "Captain Swing," thus reviving the phenomenon of anonymous letters demanding money and threatening arson that were common practice in many parts of Europe throughout the pre-industrial era (Hobsbawm & Rudé 1973; Jones 1989). Similarities of this unrest to the Luddite movement have often been emphasized: in 1811–1812, textile workers in Nottinghamshire, Yorkshire, and Lancashire destroyed stocking frames, spinning frames, gig mills, and other power looms. More threatening letters, signed by Ned Ludd, were sent to factory owners with demands that included increases in salaries. However, the Luddite movement exceeded the Swing Riots in intensity, particularly during the summer of 1812, when it organized an insurgency that was quashed by the authorities in a violent crackdown.

The Luddite movement of 1811–1812 represented the culmination of a broader rejection of mechanization. It marked the beginning of the Industrial Revolution and the difficult transition from craftsmanship to factory work. Similar episodes have been identified across Europe over a much longer period: in 1769, jennies were destroyed in Lancashire; in 1821, Catalan peasants, who supplemented their income by working with wool, smashed seventeen machines in the town of Alcoy; in June 1844, banner-printing machines were broken in the suburbs of Prague; and in 1867, the weavers of Roubaix (in the north of France) vandalized factories. In all regions where textile work with wool and cotton was widespread, the introduction of new machines provoked rebellious movements.

Initially interpreted as the archaic resistance of peasant workers to progress, these machine-breakers were rehabilitated by Hobsbawm as closely related to social bandits and other "primitive rebels" (1959). The threat of destroying machinery was one of the tools used by the oppressed to force employers to improve salaries and negotiate new working conditions. E. P. Thompson (1963) saw the Luddism of 1811–1812 as an expression of popular radicalism that exceeded mere issues of work. More recently, researchers such as Adrian Randall (1991) and François Jarrige (2009) have included the breaking of machinery in a broader reflection on the social history of the adoption of technology. They base their analyses on studies of local confrontations, the impact of economic development, and the conditions of the poor. The violence of craftsmen and peasant workers during the early Industrial Revolution is therefore no longer a subject viewed in isolation, but is now combined with new and less teleological approaches to economic history. After 1850–1860, this type of violence almost completely disappeared from working-class culture, which became used to mechanical work, and in which trade unions offered alternative forms of negotiation and collective protest.

IV. Complex General Processes

Any overall explanation of changes in crime comes up against the methodological problems raised in the previous chapters of this book. No automatic correlation can be established between variations in crime and long-term phenomena such as industrialization and urbanization. Although it is easy to explain the disappearance in the late nineteenth century of some typically rural forms of crime by the decline of rural communities in an increasingly urbanized world, historians have been unable to reach an agreement on the relative distribution of rural and urban crime, differences in their character, and their relative development over time. Every theory put forward in a particular direction is almost immediately met by counterexamples. At most, hypotheses and remarks can be proposed.

Alongside extensive sociological, economic, and anthropological theories, more attention should be paid to contingent political explanations. Although England saw a particularly early decline in homicide in the sixteenth century, this was perhaps not entirely linked to the modernity of its socioeconomic structure as compared to other European countries, but also resulted from the control by its rulers of the religious differences that in continental Europe resulted in protracted civil wars. The link between war and interpersonal violence cannot be overlooked, even in terms of indirect effects, as has been shown with regard to the burden placed by the Thirty Years' War on the rural male population of Sweden, or to the "crime waves" seen in large cities following other wars of the same period.

The role of the state must also be reintroduced into the debate, not as an abstract entity, but through an examination of the institutions themselves and the men responsible for their functioning. Historians of criminal justice have played a pioneering role in analyzing the interactions between individuals on trial and the judiciary (Castan 1980). The judicial archives could be interpreted in two different ways with respect to the state. On the one hand, intrusive new regulations from the judiciary and the police that upset social relations may have generated new forms of crime, such as desertion when universal military duty was imposed. On the other hand, the same judicial and police institutions may also have contributed to the increase in crime rates by changing the definition of certain acts and behaviors that were formerly accepted by the society, but later were no longer acceptable to the state authorities (e.g., charivari's disorders). The sharp growth in rural banditry in Europe in the late eighteenth century points as much to a weakening of the state during the politically unstable period of the Directory during the French Revolution (1795–1799) as it does to the construction by the same government of a new criminal category that justified repression (the relation of "bandits" to political opponents, such as priests or aristocrats). Political contingencies and interactions between society and the state can probably better explain phenomena such as the Sicilian Mafia, the durability and expansion of which, in both urban and rural areas, defies socioeconomic as well as culturalist analysis. The birth of the Mafia was directly linked to the history of nineteenth-century Italy. The difficulty of establishing the institutions of the unified Italian state in Sicily and the failure by that state to find allies in the local society reinforced the preeminence of a culture of violence. There is no need to rehash the folklore of "men of honor" or to blame the Sicilians for a particular cultural tropism, when it was simply a case of a balance of power and terror. The ease with which the Mafia took root in American cities in the early twentieth century, and its subsequent refocusing on drug trafficking as its most international and profitable economic activity, shows that the phenomenon went well beyond the supposed archaisms of rural Mediterranean culture.

Similarly, there is no consensus on the question of how the mass urbanization of European populations between 1750 and 1950 impacted changes in crime. Although homicide rates declined over the long term, Peter King (2013) and others have pointed out that the booming towns of the early period of industrialization experienced significant increases in homicide rates between the 1800s and the 1840s. Moreover, historians have emphasized that there was a rise in urban crime between the 1890s and the 1910s. This can be directly linked to the influx of young male migrant workers into the cities, especially from neighboring countries. However, immigration, even on an international scale, was nothing new to urban societies. Information relating to this issue should perhaps be turned on its head, directing less attention to the immigrants themselves and more toward the mechanisms by which the city integrated these new arrivals. This is, after all, the position taken by Eric A Johnson (1996), who has noted very low levels of violent crimes in German cities throughout the nineteenth century and has rejected the idea that urbanization had any influence on regional developments in crime rates across the German states. According to Johnson (1992), the variations among these regional rates correlated directly to the stigmatization of Polish and Lithuanian immigrants in German cities in contrast with the ease of integration into German society experienced by immigrants from Western Europe.

Mechanisms for the integration of immigrants are in fact as old as cities themselves, as most urban areas would not be able to support themselves without this demographic contribution. Regulation by neighborhood organizations, sociability at work, and police surveillance formed the basis for this integration (Van Dijck 2006). High levels of crime perpetrated by migrants in industrial cities may simply be a reflection of the high proportions of youths in these conurbations or of the isolation of working-class neighborhoods that were badly integrated into the older urban space, as was often the case in suburbs and industrial outskirts (Merriman 1991). The fact that crime rates in these industrializing cities eventually declined to similar levels as other cities after 1840 points to the fact that these emerging cities were experiencing a kind of "growing pains." Variations in urban violence may therefore be closely linked to the attention paid by municipal authorities to urban planning. In Birmingham, interethnic violence between street gangs in the 1870s is evidence of how a municipal council that was otherwise committed to major urban reform abandoned any commitment to unskilled youths (Weinberger 1991). As for explosions of violence between workers themselves, these were not an exclusively urban phenomenon; clashes between seasonal farmworkers from neighboring regions were sometimes very intense, such as the massacre of eight Italians in the salt marshes at Aigues-Mortes in France on 17 August 1893 (Noiriel 2010).

An overall comparison of urban and rural crime makes little sense, as the town and country have differing structures. Urban typologies may evoke specific patterns of crime beyond the simple focus on industrial cities. Unruly students in university towns played a significant role in maintaining the high homicide rate of the premodern period, and Oxford was still experiencing violent clashes between students and workers as late as the nineteenth century. Port cities also attracted particular types of crime. Capital cities are particularly interesting laboratories when it comes to comparing the effects of urban overcrowding and the early establishment of strict police surveillance, but although we know a lot about certain capital cities, particularly London, many European capitals remain unevenly studied. It is also difficult to assess the different impacts of the redefinition of public/private space, as well as of the development of domestic values, on intra-family crime and the decline in public violence in towns and rural areas. This is due not least to the wide variation in the recording of these cases.

Crime statistics are of limited help in identifying differences between types of crime in towns and villages. The increasing research into policing practices, on the other hand, provides a better understanding of the social construction of crime. Towns and countrysides often experienced different policing systems: municipal or state police and civil guards on the one hand, and gendarmerie forces on the other. Barbara Weinberger (1996) has shown how varying methods of policing in Warwickshire, located between Birmingham and the wider county, can explain the differences in statistics for the same crimes. Alcoholism was often repressed more harshly in the countryside than in the town, probably because it was an offense that was easily solved by understaffed rural police forces; conversely, small everyday offenses were much more controlled in towns, as the municipal authorities required police officers to closely monitor the implementation of urban regulations. However, these differences do not affect the trends in rates for the two environments: whatever the nature of offenses and crimes recorded, the rates decreased over the nineteenth century, confirming a certain pacification of interpersonal relationships in both town and countryside.

The dichotomy between towns and rural areas is not the only geographical approach to crime. Relationships between other areas, such as regions or continents, can also be taken into account. Digital tools, such as databases and geographic information systems, have opened new fields of research for urban crime mapping. The development of global history as a field of research also invites researchers to broaden the historical perspective of crime beyond European borders and to study international links between crime and justice. As Barry Godfrey has suggested (2014, pp. 105–08), a geographical history of crime should take into account the changing characteristics of places over time, evolutions in the relationship of crime to the local environment, and the movement of criminals.

References

Ager, Adrian W. 2014. *Crime and Poverty in 19th-Century England: The Economy of Makeshifts.* London: Bloomsbury.

Agulhon, Maurice. 1970. *La République au village: les populations du Var de la Révolution à la Seconde République.* Paris: Plon.

Archer, John E. 1990. *"By a Flash and a Scare": Arson, Animal Maiming, and Poaching in East Anglia, 1815–1870.* Oxford: Clarendon Press.

Archer, John E. 1999. "Poaching Gangs and Violence: The Urban-Rural Divide in Nineteenth Century Lancashire." *British Journal of Criminology* 39 (1): 25–38.

Baby, François. 1972. *La Guerre des demoiselles en Ariège (1829–1872).* Laroque d'Olmes, France: Montbel.

Bailey, Victor. 1977. "Salvation Army Riots, the 'Skeleton Army' and Legal Authority in the Provincial Town." In *Social Control in 19th Century Britain*, ed. A. P. Donajgrodzki. London: Croom Helm.

Blok, Anton. 1991. *De Bokkerijders. Roversbenden en geheime genootschappen in de landen van Oversmaas (1730–1774).* Amsterdam: Prometheus.

Castan, Nicole. 1980. *Justice et répression en Languedoc à l'époque des Lumières.* Paris: Flammarion.

Chassaigne, Philippe. 2005. *Ville et violence: Tensions et conflits dans la Grande-Bretagne victorienne (1840–1914).* Paris: Presses de l'université Paris-Sorbonne.

Chauvaud, Frédéric. 1995. *Les passions villageoises au XIXe siècle: les émotions rurales dans les pays de Beauce, du Hurepoix et du Mantois.* Paris: Publisud.

Chevalier, Louis. 1958. *Classes laborieuses et classes dangereuses à Paris dans la première moitié du XIXe siècle.* Paris: Plon.

Claverie, Elisabeth, & Pierre Lamaison. 1982. *L'impossible mariage. Violence et parenté en Gévaudan, 17e–18e–19e siècles.* Paris: Hachette.

Cobb, Richard. 1972. "La Bande d'Orgères." In *Reactions to the French Revolution*, ed. Richard Cobb, 181–215. Oxford: Oxford University Press.

Corbin, Alain. 1979. *Les filles de noces, misère sexuelle et prostitution aux XIXe et XXe siècles.* Paris: Aubier.

Corbin, Alain. 1990. *Le village des cannibales.* Paris: Aubier.

Corvol, Andrée. 1987. *L'homme aux bois: histoire des relations de l'homme et de la forêt, XVIIe– XXe siècle.* Paris: Fayard.

Danker, Uwe. 2001. *Die Geschichte der Räuber und Gauner.* Düsseldorf: Artemis & Winkler.

Denys, Catherine, Brigitte Marin, & Vincent Milliot, eds. 2009. *Réformer la police. Les mémoires policiers en Europe au XVIIIe siècle.* Rennes, France: Presses universitaires de Rennes.

Egmond, Florike. 1993. *Underworlds: Organized Crime in the Netherlands, 1650–1800.* Cambridge: Polity Press.

Eisner, Manuel. 2003. "Long-Term Historical Trends in Violent Crime." *Crime and Justice* 30: 83–142.

Emsley, Clive. 2007. *Crime, Police, & Penal Policy: European Experiences, 1750–1940.* Oxford: Oxford University Press.

Farge, Arlette, & Jacques Revel. 1988. *Logiques de la foule. L'affaire des enlèvements d'enfants, Paris, 1750.* Paris: Hachette.

Godfrey, Barry. 2014. *Crime in England, 1880–1945: The Rough and the Criminal, the Policed and the Incarcerated.* London: Routledge.

Hobsbawm, Eric. 1959. *Primitive Rebels: Studies in Archaic Forms of Social Movement in the 19th and 20th Centuries.* Manchester, UK: Manchester University Press.

Hobsbawm, Eric. 1969. *Bandits.* London: Weidenfeld and Nicolson.

Hobsbawm, Eric, & George Rudé. 1973. *Captain Swing.* London: Harmondsworth.

Jarrige, François. 2009. *Au temps des "tueuses de bras." Les bris de machines à l'aube de l'ère industrielle.* Rennes, France: Presses universitaires de Rennes.

Johnson, Eric A. 1992. "Cities Don't Cause Crime: Urban-Rural Difference in Late 19th and Early 20th Century German Criminality." *Social Science History* 16: 129–76.

Johnson, Eric A. 1996. "Urban and Rural Crime in Germany, 1871–1914." In *The Civilization of Crime: Violence in Town and Country since the Middle Ages,* ed. Eric A. Johnson & Eric Monkkonen, 217–57. Chicago: University of Illinois Press.

Johnson, Eric A., & Eric Monkkonen, eds. 1996. *The Civilization of Crime: Violence in Town and Country since the Middle Ages.* Chicago: University of Illinois Press.

Jones, David. 1989. *Rebecca's Children: A Study of Rural Society, Crime, and Protest.* Oxford: Oxford University Press.

Kalifa, Dominique. 1995. *L'Encre et le sang. Récits de crime et société à la Belle Epoque.* Paris: Fayard.

Kaplan, Steven L. 1976. *Bread, Politics and Political Economy in the Reign of Louis XV.* The Hague: Nijhoff.

King, Peter. 2013. "Exploring and Explaining the Geography of Homicide: Patterns of Lethal Violence in Britain and Europe, 1805–1900." *European Review of History* 20: 967–87.

Kwass, Michael. 2014. *Contraband, Louis Mandrin and the Making of a Global Underground.* Cambridge & London: Harvard University Press.

Lefebvre, Georges. 1932. *La Grande Peur de 1789.* Paris: Armand Colin.

Lenclud, Gérard. 1983. "Une société prise à son piège. Reproduction sociale et violence en Haut-Gévaudan." *Etudes rurales* 89–91: 299–308.

Lignereux, Aurélien. 2008. *La France rébellionnaire. Les résistances à la gendarmerie (1800–1859).* Rennes, France: Presses universitaires de Rennes.

Luddy, Maria. 2007. *Prostitution and Irish Society, 1800–1940.* Cambridge: Cambridge University Press.

Lupo, Salvatore. 1993. *Storia della Mafia, Dalle origini ai nostri giorni.* Rome: Donzelli.

Merriman, John. 1991. *The Margins of City Life: Explorations on the French Urban Frontier, 1815–1851.* Oxford: Oxford University Press.

Milliot, Vincent. 2011. *Un policier des Lumières.* Seyssel, France: Champ Vallon.

Neale, Frank. 1988. *Sectarian Violence: The Liverpool Experience.* Manchester, UK: Manchester University Press.

Nicolas, Jean. 2002. *La rébellion française. Mouvements populaires et conscience sociale: 1661–1789.* Paris: Seuil.

Noiriel, Gérard. 2010. *Le massacre des Italiens. Aigues-Mortes, 17 août 1893.* Paris: Fayard.

Ortalli, Gherardo. 1986. *Bande armate, banditi, banditismo e repressione di giustizia negli stati europei di antico regime.* Rome: Jouvence.

Perrot, Michelle. 1979. "Dans la France de la Belle Epoque, les Apaches, premières bandes de jeunes." In *Les marginaux et les exclus dans l'histoire*, ed. Bernard Vincent, 387–407. Paris: Union Générale d'Edition.

Péveri, Patrice. 1997. "'Cette ville était alors comme un bois. . .': Criminalité et opinion publique à Paris dans les années qui précèdent l'affaire Cartouche (1715–1721)." *Crime, Histoire & Sociétés* 1 (2): 51–73.

Pitou, Frédérique. 2000. "Jeunesse et désordre social: les 'coureurs de nuit' à Laval au XVIIIe siècle." *Revue d'histoire moderne et contemporaine* 47 (1): 69–92.

Ploux, François. 2002. *Guerres paysannes en Quercy. Violences, conciliations et répression pénale dans les campagnes du Lot, 1810–1860*. Paris: La Boutique de l'histoire.

Randall, Adrian. 1991. *Before the Luddites: Custom, Community and Machinery in the English Woolen Industry, 1776–1809*. Cambridge: Cambridge University Press.

Regnard-Drouot, Céline. 2009. *Marseille la violente: Criminalité, industrialisation et société (1851–1914)*. Rennes, Frances: Presses universitaires de Rennes.

Rousseaux, Xavier. 2000. "Espaces de désordres, espace d'ordre: le banditisme aux frontières Nord-Est de la France (1700–1810)." In *Frontière et criminalité (1715–1815)*, ed. Catherine Denys, 131–74. Arras, France: Artois presses université.

Rousseaux, Xavier. 2013. "Un 'long 19e siècle': Banditisme, protestation populaire et violence dans les territoires belges (1750–1919)." *European Review of History-Revue européenne d'histoire* 20 (6): 989–1009.

Sahlins, Peter. 1994. *Forest Rites: The War of the Demoiselles in Nineteenth-Century France*. Cambridge, MA: Harvard University Press.

Schulte, Regina. 1994. *The Village in Court: Arson, Infanticide and Poaching in the Court Records of Upper Bavaria, 1848–1914*. Cambridge: Cambridge University Press.

Sharpe, James. 2005. *Dick Turpin: The Myth of the English Highwayman*. London: Profile.

Shoemaker, Robert. 2004. *The London Mob: Violence and Disorder in Eighteenth-Century England*. London: Hambledon.

Shore, Heather. 1999. *Artful Dodgers: Youth and Crime in Early Nineteenth-Century London*. Woodbridge, UK: Boydell Press.

Shore, Heather. 2010. "Criminality, Deviance and the Underworld since 1750." In *Histories of Crime: Britain, 1600–2000*, ed. David Nash & Anne-Marie Kilday, 120–40. London: Palgrave Macmillan

Sindall, Rob. 1987. "The London Garroting Panics of 1856 and 1862." *Social History* 12 (3): 351–59.

Sindall, Rob. 1990. *Street Violence in the Nineteenth Century: Media Panic or Real Danger?* Leicester, UK: Leicester University Press.

Soulet, Jean-François. 1988. "Une nouvelle approche de la France rurale au XIXe siècle." *Revue Historique* 566:381–92.

Taylor, David. 2010. *Hooligans, Harlots, and Hangmen: Crime and Punishment in Victorian Britain*. Santa Barbara, CA: Praeger.

Thibon, Christian. 1988. *Pays de Sault. Les Pyrénées audoises au XIXe siècle: les villages et l'Etat*. Paris: CNRS.

Thompson, Edward P. 1963. *The Making of the English Working Class*. London: Victor Gollancz.

Thompson, Edward P. 1971. "The Moral Economy of the English Crowd in the Eighteenth Century." *Past & Present* 50:76–136.

Thompson, Edward P. 1975. *Whigs and Hunters: The Origin of the Black Act*. London: Allen Lane.

Van Dijck, Maarten. 2006. "De Stad als onafhandelijke variabele en centrum van moderniteit. Langtermijnstrends in stedelijke en rurale criminaliteitspatronen in de Nederlanden (1300–1800)." *Stadsgeschiedenis* 1:7–26.

Walkowitz, Judith. 1980. *Prostitution and Victorian Society: Women, Class and the State.* Cambridge: Cambridge University Press.

Weber, Eugen. 1977. *Peasants into Frenchmen: The Modernization of Rural France, 1870–1914.* London: Chatto and Windus.

Weinberger, Barbara. 1991. "L'anatomie de l'antagonisme racial et de la violence urbaine. Les bandes à Birmingham dans les années 1870." *Déviance et société* 15:407–18.

Weinberger, Barbara. 1996. "Urban and Rural Crime Rates and Their Genesis in Late Nineteenth-and Early Twentieth-Century Britain." In *The Civilization of Crime: Violence in Town and Country since the Middle Ages*, ed. Eric A. Johnson & Eric Monkkonen, 198–216 Chicago: University of Illinois Press.

Yvorel, Jean-Jacques. 2005. "Esquisse d'une histoire de la prise en charge de l'enfance délinquante aux XIXe et XXe siècles." In *Eduquer et punir: La colonie agricole et pénitentiaire de Mettay (1839–1937)*, ed. Luc Forlivesi, Georges-François Pottier, & Sophie Chassat, 9–25. Rennes, France: Presses universitaires de Rennes.

Zysberg, André. 1985. *L'Affaire d'Orgères 1790–1800.* Chartres, France: Société archéologique d'Eure et Loir.

PART TWO

FORMS OF CRIME

CHAPTER 5

HISTORIES OF INTERPERSONAL VIOLENCE IN EUROPE AND NORTH AMERICA, 1700–PRESENT

RICHARD MC MAHON

INTRODUCTION

THE history of violence is, for some, a history of progress. Steven Pinker (2011) identifies a "humanitarian revolution" in the eighteenth century that, over the last three centuries, has led to a profound change in the extent, nature, and practice of interpersonal violence in Western cultures. For Pinker, the rise of the modern city, the spread of capitalism, the increased intervention of the state in daily life have—alongside the acquisition of literacy, the diffusion of Enlightenment thought, and the increasing influence of reason, education, and science on the conduct of human affairs—led to a marked decline in the resort to and use of violence. This revolution, moreover, was built on a much longer process of civilization rooted in processes of state formation, the growth of economic and social interdependence, and the imposition of new standards of personal behavior. Here, it is the grand alliance between the state, "gentle commerce," and Enlightenment reason that provides the impetus for a radical decline in the resort to interpersonal violence. All, however, is not change. Patterns of violence are, for Pinker, also shaped by dispositions that are rooted in evolutionary processes and account for male predominance among the perpetrators of violence and the tendency for men to use violence to assert position and status. Such tendencies have, it is suggested, been controlled and ameliorated by the profound changes in sociocultural life that have occurred since the eighteenth century.

For others, the history of violence is a history, if not of progress, then certainly of profound change. Indeed, there is much support within the historiography for Pinker's claims of substantial change in violent activity since the eighteenth century. Pieter Spierenburg (1996; 2008) has, for instance, claimed that there has been a marginalization of interpersonal violence within European life since the eighteenth century, underpinned by increasing urbanization, the establishment of national police forces, and a shift in conceptions of male honor. For Spierenburg, this marginalization can be located within a wider civilizing process with deep roots in European culture from the late Middle Ages onward. Unlike Pinker, however, Spierenburg is reluctant to locate patterns of violence within a biological framework or one derived from evolutionary psychology, preferring instead to maintain a focus on social and cultural contexts for violent activity. Manuel Eisner (2014), too, identifies a range of socioeconomic and cultural factors that he argues have significantly altered patterns of violent activity. In the context of the nineteenth century, he notes a range of forces and phenomena that, as part of a "bourgeois civilizing offensive," imposed new standards of behavior and reduced the extent of violent action. These include the disciplining of workers in factories; the adoption of universal schooling and the creation of mass conscription armies; the establishment of national police forces; the rise of temperance movements; the channeling, particularly of male aggression, into "civilized leisure activities"; and, ultimately, the reshaping of concepts of masculinity to emphasize domesticity and the importance of self-control (p. 97). Unlike Spierenburg, he shows more enthusiasm for biological explanations for violent behavior over time and across cultures—noting, in particular, that the predominance of male homicide perpetrators appears "resistant to all cultural and economic change" (Eisner 2011, p. 473).

Historians of early modern England, France, and Germany such as Robert Shoemaker, Robert Muchembled, and Joachim Eibach, although skeptical or even openly hostile to the idea of understanding the history of violence within a wider civilizing process, have also pointed to a change in interpersonal violence in the eighteenth century and related this to profound changes in conceptions of masculinity and personal honor. For these historians, it is, in particular, the development of the modern city and specific cultural formations arising from city life that have been fundamental to the reshaping and eventual transformation of practices of violence since the eighteenth century (Eibach 2008; Shoemaker 2001; Muchembled 2011).

A number of historians of violence in North America also see the city as a key agent of pacification. Roger Lane's account of violence in nineteenth-century Philadelphia argues strongly that life in that city served to impose new standards of self-control on adults and children through the work practices of the developing factory system and the disciplining effect of public schooling. This, he claims, led eventually to a decline in the resort to violence as a means of managing conflicts in the city. Moreover, those who failed to integrate or who were denied the possibility of assimilation, such as African Americans, were condemned to endure higher rates of lethal interpersonal violence (Lane 1986; Lane 1997; Lane 1999). Kevin Mullen (2005) has made similar claims for San Francisco in the latter half of the nineteenth century. Mullen notes how the influence of the police and other disciplining forces in the city served to inhibit enthusiasm for violent action.

Some historians are also sympathetic to the application of the civilizing process thesis to the American circumstance and explicitly locate changes in patterns of violence
within an "American civilizing process." Stephen Mennell (2007) has argued that the
general pattern of American violence can be seen as part of an overall downward trend
in Western societies that is best understood within the framework of Elias's civilizing process thesis. Spierenburg (2006) has argued provocatively that the civilizing process was somewhat inhibited in North America, relative to Europe, by the failure of
the state to achieve a more comprehensive monopoly over violence. This he attributes
to the strength of the self-help ethic in American culture and to democracy coming
"too early." He maintains, however, that Elias's thesis provides a viable framework for
understanding the American experience. Pinker (2011, p. 106), too, has integrated the
American experience within a wider civilizing process, albeit one that took different
paths in different parts of the country. On the whole, the American pattern of violence
is portrayed as a less complete manifestation of a process of civilization that is found
across Western cultures.

This view has not gone unquestioned. Randolph Roth (2009) has argued persua-
sively that the civilizing process thesis does not apply to the American experience of
interpersonal violence. In its stead, he argues that American differences in experiences
of violence should be understood primarily in light of a failure of nation building that
emerged particularly in mid- to late nineteenth-century America. In a specifically
European context, a number of historians have also offered critiques of the applicabil-
ity of the civilizing process thesis as a means of understanding changes in homicide
rates and have argued that this approach serves to impose unnecessary distinctions
between practices of violence in particular places and periods, while drawing attention
away from their often-profound continuities (Mc Mahon, Eibach, & Roth 2013; Eibach,
2016). Those working outside the field of social and cultural history have also been
highly critical of the interpretation offered by authors such as Pinker. John Gray (2011)
views the "progress" extolled by Pinker as simply a comforting but dangerous illusion.
For Gray, some of the key changes shaping the decline in violence identified by Pinker,
such as the spread of democracy and the increase in wealth, are highly problematic
agents of pacification. The formation of democratic nation-states was, Gray argues, a
key engine driving violent activity in the twentieth century that in some areas produced
acts of ethnic cleansing. He notes, too, the fragility of norms that might inhibit violent
action, pointing out that growing prosperity is reversible and that economic collapse
can lead to an upsurge in violence.

We are then confronted by a variety of histories in Europe and North America that
offer fundamentally different interpretations of change and continuity in patterns of
violence and, more particularly, interpersonal violence. This essay offers an overview
of the key debates by examining both quantitative and contextual research on interpersonal violence. The first section examines the findings of, and debates among, historians on homicide rates and reflects briefly on the relationship between lethal and
nonlethal interpersonal violence. The second section offers an assessment of the shifting contexts for violent activity and explores patterns of continuity and change in the

profiles and actions of perpetrators. The essay concludes with some wider reflections on the place of interpersonal violence in Western cultures since the eighteenth century.

I. Homicide Rates

Do changes in homicide rates in Europe and North America from the eighteenth century to the present day reflect an increasing marginalization of interpersonal violence in social and cultural life, and can such changes be interpreted as a consequence of the benefits of specifically modern forms of economic organization and social interaction, as well as profound alterations in cultural and political life? This is a question that has exercised historians, on both sides of the Atlantic, for at least the last forty years. Studies of Europe, and, in particular, northwestern Europe, from a range of different scholars, sometimes working within different methodological frameworks, have dominated the field. American studies are less plentiful, although Roth's (2009) study offers a state-of-the-art approach to the subject that has no Europe-wide equivalent.

A. Europe

There is evidence in support of changing patterns of lethal violence from the eighteenth century to the present day. For the first half of the eighteenth century, Eisner (2014, pp. 80–81) has calculated an average European homicide rate of around 5.5 per 100,000 based on samples taken from eleven regions of Europe. By the second half of the century, the average homicide rate had fallen to 3.8 per 100,000, and in the nineteenth century rates appear to have declined further, with an average rate of 2.9 per 100,000 over the course of the century. In the first half of the twentieth century, the average rate dropped again to 1.6 per 100,000, and in the 1950s and 1960s reached an extraordinarily low rate of 0.8 per 100,000 before increasing again to a still relatively low rate of 1.2 for the closing decades of the millennium. By the beginning of the twenty-first century, the average rate was less than one-fifth of that estimated for the early decades of the eighteenth century.

There is also evidence of considerable regional variations in experiences of lethal violence in the eighteenth and nineteenth centuries. Eisner points to low rates in areas of northern Europe relative to southern Europe. Rates in England and Wales in the latter half of the eighteenth century were estimated at 1.4 per 100,000, while those estimated for Spain were three times higher, at 4.2 per 100,000. Rates in Sweden in the first half of the nineteenth century were 1.6 per 100,000, while those calculated for Italy were five times higher, at 8 per 100,000 of the population. Variations within regions are also evident. In northern Europe, rates in Ireland in the first half of the eighteenth century are presented as being close to three times those found in England and Wales during the same period. Rates in what Eisner identifies as Central Western Europe (including samples from France, Belgium, the Netherlands, and Germany), while relatively low, also include some variation, with France, for instance, appearing to have had consistently lower rates than those found in Germany (2014, pp. 80–81).

There is also evidence, however, of considerable convergence over time. By the mid-twentieth century, homicide rates in the regions covered in Eisner's study were all below 1.5 per 100,000. In some cases, this seems to have reflected a remarkable change in the incidence of lethal violence. This is most obvious in southern Europe. For Sardinia in the early years of the nineteenth century, there was an estimated homicide rate of 22.8 per 100,000, but by the closing decades of the twentieth century, this rate had fallen to 2.5 per 100,000. In Spain, the national homicide rate is estimated as 8.3 per 100,000 for the mid-nineteenth century, but this figure fell to a rate of 0.9 per 100,000 by the dawn of the twenty-first century. The impression offered by such a convergence in homicide figures is that countries such as England, the Netherlands, Belgium, and France were at the vanguard of a process of declining rates of interpersonal violence and set the trends that were eventually followed by more peripheral areas of Europe (2014, pp. 80–81).

There has, indeed, been a general tendency to locate the epicenter of the apparent transformation in modern homicide rates within urban and industrial centers. For Pinker in the late nineteenth century, "Europe had a peaceable bull's eye in the northern industrialized countries (Great Britain, France, Germany, Denmark and the Low Countries)," which were, in turn, bordered by "slightly stroppier" countries such as Ireland, Finland, and Austria-Hungary and then "surrounded" by more violent countries such as Spain, Italy, and Greece (2011, p. 87). There is a sense that from the eighteenth century to at least the mid-twentieth century rates were lowest in those areas where the forces of "modernity" were to the fore.

There are, however, problems with this view. There are difficulties in using eighteenth-century records to compare homicide rates across time and territories. This is evident even when the countries share a similar legal framework for the prosecution of crime. In comparing Irish and English rates in the eighteenth century, for instance, we need to be aware of the limitations of the available records. To begin with, there are the possible distortions that arise from comparing small samples from one country with relatively large samples from another. Eisner's (2014) homicide rate for Ireland in the first half of the eighteenth century is based on three "local estimates," while the English rates are drawn from a sample of twenty local estimates. The difficulty with the Irish sample is that there is potential for distortion in the limited time period for which records are available (for the period 1700–1750, records are only available from 1732 onward, that is, for less than twenty of the fifty years covered by the estimated rate). This immediately gives rise to some fairly obvious questions. Is the sample drawn from a particularly violent time? How representative is the local or county estimate? In the Irish case, the country experienced widespread and severe famine in the early 1740s, and this might have led to an increase in violence, which may, in turn, render the period unrepresentative of experiences in earlier decades. It is also impossible, based on current research, to determine whether experiences in Ulster (from which the sample is largely drawn) were different from those in the rest of the country. It is striking that when national data become available in the nineteenth century, the major difference in the rates between the two countries largely disappears (Mc Mahon 2013). This is not to deny the importance of county and local studies, but rather to urge caution in drawing too neat a distinction between modernizing centers and more "traditional" peripheries based on potentially unrepresentative samples.

The use of court records to posit fundamental change in patterns of lethal violence over the course of the eighteenth century within particular countries has also been questioned. Spierenburg (2011), for instance, has queried the validity of basing homicide rates for the eighteenth century on indictments, arguing that these figures miss many cases that did not come before the courts. It is difficult to assess the impact of this factor on homicide rates, but Spierenburg's point is well made that court records, on their own, are not an ideal guide to establishing overall homicide rates and trends. Some form of substantial corroborating evidence is usually needed when using homicide indictment rates to reach broad conclusions about the changing nature of patterns of lethal interpersonal violence and to confidently compare rates across time and territory. There are, indeed, definite risks in using homicide indictment rates to posit fundamental social change. This certainly applies to eighteenth-century England, where homicide indictment rates have been employed to bolster the case not only for a marked decline in the resort to interpersonal violence over time, but also for a profound change in prevailing ideas of civility, masculinity, and personal honor (see Shoemaker 2001). Such a case rarely takes account of the apparent rise in homicide that occurred in the late eighteenth and early nineteenth centuries, when, according to some estimates, English homicide rates "doubled" (Roth 2009, p. 146).

Even allowing for such problems with the sources, the evidence for radical change in much of Europe between the eighteenth century and the present day is, on a simple reading of the rates, limited. In mid- to late eighteenth-century England and Wales, the homicide rate calculated by Eisner based on nineteen local estimates was 1.4 per 100,000, while that for England and Wales in the early twenty-first century was slightly higher, but not radically different, at 1.5 per 100,000. There were fluctuations in the rates over time, but, over the course of this period, national rates remained, on average, below 2 per 100,000 (Eisner 2014, pp. 80–81). It could be that the eighteenth-century court records based on indictments miss a significant number of cases. Yet the rates from the present day are also shaped by developments such as improvements in medical care and emergency services. Current estimates by both Eckberg (2010) and Eisner (2014, p. 76) suggest that in 50 percent of cases prior to the twentieth century, the victim would have survived if he or she had had access to modern health care and emergency services. If we were to take account of improvements in medical care, the rate in the present day would be double that found in the eighteenth-century records and, indeed, those found in national statistics for the nineteenth century—suggesting an upsurge in lethal violence in recent decades rather than a marked decline from the eighteenth century onward.

A similar pattern is evident over time in Ireland, where rates based on national statistics in the nineteenth century are in line with those found in the present day, and, if we allow for improvements in medical care, would actually be lower than in contemporary Ireland (Mc Mahon 2013). Recent evidence from Scotland offers a similar picture, albeit with even lower rates in the eighteenth century. Knox finds homicide indictment rates of 0.5 or less per 100,000 across much of the eighteenth century—close to one-eighth, or, taking improvements in medical care into account, one-fifteenth, of the rates in early twenty-first-century Glasgow (Knox with Thomas 2015; United Nations Office on Drugs and Crime [UNODC] 2013). Outside of Britain and Ireland, similar patterns can be found. In Sweden, the homicide rate based on national statistics moved from 1.1 per 100,000 in the mid to late eighteenth century to 1.2 per 100,000 at the close of the twentieth century, with some relatively minor fluctuations over the intervening centuries (Eisner 2014, pp. 80–81). There are also areas of Europe that experienced a marked increase in homicide rates. This is most obvious in Finland, where homicide rates increased in the late nineteenth and early twentieth centuries, reaching a high of over 8 per 100,000 in the 1920s and remaining above the European average for much of the remainder of the century (Savolainen, Lehti, & Kivivuori 2008, p. 76). For much of Europe outside of its southern regions, then, the evidence for a radical decline in homicide is limited. The evidence from the eighteenth century to the present day offers little hint of a radical transformation in homicide rates in much of Europe, with many areas remaining below a relatively low rate of 2 per 100,000. There were particular surges in homicide rates in some areas of Europe during and/or after times of severe conflict, such as the First and Second World Wars, but, on the whole, we are confronted with a remarkable stability in rates throughout much of Northern and Western Europe.

B. North America

The evidence from North America also complicates claims of a general decline in homicide rates over time. The picture that emerges from North America is one of relatively low and declining rates in the early to mid-eighteenth century disrupted by a marked increase in its closing decades. This, in turn, was followed by a decline in rates in much of the newly-formed United States in the early nineteenth century, followed by a radical upsurge, in many areas, in the mid- to late nineteenth century. This placed the country above, and in some areas well above, average European homicide rates and established a pattern that persists to the present day, with the United States becoming, in Roth's (2009) words, a "homicidal nation."

In the early years of the eighteenth century there is little evidence of American exceptionalism. Homicide rates appear to have generally declined among "European Americans" and to have been lower, as they were in Europe, than those in the seventeenth century. New England had remarkably low rates of 1 per 100,000, which would place it among the least homicidal societies in modern history (Roth 2009, ch. 2). During the Revolutionary period, however, homicide rates increased in many regions, with those divided between Tory and Rebel groupings being particularly prone to high rates. This is evident in rural areas surrounding the major cities of New York and

Philadelphia, as well as in the Ohio Valley and the backcountry areas stretching from southwestern Virginia to northwestern Georgia (Roth 2009, p. 146). Frontier areas in the south and west were particularly prone to acts of serious violence, and, in some areas, rates might have reached as high as 200 or more per 100,000 (Roth 2009, p. 162). When homicide rates are considered alongside attacks on Native Americans and the activities of often-homicidal criminal gangs, there can be little doubt that this was an extraordinarily violent time in much of the country.

In the decades after the Revolution there was a marked divergence in experiences of lethal violence in the United States. Homicide rates decreased in the North and mountainous regions of the South, but in slaveholding regions rose considerably to levels that exceeded those of the mid-eighteenth century (Roth 2009, p. 180). There were areas of the North where homicide rates were relatively high—this is most obvious in cities such as Boston, New York, and Philadelphia (Roth 2009, pp. 187–88, 196–98), but, in the main, rates remained low. By contrast, in the slave South, between the Revolution and the Civil War, rates were around 10 to 25 per 100,000 adults per year, which was "double the rate in cities like Philadelphia and New York, which were the most homicidal places in the North" (Roth 2009, p. 200). The picture that emerges from the eighteenth and early nineteenth centuries is thus one of fluctuation over time and variation across region in response to varied circumstance, rather than one of obvious decline.

Some, however, have queried the picture of relatively low rates in the early and mid-eighteenth and early nineteenth centuries. The evidence of relatively low rates has, for instance, been questioned by Spierenburg, who, as noted earlier, is skeptical about the validity of homicide rates derived from court records. He asserts that Roth's estimates may be unreliable because they may be based primarily on surviving indictments (Spierenburg 2011). Although Roth does, at times, rely on indictment rates, he points out that his primary American data are not based solely on court records, and that he has used a range of other sources to refine the data and develop more reliable rates for this period (Roth 2011). Unless contradictory studies emerge, there is no plausible reason to deny the validity of the trends evident in Roth's figures.

From the mid-nineteenth century, Roth identifies a marked divergence between European and U.S. experiences of lethal violence. In the late 1840s and 1850s, homicide rates "exploded across the nation," and parts of the United States were transformed from being among the least to the most homicidal areas in the Western world (Roth 2009, p. 299). This increase, moreover, was felt across social, ethnic, and racial groups, with rural, often-prosperous native-born populations seeing a marked increase in homicide rates alongside rises in rates in urban areas where immigration and difficult economic circumstances prevailed. Rates also rose substantially in much of the South, in both urban and rural areas, in the lead-up to the Civil War. During that war, rates reached new heights in borderland areas, such as north Texas, where they rose to 100–200 per 100,000 adults per year. In the mountainous regions of the South, where the population was often deeply divided over the war, rates could reach simply staggering heights, and high rates persisted here in the decades after the war, reaching as high as 250 per 100,000 and indicating a profound transformation in experiences of lethal violence in the region (Roth 2009, pp. 332–39). It was, however, the southwestern part of the United States that became the most homicidal region in the Western world in the latter half of the nineteenth century. Here, homicide rates "ranged at a minimum from 140 per 100,000 adults per year in Colorado and 250 per 100,000 in New Mexico and in south west Texas to 600 per 100,000 in Arizona" (Roth 2009, p. 354).

There was a drop in homicide rates in many areas of the United States following the Civil War and Reconstruction, but they began to rise again in the North in the late 1890s and to "soar" in the rural South in the late 1880s and 1890s (Roth 2009). Rates among African Americans also overtook those of whites in both the North and the South and established a pattern of higher black homicide rates that persists to the present day (Roth 2009, p. 387). The exception to this was California, where racial discrimination against African Americans was less acute and, as a consequence, black homicide rates remained below those of whites. Rates among other, more prominent, minorities such as the Chinese were, however, high (Roth 2009; Mullen 2005; McKanna 2002). In the southwestern regions of the country, homicide rates declined in many, although not all, areas in the late nineteenth and early twentieth centuries, and the South reemerged, fueled to a large degree by the insecurities of white supremacists, as the most homicidal region in the United States and, indeed, probably in the Western world (for rates in the South at this time, see Roth 2009, p. 420).

In the twentieth century, homicide rates, while enjoying some significant fluctuations over time and varying by region as well as by ethnic and racial group, remained consistently higher than those in Europe. Although the data for this century remain to be refined, the national rates ranged between 6 and 9 per 100,000 for much of the century (Roth 2009)—placing the United States well above European averages of around 1 or, at worst, 2 per 100,000. The American experience thus clearly diverged from that of Europe in the post–Civil War period, and its rates remained above those seen elsewhere in the Western world and, indeed, above those seen in some earlier periods of American history. The reasons for such a divergence would require a separate article (for a discussion, see Monkkonen 2006), but what is clear is that the evidence from the United States does little to suggest a radical transformation in the extent of lethal interpersonal violence that might be understood in the context of either a humanitarian revolution or a wider civilizing process. Outside of Europe and North America, it becomes more difficult to identify clear patterns in homicidal violence because of the lack of research and the often-difficult nature of the available sources. There are areas outside of Europe where homicide rates are particularly high. There is also evidence, however, to suggest that low homicide rates are by no means a purely European or North American phenomenon, with, for instance, relatively low rates reported for India and Japan (see Archer & Gartner 1984).

The history of homicide rates is therefore less one of overall decline, but rather one of variation and fluctuation without a pattern that allows for overly-neat distinctions to be drawn between rates in the eighteenth century and rates in the present day, or between those in Western and non-Western cultures. It would also be a mistake to assume a neat or simple relationship between patterns of lethal and nonlethal violence. These rates provide us with a clear indication of the degree to which violence was—or was not—kept within certain bounds and limits, but they cannot be used to offer an indication of overall levels of violence in a given society (Mc Mahon, Eibach, & Roth 2013). To posit a fundamental shift in social and cultural practices of and attitudes towards violence on the basis of these rates would be unwise.

II. Contexts

Homicide rates are, of course, not the only index of marginalization or even civilization; rather, it is necessary to look also at the shifting contexts in which interpersonal violence has taken place and, in particular, to explore the meaning of both continuity and change in the nature of the participants in, practices of, and circumstances for violent action. Central to the idea of the marginalization of violence in modern European and North American life is the connection between urbanization; greater state intervention; and the withdrawal not only of elite society, but also of the mass of the population from practices of interpersonal violence. In this view, interpersonal violence, or at least serious violence, is no longer acceptable within the mainstream of Western culture and is a practice primarily restricted to those on the margins of social and cultural life, particularly within the economically deprived areas (or "de-civilized islands") of major cities. This marks a major shift away from practices at the beginning of the eighteenth century, where violence is often portrayed by some historians as being central to conceptions of masculinity and personal honor across social classes. Such a cultural shift is also generally seen as being driven by forces similar to those used to account for changes in homicide rates, namely, the abandonment of violence by political and social elites, processes of urbanization, and greater state intervention in sociocultural life over time. It is necessary, therefore, to explore the impact of the city and the state alongside changing patterns of participation in violent activity to place the use of interpersonal violence in its proper contexts.

A. The City and the State

The city, for many, has been central to the shaping of violent activity since the eighteenth century. It was here that new and more effective controls were placed on the behavior of individuals, and particularly on the violent tendencies of young men, and that rural migrants absorbed new standards of restraint in dealing with interpersonal conflicts (Johnson & Monkkonen 1996; Muchembled 2011). In North America, too, as noted earlier, the urban environment is portrayed as a central driver in the imposition of new standards of behavior, with Roger Lane (1999) noting how homicide rates decreased in Philadelphia as the city's inhabitants were subjected to the disciplining effects of factory work and public schooling, and Mullen (2005) stressing the impact of policing on the inhibition of violence.

Recent research suggests, however, that the placement of the city as an agent of pacification since the eighteenth century has been exaggerated. Peter King (2010; 2011) has demonstrated that homicide rates were often higher in urban than rural areas of Britain in the nineteenth century, and that any clear link between urbanization and declining homicide rates is problematic. He has also demonstrated how rates in rural areas such as the southwest of England or the highlands of Scotland were often much lower than in the industrial heartlands of northwestern England and the central belt of Scotland (King 2010, p. 697). King's research clearly demonstrates that the city, rather than inhibiting violence, could actually witness an increase in rates of interpersonal violence. In a broader study of European trends, King (2013, p. 980) also points out that, aside from areas such as Corsica, which had a tradition of feuding, homicide rates in rural France were often lower than in their urban and industrial counterparts. Evidence from nineteenth-century Ireland also suggests that rural, economically underdeveloped regions often had relatively low rates of homicide, and that there is no necessary connection between urban life and low rates of lethal interpersonal violence (Mc Mahon 2013).

In a North American context, Roth (2009, ch. 8) has also called into question the notion of the industrial city as an agent of pacification in the nineteenth century. He points out that the decline in homicide rates noted by Lane (1999) for Philadelphia in the late nineteenth century was not simply restricted to industrial cities. Small towns and rural areas throughout the northern United States also saw a decline in homicide rates that had little to do with the "benefits" of the disciplining influence of factory work or public schooling (Roth 2009, p. 391). Roth's study clearly serves to warn against any simple relationship between declining homicide rates and urbanization.

Cities, in the closing decades of the twentieth century, also became central points of serious violent crime in Western countries. Organized crime and urban deprivation increasingly shape experiences of violent activity, with the gentle hand of commerce often encouraging the pulling of a trigger to secure control of drug markets and to ensure the acquisition of wealth in places where legitimate avenues are closed off or extremely hard to negotiate. Homicide rates of around 25 per 100,000 in the present day in a city such as Philadelphia certainly exceed rates found in many urban areas of the northern United States in the nineteenth century.[1] Rates can, in certain crisis or postcrisis situations, reach staggeringly high rates, such as the rate of 96 per 100,000 recorded for New Orleans in 2006 after Hurricane Katrina (Roth 2009, p. 467). Homicide rates in some deprived areas of European cities also rival or exceed those found in earlier centuries.

The idea of the interventionist state as simply a guarantor of personal safety and a key driver of declining homicide rates might also be questioned. In many countries, the evidence of a radical decline in rates is limited, and there is no clear correlation between growing state intervention and declining homicide rates. There is also remarkably little research on the actual impact of the state—and, more particularly, the criminal justice system—on the extent of interpersonal violence. This is, in some respects, understandable, as it is difficult to trace the impact of a single variable such as policing or prosecutions on wider social behavior. Studies have tended to rely on the coincidence of greater state intervention with an apparent (but as yet unproven) decline in homicide rates from the eighteenth century onward. Other, more direct, studies of the relationship between forms of greater state intervention and violent activity suggest that the impact of the former on the latter may be limited. There does not appear to be any clear correlation between high or increasing levels of policing and low or declining homicide rates. In Ireland, the number of police per head of population rose dramatically in the mid- to late nineteenth century, but the impact of this rise on homicide rates was minimal. While the number of police held relatively steady in the country between the 1840s and the 1890s, the population declined from a high of around 8.5 million to around 4.5 million by 1900 without having more than a limited impact on homicide rates, with a rate in the 1840s of 1.97 per 100,000 and a rate in the 1890s of 1.86 per 100,000 (Mc Mahon 2013; O'Donnell 2005). Thus, under the impact of an increase in the number of police per head of population, Ireland moved from a position of relatively low homicide rates by European standards at mid-century to only slightly lower rates by the century's end. The growing prominence of the police in the control of violence in Europe since the eighteenth century probably reveals a slow fracturing of the capacity of communities to regulate violence, rather than a reflection of the transformative impact of state agents. In North America, Roth also points out that the police "had little to do with the decline in homicide among northern whites" in the late nineteenth century. (Roth 2009, p. 392). Indeed, he argues that "historically, homicide problems have always been more likely to engulf law enforcement officials than be solved by them" (p. 10).

Nor can the collapse of law and order in early modern and modern societies somehow be simply equated with a return to a pre-state condition in which a Hobbesian war of all against all emerges. The breakdown of modern forms of state control is not a warning that a lack of state intervention will return people to a "state of nature" so much as a phenomenon or fault line that is inherent to modern state organizations that both foster new conflicts and provide only limited security against their impact. States, it might go without saying, are not simply agents of control, but can also sustain and, indeed, generate conflict both internally and with other states. They can seek to maintain often-untenable situations through support for gross inequalities and injustices that can provoke as much as they inhibit violent action. The state can, in essence, spend much of its time and energy containing conflicts of its own making. This is most obvious in, but hardly unique to, colonial societies where the provocation to conflict shares the stage with an intolerant bewilderment at the ingratitude of the "natives" in rejecting the benefits of "civilization" brought through imperial intervention. This is also evident, in a European context, in nineteenth-century Ireland, where two prominent causes of conflict, land disputes and sectarian animosity, undoubtedly had their roots in patterns of conquest in the sixteenth and seventeenth centuries (Mc Mahon 2013). The state played a key role in sustaining, albeit with diminishing enthusiasm, the underlying social and political conditions that provoked such conflicts while simultaneously putting in place more interventionist measures for their control. Here, we can clearly see the double bind of the state as both a force which seeks to control conflict while also sustaining the underlying causes of conflict through support for an iniquitous land system and a partial state apparatus that was dominated by one religious grouping. It was only as these conditions became increasingly untenable over the course of the nineteenth century that reform was imposed on the state from below.

If anything, the striking feature of studies of the operation of criminal justice systems is not the imposition of new "civilized" standards of personal conduct from above, but rather the widespread use of the criminal courts, in many regions, to impose a local order and to negotiate conflict through legal rather than violent means. Studies of criminal justice in early modern and modern Europe tend to emphasize the importance of popular participation in the courts as a key factor in negotiating conflicts within local communities. Studies of early modern England, Scandinavia, the Netherlands, and Germany provide strong evidence of participation in the courts by men and women who sought to prosecute violence both inside and outside the home. Even where the evidence of resistance to the law is strong, there is also evidence of widespread participation in the court system (Mc Mahon 2008). In this sense, the state tends to meet a demand for order, albeit in forms that suit its own interests, rather than to impose new standards of behavior that are alien to the communities that it seeks to regulate.

There is little in the development of major cities or the growing intervention of the state to sustain an overt enthusiasm for the modern. Indeed, in the present day, the city and the state appear to be dubious sources of pacification. Contemporary patterns of and responses to interpersonal violence often reflect the fragmentation of communities and their inability to control violence without a punitive and often-stigmatizing state apparatus. They also reflect the increasingly baneful impact of urban deprivation from which there is often little means of escape other than through involvement in drug commerce. Deprivation and high levels of incarceration in the United States, in particular, also seem to undermine possibilities for the kind of solidarity that might allow communities to exercise greater controls on individual actions.

B. Conflicts and Participants

Alongside the impact of the city and the state on interpersonal violence, another key focus for historians has been to trace the social and gender profiles of violent offenders. Here, patterns of continuity and change are at their most striking, with both a remarkable continuity in the gender profile of perpetrators and, at the same time, an apparent change in their social composition. The changing social profile of perpetrators is most obvious in one of the most striking features of the history of interpersonal violence in Europe: the decline in interpersonal violence among political elites. For some commentators, this was a key step in the marginalization of violence in European society, with elite repudiation of interpersonal violence slowly trickling down and reaching the mass of the population in Europe by, at the latest, the early twentieth century (Pinker 2011, p. 82).

There can be little doubt that political elites have withdrawn from the practice of public acts of interpersonal violence. This is most obvious in the abandonment of the duel as a means of settling conflicts. But we need to be careful not to see this simply as an elite-driven step to marginalize violence or, indeed, to attribute this to the rise of empathy, revulsion at the sight of violence, or an increase in self-control. To begin with, the duel was never ubiquitous among European elites, with many countries largely abstaining from the practice. Within Europe, for instance, Spain, Italy, Germany, the Dutch Republic, Scandinavia, and Switzerland were all "lukewarm adherents" to the practice of dueling prior to the eighteenth century, and in some regions the practice never gained a firm hold (Mc Mahon, Eibach, & Roth 2013, p. 21). Across the Atlantic, many areas showed little enthusiasm for the duel, which had largely disappeared from British North America by the late seventeenth and early eighteenth centuries. In the eighteenth century, it was widely accepted that "colonial gentlemen settled their differences peacefully" (Roth 2009, p. 158). The practice did reemerge during the Stamp Act crisis of 1765, but, in the northern states at least, by the early years of the nineteenth century "anyone who killed a man in a duel would be drummed out of public life" (Roth 2009, p. 181).

The decline in the duel was also by no means a straightforward or linear process (see Eibach 2016). Some countries and regions, most notably Germany and the American South, showed renewed enthusiasm for the practice in the nineteenth century, whereas elites in both Ireland and Britain, following the pattern seen in the northern United States, largely abandoned the practice by mid-century. There is also little sense that the abandonment of the duel reflects a growing revulsion toward violence or a marked increase in empathy for others. While it is clear that the practice of interpersonal violence became increasingly inconsistent with the practice of political power, it is less certain that this shift reflects a transformation in elite sensitivities so much as it indicates a drive from below to ensure that elites were accountable and could not simply employ violence to pursue their personal and political interests in the face of popular opposition. A study that traces the decline of the duel in light of the growth of representative democracies is long overdue.

The apparent withdrawal of the middle orders from ostentatious acts of public violence is also a prominent theme within the historiography. For many historians the nature of male involvement in acts of violence has changed radically over the last three centuries. Studies of cities in England, Germany, and the Netherlands have all suggested that there was a profound change in concepts of masculinity and personal honor over the course of the eighteenth century. In this view, new forms of sociability and behavior among men worked to marginalize violence, particularly among the middle orders, and to ensure that it was not the dominant means of resolving conflicts (Eibach 2008; Shoemaker 2001; Spierenburg 2008). This view of the rejection of public violence is also supported by studies that show the persistence of public acts of lethal interpersonal violence in the present day to be primarily a lower-class phenomenon (Brookman 2005).

We need, however, to be cautious here. While the present-day middle classes of Europe and North America do not rely on interpersonal violence as a central or dominant means of resolving conflict, it is difficult to establish the centrality of violence for the middle orders in the eighteenth century. We lack detailed studies of the class basis of violence in the eighteenth and nineteenth centuries, and much of our evidence remains limited (particularly to cities). Evidence from Scotland, the one national study available, suggests that there was no radical change in the behavior of middle-order groups over the course of the eighteenth century (Knox 2015, p. 68). There has undoubtedly been a significant change in the rhetoric surrounding male violence over the last three centuries, but it remains unproven that this reflects a fundamental shift in the extent and practice of lethal violence. It may be that the new rhetoric and apparently new standards simply provided new ways of controlling and containing old problems rather than eliminating or transforming them, especially as older rituals surrounding violence began to lose their force (see Eibach 2016). There is also evidence of considerable continuities in the nature of violence over time. While serious public acts of violence may be less prominent in the present, there is little evidence that this reflects a fundamental diminution in violence in the private sphere between the eighteenth and twentieth centuries. Indeed, domestic violence remains an intractable and persistent problem across all social classes. A 2014 study revealed that over one in three women within the European Union had experienced physical and/or sexual violence, with many cases arising within familial and intimate relationships and violence often perpetrated by male partners or family members (European Union Agency for Fundamental Rights 2014, p. 21). Such evidence suggests that a certain skepticism must be maintained when entertaining the idea of a radical change in the behavior of men or in the social background of violent offenders.

While shifts in the social composition of offenders over time remain complex, there has been a remarkable continuity in the nature of lethal interpersonal violence and the gender profile of the perpetrators of such violence. Studies of homicide consistently reveal the predominance of men among the perpetrators of violence, a finding that holds true for the eighteenth as well as the twenty-first century. In the United States, Roth points out that 95 percent of homicides among nonrelatives are perpetrated by men, and that this rate has "held steady for four and a half centuries" (Roth 2009, p. 16).

There is also a remarkable similarity across nations and races in the prominence of petty disputes as a leading proximate cause of interpersonal violence. In the context of the American South, Roth points out that white and black men "killed their peers for the pettiest of reasons," including "a 9-cent debt, a hat, [or] a set of lobster traps" (2009, p. 227). In the North in the mid- to late nineteenth century, homicides were sparked by a range of petty disputes over such reasons as "throwing a watermelon rind in fun" or "teasing a dog" (p. 312). Marvin Wolfgang, in his study of homicidal violence in mid-twentieth-century Philadelphia, also identified "altercations of relatively trivial origin; insult, curse, jostling etc." as the single-largest cause of homicide in the city at that time (cited in Daly & Wilson 1988, p. 174; Wolfgang, 1958).

Studies of nineteenth-century Ireland also reveal a willingness to use violence to resolve ostensibly petty disputes. Here, disputes over a blackbird, a pipe, and a halfpenny all led to lethal violent conflict, and ostensibly petty and personal disputes among men were the leading proximate cause of lethal violence (Mc Mahon 2013, ch. 2). Similar disputes have also been found to predominate in eighteenth-century Scotland (Knox 2015). In Sri Lanka in the late nineteenth and early twentieth centuries, the single-largest "proximate cause" of homicide was a "sudden quarrel," with most cases arising from "insecurity over personal status" (Rogers 1987, pp. 135, 153). Such petty disputes also persist in the present. In England between 1992 and 2003, 45.6 percent of known homicides arose from "quarrel, revenge or loss of temper" (Povey 2004, p. 16). Such cases were more likely to emerge among men and between those who knew each other before the incident. Across three continents and, indeed, three centuries, we see at least a superficial similarity in the patterns of male violence and the predominance of men as perpetrators of lethal violence.

How might such continuities and cross-cultural similarities be explained? Historians are just beginning to grapple with this question in a serious manner. The most prominent explanation is that offered by those drawing on evolutionary psychology as an explanatory framework. This is evident in not only Pinker's (2011) work but also that of historians such as John Carter Wood (2011) and Gregory Hanlon (2013; for a summary, see also Eibach 2016). In this approach, the application of evolutionary psychology to the history of violence provides a major challenge for cultural historians. Hanlon (2013), for instance, is highly critical of cultural historians for ignoring the biological sciences and, in doing so, failing to fully recognize the limitations placed on human behavior by processes of evolution. Indeed, he calls for a form of postcultural history that will transcend the outmoded assumptions of cultural historians. Cultural history, he argues, often reveals an ignorance of the biological sciences and is rooted in a perspective that has evolved little since the 1970s (for a perspective that is more inclusive of cultural approaches, see Wood 2007).

For Hanlon (2013), cultural historians pursue diversity in human behavior at the expense of acknowledging underlying consistencies. In contrast, evolutionary psychology, in the view of Hanlon (2013), Pinker (2011), Wood (2007; 2011), and others, offers a framework for understanding human behavior by relating it to an underlying mental architecture that is common to all human societies; in doing so, these researchers seek to identify recurrent regularities in patterns of human activity without dismissing variations in behavior rooted in economic, social, political, and environmental conditions. In this sense, evolutionary psychology allows for considerable variability and diversity across time and space while asserting that there are deep biological roots that shape the nature of aggressive behavior in all human societies.

This, in turn, leads to a number of expectations concerning patterns of violent behavior: for example, men are more likely than women to engage in violent competition for access to sexual partners and to engage in violent activity with other unrelated rivals of the same sex in order to maintain, assert, or advance their status or position in society. These tendencies are most likely to find expression in the kind of apparently spontaneous "honor contests" noted previously, in which men appear to kill for the pettiest of motives (Daly & Wilson 1988).

There is strong support for evolutionary psychology when it comes to the preponderance of men among the perpetrators of violence and particularly to the understanding of violence among unrelated males. The predominance of men as perpetrators of lethal violence across cultures is an incontestable fact. Furthermore, the use of interpersonal violence by men against other men over issues of status—however rare or common in a given society—is also found across many cultures. More broadly, the pursuit of status, however managed, is undoubtedly a key factor in any understanding of human history. Is this behavior then shaped by forces that lie beyond the limits of culture, and should we look to a form of postcultural history to explain patterns of violence?

There are difficulties in doing so. Looking beyond culture or to a form of "postcultural" history to examine sociocultural behavior leads us into the realm of speculation. The fact that behavior is found across cultures does not necessarily imply that the behavior has its roots outside culture—common patterns do not necessarily imply common causes. It is unlikely also that historians, at least, can identify or adequately discuss causes that lie beyond the realm of culture. It is also problematic to argue that theories (such as evolutionary psychology) that are the product of culture and need to be interpreted within a cultural framework can offer insight into a realm "beyond culture" that, in turn, provides the fundamental basis for both exploring and defining cultural life. We also need to avoid the assumption that cultural historians posit the possibility of infinite varieties of human society. There is a difference between arguing for infinite possibilities and demonstrating a reluctance to place unnecessary limits on the possible range of human action.

Ultimately, evolutionary psychology tends to create a false distinction between biology and culture. Biology is presented as shaping the fundamentals of human behavior, with economic, social, cultural, and political forces determining the extent of that behavior and its manifestation in particular contexts. This, in some respects, reinforces a binary opposition between biology and culture that evolutionary psychology claims to break down and, in doing so, offers a form of determinism by the back door. We risk presenting biology as a prior and fundamental factor shaping central aspects of behavior rather than as one factor, albeit a highly significant one, among others. We also risk, through an undue emphasis on lethal violence, drawing overly crude distinctions between the nature of male and female violence. While women may be underrepresented in the homicide statistics, there is considerable evidence that in the case of nonlethal violence, women could play a more prominent role, and that the nature of such female violence is not radically different from that of their male counterparts (see Eibach 2016).

Ultimately, we need, as historians, to rid ourselves of crude distinctions between the "biological" and the "cultural" and to critically engage more, not less, with the biological sciences—particularly as awareness grows of how environment and culture shape biology. In doing so, however, we should not be bound or confined within the parameters of a particular theoretical framework such as that offered by evolutionary psychology; rather, we need to explore how the shaping hand of culture impinges on, and relates to, the history of the body and the underlying social practices that at least appear to endure across cultures. We need, in essence, a cross-cultural and deep history of violence rather than a postcultural one (on deep history, see Shryock & Smail 2011).

Conclusion

Many commentators have used the history of violence to either extol the virtues or condemn the inequities and delusions of modernity. In the context of the history of interpersonal violence, both views are misplaced: neither a faith in progress nor a fondness for pessimism is sustainable. Histories of violence that posit a transformation in patterns of violence rooted in the withdrawal of elites, processes of urbanization, and greater state intervention are flawed. Those that hold the modern responsible for spiraling rates of violence, although admittedly few in number, are also mistaken. While we may have to abandon a Homais-like enthusiasm for the impact of the "modern" on the extent and practice of interpersonal violence, this should not lead to a sentimental longing for the supposed securities of traditional societies. While the impact of new forms of social and cultural life on lethal interpersonal violence have been exaggerated, the evidence points not to a spiraling rise in violence as a result of specifically "modern" conditions, but to a rather surprising continuity in practice. It might even, if an optimistic note is permitted, be suggested that more "modern" forms of social and cultural life, albeit not as currently constituted, offer greater potential for the amelioration of violent conflict than do those bound by more traditional norms.

Changes in economic, social, cultural, and political forms since the eighteenth century have not radically transformed patterns of lethal interpersonal violence. This is not to deny change but rather to draw attention to profound continuities in behavior that are rooted deeply in the past and persist in the present. Such continuities point to a deeper history that is not so easily altered by the movements and fluctuations in economic, social, political, and cultural life that have occurred over the last three centuries. This deep history cannot, however, be adequately charted within the kind of framework provided by evolutionary psychology, nor can it be understood within some other versions of Darwinism that see violence as an almost defining feature of human existence. John Gray (2011) might be right that "recurrent violence is a result of the normal disorder of human life," but it is also clear that the marginalization and control of violence are generally key features of social organization. We tolerate inequalities and even personal and communal humiliations in order to avoid threats to the integrity of our bodies. We remain, by and large, unconvinced that we, and the world at large, would be better off if we were injured or dead. It is this that makes the threat of violence an effective political weapon and renders it essential to the maintenance of political and social orders, as well as a real and effective, albeit crude and damaging, means of challenging existing orders. It also means that much effort is expended to ensure that violence is marginalized within human societies. Such efforts are obviously not always successful or considered rewarding. There are times when, and places where, violence moves close to the center of social and cultural life. In such circumstances, violence might be practiced with relative impunity and can also be enjoyed and embraced by its perpetrators. Yet such moments remain the exception and can rarely, if ever, be sustained. Ultimately, violence does not shape social life, but rather, it is the control and containment of violence that determines how we organize our social existence. The importance of violence lies not in our desire to practice it, but our desire to avoid it.

NOTE

1. This figure is based on a reported 7,824 cases between 1990 and 2010 (Philadelphia Police Department 2011, p. 5).

REFERENCES

Archer, Dane, & Rosemary Gartner. 1984. *Violence and Crime in Cross-National Perspective.* New Haven, CT, & London: Yale University Press.

Brookman, Fiona. 2005. *Understanding Homicide.* London: Sage Publications.

Daly, Martin, & Margo Wilson 1988. *Homicide.* New York: Gruyter.

Eckberg, Douglas. 2010. "Historical Homicide Versus Historical Violence: Estimates of Survivable Homicide Deaths in Charleston, South Carolina, 1878–1912." Paper presented at the annual meeting of the Social Science History Association, Chicago, 19 November 2010.

Eibach, Joachim. 2008. "The Containment of Violence in Central European Cities, 1500–1800." In *Crime, Law and Popular Culture in Europe, 1500–1900,* ed. Richard Mc Mahon, 52–73. Cullompton, UK: Willan.

Eibach, Joachim. 2016. "Violence and Masculinity." In *The Oxford Handbook on the History of Crime and Criminal Justice, 1750–1945,* ed. Paul Knepper & Anja Johansen, 229–49. Oxford: Oxford University Press.

Eisner, Manuel. 2011. "Human Evolution, History and Violence: An Introduction." *British Journal of Criminology* 51 (3): 473–78.

Eisner, Manuel. 2014. "From Swords to Words: Does Macro-Level Change in Self-Control Predict Long-Term Variation in Levels of Homicide?" *Crime and Justice* 43 (1): 65–134.

Elias, Norbert. [1939] 2000. *The Civilizing Process: Sociogenetic and Psychogenetic Investigations* (revised ed.), Oxford: Blackwell.

European Union Agency for Fundamental Rights 2014. *Violence Against Women: An EU-Wide Survey.* Luxembourg: Publications Office of the European Union.

Gray, John 2011. "Delusions of Peace," *Prospect Magazine,* October 2011. http://www.prospect-magazine.co.uk/features/john-gray-steven-pinker-violence-review.

Hanlon, Gregory. 2013. "The Decline of Violence in the West: From Cultural to Post-Cultural History." *English Historical Review* 128: 367–400.

Johnson, Eric A., & Eric H. Monkkonen, eds. 1996. *The Civilization of Crime: Violence in Town and Country since the Middle Ages.* Urbana: University of Illinois Press.

King, Peter. 2010. "The Impact of Urbanization on Murder Rates and on the Geography of Homicide in England and Wales, 1780–1850." *Historical Journal* 53 (3): 671–98.

King, Peter. 2011. "Urbanization, Rising Homicide Rates and the Geography of Lethal Violence in Scotland, 1800–1860." *History* 96: 231–59.

King, Peter. 2013. "Exploring and Explaining the Geography of Homicide: Patterns of Lethal Violence in Britain and Europe, 1805–1900." *European Review of History* 20 (6): 967–87.

Knox, William J., with L. Thomas. 2015. "Homicide in Eighteenth-Century Scotland: Numbers and Theories." *Scottish Historical Review* 94 (1): 48–73.

Lane, Roger. 1986. *Roots of Violence in Black Philadelphia*. Cambridge, MA: Harvard University Press.

Lane, Roger. 1997. *Murder in America: A History*. Columbus: Ohio State University Press.

Lane, Roger. 1999. *Violent Death in the City: Suicide, Accident, and Murder in Nineteenth-century Philadelphia*, 2nd ed. Columbus: Ohio State University Press.

McKanna, Clare V. 2002. *Race and Homicide in Nineteenth-Century California*. Reno: University of Nevada Press.

Mc Mahon, Richard. 2013. *Homicide in Pre-Famine and Famine Ireland*. Liverpool: Liverpool University Press.

Mennell, Stephen. 2007. *The American Civilizing Process*. Cambridge: Polity Press.

Monkkonen, Eric. 2006. "Homicide: Explaining American Exceptionalism." *American Historical Review* 111 (1): 76–94.

Muchembled, Robert. 2011. *A History of Violence: From the End of the Middle Ages to the Present*. Cambridge: Polity Press.

Mullen, Kevin J. 2005. *Dangerous Strangers: Minority Newcomers and Criminal Violence in the Urban West, 1850–2000*. New York: Palgrave Macmillan.

O'Donnell, Ian. 2005. "Lethal Violence in Ireland, 1841–2003: Famine, Celibacy and Parental Pacification." *British Journal of Criminology* 45: 671–95.

Philadelphia Police Department 2011. *Murder Analysis: Philadelphia Police Department, 2007–2010*. Philadelphia: Police Department Research and Planning Unit.

Pinker, Steven. 2011. *The Better Angels of Our Nature: The Decline of Violence in History and Its Causes*. London: Allen Lane.

Povey, David, ed. 2004. *Crime in England and Wales 2002/2003*, Suppl. Vol. 1, *Homicide and Gun Crime*. London: Home Office.

Rogers, John D. 1987. *Crime, Justice and Society in Colonial Sri Lanka*. London: Curzon.

Roth, Randolph. 2009. *American Homicide*. Cambridge, MA: Harvard University Press.

Roth, Randolph. 2011. "Yes We Can: Working Together Toward a History of Homicide that Is Empirically, Mathematically, and Theoretically Sound." *Crime, History & Societies* 15 (2): 131–45.

Savolainen, Jukka, Martti Lehti, & Janne Kivivuori. 2008. "Historical Origins of a Cross-National Puzzle: Homicide in Finland, 1750 to 2000." *Homicide Studies* 12 (1): 67–89.

Shoemaker, Robert. 2001. "Male Honour and the Decline of Public Violence in Eighteenth-Century London." *Social History* 26: 190–208.

Shryock, Andrew, & Daniel Lord Smail. 2011. *Deep History: The Architecture of Past and Present*. Berkeley: University of California Press.

Spierenburg, Pieter. 1996. "Long-Term Trends in Homicide: Theoretical Reflections and Dutch Evidence, Fifteenth to Twentieth Centuries." In *The Civilization of Crime: Violence in Town and Country since the Middle Ages*, ed. Eric A. Johnson & Eric H. Monkkonen, 63–105. Urbana: University of Illinois Press.

Spierenburg, Pieter. 2006. "Democracy Came Too Early: A Tentative Explanation for the Problem of American Homicide." *American Historical Review* 111 (1): 104–14.

Spierenburg, Pieter. 2008. *A History of Murder: Personal Violence in Europe from the Middle Ages to the Present.* Cambridge: Polity Press.

Spierenburg, Pieter. 2011. "American Homicide: What Does the Evidence Mean for Theories of Violence and Society?" *Crime, History & Societies* 15 (2): 123–29.

United Nations Office on Drugs and Crime. 2013. *Intentional Homicide Count and Rate per 100,000 Population in the Most Populous City, by Country/Territory (2005–2012).* UNODC.

Wolfgang, Marvin E. 1958. *Patterns in Criminal Homicide.* Philadelphia, PA: University of Pennsylvania Press.

Wood, John Carter. 2011. "A Change of Perspective: Integrating Evolutionary Psychology into the Historiography of Violence." *British Journal of Criminology* 51 (3): 479–98.

CHAPTER 6

IDEAS AND PRACTICES OF PROSTITUTION AROUND THE WORLD

MAGALY RODRÍGUEZ GARCÍA

INTRODUCTION

THIS essay provides a global overview of prostitution from the early modern period to the present. The focus on female prostitution in urban settings is justified by the fact that commercial sex has nearly always been a city-based phenomenon involving women servicing men. Although the distinction between "premodern" and "modern" prostitution is not necessarily sharp, the profound political, military, and socioeconomic changes that occurred from around 1600 onward had an important impact on the sale of sex. Worldwide, the practice of prostitution and the societal reactions to it were influenced by processes of colonization, industrialization, urbanization, the rise of nation-states, military modernization, nationalism, and war, as well as by revolutions in the realms of politics, agriculture, transportation, and communication.

A long historical and broad geographical perspective permits us to observe the continuities and discontinuities in the way commercial sex was practiced, perceived, and policed. The necessities that accompanied nationalist and imperialist projects from the late eighteenth century onward had a profoundly negative impact on the understanding of prostitution but did not really alter the motivations of women to engage in the sex trade. Evidence derived from classic works on prostitution and studies collected for the project "Selling Sex in the City"[1] proves that while the efforts of authorities to control, repress, or prohibit prostitution crescendoed, more diverse and inventive methods of carrying out the trade were developed by the men and women involved in it. Similarly, the growing involvement of non-state actors in debates on prostitution—particularly whether to condemn it or to redefine it as sex work—led to the development of alternative ways to sell sex and to an increased vocalization of the workers concerned.

This contribution approaches prostitution from a double (top-down and bottom-up) perspective that integrates criminology and labor theory. On the one hand, it presents the point of view of authorities, antivice campaigners, and society at large. As these groups perceived prostitution in terms of sin, deviancy, crime, or victimhood, their responses to commercial sex variously attempted to control, conceal, or repress it. On the other hand, this essay studies prostitution as an integral part of labor history. If we follow Marcel van der Linden's "very simple definition," of work as "the purposive production of useful objects or services" (van der Linden 2011, p. 27), then prostitution can be defined as work. The trade's structure and working conditions are therefore included in this analysis. Furthermore, analyses focusing on the women's profiles and motivations for prostitution are integrated in the narrative, as they are considered essential for a more comprehensive understanding of this type of work. In so doing, this essay attempts to contribute to contemporary debates and to warn against the dangerous generalizations, myths, and gendered misconceptions that often emerge whenever prostitution (and migration for prostitution) is discussed. In particular, the popular image of young females forced into the prostitution milieu by malevolent (male) traffickers calls for a more nuanced analysis.

The essay unfolds in five sections. Section I discusses the legal and cultural definitions of prostitution across time and space. In section II, I examine the societal reactions toward prostitution and de facto or legal regimes governing commercial sex, including tolerance, regulation, abolition, and prohibition. Related to these themes is the real or imaginary link made between prostitution, deviancy, and crime, which constitutes the focus of section III. The spatial organization of the trade and the working conditions of women engaged in it are described in section IV. The final section examines the demography and causes of prostitution.[2]

I. Definitions

The online Cambridge Dictionary defines prostitution as "the work of a prostitute," and the latter as "a person who has sex with someone for money."[3] Although commonly accepted, these definitions do not permit identification of the immense range of remunerated sex activities that exists. Moreover, if taken literally, these definitions can include practices that have most often been accepted as mainstream and very different from prostitution. Marriages or other forms of intimate relationships, for example, have often involved sexual exchanges for livelihood, but society—except for radical feminists—has never linked them to commercial sex. Perhaps the metaphoric definition of prostitution provided by the online Oxford Dictionary will give us a clearer clue to its symbolic meaning across time and space: here, prostitution is "the *unworthy* or *corrupt* use of one's talents for personal or financial gain" (emphasis mine).[4] Indeed, it is the moral or status connotation attached to it, and not so much the exchange of sexual favors for money or in-kind goods or services, that has characterized the understanding of prostitution in most societies.

In Europe and the Americas, common prostitutes were identified with marginality and were arrested under regulations against "disorderly people," lewdness, and vagrancy until the first half of the twentieth century (Rosen 1982; Svänstrom 2006). Slave or pawned prostitutes in American colonies or from African and Asian countries belonged to the lowest rank of society. On the other end of the spectrum, some early forms of prostitution were linked to high prestige and were characterized by a range of entertainment services much broader than pure sexual intercourse. But although commercial sex was legal and regulated in several places in Renaissance Europe and precolonial Asia, high-level courtesans refused to be identified as prostitutes. Furthermore, early regulations always included more than the exchange of sex for money (Gronewold 2013). Premarital sex, adultery, or "indiscriminate availability" (Karras 1996, p. 17) were encompassed in the more commonly used term "whoredom." In Europe and the Americas, a clear distinction between "whores," "harlots," "mistresses," and "prostitutes" was nonexistent. From the mid-eighteenth century onward the terms "prostitution" and "prostitute" became more widely used to differentiate them from fornication and adulterous women, respectively (Nuñez & Fuentes 2013; Laite 2011).

The reinstallation of systems of regulation in the nineteenth century required a clearer categorization of prostitution. Henceforth, the monetary transaction became central to the legal definition of prostitution. Sexual barter, however, has remained difficult to categorize. During the twentieth century, the so-called "charity girls" in the United States exchanged sex for entertainment expenses but made a clear distinction between their acts and prostitution, which they considered immoral. The figure of the "cocotte" in Paris and Berlin at the turn of the century also defied easy categorization. In some African and Asian cities, too, sexual bartering for material goods or privileges seems to have been—and to still be—common. As in Europe, the identification of "real" prostitutes was problematic in colonies or countries that had introduced regulation systems in their territories. Often, any suspect woman was registered as a prostitute and exposed to intrusive medical examinations (Clement 2005; Guigon 2012; Smith 2013; Ekpootu 2013).

Colonization brought a radical shift to the conceptualization of prostitution. Women who in precolonial periods had provided more spiritual than sexual services (e.g., temple dancing girls in India and courtesans in China, Japan, and other parts of Asia) became automatically identified as prostitutes by European colonists. In places like Australia or New Zealand, European colonization laid the foundations for prostitution, and although little is known about the sexual practices of precolonial populations in Africa and the Americas, it is clear that prostitution as we know it today took off after the European conquest (Absi 2013; Frances 2011; Frances 2007; Lauro 2005; Levine 2003; White 1990).

The terms "prostitution" and "prostitute" were commonly used by officialdom during the twentieth century, but more insulting words like "whore" and its foreign equivalents were and are still popular in common parlance. However, with the development of the prostitutes' rights movement from the 1970s onward, the pejorative names came under attack. A restructuring of the trade's language took place in which prostitution came to be defined as "sex work." The new usage of the terms "sex work" and "sex worker" was an important semantic shift that signified the strengthening of a movement that understands prostitution in terms of labor and human rights (Bindman 1997; Delacoste & Alexander 1988; Pheterson 1989). For their part, radical feminists are virulently against the idea of prostitution as sex work. Instead, they define prostitution as "sexual slavery" and prefer to speak of "prostituted woman" rather than "prostitute" or, worse still, "sex worker," as the former term "brings the perpetrator into the picture" (Jeffreys 1997, p. 5; Barry 1979; Barry 1995).

II. Societal Reaction
and Legal Situation

The definition of prostitution and societal reactions to it have had an important impact on the legal regimes that have aimed to control, repress, or regulate the sale of sex. Nearly everywhere, and during much of the period studied here, legal and cultural attitudes toward prostitution have overlapped. Although some forms of high-level prostitution in earlier times commanded respect and prestige, most societies have despised it (Stearns 2009). Most cultures have at one time or another tolerated or regulated prostitution, but more often than not non-elite prostitutes have been perceived as low status or outcasts. The view of prostitution as "an evil"—a necessary one for some and an unwarranted one for others—seems to be ubiquitous. During most of Chinese history, prostitution was legal and monitored by the imperial or local state. Within a highly patriarchal society, commercial sex was recognized as an occupation, but one that was meant to protect "good" women from those who provided social companionship and sexual services to men (Gronewold 2013). For hundreds of years in precolonial India, common prostitutes formed part of the mainstream labor population but were perceived as "sinners." Furthermore, the caste-based, hierarchical society accorded them a low social status, placing them just above sweepers (Frances 2011). In medieval Europe, too, the municipal authorities of most large cities (with the exception of London) regulated prostitution and accepted prostitutes because they supposedly served as outlets for male sexual drives and protected "honest" women from rape (Karras 1996; Perry 1990; Trexler 1981). In cities of the United States, prostitution was quietly tolerated during the late eighteenth and nineteenth centuries, but whorehouse riots and violence against prostitutes were common (Rosen 1982).

Cultural, politico-military and socioeconomic changes from the late fifteenth century onward altered the perception of prostitution and, above all, the government responses to it. Parallel to the religious revival of the time, an increased number of unregulated prostitutes became visible. As the early modern state and its large military apparatus developed, independent prostitutes started to follow the armies. The new situation led to a spread of venereal diseases, to which authorities reacted with the adoption of ordinances prohibiting prostitution and confining women in hospitals or prisons. Religious societies became increasingly involved in campaigns against prostitution and in rehabilitation programs for "fallen women." During much of the seventeenth and part of the eighteenth centuries, prostitution was linked to sin (Conner 2013; Nuñez & Fuentes 2013).

But the negative effects of agricultural disruptions, urbanization, and industrialization on the working population led once again to a fairly tolerant attitude toward prostitutes. Parallel to the language of sin, a view of prostitution as a social or pathological condition became increasingly popular. And, as uncontrolled sexuality and sexually transmitted diseases became a constant preoccupation of bourgeois society (Foucault 1976), more and more persons called for the regulation of prostitution. Embryonic forms of regulation appeared in the late 1700s in Berlin and Paris. By the early 1800s, Napoleon had installed a regulatory system that included the licensing of brothels, registration of prostitutes, and compulsory health examinations. In the 1830s, the sanitary engineer Alexandre Jean-Baptiste Parent-Duchâtelet developed a comprehensive and virtually carceral system of regulation consisting of legal and regulated brothels, hospitals, prisons, and reformatories. Known as the "French system," regulation itself spread to cities around the world over the course of the nineteenth century (Bliss 2001; Corbin 1990; Guy 1991; Schaepdrijver 1986). Moreover, amid a period of nationalist fervor, political considerations motivated authorities to regulate the sex trade in many places. State control of brothels and medical examination of prostitutes were seen as ways to protect citizens, the military, the family, and the nation from political threats, disease, and homosexuality (Bernstein 1995; Gilfoyle 1999; Guy 1991). Among large cities, London and New York remained exceptions, as they never implemented the modern regulatory system. Yet there, too, prostitution was tolerated and informally regulated. Prostitution as such was not illegal, but women could be arrested under laws against "nightwalking," soliciting, public disorder, or vagrancy (Gilfoyle 1992; Laite 2011; Walkowitz 1980). In Rio de Janeiro, an extralegal form of regulation, in which the police possess a strong authority but lack a specific legal mandate to control and organize the sex trade, has characterized the history of prostitution (Blanchette & Schettini 2013).

In the colonies, the expansion of prostitution posed a serious threat to the imperial project. Interracial sex and prostitution of white women could undermine colonial power and prestige, while the spread of venereal disease could cripple colonial administrators and troops. The Contagious Diseases Acts of the 1860s were not meant to regulate prostitution in all British cities, but, as legal instruments designed to protect the empire's army, were confined to ports and garrison towns and therefore never applied to London (Levine 2003). They created a great controversy, not only because any woman suspected of being a prostitute had to undergo a compulsory genital inspection, but also because they targeted women only. Although men were equally responsible for the spread of diseases, the blame fell on women only. Of the case studies of the "Selling Sex in the City" project, Nigeria was the only country where males (soldiers) were the target of measures against venereal disease. Hence the issue generated an intense debate in Britain on the double standards governing men and women (Walkowitz 1980). But generally, the various forms of regulation that were introduced in the colonies were tougher than the system adopted in England. Colonial legislation of prostitution applied to the whole territory, was more invasive in women's lives, and was tougher on poorer and nonwhite prostitutes. Regulationist countries like Belgium, France, and the Netherlands also introduced strict methods of control in their colonies. And, while some U.S. states experimented briefly with regulation, moving toward a more muscular repression of brothel prostitution, the Americans in the Philippines took over the official system of regulation that the prior colonial authorities had introduced in the last years of Spanish rule (Corbin 1990; Frances 2011; Howell 2004; Lauro 2005).

But increasingly, public opinion turned against the official regulation of prostitution. As the number of unregistered prostitutes grew and the failure of the regulation system to control the spread of venereal disease became apparent from the 1850s onward, an abolitionist movement became stronger. Abolitionism, the movement to eliminate state-regulated prostitution, appeared for the first time in Great Britain under the leadership of Josephine Butler. Opponents of regulation viewed this form of state control of women not only as morally unacceptable but also as inefficient, because clandestine prostitutes and male clients were not part of the system. Vigorous antiregulation campaigns resulted in the repeal of the Contagious Diseases Acts in England in 1886 and in the annulment of various regulation laws in British colonies in the late 1880s. Yet in several colonies, the authorities refused to repeal their legislation or opted for an unofficial continuation of the regulation system. As in the mother country, regulation in French colonies went undisturbed until deep in the twentieth century (Corbin 1900; Levine 2003).

From the end of the nineteenth century onward, a frontal attack on regulation of prostitution and, above all, the obvious failure of the system led to the passage of municipal and national laws against brothel keeping, procuring, and soliciting, as well as stringent migration legislation in Europe, Asia, and the Americas. The First and Second World Wars saw a brief revival of regulation of prostitution, but soon after both 1919 and 1945, abolition became more widespread. In countries such as Argentina, China, Japan, and the Soviet Union, abolition or the outright prohibition of prostitution was associated with the construction of a modern twentieth-century state. Latecomers in the official abolition of regulation were Belgium, Japan, Mexico, and the preeminent regulationist country, France, which criminalized brothel keeping in 1946 and procuring, pimping, soliciting, and organized prostitution in 1960 (Conner 2013; Gilfoyle 1999; Hershatter 1997). In abolitionist countries, prostitution itself is not illegal but the activities surrounding it are. There, prostitutes are not criminalized, but because activities that facilitate the trade are included in the penal code, they become immersed in a criminal circuit.

By the latter part of the twentieth century, calls for the recognition of prostitution as sex work had led to liberalization in countries like Germany, the Netherlands, and New Zealand. In Istanbul, too, where the system of regulation existed for most of the twentieth century, prostitution is today legal and regulated. Since the nineteenth century, however, the trend in most countries has been toward a strong moral condemnation of the sex trade. Worldwide, the number of countries where prostitution is outlawed, or where prostitution is legal but procuring and soliciting are not, is much larger than the number of countries that do not criminalize prostitution or activities related to it (Country Report on Human Rights Practices 2008). Yet, in spite of the official position, municipal authorities of many abolitionist countries tolerate and regulate prostitution under public order or hospitality industry laws. This reflects the ambiguity surrounding prostitution, which leaves the persons active in the sector in a legal limbo.

III. PROSTITUTION, DEVIANCY, AND CRIME

To varying degrees, the last two centuries have been characterized by a strong identification of prostitution with deviancy and crime. Until the late 1700s, some forms of social disorder like prostitution were accepted as sinful but inevitable or even vital behavior, as they would prevent worse evils. Advocates of regulation of prostitution followed this Augustinian logic.[5] However, the nineteenth-century system of regulation, with its enclosed brothels, compulsory registration, harsh medical treatment, confinement to specialized hospitals for the treatment of venereal diseases,[6] or imprisonment for clandestine prostitutes, handled women not as sinners or fallen women, but as quasi-criminals.

Writing in a period during which public transgressions were perceived as potential threats to the social order and as a problem that called for intervention (Lee 2013), the ideas of Cesare Lombroso, the Italian founder of positivist criminology, reinforced the perception of prostitutes as deviants and offenders. In spite of the contemporary criticism of the scientific validity of his theory of the atavistic, born, or genetic criminal, Lombroso's book *La donna delinquente, la prostituta e la donna normale* (1893)[7] continued to influence interpretations of female crime until deep in the twentieth century; some of its ideas are still discernable in some contemporary representations of prostitutes. Lombroso and his co-author, Guglielmo Ferrero, were convinced that lawbreakers constituted a throwback to a more primitive form of human being, who could be distinguished from "normal" persons by physical imperfections and abnormalities, the so-called stigmata of degeneration. They classified women into three groups: criminals, prostitutes, and normal. Generally, they found that all women were less evolved than men but stressed that female criminals and prostitutes were more anomalous than "honest women and even lunatics" (Lombroso & Ferrero 2004, p. 112; Rafter & Gibson 2004). If prostitutes did not show as many anomalies as other criminals, it was because their youth and use of makeup helped them to minimize their degenerative characteristics.

Since Lombroso and his positivist colleagues focused on the physiological traits of criminals, they understood crime as a disease, not as a rational individual choice. Although offenders could not be held responsible for their acts, society had the right to protect itself from them. Incurable born criminals and innate prostitutes were to be incarcerated or locked up in brothels, but occasional offenders were viewed as having the capacity for reform, and, because born female criminals were in Lombroso's view rare, he proposed alternatives to prison for most female offenders. Furthermore, he distinguished between "born" and "occasional" prostitutes. The former resembled both female and male criminals. Moral insanity characterized the innate prostitute, as well as a lack of maternal and family feelings, aggressive or masculine behavior, a passion for liquor, unrestrained greed, a lack of decency, sexual frigidity, laziness, a passion for dancing, and a propensity for lying. These women were considered "mildly criminalistic" (Lombroso & Ferrero 2004, p. 216) but as rarely committing serious crimes because of their physical weakness or intellectual backwardness. Theft and blackmail were the most common offenses among them. Hence Lombroso and Ferrero concluded that, "in women, criminality generally takes the form of prostitution." Occasional prostitutes showed less degenerative traits but remained "notably abnormal" (pp. 221–22). They were pushed into prostitution by external factors such as early loss of virginity, coercion, poverty, or bad examples.

During the first part of the twentieth century, more sophisticated theories on female crime and prostitution became increasingly popular. Contrary to Lombroso, they embraced psychological and social-structural factors but still relied on implicit assumptions about the "distinct" nature of women (Klein 1973). The concept of "feeble-mindedness" entered the debate as a major cause of prostitution. Whereas Lombrosian practitioners set out to measure cranial and other physical traits of presumed criminals, antivice authorities and reformers who relied on psychiatrists' and eugenecists' theories subjected women accused of prostitution to mental tests and humiliating examinations (Rosen 1982). Long and impertinent questioning on their family background, education level, sexual life, habits, and employment history sought to distinguish "normal" from sexually "deviant" women. Even international organizations such as the League of Nations viewed social profiling as a useful tool to obtain indications as to the best methods of rehabilitation (Rodríguez García 2012). Indeed, many persons concerned with the issue of prostitution did not believe in punishment but called instead for rehabilitative and preventive measures that sought in extreme cases to suppress the number of prostitutes through sterilization, or, more often, to control minds through socialization (Klein 1973).

However, benevolent societies provided rehabilitation programs that women often experienced as being similar to or worse than prison terms. In colonial Mexico, so-called *Recogimientos* (seclusion institutions) attempted to safeguard women from sinful life but turned into virtual prisons for those (suspected of) practicing prostitution. Although Magdalen Homes had already existed in thirteenth-century Europe, asylums aimed at reform and control of women's sexuality spread after the mid-1700s in England, Ireland, Scotland, and the United States. Magdalen Homes' methods for the reform of prostitutes and other "fallen women" were penitence, hard work, and prayer. The importance of laundry work was emphasized, as it was seen as symbolizing the spiritual cleansing of the inmates. In early twentieth-century American cities, women accused of prostitution were not jailed but were put on probation or sent to reformatories or workhouses. Many women preferred fines or prison sentences in order to avoid officers' scrutiny during probation. French feminist Avril de Sainte-Croix was a fervent defender of rehabilitation institutions. During a meeting of the Committee of Social Questions of the League of Nations, she reported that in one of the institutions in which she was active, successful rehabilitation of young women had been achieved through "skillful administration of drugs," which "very speedily brought calm to their souls and bodies."[8] In general, rehabilitation was not attractive to women because life in a reformatory meant entrapment in programs in which they were trained in feminine "domesticity" and taught low-paid occupations such as sewing, embroidery, scrubbing, spinning, and cooking. What made reformatories even worse was the fact that the individual reform at which they aimed was not sentence-based, meaning that women could be detained for years instead of days or months in a prison (Nuñez & Fuentes 2013; Rosen 1982).

Ultimately, those who focused on the consequences rather than the causes of prostitution prevailed in the United States. During the so-called Progressive era (ca. 1890s–1920s) reformers became increasingly preoccupied with all kinds of "social evils" and their link to politicians and policemen. Like drug consumption or gambling, prostitution came to be viewed as a victimless crime, but one that could harm society through moral degeneration, public disorder, corruption, delinquency, violence, and venereal disease (Weitzer 2010). After many failed attempts to repress prostitution, authorities opted for a frontal attack. A few weeks after the American entrance into the First World War, the Commission on Training Camp Activities was created to repress prostitution and liquor sales among troops; in 1917, the Chamberlain-Kahn Act created a Division of Venereal Diseases; and in 1918, President Wilson established an Interdepartmental Social Hygiene Board. In 1919, the latter communicated to the Appropriations Committee of the House of Representatives that the board had helped to close down more than a hundred red-light districts near military camps and had incarcerated 30,000 women and girls. Whereas the international armed conflict came to an end, the federal, state, and municipal authorities continued to pursue their war against commercial sex. Prostitution has been outlawed in the United States since the Standard Vice Repression Act of 1919, after which every state enacted laws prohibiting prostitution (Clement 2006). Only some counties of the state of Nevada have legalized brothels since the 1970s, with most of them today isolated in rural areas.

Socialist revolution in various countries also led to the (de facto) criminalization of prostitution. In the Soviet Union, for example, prostitution was perceived as a symbol of capitalism and gender inequality. Instead of reintroducing criminal measures or medical supervision of women, the Bolsheviks tried to rehabilitate and educate former prostitutes. But the labor camps that were installed for this purpose became punitive institutions against women. Former prostitutes were regarded as "social parasites" harmful to society, and many were shot in the 1930s under Stalin (Alexopoulos 2003). Also in China after 1949, the Maoist regime sought to completely eradicate prostitution and the sale and use of opium, which were seen as the ultimate symbols of capitalist vice. Prostitution was harshly punished until 1958, when it was (wrongly) considered totally eradicated (Hershatter 1997).

Yet a perception of prostitutes as outright criminals has never been prevalent among the public. The idea of the fallen woman was used to refer not only to sinful or unruly behavior for which she was responsible, but also to situations of vulnerability in which women fell prey to malevolent men. Starting in the second half of the nineteenth century, women involved in prostitution became increasingly perceived as victims. In Great Britain, feminists and libertarians helped to publicize a series of sexual scandals in the 1880s, which ended with the reporting of Jack the Ripper and the murder of five prostitutes. W. T. Stead's newspaper publication on the abduction of English girls sold to continental brothels, as well as the media attention given to the Ripper murders rendered all men suspect and strengthened the notions of urban danger and female fragility (Walkowitz 1982). The link between (migration for) prostitution, male violence, and traffic was established then; by the late 1890s, a movement for the suppression of "white slave traffic" had emerged in Britain and spread internationally. From the early twentieth century onward, national and international initiatives to curtail the traffic in prostitution mushroomed[9] (Limoncelli 2010; Rodríguez García 2012), in spite of the fact that empirical evidence of widespread trafficking or appropriate tools to measure it are lacking (Knepper 2013).

The idea of prostitution as a harmful activity in which women are the main victims has become increasingly influential since the last decades of the twentieth century. As at the turn of the century, supporters of this interpretation of prostitution are of the opinion that commercial sex fuels human trafficking. In the United States, feminists have called into question the notion of prostitution as a victimless crime. Since they view prostitution as a "blatant example of the sexual oppression of women" (Bennetts & Carlton 1973, p. 137), they demand the decriminalization[10] of prostitutes as a short-term solution and the radical transformation of the socioeconomic structure of society to eliminate prostitution in the long run. In Sweden, a similar logic but a different approach has been applied. Focusing on the demand side of prostitution, Swedish feminists called for the criminalization of clients. After a long debate, the purchase of sex became illegal in Sweden in 1999 (Svänstrom 2004). Prostitution is thus viewed as a crime, but one committed by men upon women—strengthening the idea of male clients as predators. With some variations, the so-called Swedish model spread to several European countries. In February 2014, the European Parliament approved a nonbinding resolution that recommends that EU countries reevaluate their sex work policies in order to reduce the demand for prostitution and trafficking by punishing the clients. Since commercial sex is seen as inherently exploitative and as a violation of human rights, supporters of the Swedish model make no distinction between voluntary and forced prostitution. In their view, most women involved in prostitution are forced into the trade by third parties and/or poverty. As the following sections will illustrate, the structure of the trade, its working conditions, and the motivations of women involved in it are more complex than that described by pure harm-based analyses of prostitution.

IV. Trade Structure and Working Conditions

The structure of the sex trade and the working conditions within it are influenced by governmental and societal attitudes toward prostitution, as well as by the (extra-) legal, market, technological, and medical forces that govern female labor in general. Gender segmentation in the labor market in most places during much of the period studied here resulted in a general marginalization of women and led many into full-time or casual prostitution. During the early modern period, brothel and street prostitution were the most common forms of the trade. Brothels entrapped women in a system of financial exploitation, and often physically in enclosed buildings and segregated zones, but they also protected prostitutes from aggressive clients or police extortion. Although women had to divide their earnings with madams,[11] income from prostitution was always higher than in other branches of the economy. Furthermore, women often developed strategies to increase their revenues. In colonial Casablanca, for instance, prostitutes were not allowed to leave the walled brothel district (Bousbir) without permission, but when permitted to go out, they sometimes used their free time to engage in clandestine encounters in other parts of the city (Kozma 2013).

Registered women bore the stigma of prostitution but had more opportunities to use official institutions (e.g., courts) than did independent prostitutes or other females who had to rely on men to have access to public services. In Cairo, state-run brothels did not exist until the late nineteenth century, but prostitutes were taxed, had access to the courts, and were allowed to participate in guild processions—albeit at the end of the parade (Hammad & Biancani 2013). Other benefits of brothel prostitution were the familiar environment and the relative comfort for women who had no ties with kin and friends because of either death, family ruptures, or the ostracism that derived from involvement in the sex trade (Clement 2006; Nuñez & Fuentes 2013). Many women scorned the mandatory health controls and treatment of the regulated brothels of the nineteenth and twentieth centuries, but they sometimes used the system for their own purposes. While some used the health checkups to solve problems other than venereal disease, others asked medical staff for help when they wished to get out of prostitution (Absi 2013; Frances 2013).

The stigma attached to registered prostitutes, as well as accumulated debts or (induced) drug addictions, often impeded women from leaving the bordellos, but their working conditions were also dependent on their position within society. Legal systems that allowed for the sale and pawning of women, such as those in existence in China, India, Japan, Singapore, and Turkey, often led to dire working conditions, as women had little control over the number and kind of clients they received, or the services they were to provide. But young women could also be sold to luxurious brothels or wealthy men. In these cases, services were provided in sumptuous surroundings and in much better conditions, but always at the cost of personal freedom (Henriot 2001; Hershatter 1997; Tong 1994; White 1990).

New spaces and working conditions developed with the politico-military, socioeconomic, and cultural transformations from the 1600s onward. Women wanting to avoid the strict municipal or unofficial brothel rules increasingly opted for independent prostitution. With the development of large armies, independent prostitutes moved to garrison towns to provide soldiers with their services. With the further growth of the entertainment and hospitality industry starting in the nineteenth century, many prostitutes began to work in cafés, restaurants, taverns, massage parlors, theaters, saloons, hotels, and speakeasies, or took their clients to their own rooms and apartments. Until the mid-1950s, London prostitution was primarily street-based. Everywhere, self-employed prostitutes were often better placed than their counterparts in brothels to negotiate their working conditions with clients and the owners of the establishments where they practiced their trade. Also, when working in secrecy, they avoided stigmatization. Yet women working outside the official or de facto regulated system always risked punishment or extortion from authorities. In such cases, the involvement of third parties to help women escape police harassment, provide money for bail or lawyers, and to attract trustworthy clients often became necessary (Clement 2006; Gilfoyle 1992; Laite 2011).

A particularly interesting case of independent prostitution that developed in colonial times was that of Nairobi. *Malaya* prostitutes rented rooms and waited discreetly for men to purchase access from the house owner. This method allowed women to avoid arrest and societal condemnation, but with the disadvantage that they could not choose their clients. Like elite courtesans in China or the geishas of Japan, *malaya* women offered much more than sexual services (conversation, food, baths, cleaning, etc.); they claimed that their work mimicked marriage. In economic terms, *malaya* prostitution was a form of long-term investment—not a survival strategy, but a way to accumulate capital and to prosper independently. In contrast, *wazi-wazi* women solicited from the windows, doors, or porches of the houses where they rented a room. They had much more control over the clients that came in and the time they spent with them. Contrary to the *malaya* prostitutes, *wazi-wazi* women provided brief encounters and usually sexual services only. Most of them worked only temporarily in prostitution. Typically, they were daughters helping their parents to reestablish themselves in smallholdings or in trade. Finally, *watembezi* were streetwalkers or prostitutes soliciting in public places like bars or hotel lobbies. They cherished their independence to choose clients and determine the labor time, and mocked *malaya* prostitutes for their passivity and marriage-like practices. Their profits were used for family support and not so much for independent accumulation, as in the case of *malaya* women. Like streetwalkers in other parts of the world, *watembezi* developed strong ties, shared rooms, and helped each other in difficult times (White 1990).

Luise White's (1990) study of prostitution in Nairobi helps us to rethink the assumptions and myths that often surround prostitution, like strict hierarchies and limited room for agency. In such hierarchies, elite courtesans in Asia, *malaya* prostitutes in Nairobi, or high-class escorts and call girls are typically placed at the top, with other indoor and outdoor prostitutes being assigned a lower status. However, freedom and the capacity to control working conditions was (and is) in all cases relative and dependent on the locations where and the types of clients with whom women worked. With a much larger pool of middle- or low-class clients, outdoor prostitutes were able to pick and choose. Past and present elite prostitutes, self-employed or not, are in the position to entertain clients in luxurious surroundings and to live in considerably more comfortable circumstances than regular ones, but they probably have less control over the services they provide—ranging from working hours spent in nonsexual entertainment to the provision of extreme sexual favors. A high-class prostitute dependent on a few wealthy men may be less inclined to refuse certain demands than a common prostitute who provides fast and unceremonious intercourse or only manual or oral sex to ten, fifteen, or twenty customers a day (Laite 2011). Whereas upper-class prostitutes are expected to follow patriarchal rules and protocol, common prostitutes often reverse the gender roles. Ethnographic research in Bolivian brothels shows the ways in which men there are humiliated by prostitutes, with clients being robbed or induced to spend more than they have in food and drinks, thereby reversing the traditional roles by making clients indebted to women. By making fun of men's appearance or way of talking, prostitutes make sure that clients do not view them as submissive women willing to do anything for money (Absi 2013).

The issue of violence and health in relation to prostitution also needs careful reevaluation, as there exists no reliable empirical evidence on the matter. Until the twentieth century, rates of venereal diseases were extremely difficult to determine. Whether prostitutes in the past suffered more from these diseases than other sexually active persons is unclear. Nowadays, HIV/AIDS has replaced syphilis and gonorrhea as the most dangerous sexually transmitted disease, but it remains unclear whether persons active in the sex industry get infected during sexual contacts at work or in private, or whether it is transmitted through intravenous drug use. Julia Laite's (2013, p. 15) conclusion with regard to the situation in London can be applied to other cases: "It remains difficult to separate the actual health experiences of prostitutes from their pathologization within criminal justice and social work systems".

Generally, it has been assumed that prostitution leads to poor physical and psychological health, particularly among low-class prostitutes. The question is whether prostitutes suffer(ed) more than other workers engaged in substandard jobs, and whether brutal clients are (or were) the rule in the commercial sex exchange. Some contemporary case studies point to physical and mental problems as being the result of stigma and state repression, not an outcome of the sale of sex as such. Indeed, ego-documents and other sources containing firsthand accounts testify that prostitutes have been as (if not more) afraid of the police as customers' or pimps' violence. The paradox of state repression of prostitution is that it has never succeeded in abolishing the trade, but it has produced sufficient material evidence of the high incidence of official abuse and violence against prostitutes. Execution, drowning, mutilation, compulsory separation from children, flogging, forced sterilization, torture, and forced (sex) labor have occurred in places as varied as Turkey, colonial Egypt, France, England, Sweden,

Austria, China, Nazi Germany, and the Soviet Union. Historical data also sustain the contention that streetwalkers were not necessarily more vulnerable to male violence than were indoor prostitutes (Frances 2013; White 1990).

Official and unofficial abuse of prostitutes led to increased protests not only by feminists but also by the affected women. Although formal organizations appeared only in the second half of the twentieth century, prostitutes' protests took place sporadically in the late 1800s and early 1900s in such places as India, Russia, and Argentina (Bernstein 1995; Guy 1990; Levine 2003). With the development of the feminist movement, cultural changes, and new attitudes toward sex in the 1960s, prostitutes from different parts of the world became more vocal and started to organize themselves. The first well-known demonstration was organized by French prostitutes who occupied a church in Lyon in 1975 to protest police harassment and a lack of state protection. The initiative spread to the rest of France and inspired many other women worldwide. Factors that contributed to the militancy and mushrooming of sex workers' organizations were increased travel opportunities and the growth of the Internet, which facilitated connections between women (Janssen 2011).

Indeed, technological developments in communication and transport have had an important impact on the working spaces and conditions of prostitution. Just like the more widespread use of the telephone in the early twentieth century, the Internet and mobile phones have enabled women to engage in full-time or casual prostitution. These technologies have increased the independence and invisibility of prostitutes, but procurers and pimps have not become totally absent. In early twentieth-century New York, for example, the increased use of the telephone facilitated the operations of call girls and of male "bookies" who controlled, booked, and moved women and madams to different houses and flats on a weekly basis (Clement 2006). Nowadays, too, the secrecy of sexual encounters can lead to unsafe situations. And, as in past venues for prostitution, websites for sexual commerce are often constructed on an ethnic basis. Racial segregation of red-light districts was institutionalized in many colonial settings, but an ethnic hierarchy was also common in many other cities of the world. The demand for certain types of women, as well as the socioeconomic factors that led to the further development of the sex industry, has contributed to increased female mobility and a more diversified prostitution population over the last centuries.

Although foreign migration of women was not an unknown phenomenon in the early modern period, the rate of interstate female migration increased with the development of the transport infrastructure from the late eighteenth century onward. Parallel to voluntary migration, a trade in women for prostitution also existed in African, Middle Eastern, and Asian cities (van Voss 2012). This led to a more marked presence of foreign women in the worldwide sex trade, and to the conflation of migration for prostitution and white slavery or human trafficking. But the rates of foreign prostitution are uncertain. Moreover, the demography and causes of prostitution have always been more complex than the narrative of foreign or rural women being forced into the sex trade.

V. Demography and Causes
of Prostitution

Estimates of the number of women active in prostitution, as well as data on their backgrounds, are problematic. To nineteenth-century urban observers, prostitution appeared to be a growing problem, although this assertion cannot always be proven. In colonial cities, it is clear that the number of prostitutes increased along with the development of new economic activities and the huge male labor migration that supported them. Women became heavily affected by the breakdown of traditional means of survival and social norms. Because the new urban economies offered few labor opportunities for women, and as human relations became increasingly commodified and commercialized, women turned in large numbers to the sex trade (Frances 2011; van Voss 2012).

In noncolonial cities where prostitution had existed for a long time, it is much more difficult to establish the extent to which the sex trade increased as a result of industrialization and urbanization. As Christine Stansell (1986, p. 173) noticed for nineteenth-century New York, "there were more prostitutes simply because there were more people." In other cities, too, the amount of prostitution is virtually impossible to establish because of the groups that were often included in (e.g., unmarried, "unchaste," or "promiscuous" women) or excluded from (e.g., disguised or part-time prostitutes) the category of prostitution (Clement 2006; Laite 2011).

For the same reasons, data on the nativity of prostitutes are inconclusive. Past and present reports, popular writings, and media stories often stress the share of foreign-born women in prostitution. Undoubtedly, large capital cities and hubs of international migration have always attracted foreign men and women to the sex trade, but because of its furtive nature, it is not possible to state with certainty how large the foreign population in prostitution was and is in relation to the local one. For instance, a 2009 TAMPEP report on the prostitution population in Europe states that most sex workers are (foreign) migrants. Yet, as its authors admit, these results "should not be considered as absolute 'data' or as entirely representative of the actual situation." As in the past, the quantification of the sex industry and its workers remains extremely difficult, as clandestine or hidden prostitution is not reported, and many prostitutes successfully evade controls (TAMPEP 2009, pp. 8–9). Often, migrant prostitutes and women from minority groups become involved in the most visible forms of the sex trade, which possibly explains their overrepresentation in the statistics. This does not mean that the presence of foreign or minority women in prostitution was or is negligible. The available sources do confirm a strong presence among prostitutes of women (and men) of foreign origin or from ethnic minority groups. Particularly during the 1800s and early 1900s, and again from the late twentieth century onward, the growth of the global economy and increased labor migration propelled more women into interstate migration (Henderson 1999; Laite 2011; Mechant 2013; van Voss 2012).

As well, racial discrimination in the labor market pushed many women into the sex trade. In colonial and many noncolonial cities, subordinate women only had access to a limited number of badly remunerated menial factory or domestic occupations. In New York City, for example, where the share of black women in the population was low (2 percent in 1910; 5 percent in 1930), they accounted for 13 percent of the detentions at the state reformatory for women at Bedford Hills in 1910, and for 54 percent of all arrests recorded in the Women's Court in the second half of the 1930s (Clement 2006; Gilfoyle 1992).

But not all racially, socially, or economically discriminated women turn(ed) to prostitution, so the question of what motivates women to become involved in the sex trade remains. Across time and space, prostitution has offered many economic and non-economic advantages. Although it is impossible to compile and compare the different payments for prostitution in different societies in this study, it is clear that the sale of sex was (and in many cases still is) significantly more lucrative than most occupations available to women. The literature on the history of prostitution contains sufficient evidence of women who appear to have become engaged in the trade to ameliorate their personal living conditions. Many others seem in the first place to have had the maintenance of their underage, ill, or unemployed relatives in mind as a strong motivation to become and stay involved in prostitution. Everywhere, prostitution often formed part of the family economy. Hence, economic hardship is certainly discernable in most cases, and in several instances the fear of starvation or sheer want also appears. As Kingsley Davis (1937, p. 149) argued, "prostitution embraces an economic relation, and is naturally concerned with the entire system of economic forces".

Yet the economic motivation does not answer the question of why so many women with similar socioeconomic backgrounds did or do not become attracted to prostitution. The available literature evidences numerous noneconomic motivations for prostitution. A crucial one was the negative perception of conventional jobs available to women. Whereas domestic service, waitressing, peddling, or factory work were considered burdensome, discriminatory, tedious, and/or dangerous, prostitution was often linked to the idea of a more flexible and independent life. Contrary to what former authorities, doctors, social workers, antiprostitution reformers, or society at large often thought, prostitutes do not reveal any particular psychological or physical defect that makes them different from "normal" women (Corbin 1990). Generally, they were not less educated than other working-class women, and although most prostitutes came from the (heterogeneous) laboring classes, not all of them were part of destitute families. Hence, "if there are any discernable patters," Eileen McLeod affirms (1982, p. 31), they are "an independent stance" and the wish for "distance from family controls." Case studies of cities as varied as Lagos, London, Moscow, Nairobi, Rio de Janeiro, and Shanghai provide evidence of thousands of women making use of the sex trade to evade the limitations of the patriarchal order and enter the consumption society independently.

Popular narratives of prostitution also tend to portray the sector as being overpopulated by young girls. Certainly the sex industry has always been dominated by the demand for young women, but empirical studies demonstrate that nearly everywhere the mean age of prostitutes has been between twenty and twenty-five. Child prostitution was already heavily debated in Victorian England by the end of the nineteenth century, but the available literature indicates that extremely young girls were very rare. Children in prostitution also seems to have been infrequent in cities like Amsterdam, New York, Perth, and Sydney (Mechant 2013; Walkowitz 1980).[12]

This does not mean that exploitative third parties and trafficking were merely the fantasy of moral antiprostitution crusaders. Many women, particularly those from Africa, Asia, and the Middle East, were sold, pawned, or led by false promises of marriage or employment to brothels. Often, young women were sold to procurers by parents trying to escape starvation after the social turmoil and socioeconomic transformations of the colonial period. In many cases, however, women seem to have been aware of the situation and to have accepted this as a survival strategy for their families and themselves. Moreover, the traffic in Asian women between the 1850s and the 1950s seems to have been only supplementary to the much larger voluntary migration of seasoned prostitutes (van Voss 2012).

Although an almighty white slave conspiracy and trade has never been satisfactorily proven, some evidence of forceful or deceptive recruitment for prostitution in Western cities does exist. Cases of coercion seem to have been infrequent and unconnected to the larger networks of intermediaries of prostitution throughout the nineteenth and twentieth centuries. Ruth Rosen (1982) estimates that during the first decades of the twentieth century, less than 10 percent of the whole prostitute population of the United States experienced situations that fell under the white slavery label. Findings of the studies collected for the "Selling Sex in the City" project also sustain the contention that cases of women being forced or tricked into prostitution existed but were rare. Most often, third parties did not constitute the main cause of prostitution, but they did play an important part in the recruitment of women and the organization of the trade. The more risky and secretive commercial sex became, the more important a role pimps and other intermediaries played in the management of prostitution from the late nineteenth century onward. As labor migration increased, a diverse range of intermediaries (e.g., procurers; madams; brothel keepers; escort agents; owners of theaters, massage parlours, barber shops, or apartments; and female relatives, friends, or acquaintances active in the sex trade) became involved in arranging the movement of females to overseas brothels or into other forms of prostitution. Their methods included smuggling; fictitious marriages; employment contracts; facilitation of boat, train, or plane tickets; and provision of forged documents (Clement 2006).

The tripartite organization of prostitution seems to have been typical when or where women had (or have) not yet acquired sufficient political and socioeconomic power to work as independent prostitutes. Migratory impediments and labor restrictions, as well as stigma, marginalization, and violence, encourage the involvement of third parties. The available literature and source material for the late nineteenth and twentieth centuries provide evidence of pimps and procurers moving from city to city to secure recruits, but also of women actively looking for intermediaries to help them out with travel tickets, loans, documents, contacts with clients, and so on, a situation that turns the traditional view of recruiting for prostitution upside down (Rodríguez García 2012; Ekpootu 2013). French police and emigration officials interviewed by members of a travel committee conducting an international inquiry on human trafficking for the League of Nations in the mid-1920s stated that recruitment often went in two directions. The recruitment of girls for prostitution was well known to the police of all countries and to the public in general, they said—but "what is not so well known is the influence which professional prostitutes have in the recruitment of souteneurs."[13] Instances of female agency like this still need to be unveiled for a more comprehensive narrative on prostitution.

Conclusion

The study of prostitution in a long historical and broad geographical perspective permits us to understand commercial sex in terms of labor and to overturn the myths that often surround it. Among the commonalities that can be observed in the history of prostitution are the quasi-universal view of the trade as a substandard activity, a continuous effort by municipal (and later also state) authorities to control commercial sex, and a constant supply of women. Indeed, despite the stigma, thousands of women worldwide have viewed prostitution as a logical option compared to the other work alternatives available to them. Scientific studies that include the points of view of the persons concerned provide sufficient evidence of a large group of women entering prostitution voluntarily and experiencing the activities of the trade as less traumatic than generally assumed. In all the works consulted for this essay, prostitution is linked not only to higher wages but also to flexible hours; freedom from abusive employers or family members; liberation from conventional but monotonous, degrading, and exploitative jobs; and exciting experiences such as contact with persons from different classes or origins whom many women would otherwise never meet. Throughout time and space, prostitutes seem to have been as or more afraid of official repression than of violent clients or pimps. Admittedly, a lot of prostitution in different times and societies remained and remains hidden, but one can assume that independent sex work is easier to conceal than are forced activities involving one or more intermediaries.

Harsh measures to regulate prostitution in some cities and to eliminate it in others stimulated women to hide their activities, a situation that strengthened the involvement of exploitative third parties in the trade. The legalization experiments that have occurred in Germany and the Netherlands have not proven ideal (for reasons that go beyond the scope of this study), but have at least awakened the debate on the best way to provide protection to the persons involved in the sector (Aronowitz 2014). The logic behind the legalization of the sex trade is that every (adult) person has the right to use his or her body and sexuality to make a living. Interestingly, the human rights approach is also used by advocates of the criminalization of clients. In their view, prostitution violates human dignity and human rights, regardless of whether it is forced or voluntary.

The contemporary debate demonstrates that neither the decline in religion nor the spread of secularism has changed societal attitudes toward prostitution. Even in countries where prostitution is legal, the main actors (prostitutes, clients, and intermediaries) continue to be stigmatized. According to Belgian sexologist Alexander Witpas,[14] the reason why the stigma around prostitution is so resilient is because sex—especially female sex—continues to be taboo, even in oversexualized societies. This helps to explain why so many prostitutes in past and present societies have opted to hide the nature of their work, and why misconceptions about prostitution often dictate public policy.

NOTES

1. This project was organized by the author in cooperation with Elise van Nederveen Meerkerk (Wageningen University), Lex Heerma van Voss (Huygens Institute for the History of the Netherlands), and Marcel van der Linden (International Institute of Social History). A selection of papers has been compiled in an edited volume that will be published in 2016. See http://socialhistory.org/en/projects/selling-sex-city.

2. In this essay, I use the terms "prostitute" and "prostitution" instead of "sex work" and "sex worker," as the latter encompass more than the exchange of sex for monetary or material compensation. The negative connotation attached to the former terms reflects the stigma that has characterized most of the history of prostitution and does not imply a judgmental interpretation of it on the part of the author.

3. For the definition of "prostitution," see http://dictionary.cambridge.org/dictionary/british/prostitution?q=prostitution; for "prostitute," see http://dictionary.cambridge.org/dictionary/british/prostitute_1?q=prostitute.

4. See http://www.oxforddictionaries.com/definition/english/prostitution.

5. The fourth-century Christian theologian Augustine of Hippo once wrote: "Suppress prostitution, and capricious lusts will overthrow society" (quoted in Meier and Geis 1997, p. 28).

6. Most famous were the so-called Lock hospitals, which operated in Britain and its territories abroad from the mid-1700s until the twentieth century.

7. The book was translated into English in 1895 as *The Female Offender*. This first translation, however, omitted much of the information on prostitutes and "normal" women. The version used in this study was translated by Nicole Hahn Rafter and Mary Gibson (Lombroso & Ferrero 2004).

8. This report can be found in the records of the Committee of Social Questions, Geneva, 27 April 1937, League of Nations archives, United Nations Office, Geneva (hereafter "LN archives"), CQS/A.10.

9. In 1921, the League of Nations replaced the racialized term "white slavery" with "traffic in women and children."

10. Advocates of decriminalization are not in favor of the legalization of prostitution. Many radical feminists oppose legalization because it would normalize prostitution.

11. Usually 50 percent of the woman's earnings went to the brothel owner or madam. Interestingly, this rate has remained more or less constant throughout space and time.

12. The issue of child prostitution in contemporary Asia, particularly Thailand and the Philippines, is an extremely complex one that goes beyond the scope of this essay. To understand this phenomenon, not only the age of the persons concerned should be discussed, but also the various definitions and societal attitudes toward childhood, sexuality, filial duty, and child labor in general.
13. French report, December 1924–January 1925, pp. 10–11, LN archives, Box S174.
14. Debate during the international colloquium "Reframing Prostitution: From Discourse to Description, from Moralisation to Normalisation?", Ghent, University of Ghent, 27 March 2014.

References

Absi, P. 2013. "The Future of an Institution from the Past: Accommodating Regulationism in Bolivia, from the Nineteenth to the Twenty-First Century." Paper presented at the conference "Selling Sex in the City: Prostitution in World Cities, 1600 to the Present," Amsterdam, 25–27 April.

Alexopoulos, Golfo. 2003. *Stalin's Outcasts: Aliens, Citizens, and the Soviet State, 1926–1936*. Ithaca, NY: Cornell University Press.

Aronowitz, A. A. 2014. "To Punish or Not to Punish: What Works in the Regulation of the Prostitution Market?" In *Reframing Prostitution: From Discourse to Description, from Moralisation to Normalisation?* ed. N. Peršak & G. Vermeulen, 185–213. Antwerp: Maklu.

Barry, K. 1979. *Female Sexual Slavery*. Englewood Cliffs, NJ: Prentice-Hall.

Barry, K. 1995. *The Prostitution of Sexuality*. New York: New York University Press.

Bennetts, L., & E. Carlton, 1973. "Prostitution—A Non-Victim Crime?" *Issues in Criminology* 8 (2): 137–62.

Bernstein, L. 1995. *Sonia's Daughters: Prostitutes and Their Regulation in Imperial Russia*. Berkeley: University of California Press.

Bindman, J. 1997. "Redefining Prostitution as Sex Work on the International Agenda." Accessed at http://www.walnet.org/csis/papers/redefining.html#text1.

Blanchette, T., & C. Schettini. 2013. "Sex Work in Rio de Janeiro: 'More than Tolerated—Effectively Managed.' " Paper presented at the conference "Selling Sex in the City: Prostitution in World Cities, 1600 to the Present," Amsterdam, 25–27 April.

Bliss, K. E. 2001. *Compromised Positions: Prostitution, Public Health and Gender Politics in Revolutionary Mexico City*. University Park: Pennsylvania State University Press.

Clement, E. A. 2005. *Trick or Treat: Prostitutes, Charity Girls, Courting Couples, and the Creation of Modern Heterosexuality*. Chapel Hill: University of North Carolina Press.

Clement, E. A. 2006. "Prostitution." In *The Modern History of Sexuality*, ed. H. G. Cooks & M. Houlbrook, 206–30. New York: Palgrave Macmillan.

Conner, S. 2013. "Selling Sex in the City: Paris." Paper presented at the conference "Selling Sex in the City: Prostitution in World Cities, 1600 to the Present," Amsterdam, 25–27 April.

Corbin, A. 1990. *Women for Hire: Prostitution and Sexuality in France after 1850*. Cambridge, MA: Harvard University Press.

Davis, K. 1937. "The Sociology of Prostitution." *American Sociological Review* 2:744–55.

Delacoste, F., & P. Alexander. 1988, *Sex Work: Writings by Women in the Sex Industry*. London: Women's Press.

Ekpootu, M. 2013. "Sexualizing the City: Female Prostitution in Nigeria's Urban Centers in Historical Perspective." Paper presented at the conference "Selling Sex in the City: Prostitution in World Cities, 1600 to the Present," Amsterdam, 25–27 April.

Foucault, M. 1976. *Histoire de la sexualité: La volonté de savoir*. Paris: Gallimard.

Frances, R. 2007. *Selling Sex: A Hidden History of Prostitution*. Sydney, Australia: Allen & Unwin.

Frances, R. 2011. "Prostitution: The Age of Empires." In *A Cultural History of Sexuality in the Age of Empire*, ed. C. Beccalossi & I. Crozier, 145–70. Oxford, UK: Berg.

Frances, R. 2013. "Working and Living Conditions." Paper presented at the conference "Selling Sex in the City: Prostitution in World Cities, 1600 to the Present," Amsterdam, 25–27 April.

Gilfoyle, T. J. 1992. *City of Eros: New York City, Prostitution, and the Commercialization of Sex, 1790–1920*. New York: W.W. Norton & Company.

Gilfoyle, T. J. 1999. "Prostitutes in History: From Parables of Pornography to Metaphors of Modernity." *American Historical Review* 104 (1): 117–41.

Gronewold, S. 2013. "Prostitution in Shanghai, China, 1600 to the Present." Paper presented at the conference "Selling Sex in the City: Prostitution in World Cities, 1600 to the Present," Amsterdam, 25–27 April.

Guigon, C. 2012. *Les Cocottes: reines du Paris, 1900*. Paris: Parigramme.

Guy, D. J. 1991. *Sex and Danger in Buenos Aires: Prostitution, Family, and Nation in Argentina*. Lincoln: University of Nebraska Press.

Hammad, H., & F. Biancani. 2013. "Prostitution in Cairo, 1600 to the Present: An Urban Overview." Paper presented at the conference "Selling Sex in the City: Prostitution in World Cities, 1600 to the Present," Amsterdam, 25–27 April.

Henderson, T. 1999. *Disorderly Women in Eighteenth Century London: Prostitution and Control in the Metropolis, 1730–1830*. London: Longman.

Henriot, C. 2001. *Prostitution and Sexuality in Shanghai: A Social History, 1849–1949*. Cambridge, UK: Cambridge University Press.

Hershatter, G. 1997. *Dangerous Pleasures: Prostitution and Modernity in Twentieth Century Shanghai*. Berkeley: University of California Press.

Howell, P. 2004. "Race, Space and the Regulation of Prostitution in Colonial Hong Kong." *Urban History* 31 (2): 229–48.

Janssen, M-L. 2011. "Prostitution." In *A Cultural History of Sexuality in the Modern Age*, ed. G. Hekma, 177–202. New York: Berg.

Jeffreys, S. 1997. *The Idea of Prostitution*. North Melbourne, Australia: Spinifex Press.

Karras, R. M. 1996. *Common Women: Prostitution and Sexuality in Medieval England*. New York: Oxford University Press.

Klein, D. 1973. "The Etiology of Female Crime." *Issues in Criminology* 8 (2): 3–30.

Knepper, P. 2012. "Measuring the Threat of Global Crime: Insights from Research by the League of Nations into the Traffic in Women." *Criminology* 50 (3): 777–809.

Kozma, L. 2013. "Casablanca: An Urban Overview." Paper presented at the conference "Selling Sex in the City: Prostitution in World Cities, 1600 to the Present," Amsterdam, 25–27 April.

Laite, J. 2011. *Common Prostitutes and Ordinary Citizens: Commercial Sex in London, 1885–1960*. New York: Palgrave Macmillan.

Laite, J. 2013. "A Global History of Prostitution: London." Paper presented at the conference "Selling Sex in the City: Prostitution in World Cities, 1600 to the Present," Amsterdam, 25–27 April.

Lauro, A. 2005. *Coloniaux, ménagères et prostituées au Congo belge (1885–1930).* Loverval, Belgium: Editions Labor.

Lee, C. 2013. *Policing Prostitution, 1856–1886: Deviance, Surveillance and Morality.* London: Pickering & Chatto.

Levine, P. 2003. *Prostitution, Race and Politics: Policing Venereal Disease in the British Empire.* New York: Routledge.

Limoncelli, S. 2010. *The Politics of Trafficking: The First International Movement to Combat the Sexual Exploitation of Women.* Stanford, CA: Stanford University Press.

Lombroso, C., & G. Ferrero. 2004. *Criminal Woman, the Prostitute, and the Normal Woman.* Trans. and ed. N. H. Rafter & M. Gibson. Durham, NC: Duke University Press.

McLeod, E. 1982. *Women Working: Prostitution Now.* London: Croom Helm.

Mechant, M. 2013. "The Social Profiles of Prostitutes." Paper presented at the conference "Selling Sex in the City: Prostitution in World Cities, 1600 to the Present," Amsterdam, 25–27 April.

Meier, R. F., & G. Geis. 1997. *Victimless Crime? Prostitution, Drugs, Homosexuality, Abortion.* Los Angeles: Roxbury Publishing Company.

Nuñez, F., & P. Fuentes. 2013. "Selling Sex in Mexico City." Paper presented at the conference "Selling Sex in the City: Prostitution in World Cities, 1600 to the Present," Amsterdam, 25–27 April.

Perry, M. E. 1990. *Gender and Disorder in Early Modern Seville.* Princeton, NJ: Princeton University Press.

Pheterson, G., ed. 1989. *A Vindication of the Rights of Whores.* Seattle: Seal Press.

Rafter, N. H., & M. Gibson. 2004. "Editors' Introduction." In *Criminal Woman, the Prostitute, and the Normal Woman,* trans. and ed. N. H. Rafter & M. Gibson, 3–33. Durham, NC: Duke University Press.

Rodríguez García, M. 2012. "The League of Nations and the Moral Recruitment of Women." *International Review of Social History* 57:97–128.

Schaepdrijver, S. 1986. "Regulated Prostitution in Brussels, 1844–1877: A Policy and Its Implementation." *Historical Social Research* 37:89–108.

Smith, J. S. 2013. *Berlin Coquette: Prostitution and the New German Woman, 1890–1933.* Ithaca, NY: Cornell University Press.

Stansell, C. 1986. *City of Women: Sex and Class in New York, 1789–1860.* Chicago: University of Illinois Press.

Stearns, P. 2009. *Sexuality in World History.* New York: Routledge.

Svänstrom, Y. 2004. "Criminalising the John: A Swedish Gender Model?" In *The Politics of Prostitution: Women's Movements, Democratic States and the Globalisation of Sex Commerce,* ed. Joyce Outshoorn, 225–44. Cambridge, MA: Cambridge University Press.

Svänstrom, Y. 2006. "Prostitution as Vagrancy: Sweden, 1926–1964." *Journal of Scandinavian Studies in Criminology and Crime Prevention* 7:142–63.

TAMPEP. 2009. "Sex Work in Europe: A Mapping of the Prostitution Scene in 25 European Countries." Accessed at http://tampep.eu/documents/TAMPEP%202009%20European%20Mapping%20Report.pdf.

Tong, B. 1994. *Unsubmissive Women: Chinese Prostitutes in Nineteenth Century San Francisco.* Norman: University of Oklahoma Press.

Trexler, R. 1981. "La prostitution Florentine au XVe siècle: patronages et clienteles." *Annales: economies, sociétés, civilisations* 36:983–1015.

U.S. State Department. 2008. "Country Reports on Human Rights Practices." Accessed at http://www.state.gov/j/drl/rls/hrrpt/2008/index.htm.

van der Linden, M. 2011. "Studying Attitudes to Work Worldwide, 1500–1650: Concepts, Sources, and Problems of Interpretation." *International Review of Social History* 56:25–43.

van Voss, L. H. 2012. "The Worst Class of Workers: Migration, Labor Relations and Living Strategies of Prostitutes Around 1900." In *Working on Labor: Essays in Honor of Jan Lucassen*, ed. M. van der Linden & L. Lucassen, 153–70. Leiden, The Netherlands: Brill.

Walkowitz, J. 1980. *Prostitution and Victorian Society: Women, Class, and the State.* New York: Cambridge University Press.

Walkowitz, J. 1982. "Jack the Ripper and the Myth of Male Violence." *Feminist Studies* 8 (3): 542–74.

Weitzer, R. 2010. "The Movement to Criminalize Sex Work in the United States." *Journal of Law and Society* 37 (1): 61–84.

White, L. 1990. *The Comforts of Home: Prostitution in Colonial Nairobi.* Chicago: University of Chicago Press.

CHAPTER 7

FORMS OF CRIME

Crime and Retail Theft

TAMMY WHITLOCK

INTRODUCTION

RETAIL crimes include those dealing with shops and shopkeeping, along with crimes at other points of sale like wholesalers, bazaars, and open markets. In many ways, these crimes of fraud, theft, and shoplifting seem like the least serious types of property crime. Shoplifting is, after all, a favorite of the petty criminal. These types of crimes rarely involve violence, instead depending on deception for their successful execution. If we look at the costs of crime in terms of value instead of just personal violence, however, the crimes of the retail world dwarf those of muggings and pub brawls in the police courts.

Theft is certainly one of the oldest crimes, hailing back to King Edmund's Code in the tenth century and further still to more ancient law codes. The establishment of stationary retail establishments in the early modern period in Europe simply made this type of crime much easier to commit and introduced a new variety of crimes to property theft. The burgeoning expansion of consumer culture in the eighteenth and nineteenth centuries turned those opportunities into a bonanza of fraud, bad debt, and serial shoplifting alongside the old outright swiping of goods. On the part of the retailer looking for a quick profit in a fluctuating market, misrepresenting goods, bait-and-switch techniques, false fire sales, and cheaply made goods masquerading as quality material made the motto *caveat emptor*—"Let the buyer beware"—more important than ever for the Georgian or Victorian shopper. As consumer culture continues to expand, our ability to control violence as a society overall has increased, but retail crime continues to expand and cost both the retailer and honest shopper dearly.

I. The History of Shopping and Retail Crime in England

A. Retail Establishments

Although the obsession with the birth of the department store has subsided somewhat in the work of retail historians, much of the scholarship is still marked by this "before" and "after" division of consumer culture and retail crime. For modern historians especially, this innovation in the way goods were displayed, distributed, and sold defines how we explain the crime that occurred in earlier eras. In the historical record and our imaginations, the metropolitan department store looms large and tends to overshadow the more mundane continuum of retail establishments that persisted and continued to thrive well into the twentieth century and beyond (Benson & Uglioni 2003, pp. 2–3; Williams 1982; Lancaster 1995). However, crime seems to be "always with us," and trends in retail crime predate the establishment of the *grand magasin*. Likewise, our notion of a golden era in the early modern period of bow-fronted shops with their honest, locally invested purveyors falls apart quickly when we examine trial after trial of retail crimes committed in the glorious era of the single-owner shop (Mui & Mui 1989). From legal records to popular culture, the evidence reveals a much more Hobbesian world of thieving customers and cheating shopkeepers determined to best one another in the quest for personal gain, as in the following description by Daniel Defoe's fictional antiheroine Moll Flanders from the 1722 edition of the novel:

> However I have said it made me the more wary, and particularly I was shie of Shop-lifting, especially among the *Mercers* and *Drapers* who are a Set of Fellows that have their Eyes very much about them: I made a Venture or two among the Lace Folks and the Mileners, and particularly at one Shop, where two young Women were newly set up, and not been bred to Trade: There, I carried off a Peice of Bonelace, worth six or seven Pound, and a Paper of Thread; but this was but once, it was a Trick that would not serve again. (Defoe 1722, p. 217)

To understand the history of retail crime in England, one has to examine the evolution of shops and shopkeeping. Mercers, drapers, and others in the retail cloth trade were the most competitive, innovative, and risky businesspeople of the early modern period. Experimenting with new techniques like large shops, combined wholesale and retail businesses, and discounts for ready money exposed them to the risk of what modern retailers refer to as "shrinkage" (see Edwards 1958; Mui & Mui 1989, pp. 234–36; Whitlock 2004). Decades ahead of their retail contemporaries, they laid the foundation for the consumer culture that swept the nineteenth century. A century after Defoe penned *Moll Flanders*, White and Greenwell of Oxford Street touted that their shop: "has since undergone the considerable alterations, rendering it very commodious, and adapting it for the most extensive Trade . . . with a very choice, elegant and fashionable assortment of every description of Goods, usually kept by LINEN DRAPERS, MERCERS, HOSIERS, HABERDASHERS, and LACEMEN."[1] Controlling stock in this kind of environment was difficult at best. For the unwary shopkeeper, rolls of expensive fabric like silk could simply walk away.

By the 1840s and 1850s, these bloated drapery shops had become the new "emporiums," marked by their emphasis on multiple departments, cheap prices—often clearly marked—and ready-money sales that drew in even upper-working-class shoppers (Lancaster 1995, pp. 3–14; Adburgham 1964, p. 43; Whitlock 2004, pp. 33–34). Large-scale emporia tended to spring from two particular branches of the retail clothing trade. Haberdashers had begun as small-scale shops specializing in the odds and ends of the trade. Drapers sold the larger and more valuable cloth pieces like silk, muslin, and wool. However, in larger cities by the 1800s, both haberdashery and drapery shops had grown into massive affairs with multiple departments. Cash payment, or ready money, was a natural development for these larger shops (Ablett 1876, pp. 60, 108; Whitlock 2004, pp. 27–28). As the clear lines defining specialties blurred, the bigger stores found that they needed new methods to push more products. Leaving behind the era of credit and privilege when London shopping was dominated by the aristocracy and gentry, the new stores used quick cash payment systems and open-ticket pricing to appeal to a wider clientele. Shoppers were no longer embarrassed by the possibility of asking about items they could never afford. The advantage for the new emporia of these changes included helping the many assistants keep track of the pricing of the quickly sold goods and helping the store avoid the cost of credit, estimated by an 1860s guide for drapers and haberdashers to be 8 percent per year for the purveyor (Anonymous 1864, p. 31; Whitlock 2004, pp. 30–32). From the 1840s to the 1870s larger premises on the new model opened the way for the fabulous department stores of the turn of the century.

Other innovations in retail that affected the possibilities of retail crime came from an adaptation of Eastern markets to European tastes. Whether they were commercial affairs, held for charity, or a combination of both, bazaars revolutionized the way people understood consumption in the 1800s. Bazaars also utilized cash payment but added an even more open atmosphere to the previous methods of keeping goods safely ensconced behind the counter until requested by patrons (Mui & Mui 1989). Stalls of independent sellers joined together to offer hundreds of feet of open counter lushly stocked with a variety of goods that few independent stores could provide. One of the earliest and most famous of these establishments, the Soho Bazaar in London, was the brainchild of John Trotter in 1815 (Dyer 1991, p.196; Whitlock 2004, p. 43). After the Napoleonic wars, the profiteer had little use for his Soho warehouse until he came up with this new scheme that proved wildly popular. Patrons could peruse items ranging from toys to guns to exotic plants. Trotter also liked to stress how his bazaar provided opportunities for women, especially those widowed by the war, to make an honest living in a respectable environment at a daily rate of a mere three pence per foot (*Gentlemen's Magazine* 1816, p. 272; Nightingale 1816, p. 7; Whitlock 2004, pp. 41–43, 50). Success bred scores of imitators, including the Lowther Bazaar across from the

Lowther Arcade, the Oxford Street Bazaar, and the Pantechnicon in the 1820s, 1830s, and 1840s (Whitlock 2004, pp. 46–47). The term "bazaar" became synonomous with open display and a large variety of fancy articles. Charitable organizations soon began to use the term for their own charity fairs, or fancy fairs, as they were previously known (Whitlock 2004, pp. 55–56). The open display of these marts, despite the sharp eyes of many stallkeepers, made shoplifting an ever-present danger.

The department store that so characterized the late nineteenth and early twentieth centuries combined many of these earlier techniques, including the emphasis on display that drew shoppers into emporia, bazaars, and charity fairs. With Whiteley's opening in 1863 in Bayswater, the French-style department store began to dominate the London shopping scene (Rappaport 2001; Whitlock 2004, pp. 214–16). Like the earlier bazaars, these stores were staffed by mainly younger women. Emile Zola's heroine in 1883's *The Ladies' Paradise* provides a perfect example of the typical origins and rise of the shopgirl in the era of the department store (Zola 2008). With an even greater emphasis on respectability to draw in the middle-class shopper, one might expect that the clientele of the department store would be less likely to steal than those people who perused the bargain shops or open bazaars of early to mid-nineteenth-century London and the northwest. Much to the consternation of the new-style purveyors, mass of scale and open display combined to make them a haven for shoplifters of both the professional and "kleptomaniac" varieties (see Pinch 1997).

II. Types of Retail Crime

Shoplifting is the most obvious crime associated with retail sales; however, retail crime includes fraud, especially those involving credit and debt, outright theft not involving secretly stealing goods, and, when the lines between wholesale and retail blur, scams like those of the widow Madame Doodewaarde, who, along with her lover Laars, cheated wholesalers into giving her around 30,000 pounds of goods on credit only to abscond after auctioning off the merchandise for a small percentage of its worth in 1870 ("Extraordinary Frauds in the Drapery Trade," The Draper [London] 14 January 1870; Whitlock 2004, p. 79) How is it that respectable Englishmen and women broke one of the most basic commandments repeatedly in their dealings with shopkeepers?

A. Theft

Secretly stealing goods from respectable tradesmen and the practice of such deception as theft required merited particular derision dating back to the early modern period. The Elizabethans, living in the same era that gave us the sumptuary codes (Hooper 1915), recognized "Lifts," in which the criminal masqueraded as a customer, as being a separate variety of theft against which they attempted legislation in the late 1500s (Edwards 1958,

p. 4; Murphy 1986, p. 85; Whitlock 2004, p. 130). After the Glorious Revolution, concern grew until a parliamentary act passed in 1698 that set execution as the harsh but logical punishment for "the Crime of stealing Goods privately out of Shops and Warehouses, commonly called Shop-lifting" (Beattie 1986, pp. 178–179; *Morning Chronicle*, 27 March 1813; Whitlock 2004, p. 130). The idea of the ultimate punishment for such an offense held sway until the reforming era of Sir Samuel Romilly. However, as with much of the Bloody Code, juries were loath to enforce such punishment for what seemed a petty offence. The 1699 Act of William and Mary called for the execution of convicted shop-lifts who stole up to five shillings' worth of merchandise; however, Beattie found that this sentence was rarely applied in court. On average, fewer than two offenders per year were hanged, with most shoplifts suffering transportation at worst (Beattie 1986, pp. 178–79). It was the low success rate of convictions more than the law's barbaric nature that led parliament to finally follow Romilly's lead and make shoplifting a noncapital offence. In 1813 Romilly cited the tiny conviction rate of only 18 of the 188 offenders tried in the previous year (*Morning Chronicle*, 27 March 1813; Whitlock 2004, pp. 132–33). Another seven years passed before Romilly and his fellow reformers could convince the House of Lords to lessen the punishment. By this time, transportation had replaced the threat of death, especially for repeat offenders (Zedner 1991, pp. 174–77; Whitlock 2004, p. 133; for overall trends in punishment, see Wiener 1990). In the remaining years of the transportation policy, "theft of wearing apparel" remained one of the most common categories meriting that forced vacation to the Antipodes. When transportation to Australia ended in 1852, prison sentences remained the only option available to the courts (Zedner 1991, pp. 174–77; Robson 1965, p. 203). Judges had little choice but to sentence repeat offenders to a few years in prison. Upon hearing her four-year sentence pronounced in 1860, Caroline Harris told her sentencing judge, "That's only half of what I expected, so I am glad" (*Times* [London], 11 January 1860).

B. Fraud

Lifting the Bloody Code may have saved the working poor from the gallows, but neither transportation nor prison sentences saved shopkeepers from the depredations of thieves in the nineteenth century. Along with thieves posing as customers, shopkeepers had to face increasing problems with fraud. Successful shoplifting depended on the performance or respectability of the thief (Stern 1996; Stern 2008; O'Brien 1983; Abelson 1989a; Abelson 1989b). Successful fraud depended on the same pretense, and was often more difficult to prosecute. The dashing and flashy swindler of novels was much less of a threat than the seemingly respectable widow receiving goods for which she never intended to pay. The crime of fraud also dealt with the *intent* of the criminal more than the transaction itself. Defrauders who ordered goods under their own names could simply claim it was an honest case of debt gone sour (Bow Street Officer 1829, pp. 3, 12; Whitlock 2004, p. 154). A mobile society provided plenty of opportunity for such acts.

One popular type of fraud involved female servants contracting for goods on behalf of imagined or real mistresses but never intending to pay for them. A trusted servant could act and shop on behalf of his or her mistress or master. In 1814 Jane Mead falsely ordered goods at an ironmonger's shop in Downing Street under the name of her purported mistress, Miss Vansittart. It was the second time she found herself in court in less than a year. She had never actually worked for Vansittart and had worked merely two weeks for another mistress, Miss Craddock, before absconding and placing orders in a variety of shops under Craddock's name in July of the same year (*Times* [London], 2 December 1814). Some criminals would not even bother to appropriate an actual identity and would create a fictitious employer with a random, but respectable, address. "A Bow Street Officer" warned purveyors in his 1829 *The Frauds of London* to always get orders in writing (1829, pp. 12–13; see also Whitlock 2004, pp. 160–63). Robert Peel's sister-in-law Lady Alice Peel suffered such a crime at the hands of a dismissed housemaid, Mary Ann Bell. After losing her position in January of 1828, Bell used her ex-mistress's name to procure seventy pounds' worth of goods from the famous Howell and James of Oxford Street. Despite Lady Alice's refusal to appear in court, the shopkeepers were able to get Bell sentenced to seven years' transportation for the offence (*Times* [London], 5 March 1828; 8 March 1828; April 1828; Whitlock 2004, p. 163). Servant fraud remained common in the 1800s, and cases appear in court records throughout the century.

Along with servants faking orders from real or imagined masters, frauds often pretended to be the wealthy customers themselves. With acumen for current fashion and some dubiously obtained trappings like a "sable tippet, boa and muff" (Whitlock 2004, p. 163), frauds who dressed the part often convinced wary tradespeople. The creative stories told by these frauds varied from young women with rich uncles "investing in the funds" to widows waiting on a beneficent inheritance from a loving spouse. The initial story would often be used to gain sympathy and respectable lodgings from an unsuspecting dupe, as a respectable address was another weapon in the fraud's arsenal. In the late 1830s and throughout the 1840s Mary Rowley, whose husband was also convicted of fraud, committed an estimate of over 500 acts of fraud based on her inheritance of nonexistent property in Leicester and an equally fictitious chancery proceeding to win it back. Alas for her creditors, her death in 1848 with debts unpaid was quite real (*City of London Trade Protection Circular*, 19 June 1848; Whitlock 2004, p.169). Another young woman, Mary Elizabeth Johnson, faked banknotes owed to her by *Blackwood's Magazine* for authoring short stories (*Times* [London], 27 June–14 July 1851; Whitlock 2004, p. 176). No matter how false the story used to gain the credit, women who used their real names were nearly impossible to successfully prosecute. The concept of coverture and the law of necessaries also came in handy as ways to contract for debt and receive a fraudulent alimony of sorts from local shopkeepers.

If the ease with which women committed fraud exposed the cracks in coverture and the concept of *femme covert*, the use of fraud as a means to force spousal support demonstrates how women exploited the idea of necessaries under the law. Shopkeepers who contracted with respectable married women of good means all too often found that husbands were not willing to pay for the goods—as a result of separation, marital strife, or simple disagreement over the goods their wives deemed necessary to living. Initially, the law developed under the reign of Henry VI as a way to protect women from being left bereft of support by their husbands. Over time the concept of necessaries expanded to include items not essential to life (Finn 1996, pp. 703–22; Leach 1984). Lengthy or even short marriages that ended badly could leave the shopkeeper unknowingly supporting a former spouse. Divorce was expensive and difficult to obtain in the 1800s. This effective lack of legal separation could be used as a premise to go into debt for goods and services, leaving an ex-husband to pay the bill. Many refused, and shopowners then had the difficulty of suing the husbands in court for the debts of their estranged wives. After the breakup of her seventeen-year marriage to an Exeter surgeon, Mrs. DeNiceville lived with her spinster sister and took in boarders in London. When the sister died in 1871, she was forced to start charging items to her husband, who no longer recognized their legal connection. Her draper in Regent Street successfully sued Mr. DeNiceville for thirty pounds (*Times* [London], 13 May 1871; Whitlock 2004, pp. 171–74). In this case and in others, fraud, although prosecuted in the court system, was not so much a problem of crime as a stopgap in uneven divorce laws.

C. Crime by the Retailer

Just as there was a murky divide between crime and obtaining consumer goods as a means of support for wives separated from their husbands, the line between criminal fraud and good salesmanship was muddy indeed. Retailers used various methods to draw in customers in the 1800s. As competition increased and factory output exploded, retailers adapted older methods and used new and inventive ways to move goods. Alison Adburgham calls the 1830s and 1840s the "Era of Retail Adventurers" (Adburgham 1964). The new emporia and monstrous drapery shops resorted to borderline fraud and outright fraudulent practices to draw in shoppers to move their goods. Bankruptcy, although a cold, hard fact of English capitalism (Weiss 1986), was also a convenient advertising technique to convince shoppers that bargains were to be had. Some stores went "out of business" repeatedly, claiming to sell off their stock, while others professed to benefit from the misfortunes of other bankrupted tradesmen, allowing their shops to offer goods at scandalously low prices. Along with benefiting from the bankruptcies of others, tragedies of a different kind—including fires and shipwrecks—made for convincing sales. Wet or singed fabrics sold quickly to an eager public expecting bargain prices (Ablett 1876, pp. 31–32; Whitlock 2004, pp. 81–83). The John Johnson Collection at the Bodleian Library contains an 1853 poster of one of these fire sales claiming to sell over 80,000 pounds of water-damaged fabrics at less than half their normal cost (Figure 3.1, Whitlock 2004, p. 91).[2] As these slightly toasted or damp sale goods show, the longstanding belief of the English court system in *caveat emptor* remained the rule of trade as a common law concept. Originating in the 1500s, this legal concept notoriously favored the seller. Laws requiring consumer protection against adulteration or other false practices began to develop in the nineteenth century; however, the general interpretation remained in favor of *caveat emptor* until Lord Chalmers helped draft the English Sale of Goods Act in 1893 (Hamilton 1915, p. 1164; Pistis 2006). In a society ruled by such a warning, legal proof of the defrauding of customers with goods that could be closely inspected before purchase was difficult indeed.

III. SOLVING THE EVER-PRESENT PROBLEM OF RETAIL CRIME

A. Self-Policing: Trade Protection Societies

Of course, traders were just as vulnerable for their part. Customers in an urban environment were numerous, particularly mobile, and often fraudulent. In 1776 the Guardians, or the Society for the Protection of Trade Against Swindlers and Sharpers, formed in the City of London as an attempt to expose criminals who posed as customers and spread the word of their misdeeds to other retail establishments. They also banded together to finance the often-daunting cost of prosecuting repeat offenders who perpetrated retail crimes like shoplifting and fraud. Mirroring the societies formed by landowners to protect property in the face of hesitant juries unwilling to institute the Bloody Code of the eighteenth century, the urban societies were almost exclusively concerned with retailers and other business owners (Whitlock 2004, pp. 156–58). In 1816 the Guardians promised rewards of fifty shillings for the apprehension of perpetrators of robbery and up to forty shillings for those engaging in the common crime of shoplifting (PRO C114/34, 1826). The clothing trades, including woolen drapers, tailors, haberdashers, and hosiers, were strongly represented in the Society.[3] When a fraud was detected, the person's name, description, and method of fraud would be publicized in the organization's circular (Whitlock 2004, p. 158). The idea was to stop not the occasional pilfering customer, but the serial shoplifter and fraud by exposing their methods and areas of operation.

B. Medicalization

The effects of the successful medicalization of the courts in the nineteenth century are as apparent for retail crime as they are for more serious violent offenses such as murder. In her 2004 text *Medicine On Trial: A Sourcebook with Cases, Laws, and Documents*, Elisabeth Cawthon details the rise of the medical professional in Anglo-American courts. The habitual fraud or "professional" shoplifter was easy enough to understand in terms of poorer women and men using crime to obtain a livelihood, but the middle-class or wealthier retail criminal puzzled contemporaries. Early cases of wealthy shoplifters from the eighteenth and nineteenth centuries demonstrate how respectability allowed for individual denial. In cases such as that of Jane Leigh Perrot, Jane Austen's aunt living in Bath in 1799, blaming the shopkeeper for planting the goods on the customer or an outright denial often served to exonerate him or her (*Trial of Jane Leigh Perrot*; Whitlock 2004, pp. 1–3). It often came down to one individual's word against another, and respectable ladies could easily walk away in cases in which goods not sold to them found their way into pockets and packages. However, shopkeepers tired of the losses they suffered and, as the rise in trade protection societies demonstrates, became more aggressive in their efforts to prosecute the serial shoplifter (Whitlock 2004, p. 189).

Kleptomania, an irresistible impulse to steal, provided an alternative explanation in the cases of respectable shoppers stealing from retailers. This concept developed along with the professionalization of psychiatry in the nineteenth century and joined the medico-legalization of other crimes like drunkenness. In 1816 Dr. André Matthey of Switzerland named the diagnosis "klopemanie," but the name "kleptomania" or "cleptomania" had stuck by the 1880s (Miller 1981, pp. 197–200; O'Brien 1989, p. 70; Ellis 1936, pp. 477–78; Whitlock 1999; Whitlock 2004, p. 189). Perhaps the nineteenth century's most famous medical jurisprudence specialist, the American Dr. Isaac Ray in 1839 described both men and women suffering from this condition in an internationally influential treatise on insanity (Ray 1839, pp. v–x, 171–74; Whitlock 2004, p. 190). Early nineteenth-century cases were connected to head injury; however, as the century progressed, women and their particularly troublesome physiology came to dominate discussions of kleptomania, mirroring similar developments in the understanding of other types of madness (Ellis 1936, p. 486; O'Brien 1983, pp. 66–72; Abelson 1989b, pp. 173–96; Whitlock 2004, p. 191). By the 1880s the popular conception of the typical kleptomaniac was that of a wealthy, middle-class female shoplifter—one who was often experiencing some sort of hormonal change like pregnancy or menopause. In England in the spring of 1855, the case of Mary Ramsbotham, the wife of a doctor living in Portman Square in London, captured headlines. After purchasing six yards of fabric at a drapery shop that she often frequented in Baker Street, she secreted four handkerchiefs in her pocket when she thought the shopman was not looking. The draper, Mr. Moule, had her followed, arrested, and taken to police court for shoplifting. Her deft counsel, Mr. Ballantine, presented the jury at the Middlesex Sessions with a medico-legal defense of the thieving mania brought on by "constitutional changes." His argument split the jury six and six, and the judge dismissed them without a verdict (*Times* [London], 28 March–12 April 1855; Whitlock 2004, pp. 193–98). Although widely criticized at the time as a case of inequality in the practice of the law, and decried in canting ballads, the Ramsbotham case signaled the acceptance of the idea of kleptomania as a possible defense in court. Isaac Ray's revised 1860 edition of his 1839 text on medical jurisprudence contained direct references to the case in his enlarged description of kleptomania (Ray 1860; Whitlock 2004, p. 198). Initially met with criticism in legal circles and medical journals, by the 1870s and 1880s journals like the *Lancet* were calling for the introduction of more medical specialists in the courtroom to deal with kleptomania cases (*Lancet*, 24 March 1877, p. 435; *Lancet*, 27 August 1881, p. 390). As kleptomania gained acceptance in the courtroom, department stores were evolving to become the pinnacle of retail trade. Middle-class and wealthy women who stole from the new stores, like Ella Castle in 1896, were labeled as mad rather than bad (*Times* [London], 16 December 1896; Abelson 1989a; Whitlock 2004, p. 220).

C. The Scholars Weigh In

Shoplifting, kleptomania, and the rise of the department store remain the dominant historiographic trio explaining retail crime. The middle-class female criminal dominates the debate over retail crime for historical as well as intellectual reasons. With open displays and an emphasis on democratizing the luxury of pleasure shopping, department stores became not only a haven for the female shopper, but a center of retail crimes committed largely by women. William Whiteley asserted that for every man caught shoplifting at Whiteley's, there were 300 women apprehended committing the same crime. In Paris's *Bon Marché* in 1893 over 600 cases of shoplifting made it to the law courts (Miller 1981, p. 197; Lancaster 1995, p. 185; Whitlock 2004, p. 215). The trick was successfully prosecuting them. The "dark figure" in reported shoplifting crimes remains high because of stores' wish to avoid the bad publicity garnered by prosecuting respectable women. In this way, the department store managers and owners were no better off than the drapers at mid-century who had to resort to more subversive tactics like adding stolen items quietly to the bill of well-known customers (Brown 1855, p. 269; Whitlock 2004, pp. 197–98). As historians, we must ask why this uncommon explanation so dominates the discussion of what was arguably one of the most common types of crime—stealing from or defrauding the retail trader.

The stereotype of the kleptomaniacal shoplifter dominates the debates over retail crime in the late nineteenth and twentieth centuries. A combination of the rise of the medico-legal professional in court, late Victorian developments in psychology emphasizing desire, and a clear bias in the historical record highlighting the celebrated cases of wealthy shoplifters led to the development of an explanation for the rise of shoplifting that focuses on the expansion of consumer culture into the department store. Michael Miller's (1981) study of the *Bon Marché* from 1869 to 1920 is one of the first texts to emphasize the connection. In the ensuing decade of "greed is good," more studies emerged pinpointing the department store as the key development in understanding the history of shoplifting. In 1989 Elaine Abelson looked mainly at the American case in her book *When Ladies Go A-Thieving: Middle Class Shoplifters in the Victorian Department Store*. Abelson argues that the focus on such ladylike thieves avoided uncomfortable criticisms of consumer culture itself. Published six years earlier, Patricia O'Brien's (1983) work on shoplifting and the department store in France connected the kleptomania diagnosis with the rise of the medical professional in the courtroom. Leslie Camhi's (1993) study on feminine identity, kleptomania, and French department stores tied the rise of the kleptomania defense specifically to the late Victorian era of the exponential growth of consumer culture. However, the problem of consumer crime cannot be laid entirely at the feet of Aristide Boucicaut, William Whiteley, or even Gordon Selfridge.

Although much of the history of consumption in the West revolves around the star of the department store, including the works of Michael Miller (1981), T. J. Jackson Lears (1994), William Lancaster (1995), William R. Leach (1984), and Rosalind Williams (1982), only a few of these authors explore the connections between crime and retail culture. Erika Rappaport's (2001) *Shopping for Pleasure: Women and the Making of London's West End* more explicitly traces the aura of danger and culture of fraud that colors the experience of the female shopper and shoplifter. More instructively for our understanding of the long-term developments in retail is the more tamely titled book of John Benson and Gareth Shaw *The Evolution of Retail Systems, 1800–1914*, which was published in 1991 and emphasized that the history of the department store was nowhere near the whole story of retail trade. Benson and Laura Uglioni's ambitious 2003 collection of essays covering five centuries of English retail further the argument that the roots of understanding retail history and retail crime predate the singular development of the department store. Convincing essays by Nancy Cox (2003) and Claire Walsh (2003) contribute to the tracing of consumer culture innovations to the early modern period, with Cox's essay in particular demonstrating how hostile reactions to retail innovation have their origins as far back as the sixteenth century. The earlier we look for the distrust and suspicion of "cheap" shops and shopkeepers, the earlier we seem to find it, although, as Cox (2003) clearly shows, in the early modern era the bias was not always against the light-fingered customer, but sometimes against the shopkeepers themselves.

IV. Modern Costs of Retail Crime

In an era of self-cashiering and other cuts to customer service, shoplifting continues to cost the retailer and the honest consumer dearly. Reporters Helen Pid and Hatty Collier (2013), citing statistics from the British Retail Consortium (a modern trade association), put the losses from shoplifting at over 500 million pounds in 2013 in Great Britain alone. These numbers are tiny compared to the United States, which boasted over $11 billion in losses in 2012, and global losses, which are estimated in the $30 billion range, but the crime is difficult to track (Hayes International 2013). Retail crime in its various incarnations staggers us with its sheer numbers and frequency.

A. The Future of Scholarship

From popular histories like Rachel Shteir's 2011 *The Steal* to more academic studies like the recent work of William Meier, the analysis of retail crime is taking new directions.

Meier's overall thesis that crime in the late Victorian to early 20th century period was the product of socialization into a consumer economy and that professional criminals were created by the institutionalization of punishment and reform begun by the Victorians places him against those historians who see crime as either a rebellion against an increasing police state or, as in the eighteenth century, as a reassertion of tradition against creeping modernity (Meier 2011b, pp. 166–67; Meier 2011a). Meier also puts the focus back on the working classes, including gangs of shoplifters in early to mid-twentieth-century London. Whereas Shteir's (2011) study was inspired by the public fascination with the celebrity shoplifting case of Winona Ryder in 2001 and stresses the realities of upper-middle-class and privileged criminals, Meier (2011a) concentrates on the professional criminal and the connections to women's underpaid work in the context of an expanding consumer culture. Also focusing largely on the working classes, Louise Jackson and Angela Bartie's (2011) work on juvenile crime in mid-twentieth-century Britain shows that juvenile patterns of shoplifting in areas like Manchester bear out the old association with "large central self-service and department stores," as the young women in postwar Manchester stole mainly clothing items. Overall, however, one has to agree with Anthea Christodoulou (2007), who examines shoplifting and other theft from stores as a business issue, taking into account the history of retail crime, to better understand the context. She notes that although groundbreaking studies like Abelson's (1989b) work brought the topic into the academic mainstream, there is still little agreement on the real causes of shoplifting or even the gender of most offenders (pp. 89–93). In some ways, recent work signals a return to the former focus on the working classes in relationship to crime. The difference between these new interpretations and older ones is that historians now recognize that the working classes are operating within consumer culture and not necessarily against it.

NOTES

1. See "Trade Cards," 16 February 1819, Box XII, John Johnson Collection, Bodleian Library, Oxford.
2. See "FIRE! In St. Paul's Churchyard" (poster), 1853. Box: Bazaars and Sales, John Johnson Collection, Bodleian Library, Oxford.
3. The Guardians: or Society for the Protection of Trade Against Swindlers and Sharpers, Rules and Orders (Northumberland Street, Strand, London: G. Sidney, 1816); *City of London Trade Protection Circular* 1825-1849.PRO C114/34.

REFERENCES

Abelson, Elaine. 1989a. "The Invention of Kleptomania." *Signs* 15 (1): 123–43.

Abelson, Elaine. 1989b. *When Ladies Go A-Thieving: Middle-Class Shoplifters in the Victorian Department Store*. New York: Oxford University Press.

Ablett, William. 1876. *Reminiscences of an Old Draper*. London: Sampson Low, Marston, Searle, and Rivington.

Adburgham, Alison. 1964. *Shops and Shopping, 1800–1914: Where and in What Manner the Well-Dressed Englishwoman Bought Her Clothes.* London: Barrie and Jenkins.

Anonymous. 1864. *A Handy Guide for the Draper and Haberdasher.* London: F. Pitman.

Beattie, J. M. 1986. *Crime and the Courts in Early Modern England, 1660–1800.* Princeton, NJ: Princeton University Press.

Benson, John, & Gareth Shaw. 1991. *The Evolution of Retail Systems, 1800–1914.* Leicester, UK: Leicester University Press.

Benson, John, & Laura Uglioni, eds. 2003. *A Nation of Shopkeepers: Five Centuries of British Retailing.* London: I. B. Tauris.

Bow Street Officer, A. 1829. *The Frauds of London: Displaying the Numerous and Daring Cheats and Robberies Practised Upon the Stranger and the Unwary.* London: William Cole.

Brown, John. 1855. "On Genteel Thieves." *Tait's Edinburgh Magazine* Vol. 26 o.s., Vol. 22 n.s.: 269.

Camhi, Leslie. 1993. "Stealing Femininity: Department Store Kleptomania as Sexual Disorder." *Differences* 5 (2): 27–50.

Cawthon, Elisabeth A. 2004. *Medicine on Trial: A Sourcebook with Cases, Laws, and Documents.* Indianapolis, IN: Hackett Publishing.

Christodoulou, Anthea. 2007. "The World of Stolen Goods: A Psychological Perspective of Illicit Consumption." Ph.D. diss., Durham University. Accessed at http://etheses.dur.ac.uk/2493/.

Cox, Nancy. 2003. "'Beggary of the Nation': Moral, Economic and Political Attitudes to the Retail Sector in the Early Modern Period." *In A Nation of Shopkeepers: Five Centuries of British Retailing,* ed. John Benson & Laura Uglioni, 26–51. London: I. B. Tauris.

Defoe, Daniel. 1722. *The Fortunes and Misfortunes of the Famous Moll Flanders.* London: W. Chetwood. Gale-Cengage Eighteenth Century Collections Online, released 1 June 2004.

Dyer, Gary.1991. "The 'Vanity Fair' of Nineteenth-Century England: Commerce, Women and the East in the Ladies' Bazaar." *Nineteenth-Century Literature* 46 (2): 196–222.

Edwards, Loren E. 1958. *Shoplifting and Shrinkage Protection.* Springfield, IL: Charles C. Thomas.

Ellis, Havelock. 1936. *Studies in the Psychology of Sex,* Vol. 2. New York: Random House.

Finn, Margot. 1996. "Women, Consumption and Coverture in England, c. 1760–1860." *Historical Journal* 39: 703–22.

Gentlemen's Magazine. 1816. "The Bazaar." 86: 272.

Hamilton, Walton H. "The Ancient Maxim of Caveat Emptor." *Yale Law Journal* 40 (8): 1133–87.

Hayes International. 2013. "25th Annual Retail Theft Survey." Accessed at http://hayesinternational.com/wp-content/uploads/2013/06/SURVEY-2013-25th-Annual-Retail-Theft-Survey-Hayes-International-Thoughts-Behind-Numbers-Final.pdf.

Hooper, Wilfrid. 1915. "The Tudor Sumptuary Laws." *English Historical Review* 30 (119): 433–49.

Jackson, Louise A., & Angela Bartie. 2011. "'Children of the City': Juvenile Justice, Property, and Place in England and Scotland, 1945–60." *Economic History Review* 64 (1): 88–113.

Lancaster, William. 1995. *The Department Store: A Social History.* London: Leicester University Press.

Leach, William R. 1984. "Transformations in a Culture of Consumption: Women and Department Stores, 1890–1925." *Journal of American History* 71: 319–42.

Lears, T. J. Jackson. 1994. *Fables of Abundance: A Cultural History of Advertising in America.* New York: Basic Books.

Nightingale, Joseph. 1816. *The Bazaar, Its Origins, Nature and Objects Explained, and Recommended as an Important Branch of Political Economy; In a Letter to the Rt. Hon. George Rose*, M.P. London: Davies Michael and Hudson.

Meier, William M. 2011a. "Going on the Hoist: Women, Work, and Shoplifting in London, ca. 1890—1940." *Journal of British Studies* 50 (2): 410–33.

Meier, William M. 2011b. *Property Crime in London, 1850 to the Present*. New York: Palgrave MacMillan.

Miller, Michael B. 1981. *The Bon Marché: Bourgeois Culture and the Department Store, 1869–1920*. Princeton, NJ: Princeton University Press.

Mui, Hoh-cheung, & Lorna H. Mui. 1989. *Shops and Shopkeeping in Eighteenth Century England*. Montreal: McGill-Queen's University Press.

Murphy, Daniel J. I. 1986. *Customers and Thieves: An Ethnography of Shoplifting*. Brookfield, VT: Gower.

O'Brien, Patricia. 1983. "The Kleptomania Diagnosis: Bourgeois Women and Theft in Late Nineteenth-Century France." *Journal of Social History* 17: 65–67.

Pid, Helen, & Hatty Collier. 2014. "Shoplifting on the Increase as Overall Crime Figures Fall." *Guardian* (Manchester), 25 April. Accessed at http://www.theguardian.com/uk-news/2014/apr/25/shoplifting-increase-overall-crime-figures-fall-england-wales.

Pinch, Adela. 1997. "Stealing Happiness: Shoplifting in Early Nineteenth-Century England." In *Border Fetishisms: Material Objects in Unstable Space*, ed. Patricia Spyer, 122–49. New York: Routledge.

Pistis, Mario. 2006. "From Caveat Emptor to Caveat Venditor: A Brief History of English Sale of Goods Law." *Abbatescianni Studio Legale e Tributario*, 4 June. Accessed at http://www.mondaq.com/content/company.asp?article_id=40206&company_id=2457.

Rappaport, Erika D. 2001. *Shopping for Pleasure: Women in the Making of London's West End*. Princeton, NJ: Princeton University Press.

Ray, Isaac M. D. 1839. *A Treatise on the Medical Jurisprudence of Insanity*. London: G. Henderson.

Ray, Isaac M. D. 1860. *A Treatise on the Medical Jurisprudence of Insanity*. Boston: Little, Brown.

Robson, L. L. 1965. *The Convict Settlers of Australia: An Enquiry into the Original Character of the Convicts Transported to New South Wales and Van Dieman's Land, 1787–1852*. Melbourne: Melbourne University Press.

Shteir, Rachel. 2011. *The Steal: A Cultural History of Shoplifting*. New York: Penguin.

Stern, Rebecca. 1996. "Historicizing Performativity: Constructing Identities in Victorian England." Ph.D. diss., Rice University.

Stern, Rebecca. 2008. *Home Economics: Domestic Fraud in Victorian England*. Columbus: Ohio State University Press.

Trial of Jane Leigh Perrot, at Taunton Assizes, on Saturday the 29th of March, 1800; Charged With Stealing a Card of Lace, in the Shop of Elizabeth Gregory, Haberdasher & Milliner, of the City of Bath. 1800. Bath: W. Gye.

Walsh, Claire. 2003. "Social Meaning and Social Space in the Shopping Galleries of Early Modern London." In *In A Nation of Shopkeepers: Five Centuries of British Retailing*, ed. John Benson & Laura Uglioni, 52–79. London: I. B. Tauris.

Weiss, Barbara. 1986. *The Hell of the English: Bankruptcy and the Victorian Novel*. Lewisburg, PA: Bucknell University Press.

Whitlock, Tammy C. 1999. "Gender, Medicine and Consumer Culture in Victorian England: Creating the Kleptomaniac." *Albion* 31 (3): 413–37.

Whitlock, Tammy C. 2004. *Crime, Gender and Consumer Culture in Nineteenth-Century England*. Hampshire, UK: Ashgate.

Wiener, Martin J. 1990. *Reconstructing the Criminal: Culture, Law, and Policy in England, 1830–1914*. New York: Cambridge University Press.

Williams, Rosalind H. 1982. *Dream Worlds: Mass Consumption in Late Nineteenth-Century France*. Berkeley: University of California Press.

Zedner, Lucia. 1991. *Women, Crime, and Custody in Victorian England*. Oxford: Clarendon Press.

Zola, Emile. 2008. *The Ladies' Paradise*. Oxford World Classics. Oxford: Oxford University Press.

CHAPTER 8

A BRIEF HISTORY OF THE UNDERWORLD AND ORGANIZED CRIME, C. 1750–1950

HEATHER SHORE

INTRODUCTION

IN 1969, the American penologist and criminologist Donald R. Cressey invented an organized crime model for a modern audience (2008 [1969]). Two years before, he had been a consultant on organized crime for the President's Commission on Law Enforcement and Administration of Justice convened by Lyndon Johnson to address the threat of organized crime in the United States. Cressey's research, and his subsequent book, *The Theft of the Nation*, would inform U.S. government policies on organized crime for the following decades. In the 1960s Cressey spearheaded the movement of criminologists to attempt to formally define what organized crime was (Maltz, 1976). In doing so they looked back to the recent history of those North American cities in which crime groups were understood to have clawed their way into politics, economics, and society. History, and its impact on the present, was central to many of these attempts to define organized crime. As Attorney General Ramsey Clark remarked in an address to the National Emergency Committee of the National Council on Crime and Delinquency in New York in November 1967, "Many find it difficult to believe there is organized crime, but its existence is confirmed by history, experience and reason. It surfaced in the United States in the last decades of the nineteenth century and during the prohibition era" (U.S. Congress 1967, p. 359). This essay will rewind from that moment in the postwar era when academics and politicians embarked on the "modeling" of organized crime in the United States and other Western nations to consider its long evolution over the previous two centuries. The notion that the Western world has an organized crime problem, and, indeed, that the "underworld" exists as an entity and a space, has become orthodoxy. Thus, in the late modernity of the twenty-first century, organized crime and the underworld are fully entrenched in our understanding and perception of criminality.

This essay is an attempt to break down this orthodoxy and to try to understand how we came to be in this position by the postwar period. It will focus on the two centuries between 1750 and 1950, and cut a broad swathe across Europe and North America. Coverage is limited to the more well-known texts and histories, and those published in English. As a result, material on North America, Britain, and Italy predominates. The essay is constructed of two sections. Section I will provide an overview of organized crime activity, mapping out the chronology and geography of what historians know about this subject in the past. Section II will explore the founding literature, returning to the American criminologists of the 1960s and 1970s alongside the work of British criminologists. For historians, social science/criminology methodology has been useful in helping us to understand the historical development of organized crime. However, we have to draw on a wider set of cultural and social histories in order to appreciate the key role of print culture and literature in shaping our knowledge of the criminal past. Therefore, this section will consider the problems faced by historians in attempting to understand organized crime in past societies and some of the directions recent research has taken.

Before moving on to the first section, it seems appropriate to consider some problems of language and etymology. The term "organized crime" was rarely used before the mid-twentieth century. Clive Emsley notes that, in England, "'organised crime' was a term not much used in the first two-thirds of the twentieth century. But from the close of the nineteen century policemen and others were beginning to speak and to write of the professional criminal" (2011, p. 87). Certainly, for much of the late Victorian and Edwardian eras, specific references to organized crime and criminality were used predominately in a political context in the British press, most commonly in relation to events in Ireland, although occasional references to organized crime groups in Naples and Paris can be found (*Times* [London], 22 October 1880; 10 January 1881; 21 May 1920; *Observer*, 10 February 1907; *Manchester Guardian*, 12 July 1911). Starting in the early twentieth century, references to British organized and professional crime would become more common in public and print discourses. In Italy, and particularly in Sicily, from where the organized crime clan known as the Cosa Nostra or Mafiosi emerged in the early nineteenth century, the term "Mafia" was first used in an official document in 1865, in a letter about an arrest from the *delegato di pubblica sicurezza* near Palermo. As Diego Gambetta notes, "in reference to a man, *mafiusu* in nineteenth-century Sicily was ambiguous, signifying a bully, arrogant but also fearless, enterprising and proud" (1996, p. 136). The "underworld" as a term used in Western countries to specifically describe the alternative habitat of the criminal, the deviant, and the dangerous outsider was not common until the turn of the century. The earliest usage of the term was in reference to prostitution in New York, reflected in titles such as *The Women of New York; or, The Under-World of the Great City* (Ellington 1869; Gilfoyle 1992) and *Darkness and*

Daylight; or, Lights and Shadows of New York Life ... in the Underworld of the Great Metropolis (Campbell 1899). In England, Thomas Holmes, secretary of the Howard Association for penal reform, published *London's Underworld* (1912), and by the early twentieth century the use of the term was increasingly invoked in accounts of urban criminality. For example, British writer and former conman Netley Lucas wrote about the women of the underworld "the world over" (1926; Houlbrook 2013), and Alfred Morain, formerly a prefect of police of Paris, wrote about the underworld in his city (1930). Nevertheless, a terminology and discourse that described the slums, rookeries, dives, sinks, and netherworlds of urban spaces had long roots. Many European countries had a tradition of rogue literature and criminal print cultures that can be traced back at least to the sixteenth century, if not earlier (Kinney 1973; McMullan 1986). However, there are significant problems with the terminology of the "underworld" and "organized crime." Florike Egmond, in her work on the Netherlands in the early modern period, recognized this when she argued: "The term 'organized crime' immediately evokes drug-dealing, mafia-like organization and international connections. Yet, as Mary McIntosh has shown, in spite of these modern connotations, it can be used to cover historical types of crime as well. After all, criminal organization existed before the twentieth century and it would be confusing not to call it thus" (1993, pp. 4–5).

I. Chronology and Geography of the Underworld

This section will provide an overview of those crime groups that have been identified from the eighteenth century. This accounting is necessarily tentative. Unlike histories of criminal law or of penal institutions and reforms, the history of the underworld and of organized crime is much less opaque. Charting the early roots of "modern" organized crime, this section will further encompass the developments of organized crime groups in the United States, Italy, and Britain from the later nineteenth century. It is from this period that it can be argued that more "modern" conceptions of organized crime would emerge.

A. From "Bandits" to Criminal Gangs: c. 1750 to c. 1850

In 1975, Mary McIntosh was one of the earliest theorists of organized crime to attempt to historicize the underworld, its hierarchies and practices (1975). McIntosh, like many historians and criminologists since, looked back to the role of banditti, brigands, and outlaws in early modern peasant society, an approach shaped by the work of Eric Hobsbawm. His seminal text *Bandits*, published in the late 1960s, attempted to explain the role of separate societies or counter-societies that emerged as a means of protecting local interests against the authorities (the gentry, clergy, or state) (Hobsbawm 1969).

According to Hobsbawm, the "bandit" was faced with a choice and had to decide whether to become a criminal or a revolutionary. Thus the two could not coexist: "The underworld (as its name implies) is an anti-society, which exists by reversing the values of the 'straight' world—it is, in its own phrase, 'bent'—but is otherwise parasitic on it" (Hobsbawm 1969, p. 84). In an earlier book Hobsbawm had characterized the Mafia as developing from the antipathy to feudalism in rural Italy (1959, pp. 30–56). More recently, accounts of the development of groups such as the Sicilian Mafia have been much more nuanced. In his useful summary Howard Abadinsky describes the evolution of four Italian criminal organizations: the Sicilian Mafia, the Neapolitan *Camorra*, the *'Ndrangheta* ("Brotherhood") of Calabria, and the *Sacra Corona Unita* of the Puglia region (2003, p. 146). The most well-known of these, the Mafia and the Camorra, had very different roots, according to Abadinsky. He argues that the Mafia developed from the emergence of middlemen called *Gabelloti*, who ruled over the estates that had previously been controlled by the aristocracy. This aristocracy had increasingly come under attack during the nineteenth century, and ultimately, the land was "freed" through the campaigns of Giuseppe Garibaldi (Abadinsky 2003, p. 147). As Alan Wright notes, "the collapse of the feudal system after the rise and fall of Napoleon in the early nineteenth century marked the emergence of the Mafia into a *società* (society) of families that mediated between the landowners and the masses" (2006, p. 104). The Camorra, according to Abadinsky, was deliberately structured as a secret society (2003, p. 158) and was more organized and disciplined than the Mafia, although other research suggests that this is far from clear-cut. Tom Behan has stressed the mythology that surrounds the development of the Camorra in Naples, referring instead to the group's emergence in the early nineteenth century as what was effectively a criminal organization, with its roots in popular resistance and anti-authoritarianism: "The official news of the Camorra as an organization dates from 1820, when police records detail a disciplinary meeting of the Camorra. Such an event indicates a qualitative change: the Camorra and *camorristi* were no longer simply local gangs living off theft and extortion; they now had a fixed structure and some sort of hierarchy" (1995, p. 12).

In other European countries, organizations or groups with similar profiles to the Italian societies are likely to have existed. In Germany there was increasing reference to societies or gangs of crooks from the eighteenth century on. Katrin Lange has stressed that the contemporary debates about such gangs were vague and often arbitrary, allowing the authorities to target offenders variously labeled as beggars, tramps, gypsies, cheats, robbers, and bandits, or using the term *Gauner* (crooks) (2004, p. 109). While a number of publications referred to such "gangs," the term was used loosely. Lange refers to Johann Zedler's *Universal Lexikon*, published in 1741, which described gangs of robbers but provided no information on their organization or structure. A further set of writings known as the *Official Stories* (*Aktenmäßige Geschichten*), which were published in the early nineteenth century by the law enforcement and judges in charge of gang trials, also emphasized the loose structures of such gangs (Lange 2004, p. 110). Nevertheless, other German historians have been less critical of the concept of an underworld in eighteenth- and nineteenth-century Germany. Carsten Küther (1976) argues that the problem of gangs and bandits was one of poor control. The eighteenth-century judicial system was not well equipped to deal with the subcultural nature of such groups, and, he argues, the state failed to deal effectively with them. To some extent this may have been due to the lack of unification in German territories that left borders permeable and law enforcement structures far from centralized. Arguably, it was only after the Napoleonic wars, and the adoption of the Napoleonic Code in some parts of Germany (such as the regions of the west bank of the Rhine and the Grand Duchy of Baden), that the judicial system was to become more effective (Lindström 2004, p. 142).

Florike Egmond has researched organized crime in the Netherlands, focusing on various marginal groups in the early modern Dutch republic. She particularly notes the role of ethnic groups such as Jews and gypsies, as well as their links with organized crime by the late eighteenth century and the rise of vagrancy and dearth from the 1740s (Egmond 1993, pp. 184–85). Similarly, Uwe Danker's studies of gangs of robbers in eighteenth-century Coburg found that the gangs there included a significant number of Jewish vagrants (2001, pp. 96–97). On the other hand, Danker also found groups that were made up of farmers and artisans from the local area. While the eighteenth century seems to have been crucial in the Dutch and German examples, Egmond suggests that it would be unwise to impose any neat chronology onto the development of organized crime in the Netherlands: "To put it briefly: Organized rural crime did not become more (or less) professional in the period 1650–1800" (1993, p. 180). Richard Evans's discussion of the underworld in nineteenth-century Germany demonstrates how "criminal careers" unraveled and the ways in which German commentators increasingly portrayed such individuals as members of an organized criminal underworld (1998, p. 6). Here Evans draws attention to the important role of the social commentators and reformers of the nineteenth century, who would use the burgeoning print culture of newspapers, periodicals, pamphlets, and books to "discover" the underworld. Moreover, while many of the accounts of gangs in continental Europe stress the disorganized, marginal, and fluid nature of the groups, it may be that in nineteenth-century Europe, the "underworld" become more anchored to growing urban spaces.

In Britain the relationship between print culture and representations of organized crime flourished in the early to mid-eighteenth century. By 1750 the legacy of the thief-taker Jonathan Wild was still marked (Howson 1970). Wild's activities in controlling crime in early eighteenth-century London, and his collusion with the authorities, have been well documented. Perhaps in common with some of the later European incarnations of organized crime, Wild was notable for seizing opportunities created by the authorities. In this case, the rise of a statutory award system from the 1690s facilitated the creation of a significant crime culture in the early eighteenth century (Beattie 2001, pp. 376–422). Other historians of the eighteenth-century metropolis have drawn attention to criminal gangs and networks that seem to have come into being at least in part as a result of "moral panics" (Ward 2014). The extent to which any pervasive organized crime networks actually existed in eighteenth-century Britain is debatable. Once illegal markets are accessed for the disposal of stolen goods, such criminal activity becomes inherently organized. However, it would take the modernizing aspects of society for more recognizable models of organized crime to evolve: the creation and circulation of financial instruments; new technologies in firearms, safes, and transport infrastructures; the development of a strong surveillance culture that legislated the "habitual criminal" into being; the growth of global networks via colonialism; and the creation of the "underworld" in texts and literatures that could be accessed by a wide range of readers (Shore 2015).

B. Urbanization, Immigration, and Organized Crime, c. 1850 to c. 1900

As was suggested earlier, there is a crucial relationship between organized crime and print culture and the publicity it affords. Leitizia Paoli has drawn attention to the important role of historical discourses in the Italian example: "To a larger extent than in any other European country, organized crime has been a relevant topic of the public and scientific discourse in Italy since the mid-nineteenth century" (2004, p. 263). After the unification in 1861 the government focused its crime policies around the idea of the existence of stable organized crime groups, in Sicily in particular. In other words, because the government tended to associate organized crime specifically with the southern Italy region, this view was reinforced by the media and public opinion. As Paoli notes, the image of the Sicilian Mafia as a secret and powerful organization was elaborated beginning in the later nineteenth century by "'moral entrepreneurs' who published newspaper articles and romanticised reports on the mafia" (2004, p. 264). While other European countries undoubtedly had social and political groups similar to those in Italy, it is the movement of the Italian groups outside their own territory—during the nineteenth and early twentieth centuries—that arguably escalated their activities and made them more visible and threatening to the authorities. Thus, although criminal groups may well have existed in other countries, they were not necessarily known about on the global stage, while there was international reporting of the Mafia and Camorra as early as the later nineteenth century. This may have been a reflection of political events in Italy: the right-wing government was under threat during the 1870s, and it had accused the left of corruption involving the Mafiosi. Legislation was passed that, according to John Dickie, "proposed that suspected members of criminal associations and their political patrons could be imprisoned without trial for as much as five years" (2004, p. 70). In 1874, the *Times*, for example, reported on "the Mafia in Sicily" and on "Neapolitan Brigandage" (*Times* [London], 15 October 1874; 18 November 1874). The paper first referred to the Mafia in the United States in 1890, when it reported the assassination of David Hennessey, the chief of police of New Orleans. According to its report, Hennessey had been investigating Italian and Sicilian societies: "The vendetta, of which the murder of Mr. Hennessey is the latest outcome, originated in Sicily, and was transferred to New Orleans nearly 30 years ago. The opposing societies are the Mafia and the Stoppaghera" (18 October 1890).

The nineteenth century witnessed the making of the underworld across Western Europe. Thus, in many metropolises, the underworld was "discovered" as a literary, cultural, and political issue. Paris, London, and Berlin became nighttime cities, according to Joachim Schlor (1998), a phenomenon that can be seen in the parade of texts that dealt with the problems of crime and poverty. While deviance was not confined to the night, darkness came to symbolize the journey into the spaces of the underworld in Victorian cities, reflected in titles about London such as *The Night Side of London* (Ewing Ritchie 1858), *London at Midnight* (Vigar Harris 1885), and *The Hooligan Nights* (Rook 1899). Similar titles dealing with crime, poverty, and vice abounded for New York, including *The Nether Side of New York* (Crapsey 1872), *Lights and Shadows of New York Life* (McCabe 1872), and *The Night Scenes of City Life* (De Witt Talmage 1891). In London, the development of the underworld as a distinct space with its own dwellers had been cultivated through the social journalism of individuals like Henry Mayhew, John Greenwood, and Andrew Mearns and by authors of fiction like Charles Dickens and G. W. M. Reynolds. In such texts, the line between fiction and reality was increasingly blurred, and by the turn of the century the underworld had fully emerged as a marginal and "other" landscape, not only in the metropolis of London, but in many other cities and regions of Europe and North America. For example, Dominique Kalifa has explored how representations of the underworld developed in Paris during the nineteenth century, commenting that "it is often in the urban topography—streets, *places*, or *impasses*—that fear or obsession with crime crystallizes" (2004, p. 175). Novelists and journalists such as Eugène Sue shaped the reputation of the Left Bank as a "sinister and dangerous" place in the first half of the century. Indeed, Sue's *Les Mystères de Paris* (1842) would directly influence Reynolds's *The Mysteries of London*, which was published two years later (Kalifa 2004, p. 177; Reynolds 1844).

Texts such as these fundamentally shaped contemporary and later portrayals of the cultures of crime. In Western Europe, particularly from the later nineteenth century on, often-well-meaning concerns about poverty and slum life merged with new ways of thinking about criminality, physiology, and human behavior. Influential thinkers such as Francis Galton in England, Bénédict Morel in France, and Cesare Lombroso in Italy shaped and contributed to a new language that aimed to describe what were seen as inherited characteristics of populations and adopted medical and pathological rhetoric to explain criminality (Pick 1989). While these theories did not completely reject environmental explanations for crime, the increasingly deterministic way of explaining criminal behavior within certain parts of the population was attractive to many commentators. Arguably, these explanations were paralleled with the emergence of legislation that would make "the criminal" a more visible social problem. In Britain, the Habitual Criminals Act was passed in 1869, and the passage of new police legislation, and particularly the establishment of the Detective Department in 1842 and its reorganization as the Criminal Investigation Department in 1878, drew attention to the "criminal class" (McGowen 1990; Petrow 1993). In France, the Relegation Law of 1885 exemplified a harsh approach toward recidivists, deporting those who were found guilty of habitual criminality (Toth 2006, p. 21). Godfrey, Cox, & Farrall have suggested that habitual offender legislation in the nineteenth century was also influenced by colonial practices such as the Criminal Tribes Act of 1871, which was passed by the British in India to deal with the problem of habitual crime (2010, p. 197). The colonial context is key, Simon Cole notes, in understanding attitudes toward crime in colonial India: "Put in terms of caste, the habitual criminal became a 'hereditary criminal,' a member of a genetically determined criminal group. Criminality became ethnic" (2001, p. 67). In the later nineteenth and early twentieth centuries, this overly deterministic understanding of habitual criminality would arguably find its expression in the connections made between immigration and crime.

From the later nineteenth century on, the interest in the "professional" and the "habitual" criminal grew, along with the belief that such criminals inhabited a separate underworld, one that would be associated spatially with the growing urban spaces of Western Europe and North America. Unsurprisingly, it would be the new arrivals in these areas who would be accused of importing criminality into the metropolises of the late nineteenth and early twentieth centuries. Outside Western Europe, other secret societies and criminal groups had long pedigrees. It is worth mentioning the major Chinese and Japanese crime groups briefly here, as they were eventually to be imported to Western countries. The Triads had roots in the British colonies of Hong Kong, Malaysia, and Singapore, and were involved in criminal activities such as gambling, extortion, and opium trafficking (Abadinsky 2003, pp. 212–13; Booth 1990). The Chinese Tong, in contrast, were first established in San Francisco as immigrant benevolent societies in the 1850s but became increasingly associated with prostitution and gambling from the late nineteenth century on (Abadinsky 2003, p. 216; Huston 1995). The Yakuza date from at least the seventeenth century, when they were linked to a group of samurai warriors called the *hatamoto-yakko*, itinerant peddlers known as the *tekiya*, and illegal gambling gangs called the *bakuto* (Kaplan & Dubro 2003, pp. 5–6; Hill 2005). However, the Yakuza did not make any impact in the United States until the 1950s, outside the bounds of this survey (Mallory 2012, p. 145). Perhaps the most distinct immigrant groups to be considered in the context of emerging discourses of organized crime were those that had migrated from Italy. The United States was home to many groups of immigrants that would be linked to racketeering, protection, and other illegal activities in its major cities. These groups were overwhelmingly from migrant communities, including those of Irish, Jewish, and Italian origin (Wright 2006, p. 118). The most well-known of these were the Mafia and Cosa Nostra "families" that came to prominence in the late nineteenth century and had become a global reported issue by the interwar period. Many criminologists have drawn on the "alien conspiracy thesis" to explain the rise of organized crime in American society. This thesis is particularly associated with the work of criminologist Dwight Smith, who argues that American society has been historically preoccupied with placing the blame for crime on immigrant groups:

> It remains painfully obvious that Americans are susceptible to the lures of conspiracy advocates when their accusations touch the right cultural anxieties. In four instances since 1798, charges of a secret alien conspiracy have captured sufficient public attention to affect public opinion and public policy well beyond the scope of events triggering the original cry. (1976, p. 76)

For Smith, the reporting on the Mafia in the early 1890s was a clear illustration of the alien conspiracy theory. He argues that in this case evidence was used to suggest a criminal "bent" in the southern European immigrant population as a means of restricting immigration (p. 81).

Other writers have linked the growth of organized crime to the relationship between immigrant groups and urban politics in American cities. Thus, with the migration of about a quarter of a million Irish people at the mid-century, and continued migration after that, Irish immigrants found that their entry into society and ability to chase the American dream was blocked by the existing Protestant community. In order to gain power and social mobility, Irish immigrants colonized local politics. This process was exemplified by the rise of Tammany Hall, a political organization that was founded in 1786 but gained the loyalty of the Irish immigrant population in the nineteenth century. Its name became a byword for corruption, particularly under the leadership of "Boss" Tweed (Golway 2014), and it became particularly noted for its association with gangs, which were used by politicians on election days but would also work in the gambling houses and brothels that were under the control of the machine (Abadinsky 2003, p. 76). These gangs, described by Herbert Asbury in *The Gangs of New York* (1928), included the Five Points, the Plug Uglies, and the Bowery Boys among their number. However, the extent to which these gangs were involved in systematic organized crime activity remains debatable according to the historian Tyler Anbinder. In his study of the Five Points, he argues that the area's reputation has taken on "mythic proportions" (Anbinder 2001, p. 68). Nevertheless, the Five Points gang included in its ranks a young Al Capone before he left for Chicago and the Sicilian-born Lucky Luciano (Kobler 1971 p. 31). The other historical "gang" that has been connected to the origins of the Mafia in America was the Black Hand, small groups of extortionists who preyed on Italian immigrants and committed "outrages," according to the international press (*Times* [London], 10 February 1908). While Black Hand activity apparently had Italian origins, it is often problematically lumped together with Mafia activity, argues historian David Critchley, who has stressed the difficulty of untangling the history of early organized crime groups (Critchley 2009, pp. 20–23). Nevertheless, during the interwar period, Asbury (1928; 1936; 1940) made some attempt to reveal these early histories of the underbelly of American cities. What is clear is that organized crime groups became an undeniable feature of New York and other American cities between the late nineteenth and early twentieth centuries.

C. Organized Crime c. 1918 to c. 1950: Italy, North America, and Britain

Reports of organized crime activity escalated from the interwar period, particularly in North America, Italy, and Britain. In the case of American organized crime, this was linked in part to the fluctuating fortunes of Italian society during the late nineteenth and early twentieth centuries. Italian organized crime in North America would come to be most strongly associated with New York. Starting in the later nineteenth century there was a flood of emigration from southern Italy to America. By the 1930 census, New York had around 440,000 Italian immigrants. The largest proportion of these (around 237,000) had arrived by 1910. However, in the period up to 1930 that number almost doubled (Rosenwaike 1972, p. 94). It was the demands of this largely peasant-origin community that shaped the development of the Italian Mafia in New York during the twentieth century. Thus, according to sociologist Randall Collins, it was a combination of factors that led to the prominence of Italian organized crime in American cities, including "the arrival of large numbers of European immigrants from peasant backgrounds who demanded cultural services that the dominant Anglo-Protestant society made illegal; the availability of a patrimonial form of military organization that could be applied to protecting such services; and the relatively late arrival of the Italians in comparison with other ethnic groups" (1975, p. 463; cited in Abadinsky 2003, pp. 86–87). The resulting rivalry between the Italian, Irish, and Jewish groups for the control of resources meant that the Sicilians often resorted to the forms of illegal organization that they had adopted in their own country.

By the mid-1920s these organizations were on the wane in Italy, and particularly in Sicily. With the rise to power of Mussolini, the southern regions would increasingly turn to Fascism. Once the regime gained power, it was quick to move to repress the Mafia, however. As Judith Chubb has noted, "individual Mafiosi became easy targets for the fierce campaign of repression unleashed by Mussolini under the direction of the Prefect Cesare Mori, for, once its dominance was secured, Fascism tolerated no rival power structures" (1982, p. 26). Prefect Mori, Mussolini's local man in Sicily, had originally led police operations against brigands after the First World War, when a number of war veterans were believed to have joined bandit gangs. He was called out of his retirement in the mid-twenties, when Mussolini appointed him prefect of Palermo, and it was this appointment that marked the beginning of the sustained campaign to repress the mafia (Finkelstein 1998, p. 19). Mori set out to purge the island of Mafiosi, arresting 11,000 people who were believed to be either members or associates of the Mafia (Dickie 2004; Abadinsky 2003, p. 112). Moreover, the more influential Mafia leaders were essentially absorbed into the Fascist political organization. The authoritarian hand of the totalitarian state impacted Sicily far more effectively than any previous interventions had managed. As Gaia Servadio notes, Sicily had historically resisted any external interference, and the Mafia had flourished as a result of weak central government (1978, p. 3). As a result of Mori's campaign, the Italian and Sicilian Mafia would be driven underground for much of the interwar period, only resurging during the Second World War (Wright 2006, pp. 104–05). Many of the Mafiosi who were not imprisoned, absorbed into the regime, or killed would emigrate to America.

In interwar America the Mafia flourished through the enabling prism of Prohibition. While the temperance movement in America had thrived in the later nineteenth century, it would not be until 1919 that the National Prohibition Act (the Volstead Act) was passed as the Eighteenth Amendment to the Constitution, providing for federal enforcement of the law and establishing a Prohibition Bureau. Thus, the evolution of organized crime in American cities during this era was closely connected to the enforcement of Prohibition, and to the opportunities presented by the illegal liquor trade. While organized crime groups certainly existed before Prohibition, their main enterprises were concerned with prostitution, gambling, and theft. Moreover, in terms of local and civic power structures, the gangsters rested somewhere near the bottom of a "highly stratified social milieu" (Abadinsky 2003, p. 67). Alan Block has pointed to the role of the racketeer in working with local unions and industry bosses, utilizing violent skills in order to control workers and keep down labor costs for employers (1994, p. 52). However, it would be the reforming impulse of Prohibition that would really enable the proliferation of organized crime in American cities through the enterprise of bootlegging, which, "with an enormous consumer base in place, with little opprobrium attached to drinking outside of fundamentalist religious groups, . . . did provide a vital new enterprise for those inclined to organized criminality" (pp. 53–54). The bootlegging of liquor required large-scale organization. Nevertheless, it was not predominately the old-style racketeers who made the most of these new business opportunities, but rather the rising generation of immigrants from Jewish and Italian backgrounds (Haller 1976, cited in Block 1994, p. 54).

With Prohibition, the character and activities of criminal gangs shifted. It has been argued by historians that in this period gangs became much more organized, and their impact was much wider than it had been prior to Prohibition (Abadinsky 2003, p. 67). Mark Haller, writing about Chicago, has noted, "Organized crime was important because of the relatively great wealth of the most successful criminals, because of the large numbers of persons directly employed by organized crime, and because of the still larger numbers who supplemented their income through various part time activities" (1971–1972, pp. 222–23). Indeed, not only did criminals reap the benefits of the restrictions on alcohol, but so did those public officials, police, and politicians who developed venal relationships with the gangsters. Michael Woodiwiss has argued that federal enforcement agents in the Federal Prohibition Unit, renamed the Prohibition Bureau in 1927, were known to support the activities of liquor smugglers by granting them permits, escorting liquor trucks, or giving them advance warning about raids (2001, p. 190). Consequently this period, up to the repeal of Prohibition in 1933, became the classic era of organized crime development, associated in the minds of many with the activities of figures such as Al Capone, Johnny Torrio, and Bugs Moran in Chicago, and Charles "Lucky" Luciano and Meyer Lansky in New York. Moreover, while the impact of the Wall Street crash and the subsequent Great Depression starting in 1929 may have narrowed the financial gains to be made from Prohibition, those who were not dead or in prison managed to diversify by the 1930s and 1940s into other spheres of business, including restaurants, night clubs, and gambling (Haller 1974, 5–6, cited in Abadinsky 2003, p. 68). As Nancy Lubin has noted, "although the Prohibition in 1933 marked the close of an era, it did not end organized crime. Instead, it merely forced the entities to diversify and use their new sophistication and capabilities in a variety of new schemes" (1994, p. 702). Finally, it is important to remember that the Prohibition era may have skewed discussions about the historical development of organized crime. Philip Bean (2010) believes that the impact of Prohibition on organized crime has been overstated, and that violent crime did not significantly increase during this period, but rather became more visible (p. 70). He suggests that the view that Prohibition was the major fuel for organized crime is a myth that has been promoted by Hollywood: "Its guns and gangster depiction is wildly inaccurate" (p. 69). Arguably, a similar increased visibility occurred in relation to concerns about gang crime in interwar Britain.

The British experience of organized crime in the first half of the twentieth century has been subject to little rigorous investigation. While a "narrative" of some of the best-known crime groups exists, it is highly problematic (McDonald 2010; Morton 1992). The criminologists Dick Hobbs and Alan Wright have both been cautious about accepting the descriptions of family groups like the Sabinis, who were active in London in the 1920s, as systematically organized. Hobbs sees the groups that can be identified in Britain starting in the late nineteenth century as "precursors" to the "creation of the organized crime menace and its subsequent institutionalization" (2013, p. 41). Wright notes, "In relation to the interwar criminal groups, it is not possible to claim with any legitimacy that the gangs described were formal-rational organizations" (2006, p. 167). Nevertheless, the gang activity in this period does have some shared features with that of Europe and North America. References to criminal gangs were made throughout the nineteenth century, but references to gangs that combined physical violence with illegal activities only became common in the interwar period (Shore 2014). These groups were distinct in that their involvement in forms of gambling, betting, and the associated protection business was clearly organized to some extent. Moreover, territory was not only linked to residence and/or leisure, but to the racecourses and their environs, where business took place.

The "racecourse-gangs" of this period were widely reported in the press (Shore 2014). Their activities revolved around the gambling and protection business, centered on horseracing tracks during the 1920s and moving into greyhound-racing tracks by the later 1920s and the 1930s. After the First World War, there was a significant surge in attendance at the races, leading to concerns about racecourse crime. However, there was also significant anxiety about violence and criminality in the postwar metropolis (Emsley 2008; Lawrence 2003). When territorial conflicts between the gangs involved in betting and protection activities spilled over onto metropolitan streets, reporting on such crime became more intense. Reports of the "racecourse wars," as they had become known, escalated in the mid-twenties, when a series of newspapers took interest in such gang violence on the streets of London and at various stations that were carrying passengers to the races (Shore 2014, pp. 359–60). At this point the controversial Home Secretary William Joynson Hicks became more vocally and visibly involved and "made a declaration of war on the race-gangs" (Shore 2011, pp. 21–22). To a large extent, race-gang activity seemed to recede from the public view after the mid-decade. While clearly some of these groups' activities continued, they were no longer reported with the same vigor by the press. During the 1930s, there was a brief revival of racing-related violence after a violent fracas involving men from the East London race-gangs took place at the Lewes races in Sussex (Shore 2014, pp. 361–62). It was this event that, according to film historian Steven Chibnall, was the influence for Graham Greene's 1938 novel *Brighton Rock* (2005, p. 17). A number of other individuals gained prominence in this period and have been the subject of both criminal biography and autobiography, and academic study. John "Ruby" Sparks's career as a "smash-and-grab" gangster, for example, has been examined by Alyson Brown (2011; Sparks 1961). As her work demonstrates, Sparks's criminal career as a "motor-bandit" reflected contemporary fears about new forms of organized criminality that were associated with the rise of gangsterism in North American cities in this period. Other individual criminals also gained some sort of distinction in the 1930s and during the Second World War. Two of the most well-known British criminals in this period were Billy Hill—the self-styled "Boss of Britain's Underworld"—and Jack "Spot" Comer. Both men, who were associates, exploited the black market opportunities of wartime Britain (Roodhouse 2013, pp. 15, 95; Murphy 1993).

During the early twentieth century, discussion of "professional" or organized criminality was frequently shaped by fears of external threats. Thus distinct discourses about alien criminality were common in the interwar period, and the foreign criminal was seen as an invasive force, with "foreign Jews" and Italians singled out not only by the press but also by some law enforcers who relied on easily perpetuated stereotypes when dealing with such groups of criminals. For example, in early 1923, at the Old Bailey trial of the Cortesi brothers, who had been charged with the attempted murder of Charles and Harry Sabini at the Fratellanza Club in Clerkenwell, Justice Darling remarked in his summing up that "the case reminded him of the old Italian feuds of the Montagues and Capulets and the 'Whites' and 'Blacks.' Although these parties could combine against people who they held to be a common enemy, they were always quarrelling among themselves" (*Times* [London], 18 January 1923). The connections between other forms of illegality and immorality and those perceived as foreigners was also apparent in the moral panics about drugs that have been examined by Marek Kohn (1992) and Lucy Bland (2013). In particular, the descriptions and treatment of the Anglo-Chinese Billy "Brilliant" Chang, who was prosecuted in 1924 for drug dealing and later deported, reflect the problematic connections made by contemporaries between drugs, illicit sexuality, and alien criminality (Bland 2013, pp. 65–69). The latter two factors were again linked in the vice empire of the Messina brothers, who were of Sicilian and Maltese descent. The brothers were involved with the London vice trade from the 1930s until the conviction of two of their number, Eugenio and Carmelo, for procuring in 1956 (*Times* [London], 7 July 1956; Slater 2007). Criminal groups like the Sabinis and the Messinas were easy to fit into the stereotypes of "hot-blooded" foreigners in interwar Britain. As Dick Hobbs has noted of the Messinas and their exposé by the *Sunday People* journalist Duncan Webb, "they were exotic and photogenic, prospering during the career of a publicity-hungry crusading journalist at a period in British history when, in a repeat of the racism that singled out the degenerate threat of alien sexuality in the aftermath of the First World War, traditional forces were trying to reassert themselves" (2013, p. 55).

II. Foundational Texts and Historical Approaches

As the preceding section might suggest, the study of organized crime is a wide and varied field, intersecting not only with the history of crime, policing, and the law, but also with histories of local government, politics, and immigration. A reader seeking historical perspectives on organized crime is faced with this somewhat amorphous field in terms of texts dealing directly with the issues of the historical underworld, organized banditry, and the development of "modern" incarnations of organized crime. Thus, in this section I will focus on two approaches. The first will survey the definitional texts on organized crime, many of which belong to the field of criminology rather than history. The second part will focus on more specifically historical approaches to the development of organized crime.

A. Foundational Texts

For the reader coming to the concept of historical organized crime for the first time, the North American texts remain the key canon. While definitions of organized crime continue to evolve, the writers of the 1960s and 1970s who first grappled theoretically with the "problem" of organized crime in the United States still shape our understanding today. The British criminologist Dick Hobbs has noted the problems in the study of organized crime, in this case in reference to Britain, as follows:

> In the face of a dearth of indigenous data, material from the USA is used extensively. Cross cultural applications are problematic in that much of this literature, from a range of sources, refers to phenomena that are culturally specific; this is particularly true of American studies of organized crime, which in their classic form tend to refer to large-scale organized criminality of the syndicated variety. (1994, p. 444)

Nevertheless, these texts remain the foundation for many studies of organized crime in the Western world. As we saw at the start of this chapter, Donald Cressey's work from the late 1960s and 1970s remains influential, despite its many detractors. Cressey (2008 [1969]) established the syndicate model of organized crime, claiming that organized crime in North America was composed of an alliance of twenty-four Mafia families, and was highly structured, tight-knit, and hierarchical. This view has been popularized in popular culture, particularly through Mario Puzo's novel *The Godfather* (1969) and the films of the 1970s. According to Cressey, the highest Mafia authority was the "Commission," which was made up of the rulers of the most powerful "families" (p. 111). Cressey's detailed reconstruction of the structures and management of the "Commission," "families," and geographically based "councils" depicts nothing less than a bureaucracy. This, then, is the business model of the Mafia, seductively echoed in early paradigms of criminal organization, such as that of Jonathan Wild, who was accused by contemporaries of having "form'd a Kind of Corporation of Thieves, of which he was the Head or Director" (Howson 1970, p. 238). While most criminologists and historians of American organized crime recognize the significance of Cressey's work, many have found problems with his model, not least in its limited application. Contemporaries such as Joseph Albini disagreed that organized crime was hierarchical. Instead, he understood it to consist of networks of clients and patrons in a system of "loosely structured relationship" (Albini 1971, p. 288; Wright 2006, pp. 4–5). Albini was part of a group of revisionists who would challenge Cressey's model and the dominant governmental definitions of organized crime over the following decades. This group included Francis and Elizabeth Ianni (1972), who argued that kinship groups formed the basis of organized crime rather than Cressey's corporations; Peter Reuter (1983), who put forward the theory of disorganized crime in response to a study of illegal markets in New York that demonstrated the diverse and fragmented nature of organized crime; and Alan Block (1982), whose historical analysis of organized crime in New York again found fragmentation and chaos rather than hierarchy and structure.

Other authors have looked more closely at the specialization and function of underworld roles. Most notable in this regard is the work of the American criminologist Carl B. Klockars, whose study *The Professional Fence*, published in 1974, has been profoundly influential. What distinguished Klockars from many of his contemporaries was his willingness to engage with historical precursors to modern organized crime, the approach adopted in his study of the eighteenth-century thief-taker Jonathan Wild. This sense of the longer historical trajectory can also be found in an early British writer of organized crime definitions, Mary McIntosh. Her book *The Organisation of Crime* (1975) was a pioneering text in which she identified four types of professional and organized crime: picaresque, craft, project, and business. The picaresque she described as a fairly permanent gang under the leadership of one man, corresponding approximately to the brigand or bandit gang. The craft organization included people committing skilled but small-scale thefts and cons. The project crime was typical of burglars, robbers, smugglers, or fraudsters, and involved more complex techniques and planning by a team of "specialists." The business organization was typical of those criminals who practised extortion and supplied illegal goods but had some degree of protection from the law (pp. 28–29). Like Klockars, McIntosh had a keen sense of historical precedents and included in her study references to banditry, a consideration of the "cant" language, and a short discussion of the career of the notable burglar of the 1870s Charlie Peace (pp. 18–27). Both McIntosh and Klockars were undoubtedly influenced by the work of Edwin Sutherland, who wrote his seminal study of the "professional thief" in 1937. This work, which followed the career of a professional thief named Chic Conwell, was a "monograph which tells how groups of men made a living by stealing, primarily by picking pockets, shoplifting and operating confidence games" (Snodgrass 1973, p. 3). Sutherland's work is regarded as a foundational text of the Chicago school of sociology and also of the development of theoretical writing about organized crime ever since.

B. Historical Approaches

Beyond these important foundational texts, a valuable survey can be found in the work of the criminologist Alan Wright, who covers British, American, and some European organized crime groups in his aptly titled survey *Organized Crime* (2006). Wright has a strong sense of historical context that makes this book useful for the student of organized crime in past societies. Similarly, the extensive work of Dick Hobbs on organized crime (1994; 1995) has much to offer. His *Lush Life: Constructing Organized Crime in the UK* (2013) blends ethnographic study with a detailed historical survey of organized crime groups in London from the later nineteenth century. A starting point for those seeking some understanding of continuity and change in British organized crime is the article by Jenkins and Potter (1988) that deals with the precursors to the "family firms" of the era following the Second World War. British historians other than those already mentioned in section I have not embraced the critical study of organized crime. Perhaps because clear definitions are elusive, few historians have attempted to come to grips with the underworld in anything but a cursory manner. Part of the problem, in British as well as more global crime-writing cultures, is the predominance of "true crime" texts and popular histories that have tended to perpetuate a highly problematic and uncritical approach to the sources (Thomas 1998; Thomas 2005; Chesney 1970). However, historians of crime have started to problematize historical ideas about and attitudes toward criminal organization and to think about the role of local institutions— such as the police and other law enforcers—and the media in constructing the underworld "myth" (Slater 2009; Shore 2015). Recent work on criminal individuals and crime groups associated with organized crime is rooted in careful scholarly research (Brown 2011; Davies 2013; Roodhouse 2011; Shore 2015). For example, Andrew Davies's (2013) work on Glasgow and the rise of the gangster during the 1920s and 1930s combines the ethnographic approach of scholars such as Sutherland with a strong sense of historical context and sensitivity to the source material.

While other countries, as we have seen in section I, do have a range of texts dealing with organized crime history, many have not been published in English. Diego Gambetta (1996) and Judith Chubb (1982) have written with great authority on the development of Italian organized crime from its peasant roots in the south. At least a cursory understanding of Italian, and particularly Sicilian, crime groups would seem important to those who want to understand the evolution of organized crime in North America. Other authors have sought to develop a more global understanding of organized crime history. For example, the varied collection edited by Mark Galeotti (2008) ranges across a broad spectrum of time and space, including studies on organized crime in tsarist Russia as well as in occupied France. A useful study that includes some historical overview of European and North American organized crime is that of Howard Abadinsky (2003), whose broad survey includes chapters on Italy, Russia, Latin America, and Asian gangs alongside studies of organized crime in New York and Chicago. There is also a well-established literature dealing with iterations of organized gangs of bandits and brigands in early modern Europe, but the later eighteenth century onward is less well served. Individual country studies suggest that this is a thriving field; however, an accessible survey or monograph text that would provide those new to the field with some overview of historical developments has yet to be written. There are some useful accounts that consider European perspectives. For example, Alan A. Block's (1994) work on American organized crime is very strongly rooted in the broader European experience. And, while it does not specifically deal with historical analyses, the collection edited by Cyrille Fijnaut and Letizia Paoli entitled *Organized Crime in Europe: Concepts, Patterns and Control Policies in the European Union and Beyond* (2004) includes an excellent set of papers on the history of organized crime in different European countries, although the earlier period dominates here. Finally, Paul Knepper's (2009) work on white slave trading, alien criminality, and the evolution of international crime networks is particularly useful in helping to understand how changes in rhetoric and concepts of organized crime had shifted from local and regional disputes to a transnational theater by the late nineteenth and early twentieth centuries. Moreover, Knepper has also investigated the League of Nations in the interwar period, particularly in relation to its crime remit and the establishment of the Advisory Committee on the Traffic in Women and Children in 1921 (2011; 2014, pp. 405–06).

CONCLUSION

Knepper's work shows us how the paradigm of organized crime has shifted, for law enforcers as well as for historians and criminologists, to a more global stage in recent decades (2009; 2011). Talking about the development of organized crime in the twentieth and twenty-first centuries, Mark Galeotti has identified the key activities of organized crime as narcotics, people trafficking, and cyberspace (2005, pp. 2–4). Moreover, the "underworld" has become increasingly transnational, particularly with the rise of Russian and other Eastern European crime groups since the 1980s. Hence future historians may well move away from the more rural and urban studies that have dominated the histories of organized crime and the underworld for our period. While early twentieth-century studies of the Mafia, and particularly of the cross-fertilization of such organizations between Europe and the United States, arguably mark the beginning of the identification of these groups as a more global threat, for much of our period, criminal organization remained regional and local. Indeed, Dick Hobbs has stated that the role of transnationalism has been overstated, and that much organized crime remains a local phenomenon characterized by alliances with global (or, as he coins it, "glocal") markets (2013, p. 223). The nineteenth-century "underworld" as a serious area of study still remains problematic. While, as this chapter has demonstrated, there has been significant exploration of the cultural and social constructions of the underworld, there are few detailed studies of extensive criminal networks. Of course, eighteenth- and nineteenth-century criminal networks, even if we accept that such networks existed in any sort of organized form, are fundamentally elusive. Even in the arguably better-documented twentieth century, the "myth" of organized crime and the influence impact of its networks have troubled some commentators (Smith 1975; Bean 2010, pp. 69–70). Thus the "underworld" remains hidden. Moreover, in the late twentieth and twenty-first centuries, the reach of the underworld is aided by the ever-stretching tentacles of the Internet, and our understanding of what it really constitutes remains flawed.

REFERENCES

Abadinsky, Howard. 2003. *Organized Crime*. Belmont, CA: Wadsworth.

Albini, Joseph. 1971. *The American Mafia: Genesis of a Legend*. New York: Appleton Century Crofts.

Anbinder, Tyler. 2001. *Five Points: The 19th-Century New York City Neighbourhood that Invented Tap Dance, Stole Elections and Became the World's Most Notorious Slum*. New York: Free Press.

Asbury, Herbert. 1928. *The Gangs of New York: An Informal History of the Underworld*. New York: Paragon House.

Asbury, Herbert. 1936. *The French Quarter: An Informal History of the New Orleans Underworld*. London: Jarrolds.

Asbury, Herbert. 1940. *Gem of the Prairie: An Informal History of the Chicago Underworld*. New York: Knopf.

Bean, Philip. 2010. *Legalising Drugs: Debates and Dilemmas*. Bristol, UK: Policy Press.

Beattie, John. 2001. *Policing and Punishment in London, 1660–1750: Urban Crime and the Limits of Terror*. Oxford: Oxford University Press.

Behan, Tom. 1995. *The Camorra: Political Criminality in Italy*. Abingdon, UK: Routledge.

Bland, Lucy. 2013. *Modern Women on Trial: Sexual Transgression in the Age of the Flapper*. Manchester, UK: Manchester University Press.

Block, Alan A. 1982. *East Side—West Side: Organizing Crime in New York, 1930–1950*. New Brunswick, NJ: Transaction.

Block, Alan A., ed. 1994. *Space, Time and Organised Crime*. New Brunswick, NJ: Transaction.

Booth, Martin.1990. *The Triads: The Chinese Criminal Fraternity*. London: Grafton.

Brown, Alyson. 2011. "Crime, Criminal Mobility and Serial Offenders in Early Twentieth Century Britain." *Contemporary British History* 25 (4): 551–68.

Campbell, Helen. 1899. *Darkness and Daylight; or, Lights and Shadows of New York Life with Thrilling Personal Experiences in the Underworld of the Great Metropolis*. Hartford, CT: Hartford Publishing Company.

Chesney, Kellow. 1970. *The Victorian Underworld*. London: Temple Smith.

Chibnall, Steve. 2005. *Brighton Rock*. London: Tauris.

Chubb, Judith. 1982. *Patronage, Power and Poverty in Southern Europe: A Tale of Two Cities*. Cambridge: Cambridge University Press.

Cole, Simon A. 2001. *Suspect Identities: A History of Fingerprinting and Criminal Identification*. Cambridge, MA: Harvard University Press.

Collins, Randall. 1975. *Conflict Sociology*. New York: Academic Press.

Crapsey, Edward. 1872. *The Nether Side of New York: Or, the Vice, Crime and Poverty of the Metropolis*. New York: Sheldon & Company.

Cressey, Donald R., ed. 2008 [1969]. *Theft of the Nation: The Structure and Operations of Organised Crime in America*. New Brunswick, NJ: Transaction.

Critchley, David. 2009. *The Origins of Organized Crime in America: The New York City Mafia, 1891–1931*. Abingdon, UK: Routledge.

Danker, Uwe. 2001. *Die Geschichte der Räuber und Gauner*. Berlin: Artemis & Winkler.

Davies, Andrew. 2013. *City of Gangs: Glasgow and the Rise of the British Gangster*. London: Hodder and Stoughton.

De Witt Talmage, Thomas. 1891. *The Night Scenes of City Life*. Chicago: Donohue, Henneberry & Co.

Dickie, John. 2004. *Cosa Nostra: A History of the Sicilian Mafia*. Basingstoke, UK: Palgrave Macmillan.

Egmond, Florike. 1993. *Underworlds: Organized Crime in the Netherlands, 1650–1800*. Cambridge: Polity.

Ellington, George. 1869. *The Women of New York; or, the Under-world of the Great City. Illustrating the Life of Women of Fashion, Women of Pleasure, Actresses and Ballet Girls, Saloon Girls, Pickpockets and Shoplifters, Artists' Female Models, Women-of-the-Town, Etc.* New York: New York Book Company.

Emsley, Clive. 2008. "Violent Crime in England in 1919: Post-War Anxieties and Press Narratives." *Continuity and Change* 23:173–95.

Emsley, Clive. 2011. *Crime and Society in Twentieth-Century England*. Harlow, UK: Pearson.

Evans, Richard J. 1998. *Tales from the German Underworld: Crime and Punishment in the Nineteenth Century*. New Haven, CT: Yale University Press.

Ewing Ritchie, James. 1858. *The Night Side of London*. London: William Tweedie.

Fijnaut, Cyrille, & Letizia Paoli, eds. 2004. *Organized Crime in Europe: Concepts, Patterns and Control Policies in the European Union and Beyond*. Dordrecht, The Netherlands: Springer.

Finkelstein, Monte S. 1998. *Separatism, the Allies and the Mafia: The Struggle for Sicilian Independence, 1943–1948*. Cranbury, NJ: Associated University Presses.

Galeotti, Mark, ed. 2005. *Global Crime Today: The Changing Face of Organised Crime*. Oxford: Routledge.

Galeotti, Mark, ed. 2008. *Organised Crime in History*. London: Routledge.

Gambetta, Diego. 1996. *The Sicilian Mafia: The Business of Private Protection*. Cambridge, MA: Harvard University Press.

Gilfoyle, Timothy J. 1992. *City of Eros: New York City, Prostitution, and the Commercialisation of Sex, 1790–1920*. London: Norton.

Godfrey, Barry. S., David J. Cox, & Stephen J. Farrall. 2010. *Serious Offenders: A Historical Study of Habitual Criminals*. Oxford: Oxford University Press.

Golway, Terry. 2014. *Machine Made: Tammany Hall and the Creation of Modern American Politics*. New York: Liveright.

Haller, Mark, H. 1971–1972. "Organized Crime in Urban Society: Chicago in the Twentieth Century." *Journal of Social History* 5 (2): 210–34.

Haller, Mark, H. 1976. "Bootleggers in American Gambling, 1920–1950." In *Commission on Review of National Policy Toward Gambling: Gambling in America*, Appendix 1: 108–115. Washington, D.C.: Government Printing Office.

Hill, Peter. 2005. "The Changing Face of the Yakuza." *Global Crime* 6 (1): 97–116.

Hobbs, Dick. 1994. "Professional and Organized Crime in Britain." In *The Oxford Handbook of Criminology*, ed. Mike Maguire, Rod Morgan, & Robert Reiner, 441–68. Oxford: Oxford University Press.

Hobbs, Dick. 1995. *Bad Business: Professional Crime in Modern Britain*. Oxford: Oxford University Press.

Hobbs, Dick. 2013. *Lush Life: Constructing Organized Crime in the UK*. Oxford: Oxford University Press.

Hobsbawm, Eric. 1969. *Bandits*. London: Weidenfield & Nicolson.

Hobsbawm, Eric, ed. 1981 [1959]. *Primitive Rebels*. Manchester, UK: Manchester University Press.

Holmes, Thomas. 1912. *London's Underworld*. London: Dent & Sons.

Houlbrook, Matthew. 2013. "Fashioning an Ex-Crook Self: Citizenship and Criminality in the work of Netley Lucas." *Twentieth Century British History* 24 (1): 1–30.

Howson, Gerald. 1970. *Thief-Taker General: The Rise and Fall of Jonathan Wild*. London: Hutchinson.

Huston, Peter. 1995. *Tongs, Gangs, and Triads: Chinese Crime Groups in North America*. Boulder, CO: Paladin.

Ianni, Francis A. J., & Elizabeth R. Ianni. 1972. *A Family Business: Kinship and Social Control in Organized Crime*. New York: Russell Sage Foundation.

Jenkins, Phillip, & Potter Gary. W. 1988. "Before the Krays: Organized Crime in London, 1920–1960." *Criminal Justice History* 9:209–30.

Kaplan, David E., & Alec Dubro, eds. 2012 [2003]. *Yakuza: Japan's Criminal Underworld*. Berkeley: University of California Press.

Kinney, Arthur F. 1973. *Rogues, Vagabonds, and Sturdy Beggars: A New Gallery of Tudor and Early Stuart Rogue Literature*. Amherst: University of Massachusetts Press.

Klockars, Carl B. 1974. *The Professional Fence*. New York: Free Press.

Knepper, Paul. 2009. *The Invention of International Crime: A Global Issue in the Making, 1881–1914*. Basingstoke, UK: Palgrave Macmillan.

Knepper, Paul. 2011. *International Crime in the Twentieth Century: The League of Nations, 1919–1939*. London: Palgrave Macmillan.

Knepper, Paul. 2014. "International Criminals: The League of Nations, the Traffic in Women, and the Press." *Media History* 20 (4): 400–15.

Kobler, John. 1971. *Capone: The Life and World of Al Capone*. Boston: Da Capo Press.

Kohn, Marek. 1992. *Dope Girls: The Birth of the British Drug Underground*. London: Granta.

Küther, Carsten. 1976. *Robbers and Crooks in Germany: The Organized Gangs in the 18th and 19th Centuries*. Göttingen, Germany: Vandenhoeck & Ruprecht.

Lange, Katrin. 2004. "Many a Lord Is Guilty, Indeed for Many a Poor Man's Dishonest Deed: Gangs of Robbers in Early Modern Germany." In *Organised Crime in Europe: Concepts, Patterns and Control Policies in the European Union and Beyond*, ed. Cyrille Fijnaut & Letizia Paoli, 109–49. Dordrecht, The Netherlands: Springer.

Lawrence, Jon. 2003. "Forging a Peaceable Kingdom: War, Violence, and Fear of Brutalisation in Post-First World War Britain." *Journal of Modern History* 75:557–89.

Lindström, Dag. 2004. "Historical Perspectives: Swedish and International Examples." In *New Perspectives in Economic Crime*, ed. Hans Sjögren & Göran Skogh, 127–57. Cheltenham, UK: Edward Elgar.

Lubin, Nancy. 1994. "Organized Crime." In *Encyclopedia of Social History*, ed. Peter N. Stearns, 700–03. New York: Garland.

Mallory, Stephen L. 2012. *Understanding Organized Crime*. Sudbury, MA: Jones & Barlett.

Maltz, Michael. 1976. "On Defining Organized Crime: The Development of a Definition and Typology." *Crime and Delinquency* 22 (3): 338–46.

McCabe, James D. 1872. *Lights and Shadows of New York Life*. Philadelphia: National Publishing Company.

McDonald, Brian. 2010. *The Gangs of London: 100 Years of Mob Warfare*. Wrea Green, UK: Milo Books.

McGowen, Randall. 1990. "Getting to Know the Criminal Class in Nineteenth Century England." *Nineteenth Century Contexts* 14:33–54.

McIntosh, Mary. 1975. *The Organisation of Crime*. London: Macmillan.

McMullan, John L. 1986. *The Canting Crew: London's Criminal Underworld, 1550–1700*. New Brunswick, NJ: Rutgers University Press.

Morain, Alfred. 1930. *The Underworld of Paris: Secrets of the Sûreté*. London: Jarrolds.

Morton, James. 1992. *Gangland: London's Underworld*. London: Little Brown.

Murphy, Robert. 1993. *Smash and Grab: Gangsters in the London Underworld*. London: Faber and Faber.

Paoli, Letizia. 2004. "Organised Crime in Italy: Mafia and Illegal Markets—Exception and Normality." In *Organised Crime in Europe: Concepts, Patterns and Control Policies in the European Union and Beyond*, ed. Cyrille Fijnaut & Letizia Paoli, 263–302. Dordrecht, The Netherlands: Springer.

Petrow, Stefan. 1993. "The Rise of the Detective in London, 1869–1914." *Criminal Justice History* 14:91–108.

Pick, Daniel. 1989. *Faces of Degeneration: A European Disorder, c. 1848–c. 1918*. Cambridge: Cambridge University Press.

Reuter, Peter. 1983. *Disorganised Crime: The Economics of the Visible Hand*. Cambridge, MA: MIT Press.

Reynolds, G. W. M. 1844. *The Mysteries of London*. London: George Vickers.

Roodhouse, Mark. 2011. "In Racket Town: Gangster Chic in Austerity Britain, 1939–1953." *Historical Journal of Film, Television and Radio* 31 (4): 523–41.

Rook, Clarence. 1899. *The Hooligan Nights*. London: Grant Richards.

Rosenwaike, Ira. 1972. *Population History of New York City*. Syracuse, NJ: Syracuse University Press.

Schlör, Joachim. 1998. *Nights in the Big City: Paris, Berlin, London, 1840–1930*. London: Reaktion Books.

Servadio, Gaia. 1978. *Mafioso: A History of the Mafia from Its Origins to the Present Day*. New York: Dell.

Shore, Heather. 2011. "Criminality and Englishness in the Aftermath: The Racecourse Wars of the 1920s." *Twentieth Century British History* 22:474–97.

Shore, Heather. 2014. "'Rogues of the Racecourse': Racing Men and the Press in Interwar Britain." *Media History* 20 (4): 352–67.

Shore, Heather. 2015. *London's Criminal Underworlds, c. 1720–1930: A Social and Cultural History*. Basingstoke, UK: Palgrave Macmillan.

Slater, Stefan. 2007. "Pimps, Police and Filles de Joie: Foreign Prostitution in Interwar London." *London Journal* 32 (1): 53–74.

Slater, Stefan. 2009. "Prostitutes and Popular History: Notes on the 'Underworld,' 1918–1939." *Crime, Histoire & Sociétés* 13 (1): 25–48.

Smith, Dwight, C. 1975. *The Mafia Mystique*. New York: Basic Books.

Smith, Dwight C. 1976. "Mafia: The Prototypical Alien Conspiracy." *Annals of the American Academy of Political and Social Science* 423:75–88.

Snodgrass, Jon. 1973. "The Criminologist and His Criminal: The Case of Edwin H. Sutherland and Broadway Jones." *Issues in Criminology* 8:1–17.

Sparks, Ruby. 1961. *Burglar to the Nobility*. London: Barker.

Sue, Eugène. 1842. *Les Mystères de Paris*. Paris: Gosselin.

Sutherland, Edwin. 1937. *The Professional Thief*. Chicago: Chicago University Press.

Thomas, Donald. 1998. *Victorian Underworld*. London: John Murray.

Thomas, Donald. 2005. *Villains' Paradise: Britain's Underworld from the Spivs to the Krays*. London: John Murray.

Toth, Stephen. 2006. *Beyond Papillon: The French Overseas Penal Colonies, 1854–1952*. Lincoln: University of Nebraska Press.

U.S. Congress. 1967. *Congressional Record*, vol. 113, 29 November.

Vigar Harris, Henry. 1885. *London at Midnight*. London: General Publishing Company.

Ward, Richard. 2014. *Print Culture, Crime and Justice in Eighteenth-Century London*. London: Bloomsbury.

Woodiwiss, Michael. 2001. *Organized Crime and American Power: A History*. Toronto: Toronto University Press.

Wright, Alan. 2006. *Organized Crime*. Cullompton, UK: Willan.

CHAPTER 9

TERRORISM AND ITS POLICING

Anarchists and the Era of Propaganda by the Deed, 1870s–1914

CONSTANCE BANTMAN

INTRODUCTION

BETWEEN its emergence in the 1870s and the beginning of the First World War, the public perception of the anarchist movement, as well as the theoretical and legal frameworks used to comprehend and control it, underwent a dual process of criminalization and internationalization. Anarchism evolved from being tolerated, however unsympathetically, as a manifestation of advanced political radicalism to being identified as a political crime sanctioned by extensive laws at the national level and controlled internationally through comprehensive protocols and extradition and deportation measures. The use of terrorism by anarchists was pivotal to this process, as was its reception by alarmed populations and governments faced with unprecedented forms of political violence. In order to quell what was understood as a terrorist epidemic with global ramifications, radically new steps were taken: these included specific laws to define and tackle political offenses (usually in connection with anti-immigration measures), the creation of national police forces, and, beginning at the end of the nineteenth century, the development of increasingly formal and coordinated processes of international policing. This process affected most European nations and the Americas in a considerably similar manner, making anarchism, as well as its reception and treatment in mature industrial economies (in Europe and the United States) and countries faced with soaring immigration and rapid urbanization (in Latin America), a clear instance of the globalization of militant politics.

One decisive element in the perceived depoliticization of anarchism and its categorization as a criminal pursuit was the terrorist wave that started in the late 1880s, peaked in the early 1890s, and continued to claim lives and grab headlines more sporadically up to and beyond 1918. This protracted terrorist episode was largely due to the spread of "propaganda by the deed," a theory that was interpreted as justifying the use of violence as a means of publicizing anarchist ideas and accelerating the onset of revolution. This advocacy of political violence, which was relatively short-lived and far from unanimous among anarchists, was compounded by the complex sociological makeup of their militant circles, within which minor offenders and many shady characters could easily aggregate, blurring the boundaries between radical politics and criminality. This coincided with a specific socioeconomic and cultural moment and a collective sense of crisis at the end of the Second Industrial Revolution. The rise of organized labor movements and socialist parties, along with an acute growth of inequalities and the development of mass migration, were increasingly perceived as an economic, cultural, and racial threat that created a propitious atmosphere for red scares and popular xenophobia, for which the anarchists were obvious catalysts. The development of yellow journalism set the scene for a perfect storm, fanning the fear of anarchism by capitalizing on the lurid headlines that the movement afforded. A radically new inflection was added by the geographic scale on which anarchists acted and the destructive new techniques that they could use: as a precarious yet truly global movement, the moral panic that anarchism triggered was tied in with globalization and the sense of an interconnected world where deadly danger might strike anyone at any time.

Given anarchism's era-defining connection with terrorism, this theme has loomed large in the historiography of the movement. However, important limitations in understanding anarchism solely through the lens of political violence and criminal history must also be highlighted. First, in political and philosophical terms, this approach offers a very limited and erroneous perspective on a very complex and profoundly humanist and progressive body of ideas. Anarchism did incorporate temporarily an apology of political violence and, like any terrorist movement, repeatedly treaded the very fine line between illegality and ideologically motivated violence, even after the demise of propaganda by the deed. However, most committed anarchists espoused educationalism and pacifism far more durably (Graham 2005; Kinna & Davies 2009). Recent historiographic research into classical anarchism has further debunked the terrorist stereotype by emphasizing its exemplarity as an instance of network-based transnational militancy (Bantman 2006; Turcato 2007), the anarchist contribution to national emancipation struggles (Hirsch & Van der Walt 2010), and the lasting connection of anarchism with the labor movement, notably through revolutionary syndicalism. Another flaw of the criminal perspective stems from its focus on the relatively narrow time frame of pre–First World War "heroic" anarchism, leaving aside the subtle genealogies and important influences of anarchist ideas that came before and after (Ryley 2013). These are the years on which this contribution centers too, narrowing the focus down to the peak of the anarchist terrorist scare, when the movement's perceived association with political violence reached its height. One downside of this time frame is, of course, that it replicates the traditional chronology of terrorism-themed narratives of anarchism and espouses a largely Western-centric final date to discuss a truly global movement. It also leaves out subsequent terrorist episodes in an effort to avoid conflating widely different periods. Despite these limitations, a wide criminological angle that incorporates the notion of crime as a social and legal construct, even within a relatively limited time frame, has the merit of highlighting some of the conditions in which anarchism emerged and became so dreaded by contemporaries at the end of the nineteenth century, as well as some of its transformative impacts on police systems and practices nationally and globally. Even while being very reductionist and derogatory, it does capture a significant proportion of the social, cultural, and legal history of anarchism.

The first section of this essay charts the development of the ideology of propaganda by the deed from the 1870s onward, and the wave of "anarchist" terrorist attacks that followed a decade later. The second section examines how anarchism was consequently—and largely mistakenly—constructed as a crime. This perception led to the adoption of new or extended policing practices at the regional, national, and international levels, which are examined in the third section. The conclusion assesses the benefits and limitations of understanding the history of the anarchist movement through a criminological lens.

I. Propaganda by the Deed and the Anarchist Terrorist Wave

Terrorism was the main form of crime with which anarchists were identified. This conflation was only superficially true, but it was both very pervasive and very long lasting. So deep and multifaceted was the impact of the terrorist episode that started in the early 1880s that David Rapoport has identified "the anarchist wave" as the first of "four waves of terror", born of new technological conditions and "the failure of a democratic reform program," that have continued to the present day (2004, p. 65). The reactive construction of anarchism's criminal status was an incremental and uneven process that often met with some resistance.

Anarchism, a libertarian variant of socialism, emerged as an organized (albeit anti-hierarchical) movement in the 1870s in the Jura-based sections of the First International Workingmen's Association. It is notoriously difficult to put forward a simple definition of this complex political doctrine, which is best thought of as a fluid and very rich tradition, incorporating notions from ancient philosophies, the Enlightenment, utopian socialism, and Marxism, whose boundaries remain cause for numerous controversies. The traditional anarchist pantheon is usually taken to comprise William Godwin, Pierre-Joseph Proudhon, Mikhail Bakunin, and Peter Kropotkin, and the movement's forerunners are often located in Taoism and among the seventeenth-century English Diggers and the French Revolutionary period. Post-1870s anarchism comprised three main strands: communist anarchism, individualist anarchism, and syndicalism, all of which encompassed different subgroups and affiliations and embraced many causes, from workers' rights and anticolonialism to environmental concerns and gender equality (Graham 2005). Some academics—and legislators—especially concerned with the movement's first terrorist period have also suggested a division between "violent" and "philosophical" anarchists (Kraut 2012), which does not correspond to either the actual structure of anarchist milieus or actual ideological differentiations, but has the merit of emphasizing the extent to which terrorism came and sometimes continues to be seen as the ultimate defining trait of anarchism.

In the late 1870s, when anarchist circles were starting to take shape in several countries, a theory known as "propaganda by the deed" gained ground among European anarchists. It drew on earlier insurrectionist doctrines and interventions, notably a failed attempt at igniting a peasant revolt in Italy's Calabria initiated by revolutionaries Carlo Cafiero and Errico Malatesta. The Russian anarchist Mikhail Bakunin had indeed previously advocated insurrection and violence as the first steps of the revolution; his ideas were reformulated in August 1877 by the French anarchist Paul Brousse in an article that defined propaganda by the deed as "a mighty means of rousing the popular consciousness" (Stafford 1971). At that stage the term referred to revolutionary action (France's Commune was cited as an example), and violence was not mentioned explicitly (Graham 2005, pp. 151–152); the violent inflection was added in 1880 in an article by Cafiero in the Paris-based paper *Le Révolté*: "Our action must be permanent rebellion, by word, by writing, by dagger, by gun, by dynamite. . . . We shall use every weapon which can be used for rebellion. Everything is right for us which is not legal" (Graham 2005, p. 152). Closely related to propaganda by the deed was the broader notion of anarchist "illegalism," which was defined in the early 1880s as a kind of publicity strategy for the movement, unfolding through transgressive and symbolic gestures such as swindling, moonlight flits, and robberies on various scales, which taken together can be interpreted as "a direct and violent reaction against economic and social organisation by those left behind by the system" (Manfredonia 1984, p. 400). But, of course, this espousal of illegal appropriation was also a convenient decoy for robbers and gangsters with tenuous connections with anarchist ideas, and it was soon decried by the majority of anarchists.[1] As Jose C. Moya has noted in the Argentinian context, "anarchism embraced all sorts of marginal groups. . . . Common delinquents often couched their activities in the language of anarchism and hung around anarchist centers" (2004, p. 22). Thus, adding to the fear of and disrepute to the movement brought on by terrorist involvements, the perception of anarchism as a criminal activity was compounded by the opaque sociology of anarchist circles; "sincere" militants (some of whom only briefly dabbled with anarchism) coexisted with a vast transient population of infiltrated police spies, informers, petty criminals, robbers, and pimps. One notorious example is that of the Franco-Italian gangs of robbers organized around Luigi Parmeggiani and operating between France, Italy, and Britain around 1890 (Di Paola 2013). Pimps were especially prominent among the Jewish population of Buenos Aires, and many of them were deported together. This reinforced both the real and the perceived association between anarchism and crime created by the specter of terrorism.

The movement's emphasis on violence was enshrined at the 1881 Social Revolutionary Congress held in London; by the end of the decade, ideas gave way to a wave of anarchist-inspired terrorist attacks. As with most terrorist waves, recent technological developments played a key role in this process: in this instance, bombs were the anarchists' weapon of choice, relying on Alfred Nobel's 1866 invention of dynamite.

Few Western countries were spared by the terrorist wave that started in the late 1880s. Notable precedents had been set by Max Hödel's assassination attempt against Kaiser Wilhelm I in 1878 and the assassination of Tsar Alexander II by Russian nihilists in March 1881. Richard Bach Jensen has provided a detailed analytical inventory of acts of propaganda by the deed, stressing that they were "a curious combination of the acts of ideologically committed anarchists and of the violent deeds of a miscellany of perpetrators who shared dubious or no connections with anarchism" (2013, p. 23). However, such nuances rarely penetrated public opinion. In the 1880s and early 1890s, terrorist rhetoric was omnipresent in anarchists' language: many comrades engaged in the fabrication of explosives, or boasted that they did (Bantman 2013). For a period of time, it was customary for perpetrators of terrorist acts to declare themselves anarchists and use their trials as an opportunity to publicize their beliefs (Merriman 2009). Their publications notoriously circulated instructions to that end, such as the French *Indicateur anarchiste*, which was reprinted internationally. The extent to which this was engineered by provocateurs remains to be established, however, as there is clear evidence that the most vocal advocates of terrorism on paper were often in the pay of the police. According to Jensen, "the anarchists organized very few conspiracies and many acts of 'anarchist' terrorism were not committed by the anarchists at all, but by nationalists, radicals, socialists, police spies, and the mentally unbalanced" (2013, p. 3).

The 1890s was "the decade of regicide" (Jensen 2013, p. 31), with the deaths of French president Sadi Carnot (killed at the hands of Italian anarchist Santo Caserio in 1894), Spanish prime minister Antonio Canovas (killed by Michele Angiolillo in 1897), Empress Elizabeth of Austria (1898), Italian king Umberto I and U.S. president William McKinley (1901), and King George of Greece (1913)—to name only successful attempts. Other targets included industrialists (as with Alexander Berkman's attack on Henry Clay Frick), political institutions (a bomb was thrown in the French Deputy Chamber in 1892), symbols of imperial domination (Greenwich Observatory), fashionable places attended by the upper classes and taken to symbolize bourgeois oppression and wastefulness (as with Barcelona's Liceo Theatre and Paris's Café Terminus, both of which were attacked in 1893; the former saw twenty-two fatalities), and figures of the legal system involved in the sentencing of anarchists. All in all, Jensen calculates that "for the period 1878–1914 (excluding Russia) more than 200 people died and over 750 were injured as a result of real or alleged anarchist attacks throughout the globe. This includes a number of anarchists who accidentally blew themselves up with their own bombs" (2013, p. 36). However, having examined the 1880s wave closely, Jensen concludes that actual links with anarchist were tenuous, and that the equation of anarchism and terrorism and vice versa was largely a construct of public opinion, to which anarchists who praised acts of violence contributed. There were also pacifist, nonviolent currents within anarchism, and educationalist perspectives came to prevail after 1894, but by that stage the move-ment had taken a very different turn. Another limitation to this terrorist outburst was the short-lived support that it garnered among the anarchists, and especially the move-ment's intelligentsia, with the notable exception of Elisée Reclus in France and a longer commitment in the United States, notably on the part of Emma Goldman.

While terrorism and propaganda by the deed strongly contributed to the impression of an irrepressible terrorist outburst, local circumstances and variations are also notice-able, as national movements were strongly localized in their causes and manifestations. Thus, acts of violence were closely connected with labor protests in the United States, a characteristic also observed in Latin America (Argentina). Other countries seemed immune from terrorist attacks thanks to their tolerance of anarchists (Britain), whereas more repressive states suffered the more violent attacks (France, Italy, Spain). In Spain, anarchism and its repression were tied in with the influence of clericalism in the coun-try. In the United States and in Britain, the chronological coincidence and suspected overlap of anarchist terrorism with Irish nationalism presented another specificity, which for the former would partly determine the reshaping of the police surveillance organization.

II. Constructing Anarchism as Crime

As a result of the terrorist evolution of the anarchist movement, in spite of its limited and short-lived character, and due to its connection with labor organizations and pro-test movements as well as with immigration, a decisive shift from the political to the criminal in the perception of the movement took place from the late 1880s onward.

Bombs initiated a new age of terror because of their indiscriminate, impersonal, and omnipresent nature: anyone was a potential target, and danger could strike at any time. This conveyed a different political message too: that anyone was an accomplice in the unjust order of things, whereas previous waves of political attacks had aimed for clear political targets in a specific political context. This lack of immediate intel-ligibility, combined with the brutality of the attacks, meant that they seemed bound to repeat themselves according to an indecipherable logic (Rapoport 2004; Salomé 2011, pp. 263–72). In practice, however, the anarchists' targets were highly symbolic and far from indiscriminate. Nor was the bomb their sole weapon, since daggers and pistols were used too, notably in assassinations of political figures. But in the public imagi-nation, anarchist terrorism was closely connected with technological modernity, and mass newspapers as well as police archives abounded with wild speculations regard-ing the anarchists' next invention (Porter 1992). Developments in transportation and communication were another link between the anarchist terrorist wave and technol-ogy. Through work migration, exile, and communication, they allowed the movement to become fully global in scope. New means of communication also publicized the movement's transnational nature: European newspapers frequently reported on the activities of U.S. anarchists, and the other way around. The collective imagination, greatly helped by the media, became obsessed with the idea of a global anarchist conspiracy intent on destroying civilization. This tarnished not only all of the anarchist movement, but also other socialist currents and some workers' organizations, even as these distanced themselves from anarchism. It has been noted by several historians of European anarchism that the anarchists' celebration of violence, as well as the moral panic that constituted the dominant response to the movement, were symptoms of a *fin de siècle* fascination with decadence, violence, and evil confederacies. Anarchism thrived on an apocalyptic imagination in which violence appeared as purifying, but also fed public fears of an imminent catastrophe (Melchiori 1985; Porter 1992; Rioux 1991; Salomé 2011, pp. 29–30). This betrayed widespread anxiety about immigration, unemployment, threats to imperial hegemony, the rise of an organized labor movement, and parliamentary socialism—all of which were perceived as facets of a dangerous modernity.

Testifying to the remarkable role of print media in shaping perceptions of crime, periodicals and a number of essays and semi-fictional accounts played a key part in sharpening the collective dread in the face of the anarchist peril. The anarchist frenzy coincided with the rise of "New Journalism" and the successes of cheap newspapers that were addressed to a large working-class readership and showcased crime, scandal, disaster, and sports, with bolder and more lurid headlines and subheads. Anarchism provided a golden opportunity for this young industry, offering sensationalism galore, so that international newspapers quickly capitalized on the headline-grabbing "black peril." This New Journalism constituted the main form of public discourse on anarchism. Features on the subject ranged from small inserts about anarchist meetings, reports of incidents *possibly* connected with anarchists, and random violence often described as anarchism to large-scale features about terrorist attacks, investigations into anarchist circles, and biographies of notorious individuals. These were often accompanied by striking visual illustrations (Kalifa 1995). Aside from more or less neutral reporting in the brief pieces, two types of discourse underpinned these publications: scaremongering and a reassuring celebration of law and order.

The transnational nature of anarchism, through the idea of conspiracy, was a recurring theme, both implicitly and explicitly. To what extent were anarchist attacks the product of transnational plotting? Exile as a result of repression, migration, and, in some rarer cases, ideologically led cosmopolitanism had combined to make anarchism a diasporic movement with a near-global reach. There were significant German, Italian, Eastern European, and French groupings in the United States (Zimmer 2010); Brazil hosted large Italian and French contingents; London had by the early 1890s become the main destination for European political exiles. These groups were interconnected through fragile but complex and efficient communication and circulation networks, and among the propagandist literature that was circulated through these channels featured some material promoting the use of violence. However, there is very little evidence to suggest that these militant networks actually supported either acts of propaganda by the deed or the much-vaunted "Black International" frequently mentioned in police files and the press. The French terrorist Emile Henry did find refuge in London after his Paris attack, and it was rumoured that the 1894 attack on the Greenwich Observatory had in fact been meant for Russia (Merriman 2009). However, countless rumors of transnational plotting were never confirmed or indeed substantiated, and the lives of exiled and immigrant anarchists were greatly romanticized; the claim of a French spy who infiltrated London's anarchist circles that a "London Committee" sent instructions to the whole world was common fare (Bantman 2013).[2] In most cases, terrorist attacks were designed and carried out by a small group or, more frequently, an isolated individual. Nonetheless, the narrative of transnational conspiracy remains tempting to this day. It was reactivated in the mass media following 9/11, and within academe a variation was recently set out by U.S. historian Timothy Messer-Kruse in two books focusing on the pivotal Haymarket Affair of 1886 and the subsequent 1887 trial and executions of suspected anarchist terrorists, several of whom were of German origin. Messer-Kruse contends that there existed transnational terrorist networks, although he takes the phrase to refer to networks of ideas rather than actual organizations (2011, 2012). While acknowledging occasional terrorist involvements at the fringe, most studies on exile groups have by contrast highlighted the crippling material circumstances of exiled individuals, the tendency toward profound political divisions, and, in many cases, the prevalence of depoliticization or nonviolent militancy through educationalism or trade union activism.

Learned, scientific discourses on anarchism were largely based on the work of Italian doctor and pioneering criminologist Cesare Lombroso. His landmark monograph from 1894 *Gli Anarchici* was translated into French in 1895 and disseminated internationally. Lombroso did not offer a detailed sociological or ideological explanation for the appeal of anarchism, but his approach was not deprived of empathy, even as he described anarchism as a manifestation of congenital criminality and innate fanaticism using anthropometric measurements. While laying the foundations for a more subtle understanding of anarchism, his work contributed to its classification as a crime rather than a political system: "The anarchist movement is composed for the most part (except for a very few exceptions, like Reclus and Kropotkin) of criminals and madmen, and sometimes of both together" (Lombroso 1897, para 4). He distinguished between revolutions, which were rare and followed by an entire people, and, on the other hand, revolts and seditions, which were prompted by "misoneism" (the fear of the new), placing anarchism in the sphere of the latter. Lombroso's ideas were central to international debates on political crime, which generated much discussion at the first international congress of criminal anthropology held in Rome in 1885, at which possible causes considered for revolutionary leanings were again viewed as "socio-biological." The very notion of "political crime" was attacked by some criminologists, who stressed how thin the difference with common crime was (Knepper 2009). These scientific debates soon found an echo in national and international political fora in which anti-anarchist legislation was discussed.

III. Policing Anarchism: National, Regional, and International Expansion

The sense of danger associated with anarchism prompted legal changes in all the countries affected and a new approach to policing at the local, national, and international levels. Several recurring features of these responses stand out: the extension of national legislation to deal with anarchism, the connection between anarchism and immigration, and, third, the decisive move toward international cooperation against anarchism.

Anti-anarchist measures were first implemented at the national level, where they often resulted in the extension or redeployment of existing policing and surveillance structures. Following Germany's draconian 1878 antisocialist laws (which led to the exile of Johann Most, first to London and then to New York, where he became one of the most vocal exponents of propaganda by the deed), many countries changed their legislation in the early 1880s, fearing revolutionary contagion from the French Commune, the First International, and the assassination of Alexander II. In the early 1880s, some European countries passed laws against the use of explosives (Germany in 1884, Austria in 1885, Belgium in 1886, and Switzerland in 1894); Britain had taken the lead in doing so in 1883, although it durably resisted introducing further legislative changes to control anarchism. Several countries that had once harbored refugees closed their borders to them; Belgium and Switzerland both changed their laws in the late 1880s to protect themselves against the anarchist peril, resulting in recurring tensions over anarchist exiles and deportees, notably with Britain. In the early to mid-1890s, Italy, Spain, Germany, and Denmark passed very repressive legislation to crush their own anarchist movements (and, notably in Spain, socialist groupings in general). France in 1892 passed comprehensive "Wicked Laws" (a telling name given the legislation by socialist members of Parliament), which among other things made the mere possession of anarchist literature a criminal offense. In most countries, anarchists were closely watched, harassed, arbitrarily arrested, and deported, and waves of arrests were frequent. Thus, in Brazil in 1898, many arbitrary imprisonments happened in São Paulo on the occasion of May Day and the anniversary of the Chicago executions, as well as a further wave of repression following the great strikes of 1917–1919 (Toledo & Biondi 2010).

While the "anarchist peril" resulted in the passage of a significant number of laws and changed policing practices, this was not an irresistible process, and anti-anarchist legislation was opposed in several countries or areas, or geographically circumscribed. In Spain, anti-anarchist laws passed in 1894 punishing the illicit use of explosives, conspiracy, and instigation to commit such crimes were initially limited to Madrid and Barcelona before being extended to the whole of Spain in 1897 (Jensen 2013). In 1901 proposed new Italian anti-anarchist legislation was rejected. In Britain, Conservative members of Parliament started pressing for anti-alien and anti-anarchist legislation in the early 1890s, at the height of propaganda by the deed, but the Aliens Act was not passed until 1905. Britain developed a unique model of control and soon was the only country with a significant anarchist population that still allowed anarchists into its territory or tolerated them even once foreign powers had deported them without authorization. In the United States, laws preventing the immigration of anarchists and nihilists were discussed starting in 1888 and only came to fruition in 1903 with a law explicitly refusing entry into the North American territory to anarchists. An earlier Senate bill (known as the "Hill Bill") targeting immigrant anarchists and allowing for their deportation had been put forward after the assassination of the French president Sadi Carnot in 1894 but was rejected because it was perceived to threaten socialists in general (Kraut 2012, pp. 178–79). The assassination of McKinley marked the turning point after which the country no longer felt itself to be immune from anarchist outrages, and at that time "anti-anarchist sentiment . . . penetrated the judiciary," whereas up to that point "so-called breach of the peace and unlawful assembly statutes under state police powers served as the legal basis to raid anarchist meetings, break up lectures, and suppress anarchist newspapers" (Kraut 2012, pp. 175–76). In April 1902, the New York state legislature passed the Criminal Anarchy Act, which outlawed any form of publicity for anarchist ideas (Kraut 2012). In 1903, at the request of Roosevelt, Congress passed a law restricting immigration to exclude anarchists from entering into the United States. This marked a radically new approach whereby the United States would now seek to "legislate anarchism out of existence" (Zimmer 2010, p. 310).

The depoliticization of anarchism and its reclassification as a crime underpinned this legalistic turn. In Britain, much of the debate hinged on whether anarchists should be regarded as political refugees who ought to be given asylum, in line with the nineteenth-century Liberal tradition, or whether they were potentially dangerous criminals who must be turned away. These questions informed the extradition trial of Théodule Meunier, a French comrade suspected of carrying out an attack in Paris who had sought refuge in London. His 1894 legal defense against France's extradition request argued that his attack had been a political gesture and therefore warranted the granting of political asylum, but this was declined on the basis that the attack was aimed at all governments in general rather than a specific one. This decision represented the first rejection of terrorism as a legitimate form of political protest. It established "a new and very important canon in international law, and the notion that anarchist crimes were non-political soon became a commonplace in books and reference works" (Adams 1989, pp. 213–15). The same evolution was confirmed by the debates over the Aliens Act. This legislation was passed in Britain in 1905, but unlike its counterpart in the United States, it mentioned the case of the anarchist only in an obviate way, amid a long list of "undesirable immigrants," as someone sentenced in a foreign country for a crime, but not for an offense of a political character. Similarly, in the United States, before the adoption of anti-immigration laws, revolutionary acts motivated by anarchism had come to be regarded unambiguously as "extraditable crime" rather than "protected actions." This built on various European and U.S. extradition treaties signed after 1856 that stated that "persons charged with assassinating heads of state could not claim protection under the political offense exception" (Unterman 2010).

Given the movement's diasporic nature and often "foreign" origins, anti-anarchist fears in most countries were both a manifestation and an aggravating factor of existing xenophobia, based on the erroneous belief that anarchism was exclusively imported by migrants and not homegrown; consequently, anti-anarchist laws often took the form of anti-immigration and asylum laws and special measures. Italian anarchists were deported *en masse* from France in 1894. In Argentina, the 1902 Residency Law, passed after two assassination attempts on presidents, a successful one on the chief of police, and a string of bomb attacks that killed several police officers, allowed the deportation of dangerous foreigners and specifically targeted anarchists. Brazil's 1907 "Adolfo Gordo" law authorizing the deportation of foreign activists was based on the assumption that the labor movement was of foreign origin. In the United States, the anti-anarchist Aliens Act adopted in 1903 was explicitly designed to ban foreign anarchists from entry into the United States, prevent their naturalization, and allow the deportation of immigrants found to be anarchists within three years of their landing (Kraut 2012). These laws often included anarchists among other groups of "undesirable" immigrants, such as destitute, radicalized, physically or mentally ill, and elderly people.

One of the most striking features of the period was the newly extended role of international cooperation among nation-states against anarchists, even though it proved fraught with difficulties. In the early years of the anarchist scare, informal police cooperation prevailed between most of the countries affected. In Europe, international police practices were put in place starting in the mid-nineteenth century; in Latin America, supranational cooperation (often in the form of intercity police exchanges) took shape in the early twentieth century, with international police conferences in Buenos Aires in 1905, São Paulo in 1912, and Buenos Aires again in 1920 (Galeano 2010); these gatherings increasingly focused on policing anarchism in connection with immigration (Deflem 2005). In Europe, late nineteenth-century cooperation meant diplomatic efforts as well as more or less discreet interactions among spies and police agents in charge of the surveillance of comrades (Bantman 2013). It was widely believed at the time that there existed an "international anarchist register" of anthropometric portraits that made it possible to identify anarchists when they crossed borders. In fact, the register did not exist, but lists of anthropometric portraits (with or without illustrations) were kept by separate countries and used for international police communication. The *portrait parlé* method designed by French police clerk Alphonse Bertillon was increasingly used to facilitate such inter-police cooperation. After being established in Europe, it made considerable headway into Latin America, where a competing identification system based on fingerprints eventually came to prevail; cities and regions adopted such systems from the 1880s onward (1889 in Buenos Aires, 1895 in Montevideo, 1889 in Rio de Janeiro, and 1898 in São Paulo), along with unevenly successful information exchange protocols (Galeano & Garcìa Ferrari 2011). French policing methods were also adopted in the Ottoman Empire (Yilmaz 2014).

There were countless points of friction between the different national services involved in anarchist surveillance. British agents were especially wary of their continental counterparts, whom they tended to regard as highly inefficient; incidents with Italian spies had suggested that foreign interference could jeopardize the British police's own undercover work (Di Paola 2013). British authorities repeatedly bemoaned the unilateralism of other police forces, which often gave very late or no notice when extraditing individuals to Britain. Conversely, French diplomats had wished to set up in London a *commissaire* solely in charge of organizing the surveillance of London's French exiles, but had to back down in response to the British police's distrust of formal police surveillance and involvement (Laurent 2000).

An institutional turn occurred in September 1898 when, following the assassination of the Empress Elizabeth of Austria by the Italian anarchist Lucheni, the Italian government convened an international conference in Rome in order to establish between the European powers "a practical and permanent agreement aimed to successfully fight anarchist Associations and their adepts." The conference, held between 24 November and 21 December 1898, sought "to suggest the best means of repressing anarchist work and propaganda, having due regard to the autonomy of each State." The reference to national "autonomy" may well have been a concession to the British delegation, which prior to the conference had made no secret of its reluctance to enter into a formal arrangement. The agenda started with the possible implementation of penal sanctions against those involved in the fabrication or preparation of explosive devices, or those who joined anarchist "conspiracies" or groups planning an "anarchist act," inciting others to anarchist acts, or propagating anarchist ideas in the army (Vincent 1898, pp. 1–3).[3] It advocated systematic punishment for any involvement in anarchist propaganda, as well as a complete ban on anarchist publications, including the reprinting of minutes of anarchist trials in the general press. In addition to these measures, which formalized existing practices, the allocation of new powers to judges was considered, such as sentencing individuals to house arrest or topping up any sentence with a travel interdiction without notifying administrative authorities. The conference's most innovative proposals were to create a central authority in each country devoted to the surveillance of anarchists, liaising with each country's authorities, and making the use of "*portrait parlé*" systematic for the international surveillance of suspicious individuals. An "extradition sub-committee" suggested that all anarchist acts be regarded as punishable by extradition. The final report was approved by twenty of the twenty-one countries represented in Rome. Britain was the only country to abstain on most of the clauses, which, except for minor amendments, were adopted unanimously. It insisted that its existing laws allowed for the extradition of murderers (as illustrated by the Meunier case). A few concessions were made by extending the law on explosives, and the British delegation also agreed to study the best ways to control the diffusion of anarchist writings inciting violence. The subsequent correspondence between British services was telling of the refusal to alter British methods: "Expulsion as it is understood on the continent is impossible in this country. . . . All we can do is to deal with men who do criminal acts under the ordinary criminal jurisdiction."[4]

From the British perspective, the main outcome of the Rome conference was the joint agreement to avoid deporting anarchists to London. But, despite all the dispositions of the resulting Rome Protocol, the conference was regarded as a disappointment, all the more as the signatories subsequently did very little to implement these measures (Jensen 1981; Deflem 2002).

The assassination of President McKinley by the anarchist Leon Czolgosz prompted the Russian and American governments to call for new international controls in 1902. But, again, the British government refused any further cooperation, especially regarding expulsions, the surveillance of entry points into the country, and systematic exchanges of information among the national police forces. One of the reasons for the adamant emphasis on British independence was revealed on this occasion, when internal correspondence made clear that a systematic exchange of information risked exposing Scotland Yard's informers and jeopardizing all of their work. In spite of this British refusal, a confidential protocol was signed in Saint Petersburg in March 1904 by representatives from Germany, Austria-Hungary, Denmark, Romania, Russia, Serbia, Sweden and Norway, Turkey, and Bulgaria. The United States did not take part in this conference, most likely because it had no established national police force and was therefore not in a position to enter a cooperative framework (Jensen 2001).

The 1898 and 1904 International Protocols are commonly described as forerunners of Interpol: even if few decisive measures were taken by the states involved, in the long run, the Rome and Saint Petersburg conferences led to a reinforcement of direct communication between national police forces. The anarchist wave of attacks prompted a great modernization of policing nationally and internationally, with an unprecedented degree of bureaucracy, international cooperation, new identification methods, more professional and centralized police services, and a professionalization of protective measures for heads of state (Jensen 2013).

Conclusion

The battle against propaganda by the deed marked a new era in the history of political policing. In many countries, political surveillance organizations and legislation were subsequently enshrined, marking the beginning of a more overtly interventionist approach to immigration and political radicalism, which was also a manifestation of the new conception of the state's role and bureaucratic apparatus (Noiriel 1993; Yilmaz 2014). Britain's Aliens Act was reinforced in 1914, and the "Special Branch" that had presided over anti-anarchist surveillance and operations eventually became Scotland Yard. The United States' 1903 anti-alien measures were reinforced in 1918–1919 by the Espionage Act and the 1918 Sedition Act, which greatly expanded the government's ability to police radical speech. Adopting a long-term perspective, Julia Rose Kraut (2012) has shown that the 1903 Alien Immigration Act created a legal precedent for the mass deportation of radicals after 1919, the 1950s "witch hunt," and eventually a visa denial barring entry to an Islamic scholar under the Patriot Act of 2001. A similar process of consolidation occurred at the international level.

The anarchist terror wave forms an essential chapter in the complex area of political crime and its definition. As the first political movement to have annexed highly destructive modern technology in the pursuit of a political objective, anarchism occupies a unique place in the history of modern non-state terror and its legal treatment, and led to important changes in contemporary policing practices, both nationally and internationally. The "battle against international anarchism" accelerated the exchange of policing models and techniques and was a catalyst in the development of an international criminal system. In doing so, it represented an epochal transition from the revolutionary period of the nineteenth century to the twentieth century's international integration in the field of criminal justice. The criminalization of anarchism was central to this process.

The criminal angle provides a very limited understanding of the political and philosophical richness of anarchism, but it does capture an important facet of the history of the movement, especially when it comes to public perceptions and legal treatment: namely, the impact of the anarchists' long terrorist campaign in an era of profound social inequalities, mass migration, urban life, and labor unrest, at a time when a new technological context and an expanding popular press gave the anarchist outrages unprecedented resonance. The anarchist terrorist wave is also characteristic of the late nineteenth-century "first globalization": as a manifestation of globalization "from below," transnational anarchism accelerated this process by prompting an unprecedented degree of cooperation between national police forces.

NOTES

1. See the entry for "illégalisme" in the French-language *L'Encyclopédie anarchiste*, accessed at http://www.encyclopedie-anarchiste.org/articles/i/illegalisme.
2. See also "Letter from London," 26 January 1893, Box F/7/12504, Organisation Anarchique 1882–1898, Archives Nationales, Pierrefitte-sur-Seine.
3. "Précis of the Proceedings at the Anti-Anarchist Conference Convened at Rome by the Italian Government," National Archives, 1–3.
4. Letter from the Home Office to the Foreign Office, TNA FO 412/68, Measures to be taken for the Prevention of Anarchist Crimes Correspondence, 10 January 1902.

REFERENCES

Adams, Nicholas. 1989. "British Extradition Policy and the Problem of the Political Offender (1842–1914)." Ph.D. diss., University of Hull.

Bantman, Constance. 2006. "Internationalism Without an International? Cross-Channel Anarchist Networks." *Revue belge de Philologie et d'Histoire* 84 (4): 961–81.

Bantman, Constance. 2013. *The French Anarchists in London: Exile and Transnationalism in the First Globalisation*. Liverpool: Liverpool University Press.

Deflem, Mathieu. 2002. *Policing World Society*. Oxford: Oxford University Press.

Deflem, Mathieu. 2005. "International Police Cooperation—History of." In *The Encyclopaedia of Criminology*, ed. Richard A. Wright & J. Mitchell Miller, 795–98. New York: Routledge.

Di Paola, Pietro. 2013. *The Knights Errant of Anarchy: London and the Italian Anarchist Diaspora (1880–1917)*. Liverpool: Liverpool University Press.

Galeano, Diego. 2010. "Inter-Urban Policing Networks: The Rise of South American Police Cooperation, 1905–1920." Accessed at https://www.academia.edu/5883921/Inter-Urban_Policing_Networks_The_Rise_of_South_American_Police_Cooperation_1905-1920.

Galeano, Diego, & Mercedes Garcìa Ferrari. 2011. "Le bertillonage en Amerique du Sud," *Criminocorpus*. Accessed at http://criminocorpus.revues.org/399.

Graham, Robert, ed. 2005. *Anarchism: A Documentary History of Libertarian Ideas*, Vol. 1. Montreal: Black Rose Books.

Hirsch, Steven, & Lucien Van der Walt, eds. 2010. *Anarchism and Syndicalism in the Colonial and Postcolonial World, 1870–1940: The Praxis of National Liberation, Internationalism, and Social Revolution*. Leiden: Brill.

Jensen, Richard Bach. 1981. "The International Anti-Anarchist Conference of 1898 and the Origins of Interpol." *Journal of Contemporary History* 16 (2): 323–47.

Jensen, Richard Bach. 2001. "The United States, International Policing and the War Against Anarchist Terrorism, 1900–1914." *Terrorism and Political Violence* 13 (1): 15–46.

Jensen, Richard Bach. 2013. *The Battle Against Anarchist Terrorism: An International History, 1878–1934*. Cambridge: Cambridge University Press.

Kalifa, Dominique. 1995. *L'Encre et le Sang. Récits de crimes et société à la Belle Epoque*. Paris: Fayard.

Kinna, Ruth, & Laurence Davies, eds. 2009. *Anarchism and Utopianism*. Manchester, UK: Manchester University Press.

Knepper, Paul. 2009. *The Invention of International Crime: A Global Issue in the Making, 1881–1914*. Basingstoke, UK: Palgrave Macmillan.

Kraut, Julia Rose. 2012. "Global Anti-Anarchism: The Origins of Ideological Deportation and the Suppression of Expression." *Indiana Journal of Global Legal Studies* 19 (1): 169–93.

Laurent, Sébastien. 2000. *Politiques de l'ombre: Etat, renseignement et surveillance en France*. Paris: Fayard.

Lombroso, Cesare. 1894. *Gli Anarchici*. Torino: Fratelli Bocca.

Lombroso, Cesare. 1897. *Anarchy* and *Its Heroes* [extract]. Accessed at https://www.marxists.org/subject/anarchism/lombroso.htm.

Manfredonia, Gaetano. 1984. "L'Individualisme anarchiste en France, 1880–1914." Ph.D. diss., Institut d'Etudes Politiques de Paris.

Melchiori, Barbara Arnett. 1985. *Terrorism in the Late-Victorian Novel*. London: Croom Helm.

Merriman, John. 2009. *The Dynamite Club: How a Bombing in Fin de Siecle Paris Ignited the Age of Modern Terror*. Boston: Houghton Mifflin Harcourt.

Messer-Kruse, Timothy. 2011. *The Trial of the Haymarket Anarchists: Terrorism and Justice in the Gilded Age*. Basingstoke, UK: Palgrave Macmillan.

Messer-Kruse, Timothy. 2012. *The Haymarket Conspiracy: Transatlantic Anarchist Networks*. Chicago: University of Illinois Press.

Moya, Jose C. 2004. "The Positive Side of Stereotypes: Jewish Anarchists in Early-Twentieth-Century Buenos Aires." *Jewish History* 18:19–48, 22.

Noiriel, Gérard. 1993. *La Tyrannie du national. Le droit d'asile en Europe 1793–1993*. Paris: Calmann Levy.

Porter, Bernard. 1992. *Plots and Paranoia: A History of Political Espionage in Britain, 1790–1988*, 2nd ed. London and New York: Routledge.

Rapoport, David C. 2004. "The Four Waves of Terrorism." In *Attacking Terrorism: Elements of a Grand Strategy*, ed. Audrey Kurth Cronin & James M. Ludes. Washington, D.C.: Georgetown University Press, pp. 46-73.

Rioux, Jean-Pierre. 1991. *Chronique d'une fin de siècle. France, 1889–1900*. Paris: Seuil.

Ryley, Peter. 2013. *Making Another World Possible: Anarchism, Anti-Capitalism and Ecology in Late 19th and Early 20th Century Britain*. London: Bloomsbury.

Salomé, Karine. 2011. *L'Ouragan Homicide. L'attentat politique en France au XIXe siècle*. Paris: Champ Vallon.

Stafford, David. 1971. *From Anarchism to Reformism: A Study of the Political Activities of Paul Brousse, 1870–90*. London: Weidenfeld & Nicolson London.

Toledo, Edilene, & Luigi Biondi. 2010. "Constructing Syndicalism and Anarchism Globally: The Transnational Making of the Syndicalist Movement in São Paolo, Brazil, 1895–1935." In *Anarchism and Syndicalism in the Colonial and Postcolonial World, 1870–1940: The Praxis of National Liberation, Internationalism, and Social Revolution*, ed. Steven Hirsch & Lucien van der Walt. Leiden: Brill, 363-394.

Unterman, Katherine. 2010. "One Court's Freedom Fighter Is Another Court's Terrorist: Political Crimes in Extradition at the Turn of the Twentieth Century." Accessed at iss.yale.edu/node/32/attachment.

Vincent, Howard. 1898. "Précis of the Proceedings at the Anti-Anarchist Conference Convened at Rome by the Italian Government." General: Corres. Anti-Anarchist Conference at Rome, Foreign Office: Confidential Print, FO 881/7179, The National Archives, Kew.

Yilmaz, Ilkay. 2014. "Anti-Anarchism and Security Perceptions During the Hamidian Era." Accessed at http://www.zapruderworld.org/content/ilkay-yilmaz-anti-anarchism-and-security-perceptions-during-hamidian-era.

Zimmer, Kenyon, 2010. "'The Whole World Is Our Country': Immigration and Anarchism in the United States, 1885–1940." Ph.D. diss., University of Pittsburgh.

CHAPTER 10

....

DREAMS AND NIGHTMARES

Drug Trafficking and the History of International Crime

....

PAUL KNEPPER

IN "The Adventure of the Final Problem" (1893), Arthur Conan Doyle introduced Dr. Moriarty. Moriarty, the "Napoleon of crime," was an international criminal engaged in nefarious activities, but not narcotics. In fact, in "The Sign of Four" (1890), Conan Doyle revealed that Sherlock Holmes fortified himself with cocaine, among other drugs. Some seventy years later, things had changed. In *Goldfinger* (1959), Ian Fleming mentioned James Bond's role in fighting the heroin traffic. Bond learns of his Goldfinger assignment while in the Miami airport, having just arrived from quashing an international drug ring. In other words, at some point between the late nineteenth century and the mid-twentieth century, drug trafficking became a major international crime problem that everybody knew about.

Historians have taken an interest in drugs and crime since the 1970s, when Virginia Berridge wrote a series of articles (1978a; 1978b; 1978c) dealing with drugs in Britain, and David Musto published his history of drugs in the United States (1973). Important studies followed in the 1980s and 1990s, including those by Courtwright (1982), Parssinen (1982), Berridge (1987), and Spillane (1998). The "forgotten dimension" in this work, Berridge (2001) suggested, was the international aspect. She called attention to recent work on drugs, empire, and diplomacy (Gootenberg 1999; Trocki 1999; Bewley-Taylor 1999; Meyer & Parssinen 1998; McAllister 2000). Since then, more histories of the international aspects of drugs have appeared, including those by Courtwright (2001), Carstairs (2005; 2006), Erlen and Spillane (2004), van Schendel and Abraham (2005), and Mills and Barton (2007).

The discussion here examines the imagery of drug trafficking in the context of global anxiety. The focus is on the "emergence of international society" during the interwar period (Gorman 2012), when intergovernmental organizations, specifically the League of Nations, established the international drug prohibition regime. The essay deals with

Britain, given its significant role in the League, but also the United States, which refused to join the League but chose to cooperate in drug prohibition. I will make use of documents from archives in Geneva, London, and New York,[1] as well as fiction concerning international crime, to describe not only the response to drug trafficking, but also the visions of trafficking on which these responses were based. Together, these visions form the *dreamscape* of international drug crime. Section I introduces the idea of "reverse colonization" in discussing the drug trade and the British Empire. Section II explains the vision of police cooperation that shaped the League's response to drug trafficking. Section III examines the concept of "organized crime" in relation to the League's response to drug trafficking. Finally, section IV discusses the emergence of the role of the United States in the United Nations anti-drug campaign in the 1950s, and the lingering emotions of guilt and fear left over from the colonial context.

I. Ghosts of Empire

Fewer than 1,000 Chinese resided in Britain in the late nineteenth century and most dwelt in the East End of London, in the district of Stepney and Poplar. But they caught the imagination of many other residents. Charles Dickens dramatized Chinese opium dens in *The Mystery of Edwin Drood*, left unfinished at the time of his death. The number of houses licensed for opium smoking remained small (fourteen in 1910) but attracted attention from those in favor of immigration restriction. In his speech to the British Medical Association in 1892, John Hogarth Pringle stressed the importance of eradicating opium dens from London. Medical specialists agreed that moderate recreational use of the drug was impossible. Addiction, followed by moral degradation, was inevitable. The medical concern about opium smoking, Berridge (1978, pp. 13–14) points out, was underpinned by hostility toward the Chinese and their "alien practices." The image of opium dens runs by "cunning and artful Chinamen" emerged alongside worries about the potential of Chinese opium smokers to contaminate English society (Kohn 1992; Seed 2006).

The process of linking immigrants with criminal threat seems familiar—one of many examples found not only in Britain, but in the United States and elsewhere. Timothy Hickman (2000) argues that reports of Britain's opium dens led to a stream of sensationalized accounts of opium saloons in the United States and confirmed the relationship between Chinese and opium use for many Americans. Despite new users and different drugs, the "association of Asian otherness with drug use" and its effects persisted throughout the late nineteenth-century debate surrounding narcotic addiction. The image of the "Oriental" became a metaphor for narcotic addiction in public health pamphlets and the popular press. Susan Speaker (2001) emphasizes the portrayal of the drug threat in the 1920s as a foreign threat. She concentrates on the campaign waged in the United States by nongovernmental organizations (NGOs) against the narcotics problem. Using newspaper and magazine materials, she examines the rhetoric of

Richmond P. Hobson, the war hero, former member of the U.S. Congress, and lifelong temperance crusader who led the campaign against the "dope traffic." Hobson formed several anti-narcotics organizations, including the International Narcotics Education Association. Speaker shows how Hobson and his allies threw up stock images of secret conspiracy, threats to civilization, and foreign menace in their portrayal of drug smugglers and their victims (Speaker 2001).

There certainly was concern in the United States about drugs as a foreign conspiracy, with much of the animosity directed at Chinese immigrants. In 1918, the U.S. Department of the Treasury appointed a special committee, led by Congressman Henry T. Rainey, to investigate the problem of illicit drugs. The Rainey Committee estimated there were as many as 4 million addicts in the United States, the victims of an "underground traffic" in dangerous drugs equal to the volume of legitimate trade. There appeared to be a national organization behind the smuggling of illegal drugs that recruited peddlers in cities from New York to San Francisco (Treasury Department 1919). During the First World War, newspaper and magazine stories regularly appeared about "dope rings" or "drug rings" importing large quantities of drugs. Most told about shipments from the Orient and the arrest of persons with Chinese names.[2] In 1921, a group of citizens in Seattle, alarmed by reports of Chinese drug shipments through Pacific ports, formed the American White Cross International Anti-Narcotic Society. This society lobbied the U.S. Congress for legislation prohibiting the import of narcotics, gathered information for the police about local drug peddlers and smugglers, and launched a widespread education campaign about drugs as a "world problem." The White Cross Society insisted that narcotics represented a "far greater menace to America" than alcohol and claimed many victims among law-abiding citizens.[3]

But there is something more going on here—not a timeless sociological fear of strange, inscrutable people, nor even a binary conception of "otherness," but a specific historical fear founded on a definite sequence of events. Britain's view of narcotic drugs was not a reaction to a domestic context, but rather was shaped in the British Empire. Following the Second World War, historians tended to see British history and the history of the British Empire as distinct histories. But the "new imperial history" has portrayed Britain and its overseas empire as "one big thing." It is within the British experience of empire that we see the nightmare of drug trafficking that haunted British and American imaginations for decades after the empire ceased to exist, or, in the case of the United States, when no empire had formally existed.[4]

The Chinese in Britain did not represent immigrants from a foreign land, but migrants from a corner of the empire. They were addicts not because they were Asian, but because British colonial policy had made them so. Britain imported opium from India to China in the eighteenth century and after the "Opium Wars" of the 1840s and 1850s strengthened its commercial leverage for distribution. Beginning in 1874, the Anglo-Oriental Society for the Suppression of the Opium Trade lobbied against the drug policies of the British government. The society did not object to colonial trade or Westernization, but to the abuse of Westernization and contamination of Oriental culture by Western greed. As one Member of Parliament who shared the society's view told the House of Commons in 1883, England had "introduced opium into the country by fraud, and was keeping it there by force" (Brown 1973, p. 101). The anti-drug campaign of the nineteenth century led to the first international treaties. In 1909, Britain, the United States, France, and the Netherlands met in Shanghai to discuss the opium trade in their colonies. The Shanghai Commission adopted nine recommendations, which led to conferences at the Hague in 1911 and 1912. The Hague Conference of 1912 produced provisions concerning the regulation of trade and production of opium, marijuana, and cocaine. That the European powers should be ashamed of their colonial policies presented an emotive argument, although domestic opium production in China had made the drug business less profitable anyway (De Kort & Korf 1992).

The Chinese opium den evoked both guilt of empire and fear of reprisal, an emotional cocktail that has been called "reverse colonization" (Arata 1990). This theme appears in the novels of Rudyard Kipling, Bram Stoker, and Wilkie Collins, not to mention Arthur Conan Doyle. All of them structure plots around the disturbing idea of colonizers finding themselves in the position of the colonized, the exploiters being exploited. These stories invoke the theme of decline, in which a racially and morally bankrupt empire gives way to the vigor of "primitive peoples." In *Moonstone* (1868), Collins tells about the theft of a jewel from India, a crime in the English countryside that originated with an earlier crime at a Hindu temple when the jewel was first stolen. The underlying message is that the second crime, and the misadventures surrounding it, would not have occurred had it not been for the original evil committed by the English overseas. The "crime of empire" has come full circle (Arata 1990).

The League of Nations implemented a scheme for regulating drugs ostensibly on the level of nation-states, although the culture of drugs established during the age of empire remained. Colonial conceptions of drug addicts shaped League discussions and policies (Kozma 2011). Malcolm Delevingne, Britain's leading diplomat at the League of Nations in charge of drug policy, voiced the dread of reverse colonization in a 1935 speech to the Society for the Study of Inebriety. Once, he said, the British government cultivated opium in India and forced it on China. Now the ghosts of those Chinese addicts threatened residents of London, Manchester, and Birmingham. China was now poised to reverse its nineteenth-century role vis-à-vis Britain. "The tables will indeed be turned," Delevingne warned, "with a vengeance if the Far East, which has been one of the chief victims of the illicit traffic from the West, should now, armed with the knowledge that the West has taught it, become a menace to the West itself" (Delevingne 1935, p. 145).

Conan Doyle's stories emphasized another aspect of reverse colonization. "The Boscombe Valley Mystery" (1891) and "The Adventure of the Crooked Man" (1893) feature characters who fail to succeed in the colonies and return to England, where they become perpetrators of crimes or suspects in investigations. While colonization produced a wealthy class, it also produced an underclass of poor Europeans. One class of colonials prospered while another declined. The class of persons diminished by their encounter with the colonial milieu returned home, where they threatened their well-to-do counterparts. This "imperial lumpenproletariat" could be found throughout the empire, from Australia to India to Africa (Siddiqi 2006). Paul French's micro-history of the brutal killing of a British schoolgirl in Peking in 1937 reveals the role of the colonial cesspool in criminality. Although the authorities found the girl's body outside the Legation Quarter, the residence of diplomats and wealthy colonists, detectives traced the murderers to "the Badlands," where impoverished Chinese and Russian immigrants and down-and-out British participated in an informal economy of prostitution, alcohol, and narcotics. The Badlands incorporated a criminal element the British colonizers shared with the destitute and the desperate among the colonized (French 2011).

The message embodied in the opium dens was that domestic drug crime was the price to be paid for foreign misadventure. The view of drugs as a crime problem originated overseas, not merely through the association with foreign practices, but with the exploitation of these peoples and the original sin of colonization. What made the illicit drug trade so threatening was not the specter of a superior foreign power poised to overwhelm. Rather, it was the possibility that drug trafficking would enable an otherwise inferior people to turn the tables on the imperial rulers. And, given past exploitation, these peoples were motivated to seek revenge. Thus, the response to drugs was tinged by emotions of hatred and revulsion, but also guilt and fear.

II. THE GENEVA DREAM

The concept of drug trafficking as an international crime problem grew out of the interwar period. In 1919, a Dutch police official, Marius van Houten, circulated a proposal among police executives throughout Europe for new levels of cooperation. It was necessary to form an international police organization, he said, to meet the threat of a "new class of criminal—the international criminal" (van Houten 1930, p. 482). In the aftermath of the First World War, crime had increased. Four years of conflict had given the criminal element the opportunity to learn foreign languages and become familiar with cultures in other countries. The criminal element also received a boost from technological advances, including the telephone, automobile, and airplane. Modern technology for transportation, communication, and commerce had revolutionized the nature and methods of crime (van Houten 1930).

The idea for an international criminal police commission crystallized in 1923. Johann Schober, president of the Vienna police, convened a conference that led to a permanent organization. Representatives from nineteen police organizations met to discuss the sharing of information about suspects and extradition of arrested criminals. The police believed their efforts to thwart crime were hampered by time-consuming and cumbersome diplomatic channels, and that they could do more to suppress the cross-border trade in morphine and cocaine. They agreed to form the International Criminal Police Commission (ICPC), with headquarters within the Vienna Police. Throughout the 1920s and 1930s, they held an annual conference and drew in additional members, including China, Japan, and Turkey. The Berlin Congress of 1926 adopted a resolution that pledged to set up a central service in each country that would be entrusted with the exchange of names of drug traffickers and all related documentation (Marabuto 1951, p. 3).

Mathieu Deflem proposes that the police invented the threat of international crime to justify cross-border cooperation. To understand the formation of international policing, it is necessary to "traverse the fixed national-geographic borders" of police history (Deflem 2002, p. 11). For Deflem, the internationalization of policing began with developments in Germany and the United States from 1850 to 1914. Despite early successes across German states, international policing largely failed before the First World War. Not until the founding of the ICPC did international policing become a functional reality. Deflem argues that the European initiative succeeded and the American initiative did not because Europeans articulated the threat of international crime. The founders of the ICPC talked about the rise of a new generation of criminals—currency forgers, thieves, and swindlers, white slave traders and drug traffickers—who used modern technology, transportation, and communication. The threat of cross-border crime served as a "professional myth" (Deflem 2002, p. 140).

International criminality was more than a myth invented by the police, however. It became an essential part of the rationale for the League of Nations. Under Article 23c of its constitution, agreed upon in Paris in 1919, the League assumed responsibility for monitoring treaties concluded before the war concerning the drug trade.[5] To further the ambitions of these agreements, the League of Nations established by resolution at its first assembly the Advisory Commission on Opium and Other Dangerous Drugs, also called the Opium Advisory Committee (OAC). Although a technical committee within the League's framework, the Opium Advisory Committee acquired increasing significance, particularly as the League's failure as a political organization became obvious. Advocates of the League promoted the myth of internationalism surrounding drugs, that is, that the drug trade was a problem that could only be solved through international coordination at the highest level (Bruun, Pan, & Rexed 1975). In a pamphlet entitled "The League and the Drug Traffic" (1925), the League of Nations Union argued that drug trafficking before the war had been limited to opium dens in London's Limehouse district and San Francisco's Chinatown. Since the war, however, the union claimed, everyone knew that the problem was "far too big and deep-rooted a problem to be dealt with by means of police-raids in any one country." The pamphlet explained that "a new stage in the world's war on the drug trafficker is just beginning. The fight will be hard and long."[6]

Van Houten had in fact included in his original proposal his vision for international police cooperation to take place within the structure established in Geneva, and Schober pursued a partnership between the League and the ICPC for more than ten years. Schober encouraged the League to send representatives to the international police congresses, and in 1928, Jean J. Berg, a member of the OAC, attended the congress at Berne. "It is obvious," Schober stressed, "that our ultimate aim is identical with the League itself." He presented Rachel Crowdy, head of the League's Social Section, with an ambitious program for cooperation. The ICPC could assist the League in preparing lists of known international narcotics traffickers, setting up national narcotics enforcement agencies along the lines of those dealing with counterfeiting, organizing the vigilance societies involved in the fight against the white slave trade, and coordinating a worldwide campaign against employment agencies sending women abroad, where they became trapped into prostitution. As Schober explained, the ICPC engaged in the suppression of any crime practiced on an "international professional scale" by counterfeiters, thieves, or persons engaged in traffic in women or narcotic drugs.[7]

But neither the police represented in Vienna nor the diplomats at Geneva shared Schober's enthusiasm for cooperation. For the police members, the main problem was the role of the Austrian government in the ICPC. M. Vladeta Milicevic, a representative from the government of Yugoslavia, explained that although Schober proposed a council that would serve as the ICPC's administrative or controlling body, this was not enough to separate the ICPC from the Vienna police. The office, with its leadership and its staff, would be housed in the Vienna police department, its files part of the Vienna police files.[8] For the diplomats, the fact that the ICPC received funding from the Austrian government meant that it was more "national" than "international." Nevertheless, the League agreed, at least in principle, to cooperate and invited police representatives to sit on the permanent committees concerning the traffic in women and narcotic drugs. Arthur Woods, former commissioner of police in New York City, and A. W. Sirks, chief of the Rotterdam police, served on the Opium Advisory Committee.

Most of Schober's proposals for ICPC–League coordination never really got off the ground. In 1929, the Opium Advisory Committee agreed to a proposal from Delevingne to create a "blacklist" of drug traffickers. The OAC agreed to draw up a registry of persons engaged in the traffic and to circulate this list to governments, and asked Sirks for advice. When the topic was discussed the following year, Henri Carrière of the Swiss Federal Health Service stressed that the blacklist should avoid including individuals or firms not found to be criminally involved in the drug trade. Sirks countered that to be useful, the list had to contain "not only undoubted facts, but also assumptions."[9] The blacklist was a "police document," not a public document. Everything about it—the information obtained, correspondence concerning it, even OAC discussions about it— would remain confidential. Besides, if the League waited for the legal process to take its course, the information would be meaningless.

The blacklist was still under discussion in 1931. The OAC resolved that governments would supply details about persons involved in the traffic, the methods of trafficking used, and other information obtained through investigations. Many police agencies maintained their own blacklists, the OAC decided, and the League's registry should be limited to "essentials of international interest" and should not replace police lists. Only police authorities should be allowed to contribute, and the information should be sent promptly. The League Secretariat consulted on the subject with members, a number of whom agreed with the Swiss objection. But there was another reason for their reluctance. The Secretariat already maintained a card file of traffickers taken from seizure reports submitted regularly by governments—some more than others—which served primarily as a cross-referencing tool. The Secretariat was meant to adapt this to its "new purpose" of allowing real-time police intervention, but this required additional staff resources. The OAC encouraged the Secretariat to make a start on an "experi-mental basis" but appreciated the reality that the blacklist project could only become permanent with additional staff.[10]

What the blacklist discussion did accomplish was to establish a new vocabulary of international crime. The League institutionalized the idea of "trafficking" as a criminal offense committed across national borders. This language defined drug smuggling as a problem on the scale of the worldwide trade in women, firearms, and liquor. Delevingne explained the matter this way: "The International Drug Problem is a problem of illicit traffic. In some respects it is similar to the problems of illicit traffic in arms or liquor, but it has special features which put it into a class by itself" (Delevingne 1931, p. 55). In other words, smuggling illicit drugs could only solved by international organization.

III. SMUGGLERS INC.

Although the International Criminal Police Commission was never formally incorpo-rated within the League structure, the police view certainly shaped the League's outlook concerning drugs. Woods and Sirks joined the "gentlemen's club" (Bruun, Pan, & Rexed 1975) that created the international drug prohibition regime. They gave the police a sig-nificant voice on the OAC, as did T. W. Russell Pasha, who did more than anyone else to shape the idea of drug traffickers in the minds of those in Geneva.

Born into a family in Bedfordshire and educated at Cambridge, Thomas Wentworth Russell Pasha learned about colonial service from a cousin in the Indian civil service. He served as assistant commandant of the police at Alexandria before transferring to Cairo in 1917, where he became head of the city police. In 1925, the Egyptian govern-ment enacted the first narcotics law, which gave police additional powers to arrest and detain drug offenders, and Russell Pasha made it the centerpiece of his administration. He began his investigations in Cairo and extended them to Egypt and beyond (Russell Pasha 1949, pp. 60–65). In 1929, the Egyptian prime minister authorized the formation of the Central Narcotics Intelligence Bureau and put Russell Pasha in charge. His first task was to get a grip on smuggling across the Syrian border, and he soon extended his reach. From information he obtained from smugglers (persuaded to cooperate with payments and the promise of reduced prosecution) he learned of routes into Egypt and traced these back to manufacturers in Europe. He posted confidential copies of his reports to Delevingne, who then fed them to the Opium Advisory Committee in Geneva (Russell Pasha 1949, pp. 226–27).

Almost immediately, Russell Pasha hit on the expedient of sending copies of his annual reports directly to the press. Complete with illustrations of smuggling tech-niques and accounts of successful investigations leading to arrests of prominent smug-glers, the British press said that his reports had the "fascination of a detective story" (*Manchester Guardian*, 31 March 1933, p. 10) and served as "textbooks for other countries" (*Manchester Guardian*, 4 June 1936, p. 8). Once public, these annual reports furnished observers with the conventional wisdom on international drug trafficking. Russell Pasha portrayed drug traffickers as clever individuals who devised ingenious methods of sneaking drugs past the authorities. His first report opens with his account of how he smashed the Zakarian organization, narrating how Thomas Zakarian, who may have been an Armenian, opened a small shop selling carpets across from the National Hotel in Alexandria and became one of the leading international drug traffickers. After taking control of the Alexandria market, Zakarian traveled to Europe to make arrangements directly with suppliers. In Vienna, he met two Polish Jews, the Zelinger brothers, and together they built major smuggling routes from a clandestine laboratory in Switzerland back to Egypt (Central Narcotics Intelligence Bureau 1930, p. 1–8).

Alan Block (1989) has provided a look at European drug trafficking as seen from Geneva. Despite (or because) of the creation of the OAC, drug production at clandestine factories flourished, leading to the development of smuggling routes between Europe, Asia, and the Middle East. According to reports prepared for the committee, international drug smuggling between the wars encouraged organized crime networks led by Jews and Greeks. Regrettably, Block takes Russell Pasha at face value, failing to notice the anti-Semitic element that comes through clearly in Baron Henry D'Erlanger's popularized version of Russell Pasha's reports, *The Last Plague of Egypt*. According to D'Erlanger, illegal narcotics furnished Jewish immigrants in Vienna with a "glorious opportunity" for making money without capital. Russell Pasha's agents uncovered an international ring of Jews from Poland who had established themselves as leaders of the Viennese underworld. The names of the gang in the report of the Central Narcotics Intelligence Bureau "read somewhat like the cast at one of the offerings of the Yiddish theatre" (D'Erlanger 1936, pp. 121–23).

Kathryn Meyer and Terry Parssinen (1998) deepen the story of the international narcotics business between 1907 and 1949. Using material from several national archives, particularly papers of Britain's Foreign Office, they describe how traffickers devised new methods of supply, delivery, and organization in response to the League's efforts at international regulation and control. The creation of international legal structures to regulate narcotics represent some "small successes" of the League, an organization most often remembered for its failures. Nevertheless, smugglers from the United States, Greece, and China formed networks for illicit trade through fluid networks that found weak points in the system of international law enforcement. In 1920s, much of this smuggling was done by freelance merchant sailors who purchased opium in European cities and resold it for a profit in London and New York. By the 1940s, smuggling had become a more extensive business, involving a variety of methods and groups, including spies, warlords, and soldiers.

It is tempting to see international drug trafficking in the interwar period as an illegal business. A frequent argument of campaigners was that "traffic" overlapped. Traffickers made use of their networks to move illicit drugs, women's bodies, and other products. The Special Body of Experts on the Traffic in Women, established to monitor treaties on the white slave trade agreed before the war, referenced the combined traffic in their report on the worldwide traffic: "Police experience in different countries has shown that local dealings in opium and cocaine are frequently undertaken by the same members of the underworld as are engaged in commercialised prostitution."[11] OAC members shared this view. At a session in 1929, the Italian delegate Signor Cavazzoni talked about the "connection between the drug traffic in the underworld and prostitution and the white slave traffic." A surprise visit to a brothel by the *Carabinieri* discovered that cocaine powder had been sprinkled on the clothing of girls of thirteen years of age to facilitate their entry into the white slave trade.[12]

According to the "organized crime" view of international crime popular in the interwar period, criminal syndicates were motivated primarily by financial gain and conducted their activities along the lines of a conventional business. The view of government representatives and their advisors from the police and voluntary organizations was that the illegal products traded within the "international underworld" (e.g., drugs, prostitutes, weapons) were more or less interchangeable; criminal networks engaged in one or the other activity, depending on market conditions. Henry T. F. Rhodes, a criminologist trained in France, framed international crime within organized crime. "Modern gangsterism," as he put it, "could be precisely defined as a criminal organization whose methods approximate those of a legitimate business." American and European gangsters who ran their illicit activities on business lines had brought about a "huge success in illicit traffic in drugs," with the white slave traffic being "another example of a highly efficient business organization" (Rhodes 1939, pp. 237–38). Eric Ambler invoked this image of the international criminal in his novel *The Mask of Dimitrios* (1939), in which the criminal quarry maintains various identities to cover his various crimes. Dimitrios may have been born in Greece, or the Balkans; he may be a Greek, Muslim, or Jew. He exploits the chaos of war, inferior government surveillance, and the vulnerabilities of those around him to amass a fortune as a drug dealer, pimp, thief, spy, white slaver, bully, and financier.

This view fits with historians' understanding of drug selling in cities during the interwar period. Spillane (1998; 2000) describes the changing drug market conditions in Chicago during the first half of the twentieth century. Reformers and the authorities had managed to reduce the supply of opium and cocaine into the city, which concentrated the market into vice districts. Here, an assortment of entrepreneurs and underground drug distribution networks provided drugs for the urban market. For a few, drug business brought substantial rewards. Spillane draws on work by Mark Haller (1970; 1971), who described the Chicago underworld in the early twentieth century as consisting of professional thieves, business and labor racketeers, and contributors to organized crime. Professional thieves included pickpockets, shoplifters, burglars, jewel thieves, and confidence men who shared a culture of professional crime. Racketeering took more than one form, but often these criminals took control of unions to steal from members or to arrange "sweetheart" contracts. Organized crime was in fact the most systematic aspect of underworld activity, which included the provision of illegal goods and services such as gambling, prostitution, narcotics, and alcohol.

However, we should be careful about changing the scale from local to intercontinental. Haller himself insisted on the link between the underworld and cities. He thought of the underworld, and organized crime, as fundamentally connected to city neighbor-hoods. The underworld of American cities included groups involved in theft, rack-eteering, and vice activities that challenged police forces. He stressed that organized crime represented a community-scale, less organized form of business enterprise—local entrepreneurs, not national syndicates (Yeager 2012). Such a concept of organized crime cannot simply be scaled up to an international level without exaggerating the extent of its structure and activities. This is an important point, one that determined to a large extent how successful the League was in curbing trafficking.

There is a curious document in the League of Nations archives urging the Secretariat to investigate the structure of the international underworld. In 1932, Heinrich Berl sent a letter to Geneva in which he proposed an international institute of criminology. Born in Baden-Baden, Berl settled in Karlsruhe after the First World War, where he sup-ported himself giving lectures, writing articles and managing a musical theater. He gained some fame for his *Das Judentumin der Musik* (1926), a celebration of Jewish influence in music (and refutation of Wagner's anti-Semitic attack). By 1929, his interest had turned to social politics. He founded his own press, Kairos Verlag, in 1931, for which he wrote commentary on the inadequacies of Weimar democracy, feminism, and the underclass. In 1932, he authored a booklet entitled "The Under-World State," or "What Does the League of Nations Intend to Do Against the International Organisation of Crime?" He advanced the thesis that international criminals would take over the world if national governments did not band together to defeat them.[13]

League officials did not take Berl seriously. His proposal invoked a fantasy of a secret world government, a conspiracy more powerful than national police forces. But the idea of international crime as the mirror image of the League of Nations can be read a dif-ferent way. To grasp it, we need to avoid confusing the theory of international govern-ment with reality. Picture the League of Nations as an ineffective forum for nations and empires, each pushing their own agenda, without clear hierarchy, without effective com-munication. In social affairs as in politics, the League proved incapable of coordinated action on any significant scale; it was an organization in which pockets of entrepreneurs within the bureaucracy made decisive moves without the support of the center. If the international underworld is the mirror image of this group, it means that international trafficking confronts the same problems. The drug traffickers are disorganized, uncoor-dinated, and ineffective, just like the authorities; each achieves some successes because of the incompetency of the other.

IV. The United Nations and the United States

The League of Nations carried on until 1946, when the United Nations was set up. The Economic and Social Council took over the League's work on trafficking in women, crime prevention and the treatment of offenders, and the Commisson on Narcotic Drugs (CND) replaced the Opium Advisory Committee. Those in favor of an international drug regime continued their quest to realize the principles laid down during the League era. But, as David Bewley-Taylor emphasizes, this transformation also allowed the Americans to bend the international machinery to their own model (symbolized by the construction of the new UN headquarters in New York City in 1952). The American view regarded drugs as a problem originating overseas, and the United States resolved to use the UN to cut off the source of America's domestic drug addiction problem (Bewley-Taylor 1999, pp. 59, 70).

What had been the platform for T. W. Russell Pasha now fell to Harry J. Anslinger, the American representative to the CND. Anslinger grew up in Pennsylvania, where he worked as a detective for the Pennsylvania Railroad and the Pennsylvania state police. He then served in the diplomatic corps of the State Department, with posts in the Hague and Hamburg. During the Prohibition era, Anslinger pursued a diplomatic approach to liquor control and learned about the fight against narcotics smuggling. In 1930, Congress approved creation of a new law enforcement agency, the Federal Bureau of Narcotics, and appointed Anslinger as its first commissioner (McWilliams 1990). From the beginning, Anslinger operated on a world stage. He had directed his agents to report to him information about narcotics of foreign origin and how ethnic groups were involved in smuggling. Americans with immigrant parents became suspects. The Bureau of Narcotics boasted of having smashed drug rings operated by gangsters of Italian, Chinese, and Jewish backgrounds. During the 1940s, Anslinger portrayed the bureau as a small law enforcement agency struggling against a mighty international "mafia." Although he never produced evidence of a coherent organization of Italian criminals, he claimed more than once that a large number of Italians worked in the narcotics trade, and that local Italian syndicates were linked together to form an international underworld. Crime journalists appreciated what Anslinger had to say and encouraged public acceptance of his theories (Kinder 1981; Kinder & Walker 1986).

From the beginning of his tenure at the Bureau of Narcotics, Anslinger pursued links with the International Criminal Police Commission. The head office of the ICPC was transferred from Vienna to Paris in 1946, when it became known as the "International Police," or Interpol. J. Edgar Hoover, head of the U.S. Federal Bureau of Investigation, was reluctant to join the organization, and the United States did not formally become a member until 1958. Nevertheless, Anslinger worked with other international police chiefs to gather intelligence about the drug trade. From 1931 onward, he convened secret sessions of his Committee of One Hundred, an unofficial panel of narcotics enforcement officers from London, Cairo, Ottawa, Rotterdam, Berlin, and Paris. He also dispatched his agents to infiltrate international drug rings. In the 1950s, narcotics agents identified Lebanon and Turkey as the points of origin of heroin smuggled into the United States by the Sicilian Mafia. They operated networks through Marseilles and Montreal to move the drugs into New York (McWilliams 1990).

Throughout the 1950s, Anslinger tried to convince politicians about the role of organized crime in the drug problem. To develop this concept, he drew on the visibility of the Kefauver Committee. During 1950–1951, Estes Kefauver, a senator from Tennessee, convened the Special Committee to Investigate Crime in Interstate Commerce. The committee held hearings in cities across the country, from Miami to San Francisco, New York to Chicago, and, using the new medium of television, brought their proceedings to millions of Americans. Kefauver established the view that crime had become big business. There was a "nationwide crime syndicate," he contended, led by mobs in New York and Chicago, that controlled a range of activities—racketeering, gambling, prostitution, and drugs. Behind this national syndicate, there was an "international criminal organization known as the Mafia," which had originated in Sicily and was involved in numerous fields of illegal activity, chiefly narcotics. To tackle this problem required more than local police. Federal law enforcement, including the Immigration and Naturalization Service, would be needed to deport foreign-born criminals (Kefauver 1952, pp. 23–25).

Anslinger was an effective bureaucrat and politician who played to a wider field of politics, a "Cold Warrior" who linked the drug threat with the Communist threat (Kinder 1981; Bewley-Taylor 1999). The Soviet launch of the world's first orbiting satellite, *Sputnik*, triggered anxieties about faltering U.S. military technology and growing Soviet power. The Soviet Union presented an evil empire with the tools to threaten the American way of life. But drug trafficking also evoked memories of a faded empire, as we can see in Dashiel Hammett's *The Maltese Falcon* (1929). In that story, a collection of international criminals gather in San Francisco, where they draw Sam Spade into their efforts to secure a Maltese treasure known to be en route from Hong Kong. The criminals—Caspar Gutman, Bridgette O'Shaughnessy, and Joel Cairo—are not merely foreign, but remnants of the crumbling British Empire. There is a sense that the United States, embodied by the tough but principled Spade, must deal with the mess brought to American shores by the British. But on another level, the plot can be read as an account of the passing of the baton of world political and commercial hegemony from Britain to the United States. The "black figure of a bird" embodies global commercial dominance and the criminal guilt associated with managing an empire, carried to the city by mysterious international figures who seek to profit from its power (Thomas 1997, pp. 262–64).

While Anslinger encouraged Americans to worry about Communist drug infiltration, there were worries closer to home concerning a less powerful military rival, Mexico, and a less potent drug, marijuana. In the 1930s, alarming reports from New Orleans brought national attention to marijuana as an "assassin of youth" (Blackman 2004). To gauge the extent of the problem, the commissioner of public safety of New Orleans, Frank Gomila, and city chemist Madeline Gomila Lambou sent questionnaires to public authorities across the country. The first use of marijuana in the United States, they determined, had occurred in New Orleans in 1910. New Orleans became a distribution center for the drug, which later traveled up the Mississippi to cities as far north as Cleveland. The supply came from Havana, Tampico, and Vera Cruz, with quite a few sailors traveling to Mexican ports to acquire their supply. Wholesale dealers, who consisted "mostly of Mexicans, Italians, Spanish-Americans, and drifters from ships," became prosperous (Gomila and Gomila Lambou 1938: 30). Gomila and Gomila Lambou made clear the source of the threat. Marijuana had migrated north along with Mexican labor. Mexican workers had spread the drug throughout American cities. In New Orleans, Mexicans taught schoolchildren how to smoke marijuana cigarettes. "Smoking weed" became widespread in the city among dockworkers and schoolboys, leading many of them into criminal activities. Youngsters fortified with narcotics gunned down bank clerks, the police, and bystanders. The crime wave that had taken place in New Orleans was about to break in other American cities (Gomila & Gomila Lambou 1938). The FNB files illustrated the "homicidal tendencies" that resulted from use of marijuana (Gomila & Gomila Lambou 1938, p. 22).

From the beginning of the marijuana scare, there was information to show that it had been exaggerated. In New York, Mayor LaGuardia commissioned a study to determine the hazards of the drug to health and safety. His investigation sent six plainclothes police, four men and two women, who posed as "suckers," or students, into poolrooms, dime-a-dance halls, and bar and grills where marijuana smoking had been reported. The investigators concluded that activity was limited to Harlem; that the majority of marijuana smokers were "Negroes and Latin Americans"; and that some "terminal porters, mainly Negroes," distributed the drug (Schoenfeld 1944, pp. 24–25). The report emphasized, however, that marijuana did not lead to addiction in the medical sense, or to an interest in cocaine or heroin. The marijuana user did not come from the "hardened criminal class," and there was no direct relationship between marijuana use and the commission of serious crimes. There was no organized traffic in marijuana and only limited use among schoolchildren. In short, the publicity concerning the catastrophic effects of marijuana smoking was unfounded (Schoenfeld 1944, pp. 24–25).

Yet the fear of marijuana from Mexico carried on. Dutch business traveler Hendrik De Leeuw, who wrote popular books about transnational organized crime, repeated in 1955 claims made twenty years earlier. The "unceasing stream of marijuana smuggled into this country from Mexico and from the East," he wrote, contributed to "depredations of all sorts—gang warfare, murder, prostitution, thefts from drug stores" to satisfy expensive cravings. Marijuana set off a "chain reaction no less ravaging socially than the physical destruction caused by dynamite sticks." The pernicious habit led to "disintegration of American family life and breakdown of morals" (De Leeuw 1955, pp. 165–66). Heroin and cocaine were problems, but marijuana smuggling from Mexico greatly disturbed drug authorities, whose efforts were severely constrained by the vastness of the United States–Mexico border, the widespread poverty that provided temptation, and the weakness of Mexican drug enforcement. "While Mexicans use marijuana widely, a weed that will grow anywhere in anybody's backyard, it has spread all over the country" (De Leeuw 1955, p. 170).

The nightmare of reverse colonization meant that drugs gave a weaker people the power to threaten a stronger people. Mexico was never an American possession in the same sense as a colony in the British Empire, but there was certainly enough intervention in the country to accept that Mexicans had something to feel unhappy about. Americans felt racially superior to Mexicans and displayed the arrogance of a colonial power. The

Mexican introduction of marijuana into the United States threatened the American population in the same way. Marijuana required neither sophisticated drug laboratories for its production nor intricate smuggling networks led by criminal masterminds for its dissemination. Instead, it was a weed that grew anywhere, pushed onto American families by hundreds of thousands of drug pushers streaming across the border.

CONCLUSION

In the decades between Sherlock Holmes and James Bond, drug smuggling became an international crime problem. Efforts to address the problem began before the First World War, when missionaries in China shamed colonial powers into agreeing to the first international treaties. Drugs represented not merely a foreign menace, but the specter of a colonized people armed with the power to threaten the colonizers. The guilt of exploitation, combined with the fear of what that exploitation had brought about, established the emotional framework in which drug regulation would be established.

During the interwar years, the International Criminal Police Commission, working shoulder to shoulder with the League of Nations, proposed a worldwide system of drug enforcement. To prevent traffickers from slipping through the net of regulation, there would be a blacklist shared by police authorities throughout the world. This dream of enforcement did not come true, although drug trafficking was never really the problem it was made out to be. Although League advocates encouraged the view of trafficking as a solidly organized and effectively managed criminal business, the reality is that the traffickers would have been limited by the same problems as the enforcers. It is difficult to believe that the "drug rings" established more effective management structures than the police and the diplomats. The underworld state was as ineffective as the intergovernmental organization based in Geneva.

Following the Second World War, the United States aimed to mold the international machinery for drug enforcement to suit its view of the problem. To end drug addiction in the United States, it was necessary to intervene overseas. But at the same time the United States seized control of drug policy in the United Nations, it inherited the emotional legacy of the British Empire. The sense that drugs would not have become a problem *here* if Americans had not intervened over *there* haunted the public and their representatives in government.

NOTES

1. Archives used for this essay include the League of Nations Archives at the United Nations Library in Geneva; the Women's Library, which is now part of Special Collections at the London School of Economics Library; and the Rockefeller Archives in Sleepy Hollow, New York.
2. As was the case in England (Kohn 2001).

3. White Cross, "The White Cross: How It Started, What It Has Done, and What It Is Trying to Do" (1926), pamphlet, Series 3, subseries 1, Box 1, folder 94, Bureau of Social Hygiene Collection, Rockefeller Archives, Sleepy Hollow, New York.

4. For the significance of drugs to other empires, see De Kort and Korf (1992) and Mills and Barton (2007).

5. As well as those concerning traffic in women; see Knepper (2013).

6. "The League and the Drug Traffic" (1918), League of Nations Union, Miscellaneous Pamphlets and Leaflets, 1918, British Library, London.

7. Johannes Schober, "Letter to League of Nations of 30 October 1928," 4IBS/7/5/04, Box FL132, Women's Library, London.

8. Leonard Harrison, "International Police," Series 4, Box 14, Folder 655, Rockefeller Archives, Sleepy Hollow, New York.

9. Opium Advisory Committee, "Confidential Memorandum on the Establishment by the Secretariat of a 'Black List' of Illicit Traffickers in Narcotic Drugs," p. 5, R3225, League of Nations Archives, Geneva.

10. Ibid., p. 7.

11. *Report of the Special Body of Experts on the Traffic in Women and Children.* Geneva: League of Nations, 1927, p 17.

12. *Advisory Committee on Traffic in Opium and Other Dangerous Drugs: Minutes of the Twelfth Session.* Geneva, League of Nations, 1929, p. 80.

13. See Max Habitch to Eric Ekstrand, 18 July 1932, Box R3020, League of Nations archives, Geneva.

References

Arata, Stephen. 1990. "The Occidental Tourist: *Dracula* and the Anxiety of Reverse Colonisation." *Victorian Studies* 33:621–45.

Berridge, Virginia. 1978a. "East End Opium Dens and Narcotic Use in Britain." *London Journal* 4:3–28.

Berridge, Virginia. 1978b. "Victorian Opium Eating: Responses to Opiate Use in Nineteenth-Century England" *Victorian Studies* 21:437–61.

Berridge, Virginia. 1978c. "War Conditions and Narcotics Control: The Passing of the Defence of the Realm Act Regulation 40B." *Journal of Social History* 7:285–304.

Berridge, Virginia. 1987. *Opium and the People: Opium Use in Nineteenth-Century England.* New Haven, CT: Yale University Press.

Berridge, Virginia. 2001. "Illicit Drugs and Internationalism: The Forgotten Dimension." *Medical History* 45:282–88.

Bewley-Taylor, David. 1999. *The United States and International Drug Control, 1909–1997.* London: Pinter.

Blackman, Shane. 2004. *Chilling Out: The Culture of Politics of Substance Consumption, Youth and Drug Policy.* Maidenhead, UK: Open University Press.

Block, Alan A. 1989. "European Drug Traffic and Traffickers Between the Wars: The Policy of Suppression and Its Consequences." *Journal of Social History* 23:315–37.

Brown, J. B. 1973. "Politics of the Poppy: The Society for the Suppression of the Opium Trade, 1874–1916." *Journal of Contemporary History* 8:97–111.

Bruun, Kettil, Lynn Pan, & Ingemar Rexed. 1975. *The Gentlemen's Club: International Control of Drugs and Alcohol.* Chicago: University of Chicago Press.

Carstairs, Catherine. 2005. "The Stages of the International Drug Control System." *Drug and Alcohol Review* 24:57–65.

Carstairs, Catherine. 2006. *Jailed for Possession: Illegal Drug Use, Regulation and Power in Canada, 1920–1961*. Toronto: University of Toronto Press.

Central Narcotics Intelligence Bureau. 1930. *Annual Report for the Year 1929*. Cairo: Government Printing Office.

Courtwright, David. 1982. *Dark Paradise: A History of Opiate Addiction in America*. Cambridge, MA: Harvard University Press.

Courtwright, David. 2001. *Forces of Habit: Drugs and the Making of the Modern World*. Cambridge, MA: Harvard University Press.

Deflem, Mathieu. 2002. *Policing World Society: Historical Foundations of International Police Cooperation*. Oxford: Oxford University Press.

De Kort, Marcel, & Dirk J. Korf. 1992. "The Development of Trade and Drug Control in the Netherlands: A Historical Perspective." *Crime, Law and Social Change* 17:123–44.

De Leeuw, Hendrik. 1955. *Underworld Story: The Rise of Organized Crime and Vice-Rackets in the United States*. London: Neville Spearman.

Delevingne, Malcolm. 1931. "Drug Addiction as an International Problem." *British Journal of Inebriety* 29:54–59.

Delevingne, Malcolm. 1935. "Some International Aspects of the Problem of Drug Addiction." *British Journal of Inebriety* 32:125–49.

D'Erlanger, Henry. 1936. *The Last Plague of Egypt*. London: Lovat Dickson and Thompson.

Erlen, Jonathan, & Joseph Spillane, eds. 2004. *Federal Drug Control: The Evolution of Policy and Practice*. Binghamton, NY: Haworth Press.

French, Paul. 2011. *Midnight in Peking: How the Murder of a Young Englishwoman Haunted the Last Days of Old China*. New York: Penguin.

Gomila, Frank, & Madeline Gomila Lambou. 1938. "Present Status of Marihuana Vice in the United States." in *Marihuana: America's New Drug Problem*, ed. Robert Walton, 1–14. Philadelphia: J. B. Lippincott.

Gootenberg, Paul. 1999. *Cocaine: Global Histories*. New York: Routledge.

Gorman, Daniel. 2012. *The Emergence of International Society in the 1920s*. Cambridge: Cambridge University Press.

Haller, Mark. 1970. "Urban Crime and Criminal Justice: The Chicago Case." *Journal of American History* 57:619–35.

Haller, Mark. 1971. "Organized Crime in Urban Society: Chicago in the Twentieth Century." *Journal of Social History* 5:143–63.

Hickman, Timothy. 2000. "Drugs and Race in American Culture: Orientalism in the Turn-of-the-Century Discourse of Narcotic Addiction." *American Studies* 41:71–91.

Kefauver, Estes. 1952. *Crime in America*. London: Victor Gollancz.

Kinder, Douglas. 1981. "Bureaucratic Cold Warrior: Harry J. Anslinger and Illicit Narcotics Traffic." *Pacific Historical Review* 50:169–91.

Kinder, Douglas Clark, & William O. Walker. 1986. "Stable Force in a Storm: Harry J. Anslinger and Narcotic Foreign Policy, 1930–1962." *Journal of American History* 72:908–27.

Knepper, Paul. 2013. "The International Traffic in Women: Scandinavia and the League of Nations Inquiry of 1927." *Journal of Scandinavian Studies in Criminology and Crime Prevention* 14:64–80.

Kohn, Marek. 2001. *Dope Girls: The Birth of the British Drug Underground*. London: Granta.

Kozma, Liat. 2011. "The League of Nations and the Debate over Cannabis Prohibition." *History Compass* 9:61–70.

Marabuto, Paul. 1951. "The International Criminal Police." *Bulletin on Narcotics* 3:3–15.

McAllister, William. 2000. *Drug Diplomacy in the Twentieth Century: An International History.* London: Routledge.

McWilliams, John C. 1990. *The Protectors: Harry J. Anslinger and the Federal Bureau of Narcotics, 1930–1962.* Newark: University of Delaware Press.

Meyer, Kathryn, & Terry Parssinen. 1998. *Webs of Smoke: Smugglers, Warlords, Spies, and the History of the International Drug Trade.* Lanham, MD: Rowan and Littlefield.

Mills, James, & Patricia Barton. 2007. *Drugs and Empires: Essays in Modern Imperialism and Intoxication, 1500–1930.* London: Palgrave Macmillan.

Musto, David. 1973. *The American Disease: Origins of Narcotics Control.* Oxford: Oxford University Press.

Parssinen, Terry. 1982. *Secret Passions, Secret Remedies: Narcotic Drugs in British Society, 1820–1930.* Philadelphia: Institute of Human Issues.

Rhodes, Henry T. F. 1939. *The Criminal in Society.* London: Lindsay Drummond.

Russell Pasha, T. W. 1949. *Egyptian Service, 1902–1946.* London: John Murray.

Schoenfeld, Dudley. 1944. "The Sociological Study." In *The Marihuana Problem in the City of New York*, ed. Mayor's Committee on Marijuana, 1–25. New York: Livingston Press.

Seed, John. 2006. "Limehouse Blues: Looking for Chinatown in the London Docks, 1900–40." *History Workshop Journal* 62:58–85.

Siddiqi, Yumna. 2006. "The Cesspool of Empire: Sherlock Holmes and the Return of the Repressed." *Victorian Literature and Culture* 34:233–47.

Speaker, Susan L. 2001. "'The Struggle of Mankind Against Its Deadliest Foe': Themes of Counter-Subversion in Anti-Narcotic Campaigns, 1920–1940." *Journal of Social History* 34:591–610.

Spillane, Joseph. 1998. "The Making of an Underground Market: Drug Selling in Chicago, 1900–1940." *Journal of Social History* 32:27–47.

Spillane, Joseph. 2000. *Cocaine: From Medical Marvel to Modern Menace in the United States, 1884–1920.* Baltimore, MD: Johns Hopkins University Press.

Thomas, Donald. 1997. *Detective Fiction and the Rise of Forensic Science.* Cambridge: Cambridge University Press.

Treasury Department. 1919. *Traffic in Narcotic Drugs: Report of the Special Committee Investigation.* Washington, D.C.: U.S. Government Printing Office.

Trocki, Carl. 1999. *Opium, Empire and the Global Political Economy: A Study of the Asian Opium Trade.* London: Routledge.

Van Houten, M. C. 1930. "The International Co-Operation of Criminal Police: Its History and Its Aims." *Police Journal* 3:482–97.

Van Schendel, Willem, & Itty Abraham, eds. 2005. *Illicit Flows and Criminal Things: States, Borders, and the Other Side of Globalzation.* Bloomington: Indiana University Press.

Yeager, Matthew. 2012. "Fifty Years of Research on Illegal Enterprises: An Interview with Mark Haller." *Trends in Organized Crime* 15:1–12.

PART THREE

CRIME, GENDER, AND ETHNICITIES

CHAPTER 11

....

VIOLENCE AND
MASCULINITY

....

JOACHIM EIBACH

INTRODUCTION

....

WITHIN the context of the history of crime and criminal justice, the dual aspects of violence and masculinity are without doubt of great significance. From the late Middle Ages onward, courts in Europe dealt with tens of thousands of cases that involved men as perpetrators and/or victims of violent crimes. Even in today's society, the overwhelming majority of violent felonies are committed by men. Since the emergence of the interest in crime as a historical phenomenon and, more generally, in deviant behavior during the 1970s, numerous books and articles have been written on the topic. Obviously, this is closely connected to the history of murder (see Chapter 5 by Mc Mahon). Clearly, one cannot write about masculinity and violence without reflecting on the role of women in interpersonal conflict (see Chapter 12 by van der Heijden) and on the manifold aspects of gender. The topic is complex and calls for interdisciplinary theoretical and methodological reflection. Thus, there has been considerable mutual influence between social science theories and historiography on violence. Recently, some historians have advocated the application of evolutionary psychology to historical analysis.

Although classical methods of quantification cannot be lightly dismissed, over the past years the historiographical research on masculinity and violent crime has been dominated by cultural historical approaches. It has become clear that, in the course of history, male violence has taken very different forms, functions, and meanings. This fact is partially concealed by the rather simple categorization of violent offenses in historical and current criminal codes. From a cultural historical perspective, violent action by men or women cannot be interpreted as contingent, individual acts, but rather as practices embedded in sociocultural contexts and accompanied by informal norms that mirror prevailing notions of gender and are often summarized in a specific code of honor. Many studies focus rather narrowly on physical violence as defined by criminal law. However, with regard to gender, one has to consider the fact that in predominantly oral societies, including Europe in the Middle Ages, verbal violence such as defamation and blasphemy was regarded more severely than in today's society. This is important, since female defendants often accounted for the majority of verbal crimes. Sexual crimes, which were mostly committed by men, appear to be much less well-researched than homicide and assault (Loetz 2012).

From a broad perspective, the topic of interpersonal violence and masculinity finds itself trapped between two contrary assumptions. As will be delineated in more detail later, we can observe a constant, quasi-unhistorical overrepresentation of men in recorded violent crimes and thus a certain disposition of male aggressiveness. Often after spectacularly violent incidents, reports in the media tell us that men, in particular young men, have always been inclined to turn violent and just seem to be more violent than women. This viewpoint has become "a cliché of criminology" (Wiener 2004, p. 1) and finds support in the analysis of pathological types of aggression by neurobiologists (Buckholtz & Meyer-Lindenberg 2008; Siever 2008). On the other hand, several influential historians of crime, social scientists, and psychologists, many of them equipped with Norbert Elias's (1982) theory of the civilizing process, have emphasized the scope of a general evolution of manners in the history of the Western world (Johnson & Monkkonen 1996; Spierenburg 2008; Pinker 2011). However, this optimistic perspective remains highly controversial and greatly contested. Not only historians, but also social scientists from Europe and the United States with very different approaches deny that there is a general progress in modernity toward a more peaceful society (Wieviorka 2005; Sofsky 2005; Roth 2009).

Elias's work does not specifically address the gender aspect. Nevertheless, it is evident that the thesis of the civilizing process applies first and foremost to those who needed to be civilized—namely, men! Several underlying assumptions of Elias's theory appear questionable (Mc Mahon, Eibach, & Roth 2013) and have caused intense methodological debate among historians of crime (Spierenburg 2001; Spierenburg 2002; Schwerhoff 2002). All societies, not just modern Western ones, take measures to control human aggressive behavior. The medieval feud was regulated by characteristic rituals, and the containment of violence in the premodern cities of Europe was a joint venture of the citizens and the town council (Pohl 1999; Eibach 2007a). However, we can detect several types and major shifts in the history of interpersonal male violence in the Western world. The appearance of judicial courts in medieval towns in Europe was rooted in the wish by the developing urban authorities to contain men's violent actions.

While, on the one hand, the capacity to act violently against other persons belongs to the basic equipment of humans, on the other hand, violence occurs in sociocultural contexts with many facets and very diverse meanings. Consequently, one grand theory can hardly account convincingly for the entire history of violence and masculinity. Instead, an array of approaches is more likely to shed light on specific aspects of male violence in its historical dimensions. Interestingly, shifts in the history of violence often correspond with changes to and sometimes crises of prevailing notions of masculinity.

The essay will be organized as follows. Section I provides an overview of historiography, sources, and methodology, as well as an example of male-on-male group violence from 1756. Section II explores the leading theoretical approaches. Section III examines relevant types and shifts in the European history of male violence since the early modern period.

I. Sources and Issues of Methodology

Formulating the problem of male violence in these terms, the sources relevant for the history of violence and masculinity are broadly similar to those used for the history of crime in general. A distinction needs to be drawn between normative source genres such as conduct books, moral treatises, and instructions for organized paramilitaries on the one hand, and judicial records on the other. In early research from before the late 1980s, not least that carried out by Elias, normative sources often were misleadingly read as mirrors of social practice. Furthermore, normative sources were studied in order to examine changing attitudes to and perceptions of violence. By contrast, since the 1980s, a younger generation of scholars, inspired by micro- and cultural history, have turned to the bulk of handwritten court records found in judicial archives. In particular, the minutes of court sessions that include the accounts of plaintiffs, defendants, and witnesses have proved to be a rich source of information leading to a more thorough understanding of the practices, meanings, and roles of violence in everyday life (for an overview, see Schwerhoff 2011, pp. 40–71). As for the early modern period, violent acts are frequently mentioned in reports by administrative officials or travelers about local customs, even if they were very often not recorded as crimes. These sources, just like newspaper articles, can be interpreted in two ways. While they can be used to gain additional information about the practice of violence, they also contain certain topoi, stereotypes, and thus a specific discourse on violence, such as those about the "primitive populace," "uncivilized" men from minority ethnic backgrounds, or "the rough" from the working class (King 2009; Emsley 2005, p. 75). Novels and ego-documents can offer further insights into contemporary notions and attitudes on issues such as gender roles and male honor. This is especially true for the elites who produced most of this type of sources. With regard to the United States from the mid-nineteenth century onward, newspapers are regarded as the best source (Roth 2009, pp. 477–87).

One significant advantage of analyzing series of court records is that they allow the researcher both to count the number of cases focusing on the participants' gender and to reconstruct hermeneutically the "how and why" of violent action. As for methodology, there is a crucial difference in the scope of quantitative and qualitative analysis of crime. According to the quantitative evidence from multiple micro-historical studies collected by Manuel Eisner, the imbalanced gender ratio regarding assault, robbery, and homicide has remained relatively stable throughout the centuries. In Europe from the late Middle Ages until the 1990s, female perpetrators rarely made up more than

15 percent of recorded offenses (Eisner 2003, pp. 109–12). Exceptions may be due to different categories of classification, especially those regarding verbal defamation. Crime figures since the 1990s may indicate some change. According to Eisner, in Europe and the United States during the 1990s, men were still responsible for at least 85 percent of all violent crimes, both assaults and homicides. One example of the most recent trends can be seen in Switzerland, where between 1984 and 2008 the proportion of male suspects of homicide remained fairly constant, at 89 to 90 percent. However, the percentage of male perpetrators accused of assault fell consistently over that twenty-four-year period, from 92 to 86 percent (Eidgenössisches Department des Innern 2011, p. 16). Still, by comparing these figures with the proportions of the early modern period one gets the impression of a historically constant phenomenon.

Throughout history, men seem to have acted in aggressive ways much more often than women, or at least their violent actions have been registered more frequently. The crucial questions are: What does the consistent imbalance between the genders indicate, given the significant overrepresentation of males as violent offenders? With what degree of certitude can we take these figures, based on recorded crime, as a reliable mirror of long-term consistency in actual gender distribution? Finally, in more general terms, what caused this static gender distribution, and to what extent was it a product of certain biases in recording? Eisner concludes "that sex is not a relevant variable in explaining the decline in overall levels of serious violence." He goes on to assert that "neither increasing economic prosperity, historical variation in female participation in the labor market, nor changing cultural models of the family and gender roles appear to have had a significant impact on male predominance in serious violent crime" (Eisner 2003, p. 112). Obviously, the stability of the recorded ratio does not reflect the overall transformation of society. Referring to the same figures, Pieter Spierenburg makes a different point, that "the level of female violence" is "a function of the power balance between men and women." He argues, "This balance has consistently been uneven throughout the centuries and it has changed only slightly in recent times" (2008, p. 117).

While there can be no doubt about the fact that the contents of court records intertwine with social and cultural conditions at large, it is nonetheless helpful to closely examine different types of courts and the mechanisms behind the construction of these sources. This is especially apparent in the differences emerging from the practice of crime reporting and the logic of final judicial rulings. Detailed studies of the minutes of court sessions have revealed characteristic notions of violence and gender. A further consequence of such study is that the seemingly obvious link between masculinity and violence, which appears to be deeply embedded in structures of patriarchal domination irrespective of period, becomes less convincing. To illustrate this point, I will refer first to a recent study on the use of justice in Dutch towns and then to examples from Frankfurt on Main in the second half of the eighteenth century.

Manon van der Heijden's comparison of the records of higher and lower criminal courts in Dutch towns from 1600 to 1838 reveals that the extent of gender balance depends on the type of court under observation. While the proportion of female defendants in assault cases before the higher criminal courts of Amsterdam, Leiden, and

Rotterdam remained fairly low (6–16 percent) and thus fits well with the ratio noted previously, the analysis of records from the Protestant consistories and the correctional courts reveals a different picture. These courts mostly dealt with violent acts in the domestic sphere or among neighbors. Women made up 44 percent of the defendants in cases of violence brought before the consistories. The proportion of individuals brought before the court of correction in Rotterdam for fighting who were female was just slightly lower, at 42 percent. Very often these fights took place in the neighborhood. The author concludes, "Women's violent behavior may remain invisible in the early modern higher criminal court records of Holland, but it becomes more apparent in the records of the lower courts which particularly handled fights and aggression within neighborhoods" (van der Heijden 2013, p. 95).

Following from the so-called "cultural turn," most studies in the field include short sketches of individual cases with the names of the individuals involved. Such micro-historical details appear even in studies for which the main argument is based on quantitative evidence. The purpose of the following example from eighteenth-century Frankfurt on Main is to briefly demonstrate the potential of micro-historical analyses of court records for the study of crime, and moreover to shed light on the gender-biased mechanisms of crime reporting and prosecution. The legal and administrative framework of the inquisitorial trial procedures produced extensive source material. A clerk had to take notes of all questions by and answers from anyone interrogated in court. In practice, the application of the procedures varied from territory to territory and from court to court. While in some courts, the clerk only summarized the most important testimonies and the final sentence, in other courts, we find long dossiers including witnesses' reports, supplications, and legal statements of advocates. An example of this all-encompassing type of dossier are the "Criminalia" of Frankfurt on Main, a free imperial city with around 35,000 inhabitants (Eibach 2003, pp. 29–35). I will focus on one dossier out of more than 1,000 cases from the eighteenth-century city records in which men stood accused of violence.

The case concerns a typical after-tavern fight between two groups of men from neighboring quarters that turned into a confrontation with soldiers and guards (IFSG).[1] Like many other confrontations of this kind, the conflict started in the context of jolly pub sociability from apparently insignificant banter. On a Sunday night in March 1756, five young fishermen from Unterhausen had assembled in the tavern of Hermann Klingler to drink the typical light alcohol *Äppelwein* (cider) from the Frankfurt region. As Klingler reported in court, the arrival of another group of young men, gardeners from Oberhausen, immediately resulted in tensions between the men. The argument began when 25-year-old Georg Geyer from Oberhausen allegedly "just for fun" (*aus Spaß*) stole a piece of cake from 24-year-old Friedrich Heister from Unterhausen, which Heister answered with verbal insults, calling the gardener "a rascal" (*einen Spitzbuben*).[2] According to some witnesses, Geyer threw the cake on the floor and stepped on it. After Klingler had managed to contain the dispute, the gardeners from Oberhausen left the tavern, only to equip themselves with clubs, knives, and hatchets and wait for their opponents to come out. The brawl started when the fishermen left the tavern around closing time and armed themselves with poles and rudders. A little later, when night watchmen and soldiers arrived, the fight between these men from two neighborhoods turned into a battle against the city's police force, which in the end included more than sixty men. Although the battle lasted for several hours and was fought in the dark with fists, knives, and stones, only two severe injuries were recorded. One night watchman and the wife of one gardener and fish trader suffered nonlethal head injuries. By the judicial standards of the time regarding nonfatal violence, the sentence was rather harsh. Sixteen men were sentenced to severe prison and work on the city's fortification wall for periods of two weeks to three months. The tumult had threatened urban stability and demonstrated the weakness of the town council's police force, thus challenging the honor of the patrician town council. Without a doubt, the town council, as the city's principal criminal court, also considered the fact that the disturbance had taken place in Sachsenhausen, the poor people's quarter of Frankfurt on "the other side" of the river Main, an area composed of the two neighborhoods where the fishermen and gardeners lived.

Many aspects of this case remind us of typical modern-day weekend violence. The participants were largely young, unmarried "boys" (*Purschen*) from two neighboring communities, who, according to the testimonies, were of low social status and had a long-standing rivalry that had resulted in hatred between the two groups. Moreover, they had been drinking. The fight arose in a social context, and the incident that sparked it appears rather ridiculous to observers. Nonetheless, even the combined police force of city soldiers and burgher watchmen only regained control over the tumult with extreme difficulty. In the end, both Frankfurt's burghers and the city's advocates complained about "the nuisance and the godlessness" (*der Unfug und die Gottlosigkeit*) of "the wild youths from Sachsenhausen" (*wilde Sachsenhäuser Jugend*).[3] However, in many respect the case is rather typical of interpersonal male violence in the eighteenth century. I will return to this point in more detail in section III.

One major advantage of detailed court minutes is that they allow us to follow not only the sequence of violent confrontations, but also the mechanisms of crime reporting and prosecution. It is clear that physical violence in the public sphere was perceived and treated as a male domain. Interestingly, in the previous case, one officer declared in court that the soldiers and guards had been viciously attacked not only by the gardeners and fishermen, but "especially by their women and mothers" (*insonderheit deren Weiber und Mütter*), who had thrown heavy stones upon them.[4] Although this statement was highlighted in final reports by the advocates, not one woman was prosecuted. In the same vein, several other cases from Frankfurt could also be cited. In 1742, several women were involved in a tumult in the market.[5] In 1801, upon the announcement of an increase in the price of bread, a crowd of several hundred people, incited and led by impoverished women from Sachsenhausen, devastated eight of the town's bakeries (Eibach 2007b). Although in both cases, several women were taken to court, they were never sentenced. Certainly, this micro-historical analysis does not entirely repudiate the overall evidence that men turned to physical violence more often than women. It does, however, provide evidence to support the assertion that the violent behavior of women was taken less seriously, was less likely to be taken to higher courts, was rarely punished, and was generally less frequently recorded than similar behavior by men.

Over the past years, several studies on interpersonal violence in European cities have highlighted the phenomenon of female violence against men and other women (Dinges 1991; Dean 2004; Warner 2008). The finding of a gendered bias does not apply only to violent acts in the public sphere. Similar to the lower courts in Dutch towns, the litigation of neighborhood and domestic violence by the Frankfurt courts underlines the fact that women did use physical violence in conflicts. However, in the case of domestic conflict, and, in contrast to the treatment given to the responsible male heads of the household, they were rarely accused. Against the backdrop of the "double-edged" code of honor, women could take their men to court for drunkenness and wife beating, but a husband was expected to settle conflicts in the domestic sphere himself using moderate forms of castigation. A man who went to court saying he had been beaten by his wife ran the danger of making a fool of himself. "Effectively," Gowing observes, "only men could be guilty of violence" (1996, p. 180; cf. Nolde 2003, pp. 153–58; Eibach 2007c). Needless to say, the mechanisms of crime reporting and the biased construction of gender in court did not always work in favor of women. While physical violence was perceived as a kind of male prerogative, fornication, prostitution, and child murder were seen as the female domain.

II. THEORETICAL APPROACHES

There are numerous macro- and micro-sociological theories available to explain the differences in deviant behavior of men and women in general and in interpersonal violence in particular (for an overview, see Messerschmidt 1993; Archer 1994; Franke 2000; Zitzmann 2012). No single theory can convincingly explain all the relevant aspects of the multi-faceted relationship between violence and masculinity. Instead, the topic has been covered by an array of different approaches in the humanities, the social sciences, and the sciences. Neuroscience examines violence as a result of "the complex interactions between genes, biological signals, neural circuits, and the environment" (Nelson & Trainor 2007, p. 536). So far, no clear evidence has been found that testosterone—a commonly suspected catalyst of male aggressive behavior—has an impact on impulsive violence. Another objective of neuroscience is to detect genetic variations that determine pathological aggression. In this sense, men seem to be more inclined to certain antisocial behavior: "Among violent offenders, 47 percent of men and 21 percent of women have antisocial personality disorder" (Siever 2008, p. 430; cf. Buckholtz & Meyer-Lindenberg 2008, p. 125). Although these findings need to be taken into consideration, they cannot account for changing social environments and cultural contexts that have shaped the gendered aspect of violence in history (Muchembled 2012, p. 13).

Drawing on evolutionary Darwinist psychology and Steven Pinker's (2011) theory of an evolution of human cooperation based on an increase in the capacity for empathy and self-control since the Enlightenment, recently "a post-cultural history of violence" (Hanlon 2013, p. 395; cf. Wood 2007) has been suggested. The underlying assumption is that "biology and culture coexist in everyone" (Hanlon 2013, p. 396), or, more specifically, "all behaviors, in all humans, are mediated via universal mental and emotional systems based on neurochemistry and hormones, although there are significant universal variations between the sexes, and a significant range of behaviors across individuals" (p. 395). So far, the consequences of this approach in terms of historical method remain to be explored (see also Chapter 5 by Mc Mahon). As for the link between violence and masculinity, insisting on such a connection can only serve as a first step toward observing a male "competition for social resources" across time (Wood 2007, p. 104) or pointing at "the defense of status" (Wood 2011, p. 487). More precisely, in the modern era, men seem to be inclined to use physical violence and to defend their reputation of masculine toughness, particularly when other socioeconomic resources such as employment prospects, regular income, or education are not available (Adler 2003, pp. 553–54; Wood 2007, p. 105).

For historians, the categories of labeling and gendered social control, subcultures, and male bonding are particularly promising. Because of the overarching interest of the social sciences in explaining modern society, however, considerations of historical change, if included at all, do not go back beyond the emergence of modern class-based bourgeois society.

The dissimilar social control mechanisms applying to male and female violence, as analyzed previously, fit well into the labeling approach (Becker 1963), which has been advocated by leading German researchers (Schwerhoff 2011, pp. 35–39; Dinges & Sack 2000) and more recently applied to studies on sports-related violence (Tsoukala 2009). These studies argue that historically, it was the interplay of social perceptions, crime reporting, and prosecution that produced male delinquency. In contrast to violent acts by females, male violence was both expected and perceived as dangerous. Men found themselves in a highly ambivalent position. As peasants, guild members, and heads of households, they had to live up to an informal code of honor that required them to react to certain challenges with physical violence. At the same time, they had to respect the limits set by the authorities (Roper 1992; Pohl 1999). Moreover, the social profile of impoverished men from poor neighborhoods, such as Sachsenhausen in the late eighteenth century or districts of Chicago in the late nineteenth century (Adler 2003), was reinforced by the labeling of outsiders and further confirmed by deviant behavior that corresponded to their generally bad reputation. Aggressive behavior thus could be interpreted as a self-fulfilling dynamic in their response to the continued experience of marginalization, often termed "secondary deviance."

From the late 1920s onward, many sociological studies on juvenile delinquency have worked with concepts of "subculture" (Thrasher 1947 [1927]; Wolfgang and Ferracuti 1982 [1967]). This concept argues that in modern, complex societies, underprivileged or marginalized groups develop norms and codes that to some extent differ from the values of the hegemonic middle-class culture. In particular, deviant subcultures in big cities offer adolescent males social resources that the monotonous and strictly hierarchical professional sphere and their private lives cannot sufficiently provide: appreciation and respect, status, thrill, and the emotional experience of belonging ("*Gemeinschaft*"). In terms of national differences, research in the United States has focused on gangs in inner-city ghettos that have been abandoned by the state, while British sociologists in their analysis of skinheads and hooligans have tended to rely on concepts of class, and their German counterparts have analyzed the subcultures of hooligans and urban gangs with non-German ethnic identities (Knöbl 2002). Juvenile gangs—one important type of subculture among many—often exert strict social control over their members and have a clear hierarchy, with males at the top. Collective identities are strengthened in repeated conflicts, including physical violence among members as well as between rival groups (Muchembled 2012, pp. 274–300). Some subcultures place high value on rough and aggressive behavior as a sign of true and unspoilt masculinity that is understood as an integral part of male bonding. The explanatory framework of sociological studies ranges from rational choice theory, with an emphasis on instrumental violence, to notions of male honor (Bourgois 2003).

The concept of subculture does not work for the stratified society of premodern Europe, since group cultures in that period were based on birth, family, and honor, and were legally fixed. Perhaps the extravagant habitus of the Parisian *jeunesse dorée*, which was shaped through street fighting and aggressive behavior against Jacobins in 1794 and 1795, was the first juvenile subculture in modern history (Gendron 1979). However, it is difficult to apply a term that comes with an anachronistic, somewhat exotic twentieth-century flavor to nineteenth-century working-class or rural violence. Workers and peasants certainly had specific, rather durable cultures, but because of their relative size in population terms and their growing willingness to adopt bourgeois standards, they cannot adequately be described as *sub*cultures. In studies on violence in nineteenth-century England, John Carter Wood speaks of "customary" ways of working-class violence (2004, p. 48), while Martin J. Wiener argues that certain forms of male-on-male violence in the lower classes were "entrenched in popular culture" (2004, pp. 42, 50). The concept of subculture has its strengths with regard to collective identities in the complex, highly mobile societies of the twentieth century. Consequently, Pieter Spierenburg uses the term to explain the overrepresentation of immigrant minorities involved in murder in European cities of the 1980s (Spierenburg 2008, p. 216). Earlier concepts of subculture were by and large gender-blind, which is surprising, since the vast majority of perpetrators of violence were male. Notions of tough masculinity and male bonding were and still are crucial in many of today's juvenile subcultures. However, the concept is of limited value with regard to domestic and intra-couple violence.

In spite of many years of research, the challenge is still "to gain a better understanding of the potential link between masculinity and violence" (Taylor, das Nair, & Braham 2013, p. 776). This observation, while referring to neuro-scientific research, applies just as well to the social sciences. With regard to the continuous, cross-epochal reproduction of "*la domination masculine*," Pierre Bourdieu assumes that crucial aspects of masculinity have become incorporated into the male habitus and are hence passed on endlessly from generation to generation (Bourdieu 1997, p. 156; Bourdieu 1998). The male habitus is reproduced in manifold competitive "serious games" among men, games that include women only as adulating spectators (Bourdieu 1997, p. 203). According to Bourdieu, such games of dominance and honor are still played by men in present-day political, economic, and scientific life. The basic principle behind "serious games" is the competition among equal men for recognition. Though the role of women and the possibility of change appear to be underestimated, Bourdieu's conceptualization of habitus—with its potential to consider both structure and strategy equally—is indispensable for a historical understanding of violent practice in its cultural context. In societies without functional differentiation, habitus is learned through imitation of "other people's action" and adopted through embodiment (Bourdieu 1977, p. 87). Habitus is a product and a producer of history. These assumptions can be useful in the observation of diversity and transformation. This also applies to the approach of the anthropologist David Gilmore, who studied rites of manhood in both premodern and modern societies. For Gilmore, young men do not inherit their gender, but have to earn their masculinity through trials of courage and physical challenges. The particular forms of the liminal ritual differ from society to society, but their function remains basically the same (Gilmore 1990). Men practice initiation rituals or violent "serious games" to strive for, respectively, masculinity and integration.

A relevant contribution to future research comes from the interdisciplinary field of men and masculinity studies. Adopting this perspective means abandoning the idea of a universal and stable notion of masculinity. Without doubt, the cross-epochal overrepresentation of men among recorded perpetrators of violence calls for an explanation. Behind this observable fact lies the sociocultural construction of masculinity and the social profile, practice, and meaning of male violence as well as changing attitudes toward violence from the early modern period to the late twentieth century. Moreover, from the perspective of deconstructivist feminist theory, it is highly misleading to take for granted the biological "naturalness" of gender (Butler 1990). Following R. W. Connell, who in the late 1980s initiated men and masculinity studies, we find in every society a specific pattern of hegemonic masculinity. This prevalent male habitus and strategy ensures cultural dominance over both women and other men. As Connell notes, "'hegemonic masculinity' is not a fixed character type, always and everywhere the same. It is, rather, the masculinity that occupies the hegemonic position in a given pattern of gender relations, a position always contestable" (2006, p. 76). Sometimes only a relatively small group of men performs a hegemonic pattern successfully, as illustrated by sixteenth-century conquistadors, eighteenth-century gentry, or today's top business managers. Popular "exemplars of masculinity . . . have very often been men of the frontier" (p. 185). Their practice of masculinity constitutes a normative model for other social groups. As with Bourdieu's concept of habitus, Connell sees gender patterns as "a product of history, and also a *producer* of history" (p. 81). Although his outline of the shaping of modern masculinity since the Reformation leaves many questions open (Dinges 2005), it is interesting that his approach considers competing images and different ways of "doing masculinity." Among the subordinate and marginalized groups we find women and nonhegemonic forms of masculinity. In daily routines we can observe "lived patterns of meanings" of masculinities and femininities, "which as they are experienced as practices, appear as reciprocally confirming" (Messerschmidt 1997, p. 11).

Drawing on the works of Bourdieu and Connell, the German sociologist Michael Meuser focused on "serious games" among men. His findings confirm that in homosocial groups, ritualized games of dominance are still played in order to earn the solidarity and "male honour" of peers (Meuser 2002, pp. 65–66; Meuser 2008). Fragile masculinity appears no longer to be restricted to a specific social class condition or to general social deprivation. Crossing the lines between delinquent and legally accepted behavior, Meuser's examples are taken from the male worlds of dueling student fraternities, football, and hooliganism. In these contexts, male sociability includes reciprocal violence, from which women are, by and large, excluded. Meuser argues that the early socialization of male youths in competitive "serious games" gives them an advantage in today's competition for high-level positions in politics, business, and science.

III. Historical Shifts

From a bird's-eye view, interpersonal violence among men and by men against women can be summarized as an anthropological quasi-constant of competition for social resources. A closer historical inspection, however, reveals several shifts from the early modern period onward (for continuities, see Chapter 5 by Mc Mahon). Any account of the history of male violence in the Western world must start with "the culture of dispute," which is derived from numerous thick descriptions drawn from court records. This specific practice of violence has been highlighted in particular by German researchers (Walz 1992; Schwerhoff 2004; Eriksson & Krug-Richter 2003); Spierenburg uses the term "popular duel" in the same vein (2008, p. 81). There is general consensus that the experience of physical and verbal violence in the early modern period was a normal and widely accepted aspect of everyday life. Violence was practiced openly, often even ostentatiously, by men from all social strata, albeit within well-known culturally defined limits. Violent encounters were often triggered by notions of honor: the need to defend one's reputation or one's "symbolic capital" (using Bourdieu's famous definition). The functions and meanings of honor were embedded in the communications of face-to-face societies in which men and women could not afford to lose their reputation. Honor was understood as a "limited good" (Walz 1992). Because of this informal code of honor, men had no choice but to react to certain challenges in violent or at least ostentatious ways. In spite of bans by urban authorities, male burghers up until the seventeenth or even early eighteenth centuries carried long knives as symbols of their masculinity and full citizenship. For women, the necessity of defending one's honor in an openly aggressive manner seems to have been restricted to the lower classes. In the context of households and neighborhoods, men and women often acted together.

Through ritualized insults and gestures, conflict in any matter could be transformed into a conflict about honor. However, the social resource of honor not only triggered conflict, but also shaped and regulated the practice of violence. Thus, an honorable dispute among equal men, which must be distinguished from punishment and wife beating, was reciprocal and respected limits of fairness. Likewise, the means of the *correctio domestica* were contained by certain rules observed by ecclesiastical courts.

Conflicts about honor often arose suddenly in the course of sociability. As seen from the example from Sachsenhausen, the incidents that sparked violence point to the vulnerability of honor and the fragility of masculinity (Schreiner & Schwerhoff 1995). Interestingly, in the case from 1756, between the first verbal argument over a piece of cake and the start of the brawl after the tavern's closing lay a time span of three hours, during which one party had left the tavern and waited for its rivals to come out. A break or time lag that allowed tempers to cool down is characteristic of numerous other early modern rituals of social control and conflict regulation, such as charivari, knife pulling (Schuster 2000, pp. 95–97), and house scorning—an act in which a man walked up in front of his opponent's home and challenged him to come out (Kramer 1956; Spierenburg 2008, pp. 69–70). We may conclude that the male actors were able to control their affects and that there were ways to handle conflict other than quasi-automatic "impulsive violence." Yet their code of honor demanded an answer to insults. The 1756 brawl between dozens of gardeners, fishermen, and several of their women reveals rules behind what at first sight seems to be chaos. The actors, though rather unsuspicious of being recipients of the civilizing process, respected the peace of the house (the tavern). Their violence was reciprocal aggression that followed a script of escalation and known limits. Strikingly, hardly any severe injuries occurred.

One has to add that the "culture of dispute" is an ideal type that refers to a specific practice of conflict. Religious violence and violence in wartime followed a completely different logic. Moreover, in the heat of the moment, and fueled by alcohol, many actors crossed thresholds of social acceptance. There is a narrow line between the identification of meaning and ritual on the one hand, and the hermeneutic trap of endowing violence with an overdose of sense on the other. It appears that during the eighteenth century, established rules and rituals lost some of their binding force.

The overall decline of lethal violence during the eighteenth century has to be seen against the backdrop of a transformation of masculinities. This observation applies primarily to the urban sphere. While in the fifteenth and sixteenth centuries, numerous men from the upper strata were accused of aggressive behavior, in the criminal dossiers of eighteenth-century London only a few gentlemen appear. Similarly, in medium-sized German cities like Frankfurt or Cologne we find hardly any patricians or affluent merchants, or even men from the middling levels of society (Shoemaker 2001; Shoemaker 2002; Eibach 2003, pp. 211–14, 279–82; Schwerhoff 2013, p. 40). In the course of the century, master craftsmen also refrained from participating in the popular theater of street violence. The 1756 brawl is characteristic of eighteenth-century urban violence in that the actors were legally integrated, albeit impoverished, citizens from the lower echelons. Although we can decipher the regulatory features of the "culture of dispute," elaborate rituals of conflict regulation are missing. In contrast, the elite duel became more ritualized during the same period. Hence, the eighteenth and nineteenth centuries witnessed an increasing social distinction in the formerly common practice of violent honor conflicts (Schwerhoff 2013, pp. 40–42).

Without doubt, the availability of different types of judicial courts in towns had an impact on the reduced relevance of rituals and the decrease in acceptance of violence as a means of social control. Equally important were shifts of masculinity and male honor that resulted in the formation of a new hegemonic habitus. Robert Shoemaker has pointed to "an increasing intolerance of violence, new internalized understandings of elite honor, and the adoption of 'polite' and sentimental norms governing masculine conduct" in London since the late seventeenth century (2002, p. 525). According to Shoemaker, this fundamental cultural shift was accompanied by a new appreciation of inner virtues, domesticity, refined sociability, and more reserved public behavior (2001, p. 207). In the same vein, Spierenburg observes a "spiritualization of honor" (2008, p. 110). The example of seventeenth-century London suggests that the presence of a royal court and nobility, advanced social and economic differentiation, and the vivid discourse of the Enlightenment were guiding factors in the formation of a new form of masculinity. Yet these aspects were not of major relevance in the old-style imperial town of Frankfurt, with its merchants, artisans, and urban agriculture. Still, new bourgeois standards of behavior were adopted in medium-sized towns as well. The taming of violence over the course of the eighteenth century points to the penetrating effect of the overall macro-processes of rationalization and individualization in the sense of lessening the grip of corporate honor on the actors (Drawing on Weber and Durkheim, Eisner 2001, pp. 89–95).

In the nineteenth century, things became more differentiated and also more complicated. With the polite gentleman ideal and the self-restrained habitus of the *Bürger*, the European bourgeois societies inherited new role models of masculinity from the age of the Enlightenment. At the same time, violent behavior in the street became a marginalized lower-class habitus. The aspiration toward refinement stood in opposition to customary violence: in elite discourse, violence was now relocated "outside of society" (Wood 2004, p. 140). According to Schwerhoff, as rituals of honorable dispute lost their binding force across social boundaries, "several subcultures of violence emerged" (2013, p. 41). Nevertheless, one may legitimately question the argument that from their creation in the second half of the eighteenth century until the late twentieth century, modern masculinity—and, accordingly, modern male honor—has not changed greatly (Mosse 1996). Undeniably, the new middle class, or bourgeoisie, played a leading role in defining new forms of masculinity and femininity. In the course of the nineteenth century, under the influence of warfare and military reforms such as the introduction of general conscription in most European countries, bourgeois masculinity stiffened toward self-discipline, intransigence, toughness, braveness, and propensity for violence (Dudink, Hagemann, & Tosh 2004; Schmale 2003, pp. 195–203). However, we must not overlook the emergence between the late eighteenth century and 1848 of the bourgeois avant-garde project, which cultivated a soft, emotional, privacy-bound masculinity that included a fondness for children and intellectual conversation with women (Trepp 1994). Nor can one overlook the introduction of a "masculine domesticity" toward the middle of the nineteenth century (Tosh 1999, p. 6).

In any case, the male elites of nineteenth-century Europe appear Janus-faced with their preference for rationality and refined sociability on the one hand, and their passion for ritualized duels on the other. The enthusiasm of many academics, politicians, and other elite men for dueling cannot simply be dismissed as the aftermath of premodern honor conflicts. The contrast between societies with reviving cultures of dueling like Germany, Italy, France, and the southern regions of the United States and societies with no dueling cult, like England, republican Switzerland, and the northern regions of the United States indicates that masculinities in the modern era could and did take different courses (Frevert 1995; Roth 2009, pp. 181, 213–18; Ludwig, Krug-Richter, & Schwerhoff 2012).

Surprisingly, despite low homicide rates, the nineteenth century saw a great diversity of recurrent forms and meanings of interpersonal violence. The emergence of a new type of violence that variously can be categorized as "crimes of passion" (Guillais 1990; Spierenburg 2008, pp. 184–92), "romance homicide" (Roth 2009, p. 251), or "fatalistic violence" (Cottier & Raciti 2013, p. 112) mirrors the spread of new ideals of romantic love and emotionalized family life. According to Cottier and Raciti (2013), this new type of violence corresponded with the evolution of modern troubled subjectivity. In contrast to traditional domestic violence and honor conflicts, the perpetrators—mostly males, but also females—acted out of emotional despair when attempting to kill their intimate partners or their own children, acts that were often combined with a suicide attempt. At the same time, old forms of physical confrontation continued and new forms of "serious games" gained popularity. Ritualized fistfighting on the street—typically outside the pub—became emblematic for working-class masculinity. In addition, older forms of prizefighting, boxing, and other kinds of sport fighting developed into highly merchandised commodities, enjoyed by spectators from all social classes (Wood 2004, pp. 72–80). Expressive public forms of working-class violence came under increasing scrutiny, not only from professionalized police forces but also from the labor movements in England and Germany, which advocated the "civilized" standards of bourgeois behavior (Jessen 1992; Wood 2004).

Already in the eighteenth century, lower and ecclesiastical courts were attempting to control domestic violence with the help of numerous complaints by battered wives (Gowing 1996, pp. 206–29; Eibach 2007c). Nonetheless, in Victorian England, social pacification through the criminal law gained hitherto unknown strength and vigor. Supported by economic prosperity and rising levels of education, criminal courts in England seem to have been successful in making the domestic sphere a more peaceful place. This initiative was supported by a new discourse on ideal manliness. According to Wiener, "the ideal of the 'man of honor' was giving way to that of the 'man of dignity'" (2004, p. 6; cf. Emsley 2005, pp. 57–75). Paradoxically, at the same time the domestication of Victorian men in their comfortable, private middle-class homes was occurring (Tosh 1999), the upkeep and expansion of the British Empire abroad required a more violent version of masculinity.

In the course of the twentieth century, violent "men of the frontier" were to play a vital role in the imagery of masculinity, particularly if the light versions of the "Marlboro Man" and other popular representations in the mass media are included (Hatty 2000, pp. 159–89). However, one could also argue that the crisis of masculinity, which resulted from the emergence of an industrialized, bureaucratic, and technical world during the nineteenth century and led to challenges to traditional gender roles (Arni 2004, pp. 215–24; Fout 1992), was never effectively overcome and still endures today. The ongoing discourse on manliness serves as only one example of this theory.

Beyond that, any researcher, who strives to conceptualize modernity in linear processes will be confused by the different paths of violence over the past century. The twentieth century witnessed extreme and unprecedented collective violence, the enduring persistence of intimate violence, all-time low homicide rates in the 1950s and the early 1960s, and a surprising return of honor confrontations among young men starting in the 1970s. While it is advisable—from a methodological point of view—to distinguish carefully between types of violence (e.g., military violence in wartime and interpersonal violence in peacetime), the lines between different types of violence are often blurred. Thus, the lust for physical violence among the Italian "squadristi" or the German SA can only be explained if manifold aspects are considered: the experience of war and defeat in the First World War, the ideology of fascism, aggrieved manliness and the fierce antifeminist reaction to the crisis of masculinity, male bonding and the construction of a racially determined *Volksgemeinschaft* through collective experience, and the practice of violence against political opponents and other perceived enemies. The fascist movements of the 1920s were based on male bonding, with a radical antifeminine and antibourgeois concept of intransigent, aggressive manliness (Reichardt 2009; Kühne 2006). The outcome of this conception—an ideal that denied individual responsibility—first brought violence to the street and in assembly halls, and then was followed by an extreme type of warfare and a habitus that enabled ordinary men to take part in genocide.

Interestingly, the experience of extreme violence in the trenches and on the battlefields of two world wars had no lasting decivilizing effect on the quantity of homicides. In most European countries during the war and in the postwar years, there was a temporary rise in the homicide rate followed thereafter by a steady decline (Spierenburg 2008, pp. 198–209; Roth 2009, p. 452). By the middle of the twentieth century, conflicts between intimate partners made up a large portion of homicides in the Western world. In contrast to the premodern culture of dispute and sociable violence among men from the working class, this type of violence was not driven by notions of honor, being neither reciprocal nor competitive, nor linked to places of leisure. Nonetheless, in contradiction to the classical sociological breakdown of historical developments that situates concepts of honor in the stratified societies of premodern Europe and places its final manifestations in the nineteenth century, honor conflicts had a comeback in the second half of the twentieth century. Concepts of honor had an obvious impact among marginalized immigrant communities of non-European descent with features of "traditional macho honor" (Spierenburg 2008, pp. 207, 226). However, we also have to consider wider social contexts here. Over the last decades, in the economically depressed outskirts (*banlieue*) of European cities, as in the abandoned no-go areas of several American cities, new highly confrontational face-to-face-cultures have evolved. The necessity of defending personal "respect" in face-to-face relationships and the propensity to solve conflicts through violence corresponds clearly with a lack of integration into the structures of modern middle-class society, with its high degree of functional differentiation, requirement of education, and state-based institutions. Modern masculinity is still learned and shaped through "serious games," some of them legally accepted, others not. The examples of the emergence of new violent sports such as "ultimate fighting" or the revival during the fascist era of the traditional Florentine *Calcio Storico* demonstrate that the borders of legal acceptance are constantly being contested. While instrumental violence against both men and women is characteristic of organized crime, Roberto Saviano (2007) has shown with regard to the *Camorra* that the practice of Mafia violence is not founded in a purely economic logic, but is also accompanied by specific notions of masculinity and femininity. The Sicilian Mafia, which emerged as late as in the last decades of the nineteenth century, maintains a discourse of honor and honorable men that conceals their rather raw economic interests (Dickie 2004).

Conclusion

Twentieth-century youth sub- and countercultures constitute a field of experimentation regarding new and diverse nuances of masculinity and femininity. In examining the affinity to violence, we can certainly observe a wide range of gendered identities. Ironically, the primarily male homicide rates skyrocketed in the United States at a time when Bob Dylan, John Lennon, Frank Zappa, and many others were inaugurating what were by the standards of the postwar era fairly un-masculine masculinities. In recent narratives of the long-term history of violence, the various cultural explanations for the rise in homicide since the 1960s appear rather incompatible. For Pinker (2011, pp. 110–16), the new thoroughly antibourgeois attitudes adopted by the 1960s' movement toward morals, self-control, and self-indulgence fostered the affinity to violence. Conversely, for Spierenburg, the peaceful character of the hippie movement was "the cultural corollary to the trough in violence" (2008, p. 205). By contrast, Roth explains the soaring homicide rates in the United States as related to a decrease of trust in the government and state institutions. Following Roth, it is typical for such time periods in history that "men lose hope of winning respect by legitimate means" (2009, p. 455). All in all, the history of violence and masculinity since the eighteenth century is a story of continuing changes, innovations, and recurrence.

ACKNOWLEDGMENT

I thank Maurice Cottier (Bern) and John Jordan (Bern) for their comments on this text.

NOTES

1. "Criminalia," 7245 (1756), Institut für Stadtgeschichte Frankfurt am Main (IfSG), Frankfurt on Main, Germany.
2. Ibid., p. 27.
3. Ibid., pp. 6, 52.
4. Ibid., pp. 44, 72.
5. "Criminalia," 5445 (1742), IfSG, Frankfurt on Main, Germany.

REFERENCES

Adler, Jeffrey. 2003. "'On the Border of Snakeland': Evolutionary Psychology and Plebeian Violence in Industrial Chicago, 1875–1920." *Journal of Social History* 36 (3): 541–60.

Archer, John, ed. 1994. *Male Violence*. London: Routledge.

Arni, Caroline. 2004. *Entzweiungen. Die Krise der Ehe um 1900*. Cologne, Germany: Böhlau.

Becker, Howard. 1963. *Outsiders: Studies in the Sociology of Deviance*. New York: Free Press.

Bourdieu, Pierre. 1977. *Outline of a Theory of Practice*. Cambridge: Cambridge University Press.

Bourdieu, Pierre. 1997. "Die männliche Herrschaft." In *Ein alltägliches Spiel. Geschlechterkonstruktion in der sozialen Praxis*, ed. Irene Dölling & Beate Krais, 153–217. Frankfurt, Germany: Suhrkamp.

Bourdieu, Pierre. 1998. *La domination masculine*. Paris: Seuil.

Bourgois, Phillippe. 2003. *In Search of Respect: Selling Crack in El Barrio*. 2nd ed. Cambridge: Cambridge University Press.

Buckholtz, Joshua, & Andreas Meyer-Lindenberg. 2008. "MAOA and the Neurogenetic Architecture of Human Aggression." *Trends in Neurosciences* 31 (3): 120–29.

Butler, Judith. 1990. *Gender Trouble: Feminism and the Subversion of Identity*. New York: Routledge.

Connell, Raewyn W. 2006. *Masculinities*. Cambridge: Polity.

Cottier, Maurice, & Silvio Raciti. 2013. "From Honour to Subjectivity: Interpersonal Violence in Basel 1750–1868 and Berne 1861–1944." *Crime, History & Societies* 17 (2): 101–24.

Dean, Trevor. 2004. "Gender and Insult in an Italian City: Bologna in the Later Middle Ages." *Social History* 29 (2): 217–31.

Dickie, John. 2004. *Cosa Nostra: The History of the Sicilian Mafia*. London: Hodder & Stoughton.

Dinges, Martin. 1991. "'Weiblichkeit' in 'Männlichkeitsritualen'? Zu weiblichen Taktiken im Ehrenhandel in Paris im 18. Jahrhundert. *Francia* 18 (2): 71–98.

Dinges, Martin. 2005. "'Hegemoniale Männlichkeit'—ein Konzept auf dem Prüfstand." In *Männer—Macht—Körper. Hegemoniale Männlichkeiten vom Mittelalter bis heute*, ed. Martin Dinges, 7–33. Frankfurt, Germany: Campus.

Dinges, Martin, & Fritz Sack, eds. 2000. *Unsichere Großstädte? Vom Mittelalter bis zur Postmoderne*. Konstanz, Germany: UVK.

Dudink, Stefan, Karen Hagemann, & John Tosh, eds. 2004. *Masculinities in Politics and War: Gendering Modern History*. Manchester, UK: Manchester University Press.

Eibach, Joachim. 2003. *Frankfurter Verhöre. Städtische Lebenswelten und Kriminalität im 18. Jahrhundert*. Paderborn, Germany: Schöningh.

Eibach, Joachim. 2007a. "Burghers or Town Council? Who Was Responsible for Urban Stability in Early Modern German Towns?" *Urban History* 34 (1): 14–26.

Eibach, Joachim. 2007b. "Arme Frauen—Rebellierende Frauen. Der Aufruhr gegen die Sachsenhäuser Bäcker im Jahr 1801." In *Blickwechsel. Frankfurter Frauenzimmer um 1800*, ed. Ursula Kern, 78–87. Frankfurt, Germany: Kramer.

Eibach, Joachim. 2007c. "Der Kampf um die Hosen und die Justiz—Ehekonflikte in Frankfurt im 18. Jahrhundert." In *Kriminalität in Mittelalter und Früher Neuzeit*, ed. Sylvia Kesper-Biermann & Diethelm Klippel, 167–88. Wiesbaden, Germany: Harassowitz.

Eidgenössisches Departement des Innern. 2011. *Frauen und Strafrecht. Entwicklungen der Frauenkriminalität*. Neuchâtel, Switzerland: Bundesamt für Statistik.

Eisner, Manuel. 2001. "Individuelle Gewalt und Modernisierung in Europa, 1200–2000." In *Gewaltkriminalität zwischen Mythos und Realität*, ed. Günter Albrecht, Otto Backes, & Wolfgang Kühnel, 71–100. Frankfurt, Germany: Suhrkamp.

Eisner, Manuel. 2003. "Long Term Trends in Violent Crime." In *Crime and Justice: A Review of Research*, Vol. 30, ed. Michael Tonry, 83–142. Chicago: University of Chicago Press.

Elias, Norbert. 1982. *The Civilizing Process*, 2 vols., New York: Pantheon Books.

Emsley, Clive. 2005. *Hard Men: The English and Violence since 1750*. London: Hambledon.

Eriksson, Magnus, & Barbara Krug-Richter, eds. 2003. *Streitkulturen. Gewalt, Konflikt und Kommunikation in der ländlichen Gesellschaft (16.-19. Jahrhundert)*. Cologne, Germany: Böhlau.

Fout, John. 1992. "Sexual Politics in Wilhelmine Germany: The Male Gender Crisis, Moral Purity, and Homophobia." In *Forbidden History: The State, Society, and the Regulation of Sexuality in Modern Europe*, ed. John Fout, 388–421. Chicago: University of Chicago Press.

Franke, Kirsten. 2000. *Frauen und Kriminalität. Eine kritische Analyse kriminologischer und soziologischer Theorien*. Konstanz, Germany: UVK.

Frevert, Ute. 1995. *Men of Honour: A social and Cultural History of the Duel*. Cambridge: Polity.

Gendron, François. 1979. *La Jeunesse dorée. Épisodes de la Révolution française*. Sillery, Canada: Presses de l'Université du Québec.

Gilmore, David. 1990. *Manhood in the Making: Cultural Concepts of Masculinity*. New Haven, CT: Yale University Press.

Gowing, Laura. 1996. *Domestic Dangers: Women, Words, and Sex in Early Modern London*. Oxford: Clarendon.

Guillais, Joelle. 1990. *Crimes of Passion: Dramas of Private Life in Nineteenth-Century France*. New York: Routledge.

Hanlon, Gregory. 2013. "The Decline of Violence in the West: From Cultural to Post-Cultural History." *English Historical Review* 128 (531): 367–400.

Hatty, Suzanne. 2000. *Masculinities, Violence and Culture*. London: Sage.

Jessen, Ralph. 1992. "Gewaltkriminalität im Ruhrgebiet zwischen bürgerlicher Panik und proletarischer Subkultur." In *Kirmes—Kneipe—Kino. Arbeiterkultur im Ruhrgebiet zwischen Kommerz und Kontrolle (1850-1914)*, ed. Dagmar Kift, 226–55. Paderborn, Germany: Schöningh.

Johnson, Eric, & Eric Monkkonen, eds. 1996. *The Civilization of Crime: Violence in Town and Country since the Middle Ages.* Urbana: University of Illinois Press.

King, Peter. 2009. "Making Crime News: Newspapers, Violent Crime and the Selective Reporting of Old Bailey Trials in the late Eighteenth Century." *Crime, History & Societies* 13 (1): 91–116.

Knöbl, Wolfgang. 2002. "Gewalt und Gesellschaftstheorie: Vom Wandel sozialwissenschaftlicher Perspektiven am Beispiel der Analysen zu US-amerikanischen Jugendgangs." *Handlung Kultur Interpretation* 11 (2): 225–41.

Kramer, Karl-Sigismund. 1956. "Das Herausfordern aus dem Haus." *Bayerisches Jahrbuch für Volkskunde* (no number): 121–38.

Kühne, Thomas. 2006. *Kameradschaft. Die Soldaten des nationalsozialistischen Krieges und das 20. Jahrhundert.* Göttingen, Germany: Vandenhoeck.

Loetz, Francisca. 2012. *Sexualisierte Gewalt 1500–1850. Plädoyer für eine historische Gewaltforschung.* Frankfurt, Germany: Campus.

Ludwig, Ulrike, Barbara Krug-Richter, & Gerd Schwerhoff, eds. 2012. *Das Duell. Ehrenkämpfe vom Mittelalter bis zur Moderne.* Konstanz, Germany: UVK.

Mc Mahon, Richard, Joachim Eibach, & Randolph Roth. 2013. "Making Sense of Violence? Reflections on the History of Interpersonal Violence in Europe." *Crime, History & Societies* 17 (2): 5–26.

Messerschmidt, James. 1993. *Masculinities and Crime: Critique and Reconceptualization of Theory.* Lanham, MD: Rowman & Littlefield.

Messerschmidt, James. 1997. *Crime as Structured Action: Gender, Race, Class, and Crime in the Making.* London: Sage.

Meuser, Michael. 2002. "'Doing masculinity'—Zur Geschlechtslogik männlichen Gewalthandelns." In *Gewalt-Verhältnisse. Feministische Perspektiven auf Geschlecht und Gewalt*, ed. Regina Dackweiler & Reinhild Schäfer, 53–78. Frankfurt, Germany: Campus.

Meuser, Michael. 2008. "It's a Men's World. Ernste Spiele männlicher Vergemeinschaftung." In *Ernste Spiele. Zur politischen Soziologie des Fußballs*, ed. Gabriele Klein & Michael Meuser, 113–34. Bielefeld, Germany: Transcript.

Mosse, George. 1996. *The Image of Man: The Creation of Modern Masculinity.* New York: Oxford University Press.

Muchembled, Robert. 2012. *A History of Violence from the End of the Middle Ages to the Present.* Cambridge: Polity.

Nelson, Randy, & Brian Trainor. 2007. "Neural Mechanisms of Aggression." *Nature Reviews Neuroscience* 8:536–46.

Nolde, Dorothea. 2003. *Gattenmord. Macht und Gewalt in der frühneuzeitlichen Ehe.* Cologne, Germany: Böhlau.

Pinker, Steven. 2011. *The Better Angels of Our Nature: The Decline of Violence in History and Its Causes.* London: Allen Lane.

Pohl, Susanne. 1999. "'Ehrlicher Totschlag'—'Rache'—'Notwehr.' Zwischen männlichem Ehrencode und dem Primat des Stadtfriedens (Zürich 1376–1600)." In *Kulturelle Reformation. Sinnformationen im Umbruch 1400–1600*, ed. Bernhard Jussen & Craig Koslofsky, 239–83. Göttingen, Germany: Vandenhoeck.

Reichardt, Sven. 2009. *Faschistische Kampfbünde. Gewalt und Gemeinschaft im italienischen Squadrismus und in der deutschen SA*, 2nd. ed. Cologne, Germany: Böhlau.

Roper, Lyndal. 1992. "Männlichkeit und männliche Ehre." In *Frauengeschichte—Geschlechtergeschichte*, ed. Karin Hausen & Heide Wunder, 154–72. Frankfurt, Germany: Campus.

Roth, Randolph. 2009. *American Homicide*. Cambridge, MA: Harvard University Press.

Saviano, Roberto. 2007. *Gomorrah*. London: Macmillan.

Schmale, Wolfgang. 2003. *Geschichte der Männlichkeit in Europa (1450-2000)*. Cologne, Germany: Böhlau.

Schreiner, Klaus, & Gerd Schwerhoff, eds. 1995. *Verletzte Ehre. Ehrkonflikte in Gesellschaften des Mittelalters und der Frühen Neuzeit*. Cologne, Germany: Böhlau.

Schuster, Peter. 2000. *Eine Stadt vor Gericht. Recht und Alltag im spätmittelalterlichen Konstanz*. Paderborn, Germany: Schöningh.

Schwerhoff, Gerd. 2002. "Criminalized Violence and the Process of Civilisation—a Reappraisal." *Crime, History & Societies* 6 (2): 103–36.

Schwerhoff, Gerd. 2004. "Social Control of Violence, Violence as Social Control: The Case of Early Modern Germany." In *Social Control in Europe, 1500–1800*, ed. Herman Roodenburg & Pieter Spierenburg, 220–46. Columbus: Ohio State University Press.

Schwerhoff, Gerd. 2011. *Historische Kriminalitätsforschung*. Frankfurt, Germany: Campus.

Schwerhoff, Gerd. 2013. "Early Modern Violence and the Honour Code: From Social Integration to Social Distinction?" *Crime, History & Societies* 17 (2): 27–46.

Shoemaker, Robert. 2001. "Male Honour and the Decline of Public Violence in Eighteenth-Century London." *Social History* 26 (2): 190–208.

Shoemaker, Robert. 2002. "The Taming of the Duel: Masculinity, Honour and Ritual Violence in London, 1660–1800." *Historical Journal* 45 (3): 525–45.

Siever, Larry. 2008. "Neurobiology of Aggression and Violence." *American Journal of Psychiatry* 165 (4): 429–42.

Sofsky, Wolfgang. 2005. *Traktat über die Gewalt*. Frankfurt, Germany: Fischer.

Spierenburg, Pieter. 2001. "Violence and the Civilizing Process: Does It Work?" *Crime, History & Societies* 5 (2): 87–105.

Spierenburg, Pieter. 2002. "Theorizing in Jurassic Park: A Reply to Gerd Schwerhoff." *Crime, History & Societies* 6 (2): 127–28.

Spierenburg, Pieter. 2008. *A History of Murder: Personal Violence in Europe from the Middle Ages to the Present*. Cambridge: Polity Press.

Taylor, Nadine, Roshan das Nair, & Louise Braham. 2013. "Perpetrator and Victim Perceptions of Perpetrator's Masculinity as a Risk Factor for Violence: A Meta-Ethnography Synthesis." *Aggression and Violent Behavior* 18 (6): 774–83.

Thrasher, Frederick. 1947 [1927]. *The Gang: A Study of 1313 Gangs in Chicago*. Chicago: University of Chicago Press.

Tosh, John. 1999. *A Man's Place: Masculinity and the Middle-Class Home in Victorian England*. New Haven, CT: Yale University Press.

Trepp, Anne-Charlott. 1994. "The Emotional Side of Men in Late Eighteenth-Century Germany (Theory and Example)." *Central European History* 27 (2): 127–52.

Tsoukala, Anastassia. 2009. *Football Hooliganism in Europe: Security and Civil Liberties in the Balance*. London: Palgrave.

Van der Heijden, Manon. 2013. "Women, Violence and Urban Justice in Holland c. 1600–1838." *Crime, History & Societies* 17 (2): 71–100.

Walz, Rainer. 1992. "Agonale Kommunikation im Dorf der Frühen Neuzeit." *Westfälische Forschungen* 42:215–51.

Warner, Jessica, Janine Riviere, & Kathryn Graham. 2008. "Men and Women Fighting Side by Side: Examples from an English Town, 1653–1781." *Journal of Family History* 33 (2): 156–72.

Wiener, Martin. 2004. *Men of Blood: Violence, Manliness, and Criminal Justice in Victorian England*. Cambridge: Cambridge University Press.

Wieviorka, Michel. 2005. *La Violence*. Paris: Hachette.

Wolfgang, Marvin, & Franco Ferracuti. 1982 [1967]. *The Subculture of Violence: Towards an Integrated Theory in Criminology*. Beverly Hills, CA: Sage Publications.

Wood, John C. 2004. *Violence and Crime in Nineteenth-Century England: The Shadow of Our Refinement*. London: Routledge.

Wood, John C. 2007. "The Limits of Culture? Society, Evolutionary Psychology and the History of Violence." *Cultural and Social History* 4 (1): 95–114.

Wood, John C. 2011. "A Change of Perspective: Integrating Evolutionary Psychology into the Historiography of Violence." *British Journal of Criminology* 51 (3): 479–98.

Zitzmann, Ellen. 2012. *Opfer Mann? Männer im Spannungsfeld von Täter und Opfer*. Marburg, Germany: Tectum.

CHAPTER 12

WOMEN AND CRIME, 1750–2000

MANON VAN DER HEIJDEN

INTRODUCTION

IT is generally observed by criminologists that women are responsible for a smaller proportion of indictable offenses than men: approximately 13 percent of all prosecution in Europe (Aebi et al. 2010, p. 195). This strong gender difference in criminal behavior is generally linked to the dissimilar public lifestyles of men and women: the fact that women have less freedom and fewer opportunities may cause a lower participation by women in crime and may also lead to more lenient treatment by prosecutors (Pollak 1950; Adler 1975; Arnot & Usborne 2003; Burke 2006; Silvestri & Crowther-Dowey 2008, p. 27). Furthermore, scholars generally assume that the sex differences in recorded crime have been consistent across time, stressing the continuity rather than change in men's excessive contribution to criminality (Heidensohn 1996; Burkhead 2006, p. 50; Silvestri & Crowther-Dowey 2008, pp. 26, 191). However, historical data on early modern Europe show that in France, England, and the Netherlands, between 1600 and 1800 women played a much more prominent role in crime than they did in the twentieth century (Farge 1974; Feeley 1991; Feeley 1994; King 2006; Spierenburg 2008, p. 117; Van der Heijden 2013; Van der Heijden 2014).

The high percentages of female crime in the seventeenth and eighteenth centuries and the low percentage of female crime from the nineteenth century onward have led to an academic debate about trends in male and female recorded crime. The central question is: How and why do male and female recorded crime rates vary in Europe between 1750 and 1945? Crime historians agree that various factors played an important role in gender differences in recorded crime. First, historians and criminologists generally agree that gender differences in recorded crime were determined by moral and legal norms. Value systems varied over time and space, and moral and legal norms about the behavior of men and women affected their roles and conduct in private and public and their incentive to commit crimes. Moral norms also led to biased prosecution policies, particularly those related to sexual behavior, religious matters, and violence. In the twentieth century, racial, class, and gender biases remained an important element in prosecution practices, but throughout the centuries there were shifts in the attitudes of prosecutors toward men and women. Second, crime historians have observed that women's visibility in the sources is influenced by the ways in which courts were used by authorities and the people. Different types of courts—lower and higher, local and central, secular and ecclesiastical—handled different types of crime and employed different types of procedures. Women's crime was more likely to be handled by lower courts or through less formal methods of dispute regulation than by higher courts (Schwerhoff 1991; Shoemaker 1998, p. 292; King 2006, pp. 202–10; Van der Heijden 2013). Third, urban historians have shown that urbanization offers an important explanation for the levels of female crime. Women's contribution to crime was generally much higher in cities than in rural communities or small towns. The lack of economic and social support from the traditional community caused women in towns and cities to lead more independent, public, and risky lives (Farge 1974, p. 116; Hufton 1974, pp. 278–80; Beattie 1975, p. 81; Beattie 1986; Castan 1980; Shoemaker 1991, pp. 208–09).

This essay is organized as follows. Section I discusses female crime in the early modern period (ca. 1500–1800). The debate among crime historians and criminologists about the decline in female crime from the nineteenth century onward is the topic of section II. In section III, I discuss women's small contribution to violence and changing attitudes toward violence in the eighteenth and nineteenth centuries. The final section then briefly examines the increase in women's involvement in crime in the twentieth century.

I. FEMALE CRIME IN THE EARLY MODERN PERIOD

Crime historians generally agree that there are clear indications that women played a much more prominent role in crime in the period between 1600 and 1800 compared to what became the norm in the 19th and 20th centuries. Data on France, England, Germany, and the Netherlands reveal that women's involvement in crime was not limited to distinctively female offenses such as infanticide, witchcraft, and prostitution. Women also constituted a large part of the cases that are typically associated with male crime, such as property offenses and sometimes violence. Various studies on early modern crime and gender show that between 1600 and 1850, 20 to 50 percent of property crimes were committed by women (Schwerhoff 1991, p. 178; Feeley 1994, p. 235; Walker 2003; King 2006; Eibach 2003; Wettmann-Jungblut 2009; Van der Heijden 2014). Dutch and English historians have found that in seventeenth-century Amsterdam and London, women were responsible for half of the crimes that were prosecuted by the urban courts. In other cities in Holland—such as the textile city of Leiden—female crime rates even rose in some periods to over 50 percent.

The link between high levels of female crime and urbanization in the early modern period was first explored by Beattie (1975) in his work about the criminality of women in England. Beattie found that the degree of urbanization contributed to women's opportunities for living independent and public lives, and that this led to more risky lives and higher female crime rates (Beattie 1975, p. 81; Beattie 2001, pp. 63–73). Van der Heijden argues that high urbanization levels could also explain differences between regions within Europe between 1600 and 1900. The relatively low level of urbaniza-tion and smaller towns in the German areas compared to England and Holland may explain the less public roles of women and the consequently low female crime rates during that period of time. At the end of the eighteenth century, 30 to 40 percent of the Dutch population lived in towns, compared to 20 percent in England, 18 percent in Italy, and 5.5 percent in Germany. In Holland (the western part of the Netherlands) the level of urbanization was 70 percent (De Vries & Van der Woude 1995, p. 83; Clark 2009, pp. 119–23, 128).

Historians have also pointed to the link between the relatively high level of prosecu-tion of women between 1600 and 1800 and demographic features of early modern towns. Early modern urban societies were characterized by a surplus of women, which was sub-stantially higher in flourishing seafaring towns or during wars, when a large proportion of the male urban population was moved to other areas. Consequently, a substantial part of the urban female population was—either temporarily or permanently—living alone (King 2006, p. 212; Van der Heijden & Van den Heuvel 2007; Van der Heijden, Schmidt, & Wall 2007). These women were young single women, widows, or married women who lived without their husbands for varying periods of time. At the end of the eighteenth century there was a considerable surplus of women in Amsterdam: five women for every four men (Van der Heijden & Van den Heuvel 2007, p. 298).

Urban historians have found that women's independent position in urban communi-ties was also linked to migration patterns. Early modern towns owed their population growth mainly to migrants who were looking for work and ways to make a living, and among them there were many single women. Migrant domestic maids and female tex-tile workers had to compete in the labor and marriage markets with local women who had built strong social and economic networks and were more likely to receive support from the family. For migrant women the survival opportunities were clearly less prom-ising. Shoemaker's examination of the London area shows that because of their public lifestyles and the insecurity of their employment, single women and widows in urban areas were more likely to enter into disputes and less likely to settle their disputes out of court (1991, pp. 207–16). Similar conclusions are drawn by Castan, Farge, and Lambert about eighteenth-century rural and urban France. For many young lower-class women migrating from the countryside to the city, criminal activities such as theft, burglary, and prostitution were parts of a logical survival strategy (Farge 1974, p. 116; Hufton 1974, pp. 278–80; Beattie 1975, p. 81; Beattie 1986; Castan 1980; Shoemaker 1991, pp. 208–09). Page Moch has pointed to the fact that in eighteenth-century European cities, migrant women with the least social support "paid for their vulnerability in ways that landed them in jail and saddled them with infants to raise without a husband" (2003, p. 146). In her work on early modern France, Hufton characterizes the survival strategy of many urban women living alone as an "economy of makeshift"; they were making ends meet by a combination of work and various activities, including criminal conduct (Hufton 1974, pp. 278–80; see also Moch 2003, p. 146). Taken together, the relatively independent position of women, their consequently more important public roles, and their vulnerability may explain the high rate of female violence in cities such as Amsterdam and London in the seventeenth and eighteenth centuries (Van der Heijden & Van den Heuvel 2007).

Similarly, in some periods, legal norms and double standards regarding male and female behavior led to high rates of prosecution for women. Between the sixteenth and seventeenth centuries, authorities in both Protestant and Catholic countries during the Counter-Reformation increased their control over sexual behavior and religious attitudes. Scholars generally refer to sexual and religious offenses as "soft crimes" because the definition and prosecution of such infringements depend on continuously changing moral norms. Between roughly 1560 and 1660, the widespread belief in the existence of witchcraft and sorcery resulted in some areas of Western Europe in response to a sharp rise in prosecution of women for witchcraft. There was sustained and heavy persecution of witches in the southwestern regions of the Holy Roman Empire and moderate or light persecution in the rest of Western Europe. Despite the popular fascination with and historical interest in witchcraft, the prosecution of witchcraft was a rather sporadic phenomenon (Schwerhoff 1991; Behringer 1995; Levack 1995; Durrant 2007).

Double standards regarding male and female sexual behavior also led to more sustained prosecutions of women in the early modern period. In most parts of Western Europe sexual intercourse outside marriage—fornication, prostitution, and adultery—was forbidden by the law. Although men were accused of sexual and religious offenses as well, women were more likely to be arrested on such charges and to be treated less leniently by the judges (Schwerhoff 1995; Van der Heijden 2014). In early modern societies sexual honor was an important asset of women and a matter of great concern to both secular and ecclesiastical authorities. Consequently, almost everywhere in Europe the law favored men with regard to sexual offenses. In Holland in the seventeenth century adulterous women received more serious punishments and were banished for longer times than adulterous men. While men visiting prostitutes usually got away with a financial arrangement with the public prosecutor, prostitutes were arrested and convicted (Pluskota 2011). Women were also more likely to be arrested for sexual offenses because a pregnancy made her deed of fornication visible to the whole community. Authorities' concern about the financial burden of illegitimate children led in the seventeenth and eighteenth centuries in most northwest European areas to harsher punishment of women who had given birth to a child outside wedlock.

Child murder was in the early modern period a distinctively female crime that was strongly linked to the social and economic constraints women had to deal with when having an illegitimate child. Women with bastards would lose their honor and any reasonable chance of marriage, and domestic servants would certainly lose their job. Child murder tends to have been committed by single women who concealed their pregnancy and the birth of the child, and the murder was always committed directly after the birth of a child. Commonly, it was neighbors who would bring such cases to the public prosecutor or the court and who informed doctors and midwives. For eighteenth-century England, Jackson has found that disproportionate attention to single mothers led to many unjustified accusations of newborn child murder: roughly 3 percent of women arrested for infanticide were convicted (Jackson 1996, pp. 3–4, 17).

The social and economic backgrounds of women committing infanticide were similar everywhere in Western Europe: most women were around 27 years of age when they were arrested, they often earned a living as a domestic maid or cleaner, and the child was usually born at the home of their master (Faber 1978; Jackson 1996; Hässler & Hässler 2011; Van der Heijden 2014, p. 81).

Increasing attention to illegitimacy from secular and ecclesiastical authorities from the second half of the seventeenth century onward was presumably linked to economic depression, which caused higher rates of children born outside wedlock and greater concern for the moral and financial consequences of illegitimacy (Mitteraurer 1983; Jackson 1996; Pluskota 2011, p. 12; Gerber 2012; Van der Heijden 2014, pp. 72–89).

II. The Historical Debate on the "Vanishing Female" from ca. 1800

The high percentages of female crime in the seventeenth and eighteenth centuries have led to an academic debate about trends in male and female recorded crime. Using data from several European countries, the criminologist Feeley has argued that the percentage of female crime declined dramatically during the eighteenth and nineteenth centuries (Feeley & Little 1991; Feeley 1994). Feeley claims that the high percentages of female crime were not linked to a gender bias, because women were not more likely to be arrested or convicted than men. According to Feeley, this high percentage reflects real crime rates, which declined as a result of industrialization. He called the decline of women in the criminal justice process the "vanishing Female."

Feeley—and his co-authors Little and Aviram—suggests that the decline of women in the criminal justice process was caused by a shift in patriarchal patterns and the separation of public and private spheres after the Industrial Revolution starting around 1750. This development had two important consequences. First, the male breadwinner ideology changed the attitudes of judges and public prosecutors toward women committing crimes. They began to take women's crimes less seriously, and consequently women became less likely to be arrested and convicted than men. In addition, ideologies about the public and private roles of men and women led to a real decline in female crime. Since women were removed from the public sphere and the labor market, and confined in the private sphere of the home, their opportunities and incentives to commit crime decreased.

Feeley and his co-authors based their findings on the proceedings of the Old Bailey in London between 1687 and 1912 and on secondary literature on female crime in various European countries, particularly the Netherlands. Though recognizing that factors of demography, jurisdiction, and war might have played a role in the changing proportion of women in crime rates, they dispute the relevance of such factors, arguing that demographic developments and changes in the judicial system would not be sufficient to explain long-term trends in female crime (Feeley & Little 1991, pp. 724–40; Feeley 1994, pp. 250–59). While most historians assume that a separation of private (female) and public (male) spheres in the eighteenth and nineteenth centuries may have reinforced the gendered crime pattern, other scholars have raised substantial doubts about the idea of the "vanishing female" as suggested by Feeley (Emsley 1996, p. 152; Shoemaker 1998; Arnot & Usborne 2003, p. 8; King 2006, pp. 198–99)

King maintains that the English evidence points to long-term stability in the eighteenth and nineteenth centuries rather than a long-term decline. He agrees that the female proportion of crime rates strongly fluctuated between 1750 and 1850, though he links such changes to complex short-term developments such as war and exceptional circumstances. He also raises some methodological concerns with regard to the data used by Feeley. Feeley based his findings primarily on the Old Bailey, without taking into account the significant judicial changes that occurred after 1850. King points to the relationship between changes to the patterns of prosecution and procedural practice between 1850 and 1890, and the lower proportion of women brought to trial for indictable offenses in the new statistical series after 1857. Furthermore, King finds wide variations in the proportion of offenders who were female. His findings confirm Beattie's argument of a close relationship between the degree of urban involvement in a region and its percentages of female offenders (Beattie 1975; King 2006, pp. 198–220).

Although spatial variations and the complex geography of female involvement in indictable crime make it difficult to draw general conclusions, there appears to be very little evidence of long-term decline in England, at least not until the first half of the nineteenth century. The work of Zedner on nineteenth-century England shows that there was no decline in the proportion of indicted women before around 1850. The numbers of suspected persons between 1893 and 1905 demonstrate that women's proportion of prosecuted crime declined as late as the twentieth century (Zedner 1991, p. 36). As there is for England no sign of significant long-term change, King concludes that "on closer inspection therefore, the vanishing female offender vanishes" (2006, p. 220).

Dutch historians Van der Heijden and Koningsberger have also raised methodological and conceptual concerns with regard to the Dutch sources used by Feeley and his co-authors to prove their argument. First, the evidence presented relates particularly to the seventeenth century, and there are very little data on the crucial period of the assumed change over the second half of the eighteenth century and the nineteenth century. The lack of consistent evidence on the period around 1800 is particularly problematic because Feeley links the decline of female crime to the process of industrialization between 1750 and 1850. The process of industrialization started in Holland as late as 1850, while the reliable Dutch data in Feeley's analysis cover the period before 1811.

Evidence from eighteenth- and nineteenth-century Holland confirms the pattern of female crime as described by King (2006) for England in the same period. In Holland, there was long-term stability in the female share of prosecutions and convictions between 1750 and 1838. Between 1750 and 1811 women's involvement in crime continued to be high in urban areas. Regional data between 1811 and 1838 suggest that there were extensive continuities in the proportion of female offenders among the various courts between 1750 and 1838. Low figures of women's involvement between 1839 and 1886 reflect instead jurisdictional changes; the new national data after 1838 include felony cases for women from rural as well as urban regions.

Finally, the extent to which the Industrial Revolution would have resulted in a decline in women's labor participation is not clear. Demographic historian Van Poppel suggests that the Dutch industrialization around 1850 had little impact on women's labor participation (Van Poppel 2006). In addition, the alleged disappearance of women from the public sphere did not occur, and men's and women's activities in the public sphere did not reflect prevailing ideologies of domestic and public roles. In practice, women's activities transcended the realm of the household, and many women were not able—even if they wanted—to uphold the ideal of the husband as the breadwinner.

The pathbreaking work of Feeley was undoubtedly a significant step in the debate on crime and gender. However, there are important limitations regarding the current data on male and female crime. The figures on long-term European crime rates are often inconsistent and inadequate for comparison. In addition, historians and criminologists tend to focus on either the early modern period or the period after 1900, and not much work has been done on the period of transition between 1800 and 1920. More consistent and comparative evidence that includes local and regional variations, differences between urban and rural areas, and jurisdictional differences between regions in Europe and beyond is needed to answer the question of when and why women's proportion in crime declined (Van der Heijden & Koningsberger 2013).

III. GENDER AND CHANGING ATTITUDES TOWARD VIOLENCE

While some historians attempt to find long-term trends and changes by looking at the patterns of female crime, others argue that fundamental changes in the eighteenth and nineteenth centuries are much more related to the prosecution of male crime (Van der Heijden & Pluskota 2014). Most criminal justice historians agree that from the end of the eighteenth century onward, there was a growing social disapproval of male violent behavior in Western Europe. At the same time, women came to be seen as more vulnerable and in need of protection (Muchembled 2012).

Wiener has shown for Victorian England that such constructions had a significant impact on the treatment of male violence by prosecutors and the courts. In the course of the nineteenth century, the courts increasingly began to focus more on men and less on women. According to Wiener, this change also entailed a different attitude toward men's violence against women. Wiener claims that in the early modern period, women who were maltreated by their husband could seldom count on support from the authorities, although this changed in the early nineteenth century when authorities increasingly began to protect women and children against male aggression. In addition, while homicidal women tended to be treated with more leniency, homicidal men faced harsher treatment over the nineteenth century (Wiener 1998; Wiener 2004).

Wiener's emphasis on male violence was a response to feminist theories that stressed the impact of nineteenth-century notions of domesticity, patriarchy, and separate private and public spheres on women's lives, while largely neglecting the change of attitudes toward men. Zedner (1991) argues that up to the mid-nineteenth century, women were increasingly prosecuted because their criminal acts were viewed as acts of deviance from female behavior norms. In her work on working-class women, D'Cruze (1999) demonstrates that women's and girls' reputations were increasingly judged on the basis of their sexual behavior and their household skills, and although women sometimes used the courts to vindicate their reputations, a great deal of sexual assault was not reported by them. Social constructions of class, gender, and race would have made it increasingly difficult for women to defend their sexual honor, particularly if they were working class or migrants. D'Cruze finds that Irish women—who were a significant minority in urban Lancashire and Cheshire—did appear in the courts for street fighting, but they never brought sexual violence into the courts (D'Cruze 1998; D'Cruze 1999).

Other feminist studies have assumed that in the nineteenth century violence was less often brought to court because women's lives became more confined to the domestic sphere and, consequently, domestic violence became less visible. In the early modern period, cases of domestic violence were often perceived as public issues that were discussed and solved by local intermediaries and institutions. Hardwick (2009), for instance, finds that in early modern France, women received as much, and sometimes greater, protection against violence than in the nineteenth century. Similar attitudes toward violence have been found in Germany and England (Rublack 2002). Evidence from early modern Holland demonstrates that women were often protected against domestic abuse by neighbors who were afraid that violent behavior would harm the reputation of the whole neighborhood. Furthermore, the legal pluralism of early modern societies offered various opportunities for women to act against abusive husbands, particularly in towns with a broad variety of formal and informal legal bodies. Professionalization and centralization of the legal system after 1800 resulted everywhere in Western Europe in the abolition of old institutions that had been important in conflict resolution and were accessible to women (Van der Heijden 2000; Van der Heijden 2012; Van der Heijden 2013).

Stigmatization and criminalization of violence may have resulted in a growing interest in the prosecution of assault in most parts of Western Europe, though the effects might have been different for each region. It seems that in England in the eighteenth century most cases of personal violence did not reach the courts, and if they did, they were generally perceived as essentially private matters. Wiener shows for England that the legal tolerance of interpersonal violence began to change after 1800, resulting in increasing prosecution rates for assault cases and a harsher treatment of offenders by the courts (Wiener 1998, pp. 202–209; Gatrell & Hadden 1972, pp. 392–93; Zedner 1991). Furthermore, prosecution and conviction disproportionally began to concentrate on men: between 1805 and 1842 the total prosecutions of women at the assizes and quarter session courts rose fourfold, and at the same time, the prosecution of men rose eightfold (Gatrell & Hadden 1972, pp. 392–93; Zedner 1991, pp. 316–23; Wiener 1998, pp. 202–09). The gender difference continued in the course of the nineteenth century, and as a consequence the proportion of men prosecuted at the Old Bailey rose to almost 90 percent of the total suspects at the end of the century (Feeley & Little 1991; Wiener 1998, p. 209).

Wiener has also found a growing attention by lawmakers and judges to domestic violence and rape. In England after 1800, a rise in trials involving rape and domestic violence occurred, and wife beaters received harsher punishments by the courts than before. Wiener argues that growing opportunities for women to start legal actions against abusive husbands served two purposes: to better protect women and to reform men. As a consequence, battered wives became a large group among the cases dealt with by the English courts at every judicial level. As the prosecution rate of male violence rose, so did the prosecution rates for sexual assaults on women in the course of the nineteenth century (Wiener 1998, pp. 206–07; Frost 2008).

The gender differences in the treatment of male and female violators seem to support Wiener's criminalization thesis, at least for England. In his work about crime and law in England between 1780 and 1830, King observes that female offenders accused of crime in the major courts of the late eighteenth century and early nineteenth century frequently succeeded in obtaining more lenient treatment than their male equivalents. Women who were tried by the Old Bailey court—which had jurisdiction over all capital offenses and a considerable proportion of noncapital property crimes—had much better prospects than men. The majority of men coming before the Old Bailey were convicted (61 percent), while a minority of women (44 percent) were not convicted. The Old Bailey primarily tried property offenders, but the same pattern can be found in other major courts that were responsible for murder and manslaughter. King's data on Surrey and Lancashire suggest that women accused of murder had a better chance of obtaining a lenient verdict than their male counterparts (2006, pp. 165–95). Data collected by Zedner on the penal system of Victorian England confirm King's findings: between 1857 and 1890 men were much more likely to be convicted than women, with 66 to 83 percent of men who were put on trial being convicted, compared to 53 to 77 percent of women (1991, p. 308).

The studies on the major courts in England clearly point to a gender bias in prosecuting violence, but the majority of the assault cases were brought to the lower courts. Looking at minor violence in ten English petty session courts between 1880 and 1920 (10,000 prosecutions), criminologist Godfrey has found a strong gender bias in the sentencing of assaults. Magistrates clearly deemed assaults committed by women less important, as women were more likely than men to be acquitted of assault. The findings from the English courts between 1880 and 1920 show that 62 percent of men were convicted, as opposed to 49 percent of women. The gender bias was even more evident in the proportion of acquitted charges or charges that were bound over: 38 percent of males were acquitted or bound over, as opposed to 52 percent of females. The English evidence seems to be clear-cut. Whether it concerned the Old Bailey prosecuting felonies or quarter sessions covering both urban and rural areas or petty session courts dealing with common assault, the findings confirm King's statement that in England the favorable treatment of violent women represented a national pattern (Godfrey 2003, p. 341; Godfrey, Farall, & Karstedt 2005, p. 702; King 2006, pp. 227–54).

The strong evidence of growing differences in the treatment of male and female violence in England in the late eighteenth and early nineteenth centuries has led most criminal justice historians to believe that such a change took place in the rest of Western Europe. Muchembled concludes that, as in England, the French courts became increasingly severe toward male criminals, while at the same time treating women with greater leniency (2012, p. 204). According to Spierenburg, in the Netherlands by the eighteenth century, the honor of men was increasingly linked to their roles as husbands and breadwinners (2013, p. 7). While for England, Wiener observes the first signs of a change in attitudes toward masculine behavior in the sixteenth century, Spierenburg notices that in the Netherlands the crucial turn took place in the eighteenth century. There may also have been differences between regions regarding the impact of the new ideal. Emsley notes that, in comparison to other countries, English people were particularly eager to obtain self-control (Emsley 2005, p. 13).

Several scholars have also been critical about the idea of a general decline in the acceptability of male violence. Criminologist Godfrey raises doubts about two important assumptions about the decline in violent crime in the nineteenth century. First, he questions whether the decline in violent crime—as apparent in the judicial records—actually mirrors a real decline from 1870 to 1914. Second, he raises doubt about whether these figures are indicative of a shift in the attitudes toward violence in this period. Godfrey recognizes that most scholars are aware of the limitations of crime statistics, and that most researchers see them rather as indicators of a combination of factors (e.g., prosecution policy, socioeconomic circumstances, public anxieties, jurisdictional changes, police practice). However, he also thinks that criminal justice historians should move beyond the criminal statistics and search for alternative sources, such as oral histories, that may reveal common voices about violence (Godfrey 2003). In order to explain gendered sentencing patterns, crime historians should look at the impact of contextual factors on the decisions of judges. Both the context of the offense and the life trajectories of offenders, rather than gender bias, might explain differences between sentences imposed on men and women. Godfrey finds for England in the late nine-teenth century that men received more serious penalties because male violent conflicts were deemed by judges to be more severe confrontations that deserved harsher punish-ments than conflicts involving women (Godfrey, Farall, & Karstedt 2005, pp. 712, 717).

Finally, some scholars are critical about the assumption that in the eighteenth and nineteenth centuries, violence became a working-class phenomenon that needed to be controlled by the upper and middle classes. Both late nineteenth-century Germany and France experienced an upsurge in dueling, notably among students. In their intro-duction to a special issue of *Crime, History & Societies* on interpersonal violence, Mc Mahon, Eibach, and Roth warn us against neat narratives of decline, as the evidence tends to support a trend of fluctuations and variations across time and space (Mc Mahon, Eibach, & Roth 2013).

There is much less evidence for the "criminalization of men" thesis outside England and France. Although important work has been done on Dutch violence in the early modern period by Spierenburg, there is little information about the period after 1811 when the French penal code was introduced in the Netherlands. Recent examinations by Van der Heijden and Pluskota (2014) on the prosecution of male and female vio-lence in the nineteenth-century Netherlands suggest a much more nuanced picture. The records from different types of courts (police tribunal, correctional, and criminal) in various towns and cities of the Netherlands over the period 1750–1886 demonstrate growing prosecution rates for violence, both in numbers and proportionally, as was also the case in England during the same period. However, no gender bias has been found in the sentencing and conviction of assault cases. Furthermore, physical violence was the primary target of these courts, and although rape and domestic violence were punishable by law, the prosecution rates for these crimes remained low throughout the nineteenth century. Apparently, in the judicial context, increasing prosecution rates for violence in the nineteenth century did not parallel an increased focus on male violence.

IV. A New Rise in Female Crime?

Whereas the period between 1800 and 1970 was marked by a general marginalization of interpersonal violence, particularly murder, it seems that the tables turned after the 1960s. In his long-term study on murder, Spierenburg demonstrates that homicide rates in European countries considerably rose from the 1970s onward, from approximately 0.5 to 1.4 persons per 100,000 habitants. The available statistical data show that the homicide rise is mostly due to an increase in male victimization; the majority of killers and their victims are men, and Spierenburg finds that a part of the increase in homicide rates is due to a resurgence of male fighting (2008, pp. 165–223). A second important shift occurred in the twentieth century: female crime appears to have generally risen in most parts of the Western world from the 1960s onwards. The question is whether this increase includes violence.

In her work on the crime of girls and women in the twentieth-century United States, Chesney-Lind finds that although criminal statistics still reflect the dominance of male delinquency, from the 1970s onward there has been an increasing interest in the violent crimes of girls. Girls' arrests for violent crimes between 1985 and 1994 seem to provide support for a real rise in their violent crime: U.S. crime statistics show that arrests of girls for murder have increased up to 4 percent, for robbery up to 114 percent, and for aggravated assault up to 136 percent. However, Chesney-Lind observes that on closer inspection the rise is considerably less dramatic. She argues that this pattern reflects changes in youth behavior in general, rather than fundamental shifts in the behavior of girls only (Chesney-Lind 1997, pp. 33–58).

It seems that in the United States the number of youth involved in gangs increased dramatically in the 1980s, and as a result youth gangs became a serious problem in most large cities (Chesney-Lind 1997, p. 42). There seem to have been similar problems in the cities of Europe. Studies on crime in the Paris *banlieues* show that in the 1990s duels between boys were fought before a large audience of girls and boys. Although girls fought less seriously, the fights included girls too (Spierenburg 2008, p. 213). However, it remains difficult to find substantial support for the notion that girls have become relatively more aggressive in the last decades. Scholars such as Spierenburg (2008) and Muchembled (2012) point to the growing sensitivity and intense public anxiety over violence since the 1990s, which would explain a rise in prosecution rates for assault, rather than a real increase in violence rates.

There may also be different explanations for similar trends in different parts of the Western world, or a different scholarly tradition in explaining crime patterns of men and women. American scholars often emphasize the impact of racism and class on the prosecution of violence in urban ghettos, and such explanations include the involvement of girls and women. Chesney-Lind concludes that women were always more involved in violent behavior and criminal gangs than the stereotypes of women support (Chesney-Lind 1997, p. 57). In her work on female crime in twentieth-century America, Adler has paid particular attention to the social and economic backgrounds of women and their appearance in criminal justice statistics. Economic circumstances and legitimate opportunities would make it less likely that white women would have recourse to criminal behavior. There are clear indications that—despite welfare arrangements—more black women living in American cities are dealing with social-economic difficulties, such as unemployment and bad housing, than their white counterparts. Furthermore, as a result of racial bias, the criminal justice system generally treats black women with less leniency than white women. Likewise, women from lower classes are more likely to get involved in crime and to be arrested by the police than those who are well off and well educated (Adler 1975, pp. 133–54).

More recently, sociologists Steffensmeier and Schwarz have taken a closer look at the various trends in female crime in the United States and have found different trends with regard to various types of crime committed by women. Apart from women's involvement in violent crime, there seem to be clear indications that female crime rates have been slightly increasing in both Europe and the United States from the 1960s onward. Data drawn from the FBI Uniformed Crime Report and the National Crime Victimization Survey between 1965 and 2000 reveal an increase in women's involvement in offenses traditionally committed by women, such as fraud and larceny. The data also show an increase in arrests of women for misdemeanor and assault cases, though Steffensmeier and Schwarz stress that these figures do not indicate that there was an increase in the female share in assault. They argue that the rising numbers of arrests involving women are to be explained by the more aggressive prosecution practices of the police force, which have affected both men and women (Steffensmeier & Schwarz 2004, pp. 113–126).

European criminal justice statistics on women's crime suggest that there have been shifts in the attitude toward women's criminal behavior as well. In the nineteenth century, English prosecutors and welfare institutions focused their activities on the protection of girls and young women against male (sexual) aggression, and the prosecution of male aggressors. Consequently, women's crimes were taken less seriously, and in the case of prosecution they were more likely to receive milder punishments than their male counterparts. Women and girls also became less visible in the criminal justice statistics because part of their deviant behavior was regulated by welfare institutions that were increasingly set up by the government and philanthropic societies from the early nineteenth century onward (Shore 2003, pp. 75–92; King 2006, pp. 142–61; D'Cruze & Jackson 2009, p. 160). In the late twentieth and early twenty-first centuries the paradigm of the criminalization of men seems to have been replaced by the paradigm of increasing focus on girls' deviant behavior. Worrall argues that young women are no longer perceived as victims of brutal male behavior, but instead are labelled as gang members or girls who are not afraid to use violence against others. As D'Cruze and Jackson put it: "The 'girl gang' story has been a feature of press coverage of violent youth culture in the first decade of the 2000s" (2009, p. 161). Furthermore, English prosecutors have begun to treat criminal girls similar to criminal boys, resulting in increasing numbers of young women being incarcerated. (Worrall 2001, p. 86; D'Cruze & Jackson 2009, pp. 159–60).

There have been important shifts in women's share in prosecuted crime in the last decades as well. In 2004 the Dutch Central Bureau for Statistics published alarming statistics that showed an increase in the crime rates of women and girls in the last decades, with women's proportion in prosecuted crime rising from 10 percent in 1980 to 20 percent in 2004. Furthermore, the increase involved primarily girls between 12 and 17 years of age who were prosecuted for violence, destruction, and property offenses (Eggen 2004).

Shifts in female crime rates in the last two decades have stimulated scholars to find new explanations for fluctuations in women's share in prosecuted crime. In the 1960s and 1970s feminist approaches generally linked high female crime rates to the process of emancipation in the Western parts of the world (Adler 1975; Heidensohn and Silvestri 2012). In the 1990s sociologists and criminologists began to develop more nuanced theories that included a complex mix of determinants, such as neurobiological factors, social-economic circumstances, and prosecution practices. Dutch criminologists

Slotboom and Wong found several risk factors that may have been important determinants in girls' recent criminal behavior: mental illness, traumas, early sexual behavior, and low levels of self-control. In addition, girls who had a less close relationship with their mother were more likely to engage in criminal behavior (Slotboom et al. 2011, p. 64; Slotboom 2012; Wong 2012).

CONCLUSION

Sociologist Steffensmeier and behavioral scientist Allan argue that scholars should distinguish between the types of offenses committed by women and the explanation for their crimes. They agree that there is variability across time in the female percentage of offending, though such changes are limited mainly to minor property offenses or less serious forms of delinquency (Steffensmeier & Allan 1996, p. 482). Throughout the period 1600–2000 women were most likely to be prosecuted for simple thefts, rather than offenses involving serious violence (D'Cruze & Jackson 2009, p. 31). Statistical data on various regions in Europe in the early modern period show that variation in female crime rates was often linked to specific circumstances such as changing moral norms and double standards of prosecutors, as well as to economic marginality and opportunities that were related to migration, family structures, and labor participation. The data also clearly show that women were more likely to commit crimes in urban environments than in rural areas.

As Heidensohn and Silvestri recently pointed out, "there remains much to explore and better concepts are needed to do so" (2012, p. 363). It may be much more problematic to find an explanation for serious crime committed by men and women, because there are much less systematic data available. There is need of a more systematic analysis of the various factors that determine crime rates of both males and females, including variations across time and space.

References

Adler, Freda Schaffer. 1975. *Sisters in Crime: The Rise of the New Female Criminal.* New York: McGraw-Hill.

Aebi, Marcelo F., Bruno Aubusson de Cavarlay, Gordon Barclay, Beata Gruszczyńska, Stefan Harrendorf, Markku Heiskanen, Vasilika Hysi, et al. 2010. *European Sourcebook of Crime and Criminal Justice Statistics.* Lausanne: Université de Lausanne, Institut de criminologie et de droit pénal.

Arnot, Margaret L., & Cornelie Usborne. 2003. "Why Gender and Crime? Aspects of an International Debate." In *Gender and Crime in Modern Europe*, ed. Margaret L. Arnot & Cornelie Usborne. London: Routledge.

Beattie, John Maurice. 1975. "The Criminality of Women in Eighteenth-Century England." *Journal of Social History* 8 (4): 80–116.

Beattie, John Maurice. 1986. *Crime and the Courts in England, 1680–1880*. Oxford: Oxford University Press.

Beattie, John Maurice. 2001. *Policing and Punishment in London, 1660–1750: Urban Crime and the Limits of Terror*. Oxford: Oxford University Press.

Behringer, Wolfgang. 1995. "Weather, Hunger and Fear: Origins of the European Witch-Hunts in Climate, Society and Mentality." *German History* 13 (1): 1–27.

Burke, Jill. 2006. "Visualizing Neighborhood in Renaissance Florence: Santo Spirito and Santa Maria del Carmine." *Journal of Urban History* 32 (5): 693–710.

Burkhead, Michael Dow. 2006. *The Search for the Causes of Crime: A History of Theory in Criminology*. Jefferson, NC: McFarland.

Castan, Nicole. 1980. *Les Criminels de Languedoc: Les Exigences d'ordre et les voies du ressenti- ment dans une société pré-révolutionnaire (1750–1790)*. Toulouse, France: Association des Publications de l'Université de Toulouse-Le Mirail.

Chesney-Lind, Meda. 1997. *The Female Offender: Girls, Women and Crime*. Thousand Oaks, CA: Sage.

Clark, Peter. 2009. *European Cities and Towns, 400–2000*. Cambridge: Cambridge University Press.

D'Cruze, Shani. 1998. *Crimes of Outrage: Sex, Violence and Victorian Working Women*. London: University College London Press.

D'Cruze, Shani. 1999. "Sex, Violence and Local Courts: Working-Class Respectability in a Mid-Nineteenth-Century Lancashire Town." *British Journal of Criminology* 39 (1): 39–55.

D'Cruze, Shani, & Louise A. Jackson. 2009. *Women, Crime and Justice in England since 1660*. Basingstoke, UK: Palgrave Macmillan.

De Vries, Jan, & Adrianus M. van der Woude. 1995. *Nederland 1500–1815: de eerste ronde van moderne economische groei*. Amsterdam: Balans.

Durrant, Jonathan Byran. 2007. *Witchcraft, Gender and Society in Early Modern Germany*. Leiden & Boston: Brill.

Eggen, Harry. 2004. "Geweld en vernieling door meisjes toegenomen." Accessed at http://www.cbs.nl/nl-NL/menu/themas/veiligheid-recht/publicaties/artikelen/archief/2004/2004-1568-wm.htm.

Eibach, Joachim. 2003. *Frankfurter Verhöre: Städtische lebenswelten und Kriminalität im 18. Jahrhundert*. Paderborn, Germany: Schöningh.

Emsley, Clive. 1996. *Crime and Society in England, 1750-1900*, 2nd ed. London: Longman.

Emsley, Clive. 2005. *Hard Men: The English and Violence since 1750*. London & New York: Hambledon.

Faber, Sjoerd. 1978. "Kindermoord, in het bijzonder in de achttiende eeuw te Amsterdam." *Bijdragen en Mededelingen Betreffende de Geschiedenis der Nederlanden* 93 (2): 224–40.

Farge, Arlette. 1974. *Délinquance et criminalité: le vol d'aliments à Paris au XVIIIe siècle*. Paris: Plon.

Feeley, Malcolm M. 1994. "The Decline of Women in the Criminal Process: A Comparative History." In *Criminal Justice History: An International Annual*, Vol. 15, ed. Louis A. Knafla, 235–73. Westport, CT: Greenwood Press.

Feeley, Malcolm M., & Deborah L. Little. 1991. "The Vanishing Female: The Decline of Women in the Criminal Process, 1687–1912." *Law and Society Review* 25 (4): 719–57.

Feeley, Malcolm M., & Hadar Aviram. 2010. "Social Historical Studies of Women, Crime, and Courts." *Annual Review of Law and Social Science* 6: 151–171.

Frost, Ginger. 2008. "'He Could Not Hold His Passions': Domestic Violence and Cohabitation in England (1850–1905)." *Crime, History & Societies* 12 (1): 45–63.

Gatrell, Vic A. C., & Tom B. Hadden. 1972. "Criminal Statistics and Their Interpretation." In *Nineteenth-Century Society: Essays in the Use of Quantitative Methods for the Study of Social Data*, ed. E. A. Wrigley, 336–96. Cambridge: Cambridge University Press.

Gerber, Matthew. 2012. *Bastards: Politics, Family and Law in Early Modern France.* Oxford: Oxford University Press.

Godfrey, Barry. 2003. "Counting and Accounting for the Decline in Non-Lethal Violence in England, Australia, and New Zealand, 1880–1920." *British Journal of Criminology* 43 (2): 340–53.

Godfrey, Barry, Stephen Farall, & Susanne Karstedt. 2005. "Explaining Gendered Sentencing Patterns for Violent Men and Women in the Late-Victorian and Edwardian Period." *British Journal of Criminology* 45 (5): 696–720.

Hardwick, Julie. 2009. *Family Business: Litigation and the Political Economics of Daily Life in Early Modern France.* Oxford: Oxford University Press.

Hässler, Günther, & Frank Hässler. 2011. "Infanticide in Mecklenburg and Western Pomerania: Documents from Four Centuries (1570–1842)." *History of Psychiatry* 22 (1): 75–92.

Heidensohn, Frances. 1996. *Women and Crime*, 2nd ed. Basingstoke, UK: Macmillan.

Heidensohn, Frances, & Maria Silvestri. 2012. "Gender and Crime." In *The Oxford Handbook of Criminology*, 5th ed., ed. Mike Maguire, Rod Morgan, & Robert Reiner, 336–69. Oxford: Oxford University Press.

Hufton, Olwen H. 1974. *The Poor of Eighteenth-Century France, 1750–1789.* Oxford: Clarendon.

Jackson, Mark. 1996. *New-Born Child Murder: Women, Illegitimacy and the Courts in Eighteenth-Century England.* Manchester, UK: Manchester University Press.

King, Peter. 2006. *Crime and the Law in England: Remaking Justice from the Margins.* Cambridge: Cambridge University Press.

Levack, Brian Paul. 1995. *The Witch-Hunt in Early Modern Europe*, 2nd ed. London: Longman.

Mc Mahon, Richard, Joachim Eibach, & Randolph Roth. 2013. "Introduction. Making Sense of Violence? Reflections on the History of Interpersonal Violence in Europe." *Crime, History & Societies* 17 (2): 5–26.

Mitterauer, Michael. 1983. *Ledige Mütter: zur Geschichte illegitimer Geburten in Europa.* Munich: Beck.

Moch, Leslie Page. 2003. *Moving Europeans: Migration in Western Europe since 1650*, 2nd ed. Bloomington: Indiana University Press.

Muchembled, Robert. 2012. *A History of Violence: From the End of the Middle Ages to the Present.* Cambridge: Polity.

Pluskota, Marion. 2011. "Prostitution in Bristol and Nantes, 1750–1815: A Comparative Study." Ph.D. diss., University of Leicester, Centre for Urban History.

Pollak, Otto. 1950. *The Criminality of Women.* Philadelphia: University of Pennsylvania Press.

Rublack, Ulinka, ed. 2002. *Gender in Early Modern Germany.* Cambridge: Cambridge University Press.

Schwerhoff, Gerd. 1991. *Köln im Kreuzverhör. Kriminalität, Herrschaft und Gesellschaft in einer frühneuzeitlichen Stadt.* Bonn & Berlin: Bouvier.

Shoemaker, Robert Brink. 1991. *Prosecution and Punishment: Petty Crime and the Law in London and Rural Middlesex, c. 1660–1725.* Cambridge: Cambridge University Press.

Shoemaker, Robert Brink. 1998. *Gender in English Society, 1650–1850: The Emergence of Separate Spheres?* London: Longman.

Shore, Heather. 2003. "The Trouble with Boys: Gender and the 'Invention' of the Juvenile Offender in Early Nineteenth-Century Britain." In *Gender and Crime in Modern Europe*, ed. Margaret L. Arnot & Cornelie Usborne, 5–92. London: Routledge.

Silvestri, Marisa, & Chris Crowther-Dowey. 2008. *Gender and Crime: New Approaches to Criminology.* London: Sage.

Slotboom, Anne-Marie, Thessa M. L. Wong, Carolien Swier, & T. C. van der Broek. 2011. *Delinquente meisjes: Achtergronden, risicofactoren en interventies.* Den Haag, The Netherlands: Boom Juridische Uitgeverij.

Spierenburg, Pieter Cornelis. 2008. *A History of Murder: Personal Violence in Europe from the Middle Ages to the Present.* Cambridge: Polity.

Spierenburg, Pieter Cornelis. 2013. *Violence and Punishment: Civilizing the Body Through Time.* Cambridge: Polity.

Steffensmeier, Darrell, & Emilie Allan. 1996. "Gender and Crime: Toward a Gendered Theory of Female Offending." *Annual Review of Sociology* 22: 459–87.

Steffensmeier, Darrell, & Jennifer Schwarz. 2004. "Contemporary Explanations of Women's Crime." In *The Criminal Justice and Women*, ed. Barbara Price & Nathalie Sokoloff, 113–26. New York: McGraw Hill.

Van der Heijden, Manon. 2000. "Women as Victims of Sexual and Domestic Violence in Seventeenth-Century Holland: Criminal Cases of Rape, Incest and Maltreatment in Rotterdam and Delft." *Journal of Social History* 33 (3): 623–44.

Van der Heijden, Manon. 2012. *Civic Duty: Public Services in the Early Modern Low Countries.* Newcastle, UK: Cambridge Scholars.

Van der Heijden, Manon. 2013. "Women, Violence and Urban Justice in Holland c. 1600–1838." *Crime, History and Society* 17 (2): 71–100.

Van der Heijden, Manon. 2014. *Misdadige vrouwen. Criminaliteit en rechtspraak in Holland 1600-1800.* Amsterdam: Bert Bakker, Promotheus.

Van der Heijden, Manon, & Valentijn Koningsberger. 2013. "Continuity and Change? The Prosecution of Female Crime in the Eighteenth- and Nineteenth-Century Netherlands." *Crime, History & Societies* 17 (1): 101–27.

Van der Heijden, Manon, & Marion Pluskota. 2014. "Leniency Versus Toughening? The Prosecution of Male and Female Violence in 19th Century Holland." Paper presented at the Social Science History Conference, Vienna, Austria, April 23–26.

Van der Heijden, Manon, Ariadne Schmidt, & Richard Wall. 2007. "Broken Families: Economic Resources and Social Networks of Women who Head Families." *History of the Family* 12 (4): 223–32.

Van der Heijden, Manon, & Danielle van den Heuvel. 2007. "Sailors, Families and the Urban Institutional Framework in Early Modern Holland." *History of the Family* 12(4): 296–309.

Van Poppel, Frans W. A., Hendrik P. van Dalen, Evelien Walhout. 2006. *Diffusion of a Social Norm: Tracing the Emergence of the Housewife in the Netherlands, 1812-1922.* Rotterdam: Tinbergen Institute.

Walker, Garthine. 2003. *Crime, Gender and Social Order in Early Modern England.* Cambridge: Cambridge University Press.

Wettmann-Jungblut, Peter. 2009. "Modern Times, Modern Crimes? Kriminalität und Strafpraxis im badischen Raum 1700–1850." In *Verbrechen im Blick. Perspectiven der neuzeitlichen Kriminalitätsgeschichte*, ed. Rebekka Habermas & Gerd Schwerhoff, 148–81. Frankfurt & New York: Campus.

Wiener, Martin Joel. 1998. "The Victorian Criminalization of Men." In *Men and Violence: Gender, Honor, and Rituals in Modern Europe and America*, ed. Pieter Spierenburg, 197–212. Columbus: Ohio State University Press.

Wiener, Martin Joel. 2004. *Men of Blood: Violence, Manliness and Criminal Justice in Victorian England*. Cambridge: Cambridge University Press.

Wong, Thessa M. L. 2012. "Girl Delinquency: A Study on Sex Differences in (Risk Factors for) Delinquency." Ph.D. diss., VU University Amsterdam, Faculty of Law.

Worrall, Anne. 2001. "Girls at Risk? Reflections on Changing Attitudes to Young Women's Offending." *Probation Journal* 48 (2): 86–92.

Zedner, Lucia. 1991. *Women, Crime, and Custody in Victorian England*. Oxford: Oxford University Press.

CHAPTER 13

....

POLICING MINORITIES

....

MARGO DE KOSTER AND HERBERT REINKE

INTRODUCTION

....

THE policing of minorities has been the subject of criminological and sociological research for many years. Most contemporary work has been concerned with the differential use of police powers and the criminal victimization of established ethnic minorities, including issues such as police targeting—or "overpolicing," stop-and-search procedures, racial abuse, and violence by the police. These criminological writings mostly focus on the question of how cultural, ethnic, or religious differences shape everyday police work, and they often assume that these issues are of fairly recent advent (Holdaway 2009). These are unmistakably crucial issues in today's increasingly multicultural cities, which are, as they have always been, the core sites of street-level policing and police–public interactions. From a historical point of view, however, it is important to broaden the discussion and situate the policing of minorities within its longer history of the policing of migrants. Indeed, today's urban ethnic minority groups are from successive generations of immigrants, with shifting migration patterns continuously changing the perception of those who might belong to "ethnic minorities" (Bowling & Phillips 2003). Moreover, the issue of immigration brings us to a core phenomenon in the development of modern policing: the explicit endeavor to *control* migrants has been identified as a major driving force behind the professionalization of police practices since the *ancien régime* (Blanc-Chaléard et al. 2001).

The first section of this essay will give a brief overview of how, from the sixteenth century onward, migrants and traveling groups increasingly became the subject of public and official concern and attempts to control (or *police*, in its early modern sense; see Raeff 1983) their movements through vagrancy regulation and poor laws. The second section will show how these developments constituted a crucial impetus for the expansion and professionalization of police forces, that is, the creation of specialized policing agencies and techniques aimed at controlling migrants and newcomers. The third section will consider the realities of policing and the repression of vagrancy in nineteenth- and twentieth-century Europe, starting with the point that, in terms of targets, newcomers perceived as "unrooted outsiders" were in general those most at risk of arrest and prosecution, with the intensity of police repression varying considerably from one European region to another. We then move on to a closer examination of police strategies and the reality of over- and underpolicing, as well as experiences of minorities as "police property": first, as part of the policing of minorities within nation-states; second, through the policing of "gypsies"; and third, in terms of the policing of minorities in cities. The fourth section discusses issues and perspectives in minority policing during the post–Second World War period, while the conclusion closes the chapter with reflections on the presence of minorities in the police.

I. Controlling Unwanted Newcomers and Masterless Men

A. Fears of Wandering Groups

The history of migrants is one of large-scale population movements in Europe since the sixteenth century. During this era, many types of mobile groups and individuals— including seasonal laborers, long-distance migrants, self-employed peddlers, and traveling peoples such as Roma—became the subject of growing public and official concern in several countries and regions. According to Bronislaw Geremek, who wrote a number of fundamental and influential studies on the changing attitude in Europe toward the poor in general and vagrants in particular, the stigmatization of traveling groups originated in the fourteenth century. Following the sociologist Vexliard (1956), Geremek places the first use of the term "vagabond"—a term with an unmitigated pejorative connotation—in France around 1350. Its negative connotation signified undesirable wandering behavior. Vagrancy soon came to be considered a crime in itself (Geremek 1980; Woolf 1986). This negative stereotyping culminated around the turn of the sixteenth century in the publication of popular books such as *Das Narrenschiff* (1494), the *Liber Vagatorum* (ca. 1510), and works on the secret language of rogues (Geremek 1991). These works depicted vagabonds and beggars as professional thieves, robbers, and cheats. This image strongly influenced public opinion and was supported by state and church alike. As a result, people lacking a fixed abode and labeled as beggars or vagabonds were increasingly stigmatized as lazy and prone to criminal behavior (Cubero 1998; Beier & Ocobock 2008). In Naples during the 1780s the official categories of dangerous individuals began with "the idle, vagabonds, and adventurers" (*oziosi, vagabondi, avventurieri*) (Alessi 1992, p. 7). Traveling peoples were especially afflicted by these prejudices, because such families were on the move apparently without any intention to settle down. They thereby symbolized a preeminently undesirable lifestyle of permanent wandering—and, as such, they were perceived as the ultimate aliens (Lucassen 1986).

Negative attitudes toward beggars and vagrants were common and widespread across Western Europe as early as the fifteenth and sixteenth centuries (Raphael 2008). The main explanation for this phenomenon can be linked to a major change in the organization of poor relief in early modern Europe (Sachße & Tennstedt 1998), when urban authorities made attachment to the local or religious community a key element of and precondition of support for almost all relief arrangements. As a consequence, the definition of insiders and outsiders became a matter of codification from the six-teenth century onward. The common feature of such settlement legislation was that it defined a person's settlement, that is, the local entity considered responsible to provide assistance in time of need. In many cases this was the place of birth, but transfer of settlement was provided under given conditions—for instance, after a certain length of stay in another community. Not surprisingly, this had a profound impact on migra-tion behavior and often constituted an important element of local policies that aimed to oust unwanted newcomers (Winter 2008; De Munck & Winter 2012). Restrictions on outsiders' access to relief varied considerably across space and time, however. In England and Wales, for example, the issue of settlement was of major concern as early as the seventeenth century, whereas in the Low Countries, it was only from the mid-eighteenth century onward that an acceleration of processes of population growth, agrarian change, proletarization, and geographical mobility went hand in hand with a surge in legislative and juridical activity in the domain of settlement, both in urbanized and in rural areas. Furthermore, whereas the different irremovability acts in England and Wales allowed for a de facto transfer of a person's settlement from the birthplace to the place of residence, the residential criteria for gaining settlement in the southern Low Countries and later in Belgium became more restricted over time (Winter 2008). In Germany, the main pillar of the policy for excluding allegedly poor aliens was the *Heimat* principle, under which every city or village was given the right to send aliens back to the place where they were supposed to have some sort of community affiliation, usually the place of their birth. The frequent inability of traveling individuals to assert their rights thus gave rise to a class of wandering and, to use the modern term, illegal people (Lucassen 1997a).

B. Migration Control and Vagrancy Acts

In addition to the establishment of a whole range of settlement arrangements and policies—which were much more varied and dynamic than national instructions would suggest—local authorities across Europe also devised various methods of control and repression targeted directly at migrant groups. People on the move increasingly came to be labeled and prosecuted as vagrants, *gens sans aveu* or "masterless men," through a variety of vagrancy acts and local regulations. At the same time, the label of "vagrant" was quite flexible and could encompass many different categories of mobile people.

In practice, most early modern vagrancy laws were used instrumentally to remove unwanted newcomers from a territory (Beier 1985; Fahrmeir 2007; Beier & Ocobock 2008; Lis & Soly 2012).

From the late eighteenth century onward, as the nation-state consolidated, central authorities increasingly felt the urge to control migrant and minority groups in Europe. Public order and social stability became major policy concerns, and the majority of migrants who belonged to the poor and vulnerable classes were often perceived as a potential threat to public order, given their alleged propensity to engage in begging, vagrancy, prostitution, libertinage, thieving, rioting, and other forms of dangerous or criminal behavior (De Munck & Winter 2012; Lawrence 2011). During this period, the metaphor of society as a body that could be healthy but was threatened by degeneration gained more and more importance. This stemmed not only from problems of controlling real diseases like tuberculosis, syphilis, or other venereal afflictions, but also from the perceived threat that "disorderly" or nonconventional behavior posed to social stability (Becker 1999).

The increased focus on people who were labeled as vagrants or beggars was visible during the nineteenth century in the organization of national and international conferences, the publication of numerous tracts by social observers, and the promulgation of new laws. Across Europe, migration control and the repression of vagrancy now became the subject of comprehensive bodies of legislation, which modern nation-states placed at the center of larger social and public order policies (Sagolla-Croley 1995; Dyson & King 2007; Lawrence 2011). As Clive Emsley has shown for the British Vagrancy Act of 1824, central governments generally aimed at creating a new instrument for heightened surveillance of all "casual poor" (2004). The definition of the vagrant category was thus expanded to equate such individuals with criminals. At the same time, rural crisis and mass impoverishment prompted many individuals to look for work, often in areas that had not previously been destinations for mass migration. During this period, more and more people were at risk of being defined as tramps and beggars, because their place of residence could not be established and they did not benefit from regular income (Beier 1985; Smith 1999; Fumerton 2006; Winter 2004).

In addition to the ambition of efficiently controlling migratory flux and people on the move, from the eighteenth century onward, increased migration to Europe's urban centers also generated new fears of uncontrolled settlement of newcomers within the city limits. The number of people living in European towns of more than 5,000 inhabitants increased sixfold between 1750 and 1914 (Bairoch 1985). Cities also grew exponentially. Alongside the mass migration toward cities, huge numbers of people also left those cities after a brief period of residence, which resulted in huge turnover of people. This also led to growing concerns among policymakers concerning the threats posed by overcrowded cities (Clark 2009; Smith 1999). More than ever, controlling, detecting, and correcting materially or morally dangerous behavior by low-status newcomers was a central concern of urban migration policies. Urban municipal authorities increasingly issued police ordinances and regulations targeting poor aliens, including entry regulations and passport formalities at the city gates, as well as requirements for landlords and innkeepers to inform local authorities of the characteristics and previous settlement of their lodgers (Milliot 2012; Blanc-Chaléard et al. 2001; Roche 2000). Especially in Central Europe, where the application of police ordinances was based on long-standing and extensive experience (Maier 1980), such laws and other measures of administrative policing could be used to control and penalize a large spectrum of minorities and marginal groups. The police could at any time refer to some police ordinance in order to limit the movements of marginal groups; simultaneously, local police forces were eager to get rid of such people (Spencer 1992). In the nineteenth century, concerns about public order and social stability produced further increases in municipal regulations issued for urban centers, criminalizing all kinds of "disorderly behavior" (rowdyism, drunkenness, prostitution, etc.) and directly targeting poor immigrants, who were perceived as particularly prone to such unruly and dangerous behavior (Reinke 1992; De Koster 2011; Lawrence 2011).

The regulation of migrants thus appears as a multifaceted complex of modes of migration control and repressive measures, with national, provincial, and local authorities increasingly feeling the urge to intervene, while having different, and sometimes conflicting, interests and definitions of belonging (De Munck & Winter 2012). Until well into the eighteenth century, however, the authorities issuing such new legislation, at whatever level of government, often lacked officials committed to enforcing the regulations. This was about to change drastically.

II. Controlling Migrants and the Rise of Modern Policing

A. Gendarmeries and New Urban Police Forces

Increasing mobility, state formation, and accelerated urban growth from the eighteenth century onward all brought about growing concerns with social disaffiliation and disintegration. This led to the professionalization and specialization of police and administrative forces (Blanc-Chaléard et al. 2001; Lucassen 1997b). One initial step that was crucial to this development during the early nineteenth century was the introduction in many European nation-states of the eighteenth-century French model of the *Maréchaussée*. This military-style police—the first fully centralized police force in Western Europe—was charged with rounding up vagrants and beggars. French *bayonets* and Napoleonic administration imposed similar structures of bureaucratic repression and more effective, permanent policing across much of Europe. *Gendarmerie* forces were established in many of the states that were occupied by Napoleon or were created as a result of his diplomacy and drawn tightly into his sphere of influence. Perceived as a modernized control device by central governments, the new gendarmerie forces nevertheless had to deal with exactly the same phenomenon as their predecessors. The control of so-called migrant paupers became, during the first decades of the nineteenth century, their major focus in pre-industrial continental Europe (Wirsing 1991; Jessen 1991; Emsley 1999). Furthermore, states such as France considered introducing nation-wide systems of identity certificates. In the administrative context of *ancien régime* France, the possibility of such a scheme was probably unworkable, yet in 1781 a royal decree required every worker to carry an identity booklet (*livret*) that had to be signed by his successive employers. For the next century and beyond the phrase "*Je demande à voir tes papiers*" ("I demand to see your papers") appears to have been the opening words of any conversation between gendarmes and poor men on the roads of provincial France. In the early nineteenth century, the Consulate brought in an even more stringent system: without an up-to-date *livret*, any working man or woman found on the roads could be apprehended by the Napoleonic police as a vagabond and was liable to a prison sentence (Emsley 2007; Lawrence 2011).

In the cities as well, a growing ambition to control and monitor the whereabouts and activities of newcomers favored the expansion and professionalization of urban police forces as well as the development of modern techniques of bureaucratic control and police surveillance. Indeed, this ambition helps to explain why the development of police "territorialization" was such an obsession in the eighteenth century. The division of a city into different administrative neighborhoods was one of the tools used to get a better grip on the city as a whole. Thus, the sergeant no longer had to watch over the entire town, roaming wherever he pleased, but was paid to patrol and rigorously investigate a well-defined territory (Sälter 2004; Denys 2010). In eighteenth-century Vienna, the *Polizei-Hofkommission* was linked directly with the wide-ranging Commission for Security, Poor Relief, Provisions, and Deportations (*Kommission für Sicherheits-, Armen-, Verpflegs- und Subsachen*). It became standard policy, not just in Vienna, but in cities throughout Europe, periodically to deport offenders and vagrant aliens from the city (Emsley 2007). Similarly, in Paris, where the police—supervised from 1667 onward by the *lieutenant general de police de Paris*—commanded a force of around 3,000 men in the mid-eighteenth century, when the city population was approaching half a million. This extensive police force maintained a vigorous surveillance of the lodging houses (*maisons garnies*) that were frequented by poor migrants and that acquired a sinister reputation as a haven for all kinds of thieves and scoundrels (Milliot 2012).

During the nineteenth century, the importance of local police forces for the control of migrants and vagrants increased further, given the growing body of national vagrancy acts and local police ordinances discussed earlier. Most of the legislation enacted, at whatever level of government, had to be implemented locally by the police. It was therefore no coincidence that during the second half of the nineteenth century the number of policemen per capita rose substantially in all major urban centers across Europe (Emsley 2007; De Koster 2008). Until the First World War the enforcement of police ordinances remained a main police strategy when dealing with minorities such as Roma and vagrant groups. With the growing professionalization of police forces, starting during the last decades of the nineteenth century, "scientific" methods became part of police strategies as well. Among these methods, data collection on specific categories of the population labeled as "suspect" or deviant became an important precondition for monitoring specific population groups (Lawrence 2011). In Germany, for example, systematic data collections on Roma were initiated by the police around the turn of the twentieth century and continued in different forms and with changing labels throughout the entire twentieth century. Under Nazi rule in Germany, the data collection activities were intensified and were used for the purpose of identifying Roma with the intention of sending them to concentration camps for extermination. After 1945, the German Federal Republic continued these data collection activities for almost five decades. Only in 2001 did the federal police for crime control (*Bundeskriminalpolizei*) decide to end these practices in response to multiple protests (Baumann et al. 2011).

III. Repressive Practices, Their Subjects, and Their Limits in the Nineteenth and Twentieth Centuries

A. Vulnerable Newcomers but Varying Degrees of Repression

As stated previously, legal definitions of the "vagrant" were quite vague. The central criterion was the absence of an identifiable place of residence and of a fixed income. This definition was very "elastic" and open for interpretation, and thus could encompass many types of mobile people. At the same time, an increase in levels of poverty and mobility made more and more people vulnerable to prosecution. Sigrid Wadauer has shown that in late nineteenth- and early twentieth-century Austria, for example, broad interpretations linking vagrancy with unemployment resulted in frequent arrests of itinerant artisans, who did not view themselves as unemployed at all, let alone as vagrants (Wadauer 2011). Moreover, these control patterns pertained not only to the transient poor, but also to the poor residing permanently within local communities (Finzsch 1990). During the early industrialization period in particular, the distinction between "minority" and "majority" became increasingly blurred. In many rural areas as well as in cities, the overwhelming majority of the population was poor, while only a small section of the population could be described as living above the poverty level.

Research on different periods and regions in Europe has provided ample evidence of differential treatment by institutions of control and repression—including policing and criminal tribunals—which reinforced distinctions between "insiders" and "outsiders" (Blanc-Chaléard et al. 2001; Coy 2008). Indeed, much more than cultural, religious, or ethnic distinctiveness—or mobility and poverty in general—the key factor that apparently made individuals and groups particularly vulnerable to police arrest and denunciation by local communities was the perception of them as "rootless outsiders," combined with high public visibility and lack of informal support networks (Hufton 1974; Lis & Soly 1993). This vulnerability of the newcomer who lacked informal ties within the community helps to explain why immigrants and minorities—both then and now—appear disproportionately in the criminal justice system. At the same time, it helps explain why not all individuals belonging to these vulnerable groups end up in the criminal justice system (Godfrey, Lawrence, & Williams 2008): those who manage to integrate into local networks have better chances of avoiding this fate. Notably, Roma and other traveling groups—which were perceived as ultimate and eternal outsiders by authorities and the public alike—were invariably more subject to repressive intervention (see subsection C). In contrast, established minorities in the cities did not systematically constitute "police property," as relations between the police and these groups were much more complex (see subsection D).

Although new vagrancy laws and police ordinances allowed the targeting of large and various groups of mobile people, and were indeed interpreted very broadly at times, it is important to note that in practice, persecution was much less severe and ubiquitous than some authors have asserted. Both the intentions and impacts of repressive measures could vary widely from one European region to another (Lucassen 1997a; Lawrence 2011). Two main reasons can be identified for this variation. First, despite the expansion of police institutions, the means to enforce coercive policies often remained rather limited. In the eighteenth century, only states such as France, which benefited from the *maréchaussée*, or some German principalities, as well as the eastern provinces of the Dutch Republic, seem to have been capable of organizing more generalized repression of vagrants and Roma (Lucassen 1997a). Many Italian states had police institutions in this period, but these so-called *sbirri* were increasingly unreliable the farther they got from the center of power. They acquired an unenviable reputation for brutality, corruption, and being little better than the bandits and vagrants they were supposed to repress. In many parts of continental Europe during the nineteenth century, it was a legal requirement for travelers to carry an up-to-date identification booklet (*livret*) and to register their presence on arrival in a new location. The keepers of inns, hotels, and lodging houses then had to hand over the personal details of their visitors to the local *commissaires*, who ensured a sort of surveillance that was much more bureaucratic, uniform, and significant than any form of registration in place in England. However, there is plenty of evidence to suggest that it was never particularly difficult for a determined individual either to acquire forged papers or to hoodwink the police over passports and workers' travel documents (Emsley 2007).

Another major, and equally important, explanation for the varying intensity of prosecutions for vagrancy is that, for economic reasons, authorities in certain regions were not interested in restricting or hindering immigration, and instead sought to attract able-bodied migrants as a labor force for the local economy (De Munck & Winter 2012). This might, for example, help to explain why in the city of Brussels the number of vagrants prosecuted was twice or thrice as high as that in Antwerp. While Antwerp, a port city, welcomed a flexible workforce of casual workers, with temporary unemployment as part of the normal labor cycle, Brussels as a political center was much less inclined to welcome vagrants and beggars who might disturb the public decorum and join the destitute and disorderly classes of the Belgian capital (Vercammen & Van Ruysseveldt, 2015).

B. Policing Minorities in the Nation-State

In Europe, the nineteenth century was the century when the breakthrough of the nation-state occurred. Some nation-states, such as France, got to this stage earlier, while others, such as Germany or Italy, arrived there much later. Other European states, such as the Austro-Hungarian and Russian empires, did not reach this point before the First World War. The dissolution of the Austro-Hungarian Empire at the end of the First World War gave way to the establishment of a number of new nation-states, which were confronted with significant minority policing issues.

The German Empire, founded in 1871, was one of the new nineteenth-century nation-states whose minority problems became a core policing issue. These minorities included Poles in the eastern parts of Prussia, which had been a part of Poland up to the end of the eighteenth century; Danes in a territory in the north that became attached to Prussia after 1866; and French in the western parts of the empire, attached to it after the Franco-Prussian War of 1870–1871. In the eastern provinces of Prussia, the Poles became prime objects of control strategies and practices, with the police becoming involved in wider attempts to foster German cultural and Prussian hegemony in these former Polish territories. But what had been perceived as an issue of the eastern Prussian periphery became a central problem with the migration of large numbers of ethnic Poles into the coal mining and steel regions of Upper Silesia and, in particular, the Ruhr area in the west of Prussia, which turned into the core industrial area of the empire. The migration of ethnic Poles to these industrial hotspots aggravated the perceptions among government authorities and law enforcers that Poles were "dangerous." These Polish migrants—mostly unmarried young males—became a significant minority group in these regions, with up to 300,000 in the Ruhr area by the turn of the twentieth century. They also became engaged in large numbers in the first large-scale industrial disputes at the end of the nineteenth century, which led to the establishment of Polish associations and trade unions (Saul 1974; Spencer 1992; Johansen 2005).

The police and the courts had a number of instruments at their disposal to react to these developments. In the industrial regions, these administrative tools included interventions in labor disputes, such as defining picketing as a public street disturbance, and placing meetings under police surveillance and closing them if participants used languages other than German. The police thereby became involved in maintaining cultural hegemony over a minority within the nation-state. Additionally, the Prussian police and the courts had "classic" repressive instruments at their disposal as well. Contemporary crime statistics (statistics of trials) indicate an overpolicing and enforced criminalization of the Polish minority. These statistics show significantly higher crime figures and numbers of trials in those eastern Prussian provinces where the majority of the population consisted of ethnic Poles compared to other parts of Prussia (Johnson 1995).

C. Policing Roma

Even prior to the rise of modern nation-states, Roma were a population group that attracted police surveillance and repression more than other groups. The emergence of Roma in Europe during the fifteenth century coincided with the beginning of the so-called territorialization, that is, the emergence of territories with fixed boundaries and the definition of specific populations as belonging to one territory only. The beginning of territorialization and state building were accompanied by changing attitudes and strategies as far as the poor were concerned. As previously mentioned, understandings of generalized access to poor relief underwent a change to concepts that focused on the local poor only (Sachße & Tennstedt 1998). This placed Roma—as a nonlocal vagrant minority group—in a precarious position and made them the object of an array of prosecution measures during the *ancien régime* period. In Central Europe, the growing significance of the "police science" (*Polizeywissenschaft*) as one of the main approaches to consolidating the territorial state, provided the instruments for prosecuting Roma in large parts of Europe. Police ordinances were employed to submit Roma to many forms of restrictions. Quite often, the forces of the *ancien régime* territorial state engaged in "Gypsy hunts" (*Zigeunerjagden*), sometimes with fatal consequences for the victims (Hohmann 1981; Lucassen 1997b).

Throughout the nineteenth century, administrative techniques increasingly became a core police strategy to deal with Roma and other marginal groups of the population. Using police ordinances when addressing these groups allowed the police to combine control and punishment. Roma who had newly arrived in a jurisdiction were routinely escorted to the city boundaries in order to make their entry into a city as unpleasant and difficult as possible. Similar practices were applied to beggars and vagrants. In some cities, "beggar patrols" of plainclothes patrolmen rounded up beggars, especially those found in busy downtown streets. In 1907, the Düsseldorf police in the west of Prussia tried to enhance the effectiveness of these patrols by paying patrolmen an extra amount that depended on the arrest of a minimum number of beggars per month (Spencer 1992).

D. Policing Minorities in the City

The available research on patterns of police arrests and judicial prosecution for vagrancy within nineteenth- and early twentieth-century cities suggests that persons arrested and prosecuted often shared the profile of being young labor migrants who had recently arrived in the city. Having no prearranged place to move into on arrival, or having lost their job and lacking any support networks, they often failed to quickly obtain another job and were therefore out on the street and particularly vulnerable to destitution (De Koster 2011; Lawrence 2011). In other words, they matched the classical profile of the newcomer without a network in the local community. When family or other informal social bonds were present, the situation was generally very different: the police often arrested young beggars caught in the act, but after their parents or relatives had been called to the police station and been warned, they could normally return to their homes without facing the risk of further prosecution. There was also another group that was rarely prosecuted: foreigners from other countries were simply deported to the city border after being arrested. The fact that most urban police forces used separate, standardized forms for foreigners suggests that this was standard procedure and was thus a simple continuation of early modern practices of removing poor aliens from the territory (Vercammen & Van Ruysseveldt, 2015).

Whereas urban police forces acquired considerable powers to repress vagrancy and disturbances to the public order, and were placed under increasing public and official pressures to do so, actual practices of policing were constrained by financial considerations and manpower availability. Accordingly, a blind eye was turned to certain types of criminal behavior that were deemed not to challenge the social order. Overall, practical policing focused on crime management, rather than crime elimination, for in certain areas the police still faced a hostile public until well into the twentieth century. For public order offenses, the police generally pursued a policy of containment. Police authorities realized that if they tried to eliminate disorderly activities in one district, the problem would merely move elsewhere. It was therefore better to keep disorder and vice within certain limits within a well-policed area. As a result, certain neighborhoods in the city, and the people who lived within them, were seen as more in need of control than others, and migrant neighborhoods with high concentrations of urban casual poor could become the focus of closer police surveillance (Davis 1991; Roth 1997; De Koster 2011; Slater 2012).

Nevertheless, the geographical dimensions of the control of urban space, and of newcomers in particular, varied. In several nineteenth-century cities, the police appear to have focused primarily on the patroling of "respectable" streets, trying to keep them free from disorder. The poorest urban neighborhoods appear to have been seen as a kind of no-go zone for a long time; only in the twentieth century did neighborhoods with many newcomers and high population turnover become the centers of more systematic police attention (De Koster 2011; Emsley 1997).

IV. Minority Policing after 1945: Issues and Perspectives

In the aftermath of the Second World War, a development that had already begun by the end of the First World War became part of the political agenda again: the reinforcement of the homogeneous ethnic character of the nation-state as a political strategy for handling the postwar reconstruction of Europe. Parallel to this, however, other political considerations emerged on Europe's political agenda that reshaped questions of how to handle minorities. With the rise of communist regimes in Central and Eastern Europe, minorities were no longer conceived primarily as social outsiders or as members of specific ethnic groups, but were constructed politically. Within this political construction, the working class became the majority that aimed to defend its political and economic supremacy using all means available against enemies such as the bourgeoisie, who now became a minority subject to police control and violence.

In Western Europe, other political issues soon appeared at the top of the political agenda. As a consequence of decolonization of the territories formerly governed by Western European countries (Belgium, France, Great Britain, the Netherlands), migrants from the former colonies developed into substantial minority groups within these populations. Additionally, from the late 1950s and early 1960s on, with the economy starting to boom in Western Europe, including Germany, demands for a larger workforce could only be met with immigrants from southern and southwestern Europe, and from parts of the southern fringe of the Mediterranean.

Issues that were believed to derive from these different waves of immigration were handled with considerable delay. During the 1960s and the 1970s, governments and societies in some European countries regarded this migration as only temporary and were therefore reluctant to initiate measures for integrating immigrants and settling their legal status. With the growing recognition that the migrating population was becoming permanently settled in Western Europe, particularly in its urban centers (Jaschke 1997), concerns about the handling of this group by law enforcement agencies became a major policing issue—one that was only reluctantly addressed by the police. Critics from the public, including civil rights advocates from among the migrant population, raised concerns about racist and xenophobe attitudes among police agents, police brutality, and selective targeting and intervention against minorities, but these complaints were only addressed slowly by reform strategies within the police forces.

The legacy of French colonialism in North Africa (Algeria) and the presence of large numbers of Algerians in France during the Algerian struggle for independence in the 1950s and early 1960s resulted occasionally in brutal, even fatal, police violence against Algerians in France. In one severe incident, at least forty Algerians were killed by the Paris police; according to other sources, the number was considerably larger (Blanchard 2011). Since then, police relations with minorities have improved in France, but recent incidents reveal remaining—or sometimes new—conflict lines between the police and members of minority communities. The burning of suburbs of French cities during the last years of the first decade of the twenty-first century made the lasting tensions between the police and young male members of minority groups very visible. Recent studies on the overtargeting of nonwhites by the police in public and semi-public spaces further confirm this picture (Berlière & Lévy 2011).

During the first half of the 1980s, inner-city riots and violence by the English police against members of the black community, who originated mostly from former British colonies, attested to the strain between the police and minority groups in Britain.

Research carried out by criminologists and sociologists during the 1970s and the 1980s similarly revealed the widespread character of racial prejudice and stereotyping of immigrants among members of the English police (Chan 1997; Rowe 2007). Since then, however, a lot of programs designed to improve police–minority relationships have been put into practice.

In Germany, where the political system was unaffected by decolonization problems, immigrants came into the country in large numbers from the early 1960s onward after the building of the Berlin Wall and the enforcement by East German authorities of the internal German border. This border regime stopped the influx of East German workers into the booming West German economy and made the recruitment of immigrants necessary. During the formative years of this migration, successive German governments, both at the federal level and in individual *Länder*, and German society at large refused to accept the permanence of this migration, thus also denying any phenomenon that might be labeled minority policing. In recent years, however, both a critical public and civil rights organizations have introduced this issue to the political agenda. Nevertheless, the German police have been latecomers in recognizing this issue in a timely and adequate fashion, at least in comparison to other Western European countries (Jaschke 1997).

CONCLUSION

The policing of minorities is a *longue durée* police issue that has shaped everyday police practices and strategies and fostered the professionalization of the police since the late eighteenth- and early nineteenth-century beginnings of modern policing. The various questions clustering around the policing of minorities have continued to constitute core police issues during the twentieth and twenty-first centuries. Immigration, minorities as an urban issue, and the further reshaping of the nation-state all contribute to keep minority policing in a prime position on the agenda of many police forces.

In recent decades, most European countries with minority populations have tried to improve police–minority relations by integrating members of minority groups into the police forces. In some countries, particularly in Western Europe, Germany included, the overall goal of this strategy is to adjust the relative share of members of minority groups within the police personnel to better reflect the share of these groups among the population at large. Many police forces in Europe are currently moving toward this adjustment. However, recent studies show that police personnel with what is being called a "migration background" often experience considerable pressure and difficulties at their job as a result of a double bind, in which they must be neutral police officers, expected to be "regular cops" just like the others, on the one hand, and members of a minority group overburdened with expectations about gaining better access to minorities and thus considered to be "special," on the other. Nevertheless, strategies for including minority members in the police can open up opportunities for minorities, after having been viewed as threats and risks for centuries, to change their role and their status as members of the police by becoming participants in the production of security (Hunold et al. 2010).

REFERENCES

Alessi, Giorgia. 1992. *Giustizia e Polizia: Il controllo di una capitale, Napoli 1779–1803*. Naples: Jovene.

Bairoch, Paul. 1985. *De Jéricho à Mexico. Villes et économie dans l'histoire*. Paris: Gallimard.

Baumann, Imanuel, Herbert Reinke, Andrej Stephan, & Patrick Wagner. 2011. *Schatten der Vergangenheit. Das BKA und seine Gründungsgeneration in der frühen Bundesrepublik*. Köln, Germany: Wolters Kluwer.

Becker, Peter. 1999. "Weak Bodies? Prostitutes and the Role of Gender in the Criminological Writings of 19th-Century German Detectives and Magistrates." *Crime, History & Societies* 1 (3): 45–69.

Beier, A. L. 1985. *Masterless Men: The Vagrancy Problem in England, 1560–1640*. London: Methuen.

Beier, A. L., & Paul Ocobock, eds. 2008. *Cast Out: Vagrancy and Homelessness in Global and Historical Perspective*. Athens: Ohio University Press.

Berlière, Jean-Marc, & René Lévy. 2011. *Histoire des polices en France de l'ancien régime à nos jours*. Paris: Nouveau Monde Éditions.

Blanc-Chaléard, Marie-Claude, Caroline Douki, Nicole Dyonet, & Vincent Milliot, eds. 2001. *Police et migrants. France, 1667–1939*. Rennes, France: Presses Universitaires de Rennes.

Blanchard, Emmanuel. 2011. *La police parisienne et les Algériens (1944–1962)*. Paris: Nouveau Monde Éditions.

Bowling, Ben, & Coretta Phillips. 2003. "Policing Ethnic Minority Communities." In *Handbook of Policing*, ed. Tim Newburn, 528–55. Devon, UK: Willan Publishing.

Chan, Janet. 1997. *Changing Police Culture: Policing in a Multicultural Society*. Cambridge: Cambridge University Press.

Clark, Peter. 2009. *European Cities and Towns, 400–2000*. Oxford: Oxford University Press.

Coy, Jason P. 2008. *Strangers and Misfits: Banishment, Social Control, and Authority in Early Modern Germany*. Leiden, The Netherlands: Brill.

Cubero, José. 1998. *Histoire du vagabondage du moyen age à nos jours*. Paris: Éditions Imago.

Davis, Jennifer. 1991. "Urban Policing and Its Objects: Comparative Themes in England and France in the Second Half of the Nineteenth Century." In *Policing Western Europe: Politics, Professionalism, and Public Order, 1850–1940*, ed. Clive Emsley & Barbara Weinberger, 1–17. Westport, CT: Greenwood Press.

De Koster, Margo. 2008. "Routines et contraintes de la police urbaine à Anvers, 1890–1914." In *Etre policier: Les métiers de police en Europe, XVIIIe—XXe siècle*, ed. Jean-Marc Berlière, Catherine Denys, Dominique Kalifa, & Vincent Milliot, 345–62. Rennes, France: Presses Universitaires de Rennes.

De Koster, Margo. 2011. "Politieoptredens en het dagelijks ordenen van de stad. Antwerpen, eind negentiende—begin twintigste eeuw." In *Werken aan de stad. Stedelijke actoren en structuren in de Zuidelijke Nederlanden, 1500–1900*, ed. Margo De Koster, Bert De Munck, Hilde Greefs, Bart Willems, & Anne Winter, 236–53. Brussels: VUB Press.

De Munck, Bert, & Anne Winter. 2012. "Regulating Migration in Early Modern Cities: An Introduction." In *Gated Communities: Regulating Migration in Early Modern Cities*, ed. Bert De Munck & Anne Winter, 1–24. Aldershot, UK: Ashgate.

Denys, Catherine. 2010. "The Development of Police Forces in Urban Europe in the Eighteenth Century." *Journal of Urban History* 36 (3): 332–44.

Dyson, Richard, & Steven King. 2007. "'The Streets Are Paved with Idle Beggars': Experiences and Perceptions of Beggars in Nineteenth Century Oxford." In *Bettler in der europäischen Stadt der Moderne*, ed. Beate Althammer, 71–102. Bern, Switzerland: Peter Lang Publishers.

Emsley, Clive. 1999. *Gendarmes and the State in Nineteenth-Century Europe*. Oxford: Oxford University Press.

Emsley, Clive. 2004. *Crime and Society in England, 1750–1900*, 3rd ed. Harlow, UK: Pearson Longman.

Emsley, Clive. 2007. *Crime, Police and Penal Policy: European Experiences, 1750–1940*. Oxford: Oxford University Press.

Fahrmeir, Andreas. 2007. *Citizenship: The Rise and Fall of a Modern Concept*. New Haven, CT: Yale University Press.

Finzsch, Norbert. 1990. *Obrigkeit und Unterschichten. Zur Geschichte der rheinischen Unterschichten gegen Ende des 18. und zu Beginn des 19. Jahrhunderts*. Stuttgart, Germany: Franz Steiner Verlag.

Fumerton, Patricia. 2006. *Unsettled: The Culture of Mobility and the Working Poor in Early Modern England*. Chicago & London: University of Chicago Press.

Geremek, Bronislaw. 1980. *Truands et misérables dans l'Europe moderne (1350–1600)*. Paris: Gallimard.

Geremek, Bronislaw. 1991. *Les fils de Caïn. L'image des pauvres et des vagabonds dans la littérature européenne du XVe au XVIIe siècle*. Paris: Flammarion.

Godfrey, Barry S., Paul Lawrence, & Chris A. Williams. 2008. *History and Crime*. London: Sage.

Hohmann, Joachim. 1981. *Die Geschichte der Zigeunerverfolgung in Deutschland*. Frankfurt am Main, Germany: Campus Verlag.

Holdaway, Simon. 2009. *Black Police Associations: An Analysis of Race and Ethnicity Within Constabularies*. Oxford: Oxford University Press.

Hufton, Olwen. 1974. *The Poor of Eighteenth-Century France*. Oxford: Clarendon Press.

Hunold, Daniela, Daniela Klimke, Rafael Behr, & Rüdiger Lautmann. 2010. *Fremde als Ordnungshüter? Die Polizei in der Zuwanderungsgesellschaft*. Wiesbaden, Germany: Verlag für Sozialwissenschaften.

Jaschke, Hans-Gerd. 1997. *Öffentliche Sicherheit im Kulturkonflikt. Zur Entwicklung der städtischen Schutzpolizei in der multikulturellen Gesellschaft*. Frankfurt am Main, Germany: Campus Verlag.

Jessen, Ralph. 1991. *Polizei im Industrierevier. Modernisierung und Herrschaftspraxis im westfälischen Ruhrgebiet*. Götttingen, Germany: Vandenhoeck & Ruprecht.

Johansen, Anja. 2005. *Soldiers as Police: The French and Prussian Armies and the Policing of Popular Protest, 1889–1914*. Aldershot, UK: Ashgate.

Johnson, Eric A. 1995. *Urbanization and Crime: Germany, 1871–1914*. Cambridge: Cambridge University Press.

Lawrence, Paul. 2011. "The Police and Vagrants in France and England During the Nineteenth Century." In *Polizia, ordine pubblico e crimine tra città e campagna: un confronto comparative. Stato, esercito controllo del territorio*, ed. Livio Antonielli, 49–60. Manelli: Rubbettino.

Lis, Catharina, & Hugo Soly. 1993. "Neighbourhood Social Change in West European Cities." *International Review of Social History* 38: 1–30.

Lis, Catharina, & Hugo Soly. 2012. *Worthy Efforts: Attitudes to Work and Workers in Pre-Industrial Europe*. Leiden, The Netherlands: Brill.

Lucassen, Leo. 1986. *Zigeuner. Die Geschichte eines polizeilichen Ordnungsbegriffs in Deutschland, 1700–1945*. Köln, Germany: Böhlau Verlag.

Lucassen, Leo. 1997a. "Eternal Vagrants? State Formation, Migration, and Travelling Groups in Western Europe, 1350–1914." In *Migration, Migration History, History: Old Paradigms and New Perspectives*, ed. Jan Lucassen & Leo Lucassen, 225–51. Bern, Switzerland: Peter Lang Publishers.

Lucassen, Leo. 1997b. "'Harmful Tramps': Police Professionalization and Gypsies in Germany, 1700–1945." *Crime, History & Societies* 1 (1): 29–50.

Maier, Hans. 1980. *Die ältere deutsche Staats- und Verwaltungslehre*, 2nd ed. München: C. H. Beck.

Milliot, Vincent. 2012. "Urban Police and the Regulation of Migration in Eighteenth-Century France." In *Gated Communities: Regulating Migration in Early Modern Cities*, ed. Bert De Munck & Anne Winter, 135–53. Aldershot, UK: Ashgate.

Raeff, Marc. 1983. *The Well-Ordered Police State: Social and Institutional Change Through Law in the Germanies and Russia, 1600–1800*. New Haven, CT: Yale University Press.

Raphael, Lutz, ed. 2008. *Zwischen Ausschluss und Solidarität: Modi der Inklusion/Exklusion von Fremden und Armen in Europa seit der Spätantike*. Frankfurt am Main, Germany: Lang.

Reinke, Herbert. 1992. "'. . . hat sich ein politischer und wirtschaftlicher Polizeistaat entwickelt.' Polizei und Großstadt im Rheinland vom Vorabend des Ersten Weltkrieges bis zum Beginn der zwanziger Jahre." In *"Sicherheit" und "Wohlfahrt." Polizei, Gesellschaft und Herrschaft im 19. und 20. Jahrhundert*, ed. Alf Lüdtke, 219–42. Frankfurt am Main, Germany: Suhrkamp.

Roche, Daniel, ed. 2000. *La ville promise. Mobilité et accueil à Paris (fin XVIIe–début XIXe siècle)*. Paris: Fayard.

Roth, Andreas. 1997. *Kriminalitätsbekämpfung in deutschen Großstädten 1850–1914*. Berlin: Erich Schmidt Verlag.

Rowe, Mike, ed. 2007. *Policing Beyond Macpherson: Issues in Policing, Race and Society*. Cullompton, UK: Willan.

Sachße, Christoph, & Florian Tennstedt. 1998. *Geschichte der Armenfürsorge in Deutschland*, Vol. 1, *Vom Spätmittelalter bis zum 1. Weltkrieg*, 2nd ed. Stuttgart, Germany: Kohlhammer.

Sagolla-Croley, Laura. 1995. "A Working Distinction: Vagrants, Beggars, and the Labouring Poor in Mid-Victorian England." *Prose Studies* 18 (1): 74–104.

Sälter, Gerhard. 2004. *Polizei und soziale Ordnung in Paris. Zur Entstehung und Durchsetzung von Normen im städtischen Alltag des Ancien Régime*. Frankfurt am Main, Germany: Vittorio Klostermann.

Saul, Klaus. 1974. *Staat, Industrie, Arbeiterbewegung im Kaiserreich. Zur Innen- und Außenpolitik des Wilhelminischen Deutschland 1903–1914*. Düsseldorf, Germany: Bertelsmann-Universitätsverlag.

Slater, Stefan. 2012. "Street Disorder in the Metropolis, 1905–39." *Law, Crime and History* 1: 59–91.

Smith, Timothy B. 1999. "Assistance and Repression: Rural Exodus, Vagabondage and Social Crisis in France, 1880–1914." *Journal of Social History* 32 (4): 821–46.

Spencer, Elaine Glovka. 1992. *Police and the Social Order in German Cities: The Düsseldorf District, 1848–1914*. DeKalb: Northern Illinois University Press.

Vercammen, Rik, & Vicky Vanruysseveldt. 2015. "Van centraal beleid naar lokale praktijk: het 'probleem' van landloperij en bedelarij in België (1890–1910)." *Belgisch Tijdschrift voor Nieuwste Geschiedenis* XLV (1): 120–61.

Vexliard, Alexandre. 1956. *Introduction à la sociologie du vagabondage*. Paris: Marcel Rivière.

Wadauer, Sigrid. 2011. "Establishing Distinctions: Unemployment Versus Vagrancy in Austria from the Late Nineteenth Century to 1938." *International Review of Social History* 56: 31–70.

Winter, Anne. 2004. "'Vagrancy' as an Adaptive Strategy: The Duchy of Brabant, 1767–1776." *International Review of Social History* 49: 249–77.

Winter, Anne. 2008. "Caught Between Law and Practice: Migrants and Settlement Legislation in the Southern Low Countries in a Comparative Perspective, c. 1700–1900." *Rural History* 19 (2): 137–62.

Wirsing, Bern. 1991. "Die Geschichte der Gendarmeriekorps und deren Vorläuferorganisationen in Baden, Württemberg und Bayern 1750–1850." Ph.D. diss., Konstanz University.

Woolf, Stuart. 1986. *The Poor in Western Europe in the Eighteenth and Nineteenth Centuries*. London & New York: Methuen.

··

CHAPTER 14

BLACK WOMEN, CRIMINAL JUSTICE, AND VIOLENCE

··

KALI N. GROSS

INTRODUCTION

··

MUCH has been written about the alarming rate of incarceration in the United States, particularly as upward of 2 million citizens have been imprisoned. Even though that number appears to be declining, with 2012 seeing the lowest number of prisoners admitted to state and federal facilities since 1999, racial disparities persist (Carson & Gollinelli 2013, pp. 1–2).[1] African American men and women remain among the most disproportionately represented groups in prison populations. In 2009, an estimated 841,000 black men and roughly 64,800 black women were imprisoned, even though African Americans accounted for only 13.6 percent of the total U.S. population. Although the number of female prisoners pales in comparison to that of men, under the circumstances, approximately one in every 300 black women has been incarcerated, which is roughly twice the ratio for Latinas and nearly three times that for white women (Thompson 2013, pp. 299–300).[2] Despite the overrepresentation of African American women, however, only a handful of studies concentrate on their experiences within the criminal justice system, whether historically or in our own time (LeFlouria 2015; Richie 1996; Richie 2012; Rafter 1997a; Johnson 2003; Gross 2006; Hicks 2010; Lebsock 2004; Dodge 2002; Butler 2000).

This essay will spotlight aspects of the historiography on black women and crime that merit greater scholarly attention. It will also provide a concise historical overview of black women's incarceration in the United States. Finally, it will discuss a turn-of-the-century murder to explore intraracial violence and its use by the African American woman at the center of the case.

I. History and Intraracial Criminal Violence

In his critique of "New Jim Crow" writers in 2012, James Forman Jr. noted that much of the current scholarship on race and mass incarceration largely ignored violence in favor of focusing on drug charges, despite the fact that among the nation's prisoners 50 percent were serving time for violent crime (Forman 2012, pp. 104, 123).[3] At the same time, Beth Richie's research on black women and mass incarceration pointed out that intraracial intimate partner violence was one of the leading causes of death for young black women and girls (2012, p. 26). Whereas a variety of scholars are now deigning to examine black intraracial violence, nuanced historical approaches to the black experience of intraracial crime, gender violence, and trauma remain largely forthcoming.[4] To be clear, modern historians have not as a rule shied away from examining race and violence; rather, when they have raised the subject, the tendency has been to do so in fairly innocuous ways.

Most of the existing studies fall into four overarching categories: the first two address interracial violence, and the latter two encompass representational and state violence. The first category of interracial violence is arguably the largest, as a number of studies investigating race and violence have historically concentrated on white violence against blacks, a focus that is especially true for investigations of race, gender, and violence. Research on black women's interracial sexual victimization spans enslavement through Reconstruction through the Progressive era and into the Civil Rights Movement, with recent scholarship locating the endemic rapes of black women in the 1940s and 1950s as critical motivation for black women's civil rights activism (McGuire 2011; Theoharis 2013; Glymph 2008; Rosen 2009; Hunter 1998; Lee 2005). The second interracial violence category covers retaliatory violence: those studies that concentrate on African Americans who physically fought back against racist whites. Quick examples would be Nat Turner's 1831 uprising or Gabriel Prosser's rebellion in 1800 (Turner & Greenberg 1996; Tang 1997). The third category focuses on representational violence, meaning those works that examine the racial tropes and caricatures of black violence and black womanhood (White 1999; Lubiano 1992; Gross 2006, pp. 101–107). The fourth consists of research primarily on state violence, whether through biased laws and policing, unequal justice, mistreatment in prisons, or mass incarceration (Franklin 2013; Taylor 2013; Balto 2013; Agyepong 2013; Reddy 2011).

The discussion thus far has touched upon each of the aforementioned categories, all of which address important, critical issues. They make visible those crimes against black people that would otherwise be ignored and often have gone unpunished. Yet this fairly constrained focus limits our understanding of the full complexities of racialized and gendered notions of violence and allows the historiography to remain fundamentally incomplete, which does a profound disservice to the field and our society.

Black female victimization, stemming from intimate partner or community violence, remains understudied, as does black female violence against partners and against members of their own communities. Even in the instances in which historians engage black intraracial violence, the tendency is to approach it as a numbers game, either publishing the crime and arrest statistics or decrying the statistics as fundamentally flawed.[5] More often than not, historians fall short of thoroughly interrogating the full implications of beatings, murders, and rapes. The discussions do not move far beyond poverty and racism—whether historians assert that these issues underscore black violence or whether they contend they have no bearing—and rarely do we tread into discussions about trauma or seriously interrogate misogyny in these intraracial instances of domestic and gendered violence. In explaining the need for this work, Nell Irvin Painter's call for richer historical interrogations of the costs of slavery is particularly helpful. Painter explains that the "costs that were reckoned in the currency of physical abuse and family violence, will yield a fuller comprehension of our national experience" (1995, p. 127).

Yet the reticence to go there is not without merit. African Americans have been so maligned by racist notions of inherent deviance, as well as a purported heightened propensity for violence and overall criminality, that scholars have good reason to avoid wading too deeply into these troubled waters (see Muhammad 2011, introduction and ch. 2). Moreover, although this essay is principally concerned with the carceral experiences of black women and situates the call for more examination of black intraracial violence within this context, that does not negate the fact that white intraracial violence also requires more historical and current research. The overwhelming majority of white violence is also intraracial, and new evidence suggests that white domestic violence is a potential warning sign for mass acts of violence (Charlotte Childress & Harriet Childress, "White Men Have Much to Discuss about Mass Shootings," *Washington Post*, 29 March 2013; Marc Follman, Gavin Aronsen, & Deanna Pan, "A Guide to Mass Shootings in America," *Mother Jones*, 24 May 2014; Pamela Shifman & Salamishah Tillet, "To Stop the Violence, Start at Home," *New York Times* 3 February 2015; see also Kimmel 2013).

However, for the purposes of investigating black intraracial crime, rather than continuing down the contested social history path, historians might begin to study or consider violence more broadly, perhaps considering how biased justice and policing engenders both antiblack violence and black intraracial violence. For example, it is no secret that historically black women had little access to justice and protection, particularly in the late nineteenth and early twentieth centuries, from either white or black male assailants. As a result, black women had to be prepared to defend themselves because they knew that police and the justice system would be unlikely to protect them from spousal violence (Roth 2012, p. 272). In many ways, the vagaries of the justice system engendered violence as a basic survival tactic for vulnerable black women.

Moreover, black women seem to have harbored general fears about their personal safety, as many concealed small weapons on their person before leaving their homes; records indicate that they did so with good reason. For example, Bessie Banks, an otherwise law-abiding black woman, fatally stabbed an intoxicated white man after he profanely and violently accosted her on a streetcar in the early twentieth century. By all accounts, Banks exited the car in an attempt to get away, but the man pursued her onto the street, where the violent altercation occurred. He died. She was charged with murder.[6] Her case affords a glimpse into the everyday dangers black women faced just going about their business in places such as Philadelphia, and highlights the lengths to which some had to go to protect themselves, never mind the biased nature of justice. Against this backdrop, historians might also consider using sources such as these to give voice to otherwise marginalized figures. Making those actions speak might effectively work toward overturning the historical forces that rendered them mute.

II. Historical Trends in Black Female Incarceration and Victimization

Black women's historical experience with criminal justice in the United States has been fundamentally shaped by a lack of protection and an almost-negligible access to due process of law. Statutes governing enslavement, and the treatment of African-descended women in particular, subjected black women to violence and sexual exploitation at the same time that it fomented their criminalization. Seventeenth- and eighteenth-century laws—from the decree that enslaved women's children would also be enslaved to rape laws that excluded the sexual assault of black women and girls—especially jeopardized black womanhood. Statutes such as these left black women vulnerable to sexual violence, particularly given that masters would profit from any viable pregnancies (Mitchell & Flanders 1896, p. 79; Wilf 2010, p. 121; Johnson 2003, pp. 22–23; Hine & Thompson 1998, pp. 170–71; Gross 2015). Moreover, most whites held black women responsible for their victimization and promoted stereotypes about their lasciviousness. As one Alabama planter opined, he "did not know more than one negro woman he could suppose to be chaste" (White 1999, p. 31; see also Hening 1823, p. 70; Lewis & Lewis 2011, pp. 106–09; Foster 2011; Morgan 2004, pp. 12, 68, 72). Yet when black women physically resisted and attacked abusers, the victims could be subject to severe punishments from the legal system.[7]

These dynamics coalesced in profoundly detrimental ways as black women in the justice system combated widespread beliefs about their immorality and inherent criminality (Rafter 1997a; Lombroso & Ferrero 2004; Giddings 1995, p. 416). The impact of these phenomena becomes especially visible through an examination of black women's historical rates of incarceration, beginning with the nation's first penitentiary. Founded in 1790, the establishment of the Walnut Street Prison, which comprised a jail and "Penitentiary House," followed Pennsylvania's 1780 Act for the Gradual Abolition of Slavery. Fears of black freedom together with a legislative emphasis on punishing crimes against property quickly led to blacks' disproportionate confinement (Patrick-Stamp 1995, pp. 98, 101–03; Rowe 1989, p. 704, table 5; Marietta & Rowe 2006; Meranze

1996; Teeters 1955; Teeters 1937). Yet in Philadelphia, and eventually in much of the country, black women were more disproportionately represented in prison than black men. Although African Americans were far less than 20 percent of the city's population, black women accounted for nearly half of all female prisoners, and black men represented roughly 30 percent of male prisoners (Patrick-Stamp 1995, p. 111, table 5; Nash 1988, p. 137; Steinberg 1989, p. 43). By virtue of working in white-owned homes as domestics—often the only employment available to them—black women were especially susceptible to larceny charges. Furthermore, all-white judiciaries tended to favor the word of white accusers rather than that of impoverished black servants. These underlying forces contributed to blacks' increased rates of incarceration, and black women going before Philadelphia courts found themselves convicted more often than any other group (Patrick-Stamp 1995, pp. 98, 100–01; Rowe 1989, p. 704).

After the national abolition of slavery, newly freed black men and women experienced similar patterns of imprisonment in the south. For example, whereas the black population accounted for roughly 30 percent of the total southern population between 1880 and 1920, African American men accounted for just over 70 percent of male prisoners in the late nineteenth century, and African American women accounted for roughly 86 percent (Rafter 1997b, p. 142, table 6.3). Likewise, in the Midwest in 1880, black women represented 29 percent of female prisoners, while black men accounted for 11.8 percent of the males; at that time, African Americans were only 2.2 percent of the population. Though their number in the broader population essentially held steady, by 1904 the percentage of black female prisoners in the larger prison population had risen to 48.4 percent and that of black male prisoners had grown to 22 percent. By 1923, although African Americans accounted for only 2.3 percent of the general population, they accounted for 19.7 percent of all state prisoners (Rafter 1997b, p. 142, table 6.3). By the 1960s, for felony convictions those numbers had climbed to nearly 50 percent for black men and 70 percent for black women, yet blacks made up just over 10 percent of the Illinois population.[8] In the late twentieth century, as well as in the early part of the twenty-first century, harsh antidrug policies such as the Rockefeller Drug Laws negatively impacted African American women, as their imprisonment percentage for drug-related offenses was twice that of black men (Bush-Baskette 1998, p. 113).

These statistics not only highlight endemic racial disparities but also gesture toward the inherent devaluation of black womanhood in the justice system. From black women's exclusion in the 1920s from most reformatories, institutions predicated upon the rehabilitation of young women (Odem 1995, p. 25), or segregation and experiences of discrimination in those that accepted them (Rafter 1997b, pp. 55–59, 152–54; Hicks 2010, pp. 165–66, 188–89) to their presence on southern chain gangs (where they toiled alongside men), the treatment of African American women in the carceral state reflects the overwhelming belief that as women they were fundamentally deficient (Hicks 2009, p. 419; Curtin 1994, pp. 13–14, 20, 25–26; LeFlouria 2011, p. 55; Haley 2013, p. 53; Oshinsky 1996, pp. 157–77; Ayers 1984, p. 200). This rhetoric left black women extremely vulnerable to violence and sexual assault. That the nation's legal system has played such a pivotal role in black women's sexual subjection cannot be overstated, especially since it has serious implications for criminal justice and its historical and current inability to recognize black female victims, let alone punish crimes against them.

Historians have endeavored to document sexual violence against enslaved and newly freed women—with the focus on the latter group thanks in no small part to black women's brave efforts to obtain some small measure of justice. Records of those efforts have allowed scholars to reconstruct the complexities of African American women's inability to access institutionalized justice as well as see how black women used their words and testimonies to create justice for themselves. For example, black rape victims of the 1866 Memphis riot took pains to describe how they had been assaulted. Their testimonies before a Senate committee evidence their determination to affirm their citizenship and womanhood by insisting that they did not consent—that their coercion was an unlawful violation (Rosen 2009, pp. 9, 76–80; Williams 2012; Freedman 2013).

Despite their (and other black female victims') valiant attempts, the rape and sexual harassment of black women continued, largely unabated and unpunished. Not only was justice absent for black women, but even when partners attempted to defend their honor, they faced violent outcomes and arrests. In 1912 a black man protesting his wife's sexual harassment by her white employer was himself arrested and fined. As the judge remarked, "This court will never take the word of a nigger against the word of a white man" (Gross 2006, pp. 44–46; Negro Nurse 1992 [1912]). Moreover, black women's efforts to defend themselves often made them subject to harsh punishment, even at the hands of white lynch mobs. Ada Robertson narrowly avoided being lynched in 1923 after she was arrested for shooting a white man who had broken into her home and "attempted to assault her" (Feimster 2011, pp. 172–73).

The matrix of racism, patriarchy, and sexual violence that has dogged black womanhood in America is central to black women's victimization and criminalization. Understanding this dynamic is fundamental for scholarship on black women, crime, and justice. However, it is not the only aspect of black women's historical experiences in the legal system that requires more scholarly attention. Also lacking are those histories that contemplate these themes with respect to black intraracial violence and the role that biased justice plays therein.

III. A BLACK WOMAN'S TRADE IN VIOLENCE

Just as historical examinations can unearth important clues about the relationship between unequal justice and black female incarceration, they also offer potentially transformative ways to engage black female violence outside of the binaries of victimization and punishment. In the late nineteenth and early twentieth centuries, African American women's violence encompassed actions ranging from preemptive performances of combative prowess to more muscular forms of self-defense to calculated assaults designed to advance black women's agendas, whether for financial gain or for dominance in their households and communities. For example, in certain instances black women posing as prostitutes targeted white men—specifically, would-be johns—for robbery. Their actions were fairly ingenious. Not only were most male victims not likely to report having been bested by a woman—prostitute, robber, or otherwise—in a dark alley, but because of public taboos regarding interracial sex, black women committing this particular act routinely escaped punishment even if the men reported the crimes. Justices held that white men deigning to follow black women into dark corners had asked for whatever outrages befell them (Gross 2006, pp. 77–99; Lane 1989, pp. 107–09). Other examples of violence suggest that it also allowed black women to cleave out pockets of autonomy that otherwise might not have existed.[9] The case involving a 37-year-old black southern migrant named Hannah Mary Tabbs, who at the very least participated in the murder and dismemberment of her lover, serves as a startling, illustrative example.

The brutal slaying of a young black man named Wakefield Gaines horrified blacks and whites in 1887. Gaines's assailant(s) bludgeoned him to death before hacking the 24-year-old into six pieces and sinking his remains. Shortly after the discovery of Gaines's torso near a pond just outside Philadelphia, investigators identified and captured two black suspects: Gaines's married paramour Tabbs and George Wilson, a former coworker whom Tabbs implicated after her arrest. Litigation surrounding the case spanned almost nine months, which for the era was an extraordinary length of time. The case was also front-page news in presses across the nation ("Coon Chops," *New York National Police Gazette*, 5 December 1887; "Horrible Details of the Killing and Mutilation of Wakefield Gains," *Decatur Daily Republican,* 24 February 1887; "A Foul Deed Confessed," *Newark Daily Advocate,* 24 February 1887). The case and its more lurid particulars allowed typically off-limits topics such as illicit sex, race, and intimate partner violence to occupy mainstream public discourses. Over the course of the investigation, it became clear that although Tabbs had no prior criminal record, she was regarded as a neighborhood terror. Witness statements attested to her extensive history of violence, including numerous physical assaults on her family and on a number of blacks in her community. Philadelphia authorities, not particularly known for their objectivity as far as black women were concerned, nonetheless struggled to make sense of the brutality attributed to Tabbs.[10]

Accounts of her violence ran counter to her demeanor, never mind her solid employment record, having worked in a number of white homes and businesses without incident. The details may gesture toward Tabbs's dual consciousness—she performed respectability in mainstream circles while she took advantage of the black community's dislocation from police protection and other forms of institutionalized justice. It also provides a view of how violence functioned in Tabbs's life and showcases her formidable prowess in this sphere. Furthermore, although the case took place during the post-Reconstruction era—and consequently speaks to the period's complicated interracial dynamics—for the most part the case offers a nuanced history of African Americans' internal struggles with notions of intimacy, the everyday stressors of family life, and violence. In this sense, the case's potential for recovering aspects of black women's erotic autonomy is also valuable.[11]

Tabbs's violence is unique not only because she was a woman but also because she attacked individuals without regard to age or gender. Perhaps equally telling, however, is that despite the range in her victims' characteristics, she did not transgress the color line. Tabbs did not attack whites, suggesting that she understood fully the racial power dynamics of the era as well as the severity of the backlash for such actions—even in the urban north. This aspect further suggests that her brutality, while extensive, was not without logic or rationality. Her aggression ranged from physical attacks and property damage to violent threats and verbal outbursts. Her husband, John Tabbs, was one of her primary targets, though he was hardly the only one. Residents on her street and in her neighborhood were terrified (*Philadelphia Evening Bulletin*, 24 February 1887).

So infamous was her violence that when her niece, Annie Richardson, ran away, most who knew the family believed that Tabbs had murdered the girl. Following Tabbs's arrest in the Gaines case, authorities received an anonymous letter. The writer claimed to have knowledge and proof that Tabbs was some kind of serial killer with victims throughout the Mid-Atlantic region (*Philadelphia Evening Bulletin*, 1 March 1887). When the missing girl finally came forward, she explained that her aunt had begun to beat her so unmercifully that she had fled in fear of her safety. Tabbs's attacks seem to have been largely motivated by concern about the girl's comportment with Gaines, as Annie stated that the beatings were especially brutal if her aunt believed that she had interacted with Gaines, and that this was in fact the reason she ran away (*Philadelphia Evening Bulletin*, 3 March 1887; 4 March 1887). Witnesses associated with the case intimated that Tabbs became jealous when Gaines showed her niece any attention (*Philadelphia Evening Bulletin*, 23 February 1887).

The extreme nature of Tabbs's violence notwithstanding, her actions nonetheless safeguarded her personal pursuits, namely, maintaining her affair with the young Gaines. For example, her violence effectively moved her niece, who she seems to have regarded as potential competition for Gaines's affections, out of the picture. Additionally, by terrorizing her neighbors, she compelled their silence, as Gaines visited her home daily when her husband John went to work. Whereas a significant part of black women's social maneuvers during this period revolved around dissembling their sexuality in the hope of discouraging unwanted sexual attention, Tabbs concentrated her efforts on seeking erotic pleasures.[12] According to the evidence, there was a lot of heat between her and Gaines, and she seemed fully committed. Not only was he in her home everyday, but also she did his laundry, covered his expenses, and prepared his meals.

Unfortunately, Gaines's affections proved less certain. The relationship took a turn when she learned that he was seeing someone else. "Seeing" might be considered an understatement, since it was rumored that shortly before his death, Gaines had planned to wed his new girlfriend, Annie Johnson. News of this engagement is what likely sent Tabbs over the edge, and there is little doubt that it factored into her violence against him. Two weeks before Gaines's disappearance and subsequent murder, Tabbs confronted the couple. This episode would end with the young Johnson taking flight as Tabbs cut Gaines's face with a razor. He sought refuge in his sister's home, although Tabbs assured him that she would catch him and kill him (*Philadelphia Evening Bulletin*, 23 February 1887; 24 February 1887; *Philadelphia Times*, 24 February 1887). This kind of incident must have typified the volatility in their relationship, because he apparently visited her two days before his death as well as on the day he died. When he returned home from the visit, Gaines told his landlady that he believed Tabbs had tried to poison him by giving him a drink with powder at the bottom of the glass. After consuming some of it, he became violently ill (*Philadelphia Evening Bulletin*, 25 February 1887). Although the specific details about his ultimate demise are murky, what exists is a disturbing if not powerfully demonstrative example of black intraracial violence.

Tabbs's actions not only map domestic violence as enacted by a black woman but also gesture toward the ways that African Americans' dislocation from justice and protection abetted her actions. That Tabbs lacked a criminal record in Philadelphia despite the spate of violence she inflicted on her family and acquaintances is evidence of the gulf between black citizens and the legal system. Also, most historical examinations of black women and violence demonstrate how violence is often black women's undoing; Tabbs's case suggests, at least in part, that the ways black women traded in violence might also have granted them greater access to freedoms and agency that would otherwise have been unobtainable.[13]

Still, although Tabbs's case offers a rare vantage from which to contemplate black intraracial violence, it is not representative of black women's crimes or African American women's experiences of and trade in violence writ large. Black women's criminal offending has historically been confined to nonviolent property offenses as well as prostitution and drug crimes. Most instances of black female violence were domestic skirmishes or neighborhood scraps. However, the scope of black female victimization is difficult to gauge given that for so many years few crimes against them were prosecuted, interracially or intraracially.

CONCLUSION

It is difficult to examine black women's historical experience with the American legal system and find meaningful ways to use terms such as "crime" or "justice." So much about this history calls both notions into question. African American women have been, and remain, on the receiving end of the worst vicissitudes of the criminal justice system—namely, disproportionate rates of incarceration, longer prison sentences, and dislocation from protection and due process; the latter factor is related to their use of extralegal violence. At the same time, these issues continue to cry out for broader scholarly and historical treatment. Such research is essential not only for elucidating black women's experiences of crime and justice but also because their experience speaks more broadly about the fraught contours of justice in the U.S. legal system.

NOTES

1. Although the number is declining, 609,800 prisoners were admitted to state and federal prison facilities in 2012.
2. In 2011, over 1 million women were either imprisoned or under the control of the U.S. justice system. See American Civil Liberties Union (2011).
3. New Jim Crow writers would likely refer to works such as Michelle Alexander's important 2012 book, *The New Jim Crow*, and would have well-crafted responses, but I find James Forman's argument compelling.
4. My call for scholars to find ways to interrogate this issue has been guided and shaped by Heather Thompson's important (2010) piece "Why Mass Incarceration Matters." Other studies also engage these issues. Nell Irvin Painter (1995) has begun to examine the psychological impact of enslavement on both blacks and whites. Works that engage black crime include Lane (1989), Lane (1997), Patrick-Stamp (1995), Rowe (1989), and Hicks (2010). For historical research on race and domestic violence, see Adler (2010), Adler (2003), and Roth (2012). On female violence, including the experiences of blacks and Latinas, see Butler (2000). For a model of and meditation on the impact of intraracial black violence, see Brown (2004).
5. I do not mean to discount these approaches or the critiques of them; rather, I diagram this issue to find a way to call for a more textured examination of the history. However, for salient critiques of intraracial crime coverage/scholarship, see Wilson (2005); Muhammad (2011); and Khalil Muhammad, "Playing the Violence Card," *New York Times*, 5 April 2012.
6. *Commonwealth vs. Bessie Elizabeth Minor Banks*, 6 January 1911, testimony notes, case no. 307, August 1910 Sessions files, Quarter Sessions Court records, RG 21.5: Notes of Testimony 1877–1915, Philadelphia City Archives, Philadelphia, Pennsylvania.
7. Celia, an enslaved woman in Missouri, killed the owner who had raped her since her early teens. She was tried and found guilty, as the judiciary disallowed enslaved black women protection, let alone retribution, for sexual assault. She died on the gallows at 2:30 p.m. on December 21, 1855 (McLaurin 1991, p. 135).
8. In 1910 African Americans accounted for 2.4 percent of the state population and 11.6 percent in the 1960s (Dodge 2002, p. 117, table 7).
9. Just as "Stagolee" existed as an archetype for a kind of tough black masculinity, black female violence also may have served as a means for black women to fashion a new kind of womanhood (Brown 2004, pp. 2–4, 13–14). Robin D. G. Kelley also explores how Stagolee functioned as an expression of black masculinity within working-class black culture (1994, p. 66).
10. I discussed the case briefly in *Colored Amazons* (Gross 2006), and it the subject of my forthcoming book.
11. This is also an area crying out for more scholarly attention (see, however, Spillers 2003, p. 153; Hine 1989; and Lindsey & Johnson 2014).
12. African American women masked their sexuality to stave off sexual assaults and to counter racist myths about black female morality, or lack thereof. For more on dissemblance, see Hine (1989).
13. On the violence committed by the oppressed as having cleansing properties, see Fanon (2005 [1961], p. 51).

REFERENCES

Adler, Jeffrey. 2003. "'We've Got a Right to Fight; We're Married': Domestic Homicide in Chicago, 1875–1920." *Journal of Interdisciplinary History* 34 (1): 39–48.

Adler, Jeffrey. 2010. "'Bessie Done Cut Her Old Man': Race, Common-Law Marriage, and Homicide in New Orleans, 1925–1945." *Journal of Social History* 44 (1): 123–43.

Agyepong, Tera. 2013. "In the Belly of the Beast: Black Policeman Combat Police Brutality in Chicago, 1968–1983." *Journal of African History* 98 (2): 253–76.

Alexander, Michelle. 2012. *The New Jim Crow: Mass Incarceration in the Age of Colorblindness.* New York: New Press.

American Civil Liberties Union. 2011. "Prison Rape Elimination Act of 2003 (PREA)." Accessed at https://www.aclu.org/prisoners-rights-womens-rights/prison-rape-elimination-act-2003-prea.

Ayers, Edward L. 1984. *Vengeance and Justice: Crime and Justice in the Nineteenth-Century American South.* New York: Oxford University Press.

Balto, Simon Ezra. 2013. "'Occupied Territory': Police Repression and Black Resistance in Postwar Milwaukee, 1950–1968." *Journal of African History* 98 (2): 229–52.

Brown, Cecil. 2004. *Stagolee Shot Billy.* Cambridge: Harvard University Press.

Butler, Anne M. 2000. *Gendered Justice in the American West.* Urbana: University of Illinois Press.

Carson, E. Ann, & Daniela Gollinelli. 2013. "Prisoners in 2012: Trends in Admissions and Releases, 1991–2012." Accessed at www.bjs.gov/content/pub/pdf/p12tar9112.pdf.

Curtin, Mary Ellen. 1994. *"The 'Human World' of Black Women in Alabama Prisons, 1870–1900."* In *Hidden Histories of Women in the New South,* ed. Virginia Bernhard, Betty Brandon, Elizabeth Fox-Genovese, Theda Purdue, & Elizabeth H. Turner, 11–30. Columbia: University of Missouri Press.

Dodge, L. Mara. 2002. *"Whores and Thieves of the Worst Kind": A Study of Women, Crime, and Prisons, 1835–2000.* DeKalb: Northern Illinois University Press.

Fanon, Frantz. 2005 [1961]. *The Wretched of the Earth.* New York: Grove Press.

Feimster, Crystal N. 2011. *Southern Horrors: Women and the Politics of Rape and Lynching.* Cambridge: Harvard University Press.

Forman, James, Jr. 2012. "Racial Critiques of Mass Incarceration: Beyond the New Jim Crow." *New York University Law Review* 87 (April): 45–51.

Foster, Thomas A. 2011. "The Sexual Abuse of Black Men under American Slavery." *Journal of the History of Sexuality* 20 (3): 445–64.

Franklin, V. P. 2013. "Commentary: Solitary Confinement: 'I Feel Like . . . No One Cares about Me.'" *Journal of African History* 98 (2): 197–98.

Freedman, Estelle B. 2013. *Redefining Rape: Sexual Violence in the Era of Suffrage and Segregation.* Cambridge: Harvard University Press.

Giddings, Paula. 1995. "The Last Taboo." In *Words of Fire: An Anthology of African-American Feminist Thought,* ed. Beverly Guy-Sheftall, 414–28. New York: W. W. Norton and Company.

Glymph, Thavolia. 2008. *Out of the House of Bondage: The Transformation of the Plantation Household.* Cambridge: Cambridge University Press.

Gross, Kali N. 2006. *Colored Amazons: Crime, Violence, and Black Women in the City of Brotherly Love, 1880–1910.* Durham, NC: Duke University Press.

Gross, Kali Nicole. 2015. "African American Women, Mass Incarceration, and the Politics of Protection." *Journal of American History,* 102 (1): 25–33.

Haley, Sarah. 2013. "'Like I was a Man': Chain Gangs, Gender, and the Domestic Carceral Sphere in Jim Crow Georgia." *Signs* 39 (1): 53–77.

Hening, William Waller. 1823. *The Statutes at Large; Being A Collection of All the Laws of Virginia from the First Session of the Legislature in the Year 1619.* New York: R. and W. and G. Bartow.

Hicks, Cheryl D. 2009. "'Bright and Good Looking Colored Girl': Black Women's Sexuality and 'Harmful Intimacy' in Early Twentieth-Century New York." *Journal of the History of Sexuality* 18 (3): 418–56.

Hicks, Cheryl D. 2010. *Talk with You Like a Woman: African American Women, Justice, and Reform in New York, 1890–1935.* Chapel Hill: University of North Carolina Press.

Hine, Darlene Clark. 1989. "Rape and the Inner Lives of Black Women in the Middle West." *Signs* 14 (4): 912–20.

Hine, Darlene Clark, & Kathleen Thompson. 1998. *A Shining Thread of Hope: The History of Black Women in America.* New York: Broadway Books.

Hunter, Tera W. 1998. *To 'Joy My Freedom: Southern Black Women's Lives and Labors after the Civil War.* Cambridge: Harvard University Press.

Johnson, Paula C. 2003. *Inner Lives: Voices of African American Women in Prison.* New York: New York University Press.

Kelley, Robin D. G. 1994. *Race Rebels: Culture, Politics, and the Black Working Class.* New York: Free Press.

Kimmel, Michael. 2013. *Angry White Men: American Masculinity and the End of an Era.* New York: Nation Books.

Lane, Roger. 1989. *Roots of Violence in Black Philadelphia, 1860–1900.* Cambridge: Harvard University Press.

Lane, Roger. 1997. *Murder in America: A History.* Columbus: Ohio State University Press.

Lebsock, Suzanne. 2004. *A Murder in Virginia: Southern Justice on Trial.* New York: W. W. Norton and Company.

Lee, Chana Kai. 2005. *For Freedom's Sake: The Life of Fannie Lou Hamer.* Chicago: University of Illinois Press.

LeFlouria, Talitha. 2011. "'The Hand that Rocks the Cradle Cuts Cordwood': Exploring Black Women's Lives and Labor in Georgia's Convict Camps, 1865–1917." *Labor: Studies in Working-Class History of the Americas* 8 (3): 47–64.

LeFlouria, Talitha. 2015. *Chained in Silence: Black Women and Convict Labor in the New South.* Chapel Hill: University of North Carolina Press.

Lewis, Catherine M., & Richard Lewis. 2011. *Women in Slavery: A Document Reader.* Fayetteville: University of Arkansas Press.

Lindsey, Treva B., & Jessica Marie Johnson. 2014. "Searching for Climax: Black Erotic Lives in Slavery and Freedom." *Meridian* 12 (2): 169–95.

Lombroso, Cesare, & Guglielmo Ferrero. 2004. *Criminal Woman, the Prostitute, and the Normal Woman,* trans. Nicole Hahn Rafter & Mary Gibson. Durham, NC: Duke University Press.

Lubiano, Wahneema. 1992. "Black Ladies, Welfare Queens, and State Minstrels: Ideological War by Narrative Means." In *Race-ing Justice, En-gendering Power: Essays on Anita Hill, Clarence Thomas, and the Construction of Social Equality,* ed. Toni Morrison, 323–63. New York: Pantheon Books.

Marietta, Jack D., & G. S. Rowe. 2006. *Troubled Experiment: Crime and Justice in Pennsylvania, 1682–1800.* Philadelphia: University of Pennsylvania Press.

McGuire, Danielle. 2011. *At the Dark End of the Street: Black Women, Rape, and Resistance—A New History of the Civil Rights Movement from Rosa Parks to the Rise of Black Power*. New York: Vintage Books.

McLaurin, Melton A. 1991. *Celia, a Slave: A True Story*. New York: Avon.

Meranze, Michael. 1996. *Laboratories of Virtue: Punishment, Revolution, and Authority in Philadelphia, 1760–1835*. Chapel Hill: University of North Carolina Press.

Mitchell, James T., & Henry Flanders. 1896. "An Act for the Trial of Negroes." In *The Statutes at Large of Pennsylvania from 1682 to 1801, Compiled under the Authority of the Act of May 19, 1887*, Vol. 2, *1700–1712*, 77–9. Philadelphia: Clarence M. Busch.

Morgan, Jennifer L. 2004. *Laboring Women: Reproduction and Gender in New World Slavery*. Philadelphia: University of Pennsylvania Press.

Muhammad, Khalil Gibran. 2011. *The Condemnation of Blackness: Race, Crime, and the Making of Modern Urban America*. Cambridge: Harvard University Press.

Nash, Gary. 1988. *Forging Freedom: The Formation of Philadelphia's Black Community, 1720–1840*. Cambridge: Harvard University Press.

Negro Nurse, A. 1992 [1912]. "More Slavery at the South." In *Black Women in White America*, ed. Gerder Lerner, 197–200. New York: Vintage Books.

Odem, Mary E. 1995. *Delinquent Daughters: Protecting and Policing Adolescent Female Sexuality in the United States, 1885–1920*. Chapel Hill: University of North Carolina Press.

Oshinsky, David M. 1996. *"Worse Than Slavery": Parchman Farm and the Ordeal of Jim Crow Justice*. New York: Free Press.

Painter, Nell Irvin. 1995. "Soul Murder and Slavery: Toward a Fully Loaded Cost Accounting." In *U.S. History as Women's History: New Feminist Essays*, ed. Linda K. Kerber, Alice Kessler-Harris, & Kathryn Kish Sklar, 125–46. Chapel Hill: University of North Carolina Press.

Patrick-Stamp, Leslie. 1995. "Numbers that Are Not New: African Americans in the Country's First Prison, 1790–1835." *Pennsylvania Magazine of History and Biography* 119 (January–April): 95–128.

Rafter, Nicole Hahn. 1997a. *Creating Born Criminals*. Chicago: University of Illinois Press.

Rafter, Nicole Hahn. 1997b. *Partial Justice: Women, Prisons, and Social Control*, 2nd ed. New Brunswick, NJ: Transaction Publishers.

Reddy, Chandan. 2011. *Freedom with Violence: Race, Sexuality and the US State*. Durham, NC: Duke University Press.

Richie, Beth. 1996. *Compelled to Crime: The Gender Entrapment of Battered Black Women*. New York: Routledge.

Richie, Beth. 2012. *Arrested Justice: Black Women, Violence, and America's Prison Nation*. New York: New York University Press.

Rosen, Hannah. 2009. *Terror in the Heart of Freedom*. Chapel Hill: University of North Carolina Press.

Roth, Randolph. 2012. *American Homicide*. New York: Belknap Press.

Rowe, G. S. 1989. "Black Offenders, Criminal Courts, and Philadelphia Society in the Late Eighteenth Century." *Journal of Social History* 22 (4): 685–712.

Spillers, Hortense J. 2003. *Black, White, and in Color: Essays on American Literature and Culture*. Chicago: University of Chicago Press.

Steinberg, Allen. 1989. *The Transformation of Criminal Justice: Philadelphia, 1800–1880*. Chapel Hill: University of North Carolina Press.

Tang, Joyce. 1997. "Enslaved African Rebellions in Virginia." *Journal of Black Studies* 27 (5): 598–614.

Taylor, Clarence. 2013. "Race, Class, and Police Brutality in New York City: The Role of the Communist Party in the Early Cold War Years." *Journal of African History* 98 (2): 205–28.

Teeters, Negley K. 1937. *They Were in Prison: A History of the Pennsylvania Prison Society, 1787–1937*. Philadelphia: Johnson C. Winston Company.

Teeters, Negley K. 1955. *The Cradle of the Penitentiary: The Walnut Street Jail at Philadelphia, 1773–1835*. Philadelphia: Pennsylvania Prison Society.

Theoharis, Jeanne. 2013. *The Rebellious Life of Mrs. Rosa Parks*. Boston: Beacon Press.

Thompson, Gail L. 2013. "African American Women and the U.S. Criminal Justice System: A Statistical Survey, 1870–2009." *Journal of African American History* 98 (2): 299–300.

Thompson, Heather Ann. 2010. "Why Mass Incarceration Matters: Rethinking Crisis, Decline, and Transformation in Postwar American History. *Journal of American History* 97 (December): 703–34.

Turner, Nat, & Kenneth S. Greenberg, ed. 1996. *The Confessions of Nat Turner and Related Documents*. Bedford: St. Martin's Press.

White, Deborah Gray. 1999. *Ar'n't I a Woman? Female Slaves in the Plantation South*. New York: W. W. Norton and Company.

Wilf, Steven. 2010. *Law's Imagined Republic: Popular Politics and Criminal Justice in Revolutionary America*. Cambridge: Cambridge University Press.

Williams, Kidada. 2012. *They Left Great Marks on Me: African American Testimonies of Racial Violence from Emancipation to World War I*. New York: New York University Press.

Wilson, David. 2005. *Inventing Black-on-Black Violence: Discourse, Space, and Representation*. New York: Syracuse University Press.

PART FOUR

CULTURAL REPRESENTATIONS OF CRIME

···

CHAPTER 15

CRIME NEWS AND
THE PRESS

···

JOHN CARTER WOOD

Introduction

For all of the social, cultural, and technological changes in recent centuries, "news" (in the sense of purportedly true information regarding actual events) about "crime" (referring to both law breaking and law enforcement) has continued to attract substantial attention. As many have done since, the *Daily Herald* in 1927 pondered the "strange and exceedingly widespread fascination of the sinister and the macabre," asking why "nine people out of every ten follow the meagre official details and the billowing rumours of an actual murder mystery more eagerly and breathlessly than the most devoted detective story 'fan' ever stumbled from clue to clue in the encouraging company of Sherlock Holmes or Sexton Blake or Dr. Thorndyke" (*Daily Herald*, "Murder!" 12 May 1927). From the broadsheet to the blog, the appeal of crime news has transcended all eras, formats, and national borders. But there have also been changes in the relationships among those who create news, as well as in the specific themes addressed and the methods used to present them. Between the eighteenth and late twentieth centuries, two transformations were particularly important: first, the emergence of a mass newspaper readership and the development of "New Journalism" starting in the 1850s, and, second, the rise of radio and television news after the Second World War. The first shift established newspapers as the key medium of crime news; the second saw the press not so much supplanted as supplemented by broadcast media. (The transformations related to the Internet since the 1990s are not considered here.)

In this essay, I will examine selected historical developments in nonfictional crime media ("crime news") with a particular focus on the newspaper press from the late eighteenth to the mid-twentieth centuries and a geographical concentration on Great Britain. After considering crime media historiography, I describe in section I the rise to prominence of the newspaper press. In section II, I examine how crime news shapes perceptions of crime, criminals, and criminal justice. In section III, I focus on "moral panics" and "social fears" and their relevance to public understandings of and state responses to crime. Section IV turns to paths for research development, suggesting priorities for what we still need to learn. In the conclusion, I draw together some overarching, long-term conclusions about crime news.

I. CRIME AND MEDIA: HISTORIOGRAPHY, CONTINUITY, AND CHANGE

From the earliest flowering of social historians' interest in "criminal" behavior in the 1960s and 1970s, media sources have played a key role in historical research. In pioneering studies of "bandits" or "riots," the printed sources of crime "news" were used to reconstruct real events as well as elite and popular mentalities (e.g., Hobsbawm 1969; Hay et al. 1975). Some historians have also addressed media representations of "justice" (especially those related to capital punishment) as a tool to maintain an emergent capitalist social order (Linebaugh 1992; Gatrell 1994). Historians' analytical interest in media depictions of perpetrators and victims and their construction of "deviance," as well as in the parameters of "newsworthiness," was certainly shared with criminologists (e.g., Cohen & Young 1973; Chibnall 1977); even so, criminologists and historians have tended to work separately from—and even in total ignorance of—one another (Lawrence 2012). One reason for this is that whereas crime historians have only recently begun focusing on the mid-twentieth century, most criminologists focus on trends after the Second World War. Since the 1980s historians and criminologists have nonetheless shared an increasing interest in the methods and impact of media *themselves*, a result of the broader "cultural turn" in the humanities and social sciences and the accompanying focus on "representations," "discourses," and "narratives" of crime. The development of "media history" and the increasing availability of digitized sources have also been significant.

While much research on crime news has focused on the press, the modern "newspaper" attained its dominance only through a lengthy transitional process. Substantial work has now been done on the varieties of printed crime "news" in the early modern period, which along with newspapers included woodcuts, pamphlets, broadsheets, "last dying speeches" of the condemned, and publications such as the Proceedings of the Old Bailey or the Account of the Ordinary of Newgate (Linebaugh 1977; Sharpe 1985; Devereaux 1996; McKenzie 1998; Shoemaker 2004, pp. 241–73; King 2009). Newspapers began to supersede other formats of crime news in the late eighteenth century (Devereaux 2003; Devereaux 2007; McKenzie 2005; Snell 2007). By then, "newspapers were almost certainly the most widely read source of printed information about crime and justice" (King 2007, p. 74). While other sources of crime news—broadsides, theatrical productions, material objects, and the cheap, serialized stories known as "penny bloods" or "penny dreadfuls" (Chassaigne 1999; Crone 2012), all of which often freely mixed fact and fiction—remained relevant well into the Victorian era, the second half of the nineteenth century saw the press finally emerge clearly as "the most important medium for creating the public's awareness and perception of violent crime" (Archer & Jones 2003, p. 17). By 1939 "some two-thirds of the population regularly saw a daily paper" (Bingham 2004, p. 3), a substantial portion of which would have been devoted to crime news. Newspapers' predominance as a crime medium was accompanied by their growing reliance on a "New Journalism" focusing on "human interest" stories. This approach was not entirely "new" (Wiener 1988), but there was a shift toward greater drama and personalization in reporting.

As newspaper proprietors and editors know, crime has always offered striking "human interest" stories. On average, somewhat over 10 percent of reporting in the late eighteenth and early nineteenth centuries dealt with "crime" (King 2007, p. 80). Crime-related "sensationalism" remained significant throughout the nineteenth century, and there was little difference in the amount of crime coverage, the types of crime reported upon, and the language used between the sensationalist *Lloyd's Weekly Newspaper* and the more respectable pages of the London *Times*, though the former devoted more space to discussing murder (Crone 2012, pp. 221–46). The growing market for news from the late nineteenth century onward was served by popular newspapers such as the *Daily Telegraph* (founded in 1855), *Daily Mail* (1896), *Daily Express* (1900), and *Daily Mirror* (1903). A guiding motto of *Mail* and *Mirror* founder Lord Northcliffe was "get me a murder a day" (Williams 1998), and this approach was carried on in the interwar period by his brother and successor, Lord Rothermere—along with many others—even as the official statistics of serious crime and violence remained historically moderate. Photographic methods became increasingly better, cheaper, and more central to crime news, despite the prohibition of courtroom photography and in-court sketching in England and Wales after 1925 (Nead 2005). In the late 1920s, the *Daily Mirror* devoted some 15 percent of its coverage to "law, police and accidents," a figure that rose to 23 percent over the next two decades (Bingham 2009, p. 131). After the Second World War, the media focus on mysterious deaths, bizarre crimes, and individual suffering continued, and may even have increased since the mid-1960s (Reiner, Livingstone, & Allen 2003, p. 17). Furthermore, these broad patterns were international (e.g., Siemens 2007, pp. 16, 51–52).

The rise of radio and television news after 1945 has yet to become a focus of historical work on crime and media; however, radio and television crime news reporting has shared some tendencies with that of the print press: an exaggerated focus on violence and sensation rather than structural analysis, and an emphasis on "human interest" features. This is true of both radio (Cumberbatch, Woods, & Maguire 1995) and television (Gunter, Harrison, & Wykes 2003), even if the specific nature of each medium has influenced the presentation of news. In the late 1940s and 1950s, for example, "BBC radio news bulletins shared press news values, often reporting the same crimes, but bulletin length meant that radio news covered crime stories in less detail" (Roodhouse 2013, p. 228). Alongside regular television "news," programs such as *Crimewatch UK*—which, since first broadcast in 1984, has combined dramatic reconstructions of crimes with the use of surveillance footage in an effort to elicit information from the public—have significantly contributed to shaping public impressions (and, arguably, misunderstandings) of crime (Jewkes 2010, pp. 152–68).

Recent research has made clear that crime discourses emerge from concrete interactions among individuals and institutions. In the late nineteenth and early twentieth centuries, for example, journalists developed a "uniquely symbiotic" relationship with the police that was characterized by mutual dependence, "reciprocity," and a "culture of exchange" (Shpayer-Makov 2012, pp. 156, 186, 160). The Metropolitan Police opened its press office in 1919, and while police–press relations were sometimes tense in the following few decades, many detectives maintained constructive relationships with journalists: "crime journalists" even became something of a "specialist elite" (Mawby 2002, pp. 10–15; Mawby 2010, p. 1062). Crime "experts"—psychologists, sociologists, and criminologists—increasingly shaped public crime discourses, whether in comments given directly to the press or filtered through trial testimony (Wiener 1990; Wetzell 2000). Advocacy organizations such as the Howard League for Penal Reform (founded in 1866) or groups such as the National Council for Civil Liberties (NCCL, today called merely "Liberty," founded in the early 1930s) have also used the press to influence perceptions of crime and justice. (The NCCL was actually founded by a freelance journalist, Robert Kidd [Clark 2012].) Accused and convicted "criminals" themselves have contributed to crime news through forms of "life-writing" common in the interwar press (e.g., Wood 2012a, pp. 132–51; Houlbrook 2013a; Houlbrook 2013b).

II. Contexts: "Crime," "Criminals," and "Criminal Justice"

Three specific phases in the process of criminal justice have been especially important in creating crime news: police investigations, criminal trials, and postconviction punishments. There was widespread ambivalence about the early professionalized police forces established in the 1820s, but by the early twentieth century these institutions had secured a favorable press image; in turn, the police also used the press to disseminate information about alleged perpetrators. Criminal trials, however, were the central context of crime reporting, and Daniel Vyleta's comments about *fin de siècle* Vienna are broadly applicable: "The trial was not merely the locus of where the formal truth about the criminal action was established and officially sanctioned, but also the central event where criminal and public met, where the defendants' characters were evaluated, and where the public re-experienced the crime" (2007, p. 99). While mainly focused on dealing with particular criminal charges, trials also mediated wider cultural concerns, such as perceived threats to the social order or tensions around gender roles (Brückweh 2006; Bland 2013). Crime news contributed to a process of "sense-making" in the context of mass urban "modernity" in the late nineteenth and early twentieth centuries (Elder 2010, p. 2). The punishment of the guilty, especially execution, also attracted interest. In Britain, the relocation of hanging to behind prison walls in 1868 meant that its imagery became more mediated just as newspapers were establishing their predominance: the public image of capital punishment was primarily a press construction up to its abolition in 1965 (Gatrell 1994; Tulloch 2006; Seal 2014, pp. 33–77). Some newspapers contributed to the demonization of offenders, while others generated public sympathy for some condemned prisoners and even led campaigns for mercy (Wiener 2007; Seal 2009). Imprisonment, by contrast, has been subject to a highly "ambivalent" visibility (Cheliotis 2010), and it has been argued that—apart from periodic sensationalism— "news reporting of prisons is negligible," inaccurate, and characterized by a "lazy contempt" toward inmates (Jewkes 2007, pp. 449–51). Salacious or putatively "exciting" aspects of prison life, such as violent assaults or prison riots, have been well suited to media attention (Brown 2013; Brown & Barton 2013). Taken together, the press's selective focus on the processes of investigation, trial, and punishment has played a crucial role in defining the topics of "crime," "criminals," and "criminal justice."

Crime news has consistently offered an image of crime different from that apparent in official statistics. True to what has been called the "law of opposites," the statistically least common crimes (e.g., serious violence and homicide) have tended to receive the most attention, and vice versa (Surette 1998, p. 47; Reiner, Livingstone, & Allen 2003, pp. 15–16). Criminologists have argued that the media have turned serious crime into "an ever-present part of our symbolic environment" since the 1970s (Cavender 2004, p. 346). This may be true; however, as noted previously, crime has contributed significantly to "symbolic reality" for centuries, and the "professional imperatives" and "news values" that have led to a significantly skewed image of crime's realities have a long history (Chibnall 1977, p. 23; Jewkes 2010, pp. 35–62; Mawby 2010, pp. 1069–70). Even in the late eighteenth century, the press "would have given an almost entirely false picture of crime, one that focused primarily on offences involving violence to persons or property" (King 2007, pp. 90–91).

But the failure of crime news to present objective, systematic analyses of crime has taken different forms. The late eighteenth and early nineteenth centuries were characterized by "multi-vocal, sporadic, brief and sometimes chaotic styles of reporting" that created "a kaleidoscope of different and often contradictory messages" regarding "the prevalence of violent crime, the effectiveness of policing and penal institutions, and the quality of justice meted out by the courts" (King 2007, p. 76). In the early nineteenth century legal professionals overcame their previous hostility to the press (resulting from its tendency to criticize their profession as corrupt) and moved toward "an increasingly enthusiastic collaboration" with it: by the 1860s, editors were significantly reliant upon lawyers to provide knowledgeable reportage of trials (Rowbotham, Stevenson, & Pegg, 2013 pp. 25, 29, 32, 39, 59). The final decades of the nineteenth century, however, saw the balance move away from legally informed courtroom reporting toward the investigative journalism and human interest sensationalism that has subsequently characterized the partial, partisan, prurient, and popularizing nature of crime news. In reporting on mid-twentieth-century black market criminality, for example, a crime was "newsworthy if it was unusual, fitted into the press cycle, involved well-known people and places, occurred close to home, or marked crime reaching a significant level" (Roodhouse 2013, p. 228). It has been argued that seemingly nonpolitical "human interest" stories involve "a particular way of seeing the world" and a "rejection of any attempt to explain events as having a relation to social, economic, or political forces" (Curran, Douglas, & Whannel 1980, p. 306). However, while such emphases "had the effect of obscuring underlying social structures and inequalities" (Bingham 2004, p. 9), it may be that "techniques of personalisation and sensationalism made politics more accessible to readers often alienated by traditional forms of political discourse" (Bingham 2012, p. 315). But crime news has influenced perceptions of crime by what it ignores as well as what it attends to. Despite their high social costs, for example, "white-collar" crimes, complicated financial wrongdoings, or violations of corporate regulations have been given little attention compared to "street crime," except when they involve notorious individuals or salacious details (Jewkes 2010, pp. 20–21). Mainstream media treatment of white-collar crime—in the absence of aspects that can be grasped on a more "visceral" level, such as "identity theft"—has even been described as "infotainment" focused on something other than crime itself, such as celebrity gossip or anti-establishment populism (Levi 2006).

Defining "crime" also typically involves identifying the "type" of individual or group from whom its threat is perceived to be most acute. Across history, diverse groups have borne the brunt of media opprobrium as being especially criminogenic. Crime news in the late eighteenth century was shaped by discussions about the dangers posed by a "criminal class." Often defined in terms of the "lower classes" more generally, the increasing "respectability" of wider sections of the working classes led to finer distinctions of an "unrespectable," "rough" residuum or "underworld," a tendency that lives on in the attention that some sections of the press lavish on the threat of a criminal "underclass."

Modern criminological studies have focused on the role of "race" and ethnicity in post-1945 crime reporting, with the press-driven fears of the "black mugger" in the 1970s standing as a signal example (Hall et al. 1978). The associations between ethnicity and images of crime have indeed been important, but they have also been variable. In the interwar period, the press connected Chinese or Afro-Caribbean men to the (newly criminalized) "drug underground" (Kohn 2001) and highlighted Jewish or Italian "underworld" figures (Shore 2011). Jewish and Italian stereotypes were also prominent in reporting on black marketeering between the 1930s and 1950s (Roodhouse 2013, p. 233). In eighteenth- and early nineteenth-century London, however, nonwhites (with the partial exception of "Lascar" seamen) were more likely to be seen as vulnerable than violent; the Irish population, conversely, was viewed as prone to violent offending, and Jews were associated with some property crimes (King 2013; King & Wood 2015). In the nineteenth century, press associations between crime and ethnicity also focused on the "nations" making up the United Kingdom, with the Welsh, English, Scottish, and Irish blaming each other for their local crime problems (Conley 2007).

Crime reporting has also been infused with assumptions about gender. Historical research on gender, crime, and media has emphasised the opprobrium heaped upon those women accused or convicted of murder who were seen as deviating from narrow feminine norms (Ballinger 2000; D'Cruze & Jackson 2009). The gendered depiction of women in the press has, however, been complicated, and there have been accused (or even convicted) murderesses who have been sympathetically described in the press (Frost 2004; Ballinger 2005; Seal 2010; Wood 2012a; Bland 2013). The newspaper coverage of Marguerite Fahmy's murder trial in 1923 mixed notions of gender and ethnicity: the "orientalist" nature of the "deviant" sexualities of her victim (her Egyptian husband) helped to mitigate perceptions of her guilt at her trial and in the court of public opinion (Bland 2013, pp. 132–75). Conceptions of foreignness, gender, and sexuality also merged in press depictions of French prostitutes in interwar London (Slater 2007). There has been far less research into media representations of criminal men; however, changing press images of masculinity were relevant to the late Victorian "criminalisation of men"—the decreasing tolerance for customarily accepted forms of male violence and disorder (Wiener 2004)—and sensations such as the Jack the Ripper murders (Curtis 2001). Masculinity was also a prominent issue in early twentieth-century newspaper reporting about then-criminalized homosexual acts (Houlbrook 2007), as well as in forms of crime-related "life writing" (Houlbrook 2013a; Houlbrook 2013b).

Finally, age has been a focus of research on crime news, particularly in the nineteenth and early twentieth centuries. The Victorian child—whether as perpetrator or victim (or both)—often featured in newspaper crime reports (e.g., Shore 1999; Abbott 2005). Dangerous youths have been a prominent feature of newspaper reporting over the years, whether nineteenth-century "scuttlers" (Davies 1998), turn-of-the-century "hooligans" (Pearson 1983), 1960s "mods and rockers," or the more recent "Yardies" and "Hoodies." There have been intriguing elements of transnational cultural appropriation: interwar Glasgow gangs, for example, were compared to (and willingly adopted the media image of) Chicago "gangsters" (Davies 2007).

Along with defining "crime" and "criminals," crime news has also depicted the institutions of the criminal justice system. Historians of the early modern period have emphasized how depictions of executions (and the executed) legitimized state power (Linebaugh 1992; Gatrell 1994). Publications such as the Old Bailey Proceedings gave readers a detailed (if partial) insight into trial procedure. For high-profile trials, many newspapers reported verbatim courtroom testimony, giving detailed descriptions of the appearance, demeanor, and actions of those involved. Coroner's inquests also received sensationalized coverage (Wood 2012a, pp. 29–67). These were not only British phenomena: across late nineteenth- and early twentieth-century Europe, newspapers aimed to "allow the reader to experience the drama of the courtroom at first hand" (Vyleta 2007, p. 77).

Alongside the courts, the police were the criminal justice institution most addressed in crime news. Although the "new police" received skeptical and even hostile coverage from a middle-class press concerned about expense and traditional freedoms, the growing acceptance of the police was reflected in more positive coverage (even if more radical, working-class newspapers continued to critique them). Shpayer-Makov has recently shown that cooperation between detectives and journalists raised the status of both groups, with the image of the detective being transformed from a "menacing fig-ure" (2013, p. 7) to a "national celebrity" (2013, p. 7), a key process in what Clive Emsley (1992) has called the "indulgent tradition" in Britain of seeing the police in the best possible light. The relationship between the police and the press has remained ambivalent, and the press has often criticized the police as ineffective, corrupt, or oppressive. Libertarian principles (whether radical or conservative) have also fed press critiques of policing from the late nineteenth century onward (Petrow 1994). There have been periodic press-driven scandals, some of which have led to parliamentary debate and inquiries (Johansen 2011). Concerns about police powers in the first decade of the twentieth cen-tury and in the late 1920s led to storms of press criticism, political debate, and parlia-mentary inquiry (Emsley 2005; Wood 2010; Wood 2012b; Shore 2013). A similar pattern of scandal, press sensation, and state inquiry recurred in the late 1950s. Such periodic tensions can be seen as exceptions to the rule. However, since the 1970s—despite there being no shortage of "law and order" press comment—there has also been "an undercur-rent of questioning of police practices, perceived most clearly by the police themselves," and since the mid-1980s press coverage has become "increasingly critical" of the police (Reiner 2010, pp. 184–85). Policing in recent decades has been done in an "increasingly mediated world" of scrutiny (Mawby 2010, p. 1060). Press criticism of the police—as in the early twentieth century—still remains episodic and driven by "scandals," but some sections of the press have become more willing to doubt police integrity and to critique their procedures (Reiner, Livingstone, & Allen 2003, pp. 22–24). On the other hand, while admitting the "strained and mutually hostile" media–police relationship since the 1970s, Mawby insists that the "asymmetric" relationship between the police and the media described by Chibnall (1977) in the late 1970s has "become more pronounced in terms of police dominance of the relationship" (Mawby 2010, pp. 1062, 1073).

III. The Press, "Moral Panics," and "Social Fears"

The significance of the media in creating images of "crime," "criminals," and "crimi-nal justice" is especially apparent in what have become known as "moral panics." The term "moral panic" originated in research published by Jock Young and by Stanley Cohen in the early 1970s and refers to periods of sudden dramatic increase in anxieties about a perceived social threat: in such circumstances, "moral entrepreneurs" contrib-ute to perceptions that a certain group (a type of "folk devil") poses a danger, leading to a (likely exaggerated) response by the government, the police, and/or the courts (Young 1971; Cohen 1972). The original concept was developed by other researchers (notably Hall et al. 1978), and Cohen subsequently revised the theory in response to critiques (see the discussion in Marsh & Melville 2009, pp. 49–50). Since then, the concept has been widely applied, and Martin Barker has recently labeled it "one of the great success stories of the British post-1960s socio-cultural tradition of enquiry" (Nicholas & O'Malley 2013, p. xiii). One can no longer speak of a single concept of "moral panic" but rather must acknowledge a cohort of competing (if consanguine-ous) theories (see Critcher 2003; Critcher 2013; Williams 2013). There have also been critiques. Without abandoning the concept of "moral panic," Jewkes has criticized how it is frequently used, suggesting it is often vaguely or ritualistically invoked, sometimes relies on simplistic understandings of "deviancy," underestimates the complexities and contradictions of "morality," incorrectly emphasizes youth marginalization as a causal factor, fails to take into account more diffuse forms of social anxiety, and presupposes audience naïveté with regard to news reports (2010, pp. 75–83). Chas Critcher (2013) proposes the development of a revised definition that would take into account other perspectives, especially work on "moral regulation."

Despite conceptual disputes and the fact that "moral panics" are not limited to criminal contexts, labels such as "moral panic," "folk devils," and "social fears" have strongly influenced historical research on crime news. There have been recent concep-tual evaluations of the utility of "moral panic" by historians (Rowbotham & Stevenson 2005; Nicholas & O'Malley 2013), as well as substantial consideration of its usefulness in analyzing the early modern period and the eighteenth century (Hay 1982; King 1987; Lemmings 2009; Williams 2013). The latter research has seriously undermined sug-gestions (such as those made, e.g., by Thompson 1999, pp. 1, 11, 43–44, 138) that "moral panics" are a uniquely "modern" phenomenon of "advanced" societies. Press-driven "panics" over fears of violent street robbery, for example, have been identified in the eighteenth and nineteenth centuries (Davis 1980; King 1987; King 2003; Sindall 1990), as well as in recurrent police crackdowns on young "hooligans" (Pearson 1983). Even without explicitly referring to "moral panics," historians have identified related phe-nomena. The interwar decades saw a series of press-driven concerns about potentially violent veterans, "dope fiends," "motor bandits," and "racecourse gangs" (Emsley 2008; Kohn 2001; Brown 2011; Shore 2011). King (2003) has found "tremendous similarities" among four street crime–related panics stretching across 250 years, four cities, and two countries, arguing that the notion of "moral panic" is most useful when (in opposition to its conceptual inflation since the 1970s) it is defined narrowly and applied only to particular kinds of events, such as street robberies. The role of the media in moral pan-ics has been confirmed by historical research: Nicholas and O'Malley even argue that "at least since the advent of printing, it is arguably not possible to think of the wide-spread dissemination of social fears, or the development or mobilisation of a panic, *without* the media" (2013, p. 4).

Related to "moral panics" has been a broader assumption in much crime and media research that the exaggerated risk of criminal victimization presented by the mass media has contributed to the expansion of state power (what has been termed a "culture of control" in the post–Second World War period [Garland 2001]) and a more harsh "law and order" approach to offenders generally. Clear connections cannot always be drawn between press coverage, fear of crime, and political response: in a systematic study, Williams and Dickinson argue that "people who read newspapers which contain more salient crime reports show more [fear of crime]" (1993, p. 49), but they emphasize that newspapers vary in terms of their coverage of crime and that groups of readers respond differently to it. Sensationalism itself is not necessarily decisive, and, they conclude, "readership gullibility may have been previously overstated" (1993, p. 50). Still, a research consensus has emerged that crime news has at least contributed to diffuse forms of social anxiety and at times has prepared the ground for the extension of law enforcement and criminal justice systems. Such fears, of course, can also be stoked by the press in the interest of private security providers, such as those selling (and advertising) burglary insurance or home security products (Moss 2011). But while the connection between press coverage and policy change is sometimes clear—the "Garrotting Act" in the 1860s being a classic example (Davis 1980)—other panics come and go without leaving much of a trace. Finally, it might be that periods of press-driven anxiety about elements of state power itself (such as the police) can be considered "moral panics" (Wood 2013); however, this possibility must be weighed in light of King's (2003) argument, noted previously, that "moral panic" is analytically most useful when defined most narrowly.

IV. PATHS FOR FURTHER RESEARCH

As previous sections have shown, historical research on crime news has developed substantially, and historians can now enumerate aspects of both continuity and change in the relationship between media and crime. However, there are areas in which we still know too little or in which the research agenda might be profitably reoriented. For instance, while much historical research on crime and the press has—understandably—focused on sensational cases, serious crime, and "moral panics," it would be useful to know more about "everyday" crime reporting and the press treatment of lesser offenses. As with the study of the press more generally, the local and provincial press has been relatively ignored and needs more systematic attention (Walker 2006). Placing British press discourses of crime into a more international context should also be a priority. Daniel Siemens's comparative study of Berlin, Paris, and Chicago offers a particularly useful model. Siemens finds much similarity in the sorts of anxieties surrounding urban modernity in these metropolises that can be read from the reporting of crime as well as significant distinctions in attitudes toward the justice systems in each city and what he refers to as the "local moral order" (Siemens 2007). Particular attention has been given to the efforts by police forces in the German *Kaiserreich* to respond to (and shape) public perceptions of their work (Müller 2011; Johansen 2011). Some recent studies of Weimar Germany have examined media crime discourses as expressions of anxieties about urban "modernity" and the social crises following the First World War (Herzog 2009; Elder 2010). There is more to be said about how British crime reporting fits into broader European, transatlantic, or Western patterns, and much might be gained through a comparative perspective on media discourses of sexuality, deviance, and criminality, taking into account recent work on imperial and Weimar Germany (Müller 2005; Siebenpfeiffer 2005; Siemens 2009; Elder 2010), late nineteenth-century Italy (Simpson 2010), inter-war France (Maza 2012), and the United States (Ramey 2004; Miller 2011). There is particularly a need for more studies of masculinity and crime reporting (see, e.g., McLaren 1997).

Along with a more comparative perspective, we need to know more about the pro-duction and reception of crime news. Crime historians have had little to say so far about the methods of the journalists reporting on crime or the editorial decisions that were made about presenting it. This is partly a (perhaps insoluble) evidentiary prob-lem: for newspaper reports in the late eighteenth and early nineteenth centuries, "it is often almost impossible to work out who wrote them, under what constraints and with what purposes in mind" (King 2007, p. 91). However, Haia Shpayer-Makov has recently published research on the relationship between reporters and police detectives in the late nineteenth and early twentieth centuries, and crime reporters from the mid-twentieth century onward have received some attention (2012; see also Willetts 2007). This is one area (though not the only one) in which crime historians and media his-torians may learn much from one another. For instance, crime-related autobiographi-cal "life writing" in the early twentieth century—whether by criminals themselves or by police officers—has begun to receive attention (Shpayer-Makov 2012, pp. 272–97; Houlbrook 2013a; Houlbrook 2013b), but it would be very helpful to know more about the role of journalistic practices (such as "ghostwriting") in creating such narratives. Efforts by state agencies to influence (or thwart) media reporting on crime and justice also deserve further attention.

Gaining a better understanding of the reception of crime news will be more dif-ficult: the historical evidence for reader responses to crime news is fragmentary, but it can nonetheless reveal the intensity and diversity of such responses (Wood 2009; Seal 2014). On the basis of published and unpublished reader letters to newspapers, for example, Kerstin Brückweh has highlighted the multifaceted emotional responses to German press stories about serial murder: "Here, the issue is not the direct experience of physical violence," she observes, "but rather fantasies, which became mixed with the explanations offered by the media as well as one's own fears" (2006, p. 25, my trans-lation). The role of emotion is also clear from criminological studies of more recent periods that have shown a significant (though hardly simple) relationship between the consumption of crime news and a subjective sense of "fear" (Williams & Dickinson 1993). King has suggested that "it is not hard to imagine" that press reporting on crime might have similarly stoked a fear of crime in the eighteenth century (King 2007, p. 93), a point recently reinforced by Kevin Williams with regard to "moral panics" (2013). Fear is, however, not the only emotion relevant to crime news: one must also take into account empathy and sympathy. Martin Wiener has pointed to the "twofold role" of newspapers established by the late nineteenth century: "Elite and politically conservative newspapers were ready to perceive social and moral dangers in an outburst of particularly offensive crime, and to urge firm punishment, while local, popularly-aimed and more liberal newspapers stood ready to take up the cause of mercy for those facing the gallows" (2007, p. 124; see also Tulloch 2006, p. 440). Sympathetic reporting could generate strongly empathetic reactions (Wood 2009); however, the patterning of such responses by factors such as gender and experience suggests that rather than a single "public sphere" for crime news, there have been various publics with different relationships to crime and the criminal justice system (Brückweh 2006, p. 29). As Williams and Dickinson (1993) point out, the "salience" of crime news to different readership groups varies strongly.

CONCLUSION

While the historical study of "crime news" is a diverse and evolving field of research, some clear conclusions can be drawn. In significant ways, the news has been "getting it wrong" about crime across recent centuries: the media have consistently evinced a vastly disproportionate interest in the rarest kinds of crime, such as serious and violent crime (especially homicide), and they have shown less interest in dispassionate analysis than in sensationalised storytelling and fearmongering (for contemporary citations and comment, see Jewkes 2010, p. 141). However, crime news has been "wrong" in different ways. An early modern focus on creating a moral tale of the offender's descent into criminality gave way in the later eighteenth century to a more "sporadic" and "sometimes chaotic" reporting style that often took the victim's perspective, expressed doubts about the justice system, and criticised the harshness of the "Bloody Code" (King 2007, p. 76). The direct participation of lawyers in producing crime journalism appears to have increased the accuracy of the court-based aspects of crime news by the mid-nineteenth century (Rowbotham, Stevenson, & Pegg 2013); however, the decades that followed saw a return of sorts to the focus on "explaining" the criminal offender through the "human interest" techniques of "New Journalism," but by then, religiously inspired moral tales had given way to "expert discourses" that emphasized social factors, biological predispositions, and psychological compulsions, a trend that continued through the twentieth century. Crime news was increasingly shaped in professionalized and institutional contexts: compared to earlier periods it became more specialized and less "incoherent," but it also became potentially more easily distorted by the interests and political stances of the organizations that created it. Still, the diversity of media outlets interacting in a competitive market has prevented crime news—like news more generally—from becoming fully monolithic. Finally, twentieth-century crime news—whether in print or on television—was far more dependent upon visual imagery than its text-laden precursors (Jäger 2010); this likely increased emphasis on stories with immediate emotional impact, and—when applied to crime news—the old cliché that "a picture never lies" is, at best, only half true.

Nonetheless, the different ways that crime news has "gotten it wrong" are themselves valuable for historians: from a research perspective, inaccuracy can be seen as a useful feature rather than a discouraging fault. In every historical era, crime news has contained complex, ambiguous, and competing messages, and the ways that some crime-related concerns were exaggerated (while others were downplayed) makes the phenomenon of crime reporting revealing of broader social and cultural tendencies. In the interwar period, for example, the press gave voice to a range of concerns about perceived crime threats; at the same time, however, press discourses demonstrate awareness of the comparatively low levels of serious crime in Britain (by historical and international standards) and—despite periodic scandals—apparently broad faith in the police and court systems. While the death penalty appears to have been generally accepted in principle, there were ambivalent feelings about its use, and some parts of the press expressed a striking amount of sympathy for some of the condemned. After the Second World War, rising statistics of crime, the end of capital punishment, and doubts about the justice system contributed to a greater sense of threat, a reduced compassion for serious offenders, and, ultimately, a redirection of sympathies away from offenders and toward victims (Reiner, Livingstone, & Allen 2003, p. 21).

Finally, despite getting so much "wrong" about crime, crime news—like other forms of press discourse—may nonetheless have gotten more "right" than historians have been willing to give it credit for. As Adrian Bingham has commented:

> Newspapers were more complex, diverse, and unpredictable than many critics have admitted, and they provided challenging, well-written, and informative material as well as undemanding entertainment. They were not invariably reactionary and negative, but could be progressive and generous; they did not merely pander to majority opinion, but sometimes provided a powerful voice for it against vested interests; they undermined stereotypes as well as consolidated them, and provided a platform for a wide range of contributors and causes. (2009, p. 6)

Bingham's observations are emblematic of a broader recent reconsideration of the popular press in both British and European contexts (Newman & Houlbrook 2013). Sensationalized "human interest" stories might appear to be merely apolitical entertainment, but, at times, they contain critiques of social problems cast in a more digestible language for a general readership (see, e.g., Bingham 2013, p. 653; Wood 2014), providing what Siemens has called an "inter-discourse" between expert knowledge and the broader public (2007, p. 26). More broadly, the potential for sensationalistic "tabloid" journalism—at least on some occasions—to provide an "alternative public sphere" has been intriguingly explored (see discussion and citations in Örnebring 2006). There is, clearly, much work to do. Happily, there is no sign that crime news is going to lose its fascination: whether for the press, for the public, or for historians.

REFERENCES

Abbott, Jane. 2005. "The Press and the Public Visibility of Nineteenth-Century Criminal Children." In *Criminal Conversations: Victorian Crimes, Social Panic and Moral Outrage*, ed. Judith Rowbotham & Kim Stevenson, 23–39. Columbus: Ohio State University Press.

Archer, John, & Jo Jones. 2003. "Headlines from History: Violence in the Press, 1850–1914." In *The Meanings of Violence*, ed. Elizabeth Stanko, 17–31. London: Routledge.

Ballinger, Anette. 2000. *Dead Woman Walking: Executed Women in England and Wales, 1900–1955*. Aldershot, UK: Ashgate.

Ballinger, Anette. 2005. "'Reasonable' Women Who Kill: Re-Interpreting and Re-Defining Women's Responses to Domestic Violence in England and Wales, 1900–1965." *Outlines* 7 (2): 65–82.

Bingham, Adrian. 2004. *Gender, Modernity and the Popular Press in Inter-War Britain*. Oxford: Clarendon Press.

Bingham, Adrian. 2009. *Family Newspapers?: Sex, Private Life, and the British Popular Press, 1918–1978*. Oxford: Oxford University Press.

Bingham, Adrian. 2012. "Ignoring the First Draft of History?" *Media History* 18 (3–4): 311–26.

Bingham, Adrian. 2013. "'An Organ of Uplift?' The Popular Press and Political Culture in Interwar Britain." *Journalism Studies* 14 (3): 651–62.

Bland, Lucy. 2013. *Modern Women on Trial: Sexual Transgression in the Age of the Flapper*. Manchester, UK: Manchester University Press.

Brown, Alyson. 2011. "Crime, Criminal Mobility and Serial Offenders in Early Twentieth-Century Britain." *Contemporary British History* 25 (4): 551–68.

Brown, Alyson. 2013. *Inter-War Penal Policy and Crime in England: The Dartmoor Convict Prison Riots, 1932*. Basingstoke, UK: Palgrave Macmillan.

Brown, Alyson, & Alana Barton, eds. 2013. "The Prison and the Public." Special issue of *Prison Service Journal* 210 (November).

Brückweh, Kerstin. 2006. *Mordlust. Serienmorde, Gewalt und Emotionen im 20. Jahrhundert*. Frankfurt am Main, Germany: Campus Verlag.

Cavender, Gray. 2004. "Media and Crime Policy: A Reconsideration of David Garland's The Culture of Control." *Punishment and Society* 6 (3): 335–48.

Chassaigne, Philippe. 1999. "Popular Representations of Crime: The Crime Broadside—A Subculture of Violence in Victorian Britain." *Crime, History and Societies* 3 (2): 23–55.

Cheliotis, Leonidas. 2010. "The Ambivalent Consequences of Visibility: Crime and Prisons in the Mass Media." *Crime, Media, Culture* 6 (2): 169–84.

Chibnall, Steve. 1977. *Law-and-Order News: An Analysis of Crime Reporting in the British Press*. London: Tavistock Publications.

Clark, Janet. 2012. *The National Council for Civil Liberties and the Policing of Interwar Politics: At Liberty to Protest*. Manchester, UK: Manchester University Press.

Cohen, Stanley. 1972. *Folk Devils and Moral Panics: The Creation of the Mods and Rockers*. London: MacGibbon & Kee.

Cohen, Stanley, & Jock Young. 1973. *The Manufacture of News: Deviance, Social Problems and the Mass Media*. London: Constable.

Conley, Carolyn. 2007. *Certain Other Countries: Homicide, Gender and National Identity in Late Nineteenth-Century England, Ireland, Scotland and Wales*. Columbus: Ohio State University Press.

Critcher, Chas. 2003. *Moral Panics and the Media*. Buckingham, UK: Open University Press.

Critcher, Chas. 2013. "Model Answers: Moral Panics and Media History." In *Moral Panics, Social Fears and the Media*, ed. Sian Nicholas & Tom O'Malley, 13–27. Abingdon, UK: Routledge.

Crone, Rosalind. 2012. *Violent Victorians: Popular Entertainment in Nineteenth-Century London*. Manchester, UK: Manchester University Press.

Cumberbatch, Guy, Samantha Woods, & Andrea Maguire. 1995. *Crime in the News: Television, Radio and Newspapers*. Birmingham, UK: Aston University Communications Research Group.

Curran, James, Angus Douglas, & Garry Whannel. 1980. "The Political Economy of the Human-Interest Story." In *Newspapers and Democracy: International Essays on a Changing Medium*, ed. Anthony Smith, 288–347. Cambridge, MA: MIT Press.

Curtis, L. Perry. 2001. *Jack the Ripper and the London Press*. New Haven, CT: Yale University Press.

Davies, Andrew. 1998. "Youth Gangs, Masculinity and Violence in Late Victorian Manchester and Salford." *Journal of Social History* 32 (2): 349–69.

Davies, Andrew. 2007. "The Scottish Chicago: From 'Hooligans' to 'Gangsters' in Interwar Glasgow." *Cultural and Social History* 4 (4): 511–27.

Davis, Jennifer. 1980. "The London Garotting Panic of 1862: A Moral Panic and the Creation of a Criminal Class in Mid-Victorian England." In *Crime and the Law: The Social History of Crime in Western Europe since 1500*, ed. V. A. C. Gatrell & Bruce Lenman, 190–213. London: Europa.

D'Cruze, Shani, & Louise Jackson. 2009. *Women, Crime and Justice in England since 1660*. Basingstoke, UK: Palgrave Macmillan.

Devereaux, Simon. 1996. "The City and the Sessions Paper: 'Public Justice' in London, 1770–1800." *Journal of British Studies* 35 (4): 466–503.

Devereaux, Simon. 2003. "The Fall of the Sessions Paper: The Criminal Trial and the Popular Press in Late Eighteenth-Century London." *Criminal Justice History* 18: 57–88.

Devereaux, Simon. 2007. "From Sessions to Newspaper? Criminal Trial Reporting, the Nature of Crime, and the London Press, 1770–1800." *London Journal* 32 (1): 1–27.

Elder, Sace. 2010. *Murder Scenes: Normality, Deviance, and Criminal Violence in Weimar Berlin*. Ann Arbor: University of Michigan Press.

Emsley, Clive. 1992. "The English Bobby: An Indulgent Tradition." In *Myths of the English,* ed. Roy Porter, 114–35. Cambridge: Polity.

Emsley, Clive. 2005. "Sergeant Goddard: The Story of a Rotten Apple, or a Diseased Orchard?" In *Crime and Culture: An Historical Perspective*, ed. Amy Gilman Srebnick & René Lévy, 85–104. Aldershot, UK: Ashgate.

Emsley, Clive. 2008. "Violent Crime in England in 1919: Post-War Anxieties and Press Narratives." *Continuity and Change* 23 (1): 173–95.

Frost, Ginger. 2004. "'She Is But a Woman': Kitty Byron and the English Edwardian Criminal Justice System." *Gender & History* 16 (3): 538–60.

Garland, David. 2001. *The Culture of Control*. Oxford: Oxford University Press.

Gatrell, V. A. C. 1994. *The Hanging Tree: Execution and the English People, 1770–1868*. Oxford: Oxford University Press.

Gunter, Barrie, Jackie Harrison, & Maggie Wykes. 2003. *Violence on Television: Distribution, Form, Context and Themes*. London: Lawrence Erlbaum.

Hall, Stuart, Chas Critcher, Tony Jefferson, John N. Clarke, & Brian Roberts. 1978. *Policing the Crisis: Mugging, the State and Law and Order*. London: Macmillan.

Hay, Douglas. 1982. "War Dearth and Theft in the Eighteenth Century: The Record of the English Courts." *Past and Present* 95: 117–60.

Hay, Douglas, Peter Linebaugh, John G. Rule, E. P. Thompson, & Cal Winslow, eds. 1975. *Albion's Fatal Tree: Crime and Society in Eighteenth-Century England*. New York: Pantheon.

Herzog, Todd. 2009. *Crime Stories: Criminalistic Fantasy and the Culture of Crisis in Weimar Germany*. New York: Berghahn.

Hobsbawm, Eric. 1969. *Bandits*. London: Weidenfeld and Nicholson.

Houlbrook, Matt. 2007. "'The Man with the Powder Puff' in Interwar London." *Historical Journal* 50 (1): 145–71.

Houlbrook, Matt. 2013a. "Commodifying the Self Within: Ghosts, Libels, and the Crook Life Story in Interwar Britain." *Journal of Modern History* 85 (2): 321–63.

Houlbrook, Matt. 2013b. "Fashioning an Ex-Crook Self: Citizenship and Criminality in the Work of Netley Lucas." *Twentieth Century British History* 24 (1): 1–30.

Jäger, Jens. 2010. "Polizeibild/Verbrecherbild. Zur Visualisierung von Polizei und Verbrechen im 19. und 20. Jahrhundert." In *Repräsentation von Kriminalität und öffentlicher Sicherheit: Bilder, Vorstellungen und Diskurse vom 16. bis zum 20. Jahrhundert*, ed. Gerhard Sälter, Karl Härter, & Eva Wiebel, 455–86. Frankfurt am Main, Germany: Vittorio Klostermann.

Jewkes, Yvonne. 2007. "Prisons and the Media: the Shaping of Public Opinion and Penal Policy in a Mediated Society." In *Handbook on Prisons*, ed. Yvonne Jewkes, 447–66. Cullompton, UK: Willan.

Jewkes, Yvonne. 2010. *Media and Crime*. London: Sage.

Johansen, Anja. 2011. "Keeping Up Appearances: Police Rhetoric, Public Trust and 'Police Scandal' in London and Berlin, 1880–1914." *Crime, History and Societies* 15 (1): 59–83.

King, Peter. 1987. "Newspaper Reporting, Prosecution Practice and Perceptions of Urban Crime: The Colchester Crime Wave of 1765." *Continuity and Change* 2 (3): 423–54.

King, Peter. 2003. "Moral Panics and Violent Street Crime 1750–2000: A Comparative Analysis." In *Comparative Histories of Crime*, ed. Barry Godfrey, Clive Emsley, & Graeme Dunstall, 53–71. Cullompton, UK: Willan.

King, Peter. 2007. "Newspaper Reporting and Attitudes to Crime and Justice in Late Eighteenth and Early Nineteenth Century London." *Continuity and Change* 22 (1): 73–112.

King, Peter. 2009. "Making Crime News: Newspapers, Violent Crime and the Selective Reporting of Old Bailey Trials in the Late Eighteenth Century." *Crime, History and Societies* 13 (1): 91–116.

King, Peter. 2013. "Ethnicity, Prejudice and Justice: The Treatment of the Irish at the Old Bailey, 1750–1825." *Journal of British Studies* 52 (2): 390–414.

King, Peter, & John Carter Wood. 2015. "Black People and the Criminal Justice System: Prejudice and Practice." *Historical Research* 88: 100–124.

Kohn, Marek. 2001. *Dope Girls: The Birth of the British Drug Underground*. London: Granta.

Lawrence, Paul. 2012. "History, Criminology and the 'Use' of the Past." *Theoretical Criminology* 16 (3): 313–28.

Lemmings, David. 2009. "Conclusion: Moral Panics, Law and the Transformation of the Public Sphere in Early Modern England." In *Moral Panics, the Media and Law in Modern England*, ed. David Lemmings & Claire Walker, 245–66. Basingstoke, UK: Palgrave Macmillan.

Levi, Michael. 2006. "The Media Construction of Financial White-Collar Crimes." *British Journal of Criminology* 46 (6): 1037–57.

Linebaugh, Peter. 1977. "The Ordinary of Newgate and his *Account*." In *Crime in England: 1550–1800*, ed. J. S. Cockburn, 246–69. London: Methuen.

Linebaugh, Peter. 1992. *The London Hanged: Crime and Civil Society in the Eighteenth Century*. Cambridge: Cambridge University Press.

Marsh, Ian, & Gaynor Melville. 2009. *Crime Justice and the Media*. Abingdon, UK: Routledge.

Mawby, Rob C. 2002. *Policing Images: Policing, Communication and Legitimacy*. Cullompton, UK: Willan.

Mawby, Rob C. 2010. "Chibnall Revisited: Crime Reporters, the Police and 'Law-and-Order News.'" *British Journal of Criminology* 50 (6): 1060–76.

Maza, Sarah. 2012. *Violette Nozière: A Story of Murder in 1930s Paris*. Berkeley: University of California Press.

McKenzie, Andrea. 1998. "Making Crime Pay: Motives, Marketing Strategies, and the Printed Literature of Crime in England, 1670–1770." In *Criminal Justice in the Old World and the New*, ed. Greg T. Smith, Allyson N. May, & Simon Devereaux, 235–69. Toronto: Centre of Criminology, University of Toronto.

McKenzie, Andrea. 2005. "From True Confessions to True Reporting? The Decline and Fall of the Ordinary's Account." *London Journal* 30 (1): 55–70.

McLaren, Angus. 1997. *The Trials of Masculinity: Policing Sexual Boundaries, 1870–1930*. Chicago: University of Chicago Press.

Miller, April. 2011. "Bloody Blondes and Bobbed Haired Bandits: Constructing Celebrity Criminals in the 1920s Popular Press." In *In the Limelight and Under the Microscope: Forms and Functions of Female Celebrity*, ed. Su Holmes & Diane Negra, 61–81. London: Continuum.

Moss, Eloise. 2011. "Burglary Insurance and the Culture of Fear in Britain, c. 1889–1939." *Historical Journal* 54 (4): 1039–64.

Müller, Philipp. 2005. *Auf der Suche nach dem Täter. Die öffentliche Dramatisierung von Verbrechen im Berlin des Kaiserreichs*. Frankfurt am Main, Germany: Campus Verlag.

Müller, Philipp. 2011. "Covering Crime, Restoring Order. The 'Berlin Jack the Ripper' (1909) and the Press Policy of the Berlin Criminal Investigation Department." *Crime, History and Societies* 15 (1): 85–110.

Nead, Lynda. 2005. "Courtroom Sketching: Reflections on History, Law and the Image." In *Law and Popular Culture: Current Legal Issues*, Vol. 7, ed. Michael Freeman, 173–82. Oxford: Oxford University Press.

Newman, Sarah, & Matt Houlbrook. 2013. "Introduction: The Press and Popular Culture in Interwar Europe." *Journalism Studies* 14 (5): 640–50.

Nicholas, Sian, & Tom O'Malley, eds. 2013. *Moral Panics, Social Fears, and the Media: Historical Perspectives*. London: Routledge.

Örnebring, Henrik. 2006. "The Maiden Tribute and the Naming of Monsters: Two Case Studies of Tabloid Journalism as Alternative Public Sphere." *Journalism Studies* 7 (6): 851–68.

Pearson, Geoffrey. 1983. *Hooligan: A History of Respectable Fears*. London: Macmillan Education.

Petrow, Stefan. 1994. *Policing Morals: The Metropolitan Police and the Home Office, 1870–1914*. Oxford: Clarendon Press.

Ramey, Jessie. 2004. "The Bloody Blonde and the Marble Woman: Gender and Power in the Case of Ruth Snyder." *Journal of Social History* 37 (3): 625–50.

Reiner, Robert. 2010. *The Politics of the Police*. Oxford: Oxford University Press.

Reiner, Robert, Sonia Livingstone, & Jessica Allen. 2003. "From Law and Order to Lynch Mobs: Crime News since the Second World War." In *Criminal Visions: Media Representations of Crime and Justice*, ed. Paul Mason, 13–32. Cullompton, UK: Willan.

Roodhouse, Mark. 2013. *Black Market Britain, 1939–1955*. Oxford: Oxford University Press.

Rowbotham, Judith, & Kim Stevenson, eds. 2005. *Criminal Conversations: Victorian Crimes, Social Panic and Moral Outrage*. Columbus: Ohio State University Press.

Rowbotham, Judith, Kim Stevenson, & Samantha Pegg. 2013. *Crime News in Modern Britain: Press Reporting and Responsibility, 1820–2010*. Basingstoke, UK: Palgrave Macmillan.

Seal, Lizzie. 2009. "Issues of Gender and Class in the Mirror Newspapers' Campaign for the Release of Edith Chubb." *Crime, Media, Culture* 5 (1): 57–78.

Seal, Lizzie. 2010. *Women, Murder and Femininity: Gender Representations of Women Who Kill*. Basingstoke, UK: Palgrave Macmillan.

Seal, Lizzie. 2014. *Capital Punishment in Twentieth-Century Britain*. London: Routledge.

Sharpe, James. 1985. "Last Dying Speeches: Religion, Ideology and Public Execution in Seventeenth-Century England." *Past and Present* 107: 144–67.

Shoemaker, Robert. 2004. *The London Mob: Violence and Disorder in Eighteenth-Century England*. London: Hambledon.

Shore, Heather. 1999. *Artful Dodgers: Youth and Crime in Early Nineteenth-Century London*. London: Royal Historical Society, Boydell Press.

Shore, Heather. 2011. "Criminality and Englishness in the Aftermath: The Racecourse Wars of the 1920s." *Twentieth Century British History* 22 (4): 474–97.

Shore, Heather. 2013. "'Constable Dances with Instructress': The Police and the Queen of Nightclubs in Inter-War London." *Social History* 38 (2): 183–202.

Shpayer-Makov, Haia. 2012. *The Ascent of the Detective: Police Sleuths in Victorian and Edwardian England*. Oxford: Oxford University Press.

Siebenpfeiffer, Hania. 2005. *Böse Lust. Gewaltverbrechen in Diskursen der Weimarer Republik*. Köln, Germany: Böhlau Verlag.

Siemens, Daniel. 2007. *Metropole und Verbrechen. Die Gerichtsreportage in Berlin, Paris und Chicago 1919–1933*. Stuttgart, Germany: Franz Steiner Verlag.

Siemens, Daniel. 2009. "Explaining Crime: Berlin Newspapers and the Construction of the Criminal in Weimar Germany." *Journal of European Studies* 39 (3): 336–52.

Simpson, Thomas. 2010. *Murder and Media in the New Rome: The Fadda Affair*. Basingstoke, UK: Palgrave Macmillan.

Sindall, Rob. 1990. *Street Violence in the Nineteenth Century: Media Panic or Real Danger?* Leicester, UK: Leicester University Press.

Slater, Stefan. 2007. "Pimps, Police and Filles de Joie: Foreign Prostitution in Inter-War London." *London Journal* 32 (1): 53–74.

Snell, Esther. 2007. "Discourses of Criminality in the Eighteenth-Century Press: The Presentation of Crime in The Kentish Post, 1717–1768." *Continuity and Change* 22 (1): 13–47.

Surette, Ray. 1998. *Media, Crime and Criminal Justice: Images and Realities*. Belmont, CA: Wadsworth.

Thompson, Kenneth. 1999. *Moral Panics*. London: Routledge.

Tulloch, John. 2006. "The Privatising of Pain: Lincoln Newspapers, 'Mediated Publicness' and the End of Public Execution." *Journalism Studies* 7 (3): 437–51.

Vyleta, Daniel M. 2007. *Crime, Jews and News: Vienna, 1895–1914*. New York: Berghan.

Walker, Andrew. 2006. "The Development of the Provincial Press in England c. 1780–1914: An Overview." *Journalism Studies* 7 (3): 373–86.

Wetzell, Richard F. 2000. *Inventing the Criminal: A History of German Criminology, 1880–1945*. Chapel Hill: University of North Carolina Press.

Wiener, Joel H. 1988. "How New Was the New Journalism?" In *Papers for the Millions: The New Journalism in Britain, 1850s to 1914*, ed. Joel H. Wiener, 47–72. New York: Greenwood.

Wiener, Martin. 1990. *Reconstructing the Criminal: Culture, Law and Policy in England, 1830–1914*. Cambridge: Cambridge University Press.

Wiener, Martin. 2004. *Men of Blood: Violence, Manliness, and Criminal Justice in Victorian England*. Cambridge: Cambridge University Press.

Wiener, Martin. 2007. "Convicted Murderers and the Victorian Press: Condemnation vs. Sympathy." *Crimes and Misdemeanours* 1 (2): 110–25.

Willetts, Paul. 2007. "Crime: Everything Old Is New Again." *British Journalism Review* 18 (2): 53–58.

Williams, Kevin. 1998. *Get Me a Murder a Day! A History of Mass Communication in Britain*. London: Arnold.

Williams, Kevin. 2013. "Moral Panics, Emotion and Newspaper History." In *Moral Panics, Social Fears and the Media*, ed. Sian Nicholas & Tom O'Malley, 28–45. Abingdon, UK: Routledge.

Williams, Paul, & Julie Dickinson. 1993. "Fear of Crime: Read All about It? The Relationship Between Newspaper Crime Reporting and Fear of Crime." *British Journal of Criminology* 33 (1): 33–56.

Wood, John Carter. 2009. "'Those Who Have Had Trouble Can Sympathise with You': Press Writing, Reader Responses and a Murder Trial in Interwar Britain." *Journal of Social History* 43 (2): 439–62.

Wood, John Carter. 2010. "'The Third Degree': Press Reporting, Crime Fiction and Police Powers in 1920s Britain." *Twentieth Century British History* 21 (4): 464–85.

Wood, John Carter. 2012a. *The Most Remarkable Woman in England: Poison, Celebrity and the Trials of Beatrice Pace*. Manchester: Manchester University Press.

Wood, John Carter. 2012b. "Press, Politics and the 'Police and Public' Debates in Late 1920s Britain." *Crime, History and Societies* 16 (1): 75–98.

Wood, John Carter. 2013. "Watching the Detectives (and the Constables): Fearing the Police in 1920s Britain." In *Moral Panics, Social Fears, and the Media: Historical Perspectives*, ed. Sian Nicholas & Tom O'Malley, 147–61. New York: Routledge.

Wood, John Carter. 2014. "The Constables and the Garage Girl: The Police, the Press, and the Case of Helene Adele." *Media History* 20 (4): 384–99.

Young, Jock. 1971. *The Drugtakers*. London: Paladin.

CHAPTER 16

···

CRIME, CRIMINOLOGY, AND THE CRIME GENRE

···

GRAY CAVENDER AND NANCY JURIK

INTRODUCTION

···

IN this essay, we consider the relationship between the crime genre's depictions of crime and the criminal justice system (CJS) and what criminologists and other scholars actually know about crime and criminal justice. The relationship is an important one because of the popularity of crime genre productions such as television shows, films, and novels.

Over the years, criminologists have been of two minds about the accuracy of the crime genre's depictions of crime and the workings of the CJS. A traditional opinion argues that when it comes to reality, the crime genre gets it wrong. Crime genre depictions are a fallacy according to this perspective. There are several dimensions to this *fallacy perspective*. For example, Ray Surette (2007) discusses what he calls "the law of opposites," according to which the crime genre most often depicts the least frequently occurring crimes, like murder, and rarely depicts more frequently occurring property crimes or order maintenance violations. Similarly, despite the magnitude of victimization, both fiscally and physically, corporate and organizational crime are rarely depicted in the crime genre, which focuses on individual-level street crime (Cullen et al. 2006). Crime genre depictions tend to be loaded toward the front end of the CJS, meaning that there are more depictions of the police, especially homicide detectives, fewer depictions of courts, and fewer still of corrections. Criminologists lament that misperceptions arise from these genre conventions. These depictions lead people to overestimate such matters as their likelihood of being the victim of a violent crime, the number of people who work in law enforcement, and officers' success in solving crimes (Surette 2007).

A second, more recent view observes that the themes evident in crime genre productions often parallel realistic concerns that confront the CJS. The emergence of this *concordance perspective* coincides with the rise of the cultural criminology subfield. Cultural criminology takes popular culture seriously, especially in terms of why audiences are so interested in media depictions of crime. Cultural criminologists focus on topics ranging from the public's fascination with criminals to the popularity of police dramas to public fascination with prisons like Alcatraz and concentration camps (Brown 2009; Jewkes 2011). There are several dimensions to the concordance view of the media. Some scholars suggest that police dramas in film and on television reflect actual changes in policing, including the increasing presence of women and people of color in policing (Mizejewski 2004; Cavender & Jurik 2012), shifting operational goals and management strategies (Reiner 2010; Loader & Mulcahy 2004), and the growing importance of forensics in policing (Jermyn 2010; Cavender & Deutsch 2007). Other criminologists argue that crime films reflect extant criminological theories of criminality (Rafter 2006; Rafter & Brown 2011). Some scholars note that television depictions are no longer limited to portrayals of homicide detectives, but now devote more attention to courts and corrections. Scholars suggest that there is a link between these depictions and dominant socio-political ideologies that also are manifest in criminal justice operations, and that genre depictions shift when extant ideologies shift (Rapping 2003; Lenz 2003).

In this essay, we argue that regardless of whether fictional portraits are accurate, they do provide an important window into issues and controversies within actual CJS practice and the public perceptions of it. There is and has long been a relationship between crime genre presentations and our understanding of crime and CJS operations. This relationship is a rich and nuanced one. Three thematic areas strike us as especially salient realms for comparing CJS crime genre depictions: technology, diversity, and security/insecurity. We will begin with a brief sketch of the crime genre across history and cultures in the following section, and from there we will turn to discussion of these three analytic realms.

I. The Crime Genre

A genre is a category or taxonomy of cultural production. Genres are defined by recurring, almost formulaic, elements. In the crime genre, those elements include a crime, a detective who investigates the crime, and a resolution in which the crime is solved and the criminal is brought to justice (Cawleti 1976). Ironically, although the crime genre is a historically popular genre, it is the violation of its traditional elements that attracts interest and effects changes in the genre over time. There also are numerous forms of the crime genre, including the amateur sleuth, the private investigator, the police procedural, and, more recently, the forensic police drama. Although crime news coverage is not a part of the crime genre, there are also important links between the news and fictional treatments of crime. Some crime genre stories are based on dramatized accounts of actual crime (Wilson 2000). Television "reality" crime series have so closely borrowed from fictional formats that they constitute a significant blurring of fact and fiction (Cavender & Deutsch 2007), what Leishman and Mason (2003) call "faction." This symmetry between crime fact and fiction has long characterized crime genre productions. We define the crime genre broadly to include novels; television, film, and theater productions; and even video games. We regard video games and theater as sufficiently unique that we have left them to future research. Across these various media, the crime genre has changed over time to reflect actual changes in the CJS.

One of the earliest examples of the crime genre in the English language is *The Newgate Calendar*, first published in London in 1773. It featured purportedly true stories of people who had turned to crime but later recognized the error of their ways. *The Newgate Calendar* pioneered a presentational style that still characterizes many crime genre productions today, that is, a sense of realism. Despite this and even earlier non-English-language crime stories, Edgar Allan Poe is credited as the creator of the modern detective story (Knight 1980). His short stories are classic examples of the crime genre. His protagonist, C. Auguste Dupin, uses ratiocination as his method of investigation. One of Poe's stories, "The Mystery of Marie Roget" (1842), is a fictionalized account of an actual unsolved murder and exemplifies the genre's tendency to draw upon actual events. Notwithstanding Poe's contribution, it was Sherlock Holmes who came to personify the crime genre. One of the most enduring characters in literature, Holmes appeared in fifty-six short stories and four novels penned by Sir Arthur Conan Doyle between 1887 and 1917. Along with his partner, Dr. John Watson, Holmes has been featured in plays, films, novels by other authors, and, most recently, popular television programs, such as *Sherlock* in Britain (2010–present), which was quickly followed by a U.S. version, *Elementary* (2012–present). These programs are set in modern-day London and New York City, respectively, and appeal to a younger audience worldwide.

Although the crime genre has often been criticized as a male preserve, women historically have had a significant presence in it (Klein 1995). In the 1930s and 1940s, Agatha Christie and Dorothy Sayers emerged as leading mystery writers. Agatha Christie (1890–1976) remains one of the best-selling novelists of all time. Her protagonists were the small English village wise woman Miss Jane Marple and Hercule Poirot, an eccentric Belgian detective. Her books have inspired numerous films and television series up to the present. Dorothy Sayer's (1893–1957) books featuring aristocratic amateur sleuth Lord Peter Wimsey were also very popular in her time, and both Christie and Sayers were part of what was initially a British literary tradition referred to as the "cozy."

Another subgenre also emerged in the 1930s and 1940s—the hard-boiled crime novel. This was a different literary style that was most often associated with large U.S. cities and with professional detectives or police who were tough and often-flawed heroes. This genre featured more violence and sex than the cozy novels. Women tended to be victims and/or romantic interests, or played the role of *femme fatales* luring men to do wrong (Mizejewski 2004). Hard-boiled writing was popularized by the works of Dashiell Hammett (1894–1961) and Raymond Chandler (1888–1959), whose stories initially appeared in pulp magazines and are now referred to as "pulp fiction." These stories reflected the population shift to urban areas and the dangers associated with such a setting.

More recently, crime genre productions have featured the police (Mizejewski 2004). Indeed, police detectives across media today outnumber private detectives. The police procedural is now standard fare in novels and films, but especially on television. Offering seemingly backstage glimpses of police life, early examples from the 1950s include the *87th Precinct* novels by Ed McBain and the U.S. television series *Dragnet*, which originated in radio. One of the best examples of the police procedural is *Prime Suspect* (1991–2006), produced for the United Kingdom's Granada Television; the series also aired on PBS in the United States. Starring Dame Helen Mirren as Detective Chief Inspector (DCI) Jane Tennison, the show reinforced the sense of realism (i.e., verisimilitude) associated with the genre, and writers for the series typically researched events and CJS practices to enhance that sense.

Today, a variety of protagonists can be found around the world, and these cultural productions contain many standard crime genre elements while at the same time offering diverse innovations that keep the genre changing and popular. Although comparisons to real-world CJS data make it obvious that crime genre productions are fictional, we argue that they nevertheless reflect and even influence important dimensions of actual pressures and practices in the CJS.

Perhaps more than ever, crime genre productions are among the most popular forms of entertainment media. As noted, British mystery writer Agatha Christie is reportedly the best-selling novelist of all time (Bergin 2013). Approximately one-quarter of all fictional works sold in Britain and the United States are crime stories, and in Britain over the last fifty years, about 25 percent of the most popular television programs and about 20 percent of all films have been crime stories (Allen, Livingstone, & Reiner 1998). Scandinavian author Stieg Larsson's *Millennium Trilogy* has sold 65 million copies and been adapted into three Swedish films and one U.S. film adaptation. In terms of television, the U.S. series *Law and Order* (1990–2010) was the longest-running television drama in U.S. history, while in Britain, the police procedural *The Bill* (1984–2010) had that distinction. Both programs were exported to other countries, where they enjoyed large audiences.

With increased global media exchange, the international ascendancy of the crime genre is even more apparent. Different regions not only exchange but create their own unique contributions. Geographer George Demko (n.d.) provides an overview of the popularity of the crime genre and of productions in nations that include Italy, Spain, Sweden, Russia, the Czech Republic, Japan, China, Argentina, Mexico, and Israel. Scandinavian crime genre productions, now popularly referred to as "Scandi-crime," have garnered critical acclaim and are enjoyed around the world. For example, Henning Mankell's Wallander novels—on which both Swedish and British television series have been based—and the Danish television series *The Killing* (2007–2012) have been instrumental in the dissemination of Scandi-crime. Many Scandi-crime productions (e.g., *The Killing* and *Annika Bergstrom Crime Reporter* [2012]) feature strong female protagonists and are referred to as "Femi-Krimi" (John Crace, "Move Over, Ian Rankin," *Guardian*, 22 January 2009; Bergman 2009). Furthermore, crime genre popularity has even spread beyond its own productions. Robert Reiner (2010, p. 186) notes that crime and police officers appear "in almost all fiction, from *Punch and Judy* to Dostoevsky to *Singin' in the Rain* (with Gene Kelly dancing around a bewildered cop)."

Across the various media and the various forms that comprise crime genre productions, there remains a sense that these stories, although fictional, appeal to a sense of the real, whether through narrative style or by claims that the stories reflect real events.

II. Technology

In the preceding section, we discussed the crime genre's long-standing popularity. Given this historical arc, it is not surprising that the genre has changed over the years. Of course, there have been other significant changes in society as well, including population shifts from rural to urban areas, changes in labor markets (a point that will be discussed in more depth later), socio-political shifts, and, of relevance here, innovations in science and technology. For example, when Sir Arthur Conan Doyle was initially writing his Sherlock Holmes stories, many houses in London were still illuminated by gaslight, a fact that figures into one of Holmes's deductions in "The Blue Carbuncle." Technological changes in publishing were also apparent in Doyle's day. Some scholars suggest that a new publishing technology that permitted the inclusion of Sidney Paget's illustrations of Holmes in *The Strand* magazine increased the detective's popularity. Scroll forward 150 years and we encounter the world of nanotechnology, the genome mapping project, and DNA databases. Some of these shifts are depicted in *CSI* and other television forensic police dramas. The emphasis on the importance to the CJS of keeping up with relevant changes in science and technology is a feature of the crime genre's commitment to realism and verisimilitude. Since the police adopt scientific and technological innovations into their work, so will the fictional detective.

The importance of science and technology is apparent in the Sherlock Holmes stories. These stories appeared in an era that stressed scientific rationalism, the collection and organization of data, and facts that were derived from these data and were empirically verifiable. These ideas were applied to criminological thinking. In the 1830s, Lambert-Adolphe-Jacques Quetelet, a mathematician, advocated the systematic collection and use of crime statistics to analyze the distribution of crime in society. Andre-Michel Guerry, a French lawyer and Quetelet's contemporary, also pressed for a comparison of international crime statistics. Both of these scholars were instrumental in developing the scientific study of social problems such as crime (Radzinowitz 1966).

As written by Sir Arthur Conan Doyle, Sherlock Holmes was a good fit for this era. Holmes describes himself as engaging in fact-based deductive logic; he eschews speculating on solutions before he has gathered all of the facts. Priding himself on his "encyclopedic knowledge of crime," he maintains a compendium of criminal cases (his own and other interesting cases). Holmes frequently references this compendium so that his solutions are informed by past cases. Thus, like Quetelet and Guerry, Holmes sees patterns that inform his criminal investigations.

Doyle depicts Holmes as a man of science, an expert on poisons, tropical diseases, and different types of tobacco ash. Holmes conducts chemical experiments—for example, to determine if a suspicious substance is blood (see Harrington 2007). The fictional Holmes is a contemporary of a real scholar, the criminal anthropologist Cesare Lombroso, who posited in *The Criminal Man* (1876) that criminality was attributable to innate traits and characteristics. Lombroso's account bordered on a biological explanation of crime, and indeed he argued that physiological features were indicators of criminality. Doyle, a physician, incorporated some of these ideas into the Holmes stories, referencing, for example, the significance of cranial capacity in determining intelligence (see Harrington 2007). Of course, Lombroso's scientific ideas were undermined later by a new statistical technique—Pearson's R—with which scholars demonstrated that many of his conclusions about criminals were incorrect.

The fictional Holmes lives during the era that saw the development of fingerprints. There were several attempts to develop a system of identification for police work, such as Alphonse Bertillon's 1879 anthropometric method, before Sir William Hershel published his work on fingerprints in 1880. Hershel had seen fingerprints used in Bengal and contemplated their use in England. Eight years later (1888), Sir Francis Galton suggested a formal system of fingerprinting as a method of classification (Harper 2009; also see Knepper & Norris 2009). While Holmes does not utilize fingerprints himself, the importance of this innovation figures prominently in the story "The Adventure of the Norwood Builder" (Doyle 2005 [1903], pp. 849, 851). Here, a thumbprint offers damning evidence against Holmes's client. The police are familiar with fingerprinting as an identification system and conclude that the print incriminates Holmes' client:

INSPECTOR LESTRADE: Look at that with your magnifying glass, Mr. Holmes.
HOLMES: I am doing so.
INSPECTOR LESTRADE: You are aware that no two thumb-marks are alike?
HOLMES: I have heard something of the kind.
LATER, HOLMES TO WATSON: The fact is that there is one really serious flaw in this evidence to which our friend attaches so much importance.
WATSON: Indeed, Holmes! What is it?
HOLMES: Only this—that I *know* that mark was not there when I examined the hall yesterday. (Doyle 2005 [1903], pp. 849, 851)

Sherlock Holmes is one of the most enduring characters in Western literature. As noted, there are currently two television series on air featuring the famous detective. These programs are popular among a younger audience and in countries beyond England and the United States, where they originated, such as the Czech Republic and China. In these new versions, Holmes relies on today's technology, including social media. He texts, and, in one *Elementary* episode, the format of his texts is a clue. According to comments from younger viewers, these features—updated story lines and the use of social media—explain the contemporary popularity of these series (Cavender & Jurik 2014; Frank Langfitt, "*Sherlock, House of Cards* Top China's Must-Watch List," *NPR Morning Edition*, 10 March 2014).

If Holmes used deductive logic and scientific experiments in the 1800s, fictional detectives (usually police) in the twentieth and twenty-first centuries have depended even more heavily on science and technology. This is especially the case in television police drama, in which the use of technology parallels that in real police work. While the 1970s saw *Quincy* (1976–1983), a U.S. series about a medical examiner, it was in the 1990s that police dramas featuring forensic investigations became popular. An exemplar of this trend is *Prime Suspect*, the police procedural featuring DCI Jane Tennison that we mentioned earlier. In some ways, Tennison is like Holmes a century later: her careful review of documents often discloses significant information that helps to solve a case. Moreover, Tennison utilizes the latest technologies. She may assign a detective to review relevant closed-circuit television tapes, which, of course, real police detectives do as well. Often we see the detectives awaiting lab results, and Tennison frequently visits crime scenes to examine a corpse. These latter scenes mimic real crime scene investigations, complete with busy specialized personnel gathering forensic data. Tennison's appearance at the scene is a part of the series' "backstage realism."

While few police series could replicate the accolades won by *Prime Suspect*, the program did clear the way for other popular forensic novels and television police dramas. Deborah Jermyn (2010) argues that *Prime Suspect* initiated the forensic realism trend in the crime genre. Successful continuing forensic novels include Patricia Cornwell's Kate Scarpetta, medical examiner, series and Kathy Reichs's Temperance Brennan, forensic anthropologist, series, which has been adapted for television. Today, *CSI* is the most successful television forensic police series in the United States. The program, which began in 2000 and is still on the air, has enjoyed consistently high ratings and has generated two spinoffs and numerous clones. *CSI* foregrounds forensic investigations: its investigators gather important crime scene data using measurements, technology, and scientific acumen. They conduct autopsies, carry out lab tests, and consult national crime databases. Science, the program suggests, is the guarantor of justice. Often, members of the *CSI* team note that witnesses may lie, but science does not. Science is infallible, and the police have harnessed it. In the scientific universe of *CSI*'s narratives, the law is merely ancillary and, in some episodes, is perhaps even a hindrance to solving crimes and producing justice.

We offer a caveat about science and technology in the crime genre, however: at the end of the day, it is fiction. For example, as scholars have noted, Holmes, notwithstanding his claims, does not engage in deductive so much as inductive thinking (Knight 1980). Moreover, despite his pretensions to science, events that occur in the stories are not scientifically accurate—for example, the snake in "The Adventure of the Spectacled Band" drinks milk. As Stephen Knight (1980) notes, Doyle was not as concerned with scientific accuracy as with invoking the aura of science. Similar comments can be made about *CSI*. Unlike the real world of policing, lab results in *CSI* arrive quickly and are conclusive; most cases are solved and culminate in an arrest (Deutsch & Cavender 2008). Moreover, despite constant claims that science does not lie, even scientific evidence must be interpreted by human beings. There have been reports of police laboratory personnel lying about the results of their analyses to secure convictions (Jean Ortiz, "Neb. CSI

Chief Guilty of Tampering in Murder Case," *Arizona Republic*, 24 March 2010). As one consultant to *CSI* reminds us, the show is television (cited in Deutsch & Cavender 2008). The "aura of science" is created in Holmes's cases by good writing and in *CSI* by creative camera work, or what its producers call "visual storytelling" (Deutsch & Cavender 2008). The point is that good fiction is compelling, but it may be incorrect.

Whether or not crime genre police use technology realistically, writers like Sir Arthur Conan Doyle and those who have written the teleplays in more recent programs like *Prime Suspect* or *CSI* try to emulate the techniques employed by real police. They foreground scientific technologies in a manner that makes the fiction seem to be more realistic and symbolizes the import of science as a basis for knowledge in our world today.

III. Diversity

In addition to the importance of technology, another social issue links crime genre productions with the real world: both media and the CJS face issues surrounding the diversity of their staff and the communities they serve. Scholars have noted the increasing role that social diversity and the tensions associated with it have played in crime genre productions (Cavender & Jurik 2012). These portraits range in degree of accuracy and their embrace or avoidance of traditional cultural stereotypes. Nevertheless, the crime genre's attempts to grapple with diversity reveal important cultural themes.

The police, courts, and corrections have historically been dominated by an ethos that normalizes white, heterosexual masculinity and responds negatively to deviations from these norms (Martin & Jurik 2007). Because the police are such a frequent focus of crime genre productions, the links between fictional portraits and actual police work have been frequent topics of comparison. Instances of sexism, racism, and homophobia have been documented within police organizations and in interactions between police and citizenry (Miller, Forest, & Jurik 2003; Martin & Jurik 2007; Brown & Heidensohn 2000; Wilson 1997). White women and women and men of color have faced opposition and harassment (Martin & Jurik 2007). Gay, lesbian, bisexual, and transgender (GLBT) officers have not been welcomed into police ranks, and relations between GLBT communities and police have included patterns of neglect and harassment (Miller, Forest, & Jurik 2003).

Like criminal justice agencies, entertainment industries have faced pressures to diversify their workforce and to confront the tensions and social changes produced by diversity in the larger society. Popular media have been critiqued for their white masculine bias: they have overwhelmingly featured white, male, heterosexual protagonists. White women, men and women of color, and GLBT individuals have been portrayed in ways that devalue or negatively stereotype them as "other." Individuals from these populations have most often appeared in crime genre productions as criminals or victims, and rarely as recurring, heroic characters (Gray 2004; Bernardi 2001; Gross 2001; Cavender & Jurik 2012).

Since the 1960s, there have been efforts to diversify criminal justice organizations and to improve relationships with the varied communities that they serve (Martin & Jurik 2007). Ian Loader and Aogan Mulcahy (2003) use the term "democratic cosmopolitanism" to characterize this aspirational trend in police departments. Scholars argue that crime genre productions have reflected these shifts—for example, by incorporating more diverse ensemble casts and stories about societal tensions. Allen, Livingstone, and Reiner (1998) have analyzed the changing images of police, crime, and criminal justice in newspapers, film, and television programs between 1945 and 1991. They identify three distinct periods of coverage: (1) a post–Second World War era (1945–1963), during which police were portrayed as protectors in a harmonious society; (2) a post–Vietnam War era (1964–1979), during which police were portrayed as tarnished or corrupt; and (3) a bifurcated era (1980–1991), during which productions were divided between attempts to revive harmonious portraits and more tarnished images of police and their conflict with diverse communities. Despite the predominately positive nature of police portrayals over time (Reiner 2010), what is interesting is how the imagery characteristic of each period reflects the prevailing political moods or tensions of the era. Consistent with this research, we suggest that recent portrayals reflect an awareness of diverse and conflicted police organizations and communities.

As early as the 1940s, there were crime novels that featured white female protagonists (e.g., Agatha Christie's Miss Marple) and African American men confronting a racialized society (e.g., Chester Himes's Harlem detectives Grave Digger Jones and Coffin Ed Johnson). Since the 1970s, there have been successful novels challenging the view of the crime genre as a white male preserve (e.g., Sarah Paretsky's V. I. Warshaski and Sue Grafton's Kinsey Malone). During this same period, crime genre works that confront issues of cultural diversity and racism have also increased (e.g., Walter Mosley's series featuring African American protagonist Easy Rawlins and Tony Hillerman's series featuring Navajo police officers Jim Chee and Joe Leaphorn). Other novels have increasingly illustrated intersecting issues of race and gender (e.g., Barbara Neely's Blanche White stories and criminologist Franke Bailey's Professor Lizzie Stuart stories). Issues of sexual orientation have come to be featured in crime novels as well (e.g., Katherine Forrest's Kate Delafield series and Val McDermid's Dr. Lindsay Gordon stories). Some crime novels featuring men of color and white women as chief protagonists have been adapted for television or film in ways that challenge the dominance of white male protagonists, including *Cotton Comes to Harlem* (1970), based on Himes's novel of the same name; *Devil in a Blue Dress* (1995), based on Mosley's novel of the same name; and the *American Mystery* series (2002–2004), based on Hillerman's novels. However, some adaptations have reproduced traditional gender and racial stereotypes, such as *V. I. Warshawski* (1991), based on Sarah Paretsky's protagonist.

Films and television programs have made slower progress in the diversity realm than have novels. Yet they have still made strides beginning as early as the 1960s. Some productions have featured actors of color and dealt with racism. For example, the U.S. television series *The Mod Squad* (1968–1973) featured a three-person police team composed of a white man, a white woman, and a black man. In the 1970s, racial and gender diversity became more visible on television. Two U.S. series starred women as police officers: *Police Woman* (1974–1978), starring a white actress, and *Get Christie Love* (1974–1975), starring a black actress. Both programs challenged some gender and racial stereotypes while reinforcing others (Cavender & Jurik 2012).

Over the years, the inclusion of people of color in leading crime genre roles and in nonstereotypical ways has been rare. In the 1930s and 1940s, the *Charlie Chan* film series featured a Chinese detective. However, a white actor played him in stereotypical ways. In 1967, Sydney Poitier, an Academy Award–winning African American actor, starred as a police officer in the critically acclaimed film *In the Heat of the Night*. This film dealt with the racism that confronted the protagonist in his investigation. However, men of color in leading police roles were extremely rare at this time. Since the 1970s, both television and film have more frequently included characters who are people of color. The *Beverly Hills Cop* films (beginning in 1984) featured African American actor/comedian Eddie Murphy as a Detroit police officer who follows a case to Beverly Hills. The comedic and unrealistic treatment in this film nevertheless parodies some class and racial stereotypes in police organizations. Most often, men and women of color appear in ensemble casts rather than in lead roles. A popular format in police films has been the white man–black man police buddy team that blends action-adventure and comedy with the crime genre. The U.S. *Lethal Weapon* film series (beginning in 1987) is a popular example.

The 1980s saw several popular television series featuring female police protagonists. These included *Juliet Bravo* (1980–1985) and *The Gentle Touch* (1980–1984) in the United Kingdom, and *Cagney and Lacey* (1981–1988) in the United States, all of which starred white women. These programs addressed issues of discrimination, sexual harassment, and pregnancy as they affected female officers. Yet concerns about sexual orientation permeated the entertainment industry as well as actual police organizations during this time; for example, the producers of *Cagney and Lacy* rejected for a long-term role an actress who starred in the series pilot because she had played a lesbian character in a previous film (D'Acci 1994).

In the 1990s, the British program *Prime Suspect* was significant not only for its emphasis on forensic realism, but also for its portrayal of the barriers faced by women in the 1990s and 2000s as they sought to enter the upper echelons of the police ranks. *Prime Suspect* episodes portrayed DCI Tennison's efforts to be assigned to a murder investigation and to advance in the gendered organization of male policing. Episodes conveyed the 24-7 demands on police officers and the difficulties of work–life balance, particularly for women (Cavender & Jurik 2012). Later *Prime Suspect* episodes reflect some of the organizational changes identified by Marissa Silvestri (2003) and by Cavender and Jurik (2012) that actually increased demands for the availability of police or supervisors and eroded the flexibility needed by women with family responsibilities (see Silvestri, Tong, & Brown 2013). More recent television police programs in the United Kingdom and the United States (e.g., *Murder Investigation Team* [2003, 2005], *Blue Murder* [2003–2009], and *The Closer* [2005–2012]) have featured women in lead roles and dealt with issues of work–life balance and sexism. However, women in recent programs have most often been portrayed as accepted by the police organization, unlike the Tennison character in the *Prime Suspect* series (Cavender & Jurik 2012).

In contrast to the improved treatment of race and gender in more recent television crime programs, there have been series that deal with race and gender diversity but still perpetuate stereotypes. Although *Law and Order*, which dealt with law enforcement and the processing of criminal cases in court, gradually included more white women and men and women of color in central roles, it has been criticized for overrepresenting whites and for portraying men of color primarily as criminals (Eschholz, Mallard, & Flynn 2004). In this series police frequently violated the civil rights of suspects through violence and derogatory language, and courtroom segments often portrayed due process as interfering with criminal convictions. Eschholz, Mallard, and Flynn (2004) argue that these elements convey a need for "get tough" crime control strategies and reinforce perceptions that people of color pose a threat. *Law and Order Special Victims Unit* (1999–present), a spinoff dealing with crimes against women and children, has been criticized for underrepresenting victims of color and portraying male offenders as the victims of evil or inadequate mothers (Britto et al. 2007; Cuklanz & Moorti 2006).

Television has begun to feature some men and women of color in lead roles in ways that challenge negative stereotypes. The British series *Luther* (2010–2012) featured an actor of Afro-Caribbean descent in the leading role. The thriller *Scandal* (2012–present) features an African American woman in the starring role as the chief executive officer of a company that controls scandals often involving crimes. Chinese American actress Lucy Liu costars as Dr. Watson in the U.S. Sherlock Holmes series *Elementary*. While the representation of actors and actresses of different races in crime genre series has increased, many programs and many episodes within them still adopt an assimilationist stance instead of confronting issues of racism within criminal justice organizations and between these organizations and the community. White women and men and women of color are simply accepted as part of the team, and race and gender are rarely noted in the course of their work. There are exceptions, however. The three *American Mystery* television productions of Tony Hillerman's Jim Chee and Joe Leaphorn novels featured American Indian men and women in starring roles and conveyed the complexity of American Indian life on the Navajo reservation in Arizona. Several *Prime Suspect* episodes dealt with issues of racism within the police organization and between police and the Afro-Caribbean community, as well as negative police attitudes toward immigrants. *Prime Suspect 2* dealt with issues of race and gender, and featured an Afro-Caribbean sergeant who was struggling to advance in a white-dominated organization (Cavender & Jurik 2012). Episodes of *The Closer* portrayed tensions within local Latino communities regarding gang-related policing, and between police and those communities. The U.S. television program *The Wire* (2002–2008) dealt with racism and the ways in which race and class structured opportunities in Baltimore, although it offered little hope for any resolution (Cavender & Jurik 2012). A number of films have also engaged issues of race and racism as they relate to policing. The critically acclaimed film *Fruitvale Station* (2013) confronts issues of racism and racial profiling that led to real violence and death on a San Francisco Bay Area Rapid Transit train.

More systematic analyses of the treatment of race and racism in television and film crime genre productions are clearly needed.

Although crime novels began to deal with issues of sexual orientation in less stereotyped and more complex ways in the 1970s, homophobia has persisted in many hard-boiled crime series. However, several crime novel series have featured protagonists who are gay, lesbian, or transgender. Over the past decade, television and film crime genre productions have begun to include more gay, lesbian, and transgender characters in series and/or episodes, and to treat those characters in less stereotypical ways. Several television police programs (e.g., *Prime Suspect*) have featured gay or lesbian characters who have come out during an investigation. An episode of *The Closer* featured a guest star who played a transsexual and dealt with the reaction of this character's former police partner to her new gender identity. *Law and Order: Special Victims Unit* features a recurring character who is a police psychiatrist and an out gay Asian American man. One of the lead characters in the U.S. series *Orange Is the New Black* (2013–present), a prison drama, is a transgender woman played by a transgender actor. The new BBC science fiction series *Orphan Black* (2013–present) features lesbian characters. GLBT actors in lead roles are still rare, but television series and films are beginning to introduce them and to address the homophobia that remains in police departments and the CJS generally today. The praise associated with the inclusion of these characters, however, indicates the continuing rarity of such inclusion in television (see Wilson, Longmire, & Swymeler 2009).

Thus, both the CJS and the entertainment industry struggle with representing the nature and range of diversity in the larger society. As viewers and citizens have become more aware of and sensitive to the increasing diversity in the world around us, crime genre productions have come to represent and sometimes center on a wider variety of people and the problems that they face. There are examples of novels, films, and television series that have begun to address the multifaceted and nuanced nature of human identities and people's cohabitation in the world with one another. Yet events in the year 2001 brought significant changes to the nature of crime policy, merging it with national security issues in ways that treat some cultural groups as perpetual outsiders. We will see how concerns with global security and insecurity have manifested themselves in crime genre productions in the next section.

IV. Security/Insecurity

The police were created as a social institution charged with protecting the citizenry from the threat of crime in a changing world (Loader & Mulcahy 2003). This mandate to operate in the interest of maintaining social order is evidenced in contemporary slogans such as "to protect and serve." Seen from this perspective, the police are supposed to provide security in an insecure world. In the aftermath of the 9/11 attacks on the United States, the threat of terrorism and other fears such as kidnapping and human trafficking have increased our sense of risk and the desire for state action to reduce that risk. Criminologists are increasingly analyzing the importance of perceived risk to crime policies on policing (Erickson & Haggerty 1997) and punishment (Garland 2001). Other criminologists have addressed how a sense of risk has promoted the implementation of "pre-crime strategies," that is, preemptive policies that focus more on anticipating than on reacting to crime (McCulloch & Pickering 2012). Not surprisingly, the insecurity that has permeated our post-9/11 world is manifest in the crime genre as well. Television programs like 24 (2001–2010) and *Missing* (2012) reflect fears of threats such as terrorism or kidnapping, as well as a scripted urgency to take any means necessary to confront these risks. Similar emotions emerge in films like *Vantage Point* (2008) and *Taken* (2008). These productions suggest that the risk is paramount, the clock is ticking, and, for the protagonist, the ends justify the means.

Of course, a sense of risk is not a new phenomenon in criminology or in the CJS. Just as a sense of risk is present in many genre productions today, risk was also present in the crime genre in earlier eras. For example, a backdrop of risk and anxiety is prominent in Sir Arthur Conan Doyle's Sherlock Holmes stories (Knight 2004; Harper 2009). Doyle wrote the stories during a period characterized by rapid urbanization and, later, by the threat of the First World War. Londoners in this era were anxious about internal and external threats. Internally, citizens feared the effects of rapid urban growth on a sense of "menace from the streets." They had lost the ability to quickly classify others as to whether they constituted a threat (Riley 2007; Harper 2009). Indeed, the technological classification systems noted earlier, such as Bertillon's system and fingerprinting, were attempts to classify individuals for the purposes of control amid population shifts. Londoners were anxious about crime, which they attributed to the so-called criminal or dangerous classes (Knight 1980). They evaluated the police, who were thought to be deficient in intelligence and honesty, as ineffectual in controlling this threat, and they worried about the increasing centralization of government controls even as they demanded such actions (Harper 2009). Holmes's era corresponds with criminological thinking that also attributed crime to the criminal or dangerous classes. Proponents of this view argued that the criminal classes were morally dislocated, that is, urbanization and rapid growth had resulted in what we would today call defective socialization (see Radzinowicz 1966).

Into such an anxious world entered Sherlock Holmes. Although organized crime existed in London, with the exception of those involving his archrival Professor Moriarty, Holmes's cases usually involve individual-level criminality, something Londoners could understand. Holmes salved their anxieties (Harrington 2007). The stories celebrate rationality and method. His own classification systems that allowed him to identify criminals (or simply make amazing deductions about people) were an antidote to the breakdown of common systems of observation and identification (Riley 2009). He is knowledgeable of London's streets and its underworld, but, as a private citizen, he is not aligned with the less-than-trustworthy police; in the early stories, he views them with contempt. Perhaps most importantly, the stories depict Watson as the embodiment of traditional social values and Holmes as the protector of those values at a time when traditional values were in flux (Harrington 2007). Holmes and Watson personify loyalty and patriotism. In several stories, Holmes is commissioned by the British government to recover stolen documents; in another, he acts as a British spy.

Doyle evoked external threats in the stories as well. Sometimes the external threat is merely an outsider to a community, while at other times, the outsiders are gypsies or people from America or Australia. Doyle portrayed these outsiders using stereotypes that were common at the time. For example, in several stories, gypsies are depicted as bands of untrustworthy nomads; actually, Doyle employed them as "red herrings" who served as a misdirection from the actual culprit. Scholars (Knight 2004; Harrington 2007) note that the Holmes stories acknowledge a sense of danger—that is a part of the adventure—but contain it and resuscitate dominant social values in the denouement. Harrington (2007) argues that Doyle was a part of the New Imperialism movement, a body of late-nineteenth-century literature and scientific discourse that promoted the continued need for imperialism to an increasingly divided public.

Some fifty years later, the U.S. hard-boiled tradition also reflected anxieties. Writing in the 1930s and 1940s, writers like Dashiell Hammett and Raymond Chandler reflected the public's growing concern with large corporations and their impact not merely on the economy but on many aspects of social life. Often in these stories, it is the wealthy who are criminogenic forces. In Chandler's *Murder My Sweet* (1944), for example, private detective Phillip Marlow explains his refusal to drop a case after a client is murdered by saying, "He gave me a hundred bucks to take care of him, and I didn't. I'm just a small businessman in a very messy business, but I like to follow through on a sale." As was the case in Holmes's era, the police are under the thumb of the wealthy and not to be trusted. In *Hammett* (1982), Joe Gores's parody of a Dashiell Hammett story line, when asked who runs things in San Francisco, Hammett answers, "Same as in any town," to which his partner knowingly responds, "The cops, the crooks, and the big rich."

As noted at the beginning of this section, today's crime genre responds to contemporary concerns. In an oft-quoted article, Charlotte Brunsdon (2000) refers to "the structure of anxiety" that is at the heart of the crime genre. Indeed, there is no shortage of problems in today's world, and they are manifest in television police dramas such as *NYPD Blue* (1993–2005), *Law and Order*, and *CSI*. In these stories, social institutions are depicted as failing, well-meaning people do not know what to do, and it is the police who protect us from urban chaos.

In the years since the 9/11 terrorist attacks, anxieties about the threat of terrorism have become a heightened concern. Real police departments confront these concerns, as does the crime genre. Terrorism and terrorists contribute to crime genre productions in various ways. Sometimes this threat is the essence of a production. For example, in the television thriller *24*, the terrorist threat is so serious and the urgency so immediate that Counter Terrorist Unit agent Jack Bauer is justified (according to the script) in using torture to extract vital information—and to secure it now! Other productions reflect a post-9/11 technological sensibility. *Person of Interest* (2011–present) features a computer constructed after 9/11 that can predict future terrorist attacks. Because it also can predict crimes, a former Central Intelligence Agency operative uses it to become a kind of preemptive crime fighter. The science fiction/crime film *Minority Report* (2002) depicts a similar preemptive strategy. In a different vein, the television program *Homeland* (2011–present) features protagonists who suffer from emotional baggage in the aftermath of 9/11, such as the death of family members. Television crime dramas like *CSI* that were successful programs before the 9/11 attacks now occasionally include antiterrorism plots. Crime novels also incorporate the post-9/11 world. Elliott Colla's (2014) novel *Baghdad Central* is set in Iraq after the U.S. invasion. A former Iraqi police officer is tortured in Abu Ghraib prison before being released on the condition that he will work to train new Iraqi police, but he then encounters a murder mystery. Finally, some productions use antiterrorist federal agencies in ways that resemble standard genre treatments of the Federal Bureau of Investigation, that is, federal agencies are a foil to local police efforts. In Tony Hillerman's novel *The Sinister Pig* (2003 , p. 52), Navajo tribal police officer Jim Chee muses on homeland security as follows: "The FBI bureaucrats had always been notoriously inept. And now the word was that the Homeland Security Law had laid another thick layer of political patronage on top of that—adding the chaos of a new power struggle to an already clogged system."

Whatever the era and whatever the medium, the response to anxieties reinforces crime genre writer G. K. Chesterson's 1946 description of detectives as "unsleeping sentinels who guard the outposts of society . . . from criminals, the children of chaos." For Chesterton, the detective is "the agent of justice" (quoted in Harrington 2007). Fictional detectives are designed to resemble the real police.

CONCLUSION

At the outset, we noted a tension among criminologists regarding the accuracy of crime genre depictions of crime and the CJS. According to what we called the fallacy perspective, the crime genre offers largely inaccurate portrayals, and these cause misperceptions among the public. In contrast, the concordance perspective posits a greater degree of accuracy or at least insight into important CJS and societal themes. We then proceeded to demonstrate how important issues such as technological innovation and concerns over diversity and security/insecurity—matters that affect the CJS in practice—have been manifested in the crime genre.

That the crime genre addresses these and other relevant aspects of social life is not surprising. A genre that boasts as one of its defining features a sense of realism, of verisimilitude, will incorporate into its narratives matters that affect the CJS in the real world. This was the case early on with putative "true crime stories," such as *The Newgate Calendar*; with stories that were informed by actual cases, such as Poe's "The Murder of Marie Roget"; and with the portrayals that showed the presence of women police officers at a time when women were increasingly becoming police officers.

However, we think that what is important about crime genre productions is not their accuracy—they will rarely be 100 percent accurate—so much as how they frame issues in a socially relevant style that leads to timely and critical discussions about social and legal justice. Regardless of its exactitude, the crime genre, like any good fiction, addresses important dimensions of social life. These may include problems of work–life balance among female officers, sexism and homophobia in police organizations, or the troubles caused by preemptive crime strategies.

Elsewhere (Cavender & Jurik 2012) we have developed a model of what we call "progressive moral fiction," that is, fiction that delineates unjust social arrangements and offers a guide to how individuals working alone or in concert with others can be agents for social change—justice provocateurs. Our model is informed by, among others, novelist and literary critic John Gardner (1982), who argued that good fiction, moral fiction, should inspire the audience toward virtue. Good fiction, whether great literature or a television police procedural, can accomplish this end. Indeed, the fact that the crime genre is formulaic—a crime, a detective on an investigatory quest, and a resolution—may offer advantages. Writers can draw upon, but also innovate in using the formula in ways that confront the nuances and complex realities of social life. In his acceptance speech for the Noble Prize for Literature, William Faulkner (1950) said that what drives good fiction are the "old verities and truths of the heart, the old universal truths . . . love and honor and pity and pride and compassion and sacrifice." In this sense, what makes the crime genre important is its inclusion of stories that investigate the human condition, but within the framework of crime and the CJS.

REFERENCES

Allen, J., Sonia Livingstone, & Robert Reiner. 1998. "True Lies: Changing Images of Crime in British Postwar Cinema." *European Journal of Communications* 13 (1): 53–75.

Bergin, Tiffany. 2013. "Identity and Nostalgia in a Globalised World: Investigating the International Popularity of *Midsomer Murders*." *Crime Media Culture* 9 (1): 83–99.

Bergman, Kerstin. 2009. "Crime Fiction as Popular Science: The Case of Asa Nilsonne." Paper presented at the Nordic Association for Comparative Literature, Stockholm, Sweden, 6–9 August.

Bernardi, Daniel. 2001. *Classic Hollywood, Classic Whiteness*. Minneapolis: University of Minnesota Press.

Britto, Sarah, Tycy Hughes, Kurt Saltzman, & Colin Stroh. 2007. "Does 'Special' Mean Young, White and Female? Deconstructing the Meaning of 'Special' in *Law & Order: Special Victims Unit*." *Journal of Criminal Justice and Popular Culture* 14 (1): 39–57.

Brown, Jennifer, & Frances Heidensohn. 2000. *Gender and Policing: Comparative Perspectives*. New York: St. Martin's Press.

Brown, Michelle. 2009. *The Culture of Punishment: Prison, Society, and Spectacle*. New York: New York University Press.

Brunsdon, Charlotte. 2000. "The Structure of Anxiety: Recent British Television Crime Fiction." In *British Television: A Reader*, ed. Edward Buscombe, 195–217. Oxford: Clarendon Press.

Cavender, Gray, & Sarah Deutsch. 2007. "*CSI* and Moral Authority: The Police and Science." *Crime Media Culture* 3 (1): 67–81.

Cavender, Gray, & Nancy C. Jurik. 2012. *Justice Provocateur: Jane Tennison and Policing in Prime Suspect*. Urbana: University of Illinois Press.

Cavender, Gray, & Nancy C. Jurik. 2014. "The Appeal of the Crime Genre." In *Oxford Handbooks Online in Criminology and Criminal Justice*, ed. Michael Tonry, 1–13. New York: Oxford University Press.

Cawleti, John. 1976. *Adventure, Mystery, and Romance*. Chicago: University of Chicago Press.

Cuklanz, Lisa, & Sujata Moorti. 2006. "Television's New Feminism: Prime-Time Representations of Women and Victimization." *Critical Studies in Media Communications* 23 (4): 302–21.

Cullen, Francis, Gray Cavender, William Maakestad, & Michael Benson. 2006. *Corporate Crime under Attack: The Fight to Criminalize Business Violence*, 2nd ed. Cincinnati: Anderson/Elsevier.

D'Acci, Julie. 1994. *Defining Women: Television and the Case of Cagney and Lacey*. Chapel Hill: University of North Carolina Press.

Demko, George. n.d. "The International Diffusion and Adaptation of the Crime Fiction Genre." Accessed at http://www.dartmouth.edu/~gjdemko/nyaag.htm.

Deutsch, Sarah, & Gray Cavender. 2008. "CSI and Forensic Realism." *Journal of Criminal Justice and Popular Culture* 15 (1): 34–63.

Doyle, Arthur. 2005 [1903]. "The Adventure of the Norwood Builder." In *The New Annotated Sherlock Holmes*, Vol. 2, ed. Leslie Klinger, 829–63. London: W. W. Norton and Company.

Erickson, Richard, & Kevin Haggerty. 1997. *Policing the Risk Society*. New York: Oxford University Press.

Eschholz, Sarah, Matthew Mallare, & Stacey Flynn. 2004. "Images of Prime Time Justice: A Content Analysis of *NYPD Blue* and *Law and Order*." *Journal of Criminal Justice and Popular Culture* 10 (3): 161–80.

Faulkner, William. 1950. "Noble Prize Banquet Speech." Accessed at http://www.nobelprize.org/nobel_prizes/literature/laureates/1949/faulkner-speech.html.

Gardner, John. 1982. *On Moral Fiction*. New York: Basic Books.

Garland, David. 2001. *The Culture of Control: Crime and Social Order in Contemporary Society*. New York: Oxford University Press.

Gray, Herman. 2004. *Watching Race: Television and the Struggle for Blackness*. Minneapolis: University of Minnesota Press.

Gross, Larry. *Up From Invisibility: Lesbians, Gay Men, and the Media in America*. New York: Columbia University Press.

Harper, Lila Marz. 2009. "Clues in the Street: Sherlock Holmes, Martin Hewitt, and Mean Streets." *Journal of Popular Culture* 42 (1): 67–89.

Harrington, Ellen. 2007. "Nation, Identity and the Fascination with Forensic Science in Sherlock Holmes and *CSI*." *International Journal of Cultural Studies* 10 (3): 365–82.

Hillerman, Tony. 2003. *The Sinister Pig*. New York: Harper.

Jermyn, Deborah. 2010. *Prime Suspect*. London: Palgrave Macmillan.

Jewkes, Yvonne. 2011. *Media and Crime*, 2nd ed. London: Sage.

Klein, Dorrie. 1992. "Reading the New Feminist Mystery: The Female Detective, Crime and Violence." *Women and Criminal Justice* 4 (1): 37–62.

Klein, Kathleen. 1995. *The Woman Detective: Gender and Crime*, 2nd ed. Chicago: University of Illinois Press.

Knepper, Paul, & Clive Norris. 2009. "Fingerprint and Photograph: Surveillance Technologies in the Manufacture of Suspect Social Identities." In *Urban Crime Prevention, Surveillance, and Restorative Justice*, ed. Paul Knepper, Jonathan Doak, & Joanna Shapland, 77–100. Boca Raton, FL: CRC Press.

Knight, Stephen. 1980. *Form and Ideology in Crime Fiction*. Bloomington: Indiana University Press.

Knight, Stephen. 2004. *Crime Fiction, 1800–2000: Detection, Death, Diversity*. London: Palgrave/Macmillan.

Leishman, Frank, & Paul Mason. 2003. *Policing and the Media: Facts, Fictions and Factions*. Cullompton, UK: Willan Publishing.

Lenz, Timothy. 2003. *Changing Images of Law in Film and Television Crime Stories*. New York: Peter Lang.

Loader, Ian, & Aogan Mulcahy. 2004. *Policing and the Condition of England: Memory, Politics, Culture*. Oxford: Oxford University Press.

Martin, Susan, & Nancy C. Jurik. 2007. *Doing Justice, Doing Gender: Women in Legal and Criminal Justice Occupations*, 2nd ed. Thousand Oaks, CA: Sage.

McCulloch, Jude, & Sharon Pickering. 2012. "Introduction." In *Borders and Crime: Pre-Crime, Mobility and Serious Harm in an Age of Globalization*, ed. Jude McCulloch & Sharon Pickering, 1–14. London: Palgrave/Macmillan.

Miller, Susan, Kate Forest, & Nancy Jurik. 2003. "Lesbians in Policing: Perceptions and Work Experiences within the Macho Cop Culture." *Men and Masculinities* 5 (4): 355–85.

Mizejewski, Linda. 2004. *Hardboiled and High-Heeled: The Woman Detective in Popular Culture*. New York: Routledge.

Radzinowicz, Leon. 1966. *Ideology and Crime*. New York: Columbia University Press.

Rafter, Nicole. 2006. *Shots in the Mirror: Crime Films and Society*, 2nd ed. New York: Oxford University Press.

Rafter, Nicole, & Michelle Brown. 2011. *Criminology Goes to the Movies: Crime Theory in Popular Culture*. New York: New York University Press.

Rapping, Elayne. 2003. *Law and Justice as Seen on TV*. New York: New York University Press.

Reiner, Robert. 2010. *The Politics of the Police*, 4th ed. Oxford: Oxford University Press.

Riley, Brendan. 2009. "From Sherlock to Angel: The Twenty-First Century Detective." *Journal of Popular Culture* 42 (5): 908–22.

Silvestri, Marisa. 2003. *Women in Charge: Policing, Gender and Leadership*. Cullompton, UK: Willan Publishing.

Silvestri, Marisa, Stephen Tong, & Jennifer Brown. 2013. "Gender and Police Leadership: Time for a Paradigm Shift?" *International Journal of Police Science and Management* 15 (1): 61–73.

Surette, Ray. 2007. *Media, Crime, and Criminal Justice: Images, Realities, and Policies*, 4th ed. Belmont, CA: Wadsworth.

Wilson, Christopher. 2000. *Cop Knowledge: Police Power and Cultural Narrative in Twentieth-Century America*. Chicago: University of Chicago Press.

Wilson, Franklin, Dennis Longmire, & Warren Swymeler. 2009. "The Absence of Gay and Lesbian Police Officer Depictions in the First Three Decades of the Core Cop Genre: Moving Towards a Cultivation Theory Perspective." *Journal of Criminal Justice and Popular Culture* 16 (1): 27–39.

Wilson, William Julius. 1997. *When Work Disappears: The World of the New Urban Poor*. New York: Vintage.

CHAPTER 17

CONTESTED SPACES

On Crime Museums, Monuments, and Memorials

PER JØRGEN YSTEHEDE

> It is difficult to consider Villella's skull scientifically irrelevant and thus unworthy of display in a museum. That is, unless one believes that science must destroy the traces of its past.
>
> —Silvano Montaldo, *Il cranio, il sindaco,*
> *l'ingegnere, il giudice e il comico*

> Perhaps, in the end, there are the objects.
>
> —Steven Conn, *Museums and American*
> *Intellectual Life, 1876–1926*

INTRODUCTION

ON 8 May 2010 a large group of protesters gathered outside the *museo di antropologia criminale "Cesare Lombroso"* (the Lombroso Museum) in Turin, Italy. According to the newspaper *La Stampa*, the protesters yelled, "Lombroso razzista, Mazzini terrorista"— Lombroso was a racist, Mazzini was a terrorist (Luciano Borghesan, "Siamo tutti briganti, vogliamo il Sud libero," *La Stampa*, 9 May 2010). What was it that caused this violent protest outside a museum dedicated to the founding father of criminology, Cesare Lombroso (1835–1909), a figure whose theories most criminologists consider obsolete, or, at most, only of interest to those interested in the early history of the science of criminology?

To begin to understand the indignation and public outcry against the museum, one may consult some of the media articles written at the time. For example, Beppe Grillo, the former Italian comedian and founder of *MoVimento Cinque Stelle* (the Five Star Movement; M5S), that same year wrote in his blog:

> What if there was a museum in Berlin dedicated to Alfred Rosenberg, the Nazi mastermind behind the idea of the superiority of the Arian race? And what if this Rosenberg

FIG. 17.1 The Lombroso Museum was reopened to the public on 27 November 2009. Source: Archivio storico del Museo di Antropologia criminale "Cesare Lombroso" dell'Universita di Torino (Italy).

Museum displayed the remains of the Jews that were deported to the concentration camps, including their skeletons and their skulls cut open as proof of their inferiority? What if there was a museum in Turin, which there is, dedicated to Cesare Lombroso, the mastermind behind the idea that northern Italians are superior to southern Italians? And what if this Lombroso Museum displayed, which it does, the remains of the southern Italian patriots, labelled as criminals, who were killed in their tens of thousands during Piedmont's occupation of The Kingdom of the Two Sicilies? Their skeletons and their skulls cut open as proof of their inferiority, displayed in cabinets in their hundreds, instead of being buried in their homeland as human decency would demand. This lazy, racist Italy that is unaware of its history is celebrating 150 years of unity. The Piedmont Regional Administration should shut down this museum, or at least return the southerners' remains to their places of birth.[1]

According to the protesters, Lombroso had been a loyal supporter of Piedmont's invasion and occupation of the south of Italy. They also believed that he had used his scientific findings, and inspired others to use it, to legitimize murder, oppression, and violence against southern Italians. The Lombroso Museum holds a sizeable collection of the remains of people categorized as various criminal types. Among the demonstrators were family members of the deceased who objected to the display of their ancestors' skulls and bones in the museum. However, the demonstration was not solely an expression of disgust at what are now perceived as the ghoulish practices of scientists a century ago. According to Grillo, whose sentiments were shared by the protesters on Piazza Vittorio Veneto, the Lombroso Museum was a manifestation (visual and material) of northern Italy's oppression of the south (Figure 17.2). Thus, on the 150th anniversary of the Italian state, the Lombroso Museum became emblematic of acute issues in Italian politics. It became the center for the long political campaign by political groups from the south of Italy to gain recognition of southern Italians as a persecuted group—similar, if not identical, to the Jews and the Roma minorities in Italy. The protestors' historical accuracy may have left something to be desired—Lombroso was far from being a hard-nosed supporter of Piedmontese imperialist politics and had no particular contempt for the south—nor was he a mad scientist, as portrayed in the popular late nineteenth-century stereotype. Be that as it may, the outcry did not end in the streets outside the museum, but has now become a matter for the Italian courts. On 3 October 2012 Judge Danise issued a court order authorizing Amadeo Colacino, mayor of Motta Santa Lucia, to reclaim one of the museum's most prized possessions—the skull of the brigand Giuseppe Villella, who, as mentioned in the court order, was born in Motta Santa Lucia, Calabria.[2] The autopsy of Villella's brain (now lost) is perhaps one of the most famous events in the history of criminology. Lombroso's claim that he had found the cause of crime—proof that there are born criminals—has come to be seen as the genesis of the discipline of criminology. Judge Danise, Mayor Colacino, and a body founded in 2010 called *Comitato "No Lombroso"* called for the return of Villella's skull so that it could be given a burial in Calabria. In January 2013 the University of

FIG. 17.2 The Lombroso Museum at the beginning of the twentieth century. Source: Archivio storico del Museo di Antropologia criminale "Cesare Lombroso" dell'Universita di Torino (Italy).

Turin, which owns the Lombroso Museum, filed an appeal against Judge Danise's ruling, arguing that Villella's skull is protected by the Italian cultural heritage law (Codice dei beni culturali, 2004), since it is an important cultural item and thus holds value for the history of science. The court order is currently suspended, though a final decision was supposed to be made in December of 2014, one is still awaiting the court order (Montaldo 2012). The Comitato "No Lombroso" [3] sees the museum as an affront to human dignity, claiming that its existence is a racial crime—the marker of a mass grave of southerners. (In fact, most of the bones in the museum were most likely collected on the streets of Turin.) Nevertheless, the bodies in the museum (southern or not) seem to have raised questions regarding the museum's legitimacy. The Lombroso Museum is far from being the only museum that owns contested bodies and is the focus for questions about what can now, politically or morally, be displayed in a museum.

The controversy surrounding the Lombroso Museum may be said to highlight some fundamental features of crime museums, monuments, and memorials in modern contemporary society. First of all, as the abovementioned debate shows, crime museums, monuments, and/or memorials are intimately connected with specific times, spaces, materials, and social and cultural contexts. Though one may find similarities between crime museums throughout the world, they also differ markedly from each other because of their close relationship to various questions and discourses, particularly those regarding representations of nationhood. Since the rise of the nation-state, crime museums, monuments, and memorials have been given symbolic significance and power to represent the nation's soul. As French Minister of the Interior Jean-Marie Roland (1734–1793) wrote in a letter in 1792 to the painter Jacques-Louis David (1748–1825):

> The future museum should contain the development of the whole wealth of drawings, paintings, sculptures, and other monuments of art. . . . This will be a national monument. . . . France will extend its glory over all times and all the peoples of the world; the national museum will comprise a total of the most wonderful knowledge and will command the admiration of the whole universe. . . . It will have such an influence on the mind, it will so elevate the soul, it will so excite the heart that it will be the most powerful way of proclaiming the illustriousness of the French Republic. (Duncan & Wallach 2012, p. 56)

The 2010 debate on the Lombroso Museum is just one in a long series of examples of (crime) museums (as well as monuments and memorials) that have played a central part in a political struggle and received international attention. Carol Strange and Michael Kempa (2003) describe the cases of Robben Island and Alcatraz, both of which are contested sites for the representation of national identity:

> In the "new" South Africa, the successful fight against apartheid gave the Robben Island Museum a sacred mission at its outset, largely crowding out oppositional stories and eclipsing the island's broader history. . . . Heritage site is only the latest identities for Robben Island and Alcatraz. . . . Although the islands served a variety of carceral purposes over several centuries (including the confinement of military prisoners,

lepers and the mentally ill), their preservation and reconfiguration as historic sites owes most to their penal pasts..... Once they shed their penal functions for new touristic identities, their historic relevance was interpreted within nationally distinct and dynamic cultures of memorialization. (Strange & Kempa 2003, pp. 288–89)

According to Strange and Kempa, crime museums such as the prison museums found throughout the world raise ethical questions and moral dilemmas. They may be seen as commodifying pain for touristic pleasure and consumption (2003; see also Lennon & Foley 2000). Not only may their very existence arouse controversy, but even the suggestion of a crime museum, monument, or memorial can be enough to cause public outcry. One recent example is the projected memorial to those murdered in the Utøya gun massacre outside Oslo, Norway, in 2011. The *Memory Wound*[4] designed by the Swedish artist Jonas Wahlberg has met opposition from a number of groups, some threatening legal action. As one of the parents of the victims put it: "No one should be allowed to make money out of our daughter's death, and we would rather not have her name on the memorial" ("Do Not Put My Daughter's Name on Utøya Memorial, *The Local*, 13 March 2014). One can find examples of such public objections to monuments and memorials around the world and throughout history (Gamboni 2007). What crime museums, monuments, and memorials have in common with, for instance, war memorials[5] is that they pose the challenge of reaching agreement on how the nation's pain or glory should be represented.

To understand why crime museums, monuments, and memorials have been, and often still are, contested sites, one first needs to take into account the rise of not just the crime museum, but of "the museum" as a phenomenon in itself. Second, one has to consider these museums more specifically in relation to the rise of the sciences connected with criminology and the cultural tradition of crime and punishment as spectacle. The crime museum as we know it today was born in the nineteenth century and grew out of a number of historical and cultural currents. Third, crime museums should be understood more generally in relation to the rise of the professions, professional organizations, and the nation-state. Thus, one now finds crime museums throughout the world in the form of police museums, prison museums, museums of the history of psychiatry, and so on. Some, such as the Lombroso Museum, have been modernized and opened to the public, while others are closed, or their contents are collecting dust in a governmental building. Paradoxically, is that whereas museums are generally expected to display what is elevated and considered high culture, the items found in a crime museum are categorized as relating to baser aspects of the human condition.

I. The Rise of the Crime Museum—Dark Muses of Enlightenment and Progress

The history of the museum can be traced back to the early Renaissance period. Originally, a museum was not understood as being confined spatially or temporally in the way it is now. The term museum, or *museion*, meant the "place consecrated to the

Muses," the goddesses of poetry, music, and the liberal arts. It also referred more specifically to the famous library of Alexandria. Though the forms, meanings, and functions of the museum have changed over time, museums have always been, and still are, seen as cultural resources for the community. Originally the museum was a private space, but this changed during the late Renaissance period. As Paula Findlen puts it:

> The constellation of terms used to describe collecting by the late sixteenth century created a unified conceptual sphere that fully demonstrated the museum's roles in the public and private realms. By now "study" connotes a room for private study with museum as its public counterpart. Yet the polarization of these two categories evolved only in the nineteenth and the twentieth centuries as the images of "public" and "private" have also become fixed opposites. (2012. p. 35)

The museum gradually turned into a bourgeois space. From the time of the French Revolution, museums have been "in the grips of a powerful tide of national pathos" (Meyer & Savoy 2014, p. 1; see also Kroegel 2014). As a type of museum, the crime museum is akin to, and to an extent developed from, the tradition of the cabinet of curiosities, also known as the Kunstkabinett, Kunstkammer, Wunderkammer, Cabinet of Wonder, or wonder-room. These were encyclopedic collections of objects whose categorical boundaries were, in Renaissance Europe, yet to be defined. In these cabinets one would find displayed, for instance, medical oddities, anatomical and pathological specimens, illustrations of medical deformities such as conjoined or Siamese twins, and human skulls and artifacts belonging to what were seen as primitive races, such as the Australian Aborigines. These collections often began, as did the Lombroso Museum, as teaching tools for young scientists. By the nineteenth century, which ushered in the vogue of positivism, the approach of choice for the new sciences examining crime, these cabinets of curiosities were clear proof of the Enlightenment's "perversion of reason." The late nineteenth-century crime museums heralded the fate of the later criminological sciences—on the one hand, they sought to categorize these objects of horror, terror, mystery, and wonder, while on the other hand, they fell under the spell of the sublimely horrible nature of the artifacts.

The rise of the criminal sciences resulted from a number of social, political, and cultural movements that were international as well as national. From the late nineteenth century onward one can see the establishment of a number of crime museums and bodies devoted to the study of crime and punishment. The first, and the most prominent and influential, were those in Central Europe—in Italy, France, Germany, and Spain. A major focus of these institutions was the individual criminal. The so-called Italian School, and those calling themselves criminal anthropologists and followers of Lombroso became particularly well known, and later infamous. The idea that some people are born criminal has justly been seen as part and parcel of the growing dominance of the natural sciences in the eighteenth and nineteenth centuries. Charles Darwin's work in *The Origin of Species* (1859) and *The Expression of the Emotions in Man and Animals* (1872) was accompanied by an overwhelming mass of complementary and/or competing evolutionary narratives that questioned man's place in the universe. How similar to each other were human beings? What was it that made some different?

The advent of the first crime museums must in part be seen as related to the fact that the early experts on crime had a background in the natural sciences. For instance, the Lombroso Museum sought to depict the natural history of criminal man, and in a similar way the School of Criminal Anthropology adopted a format that had been used by scientists for centuries (Figure 17.1).

Of equal importance to understanding the birth of the criminal sciences, and of the crime museum, are Romanticism and the Romantic imagination (Rafter & Ystehede 2010). With Romanticism the focus moved away from abstract, external principles and ideals, and turned inward. Attention was directed to what lay beyond the horizon or was invisible beneath the surface, hidden in human nature. Romanticism cultivated the idea that nature, as God's creation, was under the control and responsibility of man. The nation-state now became the basis of a people's identity, while nature was seen as the foundation of an individual's identity. Some individuals, such as artists and geniuses, were believed to have an intuitive insight into nature's divine spirit. Thus, genius and the divine became "naturalized" in the Romantic imagination and seen as the property of certain elite individuals. It then followed that the criminal, the lawless, the heretical, and the demonic were also found in human nature. This led to the conundrum posed by the Enlightenment *philosophes*: if men are equal, rational, and good, how is one to understand and deal with those having the opposite qualities (Halttunen 1998)? The early so-called "positivist criminal science" was to a great extent a quantification of Romantic belief systems regarding crime, the criminal, and society that gave scientific credibility to the tenet that modern man and modern society have their paired opposites—their gothic doubles. This gothic double might be found at the individual level, as in the case of Dr. Jekyll and Mr. Hyde, or in an evil twin of civil society, represented as being beyond the looking glass, a dark continent, a shadowy realm, or a criminal underworld (see also Ystehede 2008). Phrenology, the science of the relationship between man's mental capabilities and physiognomy of face, may be taken as a case in point. Originally used to measure beauty and find the sublime and the elevated, from the mid-1800s onward it was also used to detect human evil (Gray 2004).

Crime museums may be seen as material manifestations of the quantification of the Enlightenment's "perversion of reason." The first experts on crime were mostly men from the civilized and privileged classes who went on "safari" tours in the urban jungle, studying it and discovering exotic habits, goods, and merchandise among the destitute, homeless, and odd. What later came to be known as art brut, or primitivism, had its origins in material found on these excursions (Peiry 2001). Taken out of context these artifacts would serve different purposes and be imbued with new meanings in these new laboratories and museums. The Romantic notion that language reflects the soul was embraced early on by the new experts on crime, who studied criminal argot in the same way as they studied criminal art. One nowadays often thinks of a nation in terms of numbers and statistics, gross national product, geographic size, and crime statistics, but this is a relatively new historical phenomenon that emerged in the nineteenth century. Concepts such as "revolution" and methods that had previously been used by astronomers to measure distances between constellations and the like would gradually become national compasses—panoptic telescopes seeking to penetrate the soul of a nation. Within criminal science, these moral statisticians, encountering what is perhaps still the most important category in criminology—the recidivist, a term derived from Latin that means one who has fallen back into sin—created supposedly objective measurements that would be crucial in shaping images of nationhood and regional moral worth. With crime statistics, one now had a means to show a people's soul, a measure of civilization, culture, Bildung, and modernity.

These bodies devoted to the study of crime became widely known at the World Fairs, or universal exhibitions, as they were also called, at which nations not only displayed industrial, artistic, and technological advances in cultural and scientific fields, but also positioned and defined themselves as nations. Unlike war museums, crime museums such as the Lombroso Museum were originally as much laboratories as museums, but they were intended from the beginning for "touristic consumption." Even if not consciously created as the circus element of "bread and circuses," crime museums were used from the beginning as an important marketing tool by the early professionals of the new criminal sciences. Prior to the foundation in 1926 of the *Office International des Musées* (International Museums Office), one of the many international bodies created by the new *Société des Nations* (League of Nations), criminal scientists began international exchanges of collections of art produced by so-called "deviants" (but see also Knepper 2011). Emile Durkheim (1858–1917), for example, when planning an exhibition of the social sciences in Bordeaux, France, in 1895,[6] was one of the many who asked Cesare Lombroso to lend the event items from his collection. In 1885, the first International Congress of Criminal Anthropology in Rome had displayed seventy skulls of Italian criminals, thirty skulls of epileptics, the entire skeleton of a thief, samples of criminal handwriting, and criminal art—to mention only some of the artifacts on show. He was not alone. His French colleague Alexandre Lacassagne (1843–1924) did not bring skulls, but came with more than 2,000 preserved samples of tattooed skin, as well as maps and illustrations to the Paris exhibition (see also Starr 2010). A point to remember is that these exhibitions, as well as the museums themselves, could be used to generate funds that provided a financial base for the new bodies concerned with crime. As Montaldo notes in his presentation of the history of the Lombroso Museum:

> The collection was presented to the public for the first time in 1884, as part of the Anthropology Exhibition held at Turin's Esposizione Generale Italiana. The scientists claimed significant exposure in the event that celebrated Italy's early stages as a unified nation, designed and organized to show Italian and international public opinion the results achieved by unification. It was no coincidence that, when the exhibition closed after registering nearly three million visitors, the organisers stressed the ideal continuity between the event and the new higher education institutions that would spring up soon afterwards. (Montaldo 2013, p. 100)

Part of the reason for the popularity and drawing power of Lombroso's museum and the criminal anthropological exhibitions during the Belle Èpoque was that it chimed with the tradition of crime and punishment as spectacle, which for centuries had enthralled the popular imagination. Lombroso was not above exploiting the drawing power of "freaks," "monsters," and other titillating exhibits. Crime museums often staged plays in which good triumphed over evil: a narrative of progress (see also Freed 2012a, b). Prison museums often put forward a narrative of how punishment had developed from the torture of former times to the more humane and modern conditions of the present. However, in the case of the Lombroso Museum, its creator lived to see himself regarded as one of the monsters:

> Lombroso's name was coupled with Nordau's in later historical analyses of nineteenth-century culture, and some later historians argued that Lombroso had inspired Nazi policies and the Final Solution. This image of Lombroso as a specialist in death and violence took hold because it meshed well with Romantic ideas about how science and scientists could go dreadfully wrong. Lombroso was viewed as a scientist who, like Mary Shelley's Dr. Frankenstein, had created a hideous progeny. . . . Lombroso's criminal anthropology offered the masses a new, morally legitimate spectacle of suffering in which the scaffold was replaced by the discourses of photography, yellow journalism, the museum—and later the cinema. The scientific exhibits of criminal anthropology, which put on show items from the newly discovered underworlds and dark continents of crime (some distant, some close to home), mirrored the rise of consumerist society, even as they contributed to the modern colonization of the discourse on crime. . . . In the nineteenth century, discourses on crime continued to be modern morality plays, yet grew to become modern allegories par excellence for the human condition. Thus "romancing" crime led in the end to the distinctly modern notion in the scientific and popular cultural imagination that crime and the criminal are natural, physically knowable parts and aspects of everyday life. (Rafter & Ystehede 2009, pp. 186, 189–90)[7]

Most crime museums for a very long time remained a mix of "a place for study" and a museum, serving a variety of functions: as a theater for the macabre, as a library, as an educational facility for the public and experts on crime alike. Chief Constable Fredrick T. Tarry, for example, argued—when seeking to create a Central Police Museum—that "the need is for a central institution, where the scientist and practical investigator will both be at home, combing and pooling their fields of knowledge and experience, and meeting on equal terms" (Tarry 1946, p. 116). The objects exhibited, however, would also provide entertainment to the public, including suchartifacts as portraits, cartoons, historical engravings, truncheons, tipstaffs, handcuffs, uniforms and headgear, police medals, badges, buttons, and, above all, exhibits connected with famous criminal cases (Jack the Ripper, H. H. Crippen, Charles Peace, Patrick McMahon, Browne and Kennedy, etc.). Furthermore:

> The major part of the space available will rightly be devoted to the display of exhibits of recent and current interest to the public and to the police in the prevention and detection of crime. The importance of speed in communications between the public and the Police, and the Police and the Police, and particularly the importance

of inducing the public to assist the Police in their search for truth by imparting quickly and fully all possible information of or about the commission of a crime. . . . A museum performs definite services in the field of education, research and exhibition. (Tarry 1946, pp. 120–21)

Some crime museums, such as the Lombroso Museum, have been modernized and updated to bring them closer to present-day (moral and political) standards, but others, such as the Crime Museum in Vienna, still strike the visitor as what the French philosopher Michel Foucault (1926–1984) called "heterotopias of time": spaces in which objects from all times and of all styles are deposited. They exist in time, but also outside of time, because they are built and preserved so as to be physically insusceptible to time's ravages (Foucault 2008; on the Crime Museum in Vienna, see also Huey 2011).

In comparison with crime museums, crime monuments and memorials may at first glance generally seem to be destined to be more frozen in time. However, crime monuments, too, change function and meaning through the passage of time and its attendant effects.

II. Crime Monuments and Memorials

The Austrian sculptor Alfred Hrdlicka (1928–2009) once suggested erecting a statue of Fritz Haarmann (1879–1925), the infamous early twentieth-century German serial killer known in his native town as the Vampire of Hanover. Hrdlicka's provocative suggestion was not carried out; however, the reason why the Haarmann statue never came into being reveals some important aspects of the nature of crime monuments and memorials. Like tombs and gravestones, these structures serve as signs of presence after death. Crime monuments and memorials are thus intimately related to the complex history of people's attitudes toward death. In his work *Western Attitudes Toward Death: From the Middle Ages to the Present*, Phillipe Ariès maps the change in public viewpoints: in medieval times, death was part of the collective public sphere, but it gradually disappeared from the life of the living in the late eighteenth and early nineteenth centuries to become something medical, technical, and private, an event happening behind the closed doors of the hospital, retirement center, funeral home, or mortuary (Àries 1975). Certainly, in the West at least, crime monuments and memorials have replaced and supplanted older forms of allegorical representations of the inevitability of the end.

Crime monuments and memorials, like crime museums, are modern phenomena, but they do have similarities to other monuments and memorials, both ancient and contemporary. One way in which crime monuments and memorials often differ from crime museums is that they mainly focus on the victim(s) of crime and not the criminal(s) and/or criminal justice agents. Monuments to individual criminals generally relate either to people and crimes from the distant past or to people whose former status has been changed by the historical narrative from one of honor to one of notoriety. Both crime monuments and crime memorials serve as foci for remembrance, usually of an event. They are physical manifestations and reflections of modern society and changes in systems of power, particularly the rise in power of the middle classes. They form part of a ritual transaction in which the value of the citizen is acknowledged. Whereas earlier monuments often served to commemorate state leaders, nowadays monuments and memorials might generally be said to be physical manifestations of modern social contracts. As part of symbolic exchanges between the governing body and the governed, the importance of monuments and memorials lies in the fact that they are identity markers for rituals of belonging and inclusion, as well as rituals of alienation and exclusion. The case of Haarmann may be seen as an example of exclusion, since in a modern society his acts are considered too horrendous to be part of civil society. This also has bearing on what might be understood at first glance as private crime memorials, for example flowers and other tokens placed at "crime scenes," due to the fact that they are positioned in a public space and invite public memorialization. This is also the case with crime monuments and memorials that can be defined as commemorating crime. As the previously mentioned controversy surrounding the projected monument at Utøya shows, like crime museums, memorials are often contested sites for the representation of national and collective identity. As Tatar asks in her work on sexual murder during the Weimar Republic, what would the erection of a statue of Fritz Haarmann suggest about German society and culture (Tatar 1997)? Society's rejection of a statue of Haarmann reflects a long cultural tradition—stretching from Vitruvius (c. 75-15 B.C.E.), who compared the human body directly to a building, to Sigmund Freud (1856–1939) and Jacques Derrida (1930–2004)—of seeing connections between bodies and buildings, and of giving monuments corporeal dimensions (Vesely 2002). Thus, crime monuments and memorials—as understood in the Pythagorean-Aristotelian tradition—are seen as a "microcosmos" of the (individual/collective) soul/spirit. However, because of what they invoke, they frequently become more politically, morally, and emotionally contested than other types of monuments, constituting sites of representation and "body politics."

The issue of, and the status given to, crime monuments and memorials as objects that are themselves somehow morally problematic is a recurring theme in the literature on dark tourism. In particular, memorials that generate profit and may be entertaining are seen as suspect and as forms of exploitation. It is sometimes argued that this situation increases the social distance between the spectator and the spectacle (see, e.g., Walby & Piché 2011). This is an issue that largely mirrors modern discussions of the representation and aesthetics of criminality in the (fine) arts, and, according to Black, the following dilemma is created:

> Because our aesthetic sensibility often conflicts with our moral sense, we are tempted to subordinate the former as deceit and illusion to the "truth" of [the] latter. By suppressing or denying our aesthetic experiences, we create a moral "reality" that is, in fact, our supreme fiction. This grand artifice or ideology of moral reason can only maintain itself as Truth at the continued expense of the individual's own subjective

feelings, his or her aesthetic and erotic responses to the world. In societies governed by moral-rational values, these responses, and their objective embodiments as artifacts (or art-facts), are periodically stigmatized. . . . In either case, art is suspected of promoting violence, and of subverting moral order. (Black 1991, pp. 4–5)

The vision of art and the artist's interest in crime at times may further fuel the tensions among aesthetics, representations of crime, public norms, and politics (see also Eburne 2008).

III. Contested Spaces—on Crime Museums, Monuments, and Memorials

There are a number of challenges involved in furnishing a general introduction to and account of crime museums, monuments, and memorials. Many of the challenges are the same as those involved in the study of other forms of historical, social, and cultural phenomena. First, there is the problem of definition and categorization. "Crime" may be just one of the labels one could use in describing any particular museum, monument, or memorial. For example, rather than being described as a "crime museum," the Lombroso institution may perfectly well be seen as a museum dedicated to the (Italian) history of science. Instead of providing too narrow a definition, this article has taken a wider view of museums, monuments, and memorials associated with crime and has tried to describe some of their features and consider some of the issues that arise when they are studied. Despite some challenges regarding clarity of definition and categorization, crime museums, monuments, and memorials are important sources for criminological knowledge. Crime museums such as the Lombroso Museum are a source of information about the development of the discipline of criminology and criminological theory. It is not just that they are vital spaces for criminologists to learn about the development of ideas about crime and criminal justice systems, but, of even more importance, they foster a discourse that provides unique insights into past and present public ideas about crime, penal attitudes, and justice. They were—and are—a medium of mass communication and as such may be among the most popular and widely read "criminological texts" in the world. Even among criminologists, few these days have read the works of Cesare Lombroso, but his museum receives approximately 20,000 visitors every year (Montaldo 2012). The prison museum on Alcatraz Island receives 1.5 million visitors a year. It is thus also important to recognize that crime museums have always played a role in shaping the public's thinking about crime and justice.

Crime museums, monuments, and memorials are places where individual, collective, and institutional memories find themselves occupying the same ground. They are places negotiating differing and at times conflicting demands: mixing personal memory, public memory, commerce, human rights, and a sense of decorum and dignity.

Notes

1. Beppe Grillo, "The Neo-Bourbons Against Lombroso," *Beppe Grillo's Blog*, 13 May 2010, accessed at http://www.beppegrillo.it/en/2010/05/the_neobourbons_against_lombro_1.html.

2. For a query as to whether Villella was actually born in Motta Santa Lucia. see M. T. Milicia, "Il brigante che sconfisse Lombroso," *Corriere della Sera*, 14 October 2012.

3. This group also has a website asserting that Cesare Lombroso was the real criminal: "His beliefs were mainly based on the thesis that 'the born or atavistic (uncultured) offender' is an individual who presents degenerative features in his physical build that differentiate him from a normal socially accepted man. In the pursuit of fame and in favour of his suspicious and antiscientific thesis, doctor Lombroso didn't hesitate to skin corpses, cut off and dissect heads, perform the most incredibile and cruel operations on men who were believed to be criminals in order to measure parts of their skulls and bodies, underlining unbelievable theories on the physical features of the natural born criminal. His work was strongly influenced by physiognomy, developing a pseudo science that dealt with forensic and psychosomatic phrenology inducing him to speculate more like a wizard apprentice than a scientist in a context based on eugenics and on some form of scientific racism the consequences of which would be visible in the following decades. In fact these conjectures were adopted as the foundation of the theories of German doctors regarding the pureness of the Aryan race, expanding Lombroso's false theory to explain the physical features of the Hebrew and the Rom and so on, justifying their extermination." See http://www.nolombroso.org/.

4. Wahlberg intends to carve a three-and-a-half-meter-wide slice through Sørbråten, the peninsula that juts out into the Tyrifjorden toward the island, to create a permanent scar on the landscape. The names of the dead will be carved on one exposed surface, which will be viewable to visitors who come down an underground walkway.

5. One example of an extremely controversial war memorial is the Vietnam Veterans' Memorial in Washington, D.C.

6. Letter from Emile Durkheim to Cesare Lombroso, 10 February 1894, Archives of the Cesare Lombroso Museum of Criminal Anthropology, Universita di Torino, Italy.

7. Translated from the Italian: "*Il nome di Lombroso è associato a quello di Nordau nelle ultime ricostruzioni della cultura del XIX secolo, e anche storici attuali si spingono ad affermare che Lombroso ispirò la politica nazista della Soluzione finale. Questa immagine di Lombroso come specialista della morte e della violenza è sopravvissuta poiché si accordava bene con l'idea romantica che una scienza e uno scienziato potessero essere profondamente sbagliati. Lombroso, come il dottor Frankenstein di Mary Shelley, fu visto come uno studioso che aveva creato un mostro scoprendo l'esistenza di sottospecie anormali dell'umanità. . . . L'antropologia criminale lombrosiana ha afferto alle masse un nuovo spettacolo, legittimato moralmente, della sofferenza, nel quale il patibolo è stato sostituito dal discorso della fotografia, della cronaca nera, dal museo criminologico e infine dal cinema. La strumentazione dell'antropologia criminale, mostrando nuove informazioni sul continente oscuro della malavita (per certi versi distante, per altri vicinissimo), ha rispecchiato la crescita della società dei consumi, veicolando la diffusione di un moderno discorso sul crimine. . . . Nel diciannovesimo secolo i discorsi sul crimine avevano un risvolto soprattutto morale, poi hanno iniziato a diventare le allegorie per eccellenza della condizione umana. L'uso fatto dal Romanticismo del crimine ha condotto alla nozione prettamente moderna dell'immaginario popolare e scientifico che il crimine e il criminale siano fenomeni della natura, aspetti fisicamente conoscibili della vita quotidiana.*"

References

Àries, Phillippe. 1975. *Western Attitudes Toward Death: From the Middle Ages to the Present.* Baltimore: John Hopkins University Press.

Black, Joel. 1991. *The Aesthetics of Murder: A Study in Romantic Literature and Contemporary Culture.* Baltimore: John Hopkins University Press.

Conn, Steven. 1998. *Museums and American Intellectual Life, 1876-1926.* Chicago: University of Chicago.

Duncan, Carol, & Alan Wallach. 2012. "The Universal Survey Museum." In *Museum Studies: An Anthology of Contexts*, ed. Bettina Messias Carbonell, 46-61. Oxford: Wiley-Blackwell.

Eburne, Jonathan P. 2008. *Surrealism and the Art of Crime.* Ithaca, NY: Cornell University Press.

Findlen, Paula. 2012. "The Museum: Its Classical Etymology and Renaissance Genealogy." In *Museum Studies: An Anthology of Contexts*, ed. Bettina Messias Carbonell, 23-45. Wiley-Blackwell: Oxford.pp 23-45.

Foucault, Michel. 2008 [1967]. "Of Other Spaces." In *Heterotopia and the City: Public Space in a Postcivil Society*, ed. Michael Dehane & Lieven De Cauter, 13-30. New York: Routledge.

Freed, Stanley A. 2012a. *Anthropology Unmasked: Museums, Science, and Politics in New York City*, Vol. 1, *The Putnam- Boas Era.* Wilmington, DE: Orange Frazer Press.

Freed, Stanley A. 2012b. *Anthropology Unmasked: Museums, Science, and Politics in New York City*, Vol. 2, *The Wissler Years.* Wilmington, DE: Orange Frazer Press.

Gamboni, Dario. 2007. *The Destruction of Art. Iconoclasm and Vandalism since the French Revolution.* London: Reaktion Books.

Gray, Richard T. 2004. *About Face: German Physiognomic Thought from Lavater to Auschwitz.* Detroit: Wayne State University.

Halttunen, Karen. 1998. *Murder Most Foul: The Killer and the American Gothic Imagination.* Cambridge, MA: Harvard University Press.

Huey, Laura. 2011. "Crime Behind the Glass: Exploring the Sublime in Crime at the Vienna Kriminalmuseum." *Theoretical Criminology* 15 (4): 381-99.

Knepper, Paul. 2011. *International Crime in the 20th Century: The League of Nations Era, 1919- 1939.* New York: Palgrave Macmillan.

Kroegel, Alessandra Galizzi. 2014. "The Journal Mouseion as Means of Transnational Culture: Guglielmo Pacchioni and the Dawn of the 'Modern Museum' in Italy." In *The Museum Is Open: Towards a Transnational History of Museums, 1750-1940*, ed. Andrea Meyer & Bénedicte Savoy, 89-100. Berlin: DeGruyter.

Lennon, John, & Malcolm Foley. 2000. *Dark Tourism: The Attraction of Death and Disasters.* Cornwall, UK: Continuum.

Meyer, Andrea, & Bénédicte Savoy. 2014. "Towards a Transnational History of Museums." In *The Museum Is Open: Towards a Transnational History of Museums, 1750-1940*, ed. Andrea Meyer & Bénédicte Savoy, 1-24. Berlin: DeGruyter.

Montaldo, Silvano. 2012. "Il cranio, il sindaco, l'ingegnere, il giudice e il comico. Un feuilleton museale italiano." *Museologia Scientifica nuove serie* 6 (1-2): 137-46.

Montaldo, Silvano. 2013. "The Lombroso Museum from Its Origins to the Present Day." In *The Cesare Lombroso Handbook*, ed. Paul Knepper, & Per Jørgen Ystehede, 98-112. London: Routledge.

Peiry, Lucienne. 2001. *Art Brut: The Origins of Outsider Art.* Paris, Switzerland: Flammarion.

Rafter, Nicole, & Per Jørgen Ystehede. 2010. "Here Be Dragons: Lombroso, the Gothic, and Social Control." In *Sociology of Crime, Law, and Deviance*, Vol. 14, *Popular Culture, Crime, and Social Control*, ed. Mathieu Deflem, 263-84. Emerald/JAI Press.

Rafter, Nicole, & Per Jørgen Ystehede. 2009 "Lombroso e la cultura di massa in Europa (1890–1930)." In *Cesare Lombroso cento anni dopo*, ed. Silvano Montaldo & Paolo Tappero, 185–92. Torino: UTET.

Starr, Douglas. 2010. *The Killer of Little Sheperds: A True Crime Story and the Birth of Forensic Science*. New York: Alfred A. Knopf.

Strange, Carolyn, & Michael Kempa. 2003. "Shades of Dark Tourism: Alcatraz and Robben Island." *Annals of Tourism Research* 30 (2): 386–405.

Tarry, Fredrick T. 1946. "A Central Police Museum and Exhibition: Plan for a National Register, Its Objective and Scope." *Police Journal* 19 (2): 116–23.

Tatar, Maria. 1997. *Lustmord: Sexual Murder in Weimar Germany*. Princeton, NJ: Princeton University Press.

Vesely, Dalibor. 2002. "The Architectonics of Embodiment." In *Body and Building: Essays on the Changing Relation of Body and Architecture*, ed. George Dodds & Robert Tavenor, 29–43. Cambridge, MA: MIT Press.

Walby, Kevin, & Justin Piché. 2011. "The Polysemy of Punishment Memorialization: Dark Tourism and Ontario's Penal History Museums." *Punishment & Society* 13 (4): 451–72.

Ystehede, Per Jørgen. 2008. *In the Twilight of Good and Evil: Cesare Lombroso and the Criminological Imagination*. Saarbrûcken: Verlag Müeller.

....

CHAPTER 18

A HISTORICAL PERSPECTIVE ON CRIME FICTION IN MEXICO DURING THE MIDDLE DECADES OF THE TWENTIETH CENTURY

....

PABLO PICCATO

Introduction

....

DETECTIVE and murder stories were part of life in Mexico during the middle decades of the twentieth century. They gave a guilty kind of pleasure to their readers, but they also helped them understand modernization. Although their authors and consumers fully embraced the genre's cosmopolitan tradition, reading and writing these stories was a way to give meaning to a Mexican reality in which justice and the truth were difficult to come by.

Despite its central role in public culture, crime fiction in Mexico has been the object of a double neglect. Literary scholars and editors at prestigious presses have considered the novels and stories published by Mexican authors during the golden age of the genre (1940–1950s) to be products of low quality and minimal artistic value. This dismissal is largely derived from established emphases on literary values connected to nationalism, rural settings, and the search for Mexican identity. From that perspective, the unpretentious, cheap, and popular crime novels published during those decades have little interest, as they used mostly urban settings and characters, and their authors followed foreign models, both stylistic and ethical. Historians, for their part, have not read crime fiction as a document of values and attitudes of Mexican publics, on the assumption that the justice and police systems in Mexico lacked any legitimacy and thus could not support the kind of restoration of moral order found at the end of standard detective stories in the countries that created the models for the genre (France, England, and the United States). All detective stories in Mexico, according to this reasoning, were a fantasy that had little to do with everyday life—in sharp contrast with historians' extensive use of nineteenth-century and revolutionary period novels as a rich source of insight about national identity, rural life, and political mobilization.

This chapter will survey Mexican crime fiction during the middle decades of the twentieth century on the assumption that it can be a productive source to understand society and, broadly defined, politics. It will argue that, despite great differences in their styles and themes, these narratives illustrate the critical engagement of Mexican readers with the state, particularly in relation to its inability to provide justice and reach the truth through police and judicial investigations. Furthermore, I will venture that this literature, along with the police news in newspapers, describes better than any other cultural text the rules and possibilities of reality facing the inhabitants of the rapidly expanding urban centers of Mexico during these years. Crime was real, and crime fiction, better than any other scientific or literary field of knowledge, laid out the coordinates that readers had to follow in order to navigate that complex life-world.

Some of this will sound familiar: crime fiction also helped readers navigate modernization and contributed to the creation of critical publics in other countries (Herzog 2009, p. 6). Mexican writers drew from an international repertoire of topics, narrative structures, and characters. It might even be argued that they contributed nothing substantial to the canon of the genre—although this is difficult to fully prove: none of the secondary literature on Europe and the United States cited in this chapter bother to mention Latin America. Yet the Mexican case is unique and commonly held ideas concerning it are worth revising because it emerged in a context in which the legal resolution of a crime could not be assumed to take place after the detective revealed the truth. The underlying assumption of the genre, even in the hard-boiled mode, was that the truth led to punishment, and that the police and the judiciary were honorable and predictable. In Mexico, the opposite had to be assumed for a story to be plausible. Mexican writers inverted the moral distinctions at the heart of crime fiction, adopting, in some outstanding examples, the perspective of criminals, or of detectives who were also criminals. Thus, the texts discussed in the following essay had two parallel plots: a detection plot in which the conventional pursuit of the truth was centered on the detective, and a moral plot, in which the relations between characters often explained the murder that had occurred and blurred the lines between criminal and detective.

After a brief critique of the scholarship on Mexican crime fiction, the first section of this essay will point to some theoretical references that can help bridge the established distinctions between high and low culture, literature and "objective" testimonies of social life. The second section discusses the police news of newspapers, as this source provided stories, settings, and editorial infrastructure to fiction writers, while also shaping the critical engagement of readers with impunity and violence. The importance of this connection is also highlighted in the third section, which delves into the material conditions of the writing and distribution of crime fiction. Editors who knew the rules of the genre educated readers and writers, yet their single-minded devotion to the genre was constantly challenged by lack of funds. Section IV uses some examples to illustrate how these writers defined reality using shared ideas about crime, the short-comings of the Mexican state, and the right of private individuals to know the truth and, if necessary, administer justice through extrajudicial means. Finally, section V examines the question of Americanization through detective fiction, showing that the process was more than a passive adoption of U.S. cultural models and was in fact part of an undercurrent of political dissent that defied the apparent political stability of those years.

I. Reading Crime Fiction as History

Studies of crime fiction in Mexico, and, to a great extent, in Latin America, have focused on the renewal of the genre since the 1970s in the context of increasingly authoritar-ian political regimes. In Mexico, the bloody 1968 repression of a student movement in the capital signaled the extent to which the regime, in its quest to maintain political control, would deploy violence against and deny justice to citizens. The *neopoliciaco* literature that emerged at this time exemplified the politically committed, conspiracy-centered tone and narrative resources that became the object of most of the scholar-ship thereafter. The tough detectives of those late novels were clearly modeled after those found in the U.S. hard-boiled novels of Chandler, Hammett, and others, leading scholars to deem earlier works, inspired by classics like Christie or Conan Doyle, as of lesser political interest (Stavans 1997; Braham 2004; Close 2008; Torres 2003; Jacovkis 2013, pp. 116–17). The writers who preceded the *neopoliciaco*, emerging mostly in the 1940s, were pioneers perhaps, but little more in terms of literary accomplishments, dil-ettantes in contrast with the prestigious incursions into the genre by contemporaneous Argentine authors like Jorge Luis Borges (Jacovkis 2013, pp. 116–17; Monsiváis 1998). The first novel-length work in this genre, and probably the most accomplished, was *Ensayo de un crimen*, by Rodolfo Usigli. It was published in 1944 and ignored for decades, with its author achieving recognition only for his plays. The 1955 film by Luis Buñuel based on the book was more successful, although it did not meet with Usigli's approval, focus-ing as it did on psychological themes that were closer to Buñuel's surrealism.

Recent Mexican scholarship has nevertheless examined early crime fiction as more than a derivative exercise, a simple forerunner to the truly original *neopoliciaco*. Rodríguez Lozano, for example, proposes a strong continuity in Mexican production within the genre, from its beginnings until Rafael Bernal's *El complot mongol* (1969) became the paradigm for subsequent noir production. The genre was always on the margins of the literary canon despite (or perhaps because of) its ability to attract numerous readers and critically refer to social life and politics (Rodríguez Lozano 2008, pp. 5–6). Although he criticizes the imitative tendencies of the early stories, Torres documents the diverse origins of the genre in terms of themes, venues, and authors' national origins and influences, pointing to a variety of publications that in some cases left few traces for posterity (Torres 2003, pp. 23, 25, 26, 71). Author-centered notions of originality nevertheless continue to burden our contemporary reading—even though, as in Japan, Mexican authors of the first half of the twentieth century did not see influence as marking inferiority: they inhabited a cosmopolitan trade in which similarities to U.S. or European authors were the product of a shared, globally modern present (Kawana 2008, p. 19).

Literary readings of the detective novel run the risk of neglecting the rich dialogue between narratives and life while stressing influence as the main form of intertextuality. Yet novels and short stories in Mexico, just as in France and Argentina, engaged readers and assumed their familiarity with local crime stories and the dangerous spaces of their cities (Kalifa 1995, pp. 107, 270, 276; Caimari 2012). That engagement was possible not only because of crime fiction's low cost—in terms of both its cheap printing and its rapid distribution—but also because its predictable architecture and use of stereotypes facilitated writing and reading (Mandel 1984). The dialogic character of crime fiction is often summarized as a cycle of guilt and restoration of moral order: readers approach these novels expecting to be titillated by transgressions, and then to have their guilt assuaged by a resolution in which the criminal is inevitably punished (Auden 1948). Yet a strictly moral understanding of crime fiction, particularly detective and hard-boiled stories, implies a reliable sequence of crime and punishment, thus neglecting the various ways in which readers connected stories with their knowledge about actual crime and police and judicial institutions. While the moral dimension of crime fiction is a necessary axis for analysis, we should keep in mind that, in Mexico, the genre drew its popularity and impact from the fact that, along with daily journalism, it was based on a critical and textured understanding of the actual relations between crime and punishment. In Weimar Germany, a similar understanding of reality led to texts that demonstrated the blurry lines between science and fiction, criminal and noncriminal, in what Herzog calls a "criminalistics fantasy" (Herzog 2009, p. 3). In Mexico, however, the genre challenged official justice but was pragmatic at the same time: it created reality, articulating the rules that gave coherence to life—a particularly useful operation in a rapidly changing urban societies (Boltanski 2012; Close 2008, p. 21; Ruth 1996).

Another common defect of strictly literary approaches to crime fiction is the implicit assumption that the genre lacked the ability to formulate and follow its own theory—that it was a source of rather spasmodic satisfaction. In fact, the genre provoked an abundance of how-to and normative texts meant to guide anyone with the opportunity to write a good tale (Van Dine 1939; Chandler 1988; Haycraft 1946). Mexican writers and editors extracted narrative models from other authors, notably Christie and Conan Doyle, and used them to build a normative framework that was the basis of critical exercises in the form of anthologies for established writers and monetary prizes for new authors (Bermúdez 1955). That framework was useful in facilitating the writing of stories that stuck to the basic demands of suspense, style, and fair play that required that the writer not mislead the readers and give them enough information to solve the case just before the resolution. The social implications of murder were a more important focus for later, hard-boiled narratives. In these, punishment did not automatically follow the discovery of the criminal, and the detective was not just an objective intelligence full of common sense and scientific insight, like Auguste Dupin or Sherlock Holmes, but a complex hero who solved stories and engaged with clients and women out of a sense of honor, sometimes at his own expense. Suspects had to be closer to the real world of crime, and their motivations had to respond to interests and desires that would not be so different from those of readers. Only then could crime fiction hope to be plausible. The critical and dialogic possibilities of crime fiction as a form of the novel were realized through those bitter, sometimes nostalgic heroes (Chandler 1988; Bakhtin 1981, pp. 10, 36).

Mexican readers and writers were aware of a theory behind detective and noir stories. Some authors were quite normative (Bermúdez 1987). Yet the Mexican production also adapted to local conditions of impunity, corruption, and violence to an extent that challenged some of the most cherished assumptions of narratives from countries where those conditions were not so problematic. This adaptation was the specificity and the strength of the genre in Mexico, what allowed it to incorporate multiple voices while delineating the rules of reality—what was possible in life and fiction, and how best to deal with it.

II. *Nota Roja* and Literature

The most important nexus of Mexican crime fiction and the reality it helped build was the police section of newspapers. Novels constantly referred to the *nota roja*—the graphic, often-moralistic, yet engaging national version of yellow journalism. Newspapers like *La Prensa*, founded in 1929, focused almost exclusively on crime news. They reached the largest audiences in the Mexican press, with diverse readerships in terms of class, age, and gender. In contrast with more established media, *nota roja* newspapers addressed readers at both an emotional and an intellectual level. Because of their large sales, *nota roja* newspapers enjoyed, at least during their golden age in the 1930s and 1940s, a relative autonomy from the government, which was otherwise able to influence mainstream newspapers through a variety of economic incentives (Monsiváis 2009; Piccato 2014a). Crime fiction had strong material links to *nota roja*: authors like Antonio Helú and José Martínez de la Vega had been journalists, several fictional detectives were reporters, and others read the newspapers as a means of solving mysteries. In fact, the longest and probably most popular series of crime stories were the adventures of detective-journalist Chucho Cárdenas, by Leo D'Olmo, published in the Sunday comics section of *La Prensa* between 1946 and 1955.

The authority of the *nota roja* to condense reality was a premise of fiction narratives. In contrast with police reports or judicial sentences, its pages were comprehensive: everything, including events that the state did not deem criminal, was presented there; even police corruption or brutality were alluded between the lines of articles, and sometimes were referenced in explicit terms. Letters from readers and opinion pieces reinforced the critical tone. In the case of *La Prensa*, its support for the reestablishment of the death penalty expressed not only the moral indignation that permeated coverage of some infamous cases (Meade 2005), but also readers' skepticism toward state-administered punishment. These feelings were supported by the thorough, sometimes intrusive work of *nota roja* reporters (Téllez Vargas & Garmabella 1982). Newspapers invited readers to get involved in the resolution of cases, seeking their hypotheses about mysterious events and their help in the capture of fugitives. In order to do the latter, coverage of the most famous cases included a diversity of details, interviews, and illustrations, so as to provide readers with the same information available to police detectives.

In crime fiction, *nota roja* reporting provided a coded reference to facts: it worked as a synecdoche for the gritty urban life, its dangers and colorful characters; it contained the information used by characters to solve crimes; and it served as a reminder of the influence of public opinion on matters of justice. In Usigli's *Ensayo de un crimen*, the main character, Roberto de la Cruz, decides to commit a crime that will be a work of art after verifying the vulgarity of the routine murders presented in the police news of his morning paper (Usigli 1986, pp. 7–8). The rest of the novel presents his struggle to achieve the proper public recognition for his creations. To his exasperation, de la Cruz realizes that the press fails to acknowledge the artistry of his attempts yet finds consolation in his personal pursuit of "the truth, the reality of a crime" (Usigli 1986, p. 116). In fact, Usigli's novel and other crime stories of the period were inspired by famous cases reported by the press and socialized, as in France, in the form of popular memory of famous crimes (Kalifa 1995, p. 278). In contrast with the French case, however, this function of the police news did not contribute to the creation of a passive audience but encouraged the development of a critical public that challenged the divides between reporter, detective, and reader.

One effect of the sensationalist and critical coverage of the *nota roja*, and further evidence of crime fiction's intricate relationship with Mexican life, was the emergence of murderers as authors of their own stories. Often lacking education, some murder suspects were nevertheless capable of both generating the events at the center of journalistic coverage and clarifying them for the public through their confessions. In some cases, particularly those involving women, suspects did not avoid arrest but set out to explain their reasons as soon as journalists, on behalf of publics fascinated by female criminality, could interview them (Piccato 2014b; Piccato 2009; see a similar case in Kawana 2008, ch. 2). Judges often granted reporters permission to meet with suspects in their cells. *La Prensa* reproduced on its front page a facsimile of the confession (later disavowed) of Pedro Gallegos, himself the inspiration for a minor character in Usigli's novel (*La Prensa*, 4 March 1932, p. 5; 20 March 1932, p. 1). This was, in part, an effect of the habits of police investigators: physical evidence was seldom the key to solving cases, but confessions were universally regarded as the best proof of guilt. In order to extract confessions, police agents used torture and the threat of extrajudicial execution; the latter was applied against Gallegos and other suspects. Although rarely presented in book form, the life stories of Mexican criminals reproduced in the *nota roja* shared many features with similar texts in Europe and the United States as cultural productions in which subjectivity acquired public resonance thanks to transgression (Houlbrook 2013).

The most famous murderer of the century, Gregorio "Goyo" Cárdenas, was luckier than Gallegos, perhaps because he confessed and, rather than recanting, provided multiple opportunities for newspapers to explain and interpret his actions—the disturbing killing and carrying out of sexual violence against four women that cost him four decades of prison. Psychologists, reporters, and writers produced a large number of explanations for his deviance, but Cárdenas was able to call attention to his own explanations and narrative of redemption (Meade 2005; Monsiváis 2009; Ríos Molina 2010). Political authorities tried to censor *nota roja* newspapers' coverage, alleging that they were making heroes out of criminals (Piccato 2014a). It was to no avail, however: the journalistic genre not only was commercially successful but also provided the structure for broadly established perceptions of reality, the same structure that shaped the verisimilitude and narrative devices of Mexican crime fiction.

III. The Creation of Readers and Authors

Besides some isolated short stories and novels, crime fiction emerged in Mexico through cheap paperbacks, most of them translations of foreign titles, and domestic magazines devoted to the genre. A key figure on both accounts was Antonio Helú (1900–1972). He had written some detective fiction since the 1920s, but in 1946 he founded the Club de la Calle Morgue along with other admirers of Poe and Chesterton. That same year Helú created the Mexican subsidiary of *Ellery Queen's Mystery Magazine* (1944), *Selecciones Policiacas y de Misterio*. The magazine started mostly with translations of foreign short stories but soon began to introduce Spanish-writing authors like Helú himself. The enterprise was not very profitable, but Helú managed to keep it alive for decades and to turn it into the most important publication in the genre in Mexico, eventually produced under the seal of Editorial Novaro, owned by a former manager at *La Prensa*. Another title, *Aventura y Misterio*, was established in 1956, and printed 20,000 biweekly copies of just over 100 pages. These magazines had few ads; although they advertised subscription prices, they probably sold single copies in kiosks and bookstores. To complement his meager earnings as editor and author, Helú wrote scripts and directed several movies.

Selecciones was not about profit, though. In a letter to F. Dannay, editor of *Ellery Queen's*, Helú stated the goal of the Club de la Calle Morgue as follows: "Few are those that in our country write detective fiction. We want many more writers of this 'genre,' and many more readers."[1] Stories were preceded by short introductions that helped the reader achieve a pleasurable experience: foreign authors were situated in terms of their influence, Mexican writers introduced with some information about their day jobs or previous publications, and advice imparted on the strategies to follow during the reading of the story. To situate Mexican authors, editors linked them to foreign models: María Elvira Bermúdez, for example, was compared with Christie and Dorothy Sayers (*Selecciones Policiacas y de Misterio*, January 1950, p. 6), rather than highlighting her national importance as the first female author in the country, a fact that was stressed when her work was republished in the 1980s (Bermúdez 1985). These magazines assumed each story would be read independently and at its own pace, as titles were not interconnected or printed in a specific sequence.

Creating good readers also involved stimulating new authors. *Selecciones* and *Aventura y Misterio* published local writers, some recognized in other genres, but most of them new. To encourage them, the latter publication offered monetary awards to the best two stories of each issue and limited itself to publishing originals in Spanish. The brief introductions to each story also provide some glimpses into the editorial process: the rejection of manuscripts from young authors always came with advice, and their second attempt could be more successful.

With few exceptions, Mexican authors of the crime genre were not full-time writers. While Helú and Usigli engaged in diverse literary activities, others were journalists (Martínez de la Vega), judicial bureaucrats (Bermúdez), diplomats (Bernal), chemists (Roberto Cruzpiñón), actors (Ulaulume), math teachers (E. Varona, an ironic pseudonym for a female writer), or movie directors (Juan Bustillo Oro). Thus, unlike the foreign luminaries, they did not see their engagement with the genre as a job but as a source of pleasure, a vehicle to express aesthetic ideas (Irwin 2002). The exception might be the author of the adventures of Chucho Cárdenas. Nothing is known about Leo D'Olmo, leading the few scholars who have looked at these novels to believe that it was a pseudonym used by several authors. Published next to the comic strips in *La Prensa*, these stories had no literary aspirations. Their authorship offered little prestige, although it may have provided a steady income.

While Mexican authors were conscious of the tropes and stereotypes of detective fiction, some writers deployed them in the form of parody, using fictional detectives to allude to the precarious, almost amateur status of the writers themselves: in the adventures of Péter Pérez, by Martínez de la Vega, the sleuth is an impoverished bungler who solves cases with outrageous theories and methods yet imitates Sherlock Holmes's mannerisms: donning pipe and cap, whistling instead of playing the violin. Much of the humorous effect of de la Vega's stories came from the observation that the objective and precise methods of the classic detectives made no sense in Mexico because of the weaknesses of its real detectives and cops.

IV. The Construction of Reality

The ineptitude of the police and the unreliability of the justice system, as documented daily by crime news, constituted the basic fact of reality that provided unity to Mexican crime fiction—and a clear contrast with its foreign models. While Martínez de la Vega made fun of the mere idea of a Mexican detective, other authors created serious detectives who acted outside and often in opposition to the police, and who subverted the official rules of justice. Few stories had an actual policeman as protagonist.

The best example of this framework is found in the adventures of Chucho Cárdenas. Chucho is a journalist who works for a newspaper that is easy to identify with *La Prensa* itself. He solves cases in amicable but pointed confrontation with the official police investigator, Inspector Cifuentes—a silly character who only thinks about jailing the first suspect he can catch. Chucho is a man of modest means and limited education, but he uses common sense and an aptitude for navigating the ways of modern life, from travel to international intrigue, to solve his cases. He distinguishes himself by his ability to mobilize the power of public opinion to fight crime, but also to expose the mistakes of the state.

In the adventures of Chucho Cárdenas and in those of Máximo Roldán, Helú's character, fictional Mexican detectives also make sure justice is served—if necessary, outside the established channels of the law. In "El fistol de la corbata," first published in 1928, Roldán lets the murderess escape because he thinks her crime was justified by the past abuse inflicted on her by the victim (Helú 1998). Chucho Cárdenas also protects suspects, either women or their relatives, who kill in defense of their honor, and in one story sets up a situation that leads an accomplice of the seducer (and murder victim) to be killed by the trigger-happy police (D'Olmo 1954). Unlike the classics of the genre, Mexican crime fiction does not situate punishment as the inevitable product of the truth. In her essays about the rules of the genre, Bermúdez adopted an orthodox view of the author's obligation toward the reader and the genre (fundamentally, the need to achieve justice at the end of the narrative), yet she also recognized that Mexicans distrusted "abstract justice and [feel] a bitter disdain toward the actions of concrete justice." After all, the poor fled from justice and the wealthy simply bought it (Bermúdez 1955, p. 15).

Detectives' reasons to solve crimes reveal the ambiguities that defined Mexican crime fiction: disinterested professionalism was never a plausible motivation for an official investigator. In real life, few police detectives had a reputation for success, and private detectives were uncommon, mostly serving corporations. The most famous private detective of those years, Valente Quintana, was a former policeman who had been accused of corruption and torture, and moved into private practice after being fired from the Mexico City police. A detective who followed the dictates of honor, like the type Chandler proposed, was not a good index of Mexican reality: Máximo Roldán solves his first case to get away from an accusation against himself; Chucho Cárdenas is inspired by compassion toward or desire to help other characters, or by rivalry with the police and other reporters; the amateur detectives in the stories by Bermúdez simply do it for the intellectual thrill (Bermúdez 1985).

Variations of these narratives in which the murderer sat at the center of the story did not depart from the critical view of Mexican justice presented in stories told from the point of view of detectives. In Usigli's *Ensayo de un crimen*, de la Cruz plans to kill several people of objectionable morality (a decadent aristocrat, a homosexual man, a prostitute), although his motivations are purely aesthetic. Recent criticism has interpreted this selection of victims as a reflection of the modernizing will of the postrevolutionary Mexican regime and its program to cleanse society of undesirables (Sánchez 2010). In the novel, however, de la Cruz, unbeknownst to him, fails to murder his intended victims and accidentally kills his own wife. Rather than a fantasy of state power, Usigli's novel is a reflection on the vagaries of public reputation within the framework of a state that is unable to allocate criminal responsibility. Usigli's indirect references to de Quincey's *Murder Considered as One of the Fine Arts* imply that the Romantic ethos of art for its own sake is being replaced by the preeminence of public recognition of the criminal-artist.

In "Cómo murió Charles Prague" (1960), by Juan Bustillo Oro, crime is also an instrument of art. In this story, set in 1920s Hollywood, the villain of a movie poisons the handsome star in order to have the script changed and become, for once, the winner—as the producer is keen to use the footage of the hero actually dying. The movie is a success, and artistic justice is done. Some time later, the killer confesses so he can be tried and perform in his last role, that of an actual villain in a trial, with the same professionalism that had characterized his work throughout his career (Bustillo Oro 1960). In other stories, detectives solve the case in front of an audience that integrates suspects and witnesses, and their findings are confirmed in dramatic fashion by the suspect's attempt to flee or by his or her confession. These scenes were necessary because a simple arrest by the Mexican police could never be interpreted as confirmation of guilt. Trials were equally inconclusive from the point of view of these narratives, particularly after the abolition of the jury system in Mexico City in 1929 (Piccato 2009).

The moral logic of murder became the key to the resolution of narratives centered on the criminal. Unlike modernist detective novels from Weimar Germany (Herzog 2009, pp. 9, 26–27), the criminal became the focus of the narrative because his or her behavior was rational in a way that Mexican readers could understand. As noted previously, many detective-centered narratives in Mexico focused the work of elucidation on the moral reasons for the crime, often justifying it, instead of concentrating on the standard work of detection through deduction and observation offered by the classics of the genre. As in U.S. gangster stories, the moral plot of Mexican narratives provided "lessons about success and failure" in a changing world—although in Mexico, the example was a fictional criminal. This practical use of the narratives of crime expressed a shared rejection, in both countries, of the positivist notion of "the criminal" as a natural type, as it challenged the broadly shared modern knowledge that the criminal was a rational, morally responsible individual, as normal as anyone else (Ruth 1996, pp. 3, 25).

V. MODERNIZATION, AMERICANIZATION, NATIONALISM

Crime fiction ignored the focus on national themes that defined the more prestigious novels and essays of the postrevolutionary period in Mexico. Unlike canonical works like Octavio Paz's *El laberinto de la soledad* (1950), crime writers did not seek to define

the characteristics of *lo mexicano*; they did not care much either about the rural solitude of *el verdadero México* that defined Juan Rulfo's books (*El llano en llamas* [1953];
Pedro Páramo [1955]). The books by Paz and Rulfo were published by the most prestigious press funded by the Mexican government, the Fondo de Cultura Económica. By
contrast, the Secretaría de Educación Pública issued popular editions of the novels by
Usigli and Bernal only in the 1980s. In general, crime fiction seems to have received no
government support during the middle decades of the century, a period of consolidation for Mexican literature.

Crime fiction avoided the philosophical or existential questions of Mexican high culture because it drew, with true modern faith, from foreign models. The structure and
tropes of its stories were in dialogue with the literatures of the United States, England,
France, and other countries where the genre was broadly disseminated. Mexican titles
were sold and read alongside foreign productions (Monsiváis 2009, p. 22; Monsiváis
1998, p. 13). The methods used by Mexican fictional detectives often invoked those
adopted by their international counterparts. Zozaya, the detective in some of Bermúdez's
stories, likes to read North American textbooks on forensic science and often uses psy-
choanalytical arguments (Bermúdez 1985; Bermúdez 1952). Mexican detectives have
fewer resources than their American counterparts, but use their intelligence: in "La
muerte aprende a cantar," published by Arturo Perucho in 1952, Lieutenant López tells
an Italian: "You do not know how cunning we the Indians here are. . . . We lack many of
the . . . devices that the Americans have to discover liars, and the money they have. But
we have a machine that does not work bad at all: this [pointing to his brain]" (Perucho
1952). The common sense of Mexican detectives did not buttress national identity: it
simply played out the moral dilemmas of modern life in the international field of crime
investigation.

Stories were often set in environments that referred to the new connections of Mexico
with the outside world. The domestic expressions of Fascism and Communism, and
the country's newly strengthened connections with the United States at the time of the
Second World War, became central themes in newspapers, newsreels, and other media.
Crime fiction often included foreign criminals or victims; some stories were set outside
Mexico, while others examined the obscure underside of the Cold War that was playing
out in Mexico. Bernal's *El complot mongol*, for example, is the story of Filiberto García,
an aged *pistolero* whose career has included killing people on the orders of politicians
as well as engaging in his own illegal businesses. Already uncomfortable in a new age
in which his trade is not so valuable, he is ordered to investigate a foreign conspiracy.
Instead, he ends up unraveling the murder of the woman he loves and taking justice
into his own hands. Part detective story (like Bernal's early production in the genre;
see Bernal 1946a; Bernal 1946b), part international intrigue, the novel is populated by
foreign agents and Chinese immigrants: "What did they put in my drink that I am
seeing only foreigners!" exclaims García at one point (Bernal 1969, p. 40). The book
marks the end of the foundational era of the genre in Mexico and sets up the tone for
later productions: common sense is not enough to solve the puzzle of crime, because,
ultimately, power is always behind it; violence dissolves the intelligence that Mexican

detectives had optimistically applied to their quests. A basic moral certainty, however, remains: murder can take the place of official justice.

International themes in Mexican crime fiction during this period display the ambivalence of Mexican readers and authors toward the country's new place in the world. "Sin novedad en Berlín," by Raymundo Quiroz Mendoza, for example, takes place in postwar Berlin, and features an American detective (who is also a journalist) and members of the Russian military. The story centers on the imagined death of Hitler, who has survived 1945 thanks to a secret society and turns out to have been not such a bad guy after all (Quiroz Mendoza 1954). An early story by the same author placed international characters, including a bullfighter, in a cosmopolitan, upper-class setting of Mexico City (Quiroz Mendoza 1950). Similarly, the adventures of Chucho Cárdenas often involve foreign plots and characters. Chucho moves nimbly in that cosmopolitan world, traveling and interacting with foreign policemen. He also understands the complexities of modern criminals' goals and methods (espionage, sabotage, drug trafficking) much better than the simple-minded Mexican police. The prestige of the foreign is obvious. Enrique Gual, a Spanish author and art critic, published a few very cosmopolitan crime novels in Mexico. In *El caso de la formula española*, the real detective is a journalist who travels broadly, is married to a woman from the United States, and makes fun of the police inspector by saying: "What do you know about Europe! . . . You have not traveled further than Texcoco" (Gual 1947, p. 40).

In contrast with European crime fiction, the appearance of the international gang of criminals as new denizens of the Mexican crime fiction underworld is not portrayed as a result of police progress or a more intense engagement with international affairs (Knepper & Azzopardi, 2011), but as a sad reflection of Mexican cops' backwardness and victims' naïveté. Swindlers and other varieties of crooks exploit their exotic accents. International police collaboration attracted real Mexican detectives (Garmabella 2007) and figured prominently in a few of Chucho Cárdenas's stories. But there was only one short step between cosmopolitan charm and xenophobic or racist views, which were often voiced against Chinese, French, Japanese, U.S., and German nationals, as well as a mishmash of South American crooks. In "Aquí está el criminal," all suspects and victims are U.S. nationals enjoying themselves in a Mexican beach resort. Chucho's moral reasoning toward a murder that occurs among them is emblematic: "It would have been worse if they had come to kill Mexicans. As long as the issue is between them, even if loss of human life is always regrettable, the lesser of two evils is preferable!" (D'Olmo 1953, p. 18). In other stories, Mexicans complain about the excessive deference and lack of proper vigilance toward foreigners visiting the country (D'Olmo n.d.a., p. 23; D'Olmo 1988).

Sophisticated foreign criminals and witty (though fictional) Mexican detectives inhabited a cosmopolitan world that was increasingly familiar to readers. Since the early forties, consumer culture, technology, and other manifestations of imported modernization had been increasingly prominent in the media (Moreno 2003; Vaughan 2015) and found a reflection in the elegant foreign criminals of fiction. In the United States according to David Ruth, the underworld "dramatized" a new "consumption-oriented urban society" (1996, p. 2; see also Wood & Knepper 2014, p. 347). Consumption was prominent in many Mexican crime stories too, but the weakness of the justice system there set a limit to any illusion of fulfillment. Theft was often a complement of morally justifiable murder and just as often went unpunished (Bustillo Oro 1951; Helú 1998). In a more conservative variation of these concerns, the ultimate guarantee of life and property in the United States is absent in the crime fiction of Mexico: in D'Olmo's stories, U.S. characters mock the Mexican judiciary because it lacks the death penalty—a fact that Inspector Cifuentes often regrets (D'Olmo 1988), and that in real life *La Prensa* lamented in editorials (Meade 2005). Stories set in the United States worked as an inverted mirror of the Mexican justice system, one in which punishment was harsh but fair. In "La cámara de la muerte," a Mexican immigrant in Texas who happens to be a friend of Chucho's is about to be executed for a crime he did not commit. The murderer turns out to be an American lawyer, and Chucho rescues his friend in dramatic fashion, with the help of the Texas governor—a "man of conscience" who loses sleep over the rare execution in the state and is ready to run to the prison in order to save an innocent man (D'Olmo n.d.b.; D'Olmo n.d.c.). Contemporary ironies aside, the story contrasts the U.S. concerns about due process with the carelessness of Mexican authorities. The uncertain link between truth and punishment inspired crime narratives in which resolution was only as certain as the moral perspective of readers and writers.

CONCLUSIONS

By the late 1960s crime stories were quickly losing the appeal that had driven many readers and new authors to the genre. Politics, as *El complot mongol* all but spelled out, had become an exercise of authoritarian violence and impunity. Meanwhile, a growing middle class no longer saw modernity as a promise of mobility and democracy. The massacre of student protesters on 2 October 1968 was a crime of state that no amount of detective common sense or journalistic courage could clarify. While the justice system continued to be unreliable and police detectives continued to brutally seek confessions, individualistic *pistoleros* gave way to the use of military might and internal spying by the regime. The rules of reality were changing in such a way that made the *nota roja* a poorer combination of visual gore and disingenuous government support (Monsiváis 2009; Padilla & Walker 2013; Walker 2013).

The crime genre evolved toward the gritty social critique of *neopoliciaco*, a trend that in Mexico was heralded by the works of Paco Ignacio Taibo II. The hard-boiled inspiration of Chandler, Hammett, Himes, and others now made any references to the placid detective inquiries of Christie, Conan Doyle, and Sayers an impossible literary task. Taibo became an icon for a university-educated left that embraced democracy and the rule of law but never quite shed its belief in the redemptive power of violence— revolutionary in politics, heroic in the quixotic sleuthing of Taibo's main character (Taibo 1977; Braham 2004; Close 2008, p. 31; Rodríguez Lozano 2008). Parallel to the retro embrace of a noir aesthetic, other writers began to draw more systematically from real life, subordinating the structure of mystery, investigation, and resolution to a realistic effort to document the brutality and impunity that characterized crime in everyday life (Leñero 1988; Taibo & Ronquillo 1992; Piazza 1983). In recent years, bookstores and kiosks have sold large numbers of true crime books about the exploits of drug traffickers. Mostly written by journalists, these narratives ignore the rules of crime fiction, as the identity of killers is usually known without much need of investigation, and that of their numerous victims is of little import. Élmer Mendoza, however, has managed to preserve the structure and many of the tropes of the hard-boiled tradition. Even though his stories are set in his home state of Sinaloa and necessarily incorporate the violence of drug traffickers and corrupt officials, his detective, El Zurdo Mendieta, is a police agent who tries to make sense of mysteries out of an anachronistic sense of honor. Aware of the impossibility of obtaining truth and justice from institutions in a world where murder has become natural because of its frequency and impunity, Mendieta echoes the tradition of his earlier Mexican predecessors by allowing punishment to be executed outside the law (Mendoza 2008; Mendoza 2012).

Reality and imagination continue to combine in changing and mutually productive ways in Mexican crime fiction. While today, life is defined by the scale of *narco* violence, continuities with the middle decades of the twentieth century are clear in the inability of the state to reveal the truth and punish the guilty. Back then, the intellectual pleasure of solving a mystery or understanding the killer's mind was a legitimate reason to consume and contribute to the genre. Urban life presented a set of puzzles that individual common sense could solve when combined with small doses of nationalism and cosmopolitanism, and a large amount of distrust toward the police. There was a moral, if not legal, resolution to each case. Reading those early stories and novels today provides a unique way to understand the ethos of an era of modernization when the right to justice and the truth was yet to be guaranteed to Mexicans. Not much has changed in that regard, yet fiction no longer offers any solace.

NOTE

1. Antonio Helú to Frederic Dannay, Mexico City, 11 October 1946, Frederic Dannay Papers, Columbia University Libraries, New York.

REFERENCES

Auden, W. H. 1948. "The Guilty Vicarage." *Harper's Magazine*, May: 406–12.

Bakhtin, M. M. 1981. *The Dialogic Imagination: Four Essays*. Austin: University of Texas Press.

Bermúdez, María Elvira. 1952. "Crimen Para Inocentes." *Selecciones Policiacas y de Misterio* 126: 62–98.

Bermúdez, María Elvira. 1955. *Los Mejores Cuentos Policíacos Mexicanos*. Mexico City: Libro-Mex.

Bermúdez, María Elvira. 1985. *Muerte a la Zaga*. Tlahuapan, Puebla, Mexico: Premià.

Bermúdez, María Elvira. 1987. *Cuento Policiaco Mexicano, Breve Antología*. Mexico City: UNAM/Coordinación de Difusión Cultura.Dirección de Literatura.

Bernal, Rafael. 1946a. *Tres Novelas Policiacas*. Mexico City: Jus.

Bernal, Rafael. 1946b. *Un Muerto en la Tumba*. Mexico City: Jus.

Bernal, Rafael. 1969. *El Complot Mongol*. Mexico City: Joaquín Mortiz.

Boltanski, Luc. 2012. *Enigmes et Complots: Une Enquête à Propos D'enquêtes*. Paris: Gallimard.

Braham, Persephone. 2004. *Crimes Against the State, Crimes Against Persons : Detective Fiction in Cuba and Mexico*. Minneapolis: University of Minnesota Press.

Bustillo Oro, Juan. 1951. "Apuesta Al Crimen." *Selecciones Policiacas y de Misterio* 92: 44–69.

Bustillo Oro. 1960. "Cómo Murió Charles Prague." *Selecciones Policiacas y de Misterio* 175: 36–45.

Caimari, Lila. 2012. *Mientras la Ciudad Duerme: Pistoleros, Policías y Periodistas en Buenos Aires, 1920-1945*. Buenos Aires: Siglo Veintiuno Editores.

Chandler, Raymond. 1988. *The Simple Art of Murder*. New York: Vintage Books.

Close, Glen S. 2008. *Contemporary Hispanic Crime Fiction: A Ttransatlantic Discourse on Urban Violence*. New York: Palgrave Macmillan.

D'Olmo, Leo. n.d.a. *Sangre y Diamantes: Aventuras de Chucho Cárdenas*. Mexico City: La Prensa.

D'Olmo, Leo. n.d.b. *La Cámara de la Muerte. Una Aventura de Chucho Cárdenas el Detective-Reportero Mexicano. Novela Original de Leo D'Olmo Escrita Especialmente Para La Prensa*. Mexico City: La Prensa.

D'Olmo, Leo. n.d.c. *Horas de Agonía (Final de "La Cámara de La Muerte"). Una Aventura de Chucho Cárdenas. Novela Original de Leo D'Olmo. Escrita Especialmetne Para La Prensa*. Mexico City: La Prensa.

D'Olmo, Leo. 1953. *Aquí Está El Criminal*. Mexico City: La Prensa.

D'Olmo, Leo. 1954. *¿Quién Mató a Rafael?* Mexico City: La Prensa.

D'Olmo, Leo. 1988. *Aventuras de Chucho Cárdenas*. Mexico City: Populibros La Prensa.

Garmabella, José Ramón. 2007. *El Criminólogo: Los Casos Más Importantes del Dr. Quiróz Cuarón*. Mexico City: Debolsillo.

Gual, Enrique. 1947. *El Caso de la Fórmula Española*. Mexico City: Editorial Albatros-Libros y revistas.

Haycraft, Howard. 1946. *The Art of the Mystery Story: A Collection of Critical Essays, Edited, and with a Commentary*. New York: Simon and Schuster.

Helú, Antonio. 1998. *La obligación de asesinar: Novelas y cuentos policiacos*. Mexico City: M. A. Porrúa.

Herzog, Todd. 2009. *Crime Stories: Criminalistic Fantasy and the Culture of Crisis in Weimar Germany*. New York: Berghahn Books.

Houlbrook, Matt. 2013. "Commodifying the Self Within: Ghosts, Libels, and the Crook Life Story in Interwar Britain." *Journal of Modern History* 85 (2): 321–63.

Irwin, J. T. 2002. "Beating the Boss: Cain's Double Indemnity." *American Literary History* 14 (2): 255–83.

Jacovkis, Natalia. 2013. "Latin American Crime Fiction." In *Crime and Detective Fiction*, ed. Rebecca Martin, 115–31. Ipswich, MA: Salem Press, Grey House Publishing.

Kalifa, Dominique. 1995. *L'encre et Le Sang: Récits de Crimes et Société À La Belle Epoque*. Paris: Fayard.

Kawana, Sari. 2008. *Murder Most Modern: Detective Fiction and Japanese Culture.* Minneapolis: University of Minnesota Press.

Knepper, Paul, & Jacqueline Azzopardi. 2011. "International Crime in the Interwar Period: A View from the Edge." *Crime, Law and Social Change* 56 (4): 407–19.

Leñero, Vicente. 1988. *Asesinato: El Doble Crimen de Los Flores Muñoz.* Mexico: Plaza y Janés.

Mandel, Ernest. 1984. *Delightful Murder: A Social History of the Crime Story.* Minneapolis: University of Minnesota Press.

Meade, Everard Kidder. 2005. "Anatomies of Justice and Chaos: Capital Punishment and the Public in Mexico, 1917–1945." Ph.D. diss., University of Chicago.

Mendoza, Élmer. 2008. *Balas de Plata.* Barcelona: Tusquets Editores.

Mendoza. 2012. *Nombre de Perro.* Mexico City: Tusquets.

Monsiváis, Carlos. 1998. "Prólogo." In *La Obligación de Asesinar: Novelas y Cuentos Policiacos,* ed. Antonio Helú, XX–XX. Mexico City: M. A. Porrúa.

Monsiváis. 2009. *Los Mil y un Velorios: Crónica de la Nota Roja en México,* 2nd ed. Mexico City: Asociación Nacional del Libro.

Moreno, Julio. 2003. *Yankee Don't Go Home! Mexican Nationalism, American Business Culture, and the Shaping of Modern Mexico, 1920–1950.* Chapel Hill: University of North Carolina Press.

Padilla, Tanalís, & Louise E. Walker. 2013. "In the Archives: History and Politics." *Journal of Iberian and Latin American Research* 19 (1): 1–10.

Perucho, Arturo. 1952. "La Muerte Aprende a Cantar." *Selecciones Policiacas y de Misterio* 117: 88–117.

Piazza, Luis Guillermo. 1983. *Los Cómplices.* Mexico City: Diana.

Piccato, Pablo. 2009. "The Girl Who Killed a Senator: Femininity and the Public Sphere in Post-Revolutionary Mexico." In *True Stories of Crime in Modern Mexico,* ed. Robert Buffington & Pablo Piccato, 128–53. Albuquerque: University of New Mexico Press.

Piccato, Pablo. 2014a. "Murders of Nota Roja: Truth and Justice in Mexican Crime News." *Past and Present* 223 (1): 195–231.

Piccato, Pablo. 2014b. "Pistoleros, Ley Fuga, and Uncertainty in Public Debates about Murder in Twentieth- Century Mexico." In *Dictablanda: Politics, Work, and Culture in Mexico, 1938–1968,* ed. Paul Gillingham & Benjamin Smith, 321–41. Durham, NC: Duke University Press.

Quiroz Mendoza, Raymundo. 1950. "Motolinía Habla de Toros." *Selecciones Policiacas y de Misterio* 74, April: 5–58.

Quiroz Mendoza, Raymundo. 1954. "Sin Novedad En Berlín." *Selecciones Policiacas y de Misterio* 9, March: 57–98.

Ríos Molina, Andrés. 2010. *Memorias de Un Loco Anormal: El Caso de Goyo Cárdenas.* Mexico City: Editorial Debate.

Rodríguez Lozano, Miguel G. 2008. *Pistas Del Relato Policial En México Somera Expedición.* México City: Universidad Nacional Autónoma de México (UNAM), Instituto de Investigaciones Filológicas.

Ruth, David E. 1996. *Inventing the Public Enemy: The Gangster in American Culture, 1918–1934.* Chicago: University of Chicago Press.

Sánchez, Fernando Fabio. 2010. *Artful Assassins: Murder as Art in Modern Mexico.* Nashville, TN: Vanderbilt University Press.

Stavans, Ilan. 1997. *Antiheroes.* Madison, NJ: Fairleigh Dickinson University Press.

Taibo, Paco Ignacio. 1977. *Cosa Fácil.* Barcelona: Planeta.

Taibo, Paco Ignacio, & Víctor Ronquillo. 1992. *El Caso Molinet*. México City: Difusion Editorial.

Téllez Vargas, Eduardo, & José Ramón Garmabella. 1982. *¡Reportero de Policía!: El Güero Téllez*. Mexico City: Ediciones Océano.

Torres, Vicente Francisco. 2003. *Muertos de Papel: Un Paseo Por La Narrativa Policial Mexicana*. Mexico City: CNCA/Sello Bermejo.

Usigli, Rodolfo. 1986. *Ensayo de Un Crimen*. Mexico City: Secretaría de Educación Pública.

Van Dine, S.S. 1939. "Twenty Rules for Writing Detective Stories." In *The Winter Murder Case: A Philo Vance Story*, ed. S. S. Van Dine, 163–74. New York: Charles Scribner's Sons.

Vaughan, Mary Kay. 2015. *Portrait of a Young Painter: Pepe Zúñiga and Mexico City's Rebel Generation*. Durham, NC: Duke University Press.

Walker, Louise E. 2013. *Waking from the Dream: Mexico's Middle Classes after 1968*. Stanford, CA: Stanford University Press.

Wood, John Carter, & Paul Knepper. 2014. "Crime Stories: Criminality, Policing and the Press in Inter-War European and Transatlantic Perspectives." *Media History* 20 (4): 345–51.

PART FIVE

RISE OF CRIMINOLOGY

....

CHAPTER 19

THE RISE OF CRIMINOLOGY IN ITS HISTORICAL CONTEXT

....

PIETER SPIERENBURG

INTRODUCTION

....

AT the beginning of the *fin de siècle* the Hungarian writer Max Nordau laid the finishing touch to a work that was to be published in two volumes in German in 1892–93. This conservative Jewish intellectual, who easily lumped together impressionist painting and gay subcultures as equally decadent, wanted to alert his contemporaries to a danger of which they were seemingly unaware. Nordau was satisfied with the result. Admittedly, much had been written already about degenerates such as criminals, prostitutes, anarchists, and lunatics, but many failed to realize that similar types were active in the otherwise exalted realm of art and literature. To underline the relationship between all specimens of the lowest segment of humanity, Nordau dedicated his book to the famous criminologist Cesare Lombroso, who was incidentally also Jewish (van der Laarse in Laarse et al. 1998, pp. 161–88; Rafter 2009, pp. 120–21). In English, Nordau's work is usually referred to as *Degeneration*, but in the original German it was called *Entartung. Entartete Kunst.* Where have we heard this phrase before? Most of us associate the concept with a regime that hated Jews, yet one of them had invented it.

The case of Max Nordau introduces two major themes of this chapter. The first concerns the intimate connection between the rise of criminology and the contemporary cultural and social climate. The second theme is introduced somewhat indirectly. Hostile commentators often imagine a straight line from late nineteenth-century ideas about degeneration and born criminals to the racist fallacies of the Third Reich. I will argue that there is no such straight line. Along the way, my discussion will range from the beginnings of criminology until about 1940. From this period, forty-five learned men and four learned women will be mentioned. As the reader will understand, this imbalance reflects not my preferences, but contemporary realities.

I. When Did Criminology Begin?

In 1838 the Frenchman Auguste Comte coined the term "*sociologie*," which is widely considered as the beginning of the discipline with that name. This field is quite different from criminology. True, several authors cite the 1885 work by Raffaele Garofolo entitled *Criminologia* (Beirne 1993, pp. 233–38), but at the time, most scholars denoted the discipline that Garofalo represented as "criminal anthropology," and this term continued to be common until the First World War. In Germany, moreover, even in the interwar period, "criminal biology" was the usual term. Obviously, the beginnings of criminology cannot be deduced simply from the use of that name. As a consequence, various founding fathers, active from the mid-eighteenth century to the late nineteenth century, have been proposed.

The choice for a particular founding father often depends on a scholar's personal approach to criminology. For example, someone who despises measuring skulls as a retrograde and politically incorrect enterprise will be reluctant to name Lombroso as the first criminologist. Some scholars, moreover, are skeptical about the very claim of identifying the causes of crime. Thus, the criminologist Piers Beirne (1993), author of the first modern overview of the rise of criminology in Europe, wants the discipline to remain in close contact with penology and the practice of criminal justice. He calls this the "classical approach," in contrast to the positivist one. His history consists of a number of portraits, beginning with Cesare Beccaria, who consequently becomes the first criminologist.

After Beirne, research into the emergence of criminology was largely taken over by historians, usually writing about one particular country. They presented various answers to the question of the beginnings of this discipline, if they bothered about it at all. A collection covering France (Mucchielli 1995) begins in 1800, because the contributors equate the rise of criminology with the increasing involvement of nonlegal specialists in the criminal justice process, as noted by Foucault (1975). By contrast, Martine Kaluszynski (2002) considers the reception of Lombroso in France as the starting point of the field. For Germany, Richard Wetzell (2000) and Christian Müller (2004) agree in a similar vein that the reception of Lombroso caused the criminology to take off in that country. Peter Becker (2002), on the other hand, adopting a rather broad definition of what criminology comprises, traces the beginnings back to around 1800 once more. He does, however, distinguish a group of authors writing before and one writing since Lombroso, the first of whom he calls criminalists. Dealing with England, Neil Davie (2004) begins in 1860, but the variegated set of authors he discusses certainly do not constitute one discipline together. An anthology composed by Nicole Rafter (2009) covering both Europe and the United States is the most recent among the works that more or less make a statement about the beginnings of criminology. Her broad time frame takes us back to Beccaria again (likewise in Hayward et al. 2010).

This lack of consensus forms a justification for squarely making my own decision. I define a criminologist as an academically trained researcher whose work is devoted exclusively to the study of crime in the broadest sense. By that criterion, Lombroso must be considered the first criminologist, while the establishment of the Italian school initiated by him and of the opposing French school marked the professionalization of the study of crime. I will, however, make room for a number of earlier authors who either wrote about a related field or devoted themselves partially to crime but whose effort is considered by many as a contribution to the development of criminology. For these authors, I propose to reserve the term "pre-criminologists."

Let us consider Cesare Beccaria (1738–1794) the first pre-criminologist, by virtue of his designation as such by several modern scholars. His fame rests on his book *Dei delitti e delle pene* (*On Crimes and Punishments* [1764]). In it, he stressed the importance of raising offenders' chances of arrest (the two principles of the certainty and promptness of punishment) without giving a clear-cut recipe for accomplishing this. In fact, this goal was realized much later with the institution of the new police. Beccaria's third principle, that of the proportionality of punishment, perhaps comes nearest to being criminological (Friedland 2012, pp. 205–17). He made a detailed classification in which every small increase in the seriousness of the offense, measured by its damage to society, is matched by an equally small increase in the severity of punishment (Porret 2003, pp. 79–83). Despite the relevance of this principle for criminological thought, he was primarily a legal theorist. Michel Porret (2003), author of one recent study devoted entirely to Beccaria and his work, sees him exclusively as a penal reformer and Enlightenment philosopher.

II. The Early Bourgeois Image of Man and the Pre-Criminologists: Free Will

Free will has always been a central tenet of Christian doctrine, especially within Catholicism. In practice, free will is applied most often to bad behavior. God granted humans, so the argument runs, the capacity to sin if they choose to, by which they of course risk divine punishment unless they repent. It is well known that the Enlightenment *philosophes*, apart from opposing torture and frowning upon the spectacle of suffering, attacked the powerful position of the churches. Voltaire, next to promoting Beccaria's work, opposed the notion that God directly intervened in earthly affairs, ridiculing those who interpreted the Lisbon earthquake of 1755 as God's punishment for people's sins. On one point in particular, however, an essential continuity prevailed between traditional religion and the Enlightenment. The *philosophes*, too, believed in free will. Consequently, Enlightenment thinkers accepted, if not the harshness, then certainly the principle of criminal punishment.

The term "image of man" stands for the Dutch *mensbeeld* and the German *Menschbild*, which does not translate well into English. I ask the reader to realize each time that my English equivalent applies to both genders. The early bourgeois image of man was rooted in Enlightenment thought. Both systems of thought cherished the idea of human progress, and in both, the notion of free will was central. Beccaria's proportional scale, for example, assumes a calculating citizen who carefully assesses expected profits and losses: the greater the advantage of crime, the greater the (required) disadvantage of punishment. There was one slight difference, however. The early bourgeois image of man elaborated on a number of Enlightenment notions without radically calling the church into question. Hence, the new image could be embraced by skeptics and believers alike and by people with liberal and conservative leanings. This image of man represented the dominant worldview until well after the mid-nineteenth century. In one way or another, all pre-criminologists shared it.

Martin Wiener (1990) discusses this image in detail. Although he restricts himself to England, I claim that his analysis applies to all major European countries. This claim can be validated indirectly. Enthusiasm for solitary confinement was intimately related to the early bourgeois image of man, and this enthusiasm was high in nearly all European countries. As already noted, free will was the central element in the early bourgeois image of man. Although a certain type of behavior might be characteristic for a particular group, or regularities over time might be observable, ultimately every man or woman was responsible for his or her actions. A second important element of this image was self-control. In Norbert Elias's (1939) sociological theory, the degree of self-control of which individuals are capable is a function of the period and the social group into which they have been born. Nineteenth-century people, on the other hand, believed that self-control or the lack of it was a reflection of a man or woman's personal merit. Whoever broke a rule—of etiquette or the law—showed insufficient self-control and needed character building. Criminal offenders had a particularly bad character that could, however, be improved. In principle, every lawbreaker could be changed for the better or, in modern terms, resocialized.

The most suitable place for resocialization was the prison. The idea that punishment can change an offender's ways predates the period under discussion here. Many early modern magistrates, for example, believed that forced labor caused inmates to unlearn their laziness. In the early and mid-nineteenth century, however, the belief in resocialization was stronger than ever. Contemporary lawyers and politicians felt, in part erroneously, that the focus of punishment had shifted completely from the body to the mind (Spierenburg 2013, p. 78). Combined with their trust in the possibility of improving everyone's character, this produced an unprecedented faith in solitary confinement. Free from the corrupting influences of fellow prisoners, each inmate would reflect on his or her misdeeds and become a better person. Chapter 34 in this volume discusses solitary confinement in greater detail. Here I am concerned with the implications of this practice for criminological thought. The early bourgeois image of man provided a foundation for both the enthusiasm for solitary confinement and pre-criminological theorizing.

Consequently, pre-criminologists primarily inquired into individual persons' motives for breaking the law. For those caught and convicted, they favored a moral approach. A brief look at the history of insanity shows once more that this idea was in tune with the general culture of the age. Early modern madhouses kept their inmates in chains or otherwise securely bound, while attempts to cure them were rare. The much-publicized "liberation of the insane" by Philippe Pinel during the French Revolution was a turning point. During the first half of the nineteenth century, the so-called "moral treatment" prevailed among psychiatric therapies (Binneveld 1985, pp. 13–43). Significantly, later in that century biological theories were to become dominant in psychiatry, at the same time that they underwent a breakthrough in the study of crime.

With Beccaria already discussed, and other penal reformers by implication, two main currents of pre-criminological thought and research remain: the school of moral statistics and the group of authors whom Becker (2002; for a brief analysis in English, see Becker 2005) calls "criminalists," with a few representatives outside Germany. The two currents are thematically distinct; they do not neatly succeed each other in time. The heyday of moral statistics was from the late 1820s to the 1840s, whereas the criminalists were active between about 1800 and about 1870. Let me begin with them.

The criminalists belong to pre-criminology because of their amateurism. They were a heterogeneous group including police officers, lawyers, journalists, and theologians. Applying their "practical gaze," they all claimed an intimate familiarity with offenders, focusing on urban habitual criminals. One could identify these individuals not so much by bodily characteristics, they believed, as by character traits, and one in particular: they were big spenders. Their way of life was acquired rather than innate. Therefore, all criminalists favored a biographical approach to their object of study. As A. F. Thiele put it in 1840, "it is precisely the life course that characterizes the habitual offender most of all" (quoted in Becker 2002, p. 70). Each writer concentrated on the decisive moment when the offender took the wrong path. Alcohol consumption often triggered this moment, or visiting brothels. Criminalists of other countries have not been systematically studied as a group. One representative, the English prison inspector Frederic Hill, wrote in 1853 that the reduction of crime depended not only on education, particularly the teaching of self-control, but also on alleviating the misery of all social classes (Davie 2004, p. 53). The well-known study *The Criminal Prisons of London and Scenes of Prison Life* (1862), in which the journalists Henry Mayhew and John Binny sketched a set of habitual offenders, fits very well with German criminalist writing. So does *The Nether Side of New York*, published by the American journalist Edward Crapsey in 1872 (Rafter 2009, pp. 141–54).

The association of moral statistics with the early bourgeois image of man at first sight seems less evident. Indeed, Beirne (1993) refers to its foremost representative, the Belgian scholar Adolphe Quetelet (1796–1874), as the founding father of positivist criminology. Viewed from another angle, however, the connection between statistics and the image in question becomes easily apparent. Early bourgeois social commentators feared the "criminal classes," considering them irresponsible individuals in plural.

Quetelet and his colleagues made a statistical study of irresponsible individuals in plural. Moral statisticians did not deny free will. According to Quetelet, individual people did make voluntary decisions, but their effects were neutralized at the collective level (van Kerckvoorde in Mucchielli 1995, pp. 260–61). The reason for including moral statistics in *pre*-criminology lies in its very name. Its practitioners devoted themselves to the study of morality, not crime. Morality included charity and level of education, while immorality, next to crime, included having illegitimate children. Crucial for the quantitative study of criminality was the decision of several governments in the early nineteenth century to publish criminal statistics. The *Compte général de l'administration de la justice criminelle en France* was released in 1827, and several scholars immediately seized this opportunity for study.

With only a few years of data available, the study of long-term trends was reserved for later generations. An examination of these few years, moreover, shows crime rates to have been relatively constant. Quetelet concluded from this that the "dark number"—he was probably the first to realize its existence—was also constant. On the basis of this observation, Quetelet arrived at a synchronic theory of the *homme moyen* (average man), an individual typical for the group to which he belonged. Shame and modesty, according to him, lay behind the low incidence of female crime. He completed his ideas about male crime with an intriguing age model. Adolescents and young adults were prone to violence and rape, whereas mature men were more frequently thieves and burglars, and when they got older and weaker, they preferred swindling. Quetelet considered his concept of the average man applicable throughout the field of moral statistics, in particular to suicide, marriage, and crime (Beirne 1993, pp. 65–110).

The Frenchman André-Michel Guerry (1802–1866) counts as the second important moral statistician. His work resembled that of Quetelet; the major difference lay in Guerry's preference for a cartographical approach. He took advantage of the departmental classification of the *Compte Général* by mapping the crime rates for all French departments. In doing so, he discovered the now-famous line from St. Malo to Geneva, below which violence predominated and above which property offenses were most common (Beirne 1993, pp. 111–41; van Kerckvoorde in Mucchielli 1995, pp. 256–57). Representatives of the field of moral statistics outside French-speaking Europe included Joseph Fletcher, who in 1849 published a report on the moral and educational statistics of England and Wales (Rafter 2009, pp. 278–83), and Georg von Mayr (1841–1925), who in 1867 conducted an analysis of the criminal statistics of the Kingdom of Bavaria. With the possibility of examining them over a number of decades, von Mayr was the first to observe that the graphs for property offenses and grain prices, those of rye in particular, showed a positive correlation (Blasius 1976, pp. 10–12). This might have earned him the label of first criminologist, but he left the field, obtaining a professorship in economics, finance, and statistics in Munich.

In 1871, three years before his death, Quetelet suddenly came out with a new book, which lacked statistics but was full of skulls and their measures. The European mood was changing.

III. A Cultural Transformation:
The Quest for Purity

The European mood changed in various ways, yet all of them were connected. Foremost, the firm belief in self-control as a panacea for personal and social ills all but vanished. This change had repercussions for the way contemporaries saw themselves and their own social group, as well as for how they viewed others. Many persons still cherished the value of rational deliberation, but increasingly their self-image left room for a new sense of vitalism. Although men and women of all periods have loved and trusted their "we-group," such feelings became intenser at this time than ever before. The emphasis on the we-group led some to embrace an aggressive form of nationalism. More generally, a belief appeared in the fundamental inequality among human groups, whether categorized by social classes, nations, or races. Finally, optimism about the progress of humanity and the possibility of individual improvement waned. The latter touches on the image people came to hold of others. Ever fewer people believed in free will, maintaining instead that fixed structures lay at the basis of everyone's personality.

This shift from free will to determinism had definite implications for dealing with crime. Most forms of deviance, contemporaries believed, originated from the innate biological or mental weaknesses of certain people. Therapeutic intervention rather than character building was the appropriate response. Psychiatrists rejected moral treatment, replacing it with a biological scheme of mental disorders. Criminologists no longer believed in discipline, resocialization, and reaching out to an offender's mind. Instead, they set out to identify deviant constitutions. In England, Wiener (1990) additionally maintains that criminals were no longer seen as dangerous, but as pathetic "wreckage"—a thesis absent from the literature on continental Europe. For Germany, Becker (2002, p. 273) explicitly says that theorists around 1900 viewed criminals as both degenerate *and* dangerous. Whatever the degree of fear for them, criminal offenders now were essentially viewed as "others."

We have no reason to assume that the new ideas produced the professionalization of the study of crime, or vice versa for that matter; the least we can say is that the two coincided. Modern criminologists like Tim Newburn (2007) speak of a mere paradigm shift, but I argue that a much broader transformation was involved. The new approach to criminals was embedded in an emerging worldview and a novel image of man.

There is no ready answer to the question of why the transformation occurred, or even when exactly. Historians writing in the 1950s and 1960s were impressed by two world wars, brutal dictatorships, and the Great Depression. For them, the turning point came around 1900, with earlier expressions of aggressive nationalism, racism, and irrationalism no more than prefigurations of the twentieth-century cataclysms. Most modern historians, however, situate the cultural turning point around 1870. Let me first go back even further in time, to 1859. This stands out as the year in which Charles Darwin (1809–1882) published *On the Origin of Species*, and by 1870 all European intellectuals had reflected on the book's content. It is of course beyond the capacity of one man to change the entire culture of his time. Instead, I argue that Darwin's work fell on fertile soil. Several scholars comment on the fact that, afraid of criticism from the Church, Darwin did not publish his theory until he heard that another scientist had threatened to be the first to do so. Few, on the other hand, seem to realize that this long delay caused *On the Origin of Species* to appear precisely at the moment when European minds were becoming receptive to Darwin's theory and, even more, to its presumed implications.

Indeed, Darwin adopted his famous concept of the "survival of the fittest" from the philosopher and sociologist Herbert Spencer (1820–1903) (Mason 2011, p. 77). Two years before the publication of *On the Origins of Species*, moreover, the Frenchman Bénédict Morel (1809–1873) introduced the theory of degeneration—a term not used by Darwin, but to become influential soon after (Rafter 2009, p. 87). And another year earlier, the discovery of a skeleton in the Neander Valley had provoked discussion about humanity's origins. Thus, scientists and philosophers were providing building blocks for the new image of man. The notion of the survival of the fittest and its sister concept of the struggle for life revolutionized people's view of nature. The dominant image of this concept shifted from the harmony of the great chain of being to the conviction that nature meant endless struggle. In the minds of many, this had definite social repercussions. Later scholars have pinned the label of "social Darwinism" on those thinkers who most rigorously applied evolutionary theory to the development of society. Social Darwinists argued, for example, that legislation to protect the socially weak was unnatural and hence useless because human society was a theater of perpetual conflict in which the strong would inevitably win. Others used biology to justify European dominance. Thus, John Lubbock claimed in 1875 that this dominance was due to natural selection (Dickens 2000, pp. 15–16). Not every thinker was a social Darwinist, but many believed that biology played a larger role in human behavior than previous generations had assumed. In practice, moreover, everyone invoked biology, especially when it came to explaining the behavior of others.

Can we identify the social origins of the transformation in the image of man and thereby place it in an even more encompassing context? Wiener speaks of a growing discontent, from the 1870s on, with the extreme social demands of self-discipline—a discontent that raised an unsettling image of a "disabled society of ineffectual, devitalized and over-controlled individuals" (Wiener 1990, p. 12). In a similar vein, a recent textbook (Altena & van Lente 2003) maintains that bourgeois culture contained two major ideals: self-discipline and self-expression. Whereas the first, deriving from the Enlightenment, meant respecting borders, the second, deriving from Romanticism, often meant transgressing them. According to the authors, the balance between self-discipline and self-expression did not shift until the 1890s, but they also speak of a new generation of bourgeois men and women, reaching adulthood around 1870. This generation expressed their discontent with a life ideal that stressed material comfort alone and doubted the validity of the traditional bourgeois view of man (pp. 196–201).

A group of Dutch and French historians, art historians, and literary scholars (Laarse et al. 1998; Labrie 2001) offers an ingenious explanation for the cultural shift under discussion centered on the concept of *Hang naar Zuiverheid*, which I will refer to in English as the "quest for purity." Following the anthropologist Mary Douglas (1966), these scholars understand purity both in the sense of cleanliness and in a symbolic and moral sense. When fear of change is rampant, according to Douglas, sensitivity toward the distinction between the pure and the impure is also high. In post-1870 Europe, the quest for purity formed a broad cultural undercurrent, independent of political ideologies. This undercurrent was common to such variegated surface currents as racism, naturalism, hygienism, nationalism, and more. In practice, the quest for purity went in either one of two directions: the drive of a small group to maintain internal purity or the drive within a larger group to identify and ultimately eliminate the impure. The first drive was typically that of like-minded intellectuals and artists, but also of vegetarians and naturalists. The second could express itself in racism or anti-Semitism, but alternatively, it led to measures against deviants, the insane, and criminals. Arnold Labrie (2001, pp. 28–33) speaks of a crisis of bourgeois culture between 1870 and 1914 that was generated in response to practically all social movements of the day. These movements caused uncertainty and fear of change in bourgeois minds, which takes us back to Mary Douglas's theory about increased sensitivity.

The movements of the day included socialism. At first sight, socialism would seem to be the rationalist counterforce to vitalist and racist ideologies. However, the concept of the quest for purity ties socialism firmly to the new image of man. Indeed, some socialists became teetotalers or vegetarians. Conversely, some biological criminologists became socialists.

IV. Cesare Lombroso, 1835–1909

One day in 1871, Lombroso sat down to examine a skull he had acquired, that of the brigand Giuseppe Villella. Turning it to the back, Lombroso observed an anomaly that he later described in various ways. Suddenly, the pieces of a puzzle came together. The skull reminded him of, among others, fetuses, primitive savages, and certain primates. Criminals, he concluded, were a subhuman species. Lombroso was not the first to draw such conclusions from skulls or brains, but his predecessors usually wrote for a medical public, and in my scheme, they are mere precursors of the first professional criminologists. Of course, Lombroso, too, had a background in medicine, but he founded a new discipline. His sudden flash of insight, to be sure, was probably a myth created afterward (Gibson in Becker & Wetzell 2006, p. 139), much like Pinel's liberation of the insane.

The Villella story introduces two major aspects of Lombroso's work. One was his conviction that born criminals, along with the insane, Africans, and some others, represented a lower stage in human evolution. In this he drew on a particular Darwinian concept, that of atavism. Atavism is not a key concept in evolutionary theory, and present-day science has largely forgotten about it: in the index of the most recent study of Darwin to date (Workman 2014), we search in vain for atavism . . . and for criminology or Lombroso, for that matter. The concept derived from the Latin *atavus* (ancestor), and Darwin applied it almost exclusively to species other than humans. He observed that, within certain individuals, traits of their distant ancestors reappeared. According to Lombroso, such evolutionary throwbacks were numerous among humans as well—numerous because all blacks, Asians, and Native Americans were atavistic to some extent. More central to Lombroso's theory was his conviction that, within Europe, many criminals and lunatics were evolutionary throwbacks. The born criminal's body was shaped by atavism, and its marks could be seen on the outside of the body.

The second element that runs as a background through Lombroso's work refers to the deep social cleavage in Italy between north and south at the time. Born in the north, Lombroso knew the south well from working as an army physician in Calabria in the early 1860s. Inhabitants of the urbanized and industrializing Po Valley and the capital considered—and still consider—all regions to their south as backward. Although atavistic criminals lived everywhere within the Italian society and around Europe, the most notorious among them originated from the *Mezzogiorno*, the southern regions. The first population studied by Lombroso consisted mostly of dead southern bandits, acquired from anatomy rooms and anthropological museums. Although he was far from sharing all the prejudices of his fellow northerners, he pointed out that hereditary factors lay at the root of southern criminality; centuries of invasion by Arabs and Normans had contaminated their blood.

The first edition of Lombroso's *l'Uomo delinquente* (*Criminal Man*) appeared in 1876. By then he had followed up his examination of cadavers and skeletons with a study of a larger population of living offenders, selected for their depravity and notoriety, as well as of insane persons and soldiers as control groups. He identified several bodily characteristics as typical for born criminals, in particular a receding forehead and a pronounced jawbone. His classification of physical traits, however, was far from systematic. Thus, thin hair as well as thick curly hair could indicate a criminal personality (Lombroso, quoted in Beirne 1993, p. 149). To Lombroso, this came as no surprise, since a criminal might bear resemblance to either one of the nonwhite races. He lavishly illustrated his study with portraits, usually depicting such notorious individuals as a round-headed rapist who looked a bit stupid in the first edition and much more dangerous in the fourth. For the author of *Criminal Man*, these depictions were simply meant to underline his point. Atavistic criminality was a natural phenomenon that could be traced back to predation in the animal realm. He even identified carnivorous plants as atavistic. The whole enterprise of identifying the physical traits of offenders required the competent gaze of professionals, which took the place of the amateuristic familiarity of most pre-criminologists (Becker 2002, pp. 291–92). In applying his professional gaze to the criminal, Lombroso definitely represented the quest for purity characteristic of the culture of his age (Schwegman in Laarse et al. 1998, pp. 123–37).

At this point some nuance is called for. As Gibson and Rafter write in the introduction to the first complete English translation of *Criminal Man*, they began their study of Lombroso with an image of his work as simply bad and prejudice-feeding science, but then found that it contained several elements that they could view with greater appreciation (Lombroso 2006, pp. 1–4). First of all, Lombroso gradually deemphasized the all-importance of biology. Only the first edition, which outlines the idea but not the actual label of the born criminal, implicitly presents this as a monocausal explanation for the existence of crime. In the third edition, however, the author specified that 40 percent of all lawbreakers were born criminals, and in the fifth this figure was reduced to 35 percent. For the remaining 60 to 65 percent of criminals, Lombroso invented several other types, among which was the passionate criminal. Like many of his contemporaries, he could put himself in the shoes of a jealous husband committing an act of desperation, and he also sympathized with women who killed their spouses after suffering continuous physical abuse. Such offenders, as well as many political protesters, were normal people who, for a moment, gave in to their passions.

Over the course of his career, we can conclude, Lombroso reduced the role of biology in the study of crime. Understandably, his Jewish roots prevented him from mingling his criminology with anti-Semitism. When discussing the criminality of Jews, he came to the table with a historical explanation that is still in use today. Their overrepresentation in fraud and receiving, he argued, was due to their large presence in occupations such as peddling, which in its turn was due to a history of exclusion. Other nuances in the image of "bad science" concern aspects of Lombroso's work that appear modern to us. The illustrations in his books, for example, included sexually explicit drawings of tattooed bodies, anticipating modern sexology. Besides these, he collected all kinds of objects, from strange murder weapons to drawings and sculptures made by offenders and the insane, again anticipating a modern area of interest. In 1884 he showed these objects at an exhibition. For later scholars, the exhibited material presents an inside look into late nineteenth-century prison subcultures. The elements of nuance in Lombroso's ideas extended to the realm of politics, discussed in the next paragraph, and even to his view of women. Lombroso had two well-educated daughters, and at times he complained about the restricted possibilities for women in his society.

Despite this, everything he wrote about women would be classified today as plainly sexist. His writing referred, of course, not to his daughters, but mostly to lower-class women. For ten years, beginning in 1889, Italian criminologists showed an extraordinary interest in female criminality, which Gibson (2002, pp. 60–61) attributes to the contemporary debate about feminism. Perhaps their interest was also triggered by the publication that year of a study of prostitutes and female thieves by Pauline Tarnowsky. The author, a Russian-born scholar working in France, stands out both as Lombroso's only supporter there and as the only female criminologist of the period (Kaluszynski 2002, p. 67; Rafter 2009, pp. 178–82). She was often cited in a book that appeared in 1893 entitled *La donna delinquente, la prostituta e la donna normale* (*The Criminal Woman, the Prostitute and the Normal Woman*), co-authored by Lombroso and his son-in-law Guglielmo Ferrero (1871–1942). The full title reveals the program. The authors believed in the fundamental inequality of the sexes. Normal women, too, were inferior to men, prone to vanity and lying, for example, but their maternal instincts kept them from crime. It was particularly fortuitous for the authors' theory that prostitution was legal at the time. This fact solved the problem inherent in the low percentage of female offenders. Prostitution, they argued, was the female counterpart to crime. Whereas atavistic men became burglars or attackers, atavistic women had an unnaturally high sex drive, which they channeled into prostitution. Illustrations of prostitutes' feet that resembled those of apes served to underline this theory (Renneville 2003, pp. 204–05).

Strange as some elements in Lombroso's work may appear to us, it had a definite appeal to his contemporaries. In accounting for this appeal, I am distinguishing between specialists and a larger audience. For each, a general and a more specific source of attraction can be mentioned. Darwin's work and the ensuing belief in a huge biological component of human behavior had prepared specialists' minds. Ordinary people, too, found the idea that criminals were "born that way" self-evident. Many Frenchmen, for example, denounced a plan to turn male and female offenders in Guiana into colonists after serving their term and to let them raise a family—what monsters would be born from that? However, the specific sources for Lombroso's appeal to specialists and laypeople were more divergent. The first appreciated his emphasis on measurement, which confirmed that the study of crime had become a professional science. The second were convinced by his large body of supplementary evidence, ranging from proverbs to stories by Dostoievski. He popularized his work even further by writing in magazines about notorious criminals (Gibson 2005). Finally, one element largely ignored by Lombroso helped to convince nearly all contemporaries that fixed structures, whether biological or not, underlay an offender's personality: criminal statistics. These were now available for several decades, as far back as the days of Quetelet, and everyone noticed in particular the large proportion of recidivists. Recidivism was equally rampant in earlier centuries, but once again we should realize that these figures were new to people of the 1870s. They drew two related conclusions: prisons had failed to improve the character of offenders, and this was because crime is innate (Beirne 1993, p. 147).

After his death in 1909 Lombroso's head and skeleton were preserved according to his wishes. His other son-in-law, Mario Carrara, performed an autopsy, concluding that his father-in-law's brain indicated genius mixed with a few minor marks of insanity.

V. The Italian and French Schools

The foundation of the journal *Archivio di Psichiatria e Antropologia Criminale* in 1880 signaled the appearance of a real school of criminology. Besides the founder, Enrico Ferri (1856–1929) and, secondarily, Raffaele Garofalo (1851–1934) count as its major representatives. The Italians organized a conference on criminology in Rome in 1885; originally planned as a national event, eventually about one-third of the participants came from abroad. Lombroso's major opponent at that meeting was a Frenchman named Lacassagne.

For the moment, the Italians prevailed. By the time he met Lombroso, Ferri had already completed a dissertation in law, in which he rejected the notion of free will. Furthermore, it was he who provided the school's founder with the label of "born criminal," although he later moved away from a direct causal link between biology and crime. According to him, no one was born with an inevitable inclination for criminal activities. Instead, certain people had an innate criminal disposition that caused a number of them to commit illegal acts later in life but allowed others who received the right education to grow up as law-abiding citizens. Thus, whether the latent criminal disposition became manifest depended on a person's upbringing. Ferri was far from modest, comparing the achievement of contemporary criminology (he did not point directly to himself) with that of Galileo, who had shown that the earth was not the center of the universe, and Darwin, who had shown that human life did not fundamentally differ from that of animals and plants. According to Ferri, criminologists demolished the third myth, that of free will (van Ruller 1998; Gibson in Becker & Wetzell 2006, pp. 151–53).

In accordance with its rejection of free will, the Italian school frowned upon the practice of criminal justice, but the legal establishment was powerful enough to preserve its traditions. Ferri considered no offender responsible for his deeds but still found punishment socially useful. Lombroso specifically attacked the proportionality principle of his compatriot and first namesake. Whereas Beccaria had attuned punishment to the offense, Lombroso wanted to attune it to the offender. What the latter had done did not matter, but who he was did. For the prevention of ordinary crime Lombroso additionally suggested better street illumination and the use of alarm systems. Ferri likewise proposed several practical measures. At the same time, Italian criminologists' attitudes toward the most serious criminals were often uncompromising. They considered the death penalty useful, deploring its abolition in Italy in 1889. Lombroso was hesitant about the death penalty at first but later allowed that it was appropriate for the most dangerous born criminals. Garofalo was decidedly more radical than his colleagues, advocating capital punishment for the majority of born criminals as an artificial form of natural selection (Franke 1990, p. 455).

Garofalo was politically conservative indeed. The attitudes of the other two main representatives of the Italian school were quite different, however. His conviction that southerners were racially impure did not prevent Lombroso from sympathy with their plight. To alleviate poverty in the *Mezzogiorno*, he even advocated the redistribution of land. Back in the north, he became a moderate socialist. According to him, state policies should ensure that human evolution took the right direction, but he rejected action from below such as strikes and revolutions. Ferri went further, accepting Marx's theory and proclaiming its compatibility with Darwin's. Lombroso sat in the Turin council for the Italian Socialist Party, and Ferri became editor-in-chief of its journal. His political beliefs even earned him a thirteen-year banishment from academia (Carney in Hayward et al. 2010, pp. 36–42). Nevertheless, while it fits perfectly into the cultural undercurrent of the quest for purity, biological criminology was not associated with one political ideology only. Contemporaries considered it a science with a variegated potential for political application. As Gibson (2002, p. 7) puts it, "the apparent compatibility of certain types of criminology with specific political positions can shift depending on historical context or which aspect of the argument is being emphasized." It was not until Mussolini's takeover that Italian criminology turned to the service of Fascism.

Resentment that a young nation-state like Italy was leading in a new academic field was greatest in France. The differences between the French school and its main target were far from total, but they were magnified by nationalistic motives (Mucchielli 1995, pp. 189–214; Mucchielli in Becker & Wetzell 2006, pp. 207–29). Indeed, Alexandre Lacassagne (1843–1924) started his career as a Lombrosian. Like his Italian counterpart, he was originally an army physician; each time he changed universities, he needed permission from his military superiors. He eventually settled in Lyon. Shortly after 1882 Lacassagne proclaimed the school of the social milieu within criminology. Distancing himself from Lombroso, he aimed to build upon the work of Quetelet and Guerry. He criticized Lombroso's use of soldiers as a control group, calling them unrepresentative of ordinary citizens. In fact, Lacassagne continued, he knew several law-abiding citizens with round heads and the like. He concluded that all bodily characteristics observable among criminals could also be found among "decent people." In 1886, a year after his participation in the Rome congress, he founded the journal *Archives d'Anthropologie Criminelle*. Three years later the French school had become influential enough to hold the second international criminological conference in Paris.

"Societies get the offenders that they deserve!" This is Lacassagne's most often-cited maxim, and together with the label of social milieu it sounds perfectly sociological: The problem of criminality diminishes as a society is organized more effectively. Not the bodies of criminals but social circumstances produce crime. Another of Lacassagne's phrases gives cause for thought: "The social milieu is like a cultural soup in which offenders crawl as microbes." Moreover, for the French school, the social milieu was not exclusively social, as we understand it today. It was much broader, including, for example, factories and the smoke they produced (Kaluszynski 2002, pp. 41–44). From Guerry's map of departments Lacassagne concluded that the elevated rates of property crime in the industrialized northeast were due not to the miserable circumstances in which the workers lived, but to the smoke that had caused their bodies to degenerate. In this way, the French and Italians approached each other again. Lombroso, too, embraced degeneration as an additional concept in response to criticism of his reliance on atavism.

Gabriel Tarde (1843–1904) is usually considered the second major representative of the French school. He offered criticism of the Italians similar to that of Lacassagne, but from the reverse angle. After reading the works of a number of biological criminologists, Tarde noted that they identified contradictory characteristics for born offenders. According to one, criminals had larger than average skulls, whereas the other was sure that they had smaller ones. There are as many criminal types as there are criminal anthropologists, Tarde ironically concluded (Beirne 1993, pp. 143–85). The Paris congress of 1889 served as a platform for such criticism, as well as critique from a third representative of the French school, Léonce Manouvrier (1850–1927) (Renneville in Mucchielli 1995, pp. 118–24; Kaluszynski 2002, pp. 67–68; Rafter 2009, pp. 192–95). The French school's emphasis on the social milieu did not necessarily lead to a renewed faith in resocialization. Lacassagne, too, supported capital punishment for serious incorrigibles, albeit by hanging instead of the guillotine. Likewise, French criminologists were not uniform in their political beliefs. For Henri Joly (1839–1925), for example, the crime-producing social milieu included first of all broken families. As a conservative Catholic, he decried the Third Republic's legalization of divorce (Veitl in Mucchielli 1995, pp. 269–85; Kaluszynski 2002, pp. 125–27).

The fact that the differences between the Italian and French schools were not complete to begin with facilitated the gradual rapprochement of the born criminal and social milieu approaches. Just as Lombroso increasingly made room for alternative types of offenders, Tarde easily admitted that some were indeed born that way. The rapprochement was visible at the international conferences following the first two. The third to fifth were held in neutral territory, as it were: Brussels in 1892, Geneva in 1896, and Amsterdam in 1901. In Amsterdam a number of lawyers were present for the first time. As if everyone sensed that Lombroso had few years to live, the sixth conference was held in Turin in 1906. Five years later, the Cologne conference drew Germany into the picture. The meeting planned for Budapest in 1914 was canceled for obvious reasons. The criminological mixture resulting from this series of conferences is usually referred to as the biosocial approach. In it, tattoos were an intriguing element. Everyone claimed that these corroborated precisely his particular theory, which actually made a tattoo the common mark of all criminals (Caplan in Becker & Wetzell 2006, pp. 337–61).

VI. The Spread of Criminology in Europe and the United States

The series of conferences constituted a tour of continental Europe, with England conspicuously absent. This is understandable, since up to the First World War the British Isles lacked a tradition of professional criminology. The English debate about crime and its causes continued to be dominated by medical specialists and authors linked to prisons or courts. The first group included the later sexologist Havelock Ellis (1859–1939), whose *The Criminal* (1890) popularized continental criminal anthropology in his country. He agreed in large part with Lombroso, except for the latter's insistence that carnivorous plants were criminal, but he also referred positively to Lacassagne (Rafter 2009, pp. 183–87). The second group, holding on to the responsibility of offenders for their actions, rejected Lombroso's theory (Davie 2004, p. 223). On the eve of the First World War, the prison doctor Charles Goring (1870–1919) set out to investigate once and for all whether there was merit to the idea of the born criminal. His *The English Convict* (1913) contained an attack on Lombroso, one that Beirne (1993, pp. 187–224) considers failed. First, the attack focused on a compendium composed by Lombroso's daughter Gina. Second, Goring actually confirmed that some physical traits, as well as mental deficiency, were indeed characteristic for English convicts. Despite this failure, the book remained a standard work throughout the interwar period.

Goring referred to crime scientists as criminologists. Already in 1893 Arthur MacDonald had introduced Lombroso's theory to the United States through a book simply entitled *Criminology* (Rafter 2009, pp. 188–91). Thus, this term became common in the Anglo-Saxon world. Nevertheless, in the United States, too, the discipline was slow to professionalize. Two quite different traditions of discourse and research deserve to be mentioned. The first started in the 1880s as a debate about "the negro problem" and soon turned into a concern about black criminality. The overrepresentation of African Americans in crime statistics led many to view the entire black population as criminal. The counter-voices of W. E. B. DuBois and Ida B. Wells were not influential enough to counter this stereotype. Social scientists of the Progressive era maintained that, unlike blacks, new immigrants like the Irish, Italians, and Jews easily adapted to American society, and the immigrants themselves eagerly adopted this idea, stressing their whiteness. Even Sicilian mafiosi, considered racially inferior in Lombroso's Italy, could become "real" Americans. The debate about black criminality involved a broad group of social scientists, philanthropists, journalists, and prison doctors. In 1928 one of America's first professional criminologists, Thorsten Sellin (1896–1994), was also the first white scholar to attack the stereotype of a criminal race (Muhammad 2010; Hanson in Hayward et al. 2010, pp. 53–58; Melossi in Hayward et al. 2010, pp. 76–82).

The second tradition that should be mentioned involved solid research instead of questionable stereotypes. Criminologists love to claim the so-called Chicago school for their discipline. In the words of one of them: "Chicago University has a special place in the history of criminology. The reason for this dates back to 1892 when it took the decision to establish the first major *sociology* department in the United States" (Newburn 2007, p. 188; my emphasis). This sociological current admittedly was inspired by, among others, French criminologists of the social milieu orientation. Beginning with the famous study *The Polish Peasant* (1919), the Chicago school had its heyday in the 1920s and 1930s. The volumes it produced, still praised as classics today, dealt with Chicago's immigrant and minority communities, vice, organized crime, the homeless, and the makeup of the city itself. These subjects certainly included a lot of deviance and crime, so their relevance for modern criminology is plain.

When we return to Europe and examine the first four decades of the twentieth century, the contrast between Germany and the Netherlands is particularly remarkable. In the first country, a biological orientation prevailed, and even authors who took social causes into account pinned rather negative labels on lawbreakers. German criminology owed its orientation to its psychiatric roots. From before unification, psychiatrists had been influenced by the theory of degeneration. In 1880, Emil Kraepelin (1856–1926), father of the present *Diagnostic and Statistical Manual of Mental Disorders*, pleaded for the medicalization of criminal justice. In a review article published in a legal journal five years later, he introduced Lombroso's work, then unavailable in German, to his compatriots. Although he found the idea of atavism unconvincing, Kraepelin praised Lombroso's scientific approach as being free from moralism, calling this a significant innovation in the study of crime. The first major German criminologist, Gustav Aschaffenburg (1866–1944), was Kraepelin's student (Wetzell 2000, pp. 1–61; Wetzell 2004, pp. 65–68; Müller 2004; Galassi 2004).

Aschaffenburg's *Das Verbrechen und seine Bekämpfung* (*Crime and Its Repression*) was the standard work from its appearance in 1903 until the Nazi takeover. While rejecting free will, Aschaffenburg accepted the legal system. He identified the causes of criminality in the social milieu, with degeneration as a crucial intermediary. In his opening speech at the Cologne congress of 1911, he maintained that sterilization and castration, although extreme measures, in some cases were acceptable means of fighting crime (Gadebusch Bondio in Becker & Wetzell 2006, p. 204). He and his colleagues, all of whom called their discipline "criminal biology," were convinced that hereditary factors were involved in offending . They categorized habitual offenders as degenerates or *Minderwertige* (people of lesser value); in the Weimar period, these individuals came to be identified as psychopaths (Wetzell 2000, pp. 63–68, 125–78; Becker 2002, pp. 260–326).

Belief in the hereditary nature of crime was widespread in conservative Bavaria. In 1924 its government instituted a Criminal Biological Agency, directed by the former prison doctor Theodor Viernstein (1878–1949). The agency collected dossiers of prisoners from all over Bavaria with the aim of distinguishing the incorrigibles from those capable of resocialization. Even the agency's priests, officially believing in free will, found heredity a convenient explanation when a prisoner refused to listen to their sermons. The dossiers contained an intriguing contradiction. They focused on behavioral aspects such as an inmate's sexual orientation, social origins, religion, and political beliefs, but the mixture of all these elements was somehow considered hereditary. According to Oliver Liang (1999), the professionals working at the agency, many of whom were conservative Catholics, found the entire Weimar society degenerate and immoral. Biological theories served to denounce this society and acted as a vehicle for reintroducing a petty bourgeois morality. It should be added that Weimar socialists, too, embraced criminal biology.

What happened to criminology after Hitler's rise to power was not unlike the events that had unfolded in Mussolini's Italy a decade earlier. In both countries, a biologically oriented criminology that originally served various political ends was put to the service of one party. Eventually, this led to a reshuffling of the main actors. In Italy in 1927, Ferri supported the Fascist plan to introduce premarital certificates that could be refused to "abnormals," which would supposedly keep them from procreating. In 1940, with the main representatives of the original Italian school dead, Julius Evola denounced the views of "the Jew Lombroso" (Cassata 2011, pp. 100, 266). For their part, the Nazis combined the theoretically incompatible positions of heredity and personal responsibility. Along with Jews and Slavs, they considered criminals to be *Untermenschen* (sub-humans), who instead of therapy deserved harsh punishment. Several biological criminologists jumped on the bandwagon, decrying the alleged softness of the Weimar period. Viernstein cleverly joined the party. Aschaffenburg's position became untenable because he was Jewish. In 1935, at his retirement from the board of the journal he had founded, he denied that criminology had contributed to Weimar "softness." Two years later Viernstein became president of the Criminal Biological Association, and in the same year the Bavarian Criminal Biological Agency was expanded into a national one. In 1939 the criminologist Franz Exner (1881–1947) theorized that the Jews' low score for violence and theft and high score for fraud and embezzlement were in line with their racial profile (Wetzell 2000, pp. 179–235).

In contrast to this biological emphasis, Dutch criminology was overwhelmingly sociological. The sociological orientation of Dutch criminology was due mainly to the efforts of two socialists, Willem Adriaan Bonger (1876–1940) and Clara Wichmann (1885–1922). I have argued that the persistence of faith in solitary confinement in the Netherlands, as well as the relative lack of a biological orientation among its scholars and intellectuals, was due to the pillarization of Dutch society (Spierenburg 1996, pp. 31–32). Of course, this does not explain why one pillar came to dominate criminology. Before the sociological view became universally accepted, biological theories had a few adherents. Gerard Anton van Hamel (1842–1917), a lawyer influenced by Lombroso, delivered the opening speech at the Amsterdam congress of 1901. The physician and champion of gay rights Arnold Aletrino (1858–1916) equally endorsed Lombroso's theories, except for his negative view of homosexuals. For his part, the psychologist Gerard Heymans (1857–1930) reproached Lombroso for his ignorance of "the amazing complexity of woman's soul" (van Weringh 1986, pp. 31, 55–60; Bank et al. 2000, p. 314). Wichmann's reaction to this critique is unknown. She pointed out that offenders might very well possess the ugly physical traits observed by Lombroso, but that adverse social circumstances could have produced both these traits and their crimes (Wichmann 2005 [1920]). Her death in childbirth prevented her from further developing this thesis, and today she is remembered primarily as a feminist lawyer. As a pacifist and vegetarian as well, she partook of the cultural undercurrent of the quest for purity. Like Bonger, she believed in a future classless society.

Bonger, a member of the Socialist Party since 1898, completed his dissertation about criminality and economic conditions in 1905. Written in French, it remains his best-known work. Although Van Hamel supervised the dissertation, its conclusions ran opposite to his views. For Bonger, the born criminal was yesterday's idea. In a later article, written at the occasion of Lombroso's demise, he posed the rhetorical question of what was left of his theory after extensive criticism—with the answer being a plain: "Nothing" (van Weringh 1986, p. 46). Consequently, Bonger also rejected the mixed, biosocial approach that had been fashionable when he embarked on his career. He was sympathetic to the social milieu school, but he wanted to replace it with a more radically sociological approach to the study of crime. Toward this end, he could have built upon the work of Durkheim, whose theories had already inspired sociological research into crime. As a socialist, however, Bonger preferred a Marxian approach.

According to him, crime and property crime in particular were rooted in the inequalities of bourgeois society. In his dissertation he went back to Von Mayr's statistics, supplementing these with many others, to demonstrate that rates of theft and other property offenses correlated with adverse economic circumstances (van Heerikhuizen 1987, pp. 63–72).

His dissertation did not immediately earn Bonger an academic post. From 1905 to 1922 he worked at an insurance company, keeping up with the scholarly literature in his spare time. In 1916 he published a slightly revised version of his dissertation in English as part of a series in which translations of Lombroso, Ferri, and Tarde also appeared. In 1922 Bonger was appointed a professor of sociology and criminology at the University of Amsterdam occupying the first chair in the Netherlands in both fields (Aletrino had taught criminal anthropology in Amsterdam since 1899, but not with the title of professor). Within the pillarized Dutch society, the socialists hailed this appointment as a major victory. In his inaugural lecture (Bonger 2005 [1922]) Bonger invited the law students, who now had two new courses, to take these only if the subject interested them.

In contrast to pre-Fascist Italy, then, the school represented by Bonger and Wichmann was tied directly to one political program. However, the approach of criminologists identifying with either of the two religious pillars must also be considered sociological. They proclaimed the so-called spiritualist school, according to which crime was due to unbelief. Statistics showing an increase in both phenomena served as evidence. Bonger reacted by examining crime rates per province, showing instead that they were lowest in those provinces with the highest rates of nondenominationalism. Throughout the 1920s and 1930s, Bonger dominated Dutch criminology and continued to prove his points with statistics. In his later years the main opposition came from outside criminology. For a time, eugenics was counted as a separate discipline, while anthropologists wrote about the characteristics of "negroes and Indians" in a highly stereotypical fashion (Biervliet et al. 1978). Incorrectly—according to my argument here—Bonger considered everything that smacked of Nazi science to constitute a return to the long-refuted Lombroso. His last book, *Ras en misdaad* (*Race and Crime*), published in the fall of 1939, was meant to counter the German tide. He ridiculed, among others, Nazi authors who glorified the fighting spirit of Nordic peoples while statistics showed that the rates of violent crime were highest in southern Europe (van Heerikhuizen 1987, pp. 191–97).

For five years at least, the Dutch situation resembled the German and Italian one. On capitulation day (15 May 1940) Bonger and his wife took their own lives. The center of Dutch criminology shifted to Leiden University. The following year, Leiden professor J. M. van Bemmelen published a textbook quoting Exner and attributing Jewish crime to that group's racial character. It was also in 1941 that the Lombrosian principle of attuning punishment to the personality of the offender was introduced into German criminal law with respect to murder. As I am writing this chapter, the German minister of justice has proposed revising the article in question (Heribert Prantl & Robert Roßmann, "Maas will Strafrecht bei Mord und Totschlag reformieren," *Süddeutsche Zeitung*, 8 February 2014).

CONCLUSION

This chapter has focused on a few countries in particular, but criminology developed elsewhere as well. The institutionalization of the discipline in university departments and specialized schools took place at a different pace in the countries concerned. At the University of Turin, Lombroso occupied chairs in various departments from 1876 onward; it was not until 1906 that he became a professor of criminal anthropology. At about the same time, Lombroso's student Salvatore Ottolenghi (1861–1934), who later became an admirer of Mussolini, started a police school in which he applied his master's theories to scientific policing (Gibson 2002, pp. 19–20, 137–41). Lacassagne, officially a professor of legal medicine, started a course in criminal anthropology in Lyon in 1886. Initiatives were launched for the establishment of a school for justice and police officials in Hanover in the 1890s and for a similar school in Spain in 1904. The University of Brussels offered a course in criminology from 1897 on. The establishment of the Institute of Criminology at the University of Paris, within the faculty of medicine, took place in 1922 (Kaluszynski 2002, pp. 198–200), making 1922 an especially significant year for the institutionalization of criminology. In the same year Bonger got his chair in Amsterdam and Sellin started to teach at the University of Pennsylvania.

By the Second World War, criminology had become or was on its way to becoming an established discipline, both in the countries examined here and in a number of others in the Western world. After 1945 criminology reemerged as a self-evident academic discipline. Its temporary flirtation with authoritarian régimes, however, was not forgotten (van Swaaningen 2006). Consequently, post-1945, criminology was primarily Anglo-Saxon-oriented. Most European criminologists repudiated prewar scholarship, orienting themselves toward the Chicago school or other approaches from the United States or the United Kingdom. Biological criminology was discredited for a while, until it resurfaced in ideas about genes and brains rather than skulls and eyebrows.

ACKNOWLEDGMENT

I am grateful to Mary Gibson and René van Swaaningen for their comments on the draft of this essay.

REFERENCES

Altena, Bert, & Dick van Lente. 2003. *Vrijheid en rede. Geschiedenis van Westerse samenlevingen, 1750–1989.* Hilversum, The Netherlands: Verloren.

Bank, Jan & Maarten van Buuren. 2000. *1900: Hoogtij van burgerlijke cultuur.* Den Haag, The Netherlands: Sdu Uitgevers.

Becker, Peter. 2002. *Verderbnis und Entartung. Eine Geschichte der Kriminologie des 19. Jahrhunderts als Diskurs und Praxis*. Göttingen, Germany: Vandenhoeck & Ruprecht.

Becker, Peter. 2005. "Criminological Language and Prose from the Late 18th to the Early 20th Centuries." In *Crime and Culture: An Historical Perspective*, ed. Amy Srebnick & René Lévy, 23–36. Aldershot, UK: Ashgate.

Becker, Peter, & Richard F. Wetzell, eds. 2006. *Criminals and Their Scientists: The History of Criminology in International Perspective*. Cambridge: Cambridge University Press.

Beirne, Piers. 1993. *Inventing Criminology: Essays on the Rise of Homo Criminalis*. New York: SUNY Press.

Biervliet, H., B. Bun, A. J. F. Köbben, H. Tromp, K.Verrips, & G. Wekker. 1978. "Biologisme, racisme en eugenetiek in de antropologie en de sociologie van de jaren dertig." In *Toen en thans. De sociale wetenschappen in de jaren dertig en nu*, ed. Frank Bovenkerk, Henri J. M. Claessen, & Bart van Heerikhuizen, 208–35. Baarn, The Netherlands: Ambo.

Binneveld, Hans. 1985. *Filantropie, repressie en medische zorg. Geschiedenis van de inrichting-spsychiatrie*. Deventer, The Netherlands: Van Loghum Slaterus.

Blasius, Dirk. 1976. *Bürgerliche Gesellschaft und Kriminalität. Zur Sozialgeschichte Preussens im Vormärz*. Göttingen, Germany: Vandenhoeck & Ruprecht.

Bonger, Willem Adriaan. 1905. *Criminalité et conditions économiques*. Amsterdam: Maas & Van Suchtelen.

Bonger, Willem Adriaan. 2005 [1922]. "Over de evolutie der moraliteit." In *Basisteksten in de criminologie*, Vol. 3, *Historische en klassieke teksten*, ed. Gerben Jan Nicolaas Bruinsma & Willem Huisman, 115–32. Den Haag, The Netherlands: Boom Juridische Uitgevers.

Cassata, Francesco. 2011. *Building the New Man: Eugenics, Racial Science and Genetics in 20th-Century Italy*. Budapest: Central European University Press.

Davie, Neil. 2004. *Les visages de la criminalité. A la recherche d'une théorie scientifique du criminel type en Angleterre, 1860–1914*. Paris: Éditions Kimé.

Dickens, Peter. 2000. *Social Darwinism: Linking Evolutionary Thought to Social Theory*. Buckingham, UK: Open University Press.

Douglas, Mary. 1966. *Purity and Danger: An Analysis of Concepts of Polution and Taboo*. New York: Praeger.

Elias, Norbert. 1939. *Über den Prozeß der Zivilisation*. Basel: Haus zum Falken.

Foucault, Michel. 1975. *Surveiller et punir: Naissance de la prison*. Paris: Gallimard.

Franke, Herman. 1990. *Twee eeuwen gevangen. Misdaad en straf in Nederland*. Utrecht: Het Spectrum.

Friedland, Paul. 2012. *Seeing Justice Done: The Age of Spectacular Capital Punishment in France*. Oxford: Oxford University Press.

Galassi, Silviana. 2004. *Kriminologie im deutschen Kaiserreich. Geschichte einer gebrochenen Verwissenschaftlichung*. Stuttgart, Germany: Franz Steiner.

Gibson, Mary. 2002. *Born to Crime: Cesare Lombroso and the Origins of Biological Criminology*. Westport, CT: Praeger.

Gibson, Mary. 2005. "Science and Narrative in Italian Criminology, 1880–1920." In *Crime and Culture: An Historical Perspective*, ed. Amy Srebnick & René Lévy, 37–47. Aldershot, UK: Ashgate.

Hayward, Keith, Shadd Maruna, & Jayne Mooney, eds. 2010. *Fifty Key thinkers in Criminology*. London: Routledge.

Heerikhuizen, Bart van. 1987. *W. A. Bonger, socioloog en socialist*. Groningen, The Netherlands: Wolters-Noordhoff/Forsten.

Kaluszynski, Martine. 2002. *La République à l'épreuve du crime. La construction du crime comme objet politique, 1880–1920*. Paris: L. G. D. J.

Laarse, Rob van der & Arnold Labrie, eds. 1998. *De hang naar zuiverheid. De cultuur van het moderne Europa*. Amsterdam: Het Spinhuis.

Labrie, Arnold. 2001. *Zuiverheid en decadentie. Over de grenzen van de burgerlijke cultuur in West-Europa, 1870–1914*. Amsterdam: Bert Bakker.

Liang, Oliver. 1999. "La biologie de la moralité. La biologie criminelle en Bavière et en Allemagne, 1924–1945." In *Homo criminalis. Pratique et doctrines médico-légales, 16e–20e siècles*, ed. Vincent Barras & Michel Porret, 119–32. Geneva: Association de la revue Equinoxe.

Lombroso, Cesare. 2006. *Criminal Man*. Trans. and ed. Mary Gibson & Nicole Hahn Rafter. Durham, NC, & London: Duke University Press.

Mason, David S. 2011. *A Concise History of Modern Europe: Liberty, Equality, Solidarity*, 2nd ed. Lanham, MD: Rowman & Littlefield.

Mucchielli, Laurent, ed. 1995. *Histoire de la criminologie française*. Paris: L'Harmattan.

Müller, Christian. 2004. *Verbrechensbekämpfung im Anstaltsstaat. Psychiatrie, Kriminologie und Strafrechtsreform in Deutschland, 1871–1933*. Göttingen, Germany: Vandenhoeck & Ruprecht.

Muhammad, Khalil Gibran. 2010. *The Condemnation of Blackness: Race, Crime and the Making of Modern Urban America*. Cambridge MA: Harvard University Press.

Newburn, Tim. 2007. *Criminology*. Cullompton, UK: Willan.

Porret, Michel. 2003. *Beccaria. Le droit de punir*. Paris: Editions Michalon.

Rafter, Nicole, ed. 2009. *The Origins of Criminology: A Reader*. New York: Routledge.

Renneville, Marc. 2003. *Crime et folie. Deux siècles d'enquêtes médicales et judiciaires*. Paris: Fayard.

Ruller, Sibo van. 1998. "Theoretische integratie bij Lombroso en Ferri." *Tijdschrift voor Criminologie* 40 (2): 129–38.

Spierenburg, Pieter. 1996. "Four Centuries of Prison History: Punishment, Suffering, the Body and Power." In *Institutions of Confinement: Hospitals, Asylums and Prisons in Western Europe and North America, 1500–1950*, ed. Norbert Finzsch & Robert Jütte, 17–35. Cambridge: Cambridge University Press.

Spierenburg, Pieter. 2013. *Violence and Punishment: Civilizing the Body Through Time*. Cambridge: Polity.

Swaaningen, René van. 2006 "In Search of Criminology's Epistemological Threshold." In *Sociological Theory and Criminological Research: Views from Europe and the United States*, ed. Matthieu Deflem, 249–70. New York: Elsevier.

Weringh, Jac. van. 1986. *De afstand tot de horizon. Verwachting en werkelijkheid in de Nederlandse criminologie*. Amsterdam: Arbeiderspers.

Wetzell, Richard F. 2000. *Inventing the Criminal: A History of German Criminology, 1880–1945*. Chapel Hill: University of North Carolina Press.

Wetzell, Richard F. 2004. "From Retributive Justice to Social Defense: Penal Reform in Fin-de-Siècle Germany." In *Germany at the Fin de Siècle: Culture, Politics and Ideas*, ed. Suzanne Marchand & David Lindenfeld, 59–77. Baton Rouge: Louisiana State University Press.

Wichmann, Clara. 2005 [1920]. "Misdaad, straf en maatschappij." In *Basisteksten in de criminologie*, Vol. 3, *Historische en klassieke teksten*, ed. Gerben Jan Nicolaas Bruinsma & Willem Huisman, 103–14. Den Haag, The Netherlands: Boom Juridische Uitgevers.

Wiener, Martin J. 1990. *Reconstructing the Criminal: Culture, Law and Policy in England, 1830–1914*. Cambridge: Cambridge University Press.

Workman, Lance. 2014. *Charles Darwin: The Shaping of Evolutionary Thinking*. Houndmills, UK: Palgrave Macmillan.

....

CHAPTER 20

CRIMINAL MINDS

*Psychiatry, Psychopathology, and
the Government of Criminality*

....

STEPHEN GARTON

INTRODUCTION

....

IN 1906, heir to a Pittsburgh fortune Harry Kendall Thaw shot and killed society architect Stanford White in front of numerous theatergoers at Madison Square Garden. His
wealth, the fame of his victim, and the scandalous cause ensured the case was a *cause
célèbre*. Thaw believed White had drugged and seduced his wife before their marriage
and, on discovering this heinous offense, was "driven mad" by thoughts of revenge. At
trial his defense counsel argued that "Dementia Americana"—the understandable loss
of reason any right-thinking American gentleman might suffer in his desire to avenge
the seduction of innocence—was the mitigating factor (Gillman 1988). While Thaw
knew his actions were wrong, he was acquitted (at a second trial) on grounds of temporary insanity because the jury concluded, as the defense had argued, that all thought of
right and wrong were expunged at the precise moment of his act of revenge. The Thaw
trial was, in one sense, typical, with advocates arguing the merits of the insanity defense
before juries and stretching or contracting the interpretation of the long-established
M'Naghten Rules to suit their purposes. In another sense it points to the expanding
repertoire of concepts and diseases deployed in the courts, reflecting a shift away from
the Victorian framework of mania and melancholia and the explosion of new functional, psychological, psychodynamic, and psychobiological theories that accompanied
the dissemination of the work of theorists such as Freud, Adolf Meyer, William James,
Charcot, Jung, and Weir-Mitchell (Shorter 1997; Kramer 1982; Grob 1983; Scull 1993).

Around the same time as Thaw's act of revenge, these new psychodynamic approaches
also found a receptive audience outside the courts as criminologists, penologists, child
savers, and social reformers, in a range of institutional contexts, came to believe that

practices informed by psychiatry might be the key to the prevention of crime and delinquency. On both sides of the Atlantic psychiatrists were increasingly used to assist in the classification, assessment, and treatment of delinquents in juvenile courts and reformatories and of prisoners in penitentiaries and prisons. There was a widespread belief that the new psychodynamic psychiatry, with its focus on personality disorders, might explain why some turned to crime and how these tendencies might be arrested and even corrected. Psychiatric approaches became a major strand within interwar criminology and penological practice in North America, Britain, and Europe.

This essay explores the ways psychiatric approaches have been incorporated into criminal justice systems in the West, concentrating largely on the United Kingdom and the United States. Section I discusses the emergence of an explicit space for psychiatry within the criminal justice system in the nineteenth century through the codification of rules governing the insanity defense. Section II traces the emergence of a distinct discourse of criminology as the context for the increasing role of medical theories of crime and dangerousness in the governance of problem populations during the late nineteenth century, an issue further explored in section III. Continuing the development of these themes, section IV focuses on the development of psychiatric theories of criminality, in particular moral imbecility and psychopathology, and how they shaped the emergence of classification and treatment options for inmates in prisons and reformatories in the interwar years. By the late 1930s, however, disillusionment with the efficacy of psychiatry was setting in, and criminology increasingly turned to sociological theories to explain deviance, a shift discussed in section V. Finally, section VI discusses the emergence of movements against psychiatry and the popular demand for zero tolerance of crime. In this context older traditions of rehabilitation informed by psychiatry were increasingly abandoned in favor of strategies such as mandatory sentencing and the reintroduction (in the United States) of capital punishment. Nonetheless, while the aspirations of interwar psychiatrists may have disappointed many, psychiatry and psychiatrists maintained a place within the larger criminal justice system, a place they continue to inhabit in the contemporary context (Loughnan 2012; Lacey 2009; Lunbeck 1994).

I. The Insanity Defence and M'Naghten Rules

The governance of crime and criminals in the West has long worked from the presumption that there are knowable and comprehensible reasons underpinning criminal acts. Greed, envy, revenge, insult, lust, and avarice historically were oft-cited reasons and provocations for criminal behaviors, although these could be supplemented by more mystical factors, such as witchcraft. In the late eighteenth and early nineteenth centuries, as the focus of criminal law deliberations shifted gradually from a concern with the fact of a crime to the nature of the individuals committing those crimes, the standard of the "reasonable man" achieved prominence in Victorian judicial thinking (Wiener 2006). At the same time, there has always been a space, for some historians stretching back to Homeric times, for unreason, bestial inclinations, madness, or, in some contexts, demonic possession to serve as the underlying causes of particular criminal acts (Robinson 1996). Crimes caused by inflamed passions, strange compulsions, delusions, and the absence of reason were part of the canon of deliberations over guilt and punishment stretching back centuries. Starting in the late eighteenth century, however, the idea that medical practitioners might assist the courts in determining whether insanity was a factor in a criminal act gained increasing acceptance. As Joel Eigen has demonstrated, the number of English murder trials in which medical practitioners were called to give evidence grew from one in ten in the late 1700s to one in two by the 1840s (1995, p. 24).

By the mid-nineteenth century the grounds for an insanity defense were finally codified in British law through the famous M'Naghten Rules of 1848 establishing the principle that such a defense hinged on a defendant being incapable of knowing that the act was wrong at the time he or she committed the crime; this principle in turn influenced North American judicial practice (Smith 1981; Walker 1968; Moran 1981). The notion of criminal lunatics provided the basis for the establishment of special institutions for such criminals. In North America the first institution for the criminally insane, Willard (New York), was opened in 1855, with a further institution (Matteawan) opening in 1896. For Britain, the empire often served as a useful laboratory for social experiments. Thus the first asylum for the criminally insane was established in Dublin in 1850, and only later, in 1863, was a similar institution, Broadmoor, opened in England (Prior 2004; Seddon 2007).

By the late nineteenth century, however, specialists in psychological medicine, known as alienists or psychiatrists, found their role in criminal trials under the M'Naghten Rules increasingly restricted. A number argued that the rules were overly narrow and related more to legal than to medical criteria. In their view, such rules took no account of the fact that some offenders suffered debilitating psychiatric conditions over which they had no control, such that they might know that the act was wrong but be unable to restrain themselves from doing it. For some, like Frederick Norton Manning, the Inspector-General of the Insane in New South Wales, the rules were "false in theory and unsatisfactory in practice" (Manning 1892, p. 59).

There was a concerted push by psychiatrists to insist that medical opinion, and especially the new discipline of forensic psychiatry, should carry more weight in the operation of criminal justice systems on both sides of the Atlantic (Singer & Krohn 1924). Slowly they made headway. In Scotland the concept of diminished responsibility, a less stringent criterion for mitigation than the M'Naghten Rules, had become an accepted consideration within judicial thinking by the late nineteenth century. Diminished responsibility and related concepts such as irresistible impulse and automatism were gradually adopted into legal frameworks in a number of jurisdictions in the first half of the twentieth century and were enshrined in the British 1957 Homicide Act

(Loughnan 2012; Walker & McCabe 1973). This push by psychiatrists to play a more active role in criminal law proceedings and decisions about the most appropriate institution for the confinement of the criminally insane, however, did not go uncontested. Thomas Mott Osborne, a warden of Sing Sing, thought the "disease theory of crime mischievous" (Osborne 1924, p. 31). More fundamentally, the operation of medical opinion within the courts, prisons, and reformatories was still at the behest of judges, juries, government bureaucracies, and superintendents.

Focusing on the theater of the trial, however, obscures more profound shifts in the operation of psychiatric perspectives in the management of criminal justice. While psychiatry was increasingly deployed by both prosecution and defense in the courtroom, criminal justice administrators—the attorney-general, police, the judiciary, and prison administrations—also began to question whether particular criminals should be presented to the court system at all. In the early twentieth century the impact of psychiatric arguments about uncontrollable compulsions, fixations, and other mental phenomena on beliefs governing what may or may not, under questioning, have fitted the M'Naghten Rules led some jurisdictions in Britain, parts of North America, and Australia to assess more closely the fitness to plead of those arrested on criminal charges. Psychiatrists were increasingly asked by police, magistrates, and judges to assess prisoners before trial, and, if found to suffer serious mental disturbances, such prisoners were certified as insane and sent to mental hospitals under court direction. In other instances some offenders found guilty but sane were reassessed after conviction and certified as insane under less stringent criteria than the M'Naghten Rules and were then sent to criminal mental hospitals or the psychiatric sections of particular prisons. Thus, while the M'Naghten Rules remained the declared criteria for assessing mental culpability in the courts, criminal justice systems, persuaded by psychiatrists that these rules were too restrictive and not aligned with contemporary understandings of mental illness, began to stream particular offenders out of the court system and into mental health systems (Walker & McCabe 1973; Garton 1986; Seddon 2007).

II. The Emergence of Criminology

The M'Naghten Rules were nested within other profound changes in the governance of crime. The emergence of institutions such as prisons, penitentiaries, and reformatories for the punishment of offenders in the early to mid-nineteenth century (and the corresponding decline in such measures as capital punishment and transportation) set in train a number of important currents in thinking about crime and punishment in the Victorian era (Wiener 1990; Seddon 2007; Rafter 2006). One was the increasing interest in the characteristics of prison populations, a fascination ignited by Cesare Lombroso's studies of Italian prisoners, leading to his theory that there was a particular "criminal type," evident in distinctive physical characteristics that marked them out from other citizens (Gibson 2006). By the late nineteenth century this emerging science of the criminal was flourishing. Researchers throughout Europe, Britain, the United States, Canada, Australia, South America, and Asia were examining prison and reformatory populations, seeking common traits that might unlock the reasons why some people turned to crime (Becker & Wetzell 2006).

These concerns were fueled by wider fears that the social Darwinist future of a triumphant West was actually under threat. Theories of degeneracy and hereditary deficiency became popular explanations for rising rates of crime, recidivism, delinquency, alcoholism, and insanity. Evidence that birth rates were declining among the middle classes but increasing among the urban underclasses added further to the fear that Western civilization, far from thriving, was in decline. Scientific explanations for decline and the search for measures that might arrest this trend added to the interest in and significance of criminology as a domain of vital scientific inquiry (Pick 1989; Bashford & Levine 2010; Kelves 1985; Becker & Wetzell 2006). Penologists, criminologists, reformers, and medical practitioners became increasingly interested in strategies to incarcerate the unfit and equally prevent vulnerable populations from lapsing into such practices as crime, delinquency, prostitution, and alcoholism (Garton 2010; Lunbeck 1994; Castel, Castel, & Lovell 1982; Rose 1985).

While Lombroso's theories of the born criminal found many supporters in Europe and the United States, they had equally as many critics, such as the English prison medical officer Charles Goring in Britain and Alexandre Lacassagne in France. In 1913, Goring published his widely cited rebuttal of Lombroso's atavistic theories of criminality, deploying statistical analyses of the inmate population of British prisons to demonstrate that there was no defined criminal type based on physical characteristics; rather, criminals were like other "deficient" social groups, marked by inferior mental capacities—an argument that gave impetus to eugenic theories of crime and a passion for mental testing that influenced criminal justice systems in Britain, Europe, and North America (Rafter 1997; Mucchielli 2006; Goring 1972). While Lombroso and Goring may have differed over the characteristics of the criminal, both endorsed the view that particular individuals were prone to crime and, if caught early (through testing), could be permanently segregated and prevented from propagating their disease. The focus of criminology became the criminal rather than the crime, and increasingly, criminology, as an extensive historiography now attests, deployed a wide range of scientific tests and theories to identify and treat those with a supposed predisposition to crime (Becker & Wetzell 2006).

There were many strands to positivist criminology, attracting a variety of disciplines and professions. Alphonse Bertillon, a pioneering biometrics researcher, popularized anthropometric measurements of criminals as a means of ensuring their identification. Fingerprinting, also for the identification of criminals, first developed in India (by Indian researchers), was adopted in Britain for use by Scotland Yard in 1901 and spread to many police forces throughout the West in subsequent decades. Numerous scientists and reformers, such as American sociologist Charles Henderson, published influential texts on the "dependent, defective and delinquent classes." This positivist turn in criminology attracted many medical practitioners. Lombroso and Lacassagne were both physicians, as was Havelock Ellis in Britain and prominent German advocate of degeneration Max Nordau. The influential German psychiatrist Emil Kraepelin was similarly fascinated by theories of criminality. In the United States there were also many prominent medical practitioner criminologists, such as W. Duncan McKim and Moriz Benedikt (Rafter 2006; Bondio 2006).

This emergence of criminology as a distinct domain of scientific inquiry in the nineteenth century has generated a significant body of scholarship, particularly in the last forty years, fueled in large part by the impact of the work of Michel Foucault (1977). Foucault's focus on criminology as a specific discourse that constructed "the criminal," creating subjects enmeshed in complex networks of surveillance and discipline, has been very influential (Becker & Wetzell 2006). It has also spawned a vast literature on other disciplinary discourses, notably psychiatry, and how new forms of governmentality have constructed and regulated a variety of problem populations (Rose 1985). The great strength of this approach is that it opened up important insights into the ways discourses and institutional practices work, double-helix-like, to create modern forms of identity and social practice. Its weakness is that it has often worked at the level of generalized discourses and ideal practices rather than at the coalface of actual practices in specific institutional contexts. New forms of governmentality were commonly undermined and compromised by financial constraints, understaffing, overcrowding, laziness, ineptitude, and sometimes sadism and violence. More importantly, these new discourses and practices did not sweep aside older traditions of regulation, as some of this literature suggests, but had to jostle for a place within existing institutional structures, which in many instances circumscribed and constrained their impact. Psychiatric approaches to crime waxed and waned in importance, serving the administration of justice rather than supplanting it.

III. THE MEDICAL TURN

From the mid-nineteenth century onward, the medical turn in thinking about social problems became evident in many areas of social reform. By the 1840s, the idea that insanity was a moral problem best treated in asylums run by churchmen and reformers was increasingly being supplanted by the view that doctors were the only experts able to determine whether moral or medical treatments would be effective, and by the 1850s asylums in the United States, Europe, Britain, and the British dominions—Australia, New Zealand, South Africa, and Canada—had largely fallen under the superintendence of medical practitioners (Scull 1993; Grob 1983). Equally striking is the medical turn in the conception and treatment of inebriety. By the 1860s, as Brian Harrison and others have shown, moral and religious frameworks for understanding inebriety as a moral vice requiring teetotalism as its cure were being supplanted by theories of habitual drunkenness as a disease requiring medical treatment (Harrison 1971; MacLeod 1967; Garton 1987). Here the focus became the confinement of inebriates (by the 1890s this confinement had become compulsory in some jurisdictions, notably Britain, which passed such legislation in 1898) in asylums and retreats where they might be isolated from corrupting influences, prevented from accessing alcohol, and subject to various forms of drug and antitoxin treatments, most famously the use of injections of bichloride of gold and sodium at such private clinics as the Keeley Institute in the United States. The first inebriate asylum was established in Bingham, New York, in 1864, and the first Keeley Institute was established in Illinois in 1880. Starting in the 1870s inebriate asylums were also established in Canada, Australia, Sweden, France, Ireland, and Germany, and by the first decade of the twentieth century there were over a hundred such institutions in the United States and nearly fifty in Britain (Baumohl & Room 1987).

Inebriate and mental asylums were also a means of streaming inmates suffering diseases out of prisons and workhouses. Habitual drunkenness became another mitigating factor deployed in the courts to position criminal acts as products of compulsions rather than rational acts. The emergence of discourses of disease alongside those of deterrence and justice highlights complex debates about the nature and character of the dependent and delinquent classes in the late nineteenth and early twentieth centuries. Those suffering disease should, it was commonly asserted, be placed in alternatives to prison where they could receive medical treatment. In part, the emergence of criminology and associated discourses around dangerousness as a social disease represented a larger scientific effort to better define who truly was a member of the criminal class (Pratt 1997; Loughnan 2012).

Another vulnerable population was youthful offenders. Reformatories for neglected, delinquent, and orphaned children had been a feature of the Victorian charity system since the early nineteenth century, but by the end of the century increasing concern about the deleterious effects of mixing younger offenders and hardened adult offenders, with attendant concerns that impressionable youths were being inducted into criminal habits while in prisons, underpinned reform efforts to create separate juvenile systems of justice and detention. By the first decades of the twentieth century children's courts had been established in North America (first in Chicago in 1899 and soon after in New York and Boston, with thirty States having such systems by the 1920s), Britain, Canada, Australia, and Germany (Mennel 1973). Similarly, special juvenile detention centers and reformatories to stream youthful offenders out of the adult system were established throughout many parts of Europe, North America, Britain, and its empire. The 1895 Gladstone Committee recommended the establishment of a "borstal" system for juvenile offenders in Britain, and the first of these institutions was opened in 1902. The 1908 Prevention of Crime Act formalized the British juvenile court and borstal system (Seddon 2007; Finder 2006; Jones 1999).

Streaming populations who were not seen as irredeemable criminals out of prisons also influenced the treatment of adult offenders. Critical here were classification systems to differentiate among criminals, between those whose condition was so ingrained and intractable—in some views, hereditary—as to warrant permanent segregation and those unfortunates who fell into bad associations through poverty, ill luck, and misfortunate and who under the right conditions might be reformed. These currents of criminological reform underpinned legislation in many jurisdictions to facilitate early release of first offenders and the increasing use of fines for some offenses, while at the same time ensuring that habitual criminals could be detained longer than their criminal offense warranted. The first habitual criminals act was passed in Britain in 1869, but the concept of the habitual offender gained much greater currency in the context of theories of born criminals and degeneracy and emerging eugenic theories of hereditary deficiency, especially as new anthropometric tests and later fingerprinting (which allowed aliases, which were commonly used, to be uncovered) revealed that rates of recidivism were much higher than previously thought, rising in Britain from 50 percent in the 1850s to 75 percent by the Edwardian era (Wiener 1990, pp. 342–58). In the 1890s a series of inquires into prison discipline in Britain highlighted that many prisoners were suffering from mental illness, inebriety, and mental defectiveness, leading to demands for more alternatives to the prison. Some claimed that habitual criminality was a disease like lunacy that required medical intervention rather than incarceration. The intention of new habitual criminal legislation in the Edwardian era was to detain genuine criminals for as long as possible to effect a "cure" (Wiener 1990). If such cures failed, then longer terms of imprisonment would act to protect society from those not amenable to reform.

In this climate of increasing anxiety about the delinquent classes, strategies for differentiating between different types of criminals became vital. The early adoption of such measures as Bertillon measurements (from the 1890s), fingerprinting (from 1901), and the introduction of mental testing of prisoners and juvenile delinquents after 1905 were all designed to identify hardened recidivists, defective delinquents, and habitual and hereditary criminals and to subject them to new forms of penal discipline, while releasing those whose fall arose from poor social conditions. For the latter, penal reform focused on first offenders and more liberal parole conditions to spare them imprisonment or reduce their time in institutions. These offenders, it was believed, might be amenable to improvement if placed in better social contexts and monitored by an emerging profession of social workers, child guidance experts, visiting nurses, and other members of helping professions alongside the more established charity networks (Walkowitz 1999; Platt 1969; Jones 1999).

Many psychiatrists and social reformers advocated early intervention as critical to success, allowing the identification of the incipient offender when he or she was more amenable to reform. In this context psychiatrists believed they held one key to understanding and ameliorating the problem of rising crime and delinquency. The answer lay in more rigorous measurement and classification: mental testing to weed out the hereditary criminals, and psychological and psychiatric assessments to uncover those whose condition might benefit from treatment. In this effort many of the new psychiatric, psychological, and social analysis approaches blurred the boundaries between delinquency, social deprivation, and maladjustment, entangling courts, especially the new children's courts, in psychological investigations, diagnoses, and decisions (Rose 1989). It was here, in the borderlands of psychological disposition, that psychiatrists came to assert the efficacy of their methods. Nonetheless, while hardened criminals were considered beyond help, in the early twentieth century, as psychiatrists on both sides of the Atlantic began to explore the efficacy of new forms of classification and treatment, one figure emerged that troubled the distinction between redeemable and irredeemable offenders—the psychopath, or moral imbecile.

IV. MORAL IMBECILES AND PSYCHOPATHS

The belief that there were criminals of considerable guile and intelligence was a powerful one in Victorian popular culture. It found its greatest expression in Arthur Conan Doyle's criminal genius, Professor Moriarty. The scientific literature on criminals of unusual intelligence, however, can be traced back to James Cowles Pritchard's 1835 *Treatise on Insanity and Other Disorders Affecting the Mind*, in which he devoted a section to "moral insanity." This concept, which in turn drew on the earlier work of French alienist Philippe Pinel on affective insanity, described conditions in which the patient showed no defect of intelligence or mental reasoning yet had little or no moral conscience. For Pritchard, people with few scruples, little empathy for others, and the willingness to ruthlessly exploit their power over weaker intellects to advance their own selfish interests suffered a profound defect of the moral and ethical senses. In the nineteenth century Pritchard's concept of moral insanity was taken up by others, including Benjamin Rush in antebellum America and later Henry Maudsley in Britain. It remained, however, a curious chapter in Victorian psychiatry, on the margins of mainstream psychiatric discourse (Augstein 1996).

Moral insanity, however, achieved much greater currency in the early twentieth century, as new eugenic theories of hereditary deficiency were increasingly deployed in assessing prison populations. Psychiatrists and criminologists in the late Victorian and Edwardian eras found troubling instances of criminals who defied easy categorization when subjected to mental and other forms of testing: offenders who seemed intelligent and calculating rather than degenerate, deficient, and of inferior intellect. In this context Pritchard's concept of moral insanity, although in the context of eugenic theories of the time often recast as moral imbecility, entered into the lexicon of Edwardian criminology, deployed by leading practitioners such as Charles Goring and Havelock Ellis. The 1908 Royal Commission into the Care and Control of the Feebleminded described moral imbecility as characteristic of habitual criminals who seemed to suffer no marked intellectual defect. This concept was given legislative weight in the 1913 Mental Deficiency Act, and throughout the 1920s criminologists and psychiatrists sought to uncover its prevalence in criminal and delinquent populations (Jackson 2000; Thomson 1998).

On the other side of the Atlantic the idea that there were some criminals of superior intellect but impoverished moral sensibility was given powerful impetus by the work of the towering figure of early twentieth-century American psychiatry Adolf Meyer.

Meyer pioneered the detailed case history approach, seeing mental symptoms as psychological adaptations to dynamic social processes. According to his theory, it was only by uncovering the historical process of adaptation, charting the changing social and psychological responses to external stimuli, that psychiatrists could uncover the psychological forces underpinning particular symptoms (Leys & Davis 1990). In 1904, Meyer, drawing on the earlier work of German psychiatrist Robert Koch, developed the concept of "constitutional psychopathic inferiority" to describe patients whose behavior was excessively aggressive or irresponsible (Lunbeck 1994; Jones 1999; Garton 2010).

Meyer's theories found immediate favour. One such advocate was William Healy, a child psychiatrist, who established the Cook County (Chicago) Juvenile Psychopathic Institute in 1909. Healy undertook detailed social and psychiatric assessments of delinquents, using his findings to stream many out of the court system into alternative treatment facilities designed to improve their prospects for successful social reintegration. Healy's practical application of Meyer's theories influenced other psychiatrists, mental hygienists, reformatory superintendents, and criminologists, including Thomas Salmon, Victor Anderson, and Katherine Bement Davis. In the early to mid-twentieth century these new psychological testing and treatment facilities proliferated, particularly on the East and West coasts of North America and in Chicago (Walker 1980; Garton 2010).

Many of these American psychiatrists, reformers, and penologists embraced the concept of psychopathic inferiority. Healy devoted a chapter in his influential 1915 text *The Individual Delinquent* to psychopaths, arguing that such juveniles were characterized by "abnormal social and mental reactions to ordinary conditions of life" (Healy 1915, pp. 575–89). For Healy, the intractable troublemakers in the juvenile delinquent population were often psychopaths. They usually came from families that were far from the dysfunctional and impoverished families normally encountered in his work, and they often seemed to be a poor influence on other inmates. They were cunning liars and troublemakers and seemed to be less amenable to reform. A wide range of American psychiatrists, particularly those studying and treating criminals, prisoners, and juvenile delinquents, embraced the psychopath classification. It entered the psychiatric lexicon through the work of such key early twentieth-century forensic psychiatrists as Bernard and Sheldon Glueck, George Kirby, Guy Fernald, Edgar King, Victor Anderson, and Edith Spaulding.

The popularity of the psychopath concept reflected its utility in the broader landscape of Progressive social reform in early twentieth-century America. This wave of reform encompassed many areas of American social life and proved to be particularly influential in areas such as penology and juvenile and urban social reform, as late nineteenth- and early twentieth-century inquiries into and surveys of child labor, habitual drunkenness, prostitution, crime, and delinquency documented appalling urban social conditions and rising rates of moral depravity. While there was a pessimistic, increasingly hereditarian and eugenic strand to American social reform, the more optimistic Progressive strand took hold through the efforts of influential reformers such as Sophonisba Breckenridge, Charles Loring Brace, Clifford Beers, and Jane Addams.

Prominent philanthropists supported new reform efforts. John D. Rockefeller Jr., after participating in a grand jury on "white slavery," established the Bureau of Social Hygiene in 1911, which subsequently funded much of the American research into delinquency and crime and supported many of the major social and psychiatric experiments in the treatment of delinquents, prisoners, and criminals during the interwar years (Alexander 1995; Ludmerer 1972; Brown 1992; Garton 2010).

Key figures supported by the bureau were attracted to the new psychodynamic theories of Adolf Meyer and their practical application for psychiatrists working in institutional contexts such as reformatories, children's courts, and penitentiaries. The bureau actively sponsored initiatives such as the establishment in 1913 of the Laboratory of Social Hygiene at the Bedford Hills Reformatory for Women, under the superintendence of Katherine Bement Davis. A few years later it also supported the opening of a "Classification Clinic" at Sing Sing Penitentiary where Sheldon Glueck undertook detailed studies of inmates. Within a few years similar clinics were opened at the Auburn, Clinton, Attica, and Great Meadow penitentiaries. The bureau further funded and monitored similar initiatives in Chicago and California (Alexander 1995; Freedman 1981; Garton 2010). Here, theories of personality disorders as the root cause of many forms of delinquent behavior became the focus of investigation.

In practice these clinics embraced a mix of professional expertise to ensure that all aspects of an inmate's social, familial, intellectual, and emotional history could be charted to ensure that those suffering particular social or intellectual problems could be differentiated from those whose disorder was one of personality. Individual inmate profiles were developed to guide treatment decisions, with social workers interviewing friends and neighbors of inmates to gain details on the social background, family relationships, and community dynamics that framed their actions. Psychologists applied a range of intelligence tests to see if there was an underlying intellectual deficiency that might warrant transfer to one of the institutions for defective delinquents at Matteawan and Dannemora. Increasingly, however, psychologists moved away from the eugenic intelligence testing, focusing increasingly on tests that aimed to uncover underlying personality types and dynamics, including the Worcester Form Boards, Pinter-Patterson, Healy II, Rorschach, and Porteus tests, and the Minnesota Multiphasic Personality Inventory. Finally, with all of this preliminary information at hand, the resident psychiatrist carried out a psychiatric examination of the inmate to determine a diagnosis and a decision on appropriate treatment. These decisions could run counter to deliberations of the courts. Inmates in some institutions were detained for far longer than their designated sentence on the basis that they were not yet cured. In these institutional and penitentiary contexts parole decisions were increasingly based on psychiatric assessments concerning fitness for release (Rafter 1997; Garton 2010; Jones 1999).

The importance of Meyer's work in shaping the impact of psychiatry in the American criminal justice system in turn influenced developments in Britain. Increasingly, prison administrators and psychiatrists found the definition of moral imbecile, enshrined in the 1913 Mental Defectives Act, too restrictive. For some British penologists and psychiatrists the flaw in this legislative provision was that it combined mental defect (as determined by intelligence testing) with criminal propensity, even though many offenders, particularly sex offenders, were of normal intelligence and thus could not be incarcerated as moral imbeciles, leading to their release back into the community when their sentence ended. Prominent British psychiatrists such as David Henderson were attracted to the concept of the psychopath because it freed psychiatric conceptions of psychopathology from mental defect, offering opportunities for extended treatment and incarceration of sex psychopaths. These approaches were also taken up elsewhere. Australia established its first classification clinic at Long Bay Gaol in 1925. Similarly, in 1931, the Tavistock Clinic, a group of influential psychiatrists, established the Association for the Scientific Treatment of Criminals and opened a specialist "Psychopathic Clinic" for the treatment of delinquency. This clinic, under the influence of Edward Glover and Kate Friedlander, pioneered the use of psychoanalysis in the treatment of delinquency in Britain (Cordess 1992). Nonetheless, British courts were slow to adopt the language of psychopathology, with some prominent jurists fearing that it was a catchall phrase "for cases otherwise difficult to classify" (Walker & McCabe 1973, p. 215). But after the Second World War the utility of the term persuaded many to adopt it in practice, and the 1957 Homicide Act specifically linked the concept of diminished responsibility to the category of psychopathic personality (Walker & McCabe 1973).

V. The Sociological Turn

Ironically, the intense interest in personality disorders and criminal behavior between the wars contributed to its undoing. The mania for psychiatric classification and treatment of inmates in penitentiaries and juvenile reformatories led to extraordinary rates of diagnosis of psychopathic personality disorders. A 1925 New York special committee investigating the problems of psychopaths in courts, penitentiaries, prisons, and reformatories found the diagnosis rate to be as high as 38 percent in some institutions. By the early 1930s, psychopaths represented over 40 percent of the criminal population in many penitentiaries in New York (Garton 2010). More troubling for criminologists, psychiatrists, and penal reformers was the fact that crime and recidivism rates did not seem to be declining, despite nearly two decades of psychiatric reform efforts. In reality, of course, practice fell far short of the ideal. Given the number of inmates in such institutions, psychiatric assessments were, perhaps inevitably, perfunctory, and case management was driven more by the need to document as many inmates as possible than concern with intensive individual treatment. Moreover, inmates were still kept in institutions where the complex dynamics of inmate and attendant violence, rape, extortion, and corruption remained prevalent. By the mid-1930s key figures associated with the Bureau of Social Hygiene were showing signs of profound disillusion. For some, such as Max Winsor, the problem was that the approach wasn't psychiatric enough: treatment was "routine and academic," and "little serious effort [was] being made to tackle the problem."[1] Given the significant proportion of supposed antisocial personality types in the criminal justice system, this failure was a serious one.

The seeming intractability of psychiatric treatment of delinquents drove some to search for new psychiatric answers, and for many the solution lay in psychoanalysis. By the late 1930s, prominent forensic and juvenile delinquent psychiatrists, such as William Healy and Sheldon and Bernard Glueck, were increasingly turning to Freudian approaches, with their promise of theoretical rigor and greater conceptual depth. Other influential psychiatrists, such as Karl Menninger, gave impetus to the idea that childhood traumas and excessive repression were keys to later maladjustment, particularly sexual delinquency (Hale 1995). In Britain, from the 1940s onward, the work of psychoanalysts like John Bowlby on maternal deprivation and attachment inspired detailed studies into the childhood dynamics of delinquency, and influential administrators, such as Norwood East, the commissioner of prisons, incorporated Freudian theories into mainstream British criminology in the postwar years (East 1949; Holmes 1993).

For others, however, the problem was deeper than a lack of proper application of psychiatric methods: the approach itself was flawed. The key critics of the personality approach included sociologists who had been integrally involved with the Bureau of Social Hygiene, notably William Thomas (Chicago University), Thorsten Sellin (Pennsylvania), and Edwin Sutherland (Indiana). Initially these sociologists had been enthusiastic advocates of the personality approach, arguing that antisocial personalities developed in specific social, economic, familial, and mental environments. In particular, they focused on family relationships, seeing these as the seedbed for the formation of particular personality types. They created detailed case studies in which sociological, psychiatric, and, increasingly, psychoanalytic approaches could collaborate in developing a more rounded picture of mental and personality formation (Jones 1999; Ross 1991). By the mid-1930s, however, Sutherland, in particular, was increasingly finding the individual case study approach unsatisfactory. The failure of psychiatric and psychoanalytic treatment to effect improvements in recidivism rates pushed him toward investigation of the social roots of antisocial behavior, shifting the focus of criminology away from individual personality to wider dynamics such as criminal subcultures, in which, through differential association, individuals in particular social groups learned forms of criminal behavior. The individual for Sutherland became a social rather than a psychological construct (Gaylord & Galliher 1986; Geis & Goff 1986).

Starting in the 1940s, Sutherland's approach became the dominant school of American criminology for the next thirty years. It influenced a number of related theoretical approaches of importance for criminology in the postwar years, notably Robert Merton's deviance theory; neutralization theory, developed by Gresham Sykes and David Matza; and labeling theory, for which the work of Howard Becker was particularly influential. Each of these approaches stressed the social processes by which deviant behaviors were learned and transmitted and shifted the focus of criminology away from the individual offender and specific personality types amenable (or not) to psychiatric intervention to larger social processes that constructed criminality. Here, the emphasis became tackling these social processes and their underlying factors, such as poverty, urban ghettoes, and gang cultures, rather than the psychiatric amelioration of their consequences (Ross 1991; Short 2007).

Despite the significant impact of psychiatrists on interwar American criminology, it is important not to exaggerate their importance. They may have influenced criminology, but in practice, psychiatric approaches, particularly classification and treatment, were largely confined to Chicago, New York, New England, and California. In the southern states and the Midwest, where the focus of local criminal justice systems was more oriented toward the regulation of African American labor and the enforcement of existing racial hierarchies through chain gangs and capital punishment, the use of psychiatry in both court deliberations and the classification and treatment of criminals was unknown until well after the Second World War (Ayers 1984; Friedman 1993; Oshinsky 1996; Garton 2003). Similarly, while intelligence testing and, more importantly, psychiatric classification and treatment and concepts of diminished responsibility were beginning to make headway in Britain, Australia, and Canada, during the interwar years, these practices remained on the periphery of the criminal justice and penal systems in these countries (Becker & Wetzell 2006). Nonetheless, by the 1950s, the concept of diminished responsibility had been established on both the East and West coasts of the United States, and the importance of psychiatric classification had been widely accepted in many jurisdictions, even as sociological approaches began to suggest that psychiatric treatments were of limited utility in the management of offenders.

The exception to this trend was the problem of the sex psychopath. In the 1940s and 1950s, as sociological approaches began to dominate criminology, heightened concern about the threat of sex psychopaths was pervasive in public discourse, especially in North America. From the late 1930s onward, numerous American states passed sex psychopath laws to incarcerate and in some contexts chemically castrate men convicted of sex crimes, particularly homosexual crimes and sex crimes involving children. By the late 1950s, nearly thirty American states had passed sex psychopath laws, and a number of states had funded psychiatric studies into sexual deviancy. The Langley Porter Psychiatric Clinic in California received special funding to investigate sex psychopaths, and diagnostic centers and research projects were funded in New Jersey and at Sing Sing Prison in New York State (Freedman 1989). Similarly, in Canada, a sex psychopath law was passed in 1948, and the British Mental Health Act of 1959 enshrined the concept of mental and sexual psychopathy in the United Kingdom (except in Scotland) (Walker & McCabe 1973; Chenier 2003).

VI. Anti-Psychiatry

The turn to sociological interpretations of crime beginning in the 1930s was in part an argument that personality theories focused on the symptoms rather than the causes of criminal behavior. Psychiatric classification and treatment remained important with respect to assisting the courts in determining the most appropriate options for the disposition of particular cases, particularly sex crimes, and assisting prison and reformatory administrators in managing individual offenders, but if rising crime and recidivism rates were to be slowed, then the deeper social roots of criminal behavior had to be uncovered. In the 1960s, an unprecedented wave of criticism challenged the credibility of psychiatry. The critique emerged from within psychiatry itself, with psychiatrists such as Franco Basaglia in Italy, David Cooper and R. D. Laing in Britain, and Thomas Szasz in America arguing that psychiatry, far from being a therapeutic intervention, was really a form of social control that stigmatized people who didn't conform to social norms (Crossley 2013). Anti-psychiatry emerged at a time of significant challenge to conventional forms of social governance. New social movements emerged around questions of race and civil rights, prisoner rights, sexual liberation, gay rights, feminism, student movements contesting traditional forms of knowledge and pedagogy, and protests about involvement in the Vietnam War. Moreover, some of these movements, notably gay liberation and feminism, added fuel to the critical fire against psychiatry, highlighting ways in which psychiatry pathologized same-sex behavior and was integral to the construction of female behaviors as forms of mental illness.

The radical political turmoil of the 1960s and 1970s had a marked impact on criminology. On the left the emphasis shifted from the nature of the offender to the nature of the criminal justice system. Sociologists and criminologists, drawing on the work of scholars such as Stanley Cohen, Erving Goffman, and Michel Foucault, increasingly focused on such concepts as social control, moral panics, total institutions, discipline, and surveillance to uncover the modes by which institutions, such as courts, the prison, and the asylum, and discourses, such as criminology and psychiatry, constructed problem populations and subjected them to practices of confinement and discipline. At the other end of the political spectrum, however, criminologists, psychiatrists, and sociologists began to move away from the rehabilitation ethos of the interwar years, stressing instead the biological and inherent psychological dynamics of criminality (Taylor 1984). Even those who maintained a psychological basis for criminality, notably the influential British psychologist Hans Eysenck, stressed that psychopathic tendencies were formed so early in a child's development that later therapeutic interventions were largely useless (Eysenck 1977).

This determinist pessimism about criminals reflected broader shifts in psychiatry itself away from psychodynamic conceptions of personality and toward the biological basis of mental disease, with a consequent decline in interest in psychotherapy and increasing interest in psychotropic drug treatments. In the *Australian and New Zealand Journal of Psychiatry*, for example, articles on neurophysiology and neurochemistry constituted only a quarter of all articles published in the journal in the early 1970s but by the late 1990s were half of all publications. For some diseases, such as schizophrenia, the aboutface was complete. By 2001 no psychiatrist in the journal was concentrating on any social, familial, or personality factors with respect to this disease, in stark contrast to the 1970s, when such factors dominated the scientific literature (Henderson 2008). Psychoanalysis was caught in this backlash. As radical critics increasingly challenged psychological approaches, many psychiatrists abandoned contentious psychodynamic theories, such as psychoanalysis, in which the line between social control and therapeutic intervention was murky, for the safer ground of biological theories (Hale 1995).

In the 1980s and 1990s the shift in popular attitudes toward crime and punishment reflected the hereditary and determinist strands of the scientific debate. Calls for tighter controls on law and order, zero-tolerance policing, mandatory sentencing, and the winding back of provisions with respect to such mitigating factors as diminished responsibility were evident in many jurisdictions throughout the Western world. In 2000, for example, a Californian citizen's initiative, Proposition 21, proposed much tougher penalties for youth and gang crime, streaming youths back into the adult criminal justice system and removing informal probation for juveniles who committed felonies. Despite intense opposition from civil liberties and human rights organizations, the proposition passed, although elements of it were later ruled invalid in the Court of Appeal (Taylor 2002). In Britain since the 1970s, as Toby Seddon has argued, there has been a significant erosion in the "penal-welfarism" that characterized the middle years of the century, replaced by an ethos that rehabilitation didn't work and a focus on the containment of risks such as suicide, self-harm, and sexual abuse; efficient management of inmate populations; and cost effectiveness. The bureaucratic and economic rationalist approach to the management of inmates, however, has fueled a corresponding interest among the critics of criminal justice and penal administration systems in the movement for inmate human rights (Seddon 2007).

CONCLUSION

In this context of hardening public and political attitudes toward criminals and their rehabilitation, the role of psychiatrists within many criminal justice systems has contracted since the 1940s. Although now rarely enjoined to diagnose and treat inmates in the hope of rehabilitating them, psychiatrists still play an important role in providing expert testimony in criminal trials and assisting in the classification of offenders before and after trial to inform sentencing and decisions about the most appropriate institutional context in which to incarcerate the offender. Ironically, however, the closing of many mental hospitals since the 1970s has thrown many former inmates of mental hospitals back onto the streets and has imposed community treatment contexts for managing new cases of psychiatric illness. Many of these systems have been inadequate to the task, and as a result some people who might otherwise have been admitted to a psychiatric facility in the past, especially those suffering severe psychoses, are now being admitted to prisons and reformatories (Neilssen 2005). The extent of mental illness in the prison populations of many Western jurisdictions is rising and creating serious challenges for the effective management of inmates. Psychiatrists may no longer be considered a profession offering hope for the amelioration or rehabilitation of the criminal, but they remain in many contexts vital advisors on decisions and managers active in the mitigation of risk in the criminal justice system.

NOTE

1. Max Winsor, "What Is There, If Anything, of Value in Therapeutics Developed by American Psychiatrists that Might Be Applied to Prisons and Reformatories" (1935), Bureau of Social Hygiene Papers, Series 3, 4/34/469, Rockefeller Archives, Sleepy Hollow, New York.

REFERENCES

Alexander, Ruth M. 1995. *The Girl Problem: Female Sexual Delinquency in New York, 1900–1930*. Ithaca, NY: Cornell University Press.

Augstein, Hannah Franziska. 1996. "J. C. Pritchard's Concept of Moral Insanity: A Medical Theory of the Corruption of Human Nature." *Medical History* 40 (3): 311–43.

Ayers, Edward. 1984. *Vengeance and Justice: Crime and Punishment in the American South*. New York: Oxford University Press.

Bashford, Alison, & Philippa Levine, eds. 2010. *The Oxford Handbook of the History of Eugenics*. Oxford: Oxford University Press.

Baumohl, Jim, & Robin Room. 1987. "Inebriety, Doctors and the State: Alcohol Treatment Institutions Before 1940." In *Recent Developments in Alcoholism*, Vol. 5, ed. Marc Galanter, 135–74. New York: Springer.

Becker, Peter, & Richard Wetzell, eds. 2006. *Criminals and Their Scientists: The History of Criminology in International Perspective*. Cambridge: Cambridge University Press.

Bondio, Mariacarla Gadebusch. 2006. "From the 'Atavistic' to the 'Inferior' Criminal Type: The Impact of the Lombrosian Theory of the Born Criminal on German Psychiatry." In *Criminals and Their Scientists: The History of Criminology in International Perspective*, ed. Peter Becker & Richard F. Wetzell, 187–05. Cambridge: Cambridge University Press.

Brown, Jo Anne. 1992. *The Definition of a Profession: The Authority of Metaphor in the History of Intelligence Testing, 1890–1930*. Princeton, NJ: Princeton University Press.

Castel, Robert, Françoise Castel, & Anne Lovell. 1982. *The Psychiatric Society*. Trans. Arthur Goldhammer. New York: Columbia University Press.

Chenier, Elise. 2003. "The Criminal Sexual Psychopath in Canada: Sex, Psychiatry and the Law Mid-Century." *Canadian Bulletin of Medical History* 20 (1): 75–101.

Cordess, Christopher. 1992. "Pioneers in Forensic Psychiatry—Edward Glover (1888–1972): Psychoanalysis and Crime—A Fragile Legacy." *Journal of Forensic Psychiatry and Psychology* 3 (3): 509–30.

Crossley, Nick. 2013. "R. D. Laing and the British Anti-Psychiatry Movement: A Socio-Historical Analysis." *Social Science and Medicine* 47 (7): 877–89.

East, Norwood. 1949. *Society and the Criminal*. London: His Majesty's Stationery Office.

Eigen, Joel. 1995. *Witnessing Insanity: Madness and Mad-Doctors in the English Court*. New Haven, CT: Yale University Press.

Eysenck, Hans. 1977 [1964]. *Crime and Personality*. London: Routledge & Kegan Paul.

Finder, Gabriel N. 2006. "Criminals and Their Analysts: Psychoanalytic Criminology in Weimar Germany and the First Austrian Republic." In *Criminals and Their Scientists: The History of Criminology in International Perspective*, ed. Peter Becker & Richard F. Wetzell, 447–69. Cambridge: Cambridge University Press.

Foucault, Michel. 1977. *Discipline and Punish: The Birth of the Prison*. Trans. Alan Sheridan. New York: Pantheon Books.

Freedman, Estelle B. 1981. *Their Sisters' Keepers: Women's Prison Reform in America, 1830–1930*. Ann Arbor: University of Michigan Press.

Freedman, Estelle B. 1989. "Uncontrolled Desires: The Response to the Sex Psychopath, 1920–1960." In *Passion and Power: Sexuality in History*, ed. Kathy Peiss & Christina Simmons, 199–204. Philadelphia: Temple University Press.

Friedman, Lawrence M. 1993. *Crime and Punishment in American History*. New York: Basic Books.

Garton, Stephen. 1986. "The Rise of the Therapeutic State: Psychiatry and the System of Criminal Jurisdiction in New South Wales, 1890–1940." *Australian Journal of Politics and History* 32 (3): 378–88.

Garton, Stephen. 1987. "Once a Drunkard Always a Drunkard: Social Reform and the Problem of Habitual Drunkenness in Australia, 1880–1914." *Labour History* 53 (November): 38–53.

Garton, Stephen. 2003. "Managing Mercy: African Americans, Parole and Paternalism in Georgia, 1919–1945." *Journal of Social History* 36 (3): 675–99.

Garton, Stephen. 2010. "Criminal Propensities: Psychiatry, Classification and Imprisonment in New York State, 1916–40." *Social History of Medicine* 23 (1): 79–97.

Gaylord, Mark S., & John F. Galliher. 1986. *The Criminology of Edwin H. Sutherland*. New Brunswick, NJ: Rutgers University Press.

Geis, Gil, & Colin Goff. 1986. "Edwin H. Sutherland's White-Collar Crime in America: An Essay in Historical Criminology." *Criminal Justice History* 7:1–31.

Gibson, Mary S. 2006. "Cesare Lombroso and Italian Criminology: Theory and Politics." In *Criminals and Their Scientists: The History of Criminology in International Perspective*, ed. Peter Becker & Richard F. Wetzell, 137–58. Cambridge: Cambridge University Press.

Gillman, Susan. 1988. "Dementia Americana: Mark Twain, 'Wapping Alice,' and the Harry K. Thaw Trial." *Critical Inquiry* 14 (2): 296–314.

Goring, Charles. 1972 [1913]. *The English Convict: A Statistical Study*. Montclair, NJ: Patterson Smith.

Grob, Gerald. 1983. *Mental Illness and American Society, 1875–1940*. Princeton, NJ: Princeton University Press.

Hale, Nathan G, Jr. 1995. *The Rise and Crisis of Psychoanalysis in the United States: Freud and the Americans, 1917–1975*. New York: Oxford University Press.

Harrison, Brian. 1971. *Drink and the Victorians: The Temperance Question in England, 1815–1872*. London: Faber & Faber.

Healy, William. 1915. *The Individual Delinquent: A Text-Book of Diagnosis and Prognosis for All Concerned in Understanding Offenders*. Boston: Little Brown.

Henderson, Julie. 2008. "Biological Psychiatry and Changing Ideas about Mental Health Prevention: Risk and Individuality." *Health Sociology Review* 17:4–17.

Holmes, Jeremy. 1993. *John Bowlby and Attachment Theory*. London: Routledge.

Jackson, Mark. 2000. *The Borderland of Imbecility: Medicine, Society and the Fabrication of the Feeble-Minded in Late Victorian and Edwardian England*. Manchester, UK: Manchester University Press.

Jones, Kathleen W. 1999. *Taming the Troublesome Child: American Families, Child Guidance, and the Limits of Psychiatric Authority*. Cambridge, MA: Harvard University Press.

Kelves, Daniel J. 1985. *In the Name of Eugenics: Genetics and the Uses of Human Heredity*. New York: Knopf.

Kramer, Ronald C. 1982. "From 'Habitual Offenders' to 'Career Criminals': The Historical Construction and Development of Criminal Categories." *Law and Human Behavior* 6 (3–4): 273–93.

Leys, Ruth, & Rand B. Davis, eds. 1990. *Defining American Psychology: The Correspondence Between Adolf Meyer and Edward Bradford Titchener*. Baltimore: Johns Hopkins University Press.

Loughnan, Arlie. 2012. *Manifest Madness: Mental Incapacity in Criminal Law*. Oxford: Oxford University Press.

Ludmerer, Kenneth M. 1972. *Genetics and American Society: A Historical Appraisal*. Baltimore: Johns Hopkins University Press.

Lunbeck, Elizabeth. 1994. *The Psychiatric Persuasion: Knowledge, Gender, and Power in Modern America*. Princeton, NJ: Princeton University Press.

MacLeod, Roy. 1967. "The Edge of Hope: Social Policy and Chronic Alcoholism, 1870–1900." *Journal of the History of Medicine and Allied Sciences* 22 (3): 215–45.

Manning, Fredrick Norton. 1892. "Proposed New Test for Insanity." *Australasian Medical Congress Transactions* 1:59–60.

Mennel, Robert M. 1973. *Thorns and Thistles: Juvenile Delinquents in the United States, 1825–1940*. Hanover, NH: University of New England Press.

Moran, Richard. 1981. *Knowing Right from Wrong: The Insanity Defence of Daniel McNaughten*. New York: Free Press.

Mucchielli, Laurent. 2006. "Criminology, Hygienism, and Eugenics in France, 1870–1914: The Medical Debates on the Elimination of 'Incorrigible' Criminals." In *Criminals and Their Scientists: The History of Criminology in International Perspective*, ed. Peter Becker & Richard F. Wetzell, 207–29. Cambridge: Cambridge University Press.

Nielssen, Olav. 2005. "Prevalence of Psychoses on Reception to Male Prisons in NSW." *Australian and New Zealand Journal of Psychiatry* 39 (6): 453–59.

Osborne, Thomas Mott. 1924 [1916]. *Society and Prisons*. New Haven, CT: Yale University Press.

Oshinsky, David M. 1996. *Worse than Slavery: Pachman Farm and the Ordeal of Jim Crow Justice*. New York: Free Press.

Pick, Daniel. 1989. *Faces of Degeneration: A European Disorder, 1848–1918*. Cambridge: Cambridge University Press.

Platt, Anthony M. 1969. *The Child Savers: The Invention of Delinquency*. Chicago: University of Chicago Press.

Pratt, John. 1997. *Governing the Dangerous: Dangerousness, Law and Social Change*. Sydney: Federation Press.

Prior, Pauline M. 2004. "Prisoner or Patient? The Official Debate on the Criminal Lunatic in Nineteenth-Century Ireland." *History of Psychiatry* 15 (2): 177–92.

Rafter, Nicole Hahn. 1997. *Creating Born Criminals*. Urbana: University of Illinois Press.

Rafter, Nicole Hahn. 2006. "Criminal Anthropology: Its Reception in the United States and the Nature of Its Appeal." In *Criminals and Their Scientists: The History of Criminology in International Perspective*, ed. Peter Becker & Richard F. Wetzell, 159–81. Cambridge: Cambridge University Press.

Robinson, Daniel N. 1996. *Wild Beasts and Idle Humours: The Insanity Defense from Antiquity to the Present*. Cambridge, MA: Harvard University Press.

Rose, Nikolas. 1985. *The Psychological Complex: Psychology, Politics and Society in England, 1869–1939*. London: Routledge & Kegan Paul.

Rose, Nikolas. 1989. *Governing the Soul: The Shaping of the Private Self*. London: Routledge.

Ross, Dorothy, 1991. *The Origins of American Social Science*. Cambridge: Cambridge University Press.

Scull, Andrew. 1993. *The Most Solitary of Afflictions: Madness and Society in Britain, 1700–1900*. New Haven, CT: Yale University Press.

Seddon, Toby. 2007. *Punishment and Madness: Governing Prisoners with Mental Health Problems*. Milton Park, UK: Routledge-Cavendish.

Short, James F., Jr., with Lorine A. Hughes. 2007. "Criminology, Criminologists, and the Sociological Enterprise." In *Sociology in America: A History*, ed. Craig Calhoun, 605–38. Chicago: University of Chicago Press.

Shorter, Edward. 1997. *A History of Psychiatry: From the Era of the Asylum to the Age of Prozac*. New York: John Wiley & Sons.

Singer, H. D., & W. O. Krohn. 1924. *Insanity and the Law: A Treatise on Forensic Psychiatry*. Philadelphia: P. Blakiston's Son & Co.

Smith, Roger. 1981. *Trial by Medicine: Insanity and Responsibility in Victorian Trials*. Edinburgh: Edinburgh University Press.

Taylor, Jennifer. 2002. "California's Proposition 21: A Case of Juvenile Injustice." *Southern California Law Review* 75:983–1020.

Taylor, Lawrence. 1984. *Born to Crime: The Genetic Causes of Criminal Behaviour*. Westport, CT: Greenwood Press.

Thomson, Matthew. 1998. *The Problem of Mental Deficiency: Eugenics, Democracy and Social Policy in Britain, c 1870–1959*. Oxford: Clarendon Press.

Walker, Nigel. 1968. *Crime and Insanity in England*, Vol. 1, *The Historical Perspective*. Edinburgh: University of Edinburgh Press.

Walker, Nigel, & Sarah McCabe. 1973. *Crime and Insanity in England*, Vol. 2, *New Solutions and New Problems*. Edinburgh: Edinburgh University Press.

Walker, Samuel. 1980. *Popular Justice: A History of American Criminal Justice*. New York: Oxford University Press.

Walkowitz, Daniel J. 1999. *Working with Class: Social Workers and the Politics of Middle Class Identity*. Chapel Hill: University of North Carolina Press.

Wiener, Martin J. 1990. *Reconstructing the Criminal: Culture, Law, and Policy in England, 1830–1914*. Cambridge: Cambridge University Press.

Wiener, Martin J. 2006. "Murderers and 'Reasonable Men': The 'Criminology' of the Victorian Judiciary." In *Criminals and Their Scientists: The History of Criminology in International Perspective*, ed. Peter Becker & Richard F. Wetzell, 43–60. Cambridge: Cambridge University Press.

CHAPTER 21

CONTINUITY AND CHANGE

*Russian and Early Soviet Criminology
and the Criminal Woman*

SHARON A. KOWALSKY

INTRODUCTION

IN 1903 the Russian Group of the International Union of Criminologists met in Brussels, Belgium. They had reason to celebrate. Finally, criminology as a profession was becoming established in Russia. Forensic doctors and psychiatric specialists were in high demand as expert witnesses in trials. Criminology was being taught in universities. Criminologists actively participated in the writing and development of a new criminal code (and although the 1903 draft was never implemented into law, it served as the basis for the new law codes promulgated by the Soviet government some years later). Russian professionals involved themselves in international organizations, drawing from and contributing to developments in the field. The ways these professionals embraced, adapted, and reshaped European criminological theories reflected particular Russian conditions. Even after the 1917 Revolutions in Russia, criminologists considered their position secure. Their acceptance of sociological conditions as the primary motivator for criminal activity seemed to sit well with the ideological vision of Russia's new rulers. They also emphasized the central role of the state in dealing with crime and criminals, again paralleling the orientation of the new Bolshevik leaders. Indeed, criminologists generally fared better than other intellectuals and professionals in the early years of the Soviet regime. Still, and particularly when discussing female criminality, criminologists emphasized both sociological and physiological factors of crime. Such perspectives, which suggested crime could not simply wither away with the advent of socialism—an inherent assumption of Bolshevik ideology—made criminology more problematic in the Soviet Union by the late 1920s, with the result that all innovative research into the causes of crime and the conditions of offenders had ceased by the end of the decade.

This chapter examines the ways that Russian criminological professionals borrowed from and contributed to the development of European criminology in the late nineteenth and early twentieth centuries. It looks in particular at criminologists' understanding and interpretations of female crime to assess the nature of Russian criminology and the impact of both European ideas and domestic politics on criminological theories in Russia.

I. Developing Russian Criminology

Criminology as a profession emerged in Russia in the second half of the nineteenth century, a bit later than in Western Europe, in connection with several domestic legal developments. First, the Judicial Reforms of 1864, an element of Tsar Alexander II's larger Great Reforms (begun in 1861 with the emancipation of the serfs), created an independent judiciary and established adversarial jury trials to replace arbitrary (and often secret) state judgments. Prosecutors and defense lawyers in this new system increasingly relied on the testimony of expert witnesses in the courtroom. Forensic, medical, and psychiatric experts found legitimacy and application of their knowledge in the service of justice, which helped to professionalize these disciplines and give them an important social purpose (Becker 2011; McReynolds 2013). Second, increasing interest in the science and technology of criminal investigation encouraged greater professionalization, with university courses established in criminalistics, police investigation, and criminology. Additionally, Russian intellectuals (*intelligentsia*) pursued their commitment to social justice and political reform through the new legal avenues as they sought to understand, discuss, and explain the causes of crime in Russian society. By the early years of the twentieth century, Russian legal professionals had established criminology as a viable profession in Russia, drawing on Western European innovations but incorporating Russian outlooks and politics into their approaches.

In establishing a Russian criminological profession, Russian criminologists drew upon and adapted Western European criminological theories and approaches to suit Russian circumstances. The Western embrace of the classical school seemed rather unsatisfactory to Russian professionals, for many of the same reasons that by the late nineteenth century a number of Europeans were also looking to other explanations. As David Garland discusses, the classical school emphasized the free will of men, in essence suggesting the broad equality of people. In the late nineteenth century, criminology challenged that assessment, emphasizing instead the importance of the individual in determining deviant behavior according to a broad spectrum of criminal tendencies. Much of this shift in interest related to the growing visibility of the masses and professionals' desire to separate those perceived to be unruly from those who behaved properly (Garland 1985). In contrast, in Russia there was little concept or application of free will, as the authoritarian political system limited individual actions and circumscribed behaviors. Still, motivated by a similar desire as Western Europeans to maintain social order, Russian professionals embraced criminology as a way to understand and reform individuals who challenged the status quo through their deviant behavior.

Some Russians turned to elements of Cesare Lombroso's criminal anthropology, seeing it as providing a better explanation than the classical school for the continued degeneracy they identified in society. For instance, physician Praskov'ia Nikolaevna Tarnovskaia (1848–1910) drew upon and contributed to Lombroso's theories as a way to establish a scientific foundation to assert the inherent and potential criminality of the masses. Asserting that the goals of criminal anthropology were "to clarify the general biological foundations for the growing number of crimes; to identify the most probable causes leading to the appearance of people predisposed to criminality; . . . and to study measures to better prevent the tendency to commit crimes," Tarnovskaia expressed her anxieties regarding rising crime rates among the masses and the causes thereof (Tarnovskaia 1902, p. 498). While not explicitly racist, Tarnovskaia's embrace of criminal anthropology reinforced for her the sense that the ordinary Russian people (peasants) were somehow less developed, less civilized, more barbaric, and more backward than their urban counterparts. Similar to the way that Lombroso's theories helped him explain the "criminal" nature of a more "primitive" segment of Italian society (Wolfgang 1961), criminal anthropology helped Tarnovskaia to confirm the "primitiveness" of ordinary rural people. In this way, Tarnovskaia created and reinforced the division of Russia society not in terms of wealth, but rather according to geography. For her, social origin shaped criminal behavior more than social circumstance did, leading her to embrace determinism as the primary cause of criminal activity. Furthermore, Tarnovskaia famously provided Lombroso with data and photographs of Russian female murderers that he used in formulating his theories of female criminals. Her major work, *Zhenshchiny-ubiitsy* (1902) was translated into French and published in Paris as *Les femmes homicides* (1908). Of all the Russian criminologists, Tarnovskaia directed her work most specifically toward the European criminological community, and this separated her and her ideas from the main course of developments in Russian criminology, in which criminal anthropology was becoming more problematic.

Other Russian professionals incorporated some of the ideas of criminal anthropology into their work, but less enthusiastically and often with reservations that tried to mitigate some of the determinism associated with the theory. For example, Dmitrii A. Dril', a leading jurist and professor of law, embraced criminal anthropological theories as a way to establish the scientific and systematic study of crime and criminals. Lombroso's ideas, he wrote, applied "specific methods of the natural sciences" to crime studies, making criminology into a science that could increase the understanding of the human mind and human psychology (Kowalsky 2009, p. 29; Mogilner 2013, pp. 341–46). Nevertheless, Dril' disagreed with Lombroso's narrow focus on the criminal individual and what Lombroso called the "born criminal." In contrast, Dril' believed that a complete understanding of criminality and the criminal could only be achieved by considering the physiological alongside and in connection with the social conditions that influenced the criminal. With his focus on the born criminal, Dril' argued that Lombroso looked backward to the "epoch of barbarity" rather than forward. Instead, a holistic approach was needed that would consider the physiological, sociological, and environmental factors that shaped human action. Lombroso's approach appealed to Dril' because of his application of scientific methods to crime studies, but Dril' found that criminal anthropology did not tell the entire story. In fact, the determinism inherent in criminal anthropology did not sit well with many Russian intellectuals of the late nineteenth and early twentieth centuries. Indeed, many Russian intellectuals rejected established Western ideologies of development, including social Darwinism, as unsuitable for and not applicable to Russian conditions. Sparse populations and extended periods of frigid weather meant the "struggle for existence" rested on the individual's attempts to survive in harsh conditions rather than on interspecies or intergroup competition for scarce resources (Todes 1989). Russian criminologists, engaged in the political disputes of the day and looking forward to the potential for increased political representation and participation, often found the determinism of criminal anthropology antithetical to a growing awareness of and desire for individual rights and actions in Russian society.

While Lombroso's criminal anthropological theories found some adherents in Russia beyond Tarnovskaia and Dril', most Russian criminological professionals believed that social and economic influences provided a more compelling explanation than biological or anthropological determinism for the course of and development of deviance. Drawing on positivism, as advocated by Western thinkers such as Auguste Comte and Enrico Ferri, a group of Russian criminologists developed instead a "sociological school" of criminology. The sociological school emphasized the social aspects and factors shaping criminality, locating the causes of crime in the social and economic, and even environmental, conditions influencing the criminal, while also considering the role of individual and personal factors. The Russian sociological approach was first formulated by the statistician I. Ia. Foinitskii (1847–1913). Foinitskii argued in his first major criminological work, "The Influence of the Time of Year on the Distribution of Crime" (1873), that external environmental factors shaped deviant behavior to a greater extent than did internal individual personal or hereditary traits. Foinitskii thus emphasized the social causes of crime while minimizing the role of determinism in driving people to offend (Foinitskii 1898–1900).

While the sociological school emphasized the environment and the criminal's individual psychological reactions to his or her conditions, it did not go far enough for many thinking Russians concerned about the course of their nation's development and convinced of the necessity of extensive social reforms. Furthermore, new political realities—an emerging revolutionary movement aiming to overthrow the established political system and a general growing dissatisfaction for and disillusionment with the autocratic system and the tsar—encouraged criminologists to seek other explanations for criminality. By the turn of the twentieth century, a new generation of criminological professionals had emerged, constituting a "left wing" within the sociological school that not only emphasized the socioeconomic causes of crime but also articulated a path toward its elimination by integrating socialist ideology into their criminological studies.

The sociological school's left wing was led by Mikhail N. Gernet, a young and innovative criminologist who established himself with his Moscow University dissertation "The Social Causes of Crime" (1906). Gernet's biography exemplifies the orientation and outlook of the new Russian criminological professional. Born in 1874, Gernet matriculated at Moscow University's law school, where he remained to teach while pursuing his doctoral degree. Between 1902 and 1904 Gernet traveled to all the European criminological "hot spots": Germany, France, Italy, and Switzerland (Gernet 1974). His travels in European circles highlight the great extent to which Russian criminology developed in response and reaction to European criminological trends. Indeed, most Russian criminological publications took pains to point out the European as well as the Russian trends regarding the particular crime being discussed. In his groundbreaking dissertation, for example, Gernet traced the development of criminology, emphasizing its positivist and Enlightenment origins and its interest in curtailing crime through the implementation of social reforms. He noted the influence of European thinkers on crime studies and particularly embraced Enrico Ferri's positivist approach and Filippo Turati's emphasis on the need to consider crime as a result of both political and social conditions. Gernet pushed the arguments further, however, by injecting socialist ideology into the analysis. He emphasized that the sociological school neglected to consider fully the negative effects of working-class exploitation on crime. Only with the recognition of working-class conditions could crime prevention efforts be successful (Gernet 1974). In this way, Gernet integrated the politics of revolutionary socialist ideology into crime studies, making criminology relevant and indeed essential for social transformation, and an important component for understanding and transforming Russian society.

Gernet and the left wing of the sociological school laid the groundwork for the establishment and professionalization of Soviet criminology after the 1917 Bolshevik Revolution. Indeed, while many professionals and intellectuals fled Russia in the years following the revolution (Finkel 2001), left-wing criminologists thrived under the Bolshevik regime, at least initially. Their embrace of science and the study of society, their socialist orientation, and their commitment to social transformation helped to position criminology as an important element in the establishment of the new socialist society and as a vehicle of the state, separating it from developments in Western Europe. Russian criminologists themselves argued that crime rates served as a "barometer" of the status of society and the advancement of the new socialist state. Understanding the causes and reasons for crime thus became a crucial element in the creation of new social norms, particularly because socialist ideology stressed that crime would disappear with the establishment of socialism. According to this ideology, by ending exploitation and fulfilling the basic needs of all people, socialism would eliminate the motivation for and necessity of crime. Until socialism could be fully established, however, criminological studies of crime and criminals could suggest how far society had come and how much work still needed to be done to achieve full social transformation and thus eliminate crime completely.

Early Soviet criminologists took seriously their "mandate" for criminal study and established an extensive system of laboratories and institutions devoted to collecting data on criminality and assessing the motives of individual offenders. These organizations were housed in universities, prisons, mental institutions, and courts, but also existed independently, forming at the local and regional levels in different locales throughout Russia and its republics. The new Soviet government not only tolerated these institutes but actively encouraged them, and they provided professional expertise to the courts and prison system while helping to develop a better understanding of the causes of crime and the means for its elimination. The crime institutes acted as both research institutions and as state-driven and state-supported vehicles for assessing crime and criminals. They generally approached the problem of crime from multifaceted and interdisciplinary perspectives that addressed the biological, social, and psychological aspects of the criminal individual and crime in general. Indeed, one of the remarkable aspects of the crime institutes was their general commitment to exploring not only the social causes of crime, as encouraged by the state's ideology, but also its individual psychological and biological factors.

One of the most prominent of these institutes was the Moscow Bureau for the Study of the Criminal Personality and Crime, formed in 1923 by the Moscow city government to conduct research among the local prison population.[1] The work of the Moscow Bureau involved a variety of professionals, including psychiatrists, psychologists, statisticians, and even university students. Its members sought to examine the criminal personality in a working environment in which an offender's character and comprehension of social norms could be evaluated, and to provide practical expertise to the courts to assist with sentencing. Even more important was the State Institute for the Study of Crime and the Criminal, formed in 1925 as a centralized organization devoted to developing a more "Soviet" approach to crime studies and to bringing criminology in line with Bolshevik ideology. Sponsored and supported by the People's Commissariat for Internal Affairs (NKVD; in other words, the secret police), the State Institute attempted to centralize and control criminological studies along Soviet lines by emphasizing the importance of sociological factors, but it retained in its very structure, organization, and approach a deep and lasting interest in individual biological and psychological influences on crime (Kowalsky 2009, pp. 64–73). For the criminologists, these approaches were not mutually exclusive and were indeed complementary and necessary. As Gernet argued, the State Institute could be distinguished from other Western European institutes because of its focus on a holistic understanding of crime as derived from socioeconomic causes and its disregard of explanations centered on anthropological characteristics (Gernet 1925; Kowalsky 2009, p. 70). As the criminologist B. S. Utevskii pointed out: "The wide application of its tasks, the scientific-practical character of its work, its Marxist methods, the tenets at the basis of its work—all this places the State Institute for the Study of Crime as the first and so far only organization of its kind not only in our union but in Europe and even in all of the civilized world" (Utevskii 1926; Kowalsky 2009, p. 70).

Early Soviet criminologists were extremely proud of the innovation and direction of criminological studies in the early Soviet Union. As in Western Europe, much of the orientation of the criminological institutes fell under the auspices of the courts, police, and prisons, and thus they retained a more practical focus rather than an academic one.

However, the integration of socialist ideology and priorities into crime studies made the Soviet institutions unique. Indeed, the 1920s have been called a "golden era" for Soviet crime studies, as practitioners employed innovative and cutting-edge methods and multidimensional perspectives in their examination and study of individual criminals, and their explanations of criminality (Ivanov & Il'ina 1991).

One group to which Soviet criminologists paid particular attention was female criminals. It is through their discussions of female crime that we can see more clearly the extent to which early Soviet criminologists embraced the sociological approach at the same time they remained committed to biologically deterministic assessments of criminality. They continued to express their prerevolutionary understanding of women and women's place in society, while at the same time attempting to integrate a new outlook on women that reflected women's changing position in Soviet society and new Soviet realities.

II. Russian and Soviet Criminology and Female Crime

While crime in general served as a "barometer" to measure the progress of the construction of the new socialist society by the 1920s, interpretations of female crime instead reinforced traditional perceptions of women's position in society, even while that position was being challenged and redefined. In the late nineteenth century, P. N. Tarnovskaia had developed her own interpretations of female criminality that emphasized the connection between premature sexual activity and criminal deviance among the rural population. Peasant customs that encouraged marriage for girls before or just at the age of sexual development, she argued in an 1898 work, harmed the physical and intellectual development of these girls and increased the likelihood that frustrations and domestic problems would lead to the murder of their family members. According to Tarnovskaia, peasant women's inherent backwardness and predisposition to deviance was exacerbated by being forced into sexual activity and motherhood before full maturity, resulting in violent reactions to marital or familial difficulties (Tarnovskaia 1898; Kowalsky 2009, pp. 83–85). Tarnovskaia's conclusions suggested that early marriage was detrimental not only to individuals and families but even to the basic genetic viability of the population, leading to the deterioration of future generations. Her concerns reflected broader European fears about national degeneration at the end of the nineteenth century (Beer 2008). By emphasizing the role of premature sexual activity in stimulating female criminality, however, Tarnovskaia argued that biological sexuality was at the root of female deviance. Rural women's sexuality was "primitive" because they developed sexual maturity later than their more "civilized" urban counterparts. Tarnovskaia did not suggest that women needed greater freedoms, liberation, or opportunities for participation in public life; rather, she located the problem of women's criminality squarely in the home. Her discussions reinforced beliefs about women's proper domestic role but suggested some reforms were necessary to improve women's situation in the home and eliminate those factors (like early marriage) that might drive desperate women to criminal deviance.

Similarly, I. Ozerov, a political economist and professor, also found that women frequently committed crimes against their family members, often as a result of early marriage. Ozerov pointed to women's level of morality, arguing that if family conditions were not conducive to the development of morality, family and society could become destabilized. While marriage provided economic stability for women, it served to focus her attentions too narrowly on the family and the home, creating conditions that might allow women's inherently deviant sexuality to cause them to engage in violent crime as a solution to the problems they faced (Ozerov 1896). Ozerov's arguments, like Tarnovskaia's, served to reinforce the proper position of women in the home, arguing not for a radical reconsideration of women's role in society, but for reforms that would alleviate some of the more abusive practices of patriarchal tradition and allow women to better fulfill their traditional roles in the family and society.

Early marriage was only one factor seen as influencing the nature of female criminality. As statistician E. N. Tarnovskii noted at the end of the nineteenth century, "for a woman, on account of the narrower circle of her activities in general, sexual feelings and the maladies and fits of passion connected with them encompass a significantly greater part of her internal world than for men. . ... All uninvited crimes for the most part result from one or another abnormality or complication of sexual and also family life" (1899, pp. 143). Criminologist M. N. Gernet also noted that women led more monotonous lives than men, spending most of their time within the family and isolated from the "struggle for existence" (Gernet 1974, p. 253). In such prerevolutionary analyses, a woman's social position became equated with her physiology, defining the types of behavior she could exhibit and limiting the types of crimes she could commit.

While criminologists like Tarnovskaia and Ozerov focused on the need to reform and improve the conditions of women within the family, by the early twentieth century, observers increasingly recognized that women's roles in society were changing. As a consequence of increased urbanization and industrialization, more women had become engaged in what criminologists called the "struggle for existence," or the economics of the public sphere. Criminologists simultaneously believed that women's increasing presence in the public sphere and the economic life of society would benefit women by diversifying their criminality and making women more like men in the types of offenses they committed, while at the same time arguing that women would succumb more easily to the pressures of public life and engage in criminal behavior. Indeed, Ozerov described women as

> more childlike, youth-like; she quickly yields to all external influences, beneficial and not beneficial, without pondering them. In her, impressions operate like a whirlwind or a turbulent river, with a rapid current that she does not have the strength to handle, and like a rickety canoe she is quickly carried on the waves of

social life; no current—and she stops. . . . And so we see that woman is a special creature with a special mental build, and the crude reality of our economic life and the extreme abnormality of her family conditions operate on her just as disastrously as our fall frost on summer flowers. (Ozerov 1896; Kowalsky 2009, p. 89)

Despite the dangers, Russian criminologists believed that as women increasingly engaged in the "struggle for existence," the focus of their lives and, by extension, the nature of their criminality would change and would become more modern, more like male criminality, and less focused on the family.

The turn of the century seemed to offer the opportunity for women's lives and experiences, for their "struggle for existence," to be transformed. Growing urbanization and industrialization that brought women into the cities and the workforce in increasing numbers opened the possibility for women to earn their own living independent of their fathers and husbands. Their expanding economic activity meant that women were engaging in public life with greater frequency. In addition, the First World War opened even more opportunities to women for participating in public and economic life. In filling jobs left vacant by men enlisting in the army, women's scope and range of activities rapidly expanded. Women were now able and encouraged to engage in activities that had previously been considered unacceptable for their sex and limited to men, such as driving trams and fighting fires. Criminologists fully expected these new realities to be reflected in female crime rates, as women's employment in new occupations created new opportunities to commit crimes.

Crime statistics from the early twentieth century, however, did not reflect the criminologists' expected transformations of female crime. Instead, women continued to commit the same types of crimes and were still arrested for the same types of offenses. Women's rates of crime did seem to be rising by the late nineteenth century, but the nature of the offenses women committed remained consistent—women were most often charged for infanticide, spouse murder, and poisonings, and they participated less frequently in typical "male" crimes such as robbery, forgery, counterfeiting, and so on. Despite rhetoric that claimed that greater diversity should be expected from female offenders, arrest statistics and criminological assessments revealed that police and professionals still found that women acted in certain specific ways that related to and reinforced their typical domestic roles. Moreover, the professionals' focus on women's "traditional" crimes reconfirmed the anxiety that many felt about the new roles women were beginning to play in society. Women continued to be arrested most often for those very crimes that seemed to contravene their proper role and traditional function in Russian society. Indeed, it appears that women's greater visibility outside the home served mostly to threaten the established order, sometimes making women more vulnerable as crime victims.[2]

In most places in Europe, the greater public visibility of women in the early twentieth century caused considerable anxiety about the nature and course of social development. While similar tensions arose in Russian society, Russian criminologists generally regarded women's increasing engagement with the public sphere as positive, hoping that such activity would free women from the bondage of the home and make them more like men in their criminality. Nevertheless, statistics and criminologists' analyses of them reinforced the traditional and unchanging nature of female criminality, despite women's new opportunities and the expectations that they would act more like men and engage in the struggle for existence. Studies of female crime helped to reinforce belief in the accepted and traditional nature of women in a time of considerable change and adjustment. By reasserting the domestic orientation of women's deviance (which focused on victims from the woman's family and centered on issues arising out of the domestic sphere), criminologists reestablished and reiterated the link between women and the domestic sphere, helping to ease anxiety about the changing position and role of women in society.

Furthermore, despite Russian criminologists' general acceptance of sociological approaches to understanding crime, their assessments of female criminals frequently fell back on biological and physiological explanations that emphasized women's biology and sexuality. One observer, the endocrinologist A. V. Nemilov, argued that despite efforts to secure equality among men and women, biological differences prevented much change in the status of women; in fact, he claimed, "the life of women and the female soul can only be understood by starting from its biological basis." (Nemilov 1907; Kowalsky 2009, p. 97; Bernstein 2007). One V. L. Sanchov noted that for women, the phases of sexual life (specifically menstruation, pregnancy, giving birth, and menopause) shaped the mental outlook and led to criminality (Sanchov 1924; Kowalsky 2009, p. 98). Female crime thus had to be explained not only in socioeconomic terms but also in the context of the influence of the physiological functions of women's bodies on their behavior. As jurist A. A. Zhizhilenko stated, "overall it must be noted that all phenomena closely connected with the sexuality of women have an effect on their criminality. The period of pregnancy, birth, the post partem period, the period of cessation, as menopause is called—all this should be taken into consideration in the analysis of female crime" (Zhizhilenko 1922, p. 26). Nemilov further emphasized that women's experiences tended to be more emotional and more directly linked to their psychology, which was rooted in and influenced by their reproductive cycles. Zhizhilenko also added that in most cases crimes such as infanticide, child abandonment, and abortion were "committed by mothers in such a state that their physical and mental health cannot be considered completely normal. . . . This condition is characteristic only of women because of the particulars of their physical organism" (Zhizhilenko 1922, p. 26). Pregnancy and birth weakened the female body, leaving women in a helpless state in which they could not control their actions or reactions, and in which external pressures could produce criminal actions. Because women could not control these forces, they could not be held responsible for their actions under such influences.

These and other interpretations of female crime placed women's biology at the very core of their criminality and removed responsibility from them for their deviance. This emphasis on female biology established a sort of biological determinism in studies of female crime that ran counter to Russian criminologists' commitment to sociological explanations of crime and also made it harder to correct, change, or eliminate female criminality from Russian society. Indeed, while overall, Russian criminologists rejected the determinism of criminal anthropology and Lombroso's theories, when considering female crime they embraced explanations rooted in the biological and sexual nature of women and often minimized or dismissed the importance of other factors that might have shaped female criminal behavior. The experience of D., a young, educated woman whose husband abandoned her for a mistress when she was four months pregnant, is illustrative of this approach. Desperate and still in love, D. bought a gun and on 12 April 1924 gave her husband an ultimatum: live with her or she would kill herself. When he refused even to give her some money to live on and suggested instead that she sell her coat, D. pulled out the gun and shot him. While criminologist S. Ukshe, who assessed the case, did recognize the material need of D. when she committed the crime, the analysis emphasized that the pregnancy had the most significant effect on her actions (Ukshe 1926; Kowalsky 2009, pp. 99–100).

Perhaps more surprising was the assessment of the case of S., a 50-year-old woman found guilty of embezzlement, a typically male crime. S. stole money from the cash box in the office where she worked as a secretary; she took the money to a casino and gambled it away, eventually stealing more money, selling her possessions, and gambling away everything she had. Psychiatrist A. N. Terent'eva described her fall into a life of crime in sexual terms: S.'s fear and horror over losing the money were transformed into sexual excitement, so much so that a bumpy tram ride caused her to experience an orgasm. Her period of social dangerousness, however, Terent'eva argued, would end with the imminent onset of menopause. At her trial, full responsibility was removed from S. and some blame for the crime was given to her employer (who perhaps foolishly left S. in charge of the cash box). Ultimately, though, criminologists determined that S.'s unsupervised sexuality and sexual passions drove the crime. Even when committing a "male" crime like embezzlement, women remained victims of their biology, physiology, and sexuality, and thus were considered unable to bear full responsibility for their actions (Terent'eva 1927, p. 290–95; Kowalsky 2009, pp. 100–02).

Such dynamics of explanations that emphasized women's sexuality, their traditional position in society, and their lack of responsibility made up the foundation of Russian criminological discussions of infanticide. A crime typically committed by women involving the family and violence, infanticide helped reveal to criminologists the level of responsibility that could be placed upon women for their offenses. The difficulty with placing responsibility for infanticide and other crimes on female sexuality was that it made the crime inherent in the physiology of women. Accepting a biological view of female criminality could undermine the very principles of the Soviet project—that crime would disappear with the achievement of communism—and make the rehabilitation of female criminals impossible. Thus, over the course of the 1920s, criminologists and the courts placed greater responsibility on men for the crime of infanticide.

Focusing on male responsibility redirected explanations of female deviance away from women's sexuality and placed it instead on "socially irresponsible" husbands and lovers. Criminologist M. Andreev noted that infanticide by fathers was a relatively new phenomenon that reflected the enforcement of Soviet laws regarding child support. According to the 1918 Soviet Family Code, men were financially responsible for their offspring regardless of their marital status. To escape making child support payments, men would often encourage their wives or girlfriends to terminate their pregnancies or commit infanticide (Andreev 1928, p. 142; Aliavdin 1929).[3] More troubling to criminologists was a willingness they noticed among women to commit infanticide at the urging of a husband or lover. For instance, psychiatrist V. V. Brailovskii described a case in which one Anna I. decided several months before she gave birth to murder her infant because her lover would only marry her if she killed the child (Brailovskii 1929, p. 74).[4] In a similar case, 19-year-old Aleksandra Vasil'evna Gugina suffocated her newborn baby because she understood that her lover, Pavel Kiselev, did not want the child and would not marry her unless she found a way to get rid of it.[5] Local courts sentenced both parties to two years' imprisonment in strict isolation. Gugina appealed the decision to the Supreme Court, which found that she had merely reacted to the circumstances in which she found herself. Emphasizing that Kiselev instigated Gugina's crime by exploiting her helpless and desperate situation, the appeals court reduced Gugina's sentence from two years to six months and pardoned her altogether through a general amnesty declared in honor of the tenth anniversary of the October Revolution. Kiselev's sentence, however, remained in full force. Thus, in this case the court placed the responsibility for the death of the infant not with the mother who committed the crime, but with the father who encouraged it and tried to cover it up.

Criminologist B. S. Man'kovskii observed that when men were found guilty of child murder, whether they had committed the crime themselves or had encouraged a woman to do so, they generally received harsher sentences than women. He indicated that 58.6 percent of women who committed infanticide received suspended sentences, compared to 11.7 percent of men. Likewise, only 2.2 percent of women spent more than two years in prison for infanticide, compared to 70.7 percent of men (Man'kovskii 1928, p. 267).[6] Clearly, the courts understood that men who resorted to killing an infant were not fulfilling their duties as good Soviet citizens. In fact, criminologists advocated harsher punishments for men in infanticide cases. Man'kovskii concluded, "With regard to men who commit infanticide for selfish reasons, such as not wanting to pay alimony, the level of punishment must be as severe as for those committing other types of murder" (p. 267). By assuming that men were more conscious of their obligations under Soviet law, the criminologists emphasized the need for male responsibility over women and placed the agency for female criminality on men, leaving women as passive participants who could not be held liable for their own actions and reinforcing patriarchal values within Soviet social norms (Kowalsky 2003).

Despite their rather innovative interpretations of crime as being the product of multiple factors and causes, both social and individual, Russian criminologists in the early twentieth century employed their analyses of female criminality as a way to reinforce traditional interpretations of women's role and position in society. Although they seemed encouraged by the gradual emergence of women in the public sphere, they did not find any noticeable or meaningful change in the types, nature, or rates of female crime. Indeed, they reinforced the naturalness of traditional female criminality by emphasizing the biological factors of and physiological causes for women's deviance. Such assessments suggested that no matter what might change regarding women's position in society, women had essential traits rooted in their sexuality and biology that shaped their behavior more than did external considerations. Women thus remained uncivilized, backward, not responsible for their behavior, and unable to engage in the public sphere and with modernity to the same extent as men.

III. The Geography of Female Crime

Perhaps as much as they linked female crime to women's biology, physiology, and sexuality, Russian criminologists also associated women's deviance with the "backward" traditions of the countryside, contrasting the nature of their crime with that of the more "civilized" male criminal and the modernity of the city. In so doing, they reinforced gendered assumptions about society, women's deviance, and social norms, and even questioned women's ability to become conscious Soviet citizens. Indeed, regardless of where women actually committed their crimes, female deviance was seen as retaining its "rural" and "primitive" nature, driven by "primitive" impulses and outdated traditions. Criminologists highlighted the differences they perceived in rural and urban crimes. Rural crimes were more often violent in nature and driven by emotion; urban crimes, in contrast, involved skill and deception, anonymity, and secrecy. Rural crimes embodied the past, the primitive and violent impulses in society, while urban crime reflected modernity and progress. Indeed, criminologists categorized an offense as urban or rural not according to where the crime was committed but with regard to the qualities of the offense, so that violent crimes became "rural" and fraud and theft became "urban." Moreover, in their assessments, criminologists found the city itself to be a factor shaping the criminal impulse, as Gernet vividly noted: "Streets bursting with people, customers cramming stores, theaters, tram stops, omnibuses, ships, underpasses, and train cars; all this creates favorable conditions for pickpocketers. The growth of large cities as commercial centers, with their labor exchanges, colossal stores, constant street trade, and assorted markets, encourages an atmosphere of speculation that promotes fraud" (Gernet 1924; Kowalsky 2009, p. 116). Despite the tremendous anxiety about the modern city that criminologists expressed, they still saw it as the future for Soviet society and the model of values that needed to be disseminated to the general population, particularly rural residents.

Additionally, rural residents, and women in particular, were seen as less enlightened, less educated, and thus more inclined to act on their passions and emotions than urban residents. Educational levels among offenders revealed the discrepancies among men and women, urban and rural residents. Figures from 1924 indicate that 64.3 percent of rural female offenders were illiterate, while only 28.6 percent could read and write. Among men, 19.8 percent remained illiterate, but 71.3 percent knew how to read and write. Educational differences persisted in the urban environment: 42.3 percent of urban female criminals were illiterate, but only 8.8 percent of male criminals could not read and write. Most urban male criminals could read and write (82.3 percent), while the majority of female urban criminals could not (51.6 percent) (B. 1925, p. 27; Tarnovskii 1925, p. 48). These figures reinforced for Russian criminologists the divide between the city and the countryside, and placed female offenders securely within the "rural" environment, regardless of where they resided or what sort of employment they engaged in. Women remained backward, despite Soviet efforts to bring enlightenment and education to the peasant majority.

For early Soviet criminologists the nature of the crime committed revealed an offender's class and background more accurately than did their place of residence or their profession. Using the offender's awareness of the harm of their actions to Soviet society helped to establish a new "Soviet" class identity and even limited the extent of responsibility an offender could bear for his or her actions (Kowalsky 2009, p. 128). Levels of responsibility can be seen in sentencing statistics. For example, in 1924, 31.8 percent of urban men and 20.4 percent of urban women were sentenced to time in prison, while only 13.3 percent of rural men and 9.4 percent of rural women received such sentences (*Statistika osuzhdennykh* 1927), pp. 122–23; Kowalsky 2009, p. 128). Multiple factors contributed to low rates of custodial sentencing, including shortages of space in prisons; a sense that such punishments did little to correct or eliminate undesirable behavior, especially among the peasantry, whom the professionals believed understood only the language of violence (Schrader 2002); and a sense that prison sentences could be detrimental, even disastrous, for women because of their closer connection to the family and "less social adaptability" (Iakubson 1927; Kowalsky 2009, p. 130). According to the courts, police, and professionals, female offenders, and peasant offenders generally, could not be held fully responsible for their actions. This led to mitigated punishments, suspended sentences, and other noncustodial punishments for female criminals, reflecting their perceived inability to understand and take responsibility for their actions. Assessments of female deviance were shaped by preconceived notions about women's position in society that remained unchanged, despite the radical transformations early Soviet society experienced. Early Soviet crime studies reinforced the status quo, rather than revealing transformation.

CONCLUSION

Russian and Soviet criminologists found new opportunities for integrating crime studies into a broader scientific effort to understand social change and transformation in the early twentieth century. Their approaches drew on the ideas and methods developed and established by their Western European colleagues throughout the nineteenth century but were shaped and formed in significant ways by internal developments and attitudes within Russia. Specifically, the authoritarian tradition of Russian politics contributed to the acceptance of centralized state initiatives in criminology, and this outlook shaped the way that criminologists understood crime and its social significance. Furthermore, the Bolshevik Revolution provided criminologists with a new context that prioritized scientific understanding in a novel way, and they took advantage of the environment to establish innovative methods and approaches to understanding crime and deviance. Despite their innovations and their determination to assess crime in order to bring about its elimination from society, early Soviet criminologists' studies generally reinforced the status quo, particularly regarding female deviance. They concluded that even with the changes brought about by modernization, industrialization, and revolution that increased women's involvement with the "struggle for existence," female crime remained a product of backwardness, ignorance, and biophysiological norms. Their assessments helped to reassert women's traditional position in society at a time of tremendous anxiety and upheaval as the new rulers of Russia set about renegotiating social relationships and social structures in general.

Notes

1. On the foundation of the Moscow Bureau, see Tsentral'nyi gosudarstvennyi arkhiv Moskovskoi oblasti (TsGAMO) [Central State Archive of the Moscow Region], f. 66, op. 13, d. 203, l. 218 (ob). See also my discussion of the establishment of criminological institutes in Russia in the 1920s in Kowalsky (2009, pp. 55–73).
2. Eric Johnson (1985, p. 171) has argued this for the German context. In addition, Helen Borich and John Hagan (1990, p. 595) have found that women's greater visibility in public may have led to increased arrest rates as society sought to establish new networks of social control. Similar patterns seem to have existed in Russia, although this is less studied (see, e.g., Frank 1996).
3. Bychkov (1929, p. 35) noted that in 1926–1927, 11 percent of those found guilty of infanticide in the Moscow regional courts were men. On the effectiveness of the alimony laws, see Goldman (1993, pp. 237–46).
4. Brailovskii did not indicate the sentencing in this case.
5. "D. No. 216432," *Sudebnaia praktika RSFSR* no. 4 (1928), pp. 21–22. Article 136, Part d, of the 1926 Soviet Criminal Code deals with premeditated murder committed by persons who bear responsibility for the care of the victim, with a prescribed punishment of up to ten years in prison.
6. The prison terms break down as follows: for women, 17.8 percent were sentenced to up to one year in prison, 21.4 percent for one to two years, and 2.2 percent for over two years; for men, 17.6 percent were sentenced for one to two years, 29.4 percent for three to four years, 17.6 percent for five to seven years, and 23.7 percent for eight to ten years.

References

Aliavdin, P. A. 1929. "Ugolovnye prestupleniia v sviazi s alimentami v Ivanovo-Voznesenskoi gubernii." *Sudebno-meditsinskaia ekspertiza* 11: 113–15.
Andreev, M. 1928. "Detoubiistvo." *Rabochii sud* 2: 137–44.

B., Iu. 1925. "Prestupnost' goroda i derevni v 1924 g." *Administrativnyi vestnik* 6: 23–28.

Becker, Elisa M. 2011. *Medicine, Law and the State in Imperial Russia*. Budapest & New York: Central European University Press.

Beer, Daniel. 2008. *Renovating Russia: The Human Sciences and the Fate of Liberal Modernity, 1880–1930*. Ithaca, NY: Cornell University Press.

Bernstein, Francis. 2007. *The Dictatorship of Sex: Lifestyle Advice for the Soviet Masses*. DeKalb: Northern Illinois University Press.

Borich, Helen, & John Hagan. 1990. "A Century of Crime in Toronto: Gender, Class, and Patterns of Social Control, 1859 to 1955." *Criminology* 8 (4): 567–99.

Brailovskii, V. V. 1929. *Opyt bio-sotsial'nogo issledovaniia ubiits: Po materialam mest zakliucheniia Severnogo Kavkaza*. Rostov na Donu, Russia: Donskaia Pravda.

Bychkov, I. Ia. 1929. *Detoubiistvo v sovremennykh usloviiakh*. Moscow: Gosudarstvennoe meditsinskoe izdatel'stvo.

Finkel, Stuart. 2001. "'The Brains of the Nation': The Expulsion of Intellectuals and the Politics of Culture in Soviet Russia, 1920–1924." Ph.D. diss., Stanford University.

Foinitskii, I. Ia. 1898–1900. *Na dosuge. Sbornik iuridicheskikh statei i izsledovanii c 1870 goda*, 2 vols. St. Petersburg: Tip. M. M. Stasiulevicha.

Frank, Stephen. 1996. "Narratives Within Numbers: Women, Crime, and Juridical Statistics in Imperial Russia, 1834–1913." *Russian Review* 55 (4): 541–66.

Garland, David. 1985. "The Criminal and His Science: A Critical Account of the Formation of Criminology at the End of the Nineteenth Century." *British Journal of Criminology* 25 (2): 109–37.

Gernet, M. N. 1924. "Predislovie." In *Prestupnyi mir Moskvy*, ed. M. N. Gernet, i–xli. Moscow: Izdatel'stvo Pravo i zhizn'.

Gernet, M. N. 1925. "Gosudarstvennyi institute po izucheniiu prestupnosti." *Administrativnyi vestnik* 11: 30–32.

Gernet, M. N. 1974. *Izbrannye proizvedeniia*. Moscow: Iuridicheskaia literatura.

Goldman, Wendy. 1993. *Women, the State, and Revolution: Soviet Family Policy and Social Life, 1917–1936*. Cambridge: Cambridge University Press.

Iakubson, V. R. 1927. "Repressiia lisheniem svobody." In *Sovremennaia prestupnost' (Prestuplenie, pol, repressiia, retsidiv)*, ed. A. G. Beloborodov, 20–38. Moscow: Izdatel'stvo Narodnogo Komissariata Vnutrennykh Del RSFSR.

Ivanov, L. O., & L. V. Il'ina. 1991. *Puti i sud'by otechestvennoi kriminologii*. Moscow: Nauka.

Johnson, Eric. 1985. "Women as Victims and Criminals: Female Homicide and Criminality in Imperial Germany, 1873–1914." *Criminal Justice History* 6: 151–75.

Kowalsky, Sharon A. 2003. "Who's Responsible for Female Crime: Gender, Deviance and the Development of Soviet Social Norms in Revolutionary Russia." *Russian Review* 62 (3): 366–86.

Kowalsky, Sharon A. 2009. *Deviant Women: Female Crime and Criminology in Revolutionary Russia, 1880–1930*. DeKalb: Northern Illinois University Press.

Man'kovskii, B. S. 1928. "Detoubiistvo." In *Ubiistva i ubiitsy*, ed. E. K. Krasnushkin, G. M. Segal, & Ts. M. Feinberg, 249–72. Moscow: Izdatel'stvo Moszdravotdela.

McReynolds, Louise. 2013. *Murder Most Russian: True Crime and Punishment in Late Imperial Russia*. Ithaca, NY, & London: Cornell University Press.

Mogilner, Marina. 2013. *Homo Imperii: A History of Physical Anthropology in Russia*. Lincoln: University of Nebraska Press.

Nemilov, A. V. 1907. *Biologicheskaia tragediia zhenshchiny*. Leningrad: Knigoizdatel'stvo 'Seiatel'.'

Ozerov, I. 1896. "Sravnitel'naia prestupnost' polov v zavisimosti ot nekotorykh faktorov." *Zhurnal iuridicheskogo obshchestva pri Imperatorskom S-Peterburgskom universitete* 4: 45–83.

Sanchov, V. L. 1924. "Toska po domu, kak faktor prestupnosti." *Rabochii sud* 11–12: 33–42.

Schrader, Abby. 2002. *Languages of the Lash: Corporal Punishment and Identity in Imperial Russia.* DeKalb: Northern Illinois University Press.

Statistika osuzhdennykh v SSSR 1923–1924. 1927. Moscow: Izdanie TsSU SSSR.

Tarnovskaia, Praskov'ia N. 1902. *Zhenshchina-ubiitsy. Anthropologicheskoe issledovanie.* St. Petersburg: T-vo khudozhestvennoi pechati.

Tarnovskaia, Praskov'ia N. 1908. *Les femmes homicides.* Paris: F. Alcan.

Tarnovskii, E. N. 1899. *Itogi Russkoi ugolovnoi statistiki za 20 let (1874–1894 gg.).* St. Petersburg: Tip. Pravitel'stvuiushchogo Senata.

Tarnovskii, E. N. 1925. "Osnovnye cherty sovremennoi prestupnosti." *Administrativnyi vestnik* 11: 45–53.

Terent'eva, A. N. 1927. "Dva sluchaia zhenshchin-rastratchits." *Prestupnik i prestunost'* 2: 290–99.

Todes, Daniel. 1989. *Darwin Without Malthus: The Struggle for Existence in Russian Evolutionary Thought.* Oxford: Oxford University Press.

Ukshe, S. 1926. "Muzheubiitsy." *Pravo i zhizn'* 4–5: 103–105.

Utevskii, B. S. 1926. "Gosudarstvennyi institute po izucheniiu prestupnosti i prestupnika." *Ezhenedel'nik Sovetskoi iustitsii* 18: 569–70.

Wolfgang, Marvin. 1961. "Pioneers in Criminology: Cesare Lombroso (1835–1909)." *Journal of Criminal Law, Criminology, and Police Science* 52 (4): 369–70.

Zhizhilenko, A. A. 1922. *Prestupnost' i ee factory.* Petrograd: Mir znanii.

PART SIX

LAW ENFORCEMENT AND POLICING

CHAPTER 22

POLICING BEFORE THE POLICE IN THE EIGHTEENTH CENTURY

British Perspectives in a European Context

DAVID G. BARRIE

INTRODUCTION

IN older British police histories, the Metropolitan Police Act of 1829 is portrayed as a watershed in law enforcement (Reith 1943; Ascoli 1979). The statute, which established a full-time, uniformed police force to prevent crime in the metropolis of London, signified the birth of "modern" policing. According to this narrative, the "old" police—the parish constables, local justices, and watchmen who enforced the law before the advent of "modern" policing—were amateur, corrupt, and inefficient. These histories suggest that after stubborn, short-sighted fools and vested interests spent decades opposing reform, the Metropolitan Police Act swept away this old, decrepit system and established a police model that would become the standard-bearer throughout much of the "civilized" world. What is presented is a consensual, Whiggish interpretation that views the British police model as distinctively different from the arbitrary, militarized, state-controlled ones that patrolled continental Europe in that the police in Britain were unarmed, civilian, and drew their authority from the public.

While historians have continued to acknowledge the importance of the Metropolitan Police Act in influencing developments in law enforcement (Emsley 2012; Philips & Storch 1999), the last few decades have witnessed a burgeoning body of scholarship that has added nuance to and challenged the traditional narrative. The initial backlash came from left-wing scholars seeking to advance a framework of analysis based more on conflict than on consensus (e.g., Storch 1975). In linking the emergence of modern policing with the needs of a class-based capitalist society, early revisionist histories focused primarily on examining the role and impact of the "new" police rather than the performance and professionalism of their eighteenth-century predecessors. What was new about the "new" police was not their greater level of efficiency, but the fact that they were a new form of social control and a product of class antagonisms produced by the transition to urban, industrial society.

While questioning whether the "new" police functioned as an instrument of the ruling and middle classes in the way that revisionist histories suggest, recent research has put more focus on how society was policed before the introduction of the so-called "new" police. Far from being an era in which individuals and communities were resistant to reform, the eighteenth century has been shown to have ushered in innovations in policing that would establish continuity with nineteenth-century practices. Not only were London and the major provincial centers of England pioneering policing initiatives and experiments earlier than was once acknowledged (Beattie 2012; Reynolds 1998; Dodsworth 2004), so, too, were the large cities of Scotland and Ireland (Barrie 2008; Palmer 1988). Indeed, in keeping with Peter King's recent (2006) study of English criminal justice history, this body of scholarship points to the need to give greater attention to the margins (provincial centers and counties) and the important role they played in shaping modern practices. Predating the full-scale introduction of capitalist working practices and industrialization, advances in law enforcement over the long eighteenth century also speak to the greater attention that historians need to pay to broader social, demographic, intellectual, and civic influences behind the birth of modern policing than the pioneering traditional/revisionist models—for all their merits—have hitherto done. As Clive Emsley (2007) has pointed out, recent scholarship, and the new approaches it has taken, situates reform within wider changes to criminal justice systems, addresses the impact of Enlightenment thought on policing, and stresses the multifaceted nature of police work and the differing police typologies under which police officers functioned. It also emphasizes how ideas about policing were shared between reformers in Europe and the United Kingdom, which points to the need to recognize the important role of intellectual transfer in the evolution of modern law enforcement.

This essay examines how communities were policed—and how law enforcement functioned and evolved—over the long eighteenth century and assesses the significance of both for further police reform in the nineteenth century. Moreover, it does this within a broad European context in order to gauge just how distinctive, if at all, the British experience was. In doing so, it considers not just the institutional and religious pillars of law enforcement, control, and discipline, but also how ordinary people policed their own communities through the use of print culture and voluntary initiatives. The essay defines "policing" broadly to incorporate civic initiatives and the policing of behavior carried out by church officials and courts in certain parts of the British Isles, most noticeably in Scotland. While significant variations across cities, counties and countries caution against imposing one model, the essay points to the need to move beyond the immediate confines of the "old" police label and appreciate the diverse and interconnected nature of law enforcement and the changing roles that various participants—including ordinary members of the community—played in it.

The essay's main focus is on England and Wales (which had the same legal structures in the eighteenth century) and Scotland, with comparisons drawn to continental Europe. England/Wales and Scotland had, and continue to have, different legal, civic, and religious histories and traditions that enable comparisons to be drawn and wider trends unpicked. Section I examines the institutional structures of law enforcement and the people who staffed them up to the mid-eighteenth century, examining the "old" police, prosecution practices, and the influence of religion on policing. Section II considers innovations in law enforcement in Britain from the mid-eighteenth century onward and how they fit within a wider European context. This section examines in more detail the influence of print culture and private policing on the emergence of the "modern" police, as well as new scientific approaches to policing, such as preventative policing.

I. The Mechanisms of Control, c.1700–1750

The police concept has a long history in Europe, predating bureaucratic police institutions by several centuries. The word came into regular usage in the sixteenth century, when it was commonly linked with good order and civic governance (Emsley 2007, p. 61). In this era, European rulers passed police ordinances to promote well-ordered territories and communities, but often lacked the functionaries to enforce them. In France, which led the way in pioneering police reform, a centralized, armed royal constabulary known as the *Maréchaussée* patrolled rural districts and roads since at least the fourteenth century. It was not, however, until the introduction of the *lieutenant général de police de Paris* (1667) and the appointment of police lieutenants in provincial French towns (1699) that urban police institutions were established (Milliot 2006). Reform in Paris helped to further extend the authority of King Louis XIV by consolidating responsibility for policing in the hands of the *lieutenant général*. Along with his subordinates, including *commissaires du Châtelet* and *inspecteurs de police*, the *lieutenant général* was charged with managing a semi-militarized city guard and overseeing the broad governance of police issues relating to the built environment. Although many European cities in the eighteenth century would subsequently mold their police systems to reflect their own institutional structures and needs, the Parisian model would prove to be as influential in shaping international police typology in the eighteenth century as London's system would become in the nineteenth, offering a reference point for how populous cities could be administered.

In stark contrast to European innovations, the concept of "police" in England was viewed with suspicion in the first half of the eighteenth century. Observers believed "police" to be associated with continental absolute rule. The perceived intrusive, secretive, and military nature of centralized European policing practices had convinced many that police institutions were incompatible with the individual liberty and local autonomy on which the governing principles of the English state were portrayed as having been constructed. However, although England, Wales, Scotland, and Ireland did not have centralized, hierarchal police models, they were far from being "unpoliced" countries. Since time immemorial, communities had established hierarchies of power and authority to police behavior and enforce agreed-upon norms. Each country was policed in a variety of ways that reflected its political, legal, and religious values and power structures. Differing legal systems and cultural traditions ensured that there was no single model of law enforcement on mainland Britain. But, as this section shows, there were a number of similarities between them—similarities that would lay the foundations for a level of convergence in the second half of the century.

A. The "Old" Police

In the first half of the eighteenth century, English and Scottish towns and counties relied upon a variety of local officials, representatives, and institutions to enforce law and order—the so-called "old" police. Authority was vested in justices who, as legal guardians, either appointed or oversaw the election from the local community of a number of lesser local officials, including constables, town officers, and watchmen. Some positions were salaried, such as that of town officer in Scotland, but most were unpaid, most notably those of magistrate and constable. A few of the larger urban centers—such as London and Edinburgh—employed paid watch forces to guard the streets at night, but these were the exception rather than the norm. Other towns either did not bother to police the nighttime streets or obliged local householders to "watch and ward" on a rotational basis.

As in continental Europe, the entitlement to undertake policing activities was expressed through, and conditioned by, ideas of male authority (Barrie & Broomhall 2012; Dodsworth 2007). All unpaid law and order tasks in practice were reserved for men—usually "independent" men, meaning, in effect, male householders who met a property requirement. Authority to enforce the law and protect others in Britain was linked to both gender and social status and was dependent upon neoclassical notions of governance—ideals stressing that men of property had an obligation to serve their communities (Dodsworth 2004). Constables typically served for one year and carried out their duties on a part-time basis in conjunction with other employment. Far from being unreliable and of suspect character, as many older histories suggested, research has shown that the majority of constables were sober, responsible, and civic-minded individuals (Morgan & Rushton 2004). Although in principle this system of law enforcement was amateur, the arrangements it produced were not necessarily unprofessional in their workings. In some parishes, the position of constable appears to have become almost semi-permanent and salaried as the first half of the eighteenth century progressed. The role of constable, though, was limited. Such individuals would neither patrol nor seek to prevent crime by their visible presence and would only investigate crime if the victim was willing and had the financial means to pay for it.

There was, inevitably, considerable regional variation within this general pattern. London, for instance, was several decades ahead of the rest of the British Isles in pioneering reform from the mid-seventeenth century onward. As John Beattie (2001) has shown, policing and prosecution were in many ways professionalized in the City of London between 1660 and 1750, with city authorities introducing a range of new initiatives to prevent, detect, and punish crime, including the establishment of new local courts of justice. Indeed, what is particularly interesting about Beattie's seminal study is that innovations in this era were not the product of a carefully planned intentional reform of English criminal law, but rather were piecemeal, incomplete, and ad hoc responses to short-term problems—problems that collectively would have significant implications. As Beattie contends, developments in the capital played an important part in shaping much government policy regarding crime and criminal justice in England in this period. London, Emsley has pointed out, was not so different from other large European cities in that it had an extremely well-developed watching system. Unlike the arrangements in the continental cities, though, watching arrangements were not under the supervision or management of one individual or committee, but were instead invested in scores of parish vestries, which, significantly, jealously protected their independence and resisted the imposition of a centralized structure (Emsley 2007, p. 69).

In most other parts of the country policing arrangements were less advanced. Victims of crime in provincial areas—and, in most cases, London, despite the developments noted here—received little support in investigating and detecting crime. As King (2000) has shown, an extremely small percentage of the offenders who were prosecuted at the Essex quarter sessions had been detected as the result of the actions of constables. In the majority of cases, the victim was the main instigator of investigation. Those who could afford it had the option of recruiting a "thief-taker," an individual hired privately to locate and apprehend criminals. However, the cost and inconvenience of such action prevented most victims from pursuing this option. Most simply chose not to attempt to investigate or detect crime, especially petty crime that offered little prospect of property being recovered.

Watch forces likewise offered little assistance with criminal investigation. Their role was limited primarily to protecting property, assisting magistrates and constables in the exercise of their duties, and apprehending suspicious persons or those committing public order offenses. While they were effective in apprehending drunks and maintaining a decent level of public decorum, they were not expected to control large outbreaks of disorder. Furthermore, although watchmen, along with temporarily enlisted special constables, often assisted more official forces during outbreaks of rioting, they were not always the front line of defense. The military or militia forces were often deployed to quell outbreaks of violent protest, or, if the riot was a protest against rising grain prices or scarcity of meal, local elites would often intervene to ensure that grievances were addressed. Indeed, when it came to deterring food riots—one of the most common forms of rioting in the eighteenth century—preventative policing was less about utilizing the services of the "old" police and more about policing bread markets. In port towns, in particular, local magistrates deployed a policy of civic paternalism that involved supplying local markets with grain at a price people could afford in order to offset disturbances. The "moral economy," as this model has been termed, was one grounded in a premodern, paternalistic social framework that was intended to defuse social tensions (Thompson 1971). But, crucially, it was not a model that was conducive to the rise of a free market economy, which would help underpin growing demands for more effective policing as the century progressed.

B. Prosecution

In England and Wales, victims had to decide not only whether to go to the trouble of investigating crime and apprehending offenders but also whether to prosecute suspected offenders. While the Crown would initiate and fund public prosecutions for serious crimes, such as murder or forgery, it left the prosecution of the vast majority of other crimes to the discretion of victims. This was "the golden era of discretionary justice" (King 2000, pp. 17–46), and a wide array of participants—not only the landed elite, as was once argued (Hay 1975, pp. 17–63)—was able to exercise discretion. The victim had a central role in the eighteenth-century English criminal justice system—but, significantly, it was a role not shared equally. Pursuing a prosecution was expensive, complex, time consuming, and, crucially, beyond the financial reach of the laboring poor. While a number of historians have shown that all sections of society made use of the local courts, the vast majority of criminal prosecutions were brought by those from the middle and upper sections of society (King 2000; Gray 2009). Most victims preferred negotiated settlements—such as the recovery of stolen goods—to formal legal redress. Aside from the fiscal and pragmatic difficulties in pursuing legal action, there was a long-standing belief in England that severity of punishment rather than certainty of prosecution was the most effective deterrent to crime. Severe, exemplary punishment of a few offenders would, it was believed, have a greater impact on preventing crime than the liberal punishment of many, as it would send out a warning to the wider community. Indeed, such a mindset underpinned the infamous "Bloody Code," which sought to deter crime through a series of brutal and publicly visible corporal and capital punishments.

Unlike England, Scotland had a publicly funded prosecutor—the procurator fiscal— who would carry out preliminary investigations of reported crimes to establish whether a case was worth pursuing. This system, though, did not result in a larger number of criminal prosecutions, which were, in fact, typically fewer in Scotland relative to population than in England (Barrie & Broomhall 2014a, pp. 49–62). Indeed, if anything, the existence of the procurator fiscal helped to keep the number of criminal prosecutions low, given the financial constraints under which prosecutors and the courts operated. Prosecutions were very much at the discretion of procurators, who would base their decision to bring charges upon the likelihood of conviction or payment of legal fees.

With only a modest public subsidy available for criminal prosecutions, only a small number of crimes were ever prosecuted. The procurator fiscal adopted a pragmatic approach when administering the law: increasing the number of criminal prosecutions and taking a tough stance against offenders during periods of heightened unrest, but adopting a more informal, lenient approach when anxiety waned and social relations improved (Crowther 1999, pp. 225–38).

In many rural European communities, local people had a deep-rooted suspicion of justice administered by those from outside their own locality. Many peasant societies, in particular, preferred to enforce their own notions of justice through extrajudicial means rather than invite unwanted interference from legal institutions (Emsley 2007, p. 61). Even in Paris, local communities often preferred to rely upon informal neighborhood surveillance and self-policing techniques than report crimes to the local police (Garrioch 1986). A similar mindset existed in some parts of Scotland. Many Scots preferred informal, local rough justice—justice that privileged the actions of local people or local ministers over that of sheriffs, magistrates and procurators—to formally administered justice. As the next subsection shows, "godly discipline" would play a central role in the policing of Scottish communities—with Scots much more likely to be brought before a church court than a criminal one (Leneman & Mitchison 1998).

C. Godly Discipline

In premodern society, church authorities punished ecclesiastical offenses and a wide array of behaviors recognized as misdemeanors—many of which were related to sin and immorality. Within Britain and Ireland, there was considerable national, regional, religious, and periodic variation, which reflected each country's distinctive ecclesiastical and cultural heritage. While the role of ecclesiastical courts in Ireland and England diminished in response to a raft of religious, social, and demographic factors as the seventeenth and eighteenth centuries progressed, in Scotland these institutions continued to flourish. Calvinist doctrine, from which the Church of Scotland's teachings were derived, preached moral restraint and "godly discipline"—and those who transgressed the Church's strict moral code faced the wrath of its local courts. These courts, which were called kirk sessions, were chaired by a minister and populated by a collection of male elders. They imposed a system of parish discipline rarely found in the Anglican Church that enabled the Scottish Church to exert greater control over society than was the case in England (Leneman & Mitchison 1998, p. 2).

Kirk sessions, and the elders who staffed them, had a significant role to play in policing communities more broadly. Indeed, in some smaller burghs, they were as important, if not more so, than town officers, constables, and watchmen in maintaining public order. Elders—who were elected from among the local congregation—were more numerous and ubiquitous than constables and watchmen and were relentless in pursuing those who transgressed Church laws. They prosecuted profanity, religious nonconformity, and sexual and moral misconduct, and often worked hand-in-hand with town officers and constables to keep a close check on the movement and behavior of local people. They supervised activity within the community to ensure that religious customs were not profaned or laws broken, and they instructed local congregations to report behavior deemed to be suspicious and morally unacceptable. Indeed, kirk elders were an important resource for community policing—although that community was a "godly" one that had to conform to the elders' own Presbyterian ideals.

Witness testimonies before the High Court of Justiciary between 1750 and 1815 reveal that elders, along with other local justices, "regularly helped to interrogate suspects bound for the higher criminal courts" and "provided a strong moral, criminal and cultural investigative framework within Scottish society" (Kilday 2007, p. 28). This was especially so in cases of suspected infanticide, in which elders assisted in interviewing witnesses, ordered physical examinations of women's bodies, and secured confessions. Indeed, prosecutions for this crime often started out as local investigations under the direction of elders—and often following a report from the local community.

Although not everyone in Scotland adhered to the Church's moral code or accepted its religious authority, the kirk's hold over society remained strong up until the late eighteenth century. From that point on, though, its influence started to wane, especially in large urban centers (Leneman & Mitchison 1998). As towns expanded, it became increasingly difficult for the Church to control the behavior and morality of parishioners. Sabbath breaches became more common as Church provision failed to keep pace with population growth, and religious observance among the lower orders declined. Although religious values continued to be widely held, the established Church, as in England, became less effective as a mechanism of control. Its retreat would leave a vacuum that policing initiatives attempted to fill as the eighteenth and nineteenth centuries progressed.

D. Roundup: Premodern Policing in Perspective

Underpinning eighteenth-century law enforcement in Britain was the belief that the community should have a role to play in it. Early modern policing practices conferred tremendous responsibility on victims—whose capacity to seek justice was often influenced by social status, ability to pay, and, especially in the case of Scotland, the willingness of legal or public officials to pursue prosecutions on their behalf. If victims were unwilling to act, then these criminal justice systems became inert and ineffective (King 2000). Although large European cities such as Paris had established centralized police systems, these mechanisms of policing continued to have many similarities with British practice, in that most European communities preferred to rely on informal sanctions and neighborhood policing rather than state-controlled police units. Continental Europe might have had institutional police structures earlier than Britain, but differences in attitudes toward, and willingness to use the services of, the police and the courts were often less marked.

To the pioneering scholars of police history, such arrangements in Britain appeared backward and inefficient when compared to modern policing practices, but for the most part they did meet the limited needs of the time. This was a system of law enforcement that was valued by local justices because it was cheap to administer and it conveyed upon all of its participants a degree of discretion and influence. It was a system, though, that was suited to the modest expectations of law enforcement at that time and to small, sparsely populated pre-industrial towns and parishes. It was not one that could accommodate rapidly urbanizing, commercial society, higher expectations of comfort and security, and growing middle-class demands for greater legal protection from the courts and new forms of civic government. As the subsequent section examines, these social, economic, intellectual, and legal drivers would stimulate a wide array of local policing innovations and experiments throughout Britain that would ultimately lay the foundations for modern policing before the "new" police was introduced in the nineteenth century.

II. Innovations in Policing, c. 1750–1800

In Europe, the development and professionalization of municipal and state police forces became much more common in the second half of the eighteenth century (Denys 2010). In this era, many European countries and states established recognizable modern features of policing with regard to structure, control, function, and organization (Bailey 1975). Many initiatives centralized police control, often in the hands of absolute monarchs, which further added to English fears that policing went hand-in-hand with arbitrary rule. In Prussia, for instance, royal police officers were appointed beginning in the mid-eighteenth century; in Vienna, in 1753, a body of police officers was created and placed under the responsibility of a new security authority, the *Unterkommission aus der Wiener Bürgerschaft* (Emsley 2007). The power of ruling authorities was further extended by the establishment of state-controlled militarized police units—typically staffed by ex-soldiers—that patrolled provincial and rural communities in a manner similar to that of the *Maréchaussée* and, from 1791 onward, the *Gendarmerie nationale* in France. Although some of these police authorities performed crime prevention and detective functions, the majority were primarily concerned with maintaining order and extending the surveillance capacity of the central state over large territories.

While such initiatives were closely linked with attempts to improve internal security, others were designed to regulate the urban environment in a manner that reflected the wider European conception of police as a form of government and civic welfare. In many French and Dutch towns, for instance, the municipal, civilian forces that were increasingly introduced stood, in terms of organization and function, in stark contrast to the much more widely studied state military forces. Far from further centralizing control, police reform in European provincial towns was often constructed according to long-standing notions of community policing. In many cases, it stemmed from the innovation of local aldermen and resulted in the entrustment of significantly increased policing responsibilities, such as watching, lighting, and cleansing, to local communities and representatives (Denys 2010).

Across the continent, therefore, there was no single police model. Police systems in provincial towns and rural communities were often different in organization, structure, and, in many cases, purpose from those that existed in large capital cities, which points to the uneven, diverse, and complex manner in which policing developed. However, although the model of reform, and the pattern it followed, was not a historical linear process (Denys 2010); what these initiatives had in common was that they established an organized authority empowered, in the words of Bayley, with a "mandate to regulate interpersonal relations within a community" through the application of force and "coercive sanctions authorized in the name of the community" (1975, p. 47). These initiatives helped to link the conception of police with the governance, security, and well-being of the local and national state through the way in which they increased the capacity for exerting greater control over populations. They also, as Denys (2010) has pointed out, reflected a burgeoning intellectual discourse on policing. Influenced by Enlightenment thought, policing—how to improve it, what purpose it should serve, and how it should be organized—became an issue of regular debate, discussion, and deliberation in the second half of the eighteenth century, finding expression in a wide array of print culture from newspapers to memoirs. The production of writings by police officers in particular was testament to the growing autonomy of the police function that police officials were attempting to establish and impose (Milliot 2006).

Despite the claims of older police histories as to the uniqueness of English policing, the second half of the eighteenth century brought a number of similar changes in other parts of Britain. Although a centrally controlled, militarized policing system was never established on mainland Britain, the British government established an armed police force, controlled from London, in Dublin in 1786 and in provincial Ireland in 1787 in response to concerns about Irish nationalism (Palmer 1988). Moreover, while London continued to lead the way in pioneering improvements, developments in policing from this point onward were also increasingly shaped from the margins, reflecting a wider trend within the English criminal justice system in general (King 2006). Some of this reforming zeal was the product of statutory enactments from the central government in Westminster, but much of it took the form of nonstatutory voluntary measures or developments that evolved from the initiatives of discrete social groups with fairly limited, self-serving aims. As the following subsection examines, the expansion of print culture would not only help victims to investigate and detect crime, but also facilitate the dissemination of ideas about the merits of policing and prosecution that ultimately would help to shape a broader discourse on law enforcement.

A. Print Culture and Policing

In the eighteenth century, people's understanding of policing and lawlessness was often shaped more by what they read or heard than by actual experience (Snell 2007). With victims having to take the initiative for investigating and detecting crime, the printed word emerged as an important tool for marshalling, disseminating, and communicating information about crime and criminals—especially in instances in which investigative inquiries needed to extend beyond the vicinity in which the crime had occurred. Newspaper advertisements and handbills in particular were used to circulate criminal intelligence following the rise of the provincial press in the second half of the century (Styles 1989).

The most common crime-related newspaper advertisements functioned as a detective resource. These would typically record information about crime and criminals with the aim of retrieving stolen property or discovering and apprehending the suspect. Others sought to deter future criminal behavior, usually by proclaiming an intention to prosecute certain types of offenses. Although affluent men of property were those most likely to make use of this resource, the policing potential of print culture was by no means restricted to the privileged few (Styles 1989). Those from more middle-class backgrounds also made use of handbills or handwritten notices (King 2000, pp. 57–62). Local authorities, too, published notices and placed newspaper advertisements, especially relating to crimes that were perceived to have harmed the common good, such as grain theft. Indeed, as John Styles (1989) points out, the fact that such notices often sought to procure information to effect legal action suggests that they formed an aspect of premodern policing in which local officials had an important role to play.

The handbill is likely to have been the most effective of the various impersonal detective approaches used beyond personal pursuit, as it had a more specific target audience and was more accessible—not least because it could be read out loud in marketplaces— than newspaper advertisements. Although criminal advertising in newspapers grew over the course of the eighteenth century, the number of notices placed was not huge, and the number of convictions that they led to was small. Nonetheless, the fact that victims of crime were increasingly willing as the century progressed to make recourse to newspaper advertisements suggests that people at least perceived them to be effective in meeting specific objectives, especially recovering stolen property. Perhaps more importantly, the increasing use of print culture as a policing resource helped to extend the surveillance of offenders throughout the country—and, in doing so, made it more possible for victims to attempt to seek legal redress than had hitherto been the case. Moreover, the rise of crime advertising proved an inspiration to late eighteenth- and early nineteenth-century police reformers, who recognized the growing need for a more effective way of conveying information about crime and criminals in an era of significant demographic mobility and urban expansion (Styles 1989, p. 89).

Media reports of crime and criminal trials, too, were important to developments in policing. Newspapers and the Proceedings of the Old Bailey, which reported on criminal trials at London's main criminal court, had a particular thirst for reporting violent and property crime, which contributed to the perception that crimes that threatened public safety and security were increasing. Moreover, many crimes were reported as having gone unpunished, which spoke to the perceived weakness of the criminal justice system. Such reports, though, by no means always presented a dominant discourse (King 2007) and are likely to have been interpreted in different ways by readers, which should caution against overstating their potential impact. However, as Esther Snell points out, "the perpetual, steady and consistent portrayal of deviancy could not fail but to problematize it implicitly and served to present its incidence as being normative—that is, an everyday, ordinary occurrence" that strengthened the case for stronger policing measures (2007, p. 9).

The London press in the third quarter of the eighteenth century regularly reported on trial proceedings at the Bow Street Magistrates' Office—which, crucially, often recorded the important role that the Bow Street runners (see the following subsection) played in apprehending offenders, collecting evidence, and seeking out witnesses (Beattie 2012, p. 103). Similarly, newspapers often publicized policing success when offenders were detected, apprehended, and brought to justice (Ward 2014). With newspapers in different parts of the country often sharing local crime news reports, the press was instrumental in disseminating messages about the perceived merits of policing to areas that had not yet embraced reform. Local newspapers throughout Scotland, for instance, published trial proceedings in the Glasgow and Edinburgh police courts—which had been introduced in 1800 and 1805, respectively. This helped to promote calls for similar summary police powers in other parts of the country (Barrie & Broomhall 20014a). Verbatim newspaper coverage, in other words, helped to make arrangements in one part of the country appear backward when compared to those in another—and in doing so put police reform firmly on local political agendas.

B. Runners, Crime, and the Expansion of Private Policing

The second half of the eighteenth century brought greater public and private initiatives aimed at investigating and detecting crime. Arguably the most famous was the introduction in 1749 of a detective force operating from the Bow Street Magistrates' Office in Middlesex, known as the Bow Street runners. In that year the local magistrate Henry Fielding appointed a number of "runners" to investigate and detect crimes. Within a few years, the Bow Street Office had emerged as an important hub for police activity in the metropolis and a leading center for policing and prosecution (Beattie 2012). The officers appointed there were detectives in all but name; they were skilled in investigating crime, locating and arresting offenders, and securing convictions. The office helped to spread the idea that crime could be reduced through efficient and quick detection, and in doing so it offered a vision of crime control that was an alternative to exemplary punishment (Rawlings 2002). Moreover, in the 1760s, John Fielding, Henry's brother, established "rotation offices" (police offices) in Middlesex to which magistrates volunteered to provide magisterial officers at fixed times on a day-to-day basis in order to make justice more accessible and efficient (Beattie 2012, p. 86). These offices were not dissimilar to the *commissaires de police* in Paris, which heard and settled petty disputes and provided readily available and cheap justice to the masses. As Emsley points out, these initiatives were proof that police reformers in London "were thinking and writing in the broad intellectual environment of Enlightenment ideas" that were emanating from Europe and were likely to have filtered into Britain in some form (2007, pp. 61–71).

Outside of London, criminal detection in the second half of the eighteenth century was facilitated by the development of associations for the prosecution of felons that sought to help members recover stolen property and seek legal redress. Although their immediate impact in terms of securing convictions was fairly modest, the associations were indicative of a wider desire on the part of victims to use the courts. In Scotland, the public prosecutor helped to keep the level of prosecutions low, but in England and Wales recorded indictable crime rose disproportionate to population growth (Emsley 1996). Although the extent to which this upward statistical pattern reflects a real rise in crime has been subject to extensive debate, it is widely accepted that it was influenced by a growing willingness of victims to prosecute. Attitudes were changing, and certain sections of the populace were becoming more intolerant of crime. At the same time, legal and administrative changes made it easier and cheaper for victims to prosecute. Significantly, these developments occurred in an intellectual context that was slowly beginning to question not only traditional forms of policing and law enforcement but also the ethos and purpose of the criminal justice system itself and how its institutional structures should function. Ideas about the merits of preventative policing and controlling crime through patrol and surveillance were gaining popularity—which would help to underpin both nonstatutory and statutory policing and watching initiatives (Beattie 2012).

Whether they employed thief takers, private detectives, or print culture to seek redress for personal grievances, local people had long utilized their own private mechanisms for informal policing (Williams 2008). In the second half of the eighteenth century, though, private policing became more organized, professional, and collective. Increasingly, it was designed to order and demarcate spatial and temporal boundaries. Often, the aims were modest, with paid watchmen being deployed to protect specific streets or shops during periods of heightened concern about burglary (Barrie 2008). Among the more ambitious private policing schemes were those that sought to improve security in Britain's busy dockyards. Merchant traders were behind much of this reforming zeal, often in response to a perceived rise in dockland crime. The most famous of these endeavors was the Thames River Police, established in 1798 by West Indian merchants alarmed about thefts from their ships and warehouses. Many thefts in such areas were likely committed by dockworkers, who saw it as their customary right to appropriate whatever goods they could as part of their employment remuneration. While many traders and employers had in the past been willing to turn a blind eye to workers acquiring perquisites, increasingly the business community looked to clamp down upon such practices. Influenced by the pervasive free market ideology of Enlightenment thinkers such as Adam Smith, customs that in the past had been widely tolerated were increasingly criminalized. Crimes were being redefined, and employer–employee relations reconceptualized, with significant implications for developments in policing and law enforcement.

In industrial towns, private policing agencies were employed to find and prosecute workplace offenders (Godfrey & Cox 2013). In the north of England, manufacturers organized policing and prosecution agencies to control and punish embezzlement, and introduced a plethora of regulations to control workers and protect industrial capitalism. The Worsted Acts of 1777 enabled the establishment of a private police force of "inspectors" with wide-ranging powers to investigate and prosecute crime. Such private policing initiatives proved to be extremely significant. Not only did they bring the criminal law more visibly into private spaces, the manner in which the "inspectorate" functioned helped to shape the emergence of public police during the nineteenth century by facilitating a wider move toward the imposition of greater surveillance and a more intrusive disciplinary culture. Moreover, in some towns, public and private policing initiatives increasingly merged—with dock police being paid by dock companies but sworn in under the authority of magistrates—in a way that would help give rise to statutory watching initiatives and the emergence of the modern bureaucratic police (Rawlings 2002, p. 75).

C. Statutory Policing Initiatives and the Emergence of "Police"

Throughout the British Isles, local authorities in the second half of the eighteenth century established full-time watch forces under police and improvement legislation. The "police" concept—in keeping with its European origins—was defined widely in this era as a form of civic administration for the common good. Although this broad notion of "police" was known in Scotland before the mid-eighteenth century (Barrie 2008), these initiatives helped to introduce the concept into English public discourse (Dodsworth 2008) and would further help to incorporate European ideas about "police" into British civic life. They were closely linked with eighteenth-century notions of enlightenment, improvement, and civic governance and what these ideas should deliver. Often they were inspired by police initiatives in neighboring provincial towns that set new standards at home and rendered unacceptable, in light of competing models, provisions that had once been considered acceptable (Barrie 2008).

The inclusion of watching provisions in police and improvement legislation was often prefixed by concerns about a perceived rise in crime and the challenges involved in maintaining order in expanding and increasingly rowdy towns. But they were also linked with changing attitudes toward community policing in that they reflected a growing reluctance among men of property to carry out time-honored watching duties. Rather than meet watching and warding obligations, many householders preferred instead to employ paid substitutes, meaning, in effect, that the system of watching became professionalized even before police reform. Indeed, police and improvement legislation often formalized this arrangement, with some local acts in Scotland in the early 1800s including provision for watching by proxy in lieu of personal attendance.

However, although the norm of policing carried out by amateur, but engaged, citizens was being challenged, broader notions of the community, masculine authority, and civic participation continued to shape the evolving discourse on eighteenth-century policing in a manner similar to what occurred in provincial European towns (Denys 2010). The notion of community policing was reconceptualized—in some ways even institutionalized—in this era. In Scotland, in keeping with Scottish Enlightenment ideals of civic society, community policing was linked to the notion of male service through police governance. Police and improvement acts created a new sphere of public participation for men who met property qualifications in the form of police and improvement commissions—which managed police affairs—and the election of ward superintendents to keep a close eye on local people. Significantly, these measures also introduced compulsory municipal rates to fund police services—the importance of which is too often overlooked in criminal justice history (Barrie & Broomhall 2014a). In British towns, reform compelled householders and communities to pay for policing services—some new, some old—that in the past might have been provided through private means. It symbolized an intellectual shift from the principle of individual, personal service to the community toward one of collective action—and one, crucially, that was convenient for redistributing the financial burden of policing. Public men who championed the case for statutory police and improvement powers promoted their own private concerns about crime, and about the challenges they faced in controlling and prosecuting it, as public concerns. In doing so, they not only spread the cost of policing over the whole community, but effectively created a bureaucratic municipal machine from which modern policing would emerge.

Influenced by the eighteenth- and early nineteenth-century criticisms of police reformers, older police histories perceived such policing and watching arrangements as being inefficient and inadequate. It is certainly the case that watch forces in some towns were staffed by old and sometimes infirm ex-soldiers and struggled to attract good recruits because of low pay. But others were more professional and insisted upon minimum standards of age, physicality, and education for watchmen. In London, watch forces were carefully organized and performed preventative police functions through beat patrolling (Paley 1989). Some even functioned under a tiered command structure that put in place a plan for the "new" model that would be initiated in 1829. Indeed, according to Elaine Reynolds (1998), modern policing in the capital evolved out of the old watch system through the efforts of local officials rather than politicians in the central government.

The police model that was constructed under local police and improvement acts in Glasgow (1800) and Edinburgh (1805) was especially visionary. These acts, which established police forces under a disciplined, hierarchical command policing structure, heralded an important link with many of the key facets of modern policing. The inclusion of police and watching provisions formed an important bridge between the old and the new police ideas from which the concept's specialist association with law and order would eventually evolve. Moreover, police courts were set up to expand the capacity of summary justice, with senior police officers taking on the role of public prosecutors for minor crimes, offenses, and misdemeanors—a role the "new" police in many parts of England would not take on until the second half of the nineteenth century (Barrie & Broomhall 2014a; Barrie & Broomhall 2014b). These courts became integral to the smooth running of towns, the maintenance of urban order, and the development of the Scottish criminal justice system, and were an essential component of the emergence of the "policeman state" (Gatrell 1992).

D. Preventative Policing: The New Science of Policing

The most widely heralded function of the "new" police who took to the streets of London in 1829 was arguably the prevention of crime through a highly visible and pro-active system of beat patrolling (Reith 1943). Such a portrayal, though, spoke to the need to brand the "new" police: to make them seem modern and, above all, different from the European forces that had long been associated—in England at least—with continental tyranny (Emsley 1999, pp. 13–38). In fact, the concept of preventative polic-ing was being discussed, debated, and experimented with in London long before Sir Robert Peel was successful in establishing mainland Britain's largest, and most influen-tial, police force (Beattie 2007).

From the mid-eighteenth century onward, though, the concept of preventative polic-ing became more widely discussed as a concept. In 1751, Bow Street magistrate Henry Fielding published *An Enquiry into the Causes of the Late Increase of Robbers*, which is generally regarded as the first significant work on preventative police (Dodsworth 2008, p. 588). A few decades later, the London magistrate and former Scottish mer-chant Patrick Colquhoun published *Treatise of the Police of the Metropolis* (1796), which called for a "general superintendence" of local districts and a centralized police force in London to prevent and detect crime. In it, Colquhoun advocated a "new science of policing" that aimed to prevent rather than merely respond to crime. Both authors conceptualized preventative policing in a way that spoke to the "police" as an instru-ment for the common good and the better ordering of society (Neocleous 2000). Their idea of preventative policing lay not in beat patrolling—although the idea of surveil-lance was an important feature in Colquhoun's *Treatise*—but in stopping the spread of vice and temptation that had accompanied the rise of commercial society. For Colquhoun, in particular, preventing crime involved checking an offender's criminal descent through the policing and regulation of the social environment and the "dens of iniquity" that bred immorality and temptation. Preventative policing, in other words, was very much part of a wider disciplinary culture and mentality that characterized a variety of European police models around the same time (Emsley 2007).

Throughout Britain and mainland Europe, the concept of police as a means for pre-venting and detecting crime found expression and was put into practice in various types of print culture, but it was not yet projected, or accepted, as the defining feature of modern policing. Nonetheless, although attempts in the late eighteenth century to create a centralized police model in London were thwarted because of the challenge such a model posed both to the self-interest of local elites (Reynolds 1998) and to classical notions of liberty and civic governance (Dodsworth 2004, pp. 199–216), preventative policing ideas were developed through a range of initiatives. The improvements in watching articulated previously were often designed with the specific purpose of preventing crime: watchmen were to organize into patrols, with designated beats, and were expected to have intimate community knowledge. Ward superintendents were also appointed in the belief that they would help to bolster the supervisory and disciplinary apparatus that oversaw both the policed and the police (Dodsworth 2008, p. 593). In 1788, for instance, magistrates in Glasgow divided the city into nine districts, each of which had a ward superintendent charged with overseeing specially appointed police officers to "prevent and detect crime" (Barrie 2008, p. 32). Although the inclusion of superintendents built upon the concept of community supervision that had been a feature of godly discipline in early modern Scottish communities, what was novel about this, and similar, police experiments was that the idea of preventative policing not only was linked with full-time salaried officers but also was associated with ideas of hierarchy, governance, surveillance, and deterrence—features that would come to define both the structure and practice of modern policing.

Although the larger, expanding towns and cities typically led the way in such reforms, rural areas, too, saw significant developments in law enforcement before the "new" police was introduced in England. Riots and the erosion of paternal authority, allied with a perceived rise in crime and changing expectations of the criminal justice system, caused men of property in rural England in the early nineteenth century to conceive better ways to defend their property. This resulted in the introduction of new policing initiatives based on the underlying principles and ethos of the old constabulary system (Storch 1989). Indeed, far from being a radical departure from what had gone before, opposition to the introduction of the new police from the propertied ranks in rural England in the 1830s and 1840s was somewhat lessened because the reforms were not fundamentally new, but rather the product of earlier innovation and experimentation. The transition from "old" to "new" after 1829 was not, Philips and Storch (1999) contend, because of the failure of the system, but rather was a product of long-term transformations of the local state and the changing social outlook and administrative philosophy of the ruling elite toward a philosophy that prioritized, among other things, preventative policing in order to meet the new expectations of law and order associated with the Metropolitan Police.

CONCLUSION

The 1829 Metropolitan Police Act deserves its reputation as a landmark statute in police history. As Philips and Storch (1999) have argued, it established the main model for law enforcement against which others were subsequently measured in England. Indeed, in the second quarter of the nineteenth century, traditional forms of law enforcement in rural England came to be viewed as inefficient and ineffective when compared to the Metropolitan Police, even though, in practice, they were functioning effectively. Although many features of modern policing evolved from the early modern practices, the move from "old" model to "new" was by no means a seamless, even transition. Many of the ideas championed by police reformers in the eighteenth century, such as Patrick Colquhoun, were not incorporated into the "new" police. That said, the historical roots of the core features of modern policing stretch back a considerable period of time—and do so in a way that was similar in some respects to nineteenth-century patterns.

While older police histories point to the uniqueness of British police development in the face of emerging centralized policing structures in continental Europe, there were more similarities than this perspective suggests. Although a centralized, militarized police system was not imposed on the British mainland, Britain had much in common with her European neighbors when it came to the periodization, nature, pattern, and purpose of police development. Like the rest of Europe, the eighteenth century was a key period—arguably a defining one—in the emergence of modern policing in Britain, and, as in Europe, Britain saw neither an even pattern of historical development nor a single model of development. In Europe, central government—and centralized policing models—undoubtedly had more influence on police reform than did central government in Britain, but it would be misleading to believe that thinking on policing arrangements in London did not influence a wider discourse too. Likewise, while models such as the *lieutenant général de police de Paris* provided important templates for reform throughout the continent, European police models, as in Britain, were also shaped by distinctive indigenous cultures and traditions as ideas were borrowed and reshaped to suit local circumstances. Indeed, in both Europe and on mainland Britain, police reform often evolved out of local initiatives, not central direction, with local communities and ordinary people in the "margins" playing an instrumental role in determining how policing evolved.

Of course, there were some salient differences in terms of the structure of some police models, especially in rural areas where the militarized and centrally controlled police units of continental Europe stood in stark contrast to the parish constables who enforced the law in British counties. Even so, the extent of difference has been somewhat skewed by historians' overconcentration on the large state military forces of continental Europe and the parish watch forces of eighteenth-century London. Throughout the provincial towns of Europe and Britain models of police were much more closely aligned with the conception of police as a form of civic government. Moreover, even though many European capital cities had more developed, hierarchical policing structures than their British counterparts, there were many similarities between them in terms of both what watchmen and officers on the ground did and wider thinking on police. Indeed, what set London apart from the rest of Europe more than anything was not that it was sluggish in embracing reform, but rather that its extensive and increasingly professionalized watching system was under the control of numerous parish vestries rather than the central state (Emsley 2007, p. 69).

Differences in policing structures should not disguise the fact that Britain and Europe were moving in broadly similar directions in terms of recognizing the perceived need and value of establishing full-time police and watching systems, and of extending the surveillance capacity of the local state over populations and specified territories. Nor should this come as any great surprise. As recent research has pointed out, British police reformers were, in all likelihood, more receptive to European police ideas than was once thought (Emsley 2007). Given this, a greater appreciation of the extent of intellectual transfer throughout Europe, and, in particular, how widely European police practice and ideas were transported to the British Isles, is much needed. Such a conceptualization will not only help to address a major imbalance in police historiography, but also promises to add an important dimension to our understanding of the ways in which policing and the police idea developed more broadly.

References

Ascoli, David. 1979. *The Queen's Peace: The Origins and Development of the Metropolitan Police, 1829 to 1979*. London: Hamilton.

Barrie, David G. 2008. *Police in the Age of Improvement: Police Development and the Civic Tradition in Scotland, 1775–1865*. Cullompton, UK: Willan.

Barrie, David G., & Susan Broomhall, eds. 2012. *A History of Police and Masculinities, 1700–2010*. Abingdon, UK: Routledge.

Barrie, David G., & Susan Broomhall. 2014a. *Police Courts in Nineteenth-Century Scotland*, Vol. 1, *Magistrates, Media and the Masses*. Farnham, UK: Ashgate.

Barrie, David G., & Susan Broomhall. 2014b. *Police Courts in Nineteenth-Century Scotland*, Vol. 2, *Boundaries, Behaviours and Bodies*. Farnham, UK: Ashgate.

Bayley, David H. 1975. "The Police and Political Development in Europe." In *The Formation of the National State in Western Europe*, ed. Charles Tilly, 328–79. Princeton, NJ: Princeton University Press.

Beattie, John M. 2001. *Policing and Prosecution in London, 1660–1750: Urban Crime and the Limits of Terror*. Oxford: Oxford University Press.

Beattie, John M. 2012. *The First English Detectives: The Bow Street Runners and the Policing of London, 1750–1840*. Oxford: Oxford University Press.

Crowther, Anne. 1999. "Crime, Prosecution and Mercy: English Influence and Scottish Practice in the Early Nineteenth Century." In *Kingdoms United?: Great Britain and Ireland since 1500: Integration and Diversity*, ed. Sean J. Connolly, 225–38. Dublin: Four Courts Press.

Denys, Catherine. 2010. "The Development of Police Forces in Urban Europe in the Eighteenth Century." *Journal of Urban History* 36 (3): 332–44.

Dodsworth, Francis. 2004. "'Civic' Police and the Condition of Liberty: The Rationality of Governance in Eighteenth-Century England." *Social History* 29 (2): 199–216.

Dodsworth, Francis. 2007. "Masculinity as Governance: Police, Public Service and the Embodiment of Authority, c. 1700–1850." In *Public Men: Political Masculinities in Modern Britain*, ed. Matthew McCormack, 33–53. Basingstoke, UK: Palgrave Macmillan.

Dodsworth, Francis. 2008. "The Idea of Police in Eighteenth-Century England: Discipline, Reformation, Superintendence, c. 1780–1800." *Journal of the History of Ideas* 69 (4): 583–604.

Emsley, Clive. 1996. *Crime and Society in England, 1750–1900*, 2nd ed. London: Longman.

Emsley, Clive. 2007. *Crime, Police and Penal Policy: European Experiences, 1750–1940*. Oxford: Oxford University Press.

Emsley, Clive. 2012. "Marketing the Brand: Exporting British Police Models, 1829–1950." *Policing: A Journal of Policy and Practice* 6 (1): 43–54.

Garrioch, David. 1986. *Neighbourhood and Community in Paris, 1740–1790*. Cambridge: Cambridge University Press.

Gatrell, Victor A. C. 1992. "Crime, Authority and the Policeman–State." In *Cambridge Social History of Britain, 1750–1950*, ed. F. M. L. Thompson, 243–310. Cambridge: Cambridge University Press.

Godfrey, Barry, & David J. Cox. 2013. *Policing and the Factory: Theft, Private Policing and the Law in Modern England*. London: Bloomsbury.

Gray, Drew D. 2009. *Crime, Prosecution and Social Relations in London: The Summary Courts of London in the Late Eighteenth Century*. Basingstoke, UK: Palgrave Macmillan.

Hay, Douglas. 1975. "Property, Authority and the Criminal Law." In *Albion's Fatal Tree: Crime and Society in Eighteenth-Century England*, ed. Douglas Hay, Peter Linebaugh, & Edward P. Thompson, 17–63. London: Allen Lane.

Kilday, Anne-Marie. 2007. *Women and Violent Crime in Enlightenment Scotland*. Woodbridge, UK: Boydell Press.

King, Peter. 2000. *Crime, Justice and Discretion in England, 1740–1820*. Oxford: Oxford University Press.

King, Peter. 2006. *Crime and the Law in England, 1750–1840*. Cambridge: Cambridge University Press.

King, Peter. 2007. "Newspaper Reporting and Attitudes to Crime and Justice in Late-Eighteenth- and Early-Nineteenth-Century London." *Continuity and Change* 22 (1): 73–112.

Leneman, Leah, & Rosalind Mitchison. 1998. *Sin in the City: Sexuality and Social Control in Urban Scotland, 1660–1780*. Edinburgh: Scottish Cultural Press.

Milliot, Vincent, ed. 2006a. *Les Mémoires policiers, 1750–1850. Écritures et pratiques policières du siècle des Lumières au Second Empire*. Rennes, France: Presses universitaires de Rennes.

Milliot, Vincent. 2006b. "Réformer les polices urbaines au siècle des Lumières: le révélateur de la mobilité." *Crime, History and Societies* 10 (1): 25–50.

Morgan, Gwenda, & Peter Rushton. 2004. *Rogues, Thieves, and the Rule of Law: The Problem of Law Enforcement in North-East England, 1718–1800*. London: UCL Press.

Neocleous, Mark. 2000. "Social Police and the Mechanisms of Prevention: Patrick Colquhoun and the Condition of Poverty." *British Journal of Criminology* 40:710–26.

Palmer, Stanley H. 1988. *Police and Protest in England and Ireland, 1780–1850*. Cambridge: Cambridge University Press.

Paley, Ruth. 1989. "'An Imperfect, Inadequate and Wretched System?' Policing London Before Peel." *Criminal Justice History* 10:95–130.

Philips, David, & Robert D. Storch. 1999. *Policing Provincial England, 1829–56: The Politics of Reform*. London: Leicester University Press.

Rawlings, Philip. 2002. *Policing: A Short History*. Cullompton, UK: Willan Publishing.

Reith, Charles. 1943. "Preventative Principle of Police." *Journal of Criminal Law and Criminology* 34:206–09.

Reynolds, Elaine A. 1998. *Before the Bobbies: The Night Watch and Police Reform in Metropolitan London, 1720–1830*. Stanford, CA: Stanford University Press.

Snell, Esther. 2007. "Discourses of Criminality in the Eighteenth-Century Press: The Presentation of Crime in the *Kentish Post*, 1717–1768." *Continuity and Change* 22 (1): 13–47.

Storch, Robert D. 1975. "The Plague of the Blue Locusts: Police Reform and Popular Resistance in Northern England, 1840–57." *International Review of Social History* 20:61–91.

Storch, Robert D. 1989. "Policing Rural Southern England Before the Police: Opinion and Practice, 1830–56." In *Policing and Prosecution in Britain, 1750–1850*, ed. Douglas Hay & Francis Snyder, 211–66. Oxford: Clarendon.

Styles, John. 1989. "Crime Advertising in Eighteenth-Century Provincial England." In *Policing and Prosecution in Britain, 1750–1850*, ed. Douglas Hay & Francis Snyder, 55–111. Oxford: Clarendon.

Thompson, Edward P. 1971. "The Moral Economy of the English Crowd in the Eighteenth Century." *Past and Present* 50:76–136.

Ward, Richard M. 2014. *Print Culture, Crime and Justice in 18th-Century London.* London: Bloomsbury.

Williams, Chris. 2008. "Constables for Hire: The History of Private 'Public' Policing in the UK." *Policing and Society: An International Journal of Research and Policy* 18 (2): 190–205.

CHAPTER 23

THE ORIGINS OF "MODERN" POLICING

MARK FINNANE

INTRODUCTION

In 1829 the new *commissaire* of police in Paris found among the items left by his predecessor a number of volumes of ordinances and laws regulating life in the city. Among them was a four-volume work compiled by a former *commissaire*, published under the instructive title *Dictionnaire de police moderne* (Alletz 1820; Merriman 2006, p. 25). Characteristic of the manuals that guided police and magistrates in the nineteenth and twentieth centuries, the volumes were a guide to duties and powers, ranging in this case from the process of arrest and prosecution of those threatening the king to the mundane work of regulating the markets and streets of Paris and the cities and towns of France. The lengthy discussion of the regulation of sale of "*champignons*" (mushrooms) for the sake of public health and individual well-being reminds us that this volume was a particular local manifestation of a more general phenomenon, the invention of modern policing. Alletz (1820) described a "*police moderne*" as not just an institution, but a system, a way of regulating and ordering a society in a modern way. In the adjective "*moderne*," he invoked a rhetoric that would flow through many jurisdictions, national and local, in the debate over the desirability of an efficient and effective new police.

Across the Channel in 1829, the London Metropolitan Police was established by an act of the British Parliament. This was not the first urban police force, in Britain or elsewhere, but built on changes in the role of earlier police officers, the constables whose office dated back to medieval times. Yet scarcely any other institution in criminal justice history can compete with the symbolic valence of the London Metropolitan Police (Emsley 2012). Its early and enduring association with its parliamentary advocate and first minister, Robert Peel, ensured that the first policeman were called "Peelers," as they had earlier come to be called in Ireland after Peel wrought a revolution in policing there during his time as chief secretary (1813–1822). Later imaginative invention shaped the memory of what were thought to be "Peel's principles" guiding this exemplary police force. In fact, such principles were twentieth-century reconstructions, influentially adumbrated by an early English historian of police, Charles Reith, and achieving sway through their repetition in American textbooks (Lentz & Chaires 2007; Emsley 2013). Through imperial transfer of ideas and institutions, the London Metropolitan Police came to play a crucial role in shaping how modern police in many countries looked— sometimes literally—and acted. In Europe, too, the image of a civil urban police, permanent but courteous, forceful but unarmed, came to play a powerful if indeterminate rhetorical role in contests over the character of a political regime and its apparatus of security (Johansen 2013). Yet the London Metropolitan Police was but one, albeit very significant, influence in what was a much more diverse pattern of institutional and discursive formations that came to define what modern police and modern policing might look like.

Our appreciation of police history has changed very significantly in the last four decades. Both social history and cognate developments in the history of the social sciences have enriched a still-developing understanding of the context and variety of police. No less than "police," policing has become a much-studied object of research and debate. On one thing all contemporary scholarship is agreed—any account of modern police that attributes its emergence to a single idea, person, or legislative enactment founders at once on the weight of empirical evidence that demonstrates continuity more than rupture. In the language of English historiography, the "Whig" account of the emergence of modern police, one that emphasized its natural condition as an emblem of the modern state, gives way to a history of complexity and contest.

The very word "police" has itself become an object of much debate, replicating a historical reality in which police embodied a capacity of government for ensuring public well-being as integral to the security of the state (Dodsworth 2004). As if to mock the early English critics of a continental despotic police, contemporary social theory has been much interested in the historical phenomenon of the police as something other than a force devoted to either the prevention or detection of crime. The police of a consolidating early modern state, it is argued, was as much concerned with the conditions of urban life and the health of the populace as it was preoccupied with the narrower interest of protection from crime (Pasquino 1991; Zedner 2006). But the dualism of this old contest over the proper sphere of police appears misleading when one moves beyond the rhetoric that inflames debate about the creation of police forces at particular moments to study police in their practical workaday roles. Depending on geographic location and jurisdiction, the work of a modern police has ranged from the high-level work of national security in protecting the interests of the state and sovereign to the mundane activity of keeping the streets clean and enabling urban mobility. In the words of another modern sociologist of police, there is both "high" and "low" policing (Brodeur 1982)—and we can see from its early nineteenth-century beginnings why this has always been so.

This essay will approach the subject by identifying key developments in the historical context that shaped a very influential model of modern policing, while also attending to alternative models and effects. Section I considers the historical conditions for a new police in the United Kingdom, Europe, and North America, with attention to the rapidly changing urban centers and contemporaneous rural disorder in the late eighteenth and early nineteenth centuries. In section II we look at the origins and mandate of the London Metropolitan Police established in 1829, as well as examining its legacy in the diffusion of a policing model and its ideological impact. Section III considers the way in which alternative approaches to policing were shaped in the *gendarmerie* model and its colonial expressions, while a concluding discussion in section IV highlights the distinctive powers, functions, and governance models that characterize what we know as "modern" policing.

I. Conditions for a New Police

The emergence of a new police in the early decades of the nineteenth century was made possible by changes in state formation and the functions of government. The consolidation of European nation-states was expressed in expanding ambitions about what government might do at home and abroad to consolidate wealth and power. In pursuit of imperial power, European governments in the age of mercantilism sought trading advantage through protecting the interests of private entrepreneurial companies in their various enterprises across the seas. At home eighteenth-century governments were much concerned with internal security, especially in the cities that were growing as a result of the changes brought by the early industrial and agricultural revolutions.

Necessarily, these developments were articulated in ideas for change, yet there was no single idea of policing, but rather a constant expression of a need for altered institutions to cope with the conditions of rapid and even revolutionary social and political change. Innovations that shaped police forces of the future were forged by governments impelled to control widespread threats to the security of the state. But more mundane challenges to the security of persons, homes, and workplaces flowed from the rapid growth of cities in the late eighteenth century. Unchecked growth of urban populations presented significant challenges to public health and ease of transit through crowded streets and highways, as well as creating opportunities for theft and other petty crime in populations no longer distinguished by close association and local knowledge of the familiar and the dangerous. The rural disruptions and disorder associated with changing agricultural patterns and land appropriation were equally important in stimulating alternatives to the deployment of military forces. In societies that had relied heavily on local authority and informal social control mechanisms, the mobility of populations displaced by economic change and warfare helped to shape new responses to crime and disorder.

For a century before the French Revolution, France was the site of two forms of policing that are recognizable in postrevolutionary legacies. Both were the outcome of executive decisions of an absolute state. From 1667 on, Paris was placed under the command of a lieutenant of police, an office created by Louis XIV. Over the period of more than a century, up to the outbreak of the Revolution, this lieutenant controlled a variety of functionaries responsible for different aspects of guarding and regulating the city and its ports along the Seine, as well as for adjudicating offenses. The functions of the Paris police included the arrest of criminals to be brought before the courts, as well as surveillance of the population for signs of disorder and subversion (Emsley 1983).

Like Paris before this innovation, other cities and towns were governed by police whose functions extended back to the medieval period. But in rural France the aspirations of an absolutist monarchy for a more ordered state were embodied in the eighteenth-century institution of the *maréchaussée*. These companies of armed militia, stationed permanently in districts throughout the country, were coordinated under the Ministry of War beginning in 1720. They had a wide range of surveillance and crime detection functions, including the surveillance, harassment, and expulsion of vagrants and beggars from local districts. Their responsibilities overlapped with those of the police of the towns, sometimes to the point of conflict and certainly lack of cooperation. The institution was vulnerable to the local charge that it was an instrument of the central government, interfering with local custom and urban autonomy. The *maréchaussée* was also hampered in its effectiveness by the poor pay and conditions of its workforce, many members of which sought other employment to supplement their pay. From the 1770s onward, with the deterioration of political conditions in the country, the institution was formed into a more disciplined body, with its officers no longer able to be married and increasingly housed in barracks (Cameron 1977; Cameron 1981). In spite of criticism of the institution, there were those on the eve of revolution who felt it needed to be strengthened. And, indeed, in the conditions of revolutionary France, the *maréchaussée* would be succeeded by the paramilitary *gendarmerie*, an arm of the central state (Emsley 1999a).

In Britain and its North American colonies, policing before the police was the business principally of local communities. The ancient office of constable was one element of a system that focused on prevention of crime, especially at night. The securing of homes and people from personal assault, or property theft, was a responsibility of the watch, a system dependent on citizen participation. The night watch exercised a crime prevention function that was perhaps even more effective than the later police reformers wished to recognize. This was also a system that related closely to the business of prosecuting crime. Offenders caught in the act would be detained and taken before magistrates for what might be very speedy justice. The fabled idea of the constable as citizen, possessing no more and no less than the citizen's powers, is a legacy of this elementary policing that had its roots firmly in the tradition of local government and relatively small communities (Reynolds 1998).

For England at least, a decisive break in this tradition came in the middle of the eighteenth century in London. The rapid growth of population in the country's capital city was accompanied by the increasing vulnerability of both urban and provincial elites who frequented the roads in and out of the capital. Gangs of highway robbers proved to be well beyond the capacity of any local magistrates to detect and prosecute their crimes. It lay in the imagination of the novelist and magistrate Henry Fielding to propose successfully the establishment of runners, aides to the magistrate of Bow Street Court in London, who assisted in the detection and arraignment of suspected criminals. The Bow Street runners, as these magistrate's assistants became known, thus undertook functions that would in the nineteenth century be taken up by detectives. They did not displace the night watch or the constable, but aimed to make effective the powers of magistrates to prosecute crime effectively. Perhaps by doing so they would improve deterrence—so it was hoped (Beattie 2012).

The innovation of the Bow Street runners can distract from other, more consequential, developments in eighteenth-century policing that become clearer when one looks not at the deficiencies of the night watch or the constable system in London and the home counties, but at changes in the other greater urban centers of the British Isles, especially Dublin, Glasgow, and Edinburgh. In the late eighteenth century Dublin was the second-largest city after London. It was governed by a Protestant ascendancy whose power lay in landed estates and political control of the Irish Parliament, with its seat in Dublin. The disordered state of the countryside in the 1780s, wracked by emerging agrarian rebellion, was matched by the unsafe condition of the Dublin streets. For the administration based in Dublin Castle, the possibility of a radical approach to policing was highlighted by proposals that drew both on a failed London initiative of 1785 and on the attractions of French systems of policing.

In 1763 an English diplomat, long resident in Paris, had published a lengthy treatise on "The Police of France." The author, Sir William Mildmay, emphasized the potential of incorporating the "civil" elements of the French system into a police model that would be a distinct department employing dedicated officers whose sole employment would be ensuring the "peace and good order" of the city (Mildmay 1763, p. 61). Mildmay's caution about the military nature of French policing cannot disguise the attraction of his ideas to Dublin Castle, whose senior civil servant cribbed from Mildmay in proposing a Parisian police solution to Dublin's problems (Palmer 1988).

The establishment of a Dublin Metropolitan Police by statute in 1786 was an event of singular importance. Yet this force does not stand alone as a model of urban policing in this period. Beginning in Glasgow in 1800, a succession of Scottish cities and towns established their own police forces, helping define the possibilities of urban policing in Britain long before the London Metropolitan Police were created in 1829. As Barrie (2010) has shown, the Scottish developments are distinctive as a precedent standing between the Dublin statute of 1786 and the London one of 1829, but there are limits to this distinctiveness, as they share much with contemporary developments of urban improvement in provincial towns in England. These developments represent a particularly interesting third alternative to the classic opposition between the repressive state models of policing flowing out of the governance of a turbulent Ireland and the ideas of a preventative police focused on the prevention of crime later identified with the London Metropolitan Police. Developments such as those expressed in the Scottish police acts expressed an ideal of urban government in which police would play a functional role in securing the proper regulation of town life, of its markets, street-life, trade, and public health. Of course these were all models of development rather than descriptions of police work in particular locations. Under the right kind of social conditions, the civic government work of police could develop as an aspect of the duties and responsibilities of colonial police forces, as much as of Scottish self-governing towns.

These Scottish ideas of the role of police as an aid to civic government overlap with the more extensive connotations of the word "police" as it developed on continental Europe during the eighteenth century, especially in German Enlightenment thought connected to the work of jurists and philosophers on the conditions of government. In a strain of thinking closely linked by Michel Foucault to the transition from ancient regime sovereignty to modern governmentality, the security and integrity of the state was seen as embedded in the health and welfare of the population. Police referred to all those conditions within the control of government that made civil life possible. Some sense of the integrated and ambitious scope of this conception of "police" can be seen in a characteristic German text of the late eighteenth century: "If subjects are to have those attributes and capacities which are in accord with the happiness of the state, they must be (1) reasonable, (2) useful and (3) not excessively burdensome members of the commonality. In accordance with this maxim, the police have therefore to attend to (1) the moral condition of subjects, (2) civil order and (3) internal security and the control of evil and injustice" (Lüdtke 2009, p. 205).

Such a visionary conception of an all-encompassing police would prove impossible to contain within the one institution. While its absolutist connotations are self-evident, such a program nevertheless highlights the manifold work of police as the institution would develop during the nineteenth century. Emphasizing the demands of civil order would justify a wide range of police interventions in the life of the urban poor and those who spent their life on the street. The demands of internal security would come to justify not only surveillance of potential risks but a wide range of repressive sanctions against organized labor and other social protest. Yet the focus on civil order also captured a vision of society in which victims of crime would have a public remedy for the harms done to them and, perhaps even better, might hope for the prevention of such harms.

The continental idea of police was an all-embracing vision of the responsibilities of government for the welfare and security of the population, which was in turn a guarantee of the security and prosperity of the state. The breadth of this conception of police as something larger than a concern with the detection and prevention of crime found its British expression in the work of Patrick Colquhoun. While there are grounds for doubting the immediate impact of his advocacy of a new police (Beattie 2012), his extended 1806 thesis on the police of London, which went through a number of editions within a decade of its publication, set out an equally comprehensive conception of the responsibilities of police. Its debts, however, were less to the continental notion of police than to his own experience and role in the development of Scottish urban policing (Barrie 2008). We can see, then, that the sharp oppositions between English and continental policing traditions that have been represented as shaping English resistance to police reform in the early nineteenth century are rather less fixed when studied in historical context. Modern policing emerges in this way neither as a single idea nor as a single institution. Rather, it is shaped by a proliferation of discourses and practices around the demands of urban government, as well as state security, during a period of revolutionary change.

II. A Preventative Police?

No amount of revisionism can contest the historical reality that the London Metropolitan Police, established by legislation in 1829, quickly established itself as a model to emulate in a large number of (particularly) English-speaking jurisdictions. We need, however, to separate the ideological baggage of talk about Peel's principles of policing, or Whiggish accounts of it as the finest expression of an English tradition of self-government, from an understanding of the emergence of the Metropolitan Police at that particular moment and perceptions that quickly developed of what kind of police this would be (Emsley 2009).

The London Metropolitan Police Act of 1829 established a new police force supervised by two new justices (magistrates), known later as commissioners. They were responsible for recruiting a force of constables, who were distributed throughout the wards of the metropolitan district. The force was hierarchical, with senior officers including superintendents, inspectors, and sergeants, terminology that would be replicated in numerous imitations throughout the English-speaking world. Although a legacy from the earlier Dublin (and failed London) initiatives placed the Metropolitan Police under the direction of the home secretary, the police would be maintained through a tax on the districts being policed—in this way, the old watch rates were replaced by a single rate, as the old parish boundaries were in turn displaced by the ambition of the police to oversee the entire metropolis, with the City of London alone being excluded. The new statute, in fact, deserves attention as an exercise in incremental administration. Introducing the bill to the Westminster Parliament, Home Secretary Robert Peel was careful to set out the gradual nature of the extension of the new police into the many districts that made up an expanding metropolitan area. Still, he did not attempt to disguise "the necessity and advantage of having an efficient, vigilant and well-regulated patrol, both by night and day, controlled by one authority, and acting under one head" (*Times* [London], 16 April 1829, p. 2).

We have already seen that the recent historiography emphasizes the continuity between what was established in 1829 and what went before it. But it is also important to acknowledge just what a significant innovation this was in the context of an emerging liberal state. By establishing at the very heart of a burgeoning new empire of settler colonies a police force not accountable to local authorities but directed by the home secretary, the British government signaled its willingness to apply the lessons of governing a more disturbed part of the union—namely, Ireland—to the largest city of the United Kingdom. The view that this outcome of 1829 represented the defeat of British fears about a continental police has been challenged in more recent accounts. Even Stanley Palmer, in his formidable comparison of English and Irish policing developments, was inclined to interpret 1829 as the effective displacement of a "wearisome" run of committees opposing proposals for a new urban police (Palmer 1988, p. 31). More recent scholarship focused on the transformation of London policing has highlighted the degree to which the diehard opponents of a new police were being challenged and displaced by new thinking during the 1820s. Most recently, John Beattie (2012) has emphasized the innovative work of the committees inquiring into the police needs of the metropolis well before 1829, suggesting that earlier historians have misread the depth of opposition to the new police.

The 1829 act created a norm rather than mandated an exception, which was arguably what characterized the 1786 Dublin act. The former's governance arrangements, however, highlight its distinctiveness compared to the prior developments in urban policing in Scotland. As we have seen, those developments owed a great deal to the traditions of civic government and ideals of urban order closely linked to the broader cultural, legal, and political identity of the Scottish part of the union (Barrie 2010). Precisely because of its strong links to this very local, if intellectually and culturally influential, movement of the Scottish Enlightenment and its liberal political culture, Scottish policing was arguably less likely to shape the future of policing than was the London-based, central government–mandated solution to the problem of urban order.

It was indeed the actions of a central state, the British state as channeled through the Westminster Parliament, that proved to be the norm in the development of the modern public police. A modern police was a public police, not a mechanism for the security of a particular location or interest, for which various forms of private policing continued to be available (Miller 2013). One did not have to cross the Irish Sea and encounter the problems of Ireland to recognize that a modern police was a police that would serve an overarching mandate for public security, whatever other functions it might have. Hence, even in the developing era of a laissez-faire state, when English counties proved uneven in their uptake of the new institution, the Westminster Parliament enacted a measure in 1856 making it compulsory for English counties to establish a police along the lines of that mandated by the 1829 act for London. Well before this, however, the preference of political elites for a preventative police on the London model had started to win the day against those who favored continuing reliance on the older traditions of policing governed by local magistrates. Within only a few years, in the 1830s, the image of London police in English provincial discourse had signaled the very essence of what modern police might be—namely, full-time, paid, in uniform, and capable of exercising authority without a display of military force (Philips & Storch 2001).

Yet it was prevention above all that distinguished the new police. This became very clear across the Atlantic as governing authorities in American cities wrestled with their choices in the face of burgeoning crime and disorder in Jacksonian America and the years that followed. Less than a year after its establishment, the London Metropolitan Police already appeared an outstanding example of police to Philadelphia Recorder James M'Ilvaine in 1830 (Johnson 1979, pp. 16–19). Addressing a grand jury on the challenges faced by the city, M'Ilvaine channeled a generation of reform rhetoric when he represented the 1829 English initiative as a triumph of a modern system in place of ramshackle decay.

The case was all the more compelling because American urban policing was so clearly a legacy of English origins. It was characterized by a dependence on night watchmen and a tradition of locally appointed constables whose primary function was to assist in the arrest of wrongdoers for the purpose of prosecution (McConville 2005; Lane 1967; Richardson 1970). "The fundamental principles of our present police," said M'Ilvaine, "were borrowed, together with other municipal regulations, from those of England." These principles, moreover, had not been adapted "to the circumstances of a crowded metropolis, and ha[d] not kept pace with the progress of criminal art or general refinement" (*Hazard's Register of Pennsylvania*, XII, 1833, p. 284). For this Philadelphian reformer, the new police model was one that would address growing crime through its more effective system of intelligence collection and powers of arresting criminals and prosecuting them systematically. Three years later, the recorder had the chance to repeat his preferences for a more effective system of public police in a more wide-ranging report of a city commission appointed to inquire into the state of police. By that stage these American observers were noting the appeal of the new system in London, where there now prevailed "an admirable degree of order, regularity and decency," and where "the most perfect security is afforded to every person during all hours of the day and night." The attraction of the London police system to defenders of liberty was that "its effects had not arisen from any additional or arbitrary powers conferred upon the officers, but are entirely referable to its regular, organized and systematic operation" (*Hazard's Register of Pennsylvania*, XII, 1833, p. 285). The republican suspicion of central government delayed the emergence of such regularity and systematization. And when it did come, the vulnerability of police leadership to the whims of urban political factions remained a feature of the American "new" police (Johnson 1979).

We have highlighted throughout this account of the origins of modern policing the central role played by an expanding central state, which took on itself the general task of public security not through military means but through a permanent institution whose last resort was force but whose intermediate responsibilities were the exercise of an authority won through the wearing of a uniform and the use of legal warrant for public security. There was, however, nothing inevitable about a central government mandate. The policing of American cities demonstrates the possibility of another path that has been remarkably resilient. There, the persistent autonomy of self-governing communities and the jealous defense of local interests have been played out in ways that have preserved, almost in amber, the British-origin context of police structures accountable to local communities. Like other criminal justice institutions, including that of the prosecution service in the Office of District Attorney, police authority flowed from democratic election. Notoriously, in some circumstances, this delivered police into the hands of sectional interests and nurtured distinctive traditions of corruption.

The particularity of these patterns in North America was highlighted during the nineteenth century by periods in which there was a struggle between city and state governments over the control of police. For a period of some years in New York in the 1860s there were even two competing urban police forces, one mandated by the state legislature, the other controlled by the city government (Richardson 1970). Such conflict did not endure, and the tradition of urban self-government prevailed. It would be wrong, however, to highlight such examples as something uniquely American, for it has been a characteristic of the two-sided aspect of modern policing that institutions with overlapping jurisdiction have frequently clashed in other political cultures. In eighteenth- and nineteenth-century France, for example, and in Italy tension between a local police responsible for the security of townspeople and a national *gendarmerie* was not infrequent (Emsley 1999a). Indeed, any state that sought to defend its national security interests through the formation of centralized *gendarmerie* left open the possibility of conflict with local police. Even within police forces, the dual functions of crime prevention and crime detection served as a source of aggravation—for example, between a detective force and the demands of the patrol police whose everyday associations with the local community created a different set of allegiances and commitments.

III. THE SCOPE OF MODERN POLICING

The English model deserves attention for the extent of its historical, ideological, and even historiographical influence. Yet we have seen that it was far from being the only model of modern police. And, if we think of modern policing as an assemblage of techniques that are part of modern government, then each police has its own point of origin as well as its own history of borrowings, transmissions, and impositions. In a series of studies, Emsley has sought to abstract what the great variety of modes of policing and police forces in the modern world owe to their contextual conditions, developing a typology of three styles of policing: state military, state civilian, and municipal (Emsley 1999b; Emsley 2012). Such an approach not only acknowledges the breadth of policing styles and institutional forms in abstract, but also points to the political conditions that shaped the emergence of modern public policing. The scope of modern policing was not, however, simply a result of executive decision. The functions of police were also the product of those being policed, of the uses made of police powers by both local elites and the common people. Sometimes those functions fitted uneasily with what police saw as their preferred work, catching criminals or defending the security of the state. The politics of modern policing are in fact characterized by a constant battle over police priorities, with the outcomes consolidating or threatening police legitimacy (Lin 2007).

We can capture some of this scope of modern policing by examining the uptake of policing, primarily in the English-speaking world, and its transformation in a variety of settings. First, we will note what happened to change one type of *gendarmerie*, the Irish constabulary, into something much more hybrid. Second, we will consider the styles of policing that resulted from transporting the idea of police into different kinds of colonial settings.

The London police was, famously, preventative in orientation. Through its systematic patrolling of the city, every day of the year, the police putatively limited occasions for crime. It was also the case, however, that the elements of regular patrol were what spoke to the advantage of *gendarmerie* policing in its continental and its Irish modes. It was the systematic, routine practice of patrolling that rendered the Irish constabulary, as they were established in 1836, a modern police. There is no doubting the importance of rural disorder and urban conflict in the half-century from 1786 to 1836 for shaping the emergence of this force (Palmer 1988). But what made the police in Ireland different from a military was again its ambition to limit the occasions for crime by instituting a routine government of constant inspection and surveillance of the population. Such a mode of control was consistent with the ambition of Dublin Castle to manage Ireland comprehensively with all the tools of a new mode of governing (MacDonagh 1977; Andrews 1975). The constabulary was tasked not merely with the prevention and detection of crime but also with the gathering of data about the range of social conditions characterizing the people and their modes of living. Hence, and in spite of all the work of the Irish constabulary in the repressive control of agrarian outrage and political disaffection, the modern Irish police was also from its early days burdened with responsibilities that made it a cousin of its unarmed counterpart in Britain (Griffin 1997). We can see this kinship, for example, in the roles undertaken by police in the detention and processing of the poor insane into that very modern institution of nineteenth-century Ireland, the lunatic asylum, later the mental hospital (Finnane 1981). From this dual function of Dublin-directed policing aimed at protest and disorder, and a more mundane, everyday policing of welfare springs the phenomenon, observed at the end of the nineteenth century, of what has been described as a now-domesticated Irish police (Malcolm 2006).

For large parts of the contemporary world, modern policing is synonymous with the legacy of empire. This was not simply a matter of imperial imposition. The styles, functions, and impacts of modern policing were also shaped by the context of reception of imperial authority (Arnold 1986; Ahire 1991). The sharpest differences in such reception are perhaps those between the settler society colonies, largely of the British Empire, and those colonies of European colonists bent on extraction of resources and wealth from the imperial domains. These different imperial regimes, with their different modes of rule and legacies, must always be distinguished between those societies where colonists came to stay and those from which colonists imagined they would one day return home (Veracini 2010). The unpredictability of imperial enterprise means that there are fuzzy boundaries between these two models, exemplified in places like East Africa (Anderson & Killingray 1991) or the Dutch East Indies before 1945 (Cribb 2010). Moreover, the scope of influence of imperial policing cannot be restricted to European empire alone, for the modes of transmission of the modern idea of policing must be traced in East and Southeast Asia through the sophisticated and influential Japanese policing models that developed as a synthesis of aspects of French, German, and English law and policing. Perhaps no better example of diffusion and transformation of police can be found than in Japan. There, the modernizing impetus of the Meiji period looked to France, and especially the Paris police, for inspiration in establishing a Japanese police force (Westney 1987). Inflecting this model with the very localized institution of the *koban* (police box), Japanese policing in turn helped shape policing in its later colonial outposts, such as Taiwan (Myers & Peattie 1984). In turn, the evident success of Japanese neighborhood policing contributed much later to influential research and debates on the need to reshape American and British policing (Bayley 1976). For every society of the contemporary world, the origins of modern policing have in the end a very local meaning, whose scope must be understood as the product of interaction between an idea, its transmission through particular agents and institutions, and the local social and political context in which it has been applied.

Those societies that imagined themselves as outposts of Britain, such as the settlements of British North America or, above all, the Australasian colonies, brought with them the institutions of the night watch, the magistrate, and the constable. The century of origin of particular communities, which is also a proxy for the demography and political economy of the settler colonists, profoundly shaped the kinds of police that emerged in the first half of the nineteenth century. This is evident, as we have seen, in the development of policing in the American states, formerly British colonies, whose police and judicial systems are characterized by a degree of municipal organization that is quite foreign to the structures that have developed in the Australian colonies and New Zealand. The tradition of local self-government that was expressed in the institutions created by the predominantly British settlers of North America was a very powerful determinant of policing arrangements. We might emphasize this tendency even more in Canada, since there the ideologically powerful institution of the Royal Canadian Mounted Police, shaped by the demands of the colonists' westward movement into the prairies and western Canada, did not displace the assumptions of a political culture that saw public policing primarily as a local function (Marquis 1997). Since policing was a responsibility of local towns, communities, or even provinces, the policing functions of the Mounties were expected to be exercised via contractual arrangements between that institution and the local government responsible for policing (Macleod 1978; Marquis 1993).

It proved quite otherwise in the Australasian colonies, but not without a historical process that exhibits the variety of choices that faced communities and governments concerned with securing safety and justice. It might be imagined that the penal colony character of the initial British settlement of Australia brought with it the very weighty presumption of a state-centered organization of policing. But along with the convicts came not only the soldiers to guard them but free settlers whose expectations of a new start in a new land were of a kind with those brought by the British emigrants to North America. There was a tension from the beginning between the policing requirements demanded of an open society in which there were large numbers of convicts, and the pressing expectations of free settlers about their need for security and guarantees of justice of a kind that they still associated with life at home. The effect of this tension was then complicated by the increasing awareness of another kind of threat to security, that arising from the presence in all the colonies of indigenous peoples who were being dispossessed of their land (Finnane 1994).

The working out of such a tension has been considered by the principal historian of New Zealand policing to be best understood through a model of development that sees the origins of modern policing as lying along a continuum between coercion and consent (Hill 1986). At different points in the half-century after the foundational Treaty of Waitangi (1840), the New Zealand constabulary was called on to exercise its force against the Maori while simultaneously guaranteeing social order and urban amenity in the towns and emergent cities of colonial New Zealand. The unique—at least in the Australasian colonies—character of New Zealand colonization, with its ambiguous constitutional recognition of indigenous peoples, even found expression in the creation for a short period of a Maori constabulary that would prove capable of exercising force against the Pakeha settlers (Hill 2005). Such an experiment would have been unimaginable in the Australian colonies. There, indigenous people were indeed recruited into police forces, especially the native police, but for the purpose above all of suppressing or controlling Aboriginal resistance. Once the resistance had been quelled there was no longer a need for the native police forces, which were disbanded (Richards 2008).

The British legacies of local self-government, including a key role for magistrates assisted by police constables, are nevertheless very evident in the Australasian colonies during the period of the emergence and consolidation of public police forces. Even during the convict era in Sydney, long before the emergence of forms of local self-government, the creation of a Sydney police involved the appointment of a magistrate who would be assisted by constables. The control of magistrates over police constables was a model displaced only at mid-century in most colonies. By then, persuasive criticism of police inefficiency in dealing with urban public order, followed by the massive disruptions caused by the gold rushes, had brought most colonies to the point of establishing a centralized police with jurisdiction over an entire colony, including towns, cities, and rural and remote regions, and under the command of a police commissioner or inspector general. Only in Tasmania—an especially noteworthy case, since it also was originally a convict colony—did a tradition of municipal control of police continue past mid-century, being brought to an end only in 1898, as the Australian tradition of the consolidated police force brought its own normative weight to bear on this exceptional arrangement (Petrow 2005).

IV. A MODERN POLICE: POWERS, FUNCTIONS AND GOVERNANCE

The politics of contemporary policing has contributed to a revised interest in the origins of modern police (Reiner 2000). Are the police of the twenty-first century radically different from the forces created during the great changes we have discussed here? Is policing only—or primarily—the work of public police forces? What are the primary functions and responsibilities of police? What is the role of force in the exercise of police power, and how was this shaped historically? Are these functions, responsibilities, and roles a legacy of the founding moments or a significant departure from them? How are police governed, and how should they be governed? To whom are they accountable? Is a police force an agent of the central state, or is its primary responsibility to a community of citizens expecting its aid in combating crime and preventing social harms? These are the kinds of questions that have also informed the writing of police history in the last three or four decades.

To the contemporary social scientist who argues that policing is being radically transformed, historians now point to the antecedents and foundations of early nineteenth-century police. Hence Zedner (2006) argues the need for a historical corrective to the presumption that all is new, recalling earlier conceptions of police and their embodiment in the broad range of functions of the eighteenth-century police forces. Investigating the origins of modern policing brings with it a recognition that the field of policing has a richer and deeper history than can be captured in the simple statement that police were crime fighters or even street cleaners. In such arguments we see in play the overlap between the work of historical accounts of the emergence of modern police and contemporary normative discussions about what kind of police we should have today.

In addressing the very large subject of the origins of modern policing, we have emphasized the need to address the topic always in its local context, while remaining aware of the powerful effects of the diffusion of ideas, practices, and even personnel between jurisdictions and nations. We have also highlighted the important and continuing tension between two models of policing, the *gendarmerie*, with its paramilitary structures and its state-centered functions, versus the omnipresent local police, with its civic or civilian character and greater orientation toward the maintenance of domestic order, that is, the security of individuals, families, and communities in their localities of cities, towns, and even rural environs. In practice, the models are frequently expressed in hybrid form. But in order to address what makes modern policing modern, it will be important to remember not only the conditions of formation of a public police in a particular place, nation, or state but also its substantive content, namely, what police do, how they do it, and how they are governed.

The establishment of modern police forces was the affirmation by government of a particular way of exercising power outside the brute display of military force by a supreme authority. Police powers were exercised through the authority bestowed by legislation or a magistrate's warrant. The fact that such power might be exercised by officers who in some places were unarmed signaled both the self-limiting aspiration of state or municipal authority and the significant degree of consent on the part of those being policed. Such consent inevitably might be imagined more than readily discovered. In states or cities with a high degree of social conflict, the exercise of police power without force of arms might remain only an aspiration. Nevertheless, it was this aspiration to the use of limited force that distinguished civilian public policing most clearly from its military cousin. On the other hand, the extensive and influential tradition of the *gendarmerie* speaks to the ultimate sanction of police power, its exercise at the direction of state authority. The modern police can never escape the question of police power, which is at bottom a capacity to use force to achieve results, because this power lies at the very heart of the institution. What is striking about the creation of modern police is the desire to make that power more effective by limiting the need for its exercise.

From the beginning, the functions of modern police were manifold. The revived interest in eighteenth-century conceptions of police responsibilities, recognizing their wide-ranging ambition for ensuring the security and welfare of the people as the bedrock of national security, has its legacy in the often-unacknowledged degrees of modern police functions. This legacy may not have flowed from the direct application of an idea of police. Instead, rapidly changing demands on urban government drove the regulation of urban spaces, customs, and workplaces for the ends of prosperity and good order. Many mundane tasks toward this end were devolved later to other agencies of government or local government. There remained a tension between these functions of police—closely linked to the idea of a preventative force whose constant presence would limit crime and depredations—and the role of police in the detection of crime as a way to ensure a high probability of arrest and subsequent prosecution. Whether *gendarmerie* or civilian police, the new police forces of the early nineteenth century generally included a range of crime prevention and social ordering functions—for *gendarmerie*, the control of suspicious characters as well as highway robbers; for civilian police, a watch over the poor, the vagrant, and the disorderly on the streets and in the marketplaces of rapidly growing towns and cities. The crime detection functions of police developed more slowly, however much they became associated with popular representations of heroic police deeds (Emsley & Shpayer-Makov 2006). Whatever the particular array of functions possessed by any particular police institution, the characteristic mode of a modern police force was its bureaucratic. The work of police was laid out in laws and regulations and carried out through a highly routinized recording of constabulary patrols, crimes and incidents reported, matters investigated, warrants delivered, and persons arrested. In turn, these functions of police, so numbered and ordered, gave rise to the collection of official statistics as a mark of accountability for the public work performed and as a measure of the effectiveness of this modern force in ensuring order.

Finally, we should note the important question of governance. What made police modern was not only this bureaucratic organization of a body of (originally all) men with particular powers of force and a wide array of functions, but the accountability of this structure to organs of government. What distinguished and continues to distinguish modern police from the array of other bodies that carry out policing work (e.g., private police, security companies, protection officers) is their ties to executive government, whether they are democratically accountable, autocratic, or authoritarian; centralized, provincial, municipal, or local. In this sense, the prerevolutionary French police, accountable to the king, whether under the lieutenant-general of the Paris police or part of the *maréchaussée* coordinated by the Ministry of War, constitutes a decisive legacy, however much British political rhetoric once derided it. What kind of governance a modern police was subjected to was a function of the particular forms of state that existed at the point of origin. It goes without saying that this also rendered police vulnerable to changes in state formation, particularly shifts in the balance between the responsibilities and powers of local government and the tendencies toward the consolidation and strengthening of the central state, changes especially evident in the governing structures of English policing (Reiner 2000; Emsley 2009). All the same, police institutions have been remarkably resilient in form, whatever the larger changes in state formation. No better example of this can be found than the persistence in the United States of the vast number of local police forces.

CONCLUSION

The modern police is both an idea and an institution, an indispensable apparatus of state and government. It is also a fixed element of popular consciousness and politics, dominating nightly newcasts and proving indispensable even to states and governments seeking to abandon or devolve other instrumentalities of government. A half-century of research has now emphasized how integral the institutions and functions of a public police are to the structure and character of contemporary nation-states (Bayley 1969; Loader 2003). A study of the origins of modern policing highlights how attentive sovereign power was to the quality of the relation between an efficacious and legitimate police and a state watchful over the security of its people and government.

REFERENCES

Ahire, Philip Terdoo. 1991. *Imperial Policing: The Emergence and Role of the Police in Colonial Nigeria, 1860–1960*. Milton Keynes, UK: Open University Press.

Alletz, P. Julien. 1820. *Dictionnaire de police moderne*. Paris: n.p. Accessed at http://archive.org/details/dictionnairedepoo3alle.

Anderson, David M, & David Killingray. 1991. *Policing the Empire: Government, Authority, and Control, 1830–1940*. Manchester, UK: Manchester University Press.

Andrews, John Harwood. 1975. *A Paper Landscape*. Oxford: Clarendon.

Arnold, David. 1986. *Police Power and Colonial Rule, Madras, 1859–1947*. New York: Oxford University Press.

Barrie, David G. 2008. *Police in the Age of Improvement: Police Development and the Civic Tradition in Scotland, 1775–1865*. Cullompton, UK: Willan Publishing.

Barrie, David G. 2010. "A Typology of British Police: Locating the Scottish Municipal Police Model in Its British Context, 1800–35." *British Journal of Criminology* 50 (2): 259–77.

Bayley, David H. 1969. *The Police and Political Development in India*. Princeton, NJ: Princeton University Press.

Bayley, David H. 1976. *Forces of Order: Police Behavior in Japan and the United States*. Berkeley: University of California Press.

Beattie, John M. 2012. *The First English Detectives: The Bow Street Runners and the Policing of London, 1750–1840*. Oxford: Oxford University Press.

Brodeur, Jean-Paul. 1982. "High Policing and Low Policing: Remarks about the Policing of Political Activities." *Social Problems* 30:507.

Cameron, Iain A. 1977. "The Police of Eighteenth-Century France." *European History Quarterly* 7 (1): 47–75.

Cameron, Iain A. 1981. *Crime and Repression in the Auvergne and the Guyenne, 1720–1790*. Cambridge: Cambridge University Press.

Cribb, Robert. 2010. "Legal Pluralism and Criminal Law in the Dutch Colonial Order." *Indonesia* 90:47–66.

Dodsworth, Francis. 2004. "'Civic' Police and the Condition of Liberty: The Rationality of Governance in Eighteenth-Century England." *Social History* 29 (2): 199–216.

Emsley, Clive. 1983. *Policing and Its Context, 1750–1870*. London: Palgrave Macmillan.

Emsley, Clive. 1999a. *Gendarmes and the State in Nineteenth-Century Europe*. Oxford: Oxford University Press.

Emsley, Clive. 1999b. "A Typology of Nineteenth-Century Police." *Crime, History & Societies* 3 (1): 29–44.

Emsley, Clive. 2009. *The Great British Bobby: A History of British Policing from 1829 to the Present*. London: Quercus.

Emsley, Clive. 2012. "Marketing the Brand: Exporting British Police Models, 1829–1950." *Policing* 6 (1): 43–54.

Emsley, Clive. 2013. "Peel's Principles, Police Principles." In *The Future of Policing*, ed. Jennifer M. Brown, 11–22. Abingdon, UK: Routledge.

Emsley, Clive, & Haia Shpayer-Makov, eds. 2006. *Police Detectives in History, 1750–1950*. Aldershot, UK: Ashgate.

Finnane, Mark. 1981. *Insanity and the Insane in Post-Famine Ireland*. London: Croom Helm.

Finnane, Mark. 1994. *Police and Government: Histories of Policing in Australia*. Melbourne: Oxford University Press.

Griffin, Brian. 1997. *The Bulkies: Police and Crime in Belfast, 1800–1865*. Dublin: Irish Academic Press.

Hazard's Register of Pennsylvania. [1828–35]. http://hdl.handle.net/2027/hvd.32044051083897.

Hill, Richard S. 1986. *Policing the Colonial Frontier: The Theory and Practice of Coercive Social and Racial Control in New Zealand, 1767–1867*. Wellington: V. R. Ward.

Hill, Richard S. 2005. "Maori Police Personnel and the Rangatiratanga Discourse." In *Crime and Empire, 1840–1940: Criminal Justice in Local and Global Context*, ed. Barry S Godfrey & Graeme Dunstall, 174–88. Cullompton, UK: Willan.

Johansen, Anja. 2013. "Lost in Translation: The English Policeman Through a German Monocle, 1848–1914." *History* 98 (333): 750–68.

Johnson, David Ralph. 1979. *Policing the Urban Underworld: The Impact of Crime on the Development of the American Police, 1800–1887*. Philadelphia: Temple University Press.

Lane, Roger. 1967. *Policing the City: Boston, 1822–1885*. Cambridge, MA: Harvard University Press.

Lentz, Susan A., & Robert H. Chaires. 2007. "The Invention of Peel's Principles: A Study of Policing 'Textbook' History." *Journal of Criminal Justice* 35 (1): 69–79.

Lin, Zhiqiu. 2007. *Policing the Wild North-West: A Sociological Study of the Provincial Police in Alberta and Saskatchewan, 1905–32*. Calgary: University of Calgary Press.

Loader, Ian. 2003. *Policing and the Condition of England: Memory, Politics and Culture.* Clarendon Studies in Criminology. Oxford: Oxford University Press.

Lüdtke, Alf. 2009. *Police and State in Prussia, 1815–1850.* Cambridge: Cambridge University Press.

MacDonagh, Oliver. 1977. *Ireland: The Union and Its Aftermath.* London: Allen & Unwin.

Macleod, R. C. 1978. *The North West Mounted Police, 1873–1919.* Ottawa: Canadian Historical Association.

Malcolm, Elizabeth. 2006. *The Irish Policeman, 1822–1922: A Life.* Dublin: Four Courts.

Marquis, Greg. 1993. *Policing Canada's Century: A History of the Canadian Association of Chiefs of Police.* Toronto: University of Toronto Press.

Marquis, Greg. 1997. "The 'Irish Model' and Nineteenth-Century Canadian Policing." *Journal of Imperial and Commonwealth History* 25 (2): 193–218.

McConville, Michael & Chester L. Mirsky. 2005. *Jury Trials and Plea Bargaining: A True History.* Oxford: Hart.

Merriman, John M. 2006. *Police Stories: Building the French State, 1815–1851.* New York: Oxford University Press.

Mildmay, William. 1763. *The Police of France; or, An Account of the Laws and Regulations Established in That Kingdom, for the Preventing of Robberies, to Which Is Added, a Particular Description of the Police and Government of the City of Paris.* London: E. Owen & T. Harrison. Accessed at http://archive.org/details/policeoffranceoroomilduoft.

Miller, Wilbur R. 2013. "A State Within 'The States': Private Policing and Delegation of Power in America." *Crime, History & Societies* 17 (2): 125–35.

Myers, Ramon Hawley, & Mark R. Peattie eds. 1984. *The Japanese Colonial Empire, 1895–1945.* Princeton, NJ: Princeton University Press.

Palmer, Stanley H. 1988. *Police and Protest in England and Ireland, 1780–1850.* Cambridge: Cambridge University Press.

Pasquino, Pasquale. 1991. "Theatrum Politicum: The Genealogy of Capital-Police and the State of Prosperity." In *The Foucault Effect: Studies in Governmentality*, ed. Graham Burchell, Colin Gordon, & Peter Miller, 105–18. Chicago: University of Chicago Press.

Petrow, Stefan. 2005. "The English Model?: Policing in Late Nineteenth-Century Tasmania." In *Crime and Empire, 1840–1940: Criminal Justice in Local and Global Context*, ed. Barry S Godfrey & Graeme Dunstall, 121–34. Cullompton, UK: Willan.

Philips, David, & Robert D. Storch. 2001. *Policing Provincial England, 1829–1856.* Leicester, UK: Leicester University Press.

Reiner, Robert. 2000. *The Politics of the Police.* Oxford: Oxford University Press.

Reynolds, Elaine. 1998. *Before the Bobbies: The Night Watch and Police Reform in Metropolitan London, 1720–1830.* Stanford, CA: Stanford University Press.

Richards, Jonathan. 2008. *The Secret War: A True History of Queensland's Native Police/ Jonathan Richards.* St. Lucia, Australia: University of Queensland Press.

Richardson, James F. 1970. *The New York Police, Colonial Times to 1901.* New York: Oxford University Press.

Veracini, Lorenzo. 2010. *Settler Colonialism: A Theoretical Overview.* Basingstoke, UK: Palgrave Macmillan.

Westney, D. Eleanor. 1987. *Imitation and Innovation: The Transfer of Western Organizational Patterns to Meiji Japan.* Cambridge, MA: Harvard University Press.

Zedner, Lucia. 2006. "Policing Before and After the Police: The Historical Antecedents of Contemporary Crime Control." *British Journal of Criminology* 46 (1): 78–96.

....

CHAPTER 24

DETECTIVES AND FORENSIC SCIENCE

The Professionalization of Police Detection

....

HAIA SHPAYER-MAKOV

INTRODUCTION

....

THE need to identify and capture criminals after they had committed an offense was met by an array of institutions and individuals in premodern societies, but only during the eighteenth century did the detective function begin to assume a lasting organizational form, becoming the basis of what would develop into a full-time and well-established occupation. Detection had been and continued to be practiced both by official enforcement agents and by private individuals who were hired by victims to track down offenders. However, the formulation and consolidation of the detective role as a distinct expertise took shape predominantly within police forces over the course of the nineteenth century.

Surprisingly, although detectives and crime investigation have long captured the public imagination, an interest manifested in their prominence in all media formats over the last 150 years, their evolution attracted relatively little attention in modern academic literature (Brodeur 2010, pp. 3, 185). Until recently, historical accounts about police detectives were featured mainly as chapters or parts of chapters in books about the history of crime, the police, or the contemporary law enforcement scene. These books often mentioned detectives only in passing or ignored them altogether. The few books dedicated to the history of detective institutions were largely written by practitioners in the field of criminal justice. This is all the more unexpected given the massive body of innovative scholarship on the history of the police published since the 1970s and the message it conveyed, namely, that during the nineteenth century police detection became an indispensable component of the criminal justice system. Lately, however, encouraging signs that this imbalance is beginning to be redressed are evident in an increasing crop of books and articles dedicated to a new, in-depth examination of various aspects of the detective vocation.[1] Still, there is abundant scope for further research on the subject.

This essay traces, in brief, key landmarks in the evolution of the role of the detective from either criminal-turned–paid informant or nonspecialist law enforcer to a professional member of a detective unit organized within municipal police departments, from the mid-eighteenth century to the Second World War, principally in England, France,[2] and the United States. The spotlight is on these societies since their social and cultural traditions, and hence their police in general and detective institutions in particular, shared common features and followed distinctive national patterns, and because comparisons between police systems usually concentrate on this subset.

Clearly, an account of the professionalization of police detection would not be complete without highlighting the interface between detection and forensic science. While occupational norms and practices of crime investigation were gradually crystalized within police forces, individuals unconnected directly to the domain of crime control—namely, scientists and medical researchers—made criminality and the criminal the focal point of their observations, debates, and publications, thereby forging a discursive arena across national boundaries in which views and recommendations on, *inter alia*, how to obtain incriminating evidence, were articulated. Detectives and other police officers may have come across these experts when the latter assisted criminal investigations or legal proceedings, but during most of the nineteenth century, interaction between them was minimal, and the advancement of methods related to criminal inquiries within and outside the police largely followed separate paths. It was only from the late nineteenth century onward that forensic science methodologies made significant inroads into the world of police detection, thereby enhancing its professionalization, although cooperation between these two realms would only be partial.

This exploratory essay outlines various pivotal trends in the professionalization of police detection in England, France, and the United States, and draws upon the history of forensic science to illuminate major forensic techniques that were developed by or introduced into the police in the period under discussion. The first part sketches the historical shifts in the professionalization of police detectives up to the late nineteenth century, when forensic techniques began to be part and parcel of detective work. The second part charts several milestones in the history of forensic science at that time and then highlights the intersection between police detection and forensic science from the late nineteenth century through the remaining years considered in this volume. In assessing the processes of police professionalization, reference is commonly made to police's public standing and commitment to public service, standards of conduct and success in performance, formal training and distinct working conditions, specialized knowledge and skills, employment of sophisticated methods, and degree of discretion enjoyed. These will be the criteria used in the following discussion. The thesis presented here focuses on key research findings published mainly in English. Suggestions for further research on the professionalization of detection are provided at the end of the essay.

I. From Rogue to Legitimate Expert

Only rudimentary and haphazard provisions for tracking down offenders were available in law enforcement bodies in the Western world of the eighteenth and early nineteenth centuries. In England and in the United States, which during and after the colonial period bore the stamp of English policing arrangements (Lane 1967, pp. 34, 118), locally based law enforcers—primarily the justice of the peace, the constable (and, in the United States, the sheriff and the marshal), and in towns also the watchman—acted on occasion as detectives, performing duties such as following up cases, arresting and interrogating suspects, gathering evidence against perpetrators, or retrieving stolen articles (Monkkonen 1981, pp. 34–35; Beattie 1986, pp. 268–83). Overall, however, these individuals were not "likely to do more than respond to the complaints brought to them" (Beattie 1986, p. 51; Lane 1967, p. 7). In the course of discharging such tasks, some officials accumulated experience and increased their proficiency, but generally they were untrained and often part-time amateurs who enjoyed wide discretion in executing their duties (Friedman 1993, pp. 27–30). Governed by the ethos of self-help and reservations about an active central government, ordinary citizens in the Anglo-American world played a primary role in addressing issues of delinquency in their locality (Lane 1967, pp. 4, 7). In a largely rural or small town environment where the population lived in intimate communities, conflicts and complaints of foul play were for the most part settled by the community or in private without recourse to the official machinery of criminal justice (Emsley 2007, pp. 57–61). Inevitably, scores of offenders continued their lives with impunity. Yet, whereas in America a district attorney prosecuted crime on behalf of victims, in England not only were ordinary citizens authorized under common law to apprehend a person who had committed a criminal offense and take him or her before a magistrate, but, when they were victims of a crime, they were generally expected to take the initiative and use their own resources to carry through the entire process of catching and committing their offenders to trial and laying out the evidence in court (Beattie 1986, pp. 35–36).

This very limited participation of officials in crime control in England had the effect of promoting the role of thief takers, an occupation that gained momentum during the eighteenth century in response to mounting demands by aggrieved persons who were unable or unwilling to trace their offenders by themselves (Beattie 1986, pp. 55–59). The expansion of the middle classes, alongside a rise in commercial transactions, generated opportunities for white-collar offenses, while at the same time entrenching the sanctity of private property and deepening intolerance for property offenses—the bulk of committed crimes. Thief takers were offered fees or rewards for results, an incentive that may have strengthened control over wrongdoers but correspondingly had a corrupting effect on many thief takers, who anyway were not respectable members of the community (Beattie 1986, pp. 51–55; Beattie 2012, pp. 7–8). To receive the financial rewards of this work, quite a few of these private detectives relied heavily on rogues and informers with affiliations to the underworld and did not abstain from colluding with criminals and resorting to perjury, incitement to crime, and even the framing of innocent people. Such behavior gave the occupation a bad name, one inextricably bound up with malpractice and lawbreaking.

A meaningful step was taken against this entrepreneurial climate in the mid-eighteenth century by the novelist Henry Fielding, who was chief magistrate of the London Bow Street Court and police office between 1748 and 1754. To better enforce the law, he created a small cadre of detectives who helped him in his judicial and investigative functions for the benefit of the public at large, at least partially at government expense (Beattie 2006, pp. 19–20; Beattie 2012, pp. 19–24). His half-brother John Fielding, who succeeded him in this judicial role until his death in 1780, further cultivated the small coterie of about half a dozen men, who in time became known as the Bow Street Runners (Beattie 2012, pp. 25–133). Studies of eighteenth- and early nineteenth-century police detection in England have overwhelmingly concentrated on this group, widely regarded as comprising the first police detectives in England. Although to attain important leads about committed and planned crimes they, too, counted upon people in the criminal milieu (Beattie 2012, pp. 67–75), in time the Runners managed to acquire a nationwide reputation as competent and, on the whole, honest crime investigators, as was the Fieldings' intention (Beattie 2006, pp. 22, 26–32; Cox 2010, pp. 28–31). In consequence, their services were sought by official and private institutions as well as by individuals across the country (Cox 2010). As the eighteenth century neared its end, against the backdrop of the march of industry and urbanization, and under ascendant pressures to rationalize the criminal justice system and reform the police, a few dozen other detectives were attached to police courts in London along the lines modeled by the Bow Street office (Beattie 2012, pp. 159–66).

In eighteenth- and early nineteenth-century France, too, the official pursuit and arrest of lawbreakers was commonly carried out by various officers who performed other policing tasks in largely preventative law enforcement bodies operating in the cities, towns, and countryside (Williams 1979, pp. 66–67, 221–28; Emsley 2006, pp. 62–64).[3] The public police in France were much more involved in investigative functions than their counterparts in England, where private thief taking was rife. Still, in the course of executing their duties, French officers likewise kept close ties with people who lived by crime and with *mouches* or *mouchards* (informants), such that it often became difficult to distinguish between policemen and outlaws, tarnishing the reputation of the police (Stead 1983, pp. 15, 25; Brown 2006, pp. 55, 57; Emsley 2006, pp. 65, 70; Brodeur 2010, pp. 52, 192; Berlière & Levy 2013, pp. 104–08). As in England, policing arrangements and activity, and the drive for police reform, were most pronounced in the capital city, where, as in London, a group of police officers was set apart in the mid-eighteenth century to specialize in crime investigation and intelligence gathering (Williams 1979, pp. 94–100, 228–36). Staffed at first by three and, after 1776, four men, this cadre followed the custom of employing individuals who were either drawn from or had ties with the criminal fraternity (Williams 1979, pp. 100–11). The *Bureau de Sûreté* (Security Office), as the office in which they worked came to be called, acted, like the Bow Street Court, as a center for storing and accessing information about such areas of crime as suspects, offenders, and stolen goods (Stead 1983, p. 27; Emsley 2006, p. 64; Beattie 2012, pp. 12, 30–31).

However, in marked contrast to the English and American settings, the French central government, which both before and after the French Revolution gave the highest priority to the protection of the sovereign and the regime, exercised a much stronger hold on society and on the course of justice. In this climate, the French courts "did not depend on victims to press criminal charges as much as the British did," and a more complex and interventionist police machinery was constructed (Brodeur 2010, p. 51). Furthermore, to attain close control over behavior and opinion, the police pursued a strategy of all-pervasive surveillance—both clandestine and overt—with agents, some ex-convicts, spying not only on political opponents or those prone to crime, but also on ordinary citizens (Stead 1983, pp. 23, 31–32, 41–42, 46–53; Brodeur 2010, pp. 53–57, 78). All these characteristics of French law enforcement continued well into the nineteenth century and were part of the context in which the various officers engaged in criminal investigations operated.

Notwithstanding the provisions in place for the detection of both ordinary and political crime in the multifaceted French system of criminal justice, scholars who note the birth of a sustainable detective bureau in France (or in Europe) usually trace it back to the *Brigade de Sûreté* (later the famous *Sûreté*), founded in 1812 as the central detective unit of the Paris police (Brown 2006, p. 39). Its formation was inextricably associated with Eugène-François Vidocq (1775–1857), a serial ex-convict and informer who, in the course of betraying his fellow criminals to the police, was recognized as endowed with just the qualities and contacts necessary to create and lead such a body (Stead 1953, p. 28). Guided by the dictum that "it takes a thief to catch a thief," Vidocq based this cadre on ex-convicts and escaped prisoners who utilized their acquaintance with malefactors to get hold of crucial information, whether under intimidation or as a tradeoff. Despite its small number—four at the beginning and twelve by 1817 (Stead 1953, p. 57)—their record in hunting down wrongdoers was impressive (Emsley 2006, p. 66), not least because of the maneuverability, good memory, mastery of disguise, and devious behavior of Vidocq, who headed the department until 1827 and later for a brief period in 1832. With an eye to commercial success, and armed with gifts of self-promotion, Vidocq advertised himself in a four-volume memoir (as well as in other profit-making ventures surrounding his figure) as an exceedingly intelligent, resourceful, and persistent crime fighter, and his exploits as important contributions to the reduction of crime, albeit deeply embroiled in the "dangerous classes" (Brown 2006, pp. 38–39; Emsley 2006, pp. 66–67). The memoir, written partly by him and partly by ghostwriters, appeared in 1828–1829 and won immediate popularity both in France and in other countries, soon seeing a host of reprints (Morton 2004, p. vii). The enormous interest in this character, both then and subsequently, publicized the criminal and underhanded origins of the detective police while simultaneously raising detection to a pivotal occupation requiring special aptitudes.[4]

Even so, however successful Vidocq and his team were in combating crime, they provoked considerable resentment among regular police officers as well as concerns among officials who thought it imperative to clear the unsavory reputation of the squad and detach it from its linkage with dubious means of detection (Stead 1983, p. 61; Emsley 2006, pp. 65–66). Though this sensitivity to public opinion was by no means as potent as it was in England and the United States (Lane 1967, p. 84; Miller 1977, pp. 1–24; Stead 1983, p. 60), it was powerful enough for the prefect of the Paris police to dissolve the Brigade in 1832 and forbid the recruitment of officers with a criminal past to the new *Sûreté* (Morton 2004, pp. 214–15; Emsley 2006, pp. 66–67). This step did not stop subsequent heads from employing spies and ex-convicts (Stead 1983, p. 62), but the experience with Vidocq and his men led to efforts "to make the police more visible, less sinister, and generally more approachable for the population" (Emsley 2006, pp. 67, 70). Clearly, the political elite in France was aware by then, as were the Fieldings more than half a century earlier, that in an age when consent was vital to maintain the legitimacy and stability of the rising nation-state and its institutions, public representations of the police commanded considerable force (Stead 1983, p. 56). Still, even at the close of the nineteenth century, the *Sûreté* still provoked suspicions and concerns (Emsley 2006, p. 76).

Though significant sectors of informed opinion were reasonably satisfied with the existing policing configuration in their respective countries, the mid-decades of the nineteenth century saw the emergence of restructured police forces across the Western world (Emsley 2007, pp. 160–71). Naturally, national circumstances and hegemonic norms dictated the specific style of each new police system, but they were commonly structured as full-time uniformed paid patrols, working night and day and dispersed geographically across the policed territory, where they were accessible to all and fully acquainted with the neighborhood and its residents. Their primary purpose was to prevent crime and preserve public order (Lane 1967, pp. 34–35; Johnson 1979, pp. 12–40; Martin 1990, pp. 42–43; Friedman 1993, pp. 67–71; Brodeur 2010, p. 62).

Interestingly, the popular perception of the French and continental police as army-like, intrusive, corrupt, largely clandestine, enmeshed in the criminal world, and a tool of central government had profound impact on the development of the police across the Channel. Opponents of police reform in England time and again used this array of associations to warn the public that the proposed police might follow the French model and thereby undermine the sacrosanct liberties and well-being of the people (Shpayer-Makov 2011, pp. 26–30). In response to such conceptual challenges, the new police forces in Britain were molded with a view to avoiding what was considered most abhorrent in the French system. In addition to rejecting a *gendarmerie* type of organization, the reformers were careful to distance the new police from the figure of the spy, which epitomized French law enforcement in public parlance (Petrow 1994, p. 54). So incompatible with English values did an invisible police seem that when a modern police force—the Metropolitan Police of London—was finally launched in 1829, no detective department was instituted in it. Thirteen years later, when the famous unit at Scotland Yard was set up in 1842, it included only eight detectives, a figure that expanded markedly only in the last decades of the century (Shpayer-Makov 2011, pp. 33–35). Not that the English police had shunned undercover policemen and informants, especially in relation to perceived political threats (Petrow 1993, p. 99; Brodeur 2010, p. 67), but even as plainclothes policing gradually became acceptable as the century unfolded, an undercurrent of unease with the idea still lingered over the advance of the detective police in Britain (Roach 2004). Added to the scruples about detection were qualms about thief taking and its infamous record of transgression and complicity with criminals and informants.

Fears of spying and its implications were not absent from attitudes to police reform in the United States either (Morn 1982, pp. 12–13, 27–28; Marx 1988, pp. 22–25; Brodeur 2010, pp. 69–70), though in no way were they as prevalent or deep-seated as in England, nor were they necessarily connected with perceptions of the French police (Miller 1977, pp. 34–37; Kuykendall 1986, p. 179). Here a stronger factor influencing the formation of the modern police was the deep-rooted discomfort with military institutions fomented by the experience of colonialism and the War of Independence, which partly explains why, at the outset, certain police forces were not uniformed (Brodeur 2010, p. 70). In any event, there was little urge initially to prevail over these suspicions, as decision-makers responsible for law enforcement in all three countries were not at all convinced that crime investigation and the apprehension of criminals required full-time specialists or organs exclusively dedicated to these tasks—at least not more than what was already in place.

All the same, despite an overwhelming preference for preventative action and misgivings about detection, attention to the reactive function of the police became more pressing during the course of the nineteenth century. Fully fledged detective units gradually sprang up in major municipal police forces in Europe and the eastern and northern parts of the United States, though detectives consistently formed only a small proportion of the manpower in each police force, and most communities had no designated detective branch at all.[5] The factors responsible for this change of direction were rooted in broader social transformations as well as shifting police priorities. Mounting attention to crime investigation reflected a heightened appreciation in the police management that solving serious crimes called for special skills and a greater investment of energy and resources. The continuous expansion of densely populated cities where criminals could easily elude detection, compounded with the growing sophistication of criminals (Lane 1967, pp. 54, 142–46), had built up a strong impetus for improved detection. In addition, although certain forms of serious crime were actually decreasing during the second half of the century (Davis 1991, p. 1; Friedman 1993, p. 210), the prevalent perception that delinquency was on the rise at a time when obedience to the law was becoming ever more indicative of the governability of the state and the degree of security extended to its citizens seemed to demand particular efforts to quell crime. Under such pressures, detectives became an integral component of the growing urban service apparatus, as well as of the instruments of state control. Yet, for detectives to attain a professional image, the public needed to be convinced of their intrinsic value, even in countries with lesser dependence on public consent. Eliminating the aura of disrepute attached to the earlier generations of detectives was crucial to this process.

Socialist and radical commentators, prompted by their ideological position to scrutinize the police and its detective wing in depth, repeatedly pointed out instances of heavy-handed methods and the risks to justice and the common weal imbued in covert policing. Though much less frequently and fervently, other commentators articulated similar qualms, especially on occasions—which were not rare—when such suspicions were confirmed. The early police detectives in the United States, from top to bottom, were notorious for their unscrupulous dealings with the underworld, acting more like commercially minded private detectives than public servants (Lane 1967, pp. 146–48, 151–56; Richardson 1970, pp. 207–13; Johnson 1979, pp. 42–71; Monkkonen 1981, p. 48; Deakin 1988, pp. 84–85). In an atmosphere of corrupt local politics in which municipal authorities used the police for their own partisan interests (Friedman 1993, pp. 149–50), an environment characteristic of the United States in the middle decades of the nineteenth century, it was not easy for police detectives to be both effective and honest (Richardson 1970, p. 207). Even in England, where supervision over the quality of police detectives was much stricter than in the United States, the year 1877 revealed to the public that most of the senior detectives at Scotland Yard were to varying degrees implicated in fraud, bribery, suppression of evidence, and the shielding of criminals— by no means professional behavior (Shpayer-Makov 2011, p. 38).

Nonetheless, detection was increasingly accepted not only as a legitimate occupation but also as essential to the good of society (Lane 1967, p. 69; Friedman 1993, pp. 204–05; Kalifa 2005, p. 39; Morris 2006, p. 93). Many historians and literary critics point to the rise of detective fiction and detective memoirs—which put the detective center stage and on the whole sketched him as a dedicated servant of the law—as a cardinal factor in strengthening this trend (Stead 1983, p. 61; Kalifa 2005, pp. 39–40; Emsley 2006, pp. 66–71, 74; Berlière & Levy 2013, pp. 112–13). The press—for numerous people the only source of information about detective work—even if it periodically subjected detectives to criticism, on balance gave them crucial support (Berlière 1991, pp. 48–49; Shpayer-Makov 2011, pp. 187–225). The sheer impression it disseminated that police detectives devoted most of their time to fighting risky violent crimes underlined their public role and romanticized the public perception of them. It is difficult to pinpoint an exact date, but scholars concur that sometime during the second half of the nineteenth century, despite lingering suspicions, the detective was divorced from his shady beginnings and even attained a heroic stature, a process that some scholars contend began in France at the end of the First Republic, or later on with Vidocq (Brown 2006, pp. 36, 38, 40, 56–57, 60; Emsley 2006, p. 77).

As might be expected, the professionalism of detectives was measured above all by the success of their investigations. In this respect, their public image fluctuated and was ambiguous. Not only did criminal activity continue unabated, but failures in getting to the bottom of specific and usually high-profile inquiries, such as the notorious Jack the Ripper case in late 1888, not infrequently gained prominent attention in the press (Shpayer-Makov 2014, pp. 331–39). Conversely, while dramatic accomplishments were glamorized by the mainstream press and often attributed to the special talents of detectives, even when the outcome was the result of sheer luck or clues provided by the victim or members of the public, as was commonly the case (a situation that continued in the twentieth century), the more typical low-profile crimes were hardly reported. Literature, too, played an ambiguous role in shaping opinion about the efficiency of official detectives. On the one hand, volume after volume of detective fiction, especially from the late nineteenth century onward, forged an indelible connection between detection and outstanding brilliance and competence, but on the other hand, Anglo-American fiction routinely opted to depict the private detective as much more skillful than the police detective (Shpayer-Makov 2011, pp. 244–65).

Some features of detective work actually ran counter to a professional model. Not that formal training would have necessarily been decisive in unraveling crimes, but the fact that such a provision was not available for detectives in England, France, or the United States during the nineteenth century by definition undermined their professional standing (Fosdick 1920, p. 331; Berlière 1991, pp. 42–45; Shpayer-Makov 2011, p. 94). Moreover, no distinct corpus of knowledge existed to steer detectives (Lane 1967, p. 150; Morris 2006, p. 92), and their legal knowledge seems to have been usually negligible. Certain guidelines were provided in police instruction books, but they mostly covered general rules and regulations. In short, preparation for becoming a detective was informal and took place on the job—a craft model of learning (Morris 2007, p. 24). In such circumstances, detectives had to rely on cumulative insights acquired haphazardly through experience and trial and error. Veteran detectives played a central role in transmitting these insights to novice recruits (Shpayer-Makov 2011, pp. 95–96), but there was no systematic diffusion of such know-how between the different police forces.

Notably, the professionalization of police detection in the United States is said to have lagged behind that of Europe (Deakin 1988). While detective departments had been organized as early as 1846 in Boston and by 1861 in such major cities as New York, Philadelphia, and Chicago, only at the very end of the century, if not later, did the police begin to focus on crime control, a focus that went hand in hand with greater attention to demands for efficiency, honesty, and the reform of police corruption (Monkkonen 1996, pp. 207–09). Against a background of entrenched individualism, free market culture, and the push west—where large territories lacked law enforcement organs—private agents and agencies played a leading role in providing detective services to society, at least in comparison to European countries (Morn 1982; Brodeur 2010, pp. 72–75). Conceivably, this contributed to the delayed development of professional public detection.

Nevertheless, although a great deal of crime was cleared up by uniformed officers at the crime scene, by the time the nineteenth century drew to a close the detective, principally in England and France, had come to be perceived as the expert in crime control (Kalifa 2005, pp. 37–38; Emsley 2006, pp. 61, 72–73, 77; Shpayer-Makov 2011, pp. 46–48). If the media played a somewhat ambivalent role in shaping opinion about the efficacy of police detectives, it carried significant weight in instilling the view that they were in fact the authority in fighting crime.

This evolving professional image was also rooted in police practices. The sheer distinction between uniformed officers and detectives within the police, and the formation of detective departments, sharpened the separation of functions. The development of expertise among detectives, especially on the continent, and of specialist subsections inside detective departments, such as the formation of the Special Irish Branch (as part of the London Metropolitan Police's Criminal Investigation Department [CID]) in 1883 to contain crimes against state security, further underpinned their distinct standing (Kuykendall 1986, p. 188; Porter 1987). Furthermore, by granting detectives preferential treatment, police authorities elevated their status both inside the police and in the public arena: they were the beneficiaries of better wages and conditions of service than uniformed officers, and they were subject to much less control and consequently enjoyed wider latitude for discretion (Fosdick 1920, p. 330; Morris 2006, pp. 93–95; Shpayer-Makov 2011, pp. 110–26; Berlière & Levy 2013, p. 114). In addition, with the shift from private to state prosecution, and the increasing involvement of the police in processing criminal cases, the officer who caught the perpetrator and gathered evidence acceptable to the court embodied this essential role (Lane 1967, p. 66; Kuykendall 1986, p. 177; Watson 2004, pp. 179–87).

Research shows that throughout most of the nineteenth century the methods used by detectives had not changed dramatically from the old-style practices of relying on human intelligence (i.e., informants and eyewitnesses), common sense, observation, and coercive force (Lane 1967, p. 65; Davis 1991, pp. 10–12; Emsley 2006, pp. 75–76). These tactics also included proactive information gathering aimed at the identification of repeat criminals. Whereas in the past discharged offenders would on occasion be branded (a legal punishment in France until 1832) or mutilated to facilitate future recognition (Cole 2001, p. 7), with the "transfer of criminal recordkeeping from the body of the criminal himself to paper records archived by the state" (Cole 2001, p. 16), the identification of habitual criminals came to hinge on the accumulation and organization of data about them. As early as the eighteenth century, both Fielding in London and sections of the police in France had been busy keeping records on miscreants, a routine that is known to have preoccupied Vidocq in the next century (Brown 2006, pp. 36, 39–40, 50). Supplementing dependence on the retentive ability of individual detectives to memorize the physical features of criminals, different types of registers with written descriptions, usually arranged in alphabetical order, were gradually accumulated.

From about the middle of the nineteenth century onward, efforts intensified to make the storing and retrieval of information about repeat criminals more methodical, even in England and the United States, where sensitivity to privacy was deeply ingrained in the culture. A major driving force for this effort was the entrenchment of the belief in the existence of a distinct criminal class, separate from respectable society and inhabited by resourceful, increasingly mobile specialists in crime whose identification required more powerful techniques (Johnson 1979, pp. 42–45, 51–59; Davis 1991, pp. 1– 2; Petrow 1994, pp. 75–81; Kaluszynski 2001, pp. 123–24; Higgs 2011, pp. 122–26). The management of knowledge about recidivists was now regarded as of paramount importance not only for identification, deterrence, and investigative purposes, but also for supervising released prisoners and serving the expanding norm of considering the past record of a defendant when passing sentence and administering punishment (Fosdick 1969, p. 316; Hebenton 1993, pp. 13–15; Cole 2001, pp. 14–18; Stanford 2009).

The invention of photography seemed to offer an obvious memory-jogging tool and was promptly utilized by police departments and prison officers as early as the 1840s and 1850s in Europe and the United States in conjunction with the various verbal records of the appearance and other details of criminals (Nickell & Fischer, 2013, p. 7).[6] A Rogues Portrait Gallery displaying the photographed faces of criminals was established by the New York Police Department as early as 1857 (Richardson 1970, p. 122), and was soon followed by similar galleries in other police forces in the United States and Europe. Photographic albums were held in different police stations (Petrow 1994, pp. 87–88).

In the search for a more efficient administration of the databases in some police forces, the classification of records included more categories, special identification bureaus were created, and designated manpower was introduced (Hebenton 1993, pp. 15–17; Petrow 1994, pp. 83–87). However, despite these attempts, the extant research points to many deficiencies (Hebenton 1993, pp. 18–21; Higgs 2011, pp. 126–27). Registration of the data, even if classified and cross-referenced, was often unsystematic, and the accumulation of massive amounts of information made it cumbersome, if not impossible, to extract the required detail. Even when identification was successful, the time consumed and the costs incurred could make it prohibitive (Berlière & Levy 2013, pp. 142–43). In places where only a small percentage of criminals were photographically recorded, the number of photographs became unmanageably large (Jäger 2001, pp. 39–40). The fact that photographs were taken unsystematically by commercial portrait photographers only exacerbated the retrieval process (Jäger 2001, p. 44). Moreover, with time, police officials realized that the camera may lie and that reliance on it did not prevent mistakes and the conviction of an innocent person. For their part, criminals learned to outmaneuver the registers and avoid recognition by changing their appearance as well as their name and address (Fosdick 1969, p. 319; Cole 2001, pp. 26–29).

Yet, with all its shortcomings, the identification system prevailing before the 1880s did advance the professionalization of police detection, and, even if many detectives refrained from using it, preferring to resort to the old-fashioned methods of personal recognition (Higgs 2011, p. 127), they still enjoyed the collective aura of expertise associated with identification procedures.

II. The Introduction
of Forensic Methodologies
in the Detective Police

While detective measures employed by the police during most of the nineteenth century were only mildly systematic and largely unscientific, outside the police walls forensic methodologies were expanding and developing into a discipline called forensic medicine, the precursor of forensic science as we know it today.[7] At the turn of the

nineteenth century, when it first developed, forensic medicine was viewed as a specialized branch of legal medicine, which was going through a significant stage of professionalization, with the introduction of personal chairs in legal medicine in universities.
France had always been more advanced than Britain and the United States in legal
medical research (Ward 1998, p. 89), and so it is not surprising that the first chair in
legal medicine was created in France in 1794 and was followed across the Channel in
Edinburgh in 1807 and in London only in 1828. Chairs of this kind mushroomed all
over Europe over the course of the century. In the United States, the first chair was
created by the College of Physicians and Surgeons of New York in 1813, followed by the
founding of chairs in other American academic centers.

The professionalization of forensic medicine made headway during the second half of
the nineteenth century when the academic chairs in legal medicine were supplemented
by the formation of medico-legal or medical forensic institutes (Ambage & Clark 1994,
p. 293). In 1868 the Medico-Legal Institute was established in Paris, followed over the
next fifty years by state- or municipally funded institutes of forensic medicine in many
other European cities, but not in England. The body of knowledge generated in these
academic research centers produced scientific experts whose specialized advice was
increasingly sought by the criminal justice system both in the investigative phase and
during the legal process (Golan 2004; Starr 2010, pp. 16–17, 99–104, 143–44, 175–89,
203–09, 212–13).

A growing number of individuals took part in the cross-fertilization of forensic ideas
at the turn of the twentieth century. One of the most prominent was Hans Gross (1847–
1915), an Austrian professor of law and examining magistrate who laid the foundations of criminalistics, a term often used interchangeably with forensic science, and
promoted the use of a wide range of scientific disciplines, such as forensic medicine,
toxicology, serology, ballistics, anthropometry, mineralogy, ecology, and botany, in
collecting and analyzing evidence (Nickell & Fischer 2013, p. 9).[8] He was also one of
the first to emphasize the need to carefully examine the crime scene for incriminating evidence as well as to define the qualities that detectives should possess. The end
of the nineteenth century saw the creation of institutions fully devoted to forensic
issues along the lines advocated by Gross, which included both forensic laboratories
and academic forensic programs. Rudolph Archibald Reiss (1876–1929), a professor of
forensic science specializing in judicial photography at the University of Lausanne, represented these two strands in the evolution of forensic science. In 1899 he became head
of the university's photographic laboratory and in 1909 founded the Institut de Police
Scientifique at the university, the first school of forensic science, which he directed
until 1919. Edmond Locard (1877–1966), a student of Alexandre Lacassagne (1843–
1924)—who is generally regarded as the founder of modern forensic science—was a
professor of forensic medicine at the University of Lyons. Locard was famous for establishing the first police laboratory in Lyons in 1910, and for formulating the "exchange
principle," which implies that in any violent criminal encounter offenders leave traces
of their presence, thus emphasizing the crucial importance of trace evidence analysis
(Watson 2011, pp. 132–33). In the wake of the founding of forensic laboratories by Reiss

and Locard, other comprehensive forensic science laboratories were established, typically outside the police and notably in continental Europe. With the growing diversity of scientific methodologies and greater use of scientific equipment like the microscope, these laboratories offered detectives and other criminal justice agents access to state-of-the-art techniques in criminal investigation, including new opportunities to explore the crime scene.

The upsurge in forensic professionalism, albeit outside the police realm, prepared the ground for a major scientific breakthrough by the police in France. This achievement was the product of the determination of a single individual: Alphonse Bertillon (1853–1914), who epitomized the integration between contemporary forensic thinking and the search by the police for objective and more rigorous techniques to identify recidivists, a search that nevertheless coexisted with a strong strain of resistance to new modes of operation.[9] Bertillon, the son of a medical doctor who was also a pioneering demographer and anthropologist and the brother of two demographers, grew up in an environment conducive to scientific reasoning. Devoid of higher education credentials, he joined the Paris police in 1879 as an assistant clerk in the identification bureau, copying details of arrested felons. Encountering the inadequacies inherent in the existing identification methods, he resolved to surmount them. By harnessing emerging forms of statistical inquiry and drawing on anthropological observations and techniques of bodily measurement, he devised an intricate identification system based on the measurement of certain parts of the body believed to be unique to each person and unchanging in adults over time (Cole 2001, pp. 57–58; Kaluszynski 2001, pp. 125–27). These measurements were carefully recorded, together with other physical and mental descriptions of the offender and his or her peculiar marks, such as tattoos and scars. Later, full-face and side-profile photographs of the offender (mugshots) were added to the records (Ward 1998, p. 90). To overcome the challenge of easy and systematic retrieval—the most serious problem in all previous identification systems—a complicated filing system, with cross-indexed cards, was constructed and further refined by Bertillon over several years. Typically, the new method of identification was initially rejected by the prefect of police and the leadership of the Sûreté, only to be grudgingly adopted by the Paris police as an experiment in 1882. Having secured the identification of an array of delinquents for the police as well as for the penal administration, the anthropometric system (later called Bertillonage) won worldwide acclaim and was embraced by police forces around the world (Berlière & Levy 2013, p. 146). Bertillon became a well-recognized participant in the international network of forensic scientists, with close contacts with people like Lacassagne and his former students Reiss and Locard.

Bertillon is best known for the anthropometric system he crafted, but he is also considered by many to be the "father of scientific detection." With his innovative mind and knowledge of current discourses on forensic science, he designed many other scientific methods to help crime investigators, including the portrait parlé (speaking portrait)—a precise and coded description of a criminal that could be transmitted through the telegraph to another operator—and crime scene photography (for details of his innovations, see Rhodes 2013; Berlière & Levy 2013, pp. 151–54). However, Bertillon did not bask long in the glory of his achievements. While the novelty of Bertillonage was greeted with enthusiasm, it also encountered growing criticism as its cost and weaknesses were exposed. Instances of mistaken identity and failure to discover the perpetrators of crimes divulged not only the fallacy of assuming that anthropometric characteristics were not subject to change, but also the system's disregard for human error and inconsistencies in measurement and filing (for defects in the system, see Cole 2001, pp. 70–72; Berlière & Levy 2013, pp. 148–49). The emerging alternative methodology of fingerprinting—which proved over time to correct these deficiencies—soon overtook Bertillonage and eventually replaced it altogether, although not without resistance.

Although the papillary lines on the tip of the fingers had already been deployed for personal identification in ancient China, a full-fledged and practicable system of fingerprint identification based on the premise that no two fingerprints are identical was not fashioned until the second half of the nineteenth century. Unlike Bertillonage, it was the end product of inadvertent and uncoordinated efforts of scientists and law enforcement officials operating independently in different parts of the world, occasionally learning from and competing for recognition with each other (Beavan 2001; Cole 2001, pp. 60–118). The principal contributors to the development of fingerprinting were William Herschel (1833–1917), an English public servant in India; Dr. Henry Faulds (1843–1930), a Scottish physician working as a missionary in Japan; the English scientist Sir Francis Galton (1822–1911); Juan Vucetich (1858–1925), a Croatian immigrant to Argentina who worked in the Buenos Aires police; and Edward Henry (1850–1931), inspector general of police for Bengal. In Europe, the system was first introduced at Scotland Yard in 1901 by Edward Henry, who had just become assistant commissioner in charge of the detective branch of the Metropolitan Police and had a stake in the matter as the person who (together with Aziz ul Haq, his assistant in India) had perfected the system by designing an effective means of classifying fingerprint patterns. Fingerprinting was shortly to be hailed by many as the most effective tool in the hands of the police. Not only was this identification technique cheaper, easier, and quicker to learn and use than Bertillonage, but it was also superior in its accuracy, saved labor, and constituted a great leap forward in identifying criminals who had left their personal trace at the crime scene, allowing investigators to link criminals to a crime and obtain indisputable forensic evidence for securing or refuting a defendant's guilt (see Cole 2001, pp. 168–89). While until the early twentieth century it was widely accepted that Scotland Yard—the crème de la crème of British detection—lagged behind continental powers in its utilization of scientific aids, modern fingerprinting established its popular image as keeping abreast of scientific developments and the reputation of the British as particularly good at detection.

Many urban police forces around the world soon saw the advantages of the system and put it into practice, though sometimes in a modified form, first in parallel with Bertillonage and then by itself.[10] Even then, people concerned with police affairs still felt that success in detection was "too often the result of chance or accident rather than of a premeditated plan," and that although Bertillonage and fingerprinting "added greatly to the effectiveness" of detective work, their scope was limited, as they could be of use only when the fingerprints of a criminal were already on file and not for the discovery of an unknown criminal or one known only by description (Fosdick 1915, p. 560). Hardened criminals, principally those who had extended their operations outside their own localities, where they were known, still posed a concern.

While new ideas aimed at improving methods of identifying multiple offenders in England were commonly initiated or implemented at Scotland Yard, on the eve of the First World War a further significant step was taken in provincial England when the modus operandi, or MO, system was devised by Major Llewellyn William Atcherley (1871–1954), chief constable of the West Riding of the Yorkshire constabulary. The procedure embedded an old-time assumption that criminals tended to operate in a manner so peculiar to themselves as to allow their identification, an assumption that had been at the root of certain registers of criminal identification in Europe (Morris 2007, p. 24). Atcherley's special contribution was to construct a more workable system of classification that was based on distinguishing characteristics of the methods of operation of the criminal, including the point of entry into a property, time of committing the crime, and tools employed in its commission (Fosdick 1915, pp. 566–70). His book *M.O.*, with details of the scheme, was published in 1913. During the same year Atcherley set up an information clearinghouse at the West Riding headquarters at Wakefield for a number of counties and boroughs in the north of England, with the intent of allowing detectives from various forces to trace criminals who traveled from community to community. Despite several deficiencies in the system—mainly the fact that the modes of operation of criminals could change—it became a standard procedure in many police forces in England and abroad.

Despite the negative response to innovations of many detectives, and the continued use of traditional means, other indications of a professional approach to detective methods besides the introduction of forensic techniques were apparent in European police forces in the early part of the twentieth century. By the First World War, criminal record files had become more standardized and elaborate, constituting "the principal part of the equipment of every detective bureau in Europe"—most distinctively in Berlin and Vienna (Fosdick 1969, pp. 316–17). Detectives were selected more carefully, and special training programs, however elementary, were introduced (Berlière 1991, pp. 45–47; Shpayer-Makov 2011, pp. 96–98).[11] A greater degree of collaboration between different forces within a country and internationally was also becoming more common.

Naturally, there was considerable variation between the different detective branches and their attitudes to professionalism. Raymond Fosdick had a lot to say about this in his book *European Police Systems*, published in 1915. While the German police appeared to him to be the most willing to experiment with new scientific ideas, the English police, even though they had taken the lead in the introduction of fingerprinting, were described as generally apathetic, exhibiting "instinctive resistance to the introduction of new methods" (Fosdick 1969, pp. 348–49). He asserted that while the "laboratory methods of the universities" and the ideas of Reiss and Gross had been adopted by many detective departments on the continent, in England the influence of such people was not yet perceptible, and few English officials knew anything of the work that had been done on the continent (pp. 366–68). Fosdick also argued that many of the elaborate appliances for the apprehension of criminals that were available to German detectives, such as tools for chemical and physical analyses, were missing in Scotland Yard (pp. 312–13). These observations have been supported by present-day researchers, who contend that beyond the realms of fingerprinting and poisons, forensic science was largely unused by English detectives (Ambage & Clark 1994; Laybourn & Taylor 2011, p. 104).

The first quarter of the twentieth century in the United States was marked by growing criticism of the slow professionalization of the police, voiced, among others, by Fosdick, who in 1920 published a book entitled *American Police System* containing a critical appraisal of the American detective force (Fosdick 1920, pp. 326–53). Reformers aimed to eliminate corrupt practices and remove political influence on the police on the one hand, and to enhance efficiency, accountability, and a scientific approach to criminal investigation on the other (Kuykendall 1986, p. 181; Deakin 1988, pp. 19–23). Under the influence of the Progressive movement, some reform along these lines had begun in the 1890s, although in the field of forensic science developments gained momentum only during the 1920s (Deakin 1988, p. 45).

The single most influential figure to advance the professionalism of American police forces during the first half of the twentieth century was August Vollmer (1876–1955), chief of the Berkeley police from 1909 to 1923, and from 1924 to 1932 (Deakin 1988, p. 34). An avid follower of Hans Gross, he was highly instrumental in introducing scientific methodologies into police detective training and work. Among his achievements were the pioneering of a simplified version of the English modus operandi in the United States; the establishment of the first police crime laboratory in the country in 1916 at Berkeley; and the founding in 1923 of a forensic science laboratory in Los Angeles—linked to the University of California at Berkeley—that became a model copied in the following decade in other urban centers in the United States.[12] It was in Vollmer's department at Berkeley, under his encouragement, that the modern lie detector test, relying on both respiration rate and blood pressure, was developed (Ward 1998, p. 122). Notwithstanding, historians claim that overall, the basic methods of inquiry did not significantly change in the United States in the interwar period, and that the "average case did not require any scientific analysis" (Kuykendall 1986, pp. 181–83).

The federal government played a limited role in criminal justice during the nineteenth century, but it significantly broadened its activity in the twentieth century with the formation of the Bureau of Investigation in 1908 (renamed the Federal Bureau of Investigation [FBI] in 1935) and its reorganization in 1924 by the then-new director, J. Edgar Hoover (Jeffreys-Jones 2008). The FBI came to stand for the latest in forensic science, blood tests, and fingerprinting (Friedman 1993, p. 271). In 1924 it absorbed the national bureau of criminal identification and in 1932 formed what became the largest forensic science laboratory offering forensic examination services in the nation.

The most noteworthy progress in forensic science in England during the interwar period took place in the mid-1930s with the formation of large-scale forensic laboratories, years after police science laboratories had been built in continental Europe.[13] Previously, when forensic expertise was required, such as in the field of ballistics, it was provided almost exclusively by outsiders—public analysts or academic scientists. Demands for the institutionalization of forensic knowledge had been at the center of public debate in the 1920s, and even before, but only in 1935, following the preliminary findings of the Home Office Departmental Committee on Detective Work and Procedure (established 1933), was a forensic laboratory opened for the Metropolitan Police, adjacent to their college at Hendon, against internal resistance, which remained unabated for many years (Morris 2007, p. 29). In its efforts to encourage training in the field and regulate scientific investigation, the Home Office instigated the formation of a network of regional forensic laboratories, with the first established in Nottingham in 1936 (Ward 1993, p. 245). The establishment of these laboratories contributed to greater collaboration between police officers and forensic scientists, although use of external expertise continued.

Similarly to the state of affairs that characterized the police in the United States, England, and even France—which was well ahead of the other two nations in terms of forensic research and application—two conflicting trends persisted side by side. On the one hand, there was confidence that police science would provide absolute certainty in resolving crime and dispense with dependence on such disreputable measures as informants, contacts with criminals, and third-degree pressure (Berlière & Levy 2013, pp. 164–65), but on the other hand, there was a reluctance to accommodate scientific innovations in the fields of crime and justice. This reluctance was motivated by a belief in the superiority of detective experience and skill, as well as a mistrust of scientific knowledge fueled by conflicting opinions offered by experts in the courtroom, mistakes made, and the derailment of the cause of justice by charlatans (Ramsland 2007, pp. 120–21). The drive to preserve the influence and standing of detectives was also a significant factor in delays in adoption. This mindset was prevalent enough to slow down, and at times halt, the scientification of the police, not only in France but also in the other two countries.

CONCLUSION

There is no single definition of what constitutes a profession. It can be argued, however, that by the eve of the Second World War—and many scholars would say even today—police detectives fell short of many of the criteria necessary to attain full professional status. Yet they had undoubtedly come a long way since the eighteenth century and had moved closer to such a status. The process of professionalization was by no means linear or without major setbacks, and it varied widely between nations and different detective units. The interwar period witnessed more than a few scandals involving corrupt detectives, reports of inefficiency, and the use of coercive power. Criticism was leveled at the quality of personnel, their standard of education, the adequacy of record systems, and forces' openness to new technology. Detectives' training, too, left much to be desired. Yet their image as the spearhead of crime fighting and as experts committed to public service became firmly entrenched, fed by an overall supportive media (Kuykendall 1986, p. 186). A gradual body of knowledge specific to them was built up, and the manner of their operations diversified greatly. Their high degree of autonomy and unique status within the police remained unchallenged. Still, while the integration of forensic techniques into their operations and training gave their professionalism a significant lift, it in fact solved only a small percentage of crimes, and adherence to low-tech forms of investigation continued to predominate. To various degrees, these characteristics of police detection persisted during the second half of the twentieth century alongside the duality of enthusiasm for scientific policing and qualms about the utility and contribution of forensic science to criminal justice (Williams 2008).

Suggested Lines of Research

Given the scant research on the consolidation of the detective vocation and the development of criminal investigation before the mid-twentieth century, there are large gaps in our knowledge about diverse aspects of these topics. Conspicuously, detective police systems in many countries still await substantive histories, but even the more extensive research on police detection in England, France, and the United States suffers from noteworthy lacunae. In relation to our topic, broadening the focus on the modes of operation of detectives in the past and exploring shifting patterns of criminal inquiries, which obviously had far-reaching implications for the professionalization of the vocation both in practice and in perception, are required. Much more needs to be discovered about the various stages of the investigative process—and not only as it related to high-profile cases—and the tension between the pressure to attain results and reliance on means widely regarded as reprehensible (e.g., the third degree, *agents provocateurs*) or detrimental to the professional image of detectives (e.g., the use of informants, consorting with criminals). What were the standard detective practices in investigating the various crimes against a person as opposed to property offenses, or crimes with a suspect and those without, and how were suspects and witnesses treated and confessions elicited? What were the meeting points between detectives and other agents of the criminal justice system outside the police? The postarrest process, the involvement of detectives in trials, and their contribution to securing convictions also merit further exploration. More research is required, too, on detectives as knowledge workers. Other questions could address the principles and norms guiding decision-makers, such as what type of crimes to investigate, when to stop an ongoing investigation, and how to allocate resources and divide labor, authority, and responsibility between uniformed officers and detectives. How did these priorities change over time?

Unlike research on the development of police detection per se, literature—monographs, encyclopedias, articles, and chapters—on the evolution of forensic science and related disciplines is abundant, often surveying developments across national boundaries. However, a sizable proportion of this work is descriptive and fails to engage in analytical examination. Here, too, the last decade or two have seen the publication of more substantive and critical studies. Yet our knowledge of the scientification of police work in the period is still limited. With all the attention to photography, Bertillonage, fingerprinting, and the growth of police laboratories, more work should be encouraged on how these and other less researched scientific innovations were incorporated into police forces around the world and how they affected detective work. What exactly was the involvement of police detectives in the implementation of new forensic measures? How did they and other police officers regard their introduction into police service? How did they acquire professional knowledge of them? Further study into the contribution of forensic experts and police surgeons to police investigations should be conducted.

This state of the research is compounded by the disproportional concentration of existing studies on the squad at Scotland Yard, the *Sûreté*, and the FBI. However significant the performance of these bodies was for law enforcement and the prestige attached to crime investigation in their respective countries, focusing on their work alone misrepresents the experience of other detectives in each country. The history of crime would profit greatly from a shift of balance to local aspects of detective work, both at certain moments and over the long term. Provincial archives and media are a mine of information in this regard. Historians should also turn their attention to cross-national comparisons to draw parallels between the themes discussed previously. No doubt, accounts of the professionalization of police detectives would be enriched by an ongoing flow of research by social historians, and by greater collaboration between them and legal historians.

Notes

1. See, for example, recent works by Beattie (2006; 2012); Berlière and Levy (2013); Brodeur (2010); Cox (2010); Emsley and Shpayer-Makov (2006); Laybourn and Taylor (2011); Morris (2006; 2007); and Shpayer-Makov (2011; 2014). Recent handbooks, encyclopedias, and companions on policing, criminology, and criminal investigation also contain essays that have expanded our knowledge of criminal investigation in the past.

2. Note that in historical discussions of police systems, the French police are often lumped together with other continental forces as the "continental system."

3. For the French and English models of police during the eighteenth and early nineteenth centuries, the differences and similarities between them, and the importation of the English model into North America, see Brodeur (2010, pp. 43–78). Also see Emsley (1984, pp. 8–52) and Emsley (2007, pp. 57–113).

4. This intriguing figure has been the subject of several biographies and many historical accounts in both popular and academic works (see, e.g., those by Stead [1953] and Morton

[2004]). Brown maintains that Vidocq's self-representations have distorted scholarly perceptions of police detection in the early nineteenth century (2006, pp. 36, 38, 60).

5. For an exceptional overview of and comparison between the different detective forces in Europe and their respective methods of detection on the eve of the First World War, as seen through the eyes of a contemporary American attorney, see Fosdick (1969 [1915], pp. 274–368). In nineteenth-century France, aside from political policemen, no specialized detective force operated outside the Paris police, though crime investigation was conducted by the *gendarmerie* and the civil police. Only in 1907 were the *Brigades Mobiles de Police Judiciaire* created to act as regional crime squads (Stead 1983, pp. 74–76; Emsley 2006, p. 64). It should also be remembered that in France, as in most other European jurisdictions, judges directed criminal investigations.

6. Jens Jäger (2001) claims that police officials did not care about photography until the 1860s or 1870s (p. 28).

7. For the history of forensic medicine in Western society, see Watson (2011); for the history of forensic science and criminal investigation, see Ramsland (2008). For the systematic use of medical knowledge in criminal investigations during the eighteenth century, see Porret (2008), and for English forensic medicine to 1878, see Forbes (1985). For a historical perspective of forensic science in terms of ideologies and institutions, see Hamlin (2013).

8. For a historiographical appreciation of Gross's contribution to forensic science in general, and crime scene investigation in particular, see Burney and Pemberton (2013) and Ramsland (2008, pp. 93–102). For a retrospective evaluation of Gross's work, see Vyleta (2006). For an overview of the development of criminalistics, see Becker (2005).

9. For Bertillon's life and work, see Rhodes (1956) and Piazza (2011).

10. For the slow shift from anthropometry to dactyloscopy (fingerprint identification) among American law enforcement agencies, see Cole (2001, pp. 140–67).

11. For the training of detectives in the different European police forces on the eve of the First World War, see Fosdick (1969, pp. 298–304).

12. For an appreciation of Vollmer's impact on American policing, see Carte and Carte (1975) and Deakin (1988). For controversies surrounding Vollmer, see Monkkonen (1996, p. 217).

13. For detailed accounts of the state of forensic science in England in the interwar period and the background to the formation of these laboratories, see Ambage and Clark (1994), and Laybourn and Taylor (2011).

BIBLIOGRAPHY

Ambage, Norman, & Michael Clark. 1994. "Unbuilt Bloomsbury: Medico-Legal Institutes and Forensic Science Laboratories in England Between the Wars." In *Legal Medicine in History*, ed. Michael Clark & Catherine Crawford, 293–313. Cambridge: Cambridge University Press.

Beattie, J. M. 1986. *Crime and the Courts in England, 1660–1800*. Princeton, NJ: Princeton University Press.

Beattie, J. M. 2006. "Early Detection: The Bow Street Runners in Late Eighteenth-Century London." In *Police Detectives in History, 1750–1950*, ed. Clive Emsley & Haia Shpayer-Makov, 15–32. Aldershot, UK: Ashgate.

Beattie, J. M. 2012. *The First Detectives: The Bow Street Runners and the Policing of London, 1750–1840*. Oxford: Oxford University Press.

Beavan, Colin. 2001. *Fingerprints*. New York: Hyperion.

Becker, Peter. 2005. *Dem Täter auf der Spur. Eine Geschichte der Kriminalistik*. Darmstadt, Germany: Primus Verlag.

Becker, Peter, & Richard F. Wetzell, eds. 2009. *Criminals and Their Scientists: The History of Criminology in International Perspective*. Cambridge: Cambridge University Press.

Bell, Amy Helen. 2014. *Murder Capital: Suspicious Deaths in London, 1933–53*. Manchester, UK: Manchester University Press.

Bell, Suzanne. 2008. *Crime and Circumstance*. Westport, CT: Praeger.

Berlière, Jean-Marc. 1991. "The Professionalisation of the Police under the Third Republic in France, 1875–1914." In *Policing Western Europe: Politics, Professionalism, and Public Order, 1850–1940*, ed. Clive Emsley & Barbara Weinberger, 36–73. New York: Greenwood Press.

Berlière, Jean-Marc, & René Levy. 2013. *Histoire des Polices en France*. Paris: Nouveau Monde.

Brodeur, Jean-Paul. 2010. *The Policing Web*. Oxford: Oxford University Press.

Brown, Howard G. 2006. "Tips, Traps and Tropes: Catching Thieves in Post-Revolutionary Paris." In *Police Detectives in History, 1750–1950*, ed. Clive Emsley & Haia Shpayer-Makov, 33–60. Aldershot, UK: Ashgate.

Burney, Ian, & Neil Pemberton. 2013. "Making Space for Criminalistics: Hans Gross and Fin-de-Siècle CSI." *Studies in History and Philosophy of Biological and Biomedical Sciences* 44:16–25.

Cole, Simon A. 2001. *Suspect Identities: A History of Fingerprinting and Criminal Identification*. Cambridge: Harvard University Press.

Cox, David J. 2010. *A Certain Share of Low Cunning: A History of the Bow Street Runners, 1792–1839*. Cullompton, UK: Willan.

Davis, Jennifer. 1991. "Urban Policing and Its Objects: Comparative Themes in England and France in the Second Half of the Nineteenth Century." In *Policing Western Europe: Politics, Professionalism, and Public Order, 1850–1940*, ed. Clive Emsley & Barbara Weinberger, 1–17. New York: Greenwood Press.

Deakin, Thomas J. 1988. *Police Professionalism: The Renaissance of American Law Enforcement*. Springfield, IL: Charles C. Thomas.

Emsley, Clive. 1984. *Policing and Its Context: 1750–1870*. New York: Schocken Books.

Emsley, Clive. 2006. "From Ex-Con to Expert: The Police Detective in Nineteenth-Century France." In *Police Detectives in History, 1750–1950*, ed. Clive Emsley & Haia Shpayer-Makov, 61–77. Aldershot, UK: Ashgate.

Emsley, Clive. 2007. *Crime, Police, and Penal Policy: European Experiences, 1750–1940*. Oxford: Oxford University Press.

Emsley, Clive, & Haia Shpayer-Makov, eds. 2006. *Police Detectives in History, 1750–1950*. Aldershot, UK: Ashgate.

Emsley, Clive, & Barbara Weinberger, eds. 1991. *Policing Western Europe: Politics, Professionalism, and Public Order, 1850–1940*. New York: Greenwood Press.

Forbes, Thomas Rogers. 1985. *Surgeons at the Bailey: English Forensic Medicine to 1878*. New Haven, CT: Yale University Press.

Fosdick, Raymond B. 1915. "The Modus Operandi System in the Detection of Criminals." *Journal of the American Institute of Criminal Law and Criminology* 6 (November): 560–70.

Fosdick, Raymond B. 1920. *American Police Systems*. New York: Century Co.

Fosdick, Raymond B. 1969 [1915]. *European Police Systems*. Montclair, NJ: Patterson Smith.

Friedman, Lawrence M. 1993. *Crime and Punishment in American History*. New York: Basic Books.

Golan, Tal. 2004. *Laws of Men and Laws of Nature: The History of Scientific Expert Testimony in England and America*. Cambridge, MA: Harvard University Press.

Hamlin, Christopher. 2013. "Forensic Cultures in Historical Perspective: Technologies of Witness Testimony, Judgment (and Justice?)." *Studies in History and Philosophy of Biological and Biomedical Sciences* 44:4–15.

Hebenton, Bill, & Terry Thomas. 1993. *Criminal Records*. Aldershot, UK: Avebury.

Higgs, Edward. 2011. *Identifying the English*. London: Continuum.

Jäger, Jens. 2001. "Photography: A Means of Surveillance? Judicial Photography, 1850 to 1900." *Crime, History and Societies* 5:27–52.

Jeffreys-Jones, Rhodri. 2008. *The FBI: A History*. New Haven, CT: Yale University Press.

Johnson, David R. 1979. *Policing the Urban Underworld*. Philadelphia: Temple University Press.

Kalifa, Dominique, & Margaret Jean Flynn. 2005. "Criminal Investigators at the Fin-de-Siècle." *Yale French Studies* 108:36–47.

Kaluszynski, Martine. 2001. "Republican Identity: Bertillonage as Government Technique." In *Documenting Individual Identity: The Development of State Practices in the Modern World*, ed. Jane Caplan & John C. Torpey, 123–38. Princeton, NJ: Princeton University Press.

Kuykendall, Jack. 1986. "The Municipal Police Detective: An Historical Analysis." *Criminology* 24 (1): 175–201.

Lane, Roger. 1967. *Policing the City: Boston, 1822–1885*. Cambridge: Harvard University Press.

Laybourn, Keith, & David Taylor. 2011. *Policing in England and Wales, 1918–30: The Fed, Flying Squads and Forensics*. London: Palgrave Macmillan.

Levy, René. 1993. "Police and the Judiciary in France Since the Nineteenth Century." *British Journal of Criminology* 23 (Spring): 167–86.

Martin, Benjamin F. 1990. *Crime and Criminal Justice under the Third Republic*. Baton Rouge: Louisiana State University Press.

Marx, Gary T. 1988. *Undercover: Police Surveillance in America*. Berkeley: University of California Press.

Miller, Wilbur, R. 1977. *Cops and Bobbies: Police Authority in New York and London, 1830–1870*. Chicago: University of Chicago Press.

Monkkonen, Eric H. 1981. *Police in Urban America, 1860–1920*. Cambridge: Cambridge University Press.

Monkkonen, Eric H. 1996. "The Urban Police in the United State." In *Crime History and Histories of Crime*, ed. Clive Emsley & Louis A. Knafla, 201–28. Westport, CT: Greenwood Press.

Morn, Frank. 1982. *"The Eye that Never Sleeps": A History of the Pinkerton National Detective Agency*. Bloomington: Indiana University Press.

Morris, R. M. 2006. "'Crime Does Not Pay': Thinking Again about Detectives in the First Century of the Metropolitan Police." In *Police Detectives in History, 1750–1950*, ed. Clive Emsley & Haia Shpayer-Makov, 79–102. Aldershot, UK: Ashgate.

Morris, Bob. 2007. "History of Criminal Investigation." In *Handbook of Criminal Investigation*, ed. Tim Newburn, Tom Williamson, & Alan Wright, 15–40. Cullompton, UK: Willan.

Morton, James. 2004. *The First Detective*. London: Abury Press.

Nickell, Joe, & John F. Fischer. 2013. *Crime Science: Methods of Forensic Detection*. Lexington: University Press of Kentucky.

Odell, Robin. 2013. *Medical Detectives: The Lives and Cases of Britain's Forensic Five*. Stroud, UK: History Press.

Petrow, Stefan. 1993. "The Rise of the Detective in London, 1869–1914." *Criminal Justice History* 14:91–108.

Petrow, Stefan. 1994. *Policing Morals: The Metropolitan Police and the Home Office, 1870–1914.* Oxford: Clarendon.

Piazza, Pierre, ed. 2011. *Aux origines de la police scientifique: Alphonse Bertillon, précurseur de la science du crime.* Paris: Karthala.

Porret, Michel. 2008. *Sur la scène du crime. Pratique pénale, enquête et expertise judiciaires à Genève (XVIIIe–XIXe siècles).* Montréal: PUM.

Porter, Bernard. 1987. *The Origins of the Vigilant State.* London: Weidenfeld & Nicolson.

Ramsland, Katherine. 2007. *Beating the Devil's Game: A History of Forensic Science and Criminal Investigation.* New York: Berkley Books.

Rhodes, Henry T. F. 2013 [1956]. *Alphonse Bertillon, Father of Scientific Detection.* New York: Abelard-Schuman.

Richardson, James F. 1970. *The New York Police: Colonial Times to 1901.* New York: Oxford University Press.

Roach, Lawrence Thornton. 2004. "The Origins and Impact of the Function of Crime Investigation and Detection in the British Police Service." Ph.D. diss., Loughborough University.

Shpayer-Makov, Haia. 2011. *The Ascent of the Detective: Police Sleuths in Victorian and Edwardian England.* Oxford: Oxford University Press.

Shpayer-Makov, Haia, ed. 2014. *The Making of the Modern Police, 1780–1914,* Vol. 6, *The Development of Detective Policing.* London: Pickering & Chatto.

Stanford, Terry. 2009. "Who Are You? We Have Ways of Finding Out!: Tracing the Police Development of Offender Identification Techniques in the Late Nineteenth Century." *Crimes and Misdemeanours* 3:54–81.

Starr, Douglas. 2010. *The Killer of Little Shepherds: A True Story of the Birth of Forensic Science.* New York: Alfred A. Knopf.

Stead, Philip John. 1953. *Vidocq: A Biography.* London: Staples Press.

Stead, Philip John. 1983. *The Police of France.* New York: Macmillan.

Thorwald, Jürgen. 1965. *The Century of the Detective.* New York: Harcourt, Brace & World.

Vyleta, Daniel Mark. 2006. "Was Early Twentieth-Century Criminology a Science of the 'Other'? A Re-Evaluation of Austro-German Criminological Debates." *Cultural and Social History* 3:406–23.

Ward, Jennifer. 1993. "Origins and Development of Forensic Medicine and Forensic Science in England, 1823–1946." Ph.D. diss., Open University.

Ward, Jenny. 1998. *Crimebusting: Breakthroughs in Forensic Science.* London: Blandford.

Watson, Katherine D. 2004. *Poisoned Lives.* London: Hambledon.

Watson, Katherine D. 2011. *Forensic Medicine in Western Society: A History.* London: Routledge.

Williams, Alan. 1979. *The Police of Paris, 1718–1789.* Baton Rouge: Louisiana State University Press.

Williams, Robin. 2008. "Policing and Forensic Science." In *Handbook of Policing,* ed. Tim Newburn, 760–93. Cullompton, UK: Willan Publishing.

....

CHAPTER 25

POLICE–PUBLIC RELATIONS

Interpretations of Policing and Democratic Governance

....

ANJA JOHANSEN

INTRODUCTION

....

IN 1954 the Los Angeles police captain G. Douglas Gourley declared: "Under our Anglo-Saxon form of policing, in high contrast with totalitarian forms, the police and the public are in a sense identical" (Gourley 1954, p. 135). Gourley would undoubtedly have been dismayed had he known that both the Nazi regime and later the Communist German Democratic Republic would make similar rhetorical identifications between the police and the public as a basis for police legitimization (Blood 2003, p. 100; Dunnage & Rossol 2015, p. 98; Lindenberger 2003, p. 16).

The legitimization of policing has rested on a multiplicity of sources: historically, it came from above through the king, the republic, the parliament, or the law. Since the late eighteenth century, references to "the people," "the public," and "the taxpayers" have become increasingly central to the legitimization of policing in Anglo-American political cultures in which the authority of law enforcement agencies were easily vulnerable to challenge (Tomlins 2006, p. 255). Throughout the nineteenth and twentieth centuries claims that policing was "for the people" and "public-oriented"—also linked to concepts of "democratic policing"—have strongly influenced official rhetoric as well as scholarly interpretations of policing in general, and police–public relations in particular. In popular lore, this identification is inscribed in the so-called Peelite principles. In Britain and the United States, as well as in Canada, Australia, and New Zealand, these principles have developed into a set of interrelated ideas that could be described as the Anglo-American police principles: civil rather than military; serving the public rather than the central government; locally organized and controlled, and therefore responsive to local concerns; polite and respectful to all citizens rather than bossy and coercive; accountable to local communities and to the law rather than arbitrary. These principles are considered by many police scholars to be the precondition for "democratic policing" and to provide the optimal basis for popular trust and legitimacy (Monkkonen 1981, pp. 23–24). Police strategies such as "community policing" are based on a similar assumption that cooperation with local communities makes policing more effective (for critical assessments, see Brogden 2008, p. 168; Manning 2010, p. 9).

These principles form the conceptual framework that links together all other factors that historians and social scientists have identified as significant for assessing the nature of police–public relations. Such a framework focuses on the acceptability and credibility of the official narrative among the population or within different groups, including popular perceptions of the policeman as a stereotype; levels of cooperation and engagement between police and communities; policing practices and attitudes toward the population as a whole, as well as toward specific groups; police use of force and lethal weapons, as well as the extent and nature of military involvement in policing; and the strength and effectiveness of institutionalized accountability mechanisms.

Throughout the nineteenth century, Anglo-American scholarship and political discourse tended to refer to continental European policing as a "negative other," an identification broadly based on French and German policing, which was frequently described by British and American observers as centrally organized, in service of and controlled by strong centralized states, politicized and nonaccountable to the public, and armed and militarized. This dichotomy has been perpetuated by Anglo-American police and government authorities as well as by continental European police critics who have used this dichotomy as a framework for criticizing policing arrangements in their own countries (Johansen 2013).

The opposition between the "Anglo-American police principles" and "continental European policing" also forms the basis of interpretations of police by historians and sociologists. These categories are used as abstract benchmarks for critical analysis of police–public relations in Britain and the United States. On the one hand, most police scholars recognize that policing in Britain and the United States often fails to meet the standards and commitments of the official rhetoric, particularly when political and economic interests are at stake or when confronted with incompatible demands from different sections of the population (Bittner 1970, pp. 6–14; Brodeur 2010, chs. 2, 4). On the other hand, there is an assumption—often implicit—that police–public relations in Britain and America remain more "democratic" and public-oriented than their counterparts in continental Europe. Thus, according to Manning (2010), the claim that Anglo-American police principles constitute the preconditions for "democratic policing" is rarely challenged or explored in English-language scholarship (p. vii).

Sophisticated versions of this dichotomy shape many police models and typologies, which tend to focus on organizational features and aim to provide a framework for comparisons, rather than promoting normative claims about levels of "democratic" and "public-friendly" policing (Bayley 1985; Bayley 2005; Mawby 1999; Mawby 2008; Emsley 1999a; Levy 2014). Nevertheless, there is also broad recognition, particularly among comparativists, that the dichotomy between Anglo-American and continental

European systems of policing is highly questionable, and even counterproductive (Monjardet 1996, pp. 283–89; Mawby 1999, p. 51; Brodeur 2010; Denis & Denys 2012, p. 11). Lévy suggests that comparison between continental police systems would be far more fruitful, rather than insisting on their dissimilarities with Anglo-American organizational structures (Lévy 2014, p. 353).

Despite the centrality of police–public relations to the legitimization of policing, few scholars have reflected on how the concept of "the public" itself has influenced modern policing in ideological and organizational terms, and shaped the various attempts to develop a "theory of policing" (Bittner 1970, pp. 114–18; Klockars 1985; Bayley 1985; Brodeur 2010). Instead, many works contain excellent empirical studies of police–public relations in practice (Taylor 2002; Klein 2010; Berlière & Lévy 2011; Deluermoz 2012) and police legitimacy (Tankeby 2014; Bradford, Jackson & Hough 2014).

This essay analyzes the historical development of "the public" and "democratic policing" as key legitimizing concepts in official rhetoric about policing, and the implications of this process for interpretations of police–public relations in Britain, the United States, France, and Germany. It first looks at the historical construction of police legitimacy on the conceptual basis of "the people," and then at the development of the idea of British and U.S. policing as "democratic policing." This discussion is followed by an analysis of the interpretation of French and German police–public relations as the "negative other." The final sections reassess three aspects of police–public relations that are central to Anglo-American police principles: local police organization, engagement with local communities, and military features in civilian policing.

I. Policing by the People, of the People, as a Legitimizing Principle

Until the nineteenth century, community self-policing was the norm in small towns and villages across Europe. Yet it was with the American and French revolutions that the concept of "the people" acquired ideological significance in relation to policing, as well as to the wider criminal justice system and governance in general. Historians have identified three distinct approaches to policing that characterized eighteenth- and nineteenth-century law enforcement: the German bureaucratic *Polizeywissenschaft* approach; the French militarily organized *Maréchausée*, later the *gendarmerie*; and the British civilian model (Dubber 2006, pp. 107–39; Dubber 2005; Raeff 1983). Of these, only the British approach conceptualized the population as a key principle in legitimizing policing. A fourth approach to policing emerged in the late eighteenth century, namely, the populist–revolutionary idea of policing through self-regulating militias of volunteers claiming to embody the will and interests of "the people." The historical literature has only paid limited attention to this form of policing, partly because it is seen as antimodern due to its nonprofessional character, and partly because it left little impact on modern policing. However, it is the most radical form of the idea of policing through the people (Carrot 2005, pp. 246–47; Pröve 2011, pp. 61–80).

In the United States, self-policing through citizen volunteers has strong roots in the revolutionary understanding of liberty and democracy (Tocqueville 1981 [1836], p. 136; Richardson 1970, pp. 13, 37; Lane 1977, p. 7; see also Miller 2013). Accordingly, the establishment of the first professional police forces in Boston in 1837 and New York in 1845 generated considerable opposition as being incompatible with American democratic culture. Men who acted as uniformed police were likened to "servants" and derided for accepting a position that was seen as undignified for free-born American citizens (Monkkonen 1981, pp. 45–46).

The experience of self-established militias in revolutionary France claiming to enforce the law according to their own discretion, outside government control and discipline, became inextricably linked to the excesses of the Terror. Thus, throughout the nineteenth century strong aversion to policing through citizens' militias remained the politically conservative position in France and across Europe. In the German states, the demand for citizens' militias (*Bürgerwehren*) for community self-policing emerged toward the end of the Napoleonic invasion in opposition to the reestablishment under Metternich of monarchical control through extensive use of state police. The call for *Bürgerwehren* remained a recurrent demand among liberal opponents to monarchical rule and this request reemerged in full force during the 1848 revolutions. Yet the rise of socialism, with its ideological disregard for private property, raised concerns among middle-class liberals, who quickly abandoned the idea of policing through "the people." Among radicals and revolutionaries, however, the dream of policing through popular volunteer forces lingered and reemerged forcefully with the Paris Commune of 1871, and again with the communist revolts across Europe after the First World War (Leßmann-Faust 2012 [1987]; Pröve 2011).

The great novelty of the London police model established by Robert Peel in 1829 was to combine legitimization through "the public" (Tayler 1997, p. 77) with a strict system of organizational discipline controlled by the Home Office or by local elites in towns and boroughs. In the early days of the Metropolitan Police, the close identification between police and the people did not exist (Monkkonen 1981, p. 6). References to "the public" mainly implied the propertied ratepayers whose person and property were in need of protection, and whose political acceptance was needed for the future funding of police forces. During the 1850s, with the increasing acceptance of professional police in Britain and a broadening of the concept of the police's commitment to serve the entire population, the notion of "the public" came to mean respectable, law-abiding individuals with fixed abode and regular employment. Largely excluded from concepts of "the public" were individuals who were categorized as not law-abiding and belonging to the "dangerous classes" as a result of previous arrests and convictions. Similarly excluded from "the public" were groups that the police treated as comprising potential lawbreakers and sought to control rather than protect. These included the jobless—whether homeless or itinerant—the destitute, and members of certain ethnic minorities.

As the London Metropolitan Police model was adopted in Boston and New York in the formation of the first professional police forces in the United States, the Peelite approach to "the public" was merged into a political culture that saw itself as far more democratically advanced than Britain. That policing should be oriented toward "the public" was considered self-evident, and, as Klockars rightly observes, "American police have been every bit as much of a people's police as the English" (1985, p. 42). With the ambition of making policing even more public oriented than in Britain, the American rhetoric revolved around vague and ever-changing notions of community self-policing (Brogden 2008, p. 168), as well as public service and police accountability to the public.

In the German states, the bureaucratic and state-oriented *Polizeiwissenschaft* tradition continued to underpin police ideology throughout the nineteenth century (Lüdtke 1982; Funk 1986). After 1848, when new police forces were established, allegedly based on the London Metropolitan model, this imported framework was superimposed on traditional principles. The famous police articles of the Prussian *Allgemeine Landrecht* of 1794, which defined Prussian policing until 1918, described the population as a passive entity to be protected. Thus, policing in Germany continued to be legitimized on the basis of state authority, with no reference to the population as a legitimizing entity. Nor did the population benefit from any recognition of accountability or control over the police. The power to define the interests of the population according to the general well-being (*Gemeinwohl*) remained the prerogative of government, civil servants, and provincial administrators. Thus, the idea of the population as a legitimizing concept only gradually developed toward the end of the nineteenth century, awkwardly coexisting with older notions of police–public relations rooted in the *Polizeiwissenschaft* tradition.

In France, the republican and Bonapartist traditions identified the state with "the people" and thereby eliminated the opposition between government and the public that was central to the Anglo-American policing principles. In this view, the state *was* "the public." No legal texts of the nineteenth century relating to the police or *gendarmerie* make any reference to the population as legitimizing policing activities. The function of police and *gendarmerie* was described exclusively as the maintenance of public order and law enforcement. This absence of any formal recognition of the population may explain why the *gendarmerie* model was so easily applied to territories under French occupation, and later to colonies.

II. From Peel's Public-Oriented Approach to "Democratic Policing"

Peel's public-oriented legitimization of policing grew out of the political necessity of getting support from reluctant Members of Parliament whose support was continuously needed for the annual renewal of the budget for the London Metropolitan Police. In the face of considerable opposition to his program of police reform and concerns about civil liberties, Peel also drew heavily on the bad reputation of French policing that stemmed from the prerevolutionary *Maréchaussée*, Napoleon's *gendarmerie*, and Fouché's secret police. In contrast to the negative image of French police as military, violent, politicized, and corrupt, Peel presented a positive counterimage of his force as a nonmilitary, apolitical public service, enforcing the law with proportionate levels of force. The development of a reassuring narrative of police–public relations was central to Peel's approach to policing, even if practice always differed considerably from the rhetoric. According to the official rhetoric, Peel committed the force to strict respect of the rights and liberties of the public, and promised that any notification from the public of policemen failing in their duty or breaching discipline would be investigated by the chief commissioner. This made the London Metropolitan Police accountable to "the public" as well as to the law, with institutionalized procedures to challenge police decisions and behavior. Peel thereby struck a balance between three conflicting demands that tend to appear in debates on police forces: effective protection of persons and property (Silver 1967), concerns about costs, and worries about infringements on the civil liberties of individuals (Campion 2005).

As in Britain, the notion of public-oriented policing in the United States faced numerous dilemmas and was similarly wrought with inconsistencies. American police forces were, in the name of democratic principles, subject to the authority of elected politicians or magistrates. This created high levels of democratic accountability to the majority but was incompatible with any claim to political neutrality and unbiased law enforcement. U.S. police were conspicuously politicized and partisan, in contrast to the British model, which was a bureaucratic organization that claimed to be politically neutral. Accordingly, popular attitudes toward many American police forces has always been characterized by low levels of trust among minority groups, with suspicions of police being biased, corrupt, and violent (Bittner 1970, pp. 10–12; Klockars 1985, p. 42).

With time, Peel's principles came to acquire a "mythical quality" (Emsley 2014, p. 11), although the list of Peelite principles only obtained their present form in the 1950s (Reith 1952, p. 154; Lenz & Chaires 2007, pp. 69–70). The glorification of British policing as "the world's best police" reached its highpoint with the Whig interpretations that saw the British model as the emblem of democratic policing (Reith 1938; Reith 1943; Radzinowicz & Hood 1948–1968; Critchley 1967; Ascoli 1979). Coexisting with a popular image of the benign British bobby, this largely uncritically positive vision described police–public relations as evidence of the superior ethical, people-oriented, gentle, lawbound, and fair nature of the British political regime.

At the same time, the broader notion of Anglo-American policing principles became tied up with the idea of "democratic policing" and assumptions about political democratization having benign effects on the nature of policing. Yet, as Brogden observes, the projection of police as the expression of the collective will of local communities for legitimation purposes is ahistorical and often incompatible with the reality of police relations with many groups and communities in both Britain and the United States (2008, p. 168; see also Waddington 1999, pp. 23–24).

Moreover, it is not at all clear what "democratic policing" might imply. As Brodeur rightly observes, there is a tendency among twentieth-century scholars to define "democratic policing" as the way police operate in democratic societies, assuming that just because the regime is democratic, policing is democratic as well. He points to a strong and continuous tendency among British and American police scholars to see democratic policing as exemplified in Britain, the United States, and other polities growing out of a specifically English institutional tradition, such as Canada, Australia, and New Zealand (2010, pp. 135–36; see also Bayley 2005; Manning 2010, pp. 3–37).

The narrative of benign policing has been so successful in Britain because it has appeared credible to large sections of the public—notably the middle classes, who rarely had any direct dealings with the police. Disenchantment with the British police among the middle classes first became noticeable during the 1960s, with the repeated clashes between police and middle-class students. Since the 1970s, sociologists and historians have critically reevaluated the power relations around police–public relations and have dismantled many myths surrounding the British police. Social historians—often coming from a critical left-wing position—have emphasized the function of the police as an instrument of social control (Storch 1975; Storch 1976; Thompson 1981; Bailey 1981; Gatrell 1990), while detailed studies on policing have highlighted the ambiguous, conflictual, and often-violent relationship between police and the working-class population (Emsley 1983; Emsley 1996; Emsley 2005; Taylor 1997; Taylor 2002, ch. 5).

While historical studies all point to considerable discrepancies between the rhetoric and the practice of British and American policing, these scholarly revisions have had little impact on the underlying presumptions of British and American policing being—despite its imperfections—comparatively more public oriented and democratic than policing in France or Germany.

III. "Continental Policing": The Negative Other of Police–Public Relations

Throughout the nineteenth and twentieth centuries, French and particularly German critics and police scholars tended to accept the claims about the moral superiority of British and American policing. Despite the dismantling of the uncritical hailing of British police as "the best police in the world," British policing during these centuries appeared to many foreign observers as more responsive to the public and less characterized by indiscriminate violence than their counterparts in continental Europe. British police authorities were also considerably more successful than French and German authorities in forging and maintaining popular acceptance of, cooperation with, and trust in the police (Bradford & Jackson 2011). The poor reputation of French and German policing was exacerbated by repeated attempts by police and government authorities in those countries to deny and cover up clear evidence of poor professional standards and violent practices (Johansen 2011). In addition, French and German authorities also sought to appear supremely in control—even when they were struggling to contain situations—which made them doubly responsible in the eyes of the public for police failings. This appeared to confirm liberal criticism of "police states" with no respect for or engagement with the public. Furthermore, the widespread accommodation and collaboration of the German and French police under Nazi rule or occupation only strengthened this narrative.

Most French and German scholarship and historical interpretations of policing are part of Franco-French or Germano-German debates, which are intrinsically linked to wider debates about the nature of successive political regimes. When comparisons are made with policing in Britain and America, these tend to serve the purpose of critically highlighting the shortcomings of French or German policing. Nevertheless, scholars have interpreted the French and German police very differently in comparison with their Anglo-American counterparts. French scholars, in contrast to their British and American colleagues, tend to be relaxed about the strong centralized state, seeing the state as neither good nor bad in itself. While accepting the French Republic as essentially benign—even if it often fails to live up to its ideals—French police scholars often focus on how policing was influenced by successive political regimes and repeated regime change during the nineteenth and twentieth centuries. Also in contrast to British and American scholars, French police historians do not see the strong centralized state as a hindrance to democratic, accountable, citizen-oriented policing. Nor do they see the military features of the *gendarmerie* as incompatible with democratic policing (Luc 2002; Luc 2010; Berlière & Lévy 2011). While French scholars accept that nineteenth-century French police–public relations suffered from politicization, corruption, and systemic violent practices, much recent scholarship has fundamentally revised the "black legend" of French policing. Instead, a narrative has developed of difficult but gradual modernization, professionalization, and republicanization (Berlière 1996; Berlière & Lévy 2011; Anderson 2011; Deluermoz 2012; Lopez 2014).

German historians and police scholars have been far more willing to adopt the perspective of German policing as the negative opposite of the Anglo-American police principles. In the nineteenth century, the public-oriented principles behind the policing of London became an attractive brand in German states and across the European continent, with police reformers and liberal and left-leaning critics pointing to Britain as a superior model of policing, both in terms of effectiveness and in its relationship with the public (Emsley 2012). This was contrasted with the heavy-handed and militarized approach to policing that characterized most late absolutist or semi-democratic political regimes of nineteenth-century Europe. Yet, as liberal and left-wing critics often implied a wider critique of their local political regime and existing power structures governing the relationship between state and citizens, the promotion of the London Metropolitan Police model in European countries cannot be detached from wider debates about police reform and constitutional struggles (Johansen 2013).

In both Germany and France there were also police reformers working for regimes with limited democratic credentials who saw the London Metropolitan model as the emblem of modernity and efficiency in law enforcement. Making the police more acceptable and legitimate to the public—or at least the respectable sections of the public—while ensuring that the control of criticism and discipline remained firmly in the hands of police and government authorities became a goal for their police reforms (Berlière 1993a; Deluermoz 2012, pp. 318–19; Müller 2005; Johansen 2013). Accordingly, very dissimilar regimes from across Europe, some with predominantly predemocratic conceptions of the relationships between the state and the population, claimed to adopt elements of the London Metropolitan model. Yet, within these hybrids, the public-oriented aspects of the London model tended to be limited or altogether absent. In all their variety, most nineteenth-century European police forces that claimed inspiration from the London Metropolitan model do not easily fit into the dichotomy between an "Anglo-American" and a "continental European" model.

Interpretations of police legitimacy and police–public relations have been further influenced by the sympathy or antipathy among scholars toward individual political regimes. This is particularly relevant for the analyses of police malpractice in Britain and America compared with interpretations of the failings of French and German policing. The Anglo-American literature rarely links critical analysis of policing to attacks on the ideological and institutional foundations of the political regime. British and American scholars tend to explain violent and corrupt policing practices in terms of structural dysfunctions and as unfortunate consequences of the core functions of policing, inherent dilemmas of police–public relations, and police subculture. Similarly, the scholars who dismantled the positive myth of the British police did not challenge the ideological foundations of the British political system, and interpretations of American policing rarely see bad policing as negatively reflecting the fundamental ideology of the constitutional principles of the American republic.

In contrast, historians of policing under autocratic rule or dictatorship tend to judge police failings very severely and to link dysfunctions in the relationship of the public and the police to the nature of the regime. This is particularly noticeable in the interpretations of police–public relations in France and Germany, which both experienced several regime changes and periods of autocratic rule and dictatorship during the nineteenth and twentieth centuries. Modernization theories—combined with the idea of the Anglo-American police principles as a precondition for democratic policing—led many police scholars and political historians to interpret the failings of the police under the French Second Empire, the German *Kaiserreich*, or even the Nazi regime or the government of communist East Germany as a consequence of the undemocratic or semi-democratic nature of these political regimes. In German scholarship, the negative aspects of police–public relations are often understood in the broader context of specifically German power structures, and the functioning of authority, that operated both at the formal institutional level and informally in everyday policing (Lüdkte 1982; Funk 1986; Jessen 1991; Lindenberger 1995; Lindenberger 2003; see also contributions to Lüdtke, Reinke, & Sturm 2011).

During the 1960s to 1980s German interpretations saw most negative aspects of police–public relations in the German Federal Republic as inextricably linked to deep-seated power structures that are often interpreted as legacies from previous regimes, notably the Nazi dictatorship. There was little interest in the inner dynamics of police organizations and the discrepancy between the legal institutional description of policing on the one hand and the actual functioning of police–public relations in the streets on the other hand. Although the previously influential *Sonderweg* interpretation of the German path to modernity has largely been abandoned, the idea still prevails of a specifically German form of exercise of power (*Herrschaft*) that shaped German policing across successive regimes throughout the nineteenth and twentieth centuries (Lindenberger 1995; Lindenberger 2003; see also contributions to Fürmetz, Reinke, & Weinhauer 2001; and to Lüdtke, Reinke, & Sturm 2011). Close correlations are drawn between the confrontational nature of police–public relations in Germany and the underdemocratic or undemocratic nature of past political regimes. These interpretations rest on the principles set out by Liang—inspired by the Anglo-American police principles—of how democratization ought to affect the ways in which police relate to the population (Liang 1992, p. 4). German police scholars have tended to emphasize that German policing only developed a public orientation during the Weimar Republic, which was then halted by the Nazi regime and the establishment of communist East Germany. The implicit assumption is that police–public relations in Britain and the United States already met these standards during the nineteenth and twentieth centuries. As a result, German police scholars have often developed a narrative in which German police–public relations are seen as needing to catch up with the Anglo-American police principles. As comparative analyses are scarce, the features that stem from problems intrinsic to policing are often not properly distinguished from features that have specifically characterized German policing (Knöbl 1998; Deluermoz 2013; Johansen 2011; Johansen 2013).

Conversely, sympathy for the French republican regimes since 1870 and the Weimar Republic has shaped interpretations in a different direction. French and German police scholars have been willing to interpret some failings in policing standards of the French republican regime, the Weimar Republic, and the post-1949 West German Republic as systemic problems that are intrinsic to the functioning of policing, police subculture, and inherent dilemmas of police–public relations. In the case of the French Third Republic, failings in police–public relations have been explained by the inability or unwillingness of successive governments to properly control and discipline police personnel. This perspective also characterizes the current challenge to the "black legend" of French policing, emphasizing features of modernity and the gradual development toward republican values in French policing since the turn of the twentieth century (Berlière 1996; Berlière & Lévy 2011; Anderson 2011; Deluermoz 2012; Lopez 2014). Seen in comparative perspective, it appears that many of the failings in the relationship between police and public—past and present—are not specific to nondemocratic governance, but have bedeviled policing in Britain and the United States as much as policing in France and Germany under successive regimes with various democratic credentials.

IV. Police–Public Relations
in Practice: Political and Social Elite

One of the key elements of the Anglo-American police principles is the claim that locally organized police forces are more accountable to the public than centrally organized police forces under government control. Yet, as many police scholars and theorists have observed, policing is never neutral, whether controlled by the state or by local communities. Bittner rightly notes that a fundamental distinction needs to be made between the public that the police serves, whose interests the police defends, and the public that is the object of police control. As interests between groups are often conflicting, defending the interests of one group is inevitably to the detriment and restriction of another group, typically the poor, the marginal, youth, and minorities (Bittner 1970, pp. 9–15; see also Ericson 2005, p. 216; Klockars 1985, p. 42).

Locally organized police give local elites considerable scope to control policing and define priorities in their own interest, with little or no accountability to the rest of the community (Mawby 2008, pp. 19–21). The Anglo-American preference for locally organized police tends to overlook the possibility that police organized at the national level—although remote and difficult to get in contact with—might sometimes constitute a neutral and robust defender of people on the margins against the use of policing in the interests of local elites. Moreover, to people at the bottom of the social hierarchy it makes little difference whether they are controlled—and sometimes physically coerced—by a police force controlled by a central state or by local elites. Yet while British and American historians and police scholars almost never challenge the ideological preference for policing under local control, they are very aware of class and racial dimensions in police–public relations.

From a comparative perspective, the question arises of whether the more public-oriented policing ideology in Britain and the United States exacerbated class bias in policing compared to state-centered systems such as those in France and Germany. Until the First World War it seems that social elites in Britain and the United States were treated more favorably by the police than was the case in France or Germany. Throughout the nineteenth century, police in Britain were very wary of intervening against members of the middle and upper classes. People belonging to "respectable society" often related to the policeman not so much as a public servant than as any employee to be disciplined and dismissed at will (Gamon 1907, p. 21). It was only with the arrival of the motorcar that members of these social groups came into regular contact with the police as offenders (Emsley 1993). In America, policing was no less class biased, with great reticence toward intervening against members of the elite or anyone with powerful connections (Bittner 1970, p. 119; Brodeur 2010, p. 111). However, given that police in American cities were under the control of whoever held political office, local elites' influence on policing also depended on political allegiance.

In French interpretations, class has been central to the analysis of policing since the nineteenth century, although French scholars generally have not regarded the devolution of policing to the local level as a solution to class bias in law enforcement. Moreover, in France, police favoritism was not simply structured along class lines. During the nineteenth century, continuous political turmoil and multiple regime changes meant that members of the middle and upper classes could not be confident that their social status alone would shelter them from undue police interference. Police were the instrument of whoever was in power and controlled the state. Therefore, connections to powerful people in government often mattered as much as social or economic standing in sheltering members of the elite from police interference.

In the German states, police were similarly biased against the lower orders, with clashes between German authorities and workers in general, and the Social Democratic Party in particular, as the most salient example of this tendency (Hall 1977; Lindenberger 1995). Nevertheless, this did not mean that all elite groups were equally sheltered from police interference. In the nineteenth century distinctions need to be made between rising elites and those belonging to old aristocratic families, who could often disregard police because of their social standing and connections. Similarly, before 1918 the police had no authority over members of the Prussian army because military officers were superior in rank to the police. For members of the rising bourgeoisie and newly ennobled elites, the relationship with the police was very different: as in France, social status, public office, or wealth were of little use when confronted with policemen who were very conscious and proud of their status as representatives of the state and enforcers of the law. This led to multiple standoffs between police and citizens with some social capital, with both seeking to assert their superior authority over the other (Johansen 2009, pp. 136–37). In France and Germany, policing tended to be less systematically class biased than in Britain and America, because even respectable members of society could not share the confidence of the British or American middle classes of being largely above police intervention. Nor did elites have extended scope for using the police to defend personal interests, as any municipal decision on policing could be overridden by the state-appointed *Landrat* or *sub-prefect*.

V. Police and the Lower Orders: Integration and Isolation

Another central principle in the British idea of police–public relations is the importance of gaining popular acceptance and cooperation. Historians have therefore paid much attention to patterns of conflict and cooperation with the public, notably among the lower orders of society. Two major features of police–public relations underwent important transformations during the second half of the nineteenth century in all four countries examined here, although with varying chronologies and extent of change.

One was the gradual increase in the acceptance of the police, not only among the middle classes but also among the lower classes in urban areas. The second major change was the decline in levels of violence between police and the public. Although violent encounters between police and the public did not disappear entirely, they seem to have become less prevalent and less serious. While there are many similarities in these transitions between Britain, the United States, France, and Germany, historians have interpreted their causes very differently depending on the extent to which police–public relations adhered to the Anglo-American policing ideals.

From the establishment of modern police in England and the United States, police authorities sought acceptance among the population for their legitimization (Ericson 2005, p. 219). While there is a general consensus among police historians that the British middle classes fully accepted the police forces from the 1860s, major confrontations between police and the working classes still occurred in the 1870s and 1880s (Miller 1977, pp. 105–11; Weinberger 1981, p. 65). The British police only gained broad acceptance among the urban poor starting in the 1890s (Emsley 1996, pp. 80–84; Taylor 2002, p. 111; see also Klein 2010, pp. 54–62, 205–07).

In France and Germany, it was only in the 1890s that police managers began to prioritize the cultivation of good relations with the public, as some realized that low regard for the police—both among the "respectable" classes and among the lower orders of society—would negatively affect both the efficiency and the legitimacy of policing (Müller 2005; Johansen 2013; Berlière 1993; Berlière & Lévy 2011, pp. 493–96). While the popularity of the police appears to have improved among the "respectable classes" between 1890 and 1914, the relationship between police and the lower orders continued to be characterized by mutual suspicion, peaking during the interwar years in major confrontations between police and the working classes (Leβmann-Faust 2012 [1987]; Lindenberger 1995; Berlière 1996).

A. Policing by Consent

Throughout the late nineteenth and twentieth centuries British police authorities claimed to have gained acceptance among the urban poor through "policing by consent" and by being accountable to the public. This assertion was vigorously challenged in the 1960s and 1970s by social historians and police scholars who identified one of the main functions of policing as social control of the lower orders. Their analyses focused on police as the heavy arm of government, intent on keeping the lower orders of society under control by everyday correction of behavior in public (Storch 1975; Storch 1976; Miller 1977, pp. 120–25; Monkkonen 1981, p. 4; Thompson 1981; Gatrell 1990; Taylor 2002, pp. 78–99; Lindenberger 1995; see also contributions in Lüdtke 1993). To striking workers and political opponents of governments, the claim that police acted with their "consent" seemed rather meaningless. As one of the primary duties of police is to protect persons and private property and to maintain public order, police inevitably favor the interests of employers during labor conflicts and support the interest of the state when the public expresses anger and frustration through public demonstrations. Moreover, the claim that police are accountable to the public is largely meaningless for the poor, the powerless, the immigrants, the marginal, minorities, and the ghetto and slum dwellers. To people from these groups, the policeman continued to be a figure of awesome—and essentially limitless—powers, well beyond any concept of service or accountability to "the public" (Gamon 1907, pp. 21–22; Bittner 1970, p. 122; Brodeur 2010, pp. 115, 119).

Although the social control aspect of policing is central to all forces irrespective of central or local structures, research on many different communities across Europe and North America has seriously moderated the Marxist-inspired focus on policing as simply class control and repression. While recognizing that police were far from neutral, apolitical enforcers of the law or practitioners of "policing by consent," historians have presented a highly complex relationship between police and the lower orders of society. They stress the limits of law enforcement and show how policing at the street level was shaped both by cooperation and rejection from the community. In order to survive on the job, individual policemen had to strike a compromise between demands from superiors and enforcement of the law within the limits of what was achievable (Taylor 2002, pp. 78–99; Jessen 1991, pp. 179–85; Evans 1987, pp. 171–74; Deluermoz 2012, pp. 118–35). Working-class people also increasingly appealed to policemen to settle disputes between neighbors and within families (Weinberger 1981; Emsley 1996, pp. 80–84).

B. Matching Police Profiles

One strategy intended to further acceptance and cooperation among the public that has shaped interpretations of police–public relations is the idea of recruiting policemen who reflect the social and ethnic composition of local communities and live within the community they police. Many police scholars and practitioners have accepted this logic, which in the late twentieth century led to recruitment strategies in many Western democracies aimed at employing more women and officers from minority groups to match the demographics of the population. Yet studies on British policemen show that this match was always very imperfect, and, as Emsley notes, there were obvious advantages of using outsiders to police communities (1996, p. 197). Moreover, the observations by Hugh Gammon (1907, pp. 21–25) on the social isolation of London policemen within working-class communities suggests that it was the professional duties of the policeman that set him apart, and that he was often isolated and excluded from social engagements within local communities.

German interpretations of police–public relations have placed much emphasis on the preference until the Weimar Republic for men with rural backgrounds to police cities, while deliberately giving lower priority to applicants with urban working-class backgrounds. Moreover, the attempts to make previous military service a requirement for employment and to isolate policemen from the rest of the population have been widely interpreted by German scholars as one of the main causes behind conflicts between police and local communities. Nevertheless, because of the increasing need for police-men and problems of recruitment, Prussian police forces—both the *Schutzmannschaft* policing larger cities and municipal police forces—included an increasing number of men from working-class areas who had no military background (Jessen 1991, pp. 157–212; Lindenberger 1995, pp. 73–76). While the social profile of German police offi-cers moved closer to that of urban working-class populations, this did not lead to any greater acceptance on either side. Although it is very difficult to compare levels of con-flict or cooperation between police and public, the nature of policing and the duties imposed by police managers on street policing seem to have been the main causes of conflict with the public (Brogden 1991; Weinberger 1981), while the social and profes-sional profile of policemen appears to have been a secondary factor.

C. Declining Levels of Violence

In the course of the long nineteenth century there was also a notable decline in the lev-els of violence between police and the public—despite periods of heightened conflicts, popular protest, and violent clashes. Until the late nineteenth century, engagements between police and the public in poorer urban areas all over Europe and North America were characterized by considerable violence on both sides (Emsley 1983, pp. 150–60; Emsley 1996, pp. 78–84; Steedman 1984, pp. 67–68; Gatrell 1990, pp. 281–87; Taylor 1997, p. 138; Klein 2010, pp. 167–88; Jessen 1991, pp. 179–85; Lindenberger 1995; Berlière 1993b; Deluermoz 2012, pp. 239–42) in what Lindenberger describes as "everyday low-intensity warfare" (*alltägliche Kleinkrig*; 2011, p. 207). Nevertheless, the late nineteenth century also saw a significant decline in the frequency and severity of violent attacks on policemen in rough districts of urban areas.

The overarching explanations provided by historians for the decline in violence between police and the public follow similar lines in all four countries, although they note periods of eruption of violent confrontations stemming from political and social tensions. While labor historians tend to emphasize the repression of workers, recent scholarship also points to considerable violence on both sides, although with a long-term general decline in violence between police and the public that reflects fundamental changes in the relationship between these groups. The decline in vio-lence between police and the public must also be seen in the light of broader cultural shifts away from interpersonal violence, in line with Norbert Elias's theory (1939) of the civilizing process: as violence became more marginalized and unacceptable, workers began to solve conflicts without resorting to it (Muchembled 2008; Pinker 2011; Spierenburg 2013). This movement was furthered by ever-rising popular expec-tations of police acting in a professional and polite manner that was moderate in the use of coercion and respectful of the rights of individuals, irrespective of their social standing. Complaints from both the middle classes and the lower orders about "unacceptable" police behavior show a significant cultural change between 1848 and 1914 (Johansen 2009).

VI. Military Features
in Policing: Interpretations
of Violence and Legitimacy

A final key transformation in police–public relations that scholars have described is the long-term marginalization of the regular army and military symbols in civilian policing. From the establishment of the London Metropolitan Police in 1829, it was a priority to distance policing as much as possible from associations with anything martial, although distinctions between civilian and military often remained highly ambiguous. The idea that British bobbies should be unarmed was a key aspect in the projection of a benign image to the population, even if British police always carried some form of weapon, as well as cutlasses and firearms for dangerous operations (Emsley 1996, pp. 54–59; Emsley 2005). In the United States, by contrast, there was no attempt to disarm police forces, and being armed was easily justified in terms of effective protection of the public against criminals. The arming of French police and *gendarmerie*—with the forms of weapon differing between units—has been similarly uncontroversial, while German scholarship has seen the heavily armed Prussian *Schutzmann* as a prime example of the violent and threatening purpose of policing that turns against the population rather than securing its protection (Reinke 1991).

The process of limiting the involvement of regular military troops in civilian policing was already under way in Britain in the eighteenth century, with a sharp decline after the 1819 Peterloo massacre. In official rhetoric as well as in historical interpretations, the decision to refrain from involving military troops in the policing of civilians became as central to police legitimization as the principles of unarmed police committed to the use of minimal force, serving as yet another indicator of "democratic policing" (Babington 1990). Conversely, military interventions in German states during the nineteenth century have been interpreted as evidence of the political backwardness of the Prussian kingdom and imperial Germany (Wehler 1985, p. 157; Berghahn 1994, pp. 257–58).

However, the close association between military involvement in policing and pre-democratic or dictatorial regimes is far from clear-cut. The reputedly militaristic Prussia used the army less and less after 1848, with rapid decline after 1889. In contrast, the democratic French Third Republic extended the practice considerably after 1889, with extensive use of the army in riot policing continuing until after the First World War (Johansen 2005). Similarly, in the United States, militarized police forces and the involvement of troops in large-scale riot policing continued throughout the twentieth century, regardless of the impeccable democratic credentials of the political regime (Head & Mann 2009).

Historians have been far more willing to excuse the use of troops by the authorities of the United States or the French Republic than historians working on successive German regimes. Accordingly, historians of Germany have seen the three major incidents of domestic military mobilization between 1889 and 1914 as evidence of the repressive cooperation between military and bureaucratic elites against legitimate struggles for democracy and labor disputes. Historians working on the French Third Republic, by contrast, have explained the far more extensive use of troops to maintain public order as caused by undue pressure from great industrialists on police and civil administrators (Jauffret 1983; Carrot 1984; Bruneteaux 1996). Others have justified the frequent use of troops in France during the Third Republic as the necessary defense of the republic in the face of serious challenges from the far left and the far right. Nevertheless, a close comparison of military involvement in the French Third Republic and the German Empire challenges the assumption of a close causal connection between democratization and a decline in military involvement in civilian policing. It also contradicts the assumption that militarism and a strong position of the army in society and politics lead to extensive military influence in civilian policing (Johansen 2005).

Labor historians in the 1970s and 1980s also argued that military involvement in protest policing almost inevitably led to boundless and indiscriminate use of violence. However, recent studies show that strategies for large-scale crowd control and protest policing developed by British, French, and Prussian police authorities in the 1890s aimed at—and to a great extent succeeded in—containing violence and avoiding death or serious injury (Berlière 1993b; Lindenberger 1995; Johansen 2005). This was despite the heavy military involvement in the French case. These findings call into question the assumption that military involvement in protest policing leads to more serious violence than maintenance of order through civilian police.

The close correlation between military features of policing, limited democratization, and high levels of violence has also been seriously questioned by recent research on *gendarmerie* forces in France, Belgium, and the Netherlands (Emsley 1999b; Luc 2002; Luc 2010; Campion 2011; Lignereux 2002; Houte 2010; Lopez 2014). These studies have challenged the sharp distinction in the Anglo-American police ideology between civilian police as more public oriented and integrated in local communities and the more militarily organized *gendarmerie*. Most recently, interpretations of French policing have noted that the *gendarmerie* during the course of the twentieth century converged with standards for civilian police in terms of accountability to the public (Berliére & Lévy 2011; Anderson 2011).

Debates about possible correlations between military-style policing and undemocratic governance has attracted renewed interest in recent years with the opening of new research into colonial policing. As is often noted in the case of the British Empire, the civilian form of policing was reserved for Great Britain, while military-style policing was developed for Ireland and later exported in a variety of forms to British colonies. From studies of the French *gendarmerie* it seems that the factors shaping police–public relations are not so much military features in everyday policing, but rather the structures surrounding the police's relationship with the public, particularly legal boundaries, clear procedures, and robust accountability mechanisms.

Conclusion

Police–public relations include a variety of ideological statements and commitments as well as particular policing strategies and approaches designed to strengthen popular acceptance of police legitimacy. Interpretations of the nature of police–public relations have been profoundly shaped by the "myths" created by official rhetoric, particularly in Britain—and, to some extent, the United States—where the official rhetoric was broadly credible to the sections of the population that benefited from police protection. In France and Germany official rhetoric about police–public relations was at best regarded with some suspicion until at least the late twentieth century, and negative aspects of police–public relations were often interpreted as revealing the true nature not only of policing, but of the political regime itself.

Yet no easy correlation can be made between democratic regimes and the nature of police–public relations, as democracy in itself provides no guarantee of more legal, even-handed, and less violent forms of policing compared to pre-democratic or semi-democratic regimes. On the other hand, between the mid-nineteenth and the twenty-first centuries, the official rhetoric in Britain, the United States, France, and Germany has undoubtedly had a positive impact on police–public relations by raising popular expectations and by setting certain benchmarks and boundaries around police exercise of power. At the heart of police–public relations lies the issue of empowering all members of the public—collectively or individually—to meaningfully challenge police decisions and behavior. The nature of police–public relations and police legitimacy ultimately depends on how police and government authorities handle the inherently asymmetrical power relationship between police and the policed.

References

Anderson, Malcolm. 2011. *In Thrall to Political Modernity: Police and Gendarmerie in France.* Oxford: Oxford University Press.

Ascoli, David. 1979. *The Queen's Peace: The Origins and Development of the Metropolitan Police, 1829–1979.* London: Hamish Hamilton.

Babington, Anthony. 1990. *Military Intervention in Britain: From the Gordon Riots to the Gibraltar Incident.* London: Routledge.

Bailey, Victor. 1981. "The Metropolitan Police, the Home Office and the Threat of Outcast London." In *Policing and Punishment in Nineteenth-Century Britain*, ed. Victor Bailey, 94–125. London: CroomHelm.

Bayley, David H. 1985. *Patterns of Policing: A Comparative International Analysis.* New Brunswick, NJ: Rutgers University Press.

Bayley, David H. 2005. *Changing the Guard: Developing Democratic Police Abroad.* Oxford: Oxford University Press.

Berghahn, Volker. 1994. *Imperial Germany, 1871–1914: Economy, Society, Culture and Politics.* Oxford: Berghahn.

Berlière, Jean-Marc. 1993a. *Le Préfet Lépine: Vers la naissance de la police moderne*. Paris: Denoël.

Berlière, Jean-Marc. 1993b. "Du maintien de l'ordre républicain au maintien républicain de l'ordre? Réflexions sur la violence." *Genèses* 12 (May): 6–29.

Berlière, Jean-Marc. 1996. *Le monde des polices en France*. Paris: Éditions complexes.

Berlière, Jean-Marc, & René Lévy. 2011. *Histoire des polices en France de l'ancien régime à nos jours*. Paris: Nouveau monde.

Bittner, Egon. 1970. *The Functions of the Police in Modern Societies*. Chevy Chase, MD: National Institute for Mental Health.

Blood, Philip. 2003. "Kurt Daluege and the Militarisation of the *Ordnungspolizei*." In *Conflict and Legality: Policing Mid-Twentieth Century Europe*, ed. Gerard Oram, 95–120. London: Francis Boutie.

Bradford, Ben, & Jonathan Jackson. 2011. "Why Britons Trust Their Police." Accessed 15 March 2015 at *Books&Ideas.net*. http://www.booksandideas.net/Why-Britons-Trust-their-Police.html.

Bradford, Ben, Jonathan Jackson, & Mike Hough. 2014. "Police Legitimacy in Action: Lessons for Theory and Policy." In *The Oxford Handbook of Police and Policing*, ed. Michael D. Reisig & Robert J. Kane, 551–70. Oxford: Oxford University Press.

Brodeur, Jean-Paul. 2010. *The Policing Web*. Oxford: Oxford University Press.

Brogden, Mike. 2008. "Community Policing as Cherry Pie." In *Policing Across the World*, ed. Rob Mawby, 167–86. London: UCL Press

Bruneteaux, Patrick. 1996. *Maintenir l'ordre: Les transformations de la violence d'État en régime démocratique*. Paris: FNSP.

Campion, David. 2005. "'Policing the Peelers': Parliament, the Public, and the Metropolitan Police, 1829–1833." In *London Politics, 1760–1940*, ed. Matthew Cracoe & Anthony Tayor, 38–54. Basingstoke, UK: Palgrave Macmillan.

Campion, Jonas. 2011. *Les gendarmes belges, français et néerlandais à la sortie de la Seconde Guerre mondiale*. Paris: André Versaille.

Carrot, Georges. 1984. "Maintien de l'ordre depuis la fin de l'ancien régime jusqu'à 1968." Ph.D. diss., University of Nice.

Carrot, Georges. 2005. "La police et la Révolution." In *Histoire et dictionnaire de la police*, ed. Michel Aubouin, Arnaud Teyssier & Jean Tulard, 219–68. Paris: Laffont.

Critchley, Tom A. 1967. *A History of Police in England and Wales, 1900–1966*. London: Constable.

Deluermoz, Quentin. 2012. *Policiers dans la ville: La construction d'un ordre public à Paris 1854–1914*. Paris: Publications de la Sorbonne.

Deluermoz, Quentin. 2013. "Capitales policières, état-nation et civilisation urbaine: Londres, Paris et Berlin au tournant du XIXe siècle." *Revue d'histoire moderne et contemporaine* 3 (60): 55–85.

Denis, Vincent, & Catherine Denys, eds. 2012. *Polices d'empires*. Rennes, France: PUR.

Dubber, Markus. 2005. *The Police Powers: Patriarchy and the Foundations of American Government*. New York: Columbia.

Dubber, Markus. 2006. "The New Police Science and the Police Power Model of the Criminal Process." In *The New Police Science*, ed. Markus Dubber & Mariana Valverde, 107–44. Stanford, CA: Stanford University Press.

Dunnage, Jonathan, & Nadine Rossol. 2015. "Building Ideological Bridges and Inventing Institutional Traditions" *Crime, History & Societies* 19 (1): 89–111.

Elias, Norbert. 1939. *Über den Prozeß der Civilisation*. Basel, Switzerland: Haus zum Falken.

Emsley, Clive. 1983. *Policing and Its Context, 1780–1870*. London: Macmillan.

Emsley, Clive. 1993. "'Mother, What Did Policemen Do When There Weren't Any Motors?' The Law, the Police and the Regulation of Motor Traffic in England, 1900–1930." *History Journal* 36 (2): 357–81.

Emsley, Clive. 1996. *The English Police: A Political and Social History*, 2nd ed. Harlow, UK: Longman.

Emsley, Clive. 1999a. "A Typology of Nineteenth-Century Police." *Crime, History & Societies* 3 (1): 29–44.

Emsley, Clive. 1999b. *Gendarmerie and the State in Nineteenth-Century Europe*. Oxford: Oxford University Press.

Emsley, Clive. 2005. *Hard Men: Violence in England since 1750*. London: Hambledon.

Emsley, Clive. 2012. "Marketing the Brand: Exporting British Police Models, 1829–1950." *Policing: A Journal of Policy and Practice* 6 (1): 43–54.

Emsley, Clive. 2014. "Peel's Principles, Police Principles." In *The Future of Policing*, ed. Jennifer Brown, 11–22. London: Routledge.

Ericson, Richard. 2005. "The Police as Reproducers of Order." In *Policing: Key Readings*, ed. Tim Newburn, 7–24. London: Routledge.

Evans, Richard. 1987. *Rethinking German History: Nineteenth-Century Germany and the Origins of the Third Reich*. London: HarperCollins.

Funk, Albrecht. 1986. *Polizei und Rechtsstaat: Die Entstehung des Staatsrechtlichen Gewaltsmonopol in Preußen, 1848–1918*. Frankfurt am Main, Germany: Campus.

Fürmetz, Gerhard, Herbert Reinke, & Klaus Weinhauer, eds. 2001. *Nachkriegspolizei: Sicherheit und Ordnung in Ost- und West-deutschland, 1945–1969*. Hamburg, Germany: Ergebnisse Verlag.

Gamon, Hugh. 1907. *The London Police Court, Today and Tomorrow*. London: J. M. Dent.

Gatrell, V. A. C. 1990. "Crime, Authority and the Policeman-State." In *The Cambridge Social History of Britain, 1750–1950*, Vol. 3, ed. F. M. L. Thompson, 243–310. Cambridge: Cambridge University Press.

Gourley, G. Douglas. 1954. "Police-Public Relations." *Annals of the American Academy of Political and Social Science* 291 (January): 135–42.

Hall, Alex. 1977. *Scandal, Sensation and Social Democracy*. Cambridge: Cambridge University Press.

Head, Michael, & Scott Mann. 2009. *Domestic Deployment of the Armed Forces: Military Powers, Law and Human Rights*. Aldershot, UK: Ashgate.

Houte, Arnaud. 2010. *Le métier de gendarme au XIXe siècle*. Rennes, France: PUR.

Jauffret, Jean-Charles. 1983. "Armée et Pouvoir Politique: la question des troupes spécialisées charges du maintien de l'ordre en France de 1871 à 1914." *Revue Historique* 270:97–144.

Jessen, Ralph. 1991. *Polizei im Industrierevier*. Göttingen, Germany: Vandenhoeck & Ruprecht.

Johansen, Anja. 2005. *Soldiers as Police: The French and Prussian Armies and the Policing of Popular Protest, 1889–1914*. Aldershot, UK: Ashgate.

Johansen, Anja. 2009. "Complain in Vain? The Development of a 'Police Complaints Culture' in Wilhelmine Berlin." *Crime, History & Societies* 13 (2): 119–42.

Johansen, Anja. 2011. "Keeping up Appearances: Police Rhetoric, Public Trust and Police Scandal in London and Berlin, 1880–1914." *Crime, History & Societies* 15 (1): 59–83.

Johansen, Anja. 2013. "Lost in Translation: The English Bobby Through a German Monocle." *Journal History* 98 (333): 750–68.

Klein, Joanne. 2010. *Invisible Men: The Secret Lives of Police Constables in Liverpool, Manchester and Birmingham, 1900–1930*. Liverpool, UK: Liverpool University Press.

Klockars, Carl B. 1985. *The Idea of Policing.* Beverly Hills, CA: Sage.

Knöbl, Wolfgang. 1998. *Polizei und Herrschaft im Modernisierungsproceß: Staatsbildung und innere Sicherheit in Preußen, England und Amerika, 1700–1914.* Frankfurt am Main, Germany: Campus.

Lane, Roger. 1977. *Policing the City: Boston, 1822–1885.* New York: Anthenium.

Lenz, Susan, & Robert Chaires. 2007. "The Invention of Peel's Principles: A Study of Policing 'Textbook' History." *Journal of Criminal Justice* 35 (1): 69–79.

Leßmann-Faust, Peter. 2012 [1987]. *Die preußische Schutzpolizei in der Weimarer Republik.* Frankfurt, Germany: Verlag für Polizeiwissenschaft.

Lévy, René. 2014. "Police and Policing in Europe: Centralisation, Pluralisation, Europeanisation." In *The Routledge Handbook of European Criminology*, ed. Sophie Body-Gendrot, Mike Hough, Klàra Kerezsi, René Lévy, & Sonja Snacken, 353–67. London: Routledge.

Liang, Hsi-Huey. 1992. *The Berlin Police Force in the Weimar Republic.* Berkeley: University of California Press.

Lignereux, Aurélien. 2002. *Gendarmes et policiers dans la France de Napoléon.* Maison-Alfort, France: SHGN.

Lindenberger, Thomas. 1995. *Straßenpolitik und der öffentlichen Ordnung in Berlin 1900 bis 1914.* Bonn, Germany: Dietz.

Lindenberger, Thomas. 2003. *Volkspolizei: Herrschaftspraxis und öffentliche Ordnung im SED-Staat 1952–1968.* Cologne, Weimar, & Vienna, Germany & Austria: Böhlau Verlag.

Lopez, Laurent. 2014. *La guerre des polices n'a pas eu lieu: Gendarmes et policiers, co-acteurs de la sécurité sous la Troisième République (1870–1914).* Paris: PUPS.

Luc, Jean-Noël, ed. 2002. *Gendarmerie: état et société au XIXe siècle.* Paris: Sorbonne.

Luc, Jean-Noël, ed. 2010. *Soldats de la loi: la gendarmerie au XXe siècle.* Paris: PUPS.

Lüdtke, Alf. 1982. *Gemeinwohl, Polizei und Festungspraxis.* Göttingen, Germany: Vandenhoeck & Ruprecht.

Lüdtke, Alf, Herbert Reinke, & Michael Sturm, eds. 2011. *Polizei, Gewalt und Staat im 20. Jahrhundert.* Berlin, Germany: Springer.

Manning, Peter. 2010. *Democratic Policing in a Changing World.* Boulder, CO, & London: Paradigm.

Mawby, Rob. 1999. "Variations on a Theme: The Development of Professional Police in the British Isles and North America." In *Policing Across the World*, ed. Rob Mawby, 28–58. London: UCL Press.

Mawby, Rob. 2008. "Models of Policing." In *Handbook of Policing*, ed. Tim Newburn, 17–46. Cullompton, UK: Willan.

Miller, Wilbur. 1977. *Cops and Bobbies: Police Authority in New York and London, 1830–1870.* Chicago: University of Chicago Press.

Miller, Wilbur. 2013. "Authority in America." *Crime, History & Societies* 17 (2): 125–35.

Monjardet, Dominique. 1996. *Ce que fait la police: Sociologie de la force publique.* Paris: Découverte.

Monkkonen, Eric. 1981. *Police in Urban America, 1860–1920.* Cambridge: Cambridge University Press.

Muchembled, Robert. 2008. *Une Histoire de la violence de la fin du moyen âge à nos jours.* Paris: Seuil.

Müller, Philipp. 2005. *Auf der Suche nach dem Täter. Die öffentliche Dramatisierung von Verbrechen im Berlin des Kaiserreichs.* Frankfurt am Main, Germany: Campus.

Pinker, Steven. 2011. *The Better Angels of Our Nature*. London: Penguin.

Pröve, Ralf. 2011. "Bürgergewalt und Staatsgewalt. Bewaffnete Bürger und vorkonstitutionelle Herrschaft im frühen 19. Jahrhundert." In *Polizei, Gewalt und Staat im 20. Jahrhundert*, ed. Alf Lüdtke, Herbert Reinke, & Michael Sturm, 61–80. Berlin, Germany: Springer.

Radzinowicz, Leon, & Roger Hood. 1948–1968. *A History of the English Criminal Law and Its Administration from 1750*. London: Stevens.

Raeff, Marc. 1983. *The Well-Ordered Police State*. New Haven, CT: Yale University Press.

Reinke, Herbert. 1991. "'Armed As If for a War': The State, the Military and the Professionalisation of the Prussian Police in Imperial Germany." In *Policing Western Europe: Politics, Professionalism and Public Order, 1850–1940*, ed. Clive Emsley & Barbara Weinberger, 55–73. Santa Barbara, CA: Greenwood Press.

Reith, Charles. 1938. *The Police Idea*. Oxford: Oxford University Press.

Reith, Charles. 1943. *British Police and the Democratic Ideal*. Oxford: Oxford University Press.

Reith, Charles. 1952. *The Blind Eye of History: A Study of the Origins of the Present Police Era*. London: Faber & Faber.

Richardson, James F. 1970. *The New York Police: Colonial Times to 1901*. New York: Oxford University Press.

Silver, Allan. 1967. "The Demand for Order in Civil Society." In *The Police: Six Sociological Essays*, ed. David J. Bordua, 12–24. New York: Wiley.

Spierenburg, Pieter. 2013. *Violence and Punishment: Civilizing the Body through Time*. Cambridge: Polity.

Steedman, Carolyn. 1984. *Policing the Victorian Community: The Formation of English Provincial Police Forces, 1856–80*. London: Routledge & Kegan Paul.

Storch, Robert D. 1975. "The Plague of the Blue Locust: Police Reform and Popular Resistance in Northern England, 1840–1857." *International Review of Social History* 20 (1): 61–90.

Storch, Robert D. 1976. "The Policemen as Domestic Missionary: Urban Discipline and Popular Culture in Northern England, 1850–1880." *Journal of Social History* 9 (4): 481–509.

Tankeby, Justice. 2014. "Police Legitimacy." In *The Oxford Handbook of Police and Policing*, ed. Michael D. Reisig & Robert J. Kane, 238–59. Oxford: Oxford University Press.

Taylor, David. 1997. *The New Police in Nineteenth-Century England: Crime, Conflict and Control*. Manchester, UK: Manchester University Press.

Taylor, David. 2002. *Policing the Victorian Town: The Development of Police in Middlesbrough, 1840–1914*. London: Palgrave.

Thompson, F. M. L. 1981. "Social Control in Victorian Britain." *Economic History Review* 34 (2): 189–208.

Tocqueville, Alexis. 1981 [1836]. *De la Démocratie en Amérique*, Vol. 1. Paris: Flammarion.

Tomlins, Christopher. 2006. "Framing the Fragments. Police: Genealogies, Discourses, Locales, Principles." In *The New Police Science*, ed. Markus Dubber & Mariana Valverde, 248–90. Stanford, CA: Stanford University Press.

Waddington, Peter A. J. 1999. *Policing Citizens*. London: University College London Press.

Wehler, Hans-Ulrich. 1985. *The German Empire, 1871–1918*. Oxford: Berg.

Weinberger, Barbara. 1981. "The Police and the Public in Mid-Nineteenth-Century Warwickshire." In *Policing and Punishment in Nineteenth-Century Britain*, ed. Victor Bailey, 65–93. London: CroomHelm.

CHAPTER 26

....

CRIME AND POLICING
IN WARTIME

....

CLIVE EMSLEY

INTRODUCTION

....

ON 25 July 1795 the *Leicester Journal* commented briefly on the impact of the current war on some of the assize courts in the east of England: "At Lincoln there is but one prisoner for trial; at Cambridge not any; at Norwich during the last year there have been but six persons. This, at least, is one benefit arising from the war." The notion that war removes potential offenders from society by putting the most crimogenic group—unskilled young men—in the armed forces has a logic to it and has been a popular assumption for centuries in Europe, and particularly in Britain, which has not experienced war on its soil since the last Jacobite rising in 1745–1746. Equally popular is the corollary that the outbreak of peace brings a rise in crime, as men trained to kill and brutalized by battlefield experiences return and engage in robbery and other forms of violent crime, unable to settle back into civilian life and labor.

The first section of what follows focuses on changes in the understanding of masculinity and changes in recruitment into the armed forces from the mid-eighteenth to the end of the twentieth century, assessing what impact these changes had on criminal, particularly violent criminal, behavior among service personnel. This is followed by an exploration of the concerns about men returning from war, who have supposedly been brutalized by their experiences and slip into violent crime because they cannot readjust to civilian life. War crimes, particularly mass killing and rape, are the focus of the third section, and this is followed, in the fourth section, by a discussion of the way in which what might be termed "ordinary" crime is perpetrated by service personnel who find themselves with the temptation and the opportunity. The fifth section addresses the way in which war can also provide the need and/or opportunities for criminal activity among the civilian population of combatant societies, particularly exploring the apparent wartime increase in offending by women and juveniles. The final section considers the way in which war has affected the policing of criminal offending and the impact of war on both civilian and military police institutions.

I. Change Through Time

The period from the mid-eighteenth to the end of the twentieth century witnessed changes in the men who were recruited into and served in the armed forces of European states, significant changes in the ideal of masculinity, and changes in the technology and organization of warfare. Each of these changes had varying degrees of impact on such crime as was perpetrated by service personnel. Among respectable European society, masculinity moved increasingly away from an understanding of a man's reputation that depended on a strong right arm and physicality toward an ideal focusing on probity, honesty, and good works that kept tough physicality in check. The old notions, however, continued to be celebrated among the armed forces, and especially among the front-line combat troops known in the modern British army as the "teeth arms." The majority of eighteenth-century and nineteenth-century soldiers were infantrymen who required little more than the courage, fitness, and toughness that continued to be celebrated among the hard men of the poorer sections of society. Moreover, given their battlefield tasks, the teeth arms particularly needed to emphasize and develop these attributes.

For most of the eighteenth century armies and navies were made up of professionals who volunteered for service, although often the "volunteering" might be through compulsion or force. National identity could be fluid, and the evidence of soldiers and soldier criminals deported in eighteenth-century Prussia shows that some men served in several different armies (Evans 1998, pp. 20–21). Legislators during the French Revolution, however, insisted that all citizens should assist the nation in time of crisis, which led to the introduction of conscription, a system perfected by Napoleon. From the beginning of the nineteenth century, states and empires fighting to maintain the vestiges of the old regime began to employ conscription as a means of raising the required new mass armies and establishing a trained reserve, as well as of taking the opportunity to teach young men about "their" nation, state, or empire. Navies had always required large numbers of men with varying degrees of skill, but the growth of technology in war on land led to a proportionate decline in the need for infantry and the recruitment of men with more sophisticated skills and abilities; this was especially the case in the twentieth century as the military came to rely more and more on mechanized vehicles and radio communications.

The consequence of these changes was that first, the pool from which servicemen were recruited expanded enormously in time of crisis or war; and second, that more and more men were needed who possessed or who had the potential to acquire the new technical skills. Thus the recruits were drawn from societies that increasingly looked down on tough, violent male physicality, yet those in the teeth arms, and above all those who were volunteers, continued to be drawn from those sections of society that still celebrated the masculinity of the working-class hard man. Moreover, for success and survival, both the teeth arms and the more skilled arms required the traditional tough attitudes and wanted men who would work for and support each other in dangerous and extreme circumstances. It has been popular among military historians to speak in terms of the "service family," in which a soldier's platoon and regiment, a sailor's messmates and ship's company, or an airman's squadron provided for and cared for the individual. For young men from the poorer sections of society, the service family could provide the kind of family support and caring environment that they had never before experienced. But young men could also find these beneficial attributes in an otherwise undesirable street gang. Service life has always been divided into periods of high activity involving training or action and periods of extreme inaction during which the far from desirable elements of hard man masculinity are indulged, such as heavy drinking, fighting, and boasting of sexual prowess. Gangs tend to fight each other over insults imagined or real, women, and territory. The same is true of the military gang, and in the military context violence can also be sparked by an opposite gang belonging to a different platoon, a different unit or service, or another army or navy. During both world wars British troops resented troops from the "White Dominions," who were better paid, wore exotic uniforms, and appeared, in consequence, to have more success with British women. Even worse than the colonials, however, were American GIs, who were "over paid, over sexed and over here," and every opportunity was found to fight them. Men from the skilled as well as the teeth arms were also sucked into this kind of behavior regardless of their often-different social origins and the fact that their families and their formative years were more likely to subscribe to the less aggressive and violent versions of masculinity (Emsley 2013, pp. 107–11).

Property crimes have been the principal offenses that have brought people before criminal courts for centuries. Service personnel have engaged in all forms of theft, but while statistical evidence is hard to find that would prove the case once and for all, it appears that drunkenness, rowdy behavior, fighting, and violent assaults, occasionally resulting in murder or manslaughter, have been committed disproportionately by service personnel against other service personnel.

From the late eighteenth century onward, the civilian world witnessed significant shifts in the development of legal and criminal justice systems, but armed forces commonly have had their own legal systems. Military law was always geared toward the maintenance of military discipline, and the majority of courts martial conducted over the period spanning the eighteenth through the twentieth centuries dealt with absenteeism and desertion; in time of war, however, when the accused was on active service in a theater of conflict, such courts could hear the kind of case that would otherwise have come before the civilian courts. Increasingly, too, military law and military courts became more and more like their civilian equivalents (Oram 2002; Oram 2003; Emsley 2013, esp. ch. 2). Alongside these changes in criminal justice was the growth of modern bureaucratic police institutions. The ordinary civilian police were often involved in offenses committed by military personnel against civilians or disturbances to the peace of their district; this could lead to police and courts, both civilian and military, becoming embroiled in arguments about jurisdiction. At the same time, military provosts, whose origins can be found in the Middle Ages and who were responsible for the policing of soldiers and sailors, were also developed and reshaped alongside the new police and drew upon their growing expertise.

II. Bandits and Brutalized Veterans

Violent bandit gangs infested parts of rural Europe during the eighteenth century. Sometimes their ranks were swelled by deserters or stragglers from the armies of warring princes; a man with knowledge and skill in the use of weaponry was of value in these bands. Former soldiers appear to have made up the single largest Christian group (a large number of Jews were also represented) among German bandit groups in the late seventeenth and eighteenth centuries (Danke 1988, pp. 88–89). In Brabant in the early eighteenth century, the bandits organized themselves along the lines of military companies, and similar bandit companies reappeared in the Netherlands during the wars of the French Revolution (Egmond 1993; see also Egmond 1986). In France itself the soldier had long been associated with criminal behavior; indeed, the police on the main roads of eighteenth-century France, the *Maréchaussée*, had been created in the early sixteenth century to protect the king's subjects from the king's soldiers. The army generally became better disciplined during the eighteenth century, but the close of the Seven Years' War in 1763 seems to have heralded an increase in criminality arising from demobilized men seeking work and reintegration into civilian society (Gomez Pardo 2012, pp. 204–05, 552–53). The introduction of conscription in revolutionary France, and its increased efficiency under Napoleon, led to some young men leaving their villages and taking to the woods and hills as at least temporary bandits (Forrest 1989, ch. 6). For small peasant communities, however, there might be little difference between bandits, in whose ranks could be found deserters, stragglers, and recalcitrant conscripts, and a proper army. The French armies of the revolutionary and Napoleonic period generally lived off the land, and for a rural community the requisition of grain and livestock for food and horses for transport can have appeared little different from looting by those same soldiers or robbery by bandits. Some bandits may have acquired the reputation of Robin Hoods, but many more put their own desires and greed above the sorry state of the peasants whom they pillaged; even among the guerrilla bands that played a part in aggravating Napoleon's Spanish ulcer, there were men who had acted as bandits and robbed poor fellow Spaniards before the French invasion (Esdaile 2004).

   In Britain during the wars of the eighteenth century, the courts were used as a way of filling the ranks of the army and the crews of warships, as fit young offenders were given the choice, sometimes in place of a trial, of volunteering; this practice in itself added to the belief that war reduced the incidence of crime (King 2002). Unlike parts of continental Europe, marauding gangs of bandits were not a problem in eighteenth-century

Britain, but there were still concerns about demobilized men returning home and taking to crime. Indeed, these concerns were such that the Parliament moderated some laws at the end of several wars to provide opportunities for demobilized soldiers and sailors; strict apprenticeship laws, for example, were relaxed for such men, and so too, temporarily, was the law against begging, always providing that a man could prove that he had been recently demobilized (Hay 1982, p. 140). But if Britain had no bandit gangs, it still had highwaymen and footpads whose numbers were believed to increase with the end of a war. Some highwaymen carried swords and pistols like cavalrymen, and a few insisted on the title of "captain" to suggest a military background, though their right to the rank seems rarely to have been borne out by the evidence (Spraggs 2001, pp. 171–72). Much of the press in Britain, which was more open and free than its continental counterparts in terms of what it could publish, often filled space with crime stories when the opportunity for military stories declined. At least one newspaper appears largely to have fabricated a gang of robbers to attract readers in the immediate aftermath of the Seven Years' War (King 1987). While there are no crime statistics from this period, there appears to have been an increase in prosecutions, and there was an increase in executions at the end of Britain's eighteenth-century wars, particularly in the decade following the end of the American War of Independence. The increases in prosecutions and executions were fed, at least in part, by a desire to combat the perceived increase in crime by deterrence. Yet in spite of the strong contemporary belief that the outbreak of war led to a decrease in crime, while the outbreak of peace led to an increase, the evidence for such a pattern is uncertain (King 2000, ch. 2).

Bandits continued to plague parts of southern Europe throughout the nineteenth century, though without much input from armies, or their stragglers and deserters. During the early 1860s the Brigands' War in the *mezzogiorno*, which followed the unification of the south of Italy into the nation-state, saw the insurgents' ranks swollen by men from two disgruntled and disbanded armies: Garibaldi's Southern Army and, more particularly, the Neapolitan Army. The situation was aggravated still further by the Savoyard monarchy's attempt to conscript southerners into the Italian army, which prompted desertion and draft dodging on a massive scale (Dickie 1999, p. 31). The causes of the Brigands' War were rooted in long-standing problems of southern Italy, and so too was banditry elsewhere in southern Europe, such as Spain and Greece, where bandits, a few of whom had military experience, were drawn from the traditional peasant or herdsmen communities. Banditry on the other side of the Atlantic, particularly in Missouri in the aftermath of the American Civil War, also drew on former soldiers. Here, former Confederate guerrilla raiders, who suffered terrible retribution at the hands of the Union victors, demanded recognition as true soldiers of the south; the most notable of these individuals, as well as the most dangerous, violent, and unpredictable, was the legendary Jesse James (Styles 2002). More conventionally, Boston at the end of the Civil War witnessed a panic created by the fear that demobilized veterans were turning to street robbery (Adler 1996).

Almost twenty years after the demobilization following the American Civil War, Wilhelm Starke, an official in the Prussian Ministry of Justice, published a broad analysis of the Prussian crime statistics for the third quarter of the nineteenth century. Starke's conclusions were similar to those of others. He noted particularly that most crime was committed by young men, but he also detected other patterns and, among other things, concluded that the Franco-Prussian War had had a significant impact on the crime statistics of both Prussia and France. First, it appeared that petty offenses had declined during the war as large numbers of young men, and especially young men from the poorer sections of urban society, were swept up by the military; second, it seemed that there had been an increase in violent offending in the war's aftermath (Starke 1884, pp. 61, 152).

Given the growth of the new academic subject of criminology at the end of the nineteenth century and the unrivaled scale of industrial slaughter in the First World War, it is not surprising that some of the theories about war and crime were explored by exponents of the new discipline in the immediate aftermath of the conflict. Franz Exner and Moritz Liepmann published significant texts on the impact of the war on crime in Austria and Germany. Thorsten Sellin set out to assess the extent to which the conflict had led to an increase in murder across Europe. Recognizing the problems inherent in the statistics, both Exner and Liepmann nevertheless concluded that there had been a decrease in various forms of offending in the early stages of the war, though neither was convinced that the end of the war had led to an increase in violent crime by brutalized veterans; indeed, Exner went so far as to consider that returning soldiers were not especially drawn to violent crime. However, both he and Liepmann believed, as did many elsewhere, that the value of human life deteriorated during the war (Exner 1927; Liepmann 1930; Sellin 1926). One English provincial newspaper, for example, wrote at the end of 1920: "The after effect of every war is the cheapening of the value of human life. The hangman had a carnival the other morning. The men who suffered the supreme penalty were ex-soldiers. At the present time one or two others are awaiting the day of execution" (*Sheffield Mail*, 2 December 1920, p. 2). Using this assumption as his starting point, Sellin compared the available statistics of various European states and concluded that "the demobilization period saw a great increase in the rate of murders in the belligerent nations with the possible exception of England and Wales" (1926, p. 134).

There was no significant academic analysis of the impact of the war by contemporaries in Britain, though at the beginning of the conflict there were reports of a decrease in the numbers of criminal offenders appearing before the courts. The judicial statistics reveal a decline in violent crime during the war, and there were fears about violent veterans expressed by a range of authoritative individuals at the war's end. What was noticeable in postwar Britain, however, was an increase in domestic violence that appears to have sprung from men returning home to be met with reports, or clear evidence, of wives' or girlfriends' unfaithfulness. In such instances juries, magistrates, and judges were often prepared to acquit a returned serviceman against the evidence, to reduce a murder charge to one of manslaughter, or to pass a light sentence. Other studies show that ex-servicemen's violence was not directed solely against unfaithful womenfolk, but was often sparked or aggravated by drink and, at the turn of the century, by the use of drugs (MacManus et al. 2013). Significantly, however, neither a reduction in the severity of a charge nor a lenient sentence was forthcoming when a man had a previous record of violence. The defense that a man was not responsible for his actions because he was suffering from shellshock was often used, and not always with respect to violent crimes. This defense continued to be adopted throughout the interwar period, in the aftermath of the Second World War, and into the beginning of the twenty-first century (Emsley 2008; Emsley 2013, pp. 7–8, 70–72). At the end of the Second World War the term "shellshock" was largely replaced by phrases such as "battle fatigue" or, more popularly among the soldiery, "bomb-happy." By the turn of the century, the more common term was "post-traumatic stress disorder," and the problem of violent ex-servicemen was undergoing serious clinical analysis, particularly in Britain and the United States.

There is evidence of French and German men returning from the trenches of the First World War and reacting violently toward their women, and toward other men. But while murder, and especially sexual murder, figured significantly in the media of Weimar Germany, the contention that the press in France and Germany featured crimes of passion less than the media in Britain is arguable. The element of veteran violence most stressed by historians of the interwar period has been that surrounding extremist politics. Liepmann's study of the figures at the end of the war led him to conclude that those convicted of manslaughter or murder, unlike their prewar counterparts, were less likely to have previous convictions. But he also noted the large number of weapons in circulation at the end of the war and the number held illegally; these, he believed, made homicide easier to commit, and he singled out political assassinations and attempted assassinations in this respect (1930, pp. 36–38). Much criminal behavior in Germany and Austria at the end of the First World War might be attributed to the appalling economic state in which people found themselves as a result of the conflict and the internal disorder sparked by revolution. It is possible that violent political crime and the rise of violent political movements were given some impetus by experiences during the First World War, but there were almost certainly other, probably more significant, contributing factors, such as the general sense of being cheated in victory among some Italian veterans, and the fact of being defeated, through no lack of courage and effort on their part, among German and Austrian veterans (Emsley 2010).

In contrast to assumptions about the brutalized, criminal veteran, work on socially and educationally deprived young American men who already had criminal records but later served in the Second World War has suggested that military experience acted as a turning point in their lives. Firm discipline, leadership, role models, the need to work as a team, and social responsibility experienced or learned in the military, together with the GI Bill of Rights and the educational opportunities offered by military service, seem to have enhanced soldiers' occupational status, job security, and economic well-being; at the same time, these led to a desistence in offending. However the expanding economic opportunities of the 1950s and 1960s probably also contributed significantly to such individuals' postwar behavior and success. By the time the Vietnam War was drawing to a close, the economic opportunities for men drawn from this social category were fading fast; when the absence of a similar GI Bill for veterans returning from

Southeast Asia was added to the picture, the pattern of criminal desistence became far worse (Sampson & Laub 1996).

III. Service Personnel and War Crimes

Military personnel may be subject to a legal authority distinct from civilian law, particularly when on active service, but they are still drawn from and maintain links with their civilian origins. In consequence, behavior by military personnel, whether criminal or not, is commonly a reflection of civilian behavior. Criminal activity provides a good example of this linkage, though often with differences in emphasis or extremes. In wartime, sailors, soldiers, and, after the development of air-power in the twentieth century, air crew are authorized to fight and kill the enemy. There have always been norms or laws regarding warfare, and these were given an international underpinning with the various international conventions drawn up beginning in the early twentieth century, but, from the early modern period onward, it has generally been accepted that prisoners of war are not to be killed or brutally treated. Prisoners have been killed, but governments and general staffs have rarely sanctiond the killing of prisoners, and armies have rarely taken action against any of their own men who have been accused of such deeds. In May 1794 the National Convention in France adopted a decree forbidding its armies to offer quarter to any British or Hanoverian soldiers, though this appears never, or almost never, to have been acted upon by French forces, and the decree was soon repealed. During the twentieth century some armies participated in acts of murder and genocide that were ordered, though not necessarily by any legislation or by any direct written command from their government or military superiors (Fergusson 2004; for the decree of the National Convention, see von Martens 1817, p. 374). Even confident rulers and generals have shown reluctance to leave a paper trail that might lead to an accusation of war crimes.

Rape has similarities with killing in the context of crimes committed by service personnel during time of war. Armed conflict appears to provide an additional impetus to and fear of rape. Individual soldiers or sailors might rape individual women, and, much less commonly, men, because of their personal fantasies, their desire for power, or their wish to assert their masculinity. But in wartime sexual assaults can easily be linked with assertions of ethnic or national difference or superiority. In the Balkan conflicts before the First World War, rape was widespread and appears to have been systematically employed as a form of ethnic warfare. In 1914 German soldiers raped as they fought their way into Belgium and northern France. Estimates vary wildly, but one conservative assessment suggests that there were between 1,000 and 5,000 children born to French women as a result of rape during the First World War (Kramer 2007, pp. 136–39; Godfroid 2012; Rivière 2012). The fear of the rapist soldier was also a weapon used to stigmatize the enemy, and rape became a weapon of revenge for the victors. Germans in the Rhineland feared the arrival of Belgian and French troops as occupiers at the end of the war; they were especially concerned by the French deployment of colonial troops—*die Schwartze Schmach*, the Black Shame. The deployment of black or brown colonial troops, who were perceived as "savage" and aggressively sexual, was a recurring fear in twentieth-century European conflicts. In the Spanish Civil War both sides played on the use of Moroccan troops by the Nationalists— the Nationalists to terrify the Republicans and the Republicans to emphasize the brutality and barbarity of the Nationalists. The Moroccan *Goumiers* who fought with the Free French among allied armies in Italy in 1944 appear to have lived up to these fearsome assumptions and were withdrawn from the theater after less than a year (Joly 2012; Williams 2013, pp. 45–57). The Soviet Army behaved well as it advanced through Bulgaria in the concluding stages of the Second World War, but in Germany, and particularly in East Prussia, it engaged in mass rape. Much of this was probably inspired by a desire for revenge that had been whipped up by Soviet propaganda; some officers endeavored to stop the rapes and the military courts prosecuted some offenders, but these efforts appear to have had little effect (Naimark 1995). The behavior of the Red Army in Germany has been regarded as exceptional in this respect; however, recent work based largely on birth records has suggested that American, British, and French troops may have been responsible for upward of 800,000 rapes (Gebhardt 2015). The problem is that the statistics of reports, investigations, and prosecutions for rape are meager. A study of rapes by American soldiers suggests a much lower figure, with a few in Britain before the invasion of Europe and an increase as the GIs moved first into France and then into Germany. The American army's judicial system acted against offenders, though it appears to have worked with significant racial blinkers as far as the accused were concerned (Lilly 2007).

Mass killing, the killing of prisoners, and mass rape of the kinds described previously are considered "war crimes" and have been, and continue to be, subject to sanction in international law as well as, in the case of other forms of crime, the law of individual countries. Military personnel reflect the society from which they originate, and, more commonly than these war crimes, they commit the kinds of activities branded as crimes by their civilian legal systems. Offenses by military personnel have been, and still can be, subject to both military law and civilian law.

IV. The Wartime Military and "Ordinary" Crime

Military law remains primarily concerned with the maintenance of discipline, but in wartime, sometimes simply to survive, but equally at other times to make significant personal profit, absentees and deserters, as well as men still serving with their units, have been known to combine with local offenders to commit criminal offenses. The wrecked economies of Europe at the end of the Second World War provided extensive opportunities for profiteering and trafficking in all kinds of goods, and the Allied armies had extensive food, clothing, and medical supplies, as well as motor vehicles, with their spare parts, tires, and petrol. Considerable amounts of this materiel disappeared as it was loaded on to ships, offloaded in foreign "liberated" ports, and then transported to where it was needed by train or lorry. In southern Italy absentees and deserters linked up with the Honored Societies in taking and trafficking military materiel, but there were also motley bandit gangs made up entirely of deserters from different armies. At the end of the war, air crew, delivering goods and bringing home prisoners of war, smuggled chocolate, cigarettes, cloth, as well as penicillin and other medical supplies into Europe, bringing back spirits, champagne, wine, and other goods that could be sold to restaurants or just used by the men themselves (Emsley 2013, pp. 88–90, 171–73).

Much of this offending was prosecuted before military courts since the accused were on active service, but when civilians were involved in the home country of the offending soldier, sailor, or airman, it was often necessary to use a civilian court. Here there could be problems of jurisdiction and awkward moments between civilian judges and magistrates and the officers of the accused military personnel. Moreover, even when these offenses may have been subject to sanction under civilian law, it could be the case that, overseas, there were no appropriate civilian courts in the vicinity to hear such cases. This, however, was a more general civil/military problem rather than one unique to wartime.

As noted previously, the most common offense brought before the courts was generally some form of appropriation of property. Soldiers were found guilty of theft, but there was also the problem of looting. Napoleon's armies lived off the land and did not always pay for what they took. During the early nineteenth century the old notion of the French soldier as a bandit gave way in popular national culture to the notion that a bit of trickery and theft merely reflected Gallic flair (Hopkin 2002). However, some of the early French criminologists writing at the close of the century still considered the army to be a hotbed of crime (Mannheim 1941, pp. 79–80). The Duke of Wellington was exasperated by the behavior of his men in Portugal and Spain and rigorous in seeking to ensure that goods were paid for and looters apprehended and punished (Daly 2013, pp. 112–21). Even so, for much of the nineteenth century British soldiers were commonly stigmatized as the "scum of the earth enlisted for drink." The First World War brought forth a mass army that, from 1916 on, contained conscripts, and even these individuals engaged in activities deemed as looting. Rather than the verb "to loot," British soldiers during the First World War preferred to make a verb of "souvenir" or "win" to describe such activities (Brophy & Partridge 1965, pp. 183, 204). But the term "looting" could cover a range of activities from the understandable, such as the appropriation of fresh food, more comfortable clothing, and various things to make a billet or slit trench more comfortable, to the art and property thefts perpetrated under the orders of men as varied as Citizen-General Bonaparte and Nazi leaders, to ordinary soldiers taking watches and rings from prisoners of war, civilians, or even Allied civilians.

V. Civilians and Wartime Crime

Wartime crime has never been an activity confined to military personnel. Wartime crime, like crime committed in time of peace, has much to do with circumstance and opportunity, and it cannot be attributed to any group stigmatized as "criminals." Wars disrupt economies, and when men are needed for the armed forces, the maintenance of families can fall on the shoulders of wives and children. The evidence from the courts of eighteenth-century England reveals an increase in the number of women prosecuted for theft, with the numbers being particularly high when war coincided with dearth (Hay 1982, p. 135; Palk 2006, pp. 42–43, 73, 179). The cost of the war against revolutionary France led to the government empowering the Bank of England to cease payment in specie. The bank replaced cash with poorly produced notes that were easy to forge; there followed a huge and sudden surge of fraudulent notes, followed by a surge in prosecutions (Palk 2006, ch. 5). The same conflict, and the same demands for money, led the government to introduce a tax on incomes, and those so inclined made fraudulent declarations. There were worse problems in continental Europe, where Napoleon's attempts to shut out the products of Britain's developing industrial economy led to widespread smuggling as well as the destruction of the economies of seaports. This, in turn, led to appalling suffering and people seeking to make ends meet through a variety of criminal activity ranging from continued smuggling to banditry and violent confrontations between civilians and officials at customs posts (Aaslestad 2009). People in other areas of the empire sought to profit from temporary economic advantages. The *département* of the Roër, for example, on the left bank of the Rhine enjoyed good harvests in 1811 and 1812 in contrast to other regions. The Napoleonic police suspected that a few entrepreneurs in the neighboring Kingdom of Holland were acquiring grain from the Roër and exporting it to Britain. At the same time merchants in the *département* were thought to be hoarding grain until the price rose still higher. Worse still, imperial functionaries appeared to be using the situation fraudulently to line their own pockets (Horn 2013, pp. 101–03).

Profiteering by state functionaries was not something confined to the period of the Napoleonic Wars. It recurred during the First World War and shocked those accustomed to seeing state servants in the German and Austrian empires as men of integrity. Franz Exner concluded that such actions were occasioned by a reduction in the standard of those employed as the better men went away to serve in the military, pay failed to keep abreast of prices, and shortages increased (Liepmann 1930, p. 7; Exner 1927, pp. 39–42). But state officials, whether motivated by desperation, by greed, or by a combination of these and other factors, were not the only civilians to see criminal opportunities in wartime. This was particularly apparent in the world wars of the twentieth century, when massive armed forces required massive quantities of food, clothing, fuel, transport, and medical supplies, and all of these goods could find a ready market among civilians eager and able to pay. It has already been noted how, during the Second World War, plentiful military materiel provided opportunities for theft and black market activity and how, in southern Italy, local civilians, especially those linked with the Honored Societies, sought to link up with military personnel for profit. Similar rackets, though possibly not quite as extensive or violent, were to be found in northwestern Europe after D-Day. The commanding officer of the military police detective section working behind the British Second Army in eastern Belgium reported that in January 1945 his men dealt with 231 cases. These led to charges against 53 military personnel, 166 Belgian civilians, and 78 Dutch civilians; property estimated to be worth just over £7,000 was recovered, including twenty-five wheels and tires valued at £500 and £1,000 worth of clothing.[1] At about the same time, the detective section based in Lille found "a new racket . . . the making of ladies coats from W[ar] D[epartment] blankets." The blankets were being transported to Paris, where they were tailored into coats priced at 8,000 francs each.[2]

Shortages occasioned or worsened by war led to flourishing black markets in both combatant and occupied countries. Ordinary citizens might look for scapegoats; in France, for example, peasant farmers and small shopkeepers were stigmatized and denounced. But the same ordinary citizens also broke regulations and engaged in illicit barter, tipping, and under-the-counter sales while at the same time condemning major trafficking, even though the major traffickers could be providing goods for the small-scale exchanges (Grenard 2008; Roodhouse 2013). Shortages and dearth during the world wars of the twentieth century appear also to have fostered an increase in theft and receiving committed by women, a trend noted in studies of crime in both Austria and Germany during the First World War. Exner and Liepmann both conceived of a masculinization (*Vermännlichung*) of female crime, and Liepmann emphasized how women were accused of committing about 20 percent of crime before the war, but were responsible for one-third by 1915 and a little over one-half two years later. The women accused of theft were usually young and often unmarried; those accused of receiving were more likely to be married or widowed (Exner 1927, pp. 145–60; Liepmann 1930, pp. 134–35, 156–57, 162). But more serious concerns about female crime during wartime focused on sexual behavior and immorality.

Generally speaking, across the European world prostitution was not a criminal offense in itself, though Lombroso had seen the prostitute as the female equivalent of the male criminal, and the emerging bureaucratic police institutions had sections charged with ensuring the regular medical examination of prostitutes. Large military camps attracted brothels as well as women desperate for money or, perhaps in the case of some younger women, looking simply for fun and flirtation—a distinction rarely recognized by authority, especially military authority, which was concerned about venereal disease incapacitating sailors and soldiers. There were, in addition, concerns about bigamous marriages, and in Germany, while the statistics of both pregnancies and abortions declined during the war, the figures for the latter fell in a much smaller proportion. Abortion, it was suspected, was occasioned by the desire to hide an affair from a returning husband or by the fear that it was impossible to feed and house another child in the worsening wartime economy (Emsley 2013, pp. 145–47; Liepmann 1930, pp. 153–54).

Perhaps the greatest concerns about increasing crime during the two world wars, however, focused on the activity of juvenile offenders. During the First World War in both Britain and the countries of the Central Powers there were concerns that the replacement by women of men sent to the front in many key jobs and positions in munitions factories was having a detrimental impact on children and young people. Fathers and elder brothers were no longer present as role models, and the number of policemen and male teachers declined. In Germany and Austria many schools were closed or partially taken over by other government departments. Food shortages, it was believed, reduced schoolchildren's ability to concentrate and encouraged them to be unruly and to steal foodstuffs. A few older boys got work at good rates of pay, and this, it was believed, fostered disrespect and criminal behavior. Similar concerns were voiced during the Second World War. In Manchester, for example, during 1940 and again in 1941 there was talk of imposing a curfew on young people, and in the following year the medical officer of Leeds Prison expressed the belief that high wartime wages earned by adolescents could foster crime because "too much money without responsibility or the necessity of learning its value leads in some cases, where self-control is wanting, to a lack of appreciation of property rights and values" (Emsley 2011, pp. 66– 68; 71–72; quotation from Smithies 1982, p. 177).

VI. War and Police Institutions

Civilian policing institutions usually dealt with civilian offenses in wartime, but when there was an occupying power, or when citizen offenders were involved with military offenders in black market trafficking, jurisdictional problems could arise. During the world wars of the twentieth century, military demands for fit young men presented further difficulties for police, since police institutions could be significantly reduced in size and dependent on older volunteers or on men (and police were generally men) who might otherwise have retired. The shortage of men could be alleviated by the recruitment of female police, but in Britain, where women were recruited in some numbers, they tended to be confined to dealing with female and child offenders, or else given what were considered to be female, domestic tasks such as office duties. In both world wars, police in Britain became older, more tired, and beset by a myriad of war-time duties, such as seeking out deserters and enforcing rationing and blackout regulations. The situation was the same for the police of other combatant states during the First World War, while in the subsequent war many found themselves compromised by occupation or, in Italy, by a civil war as *carabinieri* and police from the Interior Ministry serving with the Allies moved into areas where former comrades had been acting, possibly reluctantly, alongside the German Army or even for Mussolini's republic.

The French *gendarmerie* had always enjoyed a military role. Even though it patrolled the roads of provincial France and was the first body to be called upon to deal with internal civilian unrest, it was part of the army and provided the provosts who dealt with military offenses. During the Napoleonic period it played a central role in the pursuit of deserters and draft dodgers, earning the hostility of the communities in which its members were deployed as police; this hostility came from local mayors as well as the general population. These military police followed Napoleon's armies and enforced conscription and various other demands across his empire and within his satellite states. When Napoleon fell, part of his legacy was the *gendarmerie*-style units, which assumed various names (*carabinieri, Guardia Civil, Landjäger*) in both states that had been his allies and those that had been his foes (Emsley 1999).

Dislike flared particularly in the First World War, when all military police were seen as pursuers of deserters and absentees. *Carabinieri* were deployed as assault troops in the summer of 1915, and the men involved suffered enormous casualties, but after that their combat role gave way to policing alone. Their role in firing squads and the summary execution of men in retreat made them particularly hated. Front-line soldiers called them *imboscati* (literally, men who evaded the front); they were shot at and stoned (Collin 1984, pp. 106–10). During the First World War, and for the only time in their history, French *gendarmes* were denied the role of a combat unit, which appears to have aggravated the *poilus'* dislike of them—a feeling that, as in Italy, continued after the war. "*Le front s'arrête au premier gendarme*" (the front ends at the first *gendarme*) was the soldier's scornful comment (Panel 2003; Panel 2013; Buchbinder 2004). British "Redcaps" were similarly criticized, and, during the Second World War, the officiousness of some near the battlefield or demanding that soldiers show leave passes at home led to abuse and shouts of "Gestapo" (Emsley 2013, pp. 61–62).

As military organizations grew larger and required ever greater and more sophisticated forms of materiel, much of which had a market in the civilian word, so too did the need for military police to investigate crimes also grow. In the British Army there appears to have been a small detective force within the military police at the end of the First World War, but it ceased to exist after the Army of Occupation was withdrawn from the Rhineland in the early 1920s. Massive pilferage and often-sophisticated thefts of material bound for the British Expeditionary Force in 1939 led to the recruitment of twenty Metropolitan Police detectives at the beginning of 1940. After some initial success they were caught up in the retreat to Dunkirk and found themselves fighting their way to the beaches. On their return from France, these detectives formed the nucleus of the new Special Investigation Branch (SIB) established to investigate crimes committed by military personnel, often in league with civilians. SIB sections, usually of about sixteen men, were attached to units of several thousand men and often covered enormous areas, which, following the invasion of Europe, constantly shifted. Understandably, senior military officers were always more concerned with fighting the war than with the work of their detective units, and SIB section commanders, who were mainly recruited from the civilian police, regularly complained about their lack of administrative assistance, and the fact that they had to do their own cooking and vehicle maintenance—especially since they were often the last in line for vehicle replacements. In May 1944 the commander of 62 Section, based in Bari, was incensed by a motor transport inspection that labeled his unit "unsatisfactory." His men, he protested, were chosen for their policing abilities, not to repair and service vehicles. They had no time to learn or practice such skills:

> I have in the past taken the view that bodily harm to a person or the chance of the recovery of perhaps £200–£300 worth of property is more important than maintenance to a vehicle valued at less than £100. I would like to point out that up to the present for this month alone, approximately £3,500 worth of property has been recovered.[3]

The commander of 62 Section was not a regular soldier but a civilian police officer, and his anger was that of a police officer. Conscription brought such men, as well as men with legal backgrounds and others who felt that military law should not be different from civilian law, into the armed forces. Things had been changing in the British Army before 1914, but the influx of conscripts who had worked in the civilian criminal justice system accelerated change and increasingly led to it becoming more transparent, less influenced by the hierarchical structure of the military, and much closer to the civilian system (Emsley 2013, esp. chs. 1 & 2). While the military legal structures of other states had different starting points, the eventual success of democratic liberalism ensured that they followed a similar track at least after the Second World War.

Conclusion

There are various pressures, temptations, and opportunities to commit criminal offenses in war as well as in peace. Similarly, as in peacetime, crime in war cannot simply be laid at the door of individuals stigmatized as "criminals." War invariably aggravates economic problems and provides opportunities for those prepared to engage in the black market, leading both civilians and service personnel who might otherwise never have broken the criminal law to become involved in criminal acts. War can foster, sometimes with the direct sanction of authority, offenses such as murder and rape; but the wartime temptation to dehumanize, or see perpetrator or victim as the other arguably breaks down boundaries in such instances. The popular notion of brutalized veterans returning from war and committing violent offenses upon demobilization appears to have little reference to reality. Yet men do return with serious psychological scars that can foster different forms of criminal behavior, usually violent or sexual offenses, with the former particularly often committed within the family. Some of these problems can be solved by care and government action, but such action can also depend on the more general shape, especially the economic shape, of the country concerned. Finally, war can also put new and serious pressures on both civilian and military criminal justice systems, and these pressures can lead to change that continues into the postwar world.

Notes

1. "War Diary," January–December 1945, TNA WO 171/7804, SIS 70 Section, National Archives, Kew, United Kingdom.
2. "War Diary," October–December 1944, TNA WO 171/3415, SIS 82 Section, National Archives, Kew, United Kingdom.
3. "War Diary," January–December 1944, TNA WO 171/3590, SIS 62 Section, National Archives, Kew, United Kingdom.

References

Aaslestad, Katherine B. 2009. "War Without Battles: Civilian Experiences of Economic Warfare During the Napoleonic Era in Hamburg." In *Soldiers, Citizens and Civilians: Experiences and Perceptions of the Revolutionary and Napoleonic Wars, 1790–1820*, ed. Alan Forrest, Karen Hagemann, & Jane Rendall, 118–36. Houndmills, Basingstoke, UK: Palgrave Macmillan.

Adler, Jeffrey S. 1996. "The Making of a Moral Panic in Nineteenth-Century America: The Boston Garrotting Hysteria of 1865." *Deviant Behaviour: An Interdisciplinary Journal* 17:259–78.

Brophy, John, & Eric Partridge. 1965. *The Long Trail: What the British Soldier Sang and Said in the Great War of 1914–1918*, rev. ed. London: Andre Deutsch.

Buchbinder, Olivier. 2004. *Gendarmerie prévôtale et maintien de l'ordre (1914–1918)*. Maisons Alfort, France: Service historique de la Gendarmerie nationale.

Collin, Richard Oliver. 1984. "The Italian Police and Internal Security from Giolitti to Mussolini." Ph.D. diss., Oxford University.

Daly, Gavin. 2013. *The British Soldier in the Peninsular War: Encounters with Spain and Portugal, 1808–1814*. Houndmills, Basingstoke, UK: Palgrave.

Danke, Uwe. 1988. "Bandits and the State: Robbers and the Authorities in the Holy Roman Empire in the Late Seventeenth and Early Eighteenth Centuries." In *The German Underworld: Deviants and Outcasts in German History*, ed. Richard J. Evans, 75–107. London: Routledge.

Dickie, John. 1999. *Darkest Italy: The Nation and Stereotypes of the Mezzogiorno, 1860–1900*. New York: St. Martin's Press.

Egmond, Florike. 1986. *Banditisme in de Franse Tijd: profile van de Grote Nederlandse Bende, 1790–99*. Amsterdam: De Bataafsche Leeuw.

Egmond, Florike. 1993. *Underworlds: Organised Crime in the Netherlands, 1650–1800*. Oxford: Polity Press.

Emsley, Clive. 1999. *Gendarmes and the State in Nineteenth-Century Europe*. Oxford: Oxford University Press.

Emsley, Clive. 2008. "Violent Crime in England in 1919: Post-War Anxieties and Press Narratives." *Continuity and Change* 22:173–95.

Emsley, Clive. 2010. "A Legacy of Conflict? The 'Brutalised Veteran' and Violence in Europe after the Great War." In *Problems of Crime and Violence in Europe, 1780–2000*, ed. Efi Avdela, Shani D'Cruze, & Judith Rowbotham, 43–64. Lampeter, UK: Edwin Mellen Press.

Emsley, Clive. 2011. *Crime and Society in Twentieth-Century England*. Harlow & London: Longman.

Emsley, Clive. 2013. *Soldier, Sailor, Beggarman, Thief: Crime and the British Armed Services since 1914*. Oxford: Oxford University Press.

Esdaile, Charles J. 2004. *Fighting Napoleon: Guerrillas, Bandits and Adventurers in Spain, 1808–1814*. New Haven, CT, & London: Yale University Press.

Evans, Richard J. 1998. *Tales from the German Underworld*. New Haven, CT, & London: Yale University Press.

Exner, Franz. 1927. *Krieg und Kriminalität in Österreich*. Vienna: Hölde-Pichler-Tempsky AG.

Fergusson, Niall. 2004. "Prisoner Taking and Prisoner Killing in the Age of Total War: Towards a Political Economy of Military Defeat." *War in History* 11 (2): 148–92.

Forrest, Alan. 1989. *Conscripts and Deserters: The Army and French Society During the Revolution and Empire*. Oxford: Oxford University Press.

Gebhardt, Miriam. 2015. *Als die Soldaten kamen: Die Vergewaltigung deutscher Frauen am Ende des Zweiten Weltskrieg*. Munich: Deutsche Verlag-Anstalt.

Godfroid, Anne. 2012. "After 'Teutonic Fury,' 'Belgian Fury'? Fact and Fiction in the Revenge of Belgian Soldiers in the Rhineland in 1923." In *Rape in Wartime*, ed. Raphaëlle Branche & Fabrice Virgili, 90–102. Houndmills, Basingstoke, UK: Palgrave Macmillan.

Gomez Pardo, Julian. 2012. *La Maréchausée et le crime en Île-de-France sous Louis XIV et Louis XV*. Paris: Les Indes savants.

Grenard, Fabrice. 2008. *La France du marché noir (1940–1949)*. Paris: Payot.

Hay, Douglas. 1982. "War, Dearth and Theft in the Eighteenth Century: The Record of the English Courts." *Past and Present* 95:117–60.

Hopkin, David M. 2002. "Military Marauders in Nineteenth-Century French Popular Culture." *War in History* 9 (3): 251–78.

Horn, Pierre. 2013. "Commissariat général et commissariats spéciaux de police dans le département annexé de la Roër-Wessel et Cologne, 1809–1813." In *Police et Gendarmerie dans l'Empire napoléonien*, ed. Jacques-Olivier Boudon, 91–110. Paris: Editions SPM.

Joly, Maud. 2012. "The Practices of War, Terror and Imagination: Moor Troops and Rapes During the Spanish Civil War." In *Rape in Wartime*, ed. Raphaëlle Branche & Fabrice Virgili, 103–14. Houndmills, Basingstoke, UK: Palgrave Macmillan.

King, Peter. 1987. "Newspaper Reporting, Prosecution Practice and Perceptions of Urban Crime: The Colchester Crime Wave of 1765." *Continuity and Change* 2:423–54.

King, Peter. 2000. *Crime, Justice, and Discretion in England, 1740–1820*. Oxford: Oxford University Press.

King, Peter. 2002. "War as a Judicial Resource: Press Gangs and Prosecution Rates, 1740–1830." In *Law, Crime and English Society, 1600–1830*, ed. Norma Landau, 97–115. Cambridge: Cambridge University Press.

Kramer, Alan. 2007. *Dynamic of Destruction: Culture and Mass Killing in the First World War*. Oxford: Oxford University Press.

Liepmann, Moritz. 1930. *Krieg und Kriminalität in Deutschland*. Stuttgart, Berlin, & Leipzig: Deutsche Verlag Anstalt.

Lilly, J. Robert. 2007. *Taken by Force: Rape and American GIs in Europe During World War II*. Houndmills, Basingstoke, UK: Palgrave Macmillan.

MacManus, Deirdre, Kimberlie Dean, Margaret Jones, Roberto J. Rona, Neil Greenberg, Lisa Hull, Tom Fahy, Simon Wessely, & Nicola T. Fear. 2013. "Violent Offending by UK Military Personnel Deployed in Iraq and Afghanistan: A Data Linkage Cohort Study." *Lancet* 318:907–17

Mannheim, Hermann. 1941. *War and Crime*. London: Watts & Co.

Martens, Georg Friedrich von. 1817. *Recueil des Traités des Puissances et Etats de l'Europe*, Vol. 5. Gottingen, Germany: Dieterich.

Naimark, Norman M. 1995. *The Russians in Germany: The History of the Soviet Occupation of Germany, 1945–49*. Cambridge, MA: Harvard University Press.

Oram, Gerard. 2002. "'The Administration of Discipline by the English Is Very Rigid': British Military Law and the Death Penalty." *Crime, History and Societies* 5 (1): 93–110.

Oram, Gerard. 2003. "'The Greatest Efficiency': British and American Military Law, 1866–1918." In *Comparative Histories of Crime*, ed. Barry S. Godfrey, Clive Emsley, & Graeme Dunstall, 159–77. Cullompton, UK: Willan Publishing.

Palk, Deirdre. 2006. *Gender, Crime and Judicial Discretion, 1780–1830*. Woodbridge, UK: Royal Historical Society/Boydell.

Panel, Louis N. 2003. "Cognes, homes noirs et grenades blanches: les enjeux de la représentation des gendarmes de la Grande Guerre." In *Sociétés et Représentations*, Vol. 16, *Figures de gendarmes*, ed. Jean-Noël Luc, 167–82. Paris: CREDHES.

Panel, Louis N. 2013. "La Grande Guerre de la Gendarmerie." In *Histoire et Dictionnaire de la Gendarmerie*, ed. Jean-Noël Luc & Frédéric Médard, 43–52. Paris: Éditions Jacob-Duvernet.

Rivière, Antoine. 2012. "'Special Decisions' Children Born as the Result of German Rape and Handed over to Public Assistance during the Great War (1914–18)." In *Rape in Wartime*, ed. Raphaëlle Branche & Fabrice Virgili, 184–200. Basingstoke, UK: Palgrave Macmillan.

Roodhouse, Mark. 2013. *Black Market Britain, 1939–1955*. Oxford: Oxford University Press.

Sampson, Robert J., & John H. Laub. 1996. "Socioeconomic Achievement in the Life Course of Disadvantaged Men: Military Service as a Turning Point, circa 1940–1965." *American Sociological Review* 61 (3): 347–67.

Sellin, Thorsten. 1926. "Is Murder Increasing in Europe?" *Annals of the American Academy of Political and Social Science* 126:29–34.

Smithies, Edward. 1982. *Crime in Wartime: A Social History of Crime in World War II*. London: George Allen & Unwin.

Spraggs, Gillian. 2001. *Outlaws and Highwaymen: The Cult of the Robber in England from the Middle Ages to the Nineteenth Century*. London: Pimlico.

Starke, Wilhelm. 1884. *Verbrechen und Verbrecher in Preußen, 1854–1878. Ein kulturgeschichtliche Studie*. Berlin: Enslin.

Styles, T. J. 2002. *Jesse James: Last Rebel of the Civil War*. New York: Alfred A. Knopf.

Williams, Isobel. 2013. *Allies and Italians under Occupation: Sicily and Southern Italy, 1943–45*. Basingstoke, UK: Palgrave Macmillan.

PART SEVEN

LAW, COURTS, AND CRIMINAL JUSTICE

CHAPTER 27

THE ROLE OF POPULAR JUSTICE IN U.S. HISTORY

ELIZABETH DALE

INTRODUCTION

FROM tarring and feathering at the end of the eighteenth century to armed vigilantes patroling the border between the United States and Mexico at the start of the twenty-first, popular justice has traced a path across the history of the United States. But if popular justice has been a recurring element of that history, its place typically has been at the margins. This is particularly true in legal history, in which extralegal acts are treated as the exception rather than a historical rule (Walker 1998; Friedman 1994).

In this essay, I argue that, far from being an anomaly, popular justice must be understood as an integral (albeit troubling) part of the legal and constitutional history of the United States. That claim builds on the law and society work of legal historians like Lawrence Friedman (1994) but pushes their ideas further by asking legal history to recognize the legal role played by people outside the institutions of law. In that respect, it complements recent work by Laura Edwards (2009) and Naomi Murakawa (2014) that has explored the intersection of private justice and public law.

This study depends on what we mean when we use the phrase "popular justice," so I offer a working definition of the term in the first section of this essay. Then, in the next two sections, I elaborate on that definition as I sketch the different ways in which popular justice has been manifested across U.S. history. The first of these sections looks at popular justice as violence, tracing the different expressions of rough justice through space and time. In the next, the focus shifts to the less familiar nonviolent varieties of popular justice. Then, in a fourth section, I pull those strains together to explore how popular justice intersects with formal law.

I. Preliminaries

Popular justice often is represented in U.S. legal history as a series of set pieces: the white crowd gathered beneath the body of an African American lynching victim in the south, a vigilance committee stringing up cattle rustlers in the western plains, a riotous mob injuring persons and property during a protest in the urban north (Hall & Karsten 2009). Viewed together, those images evoke a narrow understanding of the place of popular justice in the United States: it is communal, it is violent, and it functions in the shadows outside of law. That view conceives of popular justice as a function of actions and actors: popular justice is what happens when certain people act in specific ways. Building on scholarship focused on popular justice, this essay offers an alternative view, treating popular justice as a process that occurs whenever people take the law into their own hands to judge and punish others (Huggins 1991; Brown 1975).

Thinking of popular justice as a process clarifies and sharpens our understanding of the concept, offering a crucial boundary marker: to be an expression of popular *justice*, an act must be undertaken to judge or punish (or both) another's act. A violent and destructive riot by sports fans celebrating a championship probably is not popular justice because it gives voice to no sense of justice; it is merely an expression of emotional excess. In contrast, a violent and destructive riot that targets stores that sell goods produced by slave labor may be an expression of popular justice to the extent that it seeks to punish those who profit from an economic or social wrong.

Viewing popular justice as a process of judging and punishing tells us several other important things about the concept. First, it suggests that while popular justice may be violent, it need not be; gossip may punish as effectively as tarring and feathering. Second, it implies that popular justice need not always be carried out by a collective; individuals may take the law into their own hands in defense of person or property, or to protest what they perceive to be an unjust act. Third, it reminds us that there is a constitutional aspect to popular justice: it is "popular" because it is justice that is carried out by non-state actors. That does not, of course, mean that popular justice needs to be uniformly endorsed by people in a community, and often it has not been. All too often, one person's popular justice has been another person's domestic terrorism (Kirkpatrick 2008).

As all of these considerations indicate, popular justice is an expansive concept that may be expressed in a variety of ways. And a quick look at U.S. history demonstrates how often that has been the case.

II. Justice as Violence

The set pieces at the beginning of the previous section suggest that in the United States popular justice often is equated with deadly force. But in the United States, justice as violence exists along a spectrum. The deadliest forms lie at one end of that spectrum; at the other are forms of popular justice that violently destroy property. In the middle are acts of justice that injure people without killing them.

A. Destruction of Property

Popular justice that destroys property could be directed either at offending materials or at the buildings that house them. During the American Revolution, food rioters targeted the merchants who violated boycotts of British goods, forcibly seizing goods to redistribute them and not hesitating to break into shops to do so (Smith 1994). Other mobs looted the homes of representatives of the British government or destroyed the property of loyalists (Pashman 2013; Maier 1992).

Although mob actions diminished by the turn of the nineteenth century, they did not come to a complete end (Gilje 1980). In the 1820s, neighborhood mobs in New York City attacked and destroyed brothels (Gilfoyle 1994). In the 1830s and 1840s, groups around the country destroyed churches in which abolitionists were scheduled to speak (Hone 1889, Vol. 1, p. 341) as well as buildings, like Pennsylvania Hall, that were used by abolitionists and other, often interracial, groups (Feldberg 1980; Brown 1976). In the 1850s, anti-Catholic mobs targeted Roman Catholic churches, and pro-temperance women's groups destroyed saloons and liquor stores (Haebler 1984; Varon 1998). While buildings were popular targets, mobs also attacked and destroyed other forms of property in the name of justice. In Charleston, South Carolina, anti-abolitionists seized and burned pamphlets from the post office (Hone 1889, Vol. 1, p. 155). In Illinois, a mob destroyed Elijah Lovejoy's printing presses to protest his abolitionist tracts (Kielbowicz 2006). Workers sometimes destroyed goods produced by other workers: striking handloom weavers in Philadelphia attacked looms and goods produced by other workers (Montgomery 1972). When people in Philadelphia were unable to persuade officials that a railroad line should not be built down the middle of a major artery in their neighborhood, they took to the streets to tear up the track as soon as it was laid (Feldberg 1975).

So, too, mobs that began by targeting one kind of property sometimes expanded their targets. Not satisfied by ransacking a theater where abolitionist speakers met, an anti-abolitionist mob in New York marched on the house of Lewis Tappan, a noted leader of the cause. They forced their way into his home, broke out all the windows, and then dragged the furniture into the street, where they burned it (Hone 1889, Vol. 1, p. 109). A mob in Baltimore, angered by the economic injury done when the Bank of Maryland stopped payments, expressed its outrage by breaking all the windows in the house of one bank director. Persuaded to disperse by some leading men of the town, the mob returned to the same house a few days later and pulled it down (Hone 1889, Vol. 1, p. 153).

To the extent that they focused on precise targets, which were often closely related to the issue that sparked the protest, these mob actions resembled the protests associated with the moral economy in earlier eras (Thompson 1971). But other mobs excused their conduct in other terms. Some claimed they were protecting their community from threats to its health, its safety, or its welfare (or morals) (Grimsted 1974). Others justified their actions in legal or constitutional language: they were destroying public nuisances or acting as the sovereign people (Kirkpatrick 2008; Feldberg 1975). In effect, they were making a claim to a reserved constitutional power (Dale 2011b).

Groups continued to justify acts of popular justice in those terms across the nineteenth century. During the Civil War, food rioters in several southern cities claimed they acted out of a sense of economic justice and self-defense (Chesson 1984). A group of native New Mexicans formed an organization called the White Caps after an influx of Anglo families in the 1880s threatened customary grazing practices. In the name of protecting older economic norms, the White Caps tore down the fences the new Anglo owners had built (Larson 1975). At the turn of the century, Carrie Nation and her followers justified their destruction of taverns and saloons in terms of protecting society from moral and social decay (Hume 2002). Those rationales continued to find purchase in the twentieth century: in 1917, a mob of rioters amounting to thousands of women, according to one report, protested a sudden rise in peddlers' prices in Brooklyn, New York, by burning the offending produce and overturning vendors' pushcarts and stands (Frieburger 1984). Those justifications continued to be made into the late twentieth century, when anti-abortion activists often justified bombing clinics on the ground they were defending the rights of the unborn (Nice 1988).

White mobs were never the only groups that made these sorts of claims (Hill 2010; Waldrep 1998; Larson 1975), but appeals to morality and safety often justified ugly and racist acts. Anti-Chinese mobs in Los Angeles targeted Chinese homes and businesses (Zesch 2012), and white mobs in the south that attacked places where blacks and Republicans gathered during Reconstruction claimed that they acted to discourage unrest, in the name of morality, or in response to vague threats to the community (Kantrowitz 2000). Race riots from Tulsa, Oklahoma, to Springfield, Illinois, destroyed black homes and businesses from the last decades of the nineteenth century through 1921, often in the name of public safety (Walker 1998). In the 1920s and 1940s, whites intent on preventing the so-called Black Belt from expanding in Chicago bombed buildings that had been rented to black families on that city's south side (Drake & Cayton 1945).

B. Injury to Persons

Violent expressions of popular justice also targeted and injured people. During the Revolution, mobs in New York seized British sympathizers, stripped them, beat and kicked them, and often rode them out of town on rails to punish them for aiding the enemy or for being traitors (Pashman 2013). Several decades later, brothel owners, as well as their buildings, were targets of angry mobs in New York, who beat them as they destroyed their property (Gilfoyle 1994). During the long rent strike in upstate New York, people from the community attacked and beat sheriffs and their agents as they tried to evict tenants (McCurdy 2001).

Beatings, canings, hidings, and floggings continued to be popular in the second half of the nineteenth century. In the states of the former Confederacy, the Ku Klux Klan and similar groups enforced community norms, while the previously mentioned White Caps patrolled communities in Indiana, Mississippi, and Texas, flogging people (often whites) for immorality (Larson 1975). Claims of economic injustice also were used to justify attacks at the turn of the century, with the so-called Night Riders in Missouri targeting black laborers, who were seen as tools of a tumultuous economic shift in the decade before the First World War (Roll 2002).

Vigilante or citizens' groups, many of them either violent or with the potential for violence, continued to act in the first decades of the twentieth century. In the 1920s, both the Klan and the White Cap movement returned (Larson 1975), and similar groups of Night Riders formed in Ohio and Michigan. They flogged or tarred and feathered men and women—often Catholic, immigrant, or black—who they suspected (or at least accused) of immorality (Amann 1983). In the 1930s, one of those groups, the Black Legion, turned itself into a quasi-military organization and tried to spread from Ohio into Indiana, Illinois, and Michigan (Amann 1983). Black Legion groups burned films they viewed as immoral (including a pro-Catholic film that was going to be shown in Michigan), raided and bombed recreation centers and bookstores, and attacked individuals associated with them. Their usual targets were communists, radicals, or any other group they perceived to be a threat to the community or American values (Amann 1983), a rationale offered by minutemen groups who assign themselves to patrol the country's borders with Mexico today (Shapira 2013).

Other vigilante groups attacked labor organizers, communists, and members of other radical or reform groups (Bernstein 2010; Gilmore 2008; Schwantes 1981). A mob flogged several anticorruption Democrats in Tampa, Florida, in 1935 (Ingalls 1977). When the activist Joseph Gelders was kidnapped and then flogged in Birmingham, Alabama, in 1936, one police officer explained that public sentiment would prevent Gelder's assailants from being prosecuted. The problem, the officer explained, was that the community hoped that U.S. Steel would expand its facilities in the area and as a result opposed any labor or radical agitation that might threaten that development (Ingalls 1977). Those justifications continued (and sometimes increased) in the post-*Brown* era, when apologists for massive resistance justified their attacks on civil rights activists in terms of reserved constitutional powers and the power to protect communities (Golub 2013).

Those acts of violent justice were undertaken by groups, but individuals could, and did, also take the law into their own hands in a violent manner. When William Cullen Bryant, a newspaper editor in New York City, had a dispute with William Stone, another editor in that city, Bryant went after Stone with a cowhide. Having cornered his target, Bryant managed to get in several strokes with the cowhide before Stone grabbed the weapon and turned it on Bryant (Hone 1889, Vol. 1, p. 30). When Preston Brooks, a representative from South Carolina, determined that Charles Sumner, a senator from Massachusetts, had insulted another politician from South Carolina, he walked up to Sumner as he sat writing a letter in the Capitol and beat him with a cane (Woods 2011). Although state law increasingly set limits on the power, at least nominally, slave masters and overseers through the end of the Civil War flogged slaves to punish perceived wrongdoing (Waldrep 1998; Hindus 1980).

Others punished "transgressors" using means that were more rough and ready. When General Blair objected to materials published by Duff Green on slavery, he simply beat him (Hone 1889, Vol. 1, p. 89). Philip Hone reported that when an elected representative named Crise decided he had been insulted by another representative named Stanley, he simply attacked Stanley on the floor of the House of Representatives (1889, Vol. 2, p. 87–88). Politicians and editors were not the only people who exacted summary punishment with their fists. When a man strolling down a Philadelphia street with his wife decided that a young man on a street corner had insulted her, he administered a corrective beating there on the spot (Dale 2011b). When Eleuthere Irenee du Pont de Nemours concluded that Charles Munns had convinced a number of his employees to sell him copies of du Pont's secret equipment, he and a partner met with Munns and beat him severely (Fisk 2009).

C. Deadly Violence

Sometimes, of course, popular justice turned deadly. In 1936, the Black Legion, which had previously targeted but failed to kill a number of "enemies," murdered Charles Poole in Michigan. Poole was suspected of beating his pregnant wife, but he was also a Catholic man married to a Protestant woman (Amann 1983). In Poole's case, the deadly result was intended, while other times death was an unintended consequence of the pursuit of justice. One hundred years before Poole's murder, in 1835, a vigilante group known as the Vicksburg Volunteers organized in the name of "all honest white citizens" in Tennessee and vowed to rid their town of gamblers. They first simply demanded that the gamblers leave. When that request failed to persuade them, they organized a march on a gambling den. The gamblers opened fire and killed one of the marchers. At that point, the Volunteers ceased their peaceful attempts at justice and attacked the building, seizing several of the men inside and hanging five (Waldrep 1998). Anti-abolitionist and anti-Catholic mobs in antebellum Philadelphia likewise killed people when they attacked buildings to try to punish attitudes of which they did not approve (Dale 2011b).

Once again, the deadliest form of rough justice could be manifested in a variety of ways. It could be the act of an individual: duels were one way individuals redressed wrong in the decades before the Civil War. Many of these contests took place in the south (Wyatt-Brown 1982); Philip Hone reported duels in Virginia in that same period (1889, Vol. 2, pp. 272–73), and James Henry Hammond reported trying to help persuade several hot-headed young men (including Preston Brooks) not to fight duels in South Carolina (Bleser 1988). But there were duels in the north as well. In the 1840s, Thomas Cope (1978) reported that several young men from Philadelphia went to Delaware to kill one another in duels. In addition to these formally organized affairs, men north and south used fists, knives, and sometimes guns to kill one another as they avenged a variety of wrongs (Lane 1997). The years just before the Civil War also saw the rise of another form of individualized capital punishment, in which men and some women killed seducers. This practice of killing in the name of the "unwritten law"—more specifically, in defense of morality and the sanctity of marriage—continued into the early twentieth century (Bakken 2007; Hartog 1997; Ireland 1989).

It is hard to categorize individual acts of deadly justice, since the line between an act undertaken to avenge an injustice and a murderous assault is often subjective. In the twentieth century, the problem of drawing that distinction is further complicated by the rise of the plea bargain; while pleas make it less likely a jury will give tacit approval to an individual act of deadly justice (Dale 2008b), they also leave less record of the reason for the attack. But the recent interest in stand your ground laws suggests that the idea that individuals should be able to take the law into their own hands in defense of self or others remains salient (Stein 2012). However, the range of responses to the recent verdict acquitting George Zimmerman for the killing of Trayvon Martin also suggests both a lack of consensus and racial divisions on the issue (Jon Cohen & Dan Balz, "Zimmerman Verdict Poll: Stark Reaction Based on Race," *Washington Post*, 22 July 2013).

Most deadly acts of popular justice were not the acts of individuals. Mobs targeted and killed people before the Civil War (Pfeifer 2011; Brown 1975), and lynch mobs and vigilance committees began to work in earnest in the years after that war ended (Pfeifer 2004). While many lynchings happened in the states of the former Confederacy (Ayers 1984), rough justice was never confined to the south. Mobs lynched Chinese immigrants in the west (Zesch 2012; Pfeifer 2004) and Mexicans and Native Americans in the southwest (Carrigan & Webb 2013). There were lynchings and deadly vendettas in the Midwest, in Indiana and Wisconsin, and farther east in states like Pennsylvania (Dale 2011a; Pfeifer 2004). The victims of these groups were various. Most obviously, blacks and members of other racial minorities were frequently targets. But even in the south, labor organizers and other "radicals" could also be the focus of such attacks (Ingalls 1987). Once again, justifications were sounded in the form of claims of economic justice, self-defense, or other police powers: ranchers targeted horse thieves and cattle rustlers (Brown 1975); blacks and whites in rural areas lynched rapists and murderers (Hill 2010; Pfeifer 2004).

Thus, violent acts of popular justice spanned a spectrum. On one end was violence that targeted property—houses, places of business, taverns and brothels, meeting places, and churches—and did it damage. At the other end was deadly violence against people. In between, there were acts that caused injury short of death. These various acts of rough justice often were collective, but popular justice was not exclusively undertaken by groups; individuals took the law into their own hands as well, killing others in duels or administering floggings.

III. Nonviolent Popular Justice

Communities could and did endorse individual acts of justice. After Preston Brooks beat Charles Sumner, his constituents expressed their approval by reelecting him to the House of Representatives (Woods 2011). When Singleton Mercer killed Mahlon Heberton after Heberton seduced Mercer's sister, a jury accepted Mercer's justifications of the act and found him not guilty (Dale 2011b). At the same time, communities could withhold their approval and themselves resort to acts of popular justice to punish the perpetrator. When Matt Ward killed a schoolteacher who had whipped Ward's younger brother for lying, a jury in Kentucky found Ward not guilty. But that endorsement was quickly challenged—an indignation meeting was held, effigies of Ward and his lawyers were burned in effigy, and a mob marched from the meeting to the Ward house, where they torched more effigies and nearly burned the Ward house down in the process. Matt Ward was forced to flee Louisville in fear of his life and was never able to return from exile (Ireland 1986).

A. Shaming and Shunning

The Ward case demonstrates that there were less violent means of expressing judgments and punishing as well. In the early nineteenth century, social networks, often dominated by women, used gossip to identify instances of misconduct and shame or shun wrongdoers. When rumor had it that James Henry Hammond, governor of South Carolina, had engaged in sexually inappropriate conduct with his young nieces, those same networks then discussed the behavior to explore its scope and come to judgment about whether wrongdoing had occurred. Once judgment had been reached, those same networks were then used to punish, spreading the tale of the misconduct and shaming Hammond for engaging in it. As this example suggests, these informal courts of public opinion did not merely punish through shame. In Hammond's case, the "tea party goddesses" who dominated the gossip networks in Columbia, South Carolina, demanded that other parts of the community shun Hammond and drove him into several years of political exile (Bleser 1988).

Several famous examples of the workings of the informal courts of public opinion—including both the Hammond case and the nearly contemporary Peggy Eaton case in Washington, D.C. (Marszalek 1997)—suggest that those courts often were used to punish sexual misconduct and immorality (Dale 2008a). But other examples demonstrate that the courts of public opinion could be harnessed to punish economic wrongs. When Nicholas Biddle was implicated in a bank crisis that lost a number of people their savings, elite Philadelphia shunned him in punishment (Dale 2011b). When the contentious M. du DuPont concluded that another man, Thomas Ewell, was trying to steal his trade secrets and skilled workers, he wrote pamphlets to shame Ewell and expose his dishonorable economic conduct (Fisk 2009). In the 1830s, whites in Virginia monitored their neighbors and used gossip networks to report (and shame) those who taught their slaves to read in violation of the law (Varon 1998); at the turn of the twentieth century, striking workers in Tampa used similar tactics to maintain solidarity (Hewitt 2003).

These practices continued into the twentieth century. In the 1930s, vigilante groups organized in Maryland to shame couples who parked their cars in certain areas in order to make out ("Vigilantes to Roam at Night as Petters Upset Glen Echo," *Washington Post*, 4 November 1937). In the 1990s, university students organized campaigns to shame and shun fellow students accused of rape at college campuses (William Cellis, "Date Rape and a List at Brown," *New York Times*, 18 November 1990). Students returned to that technique for similar reasons in the second decade of the twenty-first century (Cory Weinberg, "Sexual Assault Vigilantes," *Inside Higher Ed*, 15 May 2014).

B. Exile and Silencing

Ostracism and forced exile were also options for those who sought justice. During the American Revolution, community "committees" banished and ostracized loyalists (Maier 1992). In South Carolina in the 1840s, James Henry Hammond was forced out of society for several years, a temporary exile that he was able to spend on his plantation (Bleser 1988). A few years later, Matt Ward was less fortunate: he was forced to flee Kentucky entirely and lived the rest of his life in exile on a plantation owned by his family in Arkansas (Ireland 1986). Church groups punished particularly recalcitrant members in a similar way, excommunicating them for their wrongdoings (Pease & Pease 1990).

Silencing and the heckler's veto were other popular nonviolent means of shutting down speech that violated community norms. In the early nineteenth century, groups in Boston, New York, and Ohio used the heckler's veto to silence abolitionists (Harrison 1976; Pease & Pease 1990) and speakers on women's issues (Pease & Pease 1990). Hecklers also shut down performances by actors of whom they disapproved and plays on topics to which they objected (Dale 2011b). In the early twentieth century, townspeople burst in on and shut down a meeting of the Grange in Walla Walla, Washington (Schwantes 1981). In the 1930s, vigilantes broke up meetings and silenced radicals and labor organizers in the north and south (Gilmore 2008; *Atlanta Constitution*, "Terre Haute Vigilantes Balk Browder Speech," 21 October 1936). The heckler's veto continued to be a viable, if contested, method of silencing speech into the twenty-first century (Leanza 2006).

C. Boycotts and Indignation Meetings

Boycotts are another means of enforcing popular justice that have been used to censure or advance particular, often economic, senses of justice. In the eighteenth century, committees within the colonies monitored merchants and fellow citizens to enforce boycotts of British goods, and publicized the names of those who failed to comply (Maier 1970). In the late eighteenth and early nineteenth centuries, transatlantic networks of abolitionists organized boycotts of slave-made goods, while some anti-abolitionists proposed to punish abolitionists by boycotting northern-manufactured goods (Glickman 2004; Varon 1989). During the civil rights era, African American communities boycotted white-owned businesses that would not hire or sell to blacks, and white supremacist organizations like the Black Shirts threatened to boycott businesses unless they fired black workers (Gilmore 2008; Drake & Cayton 1945).

Boycotts enacted punishment in two ways: by attempting to harm a business economically and by publicizing wrongdoing. Another form of nonviolent popular justice, the indignation meeting, likewise carried out punishment through publicity. When Matt Ward was acquitted of murder, the people of Louisville held an indignation meeting at the courthouse to denounce the verdict (Ireland 1986). When the governor of Virginia commuted the death penalty of Jordan Hatcher, a slave convicted of killing his white overseer, people in Richmond, Virginia, held an indignation meeting to protest (Woods 2011). In the second half of the nineteenth century, when the police in Chicago targeted the city's small African American community after the murder of a young white working girl in 1888, members of that community held an indignation meeting to denounce the police action and try to rally public opinion to their side (Dale 2001). Not quite fifty years later, when police in Chicago broke up a peaceful picket line and killed ten people during the "Memorial Day Massacre of 1937," labor organizers joined Progressive leaders to hold an indignation meeting calling attention to police violence. More than 4,000 people attended the session (Hogan 2014).

D. Jury Nullification

Matt Ward's acquittal points to another way that people could, and did, take the law into their own hands: as jurors. Scholars of homicide have frequently pointed out that this happened at all stages of the criminal process. Grand jurors refused to issue true bills, coroner's juries mysteriously found no cause for further investigation in cases involving seemingly violent deaths, and juries at trial acquitted or significantly reduced sentences in what appeared to be clear-cut cases of murder (Adler 2006; Monkkonen 2000; Lane 1999). The power of jury nullification, or, more literally, the power of jurors to take the law into their own hands, was explicitly recognized by law in many jurisdictions during the nineteenth century (Strange 2010; Harrington 1999; Bodenhamer 1979). The power was not limited to homicide cases; jurors nullified laws in fugitive slave cases (Knowles 2013; Cover 1975), labor cases (Lambert 2005), and domestic violence cases (Moore 2002).

As these examples suggest, nonviolent popular justice was manifested in a variety of forms. Sometimes, as was the case with jury nullification, nonviolent popular justice was used to sanction acts of violent popular justice, but shaming, shunning, and boycotting were tools that functioned on their own as well. Once again, these methods were justified in familiar constitutional or police power terms. Proponents spoke of jury nullification and indignation meetings as expressions of the people's sovereign power (Knowles 2013; Kramer 2004), while apologists excused acts of shaming or shunning as the legitimate exercise of a community's moral judgment (Dale 2008a).

IV. Law and Justice

Standard accounts of popular justice in the United States suggest that, after a fairly brief period, it was an exception to the rule. In this framework, popular justice was something that people resorted to when the law did not work, either because there was no law available or because they did not trust the law (Brown 1975). And that certainly was the rationale many people used to explain their resort to popular justice: Pitchfork Ben Tillman offered just that justification when he supported lynching in South Carolina at the turn of the century (Kantrowitz 2000), business owners in Brooklyn made a similar claim when they armed themselves to fight against thieves in the 1930s ("Crime Wave in Brooklyn Calls Out Vigilantes," *Chicago Tribune*, 16 November 1937), as advocates adopted a similar argument to defend their posting of the names of accused rapists on college campuses in the twenty-first century (Cory Weinberg, "Sexual Assault Vigilantes," *Inside Higher Ed*, 15 May 2014).

But at times, popular justice has also functioned as a system parallel to the institutions of criminal justice. Religious groups and private organizations have long claimed and exercised the power to privately judge and punish their members. Church congregations held their own trials or hearings in the colonial period and continued to do so through the nineteenth century (Juster 1994; Waldrep 1990). In the second decade of the twenty-first century, groups like the National Basketball Association owners' association have claimed the right to judge and sanction their own members (Ben Bolch, "Donald Sterling Sanctioned: Adam Silver Moves to Eject Clippers Owner," *Los Angeles Times*, 29 April 2014).

In addition, there have been moments when popular justice has functioned as part of the criminal justice system and vice versa. This was most obvious in the period up to 1840, when popular justice was part of the system of formal law (Edwards 2009). People in communities joined posses and helped investigate crimes and capture suspects, as well as helping determine what the law required when they served on juries of inquest, grand juries, and juries at trials (Edwards 2009; Steinberg 1989). While transformations of criminal justice in the late 1830s and 1840s, most notably the rise of police forces and efforts to shift power to judges (Friedman 1994), limited popular power over some parts of the criminal justice system, they did not bring all popular influence to an end (Dale 2011a). Juries continued to bring popular notions of justice into the criminal justice system in the late nineteenth and early twentieth centuries (Strange 2010; Dale 2008b), while indignation meetings and other types of mob action put pressure on the formal criminal justice system in the twentieth century (Hogan 2014; Golub

2013). Police and sheriff's offices worked with citizens' groups and vigilantes in the 1930s, sometimes deputizing them and sometimes merely inviting their aid (Bernstein 2010; "Buffalo 'Vigilantes' to Hunt for Mashers," *New York Times*, 20 February 1937). And in the early twenty-first century, federal law required colleges and universities to conduct their own hearings against students accused of sexual assault (Allie Grasgreen, "Classrooms, Courts or Neither?," *Inside Higher Ed*, 12 February 2014). Recent work by Mark Golub (2013) and Naomi Murakawa (2014) reminds us, however, that this relationship could work the other way as well: on more than a few occasions sheriffs and law enforcement officers enabled and abetted lynch mobs and rioters.

Conclusion

As the preceding summary suggests, people may engage in acts of popular justice for a number of different reasons. Often, those reasons are closely tied to the general contours of the police power: the people may take the law into their own hands to protect the health or safety of their community, or to enforce norms or moral standards. They may also engage in popular justice to express a sense of economic justice or to enforce laws that are on the books, but (to their mind) are ignored by the agents of the state.

In the process of undertaking any of these roles, the people may act in a variety of ways. They may act violently, killing or maiming people or destroying property. Their actions may be collective, but popular justice can also be expressed through the acts of individuals. For all these reasons, popular justice has a complex and dynamic relationship to formal justice and the rule of law. It may be exercised outside the systems of formal law, in parallel to the formal law, and, at times, with, or even as part of, the formal system of law. This mix of roles means that popular justice is both a display of power by the people themselves and, at least at times, a sharp restriction on the power of the state. Not only do the people claim and exercise powers that deny the state a monopoly on violence, but they act in ways that assert the exclusive power of a sovereign to define the scope of law. In any event, and any form, popular justice has been a very mixed blessing.

References

Adler, Jeffrey. 2006. *First in Violence, Deepest in Dirt*. Cambridge: Harvard University Press.

Amann, Peter H. 1983. "Vigilante Fascism: The Black Legion as American Hybrid." *Comparative Studies in Society and History*. 25: 490–524.

Ayers, Edward L. 1984. *Vengeance and Justice: Crime and Punishment in the 19th Century American South*. New York: Oxford University Press.

Bakken, Gordon. 2007. "The Limits of Patriarchy: Women's Rights and 'Unwritten Law' in the West." *Historian* 60:703–16.

Bernstein, Irving. 2010. *The Turbulent Years: A History of the American Worker, 1933–1940.* Chicago: Haymarket Books.

Bleser, Carol, ed. 1988. *Secret and Sacred: The Diaries of James Henry Hammond.* New York: Oxford University Press.

Bodenhamer, David J. 1979. "Law and Disorder on the Early Frontier: Marion County Indiana, 1823–1850." *Western Historical Quarterly* 10:323–36.

Brown, Ira. 1976. "Racism and Sexism: The Case of Pennsylvania Hall." *Phylon* 37:126–36.

Brown, Richard Maxwell. 1975. *Strain of Violence: Historical Studies of American Violence and Vigilantism.* New York: Oxford University Press.

Carrigan, William D., & Clive Webb. 2013. *Forgotten Dead: Mob Violence Against Mexicans in the United States, 1848–1928.* New York: Oxford University Press.

Chesson, Michael. 1984. "Harlots or Heroines? A New Look at the Richmond Bread Riot." *Virginia Magazine of History* 92:131–75.

Cope, Thomas. 1978. *Philadelphia Merchant: The Diary of Thomas P. Cope, 1800–1851.* South Bend, IN: Gateway Editions.

Cover, Robert. 1975. *Justice Accused: Antislavery and the Judicial Process.* New Haven, CT: Yale University Press.

Dale, Elizabeth. 2001. *The Rule of Justice: The People of Chicago Versus Zephyr Davis.* Columbus: Ohio State University Press.

Dale, Elizabeth. 2008a. "A Different Sort of Justice: The Informal Courts of Public Opinion in Antebellum South Carolina." *South Carolina Law Review* 54:627–47.

Dale, Elizabeth. 2008b. "*People v. Coughlin* and the Criminal Jury in Late Nineteenth Century Chicago." *Northern Illinois Law Review* 28:503–36.

Dale, Elizabeth. 2011a. *Criminal Justice in the United States, 1789–1939.* New York: Cambridge University Press.

Dale, Elizabeth. 2011b. "Popular Sovereignty: A Case Study from the Antebellum Era." In *Constitutional Mythologies*, ed. Alain Marciano, 81–106. New York: Springer.

Drake, St. Clair, & Horace Cayton. 1945. *Black Metropolis: A Study of Negro Life in a Northern City.* New York: Harcourt, Brace, & Company.

Edwards, Laura. 2009. *The People and Their Peace: Legal Culture and the Transformation of Inequality in the Post-Revolutionary South.* Chapel Hill: University of North Carolina Press.

Feldberg, Michael. 1975. *The Philadelphia Riots of 1844.* Westport, CT: Greenwood Press.

Fisk, Catherine. 2009. *Working Knowledge: Employee Innovation and the Rise of Corporate Intellectual Property, 1800–1930.* Chapel Hill: University of North Carolina Press.

Frieburger, William. 1984. "War Prosperity and Hunger: The New York Food Riots of 1917." *Labor History* 25:217–39.

Friedman, Lawrence M. 1994. *Crime and Punishment in American History.* New York: Basic Books.

Gilje, Paul. 1980. "The Baltimore Riots of 1812 and the Breakdown of the Anglo-American Mob Tradition." *Journal of Social History* 13:547–64.

Gilfoyle, Timothy. 1994. *City of Eros: New York City, Prostitution, and the Commercialization of Sex, 1790–1920.* New York: W. W. Norton & Co.

Gilmore, Glenda. 2008. *Defying Dixie: The Radical Roots of Civil Rights: 1919–1950.* New York: W. W. Norton & Co.

Glickman, Lawrence. 2004. "'Buy for the Sake of the Slave': Abolitionism and the Origins of American Consumer Action." *American Quarterly* 56:889–912.

Golub, Mark. 2013. "Remembering Massive Resistance to School Desegregation." *Law and History Review* 32:491–530.

Grimsted, David. 1974. "Rioting in Its Jacksonian Setting." *American Historical Review* 77:364–97.

Haebler, Peter. 1984. "Nativist Riots in Manchester." *Historical New Hampshire* 39:122–38.

Hall, Kermit L., & Peter Karsten. 2009. *The Magic Mirror: Law in American History*, 2nd ed. New York: Oxford University Press.

Harrington, Matthew. 1999. "The Law-Finding Function of the American Jury." *Wisconsin Law Journal*: 337–440.

Harrison, Theresa A. 1976. "George Thompson and the 1851 'Anti-Abolition Riot.'" *Historical Journal of Western Massachusetts* 5:36–44.

Hartog, Hendrik. 1997. "Lawyering, Husbands' Right and 'the Unwritten Law' in Nineteenth-Century America." *Journal of American History* 84:67–96.

Hewitt, Nancy. 2003. *Southern Discomfort: Women's Activism in Tampa, Florida, 1880s–1920s*. Urbana: University of Illinois Press.

Hill, Karlos K. 2010. "Black Vigilantism: The Rise and Decline of African American Lynch Mob Activity in the Mississippi and Arkansas Deltas." *Journal of African American History* 95:26–43.

Hindus, Michael Stephen. 1980. *Prison and Plantation: Crime, Justice and Authority in Massachusetts and South Carolina, 1767–1878*. Chapel Hill: University of North Carolina Press.

Hogan, John F. 2014. *The 1937 Chicago Steel Strike: Blood on the Prairie*. Charleston, SC: History Press.

Hone, Philip. 1889. *The Diary of Philip Hone, 1828–1851*, Vol. 1. Ed. Bayard Tuckerman. New York: Dodd, Mead.

Huggins, Martha K., ed. 1991. *Vigilantism and the State in Modern Latin America: Essays on Extralegal Violence*. New York: Praeger.

Hume, Janice. 2002. "Saloon-Smashing Fanatic, Corn-Fed Joan of Arc." *Journalism History* 28:38–48.

Ingalls, Robert P. 1977. "The Tampa Flogging Case: Urban Vigilantism." *Florida Historical Quarterly* 56:13–27.

Ingalls, Robert P. 1987. "Lynching and Establishment Violence in Tampa, 1858–1935." *Journal of Southern History* 53:613–44.

Ireland, Robert M. 1986. "Acquitted, Yet Scorned: The Ward Trial and the Traditions of Antebellum Kentucky Criminal Justice." *Register of the Kentucky Historical Society* 84:107–45.

Ireland, Robert M. 1989. "The Libertine Must Die: Sexual Dishonor and the Unwritten Law in the Nineteenth-Century United States." *Journal of Social History* 23:27–44.

Juster, Susan. 1994. *Disorderly Women: Sexual Politics and Evangelicalism in Revolutionary New England*. Ithaca, NY: Cornell University Press.

Kantrowitz, Stephen. 2000. *Ben Tillman and the Reconstruction of White Supremacy*. Chapel Hill: University of North Carolina Press.

Kielbowicz, Richard. 2006. "Law and Mob Law in Attacks on Antislavery Newspapers, 1833–1860." *Law and History Review* 24:559–600.

Kirkpatrick, Jennet. 2008. *Uncivil Disobedience: Studies in Violence and Democratic Politics*. Princeton, NJ: Princeton University Press.

Knowles, Helen J. 2013. "Seeing the Light: Lysander Spooner's Increasingly Popular Constitutionalism." *Law and History Review* 32:531–58.

Kramer, Larry D. 2004. *The People Themselves: Popular Constitutionalism and Judicial Review.* New York: Oxford University Press.

Lambert, Josiah Bartlet. 2005. *If the Workers Took a Notion.* Ithaca, NY: Cornell University Press.

Lane, Roger. 1997. *Murder in America.* Columbus: Ohio State University Press.

Larson, Robert. 1975. "The White Caps of New Mexico: A Study of Ethnic Militancy in the Southwest." *South Pacific Historical Review* 42:171–85.

Leanza, Cheryl A. 2006. "Heckler's Veto Case Law as a Resource for Democratic Discourse." *Hofstra Law Review* 35:1305–20.

Maier, Pauline. 1970. "Popular Uprisings and Civil Authority in Eighteenth-Century America." *William and Mary Quarterly* 27:3–35.

Maier, Pauline. 1992. *From Resistance to Revolution: Colonial Radicals and the Development of American Opposition to Britain, 1765–1776.* New York: W. W. Norton & Co.

Marszalek, John F. 1997. *The Petticoat Affair: Manners, Mutiny, and Sex in Andrew Jackson's White House.* New York: Free Press.

McCurdy, Charles W. 2001. *Anti-Rent Era in New York Law and Politics, 1839–1865.* Chapel Hill: University of North Carolina Press.

Monkkonen, Eric. 2000. *Murder in New York City.* Berkeley: University of California Press.

Montgomery, David. 1972. "The Shuttle and the Cross: Weavers and Artisans in the Kensington Riots of 1844." *Journal of Social History* 5:414–46.

Moore, Sean T. 2002. "'Justifiable Provocation': Violence Against Women in Essex County, New York." *Journal of Social History* 35:889–919.

Murakawa, Naomi. 2014. *The First Civil Right: How Liberals Built Prison America.* New York: Oxford University Press.

Nice, David C. 1988. "Abortion Clinic Bombings as Political Violence." *American Journal of Political Science* 32:178–96.

Pashman, Howard. 2013. "The People's Property Law: A Step Toward Building a Legal Order in Revolutionary New York." *Law and History Review* 32:587–626.

Pease, Jane H., & William H. Pease. 1990. *Ladies, Women and Wenches: Choice and Constraint in Antebellum Charleston and Boston.* Chapel Hill: University of North Carolina Press.

Pfeifer, Michael J. 2004. *Rough Justice: Lynching and American Society, 1874–1947.* Urbana: University of Illinois Press.

Pfeifer, Michael J. 2011. *The Roots of Rough Justice: Origins of American Lynching.* Urbana: University of Illinois Press.

Roll, Jarod. 2002. "Gideon's Band: From Socialism to Vigilantism in Southeast Missouri, 1907–1916." *Labor History* 43:483–503.

Schwantes, Carlos A. 1981. "Making the World Unsafe for Democracy: Vigilantes, Grangers and the Walla Walla Outrage of 1918." *Montana: The Magazine of Western History* 31:18–29.

Shapira, Harel. 2013. *Waiting for Jose: The Minutemen's Pursuit of America.* Princeton, NJ: Princeton University Press.

Smith, Barbara Clark. 1994. "Food Riots and the American Revolution." *William and Mary Quarterly* 51:3–39.

Stein, Joshua. 2012. "George Zimmerman and the Right to Violence." Accessed at http://ssrn.com/abstract=2138270.

Steinberg, Allen. 1989. *The Transformation of Criminal Law: Philadelphia, 1800–1880.* Chapel Hill: University of North Carolina Press.

Strange, Carolyn. 2010. "The Unwritten Law of Executive Justice: Pardoning Parricide in Reconstruction-Era New York." *Law and History Review* 28:891–930.

Thompson, E. P. 1971. "The Moral Economy of the English Crowd in the Eighteenth Century." *Past and Present* 50:76–136.

Varon, Elizabeth. 1998. *We Mean to Be Counted: White Women and Politics in Antebellum Virginia*. Chapel Hill: University of North Carolina Press.

Waldrep, Christopher. 1990. "'So Much Sin': The Decline of Religious Discipline and the 'Tidal Wave' of Crime." *Journal of Social History* 25:535–53.

Waldrep, Christopher. 1998. *Roots of Disorder: Race and Criminal Justice in the American South, 1817–1880*. Urbana: University of Illinois Press.

Walker, Samuel. 1998. *Popular Justice: A History of American Criminal Justice*. New York: Oxford University Press.

Woods, Michael E. 2011. "'The Indignation of Freedom-Loving People': The Caning of Charles Sumner and Emotion in Antebellum Politics." *Journal of Social History* 44:689–705.

Wyatt-Brown, Bertram. 1982. *Southern Honor: Ethics and Behavior in the Old South*. New York: Oxford University Press.

Zesch, Scott. 2012. *The Chinatown War: Chinese Los Angeles and the Massacre of 1871*. New York: Oxford University Press.

CHAPTER 28

POPULAR DRAMAS BETWEEN TRANSGRESSION AND ORDER

Criminal Trials and Their Publics in the Nineteenth and Twentieth Centuries in Global Perspective

DANIEL SIEMENS

INTRODUCTION

SINCE the nineteenth century, criminal trials have become an important aspect of modern life and at times widely mediatized events, first through the medium of mass-circulation newspapers and then, since the 1920s, through radio and—shortly later—television. Although rulers had long before used publicly staged criminal trials as means to demonstrate and legitimize their power (Lemmings 2012a; Rubin 2012), this process turned multidimensional in the nineteenth century, not least because of the emancipation of legal experts, the professionalization of police, and the rise of mass media. In particular, heavily sensationalized criminal trials regularly transformed into popular dramas in which a variety of actors were involved in negotiating social order— on a local, regional, or national level. Topics discussed on the occasion of these trials were, for example, questions of citizenship and race (Gross 2000), class and gender (Bailey 2006, Flaherty 2014), politics and national belonging, and youth and sexuality (Willrich 2003). Since the late nineteenth century, journalists and writers have increasingly regarded the criminal courtroom as a place where fundamental questions of law, order, and politics are discussed—and decided. In their footsteps, a number of scholars have in recent years started to explore the cultural significance of the courtroom in the nineteenth and twentieth centuries, following their colleagues of the premodern period who blazed the trail (Blauert & Schwerhoff 2000). My essay is intended to summarize the existing research in this field over the last twenty years, as well as to discuss some of the methodological questions related to it. I aim to stimulate further research by adopting a transnational and—if possible—global perspective that goes beyond the transatlantic, capitalist Western world, a geopolitical frame in which questions of mass media and society have been most notably discussed.

As will be shown in section I, a strong public interest in the handling of crimes through the judicial system that usually went hand in hand with the attribution of political meaning to these trials was not limited to Western Europe or the United States, but can also be found in prerevolutionary Russia, in the late Ottoman Empire, in Meiji Japan, and in the last years of the Qing monarchy and the early Republic of China. Section II explains how mass media starting in the middle of the nineteenth century contributed decisively to the involvement of an ever growing number of the public in criminal trials, which has to be understood not as a passive receiver of a hegemonic discourse about law and order, but rather as an active participant in the constant process of reformulating local moral orders. Section III takes a closer look at media stories as popular dramas of order and transgression and argues that one decisive factor in their popularity was the "scientification of the social" since the turn of the nineteenth century. At that time, real cases tried in court often came to be understood as a representative selection of social problems. They also helped to popularize medical expert knowledge. With regard to more recent political developments in the last three decades, section IV discusses to what extent these important functions, which added to a growing awareness of social problems and also hinted at possible solutions, might have been specific to a particular time and space. Section V critically inquires into the effects of increasingly global audiences for crime news on democracy. It is suggested that an increased visibility of criminal trials does not automatically go along with an increase in democratic rights and participation. Therefore, research on crime and criminology should pay more attention to the narratives and "emotional regimes" that are utilized to report criminal trials in the mass media. Finally, the brief conclusion summarizes the main points of the essay and challenges the assumption that highly mediatized criminal trials positively contribute to the globalization of a liberal public sphere.

I. Newspapers and Crime: Historical Perspectives

With the invention of the printing press, crime news and the subsequent trials regularly provided the basis for moral stories that overwhelmingly served to legitimize authority. In Europe and Eurasia as well as China and Japan, rulers and governments engaged in a "law and order dialogue" with the general public and were usually supported by the press (Lemmings 2012b, pp. 120, 144; Silver 2008, p. 16). At the same time, the public did not confine its role to that of a passive listener to the authoritarian message. Crime news and trials were also a form of entertainment, as hundreds of often very graphic pamphlets from the sixteenth and seventeenth centuries make clear. Ethical standards did not matter much when it came to the gathering of such "news content," and consequently a lot of what ultimately found its way into print did not please those social reformers who aimed at educating the wider public.

The public's voyeuristic fascination with those individuals guilty of legal and moral transgression has persisted to the present day (Coville & Lucanio 1999); however, as this essay will argue, the relationship between the media, the public, and the criminal system changed significantly since the middle of the nineteenth century. The growing number of newspapers that at that time started to emancipate themselves politically and economically from government authority provided the precondition for a new form of courtroom reporting that no longer confined itself to reproducing narratives of guilt and punishment that ultimately legitimized existing power relations in society, but rather embarked on a path of questioning the given legal system and the values and institutions on which it was based. Exceptions confirm the rule: in Britain, a new public sphere that allowed for more critical scrutiny of authorities' judicial actions had already emerged by the late seventeenth century (Williams 2013, p. 31), and the first weeklies that specialized in reporting on crime were founded in the 1830s (Knelman 1998, p. 36). However, even here the press's predominant tone remained semi-official until the mid-nineteenth century. Crime and courtroom news were meant to entertain and inform, not to provoke critical debates (Crone 2012). Following Alexander II's "great reforms" in the 1860s, which opened up the formerly predominantly closed court sessions based on written evidence, newspapers in nineteenth-century Russia paid more attention to criminal trials (Healey 2009, p. 19). Yet, many contemporary observers in Russia did not regard the new publicity of the criminal justice system as a counterweight to the autocratix state, but as an aid (Dahlke 2012, p. 118). At the end of the century, heated controversies about the "sensational exploitation" of the courtroom were in full swing in Russia (Oberländer 2013, pp. 114–16). In Japan, the interest in crime news likewise peaked in the 1880s and 1890s. As in Europe, it brought in its wake a substantial new interest in the origins of law and the ways in which it was implemented (Hedinger 2012, pp. 148–49), and it stimulated the genre of the detective novel (Kawana 2008, pp. 1–15).

The fundamental change of the nineteenth century toward popular participation in the evolution and application of law was inversely proportional to the trend described by Michel Foucault in his famous book *Discipline and Punish*: while the punishment of criminals transformed from a "gloomy festival," or a highly public ritual, into a disciplinary practice that increasingly happened behind the prison walls, in mental asylums, and in penitentiaries and therefore decreased in visibility (Foucault 1979, pp. 8–24), the public scrutiny of the legal system operating in the courtroom increased considerably. A telling example that illustrates both the old and the new regimes is the Cologne Communist trial from October 1852 that brought some individual members of the Communist League in the Rhineland before the court but was intended to fight "democratic tendencies" in postrevolutionary Prussia more generally (Livingstone 1971, pp.

17–30). On the one hand, the predominant news reporting of the trial sided with the authorities, as was the tradition, but on the other hand, because of the clearly recognizable political character of the trial and its predictable outcome, not only the partisan press sympathetic to democratic and socialist tendencies, but also more "respectable" liberal papers commented increasingly critically on the trial. As became known, no less than the Prussian king Frederick William IV had urged the Prussian prime minister in a handwritten letter to "weave the fabric of a conspiracy in order to perform the long awaited drama of a disclosed and (above all) penalized complot" (Bittel 1955, p. 15). What began as a political trial against a few revolutionaries quickly turned into a public controversy about political ideas and social change. This would become one of the main features in the decades to come, in Germany and elsewhere. The courtroom and courtroom journalism transformed into battlegrounds for competing social, legal, and political ideas (Grunwald 2012; Oberländer 2013; Rowbotham, Stevenson, & Pegg 2013; Siemens 2007; Hett 2004). In these battles, the public became not only a political arena, but an active contestant.

II. The Active Public

The Cologne Communist trial of 1852 opened in a "blaze of publicity." Sessions were held only in the morning hours because the authorities feared that sympathizers of the defendants would provoke "violent incidents" in and around the court in the darker evening hours (Livingstone 1971, p. 26). The Prussian authorities were powerful enough to stage such a political show trial, but they had to take the circumstances and possible public reactions into account. They also had to pay attention to the newspaper coverage. Although most of the revolutionary "March demands" from the spring of 1848 remained unfulfilled, there was no arguing that the era of repressive censorship introduced in the German lands with the "Carlsbad decrees" from 1819 were over. This development was neither confined to the German lands nor limited to Europe and the United States. The rise of mass-circulation newspapers, particularly those that created new audiences by reaching out to less well-to-do segments of the population (e.g., the penny press), was a global phenomenon in the second half of the nineteenth century that deeply influenced how courtroom news stories could be gathered, written, and circulated (Rowbotham, Stevenson, & Pegg 2013; Bleyer 1916, pp. 76–77). A German lawyer noted as early as 1914 that the telegraph and the telephone had made it possible for particular criminal trials to "thrill [. . .] half of the world." Whereas legal interest in criminal trials is always limited by time and space, they would soon have the power to entertain a global audience (Glaser 1914, pp. 8–9).

Newspaper readers quickly formed a second and much larger public that complemented those few observers who were able to attend a criminal trial in person. In the early twentieth century, the proceedings of sensationalized criminal trials mesmerized millions of newspaper readers and radio listeners in the United States, Europe,

China, and Japan alike (Hedinger 2012; He 2010; Wood 2012; Elder 2010; Lean 2007). These trials even had the potential to transcend continents and become truly global media events, as the famous Leopold and Loeb murder trial in Chicago in 1924 (which also made headlines in Europe); the trial against Samuel Schwartzbard, the assassin of the Ukrainian nationalist leader Simon Petliura, in Paris in 1927; and the Berlin-based juvenile murder trial of Paul Krantz in 1928, which also reverberated in the United States, demonstrate (Siemens 2007, pp. 113, 269–314, 369–78). Not only did the "dreadful delight" of real crimes that could be consumed in private safety prove irresistible, but their consumption—previously an alleged pleasure of the "immoral" lower classes—also lost its bad reputation. In particular, middle-class readers now came to enjoy a "voyeurism of the ordinary"—a voyeurism that also had its functional side, as it helped urban audiences in the modern metropolises to "structure" their cities and to make them intelligible (Fritzsche 2005, pp. 377–83; Walkowitz 1992; Elder 2010).

Academics initially framed the media stories based on these sensational trials with caution, presenting arguments that often reformulated the bourgeois cultural criticism of the turn of the nineteenth century. Entertainment, the "logic of the spectacle," would more and more "colonize public space," or so they claimed (Kohn 2008, p. 480). Most influential in this respect was Jürgen Habermas's book *The Structural Transformation of the Public Sphere*, originally published in 1962, in which he highlighted the capitalist mass media's negative effects as contributing to a "disintegration of the bourgeois public sphere" since the late nineteenth century. The stories run in the modern media supposedly blurred the boundaries between news reporting and literature, *raisonnement* and entertainment, and, ultimately, between fact and fiction (Habermas 1989, pp. 175–95).

Over the last two decades a more optimistic reinterpretation gained ground, a reinterpretation that stressed—contradicting Habermas's normative bourgeois public sphere approach—that any attempt to separate these two spheres (the political and the world of entertainment and consumption) would be as useless as it was practically impossible. In particular, historians of modern France early on observed that the writing style of literature and newspaper coverage of real "human interest stories" became identical in the late nineteenth century: as Berenson notes, "the two blended together and nourished each other with references and images" (1993, p. 211). Unlike Habermas, these scholars did not stress decay, but emphasized the functional consequences of this development. Newer research has therefore given up on the idea that newspaper coverage, by "mirroring" a given social reality, can be used to properly reconstruct these former realities. Rather, the aim is now to understand how contemporaries—by mixing the real and the imaginary—perceived and created reality in the first place.

Such an echo of the linguistic turn directly influences how criminal historians analyze the relationship between criminal trials, mass media, and the public today. A "new cultural history of law" that aims at integrating the development of the legal system and its cultural and social effects into general historiographical narratives (Hedinger & Siemens 2012) emphasizes the "entangled inter-dynamics" (Strath 2008, p. 6) between national legal cultures, as well as within the actors in these national or supranational contexts (Kirmse 2012, pp. 112–14, 120). One consequence of this development is the new attention devoted to the public for criminal trials. Of historical interest in this respect are not only those who were physically present in the courtroom and immediately outside the courthouse, but also the potentially much larger quantity of people who participated at the trial via mass media. Any attempt to strictly divide the audience of a criminal trial into a(n) (possibly) active part—consisting of those present—and a (potentially) much larger passive part, forced to consume certain narratives without any chance to alter them, is therefore of very limited use. The latter group, the wider public, can in fact be more actively involved than the first group in the constant process of attributing meaning to the courtroom procedures and the media stories based on them. They are not isolated spectators, "linked only by a one-way relationship to the very center that maintains their isolation from one another" (Debord 1995, p. 22), but active participants who, despite their at first glance peripheral role, have a crucial influence on the acceptance or refusal of particular narratives of law, order, and transgression (a similar point is made by Williams 2013, pp. 35–38). This holds true even for the late Ottoman Empire, as Avin Rubin has recently shown in a compelling article on the 1884 trial of Hamdi Bey. Proceedings of this trial of a former public prosecutor who had fallen from grace were printed verbatim in at least one newspaper, and for the first time in Ottoman history, the courtroom was rendered "a subject for the public gaze." Thanks to the newspaper coverage, the trial soon became the talk of the town (Rubin 2012, pp. 759, 772). In modern times, this trend seems to have global application, particularly when we are dealing with a fully commercialized mass media system: to get the public engaged is as much a democratic virtue as it is economically beneficial. By reaching out to the wider public, and especially to previously politically or socially marginalized groups, mass media not only increase profits, but—in the best of cases—help these groups to "recognize their personal identities" (He 2010, p. 4). As has been argued for the United States, Europe, China, and recently New Zealand, newspapers as early as the late nineteenth and early twentieth centuries documented as well as called for reforms of local moral orders, or "community moralities" (Brickell 2014; Wood 2009; Siemens 2007; Bailey 2006; Goodman 2006).

The importance of the active public can be illustrated by comparing sensationalized but otherwise "ordinary" criminal trials with another category of highly publicized trials: the International Military Tribunal in Nuremberg (1945–1946) and the Tokyo War Crimes Trial (1946–1948). Apart from their uncontested significance for international law and in particular their contribution to the implementation of human rights (Priemel & Stiller 2012; Griech-Polelle 2009), both trials were international events that appealed to a global audience. However, historians dealing with both trials have noticed a relative lack of emotional engagement, or "passive acceptance," from the public, particularly in those countries whose former political and military leaders were standing trial (Futamura 2011, p. 37). There are multifaceted reasons for such behavior that can't be discussed here, such as indifference resulting from the often "overly complex" and "excessively technical" nature of those trials (Wilson 2011, p. 11). However, one additional reason that is hardly mentioned by historians but highly relevant for the scope of this essay is the Japanese and German publics' lack of active participation in these trials.

In occupied Germany, it was the legal aspect—and, more precisely, the controversy about the legitimacy of the court and its right to apply of new set of rules—that seemed to provoke strong emotional responses from the German public, and not only the character and extent of the crimes against humanity that had been committed during the war years (Wilke et al. 1995, pp. 82, 122). This focus of emotion is usually explained with reference to the widespread *Schlussstrich* mentality of seeking closure that quickly became dominant in postwar Germany and Japan alike. I would argue that the lack of public participation, and the inability to alter the narratives that framed the court proceedings, likewise contributed to this relatively passive reception of the trials in the host countries. In modern societies, the potential to turn a criminal trial into a media sensation depends not only on the nature and extent of a particular crime, but also on the possibility of involving and activating a wide audience, not necessarily physically, but certainly emotionally. Taking up the idea that emotions can also be understood as practices, as new research on the history of emotions argues (Scheer 2012), it is not least the task of criminal historians to explore further the effects of the emotions in and around the courtroom drama.

III. Order and Transgression

It is a feature of modern mass media to turn the reader/listener/spectator of news content into an active consumer, one who ideally contributes to the story. The "Letters to the Editor" page is just an old form of what has since become an indispensable part of online journalism: the reader's possibility to comment on a news item and to interact with others, a participation that transforms him or her from "passive" reader into "active" user. Courtroom journalism has proven to be a particularly successful field in which several of these techniques were applied early. As crimes are ultimately transgressions of the legitimate social order that allow for speculation about how personal problems and social change might be interrelated, courtroom journalism became a diverse field of social inquiry, in the courtroom as well as in the newspaper columns, starting in the late nineteenth century. Jurists still made sure that the parties involved observed the legal rules, but an increasing number of non–legally trained experts now associated with them. The complex nature of man, as well as an increasing variety of lifestyles, particularly in the growing metropolises and with regard to sexual habits, called for expert knowledge on human behavior. Widespread anxieties and uncertainties—not only about the imminent future of the society in which one was living, but also about very personal economic, interpersonal, or intimate fears—fueled an interest in courtroom journalism, with the real cases tried in court now understood as a representative selection of social problems that concerned everyone in one way or another. At the same time, these trials informed the public of attempts to solve these conflicts— through legal means as well as scientific approaches or "social engineering." The "scientification of the social" (Raphael 1996) amplified the importance of the criminal courtroom in modern societies; it became, among other things, "a new platform from which medical knowledge was displayed." On the one hand, the "doctor in the witness box" could consolidate his authority in a contemporary way, but on the other hand, his expertise was now open to public scrutiny. The courtroom thus also turned into a "platform for confusion and embarrassment" (Healey 2009, p. 20), with the press being more than happy to report extensively about such colorful "expert battles" (Siemens 2007, pp. 305–12; Oberländer 2013).

The main effect of the increasing presence and impact of criminalists and medical and social experts in criminal trials was a growing awareness of the fact that the relatively straightforward moral stories of crime and punishment that had dominated the reporting of criminal trials until the mid-nineteenth century no longer reflected the diverse and ever-changing social reality—a reality in which questions of class, race, and gender were moving to the fore. In times when the existing public order came under closer scrutiny, courtroom news reporting provided important stories that helped to redefine the boundaries between acceptable and unacceptable behavior. These narratives also questioned the long-held belief that crime was the consequence of the perpetrator's evil will. With the social question taking center stage in Europe and the United States alike, audiences were increasingly confronted with explanations of crime that stressed environmental, social, or outright political reasons for individual misdoings (Becker, Wetzell, & Lazar 2005). Cultural critics soon lamented that while criminal judges had to sentence the criminals, the journalists increasingly sentenced the victims—thus turning the question of moral guilt and responsibility upside down (Siemens 2009, pp. 345–46).

The stories of transgression and order that appeared in newspapers were based on individual cases tried in criminal courts, but they ultimately went beyond those cases to question the "very notion of modern law itself," as Eugenia Lean has demonstrated for interwar China (2007, p. 108). Taking as a starting point the highly discussed trial of Shi Jianqiao, who in the city of Tianjin in 1935 had shot to death a former warlord she held responsible for her father's death, Lean successfully shows that such trials, in which the accused and her defense team deliberately provoked and exploited public sympathy, raised important legal questions. In this case, it was the question of the extent to which the "moral authority of human feeling (qing)" should matter in the rule of law, a discussion that was much to the distaste of Chinese legal reformers at the time (Lean 2007, pp. 106–40). Here and in many other sensational trials that caught the attention of a wider public, the "public sympathy" for the defendants could simply not be ignored—and a purely technical application of the legal rules did not happen. This observation holds true even with the reservation that these effects were limited to cases that were "framed within socially and culturally acceptable and state-sanctioned behavioral and moral codes" and therefore often stabilized a given political authority (He 2010, p. 28).

Such "adjustments" seemed most likely to occur in cases in which female culprits successfully defended themselves by presenting a highly emotional narrative of their crime that either played on traditional values of female honor (Berenson 1993, Flaherty

2014) or—on the contrary—stylized their crime as a legitimate reaction against a traditionally male-dominated society whose rules were made by and for men but did not suffice to deal with the female condition (Wood 2012). In modern France, the term *crime passionels*, passion crimes, was firmly established in such cases and was eagerly exploited by defense lawyers and journalists alike (Ambroise-Rendue 2006, pp. 35–44; Harris 1989). It can only be decided on a case-to-case basis whether such narratives stimulated a critical discourse that attempted to reform or "modernize" the law and the legal system, or whether such cases ultimately helped to legitimize the given public order and its legal framework, analogous to the function played by carnivals in allowing the temporary transgression of limits. In any case, the media played a decisive part in staging criminal trials as "authentic" plays in the *théâtre moralisateur* (Ambroise-Rendue 2006, pp. 40–41): depending on the public's changing tastes and preferences, they reported on criminal trials in the form of tragedies or comedies, farces or satires, always keen to increase the circulation of their papers.

IV. Visibility and Mass Media

It is a firmly established belief in the Western world that the openness to public scrutiny of the criminal justice system at work is one of the fundamental aspects indispensable to the legitimacy of the legal system. Since the days of the Enlightenment in the eighteenth century, a fair trial could only be an open trial—not one conducted behind closed doors. Against this tradition, a recent development is noteworthy: the gradual turning away from this fundamental principle in those legal procedures that concern suspected terrorists in the aftermath of 9/11. In response to these attacks, the U.S. administration of President George W. Bush coined a new category of "enemy combatants" to deny allegedly "unlawful combatants" (a term used to target suspected al-Qaeda terrorists) access to legal rights otherwise guaranteed by the U.S. Constitution and international conventions and agreements (Akyuz, Cihan, & Roth 2012; Zusman 2011). Instead of holding public trials that would allow for public scrutiny, all U.S. administrations since 2001 have opted for indefinite detainment of alleged terrorists, who are tried in exceptional courts (military commissions), if at all (Ní Aoláin & Gross 2013). With the exception of the trial against Zacarias Moussaoui in 2006 (Linder 2006), no "sensational" or highly mediatized "al-Qaeda trial" has taken place in federal criminal courts in the United States since 2001, although the Supreme Court has repeatedly stressed that the principle of habeas corpus also applies to U.S. prisoners of war and alleged terrorists (Akyuz, Cihan, & Roth 2012, pp. 69–70).

This judicial tendency contradicts optimistic claims that praise the Western model of a transparent criminal justice system as one that will increasingly be followed globally (Heger Boyle & Meyer 1998) in two ways: First, it raises questions about the sustainability or even irreversibility of the Western way of *Verrechtlichung* in the twenty-first century by pointing to an erosion of legal standards previously attained. Second, it forces us to think more critically about the character of those trials that are actually made available to the public. If one takes a look at those trials that made global headlines in recent decades—the O. J. Simpson murder trial in Los Angeles in 1994–1995 (Linder 2000) or the Oscar Pistorius murder trial in Johannesburg in 2013–2014 (Carlin 2014), to name just a few very well-known cases—one might ask whether the sensationalist exploitation of the *faits divers*, the "human interest story," does not obscure the fact that the bigger crimes—bigger in the sense that they have more serious political consequences for a lot more people—often go unnoticed. The selection of those criminal trials that are reported thus helps to maintain the hegemony of the ruling classes, as Marxist-inspired philosophers and historians frequently argue (Jewkes 2004, pp. 16–21). Obviously, such cultural criticism, which is frequently couched in simplistic terms, does not lead very far. Historical research of crime and criminology has long demonstrated that complaints about the exploitation of sexual and other "sensational" topics have been a constant feature of conservative press criticism, at least since large-circulation mass media have been available (for an early example, see Glaser 1914, pp. 18–19). However, the complexity of modern societies makes any attempt to deliberately deceive the public by manipulating it on the basis of a previously defined strategy unlikely to succeed. The politically important as well as academically challenging question—moving the focus from the allegedly hegemonic actors and their strategies to the narratives available—is: Do the narratives established in sensationalized crime trials during the last two centuries provide the exclusive framework in which all criminal trials must be reported, and, if so, what are the consequences?

I will discuss this point with reference to a turning point in modern Chinese legal history, as emphasized recently by Haiping Zheng and Klaus Mühlhahn: the trial against the so-called Gang of Four, a fraction of the former leading members of the Chinese Communist Party, that took place in Peking in late 1980 (Bonavia 1984). This trial is seen as a turning point because it was the first time in Communist China that long-time political leaders who had fallen from grace were exposed publicly. The Gang of Four trial was staged as a highly mediatized event, a show trial that was broadcast live on Chinese television and radio and reported widely in the national press. More than 880 "representatives of the masses" attended the proceedings in the courtroom, and more than 300 journalists—meant to represent the Chinese public— were present. The trial was obviously a "scripted" event that was held to win back legitimacy for the Communist Party by admitting some previous wrongdoings and punishing certain high-profile individuals (Mühlhahn 2009, p. 291).

However scripted, the trial took place, and however controlled the press coverage actually was, it has nevertheless been argued that the trial demonstrated an important step "forward" for modern China. The Chinese legal scholar Haiping Zheng (2010) claims that in spite of its numerous defects, the trial represented progress compared with the situation in the Cultural Revolution, when individuals could be "arrested, jailed and tortured without any formal trial." Although the verdict against two of the main defendants was prefabricated by the Politburo of the Chinese Communist Party before the public trial started, it was the visibility of the proceedings as such that indirectly improved legal proceedings in the People's Republic more broadly, or so Zheng claims. However, in the context of this essay, it is important to raise the question of whether such rather optimistic readings do not overshadow a more worrisome tendency: the increasing ability of political regimes to use the mass media to create a kind of "reality effect." In modern China, such staging of "reality" is often justified using the general aim of promoting social harmony. But visibility and genuine openness are two different things—and while it is probably correct to assume that the former is a necessary precondition for the latter, it is by no means a sufficient one.

Obviously, here is not the place to broadly discuss with Habermas the effects of mass media on the transformation of the public sphere, as this is ultimately a debate on the effects of mass media on democracy (Keane 2013, pp. 67–76, 112–21; Bohman 2004). Even if the "dominant ideology approach" (Jewkes 2004, pp. 16–18) is lacking in complexity, one should likewise avoid any uncritical glorification of the achievements of the free press and/or mass media and of the visibility of politics so characteristic in modern times. The problem is less an empirical one (for a long time, criticism, particularly from conservative thinkers, centered around "sensationalism" as a form of exploitation of the emotions and the general "lowering" of political culture), but one that has to be addressed on a theoretical level: while the last two decades have demonstrated with ever greater clarity that public debates surrounding criminal trials contribute in important ways to a growing reflexivity of societies and at times increase the ambition to launch legal reforms, the discussion of the overall narratives necessary to analyze these developments needs to take the different political regimes in which they occur into consideration and is, not least for this reason, just about to begin.

V. Global Audiences and Democracy

This brings me to my last point, which is—put briefly—the question of the limits of the public's agency in criminal trials. As has been outlined previously, it has been firmly established that audiences of criminal trials in the past were all but passive. On the contrary, they were in many cases a most lively and vital component of trials: riots in front of courthouses, emotional letters written by spectators to the judges or the parties involved, heckling and intimidation in the courtroom—all these and other forms of participation were widely commented on by witnesses of those trials at which the events occurred, as well as by historians much later. It is also well known that the rise of mass media and its interest in criminal affairs did not diminish such forms of direct participation, but instead multiplied them. Press reports, and later radio and TV coverage, not only provided an opportunity to transmit individual voices to wide and diverse audiences, but also created new forms of involvement, such as the reader-reporter, who was invited to provide his personal views on the proceedings of a trial, and the pundit, who was increasingly asked to comment on particular aspects of a trial, such as the defendant's mental capacities or the wider social impact of the proceedings (thus contributing to the effect the media initially created by its coverage).

Highly mediatized criminal trials thus blurred not only the boundaries between courtroom and society, but also the lines between defendants and audiences. Regardless of the judicial chances of a particular defendant, the attention for him or her created by spectacular trials and their media coverage provided a substantial form of social capital that the defendant could and often would exploit. It is not only the case that popular "stars" accused of serious crimes yield sensational media coverage of a particular criminal trial (as was the case with O. J. Simpson and many others), but a highly publicized criminal trial can produce its own very profitable industry; it has the power to create celebrities who can later write successful books, sell their stories to see them translated into popular movies, or start careers as actors themselves. Such careers rely heavily on the emotions provoked and the constant attention provided by mass media news coverage during criminal trials and after. They are a byproduct of an intense coverage of trial proceedings that was in premodern times widely condemned as an illegitimate interference in judicial affairs and as morally "shameful" (Nash & Kilday 2010), but in recent decades has been more openly (and maybe cynically) embraced as a judicial theater that helps visualize and contribute to addressing existing social problems.

However, from the perspective of ruling elites, such a "coming to terms" with social and political realities in the form of highly engaging and mediatized criminal trials— one might even speak of "proxy trials" when referring to the social side of such events— suffers from one very serious shortcoming: its ultimate unpredictability. While it is easy to control the judicial settings of a particular trial, and relatively easy to ensure a certain character of media coverage, it is much harder to keep the emotions created by such a trial in check. Not least because criminal trials ultimately deal with real people and real events, the public only tolerates a certain amount of (perceived) distortion. Governments that are aware of the fact that it is the public and its reactions that provide legitimacy to the judicial proceedings (and to the actions of the public sector more generally) have therefore an interest in what can be labeled as the "emotional management" or "emotional regime" of the media coverage of events (Reddy 2001).

It is here that the transnational approach proves most fruitful. A global history of the relationship between criminal trials and their public has yet to be written. The emerging picture, based on the scholarship available today, suggests that a straightforward success story narrative that equates increased visibility and a growing involvement of the public with an increase in democratic rights could be overly simplistic. It might have been the case in 1920s China that news "became a marker of truth, moral authority, and authenticity," as Bryna Goodman has claimed (2006, p. 69), but it is doubtful whether the press still enjoys such credit. In many parts of the word, we are currently witnessing the rise of a new and tight relationship between mass media and political oligarchy, a "mediacracy" (Keane 2013, pp. 171–80) that serves particular economic and political interests, but disguises its ultimate goals by producing highly modern and complex media content. Sensational criminal trials that attract a global audience might become an integral part of mediacracy's portfolio. What is of global cultural interest might, however, be of very limited political relevance.

With regard to "sensational trials" that turn into international media events, I therefore suggest that it is necessary to clearly distinguish between at least two different kinds of public spheres: local or regional public spheres on the one hand, and transnational or potentially global spheres on the other. Local publics will most likely perceive courtroom proceedings, given their deep roots in the social history and legal tradition of a particular political area, as events that are of direct social significance for the "local moral order"—a term coined by the Chicago school of sociology in the early twentieth century. In contrast, the more remote observers might form emotional bonds but otherwise not be directly affected. They will therefore read or "consume" the courtroom drama first and foremost as a moral tale, or simply as entertainment that produces scary thrills.

This idea is neither new, nor does it seem to be problematic, as "moral regulation" has for a long time been identified as a permanent process created by the mass media (Critcher 2013, p. 26). The question is, however, whether "moral regulation" in this sense means moral self-regulation (as is very likely the case in local or regional public spheres), or whether it comes in the form of entertainment that is devoid of a connection to society and therefore more open to manipulation. It might well be the case that the democratizing effects of "sensational trials" that influence limited but clearly defined public spheres were an important characteristic of a specific historical period, dating from the second half of the nineteenth century to the late twentieth century, in which the political and economic realities made it possible for modernizing societies to tolerate a relatively high level of (moderate) unpredictability. Whether future audiences, shaped by the diversity currently available through social media, will insist on relatively open coverage of real criminal trials that allows an active public to participate in them, or whether they will—on the contrary—content themselves with new forms of prearranged realities and calculated surprises—to take up Debord's (1995) language, with self-referential "spectacles" in the mode of popular entertainment—is hard to foresee. In any case, one of the central tasks of the historiography of crime and media in the years ahead will be to pay more attention to the narratives of the spectacle that have been firmly established in *telenovelas*, the "Hollywood courtroom drama" (Machura 2001; Kuzina 2001; Levi 2005), "television reality crime programs" (Fishman & Cavender 1998), and pre-scripted courtroom shows since the second half of the twentieth century, and to work out their relationship to the media coverage of authentic criminal trials.

Conclusion

This essay has provided, first, a summary of the latest research on the relationship between criminal court proceedings, the mass media, and their publics. This field of research has been growing in recent decades, but its analysis is still often confined to the national level. A more comparative and potentially global perspective, as adopted here, not only points to the fact that the abovementioned relationship developed in a surprisingly similar way in many parts of the world and was by no means confined to the transatlantic Western hemisphere, but also postulates whether those questions of power, progress, and social reform that occupied historians throughout the twentieth century remain of central importance today, or whether they have to be asked differently in the twenty-first century. In particular, the postcolonial turn, in full swing in the humanities for a little more than two decades, and the current multiplicity of public spheres, made possible not least by the Internet, have the potential to affect the research questions criminal historians ask. They alter, in other words, the analytical frames at our disposal.

All topics that have come to characterize ambitious media coverage of crime and criminal trials since the nineteenth century will very likely remain major issues in the near future as well: the interconnectedness of entertainment and participation, the struggle between authoritarianism and democracy, the tension between coercion and individual freedom. More attention, however, should be given to narratives in which these topics are addressed. Such a task is not only a scholarly exercise, but also a question of fundamental importance that reflects on the development of modern society at large. In an optimistic reading, globally mediatized criminal trials might positively contribute to the "unfinished project of globalizing the liberal public sphere" (Tully 2013, p. 181), a democratic public sphere that is based on and shaped by a common understanding of events. In a pessimistic reading, the narratives of such global crime and courtroom reporting might lack the emancipatory potential so significant in the last 150 years. Without a possibility for interaction, there is ultimately no public sphere, and certainly no democracy. The media user might again, despite all the technological achievements of the past two centuries, become a "servile servant" (Tully 2013, p. 191), a mere recipient of prefigured truths and emotionally tailored stories that might serve very different ends.

References

Akyuz, Kadir, Abdulla Cihan, & Mitchel P. Roth. 2012. "Striking a Balance Between Liberty and Security: The Debate over American Counterterrorism Policies Since 9/11." In *Flawed Criminal Justice Policies: At the Intersection of the Media, Public Fear and Legislative Response*, ed. Frances P. Reddington & Gene Bonham, 63–79. Durham, NC: Carolina Academic Press.

Ambroise-Rendue, Anne-Claude. 2006. *Crimes et délits. Une histoire de la violence de la Belle Époque à nos jours*. Paris: Nouveau Monde.

Bailey, Paul. 2006. "'Women Behaving Badly': Crime, Transgressive Behaviour and Gender in Early Twentieth Century China." *Nan Nü* 8 (1): 156–97.

Becker, Peter, Richard F. Wetzell, & David Lazar, eds. 2005. *Criminals and Their Scientists: The History of Criminology in International Perspective*. Cambridge: Cambridge University Press.

Berenson, Edward. 1993. *The Trial of Madame Caillaux*. Berkeley & Los Angeles: University of California Press.

Bittel, Karl. 1955. *Der Kommunistenprozeß zu Köln 1852 im Spiegel der zeitgenössischen Presse*. Berlin: Rütten & Loening.

Blauert, Andreas, & Gerd Schwerhoff, eds. 2000. *Kriminalitätsgeschichte. Beiträge zur Sozial-und Kulturgeschichte der Vormoderne*. Konstanz, Germany: Universitätsverlag Konstanz.

Bleyer, Willard G. 1916. *Types of News Writing*. Boston & New York: Riverside Press.

Bohman, James. 2004. "Expanding Dialogue: The Internet, the Public Sphere and Prospects for Transnational Democracy." In *After Habermas: New Perspectives on the Public Sphere*, ed. Nick Crossley & John Michael Roberts, 131–55. Oxford: Blackwell.

Bonavia, David. 1984. *Verdict in Peking: The Trial of the Gang of Four*. New York: G. P. Putnam's Sons.

Brickell, Chris. 2014. "Sensation and the Making of New Zealand Adolescence." *Journal of Social History* 47 (4): 994–1020.

Carlin, John. 2014. *The Trials of Oscar Pistorius. Chase Your Shadow*. London: Atlantic Books.

Coville, Gary, & Patrick Lucanio. 1999. *Jack the Ripper: His Life and Crimes in Popular Entertainment*. Jefferson, NC, & London: McFarland.

Critcher, Chas. 2013. "Model Answers: Moral Panics and Media History." In *Moral Panics, Social Fears, and the Media*, ed. Siân Nicholas & Tom O'Malley, 13–27. London & New York: Routledge.

Crone, Rosalind. 2012. "Publishing Courtroom Drama for the Masses, 1820–1855." In *Crime, Courtrooms and the Public Sphere in Britain, 1700–1850*, ed. David Lemmings, 193–216. Farnham/Surrey, UK: Ashgate.

Dahlke, Sandra. 2012. "Old Russia in the Dock. The Trial Against Mother Superior Mitofaniia before the Moscow Disctrict Court (1874)." *Cahier du Monde Russe* 53 (1): 95–120.

Debord, Guy. 1995. *The Society of the Spectacle*. New York: Zone Books.

Elder, Sace. 2010. *Murder Scenes: Normality, Deviance, and Criminal Violence in Weimar Berlin*. Ann Arbor: Michigan University Press.

Fishman, Mark, & Gray Cavender. 1998. *Entertaining Crime: Television Reality Programs*. New York: Aldine de Gruyter.

Flaherty, Darryl. 2014. "Burning Down the House: Gender and Jury in a Tokyo Courtroom, 1928." In *Gender and Law in the Japanese Imperium*, ed. Susan L Burns & Barbara J. Brooks, 159–86. Honolulu: University of Hawaii Press.

Foucault, Michel. 1979. *Discipline and Punish: The Birth of the Prison*. Trans. Alan Sheridan. New York: Vintage Books.

Fritzsche, Peter. 2005. "Talk of the Town: The Murder of Lucie Berlin and the Production of Local Knowledge." In *Criminals and Their Scientists: The History of Criminology in International Perspective*, ed. Peter Becker, Richard Wetzell, & David Lazar, 377–98. Cambridge: Cambridge University Press.

Futamura, Madoka. 2011. "Japanese Societal Attitude Towards the Tokyo Trial: From a Contemporary Perspective." In *Beyond Victor's Justice?: The Tokyo War Crimes Trial Revisited*, ed. Yuki Tanaka, Tim McCormack, & Gerry Simpson, 35–54. Leiden & Boston: Brill.

Glaser, Fritz. 1914. *Das Verhältnis der Presse zur Justiz unter besonderer Berücksichtigung der Berichterstattung durch die Presse und ihrer gesetzlichen Verantwortlichkeit*. Berlin: Carl Heymanns Verlag.

Goodman, Bryna. 2006. "Appealing to the Public: Newspaper Presentation and Adjudication of Emotion." *Twentieth-Century China* 31 (2): 32–69.

Griech-Polelle, Beth A., ed. 2009. *The Nuremberg War Crimes Trial and Its political Consequences Today*. Baden-Baden, Germany: Nomos.

Gross, Ariela Julie. 2000. *Double Character: Slavery and Mastery in the Antebellum Southern Courtroom*. Princeton, NJ: Princeton University Press.

Grunwald, Henning. 2012. *Courtroom to Revolutionary Stage? Performance and Ideology in Weimar Political Trials*. Oxford: Oxford University Press.

Habermas, Jürgen. 1989. *The Structural Transformation of the Public Sphere*. Trans. Thomas Burger & Frederick Lawrence. Cambridge, MA: Cambridge University Press.

Harris, Ruth. 1989. *Murders and Madness: Medicine, Law, and Society in the Fin de Siècle*. Oxford: Clarendon Press.

Healey, Dan. 2009. *Bolshevik Sexual Forensics: Diagnosing Disorder in the Clinic and Courtroom, 1917–1939*. DeKalb: Northern Illinois University Press.

He, Qiliang. 2010. "Scandal and the New Woman: Identities and Media Cultures in 1920s China." *Studies on Asia* 1 (1): 1–28.

Hedinger, Daniel. 2012. "Globalisation of Legal Cultures in the 19th Century: Criminal Trials, Gender and the Public in Meiji Japan." *Interdisciplines* 3 (2): 130–60.

Hedinger, Daniel, & Daniel Siemens. 2012. "What's the Problem with Law in History?: An Introduction." *Interdisciplines* 3 (2): 6–17.

Heger Boyle, Elisabeth, & John W. Meyer. 1998. "Modern Law as a Secularized and Global Model: Implications for the Sociology of Law." *Soziale Welt* 49 (3): 213–32.

Hett, Benjamin Carter. 2004. *Death in the Tiergarten: Murder and Criminal Justice in the Kaiser's Berlin*. Cambridge: Cambridge University Press.

Jewkes, Yvonne. 2004. *Media and Crime*. London: Sage.

Kawana, Sari. 2008. *Murder Most Modern: Detective Fiction and Japanese Culture*. Minneapolis & London: Minnesota University Press.

Keane, John. 2013. *Democracy and Media Decadence*. Cambridge & London: Cambridge University Press.

Kirmse, Stefan B. 2012. "'Law and Society' in Imperial Russia." *Interdisciplines* 3 (2): 98–129.

Knelman, Judith. 1998. *Twisting in the Wind: The Murderess and the English Press*. Toronto & London: University of Toronto Press.

Kohn, Margaret. 2008. "Homo Spectator: Public Space in the Age of the Spectacle." *Philosophy Social Criticism* 34 (5): 467–86.

Kuzina, Matthias. 2001. "The Social Issue Courtroom Drama as an Expression of American Popular Culture." *Journal of Law and Society* 28 (1): 79–96.

Lean, Eugenia. 2007. *Public Passions: The Trial of Shi Jianqiao and the Rise of Popular Sympathy in Republican China*. Berkeley, Los Angeles, & London: University of California Press.

Lemmings, David. 2012a. *Crime, Courtrooms and the Public Sphere in Britain, 1700–1850*. Farnham/Surrey, UK: Ashgate.

Lemmings, David. 2012b. "Negotiating Justice in the New Public Sphere: Crime, the Courts and the Press in Early Eighteenth-Century Britain." In *Crime, Courtrooms and the Public Sphere in Britain, 1700–1850*, ed. David Lemmings, 119–45. Farnham/Surrey, UK: Ashgate.

Levi, Ross D. 2005. *The Celluloid Courtroom: A History of Legal Cinema*. Westport, CT, & London: Praeger.

Linder, Douglas O. 2006. "The Trial of Zacarias Moussaoui: An Account." Accessed at http://law2.umkc.edu/faculty/projects/ftrials/moussaoui/zmaccount.html.

Linder, Douglas O. 2010. "The Trial of Orenthal James Simpson." Accessed at http://law2.umkc.edu/faculty/projects/ftrials/Simpson/Simpsonaccount.htm.

Livingstone, Rodney, ed. 1971. *The Cologne Communist Trial*. London: Lawrence & Wishart.

Machura, Stefan, & Stefan Ulbrich. 2001. "Law in Film: Globalizing the Hollywood Courtroom Drama." *Journal of Law and Society* 28 (1): 117–32.

Mühlhahn, Klaus. 2009. *Criminal Justice in China: A History*. Cambridge, MA, & London: Harvard University Press.

Nash, David, & Anne-Marie Kilday. 2010. *Cultures of Shame: Exploring Crime and Morality in Britain, 1600–1900*. Basingstoke, UK: Palgrave Macmillan.

Ní Aolain, Fionnuala, & Oren Gross, eds. 2013. *Guantánamo and Beyond: Exceptional Courts and Military Commissions in Comparative Perspective*. New York: Cambridge University Press.

Oberländer, Alexandra. 2013. *Unerhörte Subjekte. Die Wahrnehmung sexueller Gewalt in Russland 1880-1910*. Frankfurt am Main, Germany: Campus.

Priemel, Kim C., & Alexa Stiller, eds. 2012. *Reassessing the Nuremberg Military Tribunals: Transitional Justice, Trial Narratives, and Historiography*. New York: Berghahn.

Raphael, Lutz. 1996. "Die Verwissenschaftlichung des Sozialen als methodische und konzeptionelle Herausforderung für eine Sozialgeschichte des 20. Jahrhunderts." *Geschichte und Gesellschaft* 22 (2): 165–93.

Reddy, William. 2001. *The Navigation of Feeling: A Framework for the History of Emotions*. New York: Cambridge University Press.

Rowbotham, Judith, Kim Stevenson, & Samantha Pegg. 2013. *Crime News in Modern Britain: Press Reporting and Responsibility, 1820-2010*. Houndsmills, UK: Palgrave Macmillan.

Rubin, Avi. 2012. "The Trial of the Prosecutor Hamdi Bey: Inside and Out of the Ottoman *Nizamiye* Court." *Journal of Social History* 45 (3): 757–79.

Scheer, Monique. 2012. "Are Emotions a Kind of Practice (and Is That What Makes Them Have a History)? A Bourdieuian Approach to Understanding Emotion." *History and Theory* 51 (2): 193–220.

Siemens, Daniel. 2007. *Metropole und Verbrechen. Die Gerichtsreportage in Berlin, Paris und Chicago 1919-1933*. Stuttgart, Germany: Franz Steiner Verlag.

Siemens, Daniel. 2009. "Explaining Crime: Berlin Newspapers and the Construction of the Criminal in Weimar Germany." *Journal of European Studies* 39 (3): 336–52.

Silver, Mark. 2008. *Purloined Letters: Cultural Borrowing and Japanese Crime Literature, 1868–1937*. Honolulu: University of Hawaii Press.

Strath, Bo, & Martii Koskenniemi. 2008. "Between Restoration and Revolution, National Constitutions and Global Law: an Alternative View on the European Century 1815-1914." Accessed at http://blogs.helsinki.fi/erere-project/files/2008/11/erere_project.pdf.

Tully, James. 2013. "On the Global Multiplicity of Public Spheres: The Democratic Transformation of the Public Sphere?" In *Beyond Habermas: Democracy, Knowledge, and the Public Sphere*, ed. Christian J. Emden & David Midgley, 169–204. New York: Berghahn.

Walkowitz, Judith. 1992. *City of Dreadful Delight: Narratives of Sexual Danger in Late-Victorian London*. London: Virago.

Wilke, Jürgen, Birgit Schenk, Akiba A. Chohen, & Tamar Zemach. 1995. *Holocaust und NS-Prozesse. Die Presseberichterstattung in Israel und Deutschland zwischen Aneignung und Abwehr*. Köln, Weimar, & Wien: Böhlau.

Williams, Kevin. 2013. "Moral Panics, Emotion and Newspaper History." In *Moral Panics, Social Fears, and the Media*, ed. Siân Nicholas & Tom O'Malley, 28–45. London & New York: Routledge.

Willrich, Michael. 2003. *City of Courts: Socializing Justice in Progressive Era Chicago*. New York & Cambridge: Cambridge University Press.

Wilson, Richard Ashby. 2011. *Writing History in International Criminal Trials*. Cambridge, MA: Cambridge University Press.

Wood, John Carter. 2009. "'Those Who Have Had Trouble Can Sympathise with You': Press Writing, Reader Responses and a Murder Trial in Interwar Britain." *Journal of Social History* 43 (2): 439–62.

Wood, John Carter. 2012. *The Most Remarkable Woman in England: Poison, Celebrity and the Trials of Beatrice Pace*. Manchester, UK: Manchester University Press.

Zheng, Haiping. 2010. "The Gang of Four Trial." Accessed at http://law2.umkc.edu/faculty/projects/ftrials/gangoffour/Gangof4.html.

Zusman, Lynne K., ed. 2011. *The Law of Counterterrorism*. Chicago: American Bar Association.

....

CHAPTER 29

MERCY AND PAROLE IN ANGLO-AMERICAN CRIMINAL JUSTICE SYSTEMS FROM THE EIGHTEENTH CENTURY TO THE TWENTY-FIRST CENTURY

....

CAROLYN STRANGE

INTRODUCTION

....

FROM the ancient origins of the royal prerogative of mercy to the latest stipulations for parole, governing authorities have, through formal and informal means, accommodated discretion. Every stage and dimension of criminal proceedings involves a measure of discretion, from a victim's decision or reluctance to report an offense to a judge's choice to sentence a defendant to the full extent of the law or to moderate or suspend punishment. Yet, for criminals who face punishment, the impact of postconviction discretion is distinct: it mitigates or annuls sanctions imposed through judicial findings, from minor fines to the death penalty. In the premodern era sovereign mercy, wielded by monarchs, provided the principal means through which offenders were spared from penal sanctions. When republics and democracies emerged in the modern period, executive officeholders inherited that power. However, a new bureaucratic mode of discretionary justice—parole—arose in the late nineteenth century, and its scope expanded over the following century to provide the standard route for inmates hoping to exit prison prior to the expiration of their sentences.

The discretionary arm of justice has received surprisingly little attention from historians beyond studies of the death penalty's administration. The grisly opening passage of Foucault's *Discipline and Punish* (1977), with its vivid account of a murderer put to death after prolonged torture, in addition to other landmark works, such as V. A. C. Gatrell's *The Hanging Tree* (1994), encourage us to envisage mercy as an outdated practice, dramatized through the sovereign's capricious power over life and death. Although historians have considered pardoning and parole within the framework of convict transportation (Devereaux 2007; Ekrich 1990; Maxwell-Stewart, 2010), the broader canvas of the changing nature and forms of discretion that have modified punishment is poorly covered. This chapter responds to that challenge by sketching the debates that have shaped the practices of mercy and parole since the late eighteenth century.

In the premodern Anglo-American world, a mode of justice reliant upon penal severity and the uncertainty of its infliction transformed in the late eighteenth century into a system of predicable and equitable punishment measured in terms of time and the deprivation of liberty. Although the tide of reform pulled systems of justice toward sentencing certainty and reliance upon prisons, the royal prerogative of mercy and executive pardoning privilege remained in place in England, its colonies, and the United States,. However, the need to regulate burgeoning prison populations led to rise of discretionary release schemes and the use of pardoning as means of relief for offenders facing the pains of imprisonment. In the 1870s the goal of character reform slowly emerged as the chief object of punishment, and to achieve this aim, Progressive penologists urged legislators to introduce indeterminate sentencing and parole. This twin strategy was closely associated with American justice, but in England, Canada, and Australia similar means allowed early release through institutional appraisals of inmates' progress and prospects. In the early twentieth century, criminologists, penologists, and psychologists used their scientific credentials to claim that recidivism prediction could be rendered scientific (Laune 1931), but fear of crime overwhelmed faith in experts. A countermovement of mandatory sentencing, "truth in sentencing," and "three strikes" laws swept through Anglo-American legislatures from the 1970s onward, and incarceration rates took a steep climb. As a consequence prisoners and their advocates have recently begun to see mercy as their best hope for compensatory justice (Love 2013).

This chapter is divided into three sections. The first traces how legal and political philosophers, inspired by Enlightenment ideals of proportionality and rationality, as well as the promise of predicable penitentiary punishment, condemned the arbitrary character of pardoning. Once imprisonment became the standard mode of punishment in the nineteenth century, royal pardons, and pardons granted by elected governors in the United States, assumed a new role. No longer directed primarily toward saving death-sentenced offenders from the scaffold, executive mercy began to address the problems that penitentiaries produced: overcrowding, disorder, and madness. The second section begins with the nineteenth-century roots of administrative and institutional modes of discretion, namely, the ticket of leave, the remission of sentences, and various forms of release on license. Parole—a practice of prerelease screening and postrelease supervision—was introduced first in the United States, where it was paired with indeterminate sentencing in the late nineteenth century; England, Canada, and

Australia followed suit by the mid-twentieth century. The final section analyzes how and why parole's discretionary character fell under attack in the late twentieth century, sparking a punitive turn toward mandatory sentencing and a quest for mercy's revival.

I. The Royal Prerogative and Executive Pardoning

A. Mercy and Sovereignty in Law and Politics

Mercy sits on solid common law foundations, and its association with monarchy stretches back to the eleventh century, when William the Conqueror's Codes consolidated power over English nobility, and the king claimed the authority to determine whom to spare from punishment (Grupp 1963). With the establishment of constitutional monarchy in England in the late seventeenth century, royal power was greatly reduced, but the monarch retained the prerogative to dispense mercy (Radzinowicz 1948). Pardoning became a signal attribute of the Crown, distinct from the Parliament and the judiciary.

The religious origins of this attribute were endorsed by early modern political and moral philosopher John Locke, who claimed that Mosaic law, Christian morality, and God's mercy informed liberal democratic government, and that the administration of justice ought to abide by these norms. "The Rulers should have a Power ... to mitigate the severity of the Law, and Pardon some Offenders," he argued. Despite his firm support for the rule of law, Locke advised that executives be granted latitude to "act according to discretion, for the public good, without the prescription of law" (Laslet 1988 [1689], secs 159, 160, p. 375). So long as rulers exercised sovereign authority in ways consistent with the best interest of the broader community, this power must not be challenged.

William Blackstone, the leading jurist of the late eighteenth century, combined legal and political reasoning to uphold the legitimacy and necessity of the royal prerogative. In his authoritative 1769 *Commentaries*, he wrote of mercy as a kingly attribute passed down from the ancient concept of divine monarchy. But Blackstone was also a pragmatist, writing at a time when scores of criminals were publicly whipped and hanged each year in England (King 2000, p. 275). The wise monarch realized that discord could be avoided by softening the "rigor of the general law" in cases that merited mercy. Besides, Blackstone observed, it was in the ruler's self-interest to dispense mercy, since "repeated acts of goodness, coming immediately from his own hand, endear the sovereign to his subjects, and contribute more than anything to root in their hearts that filial affection and personal loyalty which are the sure establishment of a prince" (Blackstone 1893 [1753], Book 4, pp. 397–98). Blackstone may have erred in his assumptions about endearment (American revolutionaries certainly found George III an unendearing monarch), but his observation about the self-serving inclinations of monarchs and their representatives in dispensing pardons was sound (Hay 2011). At the time he wrote his *Commentaries*, the pardon rate for capitally convicted offenders in England averaged around 60 percent (Beattie 1996, pp. 433–35). Had Blackstone peered at the record of pardons granted by governors in colonies such as Nova Scotia and Newfoundland, he would have seen that the rate ranged from just over 50 percent in the former to 70 percent in the latter (Phillips 1992, pp. 423, 431; Bannister 2003, p. 189). The infliction of bloody justice was the exception rather than the rule, although no rigid rules dictated discretion.

Surprisingly, the royalist reasoning of Locke and Blackstone made its way into the political settlement that followed the American Revolution. Despite the patriots' revolt against monarchical tyranny and colonial governors' abuse of their delegated authority, the new nation's federal politicians settled on a republican version of the royal prerogative of mercy (Scheuerman 2005). Alexander Hamilton, one of the chief architects of the U.S. Constitution, persuaded his fellow founders that the president ought to be granted full authority to dispense mercy (Duker 1976). In his contribution to the Federalist cause, Hamilton stated in 1788: "The criminal code of every country partakes so much of necessary severity that without an easy access to exceptions in favor of unfortunate guilt, justice would wear a countenance too sanguinary and cruel" (Alexander Hamilton, "The Command of the Military and Naval Forces, and the Pardoning Power of the Executive," *New York Packet*, 25 March 1788). In the immediate postrevolutionary period the prospect of unrest and disunion were uppermost in the framers' minds, and these unsettled times highlighted the usefulness of granting the chief executive unfettered power to temper justice with mercy. In its final draft, the Constitution of 1797 vested in the president alone the power to "grant Reprieves and Pardons for Offences against the United States," including crimes that had not been prosecuted. The only exception to his power concerned the charge of impeachment, which would otherwise have allowed the president to pardon himself (Duker 1976, pp. 502–06). Thus, in the aftermath of a revolution that declared the people to be sovereign, the U.S. president inherited powers akin to those claimed before him by both William the Conqueror and medieval kings.

B. Pardoning's Rational Critics

Royal pardoning and executive discretion in its various guises drew rational critique starting in the late eighteenth century, despite mercy's enshrinement in law, politics, and custom. Rationalists in Europe, Britain, and North America considered clemency an insidious practice, tied to a cruel sham of justice that lurched between terror and leniency (King 2000). How could punishment deter potential offenders when its application was irrational and unpredictable? Why should the monarch's whim, rather than the gravity of the offense, determine the infliction of punishment?

These questions were posed by legal and political philosophers who laid bare the inequities of the *ancien régime*. In the late eighteenth century the search was on for new models of justice that would replace personal discretion with penal certainty. Marquis Cesare Beccaria's "Essay on Crimes and Punishment" (published in English in 1764) was a remarkably potent polemic that persuaded fellow rationalists that indiscriminate cruelty could be replaced by less severe, systematically imposed penalties (Lieberman 2002). "As punishments become more mild," he predicted, crime would decline, and clemency and pardons would become less necessary. If states developed codes of punishment that standardized penalties for offenses, clemency could be excluded altogether, Beccaria believed (1819 [1764], p. 158). The English utilitarian philosopher Jeremy Bentham became one of his many acolytes and the staunchest critic of mercy's irresponsible administration in early nineteenth-century England. Although Bentham allowed that the imperfections of the prevailing criminal law made pardoning necessary in "deplorable" cases, he drove home the message that "enlightened and well-ordered law" would require no "correction" through the royal prerogative, which he likened to the waving of a magic wand (Bentham 1843, pp. 406, 521). The formula for better governance and universal justice was simple and sensible: "If the punishment is necessary, it ought not to be remitted; if it is not necessary, the convict should not be sentenced to undergo it" (Bentham 1840, p. 137).

In the United States the royalist roots of clemency grew more concerning over the nineteenth century. Constitutional law authority Francis Lieber was the foremost critic of executive pardoning in the United States, and he used a series of essays, published from the 1830s to the 1860s, to argue that executive mercy was out of place in a republic in which the people were sovereign. Furthermore, petitioners who considered their access to elected officials a democratic right pestered state governors and the president for mercy on sentimental grounds. If the royalist "one-man" pardon power were replaced by advisory boards, composed of judicial officers and other men of substance, Lieber believed that the pardon process would operate openly and according to clear legal principles (Lieber 1859). Mercy had an important role to play in correcting injustice, he admitted, but in his view it was "improper to leave this important act dependent upon indefinite and vague feelings" (Lieber 1833, p. xxxii). Although the president's power to pardon remained unfettered, most states began to follow Lieber's advice, largely out of anxiety that governors were misusing their powers (Dinan 2003). Over the nineteenth and early twentieth centuries, the majority of states amended their constitutions to moderate governors' sole fiat powers through the establishment of advisory boards. By the 1920s, six states had entrusted pardon boards with full executive authority over discretionary decision-making (Jensen 1922).

Executive officeholders lost their monopoly over the authority to consider pardon petitions in many parts of the United States, but in England, its colonies, and the British dominions mercy's symbolic link to sovereign power held. The monarch and her or his representatives maintained the formal right to grant clemency, although in practice justice departments and departments of state (such as the Home Office in England) assumed the day-to-day work of reading pleas for mercy and reviewing cases (Chadwick 1992).

The enlistment of a professional class of civil servants to staff these departments fulfilled many of the functions assigned to state pardon boards. The rationalist critique of gratuitous and idiosyncratic pardoning did not extirpate the pardon power, but it did spawn new agencies of discretionary justice, which assumed the mounting clemency caseload in Britain and its dominions. These administrative reforms in the field of postconviction discretion were tied to wider efforts to rationalize justice, particularly through the introduction of penitentiary punishment, the theme of the following section (Barkow 2008).

II. The Rise of Administrative and Institutional Discretion

A. Penitential Justice and Discretionary Release

The penitentiary was the product of competing ideals: the drive to systematize penalties to fit crimes alongside the intent to inspire penitence and correction (McGowan 1995; Rothman 1980). Massive prisons built to incarcerate hundreds of inmates serving long sentences at hard labor were stone testaments to these grand ambitions. Fortress-like penitentiaries could keep prisoners in isolation, press them to face up to their failings, and force them to work. But for how long? Time served should be proportionate to the gravity of the crime, according to Beccaria and Bentham; in contrast, those who stressed redemption and spiritual change as the objects of punishment, notably Quakers, viewed penitentiaries as "laboratories of virtue," where criminals had to be kept as long as necessary to learn how to live upright lives (Meranze 1996). According to religiously motivated prison advocates, benevolent visitors and chaplains were in the best position to judge an inmate's moral state. For these reasons, neither cohort of penitentiary promoters anticipated that generous pardoning, coupled with the introduction of sentence remission schedules and, ultimately, parole, would become necessary to respond to the problems penitentiaries introduced.

Prisoners made to face years in penitentiaries, breaking rocks or picking oakum, and fed on meager diets, were prone to rebelliousness and despair, and these matters pressured executives to pardon (Kahn 2005). In Canada, the United States, and England scores of riots occurred in flagship penitentiaries over the nineteenth century (McCoy 2012, pp. 167–72; McConville 1981; Brown 2003). When arson and mutiny broke out in resistance to labor demands, authorities responded with even harsher conditions. So great were the pressures the penitentiary produced that pardons became a safety valve. Between 1791 and 1809, three-quarters of inmates at Philadelphia's Walnut Street Prison were released on pardons, a rate that dipped but remained substantial over the early nineteenth century (Teeters 1955, p. 135). Prison discipline societies, which emerged in the 1820s, attributed this practice to two worrying customs: the assumption, on the part of inmates, that serving half of their sentences earned them the right to be pardoned; and the readiness of governors to grant pardons without merit, particularly around the Christmas season (McLennan 2008, p. 46). Monarchs had long practiced such customs by granting pardons on coronation days, but executive discretion was put to more pragmatic use in the age of the penitentiary.

In the 1820s one of the most ambitious experiments in penitentiary punishment—solitary confinement without labor—highlighted the capacity of pardoning to rectify injustice. Tragic results ensued after New York's Auburn State Prison, one of the Western world's model penitentiaries from its opening in 1816, subjected eighty "hardened" inmates to complete isolation. The state legislature endorsed the practice to prevent the men from corrupting fellow inmates and to force them to "subdue" their "stubborn spirits." Yet these prisoners, facing years in solitary confinement, sank into madness. Shortly after the strategy was implemented in 1821 reports of suicides and self-mutilation surfaced, and the governor, William Yates, responded by using his discretion to pardon and release the men from Auburn Prison in 1823. There had been nothing illegal about the men's punishment, but the governor and the warden both admitted that the attempt at total isolation had been a "dangerous error" (Powers 1828, p. 85).

The desire to manage inmate behavior without relying on pardoning led to compensatory systems that harnessed prisoners' willingness to follow rules and to comply with commands to work. While compensating obedient prisoners with gratuities (such as extra rations of tobacco) was customary, this casual reward practice was formalized in the mid-nineteenth century when prison managers tied compensation to the prospect of early release. In England, the overcrowding problems that bedeviled the administration of punishment in North America did not confront Captain Joshua Jebb. Appointed director of convict prisons in 1850, he too faced the challenge of dealing with growing numbers of prisoners who would previously have been transported to Australia. His solution was to introduce a sentence remission scheme whereby prisoners could shorten their time in prison. Inmates serving long sentences could thereafter shave years from their court-ordered time behind bars, although their capacity to do so was determined by their willingness to comply, their capacity to work, and the judgment of keepers (Brown 2003, pp. 48–53).

The most famous experiment in institutionalized discretion over penal sentences occurred on a tiny island off the east coast of Australia. The transportation of felons, as a condition attached to pardons, rid Britain of many of its criminals beginning in the seventeenth century, but in the final decades of this scheme one of the system's superintendents, Alexander Maconochie, used his position to test the concept of incrementally reduced punishment leading to earned release (Ekrich 1987; Finnane 1997, pp. 1–28). When he arrived in Tasmania in 1837 Maconochie reviewed the administration of the convict system for the English Society for the Improvement of Prison Discipline. His report denounced the assignment of convicts by employers and the lack of supervision of convicts released on ticket of leave, which permitted such individuals a range of freedoms (including the privilege to earn and keep wages) while they completed their terms of imprisonment. Although Maconochie's incendiary comments embarrassed the government, they won him supporters on the English Select Committee on Transportation. With their backing, Maconochie became the superintendent of the Norfolk Island penal settlement in 1840. Despite the site's fearsome reputation, he believed that even the hardest convict could be reformed through a "mark" system of discipline and reform. This regime involved the granting of marks to convicts for their compliance and productivity and the loss of them for poor work and bad habits, creating a behavioral balance sheet that determined a convict's eligibility for early release on license (Maconochie 1846, pp. 27–28).

Because Maconochie's tenure at Norfolk Island ended in 1844, his extravagant claims of lower recidivism rates under the marks system could not be fully examined. But this did not stop the penal innovator from promoting the idea that task-oriented discipline was the only way to train men for freedom (White 1976). In Ireland, a similar system was championed by Walter Crofton, who headed the Irish Convict Prisons' Board of Directors. He justified his inducement system on the principle that prisons ought to prepare inmates for release, not out of kindness but to protect society from crime (Waite 1991). Instead of sentencing criminals to serve long periods in prison, with the hope of a pardon a constant distraction, prisoners could be encouraged through rewards to earn their way toward freedom and change their behaviour. Around the world the principle of earned release was heralded as a hallmark of Progressive penology .

The retreat from deterrence and the elevation of reform as the chief aim of punishment inspired the holding of the National Congress on Penitentiary and Reformatory Discipline in Cincinnati in 1870. This event constituted a watershed in penal thinking, and the International Prison Congress, held in London two years later, provided further endorsement of the new rationale of punishment. At Cincinnati, delegates from England, Europe and the United States worked together to prepare a Declaration of Principles, with one of them naming executive clemency a "grave" problem that must be solved: "The effect of the too free use of the pardoning power is to detract from the certainty of punishment for crimes and to divert the mind of prisoners from the means supplied for their improvement" (Wines 1871, p. 522). Yet their criticism differed from Beccaria's, uttered a century earlier. On the one hand, penal Progressives attacked the uncertainty of mercy as an impediment to reform strategies; on the other hand, they were convinced that the uncertainty of sentencing was pivotal to the project of molding criminals into law-abiding citizens.

Over the following decades, the indeterminate sentence became a centerpiece in plans to amplify imprisonment's capacity to reform in the United States, where it was linked to the introduction of parole. Both innovations hinged on institutional managers' discretion over the duration of punishment (Rothman 1980, p. xv). Britain and its colonies differed in relying more squarely on earned remission and using tickets of leave and licensed release. Despite these differences, the principle that punishment ought to fit the criminal, not the crime, was adopted in wider penal circles by the late nineteenth century and was closely linked with the rising authority of social and medical science. As criminological experts became involved in the assessment of prisoners, institutional control over prisoner release waxed and executive discretion waned, although its formidable role in capital case reviews was a reminder of its continuing significance.

B. Shortening Sentences in the Age of Reform

England, Canada, Australia, and the United States took different routes to arrive at novel means of administering discretionary release. The engine of change in the nineteenth century was the United States, which was the first to link Maconochie's marks system to indeterminate sentencing. By 1900, eleven states allowed judges to sentence certain categories of convicted criminals (mostly juveniles, females, and first offenders) to prescribe minimum or maximum periods of imprisonment (Hall 1989, p. 181). As the Cincinnati National Congress's delegates had pronounced: "Sentences limited only by satisfactory proof of reformation should be substituted for those measured by mere lapse of time" (Wines 1871, p. 551). Medical and organic metaphors were favored in justifications of indeterminacy, as one promoter explained: "The reformatory process requires time, time for inflammatory action to abate, time for old wounds and sores to heal, time for healthy tissue to grow, time in which the prisoner may recuperate his energies, in which new and better resolutions may germinate, blossom and bear fruit, and in which the genuineness of any seeming alteration in his character may be tested and confirmed" (Wines 1904, p. 434).

In the early days of indeterminate sentencing, wardens placed weight on moral rectitude and industrious work habits. For female offenders, the emphasis was on the former, with the expectation that released inmates would slot into their appropriate family roles—dutiful daughters, faithful wives, solicitous mothers, and respectable widows (Rafter 1985). For males, the capacity for self-support and the support of any dependents was critical (Simon 1994). These norms continued to influence decision-makers who judged inmates' capacity to adjust to freedom, although an array of experts would reformulate the language of character assessment in the early twentieth century, adding new assessment criteria of intelligence and psychological fitness into the mix. From its introduction, the elastic prison sentence fed contradictory objectives: the need to release prisoners before the expiration of their maximum terms to keep prison populations manageable, and the objective of realizing the full promise of institutionally based reform.

In states that introduced indeterminate sentencing, parole provided a complementary means to tie prerelease observations to postrelease scrutiny of inmates' behavior. Parole's proudest standard-bearer was Zebulon R. Brockway, whose promotion of graded punishment leading to supervised release prior to the expiration of inmates' sentences earned him the superintendency of New York's Elmira Reformatory for young males and first-time felony offenders. Brockway applied the principles of the 1870 National Congress by categorizing each inmate in regard to his commitment to schooling, his participation in military-style drills and vocational programs, his attendance at religious services, and his obedience to rules. The reformatory's Board of

Managers, headed by Brockway, reviewed reports on each applicant for release, and a transfer agent (Brockway's brother in the initial years) monitored parolees, chasing down those who violated the conditions of parole (Pisciotta 1994, p. 48). A review of the reformatory movement, prepared for the International Prison Commission in 1900, determined that close to two-thirds of the 9,865 inmates Elmira received in its first thirteen years had been released on parole (Sanborn 1900, p. 37). More impressive were Elmira parolees' low rates of recidivism. Some observers questioned Brockway's glowing accounts, however, and former inmates complained about the ways in which he and his staff exacted inmate compliance. In the early 1890s, several young inmates made public complaints that Brockway and his guards subjected the prisoners to flogging and paddling to induce compliance, and that the grading system was compromised by bribes and vindictiveness (Pisciotta 1994, pp. 52–58). Like Maconochie's widely adopted marks method, Elmira's grading system allowed keepers considerable discretion in determining inmate eligibility for early release.

Despite the scandal that flared up as a result of inmates' allegations, the Elmira "plan" became a model for similar institutions. Most U.S. states with large urban populations followed Elmira's lead as they established statewide systems of parole over the late nineteenth and early twentieth centuries (Lindsey 1925). Elmira-style parole for the general prison population was not embraced outside of the United States, but similar models were introduced for juveniles, first offenders, and reformatory prisoners. For instance, England's Gladstone Committee on prisons recommended in 1895 that the Elmira approach to minimizing prison time and maximizing inmates' capacity for social adaptation be introduced for young adults, a plan that was formally installed through the borstal system in 1908 (Forsythe 1990; Harding 1988).

From the late nineteenth century onward, parole advocates asserted that sound scientific criteria could determine which prisoners were eligible for early release and precisely when they ought to be released. Italian criminologist Enrico Ferri, a regular delegate to the International Prison Congress, was an early exponent of parole as a practice requiring expert knowledge of human nature:

> It will be understood that conditional release, as it would be organized in the positive system of indeterminate segregation, ought only to be granted after a physio-psychological examination of the prisoner, and not after an official inspection of records, So that it will be refused, no longer, as now, almost exclusively in regard to the gravity of the crime, but in regard to the greater or less readaptability of the criminal to social conditions. (Ferri 1896, p. 217)

The most up-to-date reformatories and penitentiaries claimed to live up to these aspirations, but prisoner case files and parole hearing records tell a different story, involving impressionist judgments and gender, class, and racial biases. In Progressive-era prisons for women, which conducted "scientific" assessments of inmates' sexual and moral delinquency, the move toward release on parole responded to the shortage of servants in the labor market and was bound up with long-standing efforts to control female behavior through domestic service (Odem 1995; Myers 2006). In racially segregated southern states, such as Georgia and Texas, the parole system released a surprisingly high number of African Americans, but only those whose white patrons valued their labor—domestic in the case of females, and agricultural in the case of males (Garton 2003, p. 678). Parole boards in these states rendered peonage and imprisonment barely distinguishable by considering inmate employability over and above psychosocial criteria (Bluc 2012, p. 236). Moral means of judging character for discretionary release consideration lingered well beyond the time of the penitentiary's origins (Messinger et al. 1985).

Once psychologists, psychiatrists, and social workers were hired to contribute to parole evaluations in states such as California, Massachusetts, Illinois, and New York, they found what they were looking for: mental defects, personality disorders, and social maladjustment (Rothman 1980; Garton 2010). Although such labels harmed inmates' prospects of parole (particularly if they were deemed to be "psychopaths"), members of parole boards generally reached their decisions after cursory reviews of files and brief interviews with prisoners, which raised doubts about the professionalism of discretion. In the 1920s, a period when Prohibition-related gun violence rose sharply in the United States, parole boards began to face criticism that their reviews were no more scientific than unregulated pardoning, and that they coddled criminals by turning them loose before they served their full terms (State of New York 1930, p. 19). Yet the discretionary nature of parole had undeniable financial and administrative merits that wardens relied upon, and that legislators were loath to dispense with, particularly during the lean years of the Depression, when state budgets strained to breaking point. The confidence and professional pride of parole authorities took a beating in the following four decades, but the system held up for these pragmatic reasons (Simon 1994).

C. Parole by Other Names: Tickets of Leave and Release on License

Common law tradition, the strength of British custom, and their distinct histories account for the later turn to parole in Australia, Canada, and England. The ticket of leave was formally introduced by the governor of New South Wales in 1801 as a means to manage convict liberation, and it became well entrenched as a means to grant prisoners conditional liberty prior to the expiration of their sentences. In the postconvict era, modifications to the tradition provided a bridge toward new penal objectives. For instance, in 1893 the New South Wales minister of justice reported that a ticket of leave program, introduced two years prior for the treatment of first offenders, was operating smoothly: "Licence is never issued unless the Minister is satisfied from the nature and circumstances of the offence, the prisoner's previous history, character, and mode of life, and his conduct in prison, that he seriously intends and is capable of returning to an honest life" (*Sydney Evening News*, 19 May 1893, p. 6). Assistance for schemes of this nature was supplied through Australia's constitutional assignment of policing to state governments after federation in 1901. But some things stayed the same: keeping track of men and women released on tickets of leave still depended upon the aid provided by charities and religious organizations, not behavioral scientists.

In Canada a nationwide discretionary release system was introduced with the passage in 1899 of the Ticket of Leave Act. Although this legislation was modeled on England's Penal Servitude Act of 1857, which had been passed to broaden the remit of a system previously geared toward transported convicts bound for penal colonies, the ideals of Progressive penology informed Canada's legislation. Despite the 1899 Act's rejection of indeterminate sentencing, it was more liberal than most U.S. state parole provisions, since it allowed applicants, including adults and prisoners serving lengthy sentences, to apply for release without having to serve a minimum period of imprisonment (Law Reform Commission of Canada 1977). The monarch's representative, the governor general of Canada, was technically authorized to impose conditions on released prisoners and to revoke licenses; in practice, the Remissions Branch of the federal Justice Department evaluated applications and set the terms of offenders' licenses. This branch also reviewed applications for pardon and provided advice to the federal cabinet, whose decisions required the governor general's stamp of approval (Bottomley 1990). In these respects the duties of Canada's federal Remissions Branch were similar to the functions performed by the parole and pardon advisory boards that were operating in most U.S. states by the mid-twentieth century.

In England a more complicated system of earned remission and release on license predated the introduction of parole in 1968. The borstal detention scheme for youthful offenders and the system for incarcerating so-called habitual offenders were both initiated in 1908 through the Prevention of Crime Act, which created special classes and forms of license. Juveniles could be considered for early release after serving six months (in the case of males) or three months (in the case of females), with the understanding that the balance of their sentence would be served on license under the supervision of voluntary aid organizations, such as the Penal Reform League. Habitual offenders served sentences at "his majesty's pleasure," and the home secretary decided when it was safe to order their licensed release, upon the recommendation of local review committees. When a prisoner in this special class was released, he (or, less commonly, she) was granted a license to be released into the custody of the volunteer Central Association for the Aid of Discharged Convicts (Bottomley 1990, p. 328). Prisoners imprisoned for life, most often inmates serving commuted death sentences, could also be released on license. No matter what their crimes, inmates in England's prisons served sentences that could, in most cases, be commuted (Ruggles-Brise 1921, pp. 31–34).

Because the average inmate in England could reduce her or his sentence by one-third, the prison population was kept to a more manageable level than it was in the United States. However, the encouragement of habits of industry and obedience through generous remission allowances was enforced through the looming prospect of having to serve a longer sentence. Under the English system, a prisoner's noncompliance could result in the loss of privileges or a period of earned remission, and it could also trigger a prison governor to identify a prisoner as "incorrigible" and therefore a habitual offender under the 1908 Prevention Act (Ruggles-Brise 1921, p. 254). In this respect, the promise of earned release, combined with the threat of an additional ten years' discretionary imprisonment under the Act's provisions, served as the twin tools of institutional management in the English system prior to its shift to American-style parole in the 1960s. By the mid-twentieth century, the institutional judgment of release eligibility and supervision conditions determined most prisoners' experience of leaving prisons and reformatories across the Anglo-American world.

D. Mercy and the Politics of the Death Penalty in the Twentieth Century

Public attention to the politics of parole overshadowed scrutiny of executive discretion in the twentieth century, but that spotlight never totally eclipsed the pardon. The enduring significance of clemency, unrestrained by the professional guidelines that regulated parole, at least on paper, was clearest in capital cases, especially in jurisdictions where executive officeholders retained the responsibility of making the final decision regarding the death penalty's infliction (Cobb 1998). Like the president, governors were elected politicians who recognized that every determination in a capital case carried the prospect of intense political scrutiny and even impeachment, should their use of their constitutional authority be considered corrupt. In 1876, the lieutenant governor of Mississippi was impeached after he allegedly accepted a bribe to pardon a murderer; in the early 1920s the pardons granted by Governor Miriam "Ma" Ferguson of Texas reeked of corruption, since she gave them out by the hundreds per month over her administration (Moore 1989, p. 63). Irregularities of this nature were not new, but they became newly relevant as death penalty abolitionism gained momentum over the mid-twentieth century.

In England, as in Australia and Canada, the royal prerogative of mercy remained a fundamental attribute of justice, although its administration was handled by the twentieth century by government ministers and the public servants who served them. The English home secretary, and his equivalent ministerial officers in Canada and Australia, was responsible for deciding whether death sentences were carried out. In former British colonies, the Crown's representative retained formal signing authority (Roger 1992). In postfederation New South Wales, for instance, the right of cabinet members to reach a consensus and to forward their decision for formal endorsement was respected, even though appointed lieutenant governors-in-council could have exercised their prerogative to determine the fate of individuals facing execution (Strange 1996, p. 141). Despite the behind-the-scenes character of clemency deliberations petitioners still addressed their pleas for mercy to the monarch. Along with judges' recommendations and trial transcripts, these humble, heartfelt notes were reminders that lives were at stake with every line a civil servant typed into a recommendation.

No matter how technocratic, capital justice never became a routine affair. The high stakes in capital cases provided a sobering reminder that sovereign might was no less awesome in an age of bureaucracy and private executions than it had been when justice was bloody and public. However, bureaucrats tried their best to make the processes that led up to final decisions appear thoroughly considered. In 1941, Remissions Branch officers in Canada's Department of Justice prepared a capital case procedure manual in response to questions asked in Parliament about the disposition of death penalty cases. Ministers came and went from year to year, but senior bureaucrats refined over decades a routine of ordering transcripts, gathering reports from Crown attorneys and judges, reviewing appeal court rulings, and providing concise reports for cabinet review. Yet the 1941 manual could not explain why the rate of executions had increased in the 1930s, from approximately 50 percent since confederation in 1867 to 61 percent in the 1930s, with twenty-five executions in 1931 alone (Strange 1998, pp. 190–91). As the Depression eased, the rate declined sharply again. If cases were truly evaluated equitably, abolitionists demanded, what could possibly account for such fluctuations?

Often, a single case could reveal the tangle of considerations that threaded into every capital conviction. The prospect of a woman's execution invariably drew attention to customary gender prejudices, both the notion that women are less culpable than men for their actions and, conversely, the belief that women ought to be held to higher moral standards than men. Executive authorities who pardoned female murderers were less likely to face public outrage than those who allowed their sentences to stand, although this chivalric trend weakened after suffragists' demands for political equality were met. The highly publicized and controversial executions of American Ruth Snyder in 1928 and Englishwoman Ruth Ellis in 1955 proved that the mere fact of being a white female murderer provided no guarantee of clemency in modern times. Male jurors and judges were less inclined to recommend mercy whenever women appeared to have veered from prevailing scripts of sexual propriety, and the history of executive clemency reveals the same pattern (Seal 2010, pp. 143–44). Even in the early twenty-first century the very exceptionality of the capitally convicted woman remains a product of violent women's tendency to be judged mad rather than bad (Steric 2002).

Culturally freighted understandings of culpability and desert worked to most, though not all, women's advantage, but such favorable considerations did not characterize the disposition of capital cases involving defendants from ethnic and racial minorities, both men and women. Research undertaken by groups such as the National Association for the Advancement of Colored People, initiated in the 1930s, tracked the prejudicial use of discretion, which resulted in the more severe punishment of blacks convicted of the same crimes as whites. Allegations of inequality in capital justice gained credence over the twentieth century, culminating in the U.S. Supreme Court's 1972 ruling that decision-making in death penalty cases was "arbitrary and capricious." Consequently, the Court pronounced the death penalty unconstitutional, on the grounds that it was "cruel and unusual" in its administration. This ruling, *Furman v. Georgia*, put a temporary stop to executions in the U.S. because it found capital justice to be plainly racist and classist:

We know that the discretion of judges and juries in imposing the death penalty enables the penalty to be selectively applied, feeding prejudices against the accused if he is poor and despised, and lacking political clout, or if he is a member of a suspect or unpopular minority, and saving those who by social position may be in a more protected position. (*Furman v. Georgia*, 408 U.S. 238 [1972], pp. 255)

Because the ruling came down from the highest federal court, many states, jealous of their right to formulate laws for their own jurisdictions, regarded it as an attack. Thirty-five states fought back by modifying the trial of capital cases to separate the penalty phase from the determination of guilt. After one of these new laws was tested in 1976, the *Gregg v. Georgia* decision of the Supreme Court confirmed that executions could resume, so long as jurors were properly "guided" (Nice 1992).

The Court's endorsement of the death penalty's reinstatement under these modified procedures rested on the groundless expectation that all capitally sentenced offenders would enjoy equal access to clemency through the various pardoning mechanisms in place in each state. In Georgia, the *Gregg* judgment observed, the governor worked with the State Board of Pardons and Parole to consider whether or not to commute a death sentence. The Court's expectation that pardon boards and governors would give due consideration to prejudicial prosecutions proved to be ill founded, however. It quickly became evident that elected prosecutors were inclined to bring capital charges against criminals, and that judges, also elected, urged jurors to convict them in order to appear tough on crime without having to bear the responsibility of deciding who would die and who might live (Palacios 1996). In the *Gregg* decision's wake, capital convictions rose sharply, access to legal avenues of appeal diminished, and the exercise of mercy dropped in death penalty states, leading to disproportionate execution rates among the poor and African Americans, the very cohort of prisoners the *Furman* ruling identified as most vulnerable to injustice (Amnesty International 2003).

III: The Decline of Parole and the Resurgence of the Pardon

A. Parole under Attack

Unlike the United States, where many states retained the death penalty, England, Canada, Australia, and most other liberal democratic nations abolished the death penalty by the late twentieth century. As a consequence, public scrutiny of postconviction discretion centered on parole and supervised release. Over the 1950s and 1960s, Canada, Australia, and England adopted American-style parole systems, which professionalized the aftercare and supervision of prisoners by employing trained parole officers and creating parole boards to work with institutional officials in assessing applications for early release. When Canada established a National Parole Board in 1959, and when

England and Wales followed by replacing their earlier release schemes with a parole system in 1968, the notion of reform through administrative management still commanded considerable public support. The bureaucratization of discretionary release also came with the assurance that prisoner release would be administered impartially, with public safety in mind. Yet binding guidelines proved slow in coming, and this sluggishness aroused concern in government quarters. In England, the home secretary insisted in 1975 that the Parole Board publish its criteria for the granting of parole, but he received an unsatisfactory answer when the Board reported simply that parole was a privilege, not a right (Harlow & Rawlings 1997, pp. 190–91). This push for transparency in decision-making highlighted the difficulties that had dogged parole from its early days: Should decisions be made on the basis of inmates' offenses, their prior history of offending, their behavior in prison, their keepers' evaluation of their readiness for release, or the risk they might pose to the public?

Notwithstanding reports on the merits of parole produced by criminologists, social workers, and psychologists, public trust in the expertise of parole boards and officers declined in the 1960s. The days when social scientists could wave risk of reoffending charts before reporters were long gone (Dean 1968). Judges joined the general public in complaining that custodial sentences were losing their capacity to deter crime, and rising crime rates over the 1970s and 1980s confirmed that impression. Defenders of parole faced hostility from legal quarters and from mass media, which amplified fears that violent offenders and sexual predators could commit crime with impunity, since they banked on serving only a small portion of their prison sentences (Walker 1993, p. 115). In England, the government began in the 1980s to address these anxieties by chipping away at institutional and administrative discretion over the liberation of prisoners (Bottomley 1984). In Canada, Australia, and the United States, similar moves occurred as legislators reached for "real time" and "real sentencing" solutions to calm public fears and garner votes.

Efforts to align the time inmates actually served with the period of imprisonment the courts prescribed reprised the search for certainty that had animated Enlightenment visionaries two centuries earlier. Less than two decades after Canada introduced its National Parole Board, the Law Reform Commission of Canada sounded a rationalist call when it advocated "benchmark sentences" and the replacement of the Parole Board by a "sentence supervision board" comprised of legal experts (Law Reform Commission of Canada 1977). Similarly, in 1962 the U.S. Model Penal Code strongly endorsed the use of indeterminate sentencing and parole release, a feature in place in every state at that point; in 1978; however, the updated U.S. Model Sentencing and Corrections Act dismissed discretionary sentencing and recommended that parole be abolished.

The enthusiastic support for institutional discretion over the release of offenders as a fundamental principle of reformatory punishment, first heralded at the 1870 Prison Congress, found few friends by the 1970s. Even civil rights advocates lined up against parole and called for its end. Liberal-minded critics accused authorities within prisons of abusing their power to withhold parole. Inmates without representation—overwhelmingly the poor, the ill educated, and prisoners from minority groups—were deprived of fair hearings because parole officials had too much discretionary power and too little accountability (Hood 1975; Von Hirsch 1976). Squeezed from the left and the right, faith in parole shrank in the 1980s (Tonry 1995, pp. 164–65). In 1987 the U.S. federal government passed the Sentencing Reform Act, which determined that thereafter offenders sentenced under it would be ineligible for parole. This legislation capped a wave of definite sentencing statutes that abolished discretionary early release in state after state starting in the 1970s. The rise of victims' rights lobbyists and penal populism led governments in Anglo-American jurisdictions to take an adversarial approach to criminals, despite the enormous costs that the carceral state's expansion incurred (Dubber 2006; Pratt 2008).

"Truth in sentencing" statutes constrained judicial discretion and they dealt a direct blow to the authority of parole boards, especially in regard to the release of serious offenders. In 1999, the Crimes Act in New South Wales dictated that offenders sentenced to life were thenceforth required to serve their full terms of imprisonment with no prospect of parole. In Canada, a wider range of criminals, whom forensic psychologists diagnosed as "dangerous offenders," was subjected to longer periods of detention without the prospect of parole. Once so labelled, individuals who were released faced mandatory long-term supervision, with the ever-present prospect of reincarceration for life (Petrunik, Murphy, & Fedoroff 2008, pp. 116–17). In the United States, the officially declared "war on drugs" and rising community pressure to punish sexual "predators" produced a raft of mandatory sentencing laws, including California's infamous "three strikes" law. Passed in 1994, this legislation imposed an automatic sentence of twenty-five years to life in prison for offenders found guilty of three felonies, no matter how minor. In this time of retribution and deterrence, supporting discretionary justice in association with inmates' capacity for reform was a recipe for voter rejection (Garland 2001).

The skyrocketing rate of imprisonment was the costly outcome of demands for greater certainty in sentencing. In the 1990s many countries introduced "private" prisons in the 1990s (carceral institutions operated as for-profit enterprises) in a bid to reduce the financial burden of mass incarceration, but inmate numbers kept climbing. In England and Australia the imprisonment rate jumped by approximately 50 percent from the early 1990s to the late 2000s; in the United States, it shot from 110 imprisoned individuals per 100,000 citizens to 731 in 2010 (International Centre for Prison Studies 2010). Within these grossly enlarged prison populations, the poor, members of ethnic and racial minority groups, and indigenous people, particularly in Australia and Canada, became the most highly overrepresented populations, creating incalculable social costs (Anthony 2013; Kury & Shea 2011).

Populism of a progressive character was a less predictable response to mandatory sentencing, and it emerged in opposition to overimprisonment and its devastating impact on minority communities (Petersilia 2003). In 1994, 72 percent of Californians voted in favor of the three strikes law, but activists' revelation of its inequities turned public opinion around. In 2012, 69 percent voted to revise the law so that minor and nonviolent offenders would no longer face life in prison (Stanford Law School Three

Strikes Project & NAACP Legal Defense and Education Fund 2013). In countries such as Canada and Australia, diversion programs and culturally articulated restorative justice initiatives were introduced to deal with grossly disproportionate imprisonment rates in indigenous communities (Bartels 2010). Simultaneously, activists concerned about the mass criminalization of African Americans began to galvanize broad civic support for decarceration and for demands that mandatory sentencing laws be rolled back (Alexander 2010; Tonry 2011). Perhaps most surprising of all was the pressure put upon executive authorities to use their power to pardon not just offenders under the death penalty's shadow, but the tens of thousands of prisoners whose mandatory sentences left them few other prospects of relief.

B. The Revival of the Pardon

In the nineteenth century the pioneers of parole believed that the need for pardoning was about to come to a fitting end. When the secretary of the National Prison Association was asked in 1870, "What is the best method of pardoning?" he retorted: "The best plan is to permit the prisoner to pardon himself as the effect of reasonable evidence of reformation under indefinite sentence" (Wines 1871, p. 494). But the pardon did not merely survive measures that tamed monarchs' and governors' authority over the granting of mercy: in states where individual officeholders retained their power to pardon, particularly those in which the death penalty remained legal, executive authorities began in the early twenty-first century to reassert their prerogative powers to commute sentences (Ridolfi and Gordon 2009). The power of mercy to redress possibly wrongful convictions became dramatically apparent in 2003, when Governor Ryan of Illinois pardoned four men sentenced to death and commuted the death sentences of a further 164 inmates to life without parole (Sarat and Hussain 2004, p. 1308). Evidence of dubious convictions, allegations of poor legal representation, and documentation of inmates' deficient mental capacity prompted governors of other states, sometimes in company with pardon and parole boards, to commute the sentences of over 250 inmates who faced execution after the *Gregg* decision (Death Penalty Information Center 2014). Posthumous pardons became more frequent over the same period, prompted by public demands to rectify historic miscarriages of justice (Moore 1989, pp. 136–37). The contested conviction of Derek Bentley, executed in England in 1953 for his role in the murder of a police officer during a botched robbery, provoked a prolonged public campaign for his exoneration, led by his family. In 1993, forty years after Bentley was hanged, the home secretary announced the granting of a royal pardon, but only after the Court of Appeal rebuked the minister for wrongly claiming that pardons could be granted solely in cases of actual innocence (Hare 2004). A century's shift in the moral and political climate of England, and particularly new insight into the trauma of shellshock, led to the 2006 blanket pardon of 306 servicemen whom British commanders executed for cowardice or desertion during the First World War (Pfeifer 2007).

In addition to these personal and political motivations, which have always characterized petitions for mercy, a new body of legal scholarship emerged in the 2000s in support of the judicious use of pardoning (Novak 2016). Research conducted by political scientists, historians, and lawyers exposed the dwindling use of the presidential pardon in the United States and highlighted the chief executive's power to stem the rising tide of federal imprisonment attributable to mandatory sentencing laws imposed in the 1980s and 1990s (Kobil 2003). A growing chorus of scholars, including former U.S. Pardon Attorney Margaret Colgate Love, has argued that prisoners have the right to have petitions for pardon reviewed and carefully considered, and that presidents and governors, operating in a system of checks and balances, have a duty to carry out their authority to temper the rigor of law (Love 2010; Rosenzweig 2012). The gloss of human rights distinguishes this argument from the discourse of Alexander Hamilton and his fellow founders, who vested the office of president with the "benign prerogative" of mercy. Yet it remains faithful to its logic, and to the even older Lockean definition of discretionary justice as "doing public good without a rule."

Conclusion

The history of punishment is impoverished if it fails to take into account its modification and the changing ways in which sanctions have been mitigated in the postconviction phase of criminal proceedings. The historiography of pardoning has concentrated on the distant past and the actions of powerful lords and monarchs; in contrast, histories of parole, written mainly by criminologists and penologists, have painted this modern form of discretionary release as the correctional innovation that replaced pardoning. Although Progressives who pioneered parole certainly anticipated that it would supplant executive discretion (Wittmer 1927), both means of modifying prescribed punishments continued to coexist over the twentieth century and into the twenty-first.

The rationalist critics of monarchical discretion, who claimed in the late eighteenth and early nineteenth centuries that the practice undermined even-handed justice and underwrote extremes of cruelty and leniency, would have been dismayed by the Progressive penologists and scientifically minded criminologists who argued a century later that institutional discretion over punishment, tailored for the criminal rather than the crime, was the only way to adjust the wrongdoer to society. The subsequent swing toward mandatory sentencing, and away from parole boards' discretionary powers, would have reassured thinkers such as Bentham, who advocated fairness and predictability as lynchpins of just punishment. But what would a gadfly like Francis Lieber make of the pardon's revival in the early twenty-first century, resuscitated to reduce the harms inflicted by the inflexible imposition of rules and to undo the wrongs of the past (Meyer 2010)? Perhaps the tragic consequences of law's rigidity, from the isolation experiment at Auburn Prison in the 1820s to record levels of incarceration in the "free world," would prompt him to recall Locke's endorsement of right-minded mercy: "Tis fit that the Laws, then, should in some Cases give way to the Executive Power . . . since many accidents may happen, wherein the strict and rigid observation of the Laws may do harm" (Laslet 1988 [1689], sec. 159, p. 375). Once again, expedience and ideals may combine to animate a turn back toward discretionary justice.

REFERENCES

Alexander, Michelle. 2010. *The New Jim Crow: Mass Incarceration in the Age of Colorblindness.* New York: New Press.

Amnesty International. 2003. "United States of America: Death by Discrimination—The Continuing Role of Race in Capital Cases." Accessed at http://www.amnesty.org/en/library/info/AMR51/046/2003/en).

Anthony, Thalia. 2013. *Indigenous People, Crime and Punishment.* Abingdon, UK: Routledge.

Bannister, Jerry. 2003. *The Rule of the Admirals: Law, Custom, and Naval Government in Newfoundland, 1699–1832.* Toronto: Osgoode Society for Canadian Legal History.

Barkow, Rachel E. 2008. "The Ascent of the Administrative State and the Demise of Mercy." *Harvard Law Review* 121 (March): 1333–64.

Bartels, Lorean. 2010. *Research in Practice No. 13: Diversion Programs for Indigenous Women.* Canberra: Australian Institute of Criminology.

Beattie, John M. 1996. *Crime and the Courts in England, 1660–1800.* Princeton, NJ: Princeton University Press.

Beccaria, Cesare. 1819 [1764]. *An Essay on Crimes and Punishments*, 2nd ed. Philadelphia: Philip H. Nicklin.

Bentham, Jeremy. 1840. *Theory of Legislation*, Vol. 2, *Principles of the Penal Code.* Boston: Weeks, Jordan.

Bentham, Jeremy. 1843. *The Works of Jeremy Bentham*, Vol. 1, *Principles of Morals and Legislation, Fragment on Government, Civil Code, Penal Law.* Edinburgh: William Tait.

Blackstone, William. 1893 [1753]. *Commentaries on the Laws of England in Four Books.* Philadelphia: J. B. Lippincott.

Blue, Ethan. 2012. *Doing Time in the Depression: Everyday Life in Texas and California Prisons.* New York: New York University Press.

Bottomley, A. Keith. 1984. "Dilemmas of Parole in a Penal Crisis." *Howard Journal of Criminal Justice* 23 (1): 24–40.

Bottomley, A. Keith. 1990. "Parole in Transition: A Comparative Study of Origins, Developments and Prospects for the 1990s." *Crime and Justice: A Review of Research* 12:319–74.

Brown, Alyson. 2003. *English Society and the Prison: Time, Culture and Politics in the Development of the Modern Prison, 1850–1920.* Rochester, NY: Boydell Press.

Chadwick, George Roger. 1992. *Bureaucratic Mercy: The Home Office and the Treatment of Capital Cases in Victorian Britain.* New York & London: Garland.

Cobb, Paul Whitlock, Jr. 1989. "Reviving Mercy in the Structure of Capital Punishment." *Yale Law Journal* 99 (November): 389–409.

Dean, Charles W., & Thomas J. Duggan. 1968. "Problems in Parole Prediction: A Historical Analysis." *Social Problems* 15 (Spring): 450–59.

Death Penalty Information Center. 2014. "Clemency." Accessed at http://www.deathpenalty-info.org/clemency.

Devereaux, Simon. 2007. "Imposing the Royal Pardon: Execution, Transportation, and Convict Resistance in London, 1789." *Law and History Review* 25 (1): 101–38.

Dinan, John. 2003. "The Pardon Power and the American State Constitutional Tradition." *Polity* 35 (April): 389–418.

Dubber, Marcus Dirk. 2006. *Victims in the War on Crime: The Use and Abuse of Victims' Rights*. New York: New York University Press.

Duker, William F. 1976 "The President's Power to Pardon: A Constitutional History." *William & Mary Law Review* 18 (3): 475–538.

Ekrich, Roger. 1987. *Bound for America: The Transportation of British Convicts to the Colonies, 1718–1775*. Oxford: Clarendon Press.

Ferri, Enrico. 1896. *Criminal Sociology*. New York: Appleton & Company.

Finnane, Mark. 1997. *Punishment in Australian Society*. Melbourne: Oxford University Press.

Forsythe, William James. 1990. *Penal Discipline, Reformatory Projects and the English Prison Commission, 1895–1939*. Exeter, UK: Exeter University Press.

Foucault, Michel. 1977. *Discipline and Punish: The Birth of the Prison*. Trans. Alan Sheridan. London: Allen Lane.

Garland, David. 2001. *Mass Imprisonment: Social Causes and Consequences*. New York. Sage.

Garton, Stephen. 2003. "Managing Mercy: African Americans, Parole and Paternalism in the Georgia Prison System, 1919–45." *Journal of Social History* 36 (3): 675–99.

Garton, Stephen. 2010. "Criminal Propensities: Psychiatry, Classification and Imprisonment in New York State, 1916–1940." *Social History of Medicine* 23 (1): 79–97.

Gatrell, V. A. C. 1994. *The Hanging Tree: Execution and the English People, 1770–1868*. Oxford: Oxford University Press.

Grupp, Stanley. 1963. "Some Historical Aspects of the Pardon in England." *American Journal of Legal History* 7 (January): 51–62.

Hall, Kermit. 1989. *The Magic Mirror: Law in American History*. New York: Oxford University Press.

Harlow, Carol, & Richard Rawlings. 1997. *Law and Administration*, 2nd ed. Cambridge: Cambridge University Press.

Hood, Roger. 1975. "Case Against Executive Control over Time in Custody—Rejoinder to Professor Walker's Criticism." *Criminal Law Review* 33 (October): 545–52.

Harding, Christopher. 1988. "'The Inevitable End of a Discredited System'? The Origins of the Gladstone Committee Report on Prisons, 1895." *Historical Journal* 31 (September): 591–608.

Hare, Ivan. 1994. "The Prerogative of Mercy: Judicial Review of Whether to 'Let Him Have It.'" *Cambridge Law Journal* 53 (March): 4–6.

Hay, Douglas. 2011. "Property, Authority and the Criminal Law." In *Albion's Fatal Tree: Crime and Society in Eighteenth-Century England*, rev. ed., ed. Douglas Hay, Peter Linebaugh, John G. Rule, E. P Thompson, & Cal Winslow, 17–64. London: Verso.

International Centre for Prison Studies. 2010. "World Prison Brief." Accessed at http://www.prisonstudies.org/world-prison-brief.

Jensen, Christen. 1922. *The Pardoning Power in the American States*. Chicago: University of Chicago Press.

Kann, Mark E. 2005. *Punishment, Prisoner and Patriarchy: Liberty and Power in the Early American Republic*. New York: New York University Press.

King, Peter. 2000. *Crime, Justice and Discretion in England, 1740–1820*. Oxford: Oxford University Press.

Kobil, Daniel T. 2003. "How to Grant Mercy in Unforgiving Times." *Capital University Law Review* 31 (2): 219–42.

Kury, Helmut, & Evelyn Shea, eds. 2011. *Punitivity: International Trends*, Vol. 3, *Punitiveness and Punishment*. Bochum, Germany: University Press Brockmeyer.

Laslet, Peter, ed. 1988 [1689]. *Student Edition*. Cambridge: Cambridge University Press.

Laune, Ferris F. 1931. "A Technique for Developing Criteria of Parolability." *Journal of Criminal Law and Criminology* 26 (May): 41–45.

Law Reform Commission of Canada. 1977. *The Parole Process: A Study of the National Parole Board*. Ottawa: Ministry of Supply and Services.

Lieber, Francis. 1833. "Preface." In *On the Penitentiary System in the United States and Its Application in France; with an Appendix on Penal Colonies, and also Statistical Notes*, ed. Gustave de Beaumont, Alexis de Tocqueville, & Francis Lieber, v–xxxv. Philadelphia: Carey, Lea & Blanchford.

Lieber, Francis. 1859. *On Civil Liberty and Self-Government*. Philadelphia: Lippincott.

Lieberman, David. 2002. *The Province of Legislation Determined: Legal Theory in Eighteenth-Century Britain*. Cambridge: Cambridge University Press.

Lindsey, Edward. 1925. "Historical Sketch of the Indeterminate Sentence and Parole System." *Journal of Criminal Law, Criminology, and Police Science* 16 (1): 9–69.

Love, Margaret Colgate. 2010. "The Twilight of the Pardon Power." *Journal of Criminal Law and Criminology* 100 (3): 1169–212.

Love, Margaret Colgate. 2013. "Reinvigorating the Federal Pardon Process: What the President Can Learn from the States." In *Toward a More Perfect Union: A Progressive Blueprint for the Second Term*, 3–24. Washington, D.C.: American Constitution Society for Law and Policy.

Maconochie, Alexander. 1846. *Crime and Punishment: The Mark System Framed to Mix Persuasion with Punishment, and Make Their Effect Improving, Yet Their Operation Severe*. London: Hatchard & Son.

Maxwell-Stewart, Hamish. 2010. "Convict Transportation from Britain and Ireland 1615–1870." *History Compass* 8 (11): 1221–42.

McConville, Séan. 1981. *A History of English Prison Administration*, Vol. 1, *1750–1877*. London: Routledge & Kegan Paul.

McCoy, Ted. 2012. *Hard Time: Reforming the Penitentiary in Nineteenth-Century Canada*. Lethbridge, Canada: University of Athabaska Press.

McGowan, Randall. 1995. "The Well-Ordered Prison: England, 1780–1865." In *The Oxford History of the Prison: The Practice of Punishment in Western Society*, ed. Norval Morris & David J. Rothman, 79–109. New York: Oxford University Press.

McLennan, Rebecca. 2008. *The Crisis of Imprisonment: Protest, Politics, and the Making of the American Penal State, 1776–1941.* Cambridge: Cambridge University Press.

Meranze, Michael. 1996. *Laboratories of Virtue: Punishment, Revolution, and Authority, 1760–1835*. Chapel Hill: University of North Carolina Press.

Messinger, Sheldon L., John E. Berecochea, David Rauma, & Richard A. Berk. 1985. "The Foundations of Parole in California." *Law and Society Review* 19 (1): 69–106.

Meyer, Linda. 2010. *The Justice of Mercy*. Ann Arbor: University of Michigan Press.

Moore, Kathleen Dean. 1989. *Pardons: Justice, Mercy and the Public Interest*. New York: Oxford University Press.

Myers, Tamara. 2006. *Caught: Montreal's Modern Girls and the Law, 1869–1945*. Toronto: University of Toronto Press.

Nice, David C. 1992. "The States and the Death Penalty." *Western Political Quarterly* 45 (4): 1037–48.

Novak, Andrew. 2016. *Comparative Executive Clemency: The Constitutional Pardon Power and the Prerogative of Mercy in Global Perspective.* New York and London: Routledge University Press.

Odem, Mary. 1995. *Delinquent Daughters: Protecting and Policing Adolescent Female Sexuality in the United States, 1885–1920.* Chapel Hill: University of North Carolina Press.

Palacios, Victoria J. 1996. "Faith in Fantasy: The Supreme Court's Reliance on Commutation to Ensure Justice in Death Penalty Cases." *Vanderbilt Law Review* 49 (March): 310–72.

Petersilia, Joan. 2003. *When Prisoners Come Home: Parole and Prisoner Reentry.* New York: Oxford University Press.

Petrunik, Michael, Lisa Murphy, & J. Paul Fedoroff. 2008. "American and Canadian Approaches to Sex Offenders." *Federal Sentencing Reporter* 21 (2): 111–23.

Pfeifer, Douglas Carl. 2007. "The Past in the Present: Passion, Politics, and the Historical Profession in the German and British Pardon Campaigns." *Journal of Military History* 71 (4): 1107–32.

Phillips, Jim. 1992. "The Operation of the Royal Pardon in Nova Scotia, 1749–1815." *University of Toronto Law Journal* 42 (Autumn): 401–49.

Pisciotta, Alexander W. 1994. *Benevolent Repression: Social Control and the American Reformatory-Prison Movement.* New York: New York University Press.

Powers, Gershom. 1828. *Report of Gershom Powers, Agent and Keeper of the State Prison, at Auburn: Made to the Legislature, Jan. 7, 1828.* Albany, NY: Croswell & Van Benthuysen.

Pratt, John. 2008. "Penal Populism and the Contemporary Role of Punishment." In *The Critical Criminology Companion,* ed. Thalia Anthony & Chris Cunneen, 265–77. Sydney: Hawkins Press.

Radzinowicz, Leon. 1948. *A History of English Criminal Law and Its Administration from 1750: The Emergence of Penal Policy.* London: Stevens & Sons.

Rafter, Nicole Hahn. 1985. *Partial Justice: Women in State Prisons, 1800–1935.* Boston: Northeastern University Press.

Ridolfi, Kathleen, & Seth Gordon. 2009. "Gubernatorial Clemency Powers." *Criminal Justice* 26 (3): 26–41.

Rosenzweig, Paul. 2012. "Reflections on the Atrophying Pardon Power," *Journal of Criminal Law and Criminology* 102 (3): 593–612.

Rothman, David J. 1980. *Conscience and Convenience: The Asylum and Its Alternatives in Progressive America.* Boston: Little Brown.

Ruggles-Brise, Evelyn John. 1921. *The English Prison System.* London: Macmillan.

Sanborn, Frank S. 1900. "The Elmira Reformatory." In *The Reformatory System in the United States, Reports Prepared for the International Prison Commission,* ed. Samuel J. Barrows, 28–47. Washington, D.C.: Government Printing Office.

Sarat, Austin, & Nasser Hussain. 2004. "On Lawful Lawlessness: George Ryan, Executive Clemency and the Rhetoric of Sparing Life." *Stanford Law Review* 56 (5): 1307–44.

Scheuerman, William E. 2005. "American Kingship? Monarchical Origins of Modern Presidentialism." *Polity* 37 (1): 24–53.

Seal, Lizzie. 2010. *Women, Murder and Femininity: Gender Representations of Women Who Kill.* London: Palgrave Macmillan.

Simon, Jonathan. 1994. *Poor Discipline: Parole and the Social Control of the Underclass, 1890–1990.* Chicago: University of Chicago Press.

Stanford Law School Three Strikes Project & NAACP Legal Defense and Education Fund. 2013. "Progress Report: Three Strikes Reform (Proposition 36)." Accessed at https://www. law.stanford.edu/organizations/programs-and-centers/stanford-three-strikes-project/ proposition-36-progress-report.

State of New York. 1930. *Report of the Special Committee on the Parole Problem, Appointed by Governor Franklin D. Roosevelt, January 24, 1930*. New York: State of New York.

Steric, Victor L. 2002. "Gendering the Death Penalty: Countering Sex Bias in a Masculine Sanctuary." *Ohio State Law Journal* 63 (1): 433–74.

Strange, Carolyn. 1996. "Discretionary Justice: Political Culture and the Death Penalty in New South Wales and Ontario, 1890–1920." In *Qualities of Mercy: Justice, Punishment and Discretion*, ed. Carolyn Strange, 130–65. Vancouver: University of British Columbia Press.

Strange, Carolyn. 1998. "Comment, 'Capital Case Review Manual.'" *Criminal Law Review* 41 (2): 184–97.

Teeters, Negley King. 1955. *The Cradle of Penitentiary: The Walnut Street Jail at Philadelphia, 1773–1835*. Philadelphia: Pennsylvania Prison Society.

Tonry, Michael. 1995. *Malign Neglect: Race, Crime, and Punishment in America*. New York: Oxford University Press.

Tonry, Michael. 2011. *Punishing Race: A Continuing American Dilemma*. New York: Oxford University Press.

Von Hirsch, Andrew. 1976. *Doing Justice: The Choice of Punishments*. New York: Hill & Wang.

Waite, Robert G. 1991. "From Penitentiary to Reformatory: Alexander Maconochie, Walter Crofton, Zebulon Brockway and the Road to Prison Reform: New South Wales, Ireland, and Elmira, 1840–1870." *Criminal Justice History: An International Annual* 12:85–105.

Walker, Samuel. 1993. *Taming the System: The Control of Discretion in Criminal Justice, 1950–1990*. New York: Oxford University Press.

White, Stephen. 1976. "Alexander Maconochie and the Development of Parole." *Journal of Criminal Law and Criminology* 67 (1): 72–88.

Wines, Ernest Cobb, ed. 1871. *Transactions of the National Congress on Penitentiary and Reformatory Discipline, Held at Cincinnati, Ohio, October 12–18, 1870*. Albany, NY: Argus.

Wines, Frederick H. 1904. "Treatment of the Criminal." In *Proceedings of the National Conference of Charities and Correction at the Thirty-First Annual Session Held in the City of Portland, Maine, June 15–22, 1904*, ed. Isabel C. Barrows, 422–34. Columbus, OH: Press of Fred J. Herr.

Wittmer, Helen Leland. 1927. "The History, Theory and Results of Parole." *Journal of Criminal Law and Criminology* 18 (May): 24–64.

CHAPTER 30

HISTORIES OF CRIME AND CRIMINAL JUSTICE AND THE HISTORICAL ANALYSIS OF CRIMINAL LAW

MARKUS D. DUBBER

INTRODUCTION

THE basic idea driving the history of criminal law as a form of historical analysis of law is simple: the history of criminal law is a *legal* history of crime, that is, a history of crime as a legal construct or concept. This is not to say that it is (only) a conceptual history, but merely that it is a historical analysis of crime from the perspective of law. Law, however, is itself recognized as (also) a conception, and a conception of state power in particular, that is not simply reducible to a set of practices or phenomena. In this sense, the history of criminal law as a legal history of crime may be contrasted with the *social* history of crime as a history of crime from the perspective of criminology, and the *political* (or, more precisely, though also more awkwardly, the *policial*) history of crime as a history from the perspective of criminal justice. The point here is not to lay out a disciplinary taxonomy that distinguishes and relates criminal law, criminology, and criminal justice in a particular way, but rather to differentiate among various ways of doing the history of crime.

More specifically, the legal history of crime qua historical analysis of criminal law is an instance of legal history as *critical* analysis of criminal law, which in turn is one aspect of the *critical analysis of law* in general (Dubber 2015). Under this account, the historical analysis of law appears as a form of critical analysis of law insofar as it turns on the normativity of the modern idea of law, which implies claims about the legitimacy of its use by the state as a mode of governance that invites, or at least makes possible, critique. The enterprise of historical analysis of law is, in other words, historical itself;

it is historically situated insofar as it operates with a particular ("modern") conception of law as legitimatory, the origins of which can be traced back to the Enlightenment's comprehensive critical project (in which the precise location of the Enlightenment moment, in general and in particular systems of government, can be left open). Of course, the historical analysis of law in general, and of criminal law in particular, is not limited to the past two centuries (or whenever one chooses to locate the Enlightenment moment); in fact, it may well be that the *critical* analysis of law predates the eighteenth century, though the specific normative claims (in form and in substance) made by the invocation of law as a mode of governance presumably would be different, depending on the conception of law at stake.

Whatever the scope of the critical moment in the history, and therefore the historiography, of law turns out to be, it is important to acknowledge that it is just that, a moment in time—and, as we'll see, systemic space—rather than an eternal universal point of reference that can be invoked or a permanent perspective that can be assumed. The critical analysis of law, in other words, must be historicized; not only is law historically contingent, or at least specific, but so is its critical purchase.

Take, for instance, the project of "critical legal history" (or histories; see Gordon 1984), which has made important contributions to disturbing ossified assumptions about the basic constituents of legal history and, in fact, of legal thought and scholarship, but emerges as itself insufficiently critical of its own critical perspective. If critical legal studies in general—including critical legal history as its historiographical wing—is to be regarded as more than a general exercise in the "exposure" of the outcome indeterminacy of some norms held up by some people as outcome determinative—in other words, if critical legal studies is to be seen, and see itself, as a mode of *legal* studies—then the contingency of its critical stance toward its critical object, namely, law and legal norms, might become visible. Especially since critical legal studies generally distinguishes itself from scholarly projects, including *critical* projects and critical political projects in particular, that proceed from some analytic framework or approach (e.g., Marxism), and as a result bravely comes face to face with its critical object, notably legal norms of one form or another (standards, rules) without the aid, or crutches, of some prefabricated analytic system, instead dealing directly with the legal norms held out, consciously or not, to resolve legal matters by those state officials empowered with their generation, interpretation, application, and enforcement (really, when it comes down to it, judges), critical legal studies is distinctively and insistently *legal*. The conception of law underlying its critical enterprise, however, is limited to a specific, modern, post-Enlightenment conception of law in which law makes claims to legitimacy in the first place and at least attempts (or pretends to attempt), however foolishly, simple-mindedly, and transparently futilely, to justify itself, or rather to justify the exercise of state power undertaken in its name.

In other words, the conception of law that is not only targeted by, but also frames, critical legal studies is what one might call "liberal," in the historical and systemically spatial sense of being characteristic of "modern" Western political and legal thought familiar since roughly the late eighteenth century (or earlier, depending on when and where one locates the origin of this Enlightenment conception of law). This raises the question of what pre-Enlightenment critical legal history might look like, or what distinguishes critical legal history from critical legal theory, that is, what makes it a historical exercise, rather than a critical one. In other words, is precritical critical legal history possible? What would a critical legal history of medieval law or Roman law look like? Shifting the focus not in historical length, but in comparative breadth, what would a critical legal history of Chinese law look like?

This isn't the place to explore these questions in greater detail. Raising them is enough to point out the historical (and spatial) scope of the enterprise of critical legal history. Whether—and if so, how—that enterprise might be expanded in either direction is another question.

Unlike critical legal history, the historical analysis of law as critical analysis of law is acutely aware of the limitations its operative conception of law places on, and uses to shape, its critical project. It proceeds from a historically situated account of law as a mode of governance that is seen as emerging and remaining in tension with another fundamental mode of governance, police (Dubber 2005; but see Zedner & Loader 2007). The distinction between law and police reflects, and in fact is motivated by, the former's claim to—or, if you prefer, the pretense of—legitimacy that the latter is portrayed as lacking. This "modern" or "liberal" conception of law is the mode of governance that defines the law state (the *Rechtsstaat*, or the state under the rule of law) in critical contradistinction to the police state (the *Polizeistaat*). From the perspective of this critical conception of law the police state was alegitimate: it did not recognize the need for its own legitimation. State action in the police state requires no justification; it is not subject to general norms noncompliance with which would undermine its legitimacy, that is, its raison d'être. The police state has a *raison*, the *raison d'état* (or *Staatsraison*), but its raison d'être is its very existence. It serves no external (worldly) purpose that might undercut its claim to power, and to existence in the first place. This is not to say that the sovereign, as the head of the police state, which he governs as a "great family," in Rousseau's words (1755), or as "a well-governed family," in Blackstone's (1769), may not pursue an ideal of prudence or wisdom, or even see himself as the state's first public servant (as Friedrich II of Prussia did). He may decide to consider the counsel of experts in "police science" to obtain advice on how to more effectively attain whatever goals he might set for himself and, within this framework of aims, establish a more rational, systematic, and comprehensive state apparatus for the manifestation of his sovereign will.

Since police is alegitimate, at least in this account of the distinction between law and police as modes of governance, a critical policial history or a critical analysis of police is impossible. A critical history of state power might take a broader approach and explore, for instance, the classification of certain exercises of state power as manifesting one mode of governance rather than another, in particular—but not only— when the classification is undertaken by the state itself. For instance, critical history (or critical analysis of law at any given time) might question the common assertion that a particular state action complies with "the rule of law" or reflects the ever more complete implementation of the idea of the *Rechtsstaat*. It might seek to "expose" a purported exercise of the law power as an exercise of the state's police power instead, at least in substance, if not in form. But within the realm of policial analysis, the question of legitimacy does not arise—again, given the analytic framework set up by the invention of modern law as the critical counterpoint to police. Without a pretense of legitimacy, its absence could not be exposed by critique.

I. History of Criminal Law as Critical Analysis of Law

The history of criminal law occupies a central place in the historical analysis of law as an aspect of the critical analysis of law. Both conceptually and historically, the primacy of the critique of the state's penal power reflects the intrusive and facially illegitimate nature of that power. The state's penal power is intimately connected to the state's sovereignty, so much so that it may be—and has been throughout long stretches of history—impossible to imagine one without the other. It is precisely this apparent impossibility against which the critical analysis of state power as law directs its first, most insistent, most pointed, and yet also most revolutionary challenge: How can state action that does violence to the very persons whose capacity for self-government it manifests be legitimate? How can state action that violates the very autonomy of persons whose autonomous consent legitimates its very existence be legitimate? From the perspective of modern law, then, the state action most obviously and directly connected to the idea of sovereignty—and therefore statehood and state power—itself is the very state action both in greatest need of legitimation and most apparently lacking it.

The famous account of the 1757 public execution and torture of "Damiens the regicide" at the beginning of Foucault's *Discipline and Punish* (1977) is just that, an account. It describes, in considerable detail, the way in which the French state publicly and awesomely displayed its sovereign power through the mutilation and humiliation of someone who had committed the greatest offense in a penal police regime: the murder of the king-father of the great family of the state. Regicide is merely one form—if an extreme one—of *laesa majestas*, or of treason in the "common law world." In a police state, the paradigmatic offense is, literally, an offense against the sovereign. This was the case in eighteenth-century France and England, and it is still the case, explicitly, in the criminal law of the United States, as we will see shortly.

It is important to recognize at this point that the conception of penal power reflected in the Damiens account is not limited to France, or the "civil law world" (though it is certainly the case that Foucault's analysis focuses on French penal power in particular). The very same conception underlies the English offense of treason, which goes back at least to the Treason Act of 1351—and most likely farther, since that statute was merely intended (or said to be intended) to clarify the law of treason at the time.

It is important to note here, incidentally, that this reference to "law" does not imply a claim to legitimacy or some reference to the principle of legality or some such thing. At the time, and until the Enlightenment moment, whenever and wherever located, law did not carry the connotation of a legitimacy claim; after all, the very notion of police had not yet established itself and was still centuries from functioning as modern law's alegitimate straw man. In fact, the reference to law carried a different connotation at the time, one that appears clearly in the notion of a "common law," that is, a law that was common insofar as it applied to the members of the emerging royal household, all of whom were subject to its patriarchal power under the king's peace. In the Treason Act, Edward III set out a common law of treason in statutory form, a royal law of treason that covered the entire realm. It cemented the inferior status of the very lords who had sought the clarification; they had meant to limit Edward's discretionary use of the offense of constructive treason to assert jurisdiction in cases that otherwise would have been within the local jurisdiction of some lord who would have treated the offense as a *felony*, resulting in the falling of the offender's property to him rather than to the king, the victim of *treason*. Treason here was the violation of the bond between subject and king (*laesa majestas*) as opposed to that between serf and (local) lord (*felonia*) (Pollock & Maitland 1898).

The term "law," after all, did not acquire its sharp critical edge, its distinctive normative pretension, until it was put to critical use in the Enlightenment's comprehensive challenge to established modes of thinking, acting, and governing. Law became the mode of governance that signaled the beginning of a new project of state government, one in which the state embarked on a mission to justify its power to its objects, ironically by recognizing them as subjects and thereby rethinking away the very challenge of state power it had formulated for the first time. Before the Enlightenment, premodern law was happily used as synonymous with government, rule, power, police, justice, and, what is particularly interesting, peace. The sovereign, conceived as a macro householder governing his household, incorporated human—and other—resources within his peace, which expanded beyond the realm of the traditional household (each of which had a householder and his own peace) to the peace of the land, the realm, and the empire.

For this reason, it is difficult to imagine a critical history of premodern law, unless one also develops a different conception of critique, one that does not see the Enlightenment as the age of critique, as a formative critical moment that launched a new enterprise in human thought and action. This is not to say that a critical history of law could not draw on premodern political and "legal" history, if only for setting the broader framework within which the modern history of law operates. For instance, it might turn out that the distinction, and tension, between law and police itself can be seen within the (*longue durée*) context of the relationship between autonomy and heteronomy as modes of governance reaching back to the beginnings of Western political thought and action in classical Athens, where the paradigmatically heteronomous sphere of the household (*oikos*) stood in sharp (or, in the case of Plato, not quite so sharp) contrast to the paradigm of autonomy (*agora*). A similar contrast characterized

Roman government, with the *familia* on one side, and the forum, the senate, and the *res publica* on the other. The collapse of democracy and republicanism in Greece and Rome ushered in a period of heteronomous government that extended from the Middle Ages until the Enlightenment, which rediscovered autonomous government, but in a radically different way: as the self-government of all persons as such, rather than the public self-government of *sui juris* householders who were private sovereigns at home. The Enlightenment took aim at the very core of this for centuries dominant idea of government as household, or patriarchal, governance, made most explicit and rational-ized in the police science of the police state, the study of "political economy," that is, the government of the state as a family; the transfer of the radically heteronomous mode of governing (*nomos*) the traditional *oikos* to that "great family," the state; and the pub-licization of a once-distinctively private mode of governance, now renamed "political economy" or, simply, police.

Expanding the scope of critical analysis of law beyond the Enlightenment moment, then, also brings to light the household as a central site of governance throughout Western political and legal history (not to mention the central role of traditional eco-nomics in political thought). The police power is the householder's essentially limitless discretionary power over his household, and the police state is the institutionalization—and, alongside the science of police, also the rationalization—of that power at the level of state government. The police power thus is not merely the straw man of modern law, but also itself the modern manifestation of a fundamental conception of government, stretching from the family to the corporation (including the church) to the state, a conception of government that for centuries was so dominant as to be self-evident and synonymous with the very idea of government, requiring not justification, but mere description, triggering not critique, but awe.

Which brings us back to Foucault and poor Damiens, punished for having commit-ted the household offense par excellence, the ultimate act of disobedience against the householder, and, in this case, the householder of householders, the macro householder who has incorporated once-equal households into his great Rousseauian household by reducing their householders to mere constituents of his household, transforming their original jurisdiction into delegated power. This distinction—within a shared conception of governing as householding—between the royal householder and other, micro, householders is beautifully and ironically reflected in Edward III's abovemen-tioned Treason Act, which does define treason ("at the Request of the Lords and of the Commons"), but in almost comically broad and vague strokes (to "compass or imag-ine" the death of the king), which appear all the broader and vaguer when compared to those used to define little treason (*petit treason*), which requires the actual killing of the lord of a micro household. This ultimate violation of the micro householder's peace, this ultimate act of familial disobedience, remained a separate offense from ordinary homicide in Anglo-American criminal law until the nineteenth century.

Gustav Radbruch, in fact, located "the origin of criminal law" in household disci-pline, more specifically, in the essentially heteronomous and hierarchical discipline meted out by the householder upon the unfree members of his household, that is, members of his household who were not themselves heads of their own household and, as such, capable only of being governed, but not of governing, whether themselves or others (Radbruch 1950; see also Sellin 1976; on Radbruch, see Hildebrandt 2014). Radbruch contrasted internal criminal law and external international law, which arose out of the interaction among heads of household, rather than between householder and household. Although Radbruch focused on Germanic law, he might have extended the scope of his historical essay beyond the Middle Ages to ancient Athens and Rome, where he would have found the same distinction between heteronomy and autonomy, and between internal and external relations between householder and household on the one hand, and among householders on the other hand. There, too, he would have found a distinction between modes of punishment: between corporal penal discipline meted out against the unfree and noncorporal punishment applied to citizens. The distinction between heteronomy and autonomy would appear in the procedural aspect of the exercise of penal power, as indicated, for instance, by the role of juries in facilitating the self-application of norms (if only indirectly, through one's peers) and even the opportunity for self-infliction (both of which are illustrated in the case against Socrates).

In the end, Radbruch's essay on the history of criminal law remains oddly premodern in its failure to mark the significance of the invention of a new, modern, concept of law. In fact, it is less a legal history of crime or a history of crime from a legal perspective, than a social, or sociological, history of crime (or, in fact, of punishment). Within the framework of the distinction between law and police, it appears as a policial history of crime, rather than a legal one. Oddly, the history of criminal law is distinguished from that of international law, a field of law whose legal—as opposed to political or diplomatic—credentials have been contested since its very beginning. At the same time, since Radbruch's account begins with medieval Germanic tribes whose penal practices were marked by stark heteronomy and hierarchy within each tribal household, the autonomous penal practices in Greek and Roman law remain obscured. As a result, penality origin appears to lie in heteronomy and patriarchy, rather than in practices and institutions that, from the start, displayed a tension between heteronomous and autonomous penal power.

Insofar as Radbruch operates within a premodern, precritical, conception of law that remains constant throughout, his account does not amount to a historical analysis of law as critical analysis of law. This is not to say, however, that his account might not prove useful to a critical history of criminal law as law. Radbruch's essay provides a rich and provocative account of the history of penality since the Middle Ages that powerfully exposes its policial elements. As a result, it nicely documents the deep historical and conceptual roots of the orthodox policial conception of penal power onto which the modern conception of law turned its critical gaze as the most obvious instance of state power that required legitimation, rather than manifestation, however awesome.

If Radbruch's history of criminal law remains precritical in the sense of premodern, Foucault's account is consciously modern and critical in a different sense than the critical analysis of criminal law through history. Foucault, unlike Radbruch, is interested in marking the appearance of a new conception of law, but that conception differs from the one underlying the project of critical analysis of law outlined here. Foucault's critique is not normative, or, more precisely, it does not seize upon the claim to legitimacy that is central to, and distinctive and new about, the conception of law driving critical analysis of law. Note, for instance, that the description of Damiens's public punishment is followed by another description, or rather a recitation, of the "rules for the House of young prisoners in Paris" eighty years later. This juxtaposition illustrates the shift from public to private, and from physical to psychic punishment, from body to mind, not from a manifestation of the palpable reality of sovereign power whose existence requires, and in fact allows, no justification to a penal system that opens itself up to a fundamental critique of its legitimacy in conception and execution. In fact, one might see the shift from open violence to concealed treatment precisely as a move to obscure and normalize the very exercise of state power, whose intrusive intensity more than any other demands critical scrutiny of its legitimacy. Here Foucault's account is critical, but in the sense of revealing a shift in perspective and conception marked not only by difference, but also by continuity with the preceding state of affairs. It is not critical in the sense of challenging the new liberal penal law state's claims to legitimacy.

Foucault's account also differs from Radbruch's in its time frame. Foucault is interested in a specific moment in the history of penality, and in a specific aspect of that moment: the transition from public physical spectacle to private psychological control, which in his view occurred during the short century between Damiens's execution and the posting of the rules for juvenile delinquents. Radbruch's scope of analysis is far wider, and yet not as wide as that of a *longue durée* critical analysis of law that seeks the foundations of the modes of governance that (may) continue to shape state power in general, and state penal power in particular. From this broader, and longer, perspective, in fact, Foucault's account of penal history may be more self-consciously modern than Radbruch's, but it remains firmly within the orthodox conception of state power that the modern conception subjected to critical analysis. Put another way, Foucault's analysis can be seen as making—or at least as illustrating—precisely this point, namely, that the supposed radical shift in the conception of state power, penal and otherwise, brought about by the Enlightenment with the help of a modern, critical, ideal of law in fact remained an internal adjustment within the policial realm from one type of human resource control (public and physical) to another (private and psychological). The Enlightenment, in this view, did not mark a paradigm shift, but an intra-paradigmatic development from, in traditional terms, "general deterrence" to "treatment." Another long century later, one might detect a similar intra-paradigmatic move, which also was—at the time—presented as a radical paradigm shift, namely, the move during the so-called war on crime from one side of the paradigm of "peno-correctional treatment" (rehabilitation) to another (incapacitation) (Dubber 2002).

Manipulating not only the time frame, but also the (systemic) space frame, that is, supplementing historical with comparative critical analysis, reveals that the policial conception of state power that can be seen as underlying Radbruch's and Foucault's accounts of the history of penality is not limited to "civil law" countries such as Germany and France, but is also prevalent in "common law" countries such as the United Kingdom and the United States, even if—at least in the former—the word "police" remained taboo (as being typically "French"), with some notable exceptions, including not only Blackstone, but also Bentham, Patrick Colquhoun, and Adam Smith. English legal history instead prefers the older (and quainter) term "peace," which captures the core of the idea of police as a mode of governance without the unwelcome connotations of the state as a qualitatively distinct macro household (Pollock 1885). The micro householder's peace (or *mund*) becomes the state householder's police.

Nothing better illustrates the significance of the police- or peace-based conception of state power in the Anglo-American system of government than the state's penal power. The fundamental conception of crime throughout the history of English law is that of an offense against the king's peace. The ultimate, and paradigmatic, victim of crime was the king. A crime represented an offense against the king's sovereignty, an act of disobedience or deviation from the rules of proper behavior in a "well-ordered" household. Homicide, even *se defendendo*, required a royal pardon because it constituted an offense against the king by depriving him of a human resource altogether. Maiming, too, offended the king by diminishing the value of a human resource, in this case, by rendering him incapable of military service.

In American law, the state's penal power has been closely associated with its power to police and, therefore, with the very idea of sovereign power. During the revolutionary period, which is generally thought of as a time of fundamental critique of every aspect of state power, the power to punish went notably unchallenged (Dubber 2007). Instead, the English conception of crime as an essential attribute of sovereignty was accepted without question and simply adapted to the new political environment: what once was an offense against the king's peace was now an offense against the new sovereign, be it the people, the public, or—simply—the state, or even several states at once. The U.S. Supreme Court affirmed as recently as the mid-twentieth century that an act that violates a criminal norm of two states constitutes an offense against both and therefore may be subject to prosecution in either, or both, under the so-called dual sovereignty exception to the constitutional prohibition against double jeopardy:

> The dual sovereignty doctrine is founded on the common law conception of crime as an offense against the sovereignty of the government. When a defendant in a single act violates the "peace and dignity" of two sovereigns by breaking the laws of each, he has committed two distinct "offences." As the Court explained in *Moore v. Illinois*, 14 How. 13, 19 (1852), "[a]n offence, in its legal signification, means the transgression of a law." Consequently, when the same act transgresses the laws of two sovereigns, "it cannot be truly averred that the offender has been twice punished for the same offence; but only that by one act he has committed two offences, for each of which he is justly punishable." (*Heath v. Alabama*, 474 U.S. 82 [1985])

In the American federalist compromise, states retained the police power and ceded only those limited powers specifically enumerated in the federal Constitution. The power to punish, if it attracted any attention (if not critique), was simply identified as an obvious instance of the power to police. The power to police, however, as the manifestation of sovereignty, was essentially unlimited in scope, discretionary in nature, and defined by its indefinability. To limit the state's power to punish would have meant limiting its police power and therefore, ultimately, its sovereignty.

There was never a critical moment in the history of American penality (Dubber 2007). The revolutionary generation took the state's power to punish for granted: while the state's penal authority remained unquestioned, attention instead focused on who in the new federalist system would wield it. As a central aspect of the police power, and therefore of independent, as opposed to derivative or delegated, sovereignty, the penal power remained with the states, while the federal government (as opposed to a full-fledged state at the national level) was denied a direct and general penal power; whatever penal power it might have instead had to derive from the general powers ceded to it by the states and enumerated in the Constitution. The penal power of the federal government (which, again, was not a national state) was limited not only in origin and scope, but also institutionally; unlike state courts, federal courts were said to lack the power to generate new offenses under the common law misdemeanor doctrine. Any federal penal norms had to be defined by the legislature; they had to be statutory, not common, law.

Limiting federal criminal law to statutory law did more than limit the class of its producers; it also relegated it to secondary status, given the minor interstitial role statutory norms had played during the history of English criminal law up to that point, as legislative efforts at criminal lawmaking had long been met with hostility, if not obstruction, by the judiciary, which used interpretive techniques such as the rule of strict construction and various presumptions to limit their influence.

It is also worth noting, in the present context, that the limitation of U.S. federal criminal law to statutory law reveals that the police power was not thought to be limited to the legislature, as is often supposed. It is precisely because judges, too, wielded the sovereign power to police, that is, the power to maintain the "police" in the sense of peace or good order, that denying federal judges the power to recognize new common law (as opposed to legislative, statutory) offenses was important; otherwise, the federal government, through its judges, could make an end run around the constraints placed on its legislators and indirectly assert and expand a general power to police that it had been denied directly.

Of course, this *sub rosa* exercise of a federal police power happened just the same, though not through the courts. Instead, the federal legislature took an ever more expansive view of the enumerated powers it had been granted in the federal constitutional compromise, with, in the end, remarkably little resistance from the court charged with assessing the constitutionality of its actions, the (federal) Supreme Court. The power to regulate commerce proved particularly useful in this regard, as federal criminal law underwent a dramatic expansion, especially beginning in the early twentieth century.

It is worth noting, to again expand the breadth of the historical analysis comparatively, that the same focus on secondary questions of institutional competence (or, if you like, jurisdiction) rather than on the fundamental question of legitimacy—on the who, rather than the whether or the why—is also reflected in British colonial legal and political history. For instance, the British North America Act of 1867 (now the Constitution Act) delegates royal sovereignty to a colony, notably the power of "peace, order, and good government," aspects of which it assigns to the federal government and to the provinces, thus assigning Canadian constitutional law forevermore the tedious—and subsidiary—task of classifying which aspects are federal and which provincial, rather than considering their underlying legitimation. Sovereignty just is, and the only question is to whom its various fragments are assigned. In the British North America Act's list of fragments of sovereignty also appears the "Criminal Law" power, which is assigned to the federal government. At the same time, however, the Canadian provinces have the power to impose "Punishment by Fine, Penalty, or Imprisonment for enforcing any Law of the Province made in relation to any Matter coming within any of the Classes of Subjects enumerated in this Section." The apparent tension between these clauses is resolved in terms of the proper distribution of power in the Canadian federalist system, with little, if any, concern about—or reference to—the nature or legitimation of penal power, no matter who wields it.

That the British North America Act, a delegation of English royal sovereignty to a colony, does not probe, or even elucidate, the foundations of state penal power is perhaps not surprising, given the internally administrative nature of the exercise and the unquestioned English sovereignty-based conception of penal power in particular. That the legitimation of the state's most intrusive power would have gone similarly unchallenged during the revolutionary period in the United States, which lavished such close attention on the legitimacy of other state powers, notably the power of taxation, is more remarkable. Leaving aside the Federalist Papers, which—like the British North America Act—focus to a great extent on the distribution, not the justification, of state power, the most promising effort to critically rethink penal power in light of revolutionary ideas, notably the idea of self-government as the lynchpin of legitimacy, is Thomas Jefferson's 1779 Virginia criminal law bill, drafted in the course of the comprehensive revision of Virginia law undertaken by Jefferson and a handful of others in the wake of the signing of the Declaration of Independence and Jefferson's return to Virginia (Jefferson 1779).

Aside from a promising preamble, however, Jefferson's bill manifests a startling lack of interest in, and knowledge of, its subject matter, which Jefferson incidentally only picked up after George Mason, who had originally been assigned the topic of criminal law, dropped out of the endeavor. Even the preamble, though more thoughtful than the body of the bill, does not itself reflect a great deal of original thought; its promise derives from the sort of references to Beccarian ideas that were *de rigueur* at that time for anyone addressing the question of crime and punishment. Ironically, just a few years earlier, Blackstone, whom Jefferson detested for what he saw as a lack of the sort of common law humility he thought Coke personified, had adorned his discussion of criminal law in the fourth volume of his *Commentaries on the Laws of England* with *bon mots* from the then recently published *Of Crimes and Punishments* in much the same way (Stern 2014). Also like Jefferson, despite the references to Beccaria, Blackstone never challenged the fundamental "common law" conception of crime as an offense against the sovereign's "peace and dignity." Indeed, Jefferson went out of his way to celebrate medieval criminal law, complete with extensive quotations from Anglo-Saxon dooms (in the original language) and pseudo-Cokean orthography (going back through the manuscript to change the spelling of "forfeit" to "forfiet") and marginalia. In the end, Jefferson spent more time on the criminal law than on any of the other subjects that he covered in the revision effort—not because he found the subject particularly important or complex, but because it gave him the opportunity to practice his celebrated penmanship, copying and recopying the bill to produce what even a sympathetic biographer could do no better than to describe as an "extraordinarily beautiful document" ("The penmanship is beautifully clear, and no other document that Jefferson ever drew better exhibits his artistry as a literary draftsman"; Malone 1948, pp. 269–70).

But perhaps the failure during the revolutionary period to recognize, and to address, the challenge of state penality in a political system grounded in the idea of the self-governing person merely postponed a fundamental critique of penality until a moment that is often cited as a second foundational moment in American political history: the Civil War and its aftermath, and, in particular, the civil law amendments to the U.S. Constitution (not to mention Lincoln's Gettysburg Address). This was not so, however. Roughly contemporaneous with the passage of the British North America Act north of the border, the American conception of penality remained firmly entrenched in the traditional English view of crime as an offense against sovereignty, rather than a violation of the rights of another person. The treatment of criminal offenders no more raised questions of legitimacy than it had almost a century before. Instead, criminal offenders remained outside the discourse of legitimacy and constitutional rights, even as slaves were brought within the American legal and political project, at least on paper, with the Thirteenth Amendment's abolition of slavery and involuntary servitude, "except as a punishment for crime." At the same time, prisoners were classified as rightless slaves of the state (*Ruffin v. Commonwealth*, 62 Va. 790 [1871]).

II. Histories of Crime and Histories of Law

In the remainder of this essay, I would like to return to the more general methodological issues raised in the introduction. One point that I think is worth stressing is that the legal history of crime, that is, the history of criminal law qua law, also needs a history of law; what's more, insofar as law is also an idea, and in fact an ideal that is framed, and employed, as a reason—and, importantly, a justification—for state action, the history of criminal law also needs a *theory* of law, located in historical context and subject to change (even if that theory happens to make claims to universality, temporal or otherwise). To avoid unhelpful anachronism, a critical analysis of criminal law must enunciate and deploy the (or at least a) conception of law at a given point in time. (This is not to say that the conscious attempt to apply an anachronistic conception of law may not elucidate interesting differences among regimes of law, as an exercise of *internal* comparative historiography, i.e., within a given system of government. However, the results of this deliberate exercise in comparing the incommensurable should not be confused with the critical analysis of law over time.) There likely will be any number of conceptions of law circulating in a particular historical moment, or period, and critical analysis of law from the perspective of a specific conception of law will also remain open to the charge not only that it is anachronistic but also that it is insignificant or less significant than it is held out to be, or that it is uninteresting or misleading for some other reason.

Still, the point remains that the legal historian—as a historical analyst of law—should take care to enunciate the conception of law driving his or her critical analysis of the invocation, and exercise, of law as a mode of governance at a particular historical moment, rather than to take law as a silent constant (or, if you prefer, a Holmesian brooding omnipresence across space *and time*).

It might be useful, then, to think of the history of criminal law as two interconnected but also separate histories: the history of crime and the history of law. In the history of criminal law, neither of its constituents, crime and law, remains static. If one thinks of the history of criminal law as a legal history of crime, that is, as a history of crime from a legal perspective, it is important to specify just what concept of law one has in mind at any given moment. It is obvious that the legal history of *crime* would be sensitive to the historical situatedness of its object; after all, a history of a static phenomenon would be very short: it would be a description. The historical contingency of law in a history of criminal *law* is more easily forgotten. And yet the analytic perspective requires as much attention as the object of analysis, not only across time but also at any given moment. It makes no more sense to subject "crime" in the fourteenth century to historical analysis in terms of a post-Enlightenment conception of "law" than to undertake a legal historical analysis of modern crime in terms of a modern conception of law that remains unspecified. For instance, the historical analysis of criminal law exemplified in this essay is a legal historical analysis of crime in terms of a modern conception of law as grounded in the principle of autonomy, which I take to be one (common) version of what is often called a "liberal" conception of law or a conception of law characteristic of "Western democratic societies."

There are as many histories of crime as there are conceptions of crime. As a social phenomenon, crime might attract the attention of social historians, who may generate more or less nuanced and temporally and spatially focused antiquarian accounts of attitudes toward, and conceptualizations of, crime and "criminality" in a given social milieu at a given time and in a given place, or, more dynamically, may trace the evolution of these attitudes and conceptualizations over time. Law may figure in these social histories, but it may figure mainly as one—and not necessarily a particularly important—factor in the construction of the social environment of crime, often as a means of exclusion or perhaps of oppression, depending on one's view of the significance of central, perhaps even state, power or one's general view of the role of class—or race—conflict in social life and history. There is, of course, no reason why social histories of crime should take this approach; one might even think that sophisticated social histories of crime would take into account the significance of law as a social phenomenon, or certainly as a phenomenon worthy of careful study, at any given antiquarian moment and across time.

Perhaps most important, social histories of crime are histories of crime as a social phenomenon; they do not preclude other histories of crime from other perspectives. There are many histories of crime, and each history would do well to place itself in context, either by itself considering and incorporating alternative histories or, less ambitiously, by acknowledging their existence and contribution to the multidisciplinary project of the historiography of crime.

For instance, consider a moral history of crime, that is, a history of crime as a moral phenomenon or concept (depending on your view of morality). Assuming a conception of morality that does not simply regard it as another mode of social classification—or control—a moral history of crime might concern itself with such questions as the connection between morality and criminality both in the abstract and in particular, that is, whether such a connection exists and, if so, what it consists of, again at a given time and place or across time. A moral history of crime might investigate, for instance, whether—at a particular moment and place in history, or from one moment to another—immoral behavior was thought to bear any relation to criminal behavior, and, if so, whether that relationship was thought to be more or less direct, perhaps even essential, or merely incidental, and whether there was, or could be, behavior that qualified as criminal, but not as immoral, or vice versa.

Similarly, a religious (or theological) history of crime would seek to shed light on its object from the perspective of its relation to religious beliefs, again at one point or across time. Here, as in the case of a moral history of crime, one might consider the conception of the criminal, that is, someone who commits a crime, or whose characteristics are revealed through its commission. Is crime merely the manifestation of the criminal's immoral or un-Christian or "evil" character? How have changes in religious beliefs, practices, and institutions affected the conception of crime (and criminals)? Of course, this inquiry might also be expanded comparatively, as an exercise in the study of comparative religion.

A cultural history of crime might consider crime as a cultural phenomenon, straddling the line between a social science- and a humanities-based historical analysis of crime. Here crime appears as an aesthetic concept, perhaps as manifested in literary or musical or even architectural representations or images, that allows the historian to analyze crime's static or dynamic historical meaning, role, or function. Consider, for instance, the common reference to the figure of the panopticon as an architectural representation of a particular conception of punishment, or, more generally speaking, of state processing and sanctioning of crime, or rather those who commit it, or, yet more generally still, of a fundamental conception of state power beyond the penal sphere (or, if you like, governmentality).

The much-invoked panopticon in fact illustrates two basic features of historiographies of crime that are not limited to the architectural history of crime: the attempt to access the meaning of crime through an analysis of its punishment, which parallels the analysis of those who are seen to commit it, and, more broadly, through an analysis of state action in response, or with regard, to it. Histories of crime, then, are often histories of crime (and criminals) and (its or their) punishment. In fact, one might go further and suggest that this must be so, unless it is possible to conceive of crime independently of its punishment, perhaps as just another indicator of social deviance or marker of communal exclusion.

The closer one sees the connection between crime and punishment, between crime and the threatened or actual response to it, the further one moves from the social to the political end of the perspectival spectrum. A political history of crime, then, might regard crime from a statal (or, more ambiguously and more commonly in Anglo-American thought, a "governmental") perspective, exploring the conception and construction of crime within a given power dynamic. A political history of crime might, for instance, trace the evolution of conceptions of crime within a familial (or private) context to a political (or public) context, from the *oikos* to the polis, from the *familia* to the forum. From a political perspective, the state's, or the sovereign's, or the householder's response to crime would reflect its salience, as illustrated dramatically in Foucault's reproduction of the description of the elaborate punishment for regicide (i.e., the ultimate form of patricide).

The critical analysis of state penality framed by the distinction—and interrelation—between law and police as modes of governance is thus only one possible project within which a historical-comparative analysis of criminal law and of criminal police can be located. In the end, it matters little whether a particular history of crime is pursued under one disciplinary banner or another, be it law, criminology, criminal justice, or something else. Ideally, histories of crime from various perspectives, with different but clearly identified and motivated tools of analysis and critique, will complement each other to generate a wide, varied, nuanced, and contextual field of historical inquiry.

References

Blackstone, William. 1769. *Commentaries on the Laws of England*, Vol. 4. Oxford: Clarendon Press.

Dubber, Markus D. 2002. "Policing Possession: The War on Crime and the End of Criminal Law." *Journal of Criminal Law & Criminology* 91:829–996.

Dubber, Markus D. 2005. *The Police Power: Patriarchy and the Foundations of American Government*. New York: Columbia University Press.

Dubber, Markus D. 2007. "'An Extraordinarily Beautiful Document': Jefferson's 'Bill for Proportioning Crimes and Punishments' and the Challenge of Republican Punishment." In *Modern Histories of Crime and Punishment*, ed. Markus D. Dubber & Lindsay Farmer, 115–50. Stanford, CA: Stanford University Press.

Dubber, Markus D. 2015. "New Historical Jurisprudence: Legal History as Critical Analysis of Law." *Critical Analysis of Law* 2:1–18.

Foucault, Michel. 1977. *Discipline and Punish*. Trans. Alan Sheridan. New York: Vintage.

Gordon, Robert. 1984. "Critical Legal Histories." *Stanford Law Review* 36:57–125.

Hildebrandt, Mireille. 2014. "Radbruch on the Origins of the Criminal Law: Punitive Interventions Before Sovereignty." In *Foundational Texts in Modern Criminal Law*, ed. Markus D. Dubber, 219–38. Oxford: Oxford University Press.

Jefferson, Thomas. 1950 [1779]. "A Bill for Proportioning Crimes and Punishments in Cases Heretofore Capital." In *The Papers of Thomas Jefferson*, Vol. 2, ed. Julian P. Boyd, 492–507. Princeton, NJ: Princeton University Press.

Malone, Dumas. 1948. *Jefferson and His Time*, Vol. 1, *Jefferson the Virginian*. Boston: Little, Brown.

Pollock, Frederick. 1885. "The King's Peace." *Law Quarterly Review* 1:37–50.

Pollock, Frederick, & Frederic William Maitland. 1898. *The History of English Law Before the Time of Edward I*, 2nd ed. Cambridge: Cambridge University Press.

Radbruch, Gustav. 1950. "Der Ursprung des Strafrechts aus dem Stande der Unfreien." In *Elegantiae Juris Criminalis: Vierzehn Studien zur Geschichte des Strafrechts*, 2nd ed., ed. Gustav Radbruch, 1–12. Basel, Switzerland: Verlag für Recht und Gesellschaft AG (English translation "The Origin of Criminal Law in the Status of the Unfree." In *Foundational Texts in Modern Criminal Law*, ed. Markus D. Dubber, 219–38. Oxford: Oxford University Press (2014).).

Rousseau, Jean-Jacques. 1994 [1755]. *A Discourse on Political Economy*. Oxford: Oxford University Press.

Sellin, Johan Thorsten. 1976. *Slavery and the Penal System*. New York: Elsevier.

Stern, Simon. 2014. "Blackstone's Criminal Law: Common-Law Harmonization and Legislative Reform." In *Foundational Texts in Modern Criminal Law*, ed. Markus D. Dubber, 61–78. Oxford: Oxford University Press.

Zedner, Lucia, & Ian Loader. 2007. "Police Beyond Law." *New Criminal Law Review* 10:142–52.

PART EIGHT

PUNISHMENT AND PRISONS

CHAPTER 31

THE DEATH PENALTY

RANDALL MCGOWEN

INTRODUCTION

DEATH was a familiar punishment throughout early modern Europe. The execution offered a spectacle, one possessing a compelling narrative that mingled official and religious messages with an assortment of popular beliefs. Occasionally a voice would be raised against the frequency with which the death penalty was employed. Few, however, questioned the existence of the practice. Only in the eighteenth century did people begin to consider the efficacy of or the right to impose the penalty. Thereafter, with mounting intensity, the death penalty provoked debate. The question came to belong to a small number of issues that condensed arguments about the nature and purpose of state power in Europe and North America, and it continues to do so down to the present.

The history of the death penalty is not a straightforward story. The transformation of the penalty in the nineteenth century was a product both of broad cultural developments and of heated political contests. Some of the time these different dimensions of the question pulled in the same direction. At other moments they appear to have operated independently. The growing embarrassment with the display of suffering led to the end of the public execution and the simplification of the act of killing. For the many politicians who defended the practice, however, the retreat from the spectacle in no way diminished their support for the penalty. Even as the application of the death penalty declined in frequency and was withdrawn from view, it loomed larger in the public imagination. It was less the event than the idea of the execution that demanded attention.

While it is difficult to do justice to the complexity of the issue, this essay seeks to chart the contradictory currents of thought that focus on the death penalty. Section I deals with Beccaria and the fundamental challenge he offered to the early modern practice of the execution. Section II describes the mixed results of the campaign to abolish the capital punishment, while section III discusses the resurgence of support for a transformed death penalty in the later nineteenth century. Section IV summarizes twentieth-century developments in the issue, including the moment when European and American politics around the death penalty followed different paths.

I. Attacking the Death Penalty

In 1764 Europe experienced a publishing sensation when a young Italian, Cesare Beccaria, published *On Crimes and Punishments*. The work was brief, bold, and elegant. It combined a warm advocacy of humanity with the cool reasoning of utilitarian philosophy. Its short chapters moved gracefully through a series of topics such as legal procedure, the definition of crimes, and critical commentary on existing penal practices. Although many of the ideas found in the book were not new, Beccaria assembled them in a confident and compelling fashion. For many of his contemporaries the work marked the opening of a new epoch in the history of punishment. "The merit of the essay before us," wrote a reviewer in the *Annual Register* for 1767, "is so generally known and allowed, that it may seem unnecessary to inform our readers, that it has gained the attention of all ranks of people in almost every part of Europe; and that few books on any subject have ever been more generally read, or more universally applauded." In Britain William Blackstone embraced Beccaria's conclusions as he delivered an indictment of the English criminal code for its heavy reliance on capital punishment. Voltaire celebrated the work. Urban elites and the professional classes found its message persuasive. Ultimately, Beccaria's work had the effect of internationalizing the question of punishment, even as the individual states of Europe continued to pursue their distinctive paths.

Although Beccaria applauded the progress of his "enlightened century" in commercial and political terms, he lamented how "few" had "scrutinized and fought against the savagery and the disorderliness of the procedures of criminal justice, a part of legislation which is so prominent and so neglected in almost the whole of Europe." He dismissed much of existing penal practice as little more than "cold-blooded atrocity" (Beccaria 1995, p. 8). Though it came late in his work, his chapter on the death penalty occupied a central place in his critique of early modern punishment. The penalty's frequency, brutality, and spectacular appearance, Beccaria argued, symbolized all that was wrong with the existing penal regime. While he did not propose the complete abolition of the penalty, he favored radically circumscribing its application and, just as significantly, cut away much of the justification for its existence. The death penalty failed along every dimension that counted for him: it was wasteful, it failed to deter, and it was morally unsustainable.

Beccaria mounted his assault upon a punishment that had achieved a central place in the operation of early modern justice. The execution played an important role in the campaign of the early modern state to monopolize justice, even as it also represented a confession about the limited means available to rulers to battle crime and disorder. Death was the penalty for a wide range of offenses, not only murder, but property crimes and moral misconduct as well. Death came in a variety of forms: hanging, breaking on the wheel, clubbing, burning, the sword or the axe, drawing and quartering. Some executions involved elaborate stages meant to lengthen the period of agony. These practices existed along a continuum with many other forms of punishment that made use of the body to illustrate a lesson as well as inspire fear. Whipping, the stocks, branding, and amputation were all performed in public and mingled suffering with shame and humiliation. Even death was not the end of the punishment, for the body might be left to rot as an extension of the example conveyed by the execution itself. Indeed, the narrative of the execution drama was not exhausted by death. Even as the spectacle offered one face of authority, fierce and implacable, so the ruler might display a more generous pose, as the dispenser of mercy. Pardon, English judges regularly announced, cast the sovereign in a favorable light. Mercy could take various forms, from outright pardon to the gift of a less agonizing death or even the return of the body of the condemned for Christian burial (Hay 1975; Evans 1996; Silverman 2001).

For justice to achieve its desired end in the early modern period, punishment had to be carried out in public. The execution was a spectacle; it was meant to draw a crowd. It was presided over by leading civic officials and sanctioned by the presence of the clergy. Some execution rituals were elaborate, while other states tolerated more haphazard and disorderly execution days. The English execution looks ill managed compared to the greater order that characterized a Prussian execution. Still, executions across Europe were more alike in their basic constitution than different. Above all, what united them was the belief that punishment should be exemplary: it was meant to instruct, and the lesson went beyond the goal of simple deterrence. The death penalty in particular offered a message about crime and its consequences. It appealed to, and was shaped by, fundamental religious beliefs about sin and the nature of God's justice. Clergymen not only ministered to the condemned but spoke words of warning to the spectators. The agony endured by the condemned was meant to call to mind the immeasurably greater suffering sinners would experience in hell. In this way the pain inflicted in the punishment contained a lesson that reached beyond the immediate agony experienced by the condemned and justified its presence (Merback 1999). This interplay between public execution and divine judgment made possible multiple outcomes. The clergy taught that the suffering that accompanied the execution might be a form of expiation that would earn the sinner forgiveness and the reward of salvation. At least some of the time, the authorities, the clergy, and the spectators united in the wish to see the condemned confess their crimes, ask forgiveness from their rulers and neighbors, and die reconciled to the justice of their punishment. Not all of the condemned conformed to the demands of this script; some died cursing those who killed them. But many, probably most, accepted the only form of solace offered to them. Regardless of the choice they made, they were the central actors in the theater of justice. Many in the crowd came to see what they would say and how they would act. The small measure of freedom these individuals had in deciding how they would shape their role was seen by the authorities as a small price to pay in order to secure a message of obedience and a show of penance (McKenzie 2007).

While Beccaria rejected almost every aspect of this earlier understanding of punishment, the rulers of eighteenth-century society were already moving away from reliance upon spectacular punishments. His book was such a brilliant success because it fell in line with long-developing changes in practice and synthesized shifting ideas about the means and goals of penal policy. By the late seventeenth century the number of executions across most regions of Europe was in decline. The change was gradual; it could be interrupted by temporary events. Still, the diminution was striking. Frequent executions came to be associated with ineffective government. The means employed to kill became simpler, and those responsible for administering the penalty displayed greater concern about limiting the suffering of the condemned. There were a number of causes that help to explain these developments. Rulers became more confident of their ability to control their subjects. They also expressed unhappiness at the loss of potentially valuable members of society. Increasingly, the mere presence of the crowd was held to detract from the seriousness of the occasion. Elites were also beginning to distinguish their character and conduct from those of other classes in society. The spreading culture of refinement and politeness was built upon turning away from what was seen as violent, vulgar, or inelegant. People expressed doubts about whether the crowd took the appropriate message from the execution. Instead of seeing through the body to a host of related ideas about and associations with the nature of society and the dependence upon the divine, sensitive spectators saw only the pains endured by the body (Evans 1996; McGowen 1987; Spierenburg 1984).

Beccaria's work shared many of these attitudes. In brief, forceful sentences he portrayed penalties that offended the feelings of the sensitive elite even while they failed to make an impression on those whom he called the vulgar. Such punishments provided evidence of an ill-managed and savage state of society. He complained of the "futile excess of punishments," dismissing the elaborate rituals of the executions as the mere trappings of a barbaric past, a collection of superstitions and evidence of a brutal temperament. "If our passions or the necessity of war have taught us how to spill human blood," he argued, "laws, which exercise a moderating influence on human conduct, ought not to add to that cruel example, which is all the more grievous the more a legal killing is carried out with care and pomp" (Beccaria 1995, pp. 66–70). For Beccaria the focus was no longer on the undoubted right of the ruler to demand the life of those guilty of violating divine and human law, but on the limits all authority should observe in punishment. Penalty should not celebrate through its excess the power inflicting it; rather, through its modesty and attention to utility, it should shift attention to the mundane calculation of a proportion between offense and punishment (Foucault 1977). The death penalty violated the fundamental principle that no individual could be considered to have sacrificed a right to life in joining society. Life itself was sacred. "It seems absurd to me," Beccaria wrote, "that the laws, which are the expression of the public will, and which hate and punish murder, should themselves commit one, and that to deter citizens from murder, they should decree a public murder" (Beccaria 1995, p. 70). There were other limits, he thought, that need to be observed in the operation of punishment, especially those associated with human psychology. Punishment should respect the body and impose no more pain than is necessary to achieve its ends. For Beccaria, the pain involved in punishment spoke of nothing but itself. A faulty economy of pain like that involved in the operation of the death penalty hardened those likely to commit offenses, while it weakened the support for the law among those charged with carrying it out. The irrationality of existing practice excited his contempt as much as did its brutality. A proper penal regime would respect the rights of individuals and be consistent with the principles of human psychology. If torture and death belonged to more barbarous times, confinement or servitude displayed qualities more appropriate to an enlightened age. Beccaria described these penalties in different ways, as loss of freedom, as forced public labor, or even as slavery, but their great strength was that they lent themselves to calculation and measurement. They gained plausibility because they stood opposed to the terrible extravagance of the death penalty. Punishment, Beccaria proposed, should serve and promote life. The treatment of the body became for him a measure of the extent to which it realized this goal. His project of promoting enlightenment and the progress of humanity required him to seek the overthrow of that hideous symbol of the tyranny of the past, the execution (Hunt 2007).

II. The Retreat from Capital Punishment

The widespread acclaim that greeted Beccaria's work seemed to vindicate his faith in his age. Frederick II of Prussia praised his volume, and the Habsburg emperor Joseph II was inspired by it to abolish the death penalty in his realm in 1788. The Prussian General Law Code of 1794 showed the influence of Beccarian principles, at least insofar as conservative judicial bureaucrats were willing to accept them. In revising the penal code, the authorities aimed to make it more systematic and consistent, with the severity of punishment being roughly proportionate to the seriousness of the crime. They resisted, however, any move to abolish the death penalty. They were cautious men: even as they swept away many forms of execution, they retained breaking on the wheel as well as decapitation with the sword for a considerable number of crimes. Overall, however, the execution became a rarer and more modest event. These reforms contributed to a further decline in the number of executions so that between 1828 and 1832 Prussia, for instance, saw an average of only five per year (Evans 1996).

Elsewhere in Europe, the influence of Beccaria's ideas was more mixed. Despite widespread uneasiness with the traditional spectacle of death, British authorities resisted calls to diminish the number of capital statutes. The frequency of hangings in London remained fairly consistent for much of the second half of the eighteenth century. Indeed, during the penal crisis that accompanied the disruption of transportation to the American colonies in the 1780s, the number of executions surged to levels not seen since early in the century. Even when this number returned to a lower level in the 1790s, a majority of the condemned continued to perish for having committed property offenses. Furthermore, reform of the criminal laws was an unwelcome topic in the years after the French Revolution. When Samuel Romilly in 1808 launched a campaign to diminish the number of offenses for which one could suffer death, his proposals made little headway when confronted by steady opposition from the Tory legal establishment. Defenders of the gallows saw the issue in starkly political terms; it was a question of the preservation of the traditional social order (McGowen 1983). In the 1820s the Tory home secretary Robert Peel introduced measures consolidating the criminal law and considerably reducing the number of capital offenses. Peel, however, was no abolitionist. He vigorously defended, for instance, capital punishment for a crime like forgery, and there was little actual decline in the absolute number of executed as a result of Peel's reforms. Between 1826 and 1830 British judges passed sentence of death on 6,679 individuals, while 307 died on the gallows (Gatrell 1994). It was only in the aftermath of the Reform Bill of 1832, along with the subsequent election of a Whig government, that restriction of capital punishment gained a sympathetic hearing. By 1836 murder had become, in practice, the only crime for which one could suffer death, and the number of executed declined to seventeen.

France, on the other hand, offers us less a picture of consistency in the application of the death penalty than a story of dramatic swings in penal practice. Beccaria's ideas circulated widely in late eighteenth-century France. Complaints about the criminal law figured largely in the lists of grievances submitted to the Estates General in 1789. As the Constituent Assembly in 1791 considered the creation of a penal code for all of France, serious thought was given to the abolition of capital punishment. After a heated debate, the penalty was retained, though for many fewer crimes than in the past. The idealism that marked the reforms of the early years of the Revolution was soon overwhelmed by the flood of executions that accompanied the Terror. But it says a good deal about the attractiveness of these ideals that the National Convention (the French Constituent Assembly, September 1792–November 1795), in marking the end of the Terror in 1794, decreed the end of the death penalty, even though it suspended the operation of this measure until a later date. A surge of lawlessness in the years after 1794 led to the renewal of the penalty for certain violent crimes. Napoleon, on assuming power in 1801, reversed the 1794 decree, and his Penal Code of 1810 made thirty-six offenses punishable by death. Neither he nor the restored Bourbon monarchy was reluctant to use the guillotine. Between 1826 and 1830 an average of 111 people per year were sentenced to death, and of these, an average of 72 individuals were executed. As in Britain, it was political upheaval that produced significant change. In the aftermath of the Revolution of 1830, the French Penal Code of 1832 modestly reduced the number of capital offenses and permitted consideration of extenuating circumstances in awarding this sentence. King Louis-Philippe harbored abolitionist sympathies, while literary figures like Victor Hugo contributed powerful works to an emerging abolitionist movement. As a result of these changes the annual average number of executions fell from fifty-one to thirty-two (Wright 1983).

Thus far, up to the early nineteenth century, the fall in the number of executions and the restriction of the death penalty to murder were largely produced by legislators and judicial authorities who had little complaint with the death penalty in principle. They appealed more to ideas of utility than to ideals of humanity. The 1830s and 1840s, however, saw the rise of a movement that sought the complete abolition of the death penalty. Abolitionists questioned not only the legal right of the state to take the life of a citizen, but also the moral and religious justifications for doing so. The movement was strongest in liberal circles, among people who not only doubted that the state needed the sanction of death to preserve order, but who were convinced that the continued use of capital punishment represented a danger to society by bestowing upon the state a power it should not possess. In addition, the existence of the penalty was seen as an affront to liberal beliefs in the possibility of both individual and societal improvement. The death penalty, the British abolitionist William Ewart told Parliament in 1840, depended upon "the maintenance of the old principle of revenge—the *lex talionis*—for which we were substituting repentance and reform. The ancient system had been one of vindictiveness and retaliation, while our more modern system was one of prison-discipline and amendment" (McGowen 2003, p. 233). For Beccaria, and even more for conservatives, punishment was a necessary measure whose goal was to deter individuals from committing crime by the thought of the carefully calibrated pain they would endure for breaking the law. The abolitionists tended to see in the existence of crime a symptom of social failure arising from the prevalence of ignorance and poverty. The penal reformers of the 1840s directed their attention to amendment of the causes of crime and reformation of the individual offender. For them, the question of the death penalty went to the heart of the debate about the goal of all punishment; it was an evil that had to be eradicated.

In both Britain and America, Quakers and Unitarians played pivotal roles in promoting the attack upon capital punishment. Religiously inspired abolitionists did not contest the claim that there was a link between human and divine justice; on the contrary, they argued that a benevolent deity demanded a justice grounded in principles of mercy and forgiveness rather than sanctioning a desire for revenge. They rejected notions of original sin and eternal damnation, contending instead that God used gentle means to reclaim sinners. What united secular and religiously inspired reformers was a conviction that abolition was a compelling moral cause. In their eyes, the existence of the death penalty required urgent action, and advocates for abolition hastened to form voluntary societies to press their cause. In Britain the Society for the Abolition of Capital Punishment, founded in 1846, spearheaded the drive to abolish the gallows. Similar societies appeared in New York in 1844 and Massachusetts in 1845. These societies held public meetings, printed anti–death penalty works, wrote letters to newspapers, and collected signatures for petitions that were submitted to legislative bodies. Their membership was drawn heavily from the professions of the law and medicine, though ministers of liberal congregations, as well as some merchants and manufacturers who shared their beliefs, played a large role as well. Women joined in significant numbers. The leading figures in the movement were seldom party men, but more often independents who possessed an eclectic mix of beliefs. They often supported a host of liberal causes like international peace, electoral reform, temperance, and, especially, antislavery. Success, however, was elusive. Abolitionist societies were often modest in size and strapped for funds, and their opponents usually dismissed them as naïve idealists and cranks. The general public was only intermittently attentive to the issue at best. For the cause to gain much traction, its adherents needed a political opening (Masur 1989; Gregory 2012; McGowen 2003).

The abolitionist movements succeeded in capturing the attention of several national and state legislatures around mid-century. On at least eight occasions between 1840 and 1869 the British House of Commons debated measures to abolish capital punishment. A royal commission was appointed in 1864 to conduct a lengthy review of the penalty. In the midst of the 1848 revolutions the Frankfurt Parliament conducted a full-blown debate over the desirability of abolishing the death penalty. In vote after vote the assembly supported the idea of doing away with the sanction. The initiative ultimately failed, but the prominence the issue secured during the intense political struggles pointed to the status it had achieved as a symbolic marker of political difference (Evans 1996). In the United States, the legislatures of New York and Pennsylvania repeatedly discussed the death penalty in the 1840s. More striking still was the passage of abolition in Michigan in 1846, Rhode Island in 1852, and Wisconsin in 1853. Here, for the first time, popularly elected legislatures, admittedly in states with small, homogeneous populations, opted for abolition. Yet despite these successes, more often than not the cause of abolition in Europe depended on the decision of a ruler. Leopold II of Belgium began commuting death sentences when he came to the throne in 1865, and the penalty was dropped from the Belgian Law Code in 1866. Willem II of the Netherlands declined to sign death warrants starting in 1855, and capital punishment was abolished in 1870. In 1872 the king of Sweden and Norway announced that he would commute all death sentences. The king of the newly united Italy also refused from 1863 onward to confirm death sentences, and abolition was ratified in the Criminal Code of 1888. While once the death penalty had spoken of the majesty of absolute monarchy, by the nineteenth century monarchs accepted abolition as a way of advertising their adjustment to a world dominated by liberal bourgeois institutions and culture.

The high tide of abolitionism came at different moments in different countries. It crested in Germany in 1870 in the midst of legislative debates over the creation of a new criminal code for the recently united nation. Liberal sentiment was running high, and the nature of the political divisions in the Reichstag seemed to favor the cause. Eduard Lasker, a leading liberal, expressed the conviction that inspired many abolitionists when he answered his own question: "What then is the difference between life imprisonment and capital punishment? The yawning chasm is that the person *lives* and has the opportunity to improve himself to the highest level of humanity with his moral strength, that he can die as one who is pleasing to God." Those who favored retention of capital punishment appeared on the defensive. The decisive intervention in the debate was ultimately made by Bismarck, with the tacit support of the king of Prussia, Wilhelm I. Bismarck reprised many of the arguments traditionally employed by defenders of capital punishment—that abolition was a dangerous experiment, that death was required to overawe a turbulent population, and that vengeance was a healthy response to murder. He condemned what he called "the morbid sentimentality of the times." It was not, however, Bismarck's arguments that carried the day. Rather, he succeeded in shifting the ground of the debate by making a vote for abolition seem like a threat to the cause of national unity. The vote was remarkably close, but with 127 for retention and 119 for abolition, the death penalty for murder and for treason was written into the criminal code. There would not be another major debate over capital punishment in Germany for fifty years (Evans 1996, pp. 334–35, 339).

The modern history of capital punishment has often been presented as a story of the broad advance of abolitionism, even if the general movement was marked by peculiar pulses of activity and occasional unexpected turns. This wide perspective emphasizes mounting embarrassment with public, violent punishments, combined with a moral revulsion against a penalty often portrayed as inconsistent with universal human values. Yet, as often as not, the status of the death penalty at a particular moment represented a sensitive barometer of political life. The fortunes of capital punishment spoke of the balance of power between liberal parties advocating abolition and conservative parties committed to the preservation of the penalty. The outcome often hinged upon special circumstances that conditioned the trajectory of the debate. Perhaps the special case that offers the most sobering lesson about the limits of general interpretative theories is presented by the American south. In some respects the south followed the general evolution of penal practices found in the north, even if at a distance. The number of crimes for which a white person could suffer death declined over the first half of the century. The south, however, never saw the rise of a movement to abolish capital punishment. It retained laws that punished crimes such as horse theft, arson, and rape with death, even though, in practice, whites only suffered death for murder. The region was slower to end the practice of public executions, though not uniformly so. Thus the south, at least with respect to whites, displayed roughly the features that prevailed in the north. The great exception came with respect to the treatment of blacks, who whether slave or free, faced death for a much longer list of crimes. They could be executed for arson, robbery, burglary, assault with a dangerous weapon, and, above all, rape. More blacks than whites were hanged. Both before and perhaps even more after the Civil War capital punishment was seen as a crucial instrument for maintaining the existing racial order.

III. The Transformation of the Execution

One of the most striking developments of the mid-nineteenth century, again with a few notable exceptions, was the elimination of the public execution. Reformers had for so long complained about the evil consequences of these occasions that their elimination might appear to have been inevitable. What hindered this step was in part a conviction that public punishment was necessary to secure the maximum deterrence the punishment was supposed to inspire. The authorities also shared the belief that the public was owed the sight of the execution because people might suspect the authorities of trickery if the penalty was inflicted privately. Private punishment, the London *Times* warned in 1864, "loses its popular character and wants the popular sanction" (*The Times*, November 17, 1864, p. 8). Yet in 1868 the same paper was quick to celebrate the first private English execution. Conservatives who defended capital punishment ultimately came around to the viewpoint of the reformers about the deleterious effects of public executions. They also came to the same conclusion as the *Times*, that removing the penalty from the presence of the crowd was a necessary measure to preserve it (McGowen 1994, p. 257).

Complaints about the conduct of the crowds attending executions formed a staple of calls for restriction of the penalty during the early nineteenth century. The crowds represented not only a threat to public order but also moral contamination, opponents argued. The diminished number of executions had not produced any decline in enthusiasm for attending these events. On the contrary, executions in Britain, France, and Germany attracted huge crowds, numbering sometimes in the tens of thousands. The spectators were seldom riotous, but they failed to act with the decorum that polite society demanded. People were drawn to the event by curiosity, and they were quoted voicing irreverent opinions about what they saw. Middle-class journals expressed concern about the number of women and children who attended. High public officials avoided such occasions. Overall, executions had become altogether less impressive affairs, more about the death of an individual and less about the authority authorizing it.

The change came with surprising speed over a couple of decades. Connecticut abolished public executions in 1830, and this step was soon imitated by other northern states. Prussia did so in 1851 and Bavaria in 1861. Britain once again lagged behind the group. Only with the compromise conclusion, in 1868, to the debates over abolition did public executions come to an end. France alone resisted the tide. In 1870 a motion was pressed by a republican legislator to end such public displays, but an unusual combination of abolitionists and defenders of the death penalty combined to defeat the measure.

Those countries that abolished the public execution came to announce the event in more modest ways, by a bell ringing or a flag being raised. Over time even these signals disappeared. Publicity was left to the press, and journalists were content to represent the event in terms of individuals and their crimes. Once the decision was made to end the public execution, there was little dispute about where it should take place: inside the prison. The significance of this move is hard to miss; reformers had long presented the prison as an alternative to the execution, a symbol of rehabilitation rather than retribution. Enclosing the execution within the prison walls suggested that the relationship between the two penalties was deeper and more complex than had been acknowledged (Gottschalk 2006). And while the triumph of privacy might be taken as a confession of embarrassment about putting a citizen to death, it might equally well demonstrate that capital punishment could survive if complaints about its operation could be neutralized.

Even as the authorities embraced the demand for the abolition of public executions, they also engaged in an examination of the technology of death itself. In early modern times death came in a variety of forms, with much depending on the nature of the crime and the social status of the condemned. An elaborate and long-drawn-out execution was meant to offer a vivid lesson illustrated by particular gestures or inflictions. By the early nineteenth century, with the triumph of a more utilitarian approach to punishment, the measure of legitimate punishment had become the degree of pain earned by the individual offender for committing a particular offense. Any excess suffering implied either faulty management of the penalty or tyranny on the part of the government. In 1792 the French adopted the guillotine as a quick and humane mode of execution. By the third decade of the nineteenth century most German states had stopped imposing the punishment of breaking on the wheel and substituted instead beheading with an axe (Evans 1996). The problem of executions that went awry continued to plague every country that retained capital punishment. Several gruesome hangings in Britain in the 1880s led the government to search for an alternative. What remains most surprising, however, about these discussions of the mode of inflicting capital punishment is how conservative European states proved in retaining the forms of execution that prevailed in the early nineteenth century. Symbolic issues once again loomed large in this decision. No doubt the primary motive behind the retention of traditional forms was the concern that giving too much ground over the issue of what the condemned could suffer ran the risk of conceding too much to the opponents of the death penalty. Only in America did a confidence in technology lead to experimentation with novel forms of execution. The development of the electric chair, first employed in New York State in 1890, and the gas chamber, used in Nevada in 1924, were followed in the late twentieth century with the triumph of lethal injection (Banner 2002).

The concerns that were voiced over removing the sight of death from the public and limiting the pain associated with the execution suggest a discomfort with the death penalty that became more acute over time. These issues might well appear to have operated against the survival of the penalty. One trend, however, ran in the opposite direction. As the disputes over the death penalty intensified at the end of the eighteenth century, defenders of the penalty pointed to the justice of retention of death for one crime, that of murder. They often spoke of the natural feelings that demanded revenge for the most horrific crime they could imagine. Such feelings, they argued, were healthy; they were necessary to sustain society. One consequence of the gradual retreat of capital punishment over the preceding two centuries was that the penalty came in practice to be applied largely to this one offense. There is something so apparently logical about this result that one can miss its full implications. Early modern criminal codes treated murder seriously, even if the application of the law was anything but consistent. And even as murderers came to constitute an ever-larger proportion of those executed, only a minority of those who committed homicide ever received a death sentence. Still, the fact that murder became the focus of both the practice of and the debates about the death penalty weighed upon the controversy and shaped its trajectory in ways that could not have been anticipated in advance.

It had an impact on how the public reacted at both an intellectual and an emotional level to both the crime and the punishment. The nineteenth-century press increasingly became the most influential medium for mediating the experience of all crime, but especially of murder. The papers often applied a moralizing veneer to their treatment of homicide, but what more frequently dominated reporting was a sensational tone that worked powerfully upon the public imagination. It was typically the shocking, the brutal, or the exotic murder that garnered the most attention, rather than the mundane homicide. Newspaper reporting might foster identification with the victim. It frequently played upon middle-class fears and vulnerabilities. The press promoted identification with the victims of homicide, which thus meant that murder contributed to the construction of individuals' mental map of the social world. Such accounts invoked widely shared prejudices in emotionally charged stories that demanded a cathartic resolution. These cases worked to align the public with the judicial authorities so that one felt gratified at the death of the murderer. Increasingly, the issue of the death penalty became inextricably caught up in the question of murder. Defenders of capital punishment turned back the claim of the reformers that they alone cherished life by arguing that a true respect for the sanctity of life lay in demanding the life of the murderer (Halttunen 1998; Cohen 2006).

The effect of these changes—private and less painful executions, and the heightened focus upon murder—worked together to restructure the experience of the death penalty. They heightened the degree to which both murder and the execution belonged to the imagination. The death of the murderer came to appear as a recompense for the murder of a citizen. The withdrawal of the actual execution from public view made the exchange seem that much more reasonable and satisfying. The emphasis on a quick and efficient death, with no unnecessary addition of suffering, maintained the illusion that the execution was a mechanical process that was emotionally neutral. And even as the execution came to be more centrally controlled by state governments, to most people the role of the state in administering capital justice came to appear less striking. Defenders of capital punishment often spoke as if the state was merely acting as the agent for its citizens, responding to their legitimate demands for retribution. The experience of the death penalty now matched the abstractness of the ideal; the execution was an occasion when life was in question, but the narratives proposed by press or politicians added the color calculated to sway popular opinion (Kaufman-Osborn 2002).

IV. Abolition or Retention?

The campaign for the abolition of capital punishment did not prosper in late nineteenth-century Europe, when the political and cultural environment proved less receptive to the message of the reformers. Support for the movement declined in America after the Civil War. In Britain several episodes of alarming robberies in London around mid-century produced fearful calls for harsher penalties. The Indian Revolt of 1857 further saw fierce demands in the press for severe and summary justice for those held responsible for the slaughter of English women and children. The widespread public support, which included the voices of Carlyle, Ruskin, and Dickens, for the conduct of Governor Eyre in suppressing an uprising of black peasants with frequent executions in 1865 was another straw in the wind. The rejection of abolition by so respected a liberal as John Stuart Mill signaled the shift in the intellectual climate. Anglican bishops in the House of Lords, Calvinist ministers in America, and both the Catholic and Protestant clerical hierarchies in Germany lent their support to arguments for the retention of the death penalty. Fear and righteous anger mingled in the words written by the jurist James Fitzjames Stephen in an article he wrote in 1864 in the midst of the debate over abolition in Britain. The law, Stephen wrote, was meant to tame the passions by calling to its support powerful countervailing emotions. "That putting men to death for murder," he argued, "does gratify the vindictive sentiment or desire for revenge, which most people feel on hearing of a great crime, will not be denied" (McGowen 2003, p. 245). By late in the century racial and biological theories were contributing to support for the penalty. The rise of criminology as a discipline with pretentions to scientific respectability offered a vocabulary for explaining the execution as a kind of prophylactic treatment for an incurable and degenerate population. Society had the right, as it had the duty, to defend itself against the mentally defective or morally degenerate criminal.

Despite the tide turning against them, the abolitionists were never completely silenced. Their cause might not have prospered, but it seldom disappeared. Perhaps just as significant, was that despite the force of the reaction in favor of the death penalty, the number of executions rarely increased beyond the low numbers that had marked the mid-century. Abolition seemed to be a cause that smoldered, ready to burst into flame when the political conditions favored it, as they did in Progressive-era America, when ten states, largely in the upper Midwest and the west, abolished the death penalty between 1897 and 1917. And in France in 1908, the Chamber of Deputies devoted five sessions to one of the lengthiest discussions of the penalty in French history. The government of Georges Clemenceau, with support from across the political left, pressed for abolition. It was answered by a fierce campaign in the press that featured sensational stories of murder and a poll whose outcome was overwhelmingly for retention. During the debate, Justice Minister Aristide Briand advised his colleagues not to blindly follow public opinion. The opposition to abolition warned against surrendering to the barbarians and asked deputies to "think a little less about the criminals and a little more about honest folk." Although in the end the proposal for abolition was soundly defeated, the debate showed how much life remained in the cause (Wright 1983, p. 173; Nye 2003).

The fate of abolitionism in the aftermath of the First World War revealed once again how dependent the cause was upon the peculiar political conditions that prevailed at a particular time and place. The British Labour governments of the 1920s, despite the importance of abolition to a substantial portion of the party's membership, shied away from taking up what its leaders saw as too controversial a measure. Neither was there much enthusiasm for reform in France. In 1926 Mussolini restored capital punishment to Italy and significantly increased, in 1930, the number of crimes to which it applied. In America several states that had abolished the death penalty in the years before the war now restored it. Amid the alarm created by the "Red Scare" and the outbreak of criminal violence that accompanied Prohibition, the number of executions rose steadily from 1920, reaching a high point of 199 in 1935.

It was Germany, however, that shows most vividly how rapid reverses in the fortunes of death penalty politics could be. In the unsettled state of the country in the months after 1918 the authorities turned to the death penalty in an effort to reestablish order. The number of death sentences and executions swelled beyond prewar levels, with thirty-six individuals executed in 1920. In the political turmoil of the 1920s capital punishment emerged as a highly charged marker of political allegiance. Abolition might well have been included in the constitution of the Weimer Republic, but it failed in part from a lack of consistent support from the Social Democrats. Yet even as the press resorted increasingly to the language of degeneracy to describe murderers, the actual number of executions declined sharply as the decade progressed. In 1928 the Social Democrats helped to form a coalition government, one that included a committed abolitionist as justice minister. During the next two years there were no executions in Germany. The Criminal Law Committee charged with the revision of the criminal code, however, deadlocked over the question of abolition, leaving the future of capital punishment to hover in an uncertain state. The question was resolved when a retentionist replaced the abolitionist justice minister. As renewed political turmoil accelerated in 1930, the tide turned against abolition. Conservative state governments began to execute once again. Once the Nazis came to power, they expanded the number of capital crimes and cut the time between conviction and execution. The death penalty was widely employed against political opponents as well as common criminals. At the same time the government sought to restrict information about the executions lest sympathy with the condemned be inadvertently encouraged. Thus the paradox of strong advocacy of capital punishment by the authorities combined with minimal public knowledge of actual practice was fully realized (Evans 1996).

At the end of the Second World War the status of the death penalty appeared to be much as it had been in the interwar years. The death sentences handed down to collaborators in a number of countries, and the even more widespread popular justice dealt out to such people, suggested popular acceptance of capital punishment. The death sentences awarded to German and Japanese war criminals seemed to cast a veil of respectability over the penalty. The first indication of a change in attitude came in the defeated countries, with Italy in 1947 and Austria in 1950 abolishing the death penalty. The path to abolition was more roundabout in the case of West Germany, where it took a temporary convergence of interests between the traditional left and the extreme right to end capital punishment (Evans 1996). In Europe the reaction to the horror of war, and particularly to the revelations about the death camps, produced a widespread revulsion against state-sanctioned death. Under these circumstances the death penalty stood as a potent symbol of the past. The abolition of capital punishment functioned as a way of signifying a rejection of the fascist legacy and the inauguration of societies grounded in respect for human rights. Abolition in Portugal in 1976 and Spain in 1978 operated along these lines. Still, neither Britain nor France showed much inclination to follow the lead of Germany or Italy in the 1950s. The fact that both countries were caught up in colonial wars in which the death penalty played an important role in the effort to defeat resistance movements contributed to the retention of the penalty at home. It took the triumph of parties of the left, as well as the sustained engagement of a cabinet minister—Roy Jenkins in Britain in 1964, and Robert Badinter in France in 1981—to achieve abolition in each case. By the 1990s, abolition of the death penalty had become a Europe-wide development. With the fall of the Communist regimes of Eastern Europe the abolitionist movement conquered all of the continents and helped the Council of Europe to define what it called a "community of sentiment" that distinguished European civilization as peculiarly devoted to the recognition and protection of human rights. In 1994 abolition became a condition for joining the community. Opposition to the death penalty became a principle that helped to unite an otherwise-fragmented continent, in part by giving it an ideal that distinguished Europe from other regions, particularly the United States (Girling 2005; Judt 2005).

America, in the two decades after 1945, looked much like Europe during the same period—a patchwork of death penalty practices. Under the federal system criminal justice was largely left to the states to shape. A number of states had by this time abolished capital punishment, while some had retained it in law but seldom or never used it. The death penalty was most actively employed in the south, but states like New York, California, and Ohio used it as well. The 1950s saw mounting criticism of capital punishment along with a decline in public support for the institution. There was a general fall in the number of executions, although the reduction had a variety of causes and varied in intensity from state to state. Juries showed greater reluctance to return death sentences, and judicial review of capital cases increased the number of such sentences set aside. The time between sentencing and execution increased from months to years. By the 1960s anti–death penalty momentum was building, and several states abolished it. It was a halting progress toward abolition at best, but one that encouraged proponents to point to "evolving standards of decency" as a rationale for more immediate changes to the law (Banner 2002; Garland 2010).

What revolutionized the question of the death penalty in America was the intervention of the Supreme Court. For most of its history the Court had seldom addressed penal issues. From the 1930s on, however, it began examining criminal justice more closely. An ever-increasing number of capital cases came to the courts for review, which had the effect of vastly expanding the time between conviction and execution. In 1960 there were fifty-six executions in the United States; by 1965 that number had fallen to seven. After an execution in Colorado in 1967, the practice of the death penalty in the United States came to a halt. This de facto moratorium appeared to acquire formal sanction when, in 1972, in the case of *Furman v. Georgia*, the Supreme Court declared capital punishment as then practiced to be unconstitutional. While only a minority of the justices found the death penalty itself to be unconstitutional, a bare majority determined that capital justice was so random in its application, so lacking in reasonable standards for deciding among similar cases, that it violated the Eighth Amendment's prohibition on cruel and unusual punishment. Though the Court's decision was anything but clear and decisive, the consequences of *Furman* were momentous. Death rows across the country emptied. The intervention of the Court nationalized the question of the death penalty and in the process transformed the terms of the debate from legislative and political initiatives to legal-procedural considerations (Banner 2002).

As at so many points in the history of the death penalty, contingent events played a large role in shaping the outcome. The Court's decision in *Furman*, as revealed in the separate opinions, was deeply divided. Several justices left the door ajar for a return of the penalty, even spelling out the path that might be taken. The *Furman* decision occurred at a time when the political direction of the country was shifting, encouraged in part by the mounting anxiety over rising crime rates and outbreaks of civil disorder. The Court was itself a target of complaint, for it had come to symbolize the influence of national elites—legal, intellectual, and professional—who were perceived as threatening the integrity of regional values and sentiments. In the United States such populist appeals gained traction in a way they had not in Europe for most of the postwar era. Within days of the *Furman* decision several states moved to restore the death penalty, shaping their measures to satisfy the procedural concerns of the justices. By 1976 thirty-five states had voted to approve capital punishment legislation in what amounted to an electoral tidal wave. The *Furman* decision, far from ending capital punishment, produced the strongest endorsement of the penalty the nation had ever seen. In the face of this popular outcry, and after a change in personnel, the Court decided to revisit the issue in 1976. In *Gregg v. Georgia* it declared that capital punishment, under certain circumstances, was constitutional. The number of people on death row had surged in the aftermath of the passage of remedial legislation, and in 1977 the first execution since *Furman* occurred in Utah. The numbers executed thereafter rose rapidly, surging to 98 in 1999, a figure not equaled since 101 were executed in 1951 (Banner 2002; Garland 2010).

While polling suggested uniform support for capital punishment across the entire nation, death penalty practice varied widely from state to state. The Court had opened the door to the death penalty, but it had left it to the individual states to shape their own policy. Twelve states remained abolitionist. California had the largest death row, but this result was owing to the small number of executions that took place there. Kansas, a politically conservative state, executed no one. The vast majority of the executions after *Gregg* occurred in the south, and the punishment became far more regionally specific than ever before. Although many factors lay behind this peculiar outcome—the strength of fundamentalist religion, the assertion of states' rights, the attitude toward government—race was undoubtedly the dominant motive. In America the political and legal structure enabled populist politics to frustrate initiatives that emerged at the national level, especially when the institution driving abolition was itself deeply divided (Garland 2010). The establishment of the death penalty was viewed as an empowering gesture, reinforcing a sense of solidarity in a privileged community. The cost, in terms of human life, if not expense, was modest. An individual execution was of relatively little moment if those who paid the price for this abstract principle were overwhelmingly the poor and disproportionately minorities.

The Supreme Court, in handing over the decision about the retention of the death penalty to the states, did not relinquish its own role in managing and overseeing the operation of the penalty. On the contrary, a steady stream of cases to the Court forced it to set and then revisit the guidelines the states would have to observe. The issue remained contentious, with divided judicial opinions inviting litigants to make a fresh assault on the standards proposed in any one case. Questions about the age at which an offender became eligible for death, as well as disputes over mental competence, were fiercely debated before often–sharply divided justices. Supporters of the death penalty demanded that the families of victims be permitted to testify during the sentencing phase of a trial. They complained of the suffering produced by the endless litigation. Opponents of capital punishment pointed to the disturbing incidence of death row inmates exonerated by DNA evidence or proof of police or prosecutorial misconduct. The press proved as likely to give extensive coverage to such cases or to stories of botched executions as it gave to the horrific crimes that carried the condemned to death row. The widespread adoption of lethal injection demonstrated the continuing public discomfort with the idea of an execution involving additional suffering for the condemned. Yet some relatives of the victims contended that the execution looked too little like punishment. Many of these concerns had appeared at other times in the history of capital punishment, but never before had they been so persistently explored or so elaborately developed. The institution of the death penalty in twenty-first-century America gives the appearance of being in perpetual crisis. Popular opinion is fluid in the face of competing news stories. Since 2000 the number of executions has declined sharply, and in 2007 New Jersey became the first state in thirty years to abolish the death penalty. It was joined by New Mexico in 2009. Evidence of disquiet among the public is widespread, but support for capital punishment remains strong, as revealed by the unwillingness of most politicians in most parts of the country to endorse abolition. In the context of the "war on terror," capital punishment has found a new context in which to search for justification. Currently an unstable status quo prevails that satisfies no one (Thomas Laqueur, "Festivals of Punishment," *London Review of Books*, 5 October 2000, pp. 17–24; Garland 2010). What distinguishes Europe from America today is less the triumph of abolitionist sentiment among the general population than the presence in Europe of institutional arrangements and political circumstances that promoted abolition and have, thus far, inhibited the restoration of capital punishment. What marks America, on the other hand, are racial politics and governmental structures that have not only entrenched the penalty but infused it with passions derived from a political culture remarkably sensitive to populist appeals.

Conclusion

The history of the death penalty over the past three centuries offers a striking portrait of profound shifts in the shape of capital punishment. The early modern execution was mounted by civil authorities in an attempt to overawe subjects with a spectacle of punishment meant to teach obedience and display the divine warrant for this exercise of power. Modern executions, at least in the United States, do none of these things. Where they occur at all they are carried out in private. The actual number of executions is so vanishingly small that the practice can scarcely be said to represent a significant component of penal policy. It seems that very few executions are needed to anchor commitment to the institution. Insofar as defenders of capital punishment offer a justification for the penalty, it is the presence of the victim's relatives that provides it. Even as the state remains the sole authority responsible for carrying out the sentence, it appears intent on minimizing the evidence of its participation. Far from broadcasting the violence it commits, the bleak ordinariness of every aspect of the execution process speaks of a wish to disown and disguise what is happening.

Despite the evidence of a profound break in the way in which people have thought about the death penalty over time, it is impossible to ignore the existence of deep continuities as well. In an important sense, the punishment of death remains as politically expressive today as it was in early modern Europe. The practice—the rituals, scope, and intent that have shaped the penalty—looks very different. Yet its status as a symbolic exercise, a form of communication, continues to operate powerfully in the changed circumstances of the twenty-first century (Garland 2010). The death penalty remains caught up in the drama of state power. It speaks forcefully about who owns the state and in whose interest the state governs. In doing so, the death penalty focuses and individualizes the experience of government in the modern world. The decisive moment in the emergence of this question came at some point in the nineteenth century, in both Europe and America, with the rise of electoral politics as an arena for contesting fundamental questions about the organization of society. Within the wider domain of what can be called the "politics of life," it has a distinctive status that it shares with few other questions (Foucault 1978; Meranze 2003). On the one hand, the end of the death penalty announces a limit to state power and proclaims a society's commitment to the preservation of the lives of even its most despised members. On the other hand, retention of capital punishment expresses the demand that the state defend the lives of individuals with what is still seen as the supreme act of state power, the taking of a life. In doing so it enlists and channels powerful emotions of rage and fear on the one hand, and hope on the other, promising a cathartic outcome that validates and empowers individual feelings. As executions have become increasingly rare and have disappeared from the immediate experience of the population, the debate over the death penalty has become increasingly abstract. What is left is the symbolic act, the commitment to or rejection of capital punishment. The future of capital punishment remains such an insistent question because the penalty continues to speak so forcefully about the identity of the state in the eyes of its citizens.

References

Banner, Stuart. 2002. *The Death Penalty: An American History*. Cambridge, MA: Harvard University Press.

Beccaria, Cesare. 1995. *On Crimes and Punishments and Other Writings*. Cambridge: Cambridge University Press.

Cohen, Daniel. 2006. *Pillars of Salt, Monuments of Grace: New England Crime Literature and the Origins of American Popular Culture, 1674–1860*. Amherst: University of Massachusetts Press.

Evans, Richard. 1996. *Rituals of Retribution: Capital Punishment in Germany, 1600–1987*. London: Penguin.

Foucault, Michel. 1977. *Discipline and Punish: The Birth of the Prison*. New York: Pantheon.

Foucault, Michel. 1978. *The History of Sexuality: An Introduction*. New York: Pantheon.

Garland, David. 2010. *Peculiar Institution: America's Death Penalty in an Age of Abolition*. Cambridge, MA: Harvard University Press.

Gatrell, V. A. C. 1994. *The Hanging Tree: Execution and the English People, 1770–1868*. Oxford: Oxford University Press.

Girling, Evi. 2005. "European Identity and the Mission Against the Death Penalty in the United States." In *The Cultural Lives of Capital Punishment: Comparative Perspectives*, ed. Austin Sarat & Christian Boulanger, 112–28. Stanford, CA: Stanford University Press.

Gottschalk, Maria. 2006. *The Prison and the Gallows: The Politics of Mass Incarceration in America*. Cambridge: Cambridge University Press.

Gregory, James. 2012. *Victorians Against the Gallows: Capital Punishment and the Abolitionist Movement in Nineteenth Century Britain*. London: Tauris.

Halttunen, Karen. 1998. *Murder Most Foul: The Killer and the American Gothic Imagination*. Cambridge, MA: Harvard University Press.

Hay, Douglas. 1975. "Property, Authority, and the Criminal Law." In *Albion's Fatal Tree: Crime and Society in Eighteenth-Century England*, ed. Douglas Hay, Peter Linebaugh, John Rule, Edward P. Thompson, & Cal Winslow, 17–63. New York: Pantheon.

Hunt, Lynn. 2007. *Inventing Human Rights: A History*. New York: Norton.

Judt, Tony. 2005. *Postwar: A History of Europe since 1945*. New York: Penguin.

Kaufman-Osborn, Timothy. 2002. *From Noose to Needle: Capital Punishment and the Late Liberal State*. Ann Arbor: University of Michigan Press.

Masur, Louis. 1989. *Rites of Execution: Capital Punishment and the Transformation of American Culture, 1776–1865*. New York: Oxford University Press.

McGowen, Randall. 1983. "The Image of Justice and Reform of the Criminal Law in Early Nineteenth-Century England." *Buffalo Law Review* 32 (1): 89–125.

McGowen, Randall. 1987. "The Body and Punishment in Eighteenth-Century England." *Journal of Modern History* 59 (4): 651–79.

McGowen, Randall. 1994. "Civilizing Punishment: The End of the Public Execution in England." *Journal of British Studies* 33:257–82.

McGowen, Randall. 2003. "History, Culture and the Death Penalty: The British Debates, 1840–70." *Historical Reflections* 29 (2): 229–49.

McKenzie, Andrea. 2007. *Tyburn's Martyrs: Execution in England, 1675–1775.* London: Continuum.

Meranze, Michael. 2003. "Michel Foucault, the Death Penalty and the Crisis of Historical Understanding." *Historical Reflections* 29 (2): 191–209.

Merback, Mitchell. 1999. *The Thief, the Cross, and the Wheel: Pain and the Spectacle of Punishment in Medieval and Renaissance Europe.* London: Reaktion Books.

Nye, Robert. 2003. "Two Capital Punishment Debates in France: 1908 and 1981." *Historical Reflections* 29 (2): 211–28.

Silverman, Lisa. 2001. *Tortured Subjects: Pain, Truth, and the Body in Early Modern France.* Chicago: University of Chicago Press.

Spierenburg, Pieter. 1984. *The Spectacle of Suffering: Executions and the Evolution of Repression.* Cambridge: Cambridge University Press.

Wright, Gordon. 1983. *Between the Guillotine and Liberty: Two Centuries of the Crime Problem in France.* New York: Oxford University Press.

CHAPTER 32

THE RISE AND FALL OF PENAL TRANSPORTATION

HAMISH MAXWELL-STEWART

INTRODUCTION

IT is perhaps fitting that among the first Spanish convicts to be sentenced to transportation was a grandson of Christopher Columbus. Luis Colon was dispatched to Oran in North Africa for ten years for the crime of trigamy in 1563 (Braudel 1995, p. 862). The European use of deportation and forced labor extraction as a penal sanction is particularly associated with colonization. Convict labor was initially deployed in the Mediterranean and North Africa before spreading via the Atlantic islands and West Africa to the New World. By the time the French penal colony in Guiana had closed, four centuries after Luis Colon had been sentenced to transportation by a court in Valladolid, convicts had served in an impressive array of colonies. They had been used to cultivate pepper in Sumatra, tobacco in the Chesapeake and Barbados, sugar in Port Macquarie, and wheat in Australia. They had toiled at constructing fortifications in West Africa, Cuba, and Puerto Rico and docks in Bermuda, Gibraltar, and Azov. They had been sent to work in mines in Van Diemen's Land, New South Wales, Nerchinsk, and Sakhalin, and had labored on roads, canals, and railways from one end of the Western empires to the other.

Transportation was a somewhat curious beast in that it was both a method of punishing those found guilty of committing offenses and a way of securing cheap, pliable labor that could be deployed on colonial frontiers. The Spanish, Portuguese, French, British, and Russian empires all made extensive use of convict transportation to maintain, defend, and police colonial territories in the period from 1415 to the mid-twentieth century. As a result, transportation shared many features with other systems of labor exploitation, including slavery, indenture, and conscription, and it is no coincidence that transported convicts were often put to work alongside those who had lost their freedom for reasons other than that they had been pronounced guilty of committing an offense (De Vito & Lichtenstein 2015). In the seventeenth-century Chesapeake and Barbados, for example, convicts sentenced in British and Irish courts labored alongside both slaves from West and Central Africa and European indentured servants. All three forms of labor were set to work picking tobacco. The language used to describe both serving and former convicts often betrayed the close parallels with other forms of unfreedom. In Britain's Australian penal colonies, for example, convicts still under sentence were described as in "servitude," and those that were free as "emancipists" (Atkinson 1994).

Section I of this essay explores the differences between penal transportation and a series of other closely related practices, especially slavery, conscription, and banishment. Section II examines the reason for the emergence of transportation as a judicial policy in early modern Europe and its relationship with galley service. Section III provides a brief account of the transportation systems that operated in the Portuguese, Spanish, French, British, Dutch, Swedish, Habsburg, and Russian empires. Section IV explores the relationship between transportation and evolving European judicial and penal ideologies, while section V examines the manner in which the movement of convicts to and between overseas colonies fitted into wider imperial agendas. Finally, the conclusion briefly reviews the importance of penal transportation as a colonial labor extraction device as well as exploring some of the factors that accounted for its eventual demise.

I. Defining Penal Transportation

While transportation can be difficult to distinguish from other exploitative processes, the lives of transported convicts were generally characterized by three common features—traits that individually might be shared with other unfree labor migrations systems but collectively help to distinguish the trans-global movement of convict labor from other practices used to manage bonded workers. First, the length of time that the convict was ordered to serve was fixed by a sentence passed by a court or by another state-imposed sanction. Second, the transported were removed from the place of conviction to an overseas colony or border region, where they were subjected to forced labor. Third, the children of convicts were born free—or at least were not treated as convicts. In this sense the status of being a convict was not intergenerationally transmitted, as in most forms of slavery (Eltis 1993).

In practice, these boundaries were often blurred. While it is true that the children of convicts were not treated as convicts, this does not necessarily mean that they were seen as fully free. The close relationship that has often existed between state-organized transportation systems and the private sector provided the masters of convict labor with an incentive to ensure that they were compensated for the costs of maintaining convict offspring. Thus, in seventeenth- and eighteenth-century British North America children born to convict women who had been purchased by settlers were automatically indentured to their mother's master until they reached the age of twenty-one (Jeppesen 2014). Even in state-run convict Australia, the children of serving convicts were housed in government-run orphan schools, where they could be forced to enter into labor contracts with private settlers, at least until the point at which their parents became free (Frost 2012).

Another complicating factor is that states frequently treated other individuals as convicts even though they had not been formally sentenced. Perhaps the most common example of this practice was the transportation of vagrants and "gypsies." As late as the early twentieth century, the Portuguese were still regularly sending vagrants to their Angolan colonies to work alongside convicts (Coates 2013). Prisoners-of-war or rebels were also often fed into existing transportation systems without being formally sentenced. Peter the Great, for example, made use of Turkish, Tartar, Swedish, Finnish, Estonian, and Latvian prisoners, sending them to labor alongside convicts as part of the failed attempt to colonize the Black Sea port of Azov (Boeck 2008). Between 10,000 and 20,000 Polish rebels were also transported to Siberia following the failed 1830–1831 insurrection (Beer 2013). The notion of illegal combatants is, in this sense, hardly new. While they had not been convicted in a court, such transportees were ordered to work alongside civilly convicted convicts for a stipulated length of time.

Many civil transportation systems operated in parallel with military equivalents. One of the common justifications for transportation was that it protected law-abiding citizens from the dangers associated with contact with colonial environments. The death rates for British troops in West Africa in the early nineteenth century, for example, were twenty times greater than those for troops billeted in barracks in the British Isles (Curtin 1989). Penal units composed of prisoners sentenced in military or civil courts were regularly used to garrison colonial outposts. Many European counties operated militarized penal transportation systems that functioned alongside their civilian counterparts. The Russians, for example, made use of penal labor battalions until 1860 (Gentes 2005), and the Portuguese sent convict soldiers to military *presidios* in North or West Africa, Mozambique Island, Diu, and Muscat (Coates 2015). The Spanish manned *presidios* in Florida, Louisiana, and Alta California with convict soldiers (Bense 2004). The British raised penal units for service in West Africa and the Caribbean (Maxwell-Stewart 2010), while the French made extensive use of convict soldiers in conflicts in Algeria and other colonies (Kalifa 2009).

Some of the mechanisms for securing recruits for penal units operated on the borders of what might be considered convict transportation. The *Bataillons d'Infanterie Légère d'Afrique* (better known as the BILA) were originally formed in 1832 by the government of Louis-Philippe. Used in colonial operations until disbanded by the French in 1970, these battalions' recruits were sourced from military offenders and civilian prisoners who—though discharged from jail—had yet to complete military service. While these men were not technically sentenced to transportation, convicting courts knew that colonial service in a penal unit would inevitably follow metropolitan imprisonment. A least 600,000 men, overwhelming drawn from working-class populations, served in the BILA during its 138-year existence (Kalifa 2009). This practice illustrates the difficulties involved in distinguishing convict labor from other forms of unfreedom (in this case, conscription), as well as the extent to which legal mechanisms were employed to coopt the labor of offenders within the overall process of colonization.

Penal transportation is often confused with banishment. Historically, many states have exiled those found guilty of breaking laws, codes, and customs—forcing them on pain of death to remove themselves beyond the borders of the realm. This was a common way of enforcing authority in the Zulu kingdom (Cope 1995), the Roman Empire, and the early medieval world—to provide some diverse examples. The Roman poet Ovid was banished to the Black Sea, while the Anglo-Saxon masterpiece "The Seafarer" describes the torments of an exile forced overseas, bereft of brethren and "hung with ice-shards." Banishment, however, differs from transportation in that the banished are not unfree in the sense that they are not compelled to labor for others. In the Roman Empire, such a punishment was reserved for the elite, distinguishing it from convict service, which was applied only to slaves and noncitizens (Groen-Vallinga & Tacoma 2015). Banishment is both a common and ancient practice, since it is relatively simple to enact, although—as with transportation—states sometimes experienced difficulties in identifying those who returned before their period of exile had officially ended (Morgan & Rushton 2004).

Some transportation systems operated in conjunction with the practice of banishment. This was particularly the case in the Russian Empire, where prisoners could be sentenced to penal labor (*katorga*) or merely ordered to relocate to the Siberian frontier. In the nineteenth century the number of exiles sentenced to *katorga* was a fraction of the total number banished. Thus, while on average 8,400 individuals per year were ordered to relocate to Siberia in the period from 1827 to 1846, only around 1,400 of these were *katorga* convicts (Gentes 2005).

II. The Emergence of Transportation in Early Modern Europe

While there is a tendency in the literature to assume that transportation was a practice restricted to Western postmedieval states, other societies have made use of the labor of convicted criminals. West African polities, for example, sold offenders convicted of a variety of crimes, including witchcraft, into slavery (Benton 2000). It is likely that similar practices existed wherever there was a demand for slave labor. The labor of prisoners was also utilized in large centrally organized industries that relied on ganging, especially open-cut mining. Convicts were used in China, for example, as early as the Han Dynasty (206 B.C.E.–220 C.E.) to mine iron ore and copper (Wilbur 1943), and in the Roman Empire the labor of prisoners who were not Roman citizens was utilized in road construction; copper, lead, and sulfur mines; and alabaster quarries in Spain, Greece, Gaul, Egypt, and Asia Minor (Fenoaltea 1984). While most convicts appear to have been sentenced to work within the province where they were convicted, those regions that did not possess mines exported convicted labor to other regions of the Roman Empire that did (Groen-Vallinga & Tacoma 2015). Given the scale of the Han and Roman empires, it is likely that the state facilitated the transportation of prisoners over considerable distances.

Penal enslavement was a common form of punishment in early medieval Europe. It was usually enforced only after the offender had failed to pay compensation. Its attraction was that it was relatively easy to administer as long as a buyer could be found for the convicted individual. Such sanctions became less common as the use of slavery declined in Western Europe: they were rare after the twelfth century, and thereafter penal enslavement was increasingly replaced with punishments that mutilated or otherwise marked the body of the offender (Rio 2015). Even in places where prisoners were enslaved, it was not common for the convicted to be relocated over long distances. Indeed, the widespread practice of transferring property rights in the body of the offender to the victim of the offense meant that many prisoners remained in the locale in which their original crime had been committed.

The decline in penal enslavement coincided with a general reduction in the use of slave labor in European societies. By the fifteenth century slavery had ceased to exist in England, the Netherlands, and France and was rare elsewhere in Western Europe. In the main this is because mixed agriculture does not easily lend itself to slavery. Seasonal fluctuations in labor demand meant that landowners who possessed slaves found it difficult to get a return on their considerable investment in human capital during the winter months. The introduction of horse-drawn plows exacerbated the problem by reducing the number of ganged tasks and emphasizing the importance of skilled teams of workers. Consequently, the bulk of agricultural work undertaken in Europe became more suited to the use of serf labor rather than slaves (Blackburn 1997). Feudal lords thus allowed common, and even private, ownership of land in return for labor services, which over time were increasingly substituted for rents. Exceptions included mining and mono-cultivation of plantation crops, notably sugar in the Levant and Mediterranean (Eltis 1993).

When the colonization of the New World led to an expansion in plantation agriculture and increased demand for labor on associated colonial infrastructure projects, new systems of compulsion were required in order to secure the necessary manpower in the absence of willing recruits. Simultaneous changes in the nature of warfare, particularly in the Mediterranean world, increased the demand for cheap, pliable, and expendable forms of labor.

In the Mediterranean, galley service became an acceptable use for convicted criminals at about the same time that some northern European states began to experiment with the workhouse. As in the classical world, developments in maritime technology dictated the switch from the use of free to unfree labor. It was the use of the *quinquereme* in the Second Punic War—a form of galley in which each oar was manned by five men—that enabled the use of slave crews. Only the inboard oarsman was required to be skilled—the other four, who simply followed his lead, provided mere muscle power (Libourel 1973). In the early sixteenth century some Mediterranean galley fleets abandoned the *alla sensile* system, in which a single oarsman pulled each oar, in favor of the *alla scaloccio* method, in which one skilled man called the time on each oar and three unskilled rowers provided the power (Konstam 2002).

While galley service might not technically fall within the definition of transportation, since those condemned to power the fleets of the early modern Mediterranean world were not always removed to the colonies, the practices were for all other intents and purposes indistinguishable. The French, Portuguese, Spanish, and English all sent convicts to labor in both galleys and colonies, switching between the two as needs demanded (Mawson 2013). The North African penal colonies of Tangiers, Oran, Melilla, and Ceuta were all home at one stage or another to galleys that were at least partially powered by convicts. They also received prisoners convicted in the colonies and transported back to the European center from as far away as Goa, while convicts exiting French galley service were sold as indentured servants and removed to the New World (Coates 2015; Eltis 1993). Tellingly, the Russian for convict labor, *katorga*, is derived from the Muscovite word for a Mediterranean galley (Boeck 2008).

III. Transportation and
the Western Empires

Portugal was the first early modern European state to deploy convict labor in order to facilitate the process of colonization, pressing prisoners into service as both soldiers and oarsmen during the conquest of the North African city of Ceuta in 1415. As Portugal was among the last European states to abandon penal transportation, its involvement with the practice spanned more than half a millennia (a total of 539 years). Convicts, or *degradoes*, were employed in the colonization of São Tomé, Cape Verde, Mozambique, Goa, and Brazil. They were also used to construct and man forts and factories in West Africa, including El Mina. During the sixteenth century the Portuguese deployed individuals convicted in courts in the West African islands of São Tomé and Fogo as oarsmen in the Mediterranean galley fleet, reversing the normal flow of convicts from metropole to colony (Benton 2000).

While transportation to Brazil ceased after the former colony gained its independence in 1822, *degradoes* continued to be sent to other colonies. Two transportation networks effectively operated within the Portuguese Empire: an Atlantic Ocean system based on Angola and an Indian Ocean equivalent centered on Mozambique. Convicts were transported from both metropolitan Portugal to the colonies, and between Portuguese colonies. Prisoners convicted in Angola, for example, were transported to Mozambique and vice versa. Transportation from metropolitan Portugal ceased in 1932, but colonially convicted *degradoes* continued to arrive in Angola until 1954. A conservative estimate of the number of *degradoes* transported between 1415 and the final demise of the Portuguese transportation system in the mid-twentieth century is 100,000 (Coates 2013).

The Spanish penal transportation system evolved in the first half of the seventeenth century. Like its Portuguese equivalent, the flow of convicts was far from mono-directional. Prisoners convicted in New Spain, for example, could be dispatched across the Atlantic for service in the Spanish galley fleet; sent as convict soldiers to augment garrisons in the Philippines, Alta-California, or Florida; or employed in fortress construction in Cuba or Puerto Rico. The Spanish transported convicts to more locations than any other of the Western empires, since most of the *presidios*, or fortified settlements, set up across the Spanish colonial world were manned at one time or another by convict soldiers. Hundreds of *presidios* were established along the northern borders of New Spain alone (Bense 2004). Because of the association between convict labor and these establishments, prisoners sentenced to transportation within the Spanish Empire were known as *presidiarios*.

While penal transportation to the former Spanish colonies in Central and South America ceased after 1821, convicts continued to be sent to *presidios* in North Africa until 1911. About 1,000 political prisoners from the Philippines, Cuba, and Spain were also sent to the West African island of Fernando Po between 1862 and 1899. The total number of convicts transported by the Spanish in the period 1550–1911 was at least 110,000, although further research is likely to considerably increase this estimate (Anderson & Maxwell-Stewart 2014).

While Henry VIII and Elizabeth I attempted to emulate Mediterranean practice by introducing galleys manned by convicts into the English Channel fleet, these schemes amounted to little. Outside of protected estuaries, galleys were of limited use in northern European waters, and the practice of using them as floating labor extraction devices for convicts appears to have been intermittent at best (Adair 1920). In 1675–1676, however, a small group of Wampanoag from Massachusetts and Rhode Island was transported across the Atlantic to the then–English colony at Tangiers, where they were pressed into galley service alongside slaves from the North African littoral (Aylmer 1999). By this time the English had established a system for sending European convicts in the opposite direction.

Although few convicts were sentenced to transportation by English courts prior to 1640, the expansion of tobacco plantations in the West Indies and Chesapeake led to a substantial increase in colonial demand for convicted labor. It is difficult to establish the overall number of convicts dispatched to the American colonies during the English Civil War and the subsequent Commonwealth period, although the claim that over 50,000 were sent from Ireland alone in the period 1652–1659 is almost certainly an exaggeration (O'Callaghan 2000). Court records indicate that approximately 6,000 convicts were transported from England and Wales in the period 1660–1717 (Maxwell-Stewart, 2010). Numbers increased after the passing of the 1718 Transportation Act, and an estimated 48,000 arrived in the various colonies in the period up to 1775, almost all of which were sent to Britain's North American colonies—particularly Virginia and Maryland (Ekirch 1987).

The flow of British and Irish convicts to the New World all but ceased after the American Revolution—a pattern that mirrored the experience of the Portuguese and Spanish transportation systems. After 1776 the only substantial movements of convicts to British American colonies were the transportation of convict soldiers to the

Caribbean during the Revolutionary and Napoleonic Wars and the dispatching of about 9,000 convicts to Bermuda between 1824 and 1863 to work on the construction of port facilities for the royal navy. After 1776 the British at first experimented with transportation to Africa before establishing a penal colony on the east coast of Australia. The first convicts arrived in New South Wales in 1788. Between that year and 1868 a total of 168,000 convicts were sent to New South Wales, Van Diemen's Land, and Western Australia, of whom 26,000 were women (Anderson & Maxwell-Stewart 2014).

The East India Company simultaneously established a network of penal colonies that operated in parallel to those in Australia. Between 1787 and 1942 an estimated 120,000 convicts, principally from India, were transported to a variety of different penal settlements in the Indian Ocean. These included Bencoolen, Penang, Malacca, Singapore, Mauritius, Tenasserim, Aden, and the Andaman Islands. Between 1615 and the Japanese occupation of the Andamans in 1942, at least 376,000 convicts were transported to colonies within the British Empire (Anderson & Maxwell-Stewart 2014).

The French experimented with the overseas use of convict labor from the 1550s on. While most French convicts were condemned to galley service in Marseilles, Brest, and Toulon, small numbers were transported to North America prior to the loss of New France in the Seven Years' War (Hardy 1966 & Moogk 1989). Thereafter, with the exception of a brief experimental use of transportation as a punishment for political offenders during the 1790s, convicts were primarily deployed as dock labor in metropolitan France (Redfield 2000). After the colonization of Algeria in 1830, convicts were again sent overseas, especially for service with the BILA. Following the 1848 revolution, penal colonies, or *bagnes*, for civilian convicts were established first in Algeria and then on a more permanent basis in French Guiana (O'Brien 1982; Spieler 2012). A third penal colony was established in New Caledonia in 1864, and until 1887 all European convicts were sent there, although prisoners convicted in French overseas colonies continued to be transported to Guiana (Merle 1995). After this date transportation from metropolitan France to Guiana resumed for serious offenders. Following the cessation of transportation to New Caledonia in 1897, all transportees, with the exception of prisoners conscripted into the BILA, were sent to Guiana (Toth 2006), which penal colony continued to operate until 1953. In total, at least 100,000 convicts were transported to French colonial *bagnes*, and a further 600,000 former prisoners were conscripted into penal units for military service in French colonies (Anderson & Maxwell-Stewart 2014).

The Dutch Republic experimented with sending convicts to Suriname in the seventeenth century but subsequently abandoned the policy for metropolitan, but not colonially convicted, offenders (Spierenburg 2015). The Dutch East India Company's base in Cape Town received several thousand convicts in the seventeenth and eighteenth centuries who had been convicted in Ceylon and the Dutch East Indies (Ward 2009).

Swedish courts sentenced a few convicts to transportation to North America and also sent condemned prisoners to labor in its Baltic colonies in the seventeenth century (Spierenburg 2007). The use of convict labor to colonize border zones was a practice that was also well established in Eastern Europe. While the Habsburgs delivered convicts to Venice and Genoa for galley service until their acquisition of the Port of

Naples in 1707, from the beginning of the seventeenth century onward they also used the labor of convicts in fortress construction along the militarized border with the Ottoman Empire. Following the loss of Naples in 1734, the flow of convict labor to border areas increased. Between 1744 and 1768 convicts, prostitutes, religious dissenters, and vagrants were deported via the Danube to the Banat of Timişoara, where they were subjected to penal labor. As with the pool tapped for Austrian galley service, the condemned were drawn from the length and breadth of Habsburg-controlled territories, including Brussels, Italy, Hungary, Croatia, and Slavonia, as well as Austria itself (Steiner 2015).

At times, property rights in prisoners were traded from one state to another. In the mid-1680s the French state attempted to purchase prison labor from the duke of Savoy to supply oarsmen for its galley fleet (Bamford 1956). In similar fashion Germanic states sold convicts to Italian city-states in the sixteenth and seventeenth centuries (Eltis 1993). In the early nineteenth century the Prussian government shipped a small number of convicts to the Gulf of Finland, where they were handed over to the Russians, who marched them 5,250 miles to the silver mines at Nerchinsk in Siberia (Evans 1998).

As the Prussian experiment suggests, the Russian *katorga* system was well developed by the early nineteenth century. Convicts were first transported to the Siberian frontier in 1582. Between 1692 and 1711 the flow was redirected to Azov on the Black Sea (Boeck 2008). Thereafter, *katorga* labor was used in the construction of St. Petersburg, Port Rogervik, and a number of other fortresses, particularly on the Baltic coast. From 1767 on, the Nerchinsk mining complex in Siberia became the main site of convict labor within the Russian Empire. The complex, which operated until the late 1860s, was an important producer of silver and lead. *Katorga* labor was also used in other Siberian industries including saltworks, distilling, and textile production (Gentes 2004). From 1870 to 1905 convicts were used to settle the island of Sakhalin, with some of them shipped by sea from Odessa (Stephen 1970). While it is estimated that 2 million Russians were exiled to Siberia prior to 1917, a much smaller number were sentenced to hard labor (Nicholas & Shergold 1988). If the ratio of exiles to *katorga* convicts in the period 1823–1860 was consistent throughout the entire period of forced relocation, somewhere in the region of 280,000 individuals were removed to penal colonies by the tsarist regime. Other estimates put the number at under 500,000. Of these, about 40,000 were sent to Sakhalin (Pearson & Marshall 1996).

IV. Transportation and the State

There were administrative reasons why publicly organized convict labor resurfaced in early modern Europe. While some medieval legal codes mention penal servitude, it was an option few polities had the funds or facilities to render viable. By the fifteenth century the emergence of centralized nation-states had provided the capacity to operate a system of judicial punishments that did more than merely execute offenders or mark or otherwise mutilate their bodies (Pike 1978). Galley service and transportation provided a means of extracting labor and simultaneously punishing the convicted without necessitating the commitment of large amounts of resources. While both required some central organization, the French established routes by which "chains" of convicts were delivered from regional courts to Marseilles, Toulon, and, later, Brest; the costs of such logistical operations were limited compared to the costs of establishing and maintaining a national penitentiary system (Eltis 1983; Bamford 1956), and they could be further reduced through collaboration with the private sector. In England (later Britain), France, Spain, and Portugal, the task of removing convicts from court to port was contracted out to merchant firms (Eltis 1993).

Colonial and galley penal servitude became common in the same period that some northern European states started to construct workhouses and "bridewells," or houses of correction—a form of punishment that from the mid-fifteenth century on was used to police the idle poor, including beggars and vagrants, as well as petty offenders. It is no coincidence that such institutions were pioneered by states that lacked ready access to seas suited to the maritime deployment of convict labor or overseas colonies. Like their maritime equivalents, workhouses were one of a range of early modern initiatives aimed at inculcating the habits of industry among marginalized members of society. Punishment became an exercise aimed at more than ensuring that the guilty paid a penalty for the offenses that they committed (Spierenburg 2015). The manner in which vagrants were frequently sent to the galleys or transported illustrates the extent to which these early modern modes of punishment were aimed at increasing labor participation rates (Coates 2001).

The use of work-oriented punishments was also justified on the grounds that it returned a public good. Thomas Moore, for example, argued that the use of convicts as "slave" labor was an appropriate penalty for a major crime, since it resulted in a greater benefit to society than execution (Blackburn 1997). The highly influential eighteenth-century jurist Beccaria made a similar point in 1764. He argued that the strongest deterrent to crime would be "the long and painful example of a man deprived of his freedom and become a beast of burden, repaying with his toil the society he has offended" (Sellin 1976, p. 66). Convict service was practical in that it provided a middle option between the extremes of execution and other punishments such as whipping and fining. In short, it was attractive since it was both financially and administratively viable.

Convict service can be broadly situated within the transition from punishments designed to underscore the power of the state through the public display and mutilation of the body of the offender to those based on broader prosecution processes. Yet while transportation provided a cost-effective method of punishing offenders *en masse*, it remained physical in nature. Additionally, at times it might still involve public mutilation and display. In France in the mid-1680s, for example, the punishment for desertion from the French army and navy was commuted from death to galley service, although the reprieved were ordered to have their noses and ears cut off and were branded on each cheek with a *fleur-de-lis* (Bamford 1956). As late as the nineteenth century Russian convicts were branded with a Cyrillic "C" on one cheek, a "o" on the forehead, and a "K" on the other cheek—marking them out as having been sentenced to *katorga* (Gentes 2005), while Indian convicts transported by the British were forcibly tattooed with their crimes on their foreheads (Anderson 2004).

The experience of transported convicts differed from that of those sentenced to serve time in prisons and penitentiaries in that labor services were always required of convicts. Most transported felons spent little time "behind bars"—Britain's Australian penal colonies, for example, were likened to a panopticon without walls. The reliance on the physical extraction of labor and the ganging of prisoners was frequently contrasted with penitentiary-based systems of punishment that evolved from the late eighteenth century on. Designed to impact upon the prisoners' minds rather than their bodies, the latter used architecture to separate offenders in a manner that set the penitentiary system at odds with the colonial deployment of convict labor. British and American treadmills, for example, were rarely connected to grinding mechanisms, in contrast to those installed in convict Australia. While the labor that prisoners were ordered to perform in metropolitan penitentiaries was usually futile in that it produced nothing beyond serving as a mechanism to discipline convict bodies, in the colonies convicts undergoing punishment continued to cut timber, crush aggregate, and grind wheat into flour (Maxwell-Stewart 2008).

All transportation systems encountered problems with the varying extent to which prisoners could be put to productive labor. Women, the very young and very old, and those who were physically impaired were less desirable as labor commodities than the fit and skilled. Sometimes the capacity of the individual to perform labor impacted upon sentencing outcomes. A French circular of 1672, for example, recommended that no criminal over the age of fifty-five be sent to serve in the galleys unless he or she had the "necessary health" (Bamford 1956). Transportation systems that relied on the private sector had to provide merchants with a subsidy in order to ensure that all who were condemned to colonial service were transported regardless of their sex, age, skill, or ability (Ekirch 1987). Even in state-run systems colonial and metropolitan authorities often argued about the efficacy of transporting prisoners with physical impairments. While all convicts shipped to Britain's Antipodean penal colonies were supposed to be sufficiently fit to survive the voyage, colonial administrators argued that they should also be capable of performing labor and continually railed at the number who were landed who were found to be missing limbs or suffering from other physical impairments (Earnshaw 1995).

Other mechanisms were used to position convicts within the colonial labor market. The minimum term that a British convict could be sentenced to transportation for was seven years. This was fixed not for judicial reasons, but to ensure that convicts were salable commodities. A seven-year sentence was considerably longer than the mean length of contract signed by eighteenth-century transatlantic indentured servants. While convicts' prior criminal record made them less attractive to colonial buyers, such disadvantages could be offset by the additional years they were bound to serve. Throughout the nineteenth century convicts sentenced in British and Irish courts continued to be subjected to longer terms than prisoners who received metropolitan custodial sentences in order to maximize the benefits that accrued from transportation (Maxwell-Stewart 2010).

All systems of exploitation are underpinned by ideologies that serve to rationalize the process by which labor is extracted. The knowledge that transported workers had been convicted by a court served to justify both the manner in which they were worked without wages and the high death rates to which they were often exposed as a result of the process of forced relocation. In this sense, "convictism" served the same purpose as plantation racism. What marked prisoners out was not the color of their skin but their collective guilt. Forcing convicts to work could be construed as a public good in that it ensured that they both paid for their crimes and simultaneously acquired the habits of industry. Furthermore, any attempt to resist the process of forced labor extraction merely confirmed their status as untrustworthy criminals (Maxwell-Stewart 2007).

Although for all of these reasons convicts were a logical source of labor for colonial projects, the manner in which they were worked did not always mesh with the objectives of metropolitan judicial systems. Anti-transportationists argued that the colonial deployment of convict labor constituted an ineffective punishment in that the level of pain extracted from the body of each prisoner did not always match the severity of the offense for which he or she had been transported. In other words, those who had formerly worked as quarrymen were more likely to be ordered to undertake work in the colonies that exposed them to greater exertion and risk of death than were prisoners who had clerical skills, regardless of the nature of the offense for which each had originally been transported. Many European penal reformers likened transportation to slavery for this reason. They also argued that crude labor extraction techniques, especially flogging, were ill calculated to make offenders better members of society.

A related concern was that penal transportation failed to effectively isolate offenders. This was especially the case when convicts were deployed *en masse* as ganged labor in construction, mining, timber felling, and mono-cultivation. Barrack arrangements in which large numbers of prisoners were locked up at night but left otherwise unsupervised were subject to particular criticism. As the notion that crime was akin to a disease took hold over the course of the nineteenth century, transportation was often characterized as an outmoded practice that reinforced the bestial qualities of prisoners and inhibited the application of effective treatments designed to reduce reoffending (McKenzie 2004).

Metropolitan opponents of transportation argued that it was also expensive, since the emphasis on labor exploitation led to a failure of convicts to reform. Jeremy Bentham, a particularly vocal opponent, argued for an alternative system based on a series of color-coded national penitentiaries, to be painted white for debtors, blue for lesser offenders, and black for "lifers" (Kerr 1988). Despite Bentham's arguments, the considerable cost involved in this scheme meant that, with the exception of the United States, penitentiaries were only slowly adopted. Transportation remained a favored option because it was cheap compared to confinement in a purpose-built institution.

As pressure mounted from metropolitan penal reformers to bring transportation systems in line with the precepts of the penitentiary, physical punishments such as flogging were increasingly replaced with solitary confinement. During the course of the nineteenth century, cellular accommodation facilities that separated convicts from one another at night were also constructed in several penal colonies, including New South Wales, Van Diemen's Land, Norfolk Island, the Andaman Islands, and Angola. These and other reforms were expensive, and their introduction often led to acrimonious exchanges between colonial and metropolitan administrations about who was responsible for the additional costs. They also tended to blunt the colonial utility of transportation by restricting private-sector access to convict labor and increasing overheads.

V. Transportation and Colonial Policy

One of the main advantages of penal transportation was that it provided a means of addressing colonial labor shortages. Oceanic travel in the age of sailing was dangerous, as were the disease risks associated with relocation to a distant shore. Transportation provided a means of supplying overseas colonies with a source of cheap, pliable labor. Furthermore, those convicts who survived until the end of their sentence could become settlers, thus helping to populate frontier regions. In the absence of transportation and associated systems of unfree labor migration, it is difficult to envisage how early modern European states could have attracted migrants to their New World possessions, since limited labor resources and associated high wage rates are likely to have stifled colonial growth (Nicholas 1988).

In this sense, convicts, along with slaves and indentured workers, could be seen as the shock troops of colonialism. While their presence was particularly necessary during the initial stages of colonial development, local opposition to convict transportation was always likely to increase as the expansion of overseas colonies and reductions in shipping costs provided greater opportunities for working-class migration. As a result, colonial labor markets tended to tighten as colonies developed. As they did so, transportation became increasingly unpopular with free workers because cheap convict labor undercut colonial wage rates (Christopher & Maxwell-Stewart 2013).

For this reason transportation systems tended to have a limited life, although it might be argued that at the point at which competition was sufficient to attract organized colonial working-class opposition, they had done their job. The exceptions to this rule were colonies that remained unpopular as settler destinations, largely because of the continued health risks associated with migration. It is no coincidence that penal transportation to Portuguese Angola, French Guiana, and the British Andaman Islands—all of which had high death rates—persisted into the twentieth century, whereas the supply of convict labor to the Australian penal colonies did not.

The reliance on colonial labor extraction opened transportation systems up to the charge that they were a form of slavery. While transportation was initiated by state action, it frequently involved the sale of the condemned. As a result, many convicts worked for private masters who either legally owned them until their sentence expired or leased convict labor from the state for shorter periods of time. Usually, however, the power that masters held over convicts was more circumscribed than the power that they held over slaves (Eltis 1993). Thus, in Australia private masters did not have the authority to physically chastise convicts. They could, however, bring a charge against a convict servant who—if pronounced guilty by a magistrates' bench—might be sentenced to an array of punishments, including flogging (Hirst 1983).

Despite these legal differences, the experience of being a convict might have been worse than that of a slave. Slaves were expensive. As the state did not have to purchase convicts, they were sometimes regarded as a cheap alternative. Convict labor might even be seen as a byproduct of the operation of the judicial system. As such, prisoners were relatively expendable. Thus, the Spanish replaced slave labor used to construct harbor defenses in San Juan and Havana with labor from convicts, since—in the face of high death rates— slave replacement costs were prohibitive (Pike 1978). In the seventeenth century the French galley fleet came to rely increasingly on convicts, as opposed to slaves, for similar reasons. Where "Turkish" slaves were retained, it was to perform specific skilled tasks— for example, to serve as first oarsmen and therefore set the pace and control timing of the stroke, with the remaining power being delivered by unskilled convicts (Bamford 1956).

The punishments to which slaves were subjected may have been horrific, but those punishments were calculated to increase productivity. As the loss of a slave had serious financial consequences, masters thought twice about applying sanctions that crippled or maimed expensive property or in other ways reduced outputs. At times, however, it was in the interests of the state to make an example of the convicted. Thus, in some transportation systems the delivery of pain might be seen as an output in its own right. In this sense "penal labor" differed from other forms of unfreedom. In both the Roman Empire and the British Caribbean, slaves were at times sentenced to penal servitude as a punishment—a clear indication that convict status was thought to worsen the condition of the slave (Groen-Vallinga & Tacoma 2015; Paton 2001). Convicts in Australia, for example, could be ordered to labor using tools that were heavier than those required to efficiently perform the task at hand. In most circumstances, this would make no sense. In a system calculated to produce a measure of pain, it did (Evans & Thorpe 1992).

The extent to which work was organized so as to be painful varied within penal colonies. In Portuguese Angola, the fortress of São Pedro da Barra operated a site of secondary punishment—a place that had previously been used as a barracoon for slaves awaiting shipment to Brazil (Coates 2013). Prisoners were only sent there if their conduct elsewhere had proved problematic. In Australia, labor was graded. Farmwork was considered to be relatively benign, while work in road gangs, chain gangs, penal stations, and houses of correction was generally reserved for convicts who had been sentenced to those locations by a magistrates' bench. The difference in severity between these labor regimes was sufficient to impact upon death rates. The risk of death for a male convict in a penal station punishment gang, for example, was four times that for a prisoner working in the private sector (Maxwell-Stewart 2012).

Many transportation systems directed convict labor to different colonies depending on the perceived severity of the offense. In the Portuguese system distant locations associated with high European mortality rates were reserved for serious offenders. Thus, minor offenders might be sentenced to forced labor within Portugal itself, while major offenders might be transported to Goa in India and "unpardonable" offenders to Angola or galley service (Coates 2015). In Britain some transportees served their time in hulks and were never sent overseas; others were removed to Bermuda or Gibraltar for the term of their sentence before being repatriated; still others, especially those sentenced to terms longer than seven years, were removed to the penal colonies in Australia with no prospect of a state-assisted return (Shaw 1971).

Different gradations of punishment were applied to those convicted in colonial juris-dictions. A court in colonial Brazil might sentence a minor offender to be transported to Bahia for two years, to Sacramento for five years, and to Angola for life. A paral-lel Indian Ocean system also operated in which convicts sentenced in Goa were dis-patched to Diu for minor offences, Sri Lanka for serious offenses, and Mozambique Island or distant Timor for an unpardonable offense (Coates 2015).

Many European transportation systems employed different practices for colonial and metropolitan subject populations. The East India Company and later the British government in India sentenced European soldiers serving in the subcontinent to trans-portation to Australia, while indigenous convicts were dispatched to a variety of other penal colonies in the Indian Ocean. Between 1864 and 1887 the French penal colony in Guiana was reserved for colonial subject peoples from North and West Africa and Indochina, while convicts from metropolitan France were sent to the more benign New Caledonia (Anderson 2009). From 1887 to 1897 convicts convicted in France of seri-ous offenses could be transported to Guiana (Alfred Dreyfus being the most famous example), but even when convicts from metropolitan and colonial areas were sent to the same penal colony, they were often segregated. In Luanda, male European con-victs were placed in their own companies, while those from the Atlantic colonies of Cape Verde, Guiné, São Tomé, and Mozambique were organized and worked separately (Coates 2013).

All European transportation systems developed complex flows of convicts from colony to colony. As such, they were important tools for policing subject populations. Indigenous resistance to the imposition of colonial rule could result in enforced relo-cation to other imperial frontiers—a process that effectively criminalized opposition to imperial order. The Spanish, for example, transported Apache resistors to Havana to work in fortress construction, and the British sent Khoi and Maori convicts to the Australian penal colonies (Moorhead 1975; Harman 2012). The importance of trans-portation to the maintenance of imperial rule is aptly illustrated by the distribution of metropolitan and colonially convicted convicts shipped to British penal colonies. In the period 1615–1942, more transported convicts were convicted in courts located out-side of Britain than were sentenced in England, Scotland, and Wales together.

Notwithstanding this, one of the things that set transportation apart from other unfree labor systems was the substantial number of convicts who were European in origin. The use of white unfree labor threatened at times to undermine the color bar. By the second half of the sixteenth century it was unusual for British and Irish convicts to be worked alongside slave labor. Where this did occur, Europeans tended to be employed as overseers or skilled artisans, rather than as fieldhands. Attempts by Britain to transport convicts to West African forts in the late eighteenth century were opposed by the Company of Merchants Trading out of Africa on the grounds that convict labor would undermine European authority by demonstrating that whites could be enslaved as well as Africans. Similar fears derailed an attempt in 1784–1785 to send convicts to work alongside slaves in the British settlement in Honduras. One of the reasons why convicts were sent to Australia was that it was difficult to deploy an unfree labor force that was predominantly European in the late eighteenth-century Atlantic and Indian Ocean worlds (Christopher & Maxwell-Stewart 2013).

CONCLUSION

At least 970,000 convicts were used as colonial labor by the Western empires in the period from 1415 to 1954, and that number is substantially higher if criminals forcibly conscripted into French BILA units are included in the total. Transported convicts made up 7 percent of the 14.5 million unfree migrants deployed as colonial labor by Europeans between the fifteenth and twentieth centuries. While the number of convicts was dwarfed by the volume of slaves shipped to the New World, convict transportation proved to be a more durable practice. It both pre- and postdated the transatlantic slave trade, lasting until the mid-twentieth century. Moreover, while there has been a tendency in the literature to view penal transportation as a discrete practice, flows of convict, slave, and indentured workers were often intertwined. Convict soldiers were used to garrison slave forts, and in some colonies convicts replaced slave labor. On other occasions, slaves were converted into convicts through the imposition of a court sentence.

While penal transportation had a limited life expectancy in colonies that attracted settler migrants (notably British colonial North America, Brazil, New Spain, and Australia), it proved a more durable institution in locations where high European death rates or other environmental factors restricted free migration (e.g., Angola, Guiana, Andaman Islands, Siberia). Over time transportation came under attack from penal reformers as the emphasis on labor extraction put it at odds with penitentiary-based systems of punishment. Many transportation systems attempted to adopt regulations that classified and separated convicts in line with the precepts of the penitentiary in order to make the colonial practice more acceptable to its metropolitan critics. While these reforms tended to increase the costs associated with transportation, the practice remained popular for two reasons. First, the new imperialist spirit that characterized the scramble for colonial possessions from the mid-nineteenth century on led to a substantial increase in Portuguese transportation to Luanda; French transportation to

Algeria, New Caledonia, and Guiana; and Russian transportation to Sakhalin (Coates 2013). Second, transportation provided European states with the ability to control subject populations by removing colonial offenders from one colony to another. Rather than being discontinued because it was out of step with metropolitan judicial thinking, most European transportation systems were brought to a close as a result of colonial opposition.

References

Adair, E. R. 1920. "English Galleys in the Sixteenth Century." *English Historical Review* 35 (140): 497–512.

Anderson, Clare. 2004. *Legible Bodies: Race, Criminality and Colonialism in South East*. Oxford: Berg.

Anderson, Clare. 2009. "'Weel about and Turn about and Do Jis So, Eb'ry Time I Weel about and Jump Jim Crow': Dancing on the Margins of the Indian Ocean." In *Fringes of Empire: Peoples, Places, and Spaces in Colonial India*, ed. Sameetah Agha & Elizabeth Kolsky, 169–87. Oxford: Oxford University Press.

Anderson, Clare, & Hamish Maxwell-Stewart. 2014. "Convict Labour and the Western Empires." In *Routledge History of Western Empires*, ed. Robert Aldrich & Kirsten McKenzie, 102–17. Abingdon, UK: Routledge.

Atkinson, Alan. 1994. "The Free-Born Englishman Transported: Convict Rights as a Measure of Eighteenth-Century Empire." *Past and Present* 144:88–115.

Aylmer, G. E. 1999. "Slavery under Charles II: The Mediterranean and Tangier." *English Historical Review* 14 (456): 378–88.

Bamford, Paul Walden. 1956. "The Procurement of Oarsmen for French Galleys, 1660–1748." *American Historical Review* 65 (1): 31–48.

Beer, Daniel. 2013. "Decembrists, Rebels, Martyrs in Siberian Exile: The 'Zerentui Conspiracy' of 1828 and the Fashioning of a Revolutionary Genealogy." *Slavic Review* 72 (3): 528–51.

Bense, Judith. 2004. "Presidios of the Northern Spanish Borderlands." *Historical Archaeology* 38 (3): 1–5.

Benton, Lauren. 2000. "The Legal Regime of the South Atlantic World, 1400–1750: Jurisdictional Complexity as Institutional Order." *Journal of World History* 11 (1): 27–56.

Blackburn, Robin. 1997. "The Old World Background to European Colonial Slavery." *William and Mary Quarterly* 54 (1): 65–102.

Boeck, Brian J. 2008. "When Peter I Was Forced to Settle for Less: Coerced Labour and Resistance in a Failed Russian Colony (1695–1711)." *Journal of Modern History* 80 (3): 485–514.

Braudel, Ferdinand. 1995. *The Mediterranean and the Mediterranean World in the Age of Phillip II*. Berkeley: University of California Press.

Christopher, Emma, & Hamish Maxwell-Stewart. 2013. "Convict Transportation in Global Context c. 1700–1788." In *Cambridge History of Australia*, Vol. 1, ed. Alison Bashford & Stuart McIntyre, 68–90. Cambridge: Cambridge University Press.

Coates, Timothy. 2001. *Convicts and Orphans: Forced and State-Sponsored Colonizers in the Portuguese Empire, 1550–1755*. Stanford, CA: Stanford University Press.

Coates, Timothy. 2013. *Convict Labor in the Portuguese Empire, 1740–1932: Redefining the Empire with Forced Labor and New Imperialism*. Leiden, The Netherlands: Brill.

Coates, Timothy. 2015. "The Long View of Convict Labour in the Portuguese Empire, 1415–1932." In *Global Convict Labour*, ed. Christian G. De Vito & Alex Lichtenstein, 144–67. Leiden, The Netherlands: Brill.

Cope, R. L. 1995. "Written in Characters of Blood? The Reign of King Cetshwayo ka Mpande 1872–9." *Journal of African History* 36 (2): 247–69.

Curtin, Philip D. 1989. *Death by Migration: Europe's Encounter with the Tropical World in the Nineteenth Century*. Cambridge: Cambridge University Press.

De Vito, Christian, & Alex Lichtenstein, eds. 2015. *Global Convict Labour*. Leiden, The Netherlands: Brill.

Earnshaw, Beverly. 1995. "The Lame, the Blind, the Mad, the Malingerers: Sick and Disabled Convicts Within the Colonial Community." *Journal of the Royal Australian Historical Society* 81:52–38.

Ekirch, Roger. 1987. *Bound for America: The Transportation of British Convicts to the Colonies, 1718–1775*. Oxford: Clarendon Press.

Eltis, David. 1993. "Europeans and the Rise and Fall of African Slavery in the Americas: An Interpretation." *American Historical Review* 98 (5): 1399–423.

Evans, Richard J. 1998. *Tales from the German Underworld: Crime and Punishment in the 19th Century*. New Haven, CT: Yale University Press.

Evans, Raymond, & William Thorpe. 1992. "Power, Punishment and Penal Labour: Convict Workers and Moreton Bay." *Australian Historical Studies* 22 (89): 90–111.

Fenoaltea, Stefano. 1984. "Slavery and Supervision in Comparative Perspective: A Model." *Journal of Economic History* 34 (3): 642–43.

Frost, Lucy. 2012. *Abandoned Women: Scottish Convicts Exiled Beyond the Seas*. Sydney: Allen & Unwin.

Gentes, Andrew. 2004. "Katorga, Penal Labour and Tsarist Siberia." *Australian Slavonic and East European Studies* 18 (1–2): 41–61.

Gentes, Andrew. 2005. "Katorga, Penal Labour and Tsarist Russia." In *The Siberian Saga: A History of Russia's Wild East*, ed. Eva-Maria Stolberg, 73–85. Bern, Switzerland: Peter Lang.

Groen-Vallinga, M. J., & L. E. Tacoma. 2015. "Contextualising Condemnation to Hard Labour in the Roman Empire." In *Global Convict Labour*, ed. Christian G. De Vito & Alex Lichtenstein, 49–78. Leiden, The Netherlands: Brill.

Hardy, James D., Jr. 1966. "The Transportation of Convicts to Colonial Louisiana." *Louisiana History* 7 (3): 707–20.

Harman, Kristyn. 2012. *Aboriginal Convicts: Australian, Khoisan and Maori Exiles*. Sydney: University of New South Wales Press.

Hirst, John. 1983. *Convict Society and Its Enemies*. Sydney: Allen & Unwin.

Jeppesen, Jennie. 2014. "'To Serve Longer According to Law': The Chattel-Like Status of Convict Servants in Virginia." In *Order and Civility in the Early Modern Chesapeake*, ed. Deb Myers & Melanie Perreault, 193–206. Lanham, MD: Lexington Books.

Kalifa, Dominique. 2009. *Biribi: Les Bagnes Coloniaux de l'Armée Française*. Paris: Librairie Académique Perrin.

Kerr, Joan. 1988. *Out of Sight, Out of Mind: Australia's Places of Confinement*. Sydney: National Trust of Australia.

Konstam, Angus. 2002. *Renaissance War Galley, 1470–1590*. Oxford: Osprey.

Libourel, Jan M. 1973. "Galley Slaves in the Second Punic War." *Classical Philology* 68 (2): 116–19.

Mawson, Stephanie. 2013. "Unruly Plebeians and the Forzado System: Convict Transportation Between New Spain and the Philippines During the Seventeenth Century." *Revista de Indias* 73 (259): 693–730.

Maxwell-Stewart, Hamish. 2007. "'Like Poor Galley Slaves': Slavery and Convict Transportation." In *Legacies of Slavery: Comparative Perspectives*, ed. Marie Suzette Fernandes Dias, 48–61. Newcastle, UK: Cambridge Scholars Publishing.

Maxwell-Stewart, Hamish. 2008. *Closing Hell's Gates: The Death of a Convict Station*. Sydney: Allen & Unwin.

Maxwell-Stewart, Hamish. 2010. "Convict Transportation from Britain and Ireland, 1615–1870." *History Compass* 6 (3): 1–19.

Maxwell-Stewart, Hamish. 2012. "Isles of the Dead: Convict Death Rates in Comparative Perspective." *Historic Environment* 24 (3): 26–34.

McKenzie, Kirsten. 2004. *Scandal in the Colonies: Sydney and Cape Town, 1820–1850*. Melbourne: Melbourne University Press.

Merle, Isabelle. 1995. *Expériences coloniales: La Nouvelle-Calédonie, 1853–1920*. Paris: Belin Editions.

Moogk, P. N. 1989. "Reluctant Exiles: Emigrants from France in Canada before 1760." *William and Mary Quarterly* 46 (3): 463–505.

Moorhead, Max L. 1975. "Deportation of Hostile Apaches: The Policy and Practice." *Arizona and the West* 17 (3): 205–20.

Morgan, Gwenda, & Peter Rushton. 2004. *Eighteenth-Century Criminal Transportation: The Formation of the Criminal Atlantic*. Basingstoke, UK: Palgrave Macmillan.

Nicholas, Stephen. 1988. "The Convict Labour Market." In *Convict Workers: Reinterpreting Australia's Past*, ed. Stephen Nicholas, 111–26. Cambridge: Cambridge University Press.

Nicholas, Stephen, & Peter Shergold. 1988. "Transportation as Global Migration." In *Convict Workers: Reinterpreting Australia's Past*, ed. Stephen Nicholas, 28–39. Cambridge: Cambridge University Press.

O'Brien, Patricia. 1982. *The Promise of Punishment: Prisons in Nineteenth-Century France*. Princeton, NJ: Princeton University Press.

O'Callaghan, Sean. 2000. *To Hell or Barbados: The Ethnic Cleansing of Ireland*. Dublin: Brandon Books.

Paton, Diana. 2001. "Crime and the Bodies of Slaves in Eighteenth-Century Jamaica." *Journal of Social History* 34 (4): 923–54.

Pearson, Michael, & Duncan Marshall. 1996. "Study of World Heritage Values, Convict Places." Department of the Environment, Sport and Territories, Commonwealth Government of Australia.

Pike, Ruth. 1978. "Penal Servitude in the Spanish Empire: Presidio Labor in the Eighteenth Century." *Hispanic American Historical Review* 58 (1): 21–40.

Redfield, Peter. 2000. *Space in the Tropics: From Convicts to Rockets in French Guiana*. Berkeley: University of California Press.

Rio, Alice. 2015. "Penal Enslavement in the Early Middle Ages." In *Global Convict Labour*, ed. Christian G. De Vito & Alex Lichtenstein, 79–107. Leiden, The Netherlands: Brill.

Sellin, Johan. 1976. *Slavery and the Penal System*. Amsterdam: Elsevier.

Shaw, Alan G. L. 1971. *Convicts and the Colonies*. London: Faber & Faber.

Spieler, Miranda. 2012. *Empire and Underworld: Captivity in French Guiana*. Harvard, MA: Harvard University Press.

Spierenburg, Pieter. 2007. *The Prison Experience: Disciplinary Institutions and Their Inmates in Early Modern Europe*. Amsterdam: Amsterdam University Press.

Spierenburg, Pieter. 2015. "Prison and Convict Labour in Early Modern Europe." In *Global Convict Labour*, ed. Christian G. De Vito & Alex Lichtenstein, 108–25. Leiden, The Netherlands: Brill.

Steiner, Stephan. 2015. "'An Austrian Cayenne': Convict Labour and Deportation in the Early Modern Habsburg Empire." In *Global Convict Labour*, ed. Christian G. De Vito & Alex Lichtenstein, 126–43. Leiden, The Netherlands: Brill.

Stephen, J. J. 1970. "Sakhalin Island: Soviet Outpost in Northeast Asia." *Asian Survey* 10 (12): 1090–100.

Toth, Stephen. 2006. *Beyond Papillon: The French Overseas Penal Colonies, 1854–1952*. Lincoln: University of Nebraska Press.

Ward, Kerry. 2009. *Networks of Empire: Forced Migration in the Dutch East India Company*. Cambridge: Cambridge University Press.

Wilbur, C. Martin. 1943. "Industrial Slavery in China During the Former Han Dynasty (206 B.C.–A.D. 25)." *Journal of Economic History* 3 (1): 56–69.

....

CHAPTER 33

THE MAD, THE BAD AND THE PAUPER: HELP AND CONTROL IN EARLY MODERN CARCERAL INSTITUTIONS

....

SANDRA SCICLUNA

INTRODUCTION

....

THIS essay looks at institutions of confinement in the seventeenth and eighteenth centuries, including asylums, workhouses, and hospitals. Most of the illustrations are taken from research done on relevant documents of the time as well as criticism of these institutions both in the nineteenth century, when there was widespread reform in carceral institutions and by modern authors who have studied this period. When analyzing the development of punishment and confinement, one can infer four theoretical perspectives (Scicluna 2004). Durkheim contends that confinement exists to unite society (Walker 1991). Spierenburg (1984), on the other hand, writes that it is the changes in society that bring about change in confinement, moving from the more brutal to a gentler form of punishment. Foucault (1977) believes that confinement serves as a means to control the population, while Marxist theorists like Rusche and Kirchheimer (1939) see confinement as serving to control conflict in society.

The seventeenth century saw the birth of carceral institutions or hospitals to control the mad, the sick, or any person deemed to need control or reform. Earlier, the sixteenth century saw a gradual shift in thinking about the poor. The enactment of the poor laws in England (1601) and the Poor Relief Act in 1662 led to the establishment of the "workhouse," as poverty, which was linked first to morality and later to crime (Freeman 2009) was seen as a result of laziness. Prisons tried to correct "evil conduct," "laziness," and "disreputable behaviour" (Spierenburg 1984, p. 58) rather than actual crime. As crime was seen as being caused by the poor, it was believed that it was possible to train and educate them out of their criminality. It was in this context that we see the rise of carceral institutions such as the Bridewell and Bedlam houses in Britain and most British colonies, the *Zuchthäuser* in Germany, and the *hôpitaux généraux* in France. This essay will discuss the rise and fall of these institutions, the problems they faced, and the development of carceral institutions in the eighteenth Century, looking at the treatment of women, children, debtors, and the poor. Section I will look at the role of the Inquisition in the development of prisons, followed by sections addressing the house of corrections, the workhouse, and country jails. We will conclude by looking at the treatment of women. In these discussions we will also take a snapshot view of what was happening in Malta, a small island in the middle of the Mediterranean. Governed by a number of foreign powers, which have experimented on or brought over their ideas to the island, Malta is an ideal place to examine, constituting almost a microcosm of the world. During the period under discussion, the Maltese islands were ruled by the Knights of St. John. In May 1530, Charles V of Spain, had given Malta and Gozo to the Order of Saint John; in return, the knights, who were usually the younger sons of nobles from around Europe, pledged to protect Christianity in the region and to give a falcon to the king every year as well as the right to nominate the bishop of Malta. During this time Malta had three powers: the knights, the bishop, and the inquisitor. The knights remained in Malta until 1798, at which time they were replaced by Napoleon's French troops. The French stay was short lived, with the English being invited over by the Maltese in 1800. These political shifts make Malta a crossroad of powers, religion, and culture, with a context of confinement initially more in line with that of Catholic European countries, such as Italy and France, that later (from the 1800s on) was influenced largely by the British, with the construction of a Pentonville-style prison for confinement.

It is only from the mid-1980s on that we find authors such as Freedman (1984), Rafter (1985; 1992), Strange (1985), and later Zedner (1991; 1994) and Garland (1990) giving attention to the history of imprisonment. In the sixteenth and seventeenth centuries, men and women were treated in almost the same manner. At the end of the seventeenth century this started gradually to change. Although still apparently under the same regime, in reality the two groups began to be treated differently—women were often seen as needing care and instruction and were therefore treated according to care principles, while men were seen as needing control and discipline and therefore were treated under a strict regime of control. Garland (1990) maintains that it was only from the eighteenth century on that females started being treated more leniently. People's attitudes changed from seeing women as creatures of the devil in the seventeenth century to seeing them as weaker vessels in need of help and protection in the nineteenth century.

I. The Inquisition

In Catholic countries, we see the birth of the Inquisition as the official stand of the Roman Catholic Church against the Protestant reform of 1517. The Inquisition's main role was to protect the Catholic Church from heresy, sexual crimes (such as bigamy and incest), and the practice of magic (Gambin 2004), and it exerted an overarching authority over the governing authorities and local churches. The time of the Inquisition is often portrayed as a period of unmentionable torture, with films portraying people being tortured to death or burned at the stake. However, it was also the time of the separation of men from women, first time offenders from recidivists, and children from older prisoners.

The Inquisitor's Prison in Malta was a place where male and female prisoners were separated. When in 1571 Monseigneur Pietro Dusina arrived as the first general inquisitor of Malta, the first thing he did was to repair the prison. At the time of his arrival, seven ground-floor rooms were used for male prisoners, while women were kept in a single room on the first floor. Three of the ground-floor rooms were described as being uninhabitable by the ministers of the tribunal because they had no windows, were damp, and in general were in a deplorable state (Gambin 2004). In the mid-seventeenth century Inquisitor Giovanni Battista Gori Pannellini ordered the construction of seven cells, with three overlooking the streets via high windows and four smaller cells overlooking the central courtyard. The emphasis was on the sturdy construction of the walls to prevent prisoners from escaping (Gambin 2004). Persons could be detained for punishment, for unruly behavior, pending trial, or because they were waiting for more proof. The prison complex was divided into two sections. Those detained for unruly behaviour were kept in the secret part of the prison, while those who had committed a crime were detained in the public section. The aim behind imprisonment was to help the accused concentrate on his or her guilt and erroneous behavior, as this was perceived as necessary to s the reformation process. After the age of the Enlightenment, during the seventeenth century, the idea of criminals possessing free will began to change. Crime began to be seen as an illness that could be cured; prisoners were seen as ill and in need of hospitalization. This led to the creation of hospitals and workhouses where people were kept indeterminately, until they were deemed cured and their probability for law-abiding behavior increased (Walker 1991). Such a shift was linked to changes in culture as well. The Enlightenment brought with it philosophers (such as Voltaire, Beccaria, and Bentham) who were ready to speak out against inhumane punishment. This in turn led to social movements that condemned cruelty and violence, and insisted on changes to confinement to diminish the suffering of the less fortunate (Pratt 2002). Spierenburg (1998) also sees the evolution of punishment as signifying changes in society, with the rise of the belief that people with low morals and those who did not adhere to family discipline needed to be sent to a place to forcefully change their behavior. Spierenburg's argument is influenced by Elias's (1939) theory of a civilization process, which argues that change is brought about by a cultural shift or increased sensibilities (Elias 1939; Spierenburg 1984; Spierenburg 1998; Beattie 1984; Platt 2002, p. 9). By the word "civilization," Elias does not intend to say that the present is better than the past, but merely to documents facts, showing that by the nineteenth century society had become reluctant to accept punishment of offenders in the form of violence or torture. Confinement became much more acceptable, with offenders being dealt with behind closed doors (Garland 1990).

Cassar (2000) writes about a case of witchcraft during the period of the Inquisition in Malta. Sulpitia de Lango, a former prostitute; her daughter Sperantia, who was a courtesan; Violante Vergonte, another former prostitute; and her grandson, Cesare Passalacqua, who was the son of a knight named Fra Jabobo Fiot, were all accused of witchcraft. The story goes that Sulpitia wanted to secure a rich knight for her daughter and therefore enlisted the help of her friend Violante, who owned a periwinkle plant, to help her in the magical rite. As the women did not know how to read, they enlisted Cesare's help during the ritual, which included the saying of nine masses. In the course of the act, Sulpitia was seen depositing the periwinkles under the altar of the most prominent church of the Order of St. John in Valletta. She was caught when leaving the church, which resulted in all four being arrested, tortured, and sentenced by the Inquisition tribunal (Cassar 2000). The four were handed down different sentences. Cesare and Sperantia's sentence was read privately: Cesare was exiled for a year (although he later petitioned for pardon, and his exile was changed into a fine), and Sperantia was fined 250 *scudi*. Violante and Sulpitia, in contrast, were condemned in front of a large congregation. Violante was publicly flogged in the streets of Vittoriosa, while Sulpitia, who also received a flogging, was additionally condemned to eight years in prison, as she had already been found guilty of performing magic rituals twice. Nevertheless, Sulpitia was released after two years for good behavior and was allowed to return home. After another three years she was allowed to move around the island.

This case shows that the Inquisition was not as harsh as one would think. Sulpitia's case shows a woman surviving in any manner that she could. To a certain extent it does show differential treatment of offenders, but it also shows a sense of justice. The two elder women were treated more severely because they were recidivists, while the younger offenders were treated more leniently—although one does question whether this judgment was influenced by the fact that Sperantia was a young and popular courtesan and Cesare was the son of a knight. The public display of punishment illustrates the desire of the authorities to give the population a spectacle, perhaps to divert their attention from the hardships that they were undergoing (Rusche & Kirchheimer 1939). Marxist authors maintain that during the Middle Ages, attracting the attention of the masses to witches, criminals, or outsiders deliberately diverted individuals from thinking about their plight and economic hardships to thinking about the spectacle they were witnessing and morality. They contend that it was the surplus in the labor market that allowed the authorities to regard the lives of the poor as useless, as something that could be used to distract the rest of the population (Bonnici 1993). However, another explanation could be that given by Foucault in *Discipline and Punishment* (1977), in which he maintains that punishment was intended to control the masses from revolting against the governing power.

Although women were condemned to prison sentences during the Inquisition, they rarely spent time in prison. Women's sentences were often commuted to community sentences, with some imprisoned in their homes and others condemned to stay in their city. This difference in treatment was a result of the detrimental effects that a prison

sentence often had on women's health, as well as the practical consideration that sometimes there was not enough space to keep women at the Inquisitor's Prison.

Although the Inquisition insisted that prisoners should be separated according to age,
sex, and social conditions, this was a far cry from reality. It wasn't until the eighteenth
century that this type of treatment came into effect (Johnston 2000). Sometimes prisoners were condemned to work periods of service in the community. Men were often
given some form of hard labor, including rowing on the galleys, while women were
given easier work, such as nursing the sick (Gambin 2004). However, the most common forms of punishment were banishment and fines, together with the development
of an intermediate sanction called bondage, which could take four basic forms: rowing
in the galleys, performing public work, imprisonment with forced labor, or transportation to a colony. Prisons in the sixteenth century were "industries" in which prisoners
were forced to perform "hard labor" in order to reform themselves (Spierenburg 1984).
Work bondage, which became very popular starting in the 1700s, was first established
in London in 1555, with other European towns soon following suit. Durkheim (1893)
has noted how simple societies tend to be more punitive than more advanced societies. Garland (1990) contends that punishment exists to protect society's morals. While
punishment does not create morality, its presence ensures that morals are upheld. The
practice of bondage supports Rusche and Kirchheimer's (1939) claim that the creation
of punishment is linked with the labor force. The state was seen as providing a good
opportunity for offenders to work, but its real motive increase its available pool of
workers cheaply.

II. The Birth of the House
of Corrections

Imprisonment in the sixteenth and seventeenth centuries was a result of incurring the
disfavor of the governing power, losing one's honor, undermining one's reputation, or
exhibiting disloyaly to the Crown (Freeman 2009). Foucault narrates how the seventeenth century saw the birth of great houses of correction and confinement, which
resulted in a substantial number of people (in Paris, one of every one hundred individuals) being kept under some form of control. In his analysis of France, he describes
the founding of the *hôpital général* under the guise of a medical hospital that in reality
served to control the poor and those who had gained the king's disfavor (Foucault 1961).
Honor was especially important to the upper class of nobility and gentry (Smuts 1999).
Loss of face led to disgrace, as it was impossible to keep face when viewed as a penitent
sinner (Freeman 2009). Honor was equally important to women, who could find their
reputation torn to shreds by any mention of sexual indiscretion (Gowing 1996).

The birth of the *hôpital général* in 1656 shows that the ideas behind its creation
were not medical but semi-judicial: the hospital could carry out the aims of arresting,

judging, and confining without being subjected to the necessary checks and balances found in courts of law. Once in the *hôpital general*, the person was at the mercy of the directors (Foucault 1961):

> The directors having for these purposes stakes, irons, prisons, and dungeons in the said Hôpital Général and the place thereto appertaining so much as they deem necessary no appeal will be accepted from the regulations they establish within the said hospital; and as for such regulations as intervene from without, they will be executed according to their form and tenor, notwithstanding opposition or whatsoever appeal made or to be made, and without prejudice to these, and for which notwithstanding all defence or suits for justice, no distinction will be made. (Foucault 1984, p. 125)

The directors of the *hôpital général* had absolute power. People could be confined on any excuse and left in the hospital until they died. The Church was soon to catch up, however, and church institutions soon began accepting "ill people" sent there by the king. This phenomenon was not limited to France. German-speaking countries saw the creation of the *Zuchthäuser* (Foucault 1961), which was similar to the *hôpital général*—a house of confinement that accommodated the needs of the king by controlling dissidents and the poor. These houses also served as a place where the labor force could be trained and controlled (Garland 1990). When the labor force was in abundance, these places served as a reserve for the future, housing the unemployed (called vagrants or lazy persons) until there was enough request for their labor. Confined persons served as a regime of free labor that could be exploited and kept available to help society do the work that no one else wanted to do (Rusche & Kirchheimer 1939).

During the era of the great confinement, Malta was under the reign of the Knights of St. John. Although the knights were a military power, they were also known as the "Knights Hospitallers." When they arrived in Malta, there were only two hospitals, neither of which was enough to meet the needs of the country. The knights were dedicated to taking care of the sick, foundlings, and those in need of help. Contrary to what was happening in the rest of Europe at the time, in the beginning the hospital was not used in Malta as a façade for an instrument of controlling the poor or those who disagreed with the ruling powers (i.e., the knights). In 1588, the knights issued regulations for the hospital that guaranteed the good treatment of patients. Problems soon arose with the inquisitor of the time, however, as the head of the infirmary and the most privileged knight of the order, the Grand Hospitaller over time became extremely jealous of his power, so much so that no one could enter the premises without first obtaining his permission. Regardless, sometimes the inquisitor needed to enter the infirmary, to administer confession or to provide other ministry, which led to disagreements between the inquisitor and the Grand Hospitaller (Cassar 1964).

In Malta, poverty reached massive levels in 1656, with a high proportion of people begging in the streets of Valletta. The knights of Malta at first adopted a system in which beggars were registered and given a permit to beg according to their level of

poverty and sickness. However, in 1667, Grandmaster Nicholas Cotoner decided to follow the example of the French king, Louis XIV, and opened a hospital under the same
principles that governed the *hôpital général* (Cassar 1993). These actions conflict with
Foucault's (1977) beliefs on punishment as being more utilitarian. His idea of a change
in punishment is not explained by changes in morality, but through the need of the sovereign to control the uncontrollable members of society. Punishment became private
not to protect the sensibilities of the masses, but because the ruling elite were afraid
of the possibility of a mass uprising that would jeopardize their power. In Malta, the
knights could not afford to be seen as cruel, given their vocation as members of a helping religious order. Therefore, creating a hospital to take care of the needy ensured that
they fulfilled their religious role as knights hospitallers but also ensured that the masses
were kept under control.

In England at this time, we find the creation of the Bridewells, which got their
name from the first house of correction, located on the property of Bridewell Palace
in London, England, in 1553. These were not prisons, but houses of vocational training
and religious discipline. The Bridewell was created to reform the prisoner (Freeman
2009); inmates had not necessarily committed a crime and were not usually sentenced
to a fixed term of stay. As people were locked in Bridewells to be reformed, they had
to reside in the institution until they learned to behave in a normative manner—an
aim that justified the fact that prisoners' stay in Bridewells did not have a termination
date. Bridewells mainly housed vagrants and prostitutes (Teagarden 1969) and so, from
their very beginning, were places to control the poor. However, according to Sharpe
(1999), Bridewells soon lost their distinguishable character and became similar to other
prisons used to control those parts of the masses who were seen as enemies of the
state, including prisoners of war, Catholic priests, and army deserters. Bridewells also
housed lunatics, many of whom were kept with other nonlunatic prisoners, resulting in
either ridicule or fear (Howard 1753). Finally, Bridewells were used to house ordinary
criminals. People could end up in Bridewells because they were accused of bastardy,
being abusive during a drunken quarrel, or being guilty of theft. All of these people
spent their time in these institutions doing nothing, which led to them becoming more
wayward (Howard 1753).

John Howard's (1753) report sheds important light on the situation of prisons in the
eighteenth century and before. A philanthropist and the first prison reformer in Britain,
Howard was shocked by the fact that prisoners who had completed their sentences but
could not pay the jailer's fees were dragged back to prison, while others who had not
been found guilty were still confined. Another problem that he pointed out was the
poor health of many prisoners, some of whom suffered from "gaol fever" or smallpox.
This problem was not only found among criminals who were kept in dungeons, but
also among debtors. The authorities pointed out to Howard that those prisoners who
were in ill health were regularly removed from the Bridewells, which naturally encouraged him to look at the performance of the Bridewells more closely.

While assessing the situation of English houses of corrections, Howard found
numerous problems, including health issues, especially smallpox and poor hygiene,

and widespread mismanagement, especially evident in the fact that most prisoners entered these institutions healthy, and before long their health deteriorated. Howard put the blame on the sheriffs and the gentlemen in charge of the prisons. Prisoners were not supplied with the necessities to survive life in prison, and in Bridewells, prisoners had no allowances with which to buy food. This led them to become overdependent on the jailers, with some giving prisoners bread from their own food allowance (Howard 1753). Work was another problem. In most Bridewells, prisoners spent their time idling, as there was no constructive work to be done (Howard 1753). This seems rather contradictory. If Bridewells were created to control the poor and vagrants, one would expect the institution to have a number of jobs (useful or useless) that the inmates could perform. This would be in line with Foucault's idea that carceral institutions were created to "produce bodies that were both docile and capable" (1977, p. 294); however, it seems that the Bridewells were just holding places where the poor could be kept out of sight.

The poor, convicts, and other undesirable members of society not only were kept out of sight but were seen as also expendable. When in 1813 Malta was in the grips of the plague, prisoners were made to bury the dead, despite the contagious quality of the disease and their own resistance. There are stories of prisoner protests against being pressed into such service, throwing corpses from windows and stealing objects from the homes of the deceased. Nevertheless, they were forced into submission, and by the end of the year, most of the prisoners had died. Some fifty additional prisoners had to be brought over from Sicily to do the remainder of the work (Attard 2000).

III. The Workhouse

Workhouses started to operate at the beginning of the seventeenth century. These institutions were run like a household, with the words "mother" and "father" used repeatedly to refer to the residential staff. The creation of a family life was very important, and married couples managed most workhouses. Workhouses did not change much during their existence. They were funded by magistrates, administered by nobles, managed by managers who spent little time there, and run by a residential staff who did the actual work. The staff had the role of keeping prisoners busy, feeding them, and maintaining order. Prisoners' lives revolved around hard labor, religious service, and finding a means to escape (Spierenburg 1984).

Also at the beginning of the seventeenth century another new type of prison emerged in which uncontrollable people, through a petition from their families, could be imprisoned. Those whose families could afford to pay for their detention were spared hard labor. The aim of these prisons was to separate unruly individuals from the rest of the world. Prisons during the seventeenth century faced two major crises. First, members of the upper and middle classes were reluctant to imprison their youths with lower-class individuals and serious criminals. This led to the opening of private prisons, which later became mental hospitals. Second, the sale of workhouse products was becoming less profitable, because businesspeople were less likely to buy the products of hardened criminals (Spierenburg 1984).

Bedlam was a mental asylum that aimed to address both issues. In 1681 the Board of Governors became concerned about the possibility of male servants abusing the lunatic women. Consequently, they ordered that the porter's wife take the role of matron and keep the keys of the door, with "twoe lockes . . . put on the doores to the Cells wherein the said Lunatike woemen are lodged and kept."[1]

Howard (1753) emphasized the importance of different treatment for women and men. It was especially important, he said, for those women who were breastfeeding to have a fireplace near which they could warm themselves and their infants. He also spoke about the importance of having a separate room for apprentices, well-ventilated rooms for the sick, and complete separation of women and men both during the night and in the workshops. He also recommended that in all Bridewells there should be an oven and a bath, and that inmates should be given bread and beer daily, together with a quarter-ration of warm soup made from peas, rice, milk, or barley twice daily.

IV. Country Jails and Debtors

In the mid-sixteenth century prisoners often complained of lack of food. The plight of debtors was even worst. Not only did they have no food, but, unlike the prisoner, they could not work to earn some money or have tools in their possession. Furthermore, those creditors who had pressed for their imprisonment frequently failed to supply them with the food that they were entitled to by law. The normal fare for all prisoners was bread boiled in water, and a normal chant heard in the prisons was: "We are locked up and almost starved to death" (Howard 1753, p. 6). Prisoners were imprisoned either because they were awaiting trial or because they were awaiting the execution of their sentences. Theoretically, there were two types of prisons: the jail, where felons, debtors, and those awaiting trial were kept; and the house of corrections, where petty criminals were housed. However, in reality this distinction was blurred (McGowen 1998). Corruption was rife, with bailiffs and jailers regularly demanding money of prisoners (Howard 1753). For example, prisoners were held in shackles, which rendered walking and sleeping a problem. In some London jails women were allowed to be without irons, but this was not the custom in most country jails, where the rationale was that the shackles prevented inmates from escaping. Jailers often extorted money from prisoners to remove the heavy irons from those who could afford it (Howard 1753).

The provision of water was another problem. Most prisons and Bridewells did not have water, and when water was to be found, prisoners were kept locked up and given only three pints a day, which had to be enough for both drinking and washing (Howard 1753). This led to unhygienic conditions, made worse by overcrowding, with prisoners often kept in underground cells, locked up for a period of fourteen to fifteen hours a day. Not only were these wards unsanitary; there was also an unbearable stink of bodily odors. Howard further reported that the jails were very damp and the walls of the yard low, exacerbating the problem. Overcrowding, a lack of ventilation, and insufficient water and sometimes no sewers, coupled with the fact that the walls of the yards were low, made it impossible to have ensure sanitation in the prisons. Further problems were that there was no bedding or straw on which the prisoners could sleep (Howard 1753), and prisoners with contagious diseases were kept with the others.

Prisons were regulated like business enterprises. Jailers earned their living from what they could get from the prisoners, and therefore they charged them for bedding, visitors' rights, beer, and so on. Because the aim of jailers was to keep prisoners happy, they allowed them a lot of liberty. Prisoners could do what they wanted as long as they did not escape. They were free to gamble, drink, or work, and they usually established their own rules and regulations by which they settled disputes (McGowen 1998). Customs varied from prison to prison, however. It was tradition for an incoming prisoner to "pay or strip," which meant that any newcomer had either to pay the other prisoners or give up part of his or her clothing (Howard 1753, p. 16). This meant that the poor and needy, who would have already been in dire circumstances, ended up with scarcely any clothing and were at risk of dying of cold. McGowen writes, "The plight of prisoners was described in the most heartrending terms. They were trapped in prisons, victims of diseases, hunger and jailers' greed" (1998, p. 77).

> All prisoners were kept together. As Howard reported:I have now to complain of what is pernicious to their *morals*; and that is, the confining all sorts of prisoners together: debtors and felons; men and women; the young beginner and the old offender: and with all these, in some countries such as are guilty of misdemeanours only; who should have been committed to bridewell, to be corrected by diligence and labour; but for want of food, and the means of procuring it in those prisons, are in pity sent to such county gaols as afford these offenders prison-allowance. (1753, p. 10)

In 1831 an investigation was initiated by the British colonial government to look at the Great Prison in Malta. This investigation found that the situation in Maltese jails was very similar to that of institutions in England, with a necessity to overall improve the facility and the treatment of prisoners. Separation of prisoners was seen as the top concern. Male and female prisoners were not properly segregated, which was leading to abuse. Problems also stemmed from young offenders being put with older criminals, boys being kept with men, first-time offenders with recidivists, and petty criminals with dangerous criminals. Prison discipline also left a lot to be desired. Corruption was rife, and there was no real discipline. Prisoners were left to their own devices and did what they wanted as long as they did not create any trouble. Most performed no work, and there was an absence of religious instruction.[2] The report ended with the recommendation that a new prison be constructed in order to address the abovementioned problems.

During this period, prisons were used for debtors as well as criminals, and, in fact, most persons detained in prisons or Bridewells were debtors. In 1776 in England and Wales, the prison population consisted of 2,437 debtors, 994 prisoners who had committed a type of felony, and 653 prisoners who had committed a petty offense. Unlike other offenders, debtors were similar to guests in that they could complain about their treatment and bring with them their wives and children (McGowen 1998). On average, each debtor was accompanied by two dependents, usually a wife and a child (Howard 1753, pp. 22–23). Some debtors were also visited by women of dubious morality, which reformers worried would lead to the corruption of children's morals. Creditors usually had the duty to pay for the debtors' upkeep, but this was not always the case. Therefore, the prisons were transformed into a hub of activity, where debtors sold goods to each other.

During the time of the knights in Malta, there were a number of sites that served as prisons. The two main prisons were the Castellania Prison and the Great Prison (Attard 2000). The Castellania Prison, situated between Merchant Street and St. John Street in Valletta, served as the criminal and civil courts. It also housed serious offenders, those condemned to death and those awaiting some form of guarantee to be released. Women awaiting trial were also kept there, although there were no females to guard them, and there was a worry of abuse. Those who were sentenced were sent to the Great Prison, situated on St. Christopher Street in the Lower Barakka in Valletta, which was originally built to house Turkish slaves and those sentenced to the galleys (Knepper & Scicluna 2010). Having slaves and people condemned to rowing the galleys was a necessity, as no free man wanted to do the job. Usually those offenders who were strong and healthy were condemned to galley slavery, as rowers had to be strong enough to use the oars. When their health failed, they were usually released. The frequency of this sentence increased according to demand, and it was only when ship technology changed that a change in sentencing occurred (Rusche & Kirchheimer 1939). In the eighteenth century the Great Prison was used for men and women who either had short sentences or had long sentences but were not considered to be dangerous. The crimes committed were various, but offenses of poverty, laziness, and vagabondage abounded (Attard 2000). Offenders in the Great Prison were expected to perform hard labor (Rusche & Kirchheimer 1939). Debtors, too, were kept there, although the general practice was to keep women indoors while men were allowed to roam the yards.

Another important factor at this time came into play—the economics of the state. According to Ignatieff (1978), it was the movement of people from the country to the cities that resulted in changes in confinement. With the movement of the masses from the country, social order had to be kept. Rusche and Kirchmeiner (1939) maintain that when looking at confinement, one also has to look at the economic situation, because punishment is often directed at the poor. Once a poor person is caught, he or she is processed in a system akin to that of a factory, where work is the fulcrum of everything.

If one looks at punishment historically, one notices that when there is an abundance of workers, the state can afford to use capital punishment or torture (as in the Middle Ages); however, when laborers are scarce, the ruling class will create punishment that has a work component, such as the workhouses (Rusche & Kirchheimer 1939). To ensure that people from the lower classes do not prefer to live in prison, the prison experience has to be worse than the conditions experienced by the working class (Garland 1990).

V. Women in Prison

Women in prison posed a special concern. In her inquiry about women prisoners, Bosworth (2000) mentions the *salpêtrière*, a part of the *hôpitaux généraux* in Paris that was under the influence of the church. Magdalens, or prostitutes, were always a special concern. As far back as the sixteenth century, Pope Gregory XIII ordered the Ursuline nuns in Malta to take care of the daughters of prostitutes until they married or entered the convent (Critien 1940). Once women were imprisoned, the governing powers in Malta considered it imperative that males and females be separated and that appropriate female supervision be available. What better supervision could one find than the Catholic nuns? This conclusion was reached both in Europe (O'Brien 1982) and in the rest of the known world (Knepper & Scicluna 2010).

Greig recommended that a prison for women in Malta be established within the Ospizio, a house established in 1732 by Grand Master Fra Antonio Manoel de Vilhena for the "*poveri invalidi, alle miseri pazzi e zitelle pericolanti*" (poor invalids, the unfortunate insane and the spinsters in moral danger). Here, men and women were housed in a two-tiered structure. The ground floor housed the women, while men were found on the first floor. The governor of the time decided to follow Greig's suggestion and sent the female prisoners to the Ospizio in Floriana (Knepper & Scicluna 2010). In July 1831, he declared that it was necessary to make "several new arrangements in the classification of prisoners" ("Proclamation," Government of Malta, 18 July 1831). However, Grand Master De Rohan previously, in 1795, had established the Ospizio as a *reclusorio* (cloister) for young women and women prisoners (De Rohan 1795). Its regulations stressed that the women's section should be divided from the other sections by a thick wooden door; that discipline should be under the direction of a wardress for prisoners, who would report directly to the governess in charge of the women's section; and that a woman under the authority of the chaplain and the governors had to be in charge of the dividing door. This shows that already in 1795 the knights were ensuring the separation of men and women, at least in the Ospizio.

Initially, there were problems finding a matron for the Ospizio, and therefore one was found among the residents (Knepper & Scicluna 2010). By 1835 the institution had a total of 732 inmates, comprising 280 poor men and 330 poor women, 45 lunatic men and 57 lunatic women, and 20 female prisoners (Martin 1837). When, in 1837, R. Montgomery Martin visited the Ospizio he was favorably impressed, writing, "The Ospizio is a very noble charity and its regularity and good order reflect credit on all concerned" (Martin 1837, p. 248).

The Ospizio was described by the British as a "common gaol" (Knepper & Scicluna 2010, 4). This indicates that women prisoners should have been treated in the same manner as male prisoners kept in the Great Prison. However, the fact that they were kept in a charity institution, one that catered to the mentally insane and the poor, indicates that women prisoners were treated more like inmates in need of care rather than those needing control. This cultural difference in the treatment of male and female prisoners has persisted to the present, with women often being treated more leniently than their male counterparts (Garland 1990). Furthermore, women posed certain problems to the government, especially those women who had children. Two anecdotes help to explain the situation.

In 1867, Guiseppe Mifsud wrote to Ferdinando Inglott, comptroller of charitable institutions, about his daughter-in-law, who had received a sentence of two years' imprisonment. He asked that she be allowed to keep her four-year-old son with her. Inglott refused. The women's prison was overcrowded, he said, and the presence of a boy would trouble other prisoners. "This woman might have thought of the consequences before committing the crime for which she is now under punishment," Inglott declared. "To deprive her of her children is a part of the penal system."[3] That same year, Guiseppe Schiavone asked for his wife to be pardoned so that she could take care of their children and he could leave the island. A notation indicated she had been convicted of receiving stolen goods from a girl fourteen years of age and "she deserves no commiseration." Whether the children were destitute, as the man alleged, could not be determined. Inglott responded by saying a pardon could not be granted. The children could not be brought to the prison, as this would create a great inconvenience; it would be best for them to stay with their father.[4]

From the agreement entered into by the governor of Malta and the Sisters of Charity, we have an idea of the type of women the government sought to confine and the problems that the governor faced in that effort. The Sisters of Charity were brought over to Malta to look after the sick, the poor, orphans, and prisoners in 1871. This was necessary because the heads of the charitable institutions on Malta were finding it difficult to manage the sick and take care of the other institutions. Inglott maintained that the best method to reform women prisoners was by employing Roman Catholic nuns to teach them appropriate moral behavior. The nuns would also be placed in charge of orphans, ill people, and prisoners. Finding the appropriate people in Malta was proving difficult because of "local prejudice and deficiency of education." The Sisters of Charity, Inglott maintained, were "the best qualified agents" to take care of these people as they worked from the heart, or, as Inglott put it, had "a much higher motive" than money, had "no worldly care," engaged routinely in duties requiring "great self-denial," and were used to living in a convent.[5] It was first thought that the sisters of St. Joseph of the Apparition would take care of the orphanages, but they refused, and the Sisters of Charity in Naples accepted.

In assessing the situation at the Ospizio, Inglott found that the matron of the Magdalen Asylum was adequate, and he therefore determined to keep her in employment until the Sisters arrived. The assistant matron he recommended should be transferred to the hospital of the incurables. The laundress who was acting as matron was also unfit for duty, as she was deaf; the Grand Mistress was very old and infirm, the portress was an invalid, and the matron in charge of prisoners was old and illiterate. This pointed to the fact that these women needed to be substituted.

When the Sisters arrived, they lived in quarters that had been furnished by the government. Two matrons were placed in charge of the Ospizio: one had the Magdalens under her control, and the other the prisoners.[6] The relationship between the Sisters and the governor was tenuous at best, as is shown by a letter written by the governor to the Sisters in 1891 ordering them to teach English instead of Italian. This was followed by a reply from the Mother Superior, who told him that they did not have any sister who was knowledgeable in English, that they therefore could not teach English, and that if this was a problem, they could pack and leave—a reply to which the governor apologized for the trouble caused.

The Sisters aimed to control and reform the prisoners through religion and teaching them honest labor. As stated in their agreement of 11 October 1871:

> In the Osipizio at Foriana the sisters shall endeavour to reform the Magdalens first by the all powerful influence of religion secondly by training them to a life of industrial toil and thirdly by keeping them constantly employed on work calculated to make them capable, when returning to the world, of earning their livelihood without resorting to sinful occupation.
>
> The Female criminals should be brought within the influence of religion, and made to feel that it is better—to earn a living by "honest labour" than have to bear the restraints and to perform the menial work of a prison.[7]

The Sisters taught the women to sew, knit, and crochet—female jobs that would help them in their lives outside the prison. They were also taught how to patch cloths and bed linen, and they wove and washed linen for the poorhouse. All these jobs were intended to prepare the women to act in a gender-appropriate way for an honest life once they left prison (Knepper & Scicluna 2010) while simultaneously helping other state institutions with their labor.

Conclusion

We have seen how the high morals of prison philanthropists were very far from reality. Prisons were supposed to serve as a place of reform. Foucault insisted that prisons should have a strict timetable, as these "established rhythms, imposed particular occupations, regulated the cycles of activities" (1977, p. 149). The idea was to produce reform, and therefore some form of activity that regulated behavior was necessary. However, we have seen that people were sent to these institutions to secure their invisibility to the rest of the population (Cohen 1998). Their reform was not of paramount importance; they were often free to pass the time in any way they wished, as long as they did not cause trouble.

This chapter has given an overview of the development of carceral institutions during the sixteenth and seventeenth centuries to become what is termed the modern prison. The various forms of institutions—country jails, workhouses, inquisitor's prisons, Bridewells, *Zuchthäuser*, and *hôpitaux généraux*—all had one thing in common—the control of those who did not agree with the norm. Whether individuals were poor or vagrants, did not agree with the ruling body, or were debtors or criminals, they all ended up in the same place. Foucault insists that the birth of the modern prison is a result of a quasi-revolutionary movement engineered by the higher strata of society, who saw the need to treat prisoners better in order to avoid a revolution and therefore the fall of the state.

Looking at the Malta situation, we can see that in most instances the ideas of Foucault and the Marxists can be used to explain the changes that occurred in confinement. Spierenburg (1984) is partially right in saying that confinement changes according to the changing sensibility of the people; however, the Malta situation gives more support to the idea of confinement as a method of controlling the lower classes, with the powerful inventing acceptable means to avoid revolutions. It seems confinement has always targeted the less fortunate. Through the discourse of protection from magic (the Inquisition), the building of the hospital to take care of those in need (the Knights of Malta), and the building of orphanages, houses of care, and houses of corrections (the British period), we see how confinement was used to control the poor and the needy.

The prisons of the sixteenth and seventeenth centuries received a lot of criticism. This criticism led to reform, which in turn led to more criticism and reform. However, we can also see that up to this day, prisons exist and are flourishing. Ignatieff (1978, p. 210) explains this persistence by showing how it was the same critics of prisons who convinced other people in their class that prisons were necessary to control the population. "Prisons continued to exist because the prison reformers convinced others, of the same socio-economic background, of the connection of crime to the socio-economic changes of the time . . . [and that] there was therefore a need to control and bring equilibrium back to the masses" (Scicluna 2004). They convinced the social elite that prisons needed to be reformed and not closed. This opened a new era for prison reform, that of the silent or separate system of imprisonment. It is important to see both the cultural and the social functions of punishment, as systems of correction exist not only to correct wrongdoers, but also to control society. That is, criminal actions do not really exist—what exists are systems to control certain sectors of society (Rusche & Kirchheimer 1939).

NOTES

1. Governors, "Extract from Minutes of Bridewell and Bethlem Governors," 22 April 1681, accessed at http://www.bethlemheritage.org.uk/.

2. E. Greig, "The Greig Report" (1831). National Archives, Malta.
3. Charitable Institutions, "Register of References to the Comptroller of Charitable Institutions" (1867). National Archives, Malta.
4. Ibid.
5. F. Inglott, "Report to Governor Grant,"12 October 1870, CSG 01, Vol. 58, File No. 8814, National Archives, Malta.
6. "Agreement Entered into by the Comptroller of Charitable Institutions and the Sisters of Charity" (1878). National Achives, Malta.
7. "Agreement with Sisters of Charity," 11 October 1871, Malta.

REFERENCES

Attard, E. 2000. *Il-Habs*. Bir-id-deheb, Malta: Palprint.

Beattie, J. M. 1984. "Violence and Society in Early Modern England." In *Perspectives in Criminal Law*, ed. A. Doob & E. Greenspan, 36–60. London: Aurora Press.

Bonnici, A. 1993. "Maltese Society under the Hospitallers in the Light of Inquisition Documents." In *Hospitaller Malta 1530–1798: Studies on Early Modern Malta and the Order of St. John of Jerusalem*, ed. V. Mallia-Milanes, 311–49. Zabbar, Malta: Gutenburg Press.

Bosworth, M. 2000. "Confining Femininity: A History of Gender, Power and Imprisonment." *Theoretical Criminology* 4:265–84.

Cassar, C. 2000. *Sex, Magic and the Periwinkle: A Trial at the Malta Inquisition Tribunal, 1617.* Pieta, Malta: Pin.

Cassar, P. 1964. *Medical History of Malta.* London: William Clowers & Sons Ltd.

Cassar, P. 1993. "Malta's Medical and Social Services under the Knights Hospitallers." In *Hospitaller Malta 1530–1798: Studies on Early Modern Malta and the Order of St. John of Jerusalem*, ed. V. Mallia-Milanes, 475–82. Zabbar, Malta: Gutenburg Press.

Cohen, S. 1998. "The Punitive City." In *Criminological Perspectives: A Reader*, ed. J. Muncie, E. McLaughlin, & M. Langan, 399–412. London: Sage Publications.

Critien, A. 1940. *A Convent and a Hospital of the Past.* Malta: Empire.

De Rohan, E. 1795. "Regulation of the Ospizio." In *The Regulation of the Ospizio 1795 of Grandmaster De Rohan.* Order of St. John. Malta, No. 537 Fol. 144.

Durkheim, E. 1893. *The Division of Labour in Society.* Translated by W. D. Halls (1984). London: Macmillan Press.

Elias, N. 1939. *The Civilisation Process*, Vol. II, *State Formation and Civilisation.* Oxford: Oxford University Press.

Foucault, M. 1961. *Madness and Civilization.* London: Tavistock.

Foucault, M. 1977. *Discipline and Punishment.* London: Penguin.

Foucault, M. 1984. "The Great Confinement." In *The Foucault Reader: An Introduction to Foucault's Thoughts*, ed. P. Rabinow, 124–40. London: Penguin.

Freedman, E. 1984. *Their Sister's Keepers: Women's Prison Reform in America, 1830-1930.* Ann Arbor: University of Michigan Press.

Freeman, Thomas S. 2009. "The Rise of Prison Literature." *Huntington Library Quarterly* 72 (2): 133–46.

Gambin, K. 2004. *The Prison Experience at the Inquisitor's Palace.* Marsa, Malta: Gutenberg Press.

Garland, D. 1990. *Punishment and Modern Society: A Study in Social Theory.* Oxford: Oxford University Press.

Gowing, L. 1996. *"Domestic Dangers": Women, Words, and Sex in Early Modern London.* Somerset: Bookcraft Ltd.

Howard, J. 1753. *The State of the Prisons in England and Wales with Preliminary Observations: An Account of Some Foreign Prisons and Hospitals.* Warrington, UK: Williams Eyres.

Ignatieff, M. 1978. *A Just Measure of Pain: The Penitentiary in the Industrial Revolution, 1750–1850.* London: Macmillan Press.

Johnston, N. 2000. *Forms of Constraints: A History of Prison Architecture.* Chicago: University of Illinois Press.

Knepper, P., & S. Scicluna. 2010. "Historical Criminology and the Imprisonment of Women in 19th Century Malta." *Theoretical Criminology* 14 (4): 1–15.

Martin, R. M. 1837. *History of British Possessions in the Mediterranean.* London: Whittiker & Co.

McGowen, R. 1998. "The Well-Ordered Prison: England, 1780–1886." In *The Oxford History of the Prison: The Practice of Punishment in Western Society*, ed. N. Morris & D. J. Rothman, 71–99. Oxford: Oxford University Press.

O'Brien, P. 1982. *The Promise of Punishment: Prisons in Nineteenth Century France.* Princeton, NJ: Princeton University Press.

Pratt, J. 2002. *Punishment and Civilization.* London: Sage Publications.

Rafter, N. 1985. "Gender, Prison and Prison History." *Social Science History* 9: 233–47.

Rafter, N. 1992. *Partial Justice: Women, Prisons and Social Control.* New Brunswick, NJ: Transaction.

Rusche, G., & O. Kirchheimer. 1939. *Punishment and Social Structure.* New York: Russell & Russell.

Scicluna, S. 2004. "The Prison in Malta: 1850–1870 and 1931–1951." Unpublished Ph.D. dissertation, University of Leicester, UK.

Sharpe, J. A. 1999. *Crime in Early Modern England, 1550–1750.* New York: Addison, Wesley, Longman.

Smuts, R. M. 1999. *Culture and Power in England, 1585–1685.* New York: St. Martin's Press.

Spierenburg, P. C. 1984. *The Spectacle of Suffering.* Cambridge: Cambridge University Press.

Spierenburg, P. 1998. "The Body and the State: Early Modern Europe." In *The Oxford History of the Prison: The Practice of Punishment in Western Society*, ed. N. Morris & D. J. Rothman, 151–77. Oxford: Oxford University Press.

Strange, C. 1985. "The Criminal and the Fallen of Their Sex: The Establishment of Canada's First Women's Prison, 1874–1901." *Canadian Women and the Law* 1: 79–92.

Teagarden, E. 1969. "A Victorian Prison Experiment." *Journal of Social History* 2 (4): 358–65.

Walker, N. 1991. *Why Punish? Theories of Punishment Reassessed.* Oxford: Oxford University Press.

Zedner, L. 1991. "Women, Crime and Penal Responses: A Historical Account." *Crime and Justice* 14:307–63.

Zedner, L. 1994. *Women, Crime and Custody in Victorian England.* Oxford: Clarendon Press.

CHAPTER 34

HISTORIES OF THE MODERN PRISON: RENEWAL, REGRESSION AND EXPANSION

MICHAEL MERANZE

INTRODUCTION

ALTHOUGH forms of imprisonment have been present across history, the prison as we know and imagine it is a recent invention. It assumed its present preeminence in the eighteenth century, and the ongoing crises of empire and the emergence of nation-states, I argue, have profoundly shaped its history. Linked in the first instance with crime control, the prison since the eighteenth century has repeatedly been used as a mode of government over populations the state has defined as dangerous. But precisely because it emerged as a response to crises of the old order, the prison has served as a means to legitimate states and to prove their essential modernity. It is the connection between state legitimacy and the modern prison that has so long sustained the commitment to thinking that the prison is, at its core, a necessary and reformist institution.

The modern prison—with its emphasis on reformative incarceration—combined an Enlightenment critique of excess, a statist desire for control, and a religiously grounded hope of personal transformation. Its early promoters aimed to remake individuals and cultures while avoiding the violence of the older penal system; in practice, it took up and reproduced violence while generating new forms of struggle. Although initially conceived as a transformative example of new forms of governance and dynamic improvement, the prison rapidly devolved into a seemingly fixed structure wracked by recurrent patterns of crisis, reform, regression, and crisis. But despite its deadly internal deadlocks, the prison spread across the globe during the nineteenth century and became increasingly linked to systems of racial domination and colonial intrusion. In the twentieth century, new discourses in the human sciences promised to transform the prison context and the prisoners within. But ultimately these programs failed, and the prison—especially in the United States—became increasingly punitive as states swept more and more individuals into these institutions' hands.

As such, the histories of the prison pose a series of problems for anyone trying to understand and interpret them. Wracked with almost constant struggle and upheaval, the prison has maintained a remarkable stasis as techniques, philosophies, practices, and aims have been recycled endlessly around the globe. Developed and defended in terms of its "civilized" aims and designs, it is constantly called to task for its recurrent barbarisms. Justified as a necessary tool of social order, it constantly produces new crimes and new violence. How did that history proceed, and how can we understand it?

I. The Birth of the Modern Prison Out of Empire and Revolution

The prison took up its modern importance as one of a series of eighteenth-century efforts to overcome contradictions and conflicts within the relationship of the law and the state in Britain, the United States, and on the European continent. Confinement, to be sure, was not new. Across the early modern period, European states had deployed workhouses and jails to imprison and discipline the poor and the vagrant (Spierenburg 1991). The growth of merchant capital, enclosure, and the expansion of landless proletarians had stimulated local experiments to control what, from the vantage point of elites, seemed an increasingly threatening population. But the scope and ideological importance of those efforts remained limited compared to their late eighteenth-century successors.

The crises of the British Empire that began with the Seven Years' War and continued through the American Revolution took previous efforts to modify and reform criminal punishment and transformed them into aspects of a search for reconstituted authority. At that moment, with the first British Empire in the throes of crisis, the prison began its movement from marginal element to central hub in the larger system of penalty. I am not claiming that the emergence of the prison was limited to the Anglo-American world, but it was in monarchical Britain and republican America that the movement for reformative incarceration found its strongest proponents and most lasting effects. Members of the professional classes, merchants, and religious figures pressed the state to transform punishment in accord with diverse ideological and social objectives (Ignatieff 1978; McGowen 1995; Meranze 1996).

The emergence of the prison in the Anglo-American world built upon earlier efforts to alter penal systems based on corporal, capital, and financial penalties. There is a popular view of the prison as simply a displacement of the gallows, but the historical reality is far more complex. Instead, the prison was part of a century-long search for alternatives to capital and public corporal punishment. The most important of these alternatives—for the English at least—was the use of transportation to Britain's North American colonies. From 1718 onward, and despite the spectacular presence of what contemporaries called the "Bloody Code," transportation removed thousands from the gallows and sent them overseas. In addition, there were small-scale efforts to employ punitive incarceration in the years before the American Revolution (Beattie 1986; King 2000; Maxwell-Stewart 2010). The North American colonies did not have the exact equivalent of transportation, although they did employ banishment and, in the case of the enslaved, shipment to the more brutal slave colonies of the Caribbean (Meranze 2008; Tartar & Bell 2012). In both Britain and her colonies, other secondary punishments (e.g., the whipping post, the pillory, fines) were deployed far more frequently within the criminal law than was the penalty of death. Within the slave regimes, to be sure, the situation was different—there both masters and the state used violence and display regularly and with greater force and destructiveness than was common elsewhere in the system (Meranze 2008; Morris 2006; Schwarz 1988). But as we will see, slavery and the prison have their own complex history.

In England, late eighteenth-century proponents of the ideological project of prison intertwined two related themes: greater control over space and time and the possibility of awakening individual consciousness. John Howard, a dissenter and the high sheriff of Bedfordshire, set the tone. His work *The State of Prisons in England and Wales* (1777), based on his visits to jails throughout the kingdom and on the continent, was a shockingly popular and influential work. It exposed both the arbitrary structures of authority within the jails and the failure to control either prisoners or the material conditions of the prisons. Howard publicized what those familiar with criminal justice already knew: that customary codes and informal agreements shaped the actual day-to-day life of prisons and jails. But Howard took that commonplace understanding and introduced two crucial twists. First, he effectively demonized the older prison organization, thereby persuading public opinion that the prisons were porous; that there was little classification of prisoners; that jailers—dependent as they were on fees—were prone to corruption and abuse; and that jails and prisons were sources of contagion for the society as a whole. Second, drawing upon his experiences on the continent—especially in the Netherlands—he argued that these problems could be overcome by greater regulation and oversight of institutions. For Howard, the discipline he had witnessed in Dutch workhouses convinced him that problems like jail fever could be overcome by enforced cleanliness, and that the moral contagion of criminality could be overcome by labor and regulation. If Howard emphasized the possibilities of order, regulation, and cleanliness, others urged the establishment of penitentiaries because of their belief in the power of solitude to regenerate the conscience. Jonas Hanway's *Solitude in Confinement* (1781), to give only one of many examples, drew upon both religious teaching and religious history to make the case that solitude would more powerfully transform inmates than any form of public punishment. Hanway, even more than Howard, argued that properly constructed prisons could awaken conscience and allow a prisoner's soul to improve his or her habits. Of course, certain Quakers had previously insisted that solitude would more effectively transform convicts than any public or corporal penalties. But Hanway, himself a leading figure in a host of metropolitan charitable and reform efforts, placed the problem of solitary confinement squarely on the penal agenda (Ignatieff 1978; McGowen 1995).

These ideas were not novel, but their context was. The outbreak of the American Revolution and the subsequent independence of the United States triggered a series of innovations in the ideology and practice of punishment. Most immediate was the disruption of transportation. Although the British Empire was able to reestablish transportation eventually in Australia, this practice was not an expedient open in the 1770s and 1780s. As a result, prisoners were initially held on hulks on the River Thames. Ultimately, the crisis helped stimulate national debate, culminating in the Penitentiary Act of 1779, and local initiatives such as the establishment of jails to expand imprisonment as a punishment for crime. But there was a deeper connection between American revolt and the expansion of the prison than simply the disruption of transportation. The loss of the American colonies (combined with the growing crisis in India) provoked local elites to try to find new modes of governance for England and the empire as a way of proving their right to rule (Brown 2006). Although the intensification of antislavery activism is perhaps the most famous example of this rethinking of empire, the turn to reformative incarceration would prove one of the most enduring changes to governance itself. Indeed, the years between the American and French revolutions witnessed numerous local examples of reform efforts in jails and local prisons as magistrates and justices sought to apply the lessons of Howard or the convictions of Hanway or both to the reorganization of prison life.

If the attempt to justify a monarchically governed commercial empire stimulated reformist activities in England, the effort to demonstrate that republics were more enlightened than monarchies had an even more drastic effect in the United States. Although the Americans shared the Enlightenment critique of excess and the religious focus on conscience, in the United States the identification of public, corporal, and capital punishments with monarchical government gave the experiments with imprisonment a revolutionary charge that they lacked in England (Masur 1989; Meranze 1996; Rothman 1971). As a result, imprisonment became more deeply tied to the American national project than it did elsewhere.

These dynamics were centered in Pennsylvania, followed by New York and Massachusetts. In Pennsylvania legislators sought first to transform Philadelphia into a city of legal representations, declaring that convicts would work in the streets chained to wheelbarrows. These "wheelbarrow men" were expected not only to do public works, but also to provide a constant example of the penalties of lawbreaking. But rather than serving as a source of reflection and order, the "wheelbarrow men" became mobile disruptors of social discipline as crowds flocked to chat with or taunt them, to provide them relief or provocation, and to see them not as sober warnings but as sources of entertainment. The "wheelbarrow men" for their own part resisted their chains and frequently escaped. In the light of these evident problems with public labor, Pennsylvania turned to its own version of the reformed prison.

As in England, Pennsylvania in the 1780s and 1790s did not build a new incarcerative structure so much as try to reorganize an old one. In this case, the Walnut Street Jail (originally built in the 1770s) was taken over. Penal reformers in the Philadelphia Society for Alleviating the Miseries of Public Prisons and jail officials imposed new regulations separating convicts from debtors and men from women, began a labor system within the prison that combined some craft labor with the sawing of stone, and built a new house of solitary cells for new inmates or as additional punishment for violators of prison rules. Crucially, however, the prison remained located within Philadelphia, and its reorganization was predicated on the belief that the creation of an ordered social and work life under reconstituted authority, and not a deliberately constructed physical environment, held the key to successful reformation of inmates. New York and Massachusetts quickly followed suit. Visitors from the rest of the new republic and from Europe came and praised the new regime.

Although elites in commercializing societies were most likely to turn to the prison as their prime penal instrument, we should be cautious in thinking that slave societies avoided the institution. In slave societies, however, the prison served different functions. In the American south, most states created new prison regimes (with Virginia's being the earliest, in 1798) but limited their use to whites. Nonetheless, jails continued to be used to hold the enslaved either for trial or until they could be returned to those who claimed ownership of them. In Jamaica, in contrast, beginning in the 1780s, imperial and local officials expanded the use of workhouse spaces as penal instruments. Not only did these institutions serve to hold prisoners for trial or in confinement after an escape, but increasingly prisoners were sentenced to actual terms of confinement. This movement toward the use of penal imprisonment increased in the latter days of slavery (the 1820s) and was combined with efforts to deploy some of the techniques of the reformed prison (e.g., use of labor, the treadmill, separation of men from women), albeit without the same ideology of reformation (Paton 2004).

II. Penitentiaries from Prisons and the Expansion of Discipline

Penal imprisonment was well established by the 1810s and 1820s in both England and the United States and had spread across Europe. But if the institution was established, reformative incarceration had also, by this point, clearly failed in its own terms. Prisons remained undisciplined, escapes were frequent, violence was regular, and, although we do not have good data on the issue, there is no evidence either of reduced crime or increased state discipline over the population. Importantly, leading early prisons such as Walnut Street in Philadelphia, Newgate in New York, and Milbank in England witnessed open prisoner resistance and riots. Beyond failure, the initial decades of the prison also indicated a series of continuing themes in its history: the importance of professionals and commercial forces in its spread, its recurring practice of taking over older institutions and practices rather than instituting a "clean break," and the recurrent insistence that the answer to the prison's failures was more prison (Ignatieff 1978; Lewis 1965; McGowen 1995; McLennan 2008; Meranze 1996).

This evident collapse of prison authority led—across the 1820s, 1830s, and 1840s—to the construction of the great models of nineteenth-century imprisonment. At Auburn and Sing-Sing in New York, Eastern State Penitentiary in Pennsylvania, and Pentonville in England, governments repudiated hopes that they could repurpose older institutions by imposing new personalized authority and instead turned to the power of architecture to impose order on and encourage reformation among inmates. Larger and more coercive prisons spread across the United States and continental Europe as the echoes of the three great model institutions. These new penitentiaries sought to control the smallest elements of the prisoners' environments through the power of architecture and construction (Evans 1982; Foucault 1977; O'Brien 1982). Eastern State Penitentiary at Philadelphia, opened in 1829, is illustrative in this regard. Its architect, John Haviland, designed a massive machine: a central building with seven radiating wings, each of which contained thirty-six cells, twelve feet by eight feet by ten feet in dimension. The inner walls of the wings were a foot and a half thick and extended three feet beneath the ground. The outside walls went four feet below the ground and were twenty-seven inches thick. Small windows were placed high and outside of the reach of inmates to prevent escape, and each prisoner had his or her own exercise yard that he or she could only reach by passing through two doors. There were no doors to the inner corridor—only a peephole, so that the guards could watch the inmates without being noticed, and a small feed draw for the introduction of food. At the same time, Haviland aimed to overcome the health issues of unreformed prisons by working out systems of water and air circulation and plumbing and waste removal, as well as establishing boundaries between the prison itself (whose outer walls he designed as a medieval fortress) and the larger city (Haviland 1824).

As prison officials turned to architecture to establish their power and control, they also used solitary confinement to an unprecedented extent. At Eastern State Penitentiary and Pentonville solitude lay at the heart of the prison program. Officials at these institutions pioneered what was known as the "separate system," in which inmates were subjected to solitary confinement throughout their imprisonment. Their only human contact—in theory, at least—was with prison officials or specially approved outsiders. In light of later history, though, it is important to note that in both places officials and lawmakers assumed that time spent in solitary would be limited. At Eastern State Penitentiary proponents of solitary confinement believed that solitude was so powerful that actual sentences could be shortened dramatically after its imposition; at Pentonville, solitary confinement originally was proposed as a preliminary to transportation to Australia and was limited to eighteen months (this period would grow shorter over time as the links between the prison and transportation declined). Even in the leading alternative system (known as the "silent system" and modeled at the Auburn and Sing-Sing penitentiaries at New York), inmates were placed in solitary cells whenever they were not laboring or exercising.

The expansion of solitary confinement triggered one of the great debates in nineteenth-century prison history: that between labor and solitude. The debate centered on three interrelated issues. The first was an economic issue: separate prisons were much more expensive and much less productive; the state would need to commit far more to such establishments in the way of financial support than it would to the silent system. Second was a consideration of reform: proponents of the separate system argued that the most powerful technique for individual reformation was an awakened conscience; proponents of the silent system argued that the best tool to transform inmates was labor. Third was a question of cruelty that concerned the limits of the humane: Was it crueler to force people to spend their time in almost-absolute solitude (they would still be in contact with some prison officials) or to strike at their bodies through whipping and debilitating work? These issues troubled prison officials, social reformers and activists, legislators, and the public from the birth of the Victorian penitentiaries into the early twentieth century (McConville 1995; McLennan 2008; O'Brien 1995).

Underlying both systems was the notion that Michel Foucault called "discipline." Foucault's *Discipline and Punish*, along with Michael Ignatieff's *A Just Measure of Pain* and David Rothman's *The Discovery of the Asylum*—all published during the 1970s—helped launch the contemporary historiography of the prison. Of the three, Foucault's is the most significant work and has retained the greatest influence. *Discipline and Punish* argues that the prison took its place at the heart of Western punishment not because it replaced traditional punishments with a more humane and enlightened form of punishment, but because it was the most intense example of a form of power ("discipline") that underlay the spread of the capitalist economy and the effective control of the working classes. As Foucault told the story—which focused largely, though not entirely, on France—discipline was a political technology that finely divided time, space, and human motion in order to precisely govern and train human subjects. Discipline was not limited to the prison—indeed, part of our acceptance of it in prisons was its wider penetration of everyday life, which made the restraints imposed on inmates seem reasonable—but it was discipline that made concrete the notion of prison as a space for reform and restraint. Imagined, Foucault thought, in Jeremy Bentham's panopticon but realized in practice in prisons like Pentonville and Eastern State Penitentiary, discipline became the defining characterization of what reformers and officials imagined the modern prison to be (Foucault 1978).

III. The Globalization of the Prison in an Age of Empires and Nations

Although the debate over solitude and labor dominated discourse about the prison in the metropolis, of perhaps greater significance was the prison's nineteenth-century globalization. As a sign of "modernity" and "civilization," the idea of the reformed prison transcended its roots in the North Atlantic and became deeply intertwined with the history of both empire and the building of nation-states around the globe (Gibson 2011;

Sherman 2009). The turn to solitary confinement promised an intensification of coercive power focused on individuals and individualization, and this larger history of the prison marked incarceration as a global sign of modern state forms. But the seemingly modern qualities of these new architectural wonders coexisted with another less evident development: the increasingly intertwined histories of incarceration and national and imperial racial hierarchies. As nineteenth-century prisons intensified their coercion of inmates, the histories of emancipation and colonialism helped spread prisons across the globe. The relationships between these two developments were complex and remain underconceptualized.

The relationship between colonialism and the expansion of the prison was a complex one. In some places—much of Africa, for example—the idea of the reformed prison was imposed as a tool of colonial power (Bernault 2007). In these instances, the colonial state deployed the prison project as a sign of its own civilizing and modern tendencies. In other settings, such as Turkey, modernizing states turned to the reformed prison to establish their equality with Europe and the United States and to counter claims that they were historically backward (Schull 2007). In Vietnam, French colonialists made little effort to claim modern civility, and the prison became a crucial site for the development of nationalist and communist organizations and ideologies (Zinoman 2001). But the large point holds: by the beginning of the twentieth century, the reformative prison had assumed a global status as a sign of a modern and civilized state. Of course, as in the metropolis, the gaps between ideology and practice cannot be understated. Although there were periodic efforts to improve the physical conditions of prisons and prisoners, to create classification of inmates, and to provide reformative opportunities, far more common was the claim of innovation that concealed the reality of continuity with older structures and practices of confinement. In perhaps the most striking of these redeployments, some prisons in Africa turned to the tools of slave trade punishment and discipline for use in their reformed prisons (Bernault 2007). In both the imperial and postimperial contexts, the prison was also deployed as the brute edge of the suppression of political dissent and opposition.

Three cases can help make the point more concrete: Peru, India, and Japan. I cannot here, of course, do justice to the histories involved. But even a brief discussion can give some sense of the range of ways that the modern prison became a crucial site for the development of state power in an age of empire.

In Peru, political and intellectual elites took up the idea of the prison as a tool both for confronting a perceived crisis in authority during the 1850s and early 1860s, and as a means to establish the state's claim to being a modern and legitimate holder of power. Drawing both on international discourses around criminality and on domestic languages of cultural and racial hierarchy, the Peruvian state began to reorganize old spaces of confinement and, in 1862, erected a new penitentiary in Lima. For our purposes, there are three important points in this narrative. First, the Peruvian state deployed the idea of the prison as a means of establishing its claims to modernity on the international stage; the state chose to build the penitentiary and institute reforms— these choices were not imposed from the outside by imperial powers. Second, in their continuing efforts to shape and reshape both the prison space and their understanding of punishment, the Peruvians engaged with a broad international discourse around prisons and punishments. And third, despite the imposition of new architectural forms and intellectual understandings, the prison continued to reproduce existing relations of inequality in its practices, and, as in metropolitan prisons, inmates continued to resist and undermine prison authority (Aguirre 2005; Aguirre 2007).

If Peru offers a case of the globalization of the prison as a sign of the assertion of modern statehood, India places the prison at the heart of the imperial agenda and the civilizing project. India had long practiced imprisonment of a range of individuals (Guha 1995), but it was the British who introduced the practice of generalized criminal incarceration. Beginning in the late eighteenth century the British, first under the auspices of the East India Company and later as the imperial state, began attempting to impose the tenets of reformed incarceration—separation, labor, classification, control of hygiene and time, medicalization—onto Indian prisons. Not only did the British expand the reach of incarceration, but, especially from the 1830s onward, they drew upon the languages of "prison discipline" circulating in the metropolis to conceptualize their remaking of the Indian penal system (Arnold 2007). In important ways, British authorities were simply attempting to extend their metropolitan reforms to their empire. But in practice, the imperial context made all the difference. In India, as in other colonial sites, the prison as project and ideology and the prison as practice diverged dramatically. Whereas the British thought they were introducing "modern" practices to India, in reality they challenged, yet ultimately reinforced, indigenous practices of class and religious differentiation, promoted resistance to efforts to transform Indian culture and practices, and found themselves forced into constant compromises on inherited cultural practices (e.g., food preparation, hygiene, religious observance). Perhaps even more importantly, the colonial setting made the political dimensions of the prison project inescapable. Again, we need to recognize at least two dimensions here: on the one hand, the role that prisons played in attacking common social and cultural practices made prisons sites of resistance; on the other hand, as political and religious resistance to the British increased, prisons became one of the sites through which the colonial state aimed to repress dissent. From the Great Mutiny of 1857 through the struggles of communists and nationalists in the twentieth century, imperial prisoners played important roles in the long-term opposition to British rule in India. The prison, then, came to function on a third imaginary level as a key image of British oppression (Anderson 2007; Arnold 2007; Sherman 2009).

In Japan, which was never colonized by the West but was forced to assume a subordinate status in the international system, the prison served as a sign of internal transformation, equal status on the international stage, and a means to claim its identity as a modern empire. These disparate dimensions were, for the Meiji government, interrelated. Japan's traditional systems of punishment—which were deeply complex, geared to the body, and cognizant of the symbolic differences that accompanied social distinctions—were an early target of Meiji modernizers. But their attempt to transform state punishment had more than internal dimensions. In the context of their relative international weakness, and having been forced by European powers to accept a system of extraterritorial law for foreign citizens, the Japanese government saw modern penality as an essential element in regaining control over their own territory. In order to convince European states and the United States to give up their extraterritorial claims, a movement toward imprisonment and away from corporal punishment seemed essential. In line with this project to prove itself an equal and modern state, the Meiji government began in the 1870s to construct a series of new prisons along modern lines. But, as elsewhere, where there are prisons, there is repression. The government quickly realized that the prison could be used as a tool of political as well as criminological control as it imprisoned more and more of its opponents. The increased use of prisons to stifle political resistance alongside the expansion of the number of prisons led to increased public scrutiny and debate and the emergence of native but modern criminology and prison architects. By the end of the nineteenth century Japan had established prison regimes that mirrored advanced European ones and drew upon the theories and practice of discipline—even if they might ultimately be defended by military force (Botsman 2005).

There was, though, a final turn of the screw. If Japan mobilized the prison in its effort to move beyond extraterritoriality, it soon deployed the prison in its own colonial holdings as well—particularly in Taiwan. Following its 1895 assertion of sovereignty over Taiwan, the Japanese quickly began to build several new prisons. But, just as importantly, in Taiwan (as in Korea) the Japanese colonial state also established new authority for its colonial officials to impose floggings on their Taiwanese subjects. In effect, the Japanese as they entered into empire produced the same division between metropolitan and colonial penal logics that their European counterparts had embraced (and there is evidence that the idea that flogging was acceptable because of the different cultural stage of the Taiwanese came from a British official). Japan's policies make clear a fundamental fact: by the early twentieth century the modern prison was global, but it never completely displaced other, earlier forms of punishment, nor did it preclude the development of new alternative forms of coercion over the bodies of inmates (Botsman 2005; Sherman 2009).

Peru and Japan developed their modern prison systems at a moment of not only the globalization of the prison but intensified internationalization of prison discourse and penological theory. To be sure, prison discourse had been international from its late eighteenth-century origins. Officials, reformers, and writers had maintained networks of communication and ideas, and practices had moved quickly across the Atlantic. Just as the writings of John Howard rapidly made their way to the United States, so, in the 1830s and 1840s, English and French observers (most famously William Crawford, Alexis de Tocqueville, and Charles Dickens) traveled to visit the new prisons in Pennsylvania and New York. But the late nineteenth and early twentieth centuries witnessed something new, which is perhaps most famously represented in the work of Cesare Lombroso and the emergence of Italian criminology: the increasingly dense network of criminological and penological writings and the organization of international conferences to discuss the latest trends and theories in the field. International prison conferences (e.g., London in 1872; Stockholm in 1878; Rome in 1885; St. Petersburg in 1890; Paris in 1895; Brussels in 1900) occurred with greater frequency during this era. Importantly, although both Japanese and Peruvian scholars and officials drew upon European and American models, they were not simply passive recipients—instead, they debated the relevance of these models and, especially in the case of the Japanese, argued for the importance of their own penological thinking on the international stage (Aguirre 2005; Botsman 2005). By the early twentieth century, the modern prison had not only spread far beyond its origins in the North Atlantic but had gained a place as a central object in modern political and social thought.

IV. RACE, LABOR, AND INCARCERATION IN THE AGE OF EMANCIPATION

As the modern prison became deeply intertwined with the state struggles over colonialism, it also became deeply implicated in the history of emancipation. The effects of emancipation on the place of the prison were, not surprisingly, most striking in the United States. The Thirteenth and Fourteenth Amendments to the U.S. Constitution cast penal imprisonment in a new light. When the Thirteenth Amendment made criminal conviction the only legitimate ground for penal servitude and the Fourteenth Amendment allowed the denial of legal rights to convicts, the emancipation amendments allowed states to mark convicts as peculiarly debased and other (Lichtenstein 1996; McLennan 2008). Convicts' lack of civil and political rights meant that they could be subject to increasingly powerful forms of exploitation. In a contradictory movement, convicts—and their labor—simultaneously became more important to the economy and society at precisely the moment when—as civil and political beings—they were cast into a deepened form of civil death (McLennan 2011). The decades following the American Civil War witnessed arguably the most brutal prison systems in the history of the United States—at least prior to the twenty-first century.

Indeed, despite efforts to reform and ameliorate prison conditions during Reconstruction, late nineteenth-century prisons were bastions of domination and exploitation. States and businesses across late nineteenth-century America deployed prison labor in the interests of profit and economic development. In the north, businesses and prison contractors were able to seize greater and greater control over labor within prisons. Contractors introduced new machinery to increase productivity and drove prisoners to work both faster and longer. Prison officials in effect became the agents of the contractors, a situation that legislators and judges did little to oppose. Labor had been central to antebellum penitentiaries, of course, but in the late nineteenth-century north it took on a new centrality and intensity. Rather than simply a tool for reformation, prison labor became a growing source of profits for capital and the state. One important sign of the changing significance of labor can be seen in the debates over it. In the antebellum period, the great debate between separate and silent systems concerned whether or not labor should be congregate or solitary—indeed, it was not clear that labor was anything but a supplement to solitude or separation. Now, questions of labor drove the debate over prison form, and the arguments turned on who should be the prime organizer—and economic profiteer—of labor on the industrial model—the state or business. In such a situation, although labor retained some of its earlier connotations as reformative or simply punitive, during the late nineteenth century its economic importance dominated all other concerns (McLennan 2008).

As we have seen, legal imprisonment played an important, if subsidiary, role in sustaining the coercive apparatus of slavery. But with slavery's overthrow, prisons and their offshoots took on new, more complex, roles in the American south. Criminal imprisonment, deployed in the slave south primarily for white citizens, became the anchor of a process by which southern states controlled and exploited the labor of the newly emancipated African American population. Since the Civil War had destroyed much of the material infrastructure of southern penality and most of the south's penitentiaries, southern states began to build new prisons and jails, particularly during the 1870s and 1880s. At first, most freed people did not end up in prisons per se. Instead, in the aftermath of radical Reconstruction, southern states used criminal sentencing, jails, and prisons as a mechanism to distribute convicted criminals as labor for private contractors. Just as importantly, the threat of imprisonment served to compel freedmen and freedwomen to continue to labor in rural areas for white landowners. Initially as a backstop to the system of convict leasing, and then later on the newly developed penal farms (which took up the practices of the overthrown plantation system and applied it to criminal punishment), prisons and incarceration became central both to the south's economy and to its system of racial domination. Indeed, one can trace some of the changing contours of the state through the changing role of imprisonment. Whereas under slavery criminal imprisonment had been a supplement to the private power of the slave owner, in the new south it served as a way for states (the public) to profit from African Americans' work and provide laborers to crucial sectors of the industrializing economy. Although the end result of each system was to support private power, in the old south the enslaved were property of their masters, while in the new south convicts were property of the state. (For a similar transition in Jamaica, see Paton 2004.) To be sure, the criminal law was only one of many tools of violence deployed against freedmen and freedwomen, but it was inarguably a fundamental means for sustaining white supremacy and preventing the development of an independent African American yeomanry (Ayers 1984; Lichtenstein 1996; Perkinson 2010).

The convict lease system dominated southern penality from the end of Reconstruction through the early twentieth century. Freedmen and freedwomen convicted of a wide range of offenses, ranging from vagrancy or refusal to work to resisting white attempts to seize their lands to more conventional categories of violent crime (with what justice, it is difficult to say), had their time and labor sold to private businesses or special contractors who compelled them to labor in fields, in mines, and on railroads. Cast into unsafe working conditions and driven to the limits of human endurance, and sometimes beyond, the convict lease system demonstrated a southern form of penal discipline based on labor and violence that would continue in myriad forms even after it was overthrown in the early twentieth century. And, although labor in northern prisons was highly profitable, it is difficult to argue that it was essential to northern industrial development. The situation in the south was different. There, the labor of the now-overwhelmingly African American inmate population was a crucial tool in both industrial and commercial development of the economy.

These developments soon developed wide-ranging opposition. The most immediate, and longest lasting, came from convicts and prisoners in both the north and the south; prisoners attempted escape (sometimes successfully), slowed down work, feigned illness or injured themselves, and engaged in collective protests and riots. Over time, they were joined by other critics, including Progressive-era reformers; professionals in law, medicine, and the social sciences; journalists; labor unions; and commercial and industrial interests competing with the prison labor systems. The combined weight of all of these opponents ultimately overthrew both the convict lease system in the south and the contractor system in the north. In so doing, late nineteenth- and early twentieth-century American prisons would partially join with international trends to forge a new structure of punishment. But, as we shall see, the limits of these transformations would structure the future as much as the transformations themselves.

V. Penal Welfarism and Its Global Limits

The movements against the convict lease system and prison contractors merged with a larger movement toward a more "progressive" penology in the United States and Europe (Garland 1985; Rosenblum 2008). At the same time that American prisons and penal systems had been intensifying the labor of convicts and subjecting them to increased brutality, the United Kingdom was bringing to fruition penal trends begun with the construction of Pentonville and the end of transportation in the 1850s. Unlike the United States, with its disparate system of state prisons, England over the nineteenth century moved to consolidate and centralize its authority over prisons (McConville 1995). By the 1880s, the British had set up a Victorian structure of large metropolitan prisons organized around labor and the principle of "less eligibility." Moreover, they had succeeded in establishing a national prison structure directed from the center by a commissioner of prisons.

Yet on both sides of the Atlantic these systems of industrialization and Victorian dominance were displaced and dislocated suddenly after the 1880s. Experiments with newer forms of imprisonment (most importantly, prisons for women and juveniles) and new systems of discipline and classification spread rapidly. As we saw previously, the later nineteenth century also saw the birth of criminology and a deepened effort to theorize punishment and criminality. The overthrow of the dominant labor systems combined with these experiments served to remake and reconfigure the prison's place in punishment. By the early twentieth century prison policy (if not always practice) to some extent had come under the sway of what David Garland has called "penal-welfarism," especially in the United Kingdom and Germany (Garland 1985). We should not overestimate the reach of this new penal welfarism, but its importance cannot be ignored. Although prisons still stood apart from the larger system, they were increasingly integrated into a larger web of social and psychological interventions.

Of particular importance was a growing emphasis on classification, separation, and individualization. To be sure, these techniques had been part of the prison project from the beginning. The first generation of prison reformers had sought to separate debtors from convicts, men from women, and convicts from those awaiting trial; the second generation's construction of penitentiaries ordered around solitary confinement had pressed forward individualization. But in the metropolitan countries, the late nineteenth and early twentieth centuries gave new meanings to these old impulses. In part, classification assumed new importance as some prison officials attempted to institute systems of reward and punishment that allowed for the progressive advance through stages of imprisonment. Important nineteenth-century initiatives at Norfolk Island in Britain and then, famously, at the Elmira Reformatory in New York aimed to not only provide new incentives for labor but also to allow prisoners to engage in practices of self-government in reward for labor and good behavior. Although limited (and, in the case of Elmira, contained within a larger system of abuse), these early efforts laid the groundwork for a transfiguration of the prison system—especially in the United States and Great Britain (Morris 2002; Pisciotta 1994).

For one thing, in both the United States and the United Kingdom, officials increasingly placed female convicts in prisons organized especially for women. Not all of these institutions were new constructions: for instance, Holloway Prison in England had begun as a prison holding both men and women but by the first decade of the twentieth century had been reorganized as a women's prison alone. In the late nineteenth-century United States female activists pressed state officials to create a range of incarcerative spaces (e.g., women's prisons, female reformatories) that they hoped would protect women from the abuses of the general prison and allow for female-led reformation of inmates. These new institutions did allow for innovative structures and relations of authority that were more "domestic" than either the industrial or military styles dominant in male prisons at the time. In the United States especially, they took the form of cottage organization designed to create female community and to reclaim the morals of their charges. As such, they represented one nineteenth-century flowering of a feminist legal consciousness (Freedman 1981; Rafter 1983; Zedner 1995). But the ideology and practice of women's prisons not only reinforced the notion that women were especially frail but also expanded the range of offenses for which women could be incarcerated. Just as the initial turn to imprisonment led to greater restraint on minor offenders, so too did the development of women's prisons lead to more women being caught within the net of imprisonment (Odem 1995; Rafter 1983). Nor did the movement for women's prisons remove all women from their subordinate places in prisons directed primarily at men (Butler 1997).

Similar efforts restructured juvenile punishments. Perhaps the most systematic was the creation of the borstal system—juvenile reformatories—in England. Whereas the Victorian prisons had left young offenders in common jails or large prisons, the organizers of the borstal system recognized them as a specific population with specific needs and opportunities. From its establishment in 1908, the borstal system created separate institutions for offenders between ages sixteen and twenty-one who would serve sentences of between one and three years' duration, with the specifics determined in light of their behavior at the borstal. They would also be subject to supervision after release. At the same time, the British established a system of juvenile courts for children under sixteen (Garland 1985). In the United States, juvenile courts also emerged in the early twentieth century. Although the notion of treating juveniles differently from adults was not new (there had been Houses of Refuge for that purpose since the 1820s), the juvenile courts were a dramatic example of a new allegedly scientific and Progressive penology. In its most famous version in Chicago, these institutions deployed a series of new techniques including probation in order to minimize juvenile exposure to adult prisons and to find alternative places for juveniles to be confined (Willrich 2003). From 1880 to 1930 the idea of placing young people in reform schools achieved its greatest influence and authority (Schlossman 1977; Schlossman 1995). The creation of new institutions for the young allowed a rebirth of reformist discourse—although older inmates were often viewed as beyond reformation, the young were still perceived as having the capacity to be saved. The expansion of the current form of incarceration and discipline, it was believed, would succeed where earlier forms had failed.

This increased differentiation of penal institutions intersected with new techniques for approaching adult male convicts. On the one hand, practices such as parole and probation allowed both for diversion from prison and for mechanisms to reward inmates for obeying the rules and expectations of institutions. On the other hand, the spread of indeterminate sentencing and the increased use of psychiatric and medical techniques to sort and evaluate prisoners increased the emphasis on individualized treatment in the prison itself (Garland 1985; Rothman 1980). Inmates became "cases" with individualized files, histories, and prescribed routines. Crucially, the new individualization of prisons could be justified in both of the major idioms of early twentieth-century criminology—the environmental and the eugenic. Insofar as environment caused criminality, the appeal of the individualized case under constraint was obvious: remove the offender from his or her toxic community, and the process of reformation could begin. But even in the case of the eugenic sense of the born criminal, the sorting and individualizing mechanisms of the juvenile court, parole, or probation could be justified in terms of the necessity of ensuring that the system focused on the natural criminal. Environmentalism and eugenics each provided the necessary theoretical justification for Progressive penology's effort to differentiate prisons and prisoners.

In addition, some Progressive-minded officials (e.g., Thomas Mott Osborne of New York) aimed to increase prisoner self-governance on the theory that inmates should be better prepared for their return to society. Inmates in turn pressed against and with these institutional changes to create an institutional culture of negotiation and compromise of authority. By the 1930s and 1940s, when the "Big House" prisons rose to prominence, the militaristic brutality and contract labor of the late nineteenth-century prison had been displaced by what Rebecca McLennan terms a "managerial" prison, in which the central lines of authority aimed to maintain order through systems of reward but in which power was contested by new outside experts, state authorities, and inmates who aimed for some control over everyday life and, when that failed, broke out into open riot (Bright 1996; McLennan 2008; Rothman 1980). Indeed, one of the central components of the mid-century's metropolitan prisons was the importance of inmate culture and self-organization. Despite the fact that officials and guards could draw upon the power of the state, inmates were successful in determining many of the rhythms and norms of prison society (Clemmer 1940; Kunzel 2008; Sykes 1958).

Still, it will not do to overstate the practical extent of penal welfarism. It is true that it helped establish a relatively stable set of penal strategies that succeeded, from the 1920s to the 1970s, in keeping long-term imprisonment rates (Cahalan 1986) and the legitimacy of reformative aims fundamentally stable. But even in the United Kingdom, where the system was most fully developed, the influence of the reformative and the medical never outweighed the custodian or the managerial. And in the United States, with the exception of certain moments of heightened reformative zeal, the power of doctors and psychiatrists was even less (Janssen 2005; Rothman 1980). It may well be that the most important accomplishment of the medical officials was their very presence; the necessity of meeting minimal medical standards placed some restraint on the punishments ordered by prison officials (Simon 2014).

But issues of race and the structures of colonialism presented even more fundamental limits to penal welfarism. For one thing, whereas both environmentalism and eugenics were used in the case of the native white and immigrant working classes to separate out criminality from the wider population, in the case of African Americans, crime statistics and liberal penology insisted—at least through the 1930s—that African Americans as a population were particularly prone to criminality. As the numbers of blacks in prisons or convicted of crimes grew in the late nineteenth and early twentieth centuries, these numbers were used as proof of racial failings and the impossibility of including African Americans within the confines of penal welfarism (Gross 2006; Muhammad 2010). Equally important is the lack of evidence in the southern United States that penal welfarism transformed incarceration in any significant way. Although it is true that the south also established programs for parole and probation, southern prisons—and other available forms of incarceration like prison farms and work camps—remained deeply committed to custody and restraint at minimal cost. Their overwhelmingly African American population no doubt contributed to southern states' limited commitment to individualized reformative techniques. The American southwest, furthermore, resembled the south more than the north or the Midwest.

Indeed, the reformist push in the turn-of-the-century south led primarily not to what we would consider penal welfarism, but to the introduction of the chain gang.

Although it would soon become a symbol of southern brutality, the chain gang was initially viewed as a step forward, a more humane form of punishment than the convict lease system. The introduction of the chain gang is yet another reminder of a central theme in the history of the modern prison: moments of reform repetitively turned to older practices and reconfigured them as something new. In this case, the south insisted upon what the late eighteenth century had rejected—the notion that the public display of working convicts could serve as a humane form of punishment. Of course, in the case of the south, unlike Philadelphia and elsewhere, prisoners on the chain gang performed labor essential to the development of the southern economy. The chain gang in that respect marked continuity with the convict lease system and a disjuncture with the main trends of penal welfarism (Lichtenstein 1996).

Perhaps even more importantly, the limits to penal welfarism on the global scale are striking. This is not to say that many of the ideas of scientific criminology and penology did not gain international or even global reach. As the history of Peru and Japan, among other places, reveals, leading intellectuals and officials were eager contributors to the global discourse of penology in its penal welfare phase and could even find "domestic" predecessors of reformed institutions (Aguirre 2005; Botsman 2005). But in the colonial setting, from India to Vietnam, penal welfarism had little influence. Instead, the prison continued to function largely as a place of repression (political and otherwise) and as one node of a larger militaristic strategy (Zinoman 2001) that brought to bear on society what Taylor Sherman has called "coercive networks" (Sherman 2009). As the persistence of flogging in colonial punishments during the era of penal welfarism (Sherman 2009) shows, there were real limitations to the global reach of penal modernism. Perhaps the clearest indication of this divide can be seen in Kenya, where the British deployed not only capital punishment but mass prison camps to suppress the Mau Mau uprising (Anderson 2005; Elkins 2005). After all, England had been arguably the central point for the elaboration of penal welfarism—but, when confronted with a challenge to its empire, it resorted to the most brutal tools of penal power at its disposal. Indeed, if we consider the use of imprisonment by European empires or by the United States in the Philippines as part of their efforts to maintain their power, or the wide-reaching penal efforts of Nazi Germany and the Soviet Union, it would be possible to see the era of metropolitan penal welfarism as a small exercise of individualization surrounded by a much larger carceral archipelago of collective domination.

VI. Mass Incarceration and the Return of the Colonial Repressed

Although some of the aspects of penal welfarism survived beyond the 1960s (especially on the European continent), the system as a whole was displaced by the 1980s, especially in the United States. To be sure, as with the entirety of American penal history, there was an unevenness to this transformation. But it is to the leading patterns of American penal practice that I want to turn because, to a large extent, the transformation of American penal practice dominated the history of the late twentieth- and early twenty-first century prisons. This dominance does not mean that the entire world followed the lead of the United States—far from it—although American practice and discourse did help shape penal debates elsewhere (Garland 2001). More importantly, however, the United States, in its elaboration of an advanced mass system of punishment, brought together the histories of colonial and metropolitan punishment and reinvigorated older forms of punishment and penal organization in a new, more brutal, and total context.

There was little in the 1950s to indicate that the United States would soon repudiate the fundamental tenets of penal welfarism. Following the Second World War, American prisons continued to offer psychological services. In California and elsewhere there was increased sensitivity as a result of the number of veterans who ended up incarcerated (Janssen 2005). Prison populations remained stable, parole and probation continued to be used frequently, and indeterminate sentences effectively controlled by prison professionals still determined the life courses of inmates. In California, one of the beacons of postwar penology, there were new experiments with group therapy and prisoner writing groups and classes. Of course, as with the entirety of the twentieth century, there were important regional variations. Neither the south nor the southwest shared a commitment to elaborate reformative programs (Lynch 2010; Perkinson 2010). But through the 1950s the reformative ethos of progressive penology remained the leading current of the nation.

This system did not survive past the early 1970s. Inmates in the 1960s began to rebel against the psychological pressures brought by reformative programs and the unsystematic exercise of authority enabled by indeterminate sentences. They would soon be joined by outside reformers who criticized indeterminate sentencing and psychological evaluations as denying inmates dignity (American Friends Service Committee 1971; Janssen 2005). As conflicts over civil rights and black power intensified, states incarcerated minorities in ever-greater numbers. Combined with a real increase in violent crime at the end of the 1960s and beginning of the 1970s, the social turmoil of the 1960s created a fear among many white voters and public officials that race and crime were the same (Garland 2001; Simon 2007). Beginning with the Johnson administration and accelerating thereafter, the federal government pushed forward new law and order ideologies and programs (Parenti 1999; Simon 2007). Joined by the growth of victims' rights groups, politicians in both parties formed a new consensus around the notion that imprisonment should be made harsher, and that the incarcerated population should be expanded (Gottschalk 2006). The turn to determinate sentencing, combined with greater severity in the mandated length of incarceration (symbolized most effectively by the passage of "three strikes and you're out" laws), would lead to what David Garland proposed we think of as "mass incarceration" (Garland 2001).

The most obvious result of these developments was a remarkable expansion in the size of the incarcerated population. Whereas in 1970 there were 198,831 individuals held in state and federal prisons, by 2012 there were 1,570,400 such individuals (Cahalan 1986; Bureau of Justice Statistics 2013). In 1970, 98 people were incarcerated per 100,000, while in 2012, 920 per 100,000 were (Cahalan 1986; Bureau of Justice Statistics 2013). By the early twenty-first century, the United States had the world's highest rate of incarceration (Sentencing Project n.d.). These increases did not affect all races equally, however. Although African Americans and other minorities had always been overrepresented in the prison population, the extent of their overrepresentation increased in unprecedented ways, especially through the crackdown on certain forms of drug activity (Alexander 2010). Indeed, prison became one of the main mechanism through which states chose to deal with the economic dislocations that faced minority communities after the 1970s (Gilmore 2007). The end result was a reinforcement of these communities' exclusion from the main economy (Western 2006).

But it was not simply the size of the new penal apparatus that marked it as distinctive. Just as important were the ways that it repudiated the structures and norms of penal welfarism. First, mass incarceration overturned two centuries of attempts to increase the differentiation among penal institutions. In the contemporary prison are lumped the mentally ill and the criminal, while jails have once again become a major receptacle for the poor and the ill. Second, as states found themselves committed to prison growth beyond what they could pay for, they turned increasingly to private prisons. If one of the central aims of eighteenth-century prison reform had been to separate prison governance from the economic interest of the jailer, in twenty-first century America states have once again entrusted their charges to private businesses. Finally, growing out of the sense that prisons were unable to effectively reform individuals or provide them with the skills they needed to function in society, mass incarceration severely devalued and deemphasized the very notion of reform itself. The first prisons, the great penitentiaries, progressive penology, international reform, and penal welfarism had all been predicated on the hope for reform; the proponents and managers of mass incarceration effectively rejected it.

Perhaps the greatest signifier of the meaning of mass incarceration was not the size of the population per se, but rather the return of solitary confinement in secure housing units (SHUs). Jonathan Simon has pointed to the idea of "total incapacitation" as the individual counterpart to the growth in population that marks mass incarceration. Total incapacitation has reinvented solitary confinement as a form of dungeon. Inmates (largely members of prison gangs) are sent to solitary cells, sometimes for months or years; there, they are kept in spaces of sensory deprivation and locked away from any interaction with the natural environment for up to twenty-three hours per day. SHUs make no pretense to be a tool of anything but control; they are deployed to force inmates either to suffer indefinitely or to provide information to the authorities. And, in California at least, they are linked to violent "cell extractions," denial of health care, and systemic efforts at humiliation (Simon 2014).

The joining together of mass incarceration and total incapacitation is possible because convicts today are defined as enemies of both state and society. That African Americans and Latinos are overrepresented in today's prison population only strengthens that definition within the racial imagination of the discourses of law and order. The twenty-first century SHU effectively fuses together the nineteenth-century north's emphasis on solitary confinement and the south's emphasis on punishment as a tool of racial control and an expression of skepticism about reformation. But in bringing together techniques that originated in the industrializing north with racial techniques that came to first fruition in the south, the system of mass incarceration and total incapacitation breaks down the difference between metropolitan and colonial punishment.

In the long sweep of prison history, mass incarceration looks like nothing more than the return of the colonial repressed. The continued failures of prison health care, the collapse of meaningful reform efforts, the subtle but ever-present evocation of a dangerous class that must be controlled within prisons, and the striking characterization of that dangerous class as racial all echo the efforts by colonial officials to translate metropolitan penal projects into situations in which the colonial state was attempting to control populations that were alien to the state. In the United States during the era of mass incarceration, the prison population is being made alien by the prison system rather than being alien prior to prison system. The logics of colonial incarceration have remade the metropolitan prison system.

To be sure, the world is not the United States. Europe has not followed the path of mass incarceration to the degree that the United States has. As I have suggested throughout this essay, the histories of the prison in Africa, Asia, and Latin America have their own trajectories. The United States is distinctive, one might argue, precisely because there was so little separation between the colonial and the metropolitan projects; the history of slavery and expansion meant that empire was internal to the metropolis. But the future of scholarship on modern punishment will find, I think, that the metropolitan and colonial need to be thought about together because they share a common matrix in the complicated relationships between nation-states and empires that have structured so much of the history of the last two centuries.

Acknowledgment

Michael Meranze would like to thank Elizabeth Dale, Helen Deutsch, David Garland, Avery Gordon, Steven Hahn, Julia Liss, Randall McGowen, Keramet Reiter, and especially Paul Knepper for their criticisms and suggestions on this chapter.

References

Aguirre, Carlos. 2005. *The Criminals of Lima and Their Worlds: The Prison Experience, 1850–1935*. Durham, NC: Duke University Press.

Aguirre, Carlos. 2007. "Prisons and Prisoners in Modernising Latin America (1800–1940)." In *Cultures of Confinement: A History of the Prison in Africa, Asia, and Latin America*, ed. Frank Dikotter & Ian Brown, 14–54. Ithaca, NY: Cornell University Press.

Alexander, Michelle. 2010. *The New Jim Crow: Mass Incarceration in the Age of Colorblindness*. New York: New Press.

American Friends Service Committee. 1971. *Struggle for Justice: A Report on Crime and Punishment in America*. New York: Hill & Wang.

Anderson, Clare. 2007. *The Indian Uprising of 1857–8: Prisons, Prisoners, and Rebellion*. New York: Anthem Press.

Anderson, David. 2005. *Histories of the Hanged: The Dirty War in Kenya and the End of Empire*. New York: W. W. Norton.

Arnold, David. 2007. "India: The Contested Prison." In *Cultures of Confinement: A History of the Prison in Africa, Asia, and Latin America*, ed. Frank Dikotter & Ian Brown, 147–84. Ithaca, NY: Cornell University Press.

Ayers, Edward. 1984. *Vengeance and Justice: Crime and Punishment in the Nineteenth-Century American South*. New York: Oxford University Press.

Beattie, John M. 1986. *Crime and the Courts in England, 1660–1800*. Princeton, NJ: Princeton University Press.

Bernault, Florence. 2007. "The Shadow of Rule: Colonial Power and Modern Punishment in Africa." In *Cultures of Confinement: A History of the Prison in Africa, Asia, and Latin America*, ed. Frank Dikotter & Ian Brown, 55–94. Ithaca, NY: Cornell University Press.

Botsman, Daniel. 2005. *Punishment and Power in the Making of Modern Japan*. Princeton, NJ: Princeton University Press.

Bright, Charles. 1996. *The Powers That Punish: Prison and Politics in the "Big House," 1920–1955*. Ann Arbor: University of Michigan Press.

Brown, Christopher L. 2006. *Moral Capital: Foundations of British Abolitionism*. Chapel Hill: University of North Carolina Press.

Bureau of Justice Statistics. 2013. "Correctional Populations in the United States, 2012." Accessed at http://www.bjs.gov/content/pub/pdf/cpus12.pdf.

Butler, Anne M. 1997. *Gendered Justice in the American West: Women Prisoners in Men's Penitentiaries*. Urbana & Chicago: University of Illinois Press.

Cahalan, Margaret W. 1986. *Historical Corrections Statistics in the United States, 1850–1984*. Rockville, MD: Bureau of Justice Statistics.

Clemmer, Donald. 1940. *The Prison Community*. Boston: Christopher Publishing House.

Elkins, Caroline. 2005. *Imperial Reckoning: The Untold Story of Britain's Gulag in Kenya*. New York: Henry Holt.

Evans, Robin. 1982. *The Fabrication of Virtue: English Prison Architecture, 1750–1840*. New York: Cambridge University Press.

Foucault, Michel. 1977. *Discipline and Punish: The Birth of the Prison*. New York: Pantheon.

Freedman, Estelle. 1981. *Their Sisters' Keepers: Women's Prison Reform in America, 1830–1930*. Ann Arbor: University of Michigan Press.

Garland, David. 1985. *Punishment and Welfare: A History of Penal Strategies*. Brookfield, VT: Gower Publishing Company.

Garland, David. 2001. *The Culture of Control: Crime and Social Order in Contemporary Society*. Chicago: University of Chicago Press.

Gibson, Mary. 2011. "Global Perspectives on the Birth of the Prison." *American Historical Review* 116 (4): 1040–63.

Gilmore, Ruth Wilson. 2007. *Golden Gulag: Prisons, Surplus, Crisis, and Opposition in Globalizing California*. Berkeley: University of California Press.

Gottschalk, Marie. 2006. *The Prison and the Gallows: The Politics of Mass Incarceration in America*. New York: Cambridge University Press.

Gross, Kali N. 2006. *Colored Amazons: Crime, Violence and Black Women in the City of Brotherly Love, 1888–1910*. Durham, NC: Duke University Press.

Guha, Sumit. 1995. "An Indian Penal Regime: Maharashtra in the Eighteenth Century." *Past & Present* 147:101–26.

Haviland, John. 1824. *A Description of Haviland's Design for the New Penitentiary, Now Erecting Near Philadelphia, Accompanied by a Birdseye View*. Philadelphia: R. Desilver.

Ignatieff, Michael. 1978. *A Just Measure of Pain: The Penitentiary in the Industrial Revolution, 1750–1850*. New York: Pantheon.

Janssen, Volker. 2005. "Civic Welfare: Rehabilitation in California's Prisons, 1941–1971." Ph.D. diss., University of California, San Diego.

King, Peter. 2000. *Crime, Justice, and Discretion in England, 1740–1820*. New York: Oxford University Press.

Kunzel, Regina. 2008. *Criminal Intimacy: Prison and the Uneven History of Modern American Sexuality*. Chicago: University of Chicago Press.

Lewis, W. David. 1965. *From Newgate to Dannemora: The Rise of the Penitentiary in New York, 1796–1848*. Ithaca, NY: Cornell University Press.

Lichtenstein, Alexander. 1996. *Twice the Work of Free Labor: The Political Economy of Convict Labor in the New South*. New York: Verso Press.

Lynch, Mona. 2010. *Sunbelt Justice: Arizona and the Transformation of American Punishment*. Stanford, CA: Stanford University Press.

Masur, Louis P. 1989. *Rites of Execution: Capital Punishment and the Transformation of American Culture, 1776–1865*. New York: Oxford University Press.

Maxwell-Stewart, Hamish. 2010. "Convict Transportation from Britain and Ireland, 1615–1870." *History Compass* 8 (11): 1221–42.

McConville, Sean. 1995. "The Victorian Prison: England, 1865–1965." In *The Oxford History of the Prison: The Practice of Punishment in Western Society*, ed. Norval Morris & David J. Rothman, 117–50. New York: Oxford University Press.

McGowen, Randall. 1995. "The Well-Ordered Prison: England, 1780–1865." In *The Oxford History of the Prison: The Practice of Punishment in Western Society*, ed. Norval Morris & David J. Rothman, 71–99. New York: Oxford University Press.

McLennan, Rebecca. 2008. *The Crisis of Imprisonment: Protest, Politics, and the Making of the American Penal State, 1776–1941*. New York: Cambridge University Press.

McLennan, Rebecca. 2011. "The Convict's Two Lives: Civil and Natural Death in the American Prison." In *America's Death Penalty: Between Past and Present*, ed. David Garland, Randall McGowen, & Michael Meranze, 191–219. New York: New York University Press.

Meranze, Michael. 1996. *Laboratories of Virtue: Punishment, Revolution, and Authority in Philadelphia, 1760–1835*. Chapel Hill: University of North Carolina Press.

Meranze, Michael. 2008. "Penality and the Colonial Project: Crime, Punishment, and the Regulation of Morals in Early America." In *The Cambridge History of Law in America*, Vol. 1, ed. Michael Grossberg & Christopher Tomlins, 178–210. New York: Cambridge University Press.

Morris, Norval. 2002. *Maconochie's Gentlemen: The Story of Norfolk Island and the Roots of Modern Prison Reform*. New York: Oxford University Press.

Morris, Thomas L. 2006. *Southern Slavery and the Law, 1619–1860*. Chapel Hill: University of North Carolina Press.

Muhammad, Khalil Gibran. 2010. *The Condemnation of Blackness: Race, Crime, and the Making of Modern Urban America*. Cambridge, MA: Harvard University Press.

O'Brien, Patricia. 1982. *The Promise of Punishment: Prisons in Nineteenth-Century France*. Princeton, NJ: Princeton University Press.

O'Brien, Patricia. 1995. "The Prison on the Continent: Europe, 1865–1965." In *The Oxford History of the Prison: The Practice of Punishment in Western Society*, ed. Norval Morris & David J. Rothman, 178–201. New York: Oxford University Press.

Odem, Mary E. 1995. *Delinquent Daughters: Protecting and Policing Adolescent Female Sexuality in the United States, 1885–1920*. Chapel Hill: University of North Carolina Press.

Parenti, Christian. 1999. *Lockdown America: Police and Prisons in the Age of Crisis*. New York: Verso Press.

Paton, Diana. 2004. *No Bond But the Law: Punishment, Race, and Gender in Jamaican State Formation, 1780–1870*. Durham, NC: Duke University Press.

Perkinson, Robert. 2010. *Texas Tough: The Rise of America's Prison Empire*. New York: Henry Holt.

Pisciotta, Alexander. 1994. *Benevolent Repression: Social Control and American Reformatory-Prison Movement*. New York: New York University Press.

Rafter, Nicole Hahn. 1983. "Prisons for Women: 1790–1980." *Crime and Justice* 5:129–81.

Rosenblum, Warren. 2008. *Beyond the Prison Gates: Punishment and Welfare in Germany, 1850–1933*. Chapel Hill: University of North Carolina Press.

Rothman, David J. 1971. *The Discovery of the Asylum: Social Order and Disorder in the New Republic*. Boston: Little, Brown & Co.

Rothman, David J. 1980. *Conscience and Convenience: The Asylum and Its Alternatives in Progressive America*. Boston: Little, Brown & Co.

Sentencing Project. n.d. "Fact Sheet: Trends in U.S Corrections." Accessed at http://sentencingproject.org/doc/publications/inc_Trends_in_Corrections_Fact_sheet.pdf.

Schlossman, Steven. 1977. *Love and the American Delinquent: The Theory and Practice of "Progressive" Juvenile Justice, 1825–1920*. Chicago: University of Chicago Press.

Schlossman, Steven. 1995. "Delinquent Children: The Juvenile Reform School." In *The Oxford History of the Prison: The Practice of Punishment in Western Society*, ed. Norval Morris & David J. Rothman, 325–49. New York: Oxford University Press.

Schull, Kent. 2007. "Penal Institutions, Nation-State Construction, and Modernity in the Late Ottoman Empire, 1908–1919." Ph.D. diss., University of California, Los Angeles.

Schwarz, Philip J. 1988. *Twice Condemned: Slaves and the Criminal Laws of Virginia, 1705–1865*. Baton Rouge: Louisiana State University Press.

Sherman, Taylor. 2009. "Tensions of Colonial Punishment: Perspectives on Recent Developments in the Study of Coercive Networks in Asia, Africa, and the Caribbean." *History Compass* 7 (3): 659–77.

Simon, Jonathan. 2007. *Governing Through Crime: How the War on Crime Transformed American Democracy and Created a Culture of Fear*. New York: Oxford University Press.

Simon, Jonathan. 2014. *Mass Incarceration on Trial: A Remarkable Court Decision and the Future of Prisons in America*. New York: New Press.

Spierenburg, Pieter. 1991. *The Prison Experience: Disciplinary Institutions and Their Inmates in Early Modern Europe*. New Brunswick, NJ: Rutgers University Press.

Sykes, Gresham M. 1958. *The Society of Captives*. Princeton, NJ: Princeton University Press.

Tartar, Michelle Lise, & Richard Bell. 2012. "Introduction." In *Buried Lives: Incarcerated in Early America*, ed. Michelle Lise Tarter & Richard Bell, 1–32. Athens: University of Georgia Press.

Western, Bruce. 2006. *Punishment and Inequality in America*. New York: Russell Sage Foundation.

Willrich, Michael. 2003. *City of Courts: Social Justice in Progressive Era Chicago*. New York: Cambridge University Press.

Zedner, Lucia. 1995. "Wayward Sisters: The Prison for Women." In *The Oxford History of the Prison: The Practice of Punishment in Western Society*, ed. Norval Morris & David J. Rothman, 295–324. New York: Oxford University Press.

Zinoman, Peter. 2001. *The Colonial Bastille: A History of Imprisonment in Vietnam, 1862–1940*. Berkeley: University of California Press.

Index